Business Research Methods

A South-Asian Perspective

8e

WILLIAM G. ZIKMUND

BARRY J. BABIN
Max P. Watson Professor of Business
Louisiana Tech University
Affiliate Professor, Reims Management School

JON C. CARR
Assistant Professor of Management
Texas Christian University

ATANU ADHIKARI
Assistant Professor
Indian Institute of Management, Kozhikode

MITCH GRIFFIN
Professor of Marketing
Bradley University

CENGAGE Learning®

Andover • Melbourne • Mexico City • Stamford, CT • Toronto • Hong Kong • New Delhi • Seoul • Singapore • Tokyo

CENGAGE Learning

Business Research Methods, 8e

William G. Zikmund
Barry J. Babin
Jon C. Carr
Atanu Adhikari
Mitch Griffin

Cover Image: © Thinkstock

Original Edition © 2010 South-Western, Cengage Learning
Business Research Methods, Eighth Edition
by William G. Zikmund, Barry J. Babin, Jon C. Carr, and Mitch Griffin
ISBN-13: 978-1-4390-8070-2
ISBN-10: 1-4390-8070-4

ISBN-13: 978-81-315-2036-9
ISBN-10: 81-315-2036-6

Cengage Learning India Pvt. Ltd.
418, F.I.E., Patparganj
Delhi 110092

Cengage Learning is a leading provider of customized learning solutions with office locations around the globe, including Andover, Melbourne, Mexico City, Stamford (CT), Toronto, Hong Kong, New Delhi, Seoul, Singapore, and Tokyo. Locate your local office at:
www.cengage.com/global

Cengage Learning products are represented in Canada by Nelson Education, Ltd.

For product information, visit **www.cengage.co.in**

To our families.

BRIEF CONTENTS

CONTENTS CONTENTS

PART 2: BEGINNING STAGES OF THE RESEARCH PROCESS

PART 3: RESEARCH METHODS FOR COLLECTING PRIMARY DATA

PART 5: SAMPLING AND FIELDWORK

Chapter 16 Sampling Designs and Sampling Procedures, 414

Chapter 17 Determination of Sample Size: A Review of Statistical Theory, 442

PREFACE

The world of business is certainly changing at a very fast rate. Businesses can't assume that continuing to produce the same old products, by the same old process, with the same old technology, managed in the same old way will continue to produce the same old good result. The need for intelligence supported by a connection to the real world is more important than ever. Business researchers are challenged with the job of producing just this type of intelligence. The eighth edition of *Business Research Methods* addresses the dynamic nature of today's business world while conveying the essential elements of the business research process.

Most readers understand that managers want answers to questions. What is not so obvious is that the search for the correct questions can be just as important as finding the right answers. After all, search is the biggest part of "re*search*." The researcher must have some idea of how to begin the search process, how to best search through what is now terabyte after terabyte of information to pick out those elements which best hold the possibility of turning into intelligence, and then how to communicate that intelligence in a way that helps managers make decisions. When it works right, business research is a win-win proposition. The process enables a company to identify its customers and design products and processes that maximize value for all. In return, the company receives value as the customer spends their hard earned money. As a result, customers win and businesses win! All are better off.

Trying to find just the right piece of business information via the Internet can be like searching for a needle in a haystack. This information may well be hidden beneath piles and piles of irrelevant stuff! Or how about trying to find a key piece of business information that may be hidden in the mind of a consumer or some employee? A customer may not even be consciously aware of all his or her reasons for some preference or some behavior and, consequently, can't identify or talk about it. An employee may not even realize that he or she possesses important vital information. How do you go about finding this information that could be so crucial to making a good business decision? Effective business research is like applying a CAT scan to a business problem.

That's where this text comes in: *Business Research Methods* equips students with the knowledge and skills involved in this basic research process; these will simplify and provide more accuracy to their search for business intelligence. The process we describe includes six steps. Researchers must first work together with decision makers to decide what they are looking for—that metaphorical needle in the haystack. The next two stages plot out the way to go about finding the needle. Next are two stages that focus on the actual search for the needle. The process concludes when the business researcher communicates the benefits of finding "pointed" information that can help mend problems or create something really new and special for the decision maker. Success in this process usually merits the researcher a reward that is a bit more valuable than that needle!

New to *Business Research Methods*

To ensure that students are able to conduct business research with an understanding of all the latest theories and techniques available to them, the eighth edition is very much revised and updated. Certainly, the research field is dynamic both in terms of the demands placed on it by business and in terms of the technological advances that enhance and expand the capable researcher's toolbox.

The Internet has revolutionized and is still revolutionizing research. The Internet has affected all phases of research by altering information systems, ways of gathering secondary data, survey processes, sampling, questionnaire design, primary data collection, qualitative analysis, and communication, among other things. Practically every chapter includes significant coverage of Internet-related topics, and most chapters also include review questions and activities that get students involved with the Internet in a relevant way.

Overall, here is a summary of some of the key features new to the eighth edition of *Business Research Methods*.

- Tips of the Trade—Each chapter contains a useful list of important tips that correspond to the particular stage of the research process covered. The tips provide information addressing practical questions such as interview length, question wording, interviewer involvement, sample size requirements, guides for data reliability and validity, as well as useful tips for testing hypotheses using inferential statistics.
- All New Chapter Vignettes—All of the chapter vignettes are new to the eighth edition. The vignettes set the stage for each chapter by introducing topics taken from both well-known and lesser-known companies, topical areas of interest in the current business literature, and slice-of-life business situations. The vignettes help frame the material included in each chapter and put core course concepts into a real-life and current context.
- Comprehensive Cases—The end of the book now includes a set of comprehensive cases that allow the student to get real hands-on experience doing research. The data are ready to be analyzed using Excel, SPSS, or SAS, or other software capable of reading data from a spreadsheet. Shorter and more-to-the-point cases are included at the end of each chapter. Several of these cases involve simple data analyses and are accompanied by data also available on the instructor resource disk.
- Greater Breadth of Business Coverage—The eighth edition includes examples across a broader spectrum of business activities and touches on practically all areas of business including marketing, management, finance, business ethics, and accounting. The examples better reflect the diversity of today's business world. Many of these examples are captured in the new Research Snapshot features, which tie business research together with current events, ethics, technology, and topics of particular interest to the business research student.
- A New Author Team—The new authors help bring greater breadth of coverage. Together, the team represents decades of experience performing all manner of research with particular expertise in marketing and consumer research, organizational behavior, managerial strategy, and human resources.

In addition to these new features, the eighth edition is also characterized by:

- A Simplified Approach and Style—The Research Snapshots, chapter Learning Objectives, and End-of-Chapter materials are now presented in a simplified form that allows greater focus on the truly important information. The Learning Objectives ensure an important coherence and structure to the chapters that culminate with the end-of-chapter materials.
- New Layout—A more engaging layout adds interest to the book, provides more illustrations and photos, and helps to keep students involved.
- Tagged End of Chapter Exercises—The end of chapter materials now contain an increased number of questions that pertain to either ethical issues in business research or exercises requiring students to get involved with research via the Internet. These items are each uniquely tagged with a visual symbol, making these particular exercises stand out with a clear, identifying mark.
- Increased Coverage of International Business Issues—The examples and illustrations make greater use of examples from countries around the globe. Readers of this book may end up

working outside the United States or Canada, so the prevalence of international examples will increase awareness of research issues beyond North America and open up domestic students to global dynamics. This is a particularly important addition to the text since cultural and language barriers often present challenges for the business researcher.

- Greater Attention to Qualitative Research—More and more companies are realizing the benefits of qualitative research. In response to this important phenomenon, Chapter 7, *Qualitative Research Tools*, is almost entirely rewritten in the eighth edition. The chapter focuses more exclusively on qualitative research and the corresponding interpretative techniques that turn data without numbers into meaning. Phenomenology, grounded theory, ethnography, and case study approaches are now all covered. Several other chapters also emphasize qualitative research to a greater extent. For example, the Internet is not just a way of collecting quantitative data. Qualitative research is being dramatically changed by the Internet as consumers leave more and more artifactual data behind on social networking Web sites, company chat rooms, blogs, micro-blogs (such as tweets left on Twitter), and more. Thus, qualitative research tools and approaches are highlighted throughout the text.

Organization of the Book

The organization of the eighth edition of *Business Research Methods* follows the logic of the business research process itself. The book is organized into seven parts, and each part presents the basic research concepts for one of the stages in the research process; each part also discusses how these concepts relate to decisions about conducting specific projects.

Part 1: Introduction emphasizes the interplay between research and business and how the importance and scope of research varies with different business situations. Included in this discussion is an overview of computerized data management and information systems, an outline of the entire business research process, and an explanation of how all of this is changing due to the Internet. In addition, research is a way that theory is tested and research contributes to theory. Chapter 3 is devoted to theory development and explains why theory is important to effective research.

Without high ethical standards, no business is a "good business." Thus, the introductory materials also include an emphasis on business ethics and the special ethical problems associated with business research. Chapter 5 focuses exclusively on business ethics and the interplay between organizational dynamics and research.

Part 2: Beginning Stages of the Research Process covers the essentials involved in starting to study business problems. This part emphasizes decision making, problem definition, and the process of how the business problem must be translated into research questions and/or research hypotheses. Research proposals are covered in some detail, and the reader is encouraged to see these as the written agreement that helps put the decision maker and the researcher on the same page.

Chapter 7 emphasizes qualitative research applications. One role played by qualitative research is helping to separate problem symptoms from true issues that can be attacked with business research. However, qualitative research extends far beyond problem definition; it allows greater potential for discovery as well as deeper and potentially more meaningful explanations in business research.

Part 2 concludes with a detailed discussion of secondary data and emphasizes its increasing importance in a data-rich world. Chapter 8 focuses on finding and using secondary data in today's digital age.

Part 3: Research Methods for Collecting Primary Data examines the topics involved in collecting new data for the specific problem at hand. For example, the chapters describe issues related to planning, conducting, and administering surveys, which remain a mainstay for collecting consumer and employee opinions, attitudes, and behaviors.

Additionally, Chapter 12 focuses specifically on experimental research. Experiments allow causal inferences and therefore can provide strong inferences. They can, however, be intricate to design and implement; conducting experiments that provide valid results is no simple matter. When done correctly, they provide effective business intelligence.

Part 4: Measurement Concepts are critical to research. This part of the text discusses the foundation of measurement theory. Key topics include descriptions of the different levels of scale measurement and how this affects analysis and the interpretation of results. Basic ways to measure human attitudes and practical matters dealing with questionnaire design are also discussed. An increased emphasis is placed on the use of new technologies for conducting interviews. For instance, how does asking a question in an electronic format expand the options for respondents and the researcher? Topics such as these are highlighted in Part 4.

Part 5: Sampling and Fieldwork explains the difference between a population and a sample. The reasons why sampling is needed and how it can be used to confidently allow predictions about larger numbers of people are covered. The fieldwork process is also discussed, including the importance of supervision of fieldwork. This section shows how to avoid sloppy sampling and poor field supervision which can lead to error in the business research process.

Part 6: Data Analysis and Presentation covers important processes necessary in translating raw data into business intelligence. Included among these topics are the editing and coding of the data. The coded data are then ready for analysis, and this section presents the most commonly used methods for analyzing data. For instance, basic descriptive statistics are discussed as ways of portraying key results including central tendency and dispersion.

Inferential statistics are discussed, including often-used univariate and bivariate approaches such as *t*-tests. Multivariate statistical approaches are also introduced so that the reader has an awareness of techniques that can analyze many variables simultaneously. Hands-on experience with basic multivariate procedures is also provided. The final chapter brings everything together by including a discussion of how to effectively communicate research results via a report and/or presentation.

Part 7: Comprehensive Cases with Computerized Databases make up the last section of the book. These cases provide materials that challenge students to apply and integrate the concepts they have learned throughout the course. Instructors will find that these cases provide flexibility to either expand or simplify the assignment to suit the demands of varying course assignments.

The cases provide greater variety than earlier editions, including some which involve analysis of internal organizational problems as well as an opportunity to use qualitative research. When quantitative data are included, they can be easily analyzed with basic statistical tools like SPSS. Excel files are also included with the same data. These files can be read directly by statistical programs like SAS or other programs. A new comprehensive case has been added to the eighth edition.

Superior Pedagogy

More than other research textbooks, the eighth edition of *Business Research Methods* addresses students' need to comprehend all aspects of the business research process. The following features facilitate learning throughout the book:

- **Learning Objectives.** Each chapter begins with a concise list of learning objectives that emphasize the major areas of competency that students should achieve before proceeding to the next chapter. The key is to avoid labeling everything a major learning objective and to provide instructors with flexibility for emphasizing additional material as they see fit.
- **Major Headings Keyed to Learning Objectives.** First-level headings, with the exception of those labeled "Introduction," are keyed to learning objectives. This should be an aid in developing assessment rubrics and makes the book more user friendly in terms of identifying key material.
- **Research Snapshots.** All of the box materials share a common title, Research Snapshots. Each chapter contains multiple Research Snapshots. The boxes explore business research processes in a variety of modern businesses situations, ranging from international considerations to research ethics. Some boxes also illustrate research techniques and applications in a step-by-step fashion. Every attempt is made to make the box material lively and relevant to the subject matter of the chapters.

- **Writing Style.** An accessible, interesting writing style continues to be a hallmark of this book. With a careful balance between theory and practice and a sprinkling of interesting examples and anecdotes, the writing style clarifies and simplifies the business research process. In addition, the text offers a comprehensive treatment of important and current topics.
- **Statistical Approach.** A review of statistical theory provides students with an overview of the basic aspects of statistics. However, since this text stresses managerial applications more than statistical theory, students are given tools to perform the most common business research data analysis. More sophisticated data analysis approaches are left for further reference. Thus, the readers can learn how to test simple hypotheses involving differences between means or relationships among variables. Cross-tabulation, *t*-tests, ANOVA, and regression are covered in sufficient depth to allow students to use these techniques. In addition, easy-to-follow, click-through sequences can walk students through most basic approaches to producing statistical results.
- **Key Terms.** Learning the vocabulary of business research is essential to understanding the topic, and *Business Research Methods* facilitates this with key terms. First, key concepts are boldfaced and completely defined when they first appear in the textbook. Second, all key terms and concepts are listed at the end of each chapter, and many terms are highlighted in a marginal glossary. Third, a glossary summarizing all key terms and definitions appears at the end of the book for handy reference. A glossary of frequently used symbols is also included.
- **Ethics Questions.** Identified by a special icon, **ETHICS**, ethics questions are included in most chapters. Among the compelling issues students are asked to explore is redefining the right to privacy in light of new technology. The ethical issues also provide a great opportunity for building critical thinking skills.
- **Internet Questions.** Internet questions also are identified by a special icon, **'NET**. Nearly all chapters include multiple questions and research activities that illustrate advances in Internet applications common to business research.
- **Research Activities.** The end-of-chapter materials include real-world research activities intended to provide actual research experience for the student. Most provide an opportunity for the student to gain experience in multiple content areas. Some involve ethical aspects of research, and some involve Internet usage.
- **Cases.** Cases, often taken from real-life situations, illustrate business research concepts and build knowledge and research skills. These cases offer students the opportunity to participate actively in the decision-making process, one of the most effective forms of learning.

Acknowledgments

Certainly, no list of acknowledgments will be complete. So many people have assisted in this project. Chief among these would be to the late Bill Zikmund for carrying the weight of this project for each of the seven previous editions. We are privileged to be able to carry the project along into what we hope will be many more editions as the premier business research text. Also, thanks go to members of our team—including graduate assistants Kevin James, David Shows, Melanie Gardner, and Christina Chung—who have helped with research for this text and helped share some of the workload on other endeavors, freeing up time to spend on this project. We would be remiss not to mention the support and patience of our families. All have contributed to the project and our kids are particularly helpful in judging relevance of vignettes and examples. Also, thanks go to all the great faculty who mentored us during our days in the Ph.D. program. Most notable among these are Joseph F. Hair, Jr. and the late William R. Darden.

Thanks go to all the good people at Cengage Learning who helped make this project possible. A special thanks to our publisher Mike Roche, and to Emily Nesheim, Elizabeth Lowry, and Jitendra Kumar. They provided tremendous support and guidance through the writing and production process, including assistance with proofing, permissions, photos, and exhibits.

Many colleagues contributed ideas for this book. They made many suggestions that greatly enhanced this book. For their insightful reviews of the manuscript for the eighth or previous editions of *Business Research Methods*, we would like to thank the following:

Gerald Albaum
University of Oregon
Stephen Batory
Bloomsburg University
William Bearden
University of South Carolina
Joseph A. Bellizzi
Arizona State University–West
Carol Bienstock
Radford University
James A. Brunner
University of Toledo
F. Anthony Bushman
San Francisco State University
Thomas Buzas
Eastern Michigan University
Roy F. Cabaniss
Huston-Tillotson College
Steven V. Cates
Averett University
Michael d'Amico
University of Akron
Ron Eggers
Barton College
H. Harry Friedman
City University of New York–Brooklyn
Ron Goldsmith
Florida State University
Larry Goldstein
Iona College
Karen Goncalves
Nichols College
David Gourley
Arizona State University
Jim Grimm
Illinois State University
Christopher Groening
University of Pittsburgh
Al Gross
Robert Morris College
Don Heinz
University of Wisconsin

Craig Hollingshead
Texas A&M University–Kingsville
Victor Howe
University of Kentucky
Roy Howell
Texas Tech University
Michael R. Hyman
New Mexico State University
Rhea Ingram
Columbus State University–Georgia
Robert Jaross
Florida International University
P. K. Kannan
University of Maryland
Susan Kleine
Arizona State University
David B. Klenosky
Purdue University
C. S. Kohli
California State University–Fullerton
Jerome L. Langer
Assumption College
Bob Lauman
Webster University
James H. Leigh
Texas A&M University
Larry Lowe
Bryant College
Karl Mann
Tennessee Technological University
Charles R. Martin
Wichita State University
Marlys Mason
Oklahoma State University
Tom K. Massey
University of Missouri–Kansas City
Sanjay Mishra
University of Kansas
G. M. Naidu
University of Wisconsin–Whitewater
Stephanie Noble
The University of Mississippi

Mike Parent
Utah State University

Terry Paul
The Ohio State University

Charles Prohaska
Central Connecticut State University

Rick Saucier
St. John's University

Alan Sawyer
University of Florida

Robert Schaffer
California State University–Pomona

Leon G. Schiffman
City University of New York–Baruch

David Shows
Louisiana Tech University

K. Sivakumar
Lehigh University

Mark Speece
Central Washington University

Harlan Spotts
Western New England College

Wilbur W. Stanton
Old Dominion University

Bruce L. Stern
Portland State University

James L. Taylor
University of Alabama

Gail Tom
California State University–Sacramento

Deborah Utter
Boston College

David Wheeler
Suffolk University

Richard Wilcox
Carthage College

Natalie Wood
St. Joseph's University

Margaret Wright
University of Colorado

Clifford E. Young
University of Colorado–Denver

Xin Zhao
University of Utah

William Lee Ziegler
Bethune-Cookman College

Thanks also to all of the students who have inspired us and reinforced the fact that we made a great career decision about two decades ago. Thanks also to our close colleagues Tara' Lopez, Dave Ortinau, and Jim Boles for their continued support and insight.

Barry J. Babin
Louisiana Tech University

Mitch Griffin
Bradley University

Jon C. Carr
Texas Christian University
July 2009

About the South-East Asia Edition

This edition contains significant additional input in almost every chapter of the book. It provides enhanced insights into issues from emerging countries' business. Since the business situation in emerging countries requires special attention, examples of research issues relevant for businesses in these emerging countries are addressed. This edition includes several new cases and examples which would help students comprehend the research methodologies illustrated in each chapter. This edition also contains a new comprehensive case which provides a running understanding of several concepts discussed in previous chapters. This case would help students track the entire business research process, research design, hypothesis development, data collection, data analysis, and interpretation of results. Each chapter contains several examples taken from developed as well as emerging countries. These examples provide clarity of theories and concepts discussed.

This edition significantly increases the content of Chapter 24, covering concepts and discussions on the multivariate data analysis. Each of the data analysis techniques here is strengthened by adding assumptions of each technique, testing assumptions, and performing data analysis and interpretation. Several important statistical issues related to the detection of multicollinearity, heteroscadasticity, and to validation of results are included in this chapter. This chapter also has a new analytical technique, conjoint analysis to have a larger coverage of popular multivariate data analysis techniques. This chapter also contains SPSS screenshots of certain frequently used techniques in business research, namely factor analysis and conjoint analysis. The procedure to generate orthogonal design for experimental research and conjoint analysis has also been included in this edition of the chapter. Additionally, SPSS screenshots for developing orthogonal design have also been provided.

Acknowledgments

I am grateful to my parents, wife, in-laws, brothers, sister-in-laws, and all children in my family who have continuously inspired me to do what I believed in. I sincerely thank all my students who have shared their thoughts and criticism about my work.

Atanu Adhikari
IIM, Kozhikode

ABOUT THE AUTHORS

William G. Zikmund (1943–2002)

A native of the Chicago area, William G. Zikmund was a professor of marketing at Oklahoma State University. He received a Ph.D. from the University of Colorado in business administration with a concentration in marketing. Before beginning his academic career, Bill worked in research for Conway/Millikin Company (a marketing research supplier) and Remington Arms Company (an extensive user of marketing research). He also has served as a marketing research consultant to several business and nonprofit organizations. During his academic career, Bill published dozens of articles and papers in a diverse group of scholarly journals, ranging from the *Journal of Marketing* to the *Accounting Review* to the *Journal of Applied Psychology*. In addition to *Business Research Methods*, Professor Zikmund authored *Essentials of Marketing Research*, *Effective Marketing*, and a work of fiction, *A Corporate Bestiary*. Professor Zikmund was a member of several professional organizations, including the American Marketing Association, the Academy of Marketing Science, the Association for Consumer Research, the Society for Marketing Advances, the Marketing Educators' Association, and the Association of Collegiate Marketing Educators. He served on the editorial review boards of the Journal of Marketing Education, Marketing Education Review, Journal of the Academy of Marketing Science, and Journal of Business Research.

Barry J. Babin

In addition to coauthoring four textbooks, Barry Babin has published over 70 research publications in prestigious periodicals such as the Journal of Marketing, the Journal of Consumer Research, the Journal of Business Research, the Journal of Retailing, Psychological Reports, Psychology and Marketing, and the Journal of the Academy of Marketing Science. Dr. Babin also has won numerous honors for his research, including the University of Southern Mississippi Louis K. Brandt Faculty Research Award (on three occasions), the 1996 Society for Marketing Advances (SMA) Steven J. Shaw Award, and the 1997 Omerre DeSerres Award for Outstanding Contributions to Retail and Service Environment Research. His research focuses on the effect of the service environment on employees and customers, and his expertise lies in building successful outcomes that support long-lasting, mutually beneficial relationships with employees and customers. He also has expertise in encouraging creativity in the workplace and in wine marketing. Dr. Babin's primary teaching specialties involve consumers and service quality, marketing research, and creative problem solving, and he is a popular and frequent international presenter, having lectured in Australia, South Korea, France, Germany, Canada, and the United Kingdom. Dr. Babin is current president of the Academy of Marketing Sciences, former president of the Society of Marketing Advances, and marketing editor for the Journal of Business Research.

Jon C. Carr

Jon is Assistant Professor in the Department of Management at TCU where he teaches courses in the area of New Ventures and Organizational Behavior. He previously taught at the University of Southern Mississippi. He has published articles in journals such as Entrepreneurship Theory & Practice, Journal of Management, and the Journal of Business Research.

Atanu Adhikari

Atanu Adhikari is Assistant Professor at the Indian Institute of Management, Kozhikode, India. He earned his bachelor degree in Engineering, and MBA (Gold Medalist) and Ph.D. in Marketing Management. He was selected as an Emerging Scholar in 2011 by the Academy of Marketing Science, USA. His current area of research includes consumer choice behavior, experience product marketing, pricing, and applications of Bayesian econometrics in marketing research. He is actively involved in scholarly academic research and has published his research work in many national and international peer reviewed academic journals and edited books published by leading publishers. At IIM Kozhikode, he teaches Marketing Research, Marketing Management, Strategic Marketing at postgraduate level, and Advanced Marketing Research at doctoral level. Dr. Adhikari has received several awards and honors from national and international bodies, which include recognition as an Emerging Scholar from the Academy of Marketing Science; Meritorious Teaching Award from the Marketing Management Association, USA; and Best case award from EFMD, Belgium, in addition to several research grants from international bodies. He was a Runner up in the Oikos International Case Writing Competition, Switzerland. He was a fellow member of the Royal Statistical Society, London. He is affiliated with American Marketing Association and is an editor of a few international academic publications.

Mitch Griffin

Mitch is an Associate Professor of Management at Bradley University. Mitch has previous teaching experience at Southern Illinois University, the University of Minnesota, and Louisiana State University. His current teaching interests include Principles of Marketing, Pricing and Product Strategies, Sales Management, Marketing Research, and Advanced Marketing Research. In recognition of his teaching, Dr. Griffin received the Foster College of Business Administration 1994 Midwest Grain Products Inc. Outstanding Teaching Award. His research has appeared in the Journal of Consumer Research, Journal of Retailing, Journal of the Academy of Marketing Science, Journal of Business Research, Journal of Consumer Affairs, Journal of Satisfaction, Dissatisfaction and Complaining Behavior, Journal of Nonprofit and Public Sector Marketing, and Advances in Consumer Research.

Part 1
Introduction

© PHIL KNOTT/PYMCA/JUPITER IMAGES

CHAPTER 1
THE ROLE OF BUSINESS RESEARCH

LEARNING OUTCOMES

After studying this chapter, you should be able to

1. **Understand how research contributes to business success**
2. **Know how to define business research**
3. **Understand the difference between basic and applied business research**
4. **Understand how research activities can be used to address business decisions**
5. **Know when business research should and should not be conducted**
6. **Appreciate the way that technology and internationalization are changing business research**

Chapter Vignette: "If It Quacks Like a Duck?"

"If you're hurt and you miss work": This is the tag line for one of the most popular U.S. advertising campaigns—for AFLAC Insurance. The tag line is accompanied by the familiar Pekin duck constantly reminding people with a loud "AFFLLAACKK!!" Recent polls show that the AFLAC duck has become one of America's favorite icons, coming in second only to the Mars M&M's characters. But how has the duck's favorable fan status affected AFLAC's business performance? Certainly, AFLAC's business strategy goes beyond creating the most popular duck since Donald!

PR NEWSFOTO AFLAC

Throughout its thirty-year history, AFLAC, like other firms, has faced important business decisions about how to create brand awareness, how to build consumer knowledge of the brand, and how to build sales and loyalty. Leading up to these decisions, the firm must first assess its current situation and its brand awareness relative to its competitors. Approximately two dozen AFLAC duck commercials ago, research revealed that most consumers were unaware of AFLAC. The vast majority of consumers would not list AFLAC when prompted to name insurance companies. Instead, names like Allstate, State Farm, and Prudential proved more familiar. Not surprisingly, these companies enjoyed greater market share. Based on this research, AFLAC decided to invest in a national television campaign to build awareness of the brand name—"AFFLLAAACCK!!" The phonic similarity to "QUACK" proved successful.

Today, AFLAC has built great awareness of its name, but this hasn't necessarily translated into business success. Despite the tag line, fewer than 30 percent of consumers who recognize the name know that AFLAC specializes in supplemental disability insurance. This accounts for over three-fourths of AFLAC's nearly $14 billion annual revenue. Thus, while the initial research suggested the need for building awareness, their more recent research is addressing difficulties in creating the right knowledge of AFLAC. What communication strategy is best for building knowledge? Can knowledge be built in the same way as awareness? Will knowledge lead to increased intentions to do business with AFLAC? What role does the company play compared to the AFLAC sales associates in creating company image? All of these are questions that should be answered. Business research will be directed toward answering these questions. The information will then be used to try and erase the knowledge deficit faced by AFLAC. If the answers are half as effective as those that led to the AFLAC duck, the company should enjoy tremendous success. Thus, for AFLAC, as for many firms, research is an important tool in shaping business strategy.[1]

Introduction

The recent history of AFLAC demonstrates the need for information in making informed decisions addressing key issues faced by all competitive businesses. Research can provide that information. Without it, business decisions involving both tactics and strategies are made in the dark.

We open with three examples illustrating how business decisions require intelligence and how research can provide that intelligence. The following examples focus specifically on how research can lead to innovation in the form of new products, improvements in existing goods and services, or enhancements in employee relationships. Imagine yourself in the role of business manager as you read these examples and think about the information needs you may have in trying to build success for your company.

Jelly Belly brand traditionally offered fifty official jelly bean flavors. However, research input from customers has helped that number grow and now Jelly Belly even has a variety of specialty beans. Consumers willingly submitted new flavor ideas as part of the Jelly Belly Dream Bean Contest (**http://www.dreambeancontest.com**). In return, the consumers received an opportunity to win prizes. The company receives some really off-the-wall flavor ideas. Among the strangest are flavors such as Dill Pickle, Rotten Egg, Taco, Burned Bacon, and Cream of Wheat.[2] Top suggestions were put back on the Web so that people could vote for the flavor they most wanted to see introduced. In 2008, the winning flavor was Acai Berry, which beat out other finalist flavors such as Sublime Chili Lime, Thai Iced Tea, and Mojito.

More recently, Jelly Belly is trying to capitalize on consumers' desires for sports performance products. Survey research suggests that consumers would respond favorably to food and drink products providing benefits that improve one's ability to exercise.[3] As a result, Jelly Belly has introduced Sport Beans. Sport Beans contain added electrolytes, carbohydrates, and vitamins designed to provide added energy and alertness. In addition, all the strange flavor suggestions also have spawned a new product offering for the entire jelly bean market. Bean-Boozled Jelly Beans combines a traditional flavor with an exotic flavor that look identical, so consumers never know which one they are getting. The product provides added value through the fun that comes with all the potential surprises. A Skunk Spray bean looks exactly like a Licorice bean. So, the bean lover never is sure when the bean will bamboozle! Successful companies are constantly scanning ideas in the hope of providing ways of adding value. Jelly Belly's Sports Beans and Bean-Boozled Beans offer two different ways of adding value.[4]

The coffee industry, after years of the "daily grind," has proved quite dynamic over the past decade. After years of steady decline, research on consumers' beverage purchases show that coffee sales began rebounding around 1995. Telephone interviews with American consumers estimated that there were 80 million occasional coffee drinkers and 7 million daily upscale coffee drinkers in 1995. By 2001, estimates suggested there were 161 million daily or occasional U.S. coffee drinkers and 27 million daily upscale coffee drinkers.[5]

Coffee drinking habits have also changed. In 1991 there were fewer than 450 coffeehouses in the United States. Today, it seems like places such as Starbucks, Second Cup, The Coffee Bean & Tea Leaf, and Gloria Jean's are virtually everywhere in the United States and Canada. There are more than 15,000 thousand Starbucks locations around the world with the majority of these being wholly owned stores.[6] While locating these outlets requires significant formal research, Starbucks also is researching new concepts aimed at other ways a coffee shop can provide value to consumers. One concept that has survived testing thus far is the addition of free, in-store high-speed wireless Internet access. Thus, you can have hot coffee in a hot spot! After Starbucks *baristas* began reporting that customers were asking clerks what music was playing in the stores, Starbucks began testing the sales of CDs containing their in-store music. In 2009, Starbucks began a bundled pricing promotion offering a breakfast sandwich or pastry and a tall coffee drink for $3.95 in response to the declining economy. The research that underlies the introduction of these value-added concepts could first include simply asking a consumer or a small group of consumers for their reaction to the concept. Survey research and then actual in-store tests may follow. So, the research underlying such decisions can be multilayered.

Often, business research is directed toward an element of an organization's internal operations. For example, DuPont utilizes research techniques to better understand their employees' needs. DuPont has ninety-four thousand employees worldwide and fifty-four thousand in the United States.[7] The company has conducted four comprehensive work/life needs assessment surveys of its employees since 1985. This business research provides the company with considerable insight into employee work/life behavior and allows DuPont to identify trends regarding employee needs.

The most recent survey found that, as the company's work force is aging, employees' child care needs are diminishing, but elder care needs are emerging. The survey found that 88 percent of respondents identified themselves as baby boomers. About 50 percent of the employees say that they have—or expect to have—elder care responsibilities in the next three to four years, up from 40% in 1995.

The surveys have shown that DuPont employees want to balance work and family responsibilities, feeling deeply committed to both aspects of their lives. The latest research shows that company efforts to satisfy these desires have been successful. Employee perception of support from management for work/life issues improved from the 1995 study and the results indicate employees feel less stress. Support from colleagues is rated high, and women indicated they now have more role models. The study also reported that the feeling of management support is directly connected to employees' efforts to make the company successful. Employees who use the work/life programs are willing to "go the extra mile."

These examples illustrate the need for information in making informed business decisions. Jelly Belly provides consumers with the incentive of free samples of jelly beans in return for ideas about desirable new bean flavors. The statistics about coffee demonstrate how research can track trends that may lead to new business opportunities. Starbucks's research also illustrates how research can be used to examine new concepts in progressively more complex stages, setting the stage for a more successful product introduction. DuPont's ability to track employee attitudes allows them to adjust employee benefit packages to maximize satisfaction and reduce employee turnover. These are only the tip of the iceberg when it comes to the types of business research that are conducted every day. This chapter introduces basic concepts of business research and describes how research can play a crucial role in creating and managing a successful business.

The Nature of Business Research

Business research covers a wide range of phenomena. For managers, the purpose of research is to provide knowledge regarding the organization, the market, the economy, or another area of uncertainty. A financial manager may ask, "Will the environment for long-term financing be better two years from now?" A personnel manager may ask, "What kind of training is necessary for production employees?" or "What is the reason for the company's high employee turnover?" A marketing manager may ask, "How can I monitor my retail sales and retail trade activities?" Each of these questions requires information about how the environment, employees, customers, or the economy will respond to executives' decisions. Research is one of the principal tools for answering these practical questions.

Within an organization, a business researcher may be referred to as a marketing researcher, an organizational researcher, a director of financial and economic research, or one of many other titles. Although business researchers are often specialized, the term *business research* encompasses all of these functional specialties. While researchers in different functional areas may investigate different phenomena, they are similar to one another because they share similar research methods.

It's been said that "every business issue ultimately boils down to an information problem."[8] Can the right information be delivered? The ultimate goal of research is to supply accurate information that reduces the uncertainty in managerial decision making. Very often, decisions are made with little information for various reasons, including cost considerations, insufficient time to conduct research, or management's belief that enough is already known. Relying on seat-of-the-pants decision making—decision making without research—is like betting on a long shot at the racetrack because the horse's name is appealing. Occasionally there are successes, but in the long run, intuition without research leads to losses. Business research helps decision makers shift from intuitive information gathering to systematic and objective investigation.

Business Research Defined

Business research is the application of the scientific method in searching for the truth about business phenomena. These activities include defining business opportunities and problems, generating and evaluating alternative courses of action, and monitoring employee and organizational performance. Business research is more than conducting surveys.[9] This process includes idea and theory development, problem definition, searching for and collecting information, analyzing data, and communicating the findings and their implications.

business research

The application of the scientific method in searching for the truth about business phenomena. These activities include defining business opportunities and problems, generating and evaluating ideas, monitoring performance, and understanding the business process.

This definition suggests that business research information is not intuitive or haphazardly gathered. Literally, *research* (re-search) means "to search again." The term connotes patient study and scientific investigation wherein the researcher takes another, more careful look at the data to discover all that is known about the subject. Ultimately, all findings are tied back to the underlying theory.

The definition also emphasizes, through reference to the scientific method, that any information generated should be accurate and objective. The nineteenth-century American humorist Artemus Ward claimed, "It ain't the things we don't know that gets us in trouble. It's the things we know that ain't so." In other words, research isn't performed to support preconceived ideas but to test them. The researcher must be personally detached and free of bias in attempting to find truth. If bias enters into the research process, the value of the research is considerably reduced. We will discuss this further in a subsequent chapter.

Our definition makes it clear that business research is designed to facilitate the managerial decision-making process for all aspects of the business: finance, marketing, human resources, and so on. Business research is an essential tool for management in virtually all problem-solving and decision-making activities. By providing the necessary information on which to base business decisions, research can decrease the risk of making a wrong decision in each area. However, it is important to note that research is an aid to managerial decision making, never a substitute for it.

RESEARCH SNAPSHOT

Good Fat and Bad Fat

American consumers can be seen every day scouring nutrition labels. Most likely, the item they show the most interest in recently is the amount of fat. The Food and Drug Administration (FDA) is concerned that consumers get information that is not only accurate, but that also conveys the proper message to achieve a healthy diet. But all fat is not created equal. In particular, dieticians warn of the dangers associated with excess amounts of trans fats; diet nutrition labels break fats into saturated and unsaturated fats. Among numerous factors that complicate the interpretation of the nutrition label, trans fat (hydrogenated) is technically a nonsaturated fat, but it acts more like a saturated fat when consumed. So, where should it be placed? The FDA cannot address this problem intelligently without research addressing questions such as the following:

1. If trans fats are listed as saturated fats, would consumers' beliefs about their consumption become more negative?
2. If the saturated fat amount includes a specific line indicating the amount of "saturated fat" that is really trans fat, would consumers become more confused about their diet?
3. If all amounts of fat are given equal prominence on the label, will consumer attitudes toward the different types of fats be the same?
4. Will consumers interpret foods free of trans fats as healthy?

Making this even more complicated is the fact that some consumer segments, such as teenagers in this case, may actually use the nutrition labels to select the brands that are least nutritious rather than most nutritious. So, they may actually seek out the one with the worst proportion of trans fats! The FDA specifically addressed trans fats in labeling regulations that took effect in 2006. Under these regulations, the FDA allows labels to claim zero trans fat as long as less than half a gram of hydrogenated oil per serving is contained. Simple?

Sources: "Health Labels are in the Eye of the Beholder," *Food Management* 40 (January 2005), 80; Hunter, B. T., "Labeling Transfat Is Tricky," *Consumers' Research Magazine* 86 (July 2003), 8–10; Weise, E., "Food Labels Now Required to Mention Trans Fat, Allergens," *USA Today* (January 2, 2006), H1.

Finally, this definition of business research is limited by one's definition of *business*. Certainly, research regarding production, finance, marketing, and management in for-profit corporations like DuPont is business research. However, business research also includes efforts that assist non-profit organizations such as the American Heart Association, the San Diego Zoo, the Boston Pops Orchestra, or a parochial school. Further, governmental agencies such as the Federal Emergency Management Agency (FEMA) and the Department of Homeland Security (DHS) perform many functions that are similar, if not identical, to those of for-profit business organizations. For instance, the Food and Drug Administration (FDA) is an important user of research, employing it to address the way people view and use various food and drugs. One such study commissioned and funded research to address the question of how consumers used the risk summaries that are included with all drugs sold in the United States.[10] Therefore, not-for-profits and governmental agencies can use research in much the same way as managers at Starbucks, Jelly Belly, or DuPont. While the focus is on for-profit organizations, this book explores business research as it applies to all institutions.

Applied and Basic Business Research

applied business research
Research conducted to address a specific business decision for a specific firm or organization.

basic business research
Research conducted without a specific decision in mind that usually does not address the needs of a specific organization. It attempts to expand the limits of knowledge in general and is not aimed at solving a particular pragmatic problem.

One useful way to describe research is based on the specificity of its purpose. **Applied business research** is conducted to address a specific business decision for a specific firm or organization. The opening vignette describes a situation in which AFLAC may use applied research to decide how to best create knowledge of its supplemental disability insurance products.

Basic business research (sometimes referred to as pure research) is conducted without a specific decision in mind, and it usually does not address the needs of a specific organization. It attempts to expand the limits of knowledge in general, and as such it is not aimed at solving a particular pragmatic problem. Basic research can be used to test the validity of a general business theory (one that applies to all businesses) or to learn more about a particular business phenomenon. For instance, a great deal of basic research addresses employee motivation. How can managers best encourage workers to dedicate themselves toward the organization's goals? From such research, we can learn the factors that are most important to workers and how to create an environment where employees are most highly motivated. This basic research does not examine the problem from any single organization's perspective. However, AFLAC, Starbucks, or DuPont's management may become aware of such research and use it to design applied research studies examining questions about their own employees. Thus, the two types of research are not completely independent, as basic research often provides the foundation for later applied research.

While the distinction between basic and applied is useful in describing research, there are very few aspects of research that apply only to basic or only to applied research. We will use the term *business research* more generally to refer to either type of research. The focus of this text is more on applied research—studies that are undertaken to answer questions about specific problems or to make decisions about particular courses of action or policies. Applied research is emphasized in this text because most students will be oriented toward the day-to-day practice of management, and most students and researchers will be exposed to short-term, problem-solving research conducted for businesses or nonprofit organizations.

The Scientific Method

All research, whether basic or applied, involves the scientific method. **The scientific method** is the way researchers go about using knowledge and evidence to reach objective conclusions about the real world. The scientific method is the same in social sciences, such as business, as in physical sciences, such as physics. In this case, it is the way we come to understand business phenomena.

the scientific method
The way researchers go about using knowledge and evidence to reach objective conclusions about the real world.

Exhibit 1.1 briefly illustrates the scientific method. In the scientific method, there are multiple routes to developing ideas. When the ideas can be stated in researchable terms, we reach the hypothesis stage. The next step involves testing the hypothesis against empirical evidence (facts from observation or experimentation). The results either support a hypothesis or do not support a hypothesis. From these results, new knowledge is generated.

In basic research, testing these prior conceptions or hypotheses and then making inferences and conclusions about the phenomena leads to the establishment of general laws about the phenomena. Use of the scientific method in applied research ensures objectivity in gathering facts and testing creative ideas for alternative business strategies. The essence of research, whether basic or applied, lies in the scientific method. Much of this book deals with scientific methodology. Thus, the techniques of basic and applied research differ largely in degree rather than in substance.

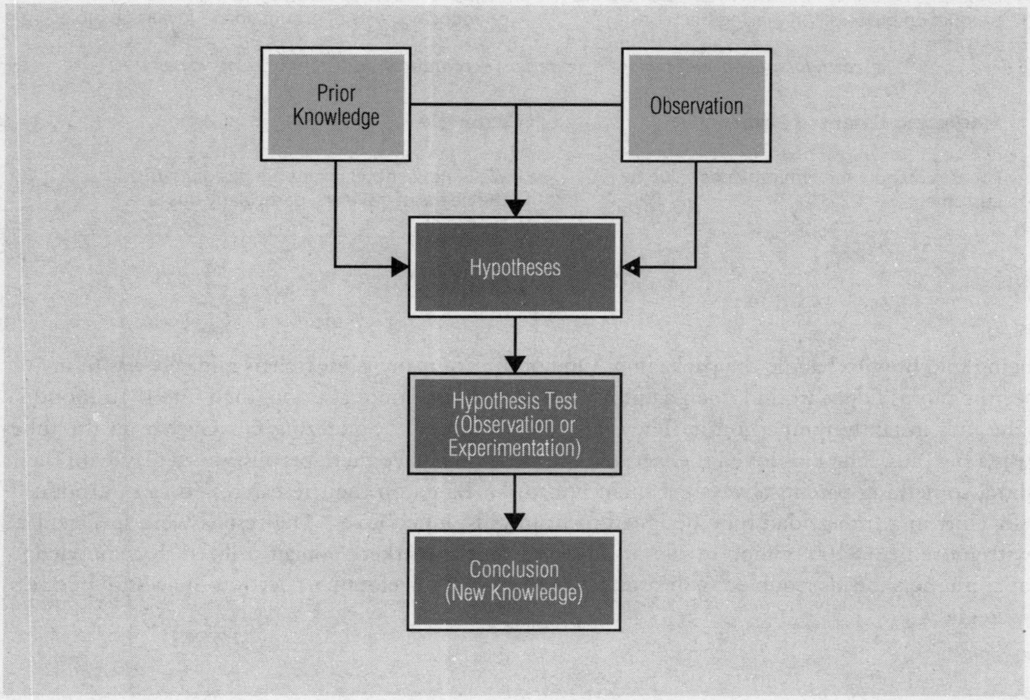

EXHIBIT 1.1
A Summary of the Scientific Method

Managerial Value of Business Research

product-oriented
Describes a firm that prioritizes decision making in a way that emphasizes technical superiority in the product.

production-oriented
Describes a firm that prioritizes efficiency and effectiveness of the production processes in making decisions.

marketing-oriented
Describes a firm in which all decisions are made with a conscious awareness of their effect on the customer.

In all of business strategy, there are only a few business orientations (see Exhibit 1.2). A firm can be **product-oriented**. A product-oriented firm prioritizes decision making in a way that emphasizes technical superiority in the product. Thus, research gathering information from technicians and experts in the field are very important in making critical decisions. A firm can be **production-oriented**. Production orientation means that the firm prioritizes efficiency and effectiveness of the production processes in making decisions. Here, research providing input from workers, engineers, finance, and accounting becomes important as the firm seeks to drive costs down. Production-oriented firms are usually very large firms manufacturing products in very large quantities. The third is **marketing-oriented**, which focuses more on how the firm provides value to customers than on the physical product or production process. With a marketing-oriented organization the majority of research focuses on the customer. Research addressing consumer desires, beliefs, and attitudes becomes essential.

We have argued that research facilitates effective management. For example, Yoplait Go-Gurt illustrates the benefit of business research. The company's consumer research about eating regular yogurt at school showed that moms and kids in their "tweens" wanted convenience and portability. Some brands, like Colombo Spoon in a Snap, offered the convenience of having a utensil as part of the packaging/delivery system. However, from what Yoplait learned about consumers, they thought kids would eat more yogurts if they could "lose the spoon" and eat yogurt anywhere, anytime. Moms and kids participating in a taste test were invited to sample different brand-on-the-go packaging shapes—long tubes, thin tubes, fat tubes, and other shapes—without

EXHIBIT 1.2
Business Orientations

Product-Oriented Firm	**Example**
Prioritizes decision making that emphasizes the physical product design, trendiness or technical superiority	The fashion industry makes clothes in styles and sizes that few can adopt.
Research focuses on technicians and experts in the field.	
Production-Oriented Firm	**Example**
Prioritizes efficiency and effectiveness of the production processes in making decisions	U.S. auto industry's assembly-line process is intent on reducing costs of production as low as possible.
Research focuses on line employees, engineers, accountants, and other efficiency experts.	
Marketing-Oriented Firm	**Example**
Focuses on how the firm provides value to customers	Well-known hotel chains are designed to address the needs of travelers, particularly business travelers.
Research focuses on customers.	

being told how to handle the packaging. One of the company's researchers said, "It was funny to see the moms fidget around, then daintily pour the product onto a spoon, then into their mouths. The kids instantly jumped on it. They knew what to do."[11] Squeezing Go-Gurt from the tube was a big plus. The kids loved the fact that the packaging gave them permission to play with their food, something parents always tell them not to do. Based on their research, Yoplait introduced Go-Gurt in a three-sided tube designed to fit in kids' lunchboxes. The results were spectacular, with more than $100 million in sales its first year on the market. Yoplait realized that knowledge of consumers' needs, coupled with product research and development, leads to successful business strategies.

As the Yoplait example shows, the prime managerial value of business research is that it provides information that improves the decision-making process. The decision-making process associated with the development and implementation of a business strategy involves four interrelated stages:

1. Identifying problems or opportunities
2. Diagnosing and assessing problems or opportunities
3. Selecting and implementing a course of action
4. Evaluating the course of action

Business research, by supplying managers with pertinent information, may play an important role by reducing managerial uncertainty in each of these stages.

Identifying Problems or Opportunities

Before any strategy can be developed, an organization must determine where it wants to go and how it will get there. Business research can help managers plan strategies by determining the nature of situations or by identifying the existence of problems or opportunities present in the organization. Business research may be used as a scanning activity to provide information about what is occurring within an organization or in its environment. The mere description of some social or economic activity may familiarize managers with organizational and environmental occurrences and help them understand a situation. Consider these two examples:

- The description of the dividend history of stocks in an industry may point to an attractive investment opportunity. Information supplied by business research may also indicate problems.
- Employee interviews undertaken to characterize the dimensions of an airline reservation clerk's job may reveal that reservation clerks emphasize competence in issuing tickets over courtesy and friendliness in customer contact.

Once business research indicates a problem or opportunity, managers may feel that the alternatives are clear enough to make a decision based on their experience or intuition. However, often they decide that more business research is needed to generate additional information for a better understanding of the situation.

Diagnosing and Assessing Problems or Opportunities

After an organization recognizes a problem or identifies a potential opportunity, business research can help clarify the situation. Managers need to gain insight about the underlying factors causing the situation. If there is a problem, they need to specify what happened and why. If an opportunity exists, they may need to explore, refine, and quantify the opportunity. If multiple opportunities exist, research may be conducted to set priorities.

Selecting and Implementing a Course of Action

After the alternative courses of action have been clearly identified, business research is often conducted to obtain specific information that will aid in evaluating the alternatives and in selecting the best course of action. For example, suppose Harley-Davidson is considering establishing a dealer network in either China or India. In this case, business research can be designed to gather the relevant information necessary to determine which, if either, course of action is best for the organization.

Opportunities may be evaluated through the use of various performance criteria. For example, estimates of market potential allow managers to evaluate the revenue that will be generated by each of the possible opportunities. A good forecast supplied by business researchers is among the most useful pieces of planning information a manager can have. Of course, complete accuracy in forecasting the future is not possible, because change is constantly occurring in the business environment. Nevertheless, objective information generated by business research to forecast environmental occurrences may be the foundation for selecting a particular course of action.

Even the best plan is likely to fail if it is not properly implemented. Business research may be conducted to indicate the specific tactics required to implement a course of action.

Evaluating the Course of Action

After a course of action has been implemented, business research may serve as a tool to tell managers whether or not planned activities were properly executed and if they accomplished what they were expected to accomplish. In other words, managers may use evaluation research to provide feedback for evaluation and control of strategies and tactics.

evaluation research
The formal, objective measurement and appraisal of the extent a given activity, project, or program has achieved its objectives

Evaluation research is the formal, objective measurement and appraisal of the extent a given activity, project, or program has achieved its objectives. In addition to measuring the extent to which completed programs achieved their objectives or whether continuing programs are presently performing as projected, evaluation research may provide information about the major factors influencing the observed performance levels.

In addition to business organizations, nonprofit organizations and governmental agencies frequently conduct evaluation research. Every year thousands of federal evaluation studies are undertaken to systematically assess the effects of public programs. For example, the General Accounting Office has been responsible for measuring outcomes of the Employment Opportunity Act, the Job Corps program, and Occupational and Safety and Health Administration (OSHA) programs.

performance-monitoring research
Refers to research that regularly, sometimes routinely, provides feedback for evaluation and control of business activity.

Performance-monitoring research is a specific type of evaluation research that regularly, perhaps routinely, provides feedback for the evaluation and control of recurring business activity. For example, most firms continuously monitor wholesale and retail activity to ensure early detection of sales declines and other anomalies. In the grocery and retail drug industries, sales research may use the Universal Product Code (UPC) for packages, together with computerized cash registers and electronic scanners at checkout counters, to provide valuable market-share information to store and brand managers interested in the retail sales volume of specific products.

United Airlines' Omnibus in-flight survey provides a good example of performance-monitoring research for quality management. United routinely selects sample flights and administers a questionnaire about in-flight service, food, and other aspects of air travel. The Omnibus survey is conducted quarterly to determine who is flying and for what reasons. It enables United to track demographic changes and to monitor customer ratings of its services on a continuing basis, allowing the airline to gather vast amounts of information at low cost. The information relating to customer reaction to services can be compared over time. For example, suppose United decided to change its menu for in-flight

Fun in the snow depends on weather trends, economic outlook, equipment, and clothing—all subjects for a business researcher.

RESEARCH SNAPSHOT

Harley-Davidson Goes Abroad

Before Harley-Davidson goes overseas, it must perform considerable research on that market. It may find that consumers in some countries, such as France or Italy, have a strong preference for more economical and practical motor bikes. There, people may prefer a Vespa Wasp to a Harley Hog! Other times, they may find that consumers have a favorable attitude toward Harley-Davidson and that it could even be a product viewed as very prestigious. Harley recently considered doing business in India based on trend analysis showing a booming economy. Favorable consumer opinion and a booming economy were insufficient to justify distributing Harleys in India. The problem? Luxury imports would be subject to very high duties which would make them cost-prohibitive to nearly all Indian consumers and India has strict emission rules for motor bikes. Thus, although research on the market was largely positive, Harley's research on the political operating environment eventually determined its decision. Even after considerable negotiation, India refused to budge on tariffs although they were willing to give on emission standards. Instead, Harley may direct its effort more toward the U.S. women's market for bikes. Research shows that motorcycle ownership among U.S. women has nearly doubled since 1990 to approximately 10 percent. Product research suggests that Harley may need to design smaller and sportier bikes to satisfy this market's desires. Perhaps these new products would also be easier to market in India. Research will tell.

Sources: "Harley Davidson Rules Out India Foray for Near Future," *Asia-Africa Intelligence Wire* (September 2, 2005); "Women Kick It into Gear," *Akron Beacon Journal* (May 22, 2005); "No Duty Cut on Harley Davidson Bikes, India to US," *The Financial Express* (February 24, 2008), www.financialexpress.com/news/No-duty-cut-on-Harley-Davidson-bikes-India-to-US/276635, accessed July 7, 2008.

meals. The results of the Omnibus survey might indicate that, shortly after the menu changed, the customers' rating of the airline's food declined. Such information about product quality would be extremely valuable, as it would allow management to quickly spot trends among passengers in other aspects of air travel, such as airport lounges, gate-line waits, or cabin cleanliness. Then managers could rapidly take action to remedy such problems.

TOTHEPOINT

The secret of success is to know something nobody else knows.

—Aristotle Onassis

When Is Business Research Needed?

The need to make intelligent, informed decisions ultimately motivates an organization to engage in business research. Not every decision requires research. Thus, when confronting a key decision, a manager must initially decide whether or not to conduct business research. The determination of the need for research centers on (1) time constraints, (2) the availability of data, (3) the nature of the decision to be made, and (4) the value of the research information in relation to costs.

Time Constraints

Systematic research takes time. In many instances, management believes that a decision must be made immediately, allowing no time for research. Decisions sometimes are made without adequate information or thorough understanding of the business situation. Although making decisions without researching a situation is not ideal, sometimes the urgency of a situation precludes the use of research. The urgency with which managers usually want to make decisions conflicts with researchers' desire for rigor in following the scientific method.

Availability of Data

Often managers already possess enough data, or information, to make sound decisions without additional research. When they lack adequate information, however, research must be considered. This means that data need to be collected from an appropriate source. If a potential source of data exists, managers will want to know how much it will cost to get the data.

RESEARCH SNAPSHOT

Business Class Success?

If you've ever checked the price of business-class airfare on a flight overseas, you were probably surprised at the price. A discounted round-trip coach ticket from Atlanta to Paris in peak season often costs just over one thousand dollars. That same business-class ticket would often cost between five and ten thousand-dollars! Typically, these flights take place in the larger passenger aircraft flown such as a Boeing 747 or a Boeing 777. A Boeing 777 can seat up to 450 passengers. However, by including three dozen business-class seats, the capacity drops to under 400 passengers.

Thus, it is easy to see that a great deal of research must assess both the product design (what service and product attributes make up a business-class experience) and pricing (in both coach and business class) to determine the best configuration of the aircraft. Research shows that business-class travelers prioritize the comfort of the seat and the ability to be able to lie flat during the flight, the quality of food, and convenience of boarding as attributes that make up the business-class experience.

In the past few years, a few start-up airlines have been trying to capitalize on this concept by starting "discount" business-class-only airlines. Maxjet estimated that consumers will exchange a little comfort for a reduction in price. They configured Boeing 737s (smaller than typical trans-ocean carriers) with 102 business-class seats that will not quite lie flat—and no coach seats! The result is a business-class- only airline with cross-Atlantic fares ranging between $1,600 and $3,800, less than half of traditional business-class fares. Taking the concept to an even smaller scale, Eos configured Boeing 757s into 48-seat all-business-class planes.

©AMIT BHARGAVA/BLOOMBERGNEWS/LANDOV

Both Maxjet and Eos received positive reviews, along with some criticisms. For example, Maxjet did not provide power outlets for laptops at their seats, considered by some to be a "fatal flaw" as far as business-class service is considered. Despite the apparent appeal, both Maxjet (December 2007) and Eos (April 2008) declared bankruptcy.

Could more effective business research have determined these were not feasible business ventures? Or, could Maxjet's "fatal flaw" of a lack of power outlets been identified? Sound business research may have enhanced the chance of success of these airlines.

Sources: McCarnety, Scott, "Start-Up Airlines Fly Only Business Class," *The Wall Street Journal* (September 20, 2005), D1; Pitock, Todd, "Getting There," *Forbes* 176 (September 2005), 30–32; Robertson, David, "Eos Bankruptcy Filing Signals End to Cheap Executive Travel," *The Times* (April 28, 2008).

© iStock

If the data cannot be obtained, or it cannot be obtained in a timely fashion, this particular research project should not be conducted. For example, many African nations have never conducted a population census. Organizations engaged in international business often find that data about business activity or population characteristics that are readily available in the United States are nonexistent or sparse in developing countries. Imagine the problems facing researchers who wish to investigate market potential in places like Uzbekistan, Macedonia, or Rwanda.

Nature of the Decision

The value of business research will depend on the nature of the managerial decision to be made. A routine tactical decision that does not require a substantial investment may not seem to warrant a substantial expenditure for research. For example, a computer company must update its operator's instruction manual when it makes minor product modifications. The research cost of determining the proper wording to use in the updated manual is likely to be too high for such a minor decision. The nature of the decision is not totally independent of the next issue to be considered: the benefits versus the costs of the research. In general, however, the more strategically or tactically important the decision, the more likely it is that research will be conducted.

Benefits versus Costs

Earlier we discussed some of the managerial benefits of business research. Of course, conducting research to obtain these benefits requires an expenditure of money. In any decision-making situation, managers must identify alternative courses of action and then weigh the value of each alternative against its cost. Business research can be thought of as an investment alternative. When deciding whether to make a decision without research or to postpone the decision in order to conduct research, managers should ask three questions:

1. Will the payoff or rate of return be worth the investment?

2. Will the information gained by business research improve the quality of the managerial decision enough to warrant the expenditure?
3. Is the proposed research expenditure the best use of the available funds?

For example, *TV-Cable Week* was not test-marketed before its launch. Although the magazine had articles and stories about television personalities and events, its main feature was program listings, channel by channel, showing the exact programs a particular subscriber could receive. To produce a custom magazine for each individual cable television system in the country required developing a costly computer system. Because that development necessitated a substantial expenditure, one that could not be scaled down by research, conducting research was judged to be an unwise investment. The value of the potential research information was not positive because its cost exceeded its benefits. Unfortunately, pricing and distribution problems became so compelling after the magazine was launched that the product was a failure. Nevertheless, without the luxury of hindsight, managers made a reasonable decision not to conduct research. They analyzed the cost of the information relative to the potential benefits of the information. Exhibit 1.3 outlines the criteria for determining when to conduct business research.

EXHIBIT 1.3 Determining When to Conduct Business Research

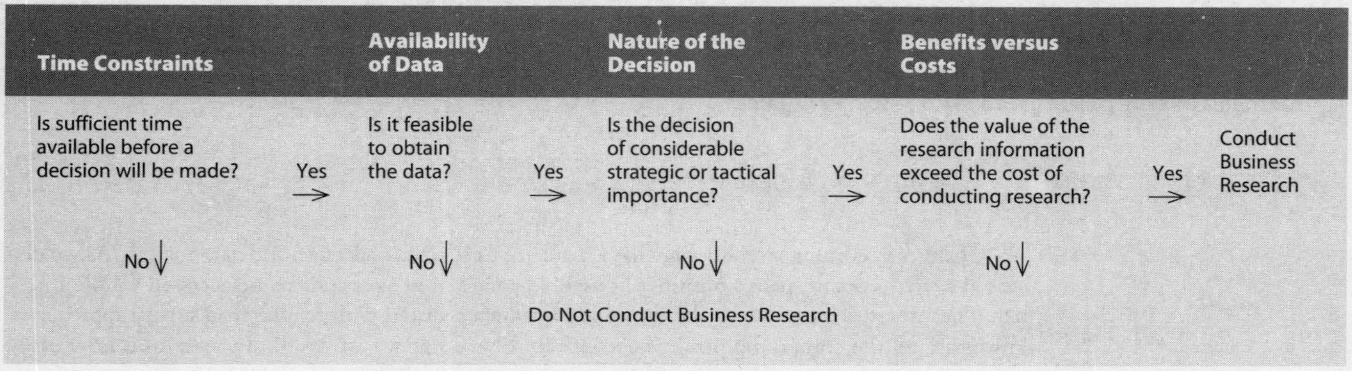

Business Research in the Twenty-First Century

Business research, like all business activity, continues to change. Changes in communication technologies and the trend toward an ever more global marketplace have played a large role in many of these changes.

Communication Technologies

Virtually everyone is "connected" today. Increasingly, many people are "connected" nearly all the time. Within the lifetime of the typical undergraduate college senior, the way information is exchanged, stored, and gathered has been revolutionized completely. Today, the amount of information formally contained in an entire library can rest easily in a single personal computer.

The speed with which information can be exchanged has also increased tremendously. During the 1970s, exchanging information overnight through a courier service from anywhere in the continental United States was heralded as a near miracle of modern technology. Today, we can exchange information from nearly anywhere in the world to nearly anywhere in the world almost instantly. Internet connections are now wireless, so one doesn't have to be tethered to a wall to access the World Wide Web. Our mobile phones and handheld data devices can be used not only to converse, but also as a means of communication that can even involve business research data. In many cases, technology also has made it possible to store or collect data for lower costs than in the past. Electronic communications are usually less costly than regular mail—and certainly less costly than a face-to-face interview—and cost about the same amount no matter how far away a respondent is from a researcher. Thus, the expressions "time is collapsing" and "distance is disappearing" capture the tremendous revolution in the speed and reach of our communication technologies.

RESEARCH SNAPSHOT

"Jacques" Daniels

Sales of U.S. distilled spirits have declined over the last 10 to 15 years as more Americans turn to wine or beer as their beverage of choice. As a result, companies like Bacardi and Brown-Forman, producers of Jack Daniels, have pursued business development strategies involving increased efforts to expand into international markets. The Brown-Forman budget for international ventures includes a significant allocation for research. By doing research before launching the product, Brown-Forman can learn product usage patterns within a particular culture. Some of the findings from this research indicate

1. Japanese consumers use Jack Daniels (JD) as a dinner beverage. A party of four or five consumers in a restaurant will order and drink a bottle of JD with their meal.
2. Australian consumers mostly consume distilled spirits in their homes. Also in contrast to Japanese consumers, Australians prefer to mix JD with soft drinks or other mixers. As a result of this research, JD launched a mixture called "Jack and Cola" sold in 12-ounce bottles all around Australia. The product has been very successful.
3. British distilled spirit consumers also like mixed drinks, but they usually partake in bars and restaurants.
4. In China and India, consumers more often chose counterfeit or "knock-offs" to save money. Thus, innovative research approaches have addressed questions related to the way the black market works and how they can better educate consumers about the differences between the real thing and the knock-offs.

The result is that Jack Daniels is now sold extensively, in various forms, and with different promotional campaigns, outside of the United States.

Sources: Swibel, Mathew, "How Distiller Brown-Forman Gets Rich by Exploiting the Greenback's Fall—and Pushing Its Brands Abroad," *Forbes* 175, no. 8 (2005), 152–155.

© iStock

Changes in computer technology have made for easier data collection and data analysis. As we discuss in a later chapter, many consumer household panels now exist and can be accessed via the Internet. Thus, there is less need for the time and expense associated with regular mail survey approaches. Furthermore, the computing power necessary to solve complicated statistical problems is now easily accessible. Again, as recently as the 1970s, such computer applications required expensive mainframe computers found only in very large corporations, major universities, and large governmental/military institutions. Researchers could expect to wait hours or even longer to get results from a statistical program involving 200 respondents. Today, even the most basic laptop computers can solve complicated statistical problems involving thousands of data points in practically a nanosecond.

Global Business Research

Like all business activities, business research has become increasingly global as more and more firms operate with few, if any, geographic boundaries. Some companies have extensive international research operations. Upjohn conducts research in 160 different countries. ACNielsen International, known for its television ratings, is the world's largest research company. Two-thirds of its business comes from outside the United States.[12] Starbucks can now be found in nearly every developed country on the earth. AFLAC offers its products on multiple continents. DuPont has a significant presence in all regions of the world.

Companies that conduct business in foreign countries must understand the nature of those particular markets and judge whether they require customized business strategies. For example, although the fifteen nations of the European Union share a single formal market, research shows that Europeans do not share identical tastes for many consumer products. Business researchers have found no such thing as a "typical" European consumer; language, religion, climate, and centuries of tradition divide the nations of the European Union. Scantel Research, a British firm that advises companies on color preferences, found inexplicable differences in Europeans' preferences in medicines. The French prefer to pop purple pills, but the English and Dutch favor white ones. Consumers in all three countries dislike bright red capsules, which are big sellers in the United States. This example illustrates that companies that do business in Europe must research throughout Europe to adapt to local customs and buying habits.[13]

Even companies that produce brands that are icons in their own country are now doing research internationally. The Research Snapshot titled "Jacques Daniels" discusses how Brown-

Forman, the parent company of Jack Daniels (the classic American "sour mash" or Bourbon whiskey), is now interviewing consumers in the far corners of the world.[14] The internationalization of research places greater demands on business researchers and heightens the need for research tools that allow us to **cross-validate** research results, meaning that the empirical findings from one culture also exist and behave similarly in another culture. The development and application of these international research tools are an important topic in basic business research.[15]

cross-validate
To verify that the empirical findings from one culture also exist and behave similarly in another culture.

Overview

The business research process is often presented as a linear, sequential process, with one specific step following another. In reality, this is not the case. For example, the time spent on each step varies, overlap between steps is common, some stages may be omitted, occasionally we need to backtrack, and the order sometimes changes. Nonetheless, some structure for the research process is necessary.

The book is organized to provide this structure, both within each chapter and in the order of the chapters. Each chapter begins with a set of specific learning objectives. Each chapter then opens with a Chapter Vignette—a glimpse of a business research situation that provides a basis of reference for that chapter. Each chapter also contains multiple Research Snapshots—specific business research scenarios that illustrate key points. Finally, each chapter concludes with a review of the learning objectives.

The book is organized into seven parts. Part 1 is the Introduction, which includes this chapter and four others. This chapter provided an introduction to business research. The next three chapters of the book give students a fuller understanding of the business research environment. Part 2, Beginning Stages of the Research Process, provides the foundation for business research, discussing problem definition and qualitative and secondary research. The third section of the book, Research Designs for Collecting Primary Data, introduces survey research, discusses observation as a research technique, and provides an overview of experimental research. Measurement Concepts, Part 4 of the book, discusses the measurement of research constructs and questionnaire design. Part 5, Sampling and Fieldwork, describes the process involved in selecting a research sample and collecting data. Part 6, Data Analysis and Presentation, explains the various approaches to analyzing the data and describes methods of presentation. The book concludes with Part 7, Comprehensive Cases with Computerized Databases, which will be integrated throughout the first six parts. Exhibit 1.4 provides an overview of the book and the research process.

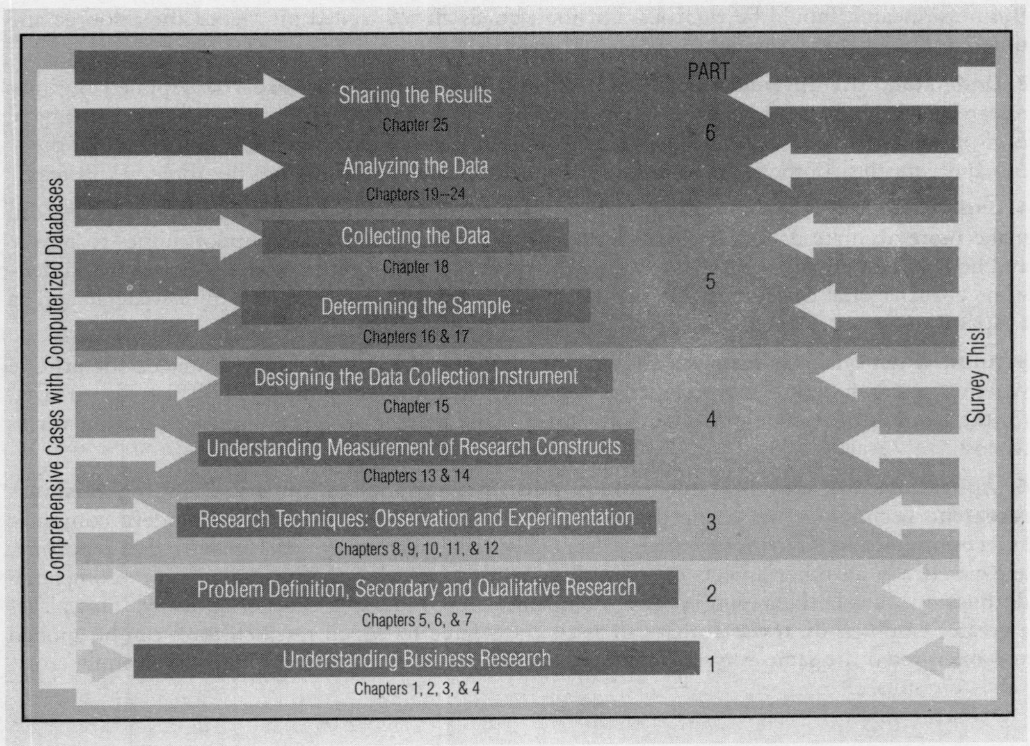

EXHIBIT 1.4
An Overview of Business Research

TIPS OF THE TRADE

- Be sure to fully understand the differing roles of exploratory, descriptive, and causal research.
  - Exploratory research provides new insights—the domain of discovery in philosophy of science terms—and often sets the groundwork for further investigation.
  - Descriptive research describes the characteristics of objects, people, or organizations. Much of business information is based on descriptive research.
  - Causal research is the only research that establishes cause and effect relationships. Most commonly, causal research takes the form of experiments such as test markets.
- A major flaw in business research is to not give due diligence to exploratory research (especially secondary data and qualitative research). Instead, researchers often move too quickly to collecting descriptive data.
- A second, and related, flaw in business research is to fail to carefully define the research objectives.

© iStock

Summary

There were six learning objectives in this chapter. After reading the chapter, the student should be competent in each area described by a learning objective.

1. Understand how research contributes to business success. While many business decisions are made "by the seat of the pants" or based on a manager's intuition, this type of decision making carries with it a large amount of risk. By first researching an issue and gathering the appropriate information (from employees, customers, competitors, and the market) managers can make a more informed decision. The result is less risky decision making.

Research is the intelligence-gathering function in business. The intelligence includes information about customers, competitors, economic trends, employees, and other factors that affect business success. This intelligence assists in decisions ranging from long-range planning to near-term tactical decisions.

2. Know how to define business research. Business research is the application of the scientific method in searching for truth about business phenomena. The research must be conducted systematically, not haphazardly. It must be objective to avoid the distorting effects of personal bias. Business research should be rigorous, but the rigor is always traded off against the resource and time constraints that go with a particular business decision.

3. Understand the difference between basic and applied business research. Applied business research seeks to facilitate managerial decision making. It is directed toward a specific managerial decision in a particular organization. Basic or pure research seeks to increase knowledge of theories and concepts. Both are important, but applied research is more often the topic in this text.

4. Understand how research activities can be used to address business decisions. Businesses can make more accurate decisions about dealing with problems and/or the opportunities to pursue and how to best pursue them. The chapter provides examples of studies involving several dimensions of managerial decision making. Thus, business research is useful both in a strategic and in a tactical sense.

5. Know when business research should and should not be conducted. Managers determine whether research should be conducted based on (1) time constraints, (2) availability of data, (3) the nature of the decision to be made, and (4) the benefit of the research information versus its cost.

6. Appreciate the way that technology and internationalization are changing business research. Technology has changed almost every aspect of business research. Modern computer and communications technology makes data collection, study design, data analysis, data reporting, and practically all other aspects of research easier and better. Furthermore, as more companies do business outside their own borders, companies are conducting research globally. This places a greater emphasis on research that can assess the degree to which research tools can be applied and interpreted the same way in different cultures. Thus, research techniques often must cross-validate results.

Key Terms and Concepts

Questions for Review and Critical Thinking

1. An automobile manufacturer is conducting research in an attempt to predict the type of car design consumers will desire in the year 2020. Is this basic or applied research? Explain.
2. Define *business research* and describe its task.
3. Comment on the following statements:
   a. Managers are paid to take chances with decisions. Researchers are paid to reduce the risk of making those decisions.
   b. A business strategy can be no better than the information on which it is formulated.
   c. The purpose of research is to solve business problems.
4. Which of the following organizations are likely to use business research? Why? How?
   a. Manufacturer of breakfast cereals
   b. Manufacturer of nuts, bolts, and other fasteners
   c. The Federal Trade Commission
   d. A hospital
   e. A company that publishes business textbooks
5. List the conditions that help a researcher decide when research should or should not be conducted.
6. Name some products that logically might have been developed with the help of business research.
7. **'NET** How do you believe the Internet has facilitated research? Try to use the Internet to find the total annual sales for Starbucks, for AFLAC, and for DuPont.
8. Is it possible to make sound managerial decisions without business research? What advantages does research offer to the decision maker over seat-of-the-pants decision making?
9. What types of tools does the researcher use more given the ever increasing internationalization of business?
10. Define a marketing orientation and a product orientation. Under which strategic orientation is there a greater need for business research?
11. How have technology and internationalization affected business research?

Research Activities

1. **'NET** Suppose you owned a jewelry store in Denton, Texas. You are considering opening a second store just like your current store. You are undecided on whether to locate the new store in another location in Denton, Texas, or in Birmingham, Alabama. Why would you decide to have some research done before making the decision? Should the research be conducted? Go to **http://www.census.gov**. Do you think any of this information would be useful in the research?
2. **'NET** Find recent examples of news articles involving the use of business research in making decisions about different aspects of business.
3. **'NET** Find an article illustrating an example of an applied research study involving some aspect of technology. How does it differ from a basic research study also focusing on a similar aspect of technology?

CHAPTER 2
INFORMATION SYSTEMS AND KNOWLEDGE MANAGEMENT

LEARNING OUTCOMES

After studying this chapter, you should be able to

1. Know and distinguish the concepts of data, information, and intelligence
2. Understand the four characteristics that describe data
3. Know the purpose of research in assisting business operations
4. Know what a decision support system is and does
5. Recognize the major categories of databases

Chapter Vignette: Data for Doughnuts!

Who makes the best doughnut in America? Which doughnut firm has the best business plan? These are two different questions to some extent. There is more to selling doughnuts than making a great doughnut.

© AP PHOTO

Krispy Kreme is the market-share leader among U.S. doughnut firms, operating hundreds of stores in practically every state in the nation; it also has operations in 15 foreign countries, with stores scheduled to open soon in China!

Although consumers may first think of the neon-laced doughnut shops when they think of Krispy Kreme, the fact is that the bulk of Krispy Kreme's revenue is generated from doughnut sales outside of its own stores. Krispy Kremes can be found in thousands of convenience and grocery stores and at practically every super store in the United States. Thus, there is a great deal of data to keep track of in terms of where doughnuts are delivered and where they are sold. Collecting these data manually would involve thousands of phone calls each time the data were needed. Clearly, this would be a labor intensive process, particularly considering that the decisions made based on these data include many day-to-day operational decisions.

While Krispy Kreme could develop systems and hardware that could track all of these data in real time, it opted to outsource this effort to a company that specializes in tracking, recording, and storing retail sales data. For Krispy Kreme, this proves more cost effective than purchasing and maintaining the technology to complete this task themselves. The data feed into software systems known as decision support systems, which allow Krispy Kreme to adjust production schedules to meet demand, adjust pricing, manage billing processes, and even track inventory-shrinkage trends. Thus, if a store's employees or customers are indulging in the Krispy Kremes without purchasing them, the system lets the executives at Krispy Kreme know. Furthermore, when Krispy Kreme needs specific data, the information provider may very well already have the data available in a data warehouse. Thus, the data provide knowledge that greatly assists Krispy Kreme business managers in day-to-day operational matters.[1]

Introduction

Krispy Kreme's use of an outside firm to manage its information illustrates the sometimes sophisticated way in which modern businesses integrate data into their decision processes. Many of the decisions that used to be made with guesswork are now supplemented with "intelligence" either automatically delivered by swome computer software or drawn from a data warehouse.

Doughnut companies certainly aren't alone in this effort. Imagine all the information that passes through a single Home Depot store each day. Every customer transaction, every empty shelf, every employee's work schedule—right down to the schedule to clean restrooms—creates potentially valuable information that can be used by researchers and decision makers. Considering that Home Depot operates thousands of stores, obviously, Home Depot needs a data depot!

Like Krispy Kreme, Home Depot has outsourced the storage and management of data inventories. In this case, IBM manages the data, allowing it to be integrated into management strategy and tactics. Data from cash registers, time clocks, shelf counts, and much more are all compiled, analyzed, and either fed automatically into management systems or supplied in the form of a research report. In a way, this type of business research is automatic![2]

This chapter discusses knowledge management and the role decision support systems play in helping firms make informed business decisions. The chapter also introduces the concept of global information systems and sources of data that exist beyond the walls of any business. Modern data technology allows businesses to more easily integrate research into strategy and operations.

Information, Data, and Intelligence

In everyday language, terms like *information* and *data* are often used interchangeably. Researchers use these terms in specific ways that emphasize how useful each can be. **Data** are simply facts or recorded measures of certain phenomena (things or events). **Information** is data formatted (structured) to support decision making or define the relationship between two facts. **Business intelligence** is the subset of data and information that actually has some explanatory power enabling effective managerial decisions to be made. So, there is more data than information, and more information than intelligence.

Think again about the thousands upon thousands of unsummarized facts recorded by Home Depot each day. Each time a product is scanned at checkout, that fact is recorded and becomes data. Each customer's transactions are simultaneously entered into the store's computerized inventory system. The inventory system structures the data in such a way that a stocking report can be generated and orders for that store can be placed. Thus, the automated inventory system turns data into information. Further, the information from each store's sales and inventory records may be harvested by analysts. The analysts may analyze the trends and prepare reports that help Home Depot buyers get the right products into each store or to even suggest places for new Home Depot locations. Thus, the analyst has now completed the transformation of data into intelligence. Exhibit 2.1 helps to illustrate the distinction between data, information, and intelligence.

data
Facts or recorded measures of certain phenomena (things).

information
Data formatted (structured) to support decision making or define the relationship between two facts.

business intelligence
The subset of data and information that actually has some explanatory power enabling effective decisions to be made.

EXHIBIT 2.1
Data, Information, Intelligence

- Products purchased are recorded by the scanner forming data.

- Inventory systems use the data to create information.
- The information tells managers what items need to be stocked.
- The information also generates and can even place orders for more products to be trucked to the store.

- Analysts analyze the data statistically and write research reports addressing important questions such as
  - What types of trends exist in customer purchases, and are there regional differences?
  - Where should new stores be located?

The Characteristics of Valuable Information

Not all data are valuable to decision makers. Useful data become information and help a business manager make decisions. Useful data can also become intelligence. Four characteristics help determine how useful data may be: relevance, quality, timeliness, and completeness.

Relevance

relevance
The characteristics of data reflecting how pertinent these particular facts are to the situation at hand.

Relevance is the characteristics of data reflecting how pertinent these particular facts are to the situation at hand. Put another way, the facts are logically connected to the situation. Unfortunately, irrelevant data and information often creep into decision making. One particularly useful way to distinguish relevance from irrelevance is to think about how things change. Relevant data are facts about things that can be changed, and if they are changed, it will materially alter the situation. So, this simple question becomes important:

Will a change in the data coincide with a change in some important outcome?

American consumers' dietary trends are relevant to Krispy Kreme. If American diets become more health-conscious, then the sales of doughnuts can be affected. This may lead Krispy Kreme to rethink its product offering. However, information on French consumers' wine preferences is probably irrelevant since it is difficult to think how a change in French wine preferences will affect U.S. doughnut preferences.

Quality

Data quality is the degree to which data represent the true situation. High-quality data are accurate, valid, and reliable, issues we discuss in detail in later chapters. High-quality data represent reality faithfully. If a consumer were to replace the product UPC from one drill at Home Depot with one from a different drill, not only would the consumer be acting unethically, but it would also mean that the data collected at the checkout counter would be inaccurate. Therefore, to the extent that the cash register is not actually recording the products that consumers take out of the stores, its quality is lowered. Sometimes, researchers will try to obtain the same data from multiple data sources as one check on its quality.[3] Data quality is a critical issue in business research, and it will be discussed throughout this text.

data quality
The degree to which data represent the true situation.

Timeliness

Business is a dynamic field in which out-of-date information can lead to poor decisions. Business information must be timely—that is, provided at the right time. Computerized information systems can record events and dispense relevant information soon after the event. A great deal of business information becomes available almost at the moment that a transaction occurs. **Timeliness** means that the data are current enough to still be relevant.

timeliness
Means that the data are current enough to still be relevant.

Computer technology has redefined standards for timely information. For example, if a business executive at Home Depot wishes to know the sales volume of any store worldwide, detailed information about any of thousands of products can be instantly determined. At Home Depot, the point-of-sale checkout system uses UPC scanners and satellite communications to link individual stores to the headquarters' computer system, from which managers can retrieve and analyze up-to-the-minute sales data on all merchandise in each store.

Completeness

Information completeness refers to having the right amount of information. Managers must have sufficient information about all aspects of their decisions. For example, a company considering establishing a production facility in Eastern Europe may plan to analyze four former Soviet-bloc countries. Population statistics, GDP, and information on inflation rates may be available on all four countries. However, information about unemployment levels may be available for only three of the countries. If information about unemployment or other characteristics cannot be obtained, the information is incomplete. Often incomplete information leads decision makers to conduct their own business research.

information completeness
Having the right amount of information.

Knowledge Management

Who has the best pizza in town? The answer to this question requires knowledge. Indeed, you, as a consumer, have stored knowledge about many products. You know the best restaurants, best theaters, best bars, and so forth. All of this knowledge helps you make decisions as a consumer. Much of it is based on personal research involving product trials or searches for information. From an individual's perspective, knowledge is simply what you have stored in memory. It helps you make decisions about a variety of things in your life.

Organizations can use knowledge in a similar way. Knowledge is accumulated not just from a single individual, however, but from many sources. Financial managers, human resource managers,

RESEARCH SNAPSHOT

RFID Technology Gets Cheaper—Business Knowledge Grows

Radio frequency identification (RFID) tags have been used by large organizations for several years now. The U.S. military makes great use of RFIDs in tracking the whereabouts of virtually all kinds of products both big and small. Logistics officers can instantly track the whereabouts of Humvees and MREs (Meals Ready to Eat). Information from the tag is transmitted to computer servers and then directly into a GTN (Global Tracking Network). Equipment and supplies can then be ordered and dispatched to needed locations with a minimal of human contact. Product consumption (ammunition, food, water, computer printers, and so forth) can also be tracked in real time. The Marines can know in real time if personnel in a desert use more food and water than personnel in a jungle.

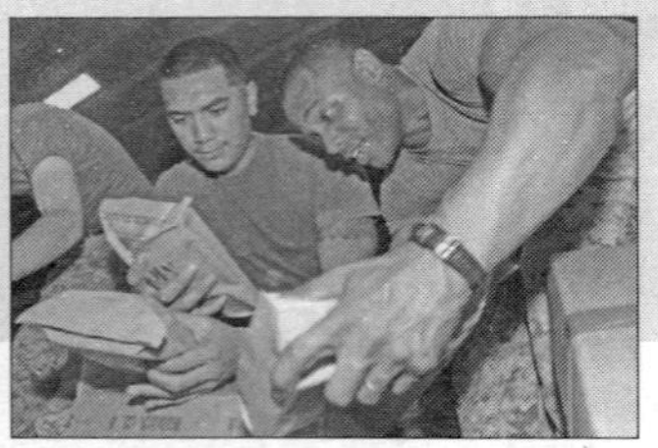

COURTESY OF DIVISION OF PUBLIC SERVICE, USMC, DEPT. OF DEFENSE, USA

Wal-Mart is pushing suppliers to adopt the technology. Not only can Wal-Mart use them in logistical operations, but the potential exists to "go into" consumers' homes and track how much and the way consumers actually consume products. Potentially, decision support systems (DSS) could tie ordering to customer consumption. However, the costs of RFIDs make it impractical for many suppliers.

Alien Technology Corporation recently announced a drop in the price of RFID tags. Now, when a company orders a million or more, the unit cost for an RFID is 12.9¢. Although this is a "basic" RFID tag, it still can store 96 bits of information. Analysts predict that the price of RFID tags will continue to drop. By 2008, the cost may drop to about 5¢, at which point the use of RFID technology in business research and operations should soar.

Sources: Clark, Don, "Alien Cuts Radio ID Tag Price to Spur Adoption by Retailers," *The Wall Street Journal* (September 12, 2005), D4; Fergueson, R. B., "Marines Deploy RFID," *e-Week* 21 (November 15, 2004), 37.

© iStock

sales managers, customer reports, economic forecasts, and custom-ordered research all contribute to an organization's knowledge base. All of this *data* forms the organization's memory. From a company's perspective, **knowledge** is a blend of previous experience, insight, and data that forms organizational memory. It provides a framework that can be thoughtfully applied when assessing a business problem. Business researchers and decision makers use this knowledge to help create solutions to strategic and tactical problems. Thus, knowledge is a key resource and a potential competitive advantage.[4]

knowledge
A blend of previous experience, insight, and data that forms organizational memory.

Knowledge management is the process of creating an inclusive, comprehensive, easily accessible organizational memory, which can be called the organization's *intellectual capital*.[5] The purpose of knowledge management is to organize the intellectual capital of an organization in a formally structured way for easy use. Knowledge is presented in a way that helps managers comprehend and act on that information and make better decisions in all areas of business. Knowledge management systems are particularly useful in making data available across the functional areas of the firm. Thus, marketing, management, and financial knowledge can be integrated. Recent research demonstrates how knowledge management systems are particularly useful in new product development and introduction.[6]

knowledge management
The process of creating an inclusive, comprehensive, easily accessible organizational memory, which is often called the organization's *intellectual capital*.

The firm's sales force plays a particularly useful role in the knowledge management process. Salespeople are in a key position to have a lot of knowledge about customers and the firm's capabilities. Thus, they are tools both for accumulating knowledge and for turning it into useful information.[7] Market-oriented organizations generally provide both formal and informal methods through which the knowledge gained by salespeople can be entered into a data warehouse to assist all decision makers, not just the sales force.

global information system
An organized collection of computer hardware, software, data, and personnel designed to capture, store, update, manipulate, analyze, and immediately display information about worldwide business activity.

Global Information Systems

Increased global competition and technological advances in interactive media have given rise to global information systems. A **global information system** is an organized collection of computer hardware, software, data, and personnel designed to capture, store, update, manipulate, analyze, and immediately display information about worldwide business activities. A global information system is a tool for providing past, present, and projected information on internal operations and external activity. Using satellite communications, high-speed microcomputers, electronic data interchanges, fiber optics, data storage devices, and other technological advances in interactive media, global information systems are changing the nature of business.

Consider a simple example. At any moment, United Parcel Service (UPS) can track the status of any shipment around the world. UPS drivers use handheld electronic clipboards called delivery information acquisition devices (DIADs) to record appropriate data about each pickup or delivery. The data are then entered into the company's main computer for record-keeping and analysis. A satellite telecommunications system allows UPS to track any shipment for a customer.

RFID stands for radio frequency identification. It is a new technology that places a tiny chip, which can be woven onto a fabric, onto virtually any product, allowing it to be tracked anywhere in the world. This can provide great insight into the different distribution channels around the world and, potentially, to the different ways consumers acquire and use products. The U.S. military uses RFID technology to assist in its logistics, and Wal-Mart is one of the leading proponents of the technology as it can greatly assist in its global information system.[8]

With so much diverse information available in a global information system, organizations have found it necessary to determine what data, information, and knowledge are most useful to particular business units.

Decision Support Systems

Business research can be described in many ways. One way is to categorize research based on the four possible functions it serves in business:

1. Foundational—answers basic questions. What business should we be in?
2. Testing—addresses things like new product concepts or promotional ideas. How effective will they be?
3. Issues—examines how specific issues impact the firm. How does organizational structure impact employee job satisfaction and turnover?
4. Performance—monitors specific metrics including financial statistics like profitability and delivery times. They are critical in real-time management and in "what-if" types of analyses examining the potential impact of a change in policy.

Of these, it is the performance category that is of most interest to decision support systems. The metrics that are monitored can be fed into automated decision-making systems, or they can trigger reports that are delivered to managers. These form the basis of a decision support system and best typify the way business research assists managers with day-to-day operational decisions.

A **decision support system (DSS)** is a system that helps decision makers confront problems through direct interaction with computerized databases and analytical software programs. The purpose of a decision support system is to store data and transform them into organized information that is easily accessible to managers. Doing so saves managers countless hours so that decisions that might take days or even weeks otherwise can be made in minutes using a DSS.

decision support system (DSS)
A computer-based system that helps decision makers confront problems through direct interaction with databases and analytical software programs.

Modern decision support systems greatly facilitate **customer relationship management (CRM)**. A CRM system is the part of the DSS that addresses exchanges between the firm and its customers. It brings together information about customers including sales data, market trends, marketing promotions and the way consumers respond to them, customer preferences, and more. A CRM system describes customer relationships in sufficient detail so that financial directors, marketing managers, salespeople, customer service representatives, and perhaps the customers themselves can access information directly, match customer needs with satisfying product offerings, remind customers of service requirements, and know what other products a customer has purchased.

customer relationship management (CRM)
Part of the DSS that addresses exchanges between the firm and its customers.

Casinos track regular customers' behavior via "players' cards" that are swiped each time a consumer conducts a transaction. This information is fed automatically into a CRM system that creates tailor-made promotional packages. The promotion may be unique to a specific customer's preferences as tracked by their own pattern of behavior. You may notice when visiting certain Web sites that they seem to be able to predict your behavior. The Research Snapshot titled "Are Businesses Clairvoyant?" tells how a CRM may be behind this clairvoyance.

RESEARCH SNAPSHOT

Are Businesses Clairvoyant?

A business traveler checks into a Wyndham hotel and finds his favorite type of pillow, favorite snacks, and a one of his favorite types of wine waiting upon arrival. Another customer daydreams of a recent golf vacation to Hawaii and wishes she could do it again. Later that day, an e-mail from Travelocity arrives with a great package deal to visit the same resort. Yet another consumer visits Barnesandnoble.com and a pop-up displays a new novel by his favorite author. Using a system called *active data warehousing,* the companies integrate data with research results that allow them to predict consumer preferences and even cyclical usage patterns quite accurately. Modern technology gives these firms a big advantage in the marketplace. Firms that don't adapt the technology may have a much harder time serving their customers. The latest technologies even provide ways for customers to voluntarily enter data or block certain data from being transmitted to the companies they do business with.

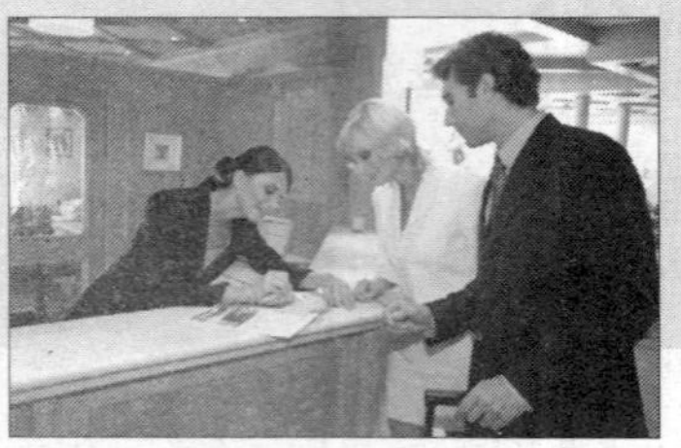

Sources: Schwarz, E., "Data Warehouses Get Active," *Infoworld* (December 8, 2003), 12; Watson, Richard T., "I Am My Own Database," *Harvard Business Review* 82 (November 2004), 18–19.

Exhibit 2.2 provides a basic illustration of a decision support system. Raw, unsummarized data are input to the DSS. Data collected in business research projects are a major source of this input, but the data may be purchased or collected by accountants, financial officers, sales managers, production managers, or company employees other than business researchers. Effective businesses spend a great deal of time and effort collecting information for input into the decision support system. Useful information is the output of a DSS. A decision support system requires both databases and software. For firms operating across national borders, the DSS becomes part of its global information system.

EXHIBIT 2.2
Decision Support System

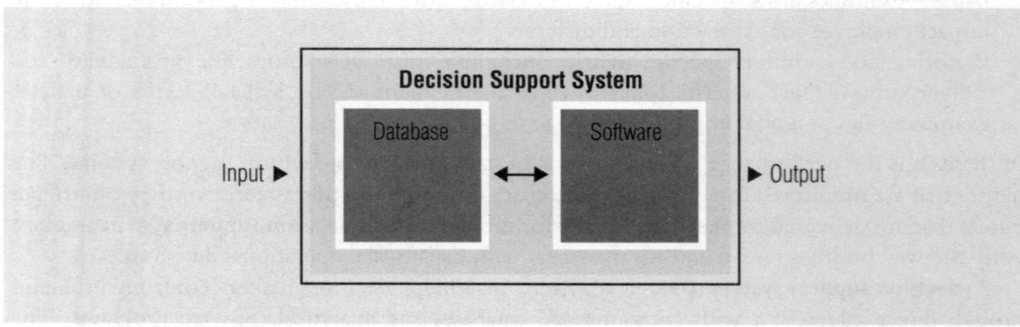

Databases and Data Warehousing

database
A collection of raw data arranged logically and organized in a form that can be stored and processed by a computer.

data warehousing
The process allowing important day-to-day operational data to be stored and organized for simplified access.

data warehouse
The multitiered computer storehouse of current and historical data.

A **database** is a collection of raw data arranged logically and organized in a form that can be stored and processed by a computer. A customer mailing list is one type of database. Population characteristics may be recorded by state, county, and city in another database. Production figures and costs can come from internal company records. Modern computer technology makes both the storage and retrieval of this information easy and convenient. Twenty years ago, the population data needed to do a retail site analysis may have required days, possibly weeks, in a library. Today, the information is just a few clicks away.

Data warehousing is the process allowing important day-to-day operational data to be stored and organized for simplified access. More specifically, a **data warehouse** is the multitiered computer storehouse of current and historical data. Data warehouse management requires that the detailed data from operational systems be extracted, transformed, placed into logical partitions (for example, daily data, weekly data, etc.), and stored in a consistent manner. Organizations with data warehouses may integrate databases from both inside and outside the company. Managing a data warehouse effectively requires considerable computing power and expertise. As a result, data warehouse companies exist that provide this service for companies in return for a fee.[9] Data warehousing allows for sophisticated analysis, such as data mining, discussed more in Chapter 8.

Input Management

How does data end up in a data warehouse where it can be used by a decision support system? In other words, how is the input managed? Input includes all the numerical, text, voice, and image data that enter the DSS. Systematic accumulation of pertinent, timely, and accurate data is essential to the success of a decision support system.

DSS managers, systems analysts, and programmers are responsible for the decision support system as a whole, but many functions within an organization provide input data. Business researchers, accountants, corporate librarians, personnel directors, salespeople, production managers, and many others within the organization help to collect data and provide input for the DSS. Input data can also come from external sources.

Exhibit 2.3 shows five major sources of data input: internal records, proprietary business research, salesperson input, behavioral tracking, and outside vendors and external distributors of data. Each source can provide valuable input.

INTERNAL RECORDS

Internal records, such as accounting reports of production costs and sales figures, provide considerable data that may become useful information for managers. An effective data collection system establishes orderly procedures to ensure that data about costs, shipments, inventory, sales, and other aspects of regular operations are routinely collected and entered into the computer.

PROPRIETARY BUSINESS RESEARCH

Business research has already been defined as a broad set of procedures and methods. To clarify the DSS concept, consider a narrower view of business research. **Proprietary business research** emphasizes the company's gathering of new data. Few proprietary research procedures and methods are conducted regularly or continuously. Instead, research projects conducted to study specific company problems generate data; this is proprietary business research. Providing managers with nonroutine data that otherwise would not be available is a major function of proprietary business research. Earlier, we discussed four categories of research. Proprietary research often involves either the testing and/or issues types of research.

proprietary business research
The gathering of new data to investigate specific problems.

SALESPERSON INPUT

Salespeople are typically a business's boundary spanners, the link between the organization and the external environments. Since they are in touch with these outside entities, they commonly provide essential business data. Sales representatives' reports frequently alert managers to changes in competitors' prices and new product offerings. It also may involve the types of complaints salespeople are hearing from customers. As trends become evident, this data may become business intelligence, leading to a change in product design or service delivery.

BEHAVIORAL TRACKING

Modern technology provides new ways of tracking human behavior. Global positioning satellite (GPS) systems allow management to track the whereabouts of delivery personnel at all times. This is the same system that provides directions through an automobile's navigation system. For example, if your delivery person takes a quick break for nine holes of golf at Weaver Ridge or decides to stop at Gorman's Pub for a couple of beers mid-afternoon, management can spot these as deviations from the appropriate delivery route. Thus, it can help track which employees are doing their jobs well.

EXHIBIT 2.3 **Six Major Sources of Input for Decision Support Systems**

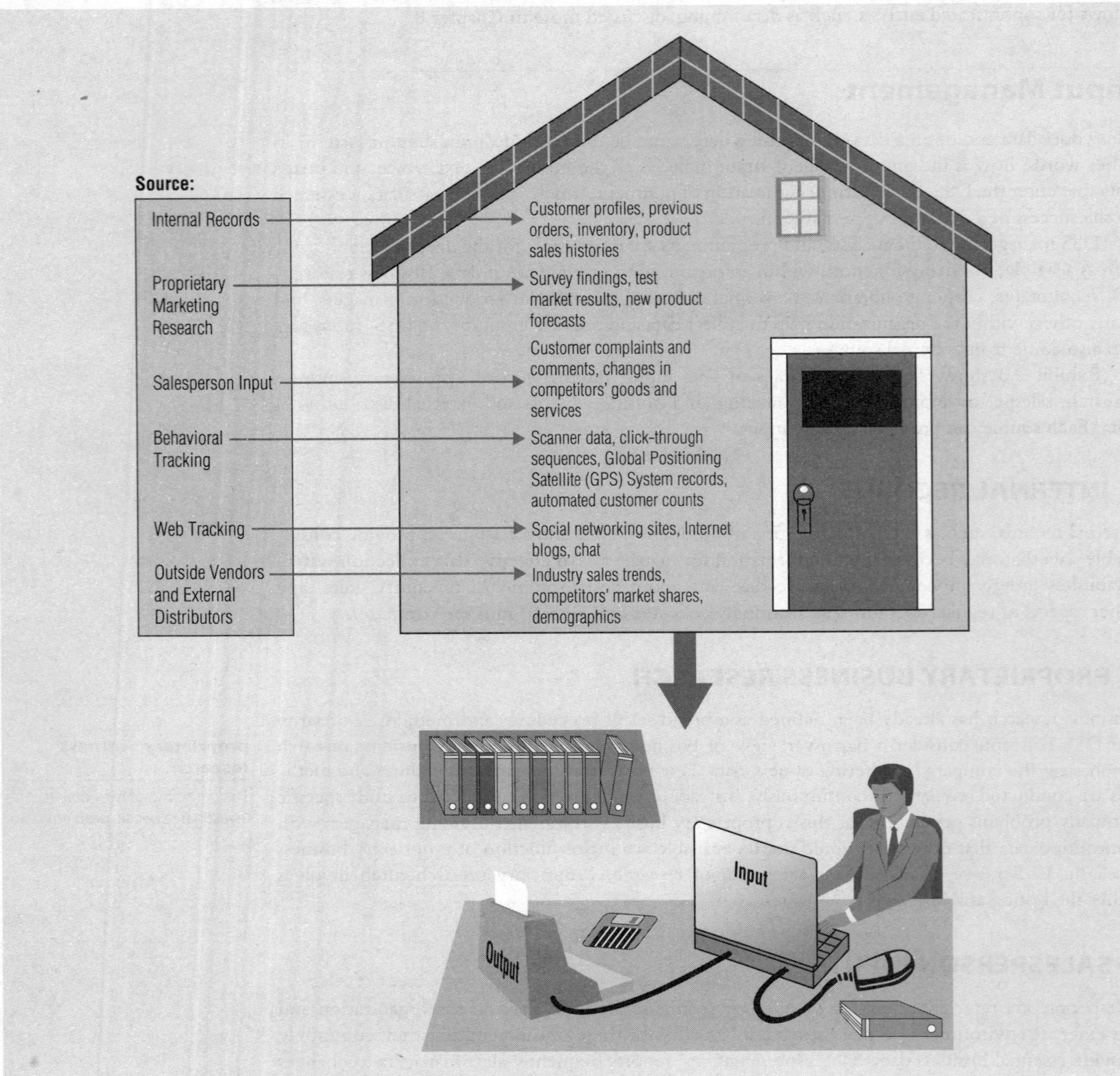

Technology also allows firms to track actual customer behavior. While it's true that GPS tracking data of customers is also sometimes possible, as the photograph suggests, the Internet also greatly facilitates customer behavior tracking. For instance, Google tracks the "click-through" sequence of customers. Therefore, if a customer is searching for information on refrigerators, and then goes to BestBuy.com, Google can track this behavior and use the information to let Best Buy know how important it is to advertise on Google and even automate pricing for advertisers.[10]

Purchase behavior can also be tracked at the point of sale. **Scanner data** refers to the accumulated records resulting from point-of-sale data recordings. In other words, each time products are scanned at a checkout counter, the information can be stored. The term *single-source* data refers to a system's ability to gather several types of interrelated data, such as type of purchase, use of a sales promotion, or advertising frequency data, from a single source in a format that will facilitate integration, comparison, and analysis.

scanner data
The accumulated records resulting from point of sale data recordings.

Staying Home at Home Depot

The DSS of any organization is no better than the quality of the data input to its data warehouse. How can firms make sure that the input remains relevant and retains a "high-touch" component in a "high-tech" world?

Home Depot has always tried to make sure its executives "stay in touch" by requiring them to spend a substantial amount of time on the sales floor of a Home Depot store, which means that one of the folks in the bright orange apron helping you choose the right flush valve may well be a six-figure executive. When Jack VanWoerkom was named new executive vice president, general counsel, and corporate secretary in 2007, his first tasks were not at the corporate headquarters in Atlanta, but rather working in the aisles of a store. Therefore, the people who decide what should go into the data warehouse and how the DSS will use it maintain an appreciation for the types of decisions faced by Home Depot store managers each and every day. Home Depot even asks outside suppliers who may be involved in information technology (IT) design to spend a few days in an actual Home Depot store. Thus, as Home Depot implements key innovations in its data networks, the people helping it to do so understand what the information needs of employees really are. Even Home Depot's outside directors meet with middle managers and conduct store visits so that they can provide more meaningful advice to senior executives. Part of this advice concerns the data needs of Home Depot managers.

Do you think such a plan would be similarly successful for a company like Krispy Kreme?

Sources: Lublin, Joanne, "Home Depot Board Gains Insight from Trenches," *The Wall Street Journal* (October 10, 2005), B3; Tucker, Katheryn Hayes , "New Home Depot GC Learns Ropes at Store" *Fulton County Daily Report* (July 18, 2007).

OUTSIDE VENDORS AND EXTERNAL DISTRIBUTORS

Outside vendors and external distributors market information as their products. Many organizations specialize in the collection and publication of high-quality information. One outside vendor, the ACNielsen Company, provides television program ratings, audience counts, and information about the demographic composition of television viewer groups. Other vendors specialize in the distribution of information. Public libraries have always purchased information, traditionally in the form of books, and they have served as distributors of this information.

GPS devices, like those used in automobile navigation systems, allow management to track delivery personnel or even actual customer behavior.

Media representatives often provide useful demographic and lifestyle data about their audiences. *Advertising Age*, *The Wall Street Journal*, *Sales and Marketing Management*, and other business-oriented publications are important sources of information. These publications keep managers up-to-date about the economy, competitors' activities, and other aspects of the business environment.

Companies called *data specialists* record and store certain business information. Computer technology has changed the way many of these organizations supply data, favoring the development of computerized databases.

Computerized Data Archives

Historically, collections of organized and readily retrievable data were available in printed form at libraries. The *Statistical Abstract of the United States,* which is filled with tables of statistical facts, is a typical example. As with many resources, the *Statistical Abstract* is now available electronically. Users can purchase it via CD-ROM or access it via the Internet. The entire 2000 U.S. census, the 2007 Economic Census, as well as projections through the current year is available at **http://www.census.gov**. More and more data are available in digitized form every day.

Numerous computerized search and retrieval systems and electronic databases are available as subscription services or in libraries. Just as a student can query the school library to find information for a term paper without leaving home, data acquisition for businesses has also become far more convenient in recent years. Today, business people access online information search and retrieval services, such as Dow Jones News Retrieval and Bloomberg Financial Markets, without leaving their offices. In fact, an increasing range of information services can be accessed from remote locations via digital wireless devices.

Modern library patrons can command a computer to search indexes and retrieve databases from a range of vendors. Just as wholesalers collect goods from manufacturers and offer them for sale to retailers who then provide them to consumers, many information firms serve as data wholesalers. **Data wholesalers** put together consortia of data sources into packages that are offered to municipal, corporate, and university libraries for a fee. Information users then access the data through these libraries. Some of the better known databases include Wilson Business Center, Hoovers, PROQUEST, INFOTRAC, DIALOG (Dialog Information Services, Inc.), LEXIS-NEXIS, and Dow Jones News Retrieval Services. These databases provide all types of information including recent news stories and data tables charting statistical trends.

data wholesalers
Companies that put together consortia of data sources into packages that are offered to municipal, corporate, and university libraries for a fee.

DIALOG, for example, maintains more than 600 databases. A typical database may have a million or more records, each consisting of a one- or two-paragraph abstract that summarizes the major points of a published article along with bibliographic information. One of the DIALOG databases, ABI/INFORM, abstracts significant articles in more than one thousand current business and management journals. Many computerized archives provide full-text downloads of published articles about companies and various research topics.

Exhibit 2.4 illustrates the services provided by two popular vendors of information services that electronically index numerous databases. For a more extensive listing, see the *Gale Directory of Databases*.[11]

Several types of databases from outside vendors and external distributors are so fundamental to decision support systems that they deserve further explanation. The following sections discuss statistical databases, financial databases, and video databases in slightly more detail.

STATISTICAL DATABASES

Statistical databases contain numerical data for analysis and forecasting. Often demographic, sales, and other relevant business variables are recorded by geographical area. Geographic information systems use these *geographical databases* and powerful software to prepare computer maps of relevant variables. Companies such as Claritas, Urban Decision Systems, and CACI all offer geographic/demographic databases that are widely used in industry.

One source for these huge data warehouses is scanner data. Substituting electronic record-keeping like optical scanners for human record-keeping results in greater accuracy and more rapid feedback about store activity.

One weakness of scanner data is that not all points of sale have scanner technology. For instance, many convenience stores lack scanner technology, as do most vending machines. Thus, those purchases go unrecorded. The Universal Product Code, or UPC, contains information on the category of goods, the manufacturer, and product identification based on size, flavor, color, and so on. This is what the optical scanner actually reads. If a large percentage of a brand's sales occur in environments without the ability to read the UPC code, the business should be aware that the scanner data may not be representative.

EXHIBIT 2.4 **Vendors of Information Services and Electronic Indexing**

Vendors	Selected Databases	Type of Data
DIALOG	ABI/INFORM	Summaries and citations from over 1,000 academic management, marketing, and general business journals with full text of more than 500 of these publications
	ASI (American Statistics Index)	Abstracts and indexes of federal government statistical publications
	PROMT (The Predicast Overview of Markets and Technologies)	Summaries and full text from 1,000 U.S. and international business and trade journals, industry newsletters, newspapers, and business research studies; information about industries and companies, including the products and technologies they develop and the markets in which they compete
	Investext	Full text of over 2 million company, industry, and geographic research reports written by analysts at more than 600 leading investment banks, brokerage houses, and consulting firms worldwide
Dow Jones News Retrieval	Business Newsstand	Articles from *New York Times, Los Angeles Times, Washington Post,* and other leading newspapers and magazines
	Historical Data Center	Historical data on securities, dividends, and exchange rates
	Web Center	Information obtained from searches of corporate, industry, government, and news Web sites

FINANCIAL DATABASES

Competitors' and customers' financial data, such as income statements and balance sheets, are of obvious interest to business managers. These are easy to access in financial databases. CompuStat publishes an extensive financial database on thousands of companies, broken down by industry and other criteria. To illustrate the depth of this pool of information, CompuStat's Global Advantage offers extensive data on 6,650 companies in more than 30 countries in Europe, the Pacific Rim, and North America.

VIDEO DATABASES

Video databases and streaming media are having a major impact on many goods and services. For example, movie studios provide clips of upcoming films and advertising agencies put television commercials on the Internet (see **http://www.adcritic.com**). McDonald's maintains a digital archive of television commercials and other video footage to share with its franchisees around the world. The video database enables franchisees and their advertising agencies to create local advertising without the need for filming the same types of scenes already archived. Just imagine the value of digital video databases to advertising agencies' decision support systems!

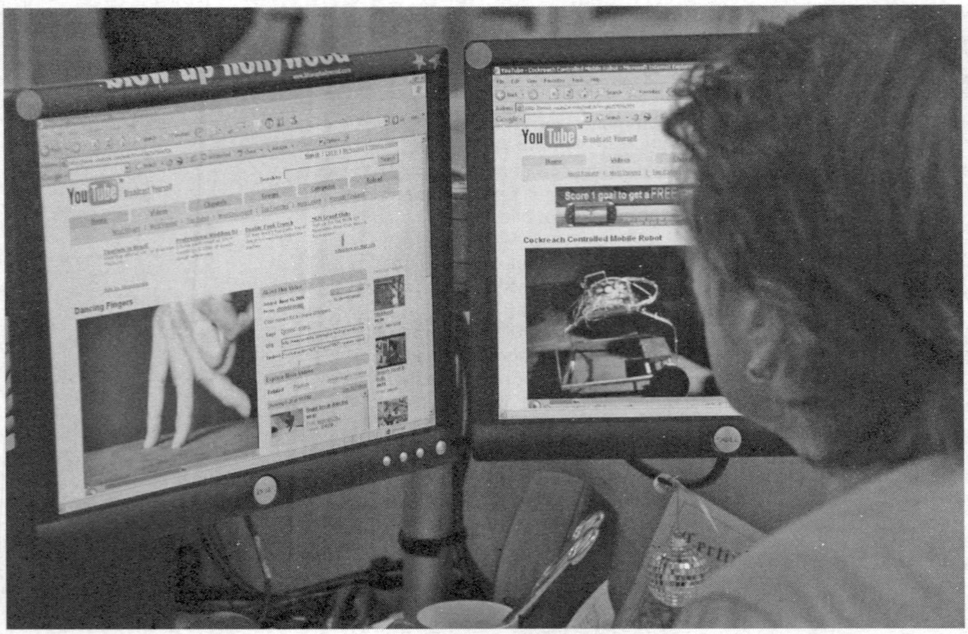

© AP PHOTO/CAMERON BLOCK

Electronic data storage is revolutionizing some research tasks. Thousands of television commercials and employee training films are available for analysis by just searching the right electronic video database.

Networks and Electronic Data Interchange

Individual personal computers can be connected through networks to other computers. Networking involves linking two or more computers to share data and software.

Electronic data interchange (EDI) systems integrate one company's computer system directly with another company's system. Much of the input to a company's decision support system may come through networks from other companies' computers. Companies such as Computer Technology Corporation and Microelectronics data services allow corporations to exchange business information with suppliers or customers. For example, every evening Wal-Mart transmits millions of characters of data about the day's sales to its apparel suppliers. Wrangler, a supplier of blue jeans, for instance, shares the data and a model that interprets the data. Wrangler also shares software applications that act to replenish stock in Wal-Mart stores. This DSS lets Wrangler's managers know when to send specific quantities of specific sizes and colors of jeans to specific stores from specific warehouses. The result is a learning loop that lowers inventory costs and leads to fewer stockouts.

The Internet and Research

electronic data interchange (EDI)
Type of exchange that occurs when one company's computer system is integrated with another company's system.

When most readers of this book were born, the Internet had yet to enter the everyday vocabulary. In fact, few people outside of a small number of universities and the U.S. Department of Defense had any clue as to what the Internet might be. In the 1960s, mainframe computers revolutionized research by allowing researchers to use research techniques involving large numbers of mathematical computations that previously would have been impossible or, at the least, impractical. In the 1980s, the mainframe computing power of the 1960s, which was available primarily in large universities, government agencies, and very large companies, was transformed into something that could go on nearly every businessperson's desktop. The personal computer (PC) and simple operating systems like DOS and eventually Windows revolutionized many business applications by making computing power relatively inexpensive and convenient. Today, the widespread usage of the Internet is perhaps the single biggest change agent in business research. Since most readers are no doubt experienced in using the Internet, we highlight a few terms and facts about the Internet that are especially useful in understanding business research.

In the following pages we discuss the World Wide Web and how to use the Internet for research. However, keep in mind that the Internet is constantly changing. The description of the Internet, especially home page addresses, may be out of date by the time this book is published. Be aware that the Internet of today will not be the Internet of tomorrow.

What Exactly Is the Internet?

Internet
A worldwide network of computers that allows users access to information from distant sources.

The **Internet** is a worldwide network of computers that allows users access to data, information, and feedback from distant sources. It functions as the world's largest public library, providing access to a seemingly endless range of data. Many people believe the Internet is the most important communications medium since television.

The Internet began in the 1960s as an experimental connection between computers at Stanford University, the University of California at Santa Barbara, the University of California at Los Angeles, and the University of Utah, in conjunction with the Department of Defense.[12] The Department of Defense was involved because it wanted to develop a communications network that could survive nuclear war. The Internet gradually grew into a nationwide network of connected computers, and now it is a worldwide network often referred to as the "information superhighway."

The Internet has no central computer; instead, each message sent bears an address code that lets a sender forward a message to a desired destination from any computer linked to the Net. Many benefits of the Internet arise because the Internet is a collection of thousands of small networks, both domestic and foreign, rather than a single computer operation.

A domain is typically a company name, institutional name, or organizational name associated with a host computer. A **host** is where the content for a particular Web site physically resides and is accessed. For example, *Forbes* magazine's Internet edition is located at **http://forbes.com**. The "com" indicates this domain is a commercial site. Educational sites end in "edu"—Louisiana Tech can be reached at **http://www.latech.edu** and Bradley University can be accessed at **http://www.bradley.edu**. The United States Marine Corps can be found at **http://www.marines.mil** (the "mil" indicating military) and many government sites, such as the U.S. House of Representatives, end with "gov," as in **http://www.house.gov** and **http://census.gov**. Many nonprofit organizations end in "org," as in **http://www.ams-web.org**, the Web home for the Academy of Marketing Science. Web addresses outside the United States often end in abbreviations for their country such as "ca," "de," or "uk" for Canada, Germany (Deutschland), and the United Kingdom, respectively.

host
Where the content for a particular Web site physically resides and is accessed.

How Is the Internet Useful in Research?

The Internet is useful to researchers in many ways. In fact, more and more applications become known as the technology grows and is adopted by more and more users. The Internet is particularly useful as a source for accessing available data and as a way of collecting data.

ACCESSING AVAILABLE DATA

The Internet allows instantaneous and effortless access to a great deal of information. Noncommercial and commercial organizations make a wealth of data and other resources available on the Internet. For example, the U.S. Library of Congress provides full text of all versions of House and Senate legislation and full text of the *Congressional Record*. The Internal Revenue Service makes it possible to obtain information and download a variety of income tax forms. Cengage Learning (**www.cengage.com**) and its college divisions (**www.cengage.com/highered/**) have online directories that allow college professors to access information about the company and its textbooks. The Gale Research Database provides basic statistics and news stories on literally thousands of companies worldwide. Thus, information that formally took a great deal of time and effort to obtain is now available with a few clicks. Further, since it can often be electronically downloaded or copied, it isn't necessary for a person to transcribe the data. Therefore, it is available in a more error-free form.

COLLECTING DATA

The Internet is also revolutionizing the way researchers collect data. Later in this text, we discuss in more detail the use of Web-based surveys. In short, questionnaires can be posted on a Web site and respondents can be invited to go to the particular URL and participate in the survey. This cuts down on the expense associated with traditional mail surveys and also reduces error since the data can be automatically recorded rather than transcribed from a paper form into an electronic format.

TOTHEPOINT

The Net is 10.5 on the Richter scale of economic change.

—Nicholas Negroponte

Furthermore, when a consumer uses the World Wide Web, his or her usage leaves a record that can be traced and observed. For instance, Zappos.com can determine how many pages were visited at their shopping site before a purchase was made. They can see if products were abandoned in the "virtual shopping cart" without a purchase being made. Online auctions provide another mechanism to track consumers' behavior. Prototype products can be offered for sale in an online auction to help assist with product design, forecasting demand, and setting an appropriate price.[13]

Navigating the Internet

World Wide Web (WWW)
A portion of the Internet that is a system of computer servers that organize information into documents called Web pages.

content providers
Parties that furnish information on the World Wide Web.

The **World Wide Web (WWW)** refers specifically to that portion of the Internet made up of servers that support a retrieval system that organizes information into documents called Web pages. World Wide Web documents, which may include graphic images, video clips, and sound clips, are formatted in programming languages, such as HTML (HyperText Markup Language) and XML (Extensible Markup Language) that allow for displaying, linking, and sharing of information on the Internet.

Parties that furnish information on the World Wide Web are called **content providers**. Content providers maintain Web sites. A Web site consists of one or more Web pages with related information about a particular topic; for example, Bradley University's Web site includes pages about its mission, courses, athletics, admissions, and faculty (see **http://www.bradley.edu**). The introductory page or opening screen is called the home page because it provides basic information about the purpose of the document along with a menu of selections or links that lead to other screens with more specific information. Thus, each page can have connections, or hyperlinks, to other pages, which may be on any computer connected to the Internet. People using the World Wide Web may be viewing information that is stored on a host computer or on a machine halfway around the world.

uniform resource locator (URL)
A Web site address that Web browsers recognize.

search engine
A computerized directory that allows anyone to search the World Wide Web for information using a keyword search.

keyword search
Takes place as the search engine searches through millions of Web pages for documents containing the keywords.

Most Web browsers also allow the user to enter a **uniform resource locator (URL)** into the program. The URL is really just a Web site address that Web browsers recognize. Many Web sites allow any user or visitor access without previous approval. However, many commercial sites require that the user have a valid account and password before access is granted.

One of the most basic research tools available via the Internet is a search engine. A **search engine** is a computerized directory that allows anyone to search the World Wide Web for information based on a keyword search. A **keyword search** takes place as the search engine searches through millions of Web pages for documents containing the keywords. Some of the most comprehensive and accurate search engines are:

Yahoo!	**http://www.yahoo.com**
Google	**http://www.google.com**
Hotbot	**http://www.hotbot.com**
Go network	**http://www.go.com**
Excite	**http://www.excite.com**
Lycos	**http://www.lycos.com**
Ask Jeeves	**http://www.ask.com**
WebCrawler	**http://www.webcrawler.com**

Google revolutionized search engines by changing the way the search was actually conducted. It searches based on a mathematical theory known as *graph theory*.[14] Google greatly improved the accuracy and usefulness of the search results obtained from a keyword search. In fact, "google" is now included as a word in many dictionaries, meaning "to search for information on the World Wide Web." Exhibit 2.5 illustrates the Google interface and expanded Google options. For instance, if one clicks on Google Scholar, a search of citations for a particular author or basic research papers on any given topic indicated by the keywords can be performed.

Interactive Media and Environmental Scanning

The Internet is an **interactive medium** because users click commands and often get customized responses. So the user and equipment can have a continuing conversation. Two or more individuals who communicate one-to-one via e-mail using an Internet service provider are also using interactive media. So are individuals who communicate with many senders and receivers via bulletin boards or chat rooms. Because of its vastness, the Internet is an especially useful source for scanning many types of environmental changes. **Environmental scanning** entails all information gathering designed to detect changes in the external operating environment of the firm. These things are usually beyond the control of the firm, but they still can have a significant impact on firm performance.

interactive medium
A medium, such as the Internet, that a person can use to communicate with and interact with other users.

environmental scanning
Entails all information gathering designed to detect changes in the external operating environment of the firm.

Ford Motor Company maintains an Internet-based relationship marketing program that, among other things, helps the automaker scan its environment using the Internet. Its dealer Web site creates a centralized communication service linking dealers via an Internet connection. Its buyer Web site allows prospective buyers to visit a virtual showroom and to get price quotes and financial information. Its owner Web site allows an owner who registers and supplies pertinent vehicle information to get free e-mail and other ownership perks. A perk might be a free Hertz upgrade or an autographed photo of one of the Ford-sponsored NASCAR drivers. In return, Ford collects data at all levels, which allow managers to scan for trends and apply what they learn at a local level.

Information Technology

pull technology
Consumers request information from a Web page and the browser then determines a response; the consumer is essentially asking for the data.

push technology
Sends data to a user's computer without a request being made; software is used to guess what information might be interesting to consumers based on the pattern of previous responses.

Data and information can be delivered to consumers or other end users via either **pull technology** or **push technology**. Conventionally, consumers request information from a Web page and the browser then determines a response. Thus, the consumer is essentially asking for the data. In this case, it is said to be pulled through the channel. The opposite of pull is push. Push technology sends data to a user's computer without a request being made. In other words, software is used to guess what information might be interesting to consumers based on the pattern of previous responses.

Smart information delivery (known by a variety of technical names, including *push phase technology*) allows a Web site, such as the Yahoo portal, to become a one-on-one medium for each individual user. Today's information technology uses "smart agents" or "intelligent agents" to deliver customized content to a viewer's desktop. **Smart agent software** is capable of learning an Internet user's preferences and automatically searching out information and distributing the information to a user's computer. My Yahoo! and MyExcite are portal services that personalize Web pages. Users can get stock quotes relevant to their portfolios, news about favorite sports teams, local weather, and other personalized information. Users can customize the sections of the service they want delivered. With push technology, pertinent content is delivered to the viewer's desktop without the user having to do the searching.

smart agent software
Software capable of learning an Internet user's preferences and automatically searching out information in selected Web sites and then distributing it.

Cookies, in computer terminology, are small computer files that record a user's Web usage history. If a person looks up a weather report by keying a zip code into a personalized Web page, the fact that the user visited the Web site and the zip code entered are recorded in the cookie. This is a clue that tells where the person lives (or maybe where he or she may be planning to visit). Web sites can then direct information to that consumer based on information in the cookie. So, someone in Hattiesburg, Mississippi, may receive pop-up ads for restaurants in Hattiesburg. Information technology is having a major impact on the nature of business research. We will explore this topic in several places throughout this book.

cookies
Small computer files that a content provider can save onto the computer of someone who visits its Web site.

Intranets

An **intranet** is a company's private data network that uses Internet standards and technology.[15] The information on an intranet—data, graphics, video, and voice—is available only inside the

intranet
A company's private data network that uses Internet standards and technology.

organization or to those individuals whom the organization deems as appropriate participants. Thus, a key difference between the Internet and an intranet is that security software programs, or "firewalls," are installed to limit access to only those employees authorized to enter the system. Intranets then serve as secure knowledge portals that contain substantial amounts of organizational memory and can integrate it with information from outside sources. For example, Caterpillar has an intranet that includes their knowledge network, a portal that provides Caterpillar employees and dealership personnel with a vast array of information about the company and its product offering. The challenge in designing an intranet is making sure that it is capable of delivering relevant data to decision makers. Research suggests that relevance is a key in getting knowledge workers to actually make use of company intranets.[16]

An intranet can be extended to include key consumers as a source of valuable research. Their participation in an intranet can lead to new product developments. Texas Instruments has successfully established an intranet that integrated communications between customers and researchers leading to the introduction and modification of its calculators.[17] An intranet lets authorized users, possibly including key customers, look at product drawings, employee newsletters, sales figures, and other kinds of company information.

Internet2

As we mentioned earlier, information technology changes rapidly. As sophisticated as the Internet and intranets are today, new technologies, such as Internet2, will dramatically enhance researchers' ability to answer business problems in the future.

Internet2 (**http://www.internet2.edu/**) is a collaborative effort involving about 250 universities, government entities (including the military), and corporate organizations. The project hopes to recreate some of the cooperative spirit that created the Internet originally. Internet2 users are limited to those involved with the affiliate organizations. The hope is to create a faster, more powerful Internet by providing multimodal access, employing more wireless technologies, and building in global trading mechanisms. Internet2 began as a research tool for the universities and organizations involved in its development.[18]

Summary

1. Know and distinguish between the concepts of data, information, and intelligence. Increased global competition and technological advances in interactive media have spurred development of global information systems. A global information system is an organized collection of computer hardware, software, data, and personnel designed to capture, store, update, manipulate, analyze, and immediately display information about worldwide business activity.

From a research perspective, there is a difference between data, information, and intelligence. Data are simply facts or recorded measures of certain phenomena (things); information is data formatted (structured) to support decision making or define the relationship between two facts. Business intelligence is the subset of data and information that actually has some explanatory power enabling effective decisions to be made.

2. Understand the four characteristics that describe data. The usefulness of data to management can be described based on four characteristics: relevance, quality, timeliness, and completeness. Relevant data have the characteristic of pertinence to the situation at hand. The information is useful. The quality of information is the degree to which data represent the true situation. High-quality data are accurate, valid, and reliable. High-quality data represent reality faithfully and present a good picture of reality. Timely information is obtained at the right time. Computerized

TIPS OF THE TRADE

- Researchers should focus on relevance as the key characteristic of useful data.
  - Do so by asking, "Will knowledge of some fact change some important outcome?"
- Focus more on getting managers the right data than the most data.
- The Internet is a valuable source of data.
  - It is a useful information collection vehicle
  - It is an exhaustive information repository
  - It is a great place for data mining

information systems can record events and present information as a transaction takes place, improving timeliness. Complete information is the right quantity of information. Managers must have sufficient information to relate all aspects of their decisions together.

3. Know the purpose of research in assisting business operations. A computer-based decision support system helps decision makers confront problems through direct interactions with databases and analytical models. A DSS stores data and transforms them into organized information that is easily accessible to managers.

4. Know what a decision support system is and does. A database is a collection of raw data arranged logically and organized in a form that can be stored and processed by a computer. Business data come from four major sources: internal records, proprietary business research, business intelligence, and outside vendors and external distributors. Each source can provide valuable input. Because most companies compile and store many different databases, they often develop data warehousing systems. Data warehousing is the process allowing important day-to-day operational data to be stored and organized for simplified access. More specifically, a data warehouse is the multitiered computer storehouse of current and historical data. Data warehouse management requires that the detailed data from operational systems be extracted, transformed, and stored (warehoused) so that the various database tables from both inside and outside the company are consistent. All of this feeds into the decision support system that automates or assists business decision making.

Numerous database search and retrieval systems are available by subscription or in libraries. Computer-assisted database searching has made the collection of external data faster and easier. Managers refer to many different types of databases.

Although personal computers work independently, they can connect to other computers in networks to share data and software. Electronic data interchange (EDI) allows one company's computer system to join directly to another company's system.

5. Recognize the major categories of databases. The Internet is a worldwide network of computers that allows users access to information and documents from distant sources. It is a combination of a worldwide communication system and the world's largest public library. The World Wide Web is a system of thousands of interconnected pages, or documents, that can be easily accessed with Web browsers and search engines.

An intranet is a company's private data network that uses Internet standards and technology. The information on an intranet—data, graphics, video, and voice—is available only inside the organization. Thus, a key difference between the Internet and an intranet is that "firewalls," or security software programs, are installed to limit access to only those employees authorized to enter the system.

A company uses Internet features to build its own intranet. Groupware and other technology can facilitate the transfer of data, information, and knowledge. In organizations that practice knowledge management, intranets function to make the knowledge of company experts more accessible throughout their organizations.

Key Terms and Concepts

business intelligence, *19*
content providers, *32*
cookies, *34*
customer relationship management (CRM), *23*
data, *19*
data quality, *21*
data warehouse, *24*
data warehousing, *24*
data wholesalers, *28*
database, *24*
decision support system (DSS), *23*
electronic data interchange (EDI), *30*
environmental scanning, *33*
global information system, *22*
host, *31*
information, *19*
information completeness, *21*
interactive medium, *32*
Internet, *30*
intranet, *34*
keyword search, *32*
knowledge, *22*
knowledge management, *22*
proprietary business research, *25*
pull technology, *33*
push technology, *33*
relevance, *20*
scanner data, *26*
search engine, *32*
smart agent software, *33*
timeliness, *21*
uniform resource locator (URL), *32*
World Wide Web (WWW), *32*

Questions for Review and Critical Thinking

1. What is data warehousing?
2. **'NET** How does data warehousing assist decision making? Visit **http://www.kbb.com**. While there, choose two cars that you might consider buying and compare them. Which do you like the best? What would you do now? What are at least three pieces of data that should be stored in a data warehouse somewhere based on your interaction with *Kelly Blue Book?*
3. What makes a decision support system successful?
4. **'NET** Give three examples of computerized databases that are available at your college or university library.
5. What type of operational questions could a delivery firm like FedEx expect to automate with the company's decision support system?
6. **'NET** What is the difference between the Internet and an intranet?
7. What types of databases might be found in the following organizations?
   a. Holiday Inn
   b. A major university's athletic department
   c. Anheuser-Busch
8. Suppose a retail firm is interested in studying the effect of lighting on customer purchase behavior. Which of the following pieces of information is the least relevant and why?
   a. Amount of natural light in the store
   b. The compensation system for store salespeople
   c. The color of the walls in the store
   d. The type of lighting: fluorescent or incandescent
9. Define *knowledge management*. What is its purpose within an organization?
10. **'NET** Imagine the data collected by eBay each day. List at least five types of data that are collected through the daily operations. Describe each in terms of it illustrating data, information, or intelligence. Make sure you list at least one of each.
11. What is the key question distinguishing relevant data from irrelevant data?
12. How could New Balance, a maker of athletic shoes, use RFID technology to collect data?
13. What are the characteristics of useful information?
14. **'NET** The Spider's Apprentice is a Web site that provides many useful tips about using search engines. Go to **http://www.monash.com/spidap.html**, then click on Search Engine FAQ to learn the ins and outs of search engines.
15. What is the difference between data, information, and intelligence?

Research Activities

1. **'NET** To learn more about data warehousing, go to **http://www.datawarehousing.org**.
2. **'NET** Use the Internet to see if you can find information to answer the following questions:
   a. What is the weather in Angers, France, today?
   b. What are four restaurants in the French Quarter in New Orleans?
   c. What is the population of Brazil?

Case 2.1 Harvard Cooperative Society

© GETTY IMAGES/ PHOTODISC GREEN

From his office window overlooking the main floor of the Harvard Cooperative Society, CEO Jerry Murphy can glance down and see customers shopping.[19] They make their way through the narrow aisles of the crowded department store, picking up a sweatshirt here, trying on a baseball cap there, checking out the endless array of merchandise that bears the Harvard University insignia.

Watching Murphy, you can well imagine the Co-op's founders, who started the store in 1882, peering through the tiny windowpanes to keep an eye on the shop floor. Was the Harvard Square store attracting steady traffic? Were the college students buying enough books and supplies for the Co-op to make a profit? Back then, it was tough to answer those questions precisely. The owners had to watch and wait, relying only on their gut feelings to know how things were going from minute to minute.

Now, more than a hundred years later, Murphy can tell you, down to the last stock-keeping unit, how he's doing at any given moment. His window on the business is the PC that sits on his desk. All day long it delivers up-to-the-minute, easy-to-read electronic reports on what's selling and what's not, which items are running low in inventory and which have fallen short of forecast. In a matter of seconds, the computer can report gross margins for any product or supplier, and Murphy can decide whether the margins are fat enough to justify keeping the supplier or product on board. "We were in the 1800s, and we had to move ahead," he says of the $55 million business.

Questions

1. What is a decision support system? What advantages does a decision support system have for a business like the Harvard Cooperative Society?
2. How would the decision support system of a business like the Harvard Cooperative Society differ from that of a major corporation?
3. Briefly outline the components of the Harvard Cooperative Society's decision support system.

CHAPTER 3
THEORY BUILDING

LEARNING OUTCOMES

After studying this chapter, you should be able to

1. **Define the meaning of *theory***
2. **Understand the goals of theory**
3. **Understand the terms *concepts, propositions, variables,* and *hypotheses***
4. **Discuss how theories are developed**
5. **Understand the scientific method**

Chapter Vignette: Theory and Practice

What if you went home tonight and turned on the light switch and nothing happened? Most of us would immediately start seeking a logical explanation: "Is the bulb burnt out?" "Did my roommate forget to pay the electric bill?" "Is the electricity out?" "Did a fuse blow?" These are common thoughts that would race through our minds. The order would probably depend on our past experience and we would try to determine the cause through a logical thought sequence. Attribution theory is one framework that helps us explain the world and determine the cause of an event (the light bulb not working) or behavior (why my girlfriend is mad at me). Simply put, this theory helps us make sense of events by providing a systematic method to assess and evaluate why things occur. Attribution theory is just one of many theoretical models that are useful to business researchers.

Introduction

The purpose of science concerns the expansion of knowledge and the search for truth. Theory building is the means by which basic researchers hope to achieve this purpose.

Students sometimes think their classes or course material are "too theoretical" or lacking "practical application." However, this should certainly not be the case. Theories are simply generalizations that help us better understand reality. Furthermore, theories allow us to understand the logic behind things we observe. If a theory does not hold true in practice, then that theory holds no value. This chapter will provide a fundamental knowledge of theory, theory development, and some terminology regarding theory necessary for business researchers.

TOTHEPOINT

There is nothing so practical as a good theory.

—Kurt Lewin

What Is a Theory?

> *Like all abstractions, the word "theory" has been used in many different ways, in many different contexts, at times so broadly as to include almost all descriptive statements about a class of phenomena, and at other times so narrowly as to exclude everything but a series of terms and their relationships that satisfies certain logical requirements.*[1]

A theory consists of a coherent set of general propositions that offer an explanation of some phenomena by describing the way other things correspond to this phenomena. Put another way, a **theory** is a formal, testable explanation of some events that includes explanations of how things relate to one another.

theory
A formal, logical explanation of some events that includes predictions of how things relate to one another.

A theory can be built through a process of reviewing previous findings of similar studies, simple logical deduction, and/or knowledge of applicable theoretical areas. For example, if a Web designer is trying to decide what color background is most effective in increasing online sales, he may first consult previous studies examining the effects of color on package design and retail store design. He may also find theories that deal with the wavelength of different colors, affective response to colors, or those that explain retail atmospherics. This may lead to the specific prediction that blue is the most effective background color for a Web site.[2]

While it may seem that theory is only relevant to academic or basic business research, theory plays a role in understanding practical research as well. Before setting research objectives, the researcher must be able to describe the business situation in some coherent way. Without this type of explanation, the researcher would have little idea of where to start. Ultimately, the logical explanation helps the researcher know what variables need to be included in the study and how they may relate to one another.

TOTHEPOINT

Theories are nets cast to catch what we call "the world": to rationalize, to explain, and to master it. We endeavour to make the mesh ever finer and finer.

—Karl R. Popper, *The Logic of Scientific Discovery*

What Are the Goals of Theory?

Suppose a researcher investigating business phenomena wants to know what caused the financial crisis. Another person wants to know if organizational structure influences leadership style. Both of these individuals want to gain a better understanding of the environment and be able to predict behavior; to be able to say that if we take a particular course of action we can expect a specific outcome to occur. These two issues—understanding and predicting—are the two purposes of theory.[3] Accomplishing the first goal allows the theorist to gain an understanding of the relationship among various phenomena. For example, a financial advisor may believe, or theorize, that older investors tend to be more interested in investment income than younger investors. This theory, once verified, would then allow her to predict the importance of expected dividend yield based on the age of her customer. Thus a theory enables us to predict the behavior or characteristics of one phenomenon from the knowledge of another phenomenon. The value of understanding and anticipating future conditions in the environment or in an organization should be obvious. In most situations, of course, understanding and prediction go hand in hand. To predict phenomena, we must have an explanation of why variables behave as they do. Theories provide these explanations.

Professor Paul R. Carlile of School of Management Boston University and Professor Clayton M. Christensen of Harvard Business School proposed cycles of theory building in management research. The author in their literature suggested that there is constant debate between inductive and deductive theory building process, and the objectivity of information collected through field related survey of large sample data. These authors have also mentioned about other authors who have opined that there is a paucity of theory that has intellectual rigor, practical usefulness, and inability to stand the test of time and changing managerial circumstances. In their researches, these two authors have proposed a model to provide a common platform for theory building and research process which seem to be more effective in practical context.

These two researchers opined that building of theory happens in two major stages. These two stages are (1) descriptive stage and (2) normative stage. Unlike other researchers, they proposed that the term "theory" is not an individual entity but a cumulative understanding of three steps in the descriptive and normative stages. These three steps, as per the researchers, are *observation, categorization/classification, and association.*

In the observation step, researchers observe the phenomenon that has happened or continuing to happen. In this state, they carefully describe this phenomenon and measure it as they see. Such careful observation and consequent measurement and documentation of the phenomenon in the beginning on the first day are important since each subsequent researcher may not agree with the description of the phenomenon and they may not be able to improve the theory or modify it. In this state, the researchers often develop the *constructs*. Constructs are lacking variables and abstractions that capture large and complicated details to understand the essence of the phenomena understudy. For instance, "utility" is one of the constructs in economic theory, which abstracts different indicators that individual value of a particular product. However, we cannot say construct of utility as theory of utility.

The second step in theory building is *classification*. After observation and description of a phenomenon, researchers need to classify this phenomenon into different categories. Classification considers the attributes of the phenomenon. In other words, the classification step in theory building can capture whether the firm will diversify or it will rely on its core competency, whether consumers rely more on objective attributes of the product that is subjective attributes. Such classification of attributes attempts to simplify the process of theory building and management researchers rely on such descriptive categorization, calling them as frameworks.

The third and the last step of theory building is defining relationships. In this step, researchers explore the interrelationship between these classified attributes and their outcomes. In descriptive theory building, researchers point out different attributes and try to find out the interrelationship between these attributes. These interrelationships are measured in terms of their magnitude as well as direction. Several techniques, many of them statistical techniques, are used to substantiate such interrelationships. The process of theory building model as opined by Carlile and Christensen (2005) is shown in Exhibit 3.1.

The theory of buying behavior of consumers is a function of their need of the merchandize that they want to buy, availability of the merchandize, price of the merchandize with respect to willingness to pay by the consumer, and consumers' motivation about the product.[4] While marketing literature has considerably dealt with different types of theories clearly related to consumer buying, however, there is very limited research on buying behavior of channel partners, namely, wholesaler and retailers. Professor Jagadish N. Sheth first introduced a theory on merchandize buying behavior. In his research, he mentioned that retailers are neither like producers nor like consumers, and hence they are to be dealt in a unique manner. The same argument is valid while building theory for any type of hypothesis. Whether the reasoning is deductive reasoning or inductive reasoning, each research is to be considered as a separate function and a theory should be proposed that would relate to different scientific aspect of behavior.

For instance, if we want to build the theory of small retail outlet (the Beatles shop, a small *kirana* store), we may consider the retail outlet in the sense of a business entity that behaves like a large business entity and has similar kind of corporate objectives. However, it may not have the multiple stakeholders that a large business entity has. Hence, its accountability, in such occasion, is more similar to an individual consumer.

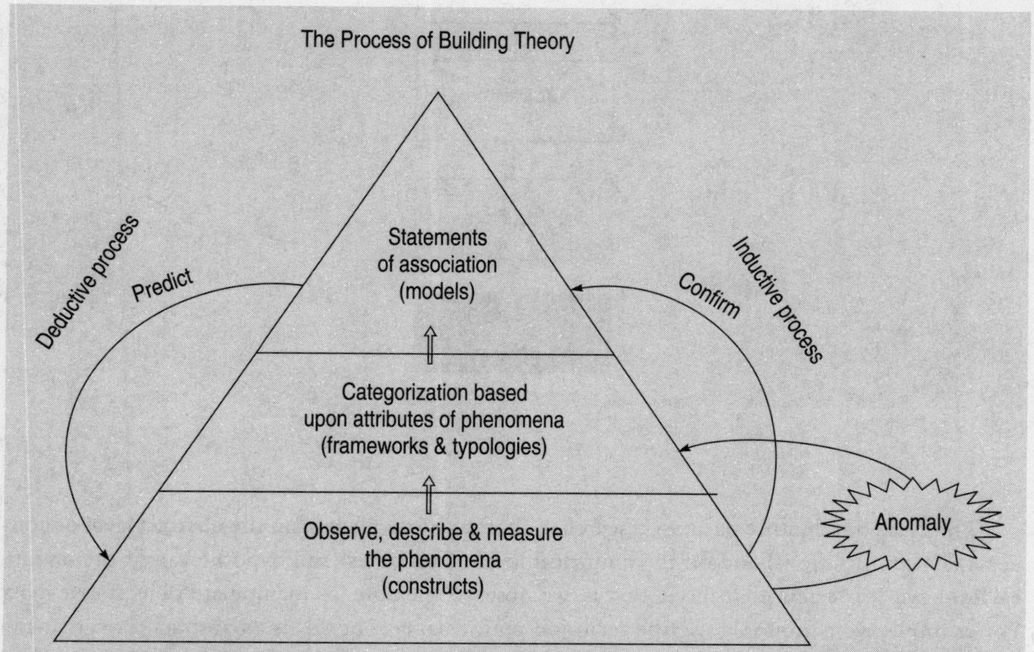

Source: The Cycles of Theory Building in Management Research by Paul R. Carlile and Clayton M. Christensen (2005) working paper.

EXHIBIT 3.1 The Process of Theory Building in Management Research

Research Concepts, Constructs, Propositions, Variables, and Hypotheses

Theory development is essentially a process of describing phenomena at increasingly higher levels of abstraction. In other words, as business researchers, we need to be able to think of things in a very abstract manner, but eventually link these abstract concepts to observable reality. To understand theory and the business research process, it will be useful to know different terminology and how these terms relate.

Research Concepts and Constructs

A **concept** or **construct** is a generalized idea about a class of objects, attributes, occurrences, or processes that has been given a name. If you, as an organizational theorist, were to describe phenomena such as supervisory behavior or risk aversion, you would categorize empirical events or real things into concepts. Concepts are the building blocks of theory. In organizational theory, leadership, productivity, and morale are concepts. In the theory of finance, gross national product, risk aversion, and inflation are frequently used concepts. Accounting concepts include assets, liabilities, and depreciation. In marketing, customer satisfaction, market share, and loyalty are important concepts.

Concepts abstract reality. That is, concepts express in words various events or objects. Concepts, however, may vary in degree of abstraction. For example, the concept of an asset is an abstract term that may, in the concrete world of reality, refer to a wide variety of things, including a specific punch press machine in a production shop. The abstraction ladder in Exhibit 3.2 indicates that it is possible to discuss concepts at various levels of abstraction. Moving up the **ladder of abstraction**, the basic concept becomes more general, wider in scope, and less amenable to measurement.

concept (or construct)
A generalized idea about a class of objects that has been given a name; an abstraction of reality that is the basic unit for theory development.

ladder of abstraction
Organization of concepts in sequence from the most concrete and individual to the most general.

EXHIBIT 3.2
A Ladder of Abstraction for Concepts

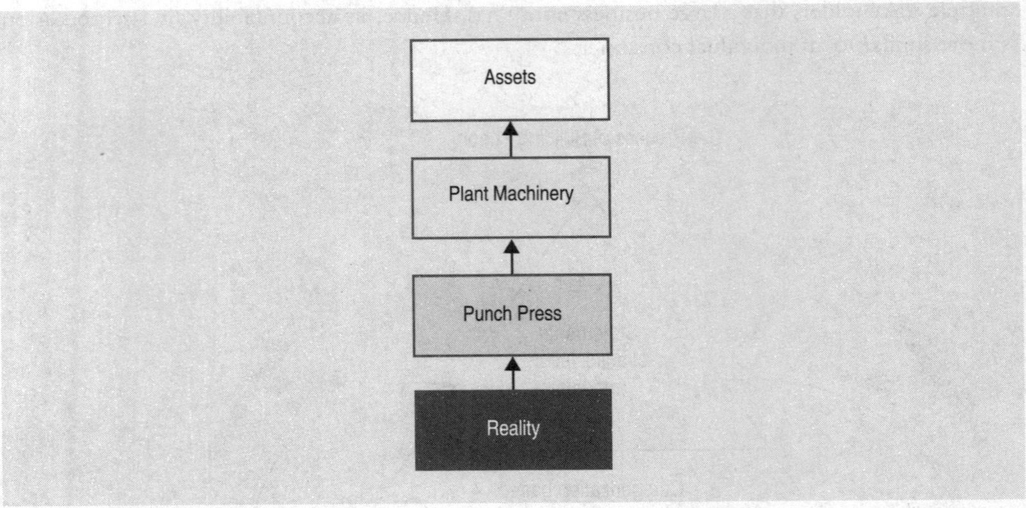

abstract level

In theory development, the level of knowledge expressing a concept that exists only as an idea or a quality apart from an object.

empirical level

Level of knowledge that is verifiable by experience or observation.

latent construct

A concept that is not directly observable or measurable, but can be estimated through proxy measures.

The basic or scientific business researcher operates at two levels: on the **abstract level** of concepts (and propositions) and on the empirical level of variables (and hypotheses). At the **empirical level**, we "experience" reality—that is, we observe, measure, or manipulate objects or events. For example, we commonly use the term job performance, but this is an abstract term that can mean different things to different people or in different situations. To move to the empirical level, we must more clearly define this construct and identify actual measures that we can assess and measure to represent job performance as shown in Exhibit 3.3. In research, we use the term **latent construct** to refer to a concept that is not directly observable or measurable, but can be estimated through proxy measures.[5] Job performance, customer satisfaction, and risk aversion are just three examples of the many latent constructs in business research. While we cannot directly see these latent constructs, we can measure them, and doing so is one of the greatest challenges for business researchers.

If an organizational researcher says "Older workers prefer different rewards than younger workers," two concepts—age of worker and reward preference—are the subjects of this abstract statement. If the researcher wishes to test this relationship, John, age 19, Chuck, age 45, and Mary, age 62—along with other workers—may be questioned about their preferences for salary, retirement plans, intrinsic job satisfaction, and so forth. Recording their ages and assessing their reward preferences are activities that occur at the empirical level. In this example, we can see

EXHIBIT 3.3
Concepts Are Abstractions of Reality

that researchers have a much easier time assessing and measuring age than the latent construct of reward preference.

In the end, researchers are concerned with the observable world, or what we shall loosely term reality. Theorists translate their conceptualization of reality into abstract ideas. Thus, theory deals with abstraction. Things are not the essence of theory; ideas are.[6] Concepts in isolation are not theories. To construct a theory we must explain how concepts relate to other concepts as discussed below.

TOTHEPOINT

Reality is merely an illusion, albeit a very persistent one.

—Albert Einstein

Research Propositions and Hypotheses

As we just mentioned, concepts are the basic units of theory development. However, theories require an understanding of the relationship among concepts. Thus, once the concepts of interest have been identified, a researcher is interested in the relationship among these concepts. **Propositions** are statements concerned with the relationships among concepts. A proposition explains the *logical* linkage among certain concepts by asserting a universal connection between concepts. For example, we might propose that treating our employees better will make them more loyal employees. This is certainly a logical link between managerial actions and employee reactions, but is quite general and not really testable in its current form.

propositions
Statements explaining the logical linkage among certain concepts by asserting a universal connection between concepts.

A **hypothesis** is a formal statement explaining some outcome. In its simplest form, a hypothesis is a guess. A sales manager may hypothesize that the salespeople who are highest in product knowledge will be the most productive. An advertising manager may hypothesize that if consumers' attitudes toward a product change in a positive direction, there will be an increase in consumption of the product. A human resource manager may hypothesize that job candidates with certain majors will be more successful employees.

hypothesis
Formal statement of an unproven proposition that is empirically testable.

A hypothesis is a proposition that is empirically testable. In other words, when one states a hypothesis, it should be written in a manner that can be supported or shown to be wrong through an empirical test. For example, using the color of the background for a Web site discussed previously, the researcher may use theoretical reasoning to develop the following hypothesis:

H1: A Web site with a blue background will generate more sales than an otherwise identical Web site with a red background.

We often apply statistics to data to empirically test hypotheses. **Empirical testing** means that something has been examined against reality using data. The abstract proposition "Treating our employees better will make them more loyal employees" may be tested empirically with a hypothesis. Exhibit 3.4 shows that the hypothesis "Increasing retirement benefits will reduce intention to leave the organization" is an empirical counterpart of this proposition. Retirement benefits and intention to leave are **variables**, reflecting the concepts of employee treatment and employee loyalty. When the data are consistent with a hypothesis, we say the hypothesis is *supported*. When the data are inconsistent with a hypothesis, we say the hypothesis is *not supported*. We are often tempted to say that we prove a hypothesis when the data conform to the prediction, but this isn't really true. Because our result is based on statistics, there is always the possibility that our conclusion is wrong. Now, at times we can be very, very confident in our conclusion, but from an absolute perspective, statistics cannot prove a hypothesis is true.

empirical testing
Examining a research hypothesis against reality using data.

variables
Anything that may assume different numerical values; the empirical assessment of a concept.

Because variables are at the empirical level, variables can be measured. In this case, retirement benefits might be measured quite easily and precisely (e.g., the actual percentage change in matching retirement funds), while the latent construct of intention to leave would be more challenging for the researcher. This step is known as **operationalizing** our variables—the process of identifying the actual measurement scales to assess the variables of interest. We will discuss operationalization in more detail in Chapter 13.

operationalizing
The process of identifying the actual measurement scales to assess the variables of interest.

EXHIBIT 3.4 **Hypotheses Are the Empirical Counterparts of Propositions**

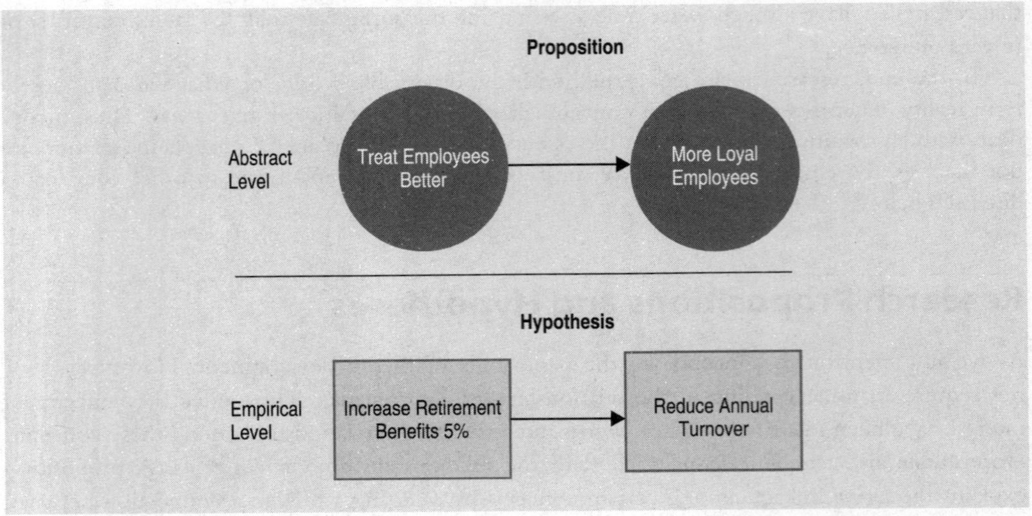

Thus, the scientific inquiry has two basic levels:

> *. . . the empirical and the abstract, conceptual. The empirical aspect is primarily concerned with the facts of the science as revealed by observation and experiments. The abstract or theoretical aspect, on the other hand, consists in a serious attempt to understand the facts of the science, and to integrate them into a coherent, i.e., a logical, system. From these observations and integrations are derived, directly or indirectly, the basic laws of the science.*[7]

Understanding Theory

Exhibit 3.5 is a simplified portrayal of a theory to explain voluntary job turnover—the movement of employees to other organizations. Two concepts—(1) the *perceived desirability of movement* to another organization and (2) the *perceived ease of movement* from the present job—are expected to be the primary determinants of *intention to quit*. This is a proposition. Further, the concept *intention to quit* is expected to be a necessary condition for the actual *voluntary job turnover behavior* to occur. This is a second proposition that links concepts together in this theory. In the more elaborate theory, *job performance* is another concept considered to be the primary determinant influencing both *perceived ease of movement* and *perceived desirability of movement*. Moreover, perceived ease of movement is related to other concepts such as *labor market conditions, number of organizations visible* to the individual, and *personal characteristics*. Perceived desirability of movement is influenced by concepts such as *equity of pay, job complexity*, and *participation in decision making*. A complete explanation of this theory is not possible; however, this example should help you understand the terminology used by theory builders.

TOTHEPOINT

If facts conflict with a theory, either the theory must be changed or the facts.

—Benedict Spinoza

Verifying Theory

In most scientific situations there are alternative theories to explain certain phenomena. To determine which is the better theory, researchers make observations or gather empirical data to verify the theories.

Maslow's hierarchical theory of motivation offers one explanation of human behavior. Maslow theorizes that individuals will attempt to satisfy physiological needs before self-esteem needs. An alternative view of motivation is provided by Freudian (psychoanalytic) theory, which suggests that unconscious, emotional impulses are the basic influences on behavior. One task of science is

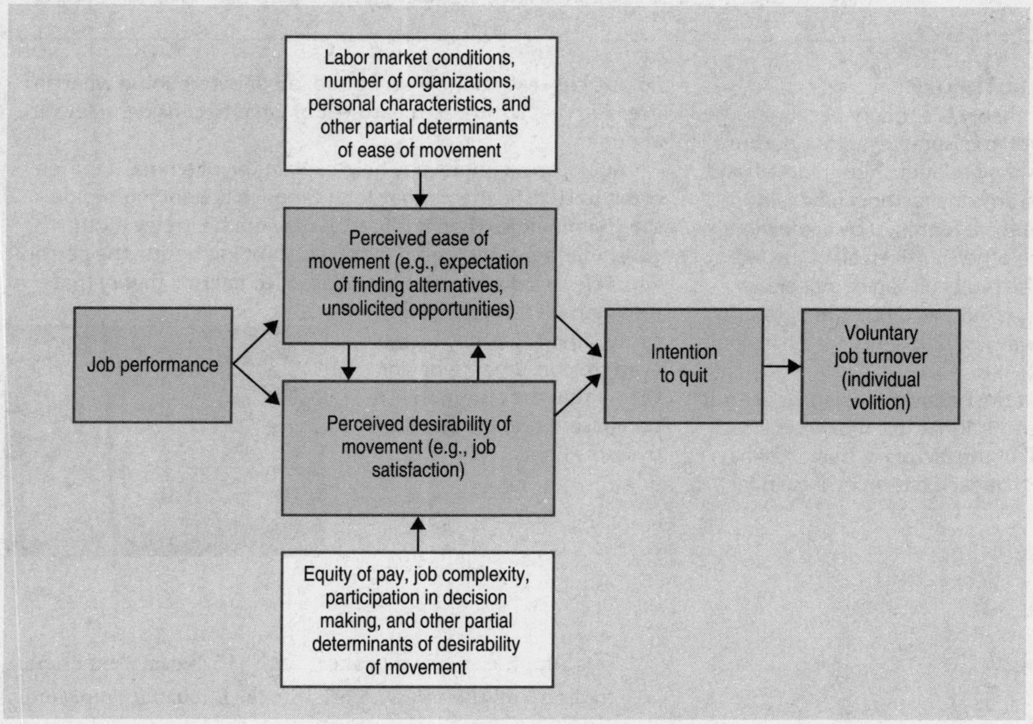

EXHIBIT 3.5 **A Basic Theory Explaining Voluntary Job Turnover**[8]

to determine if a given theoretical proposition is false or if there are inconsistencies between competing theories. Just as records are made to be broken, theories are made to be tested.

> *It must be possible to demonstrate that a given proposition or theory is false. This may at first glance appear strange. Why "false" rather than "true"? Technically, there may be other untested theories which could account for the results we obtained in our study of a proposition. At the very least, there may be a competing explanation which could be the "real" explanation for a given set of research findings. Thus, we can never be certain that our proposition or theory is the correct one. The scientist can only say, "I have a theory which I have objectively tested with data and the data are consistent with my theory." If the possibility of proving an idea false or wrong is not inherent in our test of an idea, then we cannot put much faith in the evidence that suggests it to be true. No other evidence was allowed to manifest itself.*[10]

TOTHEPOINT

Every genuine test of a theory is an attempt to falsify it, or to refute it.[9]

—Karl Popper

Theory Building

You may be wondering "Where do theories come from?" Although this is not an easy question to answer in a short chapter on theory in business research, we will explore this topic briefly. In this chapter, theory has been explained at the abstract, conceptual level and at the empirical level. Theory generation may occur at either level.

At the abstract, conceptual level, a theory may be developed with deductive reasoning by going from a general statement to a specific assertion. **Deductive reasoning** is the logical process of deriving a conclusion about a specific instance based on a known general premise or something known to be true. For example, while you might occasionally have doubts, we know that *all business professors are human beings*. If we also know that *Barry Babin is a business professor,* then we can deduce that *Barry Babin is a human being.*

At the empirical level, a theory may be developed with inductive reasoning. **Inductive reasoning** is the logical process of establishing a general proposition on the basis of observation of particular facts. All business professors that have ever been seen are human beings; therefore, all business professors are human beings.

deductive reasoning

The logical process of deriving a conclusion about a specific instance based on a known general premise or something known to be true.

inductive reasoning

The logical process of establishing a general proposition on the basis of observation of particular facts.

RESEARCH SNAPSHOT

Ballistic Theory

Ballistic theory is a theory because it deals with measurable factors, because it states their relationships in detail, and because any one factor can be fairly completely determined by a knowledge of all the others.[11] Given all of the factors except the initial speed of the projectile, an engineer can determine what that speed was. Asked to change the point of impact, he can suggest several ways in which this can be accomplished—all of which will work.

It is common knowledge that the behavioral sciences are not as advanced as the physical sciences. What this means, in effect, is that no one has yet defined all of the factors in human behavior or determined the influence that each has on events. In fact, no one has really done a very good job of determining what an event is. That is, how to measure it or what to consider relevant about it.

Again, an example may help explain the dilemma. It is irrelevant to ballistic theory that John Gingrich is standing beside the 155 mm rifle when it is fired. It may not be irrelevant to consumer behavior theory that he is standing beside the person who selects a necktie. It is not relevant to ballistic theory that the gunner's father once carried an M-1. It may be relevant to consumer behavior theory that the automobile purchaser's grandfather once owned a Ford.

© iStock

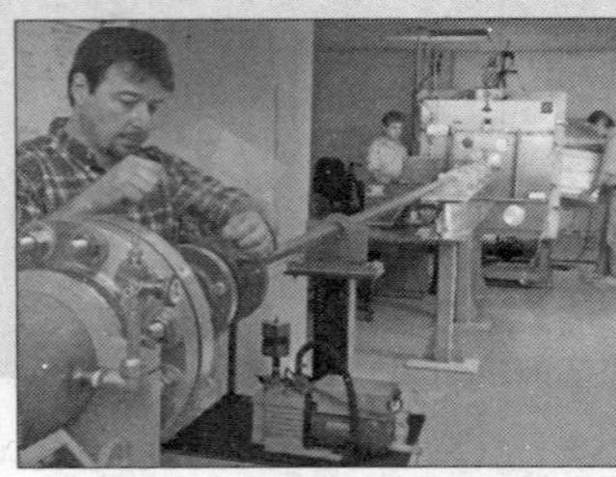

© NASA

Noting a link between changes in gold prices and political instability could be the foundation for a basic theory.

© TOMISLAV FORGO/SHUTTERSTOCK

Suppose a stockbroker with 15 years' experience trading on the New York Stock Exchange repeatedly notices that the price of gold and the price of gold stocks rise whenever there is a hijacking, terrorist bombing, or military skirmish. In other words, similar patterns occur whenever a certain type of event occurs. The stockbroker may induce from these empirical observations the more general situation that the price of gold is related to political stability. Thus, the stockbroker states a proposition based on his or her experience or specific observations: "Gold prices will increase during times of political instability." The stockbroker has constructed a basic theory.

Over the course of time, theory construction is often the result of a combination of deductive and inductive reasoning. Our experiences lead us to draw conclusions that we then try to verify empirically by using the scientific method.

The Scientific Method

scientific method
A set of prescribed procedures for establishing and connecting theoretical statements about events, for analyzing empirical evidence, and for predicting events yet unknown; techniques or procedures used to analyze empirical evidence in an attempt to confirm or disprove prior conceptions.

The **scientific method** is a set of prescribed procedures for establishing and connecting theoretical statements about events, for analyzing empirical evidence, and for predicting events yet unknown. It is useful to look at the analytic process of scientific theory building as a series of stages. While there is not complete consensus concerning exact procedures for the scientific method, we suggest seven operations may be viewed as the steps involved in the application of the scientific method:

1. Assessment of relevant existing knowledge of a phenomenon
2. Formulation of concepts and propositions
3. Statement of hypotheses
4. Design of research to test the hypotheses

5. Acquisition of meaningful empirical data
6. Analysis and evaluation of data
7. Proposal of an explanation of the phenomenon and statement of new problems raised by the research[12]

An excellent overview of the scientific method is presented in Robert Pirsig's book *Zen and the Art of Motorcycle Maintenance*:

> *Actually I've never seen a cycle-maintenance problem complex enough really to require full-scale formal scientific method. Repair problems are not that hard. When I think of formal scientific method an image sometimes comes to mind of an enormous juggernaut, a huge bulldozer—slow, tedious, lumbering, laborious, but invincible. It takes twice as long, five times as long, maybe a dozen times as long as informal mechanic's techniques, but you know in the end you're going to get it. There's no fault isolation problem in motorcycle maintenance that can stand up to it. When you've hit a really tough one, tried everything, racked your brain and nothing works, and you know that this time Nature has really decided to be difficult, you say, "Okay, Nature, that's the end of the nice guy," and you crank up the formal scientific method.*
>
> *For this you keep a lab notebook. Everything gets written down, formally, so that you know at all times where you are, where you've been, where you're going and where you want to get. In scientific work and electronics technology this is necessary because otherwise the problems get so complex you get lost in them and confused and forget what you know and what you don't know and have to give up. In cycle maintenance things are not that involved, but when confusion starts it's a good idea to hold it down by making everything formal and exact. Sometimes just the act of writing down the problems straightens out your head as to what they really are.*
>
> *The logical statements entered into the notebook are broken down into six categories: (1) statement of the problem, (2) hypotheses as to the cause of the problem, (3) experiments designed to test each hypothesis, (4) predicted results of the experiments, (5) observed results of the experiments, and (6) conclusions from the results of the experiments. This is not different from the formal arrangement of many college and high-school lab notebooks but the purpose here is no longer just busywork. The purpose now is precise guidance of thoughts that will fail if they are not accurate.*
>
> *The real purpose of scientific method is to make sure Nature hasn't misled you into thinking you know something you don't actually know. There's not a mechanic or scientist or technician alive who hasn't suffered from that one so much that he's not instinctively on guard. That's the main reason why so much scientific and mechanical information sounds so dull and so cautious. If you get careless or go romanticizing scientific information, giving it a flourish here and there, Nature will soon make a complete fool out of you. It does it often enough anyway even when you don't give it opportunities. One must be extremely careful and rigidly logical when dealing with Nature: one logical slip and an entire scientific edifice comes tumbling down. One false deduction about the machine and you can get hung up indefinitely.*
>
> *In Part One of formal scientific method, which is the statement of the problem, the main skill is in stating absolutely no more than you are positive you know. It is much better to enter a statement "Solve Problem: Why doesn't cycle work?" which sounds dumb but is correct, than it is to enter a statement "Solve Problem: What is wrong with the electrical system?" when you don't absolutely know the*

A motorcycle mechanic . . . who honks the horn to see if the battery works is informally conducting a true scientific experiment. He is testing a hypothesis by putting the question to nature.
— Robert M. Pirsig

© DBIMAGES/ALAMY

trouble is in the electrical system. What you should state is "Solve Problem: What is wrong with cycle?" and then state as the first entry of Part Two: "Hypothesis Number One: The trouble is in the electrical system." You think of as many hypotheses as you can, then you design experiments to test them to see which are true and which are false.

This careful approach to the beginning questions keeps you from taking a major wrong turn which might cause you weeks of extra work or can even hang you up completely. Scientific questions often have a surface appearance of dumbness for this reason. They are asked in order to prevent dumb mistakes later on.

Part Three, that part of formal scientific method called experimentation, is sometimes thought of by romantics as all of science itself because that's the only part with much visual surface. They see lots of test tubes and bizarre equipment and people running around making discoveries. They do not see the experiment as part of a larger intellectual process and so they often confuse experiments with demonstrations, which look the same. A man conducting a gee-whiz science show with fifty thousand dollars' worth of Frankenstein equipment is not doing anything scientific if he knows beforehand what the results of his efforts are going to be. A motorcycle mechanic, on the other hand, who honks the horn to see if the battery works is informally conducting a true scientific experiment. He is testing a hypothesis by putting the question to nature. The TV scientist who mutters sadly, "The experiment is a failure; we have failed to achieve what we had hoped for," is suffering mainly from a bad scriptwriter. An experiment is never a failure solely because it fails to achieve predicted results. An experiment is a failure only when it also fails adequately to test the hypothesis in question, when the data it produces don't prove anything one way or another.

Skill at this point consists of using experiments that test only the hypothesis in question, nothing less, nothing more. If the horn honks, and the mechanic concludes that the whole electrical system is working, he is in deep trouble. He has reached an illogical conclusion. The honking horn only tells him that the battery and horn are working. To design an experiment properly he has to think very rigidly in terms of what directly causes what. This you know from the hierarchy. The horn doesn't make the cycle go. Neither does the battery, except in a very indirect way. The point at which the electrical system directly causes the engine to fire is at the spark plugs, and if you don't test here, at the output of the electrical system, you will never really know whether the failure is electrical or not.

To test properly the mechanic removes the plug and lays it against the engine so that the base around the plug is electrically grounded, kicks the starter lever and watches the spark-plug gap for a blue spark. If there isn't any he can conclude one of two things: (a) there is an electrical failure or (b) his experiment is sloppy. If he is experienced he will try it a few more times, checking connections, trying every way he can think of to get that plug to fire. Then, if he can't get it to fire, he finally concludes that (a) is correct, there's an electrical failure, and the experiment is over. He has proved that his hypothesis is correct.

In the final category, conclusions, skill comes in stating no more than the experiment has proved. It hasn't proved that when he fixes the electrical system the motorcycle will start. There may be other things wrong. But he does know that the motorcycle isn't going to run until the electrical system is working and he sets up the next formal question: "Solve problem: What is wrong with the electrical system?"

He then sets up hypotheses for these and tests them. By asking the right questions and choosing the right tests and drawing the right conclusions the mechanic works his way down the echelons of the motorcycle hierarchy until he has found the exact specific cause or causes of the engine failure, and then he changes them so that they no longer cause the failure.

An untrained observer will see only physical labor and often get the idea that physical labor is mainly what the mechanic does. Actually the physical labor is the smallest and easiest part of what the mechanic does. By far the greatest part of his work is careful observation and precise thinking. That is why mechanics sometimes seem so taciturn and withdrawn when performing tests. They don't like it when you talk to them because they are concentrating on mental images, hierarchies, and not really looking at you or the physical motorcycle at all. They are using the experiment as part of a program to expand their hierarchy of knowledge of the faulty motorcycle and compare it to the correct hierarchy in their mind. They are looking at underlying form.[13]

Practical Value of Theories

As the above excerpt makes evident, theories allow us to generalize beyond individual facts or isolated situations. Theories provide a framework that can guide managerial strategy by providing insights into general rules of behavior. When different incidents may be theoretically comparable in

TIPS OF THE TRADE

- Theories are only relevant to research because they are useful. In that sense, nothing could be "too theoretical."
    - Theories often guide research by providing a starting place, indicating what things should be observed, and showing how these things should relate.
    - Theories become corroborated over time through testing the explanations they offer.
        - An empirical test means the theory must be compared to reality. The more that the explanations offered match reality the more the theory becomes verified.
        - The scientific method provides a way of testing theoretical propositions.
- Managerial business strategy then becomes guided by the theories that are verified through research.
    - All theories stand to be further tested, confirmed, modified, or proved to be incorrect.

some way, the scientific knowledge gained from theory development may have practical value. A good theory allows us to generalize beyond individual facts so that general patterns may be understood and predicted. For this reason it is often said there is nothing so practical as a good theory.

Summary

1. Define the meaning of *theory*. Theories are simply models designed to help us better understand reality and to understand the logic behind things we observe. A theory is a formal, logical explanation of some events that includes predictions of how things relate to one another.

2. Understand the goals of theory. There are two primary goals of theory. The first is to understand the relationships among various phenomena. A theory provides a picture of the linkages among different concepts, allowing us to better comprehend how they affect one another. The second goal is to predict. Once we have an understanding of the relationships among concepts, we can then predict what will happen if we change one factor. For example, if we understand the relationship between advertising expenditures and retail sales, we can then predict the impact of decreasing or increasing our advertising expenditures.

3. Understand the terms *concepts, propositions, variables,* and *hypotheses*. A concept or construct is a generalized idea about a class of objects, attributes, occurrences, or processes that has been given a name. Leadership style, employee turnover, and customer satisfaction are all concepts. Concepts express in words various events or objects. Propositions are statements concerned with the relationships among concepts. A proposition explains the *logical* linkage among certain concepts by asserting a universal connection between concepts: "Leadership style is related to employee turnover." A hypothesis is a formal statement explaining some outcome regarding variables of interest. Variables are the empirical reflection of a concept and a hypothesis is a proposition stated in a testable format. So, concepts and propositions are at the abstract level, while variables and hypotheses are at the empirical level.

4. Discuss how theories are developed. A theory can be built through a process of reviewing previous findings of similar studies or knowledge of applicable theoretical areas. A theory may be developed with deductive reasoning by going from a general statement to a specific assertion. Deductive reasoning is the logical process of deriving a conclusion about a specific instance based on a known general premise or something known to be true. Inductive reasoning is the logical process of establishing a general proposition on the basis of observation of particular facts.

5. Understand the scientific method. The scientific method is a set of prescribed procedures for establishing and connecting theoretical statements about events, for analyzing empirical evidence, and for predicting events yet unknown. It is useful to look at the analytic process of scientific theory building as a series of stages. We mentioned seven operations may be viewed as the steps involved in the application of the scientific method: (1) Assessment of relevant existing knowledge of a phenomenon, (2) formulation of concepts and propositions, (3) statement of hypotheses, (4) design of research to test the hypotheses, (5) acquisition of meaningful empirical data,

(6) analysis and evaluation of data, and (7) proposal of an explanation of the phenomenon and statement of new problems raised by the research. In sum, the scientific method guides us from the abstract nature of concepts and propositions, to the empirical variables and hypotheses, and to the testing and verification of theory.

Key Terms and Concepts

abstract level, *42*
concept (or construct), *41*
deductive reasoning, *45*
empirical level, *42*
empirical testing, *43*
hypothesis, *43*
inductive reasoning, *45*
ladder of abstraction, *41*
latent construct, *43*
operationalizing, *44*
propositions, *43*
scientific method, *46*
theory, *39*
variables, *43*

Questions for Review and Critical Thinking

1. How do concepts differ from variables?
2. The seventeenth-century Dutch philosopher Benedict Spinoza said, "If the facts conflict with a theory, either the theory must be changed or the facts." What is the practical meaning of this statement?
3. How do propositions and hypotheses differ?
4. Find another definition of *theory*. How is the definition you found similar to this book's definition? How is it different?
5. What are some theories offered to explain aspects of your field of business?
6. Compare and contrast *deductive logic* with *inductive logic*. Give an example of both.

Research Activities

1. **'NET** The Chapter Vignette briefly introduced *Attribution Theory*. Do a Web search regarding Attribution Theory and identify the key characteristics of this theory.
2. **'NET** The *Merriam-Webster* dictionary definition of *theory* can be found at **http://www.merriam-webster.com/dictionary/theory**. What is the definition of *theory* given at this site? How does it compare to the definition given in this chapter?
3. **'NET** *The Logic of Scientific Discovery* is an important theoretical work. Visit The Karl Popper Web site at **http://elm.eeng.dcu.ie/~tkpw/** to learn about its author and his work.

CHAPTER 4
THE BUSINESS RESEARCH PROCESS: AN OVERVIEW

LEARNING OUTCOMES

After studying this chapter, you should be able to

1. **Define decision making and understand the role research plays in making decisions**
2. **Classify business research as either exploratory research, descriptive research, or causal research**
3. **List the major phases of the research process and the steps within each**
4. **Explain the difference between a research project and a research program**

Chapter Vignette: The Changing Educational Environment

Students seeking a higher education today enjoy many more choices than did their parents. Universities offer new degree programs in varied and specific fields including areas like sports marketing and gaming management. However, it isn't simply the fields of study that may be new, but also the manner of study. Options for nontraditional students who have difficulty attending day classes or devoting years of study to obtaining a degree have grown exponentially. The University of Phoenix, Strayer University, and Nova Southeast typify institutions that specialize in catering to those seeking a nontraditional degree program. These competitive pressures have led even the most traditional universities to rethink the "sage on the stage" approach and conventional academic calendars.

The market for the MBA degree is particularly competitive. Students pursue their MBA either traditionally, in weekend-only programs, at night school, online, or in some combination. Over a quarter of a million U.S. students alone attend MBA classes of one form or another at any given time. In urban areas, such as the Dallas-Fort Worth area, there are sometimes a dozen or more institutions offering an MBA. Even in smaller communities, universities are facing decisions about their MBA offerings as the competitive set and nontraditional programs have entered the market:

- How much should they adapt to the changing environment?
- Should they offer courses online?
- If so, who are they competing with?
- Should they offer a weekend program?
- Should they offer classes in multiple locations?
- Can they better accomplish the mission of the university with an online MBA program?

- If multiple formats and locations are offered in the program, should different faculty teach?
- Is demand sufficient? That is, are there enough potential students to make this financially feasible?
- Is there a potential perceived product quality difference between a traditional and a nontraditional MBA program?

The competitive MBA market typifies the landscape of many organizations. Clearly, universities could benefit from business research addressing some of these key questions. Each university maintains its own academic standard while still trying to attract enough students to make its MBA program feasible. The competitive landscape is filled with both potential opportunities and potential problems. Decisions made by university administrators will determine how successfully each school deals with the changing environment.

Introduction

This chapter focuses on the relationship between business research and managerial decision making. Business success is determined directly by the quality of decisions made by key personnel. Researchers contribute to decision making in several key ways. These include

1. Helping to better define the current situation
2. Defining the firm—determining how consumers, competitors, and employees view the firm
3. Providing ideas for enhancing current business practices
4. Identifying new strategic directions
5. Testing ideas that will assist in implementing business strategies for the firm
6. Examining how correct a certain business theory is in a given situation

The chapter introduces the types of research that allow researchers to provide input to key decision makers. Causality and the conditions for establishing causality are presented. Last but not least, the chapter discusses stages in the business research process.

Decision Making

Young adults make many decisions that affect their future. These include important strategic decisions like whether to go to college or not. If the answer is yes, then an individual faces a decision regarding where to attend. Furthermore, the student must decide what subject to major in, what electives to take, which instructors to sign up for, whether or not to belong to a fraternity or sorority, how much to work outside of school, and so forth. The student may seek out data, usually in the form of advice provided by parents, guidance counselors, other students, or various media sources. These data may be critical in reaching decisions. Indeed, the answers to each of these questions shape a student's future, influence the way he or she is viewed by others, and ultimately determine how successful he or she will be.

Likewise, businesses face decisions that shape the future of the organization, its employees, and its customers. In each case, the decisions are brought about as the firm either seeks to capitalize on some opportunity or to reduce any potential negative impacts related to some business problem. A **business opportunity** is a situation that makes some potential competitive advantage possible. The discovery of some underserved segment presents such an opportunity. For example, eBay capitalized on a business opportunity presented by technological advances to do much the same thing that is done at a garage sale but on a very, very large scale.

business opportunity
A situation that makes some potential competitive advantage possible.

A **business problem** is a situation that makes some significant negative consequence more likely. A natural disaster can present a problem for many firms as they face potential loss of property and personnel and the possibility that their operations, and therefore their revenue, will be interrupted. Most business problems, however, are not nearly as obvious. In fact, many are not easily observable. Instead, problems are commonly inferred from **symptoms**, which are observable

business problem
A situation that makes some significant negative consequence more likely.

symptoms
Observable cues that serve as a signal of a problem because they are caused by that problem.

cues that serve as a signal of a problem because they are caused by that problem. An increase in employee turnover is generally only a symptom of a business problem, rather than the problem itself. Research may help identify what is causing this symptom so that decision makers can actually attack the problem, not just the symptom. Patients don't usually go to the doctor and point out their problem (such as an ulcer). Instead, they point out the symptoms (upset stomach) they are experiencing. Similarly, decision makers usually hear about symptoms and often need help from research to identify and attack problems. Whether facing an opportunity or a problem, businesses need quality information to deal effectively with these situations.

decision making
The process of developing and deciding among alternative ways of resolving a problem or choosing from among alternative opportunities.

Formally defined, **decision making** is the process of developing and deciding among alternative ways of resolving a problem or choosing from among alternative opportunities. A decision maker must recognize the nature of the problem or opportunity, identify how much information is currently available, how reliable it is, and determine what additional information is needed to better deal with the situation. Every decision-making situation can be classified based on whether it best represents a problem or an opportunity and where the situation falls on a continuum from absolute ambiguity to complete certainty.

Certainty

Complete certainty means that the decision maker has all information needed to make an optimal decision. This includes the exact nature of the business problem or opportunity. For example, an advertising agency may need to know the demographic characteristics of subscribers to magazines in which it may place a client's advertisements. The agency knows exactly what information it needs and where to find the information. If a manager is completely certain about both the problem or opportunity and future outcomes, then research may not be needed at all. However, perfect certainty, especially about the future, is rare.

Uncertainty

Uncertainty means that the manager grasps the general nature of desired objectives, but the information about alternatives is incomplete. Predictions about forces that shape future events are educated guesses. Under conditions of uncertainty, effective managers recognize that spending additional time to gather data that clarify the nature of a decision is needed. For instance, a university may understand that there is an objective of increasing the number of MBA students, but it may not know whether an online, weekend, or off-site MBA program is the best way to accomplish the objective. Or a firm needing operating capital may consider an initial public offering, but is not certain of demand for the stock or how to establish the price of the IPO. Business decisions generally involve uncertainty, particularly when a company is seeking new opportunities.

Ambiguity

Ambiguity means that the nature of the problem itself is unclear. Objectives are vague and decision alternatives are difficult to define. This is by far the most difficult decision situation, but perhaps the most common.

Managers face a variety of problems and decisions. Complete certainty and predictable future outcomes may make business research a waste of time. However, under conditions of uncertainty or ambiguity, business research becomes more attractive to the decision makers. Decisions also vary in terms of importance, meaning that some may have great impact on the welfare of the firm and others may have negligible impact. The more important, ambiguous, or uncertain a situation is, the more likely it is that additional time must be spent on business research.

PROBLEMS AND OPPORTUNITIES

Exhibit 4.1 depicts decision situations characterized by the nature of the decision and the degree of ambiguity.[1] Under problem-focused decision making and conditions of high ambiguity, symptoms may not clearly point to some problem. Indeed, they may be quite vague or subtle, indicating only small deviations from normal conditions. For instance, a fast-food restaurant may be experiencing small changes in the sales of its individual products, but no change in overall sales. Such a symptom may not easily point to a problem such as a change in consumer tastes. As ambiguity is lessened, the symptoms are clearer and are better indicators of a problem. A large and sudden drop in overall sales may suggest the problem that the restaurant's menu does not fare well compared to competitors' menus. Thus, a menu change may be in order. However, it is also possible the drop in sales is due to new competition, a competitor's price drop, or new promotional campaign. Thus, research is needed to clarify the situation.

Similarly, in opportunity-oriented research, ambiguity is characterized by environmental trends that do not suggest a clear direction. As the trends become larger and clearer, they are more diagnostic, meaning they point more clearly to a single opportunity.

Types of Business Research

Business research is undertaken to reduce uncertainty and focus decision making. In more ambiguous circumstances, management may be totally unaware of a business problem. Alternatively, someone may be scanning the environment for opportunities. For example, an entrepreneur may have a personal interest in softball and baseball. She is interested in converting her hobby into a profitable business venture and hits on the idea of establishing an indoor softball and baseball

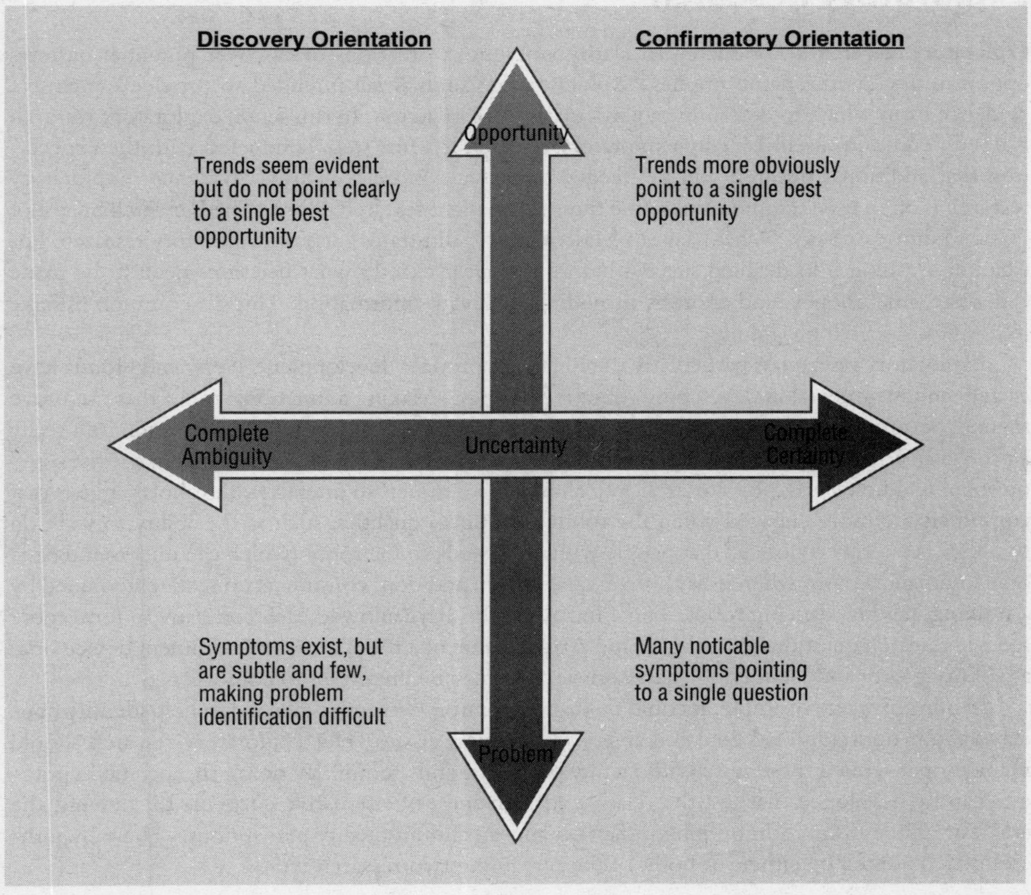

EXHIBIT 4.1
Describing Decision-Making Situations

training facility and instructional center. However, the demand for such a business is unknown. Even if there is sufficient demand, she is not sure of the best location, actual services offered, desired hours of operation, and so forth. Some preliminary research is necessary to gain insights into the nature of such a situation. Without it, the situation may remain too ambiguous to make more than a seat-of-the-pants decision. In this situation, business research is almost certainly needed.

In other situations, researchers know exactly what their problems are and can design careful studies to test specific hypotheses. For example, an organization may face a problem regarding health care benefits for their employees. Awareness of this problem could be based on input from human resource managers, recruiters, and current employees. The problem could be contributing to difficulties in recruiting new employees. How should the organization's executive team address this problem? They may devise a careful test exploring which of three different health plans are judged the most desirable. This type of research is problem-oriented and seems relatively unambiguous. This process may culminate with researchers preparing a report suggesting the relative effect of each alternative plan on employee recruitment. The selection of a new health plan should follow relatively directly from the research.

Business research can be classified on the basis of either technique or purpose. Experiments, surveys, and observational studies are just a few common research techniques. Classifying research by its purpose, such as the situations described above, shows how the nature of a decision situation influences the research methodology. The following section introduces the three types of business research:

1. Exploratory
2. Descriptive
3. Causal

Matching the particular decision situation with the right type of research is important in obtaining useful research results.

Exploratory Research

exploratory research
Conducted to clarify ambiguous situations or discover ideas that may be potential business opportunities.

Exploratory research is conducted to clarify ambiguous situations or discover potential business opportunities. As the name implies, exploratory research is *not* intended to provide conclusive evidence from which to determine a particular course of action. In this sense, exploratory research is not an end unto itself. Usually exploratory research is a first step, conducted with the expectation that additional research will be needed to provide more conclusive evidence. Exploratory research is often used to guide and refine these subsequent research efforts. The Research Snapshot "Cute, Funny, or Sexy? What Makes a Mascot Tick?" illustrates a use of exploratory research. For example, rushing into detailed surveys before it is clear exactly what decisions need to be made can waste time, money, and effort by providing irrelevant information. This is a common mistake in business research programs.

Exploratory research is particularly useful in new product development.[2] Sony and Honda have each been instrumental in developing robot technology.[3] Making a functional robot that can move around, perform basic functions, carry out instructions, and even carry on a conversation isn't really a problem. What Sony and Honda have to research is what business opportunities may exist based on robot technology. Exploratory research allowing consumers to interact with robots suggests that consumers are more engaged when the robot has human qualities, such as the ability to walk on two legs. Researchers noticed that people will actually talk to the robot (which can understand basic oral commands) more when it has human qualities. In addition, consumers do seem entertained by a walking, talking, dancing robot. These initial insights have allowed each company to form more specific research questions focusing on the relative value of a robot as an entertainment device or as a security guard, and identifying characteristics that may be important to consumers.

In our university example, it could be that exploratory research is needed to help identify concerns about nontraditional course delivery for business classes. This exploratory research should include open-ended interviews with faculty, students, and alumni. By doing so, specific hypotheses can be developed that test the relative attractiveness of alternative curricula to students, the effect of online instruction on job satisfaction and on alumni quality perceptions.[4] These hypotheses may be tested by either, or both, of the remaining two research types.

RESEARCH SNAPSHOT

Cute, Funny, or Sexy? What Makes a Mascot Tick?

Has the Pillsbury Doughboy ever changed? How old should the Brawny (paper towel) man be? What should the M&Ms characters be named? These questions all have many possible answers. In truth, a lot of research goes into answering these kinds of questions. It often begins with exploratory research. For instance, focus groups involving female consumers revealed a considerable amount of intimate discussion about the Brawny man. Thus, it seemed that a sexy Brawny man would yield a better response than a humorous or intelligent Brawny man.

Mr. Peanut, the icon for Planter's Peanuts, has actually changed very little since his introduction in the 1920s. He looks good for his age! Again, exploratory research suggests generally positive comments about Mr. Peanut, so only minor changes in the color scheme have been introduced. A few years ago, exploratory research led to some further tests of a Mr. Peanut in Bermuda shorts, but the tests proved overwhelmingly negative, sending Planters back to a more original peanut.

© iStock

Similarly, exploratory research simply asked a few consumers for their reactions to the Mars M&Ms characters. Mars was interested in discovering names for the characters. They found that most consumers simply referred to them by their colors. This piece of information became useful in shaping future research and business strategy.

Sources: Voight, Joan, "Mascot Makeover: The Risky Business of Tampering with Brand Icons," *Adweek* (July 7, 2003), 20–26; Elliot, Stuart, "Updating a Venerable Character, or Tarnishing a Sterling Reputation?" *The New York Times* (March 19, 2004), C5; "Advertising Mascots—People," TV Acres, http://www.tvacres.com/admascots_brawny.htm, accessed January 25, 2009.

PR NEWSPHOTOL/GEORGIA PACIFIC

Descriptive Research

descriptive research
Describes characteristics of objects, people, groups, organizations, or environments; tries to "paint a picture" of a given situation.

As the name implies, the major purpose of **descriptive research** is to describe characteristics of objects, people, groups, organizations, or environments. In other words, descriptive research tries to "paint a picture" of a given situation by addressing *who, what, when, where,* and *how* questions. For example, every month the Bureau of Labor Statistics (BLS) conducts descriptive research in the form of the *Current Population Survey*. Official statistics on a variety of characteristics of the labor force are derived from this survey (the *Current Population Survey* can be found at **http://www.bls.gov/CPS/**). This research describes the who, what, when, where, and how regarding the current economic and employment situation.

Unlike exploratory research, descriptive studies are conducted after the researcher has gained a firm grasp of the situation being studied. This understanding, which may have been developed in part from exploratory research, directs the study toward specific issues. Later, we will discuss the role of research questions and hypotheses. These statements help greatly in designing and implementing a descriptive study. Without these, the researcher would have little or no idea of what questions to ask. The Research Snapshot "Whines or Wines" illustrates an application of descriptive research.

Descriptive research often helps describe market segments. For example, researchers used descriptive surveys to describe consumers who are heavy consumers (buy a lot) of organic food products. The resulting report showed that these consumers tend to live in coastal cities with populations over 500,000, with the majority residing on the West Coast. The most frequent buyers of organic foods are affluent men and women of ages 45–54 (36 percent) and 18–34 (35 percent).[5] Interestingly, consumers who buy organic foods are not very brand-oriented—81 percent of them cannot name a single organic brand. Research such as this helps high-quality supermarkets such as Whole Foods make location decisions. Over half of Whole Foods' food products are organic.

Similarly, the university considering the addition of an online MBA program might benefit from descriptive research profiling the current and the potential customers. Online customers are not identical to the traditional MBA student. They tend to be older than the average 24-year-old traditional student, averaging about 30 years of age. Also, they tend to live in rural communities, be more introverted, and expect a higher workload than traditional students. Another key statistic is that the dropout rate for online students is significantly higher than for traditional MBA students. Nearly 14 percent of online students drop before completing a course as compared to 7.2 percent for traditional in-class students. For this and other reasons, online students are much more costly to serve.[6]

RESEARCH SNAPSHOT

Whines for Wines

Greg Norman is best known for performance on the golf course. However, he is also one of the most successful businesspeople to come out of sports. Among his many ventures, Norman is a well-respected vintner. Norman Estates gained fame in the wine trade with Australian wines that offered considerable quality at a fair price. More recently, Norman Estates is expanding its portfolio by purchasing vineyard properties and production capacity in California. As Norman Estates and other wineries consider diversifying production beyond their traditional boundaries, descriptive research can be vital in making these key decisions.

Descriptive research details what wine consumers like to drink in terms of where the wine is from and where the consumers are located. Consumers around the world form geographic segments with preferences for wines from certain areas. American consumers, for instance, have contributed to the growing slump in French wine sales by switching increasingly from French wines to Australian- and American-made wines. In particular, French wines at low and moderate prices have suffered, whereas higher price French wine sales remain steady. In addition, wine sales in the United States and in the United Kingdom are relatively strong compared to wine sales in France and Germany.

All of these descriptive results may allow Greg Norman a better understanding of the international wine market and therefore make better decisions about where to grow and produce wine. Do you think the choice to expand to California rather than France seems like a good decision?

Sources: Orth, U. R., M. M. Wolf, and T. Dodd, "Dimensions of Wine Region Equity and Their Impact on Consumer Preferences," *Journal of Product and Brand Management* 14, no. 2 (2005), 88–97; Conibear, Helena, "World-Wide Consumption Trends," *AIM-Digest* (2005), http://www.aim-digest.com/gateway/pages/trends/articles/trends.htm, accessed November 24, 2005.

diagnostic analysis

Seeks to diagnose reasons for business outcomes and focuses specifically on the beliefs and feelings consumers have about and toward competing products

Accuracy is critically important in descriptive research. If a descriptive study incorrectly estimates a university's demand for its MBA offering by even a few students, it can mean the difference between the program sustaining itself or being a drain on already scarce resources. For instance, if a cohort group of 25 students is predicted, but only 15 students actually sign up, the program will likely not generate enough revenue to sustain itself. Therefore, it is easy to see that descriptive research forecasting sales revenue and costs or describing consumer attitudes, satisfaction, and commitment must be accurate or decision making will suffer.

Survey research typifies a descriptive study. For example, state societies of certified public accountants (CPAs) conduct annual practice management surveys that ask questions such as "Do you charge clients for travel time at regular rates?" "Do you have a program of continuing education on a regular basis for professional employees?" "Do you pay incentive bonuses to professional staff?" Although the researcher may have a general understanding of the business practices of CPAs, conclusive evidence in the form of answers to questions of fact must be collected to determine the actual activities.

Descriptive research about consumers who buy organic food has paid off for the Whole Foods chain of stores.

A **diagnostic analysis** seeks to diagnose reasons for business outcomes and focuses specifically on the beliefs and feelings respondents have about and toward specific issues. A research study trying to diagnose slumping French wine sales might ask consumers their beliefs about the taste of French, Australian, and American wines. The results might indicate a deficiency in taste, suggesting that consumers do not believe French wines taste as fruity as do the others. Descriptive research can sometimes provide an explanation by diagnosing differences among competitors, but descriptive research does not provide direct evidence of causality.

Causal Research

If a decision maker knows what causes important outcomes like sales, stock price, and employee satisfaction, then he or she can shape firm decisions in a positive way. Causal inferences are very powerful because they lead to greater control. **Causal research** seeks to identify cause-and-effect relationships. When something *causes* an effect, it means it brings it about or makes it happen. The effect is the outcome. Rain causes grass to get wet. Rain is the cause and wet grass is the effect.

causal research
Allows causal inferences to be made; seeks to identify cause-and-effect relationships.

The different types of research discussed here are often building blocks—exploratory research builds the foundation for descriptive research, which usually establishes the basis for causal research. Thus, before causal studies are undertaken, researchers typically have a good understanding of the phenomena being studied. Because of this, the researcher can make an educated prediction about the cause-and-effect relationships that will be tested. Although greater knowledge of the situation is a good thing, it doesn't come without a price. Causal research designs can take a long time to implement. Also, they often involve intricate designs that can be very expensive. Even though managers may often want the assurance that causal inferences can bring, they are not always willing to spend the time and money it takes to get them.

CAUSALITY

Ideally, managers want to know how a change in one event will change another event of interest. As an example, how will implementing a new employee training program change job performance? Causal research attempts to establish that when we do one thing, another thing will follow. A **causal inference** is just such a conclusion. While we use the term "cause" frequently in our everyday language, scientifically establishing something as a cause is not so easy. A causal inference can only be supported when very specific evidence exists. Three critical pieces of causal evidence are:

causal inference
A conclusion that when one thing happens, another specific thing will follow.

1. Temporal Sequence
2. Concomitant Variance
3. Nonspurious Association

Temporal Sequence

Temporal sequence deals with the time order of events. In other words, having an *appropriate causal order of events,* or temporal sequence, is one criterion for causality. Simply put, the cause must occur before the effect. It would be difficult for a restaurant manager to blame a decrease in sales on a new chef if the drop in sales occurred before the new chef arrived. If a change in the CEO causes a change in stock prices, the CEO change must occur before the change in stock values.

temporal sequence
One of three criteria for causality; deals with the time order of events—the cause must occur before the effect.

Concomitant Variation

Concomitant variation occurs when two events "covary" or "correlate," meaning they vary systematically. In causal terms, concomitant variation means that when a change in the cause occurs, a change in the outcome also is observed. A correlation coefficient, which we discuss in a later chapter, is often used to represent concomitant variation. Causality cannot possibly exist when there is no systematic variation between the variables. For example, if a retail store never changes its employees' vacation policy, then the vacation policy cannot possibly be responsible for a change in employee satisfaction. There is no correlation between the two events. On the other hand, if two events vary together, one event *may* be causing the other. If a university increases its number of online MBA course offerings and experiences a decrease in enrollment in its traditional in-class MBA offerings, the online course offerings may be causing the decrease. But the systematic variation alone doesn't guarantee it.

concomitant variation
One of three criteria for causality; occurs when two events "covary," meaning they vary systematically.

Nonspurious Association

nonspurious association

One of three criteria for causality; means any covariation between a cause and an effect is true and not simply due to some other variable.

Nonspurious association means any covariation between a cause and an effect is true, rather than due to some other variable. A spurious association is one that is not true. Often, a causal inference cannot be made even though the other two conditions exist because both the cause and effect have some common cause; that is, both may be influenced by a third variable. For instance, there is a strong, positive correlation between ice cream purchases and murder rates—as ice cream purchases increase, so do murder rates.[7] When ice cream sales decline, murder rates also drop. Do people become murderers after eating ice cream? Should we outlaw the sale of ice cream? This would be silly because the concomitant variation observed between ice cream consumption and murder rates is spurious. A third variable is actually important here. People purchase more ice cream when the weather is hot. People are also more active and likely to commit a violent crime when it is hot. The weather, being associated with both may actually cause both. Exhibit 4.2 illustrates the concept of spurious association.

EXHIBIT 4.2 **The Spurious Effect of Ice Cream**

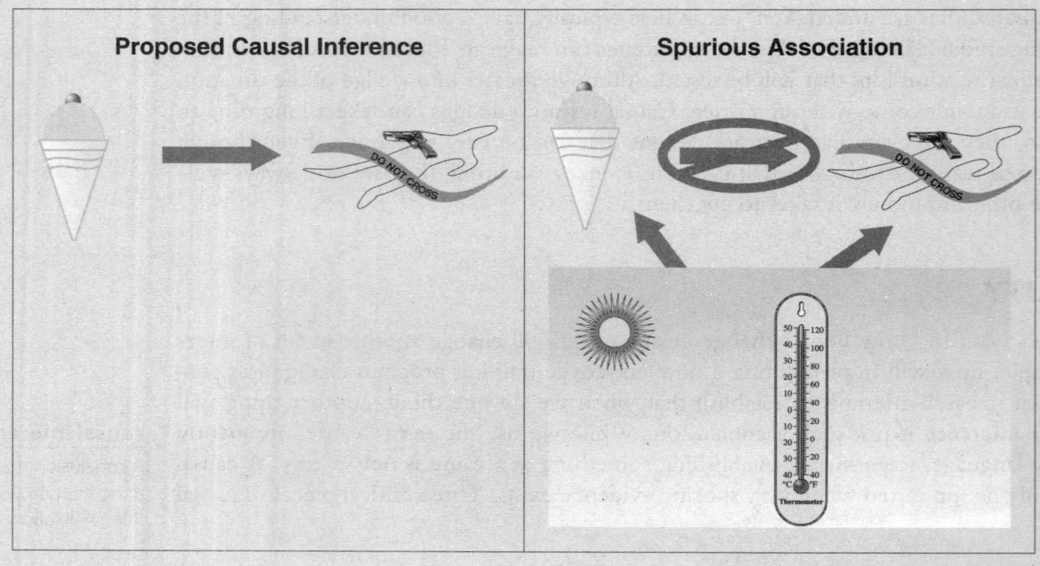

Establishing evidence of nonspuriousness can be difficult. If a researcher finds a third variable that is related to both the cause and effect, which causes a significant drop in the correlation between the cause and effect, then a causal inference becomes difficult to support. Although the researcher would like to rule out the possibility of any alternative causes, it is impossible to observe the effect of every variable on the correlation between the cause and effect. Therefore, the researcher must use logic, or a theory, to identify the most likely "third" variables that would relate significantly to both the cause and effect. The researcher must control for these variables in some way. In addition, the researcher should use theory to make sure the assumed cause-and-effect relationship truly makes sense.

In summary, causal research should do all of the following:

1. Establish the appropriate causal order or sequence of events
2. Measure the concomitant variation between the presumed cause and the presumed effect
3. Examine the possibility of spuriousness by considering the presence of alternative plausible causal factors

DEGREES OF CAUSALITY

absolute causality

Means the cause is necessary and sufficient to bring about the effect.

In everyday language, we often use the word "cause" in an absolute sense. For example, a warning label used on cigarette packages claims "smoking causes cancer." Is this true in an absolute sense? **Absolute causality** means the cause is necessary and sufficient to bring about the effect. Thus, if we find only one smoker who does not eventually get cancer, the claim is false. Although this is a very strong inference, it is impractical to think that we can establish absolute causality in the behavioral sciences.

Why do we continue to do causal research then? Well, although managers may like to be able to draw absolute conclusions, they can often make very good decisions based on less powerful inferences. **Conditional causality** means that a cause is necessary but not sufficient to bring about an effect. This is a weaker causal inference. One way to think about conditional causality is that the cause can bring about the effect, but it cannot do so alone. If other conditions are right, the cause can bring about the effect. We know there are other medical factors that contribute to cancer. For instance, genetics, lifestyle, and diet are also plausible causes of cancer. Thus, if one smokes and has a genetic disposition, diet, and lifestyle that promote cancer, smoking could be considered a conditional cause of cancer. However, if we can find someone who has contracted cancer and never smoked, the causal inference would be proven wrong.

conditional causality
Means that a cause is necessary but not sufficient to bring about an effect.

Contributory causality is the weakest form of causality, but it is still a useful concept. A cause need be neither necessary nor sufficient to bring about an effect. However, causal evidence can be established using the three factors discussed. For any outcome, there may be multiple causes. So, an event can be a contributory cause of something so long as the introduction of the other possible causes does not eliminate the correlation between it and the effect. This will become clearer when we discuss ways to test relationships later in the text. Smoking then can be a contributory cause of cancer so long as the introduction of other possible causes does not cause both smoking and cancer.

contributory causality
Means that a cause need be neither necessary nor sufficient to bring about an effect.

EXPERIMENTS

Business *experiments* hold the greatest potential for establishing cause-and-effect relationships. An **experiment** is a carefully controlled study in which the researcher manipulates a proposed cause and observes any corresponding change in the proposed effect. An **experimental variable** represents the proposed cause and is controlled by the researcher by manipulating it. **Manipulation** means that the researcher alters the level of the variable in specific increments.

experiment
A carefully controlled study in which the researcher manipulates a proposed cause and observes any corresponding change in the proposed effect.

experimental variable
Represents the proposed cause and is controlled by the researcher by manipulating it.

manipulation
Means that the researcher alters the level of the variable in specific increments.

For example, consider a manager who needs to make decisions about the price and distribution of a new video game called the Wee Box. She understands that both the price level and the type of retail outlet in which the product is placed are potential causes of sales. A study can be designed which manipulates both the price and distribution. The price can be manipulated by offering it for \$100 among some consumers and \$200 among others. Retail distribution may be manipulated by selling the Wee Box at discount stores in some consumer markets and at specialty electronics stores in others. The retailer can examine whether price and distribution cause sales by comparing the sales results in each of the four conditions created. Exhibit 4.3 illustrates this study.

An experiment like the one described above may take place in a test-market. Test-marketing is a frequently used form of business experimentation. A **test-market** is an experiment that is conducted within actual business conditions. McDonald's restaurants have a long-standing tradition of test-marketing new product concepts by introducing them at selected stores and monitoring sales and customer feedback. Recently, McDonald's extensively test-marketed McCafé specialty coffees and beverages. These products were sold at a group of McDonald's outlets and feedback was

test-market
An experiment that is conducted within actual market conditions.

EXHIBIT 4.3
Testing for Causes with an Experiment

	Wee Box Sales by Condition	
	High Price	**Low Price**
Specialty Distribution	Peoria, Illinois: Retail Price: \$200 Retail Store: Best Buy	Des Moines, Iowa: Retail Price: \$100 Retail Store: Best Buy
General Distribution	St. Louis, Missouri: Retail Price \$200 Retail Store: Big Cheap-Mart	Kansas City, Missouri: Retail Price: \$100 Retail Store: Big Cheap-Mart

Assuming that Wee Box consumers are the same in each of these cities, the extent to which price and distribution cause sales can be examined by comparing the sales results in each of these 4 conditions.

used to refine the offering including the size of the cups, prices, and what types of extras to add to the drink (including sprinkles of chocolate, whipped cream, steamed milk, and chocolate, vanilla, and caramel shots). McDonald's could then monitor the effect on overall sales, as well as cannibalization of regular coffee sales, in a real-world setting. Earlier, McDonald's had test-marketed Wi-Fi service in some outlets. Three different rival Wi-Fi service providers (the manipulation) were used in different locations and the cost, service, and customer feedback were used to select the best provider for use in McDonald's restaurants.

Most basic scientific studies in business (for example, the development of theories about employee motivation or consumer behavior) ultimately seek to identify cause-and-effect relationships. In fact, we often associate science with experiments. To predict a relationship between, say, price and perceived quality of a product, causal studies often create statistical experiments with controls that establish contrast groups.

Uncertainty Influences the Type of Research

So, which form of research—exploratory, descriptive, or causal—is appropriate for the current situation? The most appropriate type and the amount of research needed are largely a function of how much uncertainty surrounds the situation motivating the research. Exhibit 4.4 contrasts the types of research and illustrates that exploratory research is conducted during the early stages of decision making. At this point, the decision situation is usually highly ambiguous and management is very uncertain about what actions should, or even could, be taken. When management is aware of the problem but lacks some knowledge, descriptive research is usually conducted. Causal research requires sharply defined problems.

Each type of research also produces a different type of result. In many ways, exploratory research is the most productive since it should yield large numbers of ideas. It is part of the "domain of discovery," and as such, unstructured approaches can be very successful. Too much structure in this type of research may lead to more narrowly focused types of responses that could stifle creativity. Thus, although it is productive, exploratory research results usually need further testing and evaluation before they can be made actionable. At times, however, managers do take action based only on exploratory research results. Sometimes, management may not be able or may not care to invest the time and resources needed to conduct further research. Decisions made based only on exploratory research can be more risky, since exploratory research does not test ideas among a scientific sample.[8] For instance, a business school professor may ask a class of current MBA students for ideas about an online program. Although the students may provide many ideas that sound very good, even the best of them has not been tested on a sample of potential online MBA students.

EXHIBIT 4.4 **Characteristics of Different Types of Business Research**

	Exploratory Research	Descriptive Research	Causal Research
Amount of Uncertainty Characterizing Decision Situation	Highly ambiguous	Partially defined	Clearly defined
Key Research Statement	Research question	Research question	Research hypothesis
When Conducted?	Early stage of decision making	Later stages of decision making	Later stages of decision making
Usual Research Approach	Unstructured	Structured	Highly Structured
Examples	"Our sales are declining for no apparent reason." "What kinds of new products are fast-food customers interested in?"	"What kind of people patronize our stores compared to our primary competitor?" "What product features are most important to our customers?"	"Will consumers buy more products in a blue package?" "Which of two advertising campaigns will be more effective?"
Nature of Results	Discovery oriented, productive, but still speculative. Often in need of further research.	Can be confirmatory although more research is sometimes still needed. Results can be managerially actionable.	Confirmatory oriented. Fairly conclusive with managerially actionable results often obtained.

Descriptive research is typically focused around one or more fairly specific research questions. It is usually much more structured and, for many common types of business research, can yield managerially actionable results. For example, descriptive research is often used to profile a customer segment both demographically and psychographically. Results like this can greatly assist firms in deciding when and where to offer their goods or services for sale.

Causal research is usually very focused around a small number of research hypotheses. Experimental methods require tight control of research procedures. Thus, causal research is highly structured to produce specific results. Causal research results are often managerially actionable since they suggest that if management changes the value of a "cause," some desirable effect will come about. So, by changing the training program, the cause, an increase in employee productivity, can result.

The managers need information to determine customer needs and to formulate and implement marketing strategies/programs to satisfy those needs. They need to know the market with information about the customers, competitors, and other forces. Especially in emerging markets like India and China, the market factors have increased as well as changed several times and hence the need for more and accurate information. These factors are mainly multinational operations of foreign firms (different marketing strategies for different regions), and more affluent, aware, and sophisticated customers that have made competition more intense. Due to all these factors that make the environment truly dynamic, organizations need timely information that is relevant, accurate, current, reliable, and actionable. Today managers are assisted in the process of decision-making by the marketing information system and decision support systems (DSS). The information obtained from marketing research and other sources such as internal records and marketing intelligence becomes part of the firm's management information system (MIS). MIS provides information continuously rather than on an ad-hoc basis with focus on each decision maker's responsibility, style, information needs, etc. DSS enable decision makers to directly interact with databases and analysis models. Marketing research contributes data into the databases of the DSS, marketing models, specialized programs, etc.

Today, a new aspect called **competitive intelligence (CI)** is also associated with marketing research; it may be defined as a process for better understanding of a firm's competitors and the competitive environment to enhance its marketplace competitiveness. This process is obviously ethical with the legally permissible collection and analysis of competitor data, obtained from information databases, "open sources," or through ethical marketing research. CI is also a continuous process of ethical collection and analysis of information with controlled propagation of actionable intelligence to the decision makers.

competitive intelligence (CI)
A process for better understanding of a firm's competitors and the competitive environment to enhance its marketplace competitiveness.

Stages in the Research Process

Business research, like other forms of scientific inquiry, involves a sequence of highly interrelated activities. The stages of the research process overlap continuously, and it is clearly an oversimplification to state that every research project has exactly the same ordered sequence of activities. Nevertheless, business research often follows a general pattern. We offer the following research business stages:

1. Defining the research objectives
2. Planning a research design
3. Planning a sample
4. Collecting the data
5. Analyzing the data
6. Formulating the conclusions and preparing the report

Exhibit 4.5 portrays these six stages as a cyclical or circular-flow process. The circular-flow concept is used because conclusions from research studies can generate new ideas and knowledge that can lead to further investigation. Thus, there is a dashed connection between *conclusions and reporting* and *defining the research objectives*. Notice also that management is in the center of the process. The research objectives cannot be properly defined without managerial input. After all, it is the manager who ultimately has to make the decision. It is also the manager who may ask for additional research once a report is given.

EXHIBIT 4.5
Stages of the Research Process

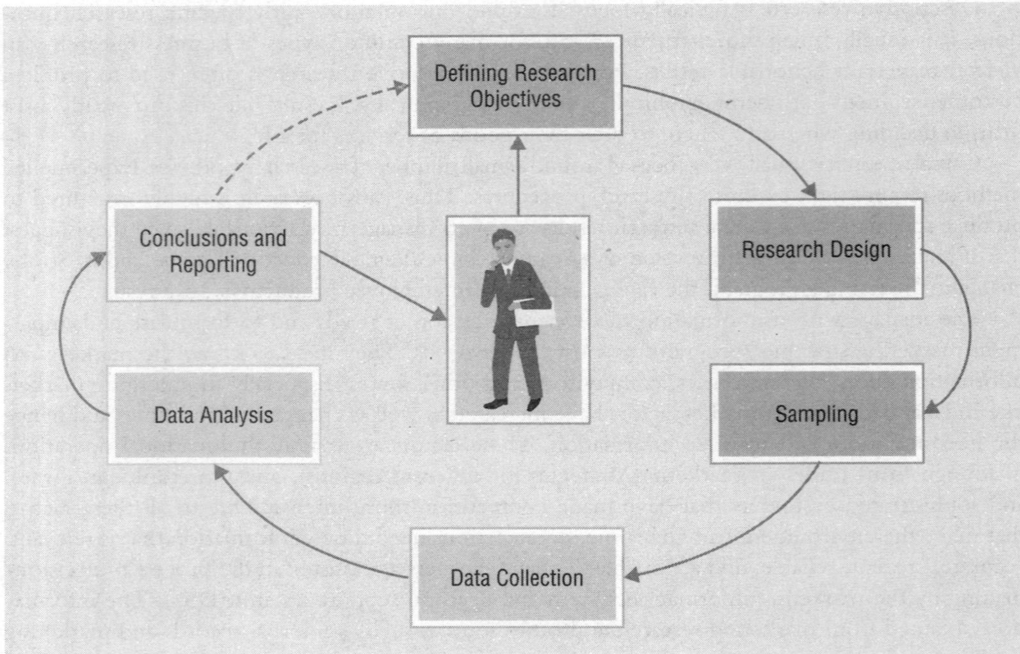

forward linkage
Implies that the earlier stages of the research process influence the later stages.

backward linkage
Implies that later steps influence earlier stages of the research process.

In practice, the stages overlap somewhat from a timing perspective. Later stages sometimes can be completed before earlier ones. The terms *forward linkage* and *backward linkage* reflect the interrelationships between stages. **Forward linkage** implies that the earlier stages influence the later stages. Thus, the research objectives outlined in the first stage affect the sample selection and the way data are collected. The sample selection question affects the wording of questionnaire items. For example, if the research concentrates on respondents with low educational levels, the questionnaire wording will be simpler than if the respondents were college graduates.

Research is sometimes directly actionable. The results may also suggest ideas for new studies.

Backward linkage implies that later steps influence earlier stages of the research process. If it is known that the data will be collected via e-mail, then the sampling must include those with e-mail access. A very important example of backward linkage is the knowledge that the executives who will read the research report are looking for specific information. The professional researcher anticipates executives' needs for information throughout the planning process, particularly during the analysis and reporting.

Alternatives in the Research Process

The researcher must choose among a number of alternatives during each stage of the research process. The research process can be compared to a map. It is important to remember that there is no single "right" path for all journeys. The road one takes depends on where one wants to go and the resources (money, time, labor, and so on) available for the trip. The map analogy is useful for the business researcher because there are several paths that can be followed at each stage. When there are severe time constraints, the quickest path may be most appropriate. When money and human resources are plentiful, more options are available and the appropriate path may be quite different.

Chapter 1 introduced the research process. Here, we briefly describe the six stages of the research process. Later, each stage is discussed in greater depth. Exhibit 4.6 shows the decisions that researchers must make in each stage. This discussion of the research process begins with research objectives, because most research projects are initiated to remedy managers' uncertainty about some aspect of the firm's business program.

Defining the Research Objectives

Exhibit 4.6 shows that the research process begins with **research objectives**. Research objectives are the goals to be achieved by conducting research. In consulting, the term **deliverables** is often used to describe the objectives to a research client. The genesis of the research objectives lies in the type of decision situation faced. The objectives may involve exploring the possibilities of entering a new market. Alternatively, they may involve testing the effect of some policy change on employee job satisfaction. Different types of objectives lead to different types of research designs.

research objectives
The goals to be achieved by conducting research.

deliverables
The term used often in consulting to describe research objectives to a research client.

EXHIBIT 4.6 **Flowchart of the Business Research Process**

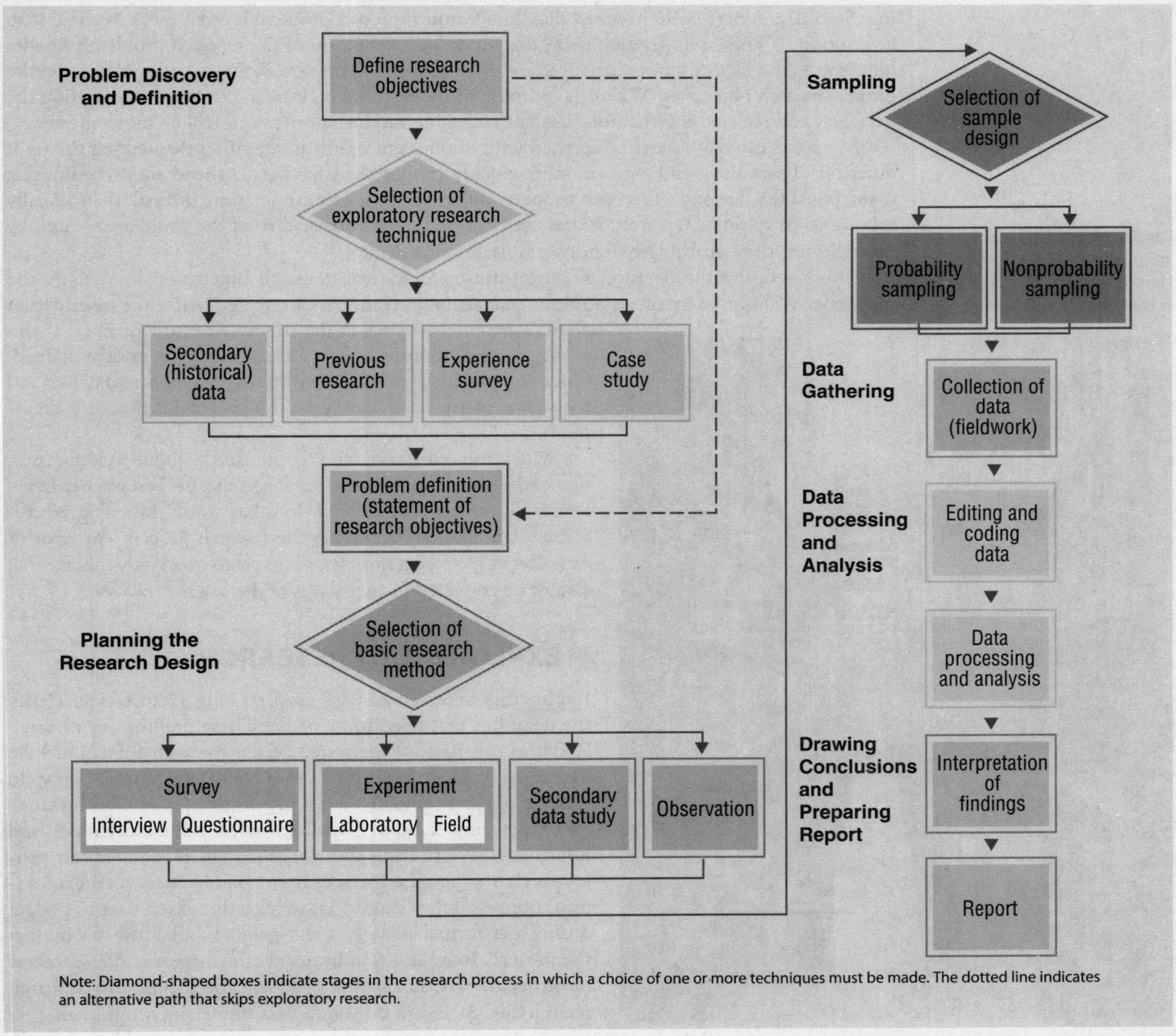

Note: Diamond-shaped boxes indicate stages in the research process in which a choice of one or more techniques must be made. The dotted line indicates an alternative path that skips exploratory research.

In applied business research, the objectives cannot really be determined until there is a clear understanding of the managerial decision to be made. This understanding must be shared between the actual decision maker and the lead researcher. We often describe this understanding as a problem statement. In general usage, the word *problem* suggests that something has gone wrong. This isn't always the case before research gets started. Actually, the research objective may be to simply clarify a situation, define an opportunity, or monitor and evaluate current business operations. The research objectives cannot be developed until managers and researchers have agreed on the actual business "problem" that will be addressed by the research. Thus, they set out to "discover" this problem through a series of interviews and through a document called a research proposal.

It should be noted that this process is oriented more toward *discovery* than *confirmation* or *justification*. Managers and researchers alike may not have a clear-cut understanding of the situation at the outset of the research process. Managers may only be able to list symptoms that could indicate a problem. For example, employee turnover is increasing, but management may not know the exact nature of the problem. Thus, the problem statement often is made only in general terms; what is to be investigated is not yet specifically identified.

DEFINING THE MANAGERIAL DECISION SITUATION

In business research, the adage "a problem well defined is a problem half solved" is worth remembering. Similarly, Albert Einstein noted that "the formulation of a problem is often more essential than its solution."[9] These phrases emphasize that an orderly definition of the research problem provides direction to the investigation. Careful attention to problem definition allows the researcher to set the proper research objectives. When the purpose of the research is clear, the chances of collecting the necessary and relevant information, and not collecting surplus information, will be much greater.

Managers often are more concerned with finding the right answer rather than asking the right question. They also want one solution quickly, rather than having to spend time considering many possible solutions. However, properly defining a problem can be more difficult than actually solving it. In business research, if data are collected before the nature of the problem is carefully thought out, they probably will not yield useful information.

The library contains a wealth of information. Studies forming a literature review can be found in the library.

© DIGITAL VISION/GETTY IMAGES

Thus, defining the decision situation must precede the research objectives. Frequently the researcher will not be involved until the management team has discovered that some information about a particular aspect of the business is needed. Even at this point the exact nature of the situation may be poorly defined. Once a problem area has been discovered, the researcher and management together can begin the process of precisely defining it.

Much too often research is conducted without a clear definition of the objectives. Researchers forget that the best place to begin a research project is at the end. In other words, knowing what is to be accomplished determines the research process. An error or omission in specifying objectives is likely to be a costly mistake that cannot be corrected in later stages of the research process.

EXPLORATORY RESEARCH

Exploratory research can be used to help identify and clarify the decisions that need to be made. These preliminary research activities can narrow the scope of the research topic and help transform ambiguous problems into well-defined ones that yield specific research objectives. By investigating any existing studies on the subject, talking with knowledgeable individuals, and informally investigating the situation, the researcher can progressively sharpen the focus of the research. After such exploration, the researcher should know exactly which data to collect during the formal phases of the project and how to conduct the project. Exhibit 4.6 indicates that managers and researchers must decide whether to use one or more exploratory research techniques. As Exhibit 4.6 indicates, this stage is optional.

The business researcher can employ techniques from four basic categories to obtain insights and gain a clearer idea of the problem: previous research, pilot studies, case studies, and experience surveys. These are discussed in detail in later chapters. This section will briefly discuss previous research and focus group interviews, the most popular type of pilot study.

Previous Research

As a general rule, researchers should first investigate previous research to see whether or not others may have already addressed similar research problems. Initially, internal research reports should be searched within the company's archives. In addition, some firms specialize in providing various types of research reports, such as economic forecasts. The *Census of Population* and the *Survey of Current Business* are each examples of previous research conducted by an outside source.

Previous research may also exist in the public domain. The first place researchers will likely look today is online. The Internet and modern electronic search engines available through most university libraries have made literature reviews simpler and faster to conduct. A **literature review** is a directed search of published works, including periodicals and books, that discusses theory and presents empirical results that are relevant to the topic at hand. While a literature survey is common in applied research studies, it is a fundamental requirement of a basic research report.

literature review

A directed search of published works, including periodicals and books, that discusses theory and presents empirical results that are relevant to the topic at hand.

Suppose, for example, that a bank is interested in determining the best site for additional automated teller machines. A logical first step would be to investigate the factors that bankers in other parts of the country consider important. By reading articles in banking journals, management might quickly discover that the best locations are inside supermarkets located in residential areas where people are young, highly educated, and earning higher-than-average incomes. These data might lead the bank to investigate census information to determine where in the city such people live. Reviewing and building on the work already compiled by others is an economical starting point for most research.

Pilot Studies

Almost all consumers take a test drive before buying a car. A pilot study serves a similar purpose for the researcher. A **pilot study** is a small-scale research project that collects data from respondents similar to those that will be used in the full study. It can serve as a guide for a larger study or examine specific aspects of the research to see if the selected procedures will actually work as intended. Pilot studies are critical in refining survey questions and reducing the risk that the full study will be fatally flawed. This is particularly true for experimental research, which depends critically on valid manipulations of experimental variables.[10] Pilot studies also often are useful in fine-tuning research objectives. Pilot studies are sometimes referred to as pretests. A **pretest** is a very descriptive term indicating a small-scale study in which the results are preliminary and intended only to assist in design of a subsequent study.

pilot study

A small-scale research project that collects data from respondents similar to those to be used in the full study.

pretest

A small-scale study in which the results are only preliminary and intended only to assist in design of a subsequent study.

Focus group interviews are sometimes used as a pilot study. A **focus group** interview brings together six to twelve people in a loosely structured format. The technique is based on the assumption that individuals are more willing to talk about things when they are able to do so within a group discussion format. Focus group respondents sometimes feed on each other's comments to develop ideas that would be difficult to express in a different interview format.

focus group

A small group discussion about some research topic led by a moderator who guides discussion among the participants.

For example, suppose a consultant is hired by Carrefour to research the way consumers react to sales promotions. Carrefour began in France over 50 years ago and pioneered the discount hypermarket format. Carrefour is now the second largest retailer in the world (behind Walmart), operating nearly 11,000 stores in 29 countries. Specifically, the researcher is asked to help Carrefour executives decide whether or not the size of promotional discounts should vary with national culture. In other words, the basic research question is whether or not culture influences consumer perceptions of sales promotions.[11] A pretest may be needed to examine whether or not differences in currency might interfere with these perceptions, or whether or not the different terms that refer to promotions and discounts can be translated into the languages of each culture. For example, is a discount expressed in Korean won interpreted the same way as a discount expressed in euros? Each euro equals about $1.28, whereas a single dollar is worth about 1,380 won.[12]

Exploratory research need not always follow a structured design. Because the purpose of exploratory research is to gain insights and discover new ideas, researchers may use considerable creativity and flexibility. Some companies perform exploratory research routinely as part of environmental scanning. If the conclusions made during this stage suggest business opportunities, the researcher is in a position to begin planning a formal, quantitative research project.

STATING RESEARCH OBJECTIVES

After identifying and clarifying the problem, with or without exploratory research, the researcher must formally state the research objectives. This statement delineates the type of research that is needed and what intelligence may result that would allow the decision maker to make informed choices. The statement of research objectives culminates the process of clarifying the managerial decision into something actionable.

A written decision statement expresses the business situation to the researcher and makes sure that managers and researchers are on the same page. The research objectives try to directly address the decision statement or statements, as the case may be. As such, the research objectives represent a contract of sorts that commits the researcher to producing the needed research. This is why they are expressed as *deliverables* in applied business research. These research objectives drive the rest of the research process. Indeed, before proceeding, the researcher and managers must agree that the objectives are appropriate and will produce relevant information.

LINKING DECISION STATEMENTS, OBJECTIVES, AND HYPOTHESES

In Chapter 3 we discussed the role of theory and research hypotheses. Our hypotheses should be logically derived from and linked to our research objectives. For example, using our opening vignette as an example, the researcher may use theoretical reasoning to develop the following hypothesis:

H1: The more hours per week a prospective student works, the more favorable the attitude toward online MBA class offerings.

Exhibit 4.7 illustrates how decision statements are linked to research objectives, which are linked to research hypotheses. Although the first two objectives each have one hypothesis, notice that the third has two. In reality, most research projects will involve more than one research objective, and each of these may often involve more than one hypothesis. Think about how you might go about trying to test the hypothesis listed in Exhibit 4.7.

EXHIBIT 4.7
Example Decision Statements, Research Objectives, and Research Hypotheses

Decision Statement	Research Objectives	Hypotheses
What should be the retail price for product X?	Forecast sales for product X at three different prices.	Sales will be higher at $5.00 than at $4.00 or at $6.99.
In what ways can we improve our service quality?	Identify the top factors that contribute to customers' perceptions.	Cleanliness is related positively to customers' service quality service perceptions.
		Crowding is related negatively to customers' service quality perceptions.
Should we invest in a training program to reduce role conflict among our employees?	Determine how much role conflict influences employee job satisfaction.	Role conflict is related positively to job satisfaction.

Planning the Research Design

research design
A master plan that specifies the methods and procedures for collecting and analyzing the needed information.

After the researcher has formulated the research problem, he or she must develop the research design as part of the research design stage. A **research design** is a master plan that specifies the methods and procedures for collecting and analyzing the needed information. A research design provides a framework or plan of action for the research. Objectives of the study determined during the early stages of research are included in the design to ensure that the information collected is appropriate for solving the problem. The researcher also must determine the sources of information, the design technique (survey or experiment, for example), the sampling methodology, and the schedule and cost of the research.

SELECTION OF THE BASIC RESEARCH METHOD

Here again, the researcher must make a decision. Exhibit 4.6 shows four basic design techniques for descriptive and causal research: surveys, experiments, secondary data, and observation. The objectives of the study, the available data sources, the urgency of the decision, and the cost of obtaining the data will determine which method should be chosen. The managerial aspects of selecting the research design will be considered later.

In business research, the most common method of generating primary data is the survey. Most people have seen the results of political surveys by Gallup or Harris Online, and some have been respondents (members of a sample who supply answers) to research questionnaires. A **survey** is a research technique in which a sample is interviewed in some form or the behavior of respondents is observed and described in some way. The term *surveyor* is most often reserved for civil engineers who describe some piece of property using a transit. Similarly, business researchers describe some group of interest (such as executives, employees, customers, or competitors) using a questionnaire. The task of writing a list of questions and designing the format of the printed or written questionnaire is an essential aspect of the development of a survey research design.

survey
A research technique in which a sample is interviewed in some form or the behavior of respondents is observed and described in some way.

Research investigators may choose to contact respondents by telephone or mail, on the Internet, or in person. An advertiser spending $3 million for 30 seconds of commercial time during the Super Bowl may telephone people to quickly gather information concerning their responses to the advertising. The economic development director for a city trying to determine the most important factors in attracting new businesses might choose a mail questionnaire because the appropriate executives are hard to reach by telephone. A manufacturer of a birth control device for men might determine the need for a versatile survey method wherein an interviewer can ask a variety of personal questions in a flexible format. While personal interviews are expensive, they are valuable because investigators can use visual aids and supplement the interviews with observations. Each of these survey methods has advantages and disadvantages. A researcher's task is to find the most appropriate way to collect the needed information in a particular situation.

The objective of many research projects is merely to record what can be observed—for example, the number of automobiles that pass by a proposed site for a gas station. This can be mechanically recorded or observed by humans. Research personnel known as mystery shoppers may act as customers to observe actions of sales personnel or do comparative shopping to learn prices at competing outlets. A mystery shopper is paid to pretend to be a customer and gather data about the way employees behave and the way they are treated in general. How often are store policies followed? Are they treated courteously? Mystery shoppers can be valuable sources for observational data.

The main advantage of the observation technique is that it records behavior without relying on reports from respondents. Observational data are often collected unobtrusively and passively without a respondent's direct participation. For instance, Nielsen Media Research uses a "people meter" attached to television sets to record the programs being watched by each household member. This eliminates the possible bias of respondents stating that they watched the president's State of the Union address rather than *Gossip Girl* on another station.

Observation is more complex than mere "nose counting," and the task is more difficult than the inexperienced researcher would imagine. While observation eliminates potential bias from interviewer interaction, several things of interest, such as attitudes, opinions, motivations, and other intangible states of mind, simply cannot be observed.

THE "BEST" RESEARCH DESIGN

It is argued that there is no single best research design. As such, the researcher often has several alternatives that can accomplish the stated research objectives. Consider the researcher who must forecast sales for the upcoming year. Some commonly used forecasting methods are surveying executive opinion, collecting sales force composite opinions, surveying user expectations, projecting trends, and analyzing environmental factors. Any one of these may yield a reliable forecast.

The ability to select the most appropriate research design develops with experience. Inexperienced researchers often jump to the conclusion that a survey methodology is usually the best

RESEARCH SNAPSHOT

Rolling Rock

Making a mark in the U.S. beer market can be difficult. American consumers tend to favor milder beers at lower price points. Some argue that most beers taste very similar. Taste tests do reveal that similarly positioned beers do taste very much the same. However, the taste rankings do not correspond to market share. For instance, Stroh's fared very well in the taste tests, but it is hardly a market leader. Rolling Rock rated 12th out of 12 beers tasted. Tasters said it tasted a bit like canned corn. Clearly, there is something more to a successful beer than taste.

For many years Rolling Rock beer was a regional brand in western Pennsylvania. Its signature package was a longneck green bottle with a white painted label featuring icons such as a horse head, a steeplechase, the number "33," and a legend about the beer being brought to you "from the glass-lined tanks of Old Latrobe." The brand, now sold by Labatt USA, expanded nationally during the 1980s by focusing on core consumers who purchased specialty beers for on-premise consumption and who were willing to pay higher prices than for national brands such as Budweiser.

As years went by, packaging options expanded to include bottles with ordinary paper labels for take-home consumption, often packaged in 12-packs. In the mid-1990s, in response to a competitive explosion from microbrews, Rolling Rock offered a number of line extensions, such as Rock Bock and amber Rock Ice. They failed. Sales stagnated. In New York and other crucial markets, price reductions to the level of Budweiser and Miller became inhibiting aspects of its marketing program. Business executives held the view that the longneck painted bottle was the heart of the brand. However, earlier efforts to develop cheaper imitations of the painted-label look had not achieved success.

PR NEWSFOTO/ROLLING ROCK

Rolling Rock executives decided to conduct a massive consumer study, recruiting consumers at shopping malls and other venues to view "live" shelf sets of beer—not just specialty beer, but beer at every price range from sub-premiums and up. Consumers given money to spend in the form of chips were exposed to "old-bundle" packages (the old graphics and the paper-label stubbies) and "new-bundle" packages (two new graphics approaches, including the one ultimately selected, and painted-label longnecks) at a variety of price points and asked to allocate chips to their next ten purchases. Some were even invited to take the "new-bundle" packages home with them for follow-up research.

As the business executives had hoped, the results did not leave any room for interpretation: Not only did the new packages meet with consumers' strong approval, but consumers consistently indicated that they would be willing to pay more for the brand in those packages. In fact, not only were they willing to pay more; they *expected* to pay more, particularly among consumers already familiar with the Rock. In three regions, the Northeast, Southeast, and West, purchase-intent among users increased dramatically both at prices 20 cents higher per 12-pack and at prices 40 cents higher per 12-pack. The increase in purchase intent was milder in the Midwest, but there Rock already commanded a solid premium over Bud and other premium beers. The sole exception to that trend was in the brand's core markets in Pennsylvania and Ohio, where Rock has never entirely escaped its shot-and-a-beer origins, but even there, purchase intent declined by only 2 percent at each of the higher prices.

Sources: Gerry Khermouch, "Sticking Their Neck Out," *BrandWeek* (November 9, 1998) 25–34, © 2006 VNU Business Media, Inc. Used with permission from Brandweek. © 1998–1999 VNU Business Media Inc.; "Which Brew for You?" *Consumer Reports* (August 2001), 10–17.

© iStock

TOTHEPOINT

You cannot put the same shoe on every foot.

—Publius Syrus

design because they are most comfortable with this method. When Chicago's Museum of Science and Industry wanted to determine the relative popularity of its exhibits, it could have conducted a survey. Instead, a creative researcher familiar with other research designs suggested a far less expensive alternative: an unobtrusive observation technique. The researcher suggested that the museum merely keep track of the frequency with which the floor tiles in front of the various exhibits had to be replaced, indicating where the heaviest traffic occurred. When this was done, the museum found that the chick-hatching exhibit was the most popular. This method provided the same results as a survey but at a much lower cost. Take a look at the research design used by Rolling Rock illustrated in the Research Snapshot "Rolling Rock."

Sampling

sampling
Involves any procedure that draws conclusions based on measurements of a portion of the population.

Although the sampling plan is outlined in the research design, the sampling stage is a distinct phase of the research process. For convenience, however, we will treat the sample planning and the actual sample generation processes together in this section.

If you take your first bite of shrimp po-boy and conclude that it needs Tabasco, you have just conducted a sample. **Sampling** involves any procedure that draws conclusions based on measurements of a portion of the population. In other words, a sample is a subset from a larger population. If certain statistical procedures are followed, a researcher need not select every item in a population because the results of a good sample should have the same characteristics as the population as a whole. Of course, when errors are made, samples do not give reliable estimates of the population.

A famous example of error due to sampling is the 1936 *Literary Digest* fiasco. The magazine conducted a survey and predicted that Republican Alf Landon would win over Democrat Franklin D. Roosevelt by a landslide in that year's presidential election. This prediction was wrong—and the error was due to sample selection. The post-mortems showed that *Literary Digest* had sampled its readers and names drawn from telephone books and auto registrations. In 1936, not everyone had a telephone or a car; thus the sample was biased toward people with means. In reality, Roosevelt received over 60 percent of the popular vote.

In 2004, early exit polls led many to believe that John Kerry would win the U.S. presidential election.[13] The exit polls were performed early on election day and done mostly in highly urban areas in the Northeast, areas that are predominantly Democratic. The resulting sample of voters responding to the early exit polls did not represent the entire U.S. population, and Kerry lost to Bush by over 3 million votes, or about 3 percent of all votes cast. Thus, the accuracy of predictions from research depends on getting a sample that really matches the population.

The first sampling question to ask is "Who is to be sampled?" The answer to this primary question requires the identification of a *target population*. Who do we want the sample to reflect? Defining this population and determining the sampling units may not be so easy. If, for example, a savings and loan association surveys people who already have accounts for answers to image questions, the selected sampling units may represent *current* customers but will not represent *potential* customers. Specifying the target population is a crucial aspect of the sampling plan.

The next sampling issue concerns sample size. How big should the sample be? Although management may wish to examine every potential buyer of a product or service, doing so may be unnecessary as well as unrealistic. Other things equal, larger samples are more precise than smaller ones. However, proper probability sampling can allow a small proportion of the total population to give a reliable measure of the whole. A later discussion will explain how large a sample must be in order to be truly representative of the universe or population. Essentially, this is a question of how much variance exists in the population.

The final sampling decision is how to select the sampling units. Simple random sampling may be the best known type, in which every unit in the population has an equal and known chance of being selected. However, this is only one type of sampling. For example, if members of the population are found in close geographical clusters, a cluster sampling procedure (one that selects area clusters rather than individual units in the population) will reduce costs. Rather than selecting 1,000 individuals throughout the United States, it may be more economical to first select 25 counties and then sample within those counties. This will substantially reduce travel, hiring, and training costs. In determining the appropriate sampling plan, the researcher will have to select the most appropriate sampling procedure for meeting the established study objectives.

Gathering Data

The data gathering stage begins once the sampling plan has been formalized. Data gathering is the process of gathering or collecting information. Data may be gathered by human observers or interviewers, or they may be recorded by machines as in the case of scanner data and Web-based surveys.

Obviously, the many research techniques involve many methods of gathering data. Surveys require direct participation by research respondents. This may involve filling out a questionnaire or interacting with an interviewer. In this sense, they are obtrusive. **Unobtrusive methods** of data gathering are those in which the subjects do not have to be disturbed for data to be collected. They may even be unaware that research is going on at all. For instance, a simple count of motorists driving past a proposed franchising location is one kind of data gathering method. However the data are collected, it is important to minimize errors in the process. For example, the data gathering should be consistent in all geographical areas. If an interviewer phrases questions incorrectly or records a respondent's statements inaccurately (not verbatim), major data collection errors will result.

unobtrusive methods
Methods in which research respondents do not have to be disturbed for data to be gathered.

Processing and Analyzing Data

EDITING AND CODING

After the fieldwork has been completed, the data must be converted into a format that will answer the manager's questions. This is part of the data processing and analysis stage. Here, the information content will be mined from the raw data. Data processing generally begins with editing and coding the data. Editing involves checking the data collection forms for omissions, legibility, and consistency in classification. The editing process corrects problems such as interviewer errors (an answer recorded on the wrong portion of a questionnaire, for example) before the data are transferred to the computer.

Before data can be tabulated, meaningful categories and character symbols must be established for groups of responses. The rules for interpreting, categorizing, recording, and transferring the data to the data storage media are called codes. This coding process facilitates computer or hand tabulation. If computer analysis is to be used, the data are entered into the computer and verified. Computer-assisted (online) interviewing is an example of the impact of technological change on the research process. Telephone interviewers, seated at computer terminals, read survey questions displayed on the monitor. The interviewer asks the questions and then types in the respondents' answers. Thus, answers are collected and processed into the computer at the same time, eliminating intermediate steps that could introduce errors.

DATA ANALYSIS

Data analysis is the application of reasoning to understand the data that have been gathered. In its simplest form, analysis may involve determining consistent patterns and summarizing the relevant details revealed in the investigation. The appropriate analytical technique for data analysis will be determined by management's information requirements, the characteristics of the research design, and the nature of the data gathered. Statistical analysis may range from portraying a simple frequency distribution to more complex multivariate analyses approaches, such as multiple regression. Later chapters will discuss three general categories of statistical analysis: univariate analysis, bivariate analysis, and multivariate analysis.

data analysis
The application of reasoning to understand the data that have been gathered.

Drawing Conclusions and Preparing a Report

One of the most important jobs that a researcher performs is communicating the research results. This is the final stage of the research project, but it is far from the least important. The conclusions and report preparation stage consist of interpreting the research results, describing the implications, and drawing the appropriate conclusions for managerial decisions. These conclusions should fulfill the deliverables promised in the research proposal. In addition, it's important that the researcher consider the varying abilities of people to understand the research results. The report shouldn't be written the same way to a group of Ph.D.'s as it would be to a group of line managers.

All too many applied business research reports are overly complicated statements of technical aspects and sophisticated research methods. Frequently, management is not interested in detailed reporting of the research design and statistical findings, but wishes only a summary of the findings. If the findings of the research remain unread on the manager's desk, the study will have been useless. The importance of effective communication cannot be overemphasized. Research is only as good as its applications.

Now that we have outlined the research process, note that the order of topics in this book follows the flowchart of the research process presented in Exhibit 4.4. Keep this flowchart in mind while reading later chapters.

The Research Program Strategy

Our discussion of the business research process began with the assumption that the researcher wished to collect data to achieve a specific organizational objective. When the researcher has only one or a small number of research objectives that can be addressed in a single study, that study is referred to as a **research project**. We have emphasized the researcher's need to select specific techniques for solving one-dimensional problems, such as identifying customer segments, selecting the most desirable employee insurance plan, or determining an IPO stock price.

research project
A single study that addresses one or a small number of research objectives.

However, if you think about a firm's business activities in a given period of time (such as a year), you'll realize that business research is not a one-shot activity—it is a continuous process. An exploratory research study may be followed by a survey, or a researcher may conduct a specific research project for each business tactical decision. If a new product is being developed, the different types of research might include studies to identify the size and characteristics of the market; product usage testing to record consumers' reactions to prototype products; brand name and packaging research to determine the product's symbolic connotations; and test-marketing the new product. Thus, when numerous related studies come together to address issues about a single company, we refer to this as a **research program**. Because research is a continuous process, management should view business research at a strategic planning level. The program strategy refers to a firm's overall plan to use business research. It is a planning activity that places a series of research projects in the context of the company's strategic plan.

research program
Numerous related studies that come together to address multiple, related research objectives.

The business research program strategy can be likened to a term insurance policy. Conducting business research minimizes risk and increases certainty. Each research project can be seen as a series of term insurance policies that makes the manager's job a bit safer.

Different Stages of Research Process with Indian Examples

Research process consists of various stages. Different stages in sequential order are shown in Exhibit 4.8.

EXHIBIT 4.8
Different Stages of a Research Process

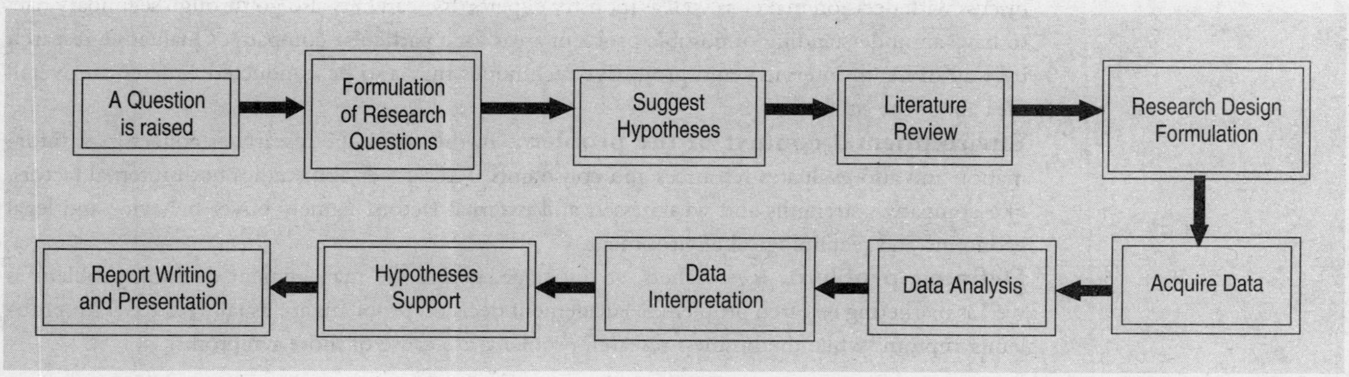

A QUESTION IS RAISED

A question can be raised from different sources. Marketers study their market share at regular intervals. Significant decrease in market share might prompt a marketer to conduct market research to figure out the reason for the decline in market share. Companies also study their competitors to know their business strategies. Understanding competitor may also trigger conducting research. There are several incidents where companies own a significant market share over their competition, however, due to external reasons the profit may decline. In such occasions companies carry out research to find out the reason of declining financial revenue. Another reason of conducting research is to know consumers' preference. Companies in FMCG and consumer durable goods industry carry out research at regular intervals to understand the taste and preference of the consumer as well as prospects. In developing countries like India where consumers are migrating from one segment to higher segment quite frequently due to availability of disposable income, consumers related studies have become essential to cater to the changing need of the consumers. Companies also engage in research to understand the external environment and their opportunities and threats to take proactive measures. Exhibit 4.9 diagram illustrates above reasons that prompt companies to conduct research.

EXHIBIT 4.9 **Reasons that Prompt a Company to Conduct Research**

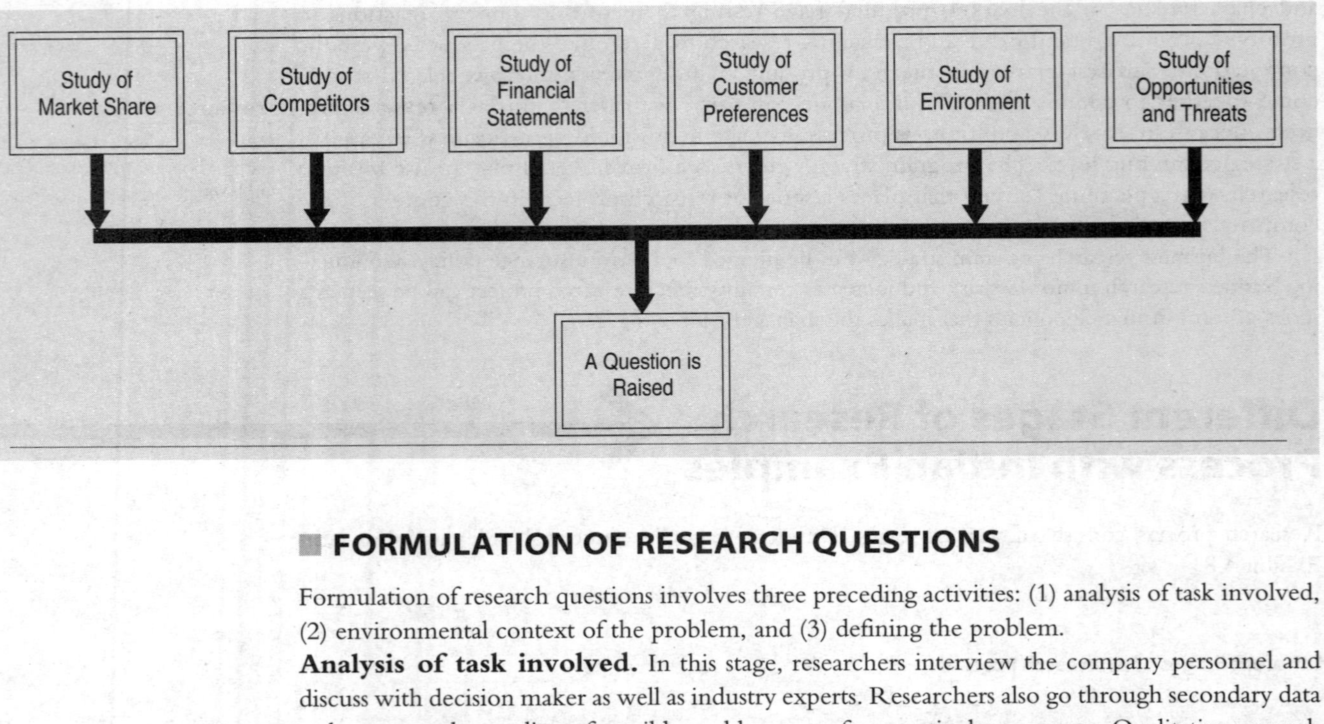

FORMULATION OF RESEARCH QUESTIONS

Formulation of research questions involves three preceding activities: (1) analysis of task involved, (2) environmental context of the problem, and (3) defining the problem.

Analysis of task involved. In this stage, researchers interview the company personnel and discuss with decision maker as well as industry experts. Researchers also go through secondary data to have an understanding of possible problem areas for a particular company. Qualitative research by way of depth interview and projective techniques may also be conducted to have an overall idea about the situation.

Environmental context of the problem. In this stage, the researcher collects past information and also evaluates resources and constraints. Researcher also studies both internal factors, like company's strengths and weaknesses, and external factors, namely buyer behavior and legal economic and technological environment.

Defining problem. Researchers, at this stage, define the management decision problem as well as marketing research problem. Management decision problems are usually related with problem symptoms while the business research problems are cause of those symptoms.

EXHIBIT 4.10 **Formulation of Research Questions**

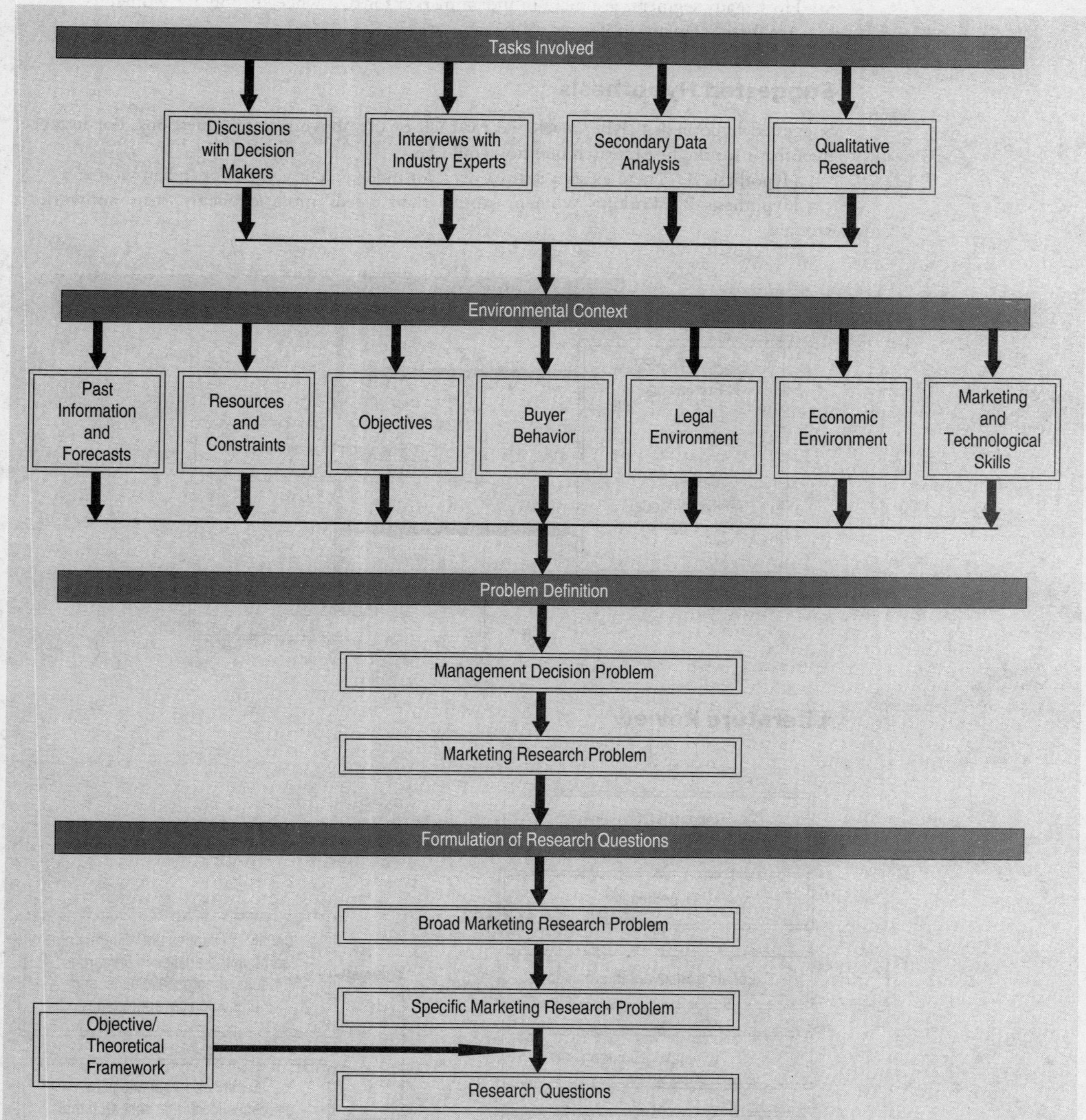

Source: Malhotra, Naresh K., "Marketing Research: An Applied Orientation," India: Pearson Education, 2010.

Research for Hero Honda Pleasure Scooter

Hero Honda, a leading two wheeler manufacturer in India, wanted to conduct a research to develop Pleasure Scooter for Indian women. The management of Hero Honda along with the research agency came up with the following research questions after a lot of deliberation:

- Are Indian women in need of an independent two wheeler?
- To what extent Indian women depend on their male family member for traveling?

- Is there a sufficient market of only two wheelers in India for women?
- How many segments are there in Indian market for two wheelers only for women?
- Are these segments motivated in the same way?

Suggested Hypothesis

Suggested hypothesis maybe developed for each of the above research questions. For instance, hypothesis for the first research question could be:

Hypothesis 1: There exists a distinct need for independent vehicle for Indian women.

Hypothesis 2: Working women express their needs more explicitly than nonworking women.

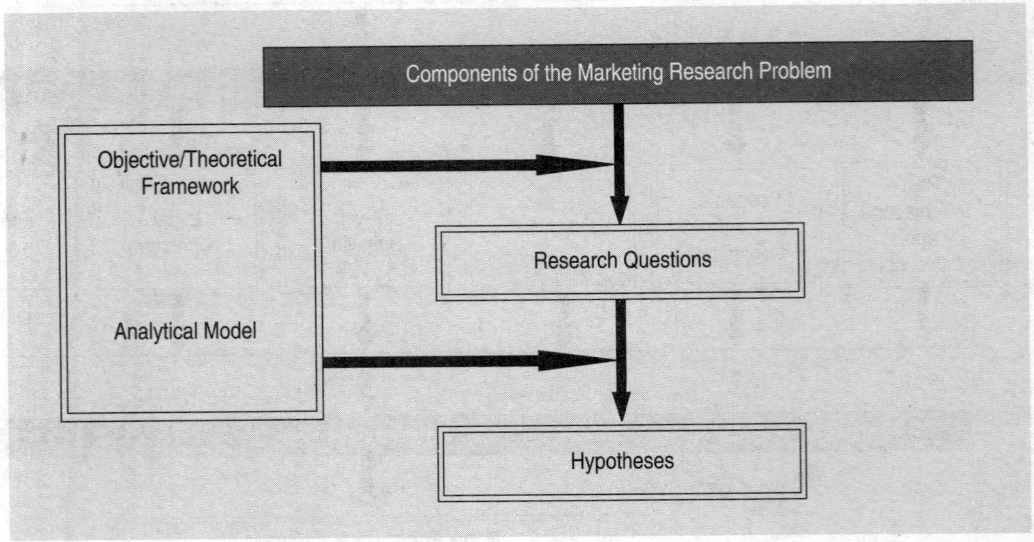

Literature Review

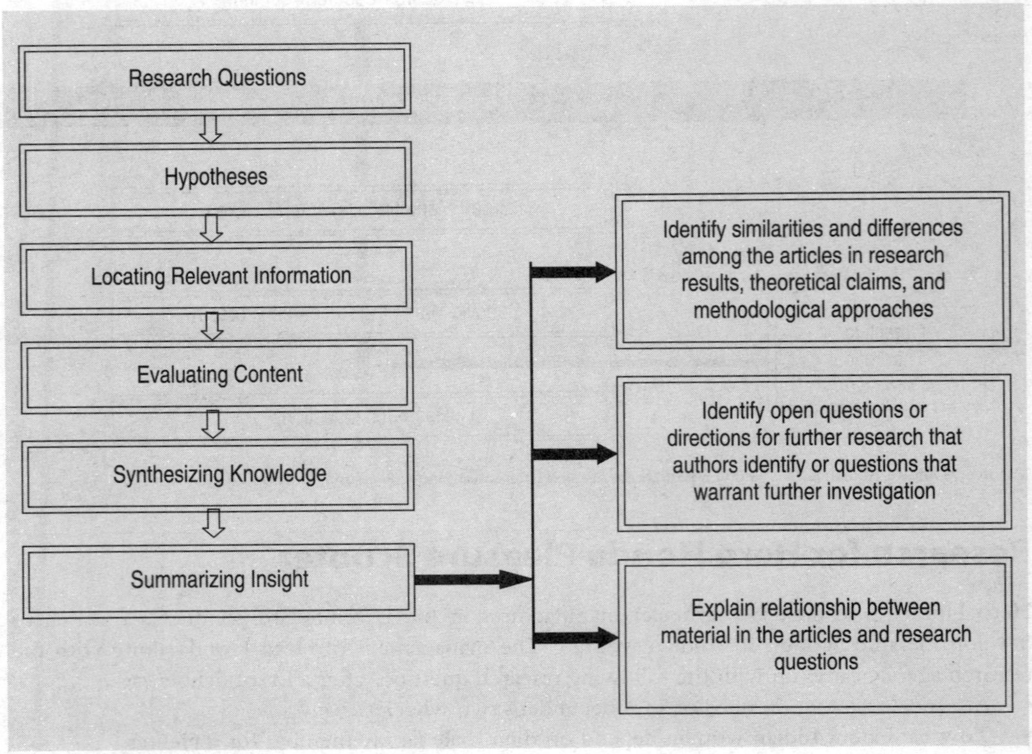

Secondary Research by Hero Honda for Pleasure Scooter

Hero Honda conducted secondary research before developing the Pleasure Scooter. The secondary research involved research done by other two wheeler manufacturers on Indian women's mobility, requirement of independent vehicle, features affecting their buying decisions, role of male members of the family in buying decision, etc. Hero Honda found that Indian women consumers provide mileage as one of the most significant factor for buying a two wheeler. Women buyers are also interested in different colors of the two wheelers as well as woman friendly features, for example, mobile phone chargers.

Research Design Formulation

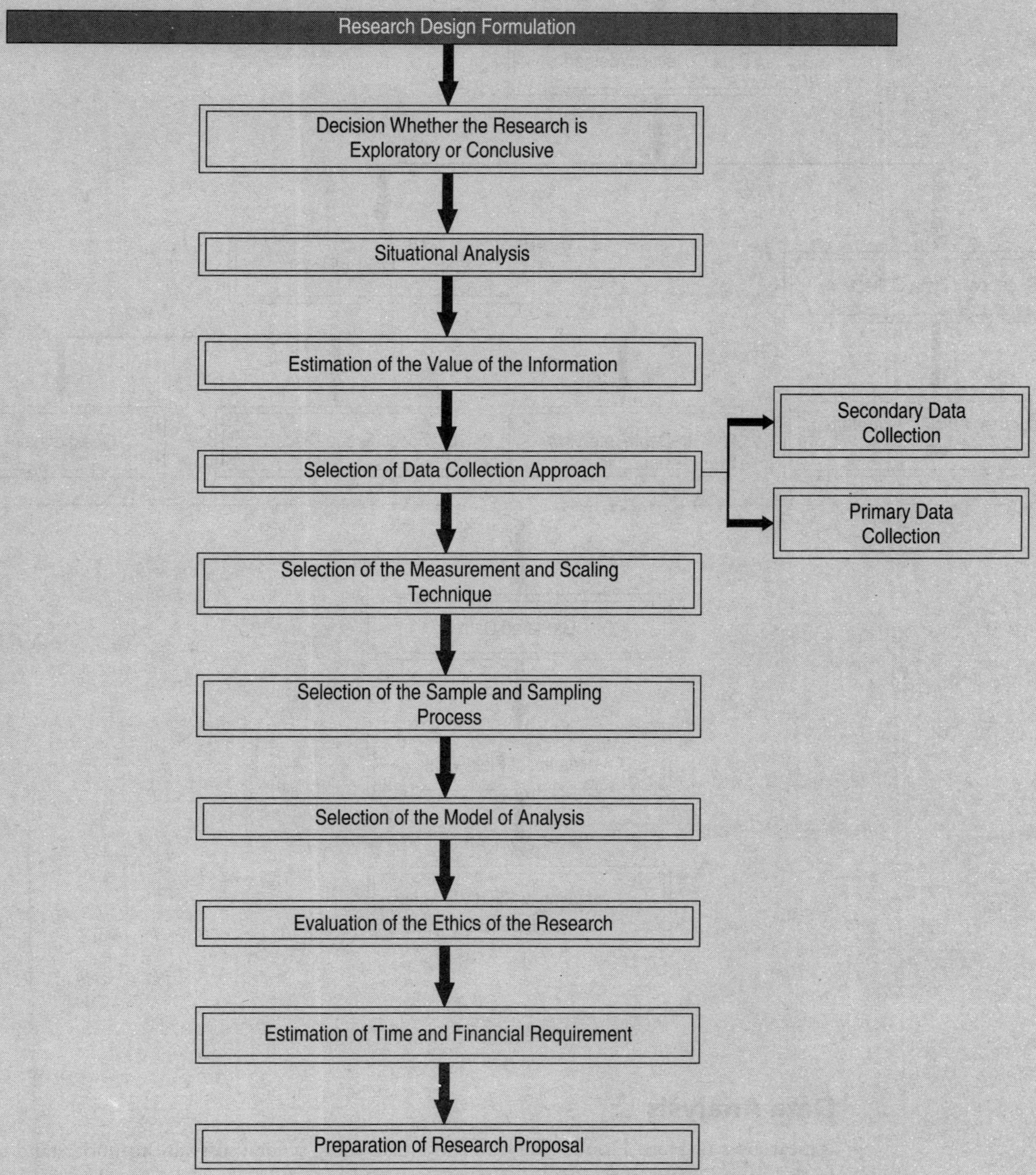

Source: Malhotra, Naresh K., "Marketing Research: An Applied Orientation," India: Pearson Education, 2010.

Acquire Data

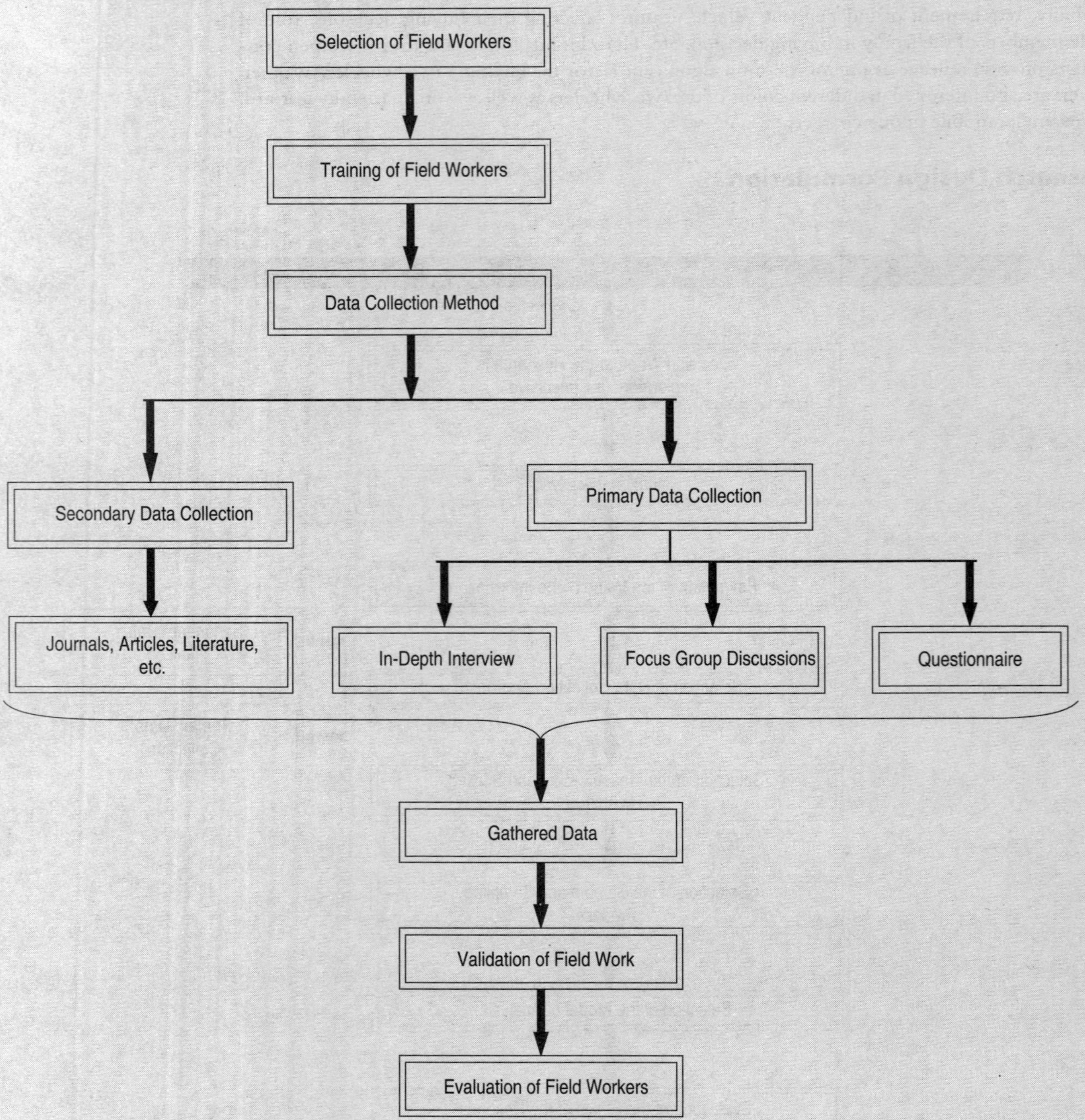

Data Analysis

Researchers in Hero Honda analyzed those data using several software to understand the pattern in the data. Descriptive analysis of the demographic profile as well as users' various needs were captured through this analysis.

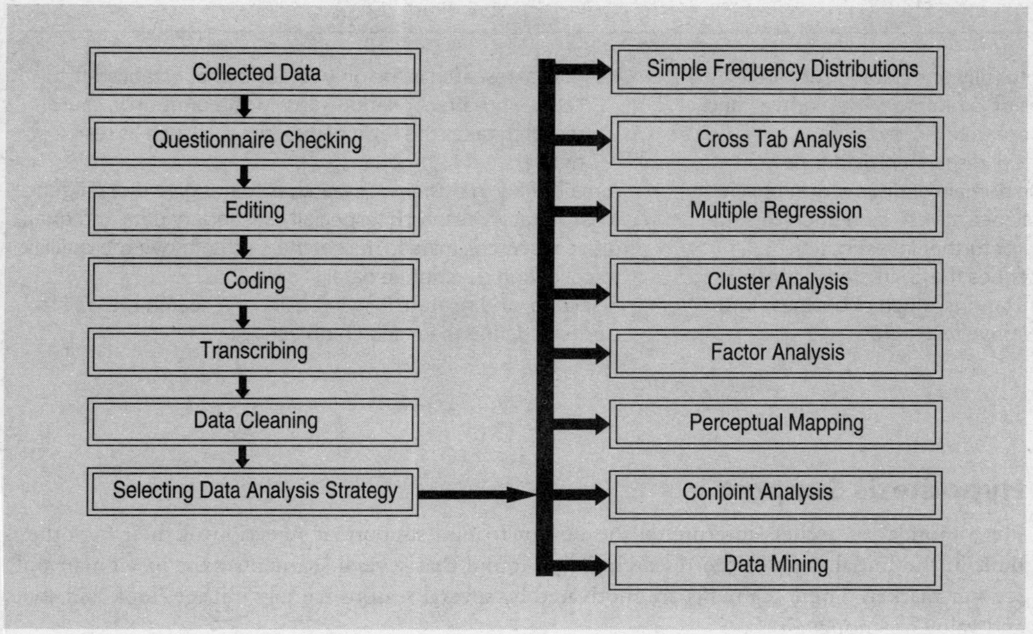

Data Interpretation

At the end of the analysis, researchers interpreted the output to understand consumers' behavior, their perception about a two wheeler, willingness to pay, buying intention, and decision-making criteria. This information tremendously helped Hero Honda to launch their first Scooter Pleasure in the market. They also came up with the idea of separate sales and service outlets "just for her."

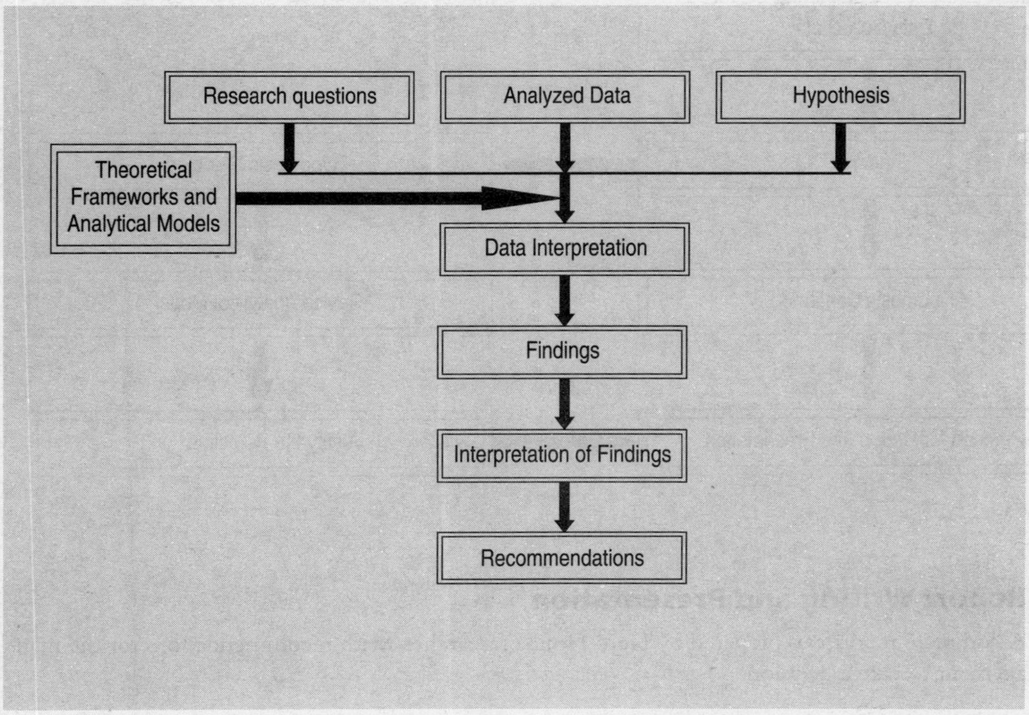

TIPS OF THE TRADE

- Be sure to fully understand the differing roles of exploratory, descriptive, and causal research:
- Exploratory research provides new insights—the domain of discovery in philosophy of science terms—and often sets the groundwork for further investigation.
- Descriptive research describes the characteristics of objects, people, or organizations. Much of business information is based on descriptive research.
- Causal research is the only research that establishes cause-and-effect relationships. Most commonly, causal research takes the form of experiments such as test markets.
- A major flaw in business research is to not give due diligence to exploratory research (especially secondary data and qualitative research). Instead, researchers often move too quickly to collecting descriptive data.
- A second, and related, flaw in business research is to fail to carefully define the research objectives.

Hypothesis Support

Hero Honda researchers interpreted the output to find support or rejection of their hypothesis built in the initial stage of the research. They found that several segments exist in woman only scooter market. These segments are motivated by several reasons namely millage, look and style, and value for money.

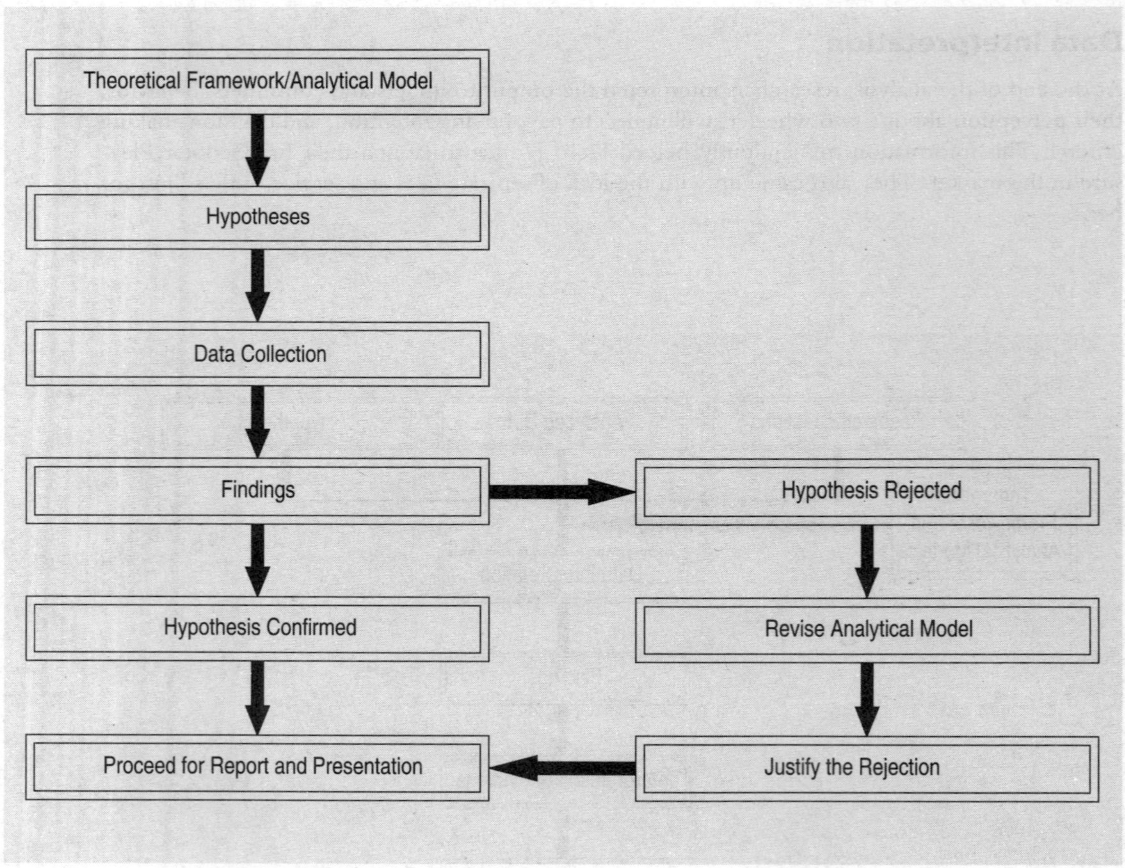

Report Writing and Presentation

A complete report was prepared by Hero Honda researchers with recommendations for the management to take a decision.

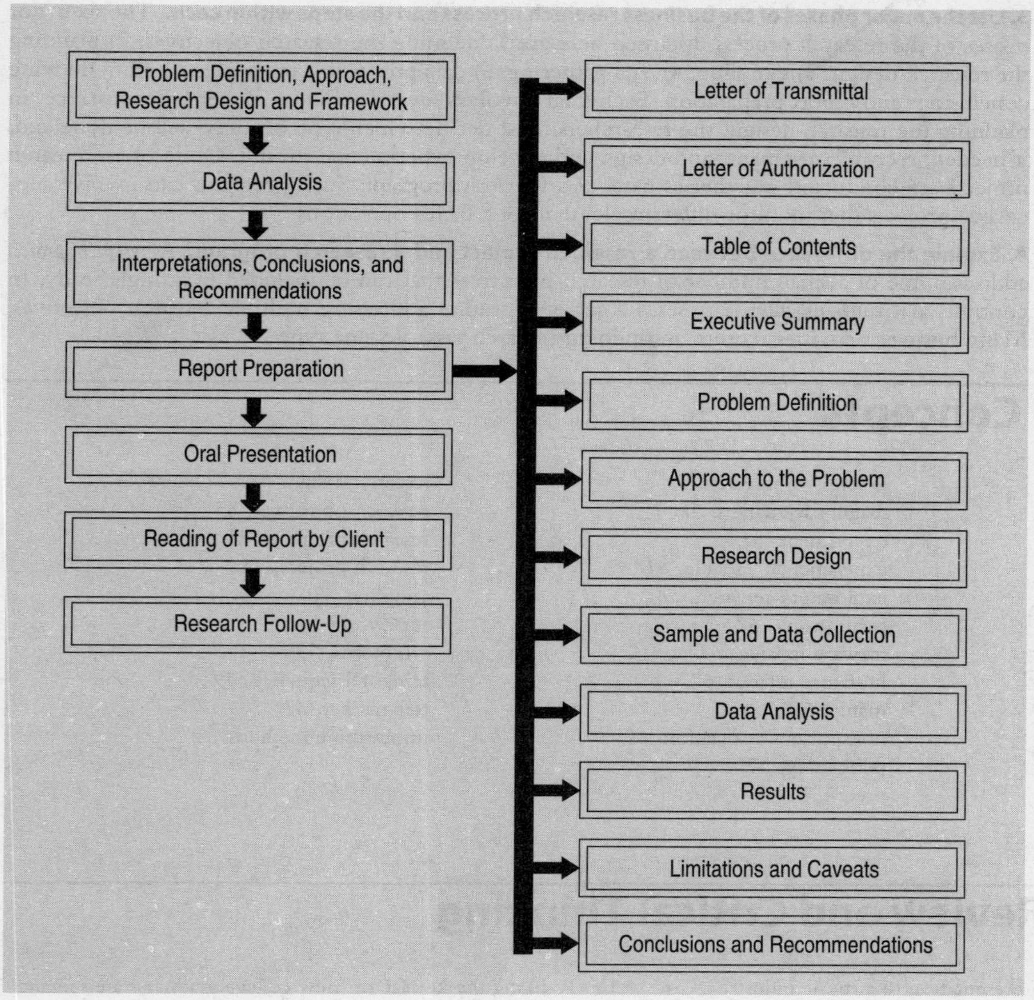

Summary

1. Define decision making and understand the role research plays in making decisions. Decision making occurs when managers choose among alternative ways of resolving problems or pursuing opportunities. Decision makers must recognize the nature of the problem or opportunity, identify how much information is available, and recognize what information they need. Every business decision can be classified on a continuum ranging from complete certainty to absolute ambiguity. Research is a way that managers can become informed about the different alternatives and make an educated guess about which alternative, if any, is the best to pursue.

2. Classify business research as either exploratory research, descriptive research, or causal research. Exploratory, descriptive, and causal research are three major types of business research projects. The clarity with which the decision situation is defined determines whether exploratory, descriptive, or causal research is most appropriate. When the decision is very ambiguous, or the interest is on discovering new ideas, exploratory research is most appropriate. Descriptive research attempts to paint a picture of the given situation by describing characteristics of objects, people, or organizations. Causal research identifies cause-and-effect relationships. Or, in other words, what change in "Y" will occur when there is some change in "X?" Three conditions must be satisfied to establish evidence of causality: 1) temporal sequence—the cause must occur before the effect; 2) concomitant variation—a change in the cause is associated (correlated) with a change in the effect; and 3) nonspurious association—the cause is true and not eliminated by the introduction of another potential cause.

3. List the major phases of the business research process and the steps within each. The six major phases of the research process discussed here are 1) defining the research objectives, 2) planning the research design, 3) sampling, 4) data gathering, 5) data processing and analysis, and 6) drawing conclusions and report preparation. Each stage involves several activities or steps. For instance, in planning the research design, the researchers must decide which type of study will be done and, if needed, recruit participants and design and develop experimental stimuli. Quite often research projects are conducted together as parts of a research program. Such programs can involve successive projects that monitor different elements of a firm's operations.

4. Explain the difference between a research project and a research program. A *research project* addresses one of a small number of research objectives that can be included in a single study. In contrast, a *research program* represents a series of studies addressing multiple research objectives. Many business activities require an ongoing research task of some type.

Key Terms and Concepts

absolute causality, *60*
backward linkage, *64*
business opportunity, *53*
business problem, *53*
causal inference, *59*
causal research, *59*
concomitant variation, *59*
conditional causality, *61*
contributory causality, *61*
data analysis, *72*
decision making, *52*
deliverables, *65*
descriptive research, *51*
diagnostic analysis, *58*
experiment, *61*
experimental variable, *61*
exploratory research, *56*
focus group, *67*
forward linkage, *64*
literature review, *67*
manipulation, *61*
nonspurious association, *60*
pilot study, *67*
pretest, *67*
research design, *68*
research objectives, *65*
research program, *73*
research project, *73*
sampling, *70*
survey, *69*
symptoms, *53*
temporal sequence, *59*
test-market, *61*
unobtrusive methods, *72*

Questions for Review and Critical Thinking

1. A business researcher gives a presentation to a music industry executive. After considering the results of a test-market examining whether or not lowering the price of in-store CDs will lower the number of illicit downloads of the same music, the executive claims: "The test-market was conducted in eight cities. In two of the cities, lowering the price did not decrease illicit downloading. Therefore, lowering the price does not decrease this behavior, and we should not decide to lower prices based on this research." Comment on the executive's conclusion. What type of inference is being made? Will the decision not to lower prices be a good one?
2. What is an experimental manipulation? A business researcher is hired by a specialty retail firm. The retailer is trying to decide what level of lighting and what temperature it should maintain in its stores to maximize sales. How can the researcher manipulate these experimental variables within a causal design?
3. We introduced the scientific method in Chapter 3. Do the stages in the research process discussed here seem to follow the scientific method?
4. Describe the type of research evidence that allows one to infer causality.
5. Why is the "define research objectives" of the research process probably the most important stage?
6. What are the three types of business research? Indicate which type each item in the list below illustrates. Explain your answers.
   a. Establishing the relationship between advertising and sales in the beer industry
   b. Ranking the key factors new college graduates are seeking in their first career position
   c. Estimating the 5-year sales potential for Cat-Scan machines in the Ark-La-Tex (Arkansas, Louisiana, and Texas) region of the United States
   d. Testing the effect of "casual day" on employee job satisfaction
   e. Discovering the ways that people who live in apartments actually use vacuum cleaners, and identifying cleaning tasks for which they do not use a vacuum
7. Suppose Auchan (**http://www.auchan.fr**), a hypermarket chain based out of France, was considering opening three hypermarkets in the midwestern United States. What role would theory play in designing a research study to track how the shopping habits of consumers from the United States differ from those in France and from those in Japan? What kind of hypothesis might be examined in a study of this topic?
8. Consider the following list, and indicate and explain whether each best fits the definition of a problem, opportunity, or symptom:
   a. A 12.5 percent decrease in store traffic for a children's shoe store in a medium-sized city mall.
   b. Walmart's stock price has decreased 25 percent between 2007 and 2009.
   c. A furniture manufacturer and retailer in North Carolina reads a research report indicating consumer trends toward Australian Jara and Kari wood. The export of these prod-

ucts is very limited and very expensive.

d. Marlboro reads a research report written by the U.S. FDA. It indicates that the number of cigarette smokers in sub-Saharan Africa is expected to increase dramatically over the next decade.

9. Define research project and research program. Referring to the question immediately above, do you think a research project or a research program is needed to provide useful input to the Auchan decision makers?
10. Define *business opportunity, business problem,* and *symptoms.* Give an example of each as it applies to a university business school.
11. What type of research design would you recommend in the situations below? For each applied business research project, what might be an example of a "deliverable?" Which do you think would involve actually testing a research hypothesis?

    a. The manufacturer of flight simulators and other pilot training equipment wishes to forecast sales volume for the next five years.
    b. A local chapter of the American Lung Association wishes to identify the demographic characteristics of individuals who donate more than $500 per year.
    c. Caterpillar Inc. is concerned about increasing inventory costs and is considering going completely to a just-in-time inventory system.
    d. A food company researcher wishes to know what types of food are carried in brown-bag lunches to learn if the company can capitalize on this phenomenon.
    e. A researcher wishes to identify who plays bingo.

12. List five ways that business research can contribute to effective business decision making.

Research Activities

1. **'NET** Look up information about the online MBA programs at the University of Phoenix (**http://www.mba-online-program.com/university_of_phoenix_online_mba.html**). Compare it to the traditional MBA program at your university. Suppose each was looking to expand the numbers of students in their programs. How might the research design differ for each?
2. **'NET** Use a Web browser to go to the Gallup Organization's home page at (**http://www.gallup.com**). The Gallup home page changes regularly. However, it should provide an opportunity to read the results of a recent poll. For example, a poll might break down American's sympathies toward Israel or the Palestinians based on numerous individual characteristics such as political affiliation or religious involvement. After reading the results of a Gallup poll of this type, learn how polls are conducted. You may need to click "about Gallup" and/or Frequently Asked Questions List (FAQ) to find this information on how the polls are conducted. List the various stages of the research process and how they were (or were not) followed in Gallup's project.
3. Any significant business decision requires input from a research project. Write a brief essay either defending this statement or refuting it.

Case 4.1 A New "Joe" on the Block

© GETTY IMAGES/ PHOTODISC GREEN

Joe Brown is ready to start a new career. After spending 30 years as a market researcher and inspired by the success of Starbucks, he is ready to enter the coffee shop business. However, before opening his first shop, he realizes that a great deal of research is needed. He has some key questions in mind.

- What markets in the United States hold the most promise for a new coffee shop?
- What type of location is best for a coffee shop?
- What is it that makes a coffee shop popular?
- What coffee do Americans prefer?

A quick trip to the Internet reveals more previous research on coffee, markets, and related materials than he expected. Many studies address taste. For example, he finds several studies that in one way or another compare the taste of different coffee shop coffees. Most commonly, they compare the taste of coffee from Starbucks against coffee from McDonald's, Dunkin' Donuts, Burger King, and sometimes a local competitor. However, it becomes difficult to draw a conclusion as the results seem to be inconsistent.

- One study had a headline that poked fun at Starbucks' high-priced coffee. The author of this study personally purchased coffee to go at four places, took them to his office, tasted them, made notes and then drew conclusions. All the coffee was tasted black with no sugar. Just cups of joe. He reached the conclusion that McDonald's Premium Coffee (at about $1.50 a cup), tasted nearly as good as Starbucks House Blend (at about $1.70 a cup), both of which were much better than either Dunkin' Donuts (at about $1.20) or Burger King (less than $1). This study argued that McDonald's was best, all things considered.
- Another study was written up by a good critic who was simply interested in identifying the best-tasting coffee. Again, he tasted them all black with nothing added. Each cup of coffee was consumed in the urban location near the inner city center in which he lived. He reached the conclusion that Starbucks' coffee had the best flavor although it showed room for improvement. McDonald's premium coffee was not as good, but better than the other two. Dunkin' Donuts coffee had reasonably unobjectionable taste but was very weak and watery. The Burger King coffee was simply not very good.
- Yet another study talked about Starbucks becoming a huge company and how it has lost touch with the common coffee shop coffee customer. The researchers stood outside a small organic specialty shop and interviewed 100 consumers as they

exited the shop. They asked, "Which coffee do you prefer?" The results showed a preference for a local coffee, tea, and incense shop, and otherwise put Starbucks last behind McDonald's, Burger King, and Dunkin' Donuts.

- Still another study compared the coffee-drinking experience. A sample of 50 consumers in St. Louis, Missouri, were interviewed and asked to list the coffee shop they frequented most. Starbucks was listed by more consumers than any other place. A small percentage listed Dunkin' Donuts but none listed McDonald's, despite their efforts at creating a premium coffee experience. The study did not ask consumers to compare the tastes of the coffee across the different places.

Joe also wants to find data showing coffee consumption patterns and the number of coffee shops around the United States, so he spends time looking for data on the Internet. His searches don't reveal anything satisfying.

As Joe ponders how to go about starting "A Cup of Joe," he wonders about the relevance of this previous research. Is it useful at all? He even questions whether he is capable of doing any primary research himself and considers hiring someone to do a feasibility study for him. Maybe doing research is easier than using research.

Sources: Shiver, J., "Taste Test: The Little Joes Take on Starbucks," *USA Today* (March 26, 2008), http://www.usatoday.com/money/industries/food/2006-03-26-coffee_x.htm, accessed July 20, 2008; Associated Press, "McDonald's Coffee Beats Starbucks, Says Consumer Reports," *The Seattle Times* (February 2, 2007), http://seattletimes.nwsource.com/html/businesstechnology/2003553322_webcoffeetest02.html, accessed July 20, 2008; "Coffee Wars: Starbucks v McDonald's," *The Economist* 386 (January 10, 2008), 58.

Questions

1. What are the top three key decisions faced by Joe?
2. What are the key deliverables that an outside researcher should produce to help Joe with the key decisions?
3. How relevant are the coffee taste studies cited above? Explain.
4. What flaws in the coffee taste studies should Joe consider in trying to weigh the merits of their results?
5. Briefly relate this situation to each of the major stages of the marketing research process.
6. Try to do a quick search to explore the question: "Are American consumer preferences the same all across the United States?"
7. Would it be better for Joe to do the research himself or have a consultant perform the work?
8. If a consultant comes in to do the job, what are three key deliverables that would likely be important to Joe in making a decision to launch the Cup of Joe coffee shop.

Case 4.2 A Small Caselet on Indian Company Explaining Research Process

© GETTY IMAGES/ PHOTODISC GREEN

This marketing research case is about the impact of e-Choupals of the Indian Tobacco Company (ITC) on decision-making ability of farmers related to agricultural practices. ITC started e-Choupal initiative in the year 2000 from Bhopal as a step to remove the intermediaries and connect the farmers directly to the mandi to make the operations more transparent. ITC started with just six Choupals and as on May 2007 reached more than 4 million farmers in about 40000 villages through more than 6500 Choupals in Uttar Pradesh, Madhya Pradesh, Rajasthan, Maharashtra, Karnataka, Andhra Pradesh, and Kerala.

ITC has plans to cover 100000 villages in the next decade by creating a low-cost IT-based interactive transaction and fulfilment channel. The e-Choupal provides various tangible and intangible benefits to the farmers. The tangible benefits include the agricultural inputs such as seeds, fertilizers, and pesticides, and the intangible benefits include information regarding weather, advance farming techniques, and other techniques to boost the per hectare productivity.

Research Question

The primary objective of this case is to empirically validate the impact of the ITC's e-Choupal initiative on improving farmer's decision-making process in agricultural practices. So, the marketing research question in this case is finding the impact of ITC's e-Choupal initiative in empowering Indian farmers.

Hypotheses

The following hypotheses are proposed to validate the impact of the ITC's e-Choupal initiative:

- Get timely price-related information regarding market price of produce before selling it
- Determine what crop to grow and when to plant and harvest
- Make more profitable crop choices
- Use good quality seeds, fertilizers, and pesticides, and more modern farm implements
- Seek out more expert opinion frequently regarding improved modern agricultural practices
- Safe storing of agricultural products can be done more effectively
- Assess weather forecast timely
- Apply effectively farming methods specific to each crop and region

Data Collection, Questionnaire Design, Sampling Process

The study population consists of the set of all farmers who could get involved with ITC through purchasing agricultural input, selling harvest, and accessing information from ITC's e-Choupal. The sampling frame consists of 28 villages from Madhya Pradesh and Uttar Pradesh. For getting a diversified sample, the listings of farmers who are associated with ITC's e-Choupal from different sanchalaks, the owners and managers of Internet kiosks, were stratified as per land size and year of association. In this way, 280 farmers were contacted for questionnaire survey.

The data has been collected by resorting to the questionnaire survey method. In addition to the demographic information of the respondents, 18 single item questions were used to gather response on the 18 decision-making aspects of farming process after and before association with ITC's e-Choupal. The questionnaire was personally administered to farmers and their responses were recorded. The response rate was found to be 89% as 248 filled-in questionnaires were received back from the respondents. After elimination of questionnaires, wherein excessive amount of data were missing, 244 responses were left with.

Data Analysis, Interpretation, and Hypothesis Support

Paired sample *t*-test was conducted in order to determine if statistical difference exists between mean scores on status of agricultural practices before and after association with ITC. It was found that there was statistically significant improvement in decision-making ability of farmers on all 18 aspects of decision-making related to farming after association with ITC. Farmers' decision-making capability increased greatly due to availability of timely price-related information regarding market price of produce before selling (mean score of 1.87 vs. 4.18; $p < 0.001$), whereas there is very little improvement (mean score 4.32 vs. 4.51; $p < 0.001$) on what crop to grow, when to plant, and when to harvest.

Results and Limitations

This marketing research case examines the impact that ICT-enabled system for information and services deliveries makes on their end users. The results clearly indicate that there is a marked improvement in the decision quality of associated farmers on all aspects of value chain, right from agricultural input selection to post-harvest management to final marketing of their produce. By providing solutions to specific queries of the farmers regarding plant diseases and expert opinion on other problems related to agriculture, ITC helps them to recognize the root cause of the problem. Once the root cause is identified, ITC helps the farmers by providing information about the alternative courses of action, and thus, an informed customer is in a better position to evaluate the alternatives and make purchase decisions. The results also indicate that the e-Choupal helps farmers throughout the production phase of the farming process.

This research has a limitation too. The fixed sampling frame and limited sample used for the study, though representative of the population, limit the scope of generalization of the results of the study. There are several other ICT-enabled governance systems which share the common objectives of empowering farmers to make the right decision related to farming practices. The study would have provided more meaningful insights if users of other ICT-enabled systems were compared with the users of ITC's e-Choupal.

Questions

1. Describe the research process done on ITC's e-Choupal.
2. How do you fromulate hypothesis for this research project.
3. Comment on data collection techniques adopted in this research project.
4. Can this research help in farmers's decision making on agricultural processes?

CASE EXHIBIT 4.2-1 **Mean Value of Several Benefits Received and Ability to Take Decisions Related to Agricultural Practices Presently and Before Association with ITC**

Agricultural Practices	Current Mean	Mean before Association with ITC
Timely price-related information regarding market price of produce before selling it	4.18	1.87
Determination of what crop to grow and when to plant and harvest	4.51	4.32
Profitable crop choices	4.47	4.14
Good quality seeds, fertilizers, and pesticides	4.52	3.42
Use more modern farm implements	3.77	2.64
Assessing expert opinion frequently regarding improved modern agricultural practices	3.07	1.91
Safe storing of agricultural products	4.15	3.32
Weather forecast	3.61	2.48
Farming methods specific to each crop and region	4.00	3.19

CHAPTER 5
THE HUMAN SIDE OF BUSINESS RESEARCH: ORGANIZATIONAL AND ETHICAL ISSUES

LEARNING OUTCOMES

After studying this chapter, you should be able to

1. **Know when research should be conducted externally and when it should be done internally**
2. **Be familiar with the types of jobs, job responsibilities, and career paths available within the business research industry**
3. **Understand the often conflicting relationship between management and researchers**
4. **Define ethics and understand how it applies to business research**
5. **Know and appreciate the rights and obligations of a) research respondents—particularly children, b) business researchers, and c) research clients or sponsors**
6. **Know how to avoid a conflict of interest in performing business research**

Chapter Vignette: They Do Want Better Pay, Right?

©AP PHOTO/JOHN S. STEWART

Amy has worked as a research analyst for an established snack food company for three years now. She was assigned as an internal consultant to the general manager of one of the manufacturing plants to assist in a salary and benefits study of the plant employees. Her partner on the project is the senior supervisor of the employees in the plant, and the data collection and analyses up to this point had gone well.

Her partner on the project, Raymond, was very supportive, and had given her access to the employees to conduct a detailed salary survey, outlining the current satisfaction with the plant supervision, salary, and health benefits. Her initial analyses and results were fairly clear—the employees were satisfied with the health and benefits associated with the plant, and they were generally satisfied with the plant management. However, the questions regarding pay were clear as well—the employees felt they were underpaid, given the work that they did for the company. When Amy examined the open-ended responses, the employee attitudes toward their pay were overwhelmingly negative. To her, this was clearly an issue that needed some follow-up.

She approached Raymond about these initial results. "Do you think we should contact HR, and see how our employees' pay stacks up with other local manufacturing companies?" She asked. Raymond's response surprised her, given his previous support of the project. "I wouldn't pay any attention to those results. Everyone wants more money. We have nothing to worry about there, and we will not contact HR regarding competitive wages around here," he stated. Amy pressed him further. "But it is very clear what their perception is. What is the problem with checking into this a little with HR? It can't hurt to just ask. I want to make sure that the results of the study are consistent with what the employees say." Raymond was adamant. "We will focus on the positive. The benefits responses look good to me. Let's not involve a bunch of other people on this. HR is fine." Amy did not know what to say. She felt that she was being steered in a particular direction. She needed some guidance, and the only person she could turn to was her supervisor.

"What am I supposed to report on this project?" Amy said to the research vice president. "I get the feeling that they don't want to hear the results. It's like they are trying to manage me on this. The employees say they want better pay. They do want better pay, right?"

Introduction

The vignette described above involves a researcher who faces a challenge in what is learned from the research process. Many companies have their own employees perform research projects and research programs. Thus, research is sometimes performed in-house, meaning that employees of the company that will benefit from the research project actually perform the research. In other cases, the research is performed by an **outside agency**, meaning that the company that will benefit from the research results hires an independent, outside firm to perform a research project.

outside agency
An independent research firm contracted by the company that actually will benefit from the research.

in-house research
Research performed by employees of the company that will benefit from the research.

While it would seem that **in-house research** would usually be of higher quality because of the increased knowledge of the researchers conducting the studies, there are several reasons why employees of the firm may not always be the best people to do the job. When the firm facing a decision encounters one of the following situations, they should consider having the research performed by an outside agency:

- An outside agency often can provide a fresh perspective. Creativity is often hindered by too much knowledge. When a firm is seeking new ideas, particularly in discovery-oriented research, an outsider is not constrained by the groupthink that often affects a company employee. In other words, employees who spend so much time together in their day-to-day work activities begin to act and think alike to a large degree. For example, history is filled with stories of products that remained unsuccessful commercially for years until someone from outside the company discovered a useful application. The technology for a microwave oven was invented in the 1940s by a company called Raytheon. Raytheon worked on radar systems for the Allied military in World War II. Not until someone from another company, Amana, tested the concept of using microwaves in a kitchen appliance did it become a commercial success. Some of the largest outside research agencies are shown in Exhibit 5.2.
- An outside agency often can be more objective. When a firm is facing a particularly sensitive situation that may even impact a large number of jobs within the company, it may be difficult for researchers to be objective. Alternatively, if a particular chief executive within the firm is in love with some new idea, researchers may feel a great deal of pressure to present results that are supportive of the concept. In these cases, outside researchers may be a good choice. Since they don't have to work for the company and interact with the players involved on a daily basis, they are less concerned about presenting results that may not be truly welcome.
- An outside agency may have special expertize. When a firm needs research requiring a particular expertize that some outside agency specializes in, it may be a good idea to use that firm to conduct the research. For example, if a company is searching for new ideas about how to use its Web site, an online focus group interview may be needed. While this is a skill that may not be prevalent within the company, there are several research firms that specialize in this particular type of research. Thus, the outside agency may have greater competency in this specific area.

TOTHEPOINT

To manage a business is to manage its future; and to manage the future is to manage information.

—Marion Harper

Likewise, there are conditions that make in-house research more attractive as well, as in the following situations:

- If the research project needs to be completed very quickly, chances are that in-house researchers can get started more quickly and get quicker or better access to internal resources that can help get the project done in short order.

- If the research project will require the close collaboration of many other employees from diverse areas of the organization, then in-house research may be preferable. The in-house research team can usually gain cooperation and more quickly ascertain just who needs to be interviewed and where those people can be found.
- A third reason for doing a project in-house has to do with economy. In-house research can almost always be done more cheaply than that done by an outside research firm.
- If secrecy is a major concern, then the research is best done in-house. Even though the outside firm might be trusted, it may take slightly less care in disguising its research efforts. Thus, other companies may pick up on signals in the marketplace that suggest the area of research for a firm. (See Exhibit 5.1.)

EXHIBIT 5.1
Should Research Be Done In-House or By an Outside Agency?

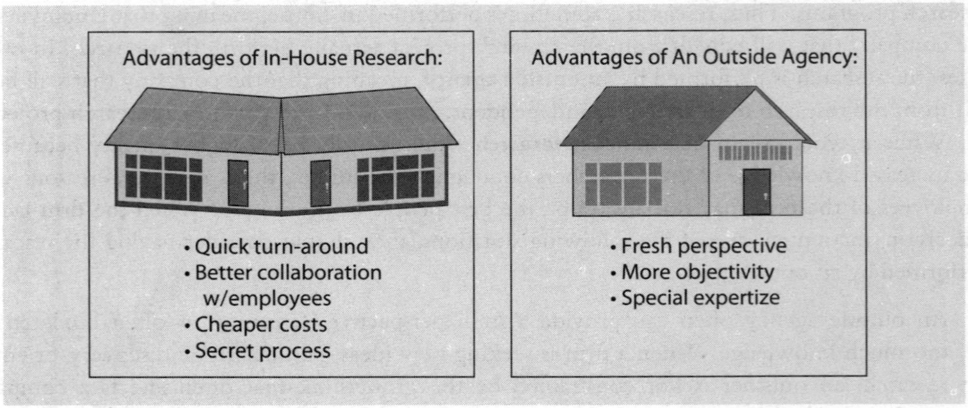

This chapter focuses on the human side of research.

Organizational Structure of Business Research

The placement of business research within a firm's organizational structure and the structure of the research department itself vary substantially, depending on the firm's acceptance of the concept of internal research and its stage of research sophistication. A research department can easily become isolated with poor organizational placement. Researchers may lack a voice in executive committees when they have no continuous relationship with management. This can occur when the research department is positioned at an inappropriately low level. Given the critically important nature of the intelligence coming out of a research department, it should be placed relatively high in the organizational structure to ensure that senior management is well informed. Research departments should also be linked with a broad spectrum of other units within the organization. Thus, they should be positioned to provide credible information both upstream and downstream within the organization.

Research departments that perform a staff function must wait for management to request assistance. Similar to Amy's situation, often the term "client" or "internal consultant" is used by the research department to refer to line management for whom services are being performed. The research department responds to clients' requests and is responsible for the design and execution of all research. It should function like an internal consulting organization that develops action-oriented, data-based recommendations.

Business Research Jobs

Research organizations themselves consist of layers of employees. Each employee has certain specific functions to perform based on his or her area of expertize and experience. A look at these jobs not only describes the potential structure of a research organization, but it also provides insight into the types of careers available as a business research specialist.

SMALL FIRMS

While it is difficult to precisely define the boundaries between small firms, mid-sized firms, and large firms, generally speaking, government statistics usually consider firms with fewer than 100 employees to be small. In small firms, the vice president of marketing may be in charge of all significant internal research projects. This officer may focus on organizational research projects that relate to staffing or stakeholder relations, or may be a sales manager who collects and analyzes sales histories, trade association statistics, and other internal data. Small companies usually have few resources and special competencies to conduct large-scale, sophisticated research projects. An advertising agency or a business consulting firm that specializes in research will be contracted if a large-scale survey is needed. At the other extreme, a large company like Procter & Gamble may staff its research departments with more than 100 people.

MID-SIZED FIRMS

Mid-sized firms can be thought of as those with between 100 and 500 employees. In a mid-sized firm, the research department may reside in the organization under the director of marketing research, as shown in Exhibit 5.3. This person provides leadership in research efforts and integrates all staff-level research activities. (This position will be discussed in greater detail in the next section.)

A **research analyst** is responsible for client contact, project design, preparation of proposals, selection of research suppliers, and supervision of data collection, analysis, and reporting activities. Normally, the research analyst is responsible for several projects simultaneously covering a wide spectrum of the firm's organizational activities. He or she works with product or division management and makes recommendations based on analysis of collected data.

Research assistants (or associates) provide technical assistance with questionnaire design, data analyses, and so forth. Another common name for this position is *junior analyst*. The **manager of decision support systems** supervises the collection and analysis of sales, inventory, and other periodic customer relationship management (CRM) data. Sales forecasts for product lines usually are developed using analytical and quantitative techniques. Sales information is provided to satisfy the planning, analysis, and control needs of decision makers. The manager of decision support systems may be assisted by a **forecast analyst** who provides technical assistance, such as running computer programs and manipulating data to forecast sales for the firm.

Personnel within a planning department may perform the research function in a mid-sized firm. At times, they may outsource some research functions, depending on the size of the project and the degree of sophistication. The planner may design research studies and then contract with outside firms that supply research services such as interviewing or data processing. They can combine the input from these outside agencies with their own work to write research reports.

research analyst
A person responsible for client contact, project design, preparation of proposals, selection of research suppliers, and supervision of data collection, analysis, and reporting activities.

research assistants
Research employees who provide technical assistance with questionnaire design, data analyses, and similar activities.

manager of decision support systems
Employee who supervises the collection and analysis of sales, inventory, and other periodic customer relationship management (CRM) data.

forecast analyst
Employee who provides technical assistance such as running computer programs and manipulating data to generate a sales forecast.

LARGE RESEARCH FIRMS

As research departments grow, they tend to specialize by product or strategic business unit. Major firms can be thought of as those with over 500 employees. Marriott Corporation has a director of research for lodging (for example, Marriott Hotels and Resorts, Courtyard by Marriott, and Fairfield Inn) and a director of research for contract services and restaurants (for example, Roy Rogers, Big Boy, and Senior Living Services). Each business unit's research director reports to the vice president of corporate marketing services. Many large organizations have managers of customer quality research who specialize in conducting surveys to measure consumers' satisfaction with product quality.

In many instances, business research units are located within a firm's marketing function. Exhibit 5.3 illustrates the organization of a typical major firm's marketing research department. Within this organization, the centralized research department conducts research for all the division's product groups. This is typical of a large research department that conducts much of its own research, including fieldwork.

EXHIBIT 5.3 **Organization of the Marketing Research Department in a Large Firm**

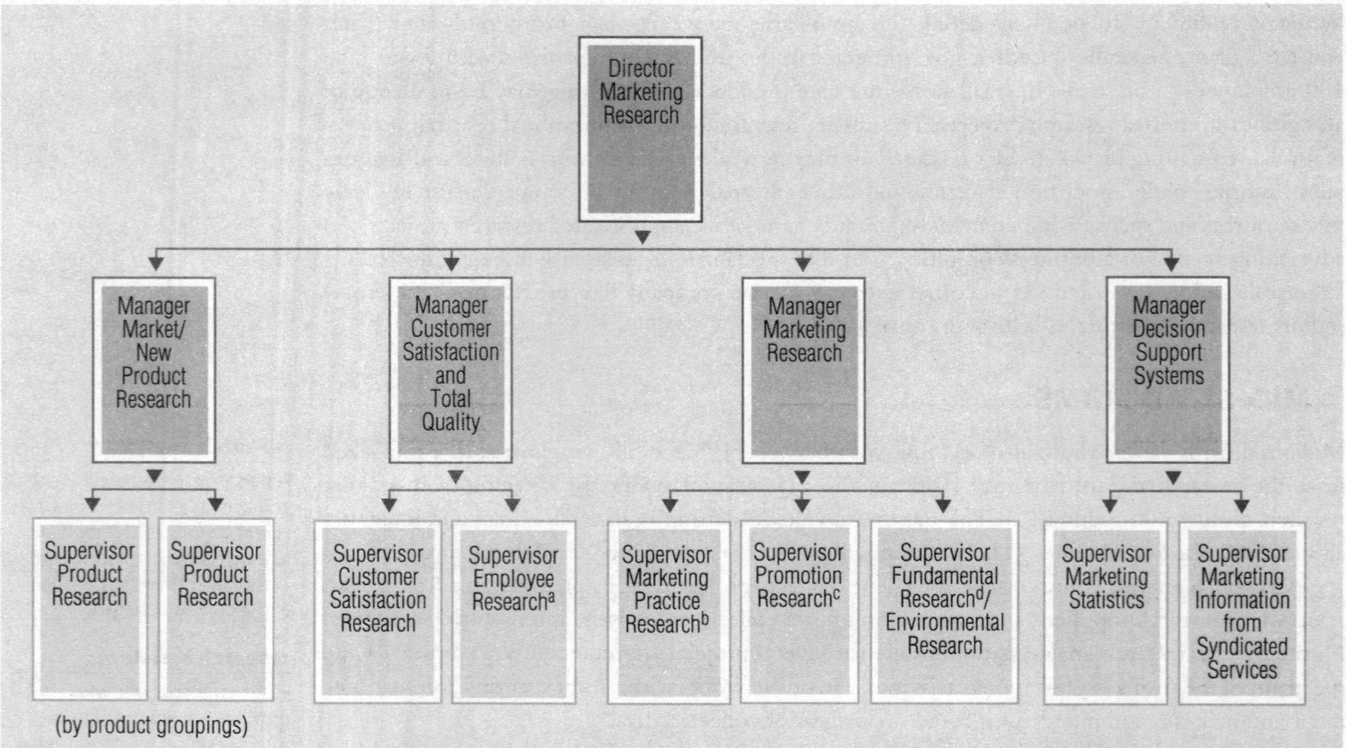

[a]Conducts research to improve total quality management in production.
[b]Conducts research that cuts across product lines or involves competitive marketing practices or characteristics of customer groups.
[c]Conducts research that cuts across product lines to measure the effectiveness of promotional activities.
[d]Conducts research aimed at gaining a basic understanding of various elements of the marketing process.

Other positions within a major firm's research department may include director of data collection (field supervisor), manager of quantitative research, focus group moderator, and manager of data processing. These are not shown in Exhibit 5.3. Even large firms sometimes outsource some research functions or even an entire project from time to time. For now, we turn our attention to the job of director of research and the interface between the research department and other departments.

The Director of Research as a Manager

A director of research plans, executes, and controls the firm's research function. This person typically serves on company executive committees that identify competitive opportunities and formulate strategies that involve customers or other organizational stakeholders. The various directors from each functional area generally make up this committee (such as finance, sales, production, and so forth). The director of research provides the research perspective during meetings. For instance, the researcher can provide input as to what types of business intelligence can be feasibly obtained given the decision being discussed. Research directors typically face problems like these:

- Skilled research professionals may like conducting research better than managing people. They pride themselves on being hands-on researchers. However, a director is a manager and spends more time in meetings and managing than actually conducting research.
- The research management role often is not formally recognized.

- Outstanding research professionals often have trouble delegating responsibility. The pride that comes with being a knowledgeable researcher makes it difficult to give up control. They may genuinely feel "I can do it better myself." As a result, they delegate only elementary or tedious tasks to subordinates. The subordinates can sometimes become disenchanted and thus become unhappy with their work.
- Finally, research is often seen as a hodgepodge of techniques available to answer individual, unrelated questions. According to this view, a research operation encompasses an array of more or less equal projects, each handled by a project director. Hence, many firms view a full-time director as unnecessary.[1]

Sources of Conflict between Senior Management and Research

In principle, the functions of research should merge harmoniously with the objectives of management for the benefit of both parties. In practice, the relationship between a research department and the users of research frequently is characterized by misunderstanding and conflict.

RESEARCH THAT IMPLIES CRITICISM

As we saw in the chapter vignette, a product manager who requests a survey of dealer loyalty will not be happy if the survey finds that the dealers are extremely critical. Similarly, a sales manager who informally projects a 5 percent increase in sales will not like hearing from the research department that the market potential indicates sales volume should be up by 20 percent. In each of these situations, the research presents information that implies criticism of a line executive's decision. In personal life, a sure way to lose a friend is to be openly critical of him or her. Things are no different in business.

MONEY

Research budgets are a source of conflict between management and researchers. Financial managers often see research as a cost rather than as an investment or a way of lowering risk. Successful decisions that are supported by research are seldom attributed to the researcher. Thus, as is often true in many areas of business, managers often want to spend as little as possible on research. In contrast, researchers often vigorously resist cutting corners in conducting research. For instance, they may feel that a large random sample is necessary to adequately address a research question using descriptive research. This approach can be very expensive and sometimes time consuming. Inevitably, management's desire to save money and the researcher's desire to conduct rigorous research conflict. Successful research projects often are those that are based on compromise. This may involve working within a budget that will produce meaningful results and sacrifice precision and rigor minimally.

TIME

Researchers say, "Good research takes time!" Managers say, "Time is money!" Like oil and water, these two views do not go together easily. A look back at the research process in the last chapter makes it clear that it can take some time to complete a research project. Simply planning one can involve days, if not weeks, of study and preparation. For instance, conducting a literature review or a review of previous studies can take weeks. Without them, the researcher may not be able to develop specific research hypotheses that would direct the project very specifically toward the current issue. Other times, the researcher may wish to interview more people than time can allow or take the time to use a more sophisticated data analysis approach.

TOTHEPOINT

The longer the title, the less important the job.

—George McGovern

Oftentimes, the more quickly the research project is done, the less likely it is to be successful. This doesn't mean it can't provide valuable information. It simply is not as certain that a quickly put-together study will provide valuable answers as would a more deliberately planned project. When studies are rushed, the following sources of error become more prominent than they would be otherwise:

RESEARCH SNAPSHOT

Marketing Research Pays

Marketing research can pay! Careers in marketing research can be very lucrative. This is particularly true if one has the right attributes. These attributes include being a good people person as well as having good quantitative skills and a good education. The fastest career tracks in marketing research are for those with at least a master's degree.

The prospects of finding a job remain good. Marketing researchers have long been in greater demand than the supply can address. The salaries also can be very lucrative. The 2002 U.S. Department of Labor Salary Survey suggests that marketing research analysts' salaries are generally between $40,000 and $80,000. These are for actual research analysts and not research directors. Beginning research employees, with little or no experience, generally enter the firm as a survey researcher. Those salaries are considerably less, generally between $20,000 and $40,000. However, they require no significant work experience.

Job opportunities in marketing research exist outside the United States as well. The salaries also are lucrative in other countries. The chart below shows salaries for non-managerial marketing research positions in the United States, Australia, Japan, and the United Kingdom. For comparison purposes, salaries for non-managerial sales employees also are provided. The salaries are expressed in thousands of U.S. dollars and reflect the latest available statistics. As can be seen, research jobs compare very favorably. In addition, researchers that move into research director positions see a substantial increase in pay. Perhaps you'll give marketing research a try?

© iStock

Common Currency ($)	Australia	UK	Japan	United States
Sales Market Analysts				
High	44.78	122.81	82.82	55.00
Low	33.58	61.40	41.41	35.00
Marketing Research				
High	55.97	78.95	82.82	76.30
Low	48.51	43.86	49.69	38.76

Sources: Enright, A., "Carve out a Niche," *Marketing News* (November 15, 2005), 17; Fellman, M. W., "Survey: Employment Levels Critically Low in MR Industry," *Marketing News* 322 (June 8, 1998), 12; U.S. Department of Labor, "Wages, Benefits and Earnings" (2006), http://www.bls.gov/bls/wages.htm, accessed May 2, 2006. Walters, Robert, "Market Research Search Results," http://www.robertwalters.com (2006), accessed January 20, 2006.

© PHOTODISC/GETTY IMAGES

- Conducting a study that is needed. Taking more time to perform a literature search, including through company and industry reports, may have provided the needed intelligence without a new study.
- Addressing the wrong issue. Taking more time to make sure the decision statement is well defined and that the research questions that follow will truly address relevant issues can lessen the chance that the research goes in the wrong direction.
- Sampling difficulties. Correctly defining, identifying, and contacting a truly representative sample is a difficult and time consuming task. However, in some types of research, the quality of results depends directly on the quality of the sample.
- Inadequate data analysis. The researcher may analyze the data quickly and without the rigor that would otherwise be taken. Therefore, certain assumptions may not be considered, and important information within the data is simply not discovered.

Sometimes a researcher will have to submit to the time pressure and do a quick-and-dirty study. A sudden event can make it necessary to acquire data quickly—but rush jobs can sometimes be avoided with proper planning of the research program. If it is necessary to conduct a study under severe time limitations, the researcher is obligated to point this out to management. The research report and presentation should include all the study limitations, including those that resulted from a shortage of time or money.

INTUITIVE DECISION MAKING

The fact of the matter is that managers are decision makers. They are action-oriented, and they often rely on gut reaction and intuition. Many times their intuition serves them well, so it isn't surprising that they sometimes do not believe a research project will help improve their decision making. At other times, they resist research because it just may provide information that is counter to their intuition or their desires. They particularly abhor being held back while waiting for some research report.

If managers do use research, they often request simple projects that will provide concrete results with certainty. Researchers tend to see problems as complex questions that can be answered only within probability ranges. One aspect of this conflict is the fact that a research report provides findings, but cannot make decisions. Decision-oriented executives may unrealistically expect research to make decisions for them or provide some type of guarantee that the action they take will be correct. While research provides information for decision making, it does not always remove all the uncertainties involved in complex decisions. Certain alternatives may be eliminated, but the research may reveal new aspects of a problem. Although research is a valuable decision-making tool, it does not relieve the executive of the decision-making task.

Presentation of the right facts can be extremely useful. However, decision makers often believe that researchers collect the wrong facts. Many researchers view themselves as technicians who generate numbers using sophisticated mathematical and statistical techniques; they may spend more time on technical details than on satisfying managerial needs. Each person who has a narrow perspective of another's job is a partial cause of the problem of generating limited or useless information.

Consider this situation: An Internet retailer (Send.com) used a television ad to try to stimulate more gift purchasing among its customers. The spot centers on several men on the golf course drinking champagne. The "punch line" comes when one of the guys is hit in the groin. The voice over exclaims, "He just got hit in the little giver!"

A male executive may like punch lines like this. However, the audience for these ads is not all male. Had research been used to test these ideas prior to spending the money to produce the ads and buy the spots, it would have revealed that men didn't respond as favorably as expected to these ads and women found them boorish.[2] Thus, intuition has its limits as a replacement for informed research intelligence.[3]

FUTURE DECISIONS BASED ON PAST EXPERIENCE

Managers wish to predict the future, but researchers measure only current or past events. In 1957, Ford introduced the Edsel, one of the classic business failures of all time. One reason for the Edsel's failure was that the research conducted several years before the car's introduction indicated a strong demand for a medium-priced car for the "man on his way up." By the time the car was introduced, however, consumer preference had shifted to two cars, one being a small import for the suburban wife. Not all research information is so dated, but all research describes what people have done in the past. In this sense, researchers use the past to predict the future.

Reducing the Conflict between Management and Researchers

Given the conflicting goals of management and research, it is probably impossible to completely eliminate the conflict. However, when researchers and decision makers work more closely together, there will be less conflict. The more closely they work together, the better the communication between decision makers and researchers. In this way, business decision makers will better understand the information needs and work requirements of researchers. It will allow for better planning of research projects and a greater appreciation for the role that research plays in minimizing the riskiness of business decision making. Exhibit 5.4 lists some common areas of conflict between research and management. Many of these can be avoided through improved understanding of the other's position.

With closer cooperation, managers are more involved with projects from the beginning. Early involvement increases the likelihood that managers will accept and act on the results. Researchers' responsibility should be made explicit by a formal job description. Better planning and an annual statement of the research program for the upcoming year will help minimize emergency assignments, which usually waste resources and demoralize personnel.

TOTHEPOINT

Someone's sitting in the shade today because someone planted a tree a long time ago.

—Warren Buffett

EXHIBIT 5.4 Areas of Conflict between Top Management and Marketing Researchers

Area of Potential Conflict	Top Management's Position	Business Researcher's Position
Research responsibility	Researchers lack a sense of accountability. The sole function of the researcher is to provide information.	The responsibility for research should be explicitly defined, and this responsibility should be consistently followed. The researcher should be involved with top management in decision making.
Research personnel	Researchers are generally poor communicators who lack enthusiasm, skills, and imagination.	Top managers are anti-intellectual. Researchers should be hired, judged, and compensated on the basis of their research capabilities.
Budget	Research costs too much. Since the research department's contribution is difficult to measure, budget cuts in the department are defensible.	"You get what you pay for." Research must have a continuing, long-term commitment from top management.
Assignments	Projects tend to be overengineered and not executed with a sense of urgency. Researchers have a ritualized, staid approach.	Top managers make too many nonresearchable or emergency requests and do not allocate sufficient time or money.
Problem definition	The researcher is best equipped to define the problem; it is sufficient for the top manager to give general direction. Top managers cannot help it if circumstances change. The researcher must appreciate this and be willing to respond to changes.	Researchers are often not given all the relevant facts about situations, which often change after research is under way. Top managers are generally unsympathetic to this widespread problem.
Research reporting	Most reports are dull, use too much jargon and too many qualifiers, and are not decision oriented. Reports too often are presented after a decision has been made.	Top managers treat research reports superficially. Good research demands thorough reporting and documentation. Top managers give insufficient time to prepare good reports.
Use of research	Top managers should be free to use research as they see fit. Changes in the need for and timing of research are sometimes unavoidable.	Top managers' use of research to support a predetermined position or to confirm or excuse past decisions represents misuse. Also, it is wasteful to request research and then not use it after it has been conducted.

*Based on John G. Keane, "Some Observations on Marketing Research in Top Management Decision Making," *Journal of Marketing*, October 1969, p. 13.

Business researchers likewise will come to understand management's perspective better. Researchers enhance company profits by encouraging better decisions. The closer together managers and researchers work, the more researchers realize that managers sometimes need information urgently. Thus, they should try to develop cost-saving research alternatives and realize that sometimes a quick-and-dirty study is necessary, even though it may not be as scientifically rigorous as might be desired. Sometimes, quick-and-dirty studies still provide usable and timely information. In other words, they should focus on results.

Perhaps most important is more effective communication of the research findings and research designs. The researchers must understand the interests and needs of the users of the research. If the researchers are sensitive to the decision-making orientation of management and can translate research performance into management language, organizational conflict will diminish.

research generalist
An employee who serves as a link between management and research specialists. The research generalist acts as a problem definer, an educator, a liaison, a communicator, and a friendly ear.

A **research generalist** can effectively serve as a link between management and the research specialist. The research generalist acts as a problem definer, an educator, a liaison, a communicator, and a friendly ear. This intermediary could work with specialists who understand management's needs and demands. The student with research skills who has a business degree seems most suited for this coordinating function.

Several strategies for reducing the conflict between management and research are possible. Managers generally should plan the role of research better, and researchers should become more decision-oriented and improve their communication skills (see Exhibit 5.5).[4]

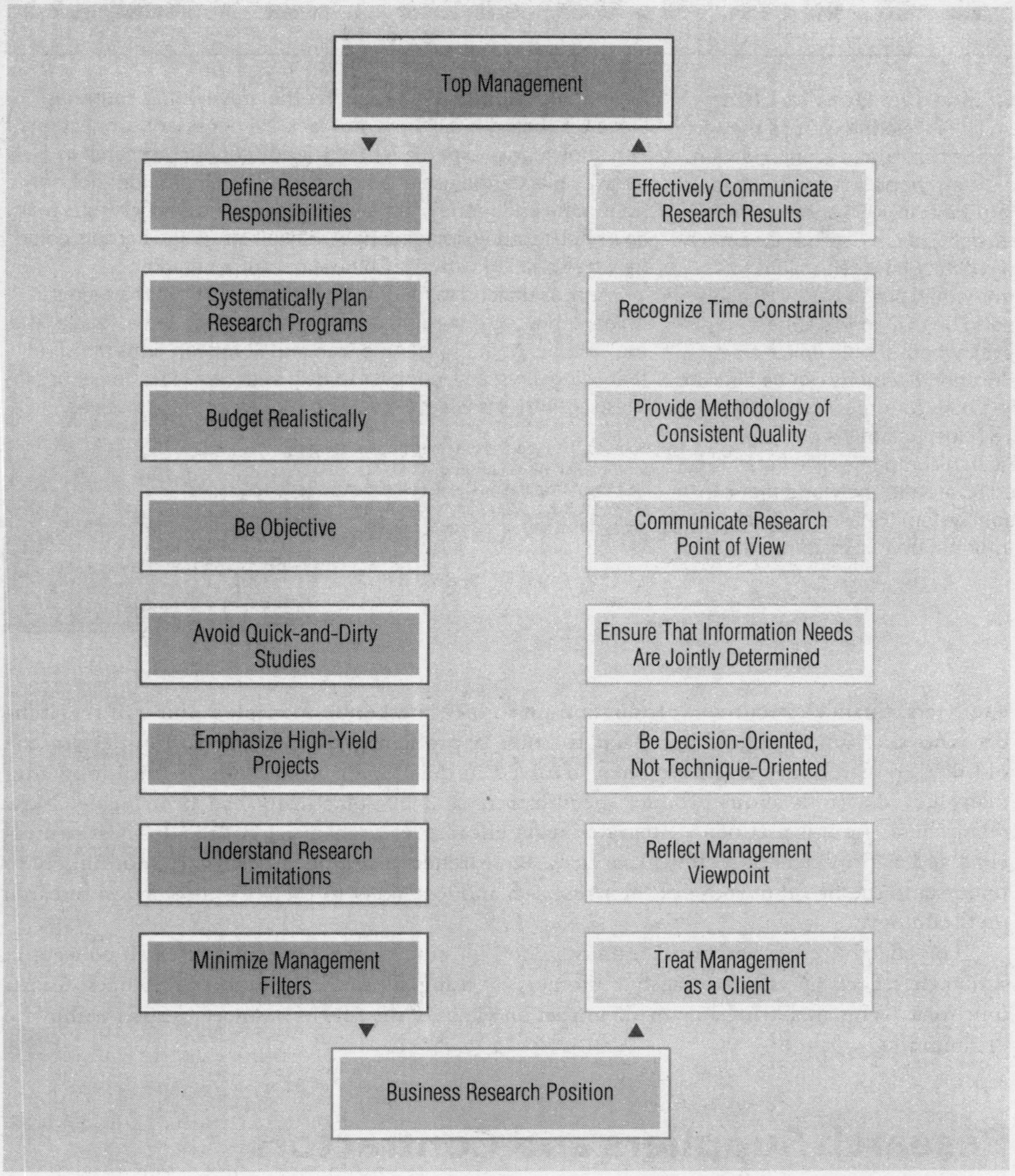

EXHIBIT 5.5
Improving Two-Way Communication to Reduce Conflict

Cross-Functional Teams

The ability to develop a successful decision making approach is often a function of the input of many different stakeholders. With improved communication, a more focused solution is possible. One way to encourage this is through cross-functional teams.

Cross-functional teams are composed of individuals from various functional areas such as engineering, production, finance, and marketing who share a common purpose. Cross-functional teams help organizations focus on a core business process, such as customer service or new-product development. Working in teams reduces the tendency for employees to focus single-mindedly on an isolated functional activity. Cross-functional teams help employees increase customer value since communication about their specific desires and opinions are better communicated across the firm.

cross-functional teams
Employee teams composed of individuals from various functional areas such as engineering, production, finance, and marketing who share a common purpose.

At trendsetting organizations, many research directors are members of cross-functional teams. New-product development, for example, may be done by a cross-functional team of

RESEARCH SNAPSHOT

Finding Häagen-Dazs in China

Ice cream lovers needn't worry if they are sent on a business trip to China. Häagen-Dazs ice cream shops first appeared in Shanghai, China, in 1996 and now there are dozens of Häagen-Dazs ice cream shops in coastal China, with plans for hundreds more. Clearly, many firms would like to follow Häagen-Dazs into China. China is expected to be the world's largest consumer market by 2020. However, where should an ice cream shop be located in China? While location decisions can be difficult enough within the borders of one's own country, imagine trying to decide where to put a shop in a huge, unfamiliar country.

Fortunately, standardized research companies like Retail Forward have resources deployed all around the world that can synthesize Geographic Information System (GIS) information with survey research and other information to assist firms with location decisions in China and in other developing countries. Since U.S.-based retail firms may lack the necessary connections and knowledge (expertize) to efficiently conduct research in faraway places, the use of an outside research provider not only saves time and money, but also yields higher quality results than an in-house study. Imagine how difficult language barriers could be when dealing with the Chinese consumer market.

And, as difficult as identifying good retail locations seems in China, other top emerging retail nations include India, Russia, and the Ukraine. As in China, American and European firms may find that using a research supplier to help with retail location issues in these countries is wiser than doing the research themselves.

© iStock

Sources: "Häagen-Dazs in China," *China Business Review* 31 (Jul/Aug 2004), 22; Hall, Cecily, "Spanning the Retail Globe," *WWD: Women's Wear Daily* 190 (July 21 2005), 11.

© CHINA FEATURES/CORBIS SYGMA

engineers, finance executives, production personnel, marketing managers, and staff researchers who take an integrated approach to solve a problem or exploit opportunities. In the old days, research may not have been involved in developing new products until long after many key decisions about product specifications and manufacturing had been made. Now researchers' input is part of an integrated team effort. Researchers act both as business consultants and as providers of technical services. Researchers working in teams are more likely to understand the broad purpose of their research and less likely to focus exclusively on research methodology.

The effective cross-functional team is a good illustration of the business research concept in action. It reflects an effort to satisfy customers by using all the organization's resources. Cross-functional teams are having a dramatic impact on views of the role of business research within the organization.

Research Suppliers and Contractors

research suppliers
Commercial providers of research services.

As mentioned in the beginning of the chapter, there are times when it makes good sense to obtain business research from an outside organization. In these cases, managers must interact with **research suppliers**, who are commercial providers of business and marketing research services. Business research is carried out by firms that may be variously classified as marketing and business research consulting companies, such as Burke, Market Facts, Inc., or Freedonia, Inc.; suppliers of syndicated research services, such as Roper Starch Worldwide; as well as interviewing agencies, universities, and government agencies.

Syndicated Service

syndicated service
A research supplier that provides standardized information for many clients in return for a fee.

No matter how large a firm's research department is, some projects are too expensive to perform in-house. A **syndicated service** is a research supplier that provides standardized information for many clients in return for a fee. They serve as a sort of supermarket for standardized research results. For example, J. D. Power and Associates sells research about customers' ratings of automobile quality and their reasons for satisfaction. Most automobile manufacturers and their advertising agencies subscribe to this syndicated service because the company provides important industry-wide information it gathers from a national sample of thousands of car buyers. By specializing in this type of customer satisfaction research, J. D. Power gains certain economies of scale.

Syndicated services can provide expensive information economically to numerous clients because the information is not specific to one client but interests many. Such suppliers offer standardized information to measure media audiences, wholesale and retail distribution data, and other forms of data.

© RHODA SIDNEY/PHOTOEDIT

Doing research in a foreign country is often better done by an outside agency with resources in those places.

Standardized Research Services

Standardized research service companies that develop a unique methodology for investigating a business specialty area. Several research firms, such as Retail Forward (**http://www.retailforward.com**), provide location services for retail firms. The Research Snapshot "Finding Häagen-Dazs in China" illustrates an interesting application for which an outside location service company may be particularly useful. Research suppliers conduct studies for multiple, individual clients using the same methods.

ACNielsen (**http://www.acnielsen.com**) collects information throughout the new-product development process, from initial concept screening through test-marketing. The BASES system can evaluate initiatives relative to other products in the competitive environment. For example, a client can compare its day-after recall scores with average scores for a product category.

Even when a firm could perform the research task in-house, research suppliers may be able to conduct the project at a lower cost, faster, and relatively more objectively. A company that wishes to quickly evaluate a new advertising strategy may find an ad agency's research department is able to provide technical expertize on copy development research that is not available within the company itself. Researchers may be well advised to seek outside help with research when conducting research in a foreign country in which the necessary human resources and knowledge to effectively collect data are lacking. The preceding Research Snapshot illustrates this situation.

standardized research service
Companies that develop a unique methodology for investigating a business specialty area.

Limited Research Service Companies and Custom Research

Limited-service research suppliers specialize in particular research activities, such as syndicated service, field interviewing, data warehousing, or data processing. Full-service research suppliers sometimes contract these companies for ad hoc research projects. The client usually controls these agencies or management consulting firms, but the research supplier handles most of the operating details of **custom research** projects. These are projects that are tailored specifically to a client's unique needs. A custom research supplier may employ individuals with titles that imply relationships with clients, such as *account executive* or *account group manager,* as well as functional specialists with titles such as *statistician, librarian, director of field services, director of tabulation and data processing,* and *interviewer.*

custom research
Research projects that are tailored specifically to a client's unique needs.

Exhibit 5.6 lists the top 25 suppliers of global marketing research and their revenues in 2008. Most provide various services ranging from designing activities to fieldwork. The services they can provide are not covered in detail here because they are discussed throughout the book, especially in the sections on fieldwork. However, here we briefly consider some managerial and human aspects of dealing with research suppliers. Clearly, the exhibit reveals that research is big business. Its growth will continue as data availability increases and as businesses desire more precision in their decision making. Therefore, attractive career opportunities are numerous for those with the right skills and desires.

Ethical Issues in Business Research

As in all human interactions, ethical issues exist in research. Our earlier discussion of potential organizational politics and the implication of different goals or perspectives introduced a situation where ethics can come into play. This book considers various ethical issues concerning fair business dealings, proper research techniques, and appropriate use of research results in other chapters. The remainder of this chapter addresses society's and managers' concerns about the ethical implications of business research.

EXHIBIT 5.6 Top 25 Global Marketing Research Firms

Organization	Headquarters	Web Site	Employees	Revenue ($M)
The Nielsen Co.	New York, NY	**nielsen.com**	33,171	$4,220.0
IMS Health Inc.	Norwalk, CT	**imshealth.com**	7,950	2,192.6
Taylor Nelson Sofres plc	London, UK	**tnsglobal.com**	15,267	2,137.2
GfK AG	Nuremberg, Germany	**gfk.com**	9,070	1,593.2
The Kantar Group	London, UK	**kantargroup.com**	7,100	1,551.4
Ipsos Group SA	Paris, France	**ipsos.com**	8,088	1,270.3
Synovate	London, UK	**synovate.com**	5,801	867.0
IRI	Chicago, IL	**infores.com**	3,655	702.0
Westat, Inc.	Rockville, MD	**westat.com**	1,906	467.8
Arbitron, Inc.	New York, NY	**arbitron.com**	1,130	352.1
INTAGE Inc.	Tokyo, Japan	**intage.co.jp**	1,666	281.1
J. D. Power and Associates	Westlake Village, CA	**jdpa.com**	875	260.5
Harris Interactive Inc.	Rochester, NY	**harrisinteractive.com**	1,336	226.8
Maritz Research	Fenton, MA	**maritzresearch.com**	806	223.3
The NPD Group Inc.	Port Washington, NY	**npd.com**	1,120	211.1
Opinion Research	Omaha, NE	**infousa.com**	1,235	202.2
Video Research, Ltd.	Tokyo, Japan	**videor.co.jp**	386	169.6
IBOPE Group	São Paulo, Brazil	**ibope.com.br**	1,743	116.5
Lieberman Research	Los Angeles, CA	**lrwonline.com**	324	87.5
comScore Inc.	Reston, VA	**comscore.com**	452	87.2
Cello Research	London, UK	**cellogroup.co.uk**	400	79.9
Market Strategies, Intl.	Livoria, MI	**marketstrategies.com**	311	61.8
BVA Group	Paris, France	**bva.fr**	620	55.6
OTX	Los Angeles, CA	**otxresearch.com**	191	54.5
Dentsu Research, Inc.	Tokyo, Japan	**dentsuresearch.co.jp**	116	54.2

Source: *Marketing News* (August 15, 2008), vol. 43 (13): H4–H50.

Ethical Questions Are Philosophical Questions

Ethical questions are philosophical questions. There are several philosophical theories that address how one develops a moral philosophy and how behavior is affected by morals. These include theories about cognitive moral development, the bases for ethical behavioral intentions, and opposing moral values.[5] While ethics remain a somewhat elusive topic, what is clear is that not everyone involved in business, or in fact involved in any human behavior, comes to the table with the same ethical standards or orientations.[6]

business ethics
The application of morals to behavior related to the exchange environment.

moral standards
Principles that reflect beliefs about what is ethical and what is unethical.

ethical dilemma
Refers to a situation in which one chooses from alternative courses of actions, each with different ethical implications.

Business ethics is the application of morals to behavior related to the business environment or context. Generally, good ethics conforms to the notion of "right," and a lack of ethics conforms to the notion of "wrong." Highly ethical behavior can be characterized as being fair, just, and acceptable.[7] Ethical values can be highly influenced by one's moral standards. **Moral standards** are principles that reflect beliefs about what is ethical and what is unethical. More simply, they can be thought of as rules distinguishing right from wrong. The Golden Rule, "Do unto others as you would have them do unto you," is one such ethical principle.

An **ethical dilemma** simply refers to a situation in which one chooses from alternative courses of actions, each with different ethical implications. Each individual develops a philosophy or way of thinking that is applied to resolve the dilemmas they face. Many people use moral standards to guide their actions when confronted with an ethical dilemma. Others adapt an ethical orientation that rejects absolute principles. Their ethics are based more on the social or cultural acceptability of behavior. If it conforms to social or cultural norms, then it is ethical. From a moral theory standpoint, idealism is a term that reflects the degree to which one accepts moral standards as a guide for behavior. **Relativism** is a term that reflects the degree to which one rejects moral standards in favor of the acceptability of some action. This way of thinking rejects absolute principles in favor of situation-based evaluations. Thus, an action that is judged ethical in one situation can be deemed unethical in another. In contrast, **idealism** is a term that reflects the degree to which one bases one's morality on moral standards. Someone who is an ethical idealist will try to apply ethical principles like the golden rule in all ethical dilemmas.

relativism
A term that reflects the degree to which one rejects moral standards in favor of the acceptability of some action. This way of thinking rejects absolute principles in favor of situation-based evaluations.

idealism
A term that reflects the degree to which one bases one's morality on moral standards.

For example, a student may face an ethical dilemma when taking a test. Another student may arrange to exchange multiple choice responses to a test via electronic text messages. This represents an ethical dilemma because there are alternative courses of action each with differing moral implications. An ethical idealist may apply a rule that cheating is always wrong and therefore would not be likely to participate in the behavior. An ethical relativist may instead argue that the behavior is acceptable because a lot of the other students will be doing the same. In other words, the consensus is that this sort of cheating is acceptable, so this student would be likely to go ahead and participate in the behavior. Researchers and business stakeholders face ethical dilemmas practically every day. The following sections describe how this can occur.

General Rights and Obligations of Concerned Parties

Everyone involved in business research can face an ethical dilemma. For this discussion, we can divide those involved in research into three parties:

1. The people actually performing the research, who can also be thought of as the "doers"
2. The research client, sponsor, or the management team requesting the research, who can be thought of as "users" of research
3. The research participants, meaning the actual research respondents or subjects

Each party has certain rights and obligations toward the other parties. Exhibit 5.7 diagrams these relationships.

Like the rest of business, research works best when all parties act ethically. Each party depends on the other to do so. A client depends on the researcher to be honest in presenting research results. The researcher depends on the client to be honest in presenting the reasons for doing the research and in describing the business situation. Each is also dependent on the research participant's honesty in answering questions during a research study. Thus, each is morally obligated

EXHIBIT 5.7
Interaction of Rights and Obligations between Parties

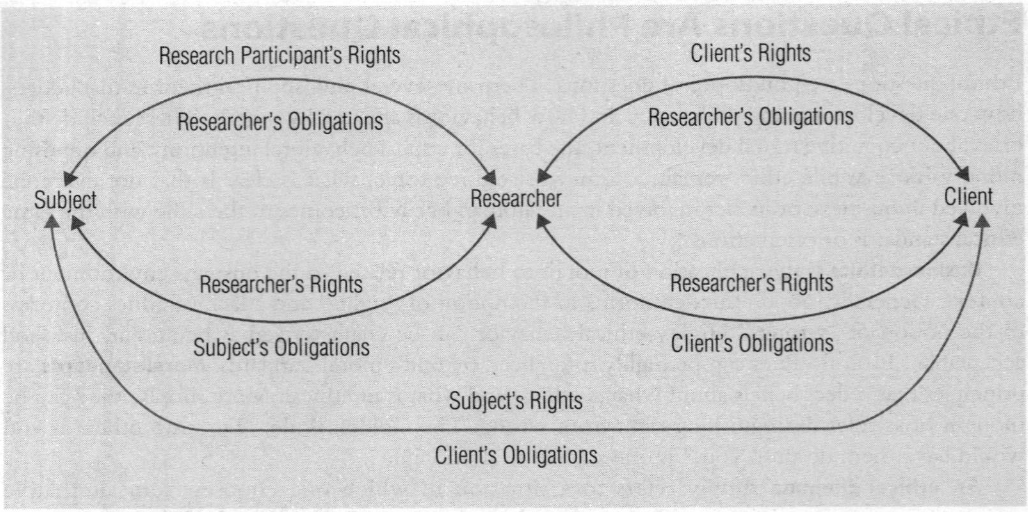

toward the other. Likewise, each also has certain rights. The following section elaborates on the obligations and rights of each party.

Rights and Obligations of the Research Participant

informed consent
When an individual understands what the researcher wants him or her to do and consents to the research study.

Most business research is conducted with the research participant's consent. In other words, the participation is active. Traditional survey research requires that a respondent voluntarily answer questions in one way or another. This may involve answering questions on the phone, responding to an e-mail request, or even sending a completed questionnaire by regular mail. In these cases, **informed consent** means that the individual understands what the researcher wants him or her to do and consents to the research study. In other cases, research participants may not be aware that they are being monitored in some way. For instance, a research firm may monitor superstore purchases via an electronic scanner. The information may assist in understanding how customers respond to promotions. However, no consent is provided since the participant is participating passively. The ethical responsibilities vary depending on whether participation is active or passive.

THE OBLIGATION TO BE TRUTHFUL

confidentiality
The information involved in a research study will not be shared with others.

When someone willingly consents to participate actively, it is generally expected that he or she will provide truthful answers. Honest cooperation is the main obligation of the research participant. In return for being truthful, the subject has the right to expect confidentiality. **Confidentiality** means that information involved in the research will not be shared with others. When the respondent truly believes that confidentiality will be maintained, then it becomes much easier to respond truthfully, even about potentially sensitive topics. Likewise, the researcher and the research sponsor also may expect the respondent to maintain confidentiality. For instance, if the research involves a new food product from Nabisco, then they may not want the respondent to discuss the idea for fear that the idea may fall into the competition's hands. Thus, confidentiality is a tool to help ensure truthful responses.

PARTICIPANT'S RIGHT TO PRIVACY

Active Research

Most people relish their privacy. Hence, the right to privacy is an important issue in business research. This issue involves the participant's freedom to choose whether to comply with the investigator's request. Traditionally, researchers have assumed that individuals make an informed choice. However, critics have argued that the old, the poor, the poorly educated, and other underprivileged individuals may be unaware of their right to choose. They have further argued that an interviewer may begin with some vague explanation of a survey's purpose, initially ask questions that are relatively innocuous, and then move to questions of a highly personal nature. It has been suggested that subjects be informed of their right to be left alone or to break off the interview at any time. Researchers should not follow the tendency to "hold on" to busy respondents. However, this view definitely is not universally accepted in the research community.

The privacy issue is illustrated by these questions:

- "Is a telephone call that interrupts family dinner an invasion of privacy?"
- "Is an e-mail requesting response to a 30-minute survey an invasion of privacy?"

Generally, interviewing firms practice common courtesy by trying not to interview late in the evening or at other inconvenient times. However, the computerized random phone number interview has stimulated increased debate over the privacy issue. As a practical matter, respondents may feel more relaxed about privacy issues if they know who is conducting the survey. Thus, it is generally recommended that field interviewers indicate that they are legitimate researchers and name the company they work for as soon as someone answers the phone. For in-person surveys, interviewers should wear official name tags and provide identification giving their name and the names of their companies.

Research companies should adhere to the principles of the "do-not-call" policy and should respect consumers' "Internet privacy." **Do-not-call legislation** restricts any telemarketing effort from calling consumers who either register with a no-call list in their state or who request not to be called. Legislators aimed these laws at sales-related calls. However, legislation in several states, including California, Louisiana, and Rhode Island, has extended this legislation to apply to "those that seek marketing information." Thus, the legislation effectively protects consumers' privacy from researchers as well as salespeople.[8]

do-not-call legislation

Restricts any telemarketing effort from calling consumers who either register with a no-call list or who request not to be called.

Consumers often are confused about the difference between telemarketing efforts and true marketing or business research. Part of this is because telemarketers sometimes disguise their sales efforts by opening the conversation by saying they are doing research. The resulting confusion contributes to both increased refusal rates and lower trust. In 1980, a public opinion poll found that 19 percent of Americans reported having refused to participate in a marketing survey within the past year. Today, that number approaches 50 percent. In 2001, only 40 percent of Americans either agreed or strongly agreed that marketers will protect their privacy. That number is down from 50 percent in 1995.[9]

Companies using the Internet to do research also face legislative changes. Much of this legislation is aimed at making sure consumers are properly notified about the collection of data and to whom it will be distributed. Researchers should make sure that consumers are given a clear and easy way to either consent to participation in active research or to easily opt out. Furthermore, companies should ensure that the information consumers send via the Internet is secure.[10]

Passive Research

Passive research involves different types of privacy issues. Generally, it is believed that unobtrusive observation of public behavior in places such as stores, airports, and museums is not a serious invasion of privacy. This belief is based on the fact that the consumers are indeed anonymous in that they are never identified by name nor is any attempt made to identify them. They are "faces in the crowd." As long as the behavior observed is typical of behavior commonly conducted in public, then there is no invasion of privacy. In contrast, recording behavior that is not typically conducted in public would be a violation of privacy. For example, hidden cameras recording people (without consent) taking showers at a health club, even if ultimately intended to gather information to help improve the shower experience, would be considered inappropriate.

Technology has also created new ways of collecting data passively that have privacy implications. Researchers are very interested in consumers' online behavior. For instance, the paths that consumers take while browsing the Internet can be extremely useful in understanding what kinds of information are most valued by consumers. Much of this information can be harvested and entered into a data warehouse. Researchers sometimes have legitimate reasons to use this data, which can improve consumers' ability to make wise decisions. In these cases, the researcher should gain the consumers' consent in some form before harvesting information from their Web usage patterns. Furthermore, if the information will be shared with other companies, a specific consent agreement is needed. This can come in the form of a question to which consumers respond yes or no, as in the following example:

> *From time to time, the opportunity to share your information with other companies arises and this could be very helpful to you in offering your desirable product choices. We respect your privacy, however, and if you do not wish us to share this information, we will not. Would you like us to share your information with other companies?*
>
> - *Yes, you can share the information*
> - *No, please keep my information private*

spyware
Software placed on a computer without consent or knowledge of the user.

Not all of these attempts are legitimate. Most readers have probably encountered spyware on their home computer. **Spyware** is software that is placed on your computer without consent or knowledge while using the Internet. This software then tracks your usage and sends the information back through the Internet to the source. Then, based on these usage patterns, the user will receive push technology advertising, usually in the form of pop-up ads. Sometimes, the user will receive so many pop-up ads that the computer becomes unusable. The use of spyware is illegitimate because it is done without consent and therefore violates the right to privacy and confidentiality.

Legislators are increasingly turning their attention to privacy issues in data collection. When children are involved, researchers have a special obligation to insure their safety. COPPA, the Children's Online Privacy Protection Act, was enacted into U.S. federal law on April 12, 2000. It defines a child as anyone under the age of 13. Anyone engaging in contact with a child through the Internet is obligated to obtain parental consent and notification before any personal information or identification can be provided by a child. Therefore, a researcher collecting a child's name, phone number, or e-mail address without parental consent is violating the law. While the law and ethics do not always correspond, in this case, it is probably pretty clear that a child's personal information shouldn't be collected.

DECEPTION IN RESEARCH DESIGNS AND THE RIGHT TO BE INFORMED

Experimental Designs

Experimental manipulations often involve some degree of deception. In fact, without some deception, a researcher would never know if a research subject was responding to the actual manipulation or to their perception of the experimental variable. This is why researchers sometimes use a placebo.

placebo
A false experimental effect used to create the perception that some effect has been administered.

A **placebo** is a false experimental effect used to create the perception of a true effect. Imagine two consumers, each participating in a study of the effect of a new herbal supplement on hypertension. One consumer receives a packet containing the citrus-flavored supplement, which is meant to be mixed in water and drunk with breakfast. The other also receives a packet, but in this case the packet contains a mixture that will simply color the water and provide a citrus flavor. The second consumer also believes he or she is drinking the actual supplement. In this way, the psychological effect is the same on both consumers, and any actual difference in hypertension must be due to the actual herbs contained in the supplement. Interestingly, experimental subjects often display some placebo effect in which the mere belief that some treatment has been applied causes some effect.

debriefing
Research subjects are fully informed and provided with a chance to ask any questions they may have about the experiment.

This type of deception can be considered ethical. Primarily, researchers conducting an experiment must generally (1) gain the willful cooperation of the research subject and (2) fully explain the actual experimental variables applied following the experiment's completion. Every experiment should include a **debriefing** session in which research subjects are fully informed and provided a chance to ask any questions that they may have about the experiment.

Descriptive Research

Researchers sometimes will even withhold the actual research questions from respondents in simple descriptive research. A distinction can thus be made between deception and discreet silence. For instance, sometimes providing the actual research question to respondents is simply providing them more information than they need to give a valid response. A researcher may ask questions about the perceived price of a product when his or her real interest is in how consumers form quality impressions.

PROTECTION FROM HARM

Researchers should do everything they can to make sure that research participants are not harmed by participating in research. Most types of research do not expose participants to any harm. However, the researcher should consider every possibility. For example, if the research involves tasting food or drink, the possibility exists that a research participant could have a severe allergic reaction. Similarly, researchers studying retail and workplace atmospherics often manipulate odors by injecting certain scents into the air.[11] The researcher is sometimes in a difficult situation. He or she has to somehow find out what things the subject is allergic to, without revealing the actual experimental conditions. One way this may be done is by asking the subjects to provide a list of potential allergies ostensibly as part of a separate research project.

Other times, research may involve some potential psychological harm. This may come in the form of stress or in the form of some experimental treatment that questions some strongly held conviction. For instance, a researcher studying helping behavior may lead a subject to believe that another person is being harmed in some way. In this way, the researcher can see how much a subject can withstand before doing something to help another person. In reality, the other person is usually a research confederate simply pretending to be in pain. Three key questions that can determine whether a research participant is being treated unethically as a result of experimental procedures are:

1. Has the research subject provided consent to participate in an experiment?
2. Is the research subject to substantial physical or psychological trauma?
3. Can the research subject be easily returned to his or her initial state?

The issue of consent is tricky in experiments because the researcher cannot reveal exactly what the research is about ahead of time or the validity of the experiment will be threatened. In addition, experimental research subjects are usually provided some incentive to participate. We will have more on this later in the book, but ethically speaking, the incentives should always be noncoercive. In other words, a faculty member seeking volunteers should not withhold a student's grade if he or she does not participate in an experiment. Thus, the volunteer should provide consent without fear of harm for saying no and with some idea about any potential risk involved.

If the answer to the second question is yes, then the research should not be conducted. If the answer to the second question is no and consent is obtained, then the manipulation does not present an ethical problem, and the researcher can proceed.

The third question is helpful in understanding how far one can go in applying manipulations to a research subject. If the answer to the third question is no, then the research should not be conducted. For example, researchers who seek to use hypnosis as a means of understanding preferences may be going too far in an effort to arrive at an answer. If the hypnotic state would cause the participant severe trauma, or if he or she cannot be easily returned to the prehypnotic state, then the research procedure should not be used. If, for instance, the consumer makes a large number of purchases under hypnosis, going deeply into debt, returning him or her to the original state may be difficult. If so, the application of hypnosis is probably inappropriate. If the answer to this question is yes, then the manipulation is ethical.

Many research companies and practically all universities now maintain a **human subjects review committee**. This is a committee that carefully reviews a proposed research design to try to make sure that no harm can come to any research participant. A side benefit of this committee is that it can also review the procedures to make sure no legal problems are created by implementing the particular design. This committee may go by some other name such as internal review board, but

human subjects review committee

Carefully reviews proposed research design to try to make sure that no harm can come to any research participant.

despite the name difference, the function remains to protect the company from doing harmful research.

Rights and Obligations of the Researcher

Research staff and research support firms should practice good business ethics. Researchers are often the focus of discussions of business ethics because of the necessity that they interact with the public. Several professional organizations have written and adopted codes of ethics for their researchers, including the American Marketing Association, the European Society for Opinion and Market Research, and the Marketing Research Society.[12]

In addition, the researchers have rights. In particular, once a research consulting firm is hired to conduct some research, they have the right to cooperation from the sponsoring client. In addition, the researchers have the right to be paid for the work they do as long as it is done professionally. Sometimes, the client may not like the results. But not liking the results is no basis for not paying. In addition, the client should pay the researcher in full and in a timely manner.

THE PURPOSE OF RESEARCH IS RESEARCH

Mixing Sales and Research

Consumers sometimes agree to participate in an interview that is purported to be pure research, but it eventually becomes obvious that the interview is really a sales pitch in disguise. This is unprofessional at best and fraudulent at worst. The Federal Trade Commission (FTC) has indicated that it is illegal to use any plan, scheme, or ruse that misrepresents the true status of a person seeking admission to a prospect's home, office, or other establishment. No research firm should engage in any sales attempts. Applied market researchers working for the sponsoring company should also avoid overtly mixing research and sales. However, the line is becoming less clear with increasing technology.

Research That Isn't Research

Consider the vignette that opened this chapter. Despite her best efforts, Amy is clearly feeling pressure to justify certain results obtained from the employee survey, while ignoring others. It's probably pretty easy to see what is actually going on. The manager really wants research that will justify a decision that already has been made. If the employees' responses contradict the decision, the manager will almost certainly disregard the research. This isn't really research so much as it is **pseudo-research** because it is conducted not to gather information for decisions but to bolster a point of view and satisfy other needs.

pseudo-research
Conducted not to gather information for marketing decisions but to bolster a point of view and satisfy other needs.

The most common type of pseudo-research is performed to justify a decision that has already been made or that management is already strongly committed to. A media company may wish to sell advertising space on Internet search sites. Even though they strongly believe that the ads will be worth the rates they will charge advertisers, they may not have the hard evidence to support this view. For example, an advertiser's sales force may provide feedback indicating customer resistance to moving their advertising from local radio to the Internet. The advertising company may then commission a study for which the only result they care to find is that the Internet ads will be effective. In this situation, a researcher should walk away from the project if it appears that management strongly desires the research to support a predetermined opinion only. While it is a fairly easy matter for an outside researcher to walk away from such a job, it is another matter for an in-house researcher to refuse such a job. Thus, avoiding pseudo-research is a right of the researcher but an obligation for the manager.

Occasionally, research is requested simply to pass blame for failure to another area. A product manager may deliberately request a research study with no intention of paying attention to the findings and recommendations. The manager knows that the particular project is in trouble but plays the standard game to cover up for his or her mismanagement. If the project fails, marketing research will become the scapegoat. The ruse may involve a statement something like this: "Well, research should have identified the problem earlier!"

RESEARCH SNAPSHOT

Is It Right, or Is It Wrong?

Sometimes, the application of research procedures to research participants can present significant ethical issues that cannot be easily dismissed by a single researcher alone. This is where a peer review process takes place. A human subjects research committee consists of a panel of researchers (and sometimes a legal authority) who carefully review the proposed procedures to identify any obvious or non-obvious ethical or legal issues. In fact, any research supported by U.S. federal funds must be subject to a peer review of this type. The peer review process for grants is described at this Web site: **http://grants.nih.gov/grants/peer/peer.htm.**

Most business research is innocuous and affords little opportunity for substantial physical or psychological trauma. However, companies involved in food marketing, dietary supplements or programs, and exercise physiology and pharmaceuticals, among others, do conduct consumer research with such possibilities. Academic researchers also sometimes conduct research with significant risks for participants. Consider research examining how some dietary supplement might make exercise more enjoyable, thus creating a better overall health and psychological effect. Clearly, a peer review by knowledgeable researchers is needed before proceeding with such research.

©LEE CELANO/REUTERS/LANDOV

As it isn't possible to completely eliminate risk from research, a human subjects review is a good safety net.

Deaths have been attributed to lack of or the breakdown of the human subjects review. Some of these have brought negative publicity to well-known universities including the University of Pennsylvania and Johns Hopkins University. At other times, the risk to research participants is not obvious. For example, recently several researchers were interested in surveying through personal interviews victims of Hurricane Katrina. The results of the research may help public entities better serve victims, allow companies to respond with more appropriate goods and services, and help build psychological theory about how consumers make decisions under conditions of high personal trauma and stress. However, is it ethical to survey participants standing in the rubble of their home? Is it ethical to survey participants who are in the process of searching for or burying relatives that did not survive the disaster? Clearly, a thorough review of the procedures involved in such situations is called for.

Corporate human subjects committees are also becoming common. These reviews also consider the possibility of legal problems with experimental or survey procedures. In addition, as technology blurs the line between research and sales, they also should review the ethics of "research" that may somehow blend with sales. In addition, research conducted on animals also needs a critical review.

Sources: Glenn, David, "Lost (and Found) in the Flood," *Chronicle of Higher Education* 52 (October 7, 2005), A14–A19; Putney, S. B. and S. Gruskin, "Time, Place and Consciousness: Three Dimensions of Meaning for U.S. Institutional Review Boards," *American Journal of Public Health* 92 (July 2002), 1067–1071.

© iStock

Also, technology is making the line between research and sales less clear. It is very likely that research data collected by companies we transact with online could be used to push products toward us that we may truly like. This is the point of push technology. What makes this ethical or not ethical? With consent, it is clearly ethical. What other ethical challenges may be faced as the technology to collect consumer information continues to develop?

Push Polls

Politicians have concocted a particular type of pseudo-research as a means of damaging opposing candidates' reputations. A **push poll** is telemarketing under the guise of research. Its name derives from the fact that the purpose of the poll is to push consumers into a predetermined response. For instance, thousands of potential voters can be called and asked to participate in a survey. The interviewer then may ask loaded questions that put a certain spin on a candidate.

push poll
Telemarketing under guise of research.

Service Monitoring

Occasionally, the line between research and customer service isn't completely clear. For instance, Toyota may survey all of its new car owners after the first year of ownership. While the survey appears to be research, it may also provide information that could be used to correct some issue with the customer. For example, if the research shows that a customer is dissatisfied with the way the car handles, Toyota could follow up with the specific customer. The follow-up could result in changing the tires of the car, resulting in a smoother and quieter ride, as well as a more satisfied customer. Should a pattern develop showing other customers with the same opinion, Toyota may need to switch the original equipment tires used on this particular car.

In this case, both research and customer service is involved. Since the car is under warranty, there would be no selling attempt. Researchers are often asked to design satisfaction surveys. These may identify the customer so they may be contacted by the company. Such practice is acceptable as long as the researcher allows the consumer the option of either being contacted or not being contacted. In other words, the customer should be asked whether it is okay for someone to follow up in an effort to improve their satisfaction. There are actually situations in which a customer could be made more satisfied by purchasing a less profitable product, as described by the Research Snapshot "Health Club Memberships: Good for Business, but Bad Ethically?"

Push polls, selling under the guise of research, and pseudo-research are all misrepresentations of the true purpose of research and should be avoided. It is important that researchers understand the difference between research and selling.

OBJECTIVITY

The need for objective scientific investigation to ensure accuracy is stressed throughout this book. Researchers should maintain high standards to be certain that their data are accurate. Furthermore, they must not intentionally try to prove a particular point for political purposes.

MISREPRESENTATION OF RESEARCH

It should go without saying, but research results should not be misrepresented. This means, for instance, that the statistical accuracy of a test should be stated precisely and the meaning of findings should not be understated or overstated. Both the researcher and the client share this obligation. There are many ways that research results can be reported in a less than full and honest way. For example, a researcher may present results showing a relationship between advertising spending and sales. However, the researcher may also discover that this relationship disappears when the primary competitors' prices are taken into account. In other words, the relationship between advertising spending and sales is made spurious by the competitors' prices. Thus, it would be questionable to say the least to report a finding suggesting that sales could be increased by increasing ad spending without also mentioning the spurious nature of this finding.

Honesty in Presenting Results

Misrepresentation can also occur in the way results are presented. For instance, charts can be created that make a very small difference appear very big. Likewise, they can be altered to make a meaningful difference seem small. Exhibit 5.9 illustrates this effect. Each chart presents exactly the same data. The data represent consumer responses to service quality ratings and satisfaction ratings. Both quality and satisfaction are collected on a 5-point strongly-disagree-to-strongly-agree scale. In frame A, the chart appears to show meaningful differences between men and women, particularly for the service-quality rating. However, notice that the scale range is shown as 4 to 5. In frame B, the researcher presents the same data but shows the full scale range (1 to 5). Now, the differences are reported as trivial.

All charts and figures should reflect fully the relevant range of values reported by respondents. If the scale range is from 1 to 5, then the chart should reflect a 1 to 5 range unless there is some value that is simply not used by respondents. If no or only a very few respondents had reported a 1 for their service quality or satisfaction rating, then it may be appropriate to show the range as 2 to 5. However, if there is any doubt, the researcher should show the full scale range.

Honesty in Reporting Errors

Likewise, any major error that has occurred during the course of the study should not be kept secret from management or the sponsor. Hiding errors or variations from the proper procedures tends to distort or shade the results. Similarly, every research design presents some limitations. For instance, the sample size may be smaller than ideal. The researcher should point out the key limitations in the research report and presentation. In this way, any factors that qualify the findings can be understood. The decision maker needs this information before deciding on any risky course of action.

EXHIBIT 5.9
How Results Can Be Misrepresented in a Report or Presentation

A) Researcher points to a "large" difference in quality ratings. Men report much higher quality service than do women. In contrast, women report only "slightly" less satisfaction than do men.

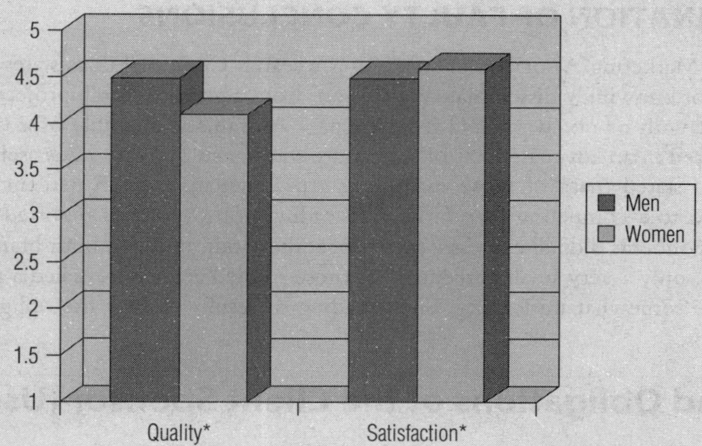

B) The researcher points to a "trivial" difference in quality perceptions between men and women. There is no difference in the satisfaction ratings of men and women.

CONFIDENTIALITY

Confidentiality comes into play in several ways. The researcher often is obligated to protect the confidentiality of both the research sponsor and the research participant. In fact, business clients value researchers' confidentiality more than any other attribute of a research firm.[13] Imagine a researcher conducting a test-market for a new high-tech Apple iPod device that allows interactive video. Just after conducting the research, the same researcher is contacted by Samsung. Samsung, which has yet to develop video capability, wants research that addresses whether or not there is a market for iPod video of any type. The researcher is now in a difficult position. Certainly, an ethical dilemma exists presenting multiple choices to the researcher, including

- Agreeing to do the research for Samsung and using some results from the Apple study to prepare a report and recommendation for Samsung
- Agreeing to sell the new concept to Samsung without doing any additional research. In other words, provide Apple's company secrets to Samsung

- Conducting an entirely new project for Samsung without revealing any of the results or ideas from the Apple study
- Turning down the chance to do the study without revealing any information about Apple to Samsung

conflict of interest

Occurs when one researcher works for two competing companies.

Which is the best choice? Obviously, both of the first two options violate the principle of maintaining client confidentiality. Thus, both are unethical. The third choice, conducting an entirely new study, may be an option. However, it may prove nearly impossible to do the entire project as if the Apple study had never been done. Even with the best of intentions, the researcher may inadvertently violate confidentiality with Apple. The last choice is the best option from a moral standpoint. It avoids any potential **conflict of interest**. In other words, actions that would best serve one client, Samsung, would be detrimental to another client, Apple. Generally, it is best to avoid working for two direct competitors.

Likewise, the researcher must also predict any confidentiality agreement with research participants. For instance, a researcher conducting a descriptive research survey may have identified each participant's e-mail address in the course of conducting the research. After seeing the results, the client may ask for the e-mail addresses as a logical prospect list. However, as long as the researcher assured each participant's confidentiality, the e-mail addresses cannot ethically be provided to the firm. Indeed, a commitment of confidentiality also helps build trust among survey respondents.[14]

DISSEMINATION OF FAULTY CONCLUSIONS

The American Marketing Association's marketing research Code of Ethics states that "a user of research shall not knowingly disseminate conclusions from a given research project or service that are inconsistent with or not warranted by the data." A dramatic example of a violation of this principle occurred in an advertisement of a cigarette smoker study. The advertisement compared two brands and stated that "of those expressing a preference, over 65 percent preferred" the advertised brand to a competing brand. The misleading portion of this reported result was that most of the respondents did *not* express a preference; they indicated that both brands tasted about the same. Thus, only a very small percentage of those studied actually revealed a preference, and the results were somewhat misleading. Such shading of results violates the obligation to report accurate findings.

Rights and Obligations of the Client Sponsor (User)

ETHICAL BEHAVIOR BETWEEN BUYER AND SELLER

The general business ethics expected between a purchasing agent and a sales representative should hold in a marketing research situation. For example, if a purchasing agent has already decided to purchase a product from a friend, it would be unethical for that person to solicit competitive bids from others because they have no chance of being accepted. Similarly, a client seeking research should only seek bids from firms that have a legitimate chance of actually doing the work. In addition, any section on the ethical obligation of a research client would be remiss not to mention that the user is obligated to pay the provider the agreed upon wage and pay within the agreed upon time.

AN OPEN RELATIONSHIP WITH RESEARCH SUPPLIERS

The client sponsor has the obligation to encourage the research supplier to objectively seek out the truth. To encourage this objectivity, a full and open statement of the decision situation, a full disclosure of constraints in time and money, and any other insights that assist the researcher should be provided. This means that the researcher will be provided adequate access to key decision makers. These decision makers should agree to openly and honestly discuss matters related to the situation. Finally, this means that the client is open to actually using the research results. Time is simply too valuable to ask a researcher to perform a project when the results will not be used.

AN OPEN RELATIONSHIP WITH INTERESTED PARTIES

Conclusions should be based on data—not conjecture. Users should not knowingly disseminate conclusions from a research project in a manner that twists them into a position that cannot be supported by the data. Twisting the results in a self-serving manner or to support some political position poses serious ethical questions. A user may also be tempted to misrepresent results while trying to close a sale. Obviously, this is also morally inappropriate.

Advocacy research—research undertaken to support a specific claim in a legal action or to represent some advocacy group—puts a client in a unique situation. Researchers often conduct advocacy research in their role as an expert witness. For instance, a researcher may be deposed to present evidence showing that a "knock-off" brand diminishes the value of a better known name brand. In conventional research, attributes such as sample size, profile of people actually interviewed, and number of questions asked are weighed against cost in traditional research. However, a court's opinion on whether research results are reliable may be based exclusively on any one specific research aspect. Thus, the slightest variation from technically correct procedures may be magnified by an attorney until a standard research result or project no longer appears adequate in a judge's eyes. How open should the client be in the courtroom?

advocacy research
Research undertaken to support a specific claim in a legal action or represent some advocacy group.

The ethics of advocacy research present a number of serious issues that can lead to an ethical dilemma:

- Lawyers' first responsibility is to represent their clients. Therefore, they might not be interested as much in the truth as they are in evidence that supports their client's position. Presenting accurate research results may harm the client.
- A researcher should be objective. However, he or she runs the risk of conducting research that does not support the desired position. In this case, the lawyer may ask the researcher if the results can somehow be interpreted in another manner.
- Should the lawyer (in this case a user of research) ask the researcher to take the stand and present an inaccurate picture of the results?

Ethically, the attorney should certainly not put the researcher on the stand and encourage an act of perjury. The attorney may hope to ask specific questions that are so limited that taken alone, they may appear to support the client. However, this is risky because the opposing attorney likely also has an expert witness that can suggest questions for cross-examination. Returning to our branding example, if the research does not support an infringement of the known brand's name, then the brand name's attorney should probably not have the researcher take the stand.

Advocacy researchers do not necessarily bias results intentionally. However, attorneys rarely submit advocacy research evidence that does not support their clients' positions.

The question of advocacy research is one of objectivity: Can the researcher seek out the truth when the sponsoring client wishes to support its position at a trial? The ethical question stems from a conflict between legal ethics and research ethics. Although the courts have set judicial standards for research methodology, perhaps only the client and individual researcher can resolve this question.

Privacy

People believe the collection and distribution of personal information without their knowledge is a serious violation of their privacy. The privacy rights of research participants create a privacy obligation on the part of the research client. Suppose a database marketing company is offering a mailing list compiled by screening millions of households to obtain brand usage information. The information would be extremely valuable to your firm, but you suspect those individuals who filled out the information forms were misled into thinking they were participating in a survey. Would it be ethical to purchase the mailing list? If respondents have been deceived about the purpose of a survey and their names subsequently are sold as part of a user mailing list, this practice is certainly unethical. The client and the research supplier have the obligation to maintain respondents' privacy.

TIPS OF THE TRADE

© iStock

- When a company faces a very emotional decision, it is usually better to have the research needed to address the related research questions done by an outside firm.
- The potential for conflict between a client/manager and a researcher can be minimized with better communication and by making sure that both parties agree on the deliverables of a research project before that project is conducted.
- Those involved in research should consider the position of others involved in the process. When considering conducting or using research in some manner, one way to help ensure fair treatment of others involved in research is to consider whether you would like to be treated in this manner or whether you would like someone to treat a close member of your family in such a manner.
- Research that creates some irreversible change in a participant can rarely be justified.
- Research with particularly vulnerable segments such as children involves special care. When doing research with children under the age of 16, parental consent is nearly always needed.

Consider another example. Sales managers know that a research survey of their business-to-business customers' buying intentions includes a means to attach a customer's name to each questionnaire. This confidential information could be of benefit to a sales representative calling on a specific customer. A client wishing to be ethical must resist the temptation to identify those accounts (that is, those respondents) that are the hottest prospects. Cyprus Market Research maintains the Sites as a service to its visitors, subject to the following terms and conditions concerning the use of the Sites. When a user uses the Site, he/she accepts the Terms of Use; if the user does not agree to the Terms of Use he/she may not use the Site. Cyprus Market Research reserves the right to modify content on its Sites and these Terms of Use periodically without prior notice.[15]

Privacy on the Internet

Privacy on the Internet is a controversial issue. A number of groups question whether Web site questionnaires, registration forms, and other means of collecting personal information will be kept confidential. Many business researchers argue that their organizations don't need to know who the user is because the individual's name is not important for their purposes. However, they do want to know certain information (such as demographic characteristics or product usage) associated with an anonymous profile. For instance, a Web advertiser could reach a targeted audience without having access to identifying information. Of course, unethical companies may violate anonymity guidelines. Research shows that consumers are sensitive to confidentiality notices before providing information via a Web site. Over 80 percent of consumers report looking for specific privacy notices before they will exchange information electronically. In addition, over half believe that companies do not do enough to ensure the privacy of personal information.[16] Thus, research users should not disclose private information without permission from the consumers who provided that information.

A Final Note on Ethics

Certainly, there are researchers who would twist results for a client or who would fabricate results for personal gain. However, these are not professionals. When one is professional, one realizes that one's actions not only have implications for oneself but also for one's field. Indeed, just a few unscrupulous researchers can give the field a bad name. Thus, researchers should maintain the highest integrity in their work to protect our industry. Research participants should also play their role, or else the data they provide will not lead to better products for all consumers. Finally, the research users must also follow good professional ethics in their treatment of researchers and research results.

Summary

1. Know when research should be conducted externally and when it should be done internally. The company that needs the research is not always the best company to actually perform the research. Sometimes it is better to use an outside supplier of some form. An outside agency is better when a fresh perspective is needed, when it would be difficult for inside researchers to be objective, and when the outside firm has some special expertize. In contrast, it is better to do the research in-house when it needs to be done very quickly, when the project requires close collaboration of many employees within the company, when the budget for the project is limited, and when secrecy is a major concern. The decision to go outside or stay inside for research depends on these particular issues.

2. Be familiar with the types of jobs, job responsibilities, and career paths available within the business research industry. The business research function may be organized in any number of ways depending on a firm's size, business, and stage of research sophistication. Business research managers must remember they are managers, not just researchers.

Research offers many career opportunities. Entry-level jobs may involve simple tasks such as data entry or performing survey research. A research analyst may be the next step on the career path. This position may involve project design, preparation of proposals, data analysis, and interpretation. Whereas there are several intermediate positions that differ depending on whether one works for a small or large firm, the director of research is the chief information officer in charge of marketing information systems and other research projects. The director plans, executes, and controls the research function for the firm.

TOTHEPOINT

He uses statistics as a drunken man uses a lamppost—for support rather than illumination.

—Andrew Lang

3. Understand the often conflicting relationship between management and researchers. Researchers and managers have different and often conflicting goals. Some of the key sources of conflict include money, time, intuition, and experience. Managers want to spend the least amount of money on research possible, have it done in the shortest period of time conceivable, and believe that intuition and experience are good substitutes for research. Researchers will exchange greater expense for more precision in the research, would like to take more time to be more certain of results, and are hesitant to rely on intuition and experience. Better communication is a key to reducing this conflict. One tool that can be useful is the implementation of cross-functional teams.

4. Define ethics and understand how it applies to business research. Business ethics is the application of morals to behavior related to the exchange environment. Generally, good ethics conforms to the notion of "right" and a lack of ethics conforms to the notion of "wrong." Those involved in research face numerous ethical dilemmas. Researchers serve clients or, put another way, the doers of research serve the users. It is often easy for a doer to compromise professional standards in an effort to please the user. After all, the user pays the bills. Given the large number of ethical dilemmas involved in research, ethics is highly applicable to business research.

5. Know and appreciate the rights and obligations of a) research respondents—particularly children, b) business researchers, and c) research clients or sponsors. Each party involved in research has certain rights and obligations. These are generally interdependent in the sense that one party's right often leads to an obligation for another party. While the rights and obligations of all three parties are important, the obligation of the researcher to protect research participants is particularly important. Experimental manipulations can sometimes expose subjects to some form of harm or involve them in a ruse. The researcher must be willing to fully inform the subjects of the true purpose of the research during a debriefing. The researcher must also avoid subjecting participants to undue physical or psychological trauma. In addition, it should be reasonably easy to return an experimental subject to his or her original, pre-experiment condition.

6. Know how to avoid a conflict of interest in performing research. A conflict of interest occurs when a researcher is faced with doing something to benefit one client at the expense of another client. One good way to avoid a conflict of interest is to avoid getting involved with multiple projects involving competing firms.

Key Terms and Concepts

advocacy research, *111*
business ethics, *99*
confidentiality, *102*
conflict of interest, *110*
cross-functional teams, *96*
custom research, *99*
debriefing, *104*
do-not-call legislation, *102*
ethical dilemma, *99*
forecast analyst, *89*
human subjects review committee, *105*
idealism, *99*
informed consent, *101*
in-house research, *87*
manager of decision support systems, *89*
moral standards, *99*
outside agency, *87*
placebo, *104*
pseudo-research, *107*
push poll, *108*
relativism, *99*
research analyst, *89*
research assistants, *89*
research generalist, *96*
research suppliers, *96*
spyware, *104*
syndicated service, *97*

Questions for Review and Critical Thinking

1. **ETHICS** What obligations does a researcher have with respect to confidentiality?
2. How should a researcher help top management better understand the functions and limitations of research?
3. **ETHICS** What is the difference between ethical relativism and ethical idealism? How might a person with an idealist ethical philosophy and a person with a relativist ethical philosophy differ with respect to including a sales pitch at the end of a research survey?
4. **ETHICS** List at least one research obligation for research participants (respondents), researchers, and research clients (sponsors)?
5. What is the difference between research and pseudo-research? Cite several examples of each.
6. **ETHICS** What is a conflict of interest in a research context? How can such conflicts of interest be avoided?
7. **ETHICS** What are business ethics? How are ethics relevant to research?
8. **ETHICS** What key questions help resolve the question of whether or not research participants serving as subjects in an experiment are treated ethically?
9. Comment on the following situation: A product manager asks the research department to forecast costs for some basic ingredients (raw materials) for a new product. The researcher asserts that this is not a research job; it is a production forecast.
10. Identify a research supplier in your area and determine what syndicated services and other functions are available to clients.
11. What are some of the basic causes of conflict between management and research?
12. **'NET** Use the Internet to find at least five research firms that perform survey research. List and describe each firm briefly.
13. What problems do research directors face in their roles as managers?
14. What actions might the business research industry take to convince the public that research is a legitimate activity and that firms that misrepresent their intentions and distort findings to achieve their aims are not true research companies?
15. What might the organizational structure of the research department be like for the following organizations?
    a. A large advertising agency
    b. A founder-owned company that operates a 20-unit restaurant chain
    c. Your university
    d. An industrial marketer with four product divisions
    e. A large consumer products company
16. **ETHICS** Comment on the ethics of the following situations:
    a. A food warehouse club advertises "savings up to 30 percent" after a survey showed a range of savings from 2 to 30 percent below average prices for selected items.
    b. A radio station broadcasts the following message during a syndicated rating service's rating period: "Please fill out your diary (which lists what media the consumer has been watching or listening to)."
    c. A sewing machine retailer advertises a market test and indicates that the regular price will be cut to one-half for three days only.
    d. A researcher tells a potential respondent that an interview will last ten minutes rather than the thirty minutes he or she actually anticipates.
    e. A respondent tells an interviewer that she wishes to cooperate with the survey, but her time is valuable and, therefore, she expects to be paid for the interview.
    f. When you visit your favorite sports team's home page on the Web, you are asked to fill out a registration questionnaire before you enter the site. The team then sells your information (team allegiance, age, address, and so on) to a company that markets sports memorabilia via catalogs and direct mail.
17. Read a recent news article from the *Wall Street Journal* or other key source that deals with a new-product introduction. Would you think it would be better for that firm to do research in-house or to use an outside agency? Explain.
18. **ETHICS** Try to participate in a survey at a survey Web site such as **http://www.mysurvey.com** or **http://www.themsrgroup.com**. Write a short essay response about your experience with particular attention paid to how the sites have protections in place to prevent children from providing personal information.
19. What are the conditions that make in-house research preferable? What are the conditions that make outside research preferable?
20. **ETHICS** Comment on the following interview:

    Interviewer: *Good afternoon, sir. My name is Mrs. Johnson, and I am with Counseling Services. We are conducting a survey concerning Memorial Park. Do you own a funeral plot? Please answer yes or no.*

    Respondent: *(pauses)*

Interviewer: *You do not own a funeral plot, do you?*
Respondent: *No.*
Interviewer: *Would you mind if I sent you a letter concerning Memorial Park? Please answer yes or no.*
Respondent: *No.*
Interviewer: *Would you please give me your address?*

Research Activities

1. Find the mission statement of Burke, Inc. (**http://www.burke.com**). What career opportunities exist at Burke? Would you consider it a small, mid-sized, or large firm?
2. **'NET—ETHICS** One purpose of the United Kingdom's Market Research Society is to set and enforce the ethical standards to be observed by research practitioners. Go to its Web site at **www.mrs.org.uk**. Click on its code of conduct and evaluate it in light of the AMA's code.

Case 5.1 Global Eating

© GETTY IMAGES/ PHOTODISC GREEN

Barton Boomer, director of marketing research for a large research firm, has a bachelor's degree in marketing from Michigan State University. He joined the firm nine years ago after a one-year stint as a research trainee at the corporate headquarters of a western packing corporation. Barton has a wife and two children. He earns $60,000 a year and owns a home in the suburbs. He is typical of a research analyst. He is asked to interview an executive with a local restaurant chain, Eats-R-Wee. Eats-R-Wee is expanding internationally. The logical two choices for expansion are either to expand first to other nations that have values similar to those in the market area of Eats-R-Wee or to expand to the nearest geographical neighbor. During the initial interviews, Mr. Big, Vice President of Operations for Eats-R-Wee, makes several points to Barton.

- "Barton, we are all set to move across the border to Ontario and begin our international expansion with our neighbor to the north, Canada. Can you provide some research that will support this position?"
- "Barton, we are in a hurry. We can't sit on our hands for weeks waiting to make this decision. We need a comprehensive research project completed by the end of the month."
- "We are interested in how our competitors will react. Have you ever done research for them?"
- "Don't worry about the fee; we'll pay you top money for a 'good' report."

Marla Madam, Barton's Director of Research, encourages Barton to get back in touch with Mr. Big and tell him that the project will get underway right away.

Question

Critique this situation with respect to Barton's job. What recommendations would you have for him? Should the company get involved with the research? Explain your answers.

Case 5.2 Big Brother Is Watching?

© GETTY IMAGES/ PHOTODISC GREEN

Technology is making our behavior more and more difficult to keep secret. Right at this very moment, there is probably some way that your location can be tracked in a way that researchers could use the information. Do you have your mobile phone with you? Is there an RFID tag in your shirt, your backpack, or some other personal item? Are you in your car, and does it have a GPS (Global Positioning Satellite) device? All of these are ways that your location and movements might be tracked.

For instance, rental cars can be tracked using GPS. Suppose a research firm contracts with an insurance firm to study the way people drive when using a rental car. A customer's every movement is then tracked. So, if the customer stops at a fast-food restaurant, the researcher knows. If the customer goes to the movie when he or she should be on a sales call, the researcher knows. If the customer is speeding, the researcher knows.

Clearly, modern technology is making confidentiality more and more difficult to maintain. While legitimate uses of this type of technology may assist in easing traffic patterns and providing better locations for service stations, shopping developments, and other retailers, at what point does the collection of such information become a concern? When would you become concerned about having your whereabouts constantly tracked?

Question

Suppose a GIS research firm is approached by the state legislature and asked to provide data about vehicle movement within the state for all cars with a satellite tracking mechanism. Based on the movement of the cars over a certain time, the police can decide when a car was speeding. They intend to use this data to send speeding tickets to those who moved too far, too fast. If you are the research firm, would you supply the data? Discuss the ethical implications of the decision.

Part 2
Beginning Stages of the Research Process

© STOCKBYTE PLATINUM/GETTY IMAGES

CHAPTER 6
PROBLEM DEFINITION: THE FOUNDATION OF BUSINESS RESEARCH

LEARNING OUTCOMES

After studying this chapter, you should be able to

1. **Explain why proper "problem definition" is essential to useful business research**
2. **Know how to recognize problems**
3. **Translate managerial decision statements into relevant research objectives**
4. **Translate research objectives into research questions and/or research hypotheses**
5. **Outline the components of a research proposal**
6. **Construct tables as part of a research proposal**

Chapter Vignette: Deland Trucking Has a "Recruitment" Problem

David Deland, who has owned his trucking business for 20 years, struggles with the spreadsheet in front of him. His recruitment specialist sits glumly across from his desk, pondering what kind of response to give to the inevitable question, "Why are our recruitment costs so high?" Next to the specialist sits James Garrett, a business research consultant who has been hired by the Deland Trucking Company to get a handle on the recruitment expenses the company has seen skyrocket over the last six months.

© COMSTOCK IMAGES/JUPITER IMAGES

"I just don't get it," David sighs in frustration. "We have seen a 45 percent increase in our trucker recruitment advertising costs, and our trucker intake and orientation expenses are killing us! James, I just don't understand what is happening here."

James and the specialist have had some initial discussions, but there is no easy way to reduce those costs without reducing the number of truckers that Deland hires. "Perhaps we can find a more efficient way of advertising our openings," suggests the recruiting specialist. "Maybe we can reduce the number of orientation sessions or travel expenses associated with the hiring process." David counters, "Well, I don't see how we are any different from our competitors. We use the same recruitment and orientation approach that they use. I have no handle on their expenses, but the fact that our expenses are skyrocketing must mean something is going on."

James stares at his copy of the spreadsheet. "There is no easy way to do this, without hurting your ability to keep drivers in your trucks," he says. "Is it that the costs for driver selection and recruitment have gone up?" "No, the costs have been the same," responds the recruiter. "It's just that we have had to do so many orientation and hiring sessions since the first of the year."

"David, it might be best if I get a look at some of your hiring statistics, as well as your driver census over the last year," comments James. Turning to the recruiter, James asks, "Can you give me some of your driver data to look through?"

"Sure," says the recruiter. "We have lots of info about our drivers, and the driver census is updated monthly. We even have some exit data we have gathered from a few drivers who have left us. I don't know exactly what the trend is with those drivers who leave, since we haven't had a chance to really analyze the data. I will send it to you through e-mail this afternoon."

James drives back to his office, reflecting on his meeting. As he passes by trucks on the way, he peeks at the drivers who are going in the same direction as he is. What do they think about their company? Would they see Deland as a great place to work? What would make Deland Trucking's recruitment costs go so high?

At his office, the e-mail with the trucker census and the hiring data has already arrived. Opening the numerous spreadsheets, James continues to wonder. Does Deland Trucking have a recruitment problem? Is the problem the company itself? What is going on?

As he examines the hiring worksheet, he compares it to the driver census figures for the last six months. "There is the problem!" he exclaims. "I think I need to put together a proposal for David on this. I'm sure he will be surprised about what his company's problem really is."

Introduction

Importance of Starting with a Good Problem Definition

The first stage of the research process introduced in the early chapters and highlighted in Chapter 4 involves translating the business decision situation into specific research objectives. While it is tempting to skip this step and go directly to designing a research project, the chances that a research project will prove useful are directly related to how well the research objectives correspond to the true business "problem." Clearly, the easiest thing for James to do in the opening vignette is to start designing a study of Deland Trucking's recruitment effectiveness. This seems to be what David and his specialist want. But is it what they really need?

This chapter looks at this important step in the research process more closely. Some useful tools are described that can help translate the business situation into relevant, actionable research objectives. Research too often takes the blame for business failures when the real failure was really management's view of its own company's situation. The Research Snapshot "Good Answers, Bad Questions?" describes some classic illustrations involving companies as big and successful as Coca-Cola, R.J. Reynolds, and Ford. While the researcher has some say in what is actually studied, remember that the client (either the firm's management team or an outside sponsor) is the research customer and the researcher is serving the client's needs through research. In other words, when the client fails to understand their situation or insists on studying an irrelevant problem, the research is very likely to fail, even if it is done perfectly.

Translating a business situation into something that can be researched is somewhat like translating one language into another. It begins by coming to a consensus on a decision statement or question. A **decision statement** is a written expression of the key question(s) that a research user wishes to answer. It is the reason that research is being considered. It must be well stated and relevant. As discussed in Chapter 4, the researcher translates this into research terms by rephrasing the decision statement into one or more research objectives. These are expressed as deliverables in the research proposal. The researcher then further expresses these in precise and scientific research terminology by creating research hypotheses from the research objectives.

decision statement
A written expression of the key question(s) that the research user wishes to answer.

In this chapter, we use the term *problem definition*. Realize that sometimes this is really opportunity seeking. For simplicity, the term **problem definition** is adapted here to refer to the process of defining and developing a decision statement and the steps involved in translating it into more precise research terminology, including a set of research objectives. If this process breaks down at any point, the research will almost certainly be useless or even harmful. It will be useless if it presents results that simply are deemed irrelevant and do not assist in decision making. It can be harmful both because of the wasted resources and because it may misdirect the company in a poor direction.

problem definition
The process of defining and developing a decision statement and the steps involved in translating it into more precise research terminology, including a set of research objectives.

Ultimately, it is difficult to say that any one step in the research process is most important. However, formally defining the problem to be attacked by developing decision statements and

EXHIBIT 6.1
Defining Problems Can Be Difficult

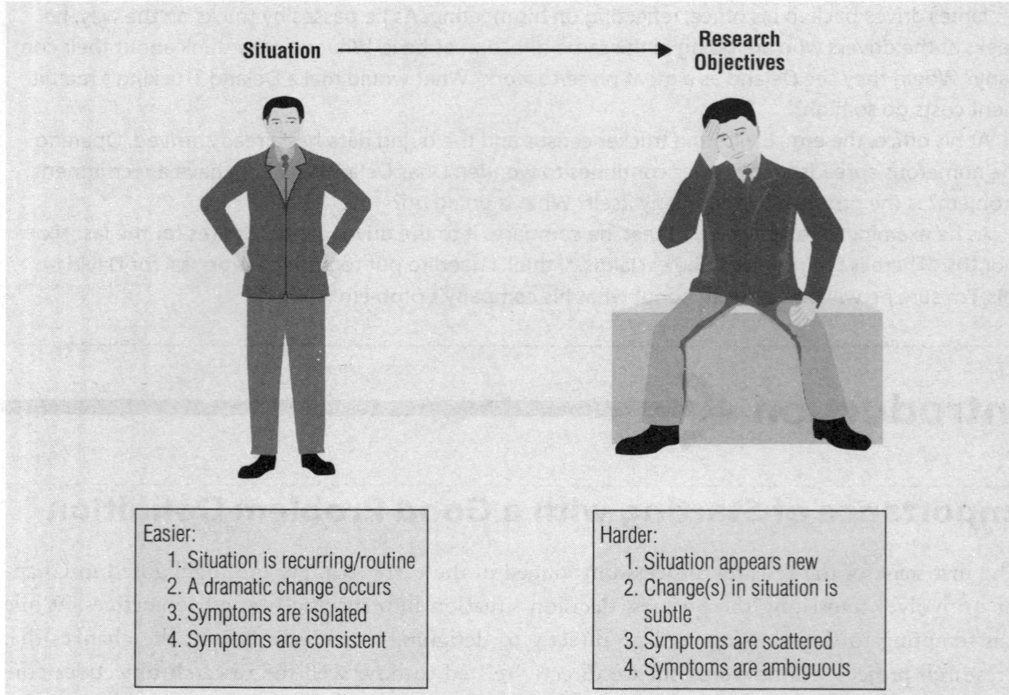

translating them into actionable research objectives must be done well or the rest of the research process is misdirected. Even a good road map is useless unless you know just where you are going. All of the roads can be correctly drawn, but they still don't get you where you want to be. Similarly, even the best research procedures will not overcome poor problem definition.

Problem Complexity

Ultimately, the quality of business research in improving business decisions is limited by the quality of the problem definition stage. This is far from the easiest stage of the research process. Indeed, it can be the most complex. Exhibit 6.1 helps to illustrate factors that influence how complex the process can be.

SITUATION FREQUENCY

Many business situations are cyclical. Cyclical business situations lead to recurring business problems. These problems can even become routine. In these cases, it is easy to define problems and identify the types of research that are needed. In some cases, problems are so routine that they can be solved without any additional research. Recurring problems can even be automated through a company's DSS.

For example, pricing problems often occur routinely. Just think about how the price of gas fluctuates when several stations are located within sight of each other. One station's prices definitely affect the sales of the other stations as well as of the station itself. Similarly, automobile companies, airline companies, and computer companies, to name just a few, face recurring pricing issues. Because these situations recur so frequently, addressing them becomes routine. Decision makers know how to communicate them to researchers and researchers know what data are needed.

Most pricing decisions in the airline industry are automated based on sophisticated demand models. The models take into account fluctuations in travel patterns based on the time of the year,

RESEARCH SNAPSHOT

Good Answers, Bad Questions?

It's amazing, but sometimes even the most successful companies make huge blunders. These blunders often are based on a misunderstanding of exactly what the brand and/or product means to consumers. Some of the famous, or infamous, examples of such blunders include RJR's introduction of Premier "Smokeless" Cigarettes, Ford's introduction of the Edsel in the 1950s, and most famous (or infamous) of all, Coca-Cola's introduction of New Coke as a replacement for regular "old" Coke.

Volumes have been written about each of these episodes. One does have to wonder, how did these great companies do such apparently dumb things? The blame is often placed at the foot of the decision makers: "Research should have revealed that product was a loser." However, researchers address the questions they are asked to address by management. Certainly, the researchers play a role in framing any decision situation into something that can be addressed by a pointed research question. The decision makers almost always start the process by asking for input from their staff, or from research consultants they have hired. Hopefully, the dialogue that results will lead to a productive research question that will provide useful results. However it isn't always the case that such research questions are self-evident.

Hindsight certainly is clearer than foresight. It seems almost unthinkable that Coke could have made its decision to replace a product with a century-long success record without considering the emotional meaning that goes along with drinking a "Coke." However, management considered Coke to be a beverage, not a brand. Thus, the focus was on the taste of Coke. Thus, researchers set about trying to decide if New Coke, which was more similar to Pepsi, tasted better than the original Coke. A great deal of very careful research suggested clearly that it did taste better. If the key question was taste, New Coke was preferred over old Coke by more consumers. In fact, there was considerable evidence that already showed a taste preference for Pepsi over old Coke. Interestingly, Coke appeared to view itself as its primary competitor. At least two very important questions were never asked or were addressed insufficiently:

Good research does not guarantee correct decisions.

1. Do consumers prefer New Coke over Pepsi?
2. When people know what they are drinking, do they still prefer New Coke to old Coke?

For a taste test to be valid, it is should be done "blindly," meaning that the taster doesn't know what he or she is drinking. Only then can one assess taste without being psychologically influenced by knowing the brand. So, Coke and Pepsi conducted a blind taste test. This is certainly a good research practice—if the question is taste. The Coke research correctly answered the taste question. The big problem is that since management didn't realize that most of the meaning of Coke is psychological, and since they were so convinced that their old product was "inferior," the dialogue between management and researchers never produced more useful questions.

In the case of Ford's Edsel, a postmortem analysis suggests that research actually indicated many of the problems that ultimately led to its demise. The name, Edsel, was never tested by research, even though hundreds of other possibilities were.

Similarly, the idea of a smokeless cigarette seemed appealing. Research addressed the question, "What is the attitude of smokers and nonsmokers toward a smokeless cigarette?" Nonsmokers loved the idea. Smokers, particularly those who lived with a nonsmoker, also indicated a favorable attitude. However, as we know, the product failed miserably. If you take the "smoke" out of "smoking," is it still the same thing? This question was never asked. Would someone who would try a smokeless cigarette replace their old brand with this new brand? Again, this wasn't asked.

Today, it is possible that some famous company could be making a very similar mistake. Consider Macy's. Macy's has acquired many regional and local department stores around the country over the past few years. Clearly, Macy's is a very recognizable name brand that brings with it considerable "equity." How important is it for Macy's to ask, "What is the best name for this department store?" If the acquisition involves taking over a local retail "institution," is a name change always a good thing? Certainly, it seems to be a good question to which research could probably provide a good answer!

Sources: Gibson, Larry, "Why the New Coke Failed," *Marketing Research* 15 (Summer 2003), 52; "Is Macy's the New Coke?" *Advertising Age* 76 (September 26, 2005), 24.

time of the day, degree of competition for that particular route, and many other factors. At one time, these decisions were based on periodic research reports. Now, the information is simply fed into a decision support system that generates a pricing schedule. It is interesting that one factor that is not very important in many of these pricing decisions is the cost involved in flying someone from point A to point B. Indeed, some passengers pay a fare much higher than the actual costs and others pay a fare much lower than the actual costs involved in getting them to their desired destination.

DRAMATIC CHANGES

When a sudden change in the business situation takes place, it can be easier to define the problem. For example, if Deland's business had increased sharply at the beginning of the year, the key factors to study could be isolated by identifying other factors that have changed in that same time period. It could be that a very large trucking contract had been obtained, or that a current customer dramatically increased their distribution needs, which Deland is benefiting from.

In contrast, when changes are very subtle and take effect over a long period of time, it can be more difficult to define the actual decision and research problems. Detecting trends that would permanently affect the recruitment challenges that Deland faces can be difficult. It may be difficult to detect the beginning of such a trend and even more difficult to know whether such a trend is relatively permanent or simply a temporary occurrence.

HOW WIDESPREAD ARE THE SYMPTOMS?

The more scattered any symptoms are, the more difficult it is to put them together into some coherent problem statement. In contrast, firms may sometimes face situations in which multiple symptoms exist, but they are all pointing to some specific business area. For instance, an automobile manufacturing company may exhibit symptoms such as increased complaints about a car's handling, increased warranty costs due to repairs, higher labor costs due to inefficiency, and lower performance ratings by consumer advocates such as *Consumer Reports*. All of these symptoms point to production as a likely problem area. This may lead to research questions that deal with supplier-manufacturer relationships, job performance, job satisfaction, supervisory support, and performance. Although having a lot of problems in one area may not sound very positive, it can be very helpful in pointing out the direction that is most in need of attention and improvement.

In contrast, when the problems are more widespread, it can be very difficult to develop useful research questions. If consumer complaints dealt with the handling and the appearance of the car, and these were accompanied by symptoms including consumer beliefs that gas mileage could be better and that dealerships did not have a pleasant environment, it may be more difficult to put these scattered symptoms together into one or a few related research questions. Later in the chapter, we'll discuss some tools for trying to analyze symptoms in an effort to find some potential common cause.

SYMPTOM AMBIGUITY

Ambiguity is almost always unpleasant. People simply are uncomfortable with the uncertainty that comes with ambiguity. Similarly, an environmental scan of a business situation may lead to many symptoms, none of which seem to point in a clear and logical direction. In this case, the problem area remains vague and the alternative directions are difficult to ascertain.

A retail store may face a situation in which sales and traffic are up, but margins are down. They may have decreased employee turnover, but lower job satisfaction. In addition, there may be several issues that arise with their suppliers, none of which is clearly positive or negative. In this case, it may be very difficult to sort through the evidence and reach a definitive decision statement or list of research objectives.

The Problem-Definition Process

Problems Mean Gaps

problem
Occurs when there is a difference between the current conditions and a more preferable set of conditions.

A **problem** occurs when there is a difference between the current conditions and a more preferable set of conditions. In other words, a gap exists between the way things are now and a way that things could be better. The gap can come about in a number of ways:[1]

RESEARCH SNAPSHOT

What Features Indian Women want in a Scooter?

Hero Honda is initiating to understand specific needs of Indian women in a vehicle that they can use. Having a tough and strong body of their vehicle was really not wanted by Indian women when they sought an independent vehicle for their use. Hero Honda, during designing Pleasure scooter found that it is difficult for Indian women to handle a scooter which is heavy. While an iron body of the vehicle would give higher strength, however, is inconvenient for a woman rider.

What could they do to address that? They conducted several researches and found that the weight of the scooter as well as the position of stand of the scooter could be designed differently so that the vehicle weights light as well as standing and de-standing becomes much easier for women. They noticed how Indian women stand a vehicle, de-stand a vehicle, move a vehicle, and start a vehicle. Additionally, they also researched what quality of material could be used to construct the body of the scooter.

On the basis of the research, Hero Honda designed the scooter which is made of plastic and changed the position and type of the stand. Instead of inclined stand, Hero Honda designed article stand in such a way that it is easier for women to stand and de-stand the vehicle.

1. Business performance is worse than expected business performance. For instance, sales, profits, and margins could be below targets set by management. This is a very typical type of problem analysis. Think of all the new products that fail to meet their targeted goals. Trend analysis would also be included in this type of problem. Management is constantly monitoring key performance variables. Previous performance usually provides a benchmark forming expectations. Sales, for example, are generally expected to increase a certain percentage each year. When sales fall below this expectation, or particularly when they fall below the previous year's sales, management usually recognizes that they have a potential problem on their hands. The Research Snapshot "Why Did Our Employees Leave?" illustrates this point.
2. Actual business performance is less than possible business performance. Realization of this gap first requires that management have some idea of what is possible. This may form a research problem in and of itself. Opportunity-seeking often falls into this type of problem-definition process. Many American and European Union companies have redefined what possible sales levels are based upon the expansion of free markets around the world. China's Civil Aviation Administration has relaxed requirements opening the Chinese air travel market to private airlines.[2] Suddenly, the possible market size for air travel has increased significantly, creating opportunities for growth.
3. Expected business performance is greater than possible business performance. Sometimes, management has unrealistic views of possible performance levels—either too high or too low. One key problem with new product introductions involves identifying realistic possibilities for sales. While you may have heard the old adage that 90 percent of all new products fail, how many of the failures had a realistic sales ceiling? In other words, did the company know the possible size of the market? In this case, the problem is not with the product but with the plan. Some product "failures" may actually have been successful if management had a more accurate idea of the total market potential. Management can close this gap through decision making. Researchers help managers make decisions by providing relevant input.

The Problem-Definition Process Steps

The problem-definition process involves several interrelated steps, as shown in Exhibit 6.2. Sometimes, the boundaries between each step aren't exactly clear. But generally, completing one step

EXHIBIT 6.2
The Problem-Definition Process

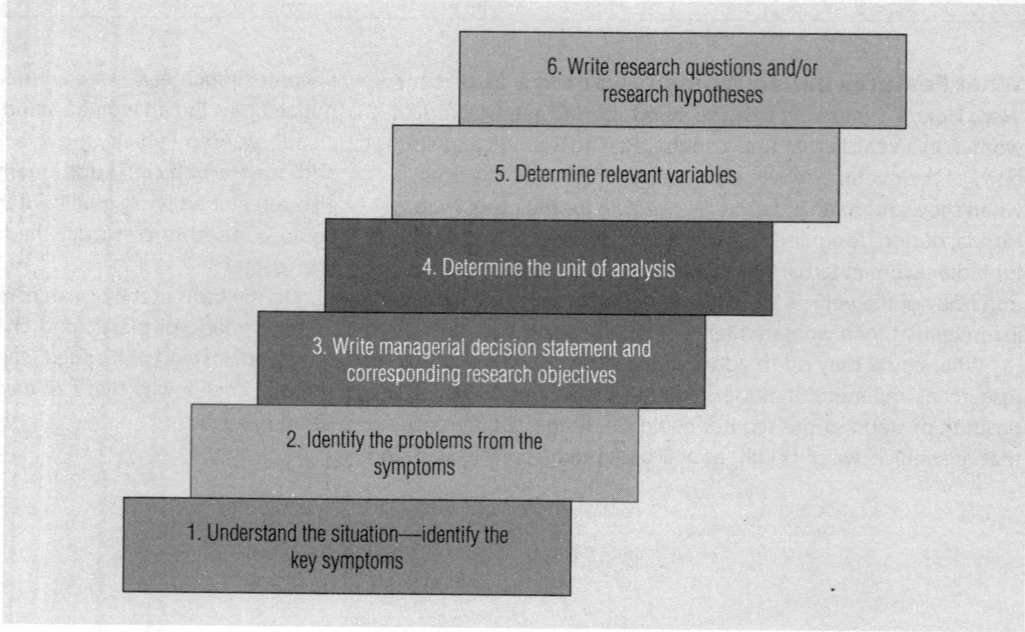

leads to the other and by the time the problem is defined, each of these steps has been addressed in some way. The steps are

1. Understand the business situation—identify key symptoms
2. Identify key problem(s) from symptoms
3. Write managerial decision statement and corresponding research objectives
4. Determine the unit of analysis
5. Determine the relevant variables
6. Write research questions and/or research hypotheses

A separate section deals with each stage below.

Understand the Business Decision

situation analysis
The gathering of background information to familiarize researchers and managers with the decision-making environment.

A **situation analysis** involves the gathering of background information to familiarize researchers and managers with the decision-making environment. The situation analysis can be written up as a way of documenting the problem-definition process. Gaining an awareness of marketplace conditions and an appreciation of the situation often requires exploratory research. Researchers sometimes apply qualitative research with the objective of better problem definition. The situation analysis begins with an interview between the researcher and management.

INTERVIEW PROCESS

The researcher must enter a dialogue with the key decision makers in an effort to fully understand the situation that has motivated a research effort. This process is critical and the researcher should be granted access to all individuals who have specific knowledge of or insight into this situation. Researchers working with managers who want the information "yesterday" often get little assistance when they ask, "What are your objectives for this study?" Nevertheless, even decision makers who have only a gut feeling that the research might be a good idea benefit greatly if they work with the researcher to articulate precise research objectives.[3] Even when there is good cooperation, seldom can key decision makers express the situation in research terms:

Despite a popular misconception to the contrary, objectives are seldom clearly articulated and given to the researcher. The decision maker seldom formulates his objectives accurately. He is likely to state his objectives in the form of platitudes which have no operational significance. Consequently, objectives usually have to be extracted by the researcher. In so doing, the researcher may well be performing his most useful service to the decision maker.[4]

Researchers may often be tempted to accept the first plausible problem statement offered by management. For instance, in the opening vignette, it is clear that David believes there is a recruitment problem. However, it is very important that the researcher not blindly accept a convenient problem definition for expediency's sake. In fact, research demonstrates that people who are better problem solvers generally reject problem definitions as given to them. Rather, they take information provided by others and re-associate it with other information in a creative way. This allows them to develop more innovative and more effective decision statements.[5]

There are many ways to discover problems and spot opportunities. There is certainly much art involved in translating scattered pieces of evidence about some business situation into relevant problem statements and then relevant research objectives. While there are other sources that address creative thinking in detail, some helpful hints that can be useful in the interview process include

1. Develop many alternative problem statements. These can emerge from the interview material or from simply rephrasing decision statements and problem statements.
2. Think about potential solutions to the problem.[6] Ultimately, for the research to be actionable, some plausible solution must exist. After pairing decision statements with research objectives, think about the solutions that might result. This can help make sure any research that results is useful.
3. Make lists. Use free-association techniques to generate lists of ideas. The more ideas, the better. Use interrogative techniques to generate lists of potential questions that can be used in the interview process. **Interrogative techniques** simply involve asking multiple what, where, who, when, why, and how questions. They can also be used to provoke introspection, which can assist with problem definition.
4. Be open-minded. It is very important to consider all ideas as plausible in the beginning stages of problem solving. One sure way to stifle progress is to think only like those intimately involved in the business situation or only like those in other industries. Analogies can be useful in thinking more creatively.

interrogative techniques
Asking multiple what, where, who, when, why, and how questions.

IDENTIFYING SYMPTOMS

Interviews with key decision makers also can be one of the best ways to identify key problem symptoms. Recall that all problems have symptoms just as human disease is diagnosed through symptoms. Once symptoms are identified, then the researcher must probe to identify possible causes of these changes. **Probing** is an interview technique that tries to draw deeper and more elaborate explanations from the discussion. This discussion may involve potential problem causes. This probing process will likely be very helpful in identifying key variables that are prime candidates for study.

probing
An interview technique that tries to draw deeper and more elaborate explanations from the discussion.

One of the most important questions the researcher can ask during these interviews is, "what has changed?" Then, the researcher should probe to identify potential causes of the change. At the risk of seeming repetitive, it is important that the researcher repeat this process to make sure that some important change has not been left out.

In addition, the researcher should look for changes in company documents, including financial statements and operating reports. Changes may also be identified by tracking down news about competitors and customers. Exhibit 6.3 provides a summary of this approach.

EXHIBIT 6.3
What Has Changed?

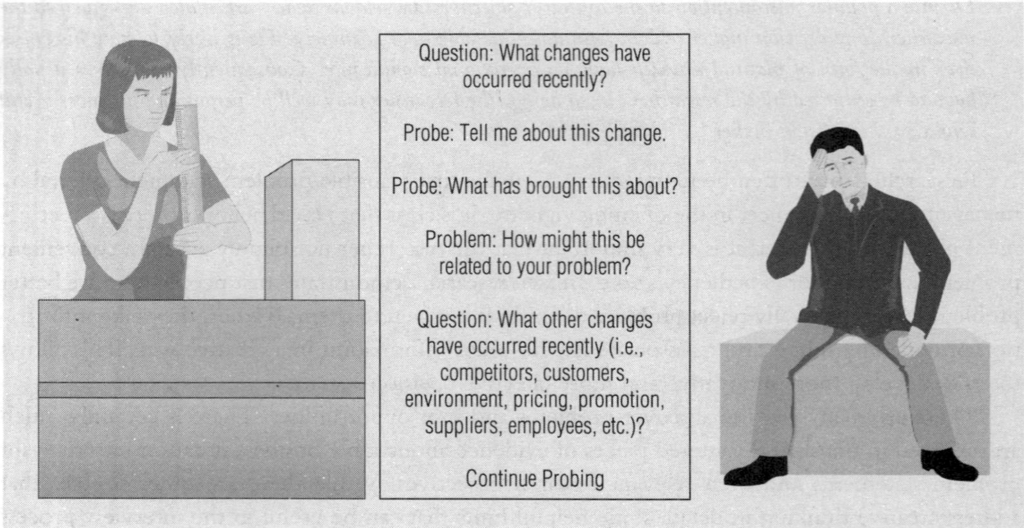

Think back to the opening vignette. Often, multiple interviews are necessary to identify all the key symptoms and gain a better understanding of the actual business situation. On a follow-up interview, the dialogue between James and David may proceed as follows:

James: *David, it is clear that your recruitment costs have been increasing since the start of the year. What other changes have occurred inside of your business within the past year?*

David: *Just a few things. We have had pressures on our bottom line, so we held back on raising the cents per mile that we give our drivers. Also, we have had to extend our long-haul trucking needs, so our drivers are on the road for a much longer period of time for each trip.*

James (probing): *Tell me, what led to this decision to extend the driver's time on the road?*

David: *It just worked out that way. Our contract just changed to allow us to do this, and our operations manager felt we could make more money per load this way.*

James: *Have you noticed changes in your customers?*

David: *We do see that they are a little irritated due to some of the problems of getting their freight delivered successfully.*

James: *Has there been a change in personnel?*

David: *Yes, we've had more than the usual share of turnover. I've turned over most personnel decisions to our new human resources manager. We've had trouble maintaining a person in that role.*

In the *change interview,* the researcher is trying to identify possible changes in the customers, the competitors, the internal conditions of the company, and the external environment. The interplay between things that have changed and things that have stayed the same can often lead to key research factors. Before preparing the proposal, James and David agree that the real decision faced is not as narrow as a recruiting problem. In this case, James is beginning to suspect that one key factor is that the increase in recruitment costs is a reflection of increased driver turnover. If driver retention could be increased, the need for larger recruitment expenses would stabilize, or even go down.

Almost any situation can be framed from a number of different perspectives. A pricing problem may be rephrased as a brand image problem. People expect high quality products to have higher prices. A quality problem may be rephrased as a packaging problem. For example, a potato chip company thought that a quality differential between their potatoes and their competitor's was the cause for the symptom showing sliding market share. However, one of the research questions that eventually resulted dealt with consumer preferences for packaging. In the end, research suggested that consumers prefer a foil package because it helps the chips stay fresher longer. Thus, the key gap turned out to be a package gap![7]

RESEARCH SNAPSHOT

Opportunity Is a "Fleeting" Thing

Have non-European automotive companies missed out on European opportunities? Europe represents a nearly $17 million annual market for new automobiles. Traditionally, the thinking is that European's prefer smaller or "light-cars." Thus, European car companies like BMW and Audi were slow to enter the SUV market. Mercedes entered the SUV market rather early on, but the emphasis was on the American market. American and Japanese companies offered little more than a token effort at selling SUVs in Europe. Thus, the SUV wars were fought in America where total volume reached 4 million shortly after 2000. Europeans were left with fewer choices if an SUV struck their fancy.

As a result, pre-2000 SUV sales in Europe were almost nonexistent. However, SUV sales in Europe have increased dramatically since then. By 2004, European SUV sales reached 16.5 million units, about one in twenty of all new autos sold in Europe. Today, Nissan, Toyota, Land Rover, and Suzuki are major players in the European SUV market. However, sales expectations for new entries from Opel, Renault, Volkswagen, Mercedes, and Audi are sluggish through 2008 with so many SUVs to choose from coupled with high fuel prices. In hindsight, could it be that several prominent automobile companies missed opportunities in Europe because they failed to know how big the market truly was?

© BIENCHEN-S/SHUTTERSTOCK

© iStock

Looking at this from the opposite direction, the tiny (by U.S. standards) two-seater SMART (**http://www.smartusa.com**) car has being introduced in the United States. Approximately 30,000 U.S. consumers have put down $99 to reserve the right to buy a SMART car since its introduction. SMART is poised to take advantage of an opportunity created by high gas prices while GM scrambles to turn production away from large SUVs like HUMMER toward new entries like the Chevrolet Volt. The relative success of these new entries against European minis like the SMART may also depend on the exchange rate which presently makes European entries expensive in the United States. Word is there may even be a SMART SUV—a miniature version of an American icon. What is the SMART future?

Sources: "The Business Week," *Business Week* 4008 (June 16, 2008), 6–10; Crain, K.C., "Analyst Sees Sales Decline for Light Vehicles in 2005," *Automotive News* 79 (January 24, 2005), 111; Meiners, Jena, "SUV Sales in Europe Will Peak in 2008," *Automotive News Europe* 9 (June 28, 2004); Marquand, R., "Euorpe's Little Smart Car to Hit U.S. Streets," *Christian Science Monitor* (2008), http://www.csmonitor.com/2008/0109/p01s01-woeu.html, accessed July 31, 2008.

Researchers should make sure that they have uncovered all possible relevant symptoms and considered their potential causes. Perhaps more interview time with key decision makers asking why people choose Coke would have helped identify some of the less tangible aspects of the Coke-Pepsi-New Coke battle. Similarly, as seen in the Research Snapshot "Opportunity Is a Fleeting Thing," the makers of automobiles in the United States should examine more carefully the possible ways that consumers make choices about the vehicles they buy. It can help avoid mistakes later.

Identifying the Relevant Issues from the Symptoms

TOTHEPOINT

The real voyage of discovery consists not in seeking new landscapes, but in having new eyes.

Anticipating the many influences and dimensions of a problem is impossible for any researcher or executive. The preceding interview is extremely useful in translating the decision situation into a working problem definition by focusing on symptoms. The probing process discussed on pages 115–116 begins this process. However, the researcher needs to be doubly certain that the research attacks real problems and not superficial symptoms.

For instance, when a firm has a problem with advertising effectiveness, the possible causes of this problem may be low brand awareness, the wrong brand image, use of the wrong media, or perhaps too small a budget. Certain occurrences that appear to be the problem may be only symptoms of a deeper problem. Exhibit 6.4 illustrates how symptoms can be translated into a problem and then a decision statement.

Writing Managerial Decision Statements and Corresponding Research Objectives

The situation analysis ends once researchers have a clear idea of the managerial objectives from the research effort. Decision statements capture these objectives in a way that invites multiple solutions. Multiple solutions are encouraged by using plural nouns to describe solutions. In other words, a decision statement that says in what "ways" a problem can be solved is better than one that says in what "way" a problem can be solved. Ultimately, research may provide evidence showing results of several ways a problem can be attacked.

Decision statements must be translated into research objectives. At this point, the researcher is starting to visualize what will need to be measured and what type of study will be needed. Exhibit 6.5 extends the examples from Exhibit 6.4, showing research objectives that correspond to each decision statement. Note that each research objective states a corresponding potential result(s) of the research project. Thus, in some ways, it is stating the information that is needed to help make the decision. Once the decision statement is written, the research essentially answers the question, "What information is needed to address this situation?"

Referring back to the opening vignette, the analysis of the symptoms has led to the conclusion that there is an employee retention problem. Perhaps drivers are dissatisfied with being away from their families for so long and this is leading to higher levels of driver turnover. Or, perhaps it is the cents per mile that is leading to driver frustration and a desire to go to a higher-paying competitor. David and James eventually agree on the following decision statement:

In what ways can Deland Trucking build driver loyalty so that retention increases and subsequent recruitment costs decrease?

What information or data will be needed to help answer this question? Obviously, we'll need to study the driver census and the number of hires needed to fill open positions. James needs to find out what might cause employee dissatisfaction and cause turnover to increase. Thinking back to the interview, James knows that there have been several changes in the company itself, many

EXHIBIT 6.4 **Symptoms Can Be Confusing**

	Firm's Situation	Symptoms	Probable Problem	Decision Statement
Research Action	Conduct Situation Analysis including interviews with key decision makers		Consider results of probing and apply creative processes	Express in actionable terms and make sure decision makers are in agreement
Situation 1	22-year-old neighborhood swimming association seeks research help	• Declining Membership for 6 years • Increased attendance at new water park • Less frequent usage among members	Swim facility is outdated and does not appeal to younger families. Younger families and children have a negative image of pool. Their "old market" is aging.	What things can be done to energize new markets and create a more favorable attitude toward the association?
Situation 2	Manufacturer of palm-sized computer with wireless Internet access believes B2B sales are too low	• Distributors complain prices are too high • Business users still use larger computers	• Business users do not see advantages of smaller units • Advantages are not outweighed by costs • Transition costs may be a drawback for B2B customers more than for B2C customers	What things can be done to improve competitive positioning of the new product in B2B markets?
Situation 3	A new microbrewery is trying to establish itself	• Consumers seem to prefer national brands over the local microbrew products • Many customers order national brands within the microbrew itself • Some customers hesitant to try new microbrew flavors	Is there a negative flavor gap? Do consumers appreciate the micro-brew approach and the full beer tasting (as opposed to drinking) experience?	How can we encourage more consumers to come to the microbrew and try our products? Should we redesign the brewery to be more inviting?

EXHIBIT 6.5 **Translating Decision Statements**

	Decision Statement	Research Objectives	Research Questions	Research Hypotheses
Research Action	Express in actionable terms and make sure decision makers are in agreement	Expresses potential research results that should aid decision-making	Ask a question that corresponds to each research objective	Specific statement explaining relationships, usually involving two variables, and including the direction of the relationship
Situation 1	What things can be done to energize new markets and create a more favorable attitude toward the association?	Determine reasons why families may choose to join or not join a "swim club."	How do the type of facilities and pricing relate to family attitudes toward a swim facility?	Child-friendly *pool designs* are positively related to *attitudes toward the facility.* Flexible *pricing policies* are positively related to *attitudes toward the facility*.
Situation 2	What product features can be improved and emphasized to improve competitive positioning of the new product in B2B markets?	List actions that may overcome the objections (switching costs) of B2B customers toward adoption of the new product.	What are the factors that most lead to perceptions of high switching costs?	*Perceived difficulty* in learning how to use the new device is related to *switching costs.* *Price* is positively related to *switching costs.* *Knowledge* of new product is positively related to *switching costs.*
Situation 3	How can we encourage more consumers to come to the microbrew and try our products? Should we redesign the brewery to be more inviting?	Describe how situational factors influence beer consumption and consumer attitudes toward beer products. List factors that will improve attitudes toward the microbrewery.	Do situational factors (such as time of day, food pairings, or environmental factors) relate to taste perceptions of beer?	Microbrew beer is *preferred* when consumed *with food.* An exciting *atmosphere* will improve consumer *attitudes toward the microbrew.*

related to saving costs. Saving costs sounds like a good idea; however, if it harms driver loyalty even slightly, it probably isn't worthwhile. Thus, the corresponding research objectives are stated as follows:

- Determine what key variables relate to driver loyalty within the company, meaning (1) how does the lower level of pay impact driver retention and (2) what does the increase in long-haul trucking do to Deland Trucking's ability to increase retention?
- Assess the impact of different intervention strategies on driver satisfaction

These research objectives are the deliverables of the research project. A research study will be conducted that (1) shows how much each of several key variables relates to loyalty and retention and (2) provides a description of likelihood of different intervention strategies on driver satisfaction.

The researcher should reach a consensus agreement with the decision maker regarding the overall decision statement(s) and research objectives. If the decision maker agrees that the statement captures the situation well and understands how the research objectives, if accomplished, will help address the situation, then the researcher can proceed. The researcher should make every effort to ensure that the decision maker understands what a research project can deliver. If there is no agreement on the decision statement or research objectives, more dialogue between decision makers and researchers is needed.

Determine the Unit of Analysis

unit of analysis
A study indicates what or who should provide the data and at what level of aggregation.

The **unit of analysis** for a study indicates what or who should provide the data and at what level of aggregation. Researchers specify whether an investigation will collect data about individuals (such as customers, employees, and owners), households (families, extended families, and so forth), organizations (businesses and business units), departments (sales, finance, and so forth), geographical areas, or objects (products, advertisements, and so forth). In studies of home buying, for example, the husband/wife dyad typically is the unit of analysis rather than the individual because many purchase decisions are made jointly by husband and wife.

Researchers who think carefully and creatively about situations often discover that a problem can be investigated at more than one level of analysis. For example, a lack of worker productivity could be due to problems that face individual employees or it could reflect problems that are present in entire business units. Determining the unit of analysis should not be overlooked during the problem-definition stage of the research.

Determine Relevant Variables

WHAT IS A VARIABLE?

variable
Anything that varies or changes from one instance to another; can exhibit differences in value, usually in magnitude or strength, or in direction.

constant
Something that does not change; is not useful in addressing research questions.

What things should be studied to address a decision statement? Researchers answer this question by identifying key variables. A **variable** is anything that varies or changes from one instance to another. Variables can exhibit differences in value, usually in magnitude or strength, or in direction. In research, a variable is either observed or manipulated, in which case it is an experimental variable.

The converse of a variable is a **constant**. A constant is something that does not change. Constants are not useful in addressing research questions. Since constants don't change, management isn't very interested in hearing the key to the problem is something that won't or can't be changed. In causal research, it can be important to make sure that some potential variable is actually held constant while studying the cause and effect between two other variables. In this way, a spurious relationship can be ruled out. At this point however, the notion of a constant is more important in helping to understand how it differs from a variable.

WHAT IS A RANDOM VARIABLE?

random variable
A variable that assumes value from a measurement process which is a random process.

Random variable is a variable that assumes value from a measurement process which is a random process. In other words, occurrence of different values of a random variable is probabilistic within a particular range, and not deterministic. For instance, age of respondent is a random variable which might take value between 18 years and 80 years for a randomly selected respondent.

TYPES OF VARIABLES

There are several key terms that help describe types of variables. The *variance* in *variables* is captured either with numerical differences or by an identified category membership. In addition, different terms describe whether a variable is a potential cause or an effect.

continuous variable
A variable that can take on a range of values that correspond to some quantitative amount.

categorical variable
A variable that indicates membership in some group.

classificatory variable
Another term for a categorical variable because it classifies units into categories.

A **continuous variable** is one that can take on a range of values that correspond to some quantitative amount. Consumer attitude toward different airlines is a variable that would generally be captured by numbers, with higher numbers indicating a more positive attitude than lower numbers. Each attribute of airlines' services, such as safety, seat comfort, and baggage handling can be numerically scored in this way. Sales volume, profits, and margin are common business metrics that represent continuous variables.

A **categorical variable** is one that indicates membership in some group. The term **classificatory variable** is sometimes also used and is generally interchangeable with *categorical variable*. Categorical variables sometimes represent quantities that take on only a small number of values (one, two, or three). However, categorical variables more often simply identify membership.

For example, people can be categorized as either male or female. A variable representing biological sex describes this important difference. The variable values can be an "M" for membership in the male category and an "F" for membership in the female category. Alternatively, the researcher could assign a "0" for men and a "1" for women. In either case, the same information is represented.

A common categorical variable in consumer research is adoption, meaning the consumer either did or did not purchase a new product. Thus, the two groups, purchase or not purchase, comprise the variable. Similarly, turnover, or whether an employee has quit or not, is a common organizational variable.

In descriptive and causal research, the terms *dependent variable* and *independent variable* describe different variable types. This distinction becomes very important in understanding how business processes can be modeled by a researcher. The distinction must be clear before one can correctly apply certain statistical procedures like multiple regression analysis. In some cases, however, such as when only one variable is involved in a hypothesis, the researcher need not make this distinction.

© AP PHOTO/ALEXANDRA BOULAT/VII

Several variables describe child consumers. Their biological sex is a categorical variable; how much they weigh, or how often they go out to the mall are continuous variables.

A **dependent variable** is a process outcome or a variable that is predicted and/or explained by other variables. An **independent variable** is a variable that is expected to influence the dependent variable in some way. Such variables are independent in the sense that they are determined outside of the process being studied. That is another way of saying that dependent variables do not change independent variables.

For example, average customer loyalty may be a dependent variable that is influenced or predicted by an independent variable such as perceptions of restaurant food quality, service quality, and customer satisfaction. Thus, a process is described by which several variables together help create and explain how much customer loyalty exists. In other words, if we know how a customer rates the food quality, service quality, and satisfaction with a restaurant, then we can predict that customer's loyalty toward that restaurant. Note that this does not mean that we can predict food quality or service quality with customer loyalty.

dependent variable

A process outcome or a variable that is predicted and/or explained by other variables.

independent variable

A variable that is expected to influence the dependent variable in some way.

Dependent variables are conventionally represented by the letter Y. Independent variables are conventionally represented by the letter X. If research involves two dependent variables and two or more independent variables, subscripts may also be used to indicate Y_1, Y_2 and X_1, X_2, and so on.

Ultimately, theory is critical in building processes that include both independent and dependent variables (see Chapter 4). Managers and researchers must be careful to identify relevant and actionable variables. *Relevant* means that a change in the variable matters and *actionable* means that a variable can be controlled by managerial action. Superfluous variables are those that are neither relevant nor actionable and should not be included in a study. Theory should help distinguish relevant from superfluous variables.

The process of identifying the relevant variables overlaps with the process of determining the research objectives. Typically, each research objective will mention a variable or variables to be measured or analyzed. As the translation process proceeds through research objectives, research questions, and research hypotheses, it is usually possible to emphasize the variables that should be included in a study (as in Exhibits 6.5 and 6.6).

Exhibit 6.6 includes some common business research hypotheses and a description of the key variables involved in each. In the first case, a regional grocery chain is considering offering a delivery service that would allow consumers to purchase groceries via the store Web site. They have conducted a trial of this in one market and have conducted a survey in that area. In the second case, a Korean automobile company is considering offering one of its models for sale in Europe. The company has also conducted a survey in two key European auto markets.

Write Research Objectives and Questions

Both managers and researchers expect problem-definition efforts to result in statements of research questions and research objectives. At the end of the problem-definition stage, the researcher

EXHIBIT 6.6 **Example Business Decision Situations, Corresponding Research Hypotheses, and Variable Descriptions**

Managerial Decision	Research Question(s)	Research Hypotheses	Categorical Variable(s)	Continuous Variable(s)
Retail grocer considering Web-based delivery service	Is there sufficient demand? How much should delivery personnel be paid? Will delivery service (new retail form) cannibalize current business?	*Projected sales volume* will exceed $5 M annually. Delivery personnel can be paid less than cashiers and achieve the same job satisfaction. Web customers express lower *intentions to visit store* than other customers.	Type of employee (delivery, cashier, etc.) Retail form (independent variable): classifies respondents based on whether they shopped (1) in store or (2) via the Web (delivery).	Sales volume: dollar amount based on a test trial in one geographic market (i.e., Phoenix/Scottsdale). Hourly wages and satisfaction with pay. Intentions to visit store (dependent variable): the percentage likelihood that a survey respondent would visit the store within the next 7 days.
What market segments should be served?	Does nationality matter? Will French and German consumers express interest in our product? Does the attitude toward Korean companies influence purchase intentions?	*French* consumers have more *interest in purchasing our product* than *German* consumers. *Attitude toward Korean companies* is related positively to *product purchase interest.*	Nationality (independent variable): represents which country a survey respondent lives in: (1) France (2) Germany.	Attitude toward Korean companies (independent variable): ratings scale that describes how favorably survey respondents view Korean companies (quality, reputation, value—higher scores mean better attitude). Product purchase interest: ratings scale that shows how interested a consumer is in buying the Korean product (higher scores = more interest).

should prepare a written statement that clarifies any ambiguity about what the research hopes to accomplish. This completes the translation process.

research questions

Express the research objectives in terms of questions that can be addressed by research.

Research questions express the research objectives in terms of questions that can be addressed by research. For example, one of the key research questions involved in the opening vignette is "Are wages and long-haul distance related to driver loyalty and retention?" Hypotheses are more specific than research questions. One key distinction between research questions and hypotheses is that hypotheses can generally specify the direction of a relationship. In other words, when an independent variable goes up, we have sufficient knowledge to predict that the dependent variable should also go up (or down as the case may be). One key research hypothesis for Deland Trucking is:

Higher cents per mile are related positively to *driver loyalty*.

TOTHEPOINT

I don't know the key to success, but the key to failure is trying to please everybody.

—Bill Cosby

At times, a researcher may suspect that two variables are related but have insufficient theoretical rationale to support the relationship as positive or negative. In this case, hypotheses cannot be offered. At times in research, particularly in exploratory research, a proposal can only offer research questions. Research hypotheses are much more specific and therefore require considerably more theoretical support. In addition, research questions are interrogative, whereas research hypotheses are declarative.

Clarity in Research Questions and Hypotheses

Research questions make it easier to understand what is perplexing managers and to indicate what issues have to be resolved. A research question is the researcher's translation of the marketing problem into a specific inquiry.

RESEARCH SNAPSHOT

Pricing Turbulence

A heavy equipment distributor sought out research because it believed there was an opportunity to increase revenues by raising prices. After several weeks of discussion, interviews, and proposal reviews, they settled on a decision question that asked, "In what ways could revenues be increased by altering pricing policies across customers?" A research project was conducted that offered the following deliverables: (1) demonstrate how much customer characteristics and environmental characteristics influence price elasticity and (2) identify market segments based on price elasticity. This led to several hypotheses including the following:

H1: The desired delivery time for equipment is negatively related to price sensitivity.
H2: The degree of market turbulence is negatively related to price sensitivity.

In addition, a research question specifically addressing market segments was asked:

RQ1: Are there market segments that can be identified based on customers' desired benefits or environmental characteristics?

© AP PHOTO

© iStock

In other words, the more critical a piece of heavy equipment is to a company, the less concerned they are with the price. Similarly, customers are less concerned with price in markets that are more turbulent, meaning there are ever-changing environmental, competitive, and political pressures.

A study of heavy equipment purchasers around the world supported both hypotheses. For business segments where delivery time is of critical importance, higher prices can be charged without the fear of losing business. Similarly, in turbulent international markets, customers have other important concerns that make them less sensitive to equipment price and more sensitive to reliability and service. In the end, the heavy equipment company was able to build customer characteristics data into a DSS system that automated prices.

Interestingly, management did not express any concerns about either market segments or market turbulence in the initial interviews. Thus, this research succeeded because good research objectives, questions, and hypotheses were developed before any study was implemented.

Sources: Smith, M.F., I. Sinha, R. Lancianai, and H. Forman, "Role of Market Turbulence in Shaping Pricing," *Industrial Marketing Management* 28 (November 1999), 637–649; Peters, G., "Combating Too Much Information," *Industrial Distribution* 94 (December 2005), 22.

A research question can be too vague and general, such as "Is advertising copy 1 better than advertising copy 2?" Advertising effectiveness can be variously measured by sales, recall of sales message, brand awareness, intention to buy, recognition, or knowledge, to name a few possibilities. Asking a more specific research question (such as, "Which advertisement has a higher day-after recall score?") helps the researcher design a study that will produce useful results, as seen in the Research Snapshot "Pricing Turbulence." Research question answers should provide input that can be used as a standard for selecting from among alternative solutions. Problem definition seeks to state research questions clearly and to develop well-formulated, specific hypotheses.

A sales manager may hypothesize that salespeople who show the highest job satisfaction will be the most productive. An advertising manager may believe that if consumers' attitudes toward a product are changed in a positive direction, consumption of the product also will increase. Hypotheses are statements that can be empirically tested.

A formal hypothesis has considerable practical value in planning and designing research. It forces researchers to be clear about what they expect to find through the study, and it raises crucial questions about data required. When evaluating a hypothesis, researchers should ensure that the information collected will be useful in decision making. Notice how the following hypotheses express expected relationships between variables:

- There is a positive relationship between *buying on the Internet* and the presence of *younger children* in the home.
- *Sales* are lower for salespeople in regions that receive less *advertising support*.
- Consumers will experience *cognitive dissonance* after the decision to *adopt* a TiVo personal video recorder.
- *Opinion leaders* are more affected by mass media communication *sources* than are non-leaders.
- Among non-exporters, the degree of perceived importance of overcoming barriers to exporting is related positively to general interest in exporting (export intentions).[8]

managerial action standard

A specific performance criterion upon which a decision can be based.

Management is often faced with a "go/no go" decision. In such cases, a research question or hypothesis may be expressed in terms of a meaningful barrier that represents the turning point in such a decision. In this case, the research involves a **managerial action standard** that specifies a specific performance criterion upon which a decision can be based. If the criterion to be measured (for example, sales or attitude changes) turns out to be higher than some predetermined level, management will do *A*; if it is lower, management will do *B*.[9] In Exhibit 6.6, the specified sales volume of $5 million represents a managerial action standard for the retail grocery chain.

Research objectives also should be limited to a manageable number. Fewer study objectives make it easier to ensure that each will be addressed fully. It becomes easy to lose focus with too many research objectives.

Exhibit 6.7 summarizes how a decision statement (corresponding to a business research problem) leads to research objectives that become a basis for the research design. Once the research has been conducted, the results may show an unanticipated aspect of the problem and suggest a need for additional research to satisfy the main objective. Accomplished researchers who have had the experience of uncovering additional aspects of a particular research problem after finishing fieldwork recommend designing studies that include questions designed to reveal the unexpected.

EXHIBIT 6.7
Influence of Decision Statement of Marketing Problem on Research Objectives and Research Designs

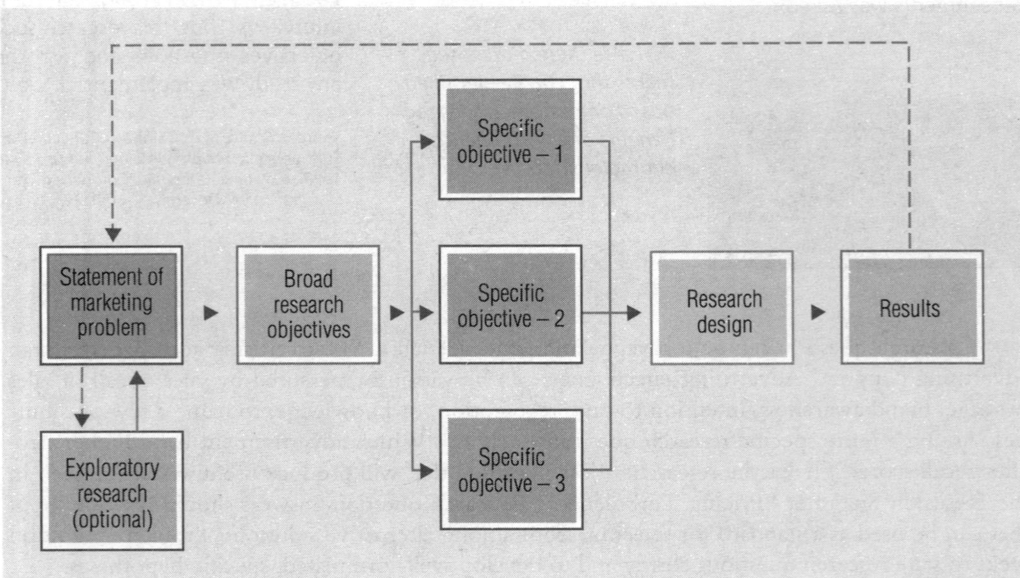

How Much Time Should Be Spent on Problem Definition?

Budget constraints usually influence how much effort is spent on problem definition. Business situations can be complex and numerous variables may be relevant. Searching for every conceivable cause and minor influence is impractical. The more important the decision faced by management, the more resources should be allocated toward problem definition. While not a guarantee, allowing more time and spending more money will help make sure the research objectives that result are relevant and can demonstrate which influences management should focus on.

Managers, being responsible for decision making, may wish the problem-definition process to proceed quickly. Researchers who take a long time to produce a set of research objectives can frustrate managers. However, the time taken to identify the correct problem is usually time well spent.

The Research Proposal

The **research proposal** is a written statement of the research design. It always includes a statement explaining the purpose of the study (in the form of research objectives or deliverables) and a definition of the problem, often in the form of a decision statement. A good proposal systematically outlines the particular research methodology and details procedures that will be used during each stage of the research process. Normally a schedule of costs and deadlines is included in the research proposal. The research proposal becomes the primary communication document between the researcher and the research user.

research proposal
A written statement of the research design.

Exhibit 6.8 illustrates an abbreviated proposal for a short research project conducted for the Internal Revenue Service (IRS) that explores public attitudes toward a variety of tax-related issues.

EXHIBIT 6.8 **An Abbreviated Version of a Research Proposal for the IRS**

Current Situation
Public perception of the IRS appears to be extremely negative. The IRS is the brunt of jokes, and the public avoids contact with any IRS entity. As a result, taxpayers are more inclined to cheat on their returns and many services provided by the IRS to assist taxpayers in preparing their tax returns and to help them understand ways they can avoid paying unnecessary taxes and penalties go unused. In addition, negative attitude lessens the Service's ability to effectively lobby for policy changes. The key decision faced by the IRS due to this situation can be stated as,

What steps could be taken to effectively improve consumer perceptions of the IRS and help design more user-friendly services?

Purpose of the Research
The general purpose of the study is to determine the taxpaying public's perceptions of the role of the IRS in administering the tax laws. In defining the limits of this study, the IRS identified the study areas to be addressed. A careful review of those areas led to the identification of the following specific research objectives:

1. To identify the extent to which taxpayers cheat on their returns, their reasons for doing so, and approaches that can be taken to deter this kind of behavior
2. To determine taxpayers' experience and level of satisfaction with various IRS services
3. To determine what services taxpayers need
4. To develop an accurate profile of taxpayers' behavior relative to the preparation of their income tax returns
5. To assess taxpayers' knowledge and opinions about various tax laws and procedures

Research Design
The survey research method will be the basic research design. Each respondent will be interviewed in his or her home. The personal interviews are generally expected to last between 35 and 45 minutes, although the length will vary depending on the previous tax-related experiences of the respondent. For example, if a respondent has never been audited, questions on audit experience will not be addressed. Or, if a respondent has never contacted the IRS for assistance, certain questions concerning reactions to IRS services will be skipped.

Some sample questions that will be asked are

Did you or your spouse prepare your federal tax return for (year)?
- ☐ **Self**
- ☐ **Spouse**
- ☐ **Someone else**

Did the federal income tax package you received in the mail contain all the forms necessary for you to fill out your return?
- ☐ **Yes**
- ☐ **No**
- ☐ **Didn't receive one in the mail**
- ☐ **Don't know**

If you were calling the IRS for assistance and no one was able to help you immediately, would you rather get a busy signal or be asked to wait on hold?
- ☐ **Busy signal**
- ☐ **Wait on hold**
- ☐ **Neither**
- ☐ **Don't know**

During the interview a self-administered questionnaire will be given to the taxpayer to ask certain sensitive questions, such as

Have you ever claimed a dependent on your tax return that you weren't really entitled to?
- ☐ **Yes**
- ☐ **No**

Sample Design
A survey of approximately 5,000 individuals located in 50 counties throughout the country will provide the database for this study. The sample will be selected on a probability basis from all households in the continental United States.

Eligible respondents will be adults over the age of 18. Within each household an effort will be made to interview the individual who is most familiar with completing the federal tax forms. When there is more than one taxpayer in the household, a random process will be used to select the taxpayer to be interviewed.

Data Gathering
The fieldworkers of a consulting organization will conduct the interviews.

Data Processing and Analysis
Standard editing and coding procedures will be utilized. Simple tabulation and cross-tabulations will be utilized to analyze the data.

Report Preparation
A written report will be prepared, and an oral presentation of the findings will be made by the research analyst at the convenience of the IRS.

Budget and Time Schedule
Any complete research proposal should include a schedule of how long it will take to conduct each stage of the research and a statement of itemized costs.

Based on *A General Taxpayer Opinion Survey*, Office of Planning and Research, Internal Revenue Service, March 1980.

The Proposal as a Planning Tool

Preparation of a research proposal forces the researcher to think critically about each stage of the research process. Vague plans, abstract ideas, and sweeping generalizations about problems or procedures must become concrete and precise statements about specific events. Data requirements and research procedures must be specified clearly so others may understand their exact implications. All ambiguities about why and how the research will be conducted must be clarified before the proposal is complete.

The researcher submits the proposal to management for acceptance, modification, or rejection. Research clients (management) evaluate the proposed study with particular emphasis on whether or not it will provide useful information, and whether it will do so within a reasonable resource budget. Initial proposals are almost always revised after the first review.

The proposal helps managers decide if the proper information will be obtained and if the proposed research will accomplish what is desired. If the problem has not been adequately translated into a set of specific research objectives and a research design, the client's assessment of the proposal will help ensure that the researchers revise it to meet the client's information needs.

An effective proposal communicates exactly what information will be obtained, where it will be obtained, and how it will be obtained. For this reason, it must be explicit about sample selection, measurement, fieldwork, and data analysis. For instance, most proposals involving descriptive research include a proposed questionnaire (or at least some sample questions).

The format for the IRS research proposal in Exhibit 6.8 follows the six stages in the research process outlined in Chapter 4. At each stage, one or more questions must be answered before the researcher can select one of the various alternatives. For example, before a proposal can be completed, the researcher needs to know what is to be measured. A simple statement like "market share" may not be enough; market share may be measured by auditing retailers' or wholesalers' sales, using trade association data, or asking consumers what brands they buy. What is to be measured is just one of many important questions that must be answered before setting the research process in motion. Exhibit 6.9 presents an overview of some of the basic questions that managers and researchers typically must answer when planning a research design.

Congress fights about everything . . . including how to spend taxpayers' money on federal research grants.

The Proposal as a Contract

When the research will be conducted by a consultant or an outside research supplier, the written proposal serves as that person's bid to offer a specific service. Typically, a client solicits several competitive proposals, and these written offers help management judge the relative quality of alternative research suppliers.

A wise researcher will not agree to do a research job for which no written proposal exists. The proposal also serves as a contract that describes the product the research user will buy. In fact, the proposal is in many ways the same as the final research report without the actual results. Misstatements and faulty

EXHIBIT 6.9 **Basic Points Addressed by Research Proposals**

Decisions to Make	Basic Questions
Problem definition	What is the purpose of the study? How much is already known? Is additional background information necessary? What is to be measured? How? Can the data be made available? Should research be conducted? Can a hypothesis be formulated?
Selection of basic research design	What types of questions need to be answered? Are descriptive or causal findings required? What is the source of the data? Can objective answers be obtained by asking people? How quickly is the information needed? How should survey questions be worded? How should experimental manipulations be made?
Selection of sample	Who or what is the source of the data? Can the target population be identified? Is a sample necessary? How accurate must the sample be? Is a probability sample necessary? Is a national sample necessary? How large a sample is necessary? How will the sample be selected?
Data gathering	Who will gather the data? How long will data gathering take? How much supervision is needed? What procedures will data collectors need to follow?
Data analysis and evaluation	Will standardized editing and coding procedures be used? How will the data be categorized? Will computer or hand tabulation be used? What is the nature of the data? What questions need to be answered? How many variables are to be investigated simultaneously? What are the criteria for evaluation of performance? What statistical tools are appropriate?
Type of report	Who will read the report? Are managerial recommendations requested? How many presentations are required? What will be the format of the written report?
Overall evaluation	How much will the study cost? Is the time frame acceptable? Is outside help needed? Will this research design attain the stated research objectives? When should the research begin?

communication may occur if the parties rely only on each individual's memory of what occurred at a planning meeting. The proposal creates a record, which greatly reduces conflicts that might arise after the research has been conducted. Both the researcher and the research client should sign the proposal indicating agreement on what will be done.

The proposal then functions as a formal, written statement of agreement between marketing executives and researchers. As such, it protects the researcher from criticisms such as, "Shouldn't we have had a larger sample?" or "Why didn't you use a focus group approach?" As a record of the researcher's obligation, the proposal also provides a standard for determining whether the actual research was conducted as originally planned.

Suppose in our Deland Trucking case, following the research, David is unhappy with the nature of the results because they indicate that higher cents per mile do, in fact, impact driver loyalty. This is something that David may not wish to face. In his despair, he complains to James saying,

> *"What I really wanted was a recruitment expense study, yet you provide results indicating my wages are too low! Why should I pay you?"*

James can refer back to the research proposal, which is signed by David. He can point right to the deliverables described above showing that David agreed to a study involving driver loyalty and the organizational characteristics that lead to loyalty. The proposal certainly protects the researcher in this case. In most cases like this, after the initial emotional reaction to unflattering results, the client comes around and realizes the report contents include information that will be helpful. Realize too that the proposal protects David in case James produced a study that addresses only research objectives not included in the proposal.

funded business research

Refers to basic research usually performed by academic researchers that is financially supported by some public or private institution, as in federal government grants.

In basic research efforts, a formal proposal serves much the same purpose. **Funded business research** generally refers to basic research usually performed by academic researchers and supported by some public or private institution. Most commonly, researchers pursue federal government grants. A very detailed proposal is usually needed for federal grants, and the agreement for funding is predicated on the research actually delivering the results described in the proposal.

One important comment needs to be made about the nature of research proposals. Not all proposals follow the same format. A researcher can adapt his or her proposal to the target audience or situation. An extremely brief proposal submitted by an organization's internal research department to its own executives bears little resemblance to a complex proposal submitted by a university professor to a federal government agency to research a basic consumer issue.

Anticipating Outcomes

As mentioned above, the proposal and the final research report will contain much of the same information. The proposal describes the data collection, measurement, data analysis, and so forth, in future tense. In the report, the actual results are presented. In this sense, the proposal anticipates the research outcome.

Experienced researchers know that research fails more often because the problem-definition process breaks down or because the research client never truly understood what a research project could or couldn't do. While it probably seems as though the proposal should make this clear, any shortcoming in the proposal can contribute to a communication failure. Thus, any tool that helps communication become as clear as can be is valued very highly.

DUMMY TABLES

dummy tables

Tables placed in research proposals that are exact representations of the actual tables that will show results in the final report with the exception that the results are hypothetical (fictitious).

One such tool that is perhaps the best way to let management know exactly what kind of results will be produced by research is the *dummy table*. **Dummy tables** are placed in research proposals and are exact representations of the actual tables that will show results in the final report with one exception: The results are hypothetical. They get the name because the researcher fills in, or "dummies up," the tables with likely but fictitious data. Dummy tables include the tables that will present hypothesis test results. In this way, they are linked directly to research objectives.

A research analyst can present dummy tables to the decision maker and ask, "Given findings like these, will you be able to make a decision?" If the decision maker says yes, the proposal may be accepted. However, if the decision maker cannot see how results like those in the dummy tables will help make the needed decision(s), it may be back to the drawing board. In other words,

TIPS OF THE TRADE

© iStock

- Researchers should allocate a substantial amount of time toward identifying and refining decision statements, research problems and questions, and research hypotheses. This is a way that the relevance of the research can be increased.
- Use qualitative research tools to probe the key decision makers during early interviews.
  - Ask what has changed.
  - Ask the decision maker to tell more about situations for clarification.
  - Ask the decision maker to compare and contrast situations.
- Express decision statements in creative terms whenever possible. For example, state them in plural form by using terms such as "what ways" might solve a problem rather than trying to find "the way" to solve a problem.
- Research questions and research hypotheses clearly identify the variables that need to be studied.
- Dummy tables are a very effective way to communicate exactly how a research problem might be linked to better decision making.

the client and researcher need to rethink what research results are necessary to solve the problem. Sometimes, examining the dummy tables may reveal that a key variable is missing or that some dependent variable is really not relevant. In other words, the problem is clarified by deciding on action standards or performance criteria and recognizing the types of research findings necessary to make specific decisions.

EXAMPLE DUMMY TABLE

Exhibit 6.10 shows a dummy table taken from the research proposal for David Deland's trucking company. From it, David can see that it shows what things most determine driver loyalty. If the results turn out as shown in the dummy table, it would suggest that David needs to perhaps increase his compensation or reduce the number of long-haul routes that his drivers must conduct.

EXHIBIT 6.10
A Dummy Table for David Deland

Regression Table: Results Showing Which Variables Determine Driver Loyalty

	Standardized Regression Coefficient	Rank (Importance)
Increase cents/mile	.50**	1
Number of long-haul routes (per month)	−.45**	2
Days off (per month)	.30**	3
Vehicle quality	.25*	4
Benefits provided	.15	5

* p-value < .01
** p-value < .05

While some tables may require some additional explanation from the researcher, every effort should be made to allow tables to stand alone and be interpreted by someone who is not an experienced researcher. In other words, the user should be able to understand the results and surmise implications that the results imply. When the final report is compiled, these tables will be included with the dummy results replaced with the actual research results.

Summary

1. Explain why proper "problem definition" is essential to useful business research. Problem definition is the process of defining and developing a decision statement and the steps involved in translating it into more precise research terminology, including a set of research objectives. While it is difficult to point to any particular research stage as the most important, a strong case can be made for this, the first stage. If this step falls apart, the entire research design is misguided. Effective problem definition helps make sure the research objectives are relevant and useful—meaning the results will actually be used. If problem definition is glossed over or done poorly, the results are likely irrelevant and potentially harmful.

2. Know how to recognize problems. Problems and opportunities are usually associated with differences. The differences can occur because of changes in some situation, or they can occur because expectations were unrealistic. Problems occur when there is a difference, or gap, between the current situation and a more ideal situation. One very common type of gap is when business performance does not match the expectations of performance in that dimension. In addition, opportunities exist when actual performance in some area does not match the potential performance. Research can supply information to help close the gap. Thus, problems are noticed by spotting these gaps. While many of these gaps may just be symptoms, further steps are taken to make sure that research addresses relevant issues, not just symptoms.

3. Translate managerial decision statements into relevant research objectives. The problem-definition process outlined in the chapter can help make sure that the research objectives are relevant. A situation analysis is helpful in this regard. In particular, interviews that identify symptoms and then probe the respondent for potential causes of these symptoms are helpful. One tool to help in this process is the "what has changed?" technique. The research objectives, once written, also indicate what variables are likely needed in the study.

4. Translate research objectives into research questions and/or research hypotheses. Research questions simply restate the research objectives in the form of a question. When the researcher has sufficient theoretical reasoning to make a more specific prediction that includes the direction of any predicted relationship, the research question can be translated into one or more research hypotheses.

5. Outline the components of a research proposal. The research proposal is a written statement of the research design that will be followed in addressing a specific problem. The research proposal allows managers to evaluate the details of the proposed research and determine if alterations are needed. Most research proposals include the following sections: decision description, purpose of the research including the research objectives, research design, sample design, data gathering and/or fieldwork techniques, data processing and analysis, budget, and time schedule.

6. Construct dummy tables as part of a research proposal. Dummy tables are included in research proposals and look exactly like the real tables that will be included in the final research report. However, they cannot actually contain results since the study has not yet been done. So, they include hypothetical results that look as much as possible like the actual results. These tables are a very good tool for communicating the value of a research project to management because they provide a real sense for implications that may result from the research.

Key Terms and Concepts

categorical variable, *130*
classificatory variable, *130*
constant, *130*
continuous variable, *130*
decision statement, *119*
dependent variable, *131*
dummy tables, *138*
funded business research, *138*
independent variable, *131*
interrogative techniques, *125*
managerial action standard, *134*
probing, *125*
problem, *123*
problem definition, *119*
random variable, *130*
research proposal, *135*
research questions, *132*
situation analysis, *124*
unit of analysis, *130*
variable, *130*

Questions for Review and Critical Thinking

1. What is a *decision statement?* How does the focus on an irrelevant decision affect the research process?
2. Define *problem recognition*. How is this process like translating text from one language into another? What role does "probing" play in this process?
3. List and describe four factors that influence how difficult the problem-definition process can be.
4. What are three types of gaps that exist, indicating that research may be needed to assist a business in making some decision?
5. Examine an article in the *Wall Street Journal* or a similar source that discusses a business situation of a company in the electronics or defense industry. Identify a problem that exists with the company. Develop some research objectives that you believe correspond to the problem.
6. What is a situation analysis? How can it be used to separate symptoms from actual problems?
7. Define unit of analysis in a marketing research context.
8. Find some business journal articles that deal with culture and international expansion. Find one that lists some hypotheses. What kinds of decisions might be assisted by the results of testing these hypotheses?
9. List and describe at least four terms that can describe the nature of a variable.
10. For each of the following variables, explain why it should be considered either continuous or categorical:
    a. Whether or not a university played in a football bowl game during 2006
    b. The average wait time a customer has before being served in a full-service restaurant
    c. Letter grades of A, B, C, D, or F
    d. The job satisfaction of a company's salespeople
    e. A consumer's age
11. Write at least three examples of hypotheses that involve a managerial action statement. Provide a corresponding decision statement for each.
12. What are the major components of a research proposal? How does a research proposal assist the researcher?
13. The chapter provides an example dummy table for the Deland Trucking vignette. Provide another example dummy table that corresponds to this same situation.
14. Evaluate the following statements of business research problems. For each provide a decision statement and corresponding research objectives:
    a. A farm implement manufacturer: Our objective is to learn the most effective form of advertising so we can maximize product line profits.
    b. An employees' credit union: Our problem is to determine the reasons why employees join the credit union, determine members' awareness of credit union services, and measure attitudes and beliefs about how effectively the credit union is operated.
    c. The producer of a television show: We have a marketing problem. The program's ratings are low. We need to learn how we can improve our ratings.
    d. A soft-drink manufacturer: The marketing problem is that we do not know if our bottlers are more satisfied with us than our competitors' bottlers are with them.
    e. A women's magazine: Our problem is to document the demographic changes that have occurred in recent decades in the lives of women and to put them in historical perspective; to examine several generations of American women through most of this century, tracking their roles as students, workers, wives, and mothers and noting the changes in timing, sequence, and duration of these roles; to examine at what age and for how long a woman enters various stages of her life: school, work, marriage, childbearing, divorce. This will be accomplished by analyzing demographic data over several generations.
    f. A manufacturer of fishing boats: The problem is to determine sales trends over the past five years by product category and to determine the seasonality of unit boat sales by quarters and by region of the country.
    g. The inventor of a tension-headache remedy (a cooling pad that is placed on the forehead for up to four hours): The purpose of this research is (1) to identify the market potential for the product, (2) to identify what desirable features the product should possess, and (3) to determine possible advertising strategies/channel strategies for the product.
15. Comment on the following statements and situations:
    a. "The best researchers are prepared to rethink and rewrite their proposals."
    b. "The client's signature is an essential element of the research proposal."
16. You have been hired by a group of hotel owners, restaurant owners, and other people engaged in businesses that benefit from tourism on South Padre Island, Texas. They wish to learn how they can attract a large number of college students to their town during spring break. Define the marketing decision statement.
17. You have been hired by a local Big Brothers and Big Sisters organization to learn how they can increase the number of males who volunteer to become Big Brothers to fatherless boys. Define your research objectives.

Research Activities

1. **'NET** Examine the Web site for International Communications Research (**http://icrsurvey.com**).[10] What services do they seem to offer that fall into the problem-definition process?
2. Consider the current situation within your local university music department. Assuming it stages musical productions to which audiences are invited and for which tickets are sold, describe the marketing situation it faces. Prepare a research proposal that would help it address a key decision. Make sure it includes at least one dummy table.

Case 6.1 E-ZPass

© GETTY IMAGES/ PHOTODISC GREEN

In the 1990s, a task force was formed among executives of seven regional transportation agencies in the New York–New Jersey area.[11] The mission of the task force was to investigate the feasibility and desirability of adopting electronic toll collection (ETC) for the interregional roadways of the area. Electronic toll collection is accomplished by providing commuters with small transceivers (tags) that emit a tuned radio signal. Receivers placed at tollbooths are able to receive the radio signal and identify the commuter associated with the particular signal. Commuters establish ETC accounts that are debited for each use of a toll road or facility, thus eliminating the need for the commuter to pay by cash or token. Because the radio signal can be read from a car in motion, ETC can reduce traffic jams at toll plazas by allowing tag holders to pass through at moderate speeds.

At the time the New York and New Jersey agencies were studying the service, electronic toll collection was already being used successfully in Texas and Louisiana. Even though several of the agencies had individually considered implementing ETC, they recognized that independent adoption would fall far short of the potential benefits achievable with an integrated interregional system.

The task force was most interested in identifying the ideal configuration of service attributes for each agency's commuters and determining how similar or different these configurations might be across agencies. The task force identified a lengthy list of attributes that was ultimately culled to six questions:

- How many accounts are necessary and what statements will be received?
- How and where does one pay for E-ZPass?
- What lanes are available for use and how they are controlled?
- Is the tag transferable to other vehicles?
- What is the price of the tag and possible service charge?
- What are other possible uses for the E-ZPass tag (airport parking, gasoline purchases, and so forth)?

From a researcher's perspective, it also seemed important to assess commuter demand for the service. However, the task force was not convinced that it needed a projection of demand, because it was committed to implementing ETC regardless of initial commuter acceptance. The task force considered its primary role to be investigating commuters' preferences for how the service should be configured *ideally.*

Questions

1. Evaluate the problem-definition process. Has the problem been defined adequately so that a relevant decision statement can be written?
2. What type of research design would you recommend for this project?
3. What research questions might be tested?
4. What might a dummy table include in this research proposal?

Case 6.2 Cane's Goes International

© GETTY IMAGES/ PHOTODISC GREEN

Raising Cane's is a fast-food chicken finger establishment based in Baton Rouge, Louisiana. Cane's restaurants are popular throughout the Gulf South. Cane's recently has been approached by people interested in opening Cane's restaurants in other countries. The best contact is an Australian. However, Cane's has also been approached about outlets in Montreal, Quebec, and in Monterrey, Mexico. Cane's prepares high-quality fried chicken fingers and has a limited menu consisting of fingers, fries, slaw, and lemonade (**http://www.raisingcanes.com**).

1. Write a decision statement for Raising Cane's.
2. Write corresponding research objectives and research questions.
3. What role would a proposal play in assisting this research effort and in assisting Cane's in improving their business situation?

Case 6.3 Deland Trucking

© GETTY IMAGES/ PHOTODISC GREEN

Based on the case scenario described throughout this chapter, prepare a research proposal that addresses this situation.

Case 6.4 Bharti Airtel Ltd. (BAL) Goes Global

© GETTY IMAGES/ PHOTODISC GREEN

Bharti Airtel Ltd. (BAL), a market leader in Indian telecommunication industry looks to expand its operations in emerging markets. It has established as a dominant player in India with its innovative business process model and as a strong brand. However, in recent times it was facing tapering growth because of increasing competition and saturation of the urban markets. While more and more players are trying to enter and capitalize the Indian market which is experiencing high growth, BAL plans to go global. The first step towards its globalization venture is the acquisition of Zain Group's telecom business in fifteen African countries in the year 2010. This it does to make a stronger hold in the African continent. The concerns around whether BAL overvalued the deal are an issue in the eyes of the industry observers. However, they are keen to see how the company performs and will it be able to use its innovative business model and establish itself as a strong brand as it is in India. Also it has to combat with the cultural differences, political forces, and socio-economic environment. So here we can see Bharti in order to shape up to the African markets facing various marketing dilemmas.

Management Questions

1. What are the critical success factors in order to tackle the new emerging market?
2. Will the cross-country differences in cultural, demographic, and market conditions affect the company?
3. How to tackle the legal and regulatory framework?
4. How to tailor market entry strategy to fit a specific industry and business environment?

Marketing Research Questions

1. Cross-country barriers: What is the acceptance for foreign companies in African markets?
2. Existing players: Who are the major competitors in the African market?
3. Consumer perception: What is the consumer perception towards new brand?

CHAPTER 7
QUALITATIVE RESEARCH TOOLS

LEARNING OUTCOMES

After studying this chapter, you should be able to

1. **List and understand the differences between qualitative research and quantitative research**
2. **Understand the role of qualitative research in exploratory research designs**
3. **Describe the basic qualitative research orientations**
4. **Prepare a focus group interview outline**
5. **Recognize technological advances in the application of qualitative research approaches**
6. **Recognize common qualitative research tools and know the advantages and limitations of their use**
7. **Know the risks associated with acting on only exploratory results**

Chapter Vignette: What's in the Van?

Is this shoe too cool? That was really the question asked by VF Corporation when they acquired Vans, the company that makes the shoe shown here.[1] Vans traditionally are synonymous with skateboarding and skateboard culture. Readers that are unfamiliar with skateboarding may well have never heard of the company. However, a reader that is part of the skateboard culture is probably looking down at his or her Vans right now!

Former Vans CEO Gary Schoenfeld points out that a decade before the acquisition (a $396 million deal), Vans was practically a dead brand.[2] However, the last ten years have seen a revival in skateboard interest and Vans has remained the number one skateboard shoe provider. Now, the incoming management team has been given the task of deciding how to raise Vans sales to $500 million per year.

COURTESY, VANS CLASSIC SLIP-ON

Where will the growth come from? Should the company define itself as a "skateboard footwear" company, a "lifestyle" company, or as the icon for the skate culture? Answering this question will require a deeper interpretation of the meaning of the "Van."

Skateboarding is a dynamic activity. A study by Board-Trac suggests that today over one in four skateboarders is female, as opposed to fewer than one in ten as recently as 2000.[3] So, what exactly is in the mind and heart of a "boarder?" Two important research questions involve "What is the meaning of a pair of Vans?" and "What things define the skateboarding experience?"

Questions like these call for qualitative research methods.[4] Not just any researcher is "fit" for this job. One way to collect this data is to hire young, energetic research employees to become "boarders" and immerse themselves into the culture.

They may have to "Kasper" like a "flatland techer" while probing for meaning among the discussion and activities of the other boarders. Here, Vans may find that their brand helps identify a boarder and make them feel unique in some ways. If so, Vans may want to investigate increasing their product line beyond shoes and simple apparel.

Depth interviews of Vans wearers in which people describe in detail why they wear Vans will also be useful. Vans shouldn't be surprised if they find a significant portion of their shoes are sold to people like Mr. Samuel Teel, a retired attorney from Toledo, Ohio. Sam is completely unaware of the connection between Vans and skateboarding. He likes them because he doesn't have to bend to tie his shoes! Maybe there are some secondary segments that could bring growth to Vans. But marketing to them could complicate things—who knows?

Introduction

Chemists sometimes use the term *qualitative analysis* to mean research that determines what some compound is made of. In other words, the focus is on the inner meaning of the chemical—its *qualities*. As the word implies, qualitative research is interested more in *qualities* than quantities. Therefore, qualitative research is not about applying specific numbers to measure variables or using statistical procedures to numerically specify a relationship's strength.

What Is Qualitative Research?

Qualitative business research is research that addresses business objectives through techniques that allow the researcher to provide elaborate interpretations of market phenomena without depending on numerical measurement. Its focus is on discovering true inner meanings and new insights. Qualitative research is very widely applied in practice. There are many research firms that specialize in qualitative research.

Qualitative research is less structured than most quantitative approaches. It does not rely on self-response questionnaires containing structured response formats. Instead, it is more **researcher-dependent** in that the researcher must extract meaning from unstructured responses, such as text from a recorded interview or a collage representing the meaning of some experience, such as skateboarding. The researcher interprets the data to extract its meaning and converts it to information.

qualitative business research
Research that addresses business objectives through techniques that allow the researcher to provide elaborate interpretations of phenomena without depending on numerical measurement; its focus is on discovering true inner meanings and new insights.

researcher-dependent
Research in which the researcher must extract meaning from unstructured responses such as text from a recorded interview or a collage representing the meaning of some experience.

Uses of Qualitative Research

Mechanics can't use a hammer to fix everything that is broken. Instead, the mechanic has a toolbox from which a tool is matched to a problem. Business research is the same. The researcher has many tools available and the research design should try to match the best tool to the research objective. Also, just as a mechanic is probably not an expert with every tool, each researcher usually has special expertise with a small number of tools. Not every researcher has expertise with tools that would comprise qualitative research.

Generally, the less specific the research objective, the more likely that qualitative research tools will be appropriate. Also, when the emphasis is on a deeper understanding of motivations or on developing novel concepts, qualitative research is very appropriate. The following list represents common situations that often call for qualitative research:[5]

1. When it is difficult to develop specific and actionable problem statements or research objectives. For instance, if after several interviews with the research client the researcher still can't determine exactly what needs to be measured, then qualitative research approaches may help with problem definition. Qualitative research is often useful to gain further insight and crystallize the research problem.
2. When the research objective is to develop an understanding of some phenomena in great detail and in much depth. Qualitative research tools are aimed at discovering the primary themes indicating human motivations and the documentation of activities is usually very complete. Often qualitative research provides richer information than quantitative approaches.
3. When the research objective is to learn how a phenomena occurs in its natural setting or to learn how to express some concept in colloquial terms. For example, how do consumers actually use a product? Or, exactly how does the accounting department process invoices? While a survey can probably ask many useful questions, observing a product in use or watching the invoice process will usually be more insightful. Qualitative research produces many product and process improvement ideas.

Qualitative researchers can learn about the skating experience by becoming immersed in the culture.

RESEARCH SNAPSHOT

Surprises at P&G!

With literally thousands of products to manage, Procter & Gamble (P&G) finds itself in the situation to conduct qualitative research almost daily. P&G doesn't introduce a product that hasn't been reviewed from nearly every possible angle. Likewise, before taking a product to a new country, you can be confident that the product has been "focus grouped" in that environment.

P&G often uses qualitative research techniques to discover potential problems or opportunities for the company's products. For example, focus groups played a major role in Herbal Essences hair care's new logo, advertising copy, reformulated ingredients, and new bottle design. The redesigned bottles for shampoo and conditioner bottles are curved in a yin and yang fashion so they can fit together. "That significantly improved conditioner sales, because consumers are now buying them as a system," claims P&G's Claudia Kotchka.

At times, P&G seeks outside help for its research. Such was the case when P&G wanted a study of its own business problems. The researchers selected began by applying qualitative research techniques including depth interviews, observational techniques (shadowing), and focus groups on P&G managers and marketing employees. These interviews gave the researchers the idea that perhaps P&G was suffering more from a management problem than from a marketing problem. It helped form a general research question that asked whether business problems were really due to low morale among the employees. After a lot of qualitative interviews with dozens and dozens of P&G employees, a quantitative study followed up these findings and supported this idea and led to suggestions for improving employee morale!

Sources: Nelson, Emily, "Focus Groupies: P&G Keeps Cincinnati Busy with All Its Studies," *Wall Street Journal* 239 (January 24, 2002), A1, Eastern Edition; Stengel, J. R., A. L. Dixon, and C. T. Allen, "Listening Begins at Home," *Harvard Business Review* (November 2003), 106–116; Chang, Julia, "Designed to Sell: Procter & Gamble," *Sales and Marketing* (April 20, 2007), http://www.salesandmarketing.com/msg/content_display/marketing/e3if5981313dc92fc1aa0356d269d91ea74 (accessed February 6, 2009).

4. When some behavior the researcher is studying is particularly context dependent—meaning the reasons something is liked or some behavior is performed depend very much on the particular situation surrounding the event. Understanding why Vans are liked is probably difficult to determine correctly outside the skating environment.
5. When a fresh approach to studying some problem is needed. This is particularly the case when quantitative research has yielded less than satisfying results. Qualitative tools can yield unique insights, many of which may lead the organization in new directions.

Each of these describes a scenario that may require an exploratory orientation. Previously, we defined exploratory research as appropriate in ambiguous situations or when new insight is needed. We indicated that exploratory research approaches are sometimes needed just to reach the appropriate problem statement and research objectives. While equating qualitative research with exploratory research is an oversimplification, the application of qualitative tools can help clear up ambiguity and provide innovative ideas.

Qualitative "versus" Quantitative Research

In social science, one can find many debates about the superiority of qualitative research over quantitative research or vice versa.[6] We'll begin by saying that this is largely a superfluous argument in either direction. The truth is that qualitative research can accomplish research objectives that quantitative research cannot. Similarly truthful, but no more so, quantitative research can accomplish objectives that qualitative research cannot. The key to successfully using either is to match the right approach to the right research context.

Many good research projects combine both qualitative and quantitative research. For instance, developing valid survey measures requires first a deep understanding of the concept to be measured and a description of the way these ideas are expressed in everyday language. Both of these are tasks best suited for qualitative research. However, validating the measure formally to make sure it can reliably capture the intended concept will likely require quantitative research.[7] Also, qualitative research may be needed to separate symptoms from problems and then quantitative

RESEARCH SNAPSHOT

Kirana Stores

In India, there are several kirana stores which are similar to convenience store in the Western countries. Management of one of the chains of such kirana store realized that the male customers are the ones who patronize kirana stores more than women. The management asked the store people to keep a record of their customers and found that there are a significant high percentage of male customers than female customers. The management checked the same across all kirana stores that they have around the country and found the same trend. Management realized that they're losing a major chunk of prospective customers and decided to study the behavior of Indian consumers whether patronize kirana stores.

Management asked our research agency to conduct research to understand the behavior of female buyers in shopping at kirana stores. They decided to conduct a qualitative research especially focus group interview and depth interview. Six focus group interviews were conducted with 8 to 12 woman participants. The focus groups were conducted by a professional moderator inside a room with glass on one side through which the management sitting outside the room can observe the discussion. The participants in the room cannot see who were sitting outside. The findings of such focus group interview were completely new to the management as they found that:

1. Women perceived that the kirana stores are for males to shop from and not designed for women buyers.
2. The layout of the kirana stores and the aisle space are narrower for women to move comfortably without having touched fellow customers.
3. Some woman respondents said that "kirana stores are made for buying cheap products and for quick shopping which male members do when it is required."

Hence through qualitative research, the management of the kirana shop chain comes to a very good understanding about the perception of consumers patronizing kirana stores in India. On the basis of such finding and through subsequent quantitative research, the management of the kirana store changed the shop layout, aisle spacing, product storage, and ambience to stimulate female buyers to visit kirana store.

research can follow up to test relationships among relevant variables. The Research Snapshot "Surprises at P&G" describes one such situation.[8]

quantitative business research
Business research that addresses research objectives through empirical assessments that involve numerical measurement and analysis.

Quantitative business research can be defined as business research that addresses research objectives through empirical assessments that involve numerical measurement and analysis approaches. Qualitative research is more apt to stand on its own in the sense that it requires less interpretation. For example, quantitative research is quite appropriate when a research objective involves a managerial action standard. For example, a salad dressing company considered changing its recipe.[9] The new recipe was tested with a sample of consumers. Each consumer rated the product using numeric scales. Management established a rule that a majority of consumers rating the new product higher than the old product would have to be established with 90 percent confidence before replacing the old formula. A project like this can involve both quantitative measurement in the form of numeric rating scales and quantitative analysis in the form of applied statistical procedures.

Contrasting Qualitative and Quantitative Methods

Exhibit 7.1 illustrates some differences between qualitative and quantitative research. Certainly, these are generalities and exceptions may apply. However, it covers some of the key distinctions. The Research Snapshot "Surprises at P&G!" also introduces qualitative research.

subjective
Results are researcher-dependent, meaning different researchers may reach different conclusions based on the same interview.

intersubjective certifiability
Different individuals following the same procedure will produce the same results or come to the same conclusion.

Quantitative researchers direct a considerable amount of activity toward measuring concepts with scales that either directly or indirectly provide numeric values. The numeric values can then be used in statistical computations and hypothesis testing. As will be described in detail later, this process involves comparing numbers in some way. In contrast, qualitative researchers are more interested in observing, listening, and interpreting. As such, the researcher is intimately involved in the research process and in constructing the results. For these reasons, qualitative research is said to be more **subjective**, meaning that the results are researcher-dependent. Different researchers may reach different conclusions based on the same interview. In that respect, qualitative research lacks **intersubjective certifiability** (sometimes called intersubjective verifiability), the ability of different individuals following the same procedures to produce the same results or come to the same

EXHIBIT 7.1
Comparing Qualitative and Quantitative Research

Qualitative Research	Research Aspect	Quantitative Research
Discover Ideas, Used in Exploratory Research with General Research Objects	Common Purpose	Test Hypotheses or Specific Research Questions
Observe and Interpret	Approach	Measure and Test
Unstructured, Free-Form	Data Collection Approach	Structured Response Categories Provided
Researcher Is Intimately Involved. Results Are Subjective.	Researcher Independence	Researcher Uninvolved Observer. Results Are Objective.
Small Samples—Often in Natural Settings	Samples	Large Samples to Produce Generalizable Results (Results That Apply to Other Situations)
Exploratory Research Designs	Most Often Used	Descriptive and Causal Research Designs

conclusion. This should not necessarily be considered a weakness of qualitative research; rather it is simply a characteristic that yields differing insights. In contrast, when a survey respondent provides a commitment score on a quantitative scale, it is thought to be more objective because the number will be the same no matter what researcher is involved in the analysis.

Qualitative research seldom involves samples with hundreds of respondents. Instead, a handful of people are usually the source of qualitative data. This is perfectly acceptable in discovery-oriented research. All ideas would still have to be tested before adopted. Does a smaller sample mean that qualitative research is cheaper than quantitative? Perhaps not. Although fewer respondents have to be interviewed, the greater researcher involvement in both the data collection and analysis can drive up the costs of qualitative research.

Given the close relationship between qualitative research and exploratory designs, it should not be surprising that qualitative research is most often used in exploratory designs. Small samples, interpretive procedures that require subjective judgments, and the unstructured interview format all make traditional hypotheses testing difficult with qualitative research. Thus, these procedures are not best suited for drawing definitive conclusions, as would be expected from causal designs involving experiments. These disadvantages for drawing inferences, however, become advantages when the goal is to draw out potential explanations because the researcher spends more time with each respondent and is able to explore much more ground due to the flexibility of the procedures.

quantitative data
Represent phenomena by assigning numbers in an ordered and meaningful way.

qualitative data
Data that are not characterized by numbers, and instead are textual, visual, or oral; focus is on stories, visual portrayals, meaningful characterizations, interpretations, and other expressive descriptions.

Contrasting Exploratory and Confirmatory Research

Philosophically, research can be considered as either exploratory or confirmatory. Most exploratory research designs produce **qualitative data**. Exploratory designs do not usually produce **quantitative data**, which represent phenomena by assigning numbers in an ordered and meaningful way. Rather than numbers, the focus of qualitative research is on stories, visual portrayals, meaningful characterizations, interpretations, and other expressive descriptions. Often, exploratory research may be needed to develop the ideas that lead to research hypotheses. In other words, in some situations the outcome of exploratory research is a testable research hypothesis. Confirmatory research then tests these hypotheses with quantitative data. The results of these tests help in decision making by suggesting a specific course of action.

TO THE POINT

The cure for boredom is curiosity. There is no cure for curiosity.

—Dorothy Parker

For example, an exploratory researcher is more likely to adopt a qualitative approach that might involve trying to develop a deeper understanding of how families are impacted by changing economic conditions or investigating how people suffering economically spend scarce resources. This may lead to the development of a hypothesis that during challenging economic times consumers seek low-cost entertainment such as movie rentals, but would not test this hypothesis. In contrast, a quantitative researcher may search for numbers that indicate economic trends. This may lead to hypothesis tests concerning how much the economy influences rental movie consumption.

Some types of qualitative studies can be conducted very quickly. Others take a very long time. For example, a single focus group analysis involving a large bottling company's sales force can likely be conducted and interpreted in a matter of days. This would provide faster results than most descriptive or causal designs. However, other types of qualitative research, such as a participant-observer study aimed at understanding skateboarding, could take months to complete. A qualitative approach can, but does not necessarily, save time.

In summary, when researchers have limited experience or knowledge about a research issue, exploratory research is a useful step. Exploratory research, which often involves qualitative methods, can be an essential first step to a more conclusive, confirmatory study by reducing the chance of beginning with an inadequate, incorrect, or misleading set of research objectives.

Orientations to Qualitative Research

Qualitative research can be performed in many ways using many techniques. Orientations to qualitative research are very much influenced by the different fields of study involved in research. These orientations are each associated with a category of qualitative research. The major categories of qualitative research include

1. Phenomenology—originating in philosophy and psychology
2. Ethnography—originating in anthropology
3. Grounded theory—originating in sociology
4. Case studies—originating in psychology and in business research

Precise lines between these approaches are difficult to draw and there are clearly links among these orientations. In addition, a particular qualitative research study may involve elements of two or more approaches. However, each category does reflect a somewhat unique approach to human inquiry and approaches to discovering knowledge. Each will be described briefly below.

Phenomenology

WHAT IS A PHENOMENOLOGICAL APPROACH TO RESEARCH?

Phenomenology represents a philosophical approach to studying human experiences based on the idea that human experience itself is inherently subjective and determined by the context in which people live.[10] The phenomenological researcher focuses on how a person's behavior is shaped by the relationship he or she has with the physical environment, objects, people, and situations. Phenomenological inquiry seeks to describe, reflect upon, and interpret experiences.

phenomenology
A philosophical approach to studying human experiences based on the idea that human experience itself is inherently subjective and determined by the context in which people live.

Researchers with a phenomenological orientation rely largely on conversational interview tools. When conversational interviews are face to face, they are recorded either with video or audiotape and then interpreted by the researcher. The phenomenological interviewer is careful to avoid asking direct questions when at all possible. Instead, the research respondent is asked to tell a story about some experience. In addition, the researcher must do everything possible to make sure a respondent is comfortable telling his or her story. One way to accomplish this is to become a member of the group (for example, becoming a skateboarder in the scenario described earlier in this chapter). Another way may be to avoid having the person use his or her real name. This might be particularly necessary in studying potentially sensitive topics such as smoking, drug usage, shoplifting, or employee theft.

Therefore, a phenomenological approach to studying the meaning of Vans may require considerable time. The researcher may first spend weeks or months fitting in with the person or group of interest to establish a comfort level. During this time, careful notes of conversations are made. If an interview is sought, the researcher would likely not begin by asking a skateboarder to describe his or her shoes. Rather, asking for favorite skateboard incidents or talking about what makes a skateboarder unique may generate productive conversation. Generally, the approach is very unstructured as a way of avoiding leading questions and to provide every opportunity for new insights.

WHAT IS HERMENEUTICS?

hermeneutics
An approach to understanding phenomenology that relies on analysis of texts through which a person tells a story about him or herself.

hermeneutic unit
Refers to a text passage from a respondent's story that is linked with a key theme from within this story or provided by the researcher.

The term hermeneutics is important in phenomenology. **Hermeneutics** is an approach to understanding phenomenology that relies on analysis of texts in which a person tells a story about him or herself.[12] Meaning is then drawn by connecting text passages to one another or to themes expressed outside the story. These connections are usually facilitated by coding the key meanings expressed in the story. While a full understanding of hermeneutics is beyond the scope of this text, some of the terminology is used when applying qualitative tools. For instance, a **hermeneutic unit** refers to a text passage from a respondent's story that is linked with a key theme from within this story or provided by the researcher.[13] These passages are an important way in which data are interpreted.

Computerized software exists to assist in coding and interpreting texts and images. ATLAS.ti is one such software package that adopts the term hermeneutic unit in referring to groups of phrases that are linked with meaning. Hermeneutic units and computerized software are also very appropriate in grounded theory approaches. One useful component of computerized approaches is a word counter. The word counter will return counts of how many times words were used in a story. Often, frequently occurring words suggest a key theme. The Research Snapshot "When Will I Ever Learn?" demonstrates the use of hermeneutics in interpreting a story about a consumer shopping for a car.

ethnography
Represents ways of studying cultures through methods that involve becoming highly active within that culture.

participant-observation
Ethnographic research approach where the researcher becomes immersed within the culture that he or she is studying and draws data from his or her observations.

Ethnography

WHAT IS ETHNOGRAPHY?

Ethnography represents ways of studying cultures through methods that involve becoming highly active within that culture. **Participant-observation** typifies an ethnographic research approach. Participant-observation means the researcher becomes immersed within the culture that he or she is studying and draws data from his or her observations. A *culture* can be either a broad culture, like American culture, or a narrow culture, like urban gangs, Harley-Davidson owners, or skateboarding enthusiasts.[14]

Organizational culture would also be relevant for ethnographic study.[15] At times, researchers have actually become employees of an organization for an extended period of time. In doing so, they become part of the culture and over time other employees come to act quite naturally around the researcher. The researcher may observe behaviors that the employee would never reveal otherwise. For instance, a researcher investigating the ethical behavior of salespeople may have difficulty getting a car salesperson to reveal any potentially deceptive sales tactics in a traditional interview. However, ethnographic techniques may result in the salesperson letting down his or her guard, resulting in more valid discoveries about the car-selling culture.

© HEMERA/THINKSTOCK

Ethnographic (participant-observation) approaches may be useful to understanding how children obtain value from their experiences with toys.

OBSERVATION IN ETHNOGRAPHY

Observation plays a key role in ethnography. Researchers today sometimes ask households for permission to place video cameras in their home. In doing so, the ethnographer can study the consumer in a "natural habitat" and use the observations to test new products, develop new product ideas, and develop strategies in general.[16]

Ethnographic study can be particularly useful when a certain culture is comprised of individuals who cannot or will not verbalize their thoughts and feelings. For instance, ethnography has advantages for discovering insights among children since it does not rely largely on their answers to questions. Instead, the researcher can simply become part of the environment, allow the children to do what they do naturally, and record their behavior.[17]

The opening vignette describing a participant-observer approach to learning about skateboarding culture represents an ethnographic approach. Here, the researcher would draw insight from observations and personal experiences with the culture.

TOTHEPOINT

I never predict. I just look out the window and see what is visible—but not yet seen.

—Peter Drucker

Grounded Theory

WHAT IS GROUNDED THEORY?

Grounded theory is probably applied less often in business research than is either phenomenology or ethnography.[18]

Grounded theory represents an inductive investigation in which the researcher poses questions about information provided by respondents or taken from historical records. The researcher asks the questions to him or herself and repeatedly questions the responses to derive deeper explanations. Grounded theory is particularly applicable in highly dynamic situations involving rapid and significant change. Two key questions asked by the grounded theory researcher are "What is happening here?" and "How is it different?"[19] The distinguishing characteristic of grounded theory is that it does not begin with a theory but instead extracts one from whatever emerges from an area of inquiry.[20]

grounded theory
Represents an inductive investigation in which the researcher poses questions about information provided by respondents or taken from historical records; the researcher asks the questions to him or herself and repeatedly questions the responses to derive deeper explanations.

HOW IS GROUNDED THEORY USED?

Consider a company that approaches a researcher to study whether or not its sales force is as effective as it has been over the past five years. The researcher uses grounded theory to discover

Qualitative research reveals that products that are perceived as "authentic" offer more value for consumers.

a potential explanation. A theory is inductively developed based on text analysis of dozens of sales meetings that had been recorded over the previous five years. By questioning the events discussed in the sales interviews and analyzing differences in the situations that may have led to the discussion, the researcher is able to develop a theory. The theory suggests that with an increasing reliance on e-mail and other technological devices for communication, the salespeople do not communicate with each other informally as much as they did five years previously. As a result, the salespeople had failed to bond into a close-knit "community."[21]

Computerized software also can be useful in developing grounded theory. In our Vans example, the researcher may interpret skateboarders' stories of good and bad skating experiences by questioning the events and changes described. These may yield theories about the role that certain brands play in shaping a good or bad experience. Alternatively, grounded theorists often rely on visual representations. Thus, the skateboarder could develop collages representing good and bad experiences. Just as with the text, questions can be applied to the visuals in an effort to develop theory.

Case Studies

WHAT ARE CASE STUDIES?

Case studies simply refer to the documented history of a particular person, group, organization, or event. Typically, a case study may describe the events of a specific company as it faces an important decision or situation, such as introducing a new product or dealing with some management crisis. Textbook cases typify this kind of case study. Clinical interviews of managers, employees, or customers can represent a case study.

The case studies can then be analyzed for important themes. **Themes** are identified by the frequency with which the same term (or a synonym) arises in the narrative description. The themes may be useful in discovering variables that are relevant to potential explanations.

case studies
The documented history of a particular person, group, organization, or event.

themes
Identified by the frequency with which the same term (or a synonym) arises in the narrative description.

HOW ARE CASE STUDIES USED?

Case studies are commonly applied in business. For instance, case studies of brands that sell "luxury" products helped provide insight into what makes up a prestigious brand. A business researcher carefully conducted case (no pun intended) studies of higher end wine labels (such as Penfold's Grange) including the methods of production and distribution. This analysis suggested that a key ingredient to a prestige brand may well be authenticity. When consumers know something is authentic, they attach more esteem to that product or brand.[22]

Case studies often overlap with one of the other categories of qualitative research. The Research Snapshot "It's Like Riding a Bike!" illustrates how observation was useful in discovering insights leading to important business changes.

A primary advantage of the case study is that an entire organization or entity can be investigated in depth with meticulous attention to detail. This highly focused attention enables the researcher to carefully study the order of events as they occur or to concentrate on identifying the relationships among functions, individuals, or entities. Conducting a case study often

RESEARCH SNAPSHOT

It's Like Riding a Bike!

Schwinn has long relied on observational research in their exploratory research studies. Here is a description of a case study documented from observational techniques:

We had a very successful dealer on the West Coast. So it occurred to me that we'd go out and find out how he's doing it. So we go out. The guy's got a nice store out in Van Nuys. We sit in the back room and we listen. The first customers come in, a man and a woman with a boy about nine or ten years old. The dad says, "Which one is it?" The son says, "This one over here." Dad looks at it. He says to the clerk, "How much is it?" The clerk says, "$179.95." The father says, "Okay, we'll take it." It blew the whole bit [there were no magic sales approaches]. Suddenly it dawned on us that it's not what they say, it's the atmosphere of the store. Here was not Joe's old, dirty bike shop—it was a beautiful store on the main street. A big sign was in front, "Valley Cyclery," inside [were] fluorescent lights, carpeting on the floor, stereo music, air-conditioning, and a beautiful display of bicycles. It was like a magnet. People came in. So, we've tried to introduce that idea to other dealers. Put a bigger investment into your store and see what happens. Some of them did, and it happened [sales improved].

More recently, researchers documented with photographs the way that most people use their bicycles. Although the vast majority of bikes available for sale are multispeed racing or mountain bikes, even a cursory observation of the photos suggested that most people clearly do not race on their bikes nor use them off-road. As a result, Schwinn reintroduced the Cruiser with much success. The Cruiser is the 1950ish touring bike with the balloon tires, big cushioned seat, and upright handlebars. In fact, the Cruiser series proved to be so successful that over 20 different 2009 Cruiser models were produced. Observation is like riding a bike—once you learn, you shouldn't ever forget!

Sources: Burch, Ray (1973), "Marketing Research: Why It Works, Why It Doesn't Work," speech to the Chicago Chapter of the American Marketing Association, 1973, reprinted with permission of the Chicago Chapter of the American Marketing Association; Curry, A. and M. Silver, "One Speed Is Enough," *U.S. News and World Report* 136 (May 10, 2004), 67–68. A complete list of the models is available at http://www.schwinnbike.com/usa/eng/Products/Cruisers/.

requires the cooperation of the party whose history is being studied. This freedom to search for whatever data an investigator deems important makes the success of any case study highly dependent on the alertness, creativity, intelligence, and motivation of the individual performing the case analysis.

Common Techniques Used inQualitative Research

Qualitative researchers apply a nearly endless number of techniques. These techniques overlap more than one of the orientations previously discussed, although each category may display a preference for certain techniques. Exhibit 7.2 lists characteristics of some common qualitative research techniques. Each is then described.

What Is a Focus Group Interview?

The focus group interview is so widely used that many advertising and research agencies do nothing but focus group interviews. In that sense, it is wrongly synonymous with qualitative research. Nonetheless, focus groups are a very important qualitative research technique and deserve considerable discussion.

focus group interview
An unstructured, free-flowing interview with a small group of around six to ten people. Focus groups are led by a trained moderator who follows a flexible format encouraging dialogue among respondents.

A **focus group interview** is an unstructured, free-flowing interview with a small group of people, usually between six and ten. Focus groups are led by a trained moderator who follows a flexible format encouraging dialogue among respondents. Common focus group topics include employee programs, employee satisfaction, brand meanings, problems with products, advertising themes, or new-product concepts.

The group meets at a central location at a designated time. Participants may range from consumers talking about hair coloring, petroleum engineers talking about problems in the "oil

EXHIBIT 7.2 **Four Common Qualitative Research Tools**

Tool	Description	Type of Approach (Category)	Key Advantages	Key Disadvantages
Focus Group Interviews	Small group discussions led by a trained moderator	Ethnography, case studies	• Can be done quickly • Gain multiple perspectives • Flexibility	• Results dependent on moderator • Results do not generalize to larger population • Difficult to use for sensitive topics • Expensive
Depth Interviews	One-on-one, probing interview between a trained researcher and a respondent	Ethnography, grounded theory, case studies	• Gain considerable insight from each individual • Good for understanding unusual behaviors	• Result dependent on researcher's interpretation • Results not meant to generalize • Very expensive
Conversations	Unstructured dialogue recorded by a researcher	Phenomenology, grounded theory	• Gain unique insights from enthusiasts • Can cover sensitive topics • Less expensive than depth interviews or focus groups	• Easy to get off course • Interpretations are very researcher-dependent
Semi-Structured Interviews	Open-ended questions, often in writing, that ask for short essay-type answers from respondents	Grounded theory, ethnography	• Can address more specific issues • Results can be easily interpreted • Cost advantages over focus groups and depth interviews	• Lack the flexibility that is likely to produce truly creative or novel explanations
Word Association/ Sentence Completion	Records the first thoughts that come to a consumer in response to some stimulus	Grounded theory, case studies	• Economical • Can be done quickly	• Lack the flexibility that is likely to produce truly creative or novel explanations
Observation	Recorded notes describing observed events	Ethnography, grounded theory, case studies	• Can be unobtrusive • Can yield actual behavior patterns	• Can be very expensive with participant-observer series
Collages	Respondents assemble pictures that represent their thoughts/feelings	Phenomenology, grounded theory	• Flexible enough to allow novel insights	• Highly dependent on the researcher's interpretation of the collage
Thematic Apperception/ Cartoon Tests	Researcher provides an ambiguous picture and respondent tells about the story	Phenomenology, grounded theory	• Projective, allows to get at sensitive issues • Flexible	• Highly dependent on the researcher's interpretation

patch," children talking about toys, or employees talking about their jobs. A moderator begins by providing some opening statement to broadly steer discussion in the intended direction. Ideally, discussion topics emerge at the group's initiative, not the moderator's. Consistent with phenomenological approaches, moderators should avoid direct questioning unless absolutely necessary.

ADVANTAGES OF FOCUS GROUP INTERVIEWS

Focus groups allow people to discuss their true feelings, anxieties, and frustrations, as well as the depth of their convictions, in their own words. While other approaches may also do much the same, focus groups offer several advantages:

1. Relatively fast
2. Easy to execute
3. Allow respondents to piggyback off each other's ideas
4. Provide multiple perspectives
5. Flexibility to allow more detailed descriptions
6. High degree of scrutiny

© SPENCER GRANT/PHOTOEDIT

Focus group facilities typically include a comfortable room for respondents, recording equipment, and a viewing room via a two-way mirror.

Speed and Ease

In an emergency situation, three or four group sessions can be conducted, analyzed, and reported in a week or so. The large number of research firms that conduct focus group interviews makes it easy to find someone to host and conduct the research. Practically every state in the United States contains multiple research firms that have their own focus group facilities. Companies with large research departments likely have at least one qualified focus group moderator so that they need not outsource the focus group.

Piggybacking and Multiple Perspectives

Furthermore, the group approach may produce thoughts that would not be produced otherwise. The interplay between respondents allows them to **piggyback** off each other's ideas. In other words, one respondent stimulates thought among the others and, as this process continues, increasingly creative insights are possible. A comment by one individual often triggers a chain of responses from the other participants. The social nature of the focus group also helps bring out multiple views as each person shares a particular perspective.

Flexibility

The flexibility of focus group interviews is advantageous, especially when compared with the more structured and rigid survey format. Numerous topics can be discussed and many insights can be gained, particularly with regard to the variations in consumer behavior in different situations. Responses that would be unlikely to emerge in a survey often come out in group interviews: "*If* the day is hot and I have to serve the whole neighborhood, I make Kool-Aid; otherwise, I give them Dr Pepper or Coke" or "Usually I work on my projects at home in the evenings, *but* when it is a team project we set aside time on Monday morning and all meet in the conference room."

piggyback

A procedure in which one respondent stimulates thought among the others; as this process continues, increasingly creative insights are possible.

If a researcher is investigating a target group to determine who consumes a particular beverage or why a consumer purchases a certain brand, situational factors must be included in any interpretations of respondent comments. For instance, in the preceding situation, the fact that a particular beverage is consumed must be noted. It would be inappropriate to say that Kool-Aid is preferred in general. The proper interpretation is situation specific. On a hot day the whole neighborhood gets Kool-Aid. When the weather isn't hot, the kids may get nothing, or if only a few kids are around, they may get lucky and get Dr Pepper. Thus, Kool-Aid can be interpreted as appropriate for satisfying large numbers of kids on a hot day while Dr Pepper is a treat for a select few. Similarly, individual assignments are worked on at home in the evenings, while team projects in the morning in the conference room.

Scrutiny

A focus group interview allows closer scrutiny in several ways. First, the session can be observed by several people, as it is usually conducted in a room containing a two-way mirror. The respondents and moderator are on one side, and an invited audience that may include both researchers and decision makers is on the other. If the decision makers are located in another city or country, the session may be shown via a live video hookup. Either through live video or a two-way mirror, some check on the eventual interpretations is provided through the ability to actually watch the research being conducted. If the observers have questions that are not being asked or want the moderator to probe on an issue, they can send a quick text message with instructions to the moderator. Second, focus group sessions are generally recorded on audio or videotape. Later, detailed examination of the recorded session can offer additional insight and help clear up disagreements about what happened.

Focus group discussion with women community by members of ASSEFA (Association for sarva seva farms) Mumbai.

FOCUS GROUP ILLUSTRATION

Focus groups often are used for concept screening and concept refinement. The concept may be continually modified, refined, and retested until management believes it is acceptable. While RJR's initial attempts at smokeless cigarettes failed in the United States, Philip Morris is developing a smokeless cigarette for the U.K. market. Focus groups are being used to help understand how the product will be received and how it might be improved.[23] The voluntary focus group respondents are presented with samples of the product and then they discuss it among themselves. The interview results suggest that the key product features that must be conveyed are the fact that it produces no ashes, no side smoke, and very little odor. These beliefs are expected to lead to a positive attitude. Focus group respondents show little concern about how the cigarette actually functioned. Smokers believe they will use the product if nonsmokers are not irritated by being near someone using the "electronic cigarette." Thus, the focus groups are useful in refining the product and developing a theory of how it should be marketed.

Imagine the differences in reactions to legislation further restricting smoking behavior that would be found among a group of smokers compared to a group of nonsmokers.

GROUP COMPOSITION

The ideal size of the focus group is six to ten people. If the group is too small, one or two members may intimidate the others. Groups that are too large may not allow for adequate participation by each group member.

Homogeneous groups seem to work best because they allow researchers to concentrate on consumers with similar lifestyles, experiences, and communication skills. The session does not become rife with too many arguments and different viewpoints stemming from diverse backgrounds. Also, from an ethnographic perspective,

RESEARCH SNAPSHOT

Overworked and Overpaid? Ethical Issues in Choosing Focus Group Respondents

Focus groups are one of the most sought-after services provided by research firms. What is a research supplier's responsibility when recruiting individuals to participate in a focus group? Practically every focus group interview requires that respondents be selected based on some relevant characteristic. For example, if the topic involves parochial school education, the group should probably not include nonparents or nonparents with no plans of having children or ever putting a child through school. Consumers that fit the desired profile sometimes make poor focus group participants. When a researcher finds good focus group participants, he or she may be tempted to use them over and over again. Is this appropriate? Should respondents be recruited because they will freely offer a lot of discussion without being overbearing or because they have the desired characteristics given the focus group topic? This is a question the focus group planner may well face.

For example, a research client observed a focus group interview being conducted by a research supplier that had previously performed several other projects for the client, each dealing with a quite unique topic. During the interview, the client noticed that some focus group respondents looked familiar.

A few days later, the client reviewed video recordings of the session alongside videotapes from two previous focus groups outsourced to the same company. She found that eight of the ten respondents in the latest focus group had appeared in one of the previous interviews as well. She was furious and considered whether or not she should pay for the interview or bother having a report prepared.

The focus group researcher had taken this approach to make sure the session went smoothly. The moderator solicited subjects who in the past had been found to be very articulate and talkative. In this case, the focus group respondents are more or less "professional," paid participants. It is questionable whether such "professional respondents" can possibly offer relevant opinions on all these topics.

The question is, has the research firm acted in an ethical manner?

the respondents should all be members of a unique and identifiable culture. Vans may benefit from a focus group interview comprised only of skateboard enthusiasts. Perhaps participants can be recruited from a local skate park. However, additional group(s) of participants that are not boarders might be useful in gaining a different perspective.

When the Centers for Disease Control and Prevention tested public service announcements about AIDS through focus groups, it discovered that single-race groups and racially diverse groups reacted differently. By conducting separate focus groups, the organization was able to gain important insights about which creative strategies were most appropriate for targeted versus broad audiences.

For example, for focus groups regarding employee satisfaction, we might want to recruit homogeneous groups based on position in the organization. The researcher may find that entry-level employees have very different perspectives and concerns than those of middle or upper-level management. Also, it is fully understandable that employees might be hesitant to criticize their supervisors. Therefore, researchers may consider interviewing different levels of employees in separate groups.

Researchers who wish to collect information from different types of people should conduct several focus groups. A diverse overall sample may be obtained by using different groups even though each group is homogeneous. For instance, in discussing household chores, four groups might be used:

- Married men
- Married women
- Single men
- Single women

Although each group is homogeneous, by using four groups, researchers obtain opinions from a wide degree of respondents.

ENVIRONMENTAL CONDITIONS

A focus group session may typically take place at the research agency in a room specifically designed for this purpose. Research suppliers that specialize in conducting focus groups operate from commercial facilities that have videotape cameras in observation rooms behind two-way mirrors and microphone systems connected to tape recorders and speakers to allow greater scrutiny as discussed above. Refreshments are provided to help create a more relaxed atmosphere conducive to a free exchange of ideas. More open and intimate reports of personal experiences and sentiments can be obtained under these conditions.

moderator

A person who leads a focus group interview and ensures that everyone gets a chance to speak and contribute to the discussion.

THE FOCUS GROUP MODERATOR

The **moderator** essentially runs the focus group and plays a critical role in its success. There are several qualities that a good moderator must possess:

1. The moderator must be able to develop rapport with the group to promote interaction among all participants. The moderator should be someone who is really interested in people, who listens carefully to what others have to say, and who can readily establish rapport, gain people's confidence, and make them feel relaxed and eager to talk.
2. The moderator must be a good listener. Careful listening is especially important because the group interview's purpose is to stimulate spontaneous responses. Without good listening skills, the moderator may direct the group in an unproductive direction.
3. The moderator must try not to interject his or her own opinions. Good moderators usually say less rather than more. They can stimulate productive discussion with generalized follow-ups such as, "Tell us more about that incident," or "How are your experiences similar or different from the one you just heard?" The moderator must be particularly careful not to ask leading questions such as "You are happy to work at Acme, aren't you?"
4. The moderator must be able to control discussion without being overbearing. The moderator's role is also to focus the discussion on the areas of concern. When a topic is no longer generating fresh ideas, the effective moderator changes the flow of discussion. The moderator does not give the group total control of the discussion, but he or she normally has prepared questions on topics that concern management. However, the timing of these questions in the discussion and the manner in which they are raised are left to the moderator's discretion. The term *focus group* thus stems from the moderator's task. He or she starts out by asking for a general discussion but usually *focuses* in on specific topics during the session.

PLANNING THE FOCUS GROUP OUTLINE

discussion guide

A focus group outline that includes written introductory comments informing the group about the focus group purpose and rules and then outlines topics or questions to be addressed in the group session.

Focus group researchers use a discussion guide to help control the interview and guide the discussion into product areas. A **discussion guide** includes written introductory comments informing the group about the focus group purpose and rules and then outlines topics or questions to be addressed in the group session. Thus, the discussion guide serves as the focus group outline. Some discussion guides will have only a few phrases in the entire document. Others may be more detailed. The amount of content depends on the nature and experience of the researcher and the complexity of the topic.

Researchers who planned the outline established certain objectives for each part of the focus group. The initial effort was to break the ice and establish rapport within the group. The logical flow of the group session then moved from general discussion about sunbathing to more focused discussion of types of warnings about danger from sun exposure.

In general, the following steps should be used to conduct an effective focus group discussion guide:

1. Welcome and introductions should take place first.
2. Begin the interview with a broad icebreaker that does not reveal too many specifics about the interview. Sometimes, this may even involve respondents providing some written story or their reaction to some stimulus like a photograph, film, product, or advertisement.

3. Questions become increasingly more specific as the interview proceeds. However, the moderator will notice that a good interview will cover the specific question topics before they have to be asked. This is preferable as respondents are clearly not forced to react to the specific issue; it just emerges naturally.
4. If there is a very specific objective to be accomplished, such as explaining why a respondent would either buy or not buy a product, that question should probably be saved for last.
5. A debriefing statement should provide respondents with the actual focus group objectives and answering any questions they may have. This is also a final shot to gain some insight from the group.

FOCUS GROUPS AS DIAGNOSTIC TOOLS

Focus groups are perhaps the predominant means by which business researchers implement exploratory research designs. Focus groups also can be helpful in later stages of a research project, particularly when the findings from surveys or other quantitative techniques raise more questions than they answer. Managers who are puzzled about the meaning of survey research results may use focus groups to better understand what survey results indicate. In such a situation, the focus group supplies diagnostic help after quantitative research has been conducted.

Focus groups are also excellent diagnostic tools for spotting problems with ideas. For instance, idea screening is often done with focus groups. An initial concept is presented to the group and then they are allowed to comment on it in detail. This usually leads to lengthy lists of potential product problems and some ideas for overcoming them. Mature products can also be "focus-grouped" in this manner.

VIDEOCONFERENCING AND FOCUS GROUPS

With the widespread utilization of videoconferencing, the number of companies using these systems to conduct focus groups has increased. With videoconference focus groups, managers can stay home and watch on television rather than having to take a trip to a focus group facility.

FocusVision (**http://www.focusvision.com/**) is a business research company that provides videoconferencing equipment and services. The FocusVision system is modular, allowing for easy movement and an ability to capture each group member close up. The system operates via a remote keypad that allows observers in a far-off location to pan the focus group room or zoom in on a particular participant. Managers viewing at remote locations can send the moderator messages during the interview.

INTERACTIVE MEDIA AND ONLINE FOCUS GROUPS

Internet applications of qualitative exploratory research are growing rapidly and involve both formal and informal applications. Formally, the term **online focus group** refers to a qualitative research effort in which a group of individuals provides unstructured comments by entering their remarks into an electronic Internet display board of some type, such as a chat-room session or in the form of a blog. Because respondents enter their comments into the computer, transcripts of verbatim responses are available immediately after the group session. Online groups can be quick and cost-efficient. However, because there is less personal interaction between participants, group synergy and snowballing of ideas may be diminished.

online focus group
A qualitative research effort in which a group of individuals provides unstructured comments by entering their remarks into an electronic Internet display board of some type.

Several companies have established a form of informal, "continuous" focus group by establishing an Internet blog for that purpose.[24] We might call this technique a **focus blog** when the intention is to mine the site for business research purposes. General Motors, American Express, and Lego all have used ideas harvested from their focus blogs. When operating, the Lego blog can be found at **http://legoisfun.blogspot.com**. While traditional focus group respondents are generally paid

focus blog
A type of informal, "continuous" focus group established as an Internet blog for the purpose of collecting qualitative data from participant comments.

$100 or more to show up and participate for 90 minutes, bloggers and online focus group respondents often participate for absolutely no fee at all! Thus, technology provides some cost advantages over traditional focus group approaches.[25]

ONLINE VERSUS FACE-TO-FACE FOCUS GROUP TECHNIQUES

A research company can facilitate a formal online focus group by setting up a private chat room for that purpose. Participants in formal and informal online focus groups feel that their anonymity is very secure. Often respondents will say things in this environment that they would never say otherwise. For example, a lingerie company was able to get insights into how it could design sexy products for larger women. Online, these women freely discussed what it would take "to feel better about being naked."[26] One can hardly imagine how difficult such a discussion might be face to face. Increased anonymity can be a major advantage for a company investigating sensitive or embarrassing issues.

Because participants do not have to be together in the same room at a research facility, the number of participants in online focus groups can be larger than in traditional focus groups. Twenty-five participants or more is not uncommon for the simultaneous chat-room format. Participants can be at widely separated locations since the Internet does not have geographical restrictions. Of course, a major disadvantage is that often the researcher does not exercise as much control in precisely who participates. In other words, a person could very easily not match the desired profile or even answer screening questions in a misleading way simply to participate.

A major drawback with online focus groups is that moderators cannot see body language and facial expressions (bewilderment, excitement, boredom, interest, and so forth). Thus, they cannot fully interpret how people are reacting. Also, moderators' ability to probe and ask additional questions on the spot is reduced in online focus groups. Research that requires focus group members to actually touch something (such as a new easy-opening packaging design) or taste something is not generally suitable for an online format.

DISADVANTAGES OF FOCUS GROUPS

Focus groups offer many advantages as a form of qualitative research. Like practically every other research technique, the focus group has some limitations and disadvantages as well. Problems with focus groups include those discussed below.

First, focus groups require objective, sensitive, and effective moderators. It is very difficult for a moderator to remain completely objective about most topics. In large research firms, the moderator may be provided only enough information to effectively conduct the interview, no more. The focus group interview obviously shouldn't reduce to, or even be influenced by, the moderator's opinion. Also, without a good moderator, one or two participants may dominate a session, yielding results that are really the opinion of one or two people, not the group. The moderator has to try very hard to make sure that all respondents feel comfortable giving their opinions and even a timid respondent's opinion is given due consideration. While many people, even some with little or no background to do so, conduct focus groups, good moderators become effective through a combination of naturally good people skills, training (in qualitative research), and experience.

Second, some unique sampling problems arise with focus groups. Researchers often select focus group participants because they have similar backgrounds and experiences or because screening indicates that the participants are more articulate or gregarious than the typical consumer (see the Research Snapshot "Overworked and Overpaid?"). Such participants may not be representative of the entire target market. Thus, focus group results are not intended to be representative of a larger population.

Third, although not so much an issue with online formats where respondents can remain anonymous, traditional face-to-face focus groups may not be useful for discussing sensitive topics. A focus group is a social setting and usually involves people with little to no familiarity with each other. Therefore, issues that people normally do not like to discuss in public may also prove difficult to discuss in a focus group.

Fourth, focus groups do cost a considerable amount of money, particularly when they are not conducted by someone employed by the company desiring the focus group. As research projects go, there are many more expensive approaches, including a full-blown mail survey using a national random sample. This may cost thousands of dollars to conduct and thousands of dollars to analyze and disseminate. Focus group prices vary regionally, but the following figures provide a rough guideline:

Renting facilities and equipment	$500
Recruiting of respondents ($75 person)	$750
Paying respondents ($100/person)	$1,000
Researcher costs	
• Preparation	$750
• Moderating	$1,000
• Analysis and report preparation	$1,500
Miscellaneous expenses	$250

TOTHEPOINT

Necessity, mother of invention.

—William Wycherley

Thus, a client can expect a professional focus group to cost over $5,000 in most situations. Further, most business topics will call for multiple focus groups. There is some cost advantage in this, as some costs will not change proportionately just because there are multiple interviews. Preparation costs may be the same for one or more interviews; the analysis and report preparation will likely only increase slightly because two or three interviews are included instead of one.

INTERPRETATION OF FGDs[27]

1. Read all the summaries obtained and note the potential trends and patterns, and strongly held or frequently aired opinions.
2. Highlight sections that correspond to the discussion guide questions and mark comments that could be used in the final report.
3. Pinpoint major ideas, allocate time to step back, and reflect on major findings.

Transcript of Focus Group Discussion

Question: Are you health conscious?
Response: Yes
Remark: It was an emphatic yes from the entire group which proves that people are very particular about their health.

Question: Do you consume carbonated drinks?
Response:
2/5 - regularly
1/5 - once or twice a week
Remark: None of the members of the group consumes carbonated drinks on a daily basis. It is reasonable to believe that there are many people out there doing this on a daily basis. Hence, the group does not cover all kinds of consumers.

Question: Are you aware of its harmful effects?
Response: 4/5 - yes
(Pesticides, not good for health/teeth, high calorie content, artificial additives, and substances)
Remark: So people are aware that what they are consuming is not right which leads us to our next question.

Question:Given a choice, would you like to shift to juices from carbonated drinks?
Response: 4/5 - yes
Remark: This shows that people are willing to shift and it is probably the lack of certain factors which is stopping them from doing it. We shall further explore those factors.

Question: What is the important factor in a juice?
Response: Taste (very imp)
Remark: Invariably, taste was a key decision element for the group.

Question: Would price be a consideration?
Response: 3/5 - yes

Question: Please write down how much are you willing to pay for a standard quantity—200-300 ml of juice?
Following prices were suggested by some members of the group. The price points were intentionally not suggested so as to allow the group to reveal how much they could pay.
Option ₹ 10-15 - (4/4 of the other members agreed to this)
Option ₹ 15-20 - (2/4 of the other members agreed to this)

Question: Does packaging matter?
Response: 3/5 - yes
Remark: Members also stressed on the need for more "grown-up" packaging like tins, cans, or tetra packs without using straws. A member suggested that in 200 ml juice tetra pack closable flops are not present. This results in spilling of the packaged juice when the tetra pack is held too tightly. They also cannot be kept for after use.

Question: Are you willing to pay extra for new and attractive packaging?
Response: Few were willing to pay extra. The exact count could not be taken because some members changed their minds after further deliberation.

Question: How many people want new packaging?
The following samples were shown:

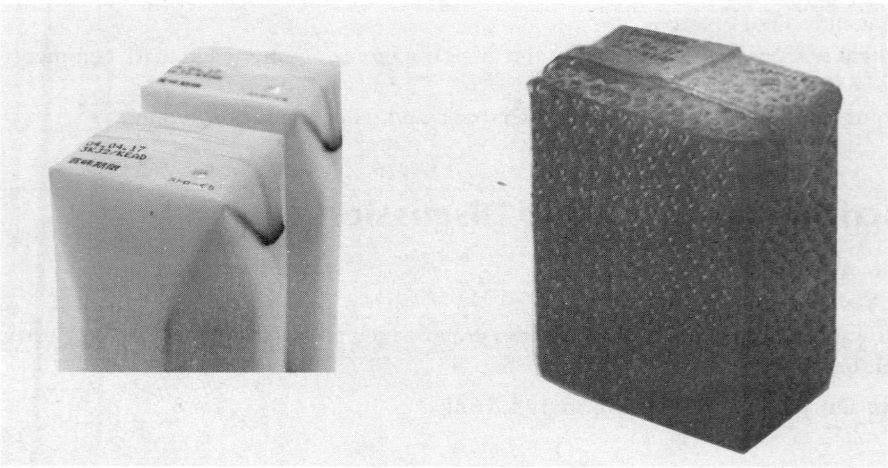

Response: 5/5 - yes

Question: Does brand matter?
Response: People associate taste with a particular brand.

Question: Do you go through the information written on the tetra pack?
Response: None of the members
Remark: The tendency to check the nutritional contents as claimed by the juice manufacturer is low among the participants. The decision to buy packaged juices is a low-involvement decision.

Question: Would you like to go to a fresh fruit juice outlet?
Response: 5/5 - yes

Question: What do you think about the local juice centers?
Response: Bad hygiene - 5/5
Bad ambience - 5/5

Question: Would you like to go to a branded juice bar offering quality service and products (fresh fruit juices) in an ambient setting, for example, like Café Coffee Day, only more healthier?

Response: Yes - 5/5

Question: Would you pay extra for a glass of juice in these outlets?

Response: Yes - 5/5

Remark: One member suggested ₹ 40-50 for a glass of juice depending on service and ambience. Also one member suggested a need for good chic ambience and healthy and fit looking waiter/waitress.

These questions formed the basis of our questionnaire session and tried to cover our topic of research which was basically to understand the consumption behavior of consumer and his/her choice of drinking in juice bars.

Analysis and Interpretations

Our findings from the FGD conducted were as follows:

i. Price only next to taste - Consumers would like to make a switch from carbonated to non-carbonated drinks like natural or flavored juices if given ample choices to pick up from. And they would prioritize taste over price and, therefore, would be ready to receive a better tasting drink even if it comes for higher price.

ii. Need to highlight benefits - Every other person today is conscious about his/her health and well aware of serious ill-effects of taking carbonated cold drinks but the belief that healthy drinks could boost their health yet needs to be ascertained, which is quite critical to gain the market share.

iii. Better packaging - Sufficient attention needs to be paid to the packaging of the product as it is one of the many critical factors which influence the purchasing decision of the consumer. Current packaging, although very attractive, has many flaws which effect consumer while drinking and storing the juices. The need for flops in the tetra packs was stressed upon by the participants. Attractive fruit-like packaging was also unanimously endorsed.

iv. Lack of "good" consumption environment - Middle class population, calculably the biggest segment of soft drinks consumers, is open to the idea of opening of juice parlors/bars like the chains Cafe Coffee Day, Coffee Beans, which have come up recently and gained huge acceptance among wide variety of people primarily for their ambience, quality of service, and consistency and hygiene of products.

v. Raise of attached "cool" quotient - Bringing up the juices as something which would be considered "cool" to consume could give a good and sustained lift to its sales, as even today youth which attends parties and college-goers would find it "uncool" to drink juices compared to carbonated beverages such as Thumps-Up or Coke.

Depth Interviews

An alternative to a focus group is a depth interview. A **depth interview** is a one-on-one interview between a professional researcher and a research respondent. Depth interviews are much the same as a psychological, clinical interview, but with a different purpose. The researcher asks many questions and follows up each answer with probes for additional elaboration.

Like focus group moderators, the interviewer's role is critical in a depth interview. He or she must be a highly skilled individual who can encourage the respondent to talk freely without influencing the direction of the conversation. Probing questions are critical.

Laddering is a term used for a particular approach to probing, asking respondents to compare differences between brands at different levels. What usually results is that the first distinctions

depth interview
A one-on-one interview between a professional researcher and a research respondent conducted about some relevant business or social topic.

laddering
A particular approach to probing, asking respondents to compare differences between brands at different levels that produces distinctions at the attribute level, the benefit level, and the value or motivation level.

are attribute-level distinctions, the second are benefit-level distinctions, and the third are at the value or motivation level. Laddering can then distinguish two brands of skateboarding shoes based on a) the materials they are made of, b) the comfort they provide, and c) the excitement they create.

Each depth interview may last more than an hour. Thus, it is a time-consuming process if multiple interviews are conducted. Not only does the interview have to be conducted, but each interview produces about the same amount of text as does a focus group interview. This has to be analyzed and interpreted by the researcher. A third major issue stems from the necessity of recording both surface reactions and subconscious motivations of the respondent. Analysis and interpretation of such data are highly subjective, and it is difficult to settle on a true interpretation.

Depth interviews provide more insight into a particular individual than do focus groups. In addition, since the setting isn't really social, respondents are more likely to discuss sensitive topics than are those in a focus group. Depth interviews are particularly advantageous when some unique or unusual behavior is being studied. For instance, depth interviews have been usefully applied to reveal characteristics of adolescent behavior, ranging from the ways they get what they want from their parents to shopping, smoking, and shoplifting.[28]

Depth interviews are similar to focus groups in many ways. The costs are similar if only a few interviews are conducted. However, if a dozen or more interviews are included in a report, the costs are higher than focus group interviews due to the increased interviewing and analysis time.

Characteristics of Depth Interviews

Depth interviews are unstructured and interactive way of collecting information for a particular research. While in focus group interview, the number of participants ranges between 8 and 12, depth interviews are conducted by the interviewer with one respondent at a time. It is about a particular product, brand, idea, etc. A depth interview usually lasts from 30 minutes to 2 hours. For a high-end product like automobile purchase where it is not possible to assemble several prospective buyers at one place at one particular time, depth interviews seem to be extremely useful. Depth interviews are also useful for personal products like contraceptives, AIDS vaccine, sanitary napkins, etc. Discussions of sensitive and confidential topics can easily be done through depth interview which otherwise is not possible in focus group interviews.

While the interviewer catalogue is a broad guideline of the interview, often a specific discussion depends upon perception and feelings of the interviewee and his responses during the time of the interview.

Depth interview has several advantages over focus group interview, since due to its individualistic nature of interviewee-interviewer interaction several important information of consumer buying behavior can be obtained. Depth interview encourages free extent of information between interviewer and interviewee which otherwise is not possible when the discussion happens in a group.

While depth interview has several advantages over focus group interview, it does have several drawbacks as well. The quality and sufficiency of information from a depth interview largely depends on the ability and expertise of the interviewer. Skilled interviewers are of high demand and quite expensive. At the same time, discussions resulted from group dynamics are absent in depth interview. Depth interviews are also not effective when marketers want to know the features of the new product that they want to develop.

conversations
An informal qualitative data-gathering approach in which the researcher engages a respondent in a discussion of the relevant subject matter.

Conversations

Holding **conversations** in qualitative research is an informal data-gathering approach in which the researcher engages a respondent in a discussion of the relevant subject matter. This approach is almost completely unstructured and the researcher enters the conversation with few expectations. The goal is to have the respondent produce a dialogue about his or her lived experiences. Meaning will be extracted from the resulting dialogue.

A conversational approach to qualitative research is particularly appropriate in phenomenological research and for developing grounded theory. In our Vans experience, the researcher may simply tape-record a conversation about becoming a "skater." The resulting dialogue can then be analyzed for themes and plots. The result may be some interesting and novel insight into the consumption patterns of skaters, for example, if the respondent said,

"I knew I was a real skater when I just had to have Vans, not just for boarding, but for wearing."

This theme may connect to a right-of-passage plot and show how Vans play a role in this process.

Technology is also influencing conversational research. Online communications such as the reviews posted about book purchases at **http://www.barnesandnoble.com** can be treated as a conversation. Companies may discover product problems and ideas for overcoming them by analyzing these computer-based consumer dialogues.[29]

A conversational approach is advantageous because each interview is usually inexpensive to conduct. Respondents often need not be paid. They are relatively effective at getting at sensitive issues once the researcher establishes a rapport with them. Conversational approaches, however, are prone to produce little relevant information since little effort is made to steer the conversation. Additionally, the data analysis is very much researcher-dependent.

SEMI-STRUCTURED INTERVIEWS

Semi-structured interviews usually come in written form and ask respondents for short essay responses to specific open-ended questions. Respondents are free to write as much or as little as they want. The questions would be divided into sections, typically, and within each section, the opening question would be followed by some probing questions. When these are performed face to face, there is room for less structured follow-ups.

The advantages to this approach include an ability to address more specific issues. Responses are usually easier to interpret than other qualitative approaches. Since the researcher can simply prepare the questions in writing ahead of time, and if in writing, the questions are administered without the presence of an interviewer, semi-structured interviews can be relatively cost-effective.

Some researchers interested in studying car salesperson stereotypes used qualitative semi-structured interviews to map consumers' cognitions (memory). The semi-structured interview began with a free-association task:

List the first five things that come into your mind when you think of a "car salesman."

This was followed up with a probing question:

Describe the way a typical "car salesman" looks.

This was followed with questions about how the car salesperson acts and how the respondent feels in the presence of a car salesperson. The results led to research showing how the information that consumers process differs in the presence of a typical car salesperson, as opposed to a less typical car salesperson.[30]

SOCIAL NETWORKING

Social networking is one of the most impactful trends in recent times. For many consumers, particularly younger generations, social networking sites like MySpace, Second Life, Zebo, and others have become the primary tool for communicating with friends both far and near and known and unknown. Social networking has replaced large volumes of e-mail and, many would say, face-to-face communications as well. While the impact that social networking will eventually have on society is an interesting question, what is most relevant to marketing research is the large portion of this information that discusses marketing and consumer related information.

Companies can assign research assistants to monitor these sites for information related to their particular brands. The information can be coded as either positive or negative. When too much negative information is being spread, the company can try to react to change the opinions. In addition, many companies like P&G and Ford maintain their own social networking sites for the purpose of gathering research data. In a way, these social networking sites are a way that companies can eavesdrop on consumer conversations and discover key information about their products. The textual data that consumers willingly put up becomes like a conversation. When researchers get the opportunity to react with consumers or employees through a social network site, they can function much like an online focus group or interview.

Free-Association/Sentence Completion Method

free-association techniques
Record respondents' first (top-of-mind) cognitive reactions to some stimulus.

Free-association techniques simply record a respondent's first cognitive reactions (top-of-mind) to some stimulus. The Rorschach or inkblot test typifies the free-association method. Respondents view an ambiguous figure and are asked to say the first thing that comes to their mind. Free-association techniques allow researchers to map a respondent's thoughts or memory.

The sentence completion method is based on free-association principles. Respondents simply are required to complete a few partial sentences with the first word or phrase that comes to mind. For example:

People who drink beer are ______________________.
A man who drinks a dark beer is ______________________.
Imported beer is most liked by ______________________.
The woman drinking beer in the commercial ______________________.

Answers to sentence-completion questions tend to be more extensive than responses to word-association tests. Although the responses lack the ability to probe for meaning as in other qualitative techniques, they are very effective in finding out what is on a respondent's mind. They can also do so in a quick and very cost-effective manner. Free-association and sentence-completion tasks are sometimes used in conjunction with other approaches. For instance, they can sometimes be used as effective icebreakers in focus group interviews.

OBSERVATION

Observation can be a very important qualitative tool. The participant-observer approach typifies how observation can be used to explore various issues. Meaning is extracted from field notes. **Field notes** are the researchers' descriptions of what actually happens in the field. These notes then become the text from which meaning is extracted.

field notes
The researcher's descriptions of what actually happens in the field; these notes then become the text from which meaning is extracted.

Observation may also take place in visual form. Researchers may observe employees in their workplace, consumers in their home, or try to gain knowledge from photographic records of one type or another. Observation can either be very inexpensive, such as when a research associate sits and simply observes behavior, or it can be very expensive, as in most participant-observer studies. Observational research is keenly advantageous for gaining insight into things that respondents cannot or will not verbalize. Observation research is a common method of data collection and is the focus of a later chapter.

COLLAGES

Business researchers sometimes have respondents prepare a collage to represent their experiences. The collages are then analyzed for meaning much in the same manner as text dialogues are analyzed. Computer software can even be applied to help develop potential grounded theories from the visual representations.

Harley-Davidson commissioned research in which collages depicting feelings about Harley-Davidson were compared based on whether the respondent was a Harley owner or an owner of a competitor's brand. The collages of "Hog" owners revealed themes of artwork and the freedom of the great outdoors. These themes did not emerge in the non-Hog groups. This led to confirmatory research which helped Harley continue its growth, appealing more specifically to its diverse market segments.[31]

Like sentence completion and word association, collages are often used within some other approach, such as a focus group or a depth interview. Collages offer the advantage of flexibility but are also very much subject to the researcher's interpretations.

PROJECTIVE RESEARCH TECHNIQUES

A **projective technique** is an indirect means of questioning enabling respondents to project beliefs and feelings onto a third party, an inanimate object, or a task situation. Projective techniques usually encourage respondents to describe a situation in their own words with little prompting by the interviewer. Individuals are expected to interpret the situation within the context of their own experiences, attitudes, and personalities and to express opinions and emotions that may be hidden from others and possibly themselves. Projective techniques are particularly useful in studying sensitive issues.

projective technique
An indirect means of questioning enabling respondents to project beliefs and feelings onto a third party, an inanimate object, or a task situation.

There is an old story about asking a man why he purchased a Mercedes-Benz. When asked directly why he purchased a Mercedes, he responds that the car holds its value and does not depreciate much, that it gets better gas mileage than you'd expect, or that it has a comfortable ride. If you ask the same person why a neighbor purchased a Mercedes, he may well answer, "Oh, that status seeker!" This story illustrates that individuals may be more likely to give true answers (consciously or unconsciously) to disguised questions, and a projective technique provides a way of disguising just who is being described.

THEMATIC APPERCEPTION TEST (TAT)

thematic apperception test (TAT)
A test that presents subjects with an ambiguous picture(s) in which consumers and products are the center of attention; the investigator asks the subject to tell what is happening in the picture(s) now and what might happen next.

A **thematic apperception test (TAT)**, sometimes called the *picture interpretation technique,* presents subjects with an ambiguous picture(s) and asks the subject to tell what is happening in the picture(s) now and what might happen next. Hence, themes (*thematic*) are elicited on the basis of the perceptual-interpretive (*apperception*) use of the pictures. The researcher then analyzes the contents of the stories that the subjects relate. A TAT represents a projective research technique.

Frequently, the TAT consists of a series of pictures with some continuity so that stories may be constructed in a variety of settings. The first picture might portray a person working at their desk; in the second picture, a person that could be a supervisor is talking to the worker; the final picture might show the original employee and another having a discussion at the water cooler. A Vans TAT might include several ambiguous pictures of a skateboarder and then show him or her heading to the store. This might reveal ideas about the brands and products that fit the role of skateboarder.

The picture or cartoon stimulus must be sufficiently interesting to encourage discussion but ambiguous enough not to disclose the nature of the research project. Clues should not be given to the character's positive or negative predisposition. A pretest of a TAT investigating why men might purchase chainsaws used a picture of a man looking at a very large tree. The research respondents were homeowners and weekend woodcutters. They almost unanimously said that they would get professional help from a tree surgeon to deal with this situation. Thus, early in pretesting, the researchers found out that the picture was not sufficiently ambiguous. The tree was too large and did not allow respondents to identify with the tree-cutting task. If subjects are to project their own views into the situation, the environmental setting should be a well-defined, familiar problem, but the solution should be ambiguous.

An example of a TAT using a cartoon drawing in which the respondent suggests a dialogue in which the characters might engage is provided in Exhibit 7.5. This TAT is a purposely ambiguous illustration of an everyday occurrence. The two office workers are shown in a situation and the respondent is asked what the woman might be talking about. This setting could be used for discussions about the organization's management, store personnel, particular software products, and so on.

Projective technique is an indirect form of extracting information while respondents project their underlying beliefs and attitudes on a particular issue. While focus group interviews and depth interviews are direct approach of qualitative research, projective technique is an indirect approach. In this procedure, respondents indirectly describe their behavior, beliefs, attribute, and feelings. There are four different techniques that researchers adopt while doing a projective technique. These are:

1. Association techniques
2. Completion techniques
3. Construction techniques
4. Expressive techniques

Association technique. In this technique, respondents are asked to describe their stimuli through words that immediately come to their mind. The respondents are given a list of words and are asked to say the word that comes to their mind for each word in the list. The words in the list, which are words for experiment, are jumbled with a few other words which are not related to the research. This is done to disguise the words that the researchers are interested to know the feelings of the respondent. Psychological reminds of association techniques that realize on the assumption that consumers reveal their perception and feelings about an issue to associative words. This methodology of analysis is done by counting the frequency of a particular word, time taken for a response, percentage of respondents who have used a particular word, and number of related

EXHIBIT 7.5

An Example of a TAT Picture

words used by respondents. A subjective evaluation from such an analysis is done by designating where the respondents have a positive, negative, or neutral view for a particular issue. Percentage of respondents who have positive views or negative views or neutral views are also calculated and used for further research.

Completion techniques. In this method of projective techniques, an incomplete sentence or story is given to the respondents and they are asked to complete the sentence or story. On the basis of words selected to complete the remaining sentence, the researchers figure out the underlying feelings and motivation of the respondent on a particular issue. The advantage of completion techniques over association technique is that sentence completion or story completion renders additional information about the issue under study.

Construction techniques. In this method of projective techniques, respondents are asked to construct their responses on a particular issue in the form of dialogue or description. While structurally this technique of qualitative research is very similar to completion techniques, however, construction techniques are more flexible to the respondent as the researchers give little prompt and structure than what they give in completion techniques. In typical construction techniques, the respondents are shown a series of pictures and are asked to tell stories on those pictures. The stories reflect individual's personality in interpreting those pictures. A commonly used taste in construction techniques is thematic appreciation test (TAT).

Expressive techniques. In this method of projective technique, the respondents are shown or described a particular situation and then asked to illustrate their opinion about other people's motivation and feeling. In other words, in this technique respondents do not express their own feelings and motivations, however, illustrate what others would feel in that particular situation. These techniques rely on the assumption that respondent, through their opinion about others, would implicitly say what respondents actually feel. One of the very commonly used expressive techniques is role playing. In role playing, respondents are asked to assume role of a particular character or stakeholder, and then express their position on that role. Researchers then consider respondents, who project about others, actually representing their own opinion into that role.

Exploratory Research in Science and in Practice

Misuses of Exploratory and Qualitative Research

Any research tool can be misapplied. Exploratory research cannot take the place of conclusive, confirmatory research. Thus, since many qualitative tools are best applied in exploratory design, they are likewise limited in the ability to draw conclusive inferences—test hypotheses. One of the biggest drawbacks is the subjectivity that comes along with "interpretation." In fact, sometimes the term *interpretive* research is used synonymously with qualitative research. When only one researcher interprets the meaning of what a single person said in a depth interview or similar technique, one should be very cautious before major business decisions are made based on these results. Is the result replicable? **Replication** means that the same results and conclusions will be drawn if the study is repeated by different researchers with different respondents following the same methods. In other words, would the same conclusion be reached based on another researcher's interpretation?

replication
The same interpretation will be drawn if the study is repeated by different researchers with different respondents following the same methods.

Indeed, some qualitative research methodologies were generally frowned upon for years based on a few early and public misapplications during what became known as the "motivational research" era. While many of the ideas produced during this time had some merit, as can sometimes be the case, too few researchers did too much interpretation of too few respondents. Compounding this, managers were quick to act on the results, believing that the results peaked

TIPS OF THE TRADE

© iStock

- Keep in mind two key differentiators between qualitative and quantitative research:
    - Qualitative research does not necessarily possess intersubjective certifiability. Two researchers can have the same experience or observe the same phenomena and have different interpretations.
    - We do not have the ability to make statistical generalizations from qualitative data. While numbers might appear—for example, we may observe that eight of the ten focus group participants mentioned the need for better on-the-job training—we cannot project this onto the population (i.e., we cannot conclude 80 percent of all employees feel we need better on-the-job training).
- It is incorrect to conclude one type of research is "better" than another, but certainly one type is more appropriate in a given set of circumstances. Qualitative research tends to be well suited for exploratory purposes, including clarifying the research objective and identifying testable hypotheses. Qualitative research is often followed up by a quantitative study for confirmation. However, there are also instances when qualitative research follows a quantitative study for "sense making" and deeper insight into numerical results.
- Focus groups and depth interviews are the most common qualitative research techniques.

inside one's subliminal consciousness and therefore held some type of extra power. Thus, often the research was flawed based on poor interpretation, and the decision process was flawed because the deciders acted prematurely. As examples, projective techniques and depth interviews were frequently used in the late 1950s and early 1960s, producing some interesting and occasionally bizarre reasons for consumers' purchasing behavior:

- A woman is very serious when she bakes a cake because unconsciously she is going through the symbolic act of giving birth.
- A man buys a convertible as a substitute mistress and a safer (and potentially cheaper) way of committing adultery.
- Men who wear suspenders are reacting to an unresolved castration complex.[32]

About two decades later, researchers for McCann-Erickson advertising agency interviewed low-income women using a form of TAT involving story completion regarding attitudes toward insecticides. Themes noted included:

- The joy of victory over roaches (watching them die or seeing them dead)
- Using the roach as a metaphor through which women can take out their hostility toward men (women generally referred to roaches as "he" instead of "she" in their stories).[33]

Certainly, some useful findings resulted. Even today, we have the Pillsbury Doughboy as evidence that useful ideas were produced. In many of these cases, interpretations were either misleading or too ambitious (taken too far). However, many companies became frustrated when decisions based upon motivational research approaches proved poor. Thus, researchers moved away from qualitative tools during the late 1960s and 1970s. Today, however, qualitative tools have won acceptance once again as researchers realize they have greater power in discovering insights that would be difficult to capture in typical survey research (which is limited as an exploratory tool).

SCIENTIFIC DECISION PROCESSES

Objectivity and replicability are two characteristics of scientific inquiry. Are focus groups objective and replicable? Would three different researchers all interpret focus group data identically? How should a facial expression or nod of the head be interpreted? Have subjects fully grasped the idea or concept behind a nonexistent product? Have respondents overstated their satisfaction because they think their supervisor will read the report and recognize them from their comments? Many of these questions are reduced to a matter of opinion that may vary from researcher to researcher and from one respondent group to another. Therefore, a focus group, or a depth interview, or TAT alone does not best represent a complete scientific inquiry.

However, if the thoughts discovered through these techniques survive preliminary evaluations and are developed into research hypotheses, they can be further tested. These tests may involve survey research or an experiment testing an idea very specifically (for example, if a certain advertising slogan is more effective than another). Thus, exploratory research approaches using qualitative research tools are very much a *part* of scientific inquiry. However, before making a *scientific* decision, a research project should include a confirmatory study using objective tools and an adequate sample in terms of both size and how well it represents a population.

But is a *scientific* decision approach always used or needed? In practice, many business decisions are based solely on the results of focus group interviews or some other exploratory result. The primary reasons for this are (1) time, (2) money, and (3) emotion.

TIME

Sometimes, researchers simply are not given enough time to follow up on exploratory research results. Companies feel an increasingly urgent need to get new products to the market faster. Thus, a seemingly good idea generated in a focus group (like Clear, Vanilla, or Cherry Dr Pepper) is simply not tested with a more conclusive study. The risk of delaying a decision may be seen as greater than the risk of proceeding without completing the scientific process. Thus, although the researcher may warn against it, there may be logical reasons for such action. The decision makers should be aware, though, that the conclusions drawn from exploratory research designs are just that—exploratory. Thus, there is less likelihood of good results from the decision than if the research process had involved further testing.

MONEY

Similarly, researchers sometimes do not follow up on exploratory research results because they believe the cost is too high. Realize that tens of thousands of dollars may have already been spent on qualitative research. Managers who are unfamiliar with research will be very tempted to wonder, "Why do I need yet another study?" and "What did I spend all that money for?" Thus, they choose to proceed based only on exploratory results. Again, the researcher has fulfilled the professional obligation as long as the tentative nature of any ideas derived from exploratory research has been relayed through the research report.

Again, this isn't always a bad approach. If the decision itself does not involve a great deal of risk or if it can be reversed easily, the best course of action may be to proceed to implementation instead of investing more money in confirmatory research. Remember, research shouldn't be performed if it will cost more than it will return.

EMOTION

Time, money, and emotion are all related. Decision makers sometimes become so anxious to have something resolved, or they get so excited about some novel discovery resulting from a focus group interview, that they may act rashly. Perhaps some of the ideas produced during the motivational research era sounded so enticing that decision makers got caught up in the emotion of the moment and proceeded without the proper amount of testing. Thus, as in life, when we fall in love with something, we are prone to act irrationally. The chances of emotion interfering in this way are lessened, but not reduced, by making sure multiple decision makers are involved in the decision process.

In conclusion, we began this section by suggesting that exploratory, qualitative research cannot take the place of a confirmatory study. However, a confirmatory study cannot take the place of an exploratory, qualitative study either. While confirmatory studies are best for testing specific ideas, a qualitative study is far better suited to developing ideas and practical theories.

Summary

1. List and understand the differences between qualitative research and quantitative research. The chapter emphasized that any argument about the overall superiority of qualitative versus quantitative research is misplaced. Rather, each approach has advantages and disadvantages that make it appropriate in certain situations. The presence or absence of numbers is not the key factor discriminating between qualitative and quantitative research. Qualitative research relies more on researchers' subjective interpretations of text or other visual material. In contrast, the numbers produced in quantitative research are objective in the sense that they don't change simply because someone else computed them. Thus, we expect quantitative research to have intersubjective certifiability, while qualitative research may not. Qualitative research typically involves small samples while quantitative research usually uses large samples. Qualitative procedures are generally more flexible and produce deeper and more elaborate explanations than quantitative research.

2. Understand the role of qualitative research in exploratory research designs. The high degree of flexibility that goes along with most qualitative techniques makes it very useful in exploratory research designs. Therefore, exploratory research designs most often involve some qualitative research technique.

3. Describe the basic qualitative research orientations. Phenomenology is a philosophical approach to studying human experiences based on the idea that human experience itself is inherently subjective and determined by the context within which a person experiences something. It lends itself well to conversational research. Ethnography represents ways of studying cultures through methods that include high involvement with that culture. Participant-observation is a common ethnographic approach. Grounded theory represents inductive qualitative investigation in which the researcher continually poses questions about a respondent's discourse in an effort to derive a deep explanation of their behavior. Collages are sometimes used to develop grounded theory. Case studies simply are documented histories of a particular person, group, organization, or event.

4. Prepare a focus group interview outline. A focus group outline should begin with introductory comments followed by a very general opening question that does not lead the respondent. More specific questions should be listed until a blunt question directly pertaining to the study objective is included. However, a skilled moderator can often lead the group without having to explicitly state these questions. It should conclude with debriefing comments and a chance for question-and-answers with respondents.

5. Recognize technological advances in the application of qualitative research approaches. Videoconferencing and online chat rooms are more economical ways of trying to do much the same as traditional focus group interviews. Some companies have even established a focus blog that is a source for continuous commentary on a company. While they are certainly cost advantageous, there is less control over who participates.

6. Recognize common qualitative research tools and know the advantages and limitations of their use. The most common qualitative research tools include the focus group interview and the depth interview. The focus group has some cost advantage per respondent because it would take ten times as long to conduct the interview portion(s) of a series of depth interviews compared to one focus group. However, the depth interview is more appropriate for discussing sensitive topics.

7. Know the risks associated with acting on only exploratory results. Companies do make decisions using only exploratory research. There are several explanations for this behavior. The researcher's job is to make sure that decision makers understand the increased risk that comes along with basing a decision only on exploratory research results.

Key Terms and Concepts

case studies, *152*
conversations, *166*
depth interview, *164*
discussion guide, *158*
ethnography, *150*
field notes, *168*
focus blog, *160*
focus group interview, *153*
free-association techniques, *167*
grounded theory, *151*
hermeneutic unit, *150*
hermeneutics, *150*
intersubjective certifiability, *147*
laddering, *164*
moderator, *158*
online focus group, *160*
participant-observation, *150*
phenomenology, *149*
piggyback, *155*
projective technique, *168*
qualitative business research, *145*
qualitative data, *148*
quantitative business research, *146*
quantitative data, *148*
replication, *170*
researcher-dependent, *145*
subjective, *147*
thematic apperception test (TAT), *168*
themes, *152*

Questions for Review and Critical Thinking

1. Define *qualitative* and *quantitative* research. Compare and contrast the two approaches.
2. Why do exploratory research designs rely so much on qualitative research techniques?
3. Why do causal designs rely so much on quantitative research techniques?
4. What are the basic orientations of qualitative research?
5. Of the four basic orientations of qualitative research, which do you think is most appropriate for a qualitative approach designed to better define a business situation prior to conducting confirmatory research?
6. What type of exploratory research would you suggest in the following situations?
   a. A product manager suggests development of a nontobacco cigarette blended from wheat, cocoa, and citrus.
   b. A research project has the purpose of evaluating potential names for a corporate spin-off.
   c. A human resource manager must determine the most important benefits of an employee health plan.
   d. An advertiser wishes to identify the symbolism associated with cigar smoking.
7. What are the key differences between a focus group interview and a depth interview?
8. **'NET** Visit some Web sites for large companies like Honda, Qantas Airlines, Target, Tesco, and Marriott. Is there any evidence that they are using their Internet sites in some way to conduct a continuous online focus blog or intermittent online focus groups?
9. What is *laddering?* How might it be used in trying to understand which fast-food restaurant customers prefer?
10. Comment on the following remark by a business consultant: "Qualitative exploration is a tool of research and a stimulant to thinking. In and by itself, however, it does not constitute business research."
11. **ETHICS** A researcher tells a manager of a wine company that he has some "cool focus group results" suggesting that respondents like the idea of a screw-cap to top wine bottles. Even before the decision maker sees the report, the manager begins purchasing screw-caps and the new bottling equipment. Comment on this situation.
12. A packaged goods manufacturer receives many thousands of customer letters a year. Some are complaints, some are compliments. They cover a broad range of topics. Are these letters a possible source for exploratory research? Why or why not?

Research Activities

1. **'NET** How might the following organizations use an Internet chat room for exploratory research?
   a. A provider of health benefits
   b. A computer software manufacturer
   c. A video game manufacturer
2. Go back to the opening vignette. What if Vans approached you to do a focus group interview that explored the idea of offering casual attire (off-board) aimed at their primary segment (skateboarders) and offering casual attire for male retirees like Samuel Teel? How would you recommend the focus group(s) proceed? Prepare a focus group outline(s) to accomplish this task.
3. Interview two people about their exercise behavior. In one interview, try to use a semi-structured approach by preparing questions ahead of time and trying to have the respondent complete answers for these questions. With the other, try a conversational approach. What are the main themes that emerge in each? Which approach do you think was more insightful? Do you think there were any "sensitive" topics that a respondent was not completely forthcoming about?

Case 7.1 Disaster and Consumer Value

© GETTY IMAGES/ PHOTODISC GREEN

In February 2009, bushfires raced across the Australian state of Victoria. This terrible tragedy resulted in the loss of over 300 lives, Australia's highest ever loss of life from a bushfire. In addition, more than 2,000 homes were destroyed and insurance losses are estimated to exceed $2 billion.[34] While rebuilding will take years, at some point after these disasters, it is time to get back to business. But major catastrophic events are likely to leave permanent changes on consumers and employees in the affected areas.

Suppose you are approached by the owner of several full-service wine stores in Victoria. It is January 2010, and they want to get back to business. But they are uncertain about whether they should simply maintain the same positioning they had previous to the bushfires. They would like to have a report from you within 60 days.

Questions

1. How could each orientation of qualitative research be used here?
2. What qualitative research tool(s) would you recommend be used and why?
3. Where would you conduct any interviews and with whom would you conduct them?
4. **ETHICS** Are there ethical issues that you should be sensitive to in this process? Explain.
5. What issues would arise in conducting a focus group interview in this situation?
6. Prepare a focus group outline.

Case 7.2 Edward Jones

© GETTY IMAGES/ PHOTODISC GREEN

Edward Jones is one of the largest investment firms in the United States, with over 4,000 branch offices in this country, Canada, and the United Kingdom. It is the only major brokerage firm that exclusively targets individual investors and small businesses, and it has nearly 6 million clients.

Edward Jones' philosophy is to offer personalized services to individual clients starting with a one-on-one interview. During the interview, investment representatives seek to identify each client's specific goals for investing. Richard G. Miller, one such representative, says that he needs to thoroughly understand what a client wants before he can build an investment strategy for that person. His initial conversation starts with, "Hey, how are you?" Gregory L. Starry, another representative, confirms the Edward Jones philosophy: "Most of my day is spent talking with and meeting clients [rather than placing stock trades]."

Only after learning these goals do the representatives design an investment strategy that will provide a client with income, growth, and safety. Each client's goals also evolve over time. Young people are focused on earning enough money to make a down payment on their first home or to buy a car. Clients in the 35 to 45 age range are concerned about getting their children through school and about their own retirement. Those in retirement want to make sure that they have an adequate income level. Miller notes, "It's not the timing in the market, but the time in the market" that will help clients achieve their goals.

Questions

1. Many people in minority groups, including African Americans, Hispanic Americans, Asian Americans, and Native Americans, do not invest. What exploratory research should Edward Jones do to develop business with these minority markets?
2. Another group with low investment activity includes those who stopped their education at the high school level. What factors should Edward Jones representatives consider in designing focus groups with these potential clients?

CHAPTER 8
SECONDARY DATA RESEARCH IN A DIGITAL AGE

LEARNING OUTCOMES

After studying this chapter, you should be able to

1. Discuss the advantages and disadvantages of secondary data
2. Define types of secondary data analysis conducted by business research managers
3. Identify various internal and proprietary sources of secondary data
4. Give examples of various external sources of secondary data
5. Describe the impact of single-source data and globalization on secondary data research

Chapter Vignette: Business Facts on a Grand Scale

A key problem that faces any business research manager is the need to constantly capture relevant data about customers, competitors, and/or market characteristics. The use of secondary data (i.e., data that has been collected previously for other purposes) has exploded with the advent of large-scale electronic information sources and the Web. One company that has taken full advantage of integrating various business related information sources is Nielsen Claritas.

©JEFF GREENBERG/PHOTOEDIT

Prior to its merge with the Nielsen Company, Claritas (which in Latin means "brightness") had a 40-year history of collecting and integrating business-related data from difference sources. Its products include (1) PRIZM, which provides market segmentation information based upon consumer behavior and geographic location; (2) Consumer Point, a target marketing analysis solution for different industry spaces; and (3) Business-Facts, which provides accurate business data for market support and strategic planning.

Business-Facts holds great promise as a secondary data source for existing companies. Using Standard Industrial Classification (SIC) and North American Industry Classification (NAICS)[1] codes developed through the Census Bureau, characteristics on business ownership, location, employment, and sales are available for 10 major industrial groupings. Data and employee counts within the Business-Facts system represent over 13 million businesses. Examples of these industry groups include construction, manufacturing, and retail sales establishments across the United States. Since business information can become quickly obsolete, Nielsen Claritas spends millions of dollars each year to verify business information on a quarterly basis.

The advantages of knowing broadly both the characteristics and location of major customer groups (or potential competitors) are very real. Using a sophisticated statistical modeling approach, The Nielsen Claritas company can link your customers to your existing or proposed locations, in a fashion such that the information is as timely and applicable as possible.

All of the information sources within Nielsen Claritas add value to business users by satisfying two very critical needs. First, Nielsen Claritas has expertise in linking different data streams into a cohesive system. This allows users to answer through secondary data sources critical existing business questions. Secondly, their information systems are geographically based, so that businesses can query data to a common point on the globe.

Truly, the integration and utilization of secondary data sources by the Nielsen Claritas Company has put business research "on the map"—both literally and figuratively!

Introduction

Research projects often begin with **secondary data**, which are gathered and recorded by someone else prior to (and for purposes other than) the current project. Secondary data usually are historical and already assembled. They require no access to respondents or subjects.

secondary data
Data that have been previously collected for some purpose other than the one at hand.

Advantages of Secondary Data

TOTHEPOINT

If I have seen farther than others, it is because I have stood on the shoulders of giants.

—Isaac Newton

The primary advantage of secondary data is their availability. Obtaining secondary data is almost always faster and less expensive than acquiring primary data. This is particularly true when researchers use electronic retrieval to access data stored digitally. In many situations, collecting secondary data is instantaneous.

Consider the money and time saved by researchers who obtained updated population estimates for a town during the interim between the 2000 and 2010 censuses. Instead of doing the fieldwork themselves, researchers could acquire estimates from a firm dealing in demographic information or from sources such as Claritas or PCensus. As in this example, the use of secondary data eliminates many of the activities normally associated with primary data collection, such as sampling and data processing.

Secondary data are essential in instances when data cannot be obtained using primary data collection procedures. For example, a manufacturer of farm implements could not duplicate the information in the *Census of Agriculture* because much of the information there (for example, amount of taxes paid) might not be accessible to a private firm.

Disadvantages of Secondary Data

An inherent disadvantage of secondary data is that they were not designed specifically to meet the researchers' needs. Thus, researchers must ask how pertinent the data are to their particular project. To evaluate secondary data, researchers should ask questions such as these:

- Is the subject matter consistent with our problem definition?
- Do the data apply to the population of interest?
- Do the data apply to the time period of interest?
- Do the secondary data appear in the correct units of measurement?
- Do the data cover the subject of interest in adequate detail?

Even when secondary information is available, it can be inadequate. Consider the following typical situations:

- A researcher interested in forklift trucks finds that the secondary data on the subject are included in a broader, less pertinent category encompassing all industrial trucks and tractors. Furthermore, the data were collected five years earlier.
- An investigator who wishes to study individuals earning more than \$100,000 per year finds the top category in a secondary study reported at \$75,000 or more per year.

- A brewery that wishes to compare its per-barrel advertising expenditures with those of competitors finds that the units of measurement differ because some report point-of-purchase expenditures with advertising and others do not.
- Data from a previous warranty card study show where consumers prefer to purchase the product but provide no reasons why.

The most common reasons why secondary data do not adequately satisfy research needs are (1) outdated information, (2) variation in definition of terms, (3) different units of measurement, and (4) lack of information to verify the data's accuracy. Furthermore, in our rapidly changing environment, information quickly becomes outdated. Because the purpose of most studies is to predict the future, secondary data must be timely to be useful.

Every primary researcher has the right to define the terms or concepts under investigation to satisfy the purpose of his or her primary investigation. This practice provides little solace, however, to the investigator of the African-American market who finds secondary data reported as "percent nonwhite." Variances in terms or variable classifications should be scrutinized to determine whether differences are important. The populations of interest must be described in comparable terms. Researchers frequently encounter secondary data that report on a population of interest that is similar but not directly comparable to their population of interest. For example, Arbitron reports its television audience estimates by geographical areas known as ADIs (Areas of Dominant Influence). An ADI is a geographic area consisting of all counties in which the home market commercial television stations receive a preponderance of total viewing hours. This unique population of interest is used exclusively to report television audiences. The geographic areas used in the census of population, such as Metropolitan Statistical Areas, are not comparable to ADIs.

Units of measurement may cause problems if they do not conform exactly to a researcher's needs as well. For example, lumber shipments in millions of board feet are quite different from billions of ton miles of lumber shipped on freight cars. Head-of-household income is not the same unit of measure as total family income. Often the objective of the original primary study may dictate that the data be summarized, rounded, or reported. When that happens, even if the original units of measurement were comparable, aggregated or adjusted, units of measurement are not suitable in the secondary study.

data conversion

The process of changing the original form of the data to a format suitable to achieve the research objective; also called data transformation.

When secondary data are reported in a format that does not exactly meet the researcher's needs, data conversion may be necessary. **Data conversion** (also called *data transformation*) is the process of changing the original form of data to a format more suitable for achieving a stated research objective. For example, sales for food products may be reported in pounds, cases, or dollars. An estimate of dollars per pound may be used to convert dollar volume data to pounds or another suitable format.

Another disadvantage of secondary data is that the user has no control over their accuracy. Although timely and pertinent secondary data may fit the researcher's requirements, the data could be inaccurate. Research conducted by other persons may be biased to support the vested interest of the source. For example, media often publish data from surveys to identify the characteristics of their subscribers or viewers, but they will most likely exclude derogatory data from their reports. If the possibility of bias exists, the secondary data should not be used.

Investigators are naturally more prone to accept data from reliable sources such as the U.S. government. Nevertheless, the researcher must assess the reputation of the organization that gathers the data and critically assess the research design to determine whether the research was correctly implemented. Unfortunately, such evaluation may be impossible without full information that explains how the original research was conducted.

cross-checks

The comparison of data from one source with data from another source to determine the similarity of independent projects.

Researchers should verify the accuracy of the data whenever possible. **Cross-checks** of data from multiple sources, similar to what Nielsen Claritas does with its Business-Facts database, should be made to determine the similarity of independent projects. When the data are not consistent, researchers should attempt to identify reasons for the differences or to determine which data are most likely to be correct. If the accuracy of the data cannot be established, the researcher must determine whether using the data is worth the risk. Exhibit 8.1 illustrates a series of questions that should be asked to evaluate secondary data before they are used.

EXHIBIT 8.1
Evaluating Secondary Data

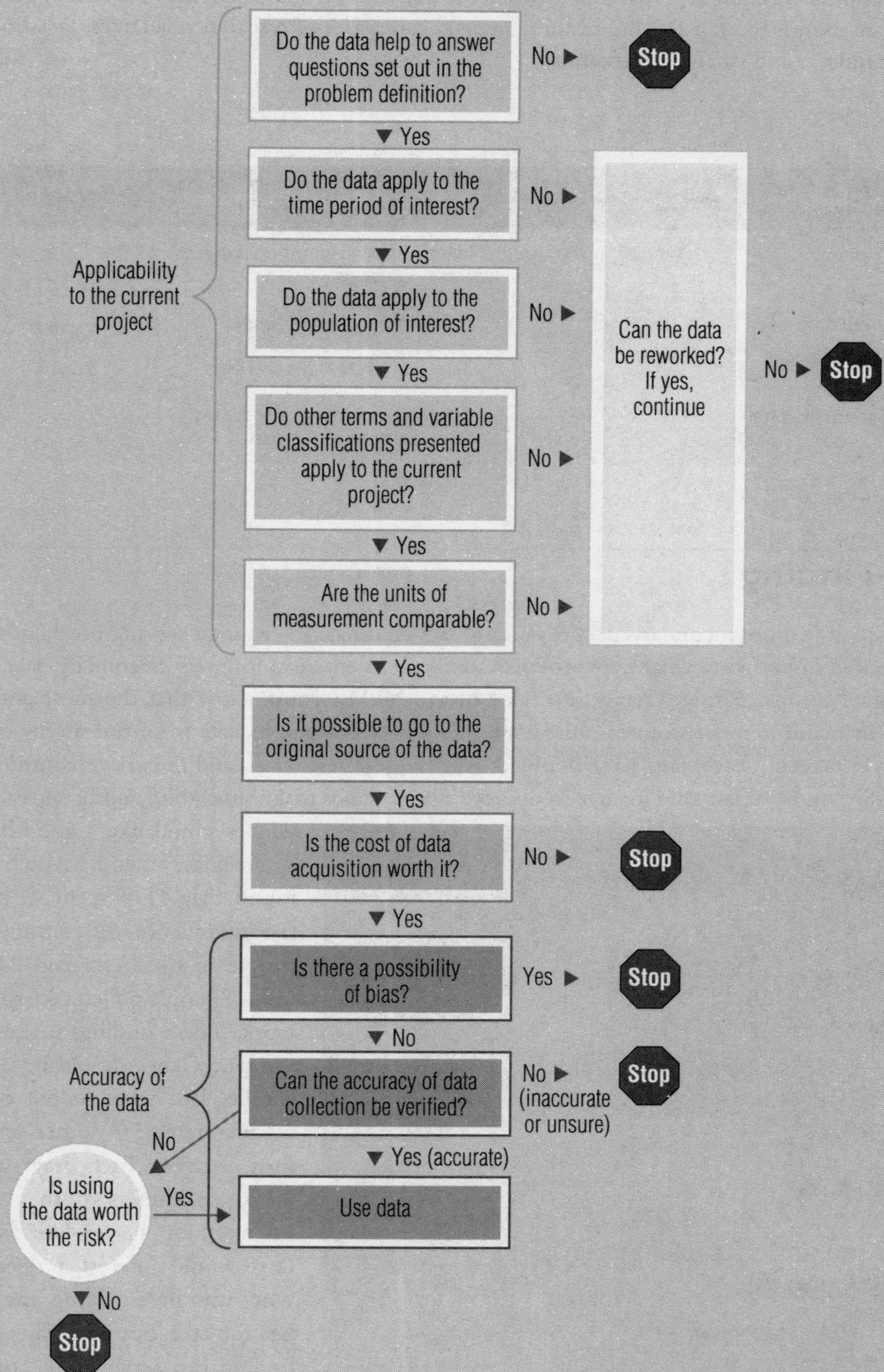

Source: The idea for Exhibit 8.1 came from Robert W. Joselyn, *Designing the Marketing Research Project* (New York: Petrocelli/Charter, 1977).

Typical Objectives for Secondary-Data Research Designs

It would be impossible to identify all the purposes of research using secondary data. However, some common business and marketing problems that can be addressed with secondary research designs are useful. Exhibit 8.2 shows three general categories of research objectives: fact-finding, model building, and database marketing.

EXHIBIT 8.2
Common Research Objectives for Secondary-Data Studies

Broad Objective	Specific Research Example
Fact-finding	Identifying consumption patterns Tracking trends
Model building	Estimating market potential Forecasting sales Selecting trade areas and sites
Database marketing	Enhancing customer databases Developing prospect lists

Fact-Finding

The simplest form of secondary-data research is fact-finding. A restaurant serving breakfast might be interested in knowing what new products are likely to entice consumers. Secondary data available from National Eating Trends, a service of the NPD Group, show that the most potential may be in menu items customers can eat on the go.[2] According to data from the survey of eating trends, take-out breakfasts have doubled over the past few years, and they have continued to surpass dine-in breakfast sales for over a decade. These trends make smoothies and breakfast sandwiches sound like a good bet for a breakfast menu. Also, NPD found that 41 percent of breakfast sandwiches are consumed by people in their cars and 24 percent of people polled take them to work. These findings suggest that the sandwiches should be easy to handle. But what to put on the biscuit or bun? Another research firm, Market Facts, says almost half of consumers say they would pay extra for cheese. These simple facts would interest a researcher who was investigating the market for take-out breakfasts. Fact-finding can serve more complex purposes as well. In the digital age we live in, the use of music as a means to notify users of a call is commonplace.

Secondary-data research supports the fact that breakfast sandwiches are at the top of the menu.

©DENNIS GOTTLIEB/JUPITER IMAGES

IDENTIFICATION OF CONSUMER BEHAVIOR FOR A PRODUCT CATEGORY

A typical objective for a secondary research study might be to uncover all available information about consumption patterns for a particular product category or to identify demographic trends that affect an industry. For example, a company called Servigistics offers software that will scan a company's own parts inventory data and compare it with marketing objectives and competitors' prices to evaluate whether the company should adjust prices for its parts. Kia Motors tried using this service in place of the usual method of marking up cost by a set fraction. By considering secondary data including internal inventory data and external data about competitors' prices, it was able to make service parts a more profitable segment of its business.[3] This example illustrates the wealth of factual information about consumption and behavior patterns that can be obtained by carefully collecting and analyzing secondary data.

TREND ANALYSIS

Business researchers are challenged to constantly watch for trends in the marketplace and the environment. **Market tracking** is the observation and analysis of trends in industry volume and brand share over time. Scanner research services and other organizations provide facts about sales volume to support this work.

market tracking
The observation and analysis of trends in industry volume and brand share over time.

Almost every large consumer goods company routinely investigates brand and product category sales volume using secondary data. This type of analysis typically involves comparisons with competitors' sales or with the company's own sales in comparable time periods. It also involves industry comparisons among different geographic areas.

Environmental Scanning

In many instances, the purpose of fact-finding is simply to study the environment to identify trends. Environmental scanning entails information gathering and fact-finding designed to detect indications of environmental changes in their initial stages of development. The Internet can be used for environmental scanning; however, there are other means, such as periodic review of contemporary publications and reports. For example, environmental scanning has shown many researchers that consumer demand in China is skyrocketing. In the case of beauty products such as cosmetics, Chinese authorities in the early 1990s stopped discouraging the use of makeup, and sales of these products took off—hitting $524 million in 2005—and were expected to grow by over one-third, reaching $705 million by 2009. Companies including Procter & Gamble, L'Oréal, and Shiseido have captured a sizable share of this market by realizing the potential and developing products to get into the Chinese market early.[4]

A number of online information services, such as Factiva and LexisNexis, routinely collect news stories about industries, product lines, and other topics of interest that have been specified by the researcher. In addition, push technology is an Internet information technology that automatically delivers content to the researcher's or manager's desktop. Push technology uses "electronic smart agents," custom software that filters, sorts, prioritizes, and stores information for later viewing.[5] This service frees the researcher from doing the searching. The true value of push technology is that the researcher who is scanning the environment can specify the kinds of news and information he or she wants, have it delivered to his or her computer quickly, and view it at leisure.

Model Building

The second general objective for secondary research, model building, is more complicated than simple fact-finding. **Model building** involves specifying relationships between two or more variables, perhaps extending to the development of descriptive or predictive equations, a technique that is used by the Nielsen Claritas Company routinely to add value to their secondary data. Models need not include complicated mathematics, though. In fact, decision makers often prefer simple models that everyone can readily understand over complex models that are difficult to comprehend. For example, market share is company sales divided by industry sales. Although some may not think of this simple calculation as a model, it represents a mathematical model of a basic relationship.

model building
The use of secondary data to help specify relationships between two or more variables; can involve the development of descriptive or predictive equations.

We will illustrate model building by discussing three common objectives that can be satisfied with secondary research: estimating market potential, forecasting sales, and selecting potential facility or expansion sites.

ESTIMATING MARKET POTENTIAL FOR GEOGRAPHIC AREAS

Business researchers often estimate their company's market potential using secondary data. In many cases exact figures may be published by a trade association or another source. However, when the desired information is unavailable, the researcher may estimate market potential by transforming secondary data from two or more sources. For example, managers may find secondary data about market potential for a country or other large geographic area, but this information may not be broken down into smaller geographical areas, such as by metropolitan area, or in terms unique to the company, such as sales territory. In this type of situation, researchers often need to make projections for the geographic area of interest.

An extended example will help explain how secondary data can be used to calculate market potential. Suppose a brewing company is looking for opportunities to expand sales by exporting or investing in other countries. Managers decide to begin by estimating market potential for the Czech Republic, Germany, Japan, and Spain. Secondary research uncovered data for per capita beer consumption and population projections for the year 2010. The data for the four countries appear in Exhibit 8.4.

To calculate market potential for the Czech Republic in 2010, multiply that country's population in the year 2010 by its per capita beer consumption:

$$10,175,000 \text{ people} \times 157 \text{ liters/person} = 1,597,475,000 \text{ liters}$$

In the Czech Republic, the market potential for beer is 1,597,475,000 liters. To get a sense of the expected sales volume, the researcher would have to multiply this amount by the price per liter at which beer typically sells in the Czech Republic. As Exhibit 8.3 reveals, Japan's population is much higher, so its market potential is greater, even though the average Czech drinks much more beer.

Of course, the calculated market potential for each country in Exhibit 8.3 is a rough estimate. One obvious problem is that not everyone in a country will be of beer-drinking age. If the researcher can get statistics for each country's projected *adult* population, the estimate will be closer. Also, you might want to consider whether each country is experiencing growth or decline in the demand for beer to estimate whether consumption habits are likely to be different in 2010. For example, beer consumption is barely growing in Europe and Japan, but it is expanding in Latin America (at about 4 percent a year) and even faster in China (by at least 6 percent a year).[6] Perhaps this information will cause you to investigate market potential in additional countries where more growth is expected.

EXHIBIT 8.3
Market Potential for Four Possible Beer Markets

Country	Population Projection for 2010 (thousands)	Annual per Capita Beer Consumption (liters)	Market Potential Estimate (k liters)
Czech Republic	10,175	157	1,597,475
Germany	82,365	116	9,554,340
Japan	127,758	48	6,132,384
Spain	45,108	84	3,789,072

Source: Population data from Population Division of the Department of Economic and Social Affairs of the United Nations Secretariat, "World Population Prospects: The 2004 Revision and World Urbanization Prospects; The 2003 Revision," http://esa.un.org/unpp, accessed February 9, 2006. Consumption data from "US Beer Consumption Reverses Decreases in 2007 - Research," http://www.just-drinks.com/article.aspx?id=95643, November 24, 2007, accessed December 10, 2008, http://galenet.galegroup.com; and "Czechs Top World Cup Beer Consumption," http://www.worldcupblog.org/world-cup-2006/czechs-top-world-beer-consumption.html, accessed December 10, 2008.

FORECASTING SALES

For any project, such as forecasting sales, you need information about the future. You will need to know what company sales will be next year and in future time periods. Sales forecasting is the process of predicting sales totals over a specific time period.

Accurate sales forecasts, especially for products in mature, stable markets, frequently come from secondary-data research that identifies trends and extrapolates past performance into the future. Researchers often use internal company sales records to project sales. A rudimentary model would multiply past sales volume by an expected growth rate. A researcher might investigate a secondary source and find that industry sales are expected to grow by 10 percent; multiplying company sales volume by 10 percent would give a basic sales forecast.

Exhibit 8.4 illustrates trend projection using a moving average projection of growth rates. Average ticket prices for a major-league baseball game are secondary data from Team Marketing Report for each year of interest (**http://www.teammarketing.com/fancost/mlb/**). The moving average is the sum of growth rates for the past three years divided by 3 (number of years). The resulting number is a forecast of the percentage increase in ticket price for the coming year. Using the three-year average growth rate of 6.4 percent for the 2008, 2007, and 2006 sales periods, we can forecast the average ticket price for 2009 as follows:

$$\$25.43 + (\$25.43 \times .064) = \$27.05$$

Using the same information, the projected price of a beer at a ballgame in 2009 is $6.43. This lets the fan know how much to take out to the old ballgame.

Moving average forecasting is best suited to a static competitive environment. More dynamic situations make other sales forecasting techniques more appropriate.

Statistical trend analysis using secondary data can be much more advanced than this simple example. Many statistical techniques build forecasting models using secondary data. This chapter emphasizes secondary-data research rather than statistical analysis, which is covered in later chapters.

EXHIBIT 8.54
Sales Forecast Using Secondary Data and Moving Averages

Year	Average Ticket Price ($)	Percentage Rate of Growth (Decline) from Previous Year	3-Year Moving Average Rate of Growth (Decline)
1996	11.20	5.2%	3.5%
1997	12.36	10.4%	5.8%
1998	13.59	10.0%	8.5%
1999	14.91	9.7%	10.0%
2000	16.67	11.8%	10.5%
2001	18.99	13.9%	11.8%
2002	18.30	−3.6%	7.4%
2003	19.01	3.9%	4.7%
2004	19.82	4.3%	1.5%
2005	21.17	6.8%	5.0%
2006	22.21	4.9%	5.3%
2007	22.70	2.2%	4.6%
2008	25.43	12.0%	6.4%

ANALYSIS OF TRADE AREAS AND SITES

site analysis techniques
Techniques that use secondary data to select the best location for retail or wholesale operations.

index of retail saturation
A calculation that describes the relationship between retail demand and supply.

Managers routinely examine trade areas and use **site analysis techniques** to select the best locations for retail or wholesale operations. Secondary-data research helps managers make these site selection decisions. Some organizations, especially franchisers, have developed special computer software based on analytical models to select sites for retail outlets. The researcher must obtain the appropriate secondary data for analysis with the computer software.

The **index of retail saturation** offers one way to investigate retail sites and to describe the relationship between retail demand and supply.[7] It is easy to calculate once the appropriate secondary data are obtained:

$$\text{Index of retail saturation} = \frac{\text{Local market potential (demand)}}{\text{Local market retailing space}}$$

For example, Exhibit 8.5 shows the relevant secondary data for shoe store sales in a five-mile radius surrounding a Florida shopping center. These types of data can be purchased from vendors of market information such as Urban Decision Systems. First, to estimate local market potential (demand), we multiply population by annual per capita shoe sales. This estimate, line 3 in Exhibit 8.5, goes in the numerator to calculate the index of retail saturation:

$$\text{Index of retail saturation} = \frac{\$14{,}249{,}000}{94{,}000} = 152$$

EXHIBIT 8.5
Secondary Data for Calculating an Index of Retail Saturation

1. Population	261,785
2. Annual per capita shoe sales	$54.43
3. Local market potential (line 1 × line 2)	$14,249,000
4. Square feet of retail space used to sell shoes	94,000 sq. ft.
5. Index of retail saturation (line 3/line 4)	152

The retailer can compare this index figure with those of other areas to determine which sites have the greatest market potential with the least amount of retail competition. An index value above 200 is considered to indicate exceptional opportunities.

Data Mining

Large corporations' decision support systems often contain millions or even hundreds of millions of records of data. These complex data volumes are too large to be understood by managers. Consider, for example, Capital One, a consumer lending company with nearly 50 million customer accounts, including credit cards and auto loans. Suppose the company collects data on customer purchases, and each customer makes five transactions in a month, or 60 per year. With 50 million customers and decades of data (the company was founded in 1988), it's easy to see how record counts quickly grow beyond the comfort zone for most humans.[8]

Two points about data volume are important to keep in mind. First, relevant data are often in independent and unrelated files. Second, the number of distinct pieces of information each data record contains is often large. When the number of distinct pieces of information contained in each data record and data volume grows too large, end users don't have the capacity to make sense of it all. Data mining helps clarify the underlying meaning of the data.

data mining
The use of powerful computers to dig through volumes of data to discover patterns about an organization's customers and products; applies to many different forms of analysis.

The term **data mining** refers to the use of powerful computers to dig through volumes of data to discover patterns about an organization's customers and products. It is a broad term that applies to many different forms of analysis. For example, **neural networks** are a form of artificial intelligence in which a computer is programmed to mimic the way that human brains process information. One computer expert put it this way:

> *A neural network learns pretty much the way a human being does. Suppose you say "big" and show a child an elephant, and then you say "small" and show her a poodle. You repeat this process with a house and a giraffe as examples of "big" and then a grain of sand and an ant as examples of "small." Pretty soon she will figure it out and tell you that a truck is "big" and a needle is "small." Neural networks can similarly generalize by looking at examples.*[9]

neural networks
A form of artificial intelligence in which a computer is programmed to mimic the way that human brains process information.

Market-basket analysis is a form of data mining that analyzes anonymous point-of-sale transaction databases to identify coinciding purchases or relationships between products purchased and other retail shopping information.[10] Consider this example about patterns in customer purchases: Osco Drugs mined its databases provided by checkout scanners and found that when men go to its drugstores to buy diapers in the evening between 6:00 p.m. and 8:00 p.m., they sometimes walk out with a six-pack of beer as well. Knowing this behavioral pattern, supermarket managers may consider laying out their stores so that these items are closer together.[11]

market-basket analysis
A form of data mining that analyzes anonymous point-of-sale transaction databases to identify coinciding purchases or relationships between products purchased and other retail shopping information.

A data-mining application of interest to some researchers is known as **customer discovery**, which involves mining data to look for patterns identifying who is likely to be a valuable customer. For example, a larger provider of business services wanted to sell a new product to its existing customers, but it knew that only some of them would be interested. The company had to adapt each product offering to each customer's individual needs, so it wanted to save money by identifying the best prospects. It contracted with a research provider called DataMind to mine its data on sales, responses to marketing, and customer service to look for the customers most likely to be interested in the new product. DataMind assigned each of the company's customers an index number indicating their expected interest level, and the selling effort was much more efficient as a result.[12]

customer discovery
Involves mining data to look for patterns identifying who is likely to be a valuable customer.

When a company knows the identity of the customer who makes repeated purchases from the same organization, an analysis can be made of sequences of purchases. The use of data mining to detect sequence patterns is a popular application among direct marketers, such as catalog retailers. A catalog merchant has information for each customer, revealing the sets of products that the customer buys in every purchase order. A sequence detection function can then be used to discover the set of purchases that frequently precedes the purchase of, say, a microwave oven. As another example, a sequence of insurance claims could lead to the identification of frequently occurring medical procedures performed on patients, which in turn could be used to detect cases of medical fraud.

Data mining requires sophisticated computer resources, and it is expensive. That's why companies like DataMind, IBM, Oracle, Information Builders, and Acxiom Corporation offer data-mining services. Customers send the databases they want analyzed and let the data-mining company do the "number crunching."

Database Marketing and Customer Relationship Management

CRM (customer relationship management) systems are a decision support system that manage the interactions between an organization and its customers. A CRM maintains customer databases containing customers' names, addresses, phone numbers, past purchases, responses to past promotional offers, and other relevant data such as demographic and financial data. **Database marketing** is the practice of using CRM databases to develop one-to-one relationships and precisely targeted promotional efforts with individual customers. For example, a fruit catalog company CRM contains a database of previous customers, including what purchases they made during the Christmas holidays.

database marketing
The use of customer databases to promote one-to-one relationships with customers and create precisely targeted promotions.

Each year the company sends last year's gift list to customers to help them send the same gifts to their friends and relatives.

Because database marketing requires vast amounts of CRM data compiled from numerous sources, secondary data are often acquired for the exclusive purpose of developing or enhancing databases. The transaction record, which often lists the item purchased, its value, customer name, address, and zip code, is the building block for many databases. This may be supplemented with data customers provide directly, such as data on a warranty card, and by secondary data purchased from third parties. For example, credit services may sell databases about applications for loans, credit card payment history, and other financial data. Several companies, such as Donnelley Marketing (with its BusinessContentFile and ConsumerContentFile services) and Claritas (with PRIZM), collect primary data and then sell demographic data that can be related to small geographic areas, such as those with a certain zip code. (Remember that when the vendor collects the data, they are primary data, but when the database marketer incorporates the data into his or her database, they are secondary data.)

Now that some of the purposes of secondary-data analysis have been addressed, we turn to a discussion of the sources of secondary data.

Sources of Secondary Data

Secondary data can be classified as either internal to the organization or external. Modern information technology makes this distinction seem somewhat simplistic. Some accounting documents are indisputably internal records of the organization. Researchers in another organization cannot have access to them. Clearly, a book published by the federal government and located at a public library is external to the company. However, in today's world of electronic data interchange, the data that appear in a book published by the federal government may also be purchased from an online information vendor for instantaneous access and subsequently stored in a company's decision support system.

internal and proprietary data
Secondary data that originate inside the organization.

Internal data should be defined as data that originated in the organization, or data created, recorded, or generated by the organization. **Internal and proprietary data** is perhaps a more descriptive term.

Sources of Internal and Proprietary Data

Most organizations routinely gather, record, and store internal data to help them solve future problems. An organization's accounting system can usually provide a wealth of information. Routine documents such as sales invoices allow external financial reporting, which in turn can be a source of data for further analysis. If the data are properly coded into a modular database in the accounting system, the researcher may be able to conduct more detailed analysis using the decision support system. Sales information can be broken down by account or by product and region; information related to orders received, back orders, and unfilled orders can be identified; sales can be forecast on the basis of past data. Other useful sources of internal data include salespeople's call reports, customer complaints, service records, warranty card returns, and other records.

Researchers frequently aggregate or disaggregate internal data. For example, a computer service firm used internal secondary data to analyze sales over the previous three years, categorizing business by industry, product, purchase level, and so on. The company discovered that 60 percent of its customers represented only 2 percent of its business and that nearly all of these customers came through telephone directory advertising. This simple investigation of internal records showed that, in effect, the firm was paying to attract customers it did not want.

Internet technology is making it easier to research internal and proprietary data. Often companies set up intranets so that employees can use Web tools to store and share data within the organization. And just as Google's search software lets people search the entire World Wide Web, Google is offering the enterprise search, which is essentially the same technology in a version that searches a corporate intranet. The enterprise search considers not only how often a particular document has been viewed but also the history of the user's past search patterns, such as how often that user has looked at particular documents and for how long. In addition, other companies have purchased specialized software, such as Autonomy, which searches internal sources plus such external sources as news and government Web sites.[13]

External Data: The Distribution System

external data
Data created, recorded, or generated by an entity other than the researcher's organization.

External data are generated or recorded by an entity other than the researcher's organization. The government, newspapers and journals, trade associations, and other organizations create or produce information. Traditionally, this information has been in published form, perhaps available from a public library, trade association, or government agency. Today, however, computerized data archives and electronic data interchange make external data as accessible as internal data. Exhibit 8.6 illustrates some traditional and some modern ways of distributing information.

Information as a Product and Its Distribution Channels

Because secondary data have value, they can be bought and sold like other products. And just as bottles of perfume or plumbers' wrenches may be distributed in many ways, secondary data also flow through various channels of distribution. Many users, such as the Fortune 500 corporations, purchase documents and computerized census data directly from the government. However, many small companies get census data from a library or another intermediary or vendor of secondary information.

LIBRARIES

Traditionally, libraries' vast storehouses of information have served as a bridge between users and producers of secondary data. The library staff deals directly with the creators of information, such as the federal government, and intermediate distributors of information, such as abstracting and indexing services. The user need only locate the appropriate secondary data on the library shelves. Libraries provide collections of books, journals, newspapers, and so on for reading and reference. They also stock many bibliographies, abstracts, guides, directories, and indexes, as well as offer access to basic databases.

The word *library* typically connotes a public or university facility. However, many major corporations and government agencies also have libraries. A corporate librarian's advice on sources of industry information or the United Nations librarian's help in finding statistics about international markets can be invaluable.

THE INTERNET

Today, of course, much secondary data is conveniently available over the Internet. Its creation has added an international dimension to the acquisition of secondary data. For example, Library Spot, at **http://www.libraryspot.com**, provides links to online libraries, including law libraries, medical libraries, and music libraries. Its reference desk feature links to calendars, dictionaries, encyclopedias, maps, and other sources typically found at a traditional library's reference desk.

Exhibit 8.7 lists some of the most popular Internet addresses where secondary data may be found.

VENDORS

The information age offers many channels besides libraries through which to access data. Many external producers make secondary data available directly from the organizations that produce the data or through intermediaries, which are often called *vendors*. Vendors such as Factiva now allow managers to access thousands of external databases via desktop computers and telecommunications systems. Hoovers (**http://www.hoovers.com**) specializes in providing information about thousands of companies' financial situations and operations.

EXHIBIT 8.6
Information as a Product and Its Distribution Channels

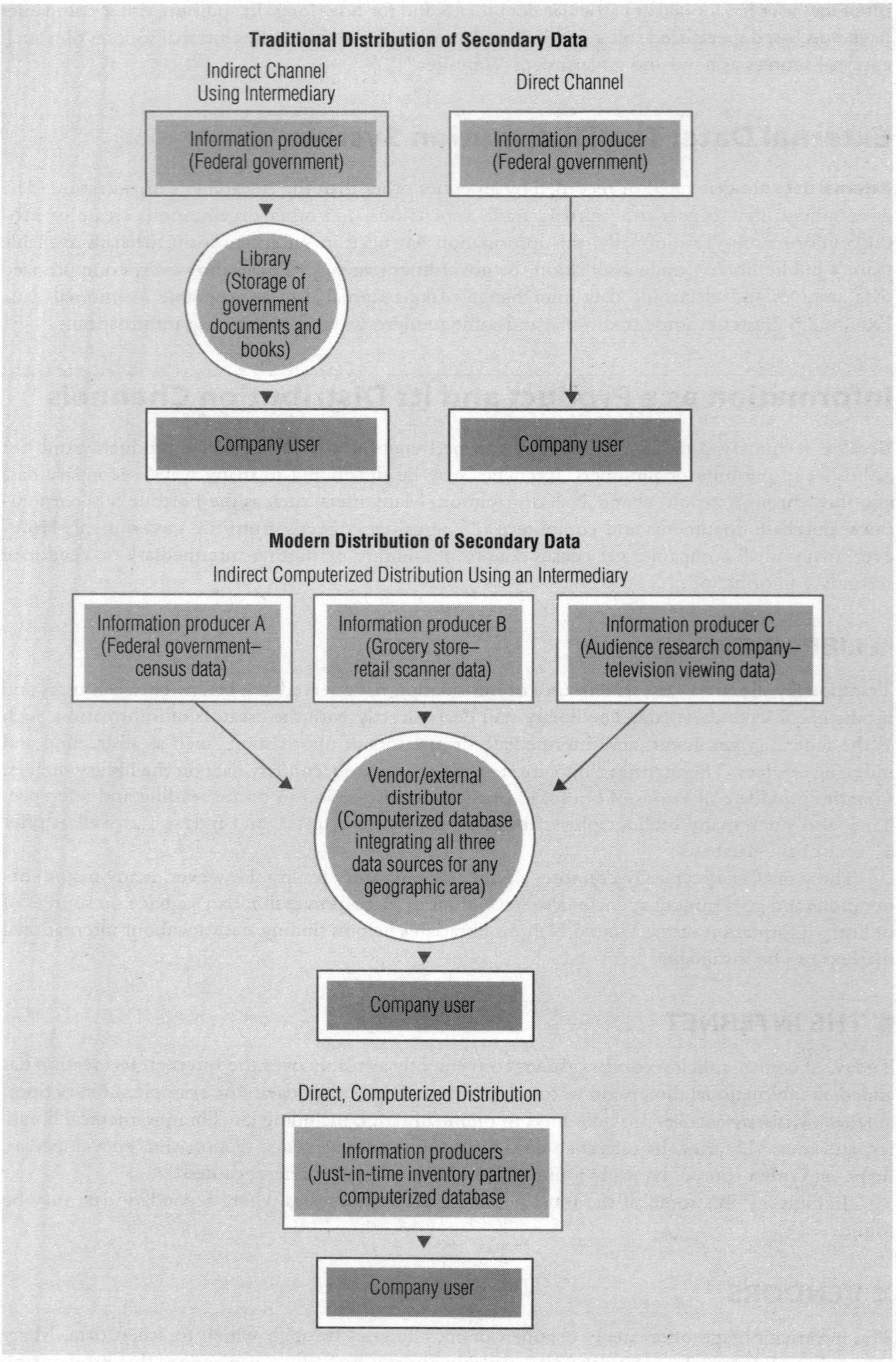

PRODUCERS

Classifying external secondary data by the nature of the producer of information yields five basic sources: publishers of books and periodicals, government sources, media sources, trade association sources, and commercial sources. The following section discusses each type of secondary data source.

EXHIBIT 8.7
Selected Internet Sites for Secondary Data

Name	Description	URL
Yahoo!	Portal that serves as a gateway to all kinds of sites on the Web.	http://www.yahoo.com
CEOexpress	The 80/20 rule applied to the Internet. A series of links designed by a busy executive for busy executives.	http://www.ceoexpress.com
The New York Public Library Home Page	Library resources and links available online.	http://www.nypl.org
Census Bureau	Demographic information from the U.S. Census Bureau.	http://www.census.gov
Statistical Abstract of the United States	Highlights from the primary reference book for government statistics.	http://www.census.gov/statab/www
STAT-USA/Internet	A comprehensive source of U.S. government information that focuses on economic, financial, and trade data.	http://www.stat-usa.gov/
Advertising Age magazine	Provides content on marketing media, advertising, and public relations.	http://www.adage.com
Inc.com	*Inc.* magazine's resources for growing a small business.	http://www.inc.com
The Wall Street Journal Online	Provides a continually updated view of business news around the world.	http://online.wsj.com
CNN Money	Provides business news, information on managing a business and managing money, and other business data.	http://money.cnn.com
NAICS—North American Industry Classification System	Describes the new classification system that replaced the SIC system.	http://www.census.gov/epcd/www/naics.html
MapQuest	Allows users to enter an address and zip code and see a map.	http://www.mapquest.com
Brint.com: The BizTech Network	Business and technology portal and global network for e-business, information, technology, and knowledge management.	http://www.brint.com

Books and Periodicals

Some researchers consider books and periodicals found in a library to be the quintessential secondary data source. A researcher who finds books on a topic of interest obviously is off to a good start.

Professional journals, such as the *Journal of Marketing, Journal of Management, Journal of the Academy of Marketing Science, The Journal of Business Research, Journal of Advertising Research, American Demographics,* and *The Public Opinion Quarterly,* as well as commercial business periodicals such as the *Wall Street Journal, Fortune,* and *BusinessWeek,* contain much useful material. *Sales and Marketing Management's Survey of Buying Power* is a particularly useful source of information about markets. To locate data in periodicals, indexing services such as the *ABI/INFORM* and *Business Periodicals Index* and the *Wall Street Journal Index* are very useful. Guides to data sources also are helpful. For

TOTHEPOINT

The man who does not read good books has no advantage over the man who cannot read them.

—Mark Twain

example, *American Statistical Index and Business Information Sources* is a very valuable source. Most university libraries provide access to at least some of these databases.

Government Sources

Government agencies produce data prolifically. Most of the data published by the federal government can be counted on for accuracy and quality of investigation. Most students are familiar with the U.S. *Census of Population,* which provides a wealth of data.

The *Census of Population* is only one of many resources that the government provides. Banks and savings and loan companies rely heavily on the *Federal Reserve Bulletin* and the *Economic Report of the President* for data relating to research on financial and economic conditions. Builders and contractors use the information in the *Current Housing Reports* and *American Housing Survey* for their research. The *Statistical Abstract of the United States* is an extremely valuable source of information about the social, political, and economic organizations of the United States. It abstracts data available in hundreds of other government publications and serves as a convenient reference to more specific statistical data.

The federal government is a leader in making secondary data available on the Internet. Visit FedWorld (**http://www.fedworld.gov**) for a central access point and links to many of these important documents. STAT-USA/Internet is another authoritative and comprehensive source of U.S. government information that focuses on economic, financial, and trade data. It contains the following types of information:

- More than 18,000 market research reports on individual countries and markets compiled by foreign experts at U.S. embassies
- Economic data series, current and historical, such as gross domestic product, balance of payment, and merchandise trade
- Standard reference works, such as the *Economic Report of the President,* the *Budget of the United States Federal Government,* and the *World Factbook*
- Worldwide listings of businesses interested in buying U.S. products

The STAT-USA/Internet Web address is **http://www.stat-usa.gov**. However, only subscribers who pay a fee have access to this service.

State, county, and local government agencies can also be useful sources of information. Many state governments publish state economic models and forecasts, and many cities have metropolitan planning agencies that provide data about the population, economy, transportation system, and so on. These are similar to federal government data but are more current and are structured to suit local needs.

Many cities and states publish information on the Internet. Many search engines have directory entries that allow easy navigation to a particular state's Web site. A researcher using Yahoo!, for example, needs only to click Regional Information to find numerous paths to information about states.

Media Sources

Information on a broad range of subjects is available from broadcast and print media. *CNN Financial News* and *BusinessWeek* are valuable sources for information on the economy and many industries. Media frequently commission research studies about various aspects of Americans' lives, such as financial affairs, and make reports of survey findings available to potential advertisers free of charge. Data about the readers of magazines and the audiences for broadcast media typically are profiled in media kits and advertisements.

Information about special-interest topics may also be available. *Hispanic Business* reports that the number of Hispanic-owned companies in the United States is expected to grow at a rate of 55 percent between 2004 and 2010, reaching 3.2 million firms, with revenue growth for the period of 70 percent. According to the magazine, most of these firms are located in 20 states, with over half in California and Florida. For researchers willing to pay a modest $85, *Hispanic Business* offers a more detailed report about Hispanic-owned businesses.[14]

Data such as these are plentiful because the media like to show that their vehicles are viewed or heard by advertisers' target markets. These types of data should be evaluated carefully, however,

RESEARCH SNAPSHOT

Water, Water Everywhere (in a bottle)

Most people would consider water to be relatively free. The ever-present bottle of water that you see in people's hands is a common sight, yet it is a relatively new trend in the beverage industry. In some ways, it does not seem to make sense that something available everywhere can represent an industry. When asked why a bottle of water which is typically priced at over a dollar per bottle is the beverage of choice, consumers routinely see it as a healthy and convenient "beverage" in today's world.

The trend for bottled water consumption is exploding—in 1976, the average person drank 1.6 gallons of bottled water per year. Thirty years later, that average is 27.6 gallons per year. As a result, researchers have begun to build data around this growing industry segment. Within this $8.3 billion industry, wholesale dollar sales and market share heavily favor familiar beverage brands such as Dasani (Coca-Cola) and Aquafina (PepsiCo), but the largest producer of bottled water is actually Nestlé Waters of North America, producer of several brands such as Ozarka and Poland Springs.

These data are useful to other researchers who wish to analyze the traditional and non-traditional beverage industry. So, the next time you "grab your water," you are contributing to a relatively new industry that has somehow made water even more a part of our lives.

Source: *Beverage World* (April 2006); International Bottled Water Association, http://www.bottledwater.org.

© iStock

because often they cover only limited aspects of a topic. Nevertheless, they can be quite valuable for research, and they are generally available free of charge.

Trade Association Sources

Trade associations, such as the Food Marketing Institute or the American Petroleum Institute, serve the information needs of a particular industry. The trade association collects data on a number of topics of specific interest to firms, especially data on market size and market trends. Association members have a source of information that is particularly germane to their industry questions. For example, the Newspaper Advertising Bureau (NAB) has catalogued and listed in its computer the specialized sections that are currently popular in newspapers. The NAB has surveyed all daily, Sunday, and weekend newspapers in the United States and Canada on their editorial content and has stored this information, along with data on rates, circulation, and mechanical requirements, in its computer for advertisers' use. As seen in the Research Snapshot "Water, Water Everywhere (in a Bottle)," trade associations are valuable sources of interesting data.

Commercial Sources

Numerous firms specialize in selling and/or publishing information. For example, the Polk Company publishes information on the automotive field, such as average car values and new-car purchase rates by zip code. Many of these organizations offer information in published formats and as CD-ROM or Internet databases. The following discussion of several of these firms provides a sampling of the diverse data that are available.

Market-Share Data. A number of syndicated services supply either wholesale or retail sales volume data based on product movement. Information Resources, Inc., collects market-share data using Universal Product Codes (UPC) and optical scanning at retail store checkouts. INFOSCAN is a syndicated store tracking service that collects scanner data weekly from more than 32,000 supermarket, drug, and mass merchandiser outlets across the United States. Sales in France, Germany, Greece, Italy, the Netherlands, Spain, and the United Kingdom also are tracked by INFOSCAN.

Although it is best known for its television rating operations, ACNielsen also has a scanner-based marketing and sales information service called ScanTrack. This service gathers sales and marketing data from a sample of more than 4,800 stores representing more than 800 retailers in 50 major U.S. markets. As part of Nielsen's Retail Measurement Service, auditors visit the stores at regular intervals to track promotions to customers, retail inventories, displays, brand distribution, out-of-stock conditions, and other retail marketing activity. Scanner data allow researchers to monitor sales data before, during, and after changes in advertising frequency, price changes, distribution of free samples, and similar marketing tactics.

Wal-Mart operates its own in-store scanner system called RetailLink. Key suppliers can have online access to relevant data free of charge.[15] The *Market Share Reporter* is produced each year, made available for sale, and provides market share data for most industries.

Many primary data investigations use scanner data to measure the results of experimental manipulations such as altering advertising copy. For example, scanning systems combined with consumer panels are used to create electronic test-markets. Systems based on UPCs (bar codes) and similar technology have been implemented in factories, warehouses, and transportation companies to research inventory levels, shipments, and the like.

Demographic and Census Updates. A number of firms, such as CACI Marketing Systems and Urban Information Systems, offer computerized U.S. census files and updates of these data broken down by small geographic areas, such as zip codes. Many of these research suppliers provide in-depth information on minority customers and other market segments.

Consumer Attitude and Public Opinion Research. Many research firms offer specialized syndicated services that report findings from attitude research and opinion polls. For example, Yankelovich provides custom research, tailored for specific projects, and several syndicated services. Yankelovich's public opinion research studies, such as the voter and public attitude surveys that appear in *Time* and other news magazines, are a source of secondary data. One of the firm's services is the *Yankelovich MONITOR,* a syndicated annual census of changing social values and an analysis of how they can affect consumer marketing. The *MONITOR* charts the growth and spread of new social values, characterizes the types of customers who support the new values and those who continue to support traditional values, and outlines the ways in which people's values affect purchasing behavior.

Harris/Interactive is another public opinion research firm that provides syndicated and custom research for business. One of its services is its ABC News/Harris survey. This survey, released three times per week, monitors the pulse of the American public on topics such as inflation, unemployment, energy, attitudes toward the president, elections, and so on.

Consumption and Purchase Behavior Data. NPD's *National Eating Trends* (NET) is the most detailed database available on consumption patterns and trends for more than 4,000 food and beverage products. This is a syndicated source of data about the types of meals people eat and when and how they eat them. The data, called *diary panel data,* are based on records of meals and diaries kept by a group of households that have agreed to record their consumption behavior over an extended period of time.

National Family Opinion (NFO), Marketing Research Corporation of America (MRCA), and many other syndicated sources sell diary panel data about consumption and purchase behavior. Since the advent of scanner data, diary panels are more commonly used to record purchases of apparel, hardware, home furnishings, jewelry, and other durable goods, rather than purchases of non-durable consumer packaged goods. More recently, services have been tracking consumer behavior online, collecting data about sites visited and purchases made over the Internet.

Advertising Research. Advertisers can purchase readership and audience data from a number of firms. W. R. Simmons and Associates measures magazine audiences; Arbitron measures radio audiences; ACNielsen Media Measurement estimates television audience ratings. By specializing in collecting and selling audience information on a continuing basis, these commercial sources provide a valuable service to their subscribers.

Assistance in measuring advertising effectiveness is another syndicated service. For example, Roper Starch Worldwide measures the impact of advertising in magazines. Readership information can be obtained for competitors' ads or the client's own ads. Respondents are classified as noted readers, associated readers, or read-most readers.

Burke Marketing Research provides a service that measures the extent to which respondents recall television commercials aired the night before. It provides product category norms, or average DAR (Day-After Recall) scores, and DAR scores for other products.

An individual advertiser would be unable to monitor every minute of every television program before deciding on the appropriate ones in which to place advertising. However, numerous clients, agencies, television networks, and advertisers can purchase the Nielsen television ratings service.

Single-Source Data-Integrated Information

ACNielsen Company offers data from both its television meters and scanner operations. The integration of these two types of data helps marketers investigate the impact of television advertising on retail sales. In other ways as well, users of data find that merging two or more diverse types of data into a single database offers many advantages.

PRIZM by Nielsen Claritas, CACI, ClusterPlus by SMI, Mediamark Research Inc., and many other syndicated databases report product purchase behavior, media usage, demographic characteristics, lifestyle variables, and business activity by geographic area such as zip code. Although such data are often called *geodemographic,* they cover such a broad range of phenomena that no one name is a good description. These data use small geographic areas as the unit of analysis.

The data and information industry uses the term **single-source data** for diverse types of data offered by a single company. Exhibit 8.8 identifies three major marketers of single-source data.

single-source data

Diverse types of data offered by a single company; usually integrated on the basis of a common variable such as geographic area or store.

EXHIBIT 8.8
Examples of Single-Source Databases

CACI Marketing Systems **http://www.caci.com**	Provides industry-specific marketing services, such as customer profiling and segmentation, custom target analysis, demographic data reports and maps, and site evaluation and selection. CACI offers demographics and data on businesses, lifestyles, consumer spending, purchase potential, shopping centers, traffic volumes, and other statistics.
PRIZM by Claritas Corporation **http://www.claritas.com**	PRIZM, which stands for Potential Rating Index for Zip Markets, is based on the "birds-of-a-feather" assumption that people live near others who are like themselves. PRIZM combines census data, consumer surveys about shopping and lifestyle, and purchase data to identify market segments. Colorful names such as Young Suburbia, Shot Guns, and Pickups describe 40 segments that can be identified by zip code. Claritas also has a lifestyle census in the United Kingdom (**http://www.claritas.co.uk**).
MRI Cable Report—Mediamark Research Inc. **http://www.mediamark.com**	Integrates information on cable television viewing with demographic and product usage information.

Panel Data

In business research, the term panel data refers to multi-dimensional data. A panel data consists of information of sampling unit (company, individual) for many dimensions across multiple time periods. In this case, a panel data has observations of both longitudinal and cross-sectional data. Cross-sectional data are special type of panel data which are uni-dimensional.

A panel data could be a balanced panel data or an unbalanced panel data. A balanced panel data would contain observations of same number of individual characteristics across a number of years for all individuals. On the contrary, an unbalanced panel data would contain observations of different individuals across different years. Exhibits 8.9 and 8.10 are the examples of balanced panel data and unbalanced panel data, respectively.

EXHIBIT 8.9
Balanced Panel Data

Person	Year	Income	Age	Gender
1	2008	10000	36	Male
1	2009	12000	37	Male
1	2010	15000	38	Male
2	2008	18000	42	Female
2	2009	20000	43	Female
2	2010	26000	44	Female

EXHIBIT 8.10
Unbalanced Panel Data

Person	Year	Income	Age	Gender
1	2008	10000	36	Male
1	2009	12000	37	Male
2	2007	15000	41	Female
2	2008	18000	42	Female
2	2009	20000	43	Female
3	2008	26000	36	Male

Scanner Panel Data

Many retail outlets, namely Reliance Fresh, Foodworld, and Wal Mart gather consumers' information at the point of billing. Electronic billing system of these retail outlets helps the management to gather individual consumer specific information of the product and brand they bought and the quantity and product size they bought in different occasions. Such information can be used by business researchers for taking several decisions related to product development, advertising, promotion, assortment size, pack size, inventory control, shelf space design as well as timeliness of the product delivery. Since the scanner data is readily available with the company as well as with the market research agencies, these data can be used for effective decision making on end of aisle display, product positioning, and shelf layout. An image of a typical scanner is shown here.[16]

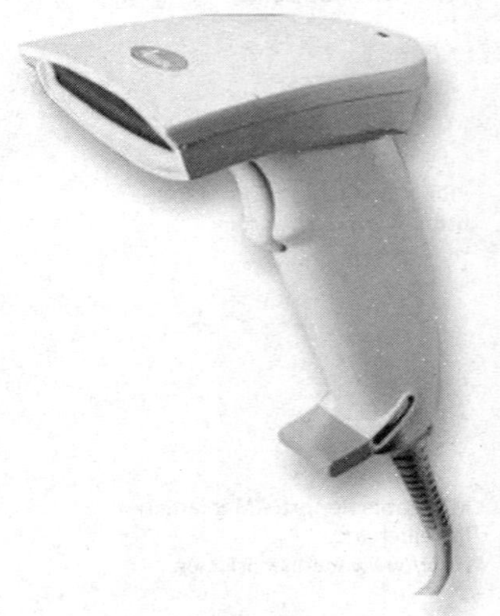

Sources for Global Research

As business has become more global, so has the secondary data industry. The Japan Management Association Research Institute, Japan's largest provider of secondary research data to government and industry, maintains an office in San Diego. The Institute's goal is to help U.S. firms access its enormous store of data about Japan to develop and plan their business there. The office in San Diego provides translators and acts as an intermediary between Japanese researchers and U.S. clients.

Secondary data compiled outside the United States have the same limitations as domestic secondary data. However, international researchers should watch for certain pitfalls that frequently are associated with foreign data and cross-cultural research. First, data may simply be unavailable in certain countries. Second, the accuracy of some data may be called into question. This is especially likely with official statistics that may be adjusted for the political purposes of foreign governments.

RESEARCH SNAPSHOT

Around the World of Data

With the Internet, we can quickly go around the world and find data. Many countries have Web sites that summarize basic characteristics with data tables. Here are just a few of the many Web sites that make finding data about different parts of the world easier:

- United States
  http://www.stat-usa.gov
- South Africa
  http://www.statssa.gov.za
- Australia
  http://www.nla.gov.au/oz/stats.html
- Japan
  http://www.stat.go.jp
- U.K.
  http://www.statistics.gov.uk
- France
  http://www.insee.fr
- South America
  http://www.internetworldstats.com/south.htm
- Norway
  http://www.ssb.no
- United Nations
  http://www.un.org/esa

Finally, although economic terminology may be standardized, various countries use different definitions and accounting and recording practices for many economic concepts. For example, different countries may measure disposable personal income in radically different ways. International researchers should take extra care to investigate the comparability of data among countries. The Research Snapshot "Around the World of Data" provides some of the many Web site locations for data from around the world.

The U.S. government and other organizations compile databases that may aid international secondary data needs. For example, *The European Union in the U.S.* (**http://www.eurunion.org**) reports on historical and current activity in the European Union providing a comprehensive reference guide to information about laws and regulations. The *European Union in the U.S.* profiles in detail each European Union member state, investment opportunities, sources of grants and other funding, and other information about business resources.

The U.S. government offers a wealth of data about foreign countries. The CIA's *World Factbook* and the *National Trade Data Bank* are especially useful. Both can be accessed using the Internet. The National Trade Data Bank (NTDB), the U.S. government's most comprehensive source of world trade data, illustrates what is available.

The National Trade Data Bank was established by the Omnibus Trade and Competitiveness Act of 1988.[17] Its purpose was to provide "reasonable public access, including electronic access" to an export promotion data system that was centralized, inexpensive, and easy to use.

The U.S. Department of Commerce has the responsibility for operating and maintaining the NTDB and works with federal agencies that collect and distribute trade information to keep the NTDB up-to-date. The NTDB has been published monthly on CD-ROM since 1990. Over one thousand public and university libraries offer access to the NTDB through the Federal Depository Library system.

The National Trade Data Bank consists of 133 separate trade- and business-related programs (databases). By using it, small- and medium-sized companies get immediate access to information that until now only Fortune 500 companies could afford.

Topics in the NTDB include export opportunities by industry, country, and product; foreign companies or importers looking for specific products; how-to market guides; demographic, political, and socioeconomic conditions in hundreds of countries; and much more. NTDB offers one-stop shopping for trade information from more than 20 federal sources. You do not need to know which federal agency produces the information: All you need to do is consult NTDB.

Some of the specific information that can be obtained from the NTDB is listed in Exhibit 8.11.

TIPS OF THE TRADE

- Always consider the possibility that secondary data may exist which can address the research question at hand.
- Only rely on secondary data that are reliable and valid. Generally, the reliability and validity are established by details the data source provides about how the data were collected and processed.
- Only rely on secondary data for which the units of measure are clear.
- Secondary data are particularly useful for trend analysis, environmental scanning, and estimating market potential for geographic areas.
- Government sites such as the Census Bureau (**www.census.gov**), the CIA Factbook (**www.cia.gov**), and STAT-USA (**www.stat-usa.gov**) are great sources for geodemographic data about locations and peoples around the world.

EXHIBIT 8.11
Examples of Information Contained in the NTDB

Agricultural commodity production and trade
Basic export information
Calendars of trade fairs and exhibitions
Capital markets and export financing
Country reports on economic and social policies and trade practices
Energy production, supply, and inventories
Exchange rates
Export licensing information
Guides to doing business in foreign countries
International trade terms directory
How-to guides
International trade regulations/agreements
International trade agreements
Labor, employment, and productivity
Maritime and shipping information
Market research reports
Overseas contacts
Overseas and domestic industry information
Price indexes
Small business information
State exports
State trade contacts
Trade opportunities
U.S. export regulations
U.S. import and export statistics by country and commodity
U.S. international transactions
World Factbook
World minerals production

Summary

1. Discuss the advantages and disadvantages of secondary data. Secondary data are data that have been gathered and recorded previously by someone else for purposes other than those of the current researcher. The chief advantage of secondary data is that they are almost always less expensive to obtain than primary data. Generally they can be obtained rapidly and may provide information not otherwise available to the researcher. The disadvantage of secondary data is that they were not intended specifically to meet the researcher's needs. The researcher must examine secondary data for accuracy, bias, and soundness. One way to do this is to cross-check various available sources.

2. Define types of secondary data analysis conducted by business research managers. Secondary research designs address many common business research problems. There are three general categories of secondary research objectives: fact-finding, model building, and database marketing. A typical fact-finding study might seek to uncover all available information about consumption patterns for a particular product category or to identify business trends that affect an industry. Model building is more complicated; it involves specifying relationships between two or more variables. The practice of database marketing, which involves maintaining customer databases with customers' names, addresses, phone numbers, past purchases, responses to past promotional offers, and other relevant data such as demographic and financial data, is increasingly being supported by business research efforts.

3. Identify various internal and proprietary sources of secondary data. Managers often get data from internal proprietary sources such as accounting records. Data mining is the use of powerful computers to dig through volumes of data to discover patterns about an organization's customers and products. It is a broad term that applies to many different forms of analysis.

4. Give examples of various external sources of secondary data. External data are generated or recorded by another entity. The government, newspaper and journal publishers, trade associations, and other organizations create or produce information. Traditionally this information has been distributed in published form, either directly from producer to researcher, or indirectly through intermediaries such as public libraries. Modern computerized data archives, electronic data interchange, and the Internet have changed the distribution of external data, making them almost as accessible as internal data. *Push technology* is a term referring to an Internet information technology that automatically delivers content to the researcher's or manager's desktop. This service helps in environmental scanning.

5. Describe the impact of single-source data and globalization on secondary data research. The marketing of multiple types of related data by single-source suppliers has radically changed the nature of secondary-data research. Businesses can measure promotional efforts and related buyer behavior by detailed customer characteristics. As business has become more global, so has the secondary-data industry. International researchers should watch for pitfalls that can be associated with foreign data and cross-cultural research, such as problems with the availability and reliability of data.

Key Terms and Concepts

cross-checks, *178*
customer discovery, *186*
data conversion, *178*
data mining, *185*
database marketing, *186*
external data, *188*
index of retail saturation, *184*
internal and proprietary data, *187*
market tracking, *181*
market-basket analysis, *185*
model building, *182*
neural networks, *185*
secondary data, *177*
single-source data, *194*
site analysis techniques, *184*

Questions for Review and Critical Thinking

1. Secondary data have been called the first line of attack for business researchers. Discuss this description.
2. Suppose you wish to learn about the size of the soft-drink market, particularly root beer sales, growth patterns, and market shares. Indicate probable sources for these secondary data.
3. What is *push technology?*
4. Identify some typical research objectives for secondary-data studies.
5. How might a researcher doing a job for a company such as Pulte Homes (**http://www.pultehomes.com**) or David Weekley Homes (**http://www.davidweekley.com**) use secondary data and data mining?
6. What would be a source for the following data?
   a. Population, average income, and employment rates for Oregon
   b. Maps of U.S. counties and cities
   c. Trends in automobile ownership
   d. Divorce trends in the United States
   e. Median weekly earnings of full-time, salaried workers for the previous five years
   f. Annual sales of the top ten fast-food companies
   g. Top ten Web sites ranked by number of unique visitors
   h. Attendance at professional sports events
7. Suppose you are a business research consultant and a client comes to your office and says, "I must have the latest information on the supply of and demand for Maine potatoes within the next 24 hours." What would you do?
8. Find the following data in the *Survey of Current Business:*
   a. U.S. gross domestic product for the first quarter of 2006
   b. Exports of goods and services for the fourth quarter of 2006
   c. Imports of goods and services for the fourth quarter of 2006
9. **ETHICS** A newspaper reporter finds data in a study that surveyed children that reports a high percentage of children can match cartoon characters with the products they represent. For instance, they can match cereal with Captain Crunch and Ronald McDonald with a Big Mac. The reporter used this to write a story about the need to place limits on the use of cartoon characters. However, the study also provided data suggesting that matching the cartoon character and the product did not lead to significantly higher consumption. Would this be a proper use of secondary data?

Research Activities

1. Use secondary data to learn the size of the U.S. golf market and to profile the typical golfer.
2. **'NET** Where could a researcher working for the U.S. Marine Corps (**http://www.marines.com**) find information that would identify the most productive areas of the United States in which to recruit? What would you recommend?
3. **'NET** PopClocks estimate the U.S. and world populations. Go to the Census Bureau home page (**http://www.census.gov**), navigate to the population section, and find today's estimate of the U.S. and world populations.
4. **'NET** Try to find the U.S. market share for the following companies within 30 minutes:
   a. Home Depot
   b. Burger King
   c. Marlboro
   d. Was this a difficult task? If so, why do you think it is this difficult?
5. **'NET** Use the Internet to learn what you can about Indonesia.
   a. Check the corruption index for Indonesia at **http://www.transparency.org**.
   b. What additional kinds of information are available from the following sources?
      - Go to **http://freetheworld.com/member.html** and view info for Indonesia.
      - Visit the CIA's *World Factbook at* **http://www.cia.gov/cia/publications/factbook.**
      - Go to Google, Yahoo! Search, or another search engine, and use "Indonesia" as a search word.
6. **'NET** Go to Statistics Norway at **http://www.ssb.no**. What data, if any, can you obtain in English? What languages can be used to search this Web site? What databases might be of interest to the business researcher?
7. **'NET** Go to Statistics Canada at **http://www.statcan.gc.ca**. What languages can be used to search this Web site? What databases might be of interest to the business researcher?
8. **'NET** Suppose you were working for a company that wanted to start a business selling handmade acoustic guitars that are reproductions of classic vintage guitars. Pricing is a big part of the decision. Secondary information is available via the Internet. Use eBay (**http://ebay.com**) to identify four key brands of acoustic guitars by studying the vintage acoustic guitars listed for sale. Since the company wishes to charge premium prices, they will model after the most expensive brand. What brand seems to be associated with the highest prices?

Case 8.1 Demand for Gas Guzzlers

© GETTY IMAGES/ PHOTODISC GREEN

In fall 2005, Hurricanes Katrina and Rita churning in the Gulf of Mexico damaged oil rigs and refineries, contributing to a spike in oil prices. Many observers expressed confidence that those events were the long-expected trigger that would kill off demand for SUVs and other gas-guzzling vehicles.[18] They were only partly right.

In the months leading up to the hurricanes, sales of SUVs had already been falling, according to data from *Automotive News*. Automakers had been shifting ad dollars away from these products. CNW Market Research said that in August 2005, consumers had for the first time placed fuel economy ahead of performance when ranking factors for choosing a new vehicle. When gas prices approached three dollars a gallon in September 2005, marketers felt sure that fuel economy would remain a top concern. Advertisers began creating more ads featuring vehicles' gas mileage.

But by the end of the year, attitudes were shifting again. The National Automobile Dealers Association surveyed consumers visiting its Web site for information about car purchases, and it learned they ranked price as most important, followed by make and model, then performance. Fuel economy ranked last, with 3 percent considering it most important and 11 percent considering it least important. What's a carmaker to do? General Motors gathers data from the shoppers who visit Web sites such as **www.kbb.com** to look up information, and it is analyzing the data to identify the price of fuel at which car buyers adjust their priorities.

Questions

1. From the standpoint of an automobile company, what sources of information in this article offer secondary data?
2. Suggest two or three other sources of data that might be of interest to auto companies interested in forecasting demand.
3. Online or at your library, look for information about recent trends in SUV purchases. Report what you learned, and forecast whether SUV sales are likely to recover or continue their decline. What role do gas prices play in your forecast?

Case 8.2 An Indian Case

© GETTY IMAGES/ PHOTODISC GREEN

ACNielsen Market Information Digest (MID) contains information of wide range of product for the companies who are interested in consumer goods market. It has both primary and secondary data of Indian consumers on 78 different product categories on retail sales and media spending and demographic as well as sociographic information. This data source provides insightful tools to the users of secondary data on Indian retail market of FMCG as well as branded goods. The data also gives information on Indian consumers' spending habit, media usage, brand preference, etc. MID is used by companies for their marketing plans and helps the companies to figure out in which category they should enter, how many segments are available in a particular product category, what is the profile of those segments, the growth potential of each segment, etc.

Question

1. What type of secondary data can be obtained from MID? In what purpose can these data be used in research?

Part 3
Research Methods for Collecting Primary Data

© JOHN LUND/THE IMAGE BANK/GETTY IMAGES

CHAPTER 9
SURVEY RESEARCH: AN OVERVIEW

LEARNING OUTCOMES

After studying this chapter, you should be able to

1. **Define surveys and explain their advantages**
2. **Describe the type of information that may be gathered in a survey**
3. **Identify sources of error in survey research**
4. **Distinguish among the various categories of surveys**
5. **Discuss the importance of survey research to total quality management programs**

Chapter Vignette: Media Phones—The Next Wave of Communication Technology?

What's next in the world of electronic communication? In just a few years, we have seen cellular phones move from simple devices to talk with someone to portable music and video players with the ability to directly download music and movies, as well as watch television. We keep our calendars and all our contact information in our cell phones. During this same time, our in-home phones have advanced little. That is about to change, according to research conducted by In-Stat (**http://www.in-stat.com**). In-Stat claims to be "the leading provider of actionable research, market analysis and forecasts of advanced communications services, infrastructure, end-user devices and semiconductors."

While you may have never heard the term *media phone,* you could very well have one in your home in the next four years:

> *The media phone represents a new category of broadband multimedia device that has the potential to become the 4th screen in the home, complementing the PC, TV, and mobile handset. The media phone delivers direct access to Internet-based entertainment and applications using a large (6–10 inch) color touchscreen display with a high-quality speakerphone. The media phone combines the power of a PC with the always-on functionality of the home telephone. Most units are configured with one or more cordless DECT voice handsets, suitable for any room in the home.*
>
> *In-Stat research has found that the most popular consumer Internet activities include viewing online information services (news updates, weather forecasts, recipes, directory searches), and accessing entertainment content (YouTube videos, movie clips, and music). Media phones offer always-on, one-touch access to this popular media content. Other applications, such as a digital picture frame, TV electronic program guide, local purchases (e.g., pizza or movie tickets) and the integration of mobile features (e.g., visual voice mail, network-based address book, and location-based services) will help make the media phone an indispensable part of every broadband household.* (**http://www.instat.com/ promos/09/dl/media_phone_3ufewaCr.pdf**)

In-Stat has conducted extensive survey research to learn consumer perceptions, attitudes, and desires regarding media phones. The company estimates the consumer market for media phones could reach nearly 50 million units and $8 billion in worldwide revenue by 2013. In addition to identifying the primary uses of the media phone noted above, In-Stat research determined the characteristics of the product customers desired across consumer age groups and geographic locations. For example, U.K. customers place much greater importance on the television component of the media phone than French customers. Further, the research shows (perhaps not surprisingly) that younger customers have a much higher level of interest in the media phone than older customers. Younger customers also planned on putting the media phone in their living room or bedroom, while older customers would place it in their home office. Older customers also show a strong preference for charging their media phone handsets in a cradle, while younger customers want to plug theirs in like a cell phone.

In-Stat's survey research obviously has significant benefits for an electronics manufacturer. Not only will this research help with product design and development, but with production planning, pricing, promotion, and distribution. An investment in this research upfront can save millions of dollars down the road. In a few years, we may all have a media phone in our home![1]

Introduction

In business research, it is important to understand consumer loyalty in the context of the competitive environment where a product or brand operates. In emerging markets, namely, in China, India, and Brazil, consumer loyalty shifts very quickly as several products and brands are launched by competitors on a regular interval. Continuous migration of consumers from one social economy class to upper social economy class has resulted in very less association of consumers with one particular brand. For instance, in just a few years mobile phone market in India has observed 26 mobile phone brands offering different features at reasonably less price providing value to the customers. These mobile phones contain features that are entertainment centric offering music, video, video conversation, and many more in addition to the basic features. Hence there are several consumer loyalty issues that companies manufacturing cell phones would like to address to design a better marketing plan. For instance, it may be important for a company to know if the consumers are loyal to a brand or they are loyal to a particular feature like size/color/weight/battery life, etc. Brands with higher loyalty are more profitable than their less loyal counterparts. Hence understanding consumer behavior is fundamental for these companies who constantly engage in survey research to better learn consumer behavior. Samsung, for instance, uses extensive survey research to learn about consumer's perception and attitude of cell phone purchase.[2]

The purpose of survey research is to collect primary data—data gathered and assembled specifically for the project at hand. This chapter, the first of two on survey research, defines the subject. It also discusses typical research objectives that may be accomplished with surveys and various advantages of the survey method. The chapter explains many potential errors that researchers must be careful to avoid. Finally, it classifies the various survey research methods.

Often research entails asking people—called **respondents**—to provide answers to written or spoken questions. These interviews or questionnaires collect data through the mail, on the telephone, online, or face-to-face. Thus, a survey is defined as a method of collecting primary data based on communication with a representative sample of individuals. Surveys provide a snapshot at a given point in time. The more formal term, **sample survey**, emphasizes that the purpose of contacting respondents is to obtain a representative sample, or subset, of the target population.

respondents
People who verbally answer an interviewer's questions or provide answers to written questions.

sample survey
A more formal term for a survey.

An effective survey should have the following properties:

- **Clarity.** Goal and objective of the survey should be clearly defined.
- **Completability.** Survey questions must be easy to understand and follow.
- **Processability.** The data must be clean and valid for further processing.
- **Analyzability.** Data must be properly analyzed.
- **Timeliness.** The time gap between planning and implementation should be short for effective decision making.

Using Surveys

The type of information gathered in a survey varies considerably depending on its objectives. Typically, surveys attempt to describe what is happening or to learn the reasons for a particular business activity.

Identifying characteristics of target markets, measuring customer attitudes, and describing consumer purchase patterns are all common business research objectives. Survey research seeks to answer certain specific questions about the surveyed topic related to "why," "who," "where," "how," and "what." Most business surveys have multiple objectives; few gather only a single type of factual information. In the opening vignette, In-Stat asked questions about product use and desirable features which can help with product development and advertising messages. Geographic, demographic, and media exposure information were also collected to help plan a market segmentation strategy. A study commissioned by eBay provides another example of the information that can be gleaned from survey research. eBay learned that almost 60 percent of respondents receive unwanted gifts, and 15 percent of them had sold an unwanted gift online, suggesting a possible source of demand for eBay's auction services.[3] In addition, the survey indicated that selling unwanted gifts online was twice as common among 25- to 34-year-olds. Although consumer surveys are a common form of business research, not all survey research is conducted with the ultimate consumer. Frequently, studies focus on wholesalers, retailers, industrial buyers, or within the organization itself. For example, a survey could be used to determine an organization's commitment to the environment. Also, measuring employee job satisfaction and describing the risk aversion of financial investors may be important survey objectives.

Because most survey research is descriptive research, the term *survey* is most often associated with quantitative findings. Although most surveys are conducted to quantify certain factual information, some aspects of surveys may also be qualitative. In new-product development, a survey often has a qualitative objective of refining product concepts. Stylistic, aesthetic, or functional changes may be made on the basis of respondents' suggestions. In our example of an organization's environmental attitudes, a survey might be used to gather qualitative information regarding activities that could make the company more "green."

Evaluating the nature of advertising may also be an objective of survey research, as in the following story told to advertiser Michael Arlen about testing a rough commercial for AT&T:

> *We called it "Fishing Camp." The idea was this: These guys go off to a fishing camp in the north woods, somewhere far away, where they're going to have a terrific time together and do all this great fishing, only what happens is that it rains all the time and the fishing is a bust. Mind you, this was a humorous ad. The emphasis was on the humor. Anyway, the big moment occurs when the fishing guys are talking on the phone to their jealous friends back home—who naturally want to know how great the fishing is—and what you see are the fishing guys, huddled in this cabin, with the rain pouring down outside, and one of the guys is staring at a frying pan full of hamburgers sizzling on the stove while he says into the phone, "Boy, you should see the great trout we've got cooking here."*[4]

However, much to the advertisers' astonishment, when they tested the advertisement and gave subjects a questionnaire, respondents recalled that what was cooking was trout. To counteract this misimpression, said the advertiser, "We ended up making it, but what we had to do was, when we came to that segment, we put the camera almost *inside* the frying pan, and in the frying pan we put huge, crude chunks of hamburger that were so raw they were almost red."

Advantages of Surveys

Surveys provide a quick, inexpensive, efficient, and accurate means of assessing information about a population. The examples given earlier illustrate that surveys are quite flexible and, when properly conducted, extremely valuable to the manager.

As we discussed in Chapter 1, business research has proliferated in recent years. The growth of survey research is related to the simple idea that to find out what someone thinks, you need to ask them.[5]

RESEARCH SNAPSHOT

Intuit Gets Answers to Satisfy Customers

Intuit, maker of Quicken, QuickBooks, and Turbo Tax software for accounting and tax preparation, has enjoyed years of growth and profits, thanks in part to its efforts to learn what customers want. One of its most important marketing research tools is called a "net promoter survey." That survey is extremely simple. Researchers simply ask customers, "On a scale of 0 to 10 (with 10 being most likely), how likely is it that you would recommend our product to your friends or colleagues?" Customers who respond with a 9 or 10 are called "promoters," and customers who respond with 0 through 6 are called "detractors." Subtracting the percentage of respondents who are detractors from the percentage who are promoters yields the net promoter score.

Intuit's CEO, Steve Bennett—who says he believes that "anything that can be measured can be improved"—encourages the ongoing collection of net promoter scores as a way to improve products and customer service and thereby build revenues and profits. Of course, making improvements requires that the company not only know *whether* customers are satisfied or dissatisfied but also know *why*. To learn more, the company asks survey respondents who are promoters to go online and provide more detailed opinions. For example, Intuit learned that claiming rebates was an annoying process (the company has simplified it) and that discount stores were offering some products for less than the prices offered online to frequent buyers (the company plans to adjust prices).

For even more in-depth information, Intuit supplements survey research with direct observation of customers. One year the company sent hundreds of employees, including CEO Bennett, to visit customers as they worked at their computers. The observers learned that a significant number of small-business owners were struggling with the accounting know-how they needed to use QuickBooks and were mystified by terms such as *accounts payable* and *accounts receivable*. In response, the company introduced QuickBooks: Simple Start Edition, which replaces the financial jargon with simple terms like *cash in* and *cash out*. In the first year after its launch, Simple Start Edition sold more copies than any other accounting software except the standard QuickBooks.

This Research Snapshot not only illustrates Intuit's reliance on survey research to enhance products and monitor customer satisfaction and loyalty, but also shows the close relationship between qualitative and quantitative research. As we discussed in Chapter 7, qualitative research is often used in exploratory business research to set the stage for quantitative research, such as surveys. Qualitative research can also be used to provide richer information, to bring the quantitative research numbers to life. Intuit recognizes the value of both research approaches.

Sources: Darlin, Damon, "The Only Question That Matters," *Business 2.0* (September 2005), http://web2.infotrac.galegroup.com; Kirkpatrick, David, "Throw It at the Wall and See if It Sticks," *Fortune* (December 12, 2005), http://web2.infotrac.galegroup.com; and McGregor, Jena, "Would You Recommend Us?" *Business Week* (January 30, 2006), http://web5.infotrac.galegroup.com; Reicheld, Frederick F., "The One Number You Need to Grow," *Harvard Business Review* (December 1, 2003); Reicheld, Frederick F., "The One Number You Need to Grow: Key Ideas from the Harvard Business Review Article," *HBR in Brief*, accessed February 12, 2009.

Over the last 50 years and particularly during the last two decades, survey research techniques and standards have become quite scientific and accurate. When properly conducted, surveys offer managers many advantages. However, they can also be used poorly when researchers do not follow research principles, such as careful survey and sample design. Sometimes even a well-designed and carefully executed survey is not helpful because the results are delivered too late to inform decisions.

The disadvantages of specific forms of survey data collection—personal interview, telephone, mail, Internet, and other self-administered formats—are discussed in Chapter 10. However, errors are common to all forms of surveys, so it is appropriate to describe them generally.

Several areas in business can benefit from survey research:

- Consumer satisfaction
- Complaint identification and monitoring
- Development of preferred product features
- Measuring willingness to pay for a product
- Segmenting customer base
- Customers retention and customer integration
- Loyalty program planning
- Profile evaluation of customer or employees
- Advertising effectiveness measurement
- Interest areas of viewers/readership
- Acquisition of customers

Some aspects survey research attempts to address are:

- What is the most preferred and important to customers or employees?
- Identifying profile of customer.
- Is the customer expectation same as what company is providing? Is it above or below than what is expected by the customer?
- How to deploy resources most effectively and efficiently?
- Identifying areas that need improvement.
- Consumers' perception about a brand and competing brands.
- Brand's perceived strengths and/or weaknesses.
- Strategies that enable the organization to compete in the market most effectively.

Errors in Survey Research

A manager who is evaluating the quality of a survey must estimate its accuracy. Exhibit 9.1 outlines the various forms of survey error. They have two major sources: random sampling error and systematic error.

Random Sampling Error

random sampling error
A statistical fluctuation that occurs because of chance variation in the elements selected for a sample.

Most surveys try to portray a representative cross-section of a particular target population. Even with technically proper random probability samples, however, statistical errors will occur because of chance variation in the elements selected for the sample. These statistical problems are unavoidable without very large samples (>400). However, the extent of **random sampling error** can be estimated. Chapters 16 and 17 will discuss these errors and ways they can be estimated in more detail.

Systematic Error

systematic error
Error resulting from some imperfect aspect of the research design that causes respondent error or from a mistake in the execution of the research.

sample bias
A persistent tendency for the results of a sample to deviate in one direction from the true value of the population parameter.

The other major source of survey error, **systematic error**, results from some imperfect aspect of the research design or from a mistake in the execution of the research. Because systematic errors include all sources of error other than those introduced by the random sampling procedure, these errors or biases are also called *nonsampling errors*. A **sample bias** exists when the results of a sample show a persistent tendency to deviate in one direction from the true value of the population parameter. The many sources of error that in some way systematically influence answers can be divided into two general categories: respondent error and administrative error.

Respondent Error

respondent error
A category of sample bias resulting from some respondent action or inaction such as nonresponse or response bias.

Surveys ask people for answers. If people cooperate and give truthful answers, a survey will likely accomplish its goal. If these conditions are not met, nonresponse error or response bias, the two major categories of **respondent error**, may cause sample bias.

NONRESPONSE ERROR

nonresponse error
The statistical differences between a survey that includes only those who responded and a perfect survey that would also include those who failed to respond.

Few surveys have 100 percent response rates. In fact, surveys with relatively low response rates may still accurately reflect the population of interest. However, a researcher who obtains a 1 percent response to a five-page e-mail questionnaire concerning various brands of spark plugs may face a serious problem. To use the results, the researcher must believe that consumers who responded to the questionnaire are representative of all consumers, including those who did not respond. The statistical differences between a survey that includes only those who responded and a survey that also included those who failed to respond are referred to as **nonresponse error**. This problem is especially acute in mail and Internet surveys, but nonresponse also threatens telephone and face-to-face interviews.

EXHIBIT 9.1 **Categories of Survey Errors**

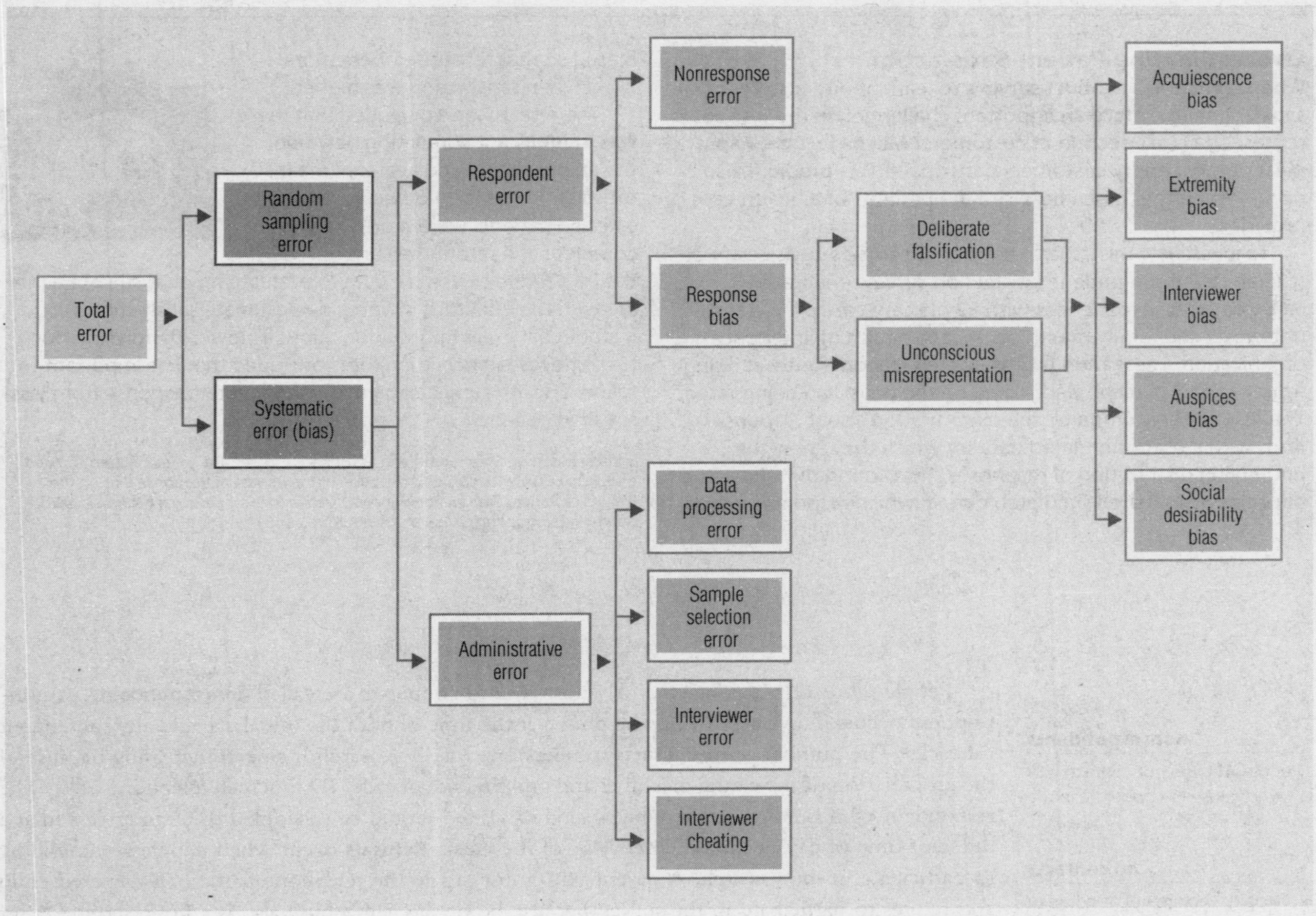

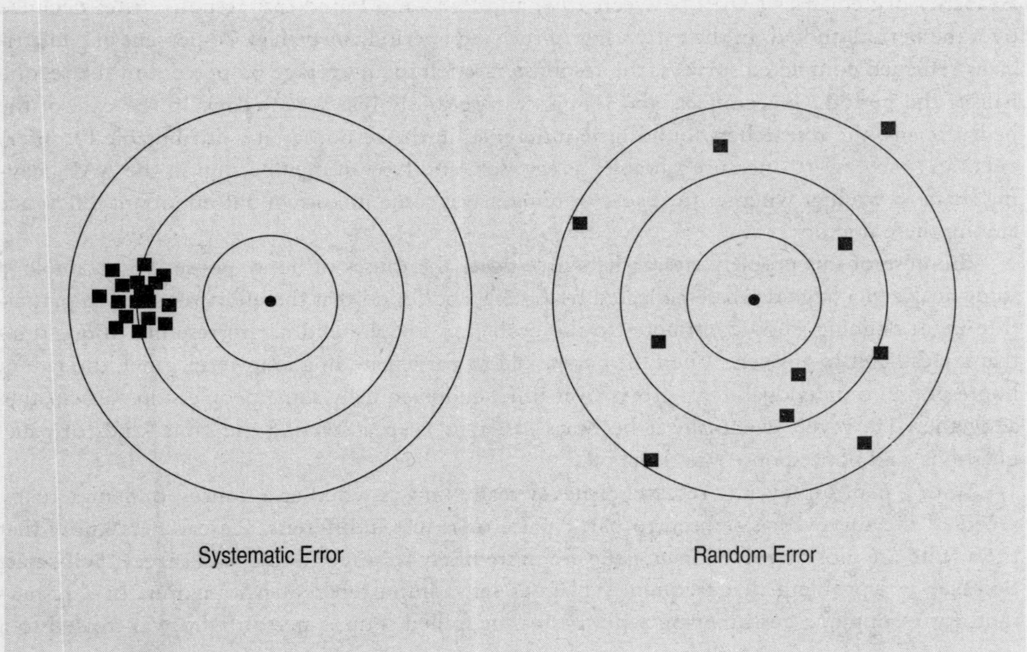

EXHIBIT 9.2
Errors in Survey

RESEARCH SNAPSHOT

Overestimating Patient Satisfaction

When companies conduct surveys to learn about customer satisfaction, they face an important challenge: do the responses represent a cross-section of customers? Maybe just the happiest or most angry customers participate. This problem also occurs when the "customers" are the patients of a health-care provider.

To investigate this issue, a group of researchers in Massachusetts studied data from patient satisfaction surveys that rated 6,681 patients' experiences with 82 primary-care physicians (internists and family practitioners) at a health maintenance organization. These ratings represented response rates ranging from 11 to 55 percent, depending on the physician being rated. The researchers compared their information about response rates with a set of simulated data for which they knew the underlying distribution of responses. They found that the actual data closely matched simulated data in which responses were biased so that responses were more likely when satisfaction was higher.

The researchers concluded that there was a significant correlation between the response rate and average (mean) satisfaction rating. In other words, more-satisfied patients were more likely to complete and return the survey. Thus, if the HMO were to use the data to evaluate how satisfied patients are with their doctors, it would overestimate satisfaction. Also, it would have less information about its lower-performing doctors. The researchers therefore concluded that it is important to follow up with subjects to encourage greater response from less-satisfied patients.

Source: Based on Mazor, Kathleen M., Brian E. Clauser, Terry Field, Robert A. Yood, and Jerry H. Gurwitz, "A Demonstration of the Impact of Response Bias on the Results of Patient Satisfaction Surveys," *Health Services Research* (October 2002), downloaded from http://galenet.galegroup.com.

nonrespondents
People who are not contacted or who refuse to cooperate in the research.

no contacts
People who are not at home or who are otherwise inaccessible on the first and second contact.

refusals
People who are unwilling to participate in a research project.

People who are not contacted or who refuse to cooperate are called **nonrespondents**. A nonresponse occurs if no one answers the phone at the time of both the initial call and any subsequent callbacks. The number of **no contacts** in telephone survey research has been increasing because of the proliferation of answering machines and growing use of caller ID to screen telephone calls.[6] The respondent who is not at home when called or visited should be scheduled to be interviewed at a different time of day or on a different day of the week. **Refusals** occur when people are unwilling to participate in the research. A parent who must juggle the telephone and a half-diapered child and refuses to participate in the survey because he or she is too busy also is a nonresponse. After receiving a refusal from a potential respondent, an interviewer can do nothing other than be polite.

A research team reviewed 50 mail surveys of pediatricians conducted by the American Academy of Pediatrics (AAP) between 1994 and 2002 and found that response rates declined over the period studied. In the early years of the study period, an average 70 percent of pediatricians returned completed surveys; the response rate fell to an average 63 percent in the second half of the period.[7] No contacts and refusals can seriously bias survey data. In the case of the pediatricians, the researchers found little difference in the response rates attributable to differences in such easy-to-measure variables as age, sex, and type of membership in the AAP, leaving them to wonder whether the cause of refusals was some unknown but important difference among these doctors.

Because of this problem, researchers investigate the causes of nonresponse. For example, a study analyzed a large database collected by AT&T and found that the effort required to participate in an ongoing study contributes to the problem.[8] People tend not to respond to questions that are difficult to answer. When they are asked to participate in a long-term panel, the rate of nonresponse to individual items grows over time, and eventually some people stop participating altogether. However, eventually it becomes easier to keep answering the same kinds of panel questions, and nonresponse rates level off.

self-selection bias
A bias that occurs because people who feel strongly about a subject are more likely to respond to survey questions than people who feel indifferent about it.

With a mail survey, the researcher never really knows whether a nonrespondent actually received the survey, has refused to participate, or is just indifferent. Researchers know that those who are most involved in an issue are more likely to respond to a mail survey. **Self-selection bias** is a problem that frequently plagues self-administered questionnaires. In a restaurant, for example, a customer on whom a waiter spilled soup, a person who was treated to a surprise dinner, or others who feel strongly about the service are more likely to complete a self-administered questionnaire left at the table than individuals who are indifferent about the restaurant. Self-selection biases distort surveys because they overrepresent extreme positions while underrepresenting responses from those who are indifferent. Several techniques will be discussed later for encouraging respondents to reply to mail and Internet surveys.

Comparing the demographics of the sample with the demographics of the target population is one means of inspecting for possible biases in response patterns. If a particular group, such as older citizens, is underrepresented or if any potential biases appear in a response pattern, additional efforts should be made to obtain data from the underrepresented segments of the population. For example, telephone surveys may be used instead of mail surveys or personal interviews may be used instead of telephone interviews in an attempt to increase participation of underrepresented segments.

©YURIARCURS/SHUTTERSTOCK

Many e-mail addresses are actually inactive. Inactive e-mails contribute to low response rates.

RESPONSE BIAS

A **response bias** occurs when respondents tend to answer questions with a certain slant. People may consciously or unconsciously misrepresent the truth. If a distortion of measurement occurs because respondents' answers are falsified or misrepresented, either intentionally or inadvertently, the resulting sample bias will be a response bias. When researchers identify response bias, they should include a corrective measure.

response bias

A bias that occurs when respondents either consciously or unconsciously tend to answer questions with a certain slant that misrepresents the truth.

Deliberate Falsification

Occasionally people deliberately give false answers. It is difficult to assess why people knowingly misrepresent answers. A response bias may occur when people misrepresent answers to appear intelligent, conceal personal information, avoid embarrassment, and so on. For example, respondents may be able to remember the total amount of money spent grocery shopping, but they may forget the exact prices of individual items that they purchased. Rather than appear ignorant or unconcerned about prices, they may provide their best estimate and not tell the truth—namely, that they cannot remember. Sometimes respondents become bored with the interview and provide answers just to get rid of the interviewer. At other times respondents try to appear well informed by providing the answers they think are expected of them. On still other occasions, they give answers simply to please the interviewer.

One explanation for conscious and deliberate misrepresentation of facts is the so-called average-person hypothesis. Individuals may prefer to be viewed as average, so they alter their responses to conform more closely to their *perception* of the average person. Average-person effects have been found in response to questions about such topics as savings account balances, car prices, voting behavior, and hospital stays.

Unconscious Misrepresentation

Even when a respondent is consciously trying to be truthful and cooperative, response bias can arise from the question format, the question content, or some other stimulus. For example, bias can be introduced by the situation in which the survey is administered. The results of two in-flight surveys concerning aircraft preference illustrate this point. Passengers flying on B-747s preferred B-747s to L-1011s (74 percent versus 19 percent), while passengers flying on L-1011s preferred L-1011s to B-747s (56 percent versus 38 percent). Managers may be tempted to conclude that the results demonstrate a preference for B-747s over L-1011s. But perhaps respondents were influenced by other factors besides the airplane or had not experience flying in the other type of plane. Respondents' satisfaction scores may simply be a simple response to their overall satisfaction with the flying experience. Also, airlines have fleets that consist predominantly of one brand of aircraft. Thus, the data appearing to support Boeing may really be showing greater satisfaction for the airlines that happen to be flying Boeing and would have higher satisfaction no matter what planes were in their fleet.[9]

Respondents who misunderstand questions may unconsciously provide biased answers. Or they may be willing to answer but unable to do so because they have forgotten the exact details. Asking "When was the last time you attended a concert?" may result in a best-guess estimate because the respondent has forgotten the exact date.

A bias may also occur when a respondent has not thought about an unexpected question. Many respondents will answer questions even though they have given them little thought. For example, in most investigations of consumers' buying intentions, the predictability of the intention scales depends on how close the subject is to making a purchase. The intentions of subjects who have little knowledge of the brand or the store alternatives being surveyed and the intentions of subjects who have not yet made any purchase plans cannot be expected to predict purchase behavior accurately.

In many cases consumers cannot adequately express their feelings in words. The cause may be questions that are vague or ambiguous. Researchers may ask someone to describe his or her frustration when using a computer. The problem is, the researcher may be interested in software problems while the respondent is thinking of hardware issues. Language differences also may be a source of misunderstanding. A survey in the Philippines found that, despite seemingly high toothpaste usage, only a tiny percentage of people responded positively when asked, "Do you use toothpaste?" As it turned out, people in the Philippines tend to refer to toothpaste by using the brand name Colgate. When researchers returned and asked, "Do you use Colgate?" the positive response rate soared.

As the time following a purchase or a shopping event increases, people become more likely to underreport information about that event. Time lapse influences people's ability to precisely remember and communicate specific factors.

Unconscious misrepresentation bias may also occur because consumers unconsciously avoid facing the realities of a future buying situation. Housing surveys record that Americans overwhelmingly continue to aspire to own detached, single-family dwellings (preferably single-level, ranch-type structures that require two to five times the amount of land per unit required for apartments). However, builders know that apartment (condo) purchases by first buyers are more common than respondents report, despite their aspirations.

Types of Response Bias

Response bias falls into four specific categories: acquiescence bias, extremity bias, interviewer bias, and social desirability bias. These categories overlap and are not mutually exclusive. A single biased answer may be distorted for many complex reasons, some distortions being deliberate and some being unconscious misrepresentations.

acquiescence bias

A tendency for respondents to agree with all or most questions asked of them in a survey.

Acquiescence bias. Some respondents are very agreeable. They seem to agree to practically every statement they are asked about. A tendency to agree (or disagree) with all or most questions is known as **acquiescence bias**. This bias is particularly prominent in new-product research. Questions about a new-product idea generally elicit some acquiescence bias because respondents give positive connotations to most new ideas. For example, consumers responded favorably to survey questions about pump baseball gloves (the pump inserts air into the pocket of the glove, providing more cushioning). However, when these expensive gloves hit the market, they sat on the shelves. When conducting new-product research, researchers should recognize the high likelihood of acquiescence bias.

Agreement or disagreement can also be influenced by a respondents' feelings toward the organization identified as conducting or sponsoring the research. Auspices bias occurs when answers reflect the person's liking or disliking of the sponsor organization rather than simply the relevant opinions.

Extremity bias. Some individuals tend to use extremes when responding to questions. For example, they may choose only "1" or "10" on a ten-point scale. Others consistently refuse to use extreme positions and tend to respond more neutrally—"I never give a 10 because nothing is really perfect." Response styles vary from person to person, and extreme responses may cause an **extremity bias** in the data.[10]

extremity bias

A category of response bias that results because some individuals tend to use extremes when responding to questions.

Interviewer bias. Response bias may arise from the interplay between interviewer and respondent. If the interviewer's presence influences respondents to give untrue or modified answers, the survey will be marred by **interviewer bias**. Many homemakers and retired people welcome an interviewer's visit as a break in routine activities. Other respondents may give answers they believe will please the interviewer rather than the truthful responses. Respondents may wish to appear intelligent and wealthy—of course they read *Scientific American* rather than *Playboy*!

interviewer bias

A response bias that occurs because the presence of the interviewer influences respondents' answers.

The interviewer's age, sex, style of dress, tone of voice, facial expressions, or other nonverbal characteristics may have some influence on a respondent's answers. If an interviewer smiles and makes a positive statement after a respondent's answers, the respondent will be more likely to give similar responses. In a research study on sexual harassment against saleswomen, male interviewers might not yield as candid responses from saleswomen as female interviewers would.

Many interviewers, contrary to instructions, shorten or rephrase questions to suit their needs. This potential influence on responses can be avoided to some extent if interviewers receive training and supervision that emphasize the necessity of appearing neutral.

If interviews go on too long, respondents may feel that time is being wasted. They may answer as abruptly as possible with little forethought.

Social desirability bias. **Social desirability bias** may occur either consciously or unconsciously because the respondent wishes to create a favorable impression or save face in the presence of an interviewer. Incomes may be inflated, education overstated, or perceived respectable answers given to gain prestige. In contrast, answers to questions that seek factual information or responses about matters of public knowledge (zip code, number of children, and so on) usually are quite accurate. An interviewer's presence may increase a respondent's tendency to give inaccurate answers to sensitive questions such as "Did you vote in the last election?" or "Do you have termites or roaches in your home?" or "Do you color your hair?"

social desirability bias

Bias in responses caused by respondents' desire, either conscious or unconscious, to gain prestige or appear in a different social role.

Social desirability bias is especially significant in the case of research that addresses sensitive or personal topics, including respondents' sexual behavior. A group of researchers recently evaluated responses to questions about homosexual sexual activity, collected by the National Opinion Research Center's long-running General Social Survey.[11] The researchers found that over time, as attitudes toward homosexual conduct have softened, the frequency of repeated female-female sexual contacts increased dramatically, suggesting the possibility that reporting levels have been subject to social desirability bias. However, the researchers noted that rates of male-male sexual contact were fairly steady over the period and that the rate of change for female-female sexual contact persisted even when adjusted for measures of greater tolerance. This evidence suggests that the data reflect more phenomena than mere social desirability bias.

The more people are susceptible to interpersonal influence, the more likely a response bias will occur. One example of this can be found in adolescents' buying behavior.

©JEFF GREENBERG/PHOTOEDIT

administrative error
An error caused by the improper administration or execution of the research task.

data-processing error
A category of administrative error that occurs because of incorrect data entry, incorrect computer programming, or other procedural errors during data analysis.

sample selection error
An administrative error caused by improper sample design or sampling procedure execution.

interviewer error
Mistakes made by interviewers failing to record survey responses correctly.

interviewer cheating
The practice of filling in fake answers or falsifying questionnaires while working as an interviewer.

Administrative Error

The result of improper administration or execution of the research task is called an **administrative error**. Administrative errors are caused by carelessness, confusion, neglect, omission, or some other blunder. Four types of administrative error are data-processing error, sample selection error, interviewer error, and interviewer cheating.

DATA-PROCESSING ERROR

Processing data by computer, like any arithmetic or procedural process, is subject to error because data must be edited, coded, and entered into the computer by people. The accuracy of data processed by computer depends on correct data entry and programming. **Data-processing error** can be minimized by establishing careful procedures for verifying each step in the data-processing stage.

SAMPLE SELECTION ERROR

Many kinds of error involve failure to select a representative sample. **Sample selection error** is systematic error that results in an unrepresentative sample because of an error in either the sample design or the execution of the sampling procedure. Executing a sampling plan free of procedural error is difficult. A firm that selects its sample from the phone book will have some systematic error, because those with only cell phones or with unlisted numbers are not included. Stopping respondents during daytime hours in shopping centers largely excludes working people or those who primarily shop by mail, Internet, or telephone. In other cases, researchers interview the wrong person. Consider a political pollster who uses random-digit dialing to select a sample, rather than a list of registered voters. Unregistered 17-year-olds may be willing to give their opinions, but they are the wrong people to ask because they cannot vote.

One problem with Web-based surveys is that there is no way of knowing who exactly responded to the questionnaire.

© ZOONAR/THINKSTOCK

INTERVIEWER ERROR

Interviewers' abilities vary considerably. **Interviewer error** is introduced when interviewers record answers but check the wrong response or are unable to write fast enough to record answers verbatim. Also, selective perception may cause interviewers to misrecord data that do not support their own attitudes and opinions.

INTERVIEWER CHEATING

Interviewer cheating occurs when an interviewer falsifies entire questionnaires or fills in answers to questions that have been intentionally skipped. Some interviewers cheat to finish an interview as quickly as possible or to avoid questions about sensitive topics. Often interviewers are paid by the completed survey, so you can see the motivation to complete a survey that is left with some questions unanswered.

If interviewers are suspected of faking questionnaires, they should be told that a small percentage of respondents will be called back to confirm whether the initial interview was actually conducted. This practice should discourage interviewers from cheating. The term *curb-stoning* is sometimes used to refer to interviewers filling in responses for respondents that do not really exist.

Rule-of-Thumb Estimates for Systematic Error

The techniques for estimating systematic, or nonsampling, error are less precise than many sample statistics. Researchers have established conservative rules of thumb based on experience to estimate systematic error. In the case of consumer research, experienced researchers might determine that only a certain percentage of people who say they will definitely buy a new product actually do so. Evidence for a mere-measurement effect suggests that in some situations, researchers might conclude that respondents' own buying behavior will exaggerate overall sales. Thus, researchers often present actual survey findings *and* their interpretations of estimated purchase response based on estimates of nonsampling error. For example, one pay-per-view cable TV company surveys geographic areas it plans to enter and estimates the number of people who indicate they will subscribe to its service. The company knocks down the percentage by a "ballpark 10 percent" because experience in other geographic areas has indicated that there is a systematic upward bias of 10 percent on this intentions question.

What Can Be Done to Reduce Survey Error?

Now that we have examined the sources of error in surveys, you may have lost some of your optimism about survey research. Don't be discouraged! The discussion emphasized the bad news because it is important for managers to realize that surveys are not a panacea. There are, however, ways to handle and reduce survey errors. For example, Chapter 15 on questionnaire design discusses the reduction of response bias; Chapters 16 and 17 discuss the reduction of sample selection and random sampling error. Indeed, much of the remainder of this book discusses various techniques for reducing bias in business research. The good news lies ahead!

Classifying Survey Research Methods

Now that we have introduced some advantages and disadvantages of surveys in general, we turn to a discussion of classification of surveys according to several criteria. Surveys may be classified based on the method of communication, the degrees of structure and disguise in the questionnaire, and the time frame in which the data are gathered (temporal classification). Chapter 10 classifies surveys according to method of communicating with the respondent, covering topics such as personal interviews, telephone interviews, mail surveys, and Internet surveys. The classifications based on structure and disguise and on time frame will be discussed in the remainder of this chapter.

Structured/Unstructured and Disguised/Undisguised Questionnaires

In designing a questionnaire (or an *interview schedule*), the researcher must decide how much structure or standardization is needed.[12] A **structured question** limits the number of allowable responses. For example, the respondent may be instructed to choose one alternative response such as "under 18," "18–35," or "over 35" to indicate his or her age. An **unstructured question** does not restrict the respondent's answers. An open-ended, unstructured question such as "Why do you shop at Wal-Mart?" allows the respondent considerable freedom in answering.

structured question
A question that imposes a limit on the number of allowable responses.

unstructured question
A question that does not restrict the respondents' answers.

The researcher must also decide whether to use **undisguised questions** or **disguised questions.** A straightforward, or undisguised, question such as "Do you have dandruff problems?" assumes that the respondent is willing to reveal the information. However, researchers know that some questions are threatening to a person's ego, prestige, or self-concept. So, they have designed a number of indirect techniques of questioning to disguise the purpose of the study.

Questionnaires can be categorized by their degree of structure and degree of disguise. For example, interviews in exploratory research might use *unstructured-disguised* questionnaires. The projective techniques discussed in Chapter 7 fall into this category. Other classifications are *structured-undisguised, unstructured-undisguised,* and *structured-disguised.* These classifications have two limitations: First, the degree of structure and the degree of disguise vary; they are not clear-cut categories. Second, most surveys are hybrids, asking both structured and unstructured questions. Recognizing the degrees of structure and disguise necessary to meet survey objectives will help in the selection of the appropriate communication medium for conducting the survey.

Temporal Classification

Although most surveys are for individual research projects conducted only once over a short time period, other projects require multiple surveys over a long period. Thus, surveys can be classified on a temporal basis.

CROSS-SECTIONAL STUDIES

cross-sectional study
A study in which various segments of a population are sampled and data are collected at a single moment in time.

undisguised questions
Straightforward questions that assume the respondent is willing to answer.

disguised questions
Indirect questions that assume the purpose of the study must be hidden from the respondent.

Do you make New Year's resolutions? A Harris Interactive survey conducted in November 2008 indicates that women (74 percent) are more likely than men (58 percent) to actually make a New Year's resolution. However, more men than women "always or often keep their resolutions" (22 percent of men compared to 14 percent of women).[13] This was a **cross-sectional study** because it collected the data at a single point in time. That is, the survey asked people to reflect on their past behavior, rather than ask them if they made a resolution, then follow up a year later to see if the resolution was kept. Such a study samples various segments of the population to investigate relationships among variables by cross-tabulation. Most business research surveys fall into this category. We can think of cross-sectional studies as taking a snapshot of the current situation.

The typical method of analyzing a cross-sectional survey is to divide the sample into appropriate subgroups. For example, if a winery expects income levels to influence attitudes toward wines, the data are broken down into subgroups based on income and analyzed to reveal similarities or differences among the income subgroups. If a manager thinks that length of time an employee has been with the organization will influence their attitudes toward corporate policies, employees might be broken into different groups based on tenure (e.g., less than 5 years, 5–9 years, 10–14 years, and 15 years or more) so their attitudes can be examined.

LONGITUDINAL STUDIES

longitudinal study
A survey of respondents at different times, thus allowing analysis of response continuity and changes over time.

In a **longitudinal study** respondents are questioned at multiple points in time. The purpose of longitudinal studies is to examine continuity of response and to observe changes that occur over time. Many syndicated polling services, such as Gallup, conduct regular polls. For example, the Bureau of Labor Statistics conducts the National Longitudinal Survey of Youth, interviewing the same sample of individuals repeatedly since 1979. (Respondents, who were "youth" at the beginning of the study, are now in their 40s.) Research scientist Jay Zagorsky recently analyzed the longitudinal data from that study to determine that those who married and stayed with their spouse accumulated almost twice as much wealth as single and divorced people in the study.[14] The Yankelovich MONITOR has been tracking American values and attitudes for more than 30 years. This survey is an example of a longitudinal study that uses successive samples; its researchers survey several different samples at different times. Longitudinal studies of this type are sometimes called *cohort studies,* because similar groups of people who share a certain experience during the same time interval (cohorts) are expected to be included in each sample. Exhibit 9.3 illustrates the results of a longitudinal study by Harris Interactive, which since 1966 has been asking five questions related to powerlessness and isolation to create an "alienation index." We can think of longitudinal studies as taking a movie of an evolving situation.

In applied business research, a longitudinal study that uses successive samples is called a **tracking study** because successive waves are designed to compare trends and identify changes in variables such as consumer satisfaction, brand image, or advertising awareness. These studies are useful for assessing aggregate trends but do not allow for tracking changes in individuals over time.

Conducting surveys in waves with two or more sample groups avoids the problem of response bias resulting from a prior interview. A respondent who was interviewed in an earlier survey about a certain brand may become more aware of the brand or pay more attention to its advertising after being interviewed. Using different samples eliminates this problem. However, researchers can never be sure whether the changes in the variable being measured are due to a different sample or to an actual change in the variable over time.

TOTHEPOINT

Time is but the stream I go a-fishing in.

—Henry David Thoreau

tracking study

A type of longitudinal study that uses successive samples to compare trends and identify changes in variables such as consumer satisfaction, brand image, or advertising awareness.

Consumer Panel

A longitudinal study that gathers data from the same sample of individuals or households over time is called a **consumer panel**. Consider the packaged-goods marketer that wishes to learn about brand-switching behavior. A consumer panel that consists of a group of people who record their purchasing habits in a diary over time will provide the manager with a continuous stream of information about the brand and product class. Diary data that are recorded regularly over an extended period enable the researcher to track repeat-purchase behavior and changes in purchasing habits that occur in response to changes in price, special promotions, or other aspects of business strategy.

consumer panel

A longitudinal survey of the same sample of individuals or households to record their attitudes, behavior, or purchasing habits over time.

Panel members may be contacted by telephone, in a personal interview, by mail questionnaire, or by e-mail. Typically respondents complete media exposure or purchase diaries and mail them back to the survey organization. If the panel members have agreed to field test new products, face-to-face or telephone interviews may be required. The nature of the problem dictates which communication method to use.

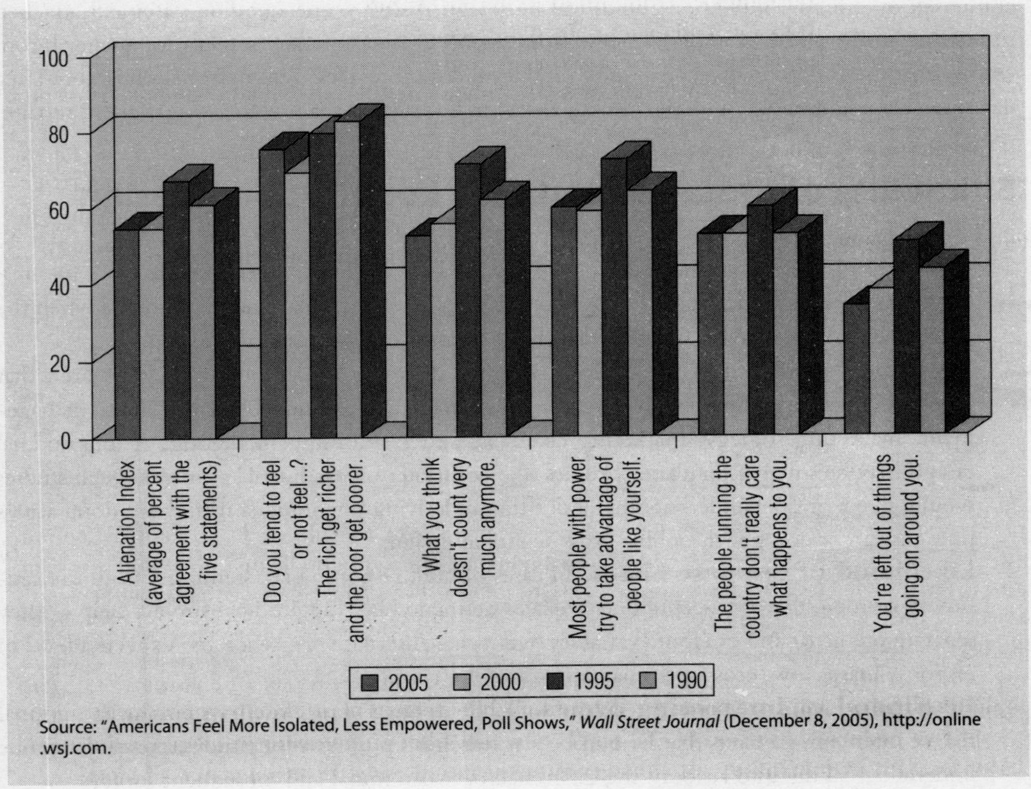

EXHIBIT 9.3
Longitudinal Research from a Harris Poll

Source: "Americans Feel More Isolated, Less Empowered, Poll Shows," *Wall Street Journal* (December 8, 2005), http://online.wsj.com.

RESEARCH SNAPSHOT

makemytrip.com Survey for Consumer Satisfaction

makemytrip.com, one of the leading online and off-line travel agents, uses survey research to understand consumer satisfaction for the service they have rendered, stay in the hotels they have bought, and travel of car rental on a regular basis. The company uses surveys to gather data and improve the satisfaction of the consumers who use their service. Immediately after a consumer welfare service makemytrip.com posts a short questionnaire to their e-mail. The survey asks the user how convenient was their purchase process, staying in the hotel, and service of the car they hired. The survey also gathers descriptive information of the consumers and also asks what services they use through makemytrip.com.

Because establishing and maintaining a panel is expensive, panels often are managed by contractors who offer their services to many organizations. A number of commercial firms, such as National Family Opinion (NFO), Inc., Market Research Corporation of America, and Consumer Mail Panels, Inc., specialize in maintaining consumer panels. In recent years Internet panels have grown in popularity. Because clients of these firms need to share the expenses with other clients to acquire longitudinal data at a reasonable cost, panel members may be asked questions about a number of different issues.

The first questionnaire a panel member is asked to complete typically includes questions about product ownership, product usage, pets, family members, and demographic data. The purpose of such a questionnaire is to gather the behavioral and demographic data that will be used to identify heavy buyers, difficult-to-reach customers, and so on for future surveys. Individuals who serve as members of consumer panels usually are compensated with cash, attractive gifts, or the chance to win a sweepstake.

Marketers whose products are purchased by few households find panels an economical means of reaching respondents who own their products. A two-stage process typically is used. A panel composed of around 15,000 households can be screened with a one-question statement attached to another project. For example, a question in an NFO questionnaire screens for ownership of certain uncommon products, such as snowmobiles and motorcycles. This information is stored in a database. Then households with the unusual item can be sampled again with a longer questionnaire.

Suitability of Cross-sectional vs. Longitudinal Design

The decision to choose a survey design can be made based on the following criteria:

1. **Start date and end date of the research.** A cross-sectional study is desirable when the researcher does not have a definite idea about starting and finishing of research.
2. **Nature of key constructs.** Cross-sectional design is suitable for survey research that employs concrete and externally oriented constructs, such as domains of sales force management, marketing strategy, marketing channels, and relationship marketing. A longitudinal design may be suitable for abstract topics like consumer or managerial attitudes. Such studies would give a greater understanding about the underlying phenomena if they are done across time instead of doing it through a cross-sectional design.
3. **Likelihood of response biases.** In cases of high response bias, stemming from the sensitivity of topic that is susceptible to socially desirable bias, longitudinal surveys help as they separate predictor and outcome variables over time. Alternatively, when the expected level of response bias is low, cross-sectional design may be used.
4. **Likelihood of intervening events.** While dealing with closed systems with minimal risk of intervening events that lie outside a researcher's purview, longitudinal research can be undertaken taking into account the difference between initial and subsequent surveys.

5. **Measurement format and scales.** Instances in which separation in formats or scales is not possible, use of a longitudinal approach can help to disrupt response biases.
6. **Theoretical foundation.** Well-established domains with strong causal relationships such as market orientation and inter-organizational trust can benefit from cross-sectional design. However, nascent theoretical domains with weak cause-effect relationships, such as marketing metrics, CRM, and brand communities, may use longitudinal designs as a means to enhance confidence in the causal statements.

Total Quality Management and Customer Satisfaction Surveys

Total quality management is a business strategy that emphasizes market-driven quality as a top priority. Total quality management involves implementing and adjusting the firm's business activities to assure customers' satisfaction with the quality of goods and services.

total quality management
A business philosophy that emphasizes market-driven quality as a top organizational priority.

Many U.S. organizations adopted total quality management in the 1980s when an increase in high-quality foreign competition challenged their former dominance. Today companies continue to recognize the need for total quality management programs. Executives and production workers are sometimes too far removed from the customer. Companies need a means to bridge this gap with feedback about quality of goods and services. This means conducting research. In an organization driven by the quality concept, business research plays an important role in the management of total product quality.

What Is Quality?

Organizations used to define quality by engineering standards. Most companies no longer see quality that way. Some managers say that having a quality product means that the good or service conforms to consumers' requirements and that the product is acceptable. Effective executives who subscribe to a total quality management philosophy, however, believe that the product's quality must go beyond acceptability for a given price range. Rather than merely being relieved that nothing went wrong, consumers should experience some delightful surprises or reap some unexpected benefits. In other words, quality assurance is more than just meeting minimum standards. The level of quality is the degree to which a good or service truly is seen as good or bad.

Obviously, a BMW 750i does not compete directly with a Kia Spectra. Buyers of these automobiles are in different market segments, and their expectations of quality differ widely. Nevertheless, managers at BMW and Kia both try to establish the quality that is acceptable given the cost of ownership.

Internal and External Customers

Organizations that have adopted the total quality management philosophy believe that a focus on customers must include more than external customers. Like Arbor, Inc., they believe that everyone in the organization has customers:

> *Every person, in every department, and at every level, has a customer. The customer is anyone to whom an individual provides service, information, support, or product. The customer may be another employee or department (internal) or outside the company (external).*[15]

Total quality management programs work most effectively when every employee knows exactly who his or her customers are and what output internal and external customers expect. Also, it is important to know how customers perceive their needs are being met. All too often differences between perceptions and reality are not understood.

RESEARCH SNAPSHOT

Fairfax Library's Survey for Satisfaction

Not only do businesses use research, but not-for-profits often engage in research activities as well. For instance, the Fairfax (Virginia) County Public Library (FCPL) uses surveys to gather data and improve the satisfaction of library users and the community at large—the taxpayers who pay the library's bills. Like most libraries, FCPL has long gathered usage data such as circulation statistics and number of patrons who visit each day, but it has more recently focused on outcomes including satisfaction with specific services and the library overall.

Every spring, FCPL posts a ten-question survey on its Web site. This Web Site User Survey asks users how easy the site is to navigate, what additional online services they would like, and whether they are satisfied with the Web site. Periodically, the library conducts face-to-face and telephone surveys of library users. These surveys gather descriptive information about visitors and ask what services they use, how aware they are of particular services, and how satisfied they are. Answers help the library correct problems and set budget priorities.

In a recent telephone survey, the library called a sample of community members to investigate whether changes it had made to its information services had affected use of the library. Answers to 33 questions helped the library pinpoint what services were being used and what attitudes they held toward the library. FCPL's librarians were pleased to learn that even nonusers of the library viewed it as a valuable part of the community.

Source: Based on Clay, Edwin S., III and Patricia Bangs, "Beyond Numbers," *Library Journal* (January 1, 2006), http://www.galenet.com.

Implementing Total Quality Management

Implementing a total quality management program requires considerable survey research. A firm must routinely ask customers to rate it against its competitors. It must periodically measure employee knowledge, attitudes, and expectations. It must monitor company performance against benchmark standards. It must determine whether customers found any delightful surprises or major disappointments. In other words, a total quality management strategy expresses the conviction that to improve quality, an organization must regularly conduct surveys to evaluate quality improvement.

Exhibit 9.4 illustrates the total quality management process. The exhibit shows that overall tracking of quality improvement requires longitudinal research. The process begins with a *commitment and exploration stage,* during which management makes a commitment to total quality assurance and researchers explore external and internal customers' needs and beliefs. The research must discover what product features customers value, what problems customers are having with the product, what aspects of product operation or customer service have disappointed customers, what the company is doing right, and what the company may be doing wrong.

After internal and external customers' problems and desires have been identified, the *benchmarking stage* begins. Research must establish quantitative measures that can serve as benchmarks or points of comparison against which to evaluate future efforts. The surveys must establish initial measures of overall satisfaction, of the frequency of customer problems, and of quality ratings for specific attributes. Researchers must identify the company's or brand's position relative to competitors' quality positions. For example, when Anthony Balzarini became food-service manager at Empire Health Services in Spokane, Washington, he became responsible for serving meals to the patients of the company's two hospitals, plus retail food service (sales to visitors and employees who eat in the hospitals). He began tracking quality according to several measures, including satisfaction scores on patient surveys and sales volume and revenue on the retail side. Sales measurements include comparing the average sale with other locations, including restaurants, in the Spokane area.[16]

The *initial quality improvement* stage establishes a quality improvement process within the organization. Management and employees must translate quality issues into the internal vocabulary of the organization. The company must establish performance standards and expectations for improvement. For Balzarini, this stage included training food-service employees in providing patient service. He began holding meetings twice daily to identify any problems to be resolved. Managers were each assigned to one floor of the hospital and charged with building a close working relationship with the nursing staff there. They are expected to visit their floor every week and conduct 15 interviews with patients to learn about what they like and dislike. On the retail side, the manager is expected to revise menus every 12 weeks to offer more variety. Waste is literally weighed and categorized to identify which types of food are rejected by patients and customers.

After managers and employees have set quality objectives and implemented procedures and standards, the firm continues to track satisfaction and quality ratings in successive waves. The purpose of tracking wave 1 is to measure trends in satisfaction and quality ratings. Business researchers

EXHIBIT 9.4 **Longitudinal Research for Total Quality Management**

Time	Marketing Research Activity with External Consumers (Customers)	Marketing Management Activity	Marketing Research Activity with Internal Consumers (Employees)
Time 1 **Commitment and exploration stage**	Exploratory study to determine the quality the customer wants, discover customer problems, and identify the importance of specific product attributes.	Establish marketing objective that the customer should define quality.	Exploratory study to determine (1) whether internal customers, such as service employees, are aware of the need for service quality as a major means to achieve customer satisfaction and (2) whether they know the quality standards for their jobs. Establish whether employees are motivated and trained. Identify road blocks that prevent employees from meeting customer needs.
Time 2 **Benchmarking stage**	Benchmarking study to measure overall satisfaction and quality ratings of specific attributes.	Identify brand's position relative to competitors' satisfaction and quality rating; establish standards for customer satisfaction.	Benchmarking to measure employees' actual performance and perceptions about performance.
Time 3 **Initial quality improvement stage**	Tracking wave 1 to measure trends in satisfaction and quality ratings.	Improve quality; reward performance.	Tracking wave 1 to measure and compare what is actually happening with what should be happening. Establish whether the company is conforming to its quality standards.
Time 4 **Continuous quality improvement**	Tracking wave 2 to measure trends in satisfaction and quality ratings.	Improve quality; reward performance.	Tracking wave 2 to measure trends in quality improvement.

determine whether the organization is meeting customer needs as specified by quantitative standards. At one of Empire's two hospitals, one of the food-service managers learned that a patient on a liquid diet disliked the broth he was being served. An investigation showed that the recipe had been changed, and a taste test confirmed that the original recipe was superior, so the hospital switched back to the original recipe.

The next stage, *continuous quality improvement,* consists of many consecutive waves with the same purpose—to improve over the previous period. Continuous quality improvement requires that management allow employees to initiate problem solving without a lot of red tape. Employees should be able to initiate proactive communications with consumers. In tracking wave 2, management compares results with those of earlier stages. Quality improvement management continues. At Empire, improvements have been reflected in rising patient satisfaction scores and growing sales in retail operations.

Management must also reward performance. At Empire, Balzarini set up a program called "You Rock." Any employee who observes an excellent action by another employee, beyond mere job requirements, acknowledges the good work with a card awarding points redeemable in the hospitals' retail areas. Balzarini also sends weekly thank-you cards to workers who showed outstanding performance.

Exhibit 9.4 shows that total quality management programs measure performance against *customers'* standards—not against standards determined by quality engineers within the company. All changes within the organization are oriented toward improvement of customers' perceptions of quality. The exhibit indicates the need for integration of establishing consumer requirements, quantifying benchmark measures, setting objectives, conducting research studies, and making adjustments in the organization to improve quality. Continuous quality improvement is an ongoing process.

The activities outlined in Exhibit 9.4 work for providers of both goods and services. However, service products and customer services offered along with goods have some distinctive aspects. We will first discuss the quality of goods and then consider the quality of services.

In general, consumer and industrial goods providers track customer satisfaction to investigate customer perceptions of product quality by measuring perceptions of the product characteristics listed in Exhibit 9.5.[17] These studies measure whether a firm's perceptions about product characteristics conform to customers' expectations and how these perceptions change over time. For example, any customer satisfaction survey will investigate a good's performance by asking, "How well does the product perform its core function?" To determine the quality of a recycling lawn mower, a researcher might ask, "How well does the mower cut grass and eliminate the need for bagging clippings?" The researcher may ask questions to determine whether the product's quality of performance was a delightful surprise, something well beyond expected performance. Similar questions will cover the other major product characteristics.

Measuring service disconfirmation involves comparing expectations with performance. Favorable quality and performance better than expected leads to satisfaction. Time after time, studies have shown differences between what customers expected and what the frontline service personnel delivered. Researchers direct a lot of effort toward assessing consumer expectations.

In organizations that wish to improve service quality, managers must identify and analyze customer service needs and then establish specifications for the level of service. They must then train frontline personnel and give them the responsibility for quality service. Frontline personnel need to be motivated and encouraged to deliver the service that goes beyond consumer expectations. Finally, regular surveys with both external customers and internal employees measure results against standards.

Researchers investigate service quality to measure customer satisfaction and perceived quality in terms of the service attributes listed in Exhibit 9.5. Considerations in the actual measurement of quality of goods and service delivery are further addressed in Chapters 13, 14, and 15.

TIPS OF THE TRADE

© iStock

- Surveys are the most widely used method of collecting primary quantitative data for business research. However, a very common error in business research is to begin questionnaire design and the survey process too soon.
    - Be sure to fully exhaust secondary research sources before undertaking primary research activities.
    - Be sure to have a clear understanding of the research issues and objectives, often gained through exploratory qualitative research, before undertaking primary research activities.
- Error exists in all survey research.
    - *Random sampling error* is present due to chance variation in the sample elements and can only be addressed through large sample size.
    - *Systematic error* is due to a flaw in the research design or execution. It is our job as a business researcher to minimize systematic error.

EXHIBIT 9.5 Quality Dimensions for Goods and Services

Quality Dimension	Characteristic	Example
Goods		
Performance	The product performs its core function.	A razor gives a close shave.
Features	The product has auxiliary dimensions that provide secondary benefits.	A motor oil comes in a convenient package.
Conformance with specifications	There is a low incidence of defects.	Napa Valley wine comes from Napa Valley.
Reliability	The product performs consistently.	A lawn mower works properly each time it is used.
Durability	The economic life of the product is within an acceptable range.	A motorcycle runs fine for many years.
Serviceability	The system for servicing the product is efficient, competent, and convenient.	A computer software manufacturer maintains a toll-free phone number staffed by technical people who can answer questions quickly and accurately.
Aesthetic design	The product's design makes it look and feel like a quality product.	A snowmobile is aerodynamic.
Services		
Access	Contact with service personnel is easy.	A visit to the dentist does not involve a long wait.
Communication	The customer is informed and understands the service and how much it will cost.	A computer technician explains needed repairs without using overly technical terms.
Competence	The service providers have the required skills.	A tax accountant has a CPA certification.
Courtesy	Personnel are polite and friendly.	Bank tellers smile and wish the customer a "good day" at the close of each transaction.
Reliability	The service is performed consistently and personnel are dependable.	Employees of the office cleaning service arrive on schedule every Friday evening after working hours.
Credibility	Service providers have integrity.	The doctor who is performing a heart transplant is trustworthy and believable.

Source: Adapted from Aaker, David A., *Managing Brand Equity* (New York: Macmillan, 1991), 90–95.

Summary

1. Define surveys and explain their advantages. The survey is a common tool for asking respondents questions. Surveys can provide quick, inexpensive, and accurate information for a variety of objectives. The term sample survey is often used because a survey is expected to obtain a representative sample of the target population.

2. Describe the type of information that may be gathered in a survey. The typical survey is a descriptive research study with the objective of measuring awareness, knowledge, behavior, opinions, and attitudes, both inside and outside of the organization. Common survey populations include customers, employees, suppliers, and distributors.

3. Identify sources of error in survey research. Two major forms of error are common in survey research. The first, random sampling error, is caused by chance variation and results in a sample that is not absolutely representative of the target population. Such errors are inevitable, but they can be predicted using the statistical methods discussed in later chapters on sampling. The second major category of error, systematic error, takes several forms. Nonresponse error is caused by subjects' failing to respond to a survey. This type of error can be identified by comparing the demographics of the sample population with those of the target population and reduced by making a special effort to contact underrepresented groups. In addition, response bias occurs when a response to a questionnaire is falsified or misrepresented, either intentionally or inadvertently. There are four specific categories of response bias: acquiescence bias, extremity bias, interviewer bias, and social desirability bias. An additional source of survey error comes from administrative problems such as inconsistencies in interviewers' abilities, cheating, coding mistakes, and so forth.

4. Distinguish among the various categories of surveys. Surveys may be classified according to methods of communication, by the degrees of structure and disguise in the questionnaires, and on a temporal basis. Questionnaires may be structured, with limited choices of responses, or unstructured, to allow open-ended responses. Disguised questions camouflage the real purpose and may be used to probe sensitive topics. Surveys may consider the population at a given moment or follow trends over a period of time. The first approach, the cross-sectional study, usually is intended to separate the population into meaningful subgroups. The second type of study, the longitudinal study, can reveal important population changes over time. Longitudinal studies may involve contacting different sets of respondents or the same ones repeatedly. One form of longitudinal study is the consumer panel. Consumer panels are expensive to conduct, so firms often hire contractors who provide services to many companies, thus spreading costs over many clients.

5. Discuss the importance of survey research to total quality management programs. Total quality management is the process of implementing and adjusting a firm's business strategy to assure customers' satisfaction with the quality of goods or services. The level of quality is the degree to which a good or service is seen as good or bad by customers. Business research provides companies with feedback about the quality of goods and services. Implementing a total quality management program requires considerable survey research, conducted routinely, to ask customers to rate a company against its competitors. It also measures employee attitudes and monitors company performance against benchmark standards. After identifying customer problems and desires, the firm tracks satisfaction and quality ratings in successive waves. Total quality management research is an ongoing process for continuous quality improvement that works for both marketers of goods and service providers.

Key Terms and Concepts

acquiescence bias, *210*
administrative error, *212*
consumer panel, *216*
cross-sectional study, *214*
data-processing error, *212*
disguised questions, *214*
extremity bias, *211*
interviewer bias, *211*
interviewer cheating, *212*
interviewer error, *212*
longitudinal study, *215*
no contacts, *208*
nonrespondents, *208*
nonresponse error, *206*
random sampling error, *206*
refusals, *208*
respondent error, *206*
respondents, *203*
response bias, *209*
sample bias, *206*
sample selection error, *212*
sample survey, *203*
self-selection bias, *208*
social desirability bias, *211*
structured question, *213*
systematic error, *206*
total quality management, *217*
tracking study, *216*
undisguised questions, *214*
unstructured question, *213*

Questions for Review and Critical Thinking

1. Name several nonbusiness applications of survey research.
2. What is *self-selection bias*? How might we avoid this?
3. Do surveys tend to gather qualitative or quantitative data? What types of information are commonly measured with surveys?
4. Give an example of each type of error listed in Exhibit 9.1.
5. In a survey, chief executive officers (CEOs) indicated that they would prefer to relocate their businesses to Atlanta (first choice), San Diego, Tampa, Los Angeles, or Boston. The CEOs who said they planned on building new office space in the following year were asked where they were going to build. They indicated they were going to build in New York, Los Angeles, San Francisco, or Chicago. Explain the difference between these two responses.
6. What potential sources of error might be associated with the following situations?
   a. In a survey of frequent fliers age 50 and older, researchers concluded that price does not play a significant role in airline travel because only 25 percent of the respondents check off price as the most important consideration in determining where and how they travel.
   b. A survey of voters finds that most respondents do not like negative political ads—that is, advertising by one political candidate that criticizes or exposes secrets about the opponent's "dirty laundry."
   c. Researchers who must conduct a 45-minute personal interview decide to offer $25 to each respondent because they believe that people who will sell their opinions are more typical than someone who will talk to a stranger for 45 minutes.
   d. A company's sales representatives are asked what percentage of the time they spend making presentations to prospects, traveling, talking on the telephone, participating in meetings, working on the computer, and engaging in other on-the-job activities.
   e. A survey comes with a water hardness packet to test the hardness of the water in a respondent's home. The packet includes a color chart and a plastic strip to dip into hot water. The respondent is given instructions in six steps on how to compare the color of the plastic strip with the color chart that indicates water hardness.
7. A researcher investigating public health issues goes into a junior high school classroom and asks the students if they have ever smoked a cigarette. The students are asked to respond orally in the presence of other students. What types of error might enter into this process? What might be a better approach?
8. A survey conducted by the National Endowment for the Arts asked, "Have you read a book within the last year?" What response bias might arise from this question?
9. Name some common objectives of cross-sectional surveys.
10. Give an example of a political situation in which longitudinal research might be useful. Name some common objectives for a longitudinal study in a business situation.
11. What are the advantages and disadvantages of using consumer panels?
12. Search either your local newspaper, the Wall Street Journal, or USA Today to find some news story derived from survey research results. Often, these stories deal with public opinions about product complaints, product consumption, job-related issues, marriage and family, public policy issues, or politics. Was the study's methodology appropriate to draw conclusions?
13. Suppose you are the research director for your state's tourism bureau. Assess the state's information needs, and identify the information you will collect in a survey of tourists who visit your state.
14. **ETHICS** A researcher sends out 2,000 questionnaires via e-mail. Fifty are returned because the addresses are inaccurate. Of the 1,950 delivered questionnaires, 100 are completed and e-mailed back. However, 40 of these respondents wrote that they did not want to participate in the survey. The researcher indicates the response rate was 5.0 percent. Is this the right thing to do?

Research Activities

1. **'NET** Go to Survey Monkey (**http://www.surveymonkey.com**). Then, visit **http://www.mysurvey.com**. What is the difference between the two Web sites in terms of the services they provide to users?
2. **'NET** The National Longitudinal Surveys (NLS) conducted by the Bureau of Labor Statistics provide data on the labor force experience (current labor force and employment status, work history, and characteristics of current or last job) of five groups of the U.S. population. Go to **http://www.bls.gov/opub/hom/homtoc.htm** to learn about the objectives and methodology for this study. How accurate do you believe the information reported here really is? What sources of error might be present in the data?
3. Ask a small sample of students at your university to report their GPA. Then, try to find the average GPA of students at your school. If you have to, ask several professors to give their opinion. Does it seem that the student data are subject to error? Explain.
4. **'NET** Located at the University of Connecticut, the Roper Center is the largest library of public opinion data in the world. An online polling magazine and the methodology and findings of many surveys may be found at **http://www.ropercenter.uconn.edu**. Report on an article or study of your choice.

Case 9.1 SAT and ACT Writing Tests

© GETTY IMAGES/ PHOTODISC GREEN

The SAT and ACT college entrance exams once were completely multiple choice, but both tests recently began including an essay portion (which is optional for the ACT). Some researchers have investigated how the essay tests are used by one group they serve: the admissions offices of the colleges that look at test results during the selection process.[18]

Early survey research suggests that some admissions officers harbor doubts about the essay tests. ACT, Inc. reported that among the schools it surveyed, only about one-fifth are requiring that applicants take the writing portion of the exam. Another one-fifth merely recommend (but don't require) the essay.

Kaplan, Inc., which markets test preparation services, conducted surveys as well. Kaplan asked 374 colleges whether they would be using the SAT writing test in screening candidates. Almost half (47 percent) said they would not use the essay at all. Another 22 percent said they would use it but give it less weight than the math and verbal SAT scores.

Kaplan also surveys students who take the exams for which it provides training. On its Web site, the company says, "More than 25 percent of students ran out of time on the essay!"

Questions

1. What survey objectives would ACT have in asking colleges how they use its essay test? What objectives would Kaplan have for its survey research?
2. If you were a marketer for the College Board (the SAT's company) or ACT, Inc., what further information would you want to gather after receiving the results described here?
3. What sources of error or response bias might be present in the surveys described here?

Case 9.2 The Walker Information Group

© GETTY IMAGES/ PHOTODISC GREEN

The Walker Information Group is among the largest research companies in the world. Walker's clients include many Fortune 500 and blue chip industry leaders such as Cummins Engine Company, Lenscrafters, Continental Cablevision, Florida Power and Light, and Oglethorpe Power Corporation.

The Indianapolis-based company was founded in 1939 as a field interviewing service by Tommie Walker, mother of Frank Walker, the current chairman and chief executive officer of the organization. In the 1920s Tommie Walker's late husband worked for a bank that was considering sponsoring an Indianapolis radio show featuring classical music. The bank wanted to know who was listening to this show. Tommie was hired to do the interviewing, and she threw herself into the work. After that, referrals brought her more interviewing work for surveys. During an interview with a woman whose husband was a district sales manager for the A&P grocery chain, she learned that A&P was looking for a surveyor in the Midwest. A&P's sales manager liked Tommie, but wouldn't hire anyone without a formal company, a field staff, and insurance. Tommie founded Walker Marketing Research on October 20, 1939, and her business with A&P lasted 17 years.

Today, the Walker Information Group specializes in business, health care, and consumer research, as well as database marketing. The company is organized into six strategic business units.

Walker Research conducts traditional market research services that range from questionnaire design and data collection to advanced analysis and consultation. Walker has expertise in helping companies measure how their actions are perceived by the audiences most important to them, and how these perceptions affect their image, reputation, corporate citizenship, recruiting, sales, and more.

Data Source is a business unit that primarily is concerned with data collection and processing data. It specializes in telephone data collection.

Customer Satisfaction Measurement (CSM), as the name implies, specializes in measuring customer satisfaction and in helping clients improve their relationship with customers.

CSM Worldwide Network spans more than 50 countries. It is the first international network of professional research and consulting businesses dedicated to customer satisfaction measurement and management. The CSM Worldwide Network assures that multicountry customer satisfaction research is consistent by taking into account local conditions and cultural norms. Network members are trained to use consistent methods that allow standardization and comparability of information from country to country.

Walker Direct designs and develops databases and implements direct-marketing programs that help generate leads for businesses and raise funds for nonprofit organizations.

Walker Clinical is a health-care product use research company. Walker helps pharmaceutical, medical-device, and consumer-product manufacturers test how well new products work and how customers like them.

Questions

1. What type of custom survey research projects might Walker Market Research and Analysis conduct for its clients?
2. What stages are involved in conducting a survey? For which stages might a client company hire a research supplier like Walker Research? Data Source?
3. What is the purpose of customer satisfaction measurement?
4. What measures, other than findings from surveys, might a company use to evaluate the effectiveness of a total quality management program?

Case 9.3 An Indian Case On Survey Research: Census Of India—"Our Census - Our Future"

© GETTY IMAGES/ PHOTODISC GREEN

Indian population census organization is one of the largest administrative networks in the world. In order to ensure full utility of the population count, Indian census attempts to collect information on various socio-economic characteristics of the entire population. The population census covering more than 1 billion people is one of the most extensive and complicated statistical operations and, thus, requires careful planning and efficient implementation The Indian census is the most credible source of information on demography (population characteristics), economic activity, literacy and education, housing and household amenities, urbanization, fertility and mortality, scheduled castes and scheduled tribes, language, religion, migration, disability, and many other socio-cultural and demographic data for the government. So it is of utmost importance that the survey errors are minimized. The delimitation/reservation of constituencies—parliamentary/assembly/panchayats, and other local bodies— is also done on the basis of the demographic data thrown up by the census. Census is the basis for reviewing the country's progress in the past decade, monitoring the ongoing schemes of the Government, and most importantly, plan for the future.

Errors

The census survey is a longitudinal study undertaken every ten years. There is no scope for sampling error as the sample and the population is one and the same. There may be coverage error, due omission or duplication in census enumeration in terms of coverage of census houses/households or individuals. This coverage error is minimized or reduced by post enumeration survey. In conducting this survey, opportunity is also taken to measure error in responses, or the content error in the recorded household characteristics, with regard to certain items canvassed in the census.

Questionnaire Design

The questionnaire is designed to collect the following information:

Location particulars
Individual particulars
General and socio-cultural characteristics
Characteristics of workers and non-workers
Migration characteristics
Fertility particulars
Land information (if the household is involved in cultivation)

The questionnaire is designed to capture all these data comprehensively. The questionnaire is administered face to face where the interviewer presents the items orally so this takes care of ambiguities or misunderstanding of the questions.

Questions

1. What are the characteristics of a census survey as opposed to sample survey?
2. What types of errors can occur in census survey? What types of errors can be eliminated through census survey?
3. What are the advantages and disadvantages of census survey over sample survey?
4. In which business context do you recommend conducting a census survey? How would it improve over sample survey in making business decisions?

CHAPTER 10
SURVEY RESEARCH: COMMUNICATING WITH RESPONDENTS

LEARNING OUTCOMES

After studying this chapter, you should be able to

1. **Summarize ways researchers gather information through interviews**
2. **Compare the advantages and disadvantages of conducting door-to-door, mall intercept, and telephone interviews**
3. **Evaluate the advantages and disadvantages of distributing questionnaires through the mail, the Internet, and by other means**
4. **Discuss the importance of pretesting questionnaires**
5. **Describe ethical issues that arise in survey research**

Chapter Vignette: Mobile Surveys Catching On, and Catching Respondents "On the Go"!

The use of cell phones as a basic communication and information management device has led to several new ways to capture the opinions of others. This has largely been a function of SMS (or short message service) text messaging. Young and old alike have developed an amazing new skill, often referred to as "texting," as a means to communicate with others via short messages through their cell phones. The implications for this new skill shared by so many have not been lost on the business research market.

Mobile surveying technologies now integrate SMS text messaging with electronic surveys. If a phone has SMS technology, recipients of a mobile survey receive an SMS text message, where they can answer single or multiple choice questions, or even provide open-ended responses to questions, anytime or anywhere. The use of these types of "instant feedback" survey responses can have many different business applications.

For example, business researchers may wish to capture consumer reactions to products over time, or may wish to get an instant "first impression," as they use a product initially. Perhaps a firm wishes to capture instant feedback from a training exercise, or may wish to capture or understand respondent attitudes to a particular part of a meeting or event. In fact, current researchers interested in experiential surveying use mobile surveys to capture people's feelings at that particular instant, and thus can create a longitudinal understanding of people's attitudes and emotional states over time.

Mobile surveying is an exciting new way to capture data on respondents, no matter where they are. Texting is here to stay—perhaps the next time you see someone furiously texting on their cell phone, they are responding to a mobile survey "on the go"!

Introduction

During most of the twentieth century, obtaining survey data involved inviting individuals to answer questions asked by human interviewers (interviews) or questions they read themselves (questionnaires). Interviewers communicated with respondents face-to-face or over the telephone, or respondents filled out self-administered paper questionnaires, which were typically distributed by mail. These media for conducting surveys remain popular with business researchers. However, as the preceding vignette suggests, digital technology is having a profound impact on society in general and on business research in particular. Its greatest impact is in the creation of new forms of communications media.

Interviews as Interactive Communication

When two people engage in a conversation, human interaction takes place. Human interactive media are a personal form of communication. One human being directs a message to and interacts with another individual (or a small group). When most people think of interviewing, they envision two people engaged in a face-to-face dialog or a conversation on the telephone.

Electronic interactive media allow researchers to reach a large audience, personalize individual messages, and interact using digital technology. To a large extent, electronic interactive media are controlled by the users themselves. No other human need be present. Survey respondents today are not passive audience members. They are actively involved in a two-way communication using electronic interactive media.

The Internet is radically altering many organizations' research strategies, providing a prominent example of the new electronic interactive media. Consumers determine what information they will be exposed to by choosing what sites to visit and by blocking or closing annoying pop-up ads. Electronic interactive media also include CD-ROM and DVD materials, touch-tone telephone systems, touch-screen interactive kiosks in stores, and other forms of digital technology.

Electronic dating services have become a popular, successful example of electronic interactive media.

Noninteractive Media

The traditional questionnaire received by mail and completed by the respondent does not allow a dialog or an exchange of information providing immediate feedback. So, from our perspective, self-administered questionnaires printed on paper are noninteractive. This fact does not mean that they are without merit, just that this type of survey is less flexible than surveys using interactive communication media.

Each technique for conducting surveys has merits and shortcomings. The purpose of this chapter is to explain when researchers should use different types of surveys. The chapter begins with a discussion of surveys that use live interviews. Then we turn to noninteractive, self-administered questionnaires. Finally, we explain how the Internet and digital technology are dramatically changing survey research.

RESEARCH SNAPSHOT

Winning the Indian Consumer

Recent survey says that Indian consumers' buying spree has not suffered a heat in the last five quarters in spite of high inflation and increasing oil price in the country. The country has shown a very high consumer confidence level consistently. A survey conducted by Nielsen India shows that Indian consumers' confidence is governed by strong growth of the country's economy and the job market. A study conducted in 51 countries, having a sample of 500 from India, shows that Indian consumers are most optimistic globally. However, Indians were concerned about high food price and oil price which has increased overall household expenditure significantly.

Source: http://inchincloser.com/2010/02/04/winning-the-indian-consumer/

Personal Interviews

To conduct interviews, the researcher may communicate with individuals in person by going door-to-door or intercepting them in shopping malls, or interviews may take place over the telephone. Traditionally, researchers have recorded interview results using paper and pencil, but computers are increasingly supporting survey research. In this section, we examine the general characteristics of face-to-face personal interviews, then compare the characteristics of door-to-door personal interviews and personal interviews conducted in shopping malls. The next section examines telephone interviews.

Gathering information through face-to-face contact with individuals goes back many years. Periodic censuses were used to set tax rates and aid military conscription in the ancient empires of Egypt and Rome.[1] During the Middle Ages, the merchant families of Fugger and Rothschild prospered in part because their far-flung organizations enabled them to get information before their competitors could.[2] Today, survey researchers typically present themselves in shopping centers and street corners throughout the United States and announce, "Good afternoon, my name is ________________. I am with ________________ Company, and we are conducting a survey on ________________."

personal interview
Face-to-face communication in which an interviewer asks a respondent to answer questions.

A **personal interview** is a form of direct communication in which an interviewer asks respondents questions face-to-face. This versatile and flexible method is a two-way conversation between interviewer and respondent.

Advantages of Personal Interviews

Business researchers find that personal interviews offer many unique advantages. One of the most important is the opportunity for detailed feedback.

OPPORTUNITY FOR FEEDBACK

Personal interviews, similar to those mentioned in the Research Snapshot "The Challenge of Assessing Adult Literacy," provide the opportunity for feedback and clarification. For example, if a consumer is reluctant to provide sensitive information, the interviewer may offer reassurance that his or her answers will be strictly confidential. Personal interviews offer the lowest chance that respondents

RESEARCH SNAPSHOT

The Challenge of Assessing Adult Literacy

The need to understand and address functional adult literacy is an important one. The term functionally literate is often misunderstood—in reality, it is the degree to which adults can adequately "function" with written materials they are exposed to in their daily lives. Illiteracy creates clear and in some instances not-so-clear challenges for adults. While it is clear that a person's literacy is certainly tied to their ability to obtain a good job, they are also challenged by the everyday use of printed and written information such as newspapers, bank statements, and even medication prescription instructions. The question is how to understand the level of illiteracy in a population when those individuals you are most interested in (i.e., the adult illiterate) may not or cannot respond to a written questionnaire in the first place.

In the United States, the 2003 National Assessment of Adult Literacy (NAAL) recognized this challenge early and developed one of the most comprehensive personal interview and assessment programs ever attempted. Using a stratified sample of over eighteen thousand adults, they conducted in-home personal interviews that took approximately 90 minutes to complete. During these interviews, a multistage assessment was conducted. Respondents were given a short and very simple screening questionnaire, which would determine if they could proceed. If the respondent could not complete the short screening tool, they were not required to go further with the literacy assessment, and were scored on a normed scale as functionally illiterate. For those that could complete the screening questions, example materials—such items as store coupons, telephone bills, and driving directions—were carefully presented, with the respondents answering a questionnaire related to those everyday items.

The direct and interactive nature of the assessment was critically important to the NAAL's success. As a result, the U.S. Department of Education was able to comprehensively understand the degree of adult illiteracy within the United States, and ultimately capture demographic and socioeconomic characteristics of those adults who were challenged from a literacy standpoint. It was the hard work of highly trained personal interviewers that helped the Department of Education address this critical national question.

Source: National Assessment of Adult Literacy, http://nces.ed.gov/NAAL/.

will misinterpret questions, because an interviewer who senses confusion can clarify the instruction or questions. Circumstances may dictate that at the conclusion of the interview, the respondent be given additional information concerning the purpose of the study. This clarification is easily accomplished with a personal interview. If the feedback indicates that some question or set of questions is particularly confusing, the researcher can make changes that make the questionnaire easier to understand.

PROBING COMPLEX ANSWERS

Another important characteristic of personal interviews is the opportunity to follow up by probing. If a respondent's answer is too brief or unclear, the researcher may request a more comprehensive or clearer explanation. In probing, the interviewer asks for clarification with standardized questions such as "Can you tell me more about what you had in mind?" (See Chapter 7 on qualitative research for an expanded discussion of probing.) Although interviewers are expected to ask questions exactly as they appear on the questionnaire, probing allows them some flexibility. Depending on the research purpose, personal interviews vary in the degree to which questions are structured and in the amount of probing required. The personal interview is especially useful for obtaining unstructured information. Skilled interviewers can handle complex questions that cannot easily be asked in telephone or mail surveys.

LENGTH OF INTERVIEW

If the research objective requires an extremely lengthy questionnaire, personal interviews may be the only option. A general rule of thumb on mail surveys is that they should not exceed six pages, and telephone interviews typically last less than ten minutes. In contrast, a personal interview can be much longer, perhaps an hour and a half, as was the case for the U.S. National Adult Literacy Assessment. However, the longer the interview, no matter what the form, the more the respondent should be compensated for their time and participation. Researchers should also be clear about how long participation should take in the opening dialog requesting participation. Online surveys should include a completion meter that shows the progress a respondent has made toward completing the task.

COMPLETENESS OF QUESTIONNAIRE

The social interaction between a well-trained interviewer and a respondent in a personal interview increases the likelihood that the respondent will answer all the items on the questionnaire. The respondent who grows bored with a telephone interview may terminate the interview at his or her discretion simply by hanging up the phone. Self-administration of a mail questionnaire requires even more effort by the respondent. Rather than write lengthy responses, the respondent may fail to complete some of the questions. **Item nonresponse**—failure to provide an answer to a question—is least likely to occur when an experienced interviewer asks questions directly.

item nonresponse
Failure of a respondent to provide an answer to a survey question.

PROPS AND VISUAL AIDS

Interviewing respondents face-to-face allows the investigator to show them new product samples, sketches of proposed advertising, or other visual aids. When Lego Group wanted to introduce new train model sets for its famous building bricks, the company targeted adults who build complex models with its product. The company invited adults who were swapping ideas at the Lego Web site to visit the New York office, where they viewed ideas and provided their opinions. The respondents wound up rejecting all the company's ideas, but they suggested something different: the Santa Fe Super Chief set, which sold out within two weeks, after being advertised only by enthusiastic word of mouth.[3] This research could not have been done in a telephone interview or mail survey.

Research that uses visual aids has become increasingly popular with researchers who investigate film concepts, advertising problems, and moviegoers' awareness of performers. Research for movies often begins by showing respondents videotapes of the prospective cast. After the movie has been produced, film clips are shown and interviews conducted to evaluate the movie's appeal, especially which scenes to emphasize in advertisements.

HIGH PARTICIPATION

Although some people are reluctant to participate in a survey, the presence of an interviewer generally increases the percentage of people willing to complete the interview. Respondents typically are required to do no reading or writing—all they have to do is talk. Many people enjoy sharing information and insights with friendly and sympathetic interviewers. People are often more hesitant to tell a person "no" face-to-face than they are over the phone or through some impersonal contact.

Disadvantages of Personal Interviews

Personal interviews also have some disadvantages. Respondents are not anonymous and as a result may be reluctant to provide confidential information to another person. Suppose a survey asked top executives, "Do you see any major internal instabilities or threats (people, money, material, and so on) to the achievement of your marketing objectives?" Many managers may be reluctant to answer this sensitive question honestly in a personal interview in which their identities are known.

INTERVIEWER INFLUENCE

Some evidence suggests that demographic characteristics of the interviewer influence respondents' answers. For example, one research study revealed that male interviewers produced larger amounts of interviewer variance than female interviewers in a survey in which 85 percent of the respondents were female. Older interviewers who interviewed older respondents produced more variance than other age combinations, whereas younger interviewers who interviewed younger respondents produced the least variance.

Differential interviewer techniques may be a source of bias. The rephrasing of a question, the interviewer's tone of voice, and the interviewer's appearance may influence the respondent's answer. Consider the interviewer who has conducted 100 personal interviews. During the next one, he or she may lose concentration and either selectively perceive or anticipate the respondent's answer. The interpretation of the response may differ somewhat from what the respondent intended. Typically, the public thinks of the person who does marketing research as a dedicated scientist. Unfortunately, some interviewers do not fit that ideal. Considerable interviewer variability exists. Cheating is possible; interviewers may cut corners to save time and energy, faking parts of their reports by dummying up part, or all, of the questionnaire. Control over interviewers is important to ensure that difficult, embarrassing, or time-consuming questions are handled properly.

LACK OF ANONYMITY OF RESPONDENT

Because a respondent in a personal interview is not anonymous and may be reluctant to provide confidential information to another person, researchers often spend considerable time and effort to phrase sensitive questions to avoid social desirability bias. For example, the interviewer may show the respondent a card that lists possible answers and ask the respondent to read a category number rather than be required to verbalize sensitive answers.

COST

Personal interviews are expensive, generally substantially more costly than mail, Internet, or telephone surveys. The geographic proximity of respondents, the length and complexity of the questionnaire, and the number of people who are nonrespondents because they could not be contacted (not-at-homes) will all influence the cost of the personal interview.

Door-to-Door Interviews and Shopping Mall Intercepts

Personal interviews may be conducted at the respondents' homes or offices or in many other places. Increasingly, personal interviews are being conducted in shopping malls. Mall intercept interviews allow many interviews to be conducted quickly. Often, respondents are intercepted in public areas of shopping malls and then asked to come to a permanent research facility to taste new food items or to view advertisements. The locale for the interview generally influences the participation rate, and thus the degree to which the sample represents the general population.

DOOR-TO-DOOR INTERVIEWS

The presence of an interviewer at the door generally increases the likelihood that a person will be willing to complete an interview. Because **door-to-door interviews** increase the participation rate, they provide a more representative sample of the population than mail questionnaires. For example, response rates to mail surveys are substantially lower among Hispanics whether the questionnaire is printed in English or Spanish.[4] People who do not have telephones, who have unlisted telephone numbers, or who are otherwise difficult to contact may be reached using door-to-door interviews. However, door-to-door interviews may underrepresent some groups and overrepresent others based on the geographic areas covered.

door-to-door interviews
Personal interviews conducted at respondents' doorsteps in an effort to increase the participation rate in the survey.

Door-to-door interviews may exclude individuals who live in multiple-dwelling units with security systems, such as high-rise apartment dwellers, or executives who are too busy to grant personal interviews during business hours. Other people, for security reasons, simply will not open the door when a stranger knocks. Telephoning an individual in one of these subgroups to make an appointment may make the total sample more representative. However, obtaining a representative sample of this security-conscious subgroup based on a listing in the telephone directory may be difficult. For these reasons, door-to-door interviews are becoming a thing of the past.

CALLBACKS

callbacks
Attempts to recontact individuals selected for a sample who were not available initially.

When a person selected to be in the sample cannot be contacted on the first visit, a systematic procedure is normally initiated to call back at another time. **Callbacks**, or attempts to recontact individuals selected for the sample, are the major means of reducing nonresponse error. Calling back a sampling unit is more expensive than interviewing the person the first time around, because subjects who initially were not at home generally are more widely dispersed geographically than the original sample units. Callbacks in door-to-door interviews are important because not-at-home individuals (for example, working parents) may systematically vary from those who *are* at home (nonworking parents, retired people, and the like).

MALL INTERCEPT INTERVIEWS

mall intercept interviews
Personal interviews conducted in a shopping mall.

Personal interviews conducted in shopping malls are referred to as **mall intercept interviews**, or *shopping center sampling*. Interviewers typically intercept shoppers at a central point within the mall or at an entrance. The main reason mall intercept interviews are conducted is because their costs are lower. No travel is required to the respondent's home; instead, the respondent comes to the interviewer, and many interviews can be conducted quickly in this way.

A major problem with mall intercept interviews is that individuals usually are in a hurry to shop, so the incidence of refusal is high—typically around 50 percent. Yet it is standard practice for many commercial research companies, who conduct more personal interviews in shopping malls than it conducts door-to-door.

In a mall interview, the researcher must recognize that he or she should not be looking for a representative sample of the total population. Each mall has its own target market's characteristics, and there is likely to be a larger bias than with careful household probability sampling. However, personal interviews in shopping malls are appropriate when the target group is a special market segment such as the parents of children of bike-riding age. If the respondent indicates that he or she has a child of this age, the parent can then be brought into a rented space and shown several bikes. The mall intercept interview allows the researcher to show large, heavy, or immobile visual materials, such as a television commercial. A mall interviewer can give an individual a product to take home to use and obtain a commitment that the respondent will cooperate when recontacted later by telephone. Mall intercept interviews are also valuable when activities such as cooking and tasting of food must be closely coordinated and timed to follow each other. They may also be appropriate when a consumer durable product must be demonstrated. For example, when video-cassette recorders and DVD players were innovations in the prototype stage, the effort and space required to set up and properly display these units ruled out in-home testing.

TOTHEPOINT

A man's feet should be planted in his country, but his eyes should survey the world.

—George Santayana

Global Considerations

Willingness to participate in a personal interview varies dramatically around the world. For example, in many Middle Eastern countries women would never consent to be interviewed by a man. And in many countries the idea of discussing grooming behavior and personal-care products with a stranger would be highly offensive. Few people would consent to be interviewed on such topics.

The norms about appropriate business conduct also influence businesspeople's willingness to provide information to interviewers. For example, conducting business-to-business interviews in Japan during business hours is difficult because managers, strongly loyal to their firm, believe that they have an absolute responsibility to oversee their employees while on the job. In some cultures when a businessperson is reluctant to be interviewed, a reputable third party may be asked to intervene so that an interview may take place.

Telephone Interviews

For several decades, landline **telephone interviews** have been the mainstay of commercial survey research. The quality of data obtained by telephone is potentially comparable to the quality of data collected face-to-face. Respondents are more willing to provide detailed and reliable information on a variety of personal topics over the phone while in the privacy of their own homes than when answering questions face-to-face.

telephone interviews
Personal interviews conducted by telephone, the mainstay of commercial survey research.

In-home phone surveys are still considered capable of providing fairly representative samples of the U.S. population. However, the "no-call" legislation dating back to the middle of the first decade of the twenty-first century has limited this capability somewhat. Business researchers cannot solicit information via phone numbers listed on the do-not-call registry. Thus, to the extent that consumers who place their numbers on these lists share something in common, such as a greater desire for privacy, a representative sample of the general population cannot be obtained. Marketers and marketing researchers can obtain the do-not-call lists of phone numbers from the FTC for $62 per area code. The entire registry can be obtained for $17,050. This information can be obtained from the FTC do-not-call Web site shown in the screenshot. Although this may seem expensive, the FTC levies fines on the order of $10,000 per violation (per call); so obtaining the registry is a wise investment for those wishing to contact consumers via telephone. AT&T faced fines of over three-quarters of a million dollars for making 78 unwanted calls to 29 consumers listed on the do-not-call list. So, the Feds do take violations very seriously.

Likewise, the Canadian government has instituted a nearly identical do-not-call program. The Canadian Radio-Television and Telecommunications Commission imposes fines up to $11,000 per call for calls made to people on the Canadian do-not-call list. Other countries in Europe and elsewhere are also considering such legislation. The advantages of privacy simply make phones less capable of obtaining representative samples than they once were. Often, however, a landline phone call is still the researcher's best option.

MOBILE PHONE INTERVIEWS

Mobile phone interviews differ from landline phones most obviously because they are directed toward a mobile (i.e., cell) phone number. However, there are other less obvious distinctions.

- In the U.S., no telemarketing can be directed toward mobile phone numbers by law. The primary reason for enacting this law was that respondents would often have to pay to receive the call. Respondents would have to "opt in" before their phone number would be made available for such calls.
- The recipient of a mobile phone call is even more likely to be distracted than with a call to someone's home or office. In fact, the respondent may be driving a car, on a subway train, or walking down a noisy street. Factors such as this are not conducive to a high-quality interview.
- The area codes for mobile phones are not necessarily tied to geography. For instance, a person who moves from Georgia to Arizona can choose to keep his or her old phone number. Therefore, a researcher may be unable to determine whether or not a respondent fits into the desired geographic sampling population simply by taking note of the area code.

The federal government provides information for both consumers and businesses through this Web site.

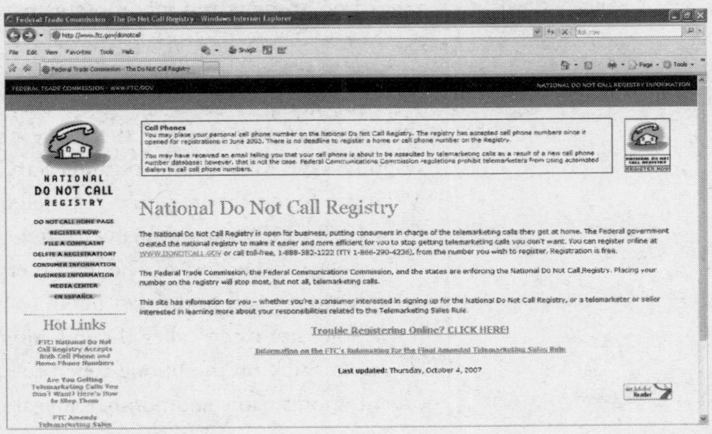

WWW.DONOTCALL.GOV

- The phones have varying abilities for automated responses and differing keypads. Some requests, such as "hit pound sign," may be more difficult to do on some keypads than on others.

Phone Interview Characteristics

Phone interviews in general have several distinctive characteristics that set them apart from other survey techniques. These characteristics present significant advantages and disadvantages for the researcher.

SPEED

One advantage of telephone interviewing is the speed of data collection. While data collection with mail or personal interviews can take several weeks, hundreds of telephone interviews can be conducted literally overnight. When the interviewer enters the respondents' answers directly into a computerized system, the data processing speeds up even more.

COST

As the cost of personal interviews continues to increase, telephone interviews are becoming relatively inexpensive. The cost of telephone interviews is estimated to be less than 25 percent of the cost of door-to-door personal interviews. Travel time and costs are eliminated. However, the typical Internet survey is less expensive than a telephone survey.

ABSENCE OF FACE-TO-FACE CONTACT

Telephone interviews are more impersonal than face-to-face interviews. Respondents may answer embarrassing or confidential questions more willingly in a telephone interview than in a personal interview. However, mail and Internet surveys, although not perfect, are better media for gathering extremely sensitive information because they seem more anonymous. Some evidence suggests that people provide information on income and other financial matters only reluctantly, even in telephone interviews. Such questions may be personally threatening for a variety of reasons, and high refusal rates for this type of question occur with each form of survey research.

Although telephone calls may be less threatening because the interviewer is not physically present, the absence of face-to-face contact can also be a liability. The respondent cannot see that the interviewer is still writing down the previous comment and may continue to elaborate on an answer. If the respondent pauses to think about an answer, the interviewer may not realize it and may go on to the next question. Hence, there is a greater tendency for interviewers to record no answers and incomplete answers in telephone interviews than in personal interviews.

COOPERATION

One trend is very clear. In the last few decades, telephone response rates have fallen. Analysis of response rates for the long-running Survey of Consumer Attitudes conducted by the University of Michigan found that response rates fell from a high of 72 percent to 67 percent during the period from 1979 to 1996 and then even faster after 1996, dropping to 60 percent.[5] Lenny Murphy of data collection firm Dialtek says he has observed a decline in survey response rates from a typical range of 30 to 40 percent in the past down to below 20 percent.[6] Fewer calls are answered because more households are using caller ID and answering machines to screen their calls, and many individuals do not pick up the phone when the display reads "out of area" or when an unfamiliar survey organization's name and number appear on the display. Also, more phone lines are dedicated to fax machines and computers. However, the University of Michigan study found that the rate of refusal actually grew faster in the more recent period than the rate of not answering researchers' calls.

One way researchers can try to improve response rates is to leave a message on the household's telephone answering machine or voice mail. However, many people will not return a call to help someone conduct a survey. Using a message explicitly stating that the purpose of the call is not sales related may improve responses. Other researchers simply hope to reach respondents when they call back, trying callbacks at different times and on different days.

Further complicating the situation is the use of wireless mobile phone services.[7] Regulations by the Federal Communications Commission make it illegal for researchers to use automated dialing equipment to call mobile phones. Even if researchers dial the calls by hand, they may not contact anyone who would have to pay for the call—that is, most cell phone users. So far, only a small share of U.S. households (less than 4 percent) have given up their landlines, but those numbers are growing, and they include a sizable segment of young adults. In fact, consumers may keep their phone numbers when they change to a new phone company, so many consumers who have abandoned landlines for cell phones may be keeping a phone number that telephone interviewers may no longer dial without penalty.

Other countries may not adopt laws restricting calls to mobile phones. In addition, consumers in other countries are more open to responding to research delivered by voice or by text messaging. Thus, the mobile phone may be a better interview tool outside of the United States than in the United States.

Refusal to cooperate with interviews is directly related to interview length. A major study of survey research found that interviews of 5 minutes or less had a refusal rate of 21 percent; interviews of between 6 and 12 minutes had 41 percent refusal rates; and interviews of 13 minutes or more had 47 percent rates. In unusual cases, a few highly interested respondents will put up with longer interviews. A good rule of thumb is to keep telephone interviews approximately 10 to 15 minutes long. In general, 30 minutes is the maximum amount of time most respondents will spend unless they are highly interested in the survey subject.

Another way to encourage participation is to send households an invitation to participate in a survey. The invitation can describe the purpose and importance of the survey and the likely duration of the survey. The invitation can also encourage subjects to be available and reassure them that the caller will not try to sell anything. In a recent study comparing response rates, the rates were highest among households that received an advance letter, somewhat lower when the notice came on a postcard, and lowest when no notice was sent.[8]

INCENTIVES TO REPOND

Respondents should receive some incentive to respond. Research addresses different types of incentives. For telephone interviews, test-marketing involving different types of survey introductions suggests that not all introductions are equally effective. A financial incentive or some significant chance to win a desirable prize will produce a higher telephone response rate than a simple assurance that the research is not a sales pitch, a more detailed description of the survey, or an assurance of confidentiality.[9]

REPRESENTATIVE SAMPLES

Practical difficulties complicate obtaining representative samples based on listings in the telephone book. About 95 percent of households in the United States have landline telephones. People without phones are more likely to be poor, aged, rural, or living in the South. Unlisted phone numbers and numbers too new to be printed in the directory are a greater problem. People have unlisted phone numbers for two reasons:

- They have recently moved
- They prefer to have unlisted numbers for privacy

Individuals whose phone numbers are unlisted because of a recent move differ slightly from those with published numbers. The unlisted group tends to be younger, more urban, and less likely to own a single-family dwelling. Households that maintain unlisted phone numbers by choice tend to have higher incomes. And, as previously mentioned, a number of low-income households are unlisted by circumstance.

random digit dialing

Use of telephone exchanges and a table of random numbers to contact respondents with unlisted phone numbers.

The problem of unlisted phone numbers can be partially resolved through the use of random digit dialing. **Random digit dialing** eliminates the counting of names in a list (for example, calling every fiftieth name in a column) and subjectively determining whether a directory listing is a business, institution, or legitimate household. In the simplest form of random digit dialing, telephone exchanges (prefixes) for the geographic areas in the sample are obtained. Using a table of random numbers, the last four digits of the telephone number are selected. Telephone directories can be ignored entirely or used in combination with the assignment of one or several random digits. Random digit dialing also helps overcome the problem due to new listings and recent changes in numbers. Unfortunately, the refusal rate in commercial random digit dialing studies is higher than the refusal rate for telephone surveys that use only listed telephone numbers.

CALLBACKS

An unanswered call, a busy signal, or a respondent who is not at home requires a callback. Telephone callbacks are much easier to make than callbacks in personal interviews. However, as mentioned, the ownership of telephone answering machines is growing, and their effects on callbacks need to be studied.

LIMITED DURATION

Respondents who run out of patience with the interview can merely hang up. To encourage participation, interviews should be relatively short. The length of the telephone interview is definitely limited.

LACK OF VISUAL MEDIUM

Because visual aids cannot be used in telephone interviews, this method is not appropriate for packaging research, copy testing of television and print advertising, and concept tests that require visual materials. Likewise, certain attitude scales and measuring instruments, such as the semantic differential (described in a later chapter), require the respondent to see a graphic scale, so they are difficult to use over the phone.

central location interviewing

Telephone interviews conducted from a central location allowing firms to hire a staff of professional interviewers and to supervise and control the quality of interviewing more effectively.

Central Location Interviewing

Research agencies or interviewing services typically conduct all telephone interviews from a central location. Such **central location interviewing** allows firms to hire a staff of professional interviewers and to supervise and control the quality of interviewing more effectively. When telephone interviews are centralized and computerized, an agency or business can benefit from additional cost economies.

computer-assisted telephone interviewing (CATI)

Technology that allows answers to telephone interviews to be entered directly into a computer for processing.

Computer-Assisted Telephone Interviewing

Advances in computer technology allow responses to telephone interviews to be entered directly into the computer in a process known as **computer-assisted telephone interviewing (CATI)**.

RESEARCH SNAPSHOT

Automated Phone Surveys of Teens

Automatic telephone surveys are a good way to reach all members of the family, not just the head of the household. What if you wanted to ask questions about holiday shopping, what's for dinner, or what kind of vacation the family would like? A short telephone survey may be the answer. One advantage is that no "real person" has to hear the answers to potentially sensitive questions.

Computer-assisted telephone interviewing (CATI) and computerized self-interviewing, in which the subjects listened to prerecorded questions and then responded by entering answers with the telephone's keypad, have been used to ask the "teen" in the house about smoking. The researchers predicted that the young people would be more likely to say they smoke in the self-administered survey than in response to a live interviewer, because pressing keys on the keypad would feel more confidential.

The interviewers were right. In the self-administered survey, the teens were more likely to say they had smoked in the past thirty days or, if they had not smoked, to lack a firm commitment not to smoke in the future. Many of them indicated a parent was present while they answered the questions, and when they did, their responses were less likely to indicate smoking desire or susceptibility. This pattern suggests that they might be underreporting their smoking behavior. These findings encourage researchers to be attentive to confidentiality when working with teenage subjects.

Sources: "Survey: Consumers Say 'Yes' to Holiday Shopping," *Stores 83*, no. 12 (December 2001), 18; also based on Moskowitz, Joel M., "Assessment of Cigarette Smoking and Smoking Susceptibility among Youth: Telephone Computer-Assisted Self-Interviews versus Computer-Assisted Telephone Interviews," *Public Opinion Quarterly* 68 (Winter 2004), 565–587.

Telephone interviewers are seated at computer terminals. Monitors display the questionnaires, one question at a time, along with precoded possible responses to each question. The interviewer reads each question as it appears on the screen. When the respondent answers, the interviewer enters the response directly into the computer, and it is automatically stored in the computer's memory. The computer then displays the next question on the screen. Computer-assisted telephone interviewing requires that answers to the questionnaire be highly structured. If a respondent gives an unacceptable answer (that is, one not precoded and programmed), the computer will reject it (see Research Snapshot "Automated Phone Surveys of Teens").

Computer-assisted telephone interviewing systems include telephone management systems that select phone numbers, dial the numbers automatically, and perform other labor-saving functions. These systems can automatically control sample selection by randomly generating names or fulfilling a sample quota. A computer can generate an automatic callback schedule. A typical call management system might schedule recontact attempts to recall no answers after two hours and busy numbers after ten minutes and allow the interviewer to enter a more favorable time slot (day and hour) when a respondent indicates that he or she is too busy to be interviewed. Software systems also allow researchers to request daily status reports on the number of completed interviews relative to quotas. CATI interviews can also be conducted by a prerecorded voice with the respondent answering by punching buttons on the phone.

Computerized Voice-Activated Telephone Interview

Technological advances have combined computerized telephone dialing and voice-activated computer messages to allow researchers to conduct telephone interviews without human interviewers. However, researchers have found that computerized voice-activated telephone interviewing works best with very short, simple questionnaires. One system includes a voice-synthesized module controlled by a microprocessor. With it the sponsor is able to register a caller's single response such as "true/false," "yes/no," "like/dislike," or "for/against." This type of system has been used by television and radio stations to register callers' responses to certain issues. One system, Telsol, begins with an announcement that the respondent is listening to a recorded message. The computer then asks questions, leaving blank tape in between to record the answers. If respondents do not answer the first two questions, the computer disconnects and goes to the next call. With this process, the entire data collection process can be automated because a recorded voice is used to both ask the questions and record answers.

computer-assisted personal interviewing (CAPI)
Either the interviewer or the respondent answers the interview by sitting at the computer terminal and recording the responses.

In computerized personal interviewing or **computer-assisted personal interviewing (CAPI),** either the interviewer or the respondent answers the interview by sitting at the computer terminal and recording the responses. In the absence of an interviewer, we call it, **computer-assisted self interviewing (CASI).**

computer-assisted self interviewing (CASI)
CAPI in the absence of an interviewer.

- The interviewer or the respondent sits at the computer terminal to answer the questionnaire using computer aids like keyboard or mouse.
- Console is used to help or assist the person during the interview.
- To capture the interest levels of the interviewee, colorful screens are used apart from screen stimuli that improve the involvement in the questionnaire.
- Though there is no personal contact between the respondent and the interviewer, it is still termed personal interview as the interviewer is at the respondent's disposal at the server end, from where he is hosting.
- This approach is extended to shopping malls, which is preceded by an intercept, followed by screening process.
- Used in conducting business-to-business research at trade shows or conventions.
- Used extensively for data collection.

ADVANTAGES

Cost-effectiveness is what makes this form of interviewing special, especially when large numbers of respondents are being interviewed.

- Recruitment costs and salaries to the interviewers are scrapped.
- Computer-programs can be designed so as to format and analyze respondents' data instead of manually analyzing it, through print-outs of responses. Statistical tools can be employed to analyze data.
- By placing the program on the web, wide number of respondents can be attracted.

DISADVANTAGES

- The major problem with this form of interviewing is that it attracts net-savvy or computer-savvy respondents and loses out some potential respondents. Also, there tends to be a bias due to the type of respondents who are answering the survey.
- The survey can miss feedback and clarification/quality control that a personal interviewer could provide (e.g., lots of respondents misinterpret the question).

Global Considerations

Different cultures often have different norms about proper telephone behavior. For example, business-to-business researchers have learned that Latin American businesspeople will not open up to strangers on the telephone. So, researchers in Latin America usually find personal interviews more suitable than telephone surveys. In Japan, respondents consider it ill-mannered if telephone interviews last more than 20 minutes.

Self-Administered Questionnaires

Many surveys do not require an interviewer's presence. Researchers distribute questionnaires to consumers through the mail and in many other ways (see Exhibit 10.1). They insert questionnaires in packages and magazines. They may place questionnaires at points of purchase or in high-traffic locations in stores or malls. They may even fax questionnaires to individuals. Questionnaires can be printed on paper, but they may be posted on the Internet or sent via e-mail. No matter how the **self-administered questionnaires** are distributed, they are different from interviews because the respondent takes responsibility for reading and answering the questions.

self-administered questionnaires

Surveys in which the respondent takes the responsibility for reading and answering the questions.

Self-administered questionnaires present a challenge to the researcher because they rely on the clarity of the written word rather than on the skills of the interviewer. The nature of self-administered questionnaires is best illustrated by explaining mail questionnaires.

EXHIBIT 10.1 **Self-Administered Questionnaires Can Be Either Printed or Electronic**

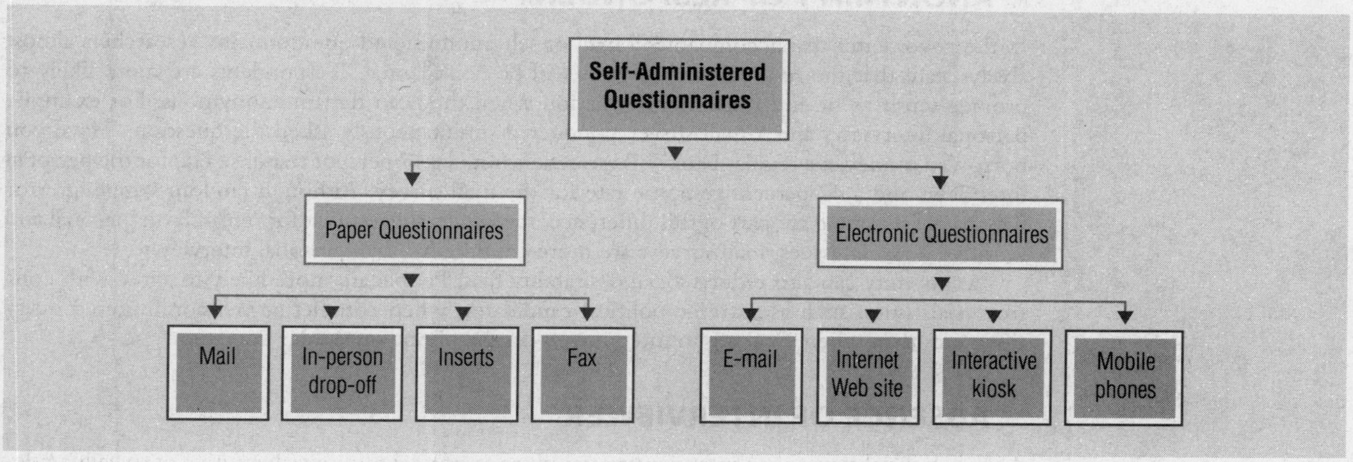

Mail Questionnaires

A **mail survey** is a self-administered questionnaire sent to respondents through the mail. This paper-and-pencil method has several advantages and disadvantages.

mail survey

A self-administered questionnaire sent to respondents through the mail.

GEOGRAPHIC FLEXIBILITY

Mail questionnaires can reach a geographically dispersed sample simultaneously because interviewers are not required. Respondents (such as farmers) who are located in isolated areas or those (such as executives) who are otherwise difficult to reach can easily be contacted by mail. For example, a pharmaceutical firm may find that doctors are not available for personal or telephone interviews. However, a mail survey can reach both rural and urban doctors who practice in widely dispersed geographic areas.

COST

Mail questionnaires are relatively inexpensive compared with personal interviews, though they are not cheap. Most include follow-up mailings, which require additional postage and printing costs. And it usually isn't cost-effective to try to cut costs on printing—questionnaires photocopied on low-grade paper have a greater likelihood of being thrown in the wastebasket than those prepared with more expensive, high-quality printing. The low response rates contribute to the high cost.

RESPONDENT CONVENIENCE

Mail surveys and other self-administered questionnaires can be filled out when the respondents have time, so respondents are more likely to take time to think about their replies. Many hard-to-reach respondents place a high value on convenience and thus are best contacted by mail. In some situations, particularly in business-to-business research, mail questionnaires allow respondents to collect facts, such as employment statistics, that they may not be able to recall without checking. Being able to check information by verifying records or, in household surveys, by consulting with other family members should provide more valid, factual information than either personal or telephone interviews would allow. A catalog retailer may use mail surveys to estimate sales volume for catalog items by sending a mock catalog as part of the questionnaire. Respondents would be asked to indicate how likely they would be to order selected items. Using the mail allows respondents to consult other family members and to make their decisions within a reasonable time span.

ANONYMITY OF RESPONDENT

In the cover letter that accompanies a mail or self-administered questionnaire, researchers almost always state that the respondents' answers will be confidential. Respondents are more likely to provide sensitive or embarrassing information when they can remain anonymous. For example, personal interviews and a mail survey conducted simultaneously asked the question "Have you borrowed money at a regular bank?" Researchers noted a 17 percent response rate for the personal interviews and a 42 percent response rate for the mail survey. Although random sampling error may have accounted for part of this difference, the results suggest that for research on personal and sensitive financial issues, mail surveys are more confidential than personal interviews.

Anonymity can also reduce social desirability bias. People are more likely to agree with controversial issues, such as extreme political candidates, when completing self-administered questionnaires than when speaking to interviewers on the phone or at their doorsteps.

ABSENCE OF INTERVIEWER

Although the absence of an interviewer can induce respondents to reveal sensitive or socially undesirable information, this lack of personal contact can also be a disadvantage. Once the respondent receives the questionnaire, the questioning process is beyond the researcher's control. Although the printed stimulus is the same, each respondent will attach a different personal meaning to each question. Selective perception operates in research as well as in advertising. The respondent does not have the opportunity to question the interviewer. Problems that might be clarified in a personal or telephone interview can remain misunderstandings in a mail survey. There is no interviewer to probe for additional information or clarification of an answer, and the recorded answers must be assumed to be complete.

Respondents have the opportunity to read the entire questionnaire before they answer individual questions. Often the text of a later question will provide information that affects responses to earlier questions.

STANDARDIZED QUESTIONS

Mail questionnaires typically are highly standardized, and the questions are quite structured. Questions and instructions must be clear-cut and straightforward. Ambiguous questions only create additional error. Interviewing allows for feedback from the interviewer regarding the respondent's comprehension of the questionnaire. An interviewer who notices that the first 50 respondents are having some difficulty understanding a question can report this fact to the research analyst so that revisions can be made. With a mail survey, however, once the questionnaires are mailed, it is difficult to change the format or the questions.

TIME IS MONEY

If time is a factor in management's interest in the research results, or if attitudes are rapidly changing (for example, toward a political event), mail surveys may not be the best communication medium. A minimum of two or three weeks is necessary for receiving the majority of the responses. Follow-up mailings, which usually are sent when the returns begin to trickle in, require an additional two or three weeks. The time between the first mailing and the cut-off date (when questionnaires will no longer be accepted) normally is six to eight weeks. In a regional or local study, personal interviews can be conducted more quickly. However, conducting a national study by mail might be substantially faster than conducting personal interviews across the nation.

LENGTH OF MAIL QUESTIONNAIRE

Mail questionnaires vary considerably in length, ranging from extremely short postcard questionnaires to multipage booklets that require respondents to fill in thousands of answers. A general rule of thumb is that a mail questionnaire should not exceed six pages in length. When a questionnaire requires a respondent to expend a great deal of effort, an incentive is generally required to induce the respondent to return the questionnaire. The following sections discuss several ways to obtain high response rates even when questionnaires are longer than average.

Response Rates

All questionnaires that arrive via bulk mail are likely to get thrown away. Questionnaires that are boring, unclear, or too complex are even more likely to get thrown in the wastebasket. A poorly designed mail questionnaire may be returned by less than 5 percent of those sampled (that is, a 5 percent response rate). The basic calculation for obtaining a **response rate** is to count the number of questionnaires returned or completed, then divide the total by the number of eligible people who were contacted or requested to participate in the survey. Typically, the number in the denominator is adjusted for faulty addresses and similar problems that reduce the number of eligible participants.

response rate

The number of questionnaires returned or completed divided by the number of eligible people who were asked to participate in the survey.

The major limitations of mail questionnaires relate to response problems. Respondents who complete the questionnaire may not be typical of all people in the sample. Individuals with a special interest in the topic are more likely to respond to a mail survey than those who are indifferent.

A researcher has no assurance that the intended subject is the person who fills out the questionnaire. The wrong person answering the questions may be a problem when surveying corporate executives, physicians, and other professionals, who may pass questionnaires on to subordinates to complete. This probably is not unique to snail mail surveys since electronic surveying suffers similarly.

Evidence suggests that cooperation and response rates rise as home value increases. Also, if the sample has a high proportion of retired and well-off householders, response rates will be lower. Mail survey respondents tend to be better educated than nonrespondents. If they return the questionnaire at all, poorly educated respondents who cannot read and write well may skip open-ended questions to which they are required to write out their answers. Rarely will a mail survey have a 50 percent or greater response rate. However, the use of follow-up mailings and other techniques may increase the response rate to an acceptable percentage. The lower the response rate, the greater the concern that the resulting sample will not adequately represent the population.

Increasing Response Rates for Mail Surveys

Nonresponse error is always a potential problem with mail surveys. Individuals who are interested in the general subject of the survey are more likely to respond than those with less interest or little experience. Thus, people who hold extreme positions on an issue are more likely to respond than individuals who are largely indifferent to the topic. To minimize this bias, researchers have developed a number of techniques to increase the response rate to mail surveys. For example, almost all surveys include postage-paid return envelopes. Using a stamped return envelope instead of a business reply envelope increases response rates even more.[10] Designing and formatting attractive questionnaires and wording questions so that they are easy to understand also help ensure a good response rate. However, special efforts may be required even with a sound questionnaire. Several of these methods are discussed in the following subsections.

COVER LETTER

cover letter
Letter that accompanies a questionnaire to induce the reader to complete and return the questionnaire.

A **cover letter** that accompanies a questionnaire or is printed on the first page of the questionnaire booklet is an important means of inducing a reader to complete and return the questionnaire. Exhibit 10.2 illustrates a cover letter and some of the points considered by a research professional to be important in gaining respondents' attention and cooperation. The first paragraph of the letter explains why the study is important. The basic appeal alludes to the social usefulness of responding. Two other frequently used appeals are asking for help ("Will you do us a favor?") and the egotistical appeal ("Your opinions are important!"). Most cover letters promise confidentiality, invite the recipient to use an enclosed postage-paid reply envelope, describe any incentive or reward for participation, explain that answering the questionnaire will not be difficult and will take only a short time, and describe how the person was scientifically selected for participation.

A personalized letter addressed to a specific individual shows the respondent that he or she is important. Including an individually typed cover letter on letterhead rather than a printed form is an important element in increasing the response rate in mail surveys.[11]

MONEY HELPS

The respondent's motivation for returning a questionnaire may be increased by offering monetary incentives or premiums. Although pens, lottery tickets, and a variety of premiums have been used, monetary incentives appear to be the most effective and least biasing incentive. Money attracts attention and creates a sense of obligation. Perhaps for this reason, monetary incentives work for all income categories. Often, cover letters try to boost response rates with messages such as "We know that the attached dollar cannot compensate you for your time but please accept it as a token of our appreciation." Response rates increase dramatically when the monetary incentive is to be sent to a charity of the respondent's choice rather than directly to the respondent.

INTERESTING QUESTIONS

The topic of the research—and thus the point of the questions—cannot be manipulated without changing the definition of the research problem. However, certain interesting questions can be added to the questionnaire, perhaps at the beginning, to stimulate respondents' interest and to induce cooperation. By including questions that are of little concern to the researchers but that the respondents want to answer, the researchers may give respondents who are indifferent to the major questions a reason for responding.

FOLLOW-UPS

Most mail surveys generate responses in a pattern like that shown in Exhibit 10.3, which graphs the cumulative response rates for two mail surveys. The response rates are relatively high for the first two weeks (as indicated by the steepness of each curve), then the rates gradually taper off.

After responses from the first wave of mailings begin to trickle in, most studies use a follow-up letter or postcard reminder, which request that the questionnaire be returned because a 100-percent return rate is important. A follow-up may include a duplicate questionnaire or may merely be a reminder to return the original questionnaire. Multiple contacts almost always increase response rates. The more attempts made to reach people, the greater the chances of their responding.[12]

Both of the studies in Exhibit 10.3 used follow-ups. Notice how the cumulative response rates picked up around week four.

EXHIBIT 10.2
A Cover Letter Requesting Participation in a Survey

MKTR **Market Research Leaders**

Component: →	111 Eustice Square, Terroir, IL 39800-7600
Respondent's Address →	Mr. Griff Mitchell 821 Shrewsbury Ave Hector Chase, LA 70809
	Dear Mr. Mitchell:
Request/Time involved →	We'd like your input as part of a study of family media habits. This study is not involved in any attempt to sell anything. Rather, the results will help provide better media options for families. The survey typically takes about 12 minutes to complete.
Selection Method →	You were selected based on a random sample of home owners living in the 70809 zip code.
Reason to Respond →	We need your opinion about many important issues involving the way modern families interact with various media including print, television, radio, and Internet sources. Companies need input to create the most appealing and useful options for consumers; and local, state, and federal agencies need input to know what types of regulations, if any, are most appropriate. Without the opinions of people like you, many of these key issues will likely not be resolved.
Confidentiality/ IRB Approval →	The information you provide, just as with all the information collected within the scope of this project, will be entirely confidential. It will only be used for the purpose of this research and no individuals will be identified within the data. Additionally, this survey and the request for you to participate has been reviewed and approved by the Institutional Review Board of MKTR which monitors all research conducted and assures that procedures are consistent with ethical guidelines for federally funded research (although this particular project is not funded federally). If you have any questions, the MKTR IRB can be contacted at (888) 555-8888.
Incentive →	Your response will improve the media choices that your family faces. In addition, a $10 check that you can cash at your personal bank is included as a token of our appreciation.
Willingness to answer questions →	Additionally, you can direct any questions about this project directly to me. The contact information is available at the top of this letter. Additionally, we will be happy to provide you a summary of the results. Simply complete the enclosed self-addressed postcard and drop it in the mail or include it with the completed questionnaire. A self-addressed, postage paid reply envelope is included for your return.
Thanks →	Again, thank you so much for your time and for sharing your opinions.
Signature →	*Laurie Thibodeaux*

ADVANCE NOTIFICATION

Advance notification, by either letter or telephone, that a questionnaire will be arriving has been successful in increasing response rates in some situations. ACNielsen has used this technique to ensure a high cooperation rate in filling out diaries of television watching. Advance notices that go out closer to the questionnaire mailing time produce better results than those sent too far in advance. The optimal lead time for advance notification is three days before the mail survey is to arrive.

SURVEY SPONSORSHIP

Auspices bias may result from the sponsorship of a survey. One business-to-business researcher wished to conduct a survey of its wholesalers to learn their stocking policies and their attitudes concerning competing manufacturers. A mail questionnaire sent on the corporate letterhead very

EXHIBIT 10.3

Plots of Actual Response Patterns for Two Commercial Surveys

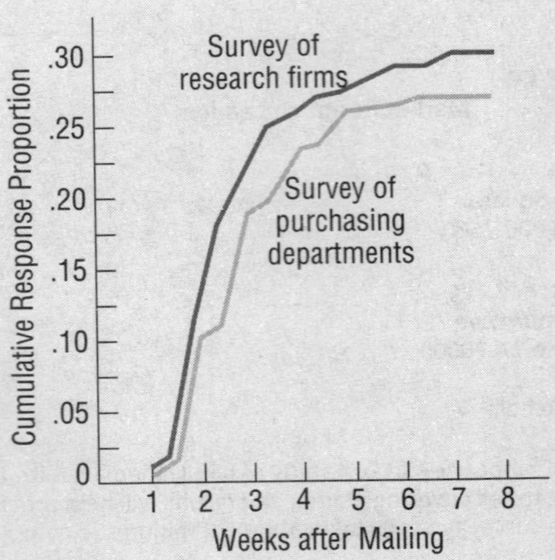

Mail surveys can reach a geographically dispersed sample and are relatively inexpensive. One disadvantage is the length of time involved in getting responses back. Response rates themselves also offer a challenge to surveyors.

likely would have received a much lower response rate than the questionnaire actually sent, which used the letterhead of a commercial marketing research firm. Sponsorship by well-known and prestigious organizations such as universities or government agencies may also significantly influence response rates. A mail survey sent to members of a consumer panel will receive an exceptionally high response rate because panel members have already agreed to cooperate with surveys.

© PHOTODISC/THINKSTOCK

OTHER TECHNIQUES

Numerous other devices have been used for increasing response rates. For example, the type of postage (commemorative versus regular stamp), envelope size, color of the questionnaire paper, and many other factors have been varied in efforts to increase response rates. Each has had at least limited success in certain situations; unfortunately, under other conditions each has failed to increase response rates significantly. The researcher should consider his or her particular situation. For example, the researcher who is investigating consumers faces one situation; the researcher who is surveying corporate executives faces quite another.

KEYING MAIL QUESTIONNAIRES WITH CODES

A researcher planning a follow-up letter or postcard should not disturb respondents who already have returned the questionnaire. The expense of mailing questionnaires to those who already have responded is usually avoidable. One device for eliminating those who have already responded from the follow-up mailing list is to mark the questionnaires so that they may be keyed to identify members of the sampling frame who are nonrespondents. Blind keying of questionnaires on a return envelope (systematically varying the job number or room number of the marketing research department, for example) or a visible code number on the questionnaire has been used for this purpose. Visible keying is indicated with statements such as "The sole purpose of the number on the last page is to avoid sending a second questionnaire to people who complete and return the first one." Ethical researchers key questionnaires only to increase response rates, thereby preserving respondents' anonymity.

Global Considerations

Researchers conducting surveys in more than one country must recognize that postal services and cultural circumstances differ around the world. Some of the issues to consider are the reliability of mail delivery, literacy rates, and trust that researchers can and will provide confidentiality. In some cases, hand delivery of surveys or door-to-door interviewing may be necessary. In other cases, consumers (especially women or children) might be discouraged from talking to an interviewer who is not a family member, so mailed questionnaires would be superior to interviews.

Self-Administered Questionnaires Using Other Forms of Distribution

Many forms of self-administered, printed questionnaires are very similar to mail questionnaires. Airlines frequently pass out questionnaires to passengers during flights. Restaurants, hotels, and other service establishments print short questionnaires on cards so that customers can evaluate the service. *Tennis Magazine, Advertising Age, Wired,* and many other publications have used inserted questionnaires to survey current readers inexpensively, and often the results provide material for a magazine article.

Many manufacturers use their warranty or owner registration cards to collect demographic information and data about where and why products were purchased. Using owner registration cards is an extremely economical technique for tracing trends in consumer habits. Again, problems may arise because people who fill out these self-administered questionnaires differ from those who do not.

Extremely long questionnaires may be dropped off by an interviewer and then picked up later. The **drop-off method** sacrifices some cost savings because it requires traveling to each respondent's location.

drop-off method
A survey method that requires the interviewer to travel to the respondent's location to drop off questionnaires that will be picked up later.

Fax Surveys

With fax surveys, potential survey respondents receive and/or return questionnaires via fax machines.[13] A questionnaire inserted in a magazine may instruct the respondent to clip out the questionnaire and fax it to a certain phone number. In a mail survey, a prepaid-postage envelope places little burden on the respondent. But faxing a questionnaire to a long-distance number requires that the respondent pay for the transmission of the fax. Thus, a disadvantage of the **fax survey** is that only respondents with fax machines who are willing to exert the extra effort will return questionnaires. Again, people with extreme opinions will be more likely to respond.

fax survey
A survey that uses fax machines as a way for respondents to receive and return questionnaires.

To address this disadvantage, marketers may use faxing as one of several options for replying to a survey. Recently, the journal *American Family Physician* carried a reader survey that gave respondents the option of either returning the reply by fax or visiting the journal's Web site to answer the same questions online.[14] For busy physicians who likely have access to office equipment, this approach would improve the response rate.

Fax machines can also be used to distribute questionnaires. These fax surveys reduce the sender's printing and postage costs and can be delivered and returned faster than traditional mail surveys. Questionnaires distributed via fax can deal with timely issues. Although few households have fax machines, when the sample consists of organizations that are likely to have fax machines, the sample coverage may be adequate.

E-Mail Surveys

e-mail surveys
Surveys distributed through electronic mail.

Questionnaires can be distributed via e-mail, but researchers must remember that some individuals cannot be reached this way. Certain projects do lend themselves to **e-mail surveys**, such as internal surveys of employees or satisfaction surveys of retail buyers who regularly deal with an organization via e-mail. The benefits of incorporating a questionnaire in an e-mail include the speed of distribution, lower distribution and processing costs, faster turnaround time, more flexibility, and less handling of paper questionnaires. The speed of e-mail distribution and the quick response time can be major advantages for surveys dealing with time-sensitive issues.

Not much academic research has been conducted on e-mail surveys. Nevertheless, some researchers have argued that many respondents feel they can be more candid in e-mail than in person or on the telephone, for the same reasons they are candid on other self-administered questionnaires. Yet in many organizations employees know that their e-mails are not secure and "eavesdropping" by a supervisor could possibly occur. Further, maintaining respondents' anonymity is difficult, because a reply to an e-mail message typically includes the sender's address. Researchers designing e-mail surveys should assure respondents that their answers will be confidential.

Not all e-mail systems have the same capacity: Some handle color and graphics well; others are limited to text. The extensive differences in the capabilities of respondents' computers and e-mail software limit the types of questions and the layout of the e-mail questionnaire. For example, the display settings for computer screens vary widely, and wrap-around of lines may put the questions and the answer choices into strange and difficult-to-read patterns.[15] Many novice e-mail users find it difficult to mark answers in brackets on an e-mail questionnaire and/or to send a completed questionnaire using the e-mail reply function. For this reason, some researchers give respondents the option to print out the questionnaire, complete it in writing, and return it via regular mail. Unless the research is an internal organizational survey, this alternative, of course, requires the respondent to pay postage.

In general, the guidelines for printed mail surveys apply to e-mail surveys. However, some differences exist, because the cover letter and the questionnaire appear in a single e-mail message. A potential respondent who is not immediately motivated to respond, especially one who

EXHIBIT 10.4
The picture shows a typical e-mail survey questionnaire of a restaurant.

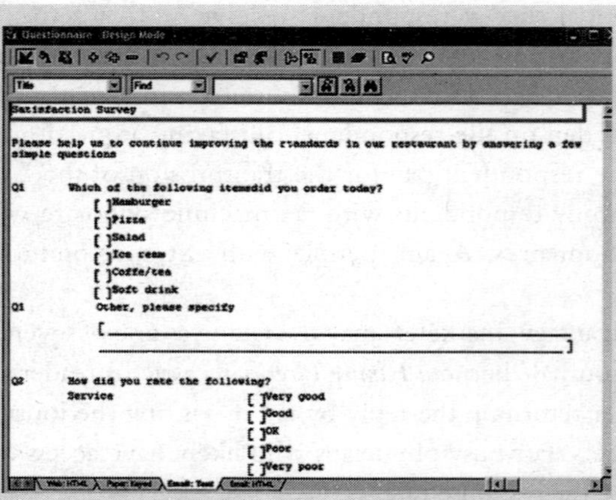

Source: http://www.snapsurveys.com/email-surveys/

considers an unsolicited e-mail survey to be spam, can quickly hit the delete button to remove the e-mail. This response suggests that e-mail cover letters should be brief and the questionnaires relatively short. The cover letter should explain how the company got the recipient's name and should include a valid return e-mail address in the "from" box and reveal who is conducting the survey. Also, if the e-mail lists more than one address in the "to" or "CC" field, all recipients will see the entire list of names. This lack of anonymity has the potential to cause response bias and nonresponse error. When possible, the e-mail should be addressed to a single person. (The blind carbon copy, or BCC, field can be used if the same message must be sent to an entire sample.)

E-mail has another important role in survey research. E-mail letters can be used as cover letters asking respondents to participate in an Internet survey. Such e-mails typically provide a password and a link to a unique Web site location that requires a password for access.

Internet Surveys

An **Internet survey** is a self-administered questionnaire posted on a Web site. Respondents provide answers to questions displayed onscreen by highlighting a phrase, clicking an icon, or keying in an answer. Like every other type of survey, Internet surveys have both advantages and disadvantages.

Internet survey
A self-administered questionnaire posted on a Web site.

SPEED AND COST-EFFECTIVENESS

Internet surveys allow researchers to reach a large audience (possibly a global one), personalize individual messages, and secure confidential answers quickly and cost-effectively. These computer-to-computer self-administered questionnaires eliminate the costs of paper, postage, and data entry, as well as other administrative costs. Once an Internet questionnaire has been developed, the incremental cost of reaching additional respondents is minimal. So, samples can be larger than with interviews or other types of self-administered questionnaires. Even with large samples, surveys that used to take many weeks can be conducted in a week or less.

VISUAL APPEAL AND INTERACTIVITY

Surveys conducted on the Internet can be interactive. The researcher can use more sophisticated lines of questioning based on the respondents' prior answers. Many of these interactive surveys utilize color, sound, and animation, which may help to increase respondents' cooperation and willingness to spend time answering the questionnaires. The Internet is an excellent medium for the presentation of visual materials, such as photographs or drawings of product prototypes, advertisements, and movie trailers. Innovative measuring instruments that take advantage of the ability to adjust backgrounds, fonts, color, and other features have been designed and applied with considerable success.

RESPONDENT PARTICIPATION AND COOPERATION

Participation in some Internet surveys occurs because computer users intentionally navigate to a particular Web site where questions are displayed. For example, a survey of more than 10,000 visitors to the Ticketmaster Web site helped Ticketmaster better understand its customer purchase patterns and evaluate visitor satisfaction with the site. In some cases, individuals expect to encounter a survey at a Web site; in others, it is totally unexpected. In some instances, the visitor cannot venture beyond the survey page without providing information for the organization's "registration" questionnaire. When the computer user does not expect a survey on a Web site and participation is voluntary, response rates are low. And, as with other questionnaires that rely on voluntary self-selection, participants tend to be more interested in or involved with the subject of the research than the average person.

For many other Internet surveys, respondents are initially contacted via e-mail. Often they are members of consumer panels who have previously indicated their willingness to cooperate. When panel members receive an e-mail invitation to participate, they are given logon instructions and a password. This security feature prevents access by individuals who are not part of the scientifically selected sample. Assigning a unique password code also allows the researchers to track the responses of each respondent, thereby identifying any respondent who makes an effort to answer the questionnaire more than once.

Panel members also need an incentive to respond. A study of German consumers showed that nothing beat financial incentives. In other words, the best way to get responses was to simply pay consumers for participating in surveys.[16]

welcome screen
The first Web page in an internet survey, which introduces the survey and requests that the respondent enter a password or pin.

Ideally, the **welcome screen** contains the name of the research company and information about how to contact the organization if the respondent has a problem or concern. A typical statement might be "If you have any concerns or questions about this survey or if you experience any technical difficulties, please contact [name of research organization]."

REPRESENTATIVE SAMPLES

The population to be studied, the purpose of the research, and the sampling methods determine the quality of Internet samples, which varies substantially. If the sample consists merely of those who visit a Web page and voluntarily fill out a questionnaire, then it is not likely to be representative of the entire U.S. population, because of self-selection error. However, if the purpose of the research is to evaluate how visitors feel about a Web site, randomly selecting every 100th visitor may accomplish the study's purpose.

Of course, a disadvantage, albeit ever decreasing, of Internet surveys is that many individuals in the general population cannot access the Internet. Even among people with Internet access, not all of them have the same level of technology. Many people with low-speed Internet connections (low bandwidth) cannot quickly download high-resolution graphic files. Many lack powerful computers or software that is compatible with advanced features programmed into many Internet questionnaires. Some individuals have minimal computer skills. They may not know how to navigate through and provide answers to an Internet questionnaire. For example, the advanced audio- and video-streaming technology of RealPlayer or Windows Media Player software can be used to incorporate a television commercial and questions about its effectiveness into an Internet survey. However, some respondents might find downloading the file too slow or even impossible, others might not have the RealPlayer or Windows Media Player software, and still others might not know how to use the streaming media software to view the commercial.

For the foreseeable future, Internet surveys sampling the general public should be designed with the recognition that problems may arise for the reasons just described. Thus, photographs, animation, or other cutting-edge technological features created on the researcher's/Web designer's powerful computer may have to be simplified or eliminated so that all respondents can interact at the same level of technological sophistication.

Because Internet surveys can be accessed anytime (24/7) from anywhere, they can reach certain hard-to-reach, busy respondents such as doctors, who would be almost impossible to reach via the telephone.

ACCURATE REAL-TIME DATA CAPTURE

The computer-to-computer nature of Internet surveys means that each respondent's answers are entered directly into the researcher's computer as soon as the questionnaire is submitted. In addition, the questionnaire software may be programmed to reject improper data entry. For example, on a paper questionnaire a respondent might incorrectly check two responses even though the instructions call for a single answer. In an Internet survey, this mistake can be interactively corrected as the survey is taking place. Thus, the data capture is more accurate than when humans are involved.

Real-time data capture allows for real-time data analysis. A researcher can review up-to-the-minute sample size counts and tabulation data from an Internet survey in real time.

CALLBACKS

When the sample for an Internet survey is drawn from a consumer panel, those who have not completed the survey questionnaire can be easily recontacted. Computer software can simply automatically send e-mail reminders to panel members who did not visit the welcome page. Computer software can also identify the passwords of respondents who completed only a portion of the questionnaire and send those people customized messages. Sometimes such e-mails offer additional incentives to those individuals who terminated the questionnaire with only a few additional questions to answer, so that they are motivated to comply with the request to finish the questionnaire.

PERSONALIZED AND FLEXIBLE QUESTIONING

Computer-interactive Internet surveys are programmed in much the same way as computer-assisted telephone interviews. That is, the software that is used allows questioning to branch off into two or more different lines depending on a respondent's answer to a filtered question. The difference is that there is no interviewer. The respondent interacts directly with software on a Web site. In other words, the computer program asks questions in a sequence determined by the respondent's previous answers. The questions appear on the computer screen, and answers are recorded by simply pressing a key or clicking an icon, thus immediately entering the data into the computer's memory. Of course, these methods avoid labor costs associated with data collection and processing of paper-and-pencil questionnaires.

This ability to sequence questions based on previous responses is a major advantage of computer-assisted surveys. The computer can be programmed to skip from question 6 to question 9 if the answer to question 6 is no. Furthermore, responses to previous questions can lead to questions that can be personalized for individual respondents (for example, "When you cannot buy your favorite brand, Revlon, what brand of lipstick do you prefer?"). Often the respondent's name appears in questions to personalize the questionnaire. Fewer and more relevant questions speed up the response process and increase the respondent's involvement with the survey.

A related advantage of using a Web survey is that it can prompt respondents when they skip over a question. In a test comparing telephone and Internet versions of the same survey, the rate of item nonresponse was less for the Internet version, which issued a prompt for each item that was left blank.[17] This was likely not a simple matter of motivation, because the rate of respondents who actually took the Web version was less than for the telephone version, even though the researchers offered a larger incentive to those who were asked to go online. (An earlier telephone screening had verified that everyone who was asked to participate had a computer.)

The ability to customize questions and the low cost per recipient also help researchers keep surveys short, an important consideration for boosting responses.[18] Jakob Nielsen, a consultant on Internet usability with the Nielsen Norman Group, emphasizes that "quick and painless" surveys generate the highest response and urges researchers to keep surveys as short as possible. He suggests that if the research objectives call for a long survey, the questions can be divided among several questionnaires, with each version sent to a different group of respondents.

Designers of Internet questionnaires can be creative and flexible in the presentation of questions by using a variety of **dialog boxes**, or windows that prompt the respondent to enter information. Chapter 15 discusses electronic questionnaire design and layout further.

dialog boxes
Windows that open on a computer screen to prompt the user to enter information.

RESPONDENT ANONYMITY

Respondents are more likely to provide sensitive or embarrassing information when they can remain anonymous. The anonymity of the Internet encourages respondents to provide honest answers to sensitive questions.

RESPONSE RATES

The methods for improving response rates for an Internet survey are similar to those for other kinds of survey research. A personalized invitation may be important. In many cases, the invitation is delivered via e-mail. The respondents may not recognize the sender's address, so the message's subject line is critical.[19] The subject line should refer to a topic likely to interest the audience, and legal as well as ethical standards dictate that it may not be deceptive. Thus, the line might be worded in a way similar to the following: "Please give your opinion on [subject matter of interest]." Researchers should avoid gimmicks like dollar signs and the word *free,* either of which is likely to alert the spam filters installed on most computers.

As mentioned earlier, with a password system, people who have not participated in a survey in a predetermined period of time can be sent a friendly e-mail reminder asking them to participate before the study ends. This type of follow-up, along with preliminary notification, interesting early questions, and variations of most other techniques for increasing response rates to mail questionnaires, is recommended for Internet surveys.

Unlike mail surveys, Internet surveys do not offer the opportunity to send a physical incentive, such as a dollar bill, to the respondent. Incentives to respond to a survey must be in the form of a promise of a future reward—for example, "As a token of appreciation for completing this survey, the sponsor of the survey will make a sizable contribution to a national charity. You can vote for your preferred charity at the end of the survey." Although some researchers have had success with promising incentives, academic research about Internet surveys is sparse, and currently there are few definitive answers about the most effective ways to increase response rates.

SECURITY CONCERNS

Many organizations worry that hackers or competitors may access Web sites to discover new product concepts, new advertising campaigns, and other top-secret ideas. Respondents may worry whether personal information will remain private. So may the organizations sponsoring the research. Recently, McDonald's conducted quality-control research in England and Scotland, automating the transmittal of data with a system in which consultants used handheld devices and sent the numbers to headquarters as e-mail messages. The system saved hours of work, but the company worried that confidential information could be compromised. McDonald's therefore purchased software that encrypted the data and allowed the handhelds to be remotely wiped clean of data if they were lost or stolen.[20]

As in the experience of McDonald's, no system can be 100 percent secure, but risks can be minimized. Many research service suppliers specializing in Internet surveying have developed password-protected systems that are very secure. One important feature of these systems restricts access and prevents individuals from filling out a questionnaire over and over again.

Kiosk Interactive Surveys

A computer with a touch screen may be installed in a kiosk at a trade show, at a professional conference, in an airport, or in any other high-traffic location to administer an interactive survey. Because the respondent chooses to interact with an on-site computer, self-selection often is a problem with this type of survey. Computer-literate individuals are most likely to complete these interactive questionnaires. At temporary locations such as conventions, these surveys often require a fieldworker to be at the location to explain how to use the computer system. This personal assistance is an obvious disadvantage.

Survey Research That Mixes Modes

For many surveys, research objectives dictate the use of some combination of telephone, mail, e-mail, Internet, and personal interview. For example, the researcher may conduct a short telephone screening interview to determine whether respondents are eligible for recontact in a more extensive personal interview. Such a **mixed-mode survey** combines the advantages of the telephone survey (such as fast screening) and those of the personal interview. A mixed-mode survey can employ any combination of two or more survey methods. Conducting a research study in two or more waves, however, creates the possibility that some respondents will no longer cooperate or will be unavailable in the second wave of the survey.

mixed-mode survey
Study that employs any combination of survey methods.

Several variations of survey research use cable television channels. For example, a telephone interviewer calls a cable subscriber and asks him or her to tune in to a particular channel at a certain time. An appointment is made to interview the respondent shortly after the program or visual material is displayed. NBC uses this type of mixed-mode survey to test the concepts for many proposed new programs.

Text-Message Surveys

Yes, surveys are even being sent via text messages. These may use the SMS (short message service) or MMS (multimedia message service). This technique is perhaps the newest survey approach. It has all the advantages of mobile phone surveys in terms of reach and it also shares the disadvantages in terms of reaching respondents who have not opted in via a mobile phone. However, text-message surveys are catching on in other countries and are ideal for surveys involving only a few very short questions. Additionally, MMS messages can include graphic displays or even short videos. This technology is likely to see more applications in the near future.

Selecting the Appropriate Survey Research Design

Earlier discussions of research design and problem definition emphasized that many research tasks may lead to similar decision-making information. There is no best form of survey; each has advantages and disadvantages. A researcher who must ask highly confidential questions may use a mail survey, thus sacrificing speed of data collection to avoid interviewer bias. If a researcher must have considerable control over question phrasing, central location telephone interviewing may be appropriate.

To determine the appropriate technique, the researcher must ask several questions: Is the assistance of an interviewer necessary? Are respondents interested in the issues being investigated? Will cooperation be easily attained? How quickly is the information needed? Will the study require a long and complex questionnaire? How large is the budget? The criteria—cost, speed, anonymity, and so forth—may differ for each project.

Exhibit 10.5 summarizes the major advantages and disadvantages of typical door-to-door, mall intercept, telephone, mail, and Internet surveys. It emphasizes the typical types of surveys. For example, a creative researcher might be able to design highly versatile and flexible mail questionnaires, but most researchers use standardized questions. An elaborate mail survey may be far more expensive than a short personal interview, but generally this is not the case.

TOTHEPOINT

Practice is the best of all instructors.

—Publius Syrus, Circa 42 BC

EXHIBIT 10.5 **Advantages and Disadvantages of Typical Survey Methods**

	Door-to-Door Personal Interview	Mall Intercept Personal Interview	Telephone Interview	Mail Survey	Internet Survey
Speed of data collection	Moderate to fast	Fast	Very fast	Slow; researcher has no control over return of questionnaire	Instantaneous; 24/7
Geographic flexibility	Limited to moderate	Confined, possible urban bias	High	High	High (worldwide)
Respondent cooperation	Excellent	Moderate to low	Good	Moderate; poorly designed questionnaire will have low response rate	Varies depending on Web site; high from consumer panels
Versatility of questioning	Quite versatile	Extremely versatile	Moderate	Not versatile; requires highly standardized format	Extremely versatile
Questionnaire length	Long	Moderate to long	Moderate	Varies depending on incentive	Moderate; length customized based on answers
Item non-response rate	Low	Medium	Medium	High	Software can assure none
Possibility for respondent misunderstanding	Low	Low	Average	High; no interviewer present for clarification	High
Degree of interviewer influence on answers	High	High	Moderate	None; interviewer absent	None
Supervision of interviewers	Moderate	Moderate to high	High, especially with central-location interviewing	Not applicable	Not applicable
Anonymity of respondent	Low	Low	Moderate	High	Respondent can be either anonymous or known
Ease of callback or follow-up	Difficult	Difficult	Easy	Easy, but takes time	Difficult, unless e-mail address is known
Cost	Highest	Moderate to high	Low to moderate	Lowest	Low
Special features	Visual materials may be shown or demonstrated; extended probing possible	Taste tests, viewing of TV commercials possible	Fieldwork and supervision of data collection are simplified; quite adaptable to computer technology	Respondent may answer questions at own convenience; has time to reflect on answers	Streaming media software allows use of graphics and animation

Note: The emphasis is on *typical* surveys. For example, an elaborate mail survey may be far more expensive than a short personal interview, but this generally is not the case.

© iStock

TIPS OF THE TRADE

- Interpretative research involving a survey generally requires an interactive approach. On occasion, respondents may simply be asked to write a story without any elaboration, but generally, particularly with phenomenology, the researcher and the respondent are actively engaged.
- The longer the questionnaire, the lower the response rate.
  - When long questionnaires are absolutely necessary, the researcher should:
    - Look for respondents who are essentially a captive audience; like students in a class
    - Offer a nontrivial incentive to respond
    - Try to target the survey toward individuals who are highly involved in the topic
    - Use a survey research panel
- E-mail surveys and Internet surveys are good approaches for most types of surveys.
  - When a panel or special interest group provides responses, the researcher should be extra vigilant for bogus response patterns.
  - Good response rates with no true special considerations such as a very high incentive or extreme levels of involvement can be expected to be between 10 and 15 percent.

Pretesting

A researcher who is surveying 3,000 consumers does not want to find out after the questionnaires have been completed or returned that most respondents misunderstood a particular question, skipped a series of questions, or misinterpreted the instructions for filling out the questionnaire. To avoid problems such as these, screening procedures, or *pretests,* are often used. **Pretesting** involves a trial run with a group of respondents to iron out fundamental problems in the instructions or design of a questionnaire. The researcher looks for such obstacles as the point at which respondent fatigue sets in and whether there are any particular places in the questionnaire where respondents tend to terminate. Unfortunately, this stage of research is sometimes eliminated because of costs or time pressures.

pretesting
Screening procedure that involves a trial run with a group of respondents to iron out fundamental problems in the survey design.

Broadly speaking, three basic ways to pretest exist. The first two involve screening the questionnaire with other research professionals, and the third—the one most often called pretesting—is a trial run with a group of respondents. When screening the questionnaire with other research professionals, the investigator asks them to look for such problems as difficulties with question wording, leading questions, and bias due to question order. An alternative type of screening might involve a client or the research manager who ordered the research. Often, managers ask researchers to collect information, but when they see the questionnaire, they find that it does not really meet their needs. Only by checking with the individual who has requested the questionnaire does the researcher know for sure that the information needed will be provided. Once the researcher has decided on the final questionnaire, data should be collected with a small number of respondents (perhaps 100) to determine whether the questionnaire needs refinement.

Ethical Issues in Survey Research

Many ethical issues apply to survey research, such as respondents' right to privacy, the use of deception, respondents' right to be informed about the purpose of the research, the need for confidentiality, the need for honesty in collecting data, and the need for objectivity in reporting data. You may wish to reexamine Chapter 5's coverage of these issues now that various survey research techniques have been discussed.[21]

Summary

1. Summarize ways researchers gather information through interviews. Interviews can be categorized based on the medium used to communicate with respondents. Interviews can be conducted door-to-door, in shopping malls, or on the telephone. Traditionally, interviews have been recorded using paper and pencil, but survey researchers are increasingly using computers. Personal interviews are a flexible method that allows researchers to use visual aids and various kinds of props. However, the presence of an interviewer may influence subjects' responses.

2. Compare the advantages and disadvantages of conducting door-to-door, mall intercept, and telephone interviews. Door-to-door personal interviews can get high response rates, but they are more costly to administer than other types of surveys. When a sample need not represent the entire country, mall intercept interviews may reduce costs. Telephone interviewing has the advantage of providing data fast and at a lower cost per interview. However, not all households have telephones, and not all telephone numbers are listed in directories. This causes problems in obtaining a representative sample, so researchers often use random digit dialing. Absence of face-to-face contact and inability to use visual materials also limit telephone interviewing. Computer-assisted telephone interviewing from central locations can improve the efficiency of certain kinds of telephone surveys.

3. Evaluate the advantages and disadvantages of distributing questionnaires through the mail, the Internet, and by other means. Traditionally, self-administered questionnaires have been distributed by mail, but self-administered questionnaires also may be dropped off to individual respondents, distributed from central locations, or administered via computer. Mail questionnaires generally are less expensive than telephone or personal interviews, but they also introduce a much larger chance of nonresponse error. Several methods can be used to encourage higher response rates. Mail questionnaires must be more structured than other types of surveys and cannot be changed if problems are discovered in the course of data collection. The Internet and other interactive media provide convenient ways for organizations to conduct surveys. Internet surveys are quick and cost-effective, but not everyone has Internet access. Because the surveys are computerized and interactive, questionnaires can be personalized and data can be captured in real time. Some privacy and security concerns exist, but the future of Internet surveys looks promising.

4. Discuss the importance of pretesting questionnaires. Pretesting a questionnaire on a small sample of respondents is a useful way to discover problems while they can still be corrected. Pretests may involve screening the questionnaire with other research professionals or conducting a trial run with a set of respondents.

5. Describe ethical issues that arise in survey research. Researchers must protect the public from misrepresentation and exploitation. This obligation includes honesty about the purpose of a research project and protection of subjects' right to refuse to participate or to answer particular questions. Researchers also should protect the confidentiality of participants and record responses honestly.

Key Terms and Concepts

callbacks, *232*
central location interviewing, *236*
computer-assisted personal interviewing (CAPI), 238
computer-assisted self interviewing (CASI), 238
computer-assisted telephone interviewing (CATI), *237*
cover letter, *242*
dialog boxes, *250*
door-to-door interviews, *231*
drop-off method, *245*
e-mail surveys, *246*
fax survey, *245*
Internet survey, *247*
item nonresponse, *230*
mail survey, *239*
mall intercept interviews, *232*
mixed-mode survey, *251*
personal interview, *228*
pretesting, *253*
random digit dialing, *236*
response rate, *241*
self-administered questionnaires, *239*
telephone interviews, *233*
welcome screen, *247*

Questions for Review and Critical Thinking

1. What type of communication medium would you use to conduct the following surveys? Why?
   a. Survey of the buying motives of industrial engineers
   b. Survey of the satisfaction levels of hourly support staff
   c. Survey of television commercial advertising awareness
   d. Survey of top corporate executives
2. A publisher offers college professors one of four best-selling mass-market books as an incentive for filling out a 10-page mail questionnaire about a new textbook. What advantages and disadvantages does this incentive have?
3. "Individuals are less willing to cooperate with surveys today than they were 50 years ago." Comment on this statement.
4. What do you think should be the maximum length of a self-administered e-mail questionnaire?
5. Do most surveys use a single communication mode (for example, the telephone), as most textbooks suggest?
6. A survey researcher reports that "205 usable questionnaires out of 942 questionnaires delivered in our mail survey converts to a 21.7 percent response rate." What are the subtle implications of this statement?
7. Evaluate the following survey designs:
   a. A researcher suggests mailing a small safe (a metal file box with a built-in lock) without the lock combination to respondents, with a note explaining that respondents will be called in a few days for a telephone interview. During the telephone interview, the respondent is given the combination and the safe may be opened.
   b. A shopping mall that wishes to evaluate its image places packets including a questionnaire, cover letter, and stamped return envelope in the mall where customers can pick them up if they wish.
   c. An e-mail message is sent to individuals who own computers, asking them to complete a questionnaire on a Web site. Respondents answer the questions and then have the opportunity to play a slot-machine game on the Web site. Each respondent is guaranteed a monetary incentive but has the option to increase it by playing the slot-machine game.
   d. A mall intercept interviewing service is located in a regional shopping center. The facility contains a small room for television and movie presentations. Shoppers are used as sampling units. However, mall intercept interviewers recruit additional subjects for television commercial experiments by offering them several complimentary tickets for special sneak previews. Individuals contacted at the mall are allowed to bring up to five guests. In some cases the complimentary tickets are offered through ads in a local newspaper.
   e. *Time* magazine opts to conduct a mail survey rather than a telephone survey for a study to determine the demographic characteristics and purchasing behavior of its subscribers.
8. What type of research studies lend themselves to the use of e-mail for survey research? What are the advantages and disadvantages of using e-mail?
9. **ETHICS** Comment on the ethics of the following situations:
   a. A researcher plans to use invisible ink to code questionnaires to identify respondents in a distributor survey.
   b. A political action committee conducts a survey about its cause. At the end of the questionnaire, it includes a request for a donation.
   c. A telephone interviewer calls at 1:00 p.m. on Sunday and asks the person who answers the phone to take part in an interview.
   d. An industrial manufacturing firm wishes to survey its own distributors. It invents the name "Mountain States Marketing Research" and sends out a mail questionnaire under this name.
   e. A questionnaire is printed on the back of a warranty card included inside the package of a food processor. The questionnaire includes a number of questions about shopping behavior, demographics, and customer lifestyles. At the bottom of the warranty card is a short note in small print that says "Thank you for completing this questionnaire. Your answers will be used for further studies and to help us serve you better in the future. You will also benefit by receiving important mailings and special offers from a number of organizations whose products and services relate directly to the activities, interests, and hobbies in which you enjoy participating on a regular basis. Please indicate if there is some reason you would prefer not to receive this information."
10. **ETHICS** How might the business research industry take action to ensure that the public believes that telephone surveys and door-to-door interviews are legitimate activities and that firms that misrepresent and deceive the public using research as a sales ploy are not true researchers?
11. Why is the mobile phone likely to be an ineffective way of reaching potential respondents in America?
12. The American Testing Institute (also known as the U.S. Testing Authority) mails respondents what it calls a "television" survey. A questionnaire is sent to respondents, who are asked to complete it and mail it back along with a check for $14.80. In return for answering eight questions on viewing habits, the institute promises to send respondents one of twenty prizes ranging in value from $200 to $2,000—among which are video recorders, diamond watches, color televisions, and two nights of hotel accommodations at a land development resort community. The institute lists the odds of winning as 1 in 150,000 on all prizes except the hotel stay, for which the odds are 149,981 out of 150,000. During a three-month period, the institute sends out 200,000 questionnaires. What are the ethical issues in this situation?
13. **'NET** Go to the Pew Internet and American Life page at **http://www.pewinternet.org.** Several reports based on survey research will be listed. Select one of the reports. What were the research objectives? What were the first three questions on the survey?
14. **'NET** Go to the NPD Group Web site (**http://www.npd.com**) and click on the Store link. What types of custom and syndicated survey research services does the company offer?
15. **'NET** Go to the CASRO (Council of American Survey Research Organizations) home page (**http://www.casro.org**). Select "About Us." What are the key aspects of this research organization's mission?

Research Activities

1. **'NET** Visit this Web site: **http://www.zoomerang.com**. What unique service does this company offer? Then visit this site: **http://www.websurveyor.com**. How does this service differ from Zoomerang? Create a short survey and e-mail it to 10 of your friends without any advance notice. At the end of the survey, ask them if they would have responded had they not noticed the survey came from you. What is the response rate? What would it have been if the respondent did not know you?

Case 10.1 National Do Not Call Registry

© GETTY IMAGES/ PHOTODISC GREEN

Citizens' annoyance with phone calls from salespeople prompted Congress to pass a law setting up a National Do Not Call Registry. The registry was soon flooded with requests to have phone numbers removed from telemarketers' lists. By law, salespeople may not call numbers listed on this registry. The law makes exceptions for charities and researchers. However, a recent poll suggests that even though phone calls from researchers may be legal, they are not always well received.[22]

In late 2005, Harris Interactive conducted an Internet survey in which almost 2,000 adults answered questions about the National Do Not Call Registry. About three-quarters of the respondents said they had signed up for the registry, and a majority (61 percent) said they had since received "far less" contact from telemarketers. In addition, 70 percent said that since registering, they had been contacted by someone "who was doing a poll or survey" and wanted them to participate. But apparently respondents weren't sure whether this practice was acceptable. Only one-fourth (24 percent) of respondents said they knew that researchers "are allowed to call," and over half (63 percent) weren't sure about researchers' rights under the law.

Questions

1. Was an online survey the best medium for a poll on this subject? What were some pros and cons of conducting this poll online?
2. How might the results have differed if this poll had been conducted by telephone?
3. As a researcher, how would you address people's doubts about whether pollsters may contact households listed on the Do Not Call Registry?

Case 10.2 Royal Bee Electric Fishing Reel

© GETTY IMAGES/ PHOTODISC GREEN

Royal Barton started thinking about an electric fishing reel when his father had a stroke and lost the use of an arm. To see that happen to his dad, who had taught him the joys of fishing and hunting, made Barton realize what a chunk a physical handicap could take out of a sports enthusiast's life. Being able to cast and retrieve a lure and experience the thrill of a big bass trying to take your rig away from you were among the joys of life that would be denied Barton's father forever.

Barton was determined to do something about it, if not for his father, then at least for others who had suffered a similar fate. So, after tremendous personal expense and years of research and development, Barton perfected what is sure to be the standard bearer for all future freshwater electric reels. Forget those saltwater jobs, which Barton refers to as "winches." He has developed something that is small, compact, and has incredible applications.

He calls it the Royal Bee. The first word is obviously his first name. The second word refers to the low buzzing sound the reel makes when in use.

The Royal Bee system looks simple enough and probably is if you understand the mechanical workings of a reel. A system of gears ties into the spool, and a motor in the back drives the gears attached to the triggering system.

All gearing of the electrical system can be disengaged so that you can cast normally. But pushing the button for "retrieve" engages two gears. After the gears are engaged, the trigger travels far enough to touch the switch that tightens the drive belt, and there is no slipping. You cannot hit the switch until the gears are properly engaged. This means that you cast manually, just as you would normally fish, then you reengage the reel for the levelwind to work. And you can do all that with one hand!

The system works on a 6-volt battery that you can attach to your belt or hang around your neck if you are wading. If you have a boat with a 6-volt battery, the reel can actually work off of the battery. There is a small connector that plugs into the reel, so you could easily use more than one reel with the battery. For instance, if you have two or three outfits equipped with different lures, you just switch the connector from reel to reel as you use it. A reel with the Royal Bee system can be used in a conventional manner. You do not have to use it as an electric reel unless you choose to do so.

Barton believes the Royal Bee may not be just for handicapped fishermen. Ken Cook, one of the leading professional anglers in the country, is sold on the Royal Bee. After he suffered a broken arm, he had to withdraw from some tournaments because fishing with one hand was difficult. By the time his arm healed, he was hooked on the Royal Bee because it increased bassing efficiency. As Cook explains, "The electric reel has increased my efficiency in two ways. One is in flipping, where I use it all the time. The other is for fishing topwater, when I have to make a long cast. When I'm flipping, the electric reel gives me instant control over slack line. I can keep both hands on the rod. I never have to remove them to take up slack. I flip, engage the reel, and then all I have to do is push the lever with my thumb to take up slack instantly."

Cook's reel (a Ryobi 4000) is one of several that can be converted to the electric retrieve. For flipping, Cook loads his reel with 20-pound test line. He uses a similar reel with lighter line when fishing a surface lure. "What you can do with the electric reel is eliminate unproductive reeling time," Cook says.

A few extra seconds may not mean much if you are out on a neighborhood pond just fishing on the weekend. But it can mean a lot if you are in tournament competition, where one extra cast might keep you from going home with $50,000 tucked in your pocket. "Look at it this way," Cook explains. "Let's suppose we're in clear water and it's necessary to make a long cast to the cover we want to fish with a topwater lure. There's a whole lot of unproductive water between us and the cover. With the electric reel, I make my long cast and fish the cover. Then, when I'm ready to reel in, I just press the retrieve lever so the battery engages the necessary gears, and I've got my lure back ready to make another cast while you're still cranking."

When Royal Barton retired from his veterinary supply business, he began enjoying his favorite pastimes: hunting, fishing, and developing the Royal Bee system. He realized he needed help in marketing his product, so he sought professional assistance to learn how to reach the broadest possible market for the Royal Bee system.

Questions

1. What business research problem does Royal Barton face? What are his information needs? Outline some survey research objectives for a research project on the Royal Bee system.
2. What type of survey—personal interview, telephone interview, or mail survey—should be selected?
3. What sources of survey error are most likely to occur in a study of this type?
4. What means should be used to obtain a high response rate?

Case 10.3 Telephonic Survey in South India

© GETTY IMAGES/ PHOTODISC GREEN

Telephonic surveys are not very popular in developing countries because of the limited coverage of networks. In the recent years, with improving telephone coverage, telephonic interviews have become a promising method of data collection. This method is less time-consuming and also incurs low cost. In order to assess the extents of telephonic survey, a survey was conducted in South India.

The study was conducted in Kurunji Nagar, an urban area of Puducherry in South India with approximately 600 households. It involved 50 telephonic and 50 face-to-face surveys. For the telephone survey, 100 telephone numbers were randomly selected (using a random number table) from 481 Bharat Sanchar Nigam Ltd. (a telecommunication company, BSNL) landline numbers of Kurunji Nagar. Of the 100 telephone numbers, 71 were dialed to cover 50 households. The survey was conducted in the evening between 5pm to 7pm on weekdays and on weekends from 10am to 12pm. Any family members older than 18 years old who answered the telephone were interviewed. Face-to face surveys were also conducted during the same time of the day as the telephone surveys.

Results

A total of 71 telephone numbers were dialed. 8 were non-existent, 2 were non residential, and there was no response from 8 numbers. Of the 53 houses contacted by telephone, three respondents did not consent for the survey. Of the 52 houses contacted during the face-to-face survey, two respondents did not consent. The average length of time taken for each questionnaire was 5.6 minutes in both the telephone survey and the face-to-face survey.

In this study, the response rate of telephone surveys was similar to that of face-to-face surveys. The higher response rate in this study may be due to the short interview time, non sensitive questionnaire, or the low frequency of telephone surveys in India. The population covered in the survey was within 1 to 2 km and the face-to-face surveys took about double the time as compared with telephone surveys. This study included only landlines. Later, during the face-to-face surveys, it was revealed that 14% of the houses selected for face-to-face surveys did not have a landline connection but had a mobile phone. Hence, mobile numbers should also be included as part of the telephone survey to reach out to more households.

CASE EXHIBIT 10.3-1 **Respondent Characteristics**

	Face-to-Face Survey ($n = 50$)	Telephone Survey ($n = 50$)	p-Value
Male: Female ratio	1:3.2	1:1.3	< 0.05*
Mean age (range)	40 years (19–62)	42 years (18–73)	0.35
Mean family size	4.3(1–8)	4.3(2–8)	1.25
Proportion of graduates and post graduates	62%	54%	0.54

* Significant p at less than 0.05

CASE EXHIBIT 10.3-2 Attitude and Knowledge on Route of Administration of Medicines

	Face-to-Face Survey *n* = 50(%)	Telephone Survey *n*= 50%	p-Value
Prefer oral medication for fever in adults	38(76)	40(80)	0.8
Prefer oral medication for diarrhea in adults	42(84)	44(88)	0.8
Prefer oral medication for fever in children	40(80)	39(78)	1.0
Prefer oral medication for diarrhea in children	40(80)	40(80)	1.0
Request for injection in place of oral medicines	9(18)	6(12)	0.6
Request for oral medicines in place of injection	16(32)	12(24)	0.6
Awareness about transmission of infection through contaminated needles	50(100)	50(100)	Not applicable
Awareness about transmission of HIV through contaminated needles	needles	45(90)	44(88)
Awareness about transmission of jaundice through contaminated needles	24(48)	25(50)	0.8

Conclusion

The response rate for the telephonic survey was found to be good. The response characteristics were found to be similar both in case of telephonic survey and face-to-face interview. Hence, telephone surveys are feasible in the Indian scenario and it is a time-saving, useful tool in a population with good telephone coverage. The method is useful for assessing markets for products and also gains feedbacks from the customer.

Questions

1. What are the advantages and disadvantages of the two interview techniques adopted in this research?
2. What is your opinion about the response rate of telephone survey vis-a-vis face to face interview of consumers in emerging economy?

CHAPTER 11
OBSERVATION METHODS

LEARNING OUTCOMES

After studying this chapter, you should be able to

1. **Discuss the role of observation as a business research method**
2. **Describe the use of direct observation and contrived observation**
3. **Identify ethical issues in observation studies**
4. **Explain the observation of physical objects and message content**
5. **Describe major types of mechanical observation**
6. **Summarize techniques for measuring physiological reactions**

Chapter Vignette: Mystery Diner at Seasons Restaurant

Mike and Marilyn, Brian and Mary Kay, and Mitch and Jill were certainly enjoying their dinner at Seasons Restaurant on the seventh floor of the Four Seasons Hotel in Chicago. The restaurant is "an extravagant affair" with mahogany paneled walls, beautiful brocade armchairs, and fresh flowers everywhere. They had started by splitting a bottle of champagne before each ordering the eight-course degustation—eight separate dishes, each with a matching wine. The three couples were enjoying the service, the food, the wine, and the company of their friends, a bit unaware of the other diners. However, they were being closely observed without even realizing it. A *mystery shopper* (or mystery diner in this case) was sitting near them, observing their dining experience, as well as the service being provided.

Mystery shoppers (or mystery diners or mystery employees) can help inspect and evaluate a variety of activities, including customer service, company operations, employee integrity, store merchandising, and product quality. Mystery shopping originated as a technique used by private investigators to identify and prevent employee theft—primarily at banks and retail stores. By posing as workers, mystery employees could become part of the organization and observe the operation and employee behavior, including identifying opportunities for theft and workers that might be stealing. The term "mystery shopping" was coined in the 1940s by WilMark, the first research firm to apply the concept beyond integrity applications. Since then, we have seen widespread application of mystery shopping. Today, over 100 companies belong to the Mystery Shopping Providers Association (MSPA) and the industry is estimated to be over $1.5 billion annually.

Mystery shoppers can prove advantageous in many ways. A mystery shopper allows an organization to view their operation through a trained customer's (or employee's) eyes. Questioning employees is certainly unlikely to reveal employee theft. Similarly, a survey of the wait staff at Seasons Restaurant would probably indicate that they are attentive to diners, keep the water glasses filled, and are consistently polite. Observing these behaviors, however, can provide a far more accurate picture and more detailed information. Mystery shoppers can report how long they waited, how they were treated, and even note that some diners are "not the typical Seasons crowd."[1]

Introduction

Mystery shoppers are just one observational approach to collecting research data. While survey data can provide some insight into future or past behavior, one can hardly argue with the power of data representing actual behavior. This chapter introduces the various techniques involved in observational methods of data gathering in business research.

Observation in Business Research

In business research, **observation** is a systematic process of recording behavioral patterns of people, objects, and occurrences as they happen. No questioning or communicating with people is needed. Researchers who use observation as a method of data collection either witness and record information while watching events take place or take advantage of some tracking system such as check-out scanners or Internet activity records. These tracking systems can observe and provide data such as whether or not a specific consumer purchased more products on discount or at regular price or how long an employee takes to complete a specific task.

observation
The systematic process of recording the behavioral patterns of people, objects, and occurrences as they are witnessed.

Observation becomes a tool for scientific inquiry when it meets several conditions:

- The observation serves a formulated research purpose.
- The observation is planned systematically.
- The observation is recorded systematically and related to general propositions, rather than simply reflecting a set of interesting curiosities.
- The observation is subjected to checks or controls on validity and reliability.[2]

TOTHEPOINT

Where observation is concerned, chance favors only the prepared mind.

—Louis Pasteur

What Can Be Observed?

Observational studies gather a wide variety of information about behavior. Exhibit 11.1 lists seven kinds of observable phenomena: *physical actions,* such as shopping patterns (in-store or via a Web interface) or television viewing; *verbal behavior,* such as sales conversations or the exchange between a worker and supervisor; *expressive behavior,* such as tone of voice, facial expressions, or a coach stomping his foot; *spatial relations and locations,* such as traffic patterns; *temporal patterns,* such as amount of time spent shopping, driving, or making a business decision; *physical objects,* such as the amount of newspapers recycled or number of beer cans in the trash; and *verbal and pictorial records,* such as the content of advertisements or the number of minorities pictured in a company brochure. (Investigation of secondary data also uses observation, but that subject was described in Chapter 8 and is not extensively discussed in this chapter.)

EXHIBIT 11.1
What Can Be Observed

Phenomenon	Example
Physical action	A worker's movement during an assembly process
Verbal behavior	Statements made by airline travelers while waiting in line
Expressive behavior	Facial expressions, tones of voices, and forms of body language
Spatial relations and locations	Proximity of middle managers' offices to the president's office
Temporal patterns	Length of time it takes to execute a stock purchase order
Physical objects	Percent of recycled materials compared to trash
Verbal and pictorial records	Number of illustrations appearing in a training booklet

While the observation method may be used to describe a wide variety of behavior, cognitive phenomena such as attitudes, motivations, and preferences cannot be observed. As a result, observation research cannot provide an explanation of why a behavior occurred or what actions were intended. Another limitation is that the observation period generally is short. Observing behavior patterns that occur over a period of several days or weeks generally is too costly or even impossible. Nonetheless, observation can provide some very interesting insights as described in the Research Snapshot "This Trend Brought to You by DDB SignBank."

The Nature of Observation Studies

Business researchers can observe people, objects, events, or other phenomena using either human observers or machines designed for specific observation tasks. Human observation best suits a situation or behavior that is not easily predictable in advance of the research. Mechanical observation, as performed by supermarket scanners or traffic counters, can very accurately record situations or types of behavior that are routine, repetitive, or programmatic.

Human or mechanical observation is generally *unobtrusive,* meaning no communication with a respondent takes place. For example, rather than asking an employee how long it takes to handle an insurance claim, a researcher might observe and record the time it takes for different steps in this process. Or, rather than ask a consumer how long they spend shopping for produce, a researcher can watch shoppers in a supermarket and note the time each spends in the produce area. As noted in the opening vignette, the unobtrusive or nonreactive nature of the observation method often generates data without a subject's knowledge. A situation in which an observer's presence is known to the subject involves **visible observation**. A situation in which a subject is unaware that observation is taking place is **hidden observation**. Hidden, unobtrusive observation minimizes respondent error. Asking subjects to participate in the research is not required when they are unaware that they are being observed.

visible observation
Observation in which the observer's presence is known to the subject.

hidden observation
Observation in which the subject is unaware that observation is taking place.

The major advantage of observation studies over surveys, which obtain self-reported data from respondents, is that the data are free from distortions, inaccuracies, or other response biases due to memory error, social desirability bias, and so on. The data are recorded when the actual behavior takes place.

Observation of Human Behavior

Whereas surveys emphasize verbal responses, observation studies emphasize and allow for the systematic recording of nonverbal behavior. Toy manufacturers such as Fisher Price use the observation technique because children often cannot express their reactions to products. By observing children at play with a proposed toy, doll, or game, business researchers may be able to identify the elements of a potentially successful product. Toy researchers might observe play to answer the following questions:

- How long does the child's attention stay with the product?
- How exactly does the child play with the toy?
- Are the child's peers equally interested in the toy?

Behavioral scientists have recognized that nonverbal behavior can be a communication process by which meanings are exchanged among individuals. Head nods, smiles, raised eyebrows, and other facial expressions or body movements have been recognized as communication symbols. Observation of nonverbal communication may hold considerable promise for the business researcher. For example, a hypothesis about customer-salesperson interactions is that the salesperson would signal status based on the importance of each transaction. In low-importance transactions, in which potential customers are plentiful and easily replaced (say, a shoe store), the salesperson may show definite nonverbal signs of higher status than the customer. When customers are scarce, as in big-ticket purchase situations, the opposite should be true. For example, real estate sales agents

RESEARCH SNAPSHOT

© iStock

This Trend Brought to You by DDB SignBank

Extending the practice of observation beyond what can clearly be done scientifically, such as counting the number of tomato soup cans in a pantry or measuring the time spent watching television, some researchers have tried to catalog behaviors that may signal the beginning of important trends. This practice, called *trend spotting,* is controversial because the observations are subjective and unsystematic. In spite of the criticism, marketers are increasingly turning to trend spotters, so researchers have an incentive to develop this method's capabilities.

Starting in its office in Copenhagen, Denmark, giant ad agency DDB Worldwide has created a service called DDB SignBank, which invites all of DDB's staff throughout the world, plus other targeted groups such as members of youth organizations, to submit their observations to managers appointed as SignBankers. Staff members are directed to identify consumer behaviors, rather than comments gathered from other research methods, that might signal a new trend in the society or culture. The SignBankers classify the observations and enter them into a corporate database. The database is updated each day, and account teams at the agency can search it for signs related to their clients' advertising objectives.

The idea behind SignBank, developed by sociologist Eva Steensig, is that the size of the database (which contained thirty thousand signs at a recent count) will allow patterns to emerge in the sheer number of observations. The data may be most useful as a source of ideas to test more rigorously. Anthon Berg, a Scandinavian brand of chocolate, used SignBank data to identify new occasions for which to promote chocolate and new uses for chocolate in health and beauty treatments.

Recently, SignBank has observed a shift in consumers from "herds" to "swarms." Herds are a single body of people that share a common view and choose a joint direction led by an opinion leader. Swarms are a group of individuals with differing opinions that go in a multitude of directions. DDB claims that the information available on the Internet has empowered consumers and they don't "believe just anything anymore." As a result, traditional institutions and media sources, such as churches, banks, newspapers, and brands, are losing power. Individuals are sharing information directly and being strengthened by becoming a member of the swarm.

Sources: Based on Creamer, Matthew, "DDB Collects 'Signs' to Identify Trends," *Advertising Age* (December 5, 2005), downloaded from http://www.adage.com, accessed June 16, 2006; Pfanner, Eric, "On Advertising: Do I Spot a Trend?" *International Herald Tribune* (January 1, 2006), www.iht.com; DDB Worldwide, "DDB Worldwide Introduces DDB SignBank, a New Consumer Knowledge Model," news release (November 29, 2005), http://www.ddbneedham.dk; "From Herds to Swarms," *Marketing Tribune* 7 (April 7, 2008), 30–31, accessed at http://www.ddbamsterdam.nl/public/en/signbank/signbank.

© LJUPCO SMOKOVSKI/SHUTTERSTOCK

may display nonverbal indicators of deference. One way to test this hypothesis would be with an observation study using the nonverbal communication measures shown in Exhibit 11.2.

Of course, researchers would not ignore verbal behavior. In fact, in certain observation studies, verbal expression is very important.

Complementary Evidence

The results of observation studies may extend the results of other forms of research by providing *complementary evidence* concerning individuals' "true" feelings. Focus group interviews often are conducted behind two-way mirrors from which executives observe as well as listen to what is occurring. This additional source allows for interpretation of nonverbal behavior such as facial expressions or head nods to supplement information from interviews.

For example, in one focus group session concerning women's use of hand lotion, researchers observed that all the women's hands were above the table while they were casually waiting for the session to begin. Seconds after the women were told that the topic was to be hand lotion, all their hands were placed out of sight. This observation, combined with the group discussion, revealed the women's anger, guilt, and shame about the condition of their hands. Although they felt they were expected to have soft, pretty hands, their housework required them to wash dishes, clean floors, and do other chores that were hard on their hands. Note, however, that without the discussion provided by the participants the researcher would only have been able to note the action of placing their hands under the table, not the explanation for this behavior.

EXHIBIT 11.2 **Observing and Interpreting Nonverbal Communication**

Behavior		Description	Example
Facial expressions		Expressions of emotion such as surprise (eyes wide open, mouth rounded and slightly open, brow furrowed)	A consumer reacts to the price quoted by a salesperson.
Body language		Posture, placement of arms and legs	A consumer crosses arms as salesperson speaks, possibly indicating a lack of trust.
Eye activity		Eye contact, staring, looking away, dilated pupils. In U.S. culture, not making eye contact is indicative of a deteriorating relationship. Dilated pupils can indicate emotion or degree of honesty.	A consumer avoids making eye contact with a salesperson knowing that he or she will not make a purchase.
Personal space	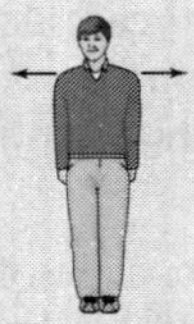	Physical distance between individuals; in the United States, people like to be about eight feet apart to have a discussion.	A consumer may back away from a salesperson who is viewed to be violating one's personal space.
Gestures		Responses to certain events with specific body reactions or gestures	A consumer who wins something (maybe at the casino or a sports contest) lifts arms, stands tall, and sticks out chest.
Manners		Accepted protocol for given situations	A salesperson may shake a customer's hand, but should not touch a customer otherwise.

direct observation
A straightforward attempt to observe and record what naturally occurs; the investigator does not create an artificial situation.

Direct Observation

Direct observation can produce detailed records of what people actually do during an event. The observer plays a passive role, making no attempt to control or manipulate a situation, instead merely recording what occurs. Many types of data can be obtained more accurately through direct observation than by questioning. For example, recording traffic counts or observing the direction of customer movement within a supermarket can help managers design store layouts that maximize the exposure of departments that sell impulse goods. A manufacturer can determine the number of facings, shelf locations, display maintenance, and other characteristics that improve store conditions. If directly questioned in a survey, most shoppers would be unable to accurately portray the time they spent in each department. The observation method, in contrast, could determine this without difficulty.

With the direct observation method, the data consist of records of events made as they occur. An observation form often helps keep researchers' observations consistent and ensures that they record all relevant information. A respondent is not required to recall—perhaps inaccurately—an event after it has occurred; instead, the observation is instantaneous.

In many cases, direct observation is the most straightforward form of data collection—or the only form possible. A produce manager for Auchan (a France-based hypermart firm) may periodically gather competitive price information from Carrefour (also a France-based hypermart firm) stores within competing areas. Both Carrefour and Auchan can monitor each other's promotions by observing promotions posted on the competitor's Web site (see **http://www.auchan.fr** and **http://www.carrefour.fr**, for example). In other situations, observation is the most economical technique. In a common type of observation study, a shopping center manager may observe the license plate (tag) numbers on cars in its parking lot. These data, along with automobile registration information, provide an inexpensive means of determining where customers live.

Certain data may be obtained more quickly or easily using direct observation than by other methods—gender, race, and other respondent characteristics can simply be observed. Researchers investigating a diet product may use observation when selecting respondents in a shopping mall.

RESEARCH SNAPSHOT

Hero Honda Research of Direct Observations Method

Hero Honda while developing Pleasure Scooter for women consumers in India conducted observation research. They wanted to understand the technique that consumers enjoyed while driving a scooter. They observed the level of comfort and pattern of use by women consumers while de-standing, starting, maneuvering, parking, and standing the scooter. Hero Honda research team concluded that a scooter with a metal body seemed heavy for Indian women and college going girls. They also found that standing a scooter was a difficult task for women as the scooter needs to be lifted on its stand. They also observed that the majority of scooter drivers carry their relatives, family members, or friends as pillion riders at some point or the other.

Overweight people may be prescreened by observing pedestrians, thus eliminating a number of screening interviews. Behaviors occurring in public places can also be easily observed, as the Research Snapshot "Clean as We Say, or Clean as We Do?".

In a quality-of-life survey, researchers asked respondents a series of questions that were compiled into an index of well-being. But interviewers also used direct observation because the researchers wanted to investigate the effect of weather conditions on people's answers. The researchers quickly and easily observed and recorded outside weather conditions on the day of the interviews, as well as the temperature and humidity in the building in which the interviews were conducted.[3]

Recording the decision time necessary to make a choice between two alternatives is a relatively simple, unobtrusive task easily accomplished through direct observation. Observing the choice time as a measure of the strength of the preference between alternatives is called **response latency**. This measure is based on the hypothesis that the longer a decision maker takes to choose between two alternatives, the closer the two alternatives are in terms of preference. In contrast, making a quick decision presumably indicates a considerable psychological distance between alternatives—that is, the choice is obvious. It is simple for a computer to record decision times, so the response latency measure has gained popularity now that computer-assisted data collection methods are common.

response latency
The amount of time it takes to make a choice between two alternatives; used as a measure of the strength of preference.

ERRORS ASSOCIATED WITH DIRECT OBSERVATION

Although direct observation involves no interaction with the subject, the method is not error-free; the observer may record events subjectively. The same visual cues that may influence the interplay between interviewer and respondent (e.g., the subject's age or sex) may come into play in some direct observation settings, such as when the observer subjectively attributes a particular economic status or educational background to a subject. A distortion of measurement resulting from the cognitive behavior or actions of the witnessing observer is called **observer bias**. For example, in a research project using observers to evaluate whether sales clerks are rude or courteous, fieldworkers may be required to rely on their own interpretations of people or situations during the observation process.

observer bias
A distortion of measurement resulting from the cognitive behavior or actions of a witnessing observer.

Also, accuracy may suffer if the observer does not record every detail that describes the persons, objects, and events in a given situation. Generally, the observer should record as much detail as possible. However, the pace of events, the observer's memory and writing speed, and other factors will limit the amount of detail that can be recorded.

Interpretation of observation data is another potential source of error. Facial expressions and other nonverbal communication may have several meanings. Does a smile always mean happiness? Does the fact that someone is standing or seated next to the president of a company necessarily indicate the person's status?

SCIENTIFICALLY CONTRIVED OBSERVATION

contrived observation
Observation in which the investigator creates an artificial environment in order to test a hypothesis.

Most observation takes place in a natural setting, but sometimes the investigator intervenes to create an artificial environment in order to test a hypothesis. This approach is called **contrived observation**. Contrived observation can increase the frequency of occurrence of certain behavior

RESEARCH SNAPSHOT

Clean as We Say, or Clean as We Do?

People know that hand washing is a fundamental way to stay healthy, not to mention simple good manners. So, when you ask them, most people say they faithfully wash their hands. But according to observational research, what people say about this behavior is not what they necessarily do.

The American Society for Microbiology and the Soap and Detergent Association together arranged for a nationwide study of hand washing by U.S. adults. In an online survey by Harris Interactive, 91 percent of adults said they always wash their hands after using a public restroom. Men were somewhat less likely to make this claim—88 percent, versus 94 percent of women. The researchers followed up on the survey results by observing adults in public restrooms in Atlanta, Chicago, New York City, and San Francisco. A 2007 tally of the percentage who washed their hands found that only 77 percent did so. About 66 percent of men were observed washing their hands after going to the restroom while women washed their hands 88 percent of the time. The difference between reporting of hand washing and actual hand washing was greater for the men (about a 22 percent difference) than for the women (6 percent). The numbers also vary geographically across the United States. Among major cities, Chicago has the cleanest hands as 81 percent of people can be observed washing after a toilet break while San Francisco scored lowest at 73 percent overall. Additionally, hand-washing is down 6 percent since 2005.

© M. THOMAS/ZEFA/CORBIS

© iStock

This research showing a divide between what individuals believe they should be doing, what they say they do, and what they actually do could be useful in helping agencies craft messages aimed at improving citizens' health. In addition, soap marketers may want to learn more about what keeps individuals from washing their hands (is it inconvenient? are public sinks a turnoff?), even while being prepared for some response bias.

The study was conducted by having observers discreetly watch and record the frequency of the number of people using a public toilet facility and the number of people who washed their hands. Observers pretended to be grooming themselves while watching the visitors. Over 6,000 people were observed in four U.S. cities. Do you think a hidden camera would reveal different results?

Source: Based on "Hygiene Habits Stall: Public Handwashing Down," Cleaning 101, www.cleaning101.com/newsroom/09-17-07.cfm; Harris Interactive, "Many Adults Report Not Washing Their Hands When They Should, and More People Claim to Wash Their Hands than Who Actually Do," news release (December 14, 2005); "Hand Washing Survey Fact Sheet" (2005), http://www.cleaning101.com, accessed February 24, 2006; and Harris Interactive, "A Survey of Hand Washing Behavior (2005 Findings)" (September 2005), accessed at "2005 ASM/SDA Hand Hygiene Survey Results," http://www.cleaning101.com (SDA Web site), February 24, 2006.

TOTHEPOINT

What we see depends mainly on what we look for.

—Sir John Lubbock

patterns, such as employee responses to complaints. An airline passenger complaining about a meal or service from the flight attendant may actually be a researcher recording that person's reactions. If situations were not contrived, the research time spent waiting and observing would expand considerably. This is one of the reasons for the growing popularity of *mystery shoppers* introduced in the opening vignette. They can effectively create a situation (such as a customer complaint) that might be very time consuming to observe if it were to occur naturally.

Combining Direct Observation and Interviewing

Some research studies combine visible observation with personal interviews. During or after detailed observations, individuals are asked to explain their actions.[4] For example, direct observation of women applying hand and body lotion identified two kinds of users. Some women slapped on the lotion, rubbing it briskly into their skin. Others caressed their skin as they applied the lotion. When the women were questioned about their behavior, the researchers discovered that women who slapped the lotion on were using the lotion as a remedy for dry skin. Those who caressed their skin were more interested in making their skin smell nice and feel soft.

Ethical Issues in the Observation of Humans

Observation methods introduce a number of ethical issues. Hidden observation raises the issue of the respondent's right to privacy. Suppose a research firm is approached by a company interested in acquiring information about how women put on their bras. The researcher considers approaching spas in several key cities about placing small cameras inconspicuously to observe women getting dressed. Obviously, this is an illegal and unethical approach. However, what if other women are hired to observe and record this activity? While to some extent the dressing room is an area where women often do dress where others can observe them, women do not expect to have their dressing behavior recorded. Therefore, unless a way can be found to have some women consent to such observation, this observational approach is unethical.

Some people might see contrived observation as entrapment. To *entrap* means to deceive or trick into difficulty, which clearly is an abusive action. The problem is one of balancing values. If the researcher obtains permission to observe someone, the subject may not act naturally. So, at times there is a strong temptation to observe without obtaining consent. In other times, such as monitoring mall traffic, obtaining consent just to observe people walking through the mall would be difficult.

So, when should researchers feel comfortable collecting observational data? While exceptions exist to every rule, here are three questions that can help address this question:

1. Is the behavior being observed commonly performed in public where it is expected that others can observe the behavior?
2. Is the behavior performed in a setting in which the anonymity—meaning there is no way to identify individuals—of the person being observed is assured?
3. Has the person agreed to be observed?

©PHOTODISC/GETTY IMAGES

Even if fashion companies could learn a lot about the types of problems consumers typically have when purchasing and wearing clothes, would observation through two-way mirrors be appropriate?

If the answers to the first two questions are *yes*, then there is not likely a violation of privacy in collecting observational research data. If the answer to the third question is *yes*, then gathering the data also is likely to be ethical.

Observation of Physical Objects

Physical phenomena may be the subject of observation study. Physical-trace evidence is a visible mark of some past event or occurrence. For example, the wear on library books indirectly indicates which books are actually read (handled most) when checked out. A classic example of physical-trace evidence in a nonprofit setting was erosion on the floor tiles around the hatching-chick exhibit at Chicago's Museum of Science and Industry. These tiles had to be replaced every six weeks; tiles in other parts of the museum did not need to be replaced for years. The selective erosion of tiles, indexed by the replacement rate, was a measure of the relative popularity of exhibits.

Clearly, a creative business researcher has many options for determining the solution to a problem. The story about Charles Coolidge Parlin, generally recognized as one of the founders of commercial business research, counting garbage cans at the turn of the twentieth century illustrates another study of physical traces.

TOTHEPOINT

What would you rather believe? What I say, or what you saw with your own eyes?

—Groucho Marx

Parlin designed an observation study to persuade Campbell's Soup Company to advertise in the *Saturday Evening Post*. Campbell's was reluctant to advertise because it believed that the *Post* was read primarily by working people who would prefer to make soup from scratch, peeling the potatoes and scraping the carrots, rather than paying ten cents for a can of soup. To demonstrate that rich people weren't the target market, Parlin selected a sample of Philadelphia garbage routes. Garbage from each specific area of the city that was selected was dumped on the floor of a local National Guard Armory. Parlin had the number of Campbell's soup cans in each pile counted. The results indicated that the garbage from the rich people's homes didn't contain many cans of Campbell's soup. Although they may not have made soup from scratch themselves, their housekeepers may have. The garbage piles

© JANINE WEIDEL PHOTOLIBRARY/ALAMY

Picking through the garbage on the side of the road can reveal behaviors of fast-food customers.

from the blue-collar area showed a larger number of Campbell's soup cans. This observation study was enough evidence for Campbell's. They advertised in the *Saturday Evening Post*.[5]

The method used in this study has since been used in a scientific project at the University of Arizona in which aspiring archaeologists have sifted through garbage for over 30 years. They examine soggy cigarette butts, empty milk cartons, and half-eaten Big Macs in an effort to understand modern life.

What is most interesting about the garbage project is that observations can be compared with the results of surveys about food consumption—and garbage does not lie. This type of observation can correct for overreporting consumption of healthful items and underreporting of, say, cigarette or alcohol consumption.

Another application of observing physical objects is to count and record physical inventories through retail or wholesale audits. This method allows researchers to investigate brand sales on regional and national levels, market shares, seasonal purchasing patterns, and so on. Business research suppliers offer audit data at both the retail and the wholesale levels.

An observer can record physical-trace data to discover information a respondent could not recall accurately. For example, measuring the number of ounces of a liquid bleach used during a test provides precise physical-trace evidence without relying on the respondent's memory. The accuracy of respondents' memories is not a problem for the firm that conducts a pantry audit. The pantry audit requires an inventory of the brands, quantities, and package sizes in a consumer's home rather than responses from individuals. The problem of untruthfulness or some other form of response bias is avoided. For example, the pantry audit prevents the possible problem of respondents erroneously claiming to have purchased prestige brands. However, gaining permission to physically check consumers' pantries is not easy, and the fieldwork is expensive. In addition, the brand in the pantry may not reflect the brand purchased most often if consumers substituted it because they had a coupon, the usual brand was out of stock, or some other reason.

Content Analysis

content analysis

The systematic observation and quantitative description of the manifest content of communication.

Besides observing people and physical objects, researchers may use **content analysis**, which obtains data by observing and analyzing the contents or messages of advertisements, newspaper articles, television programs, letters, and the like. This method involves systematic analysis as well as observation to identify the specific information content and other characteristics of the messages. Content analysis studies the message itself and involves the design of a systematic observation and recording procedure for quantitative description of the manifest content of communication. This technique measures the extent of emphasis or omission of a given analytical category. For example, content analysis of advertisements might evaluate their use of words, themes, characters, or space and time relationships. Another topic of content analysis is the frequency with which women, African-Americans, or ethnic minorities appear in mass media.

Content analysis might be used to investigate questions such as whether some advertisers use certain themes, appeals, claims, or deceptive practices more than others or whether recent consumer-oriented actions by the Federal Trade Commission have influenced the contents of advertising. A cable television programmer might do a content analysis of network programming to evaluate its competition. Every year researchers analyze the Super Bowl telecast to see how much of the visual material is live-action play and how much is replay, or how many shots focus on the cheerleaders and how many on spectators. Content analysis also can explore the information content of television commercials directed at children, the company images portrayed in ads, and numerous other aspects of advertising.

Study of the content of communications is more sophisticated than simply counting the items; it requires a system of analysis to secure relevant data. After one employee role-playing session involving leaders and subordinates, researchers analyzed videotapes to identify categories of verbal behaviors (e.g., positive reward statements, positive comparison statements, and self-evaluation requests). Trained coders, using a set of specific instructions, then recorded and coded the leaders' behavior into specific verbal categories.

Trace Analysis

Trace analysis is an observation technique where researchers collect data on the basis of physical trace and evidence of previous activities of the users. For instance by looking at the product wrappers in the waste bin one can comment on what different kinds of brands the person has used. While this analysis technique has certain disadvantages in terms of generalizability of the result, companies like Procter & Gamble and Colgate-Palmolive use trace analysis quite frequently to have initial idea about the consumption behavior of their newly launched products. Several market research companies use trace analysis in-house of their panel of consumers as well as university canteens, roadside dustbins, etc.

Mechanical Observation

In many situations, the primary—and sometimes the only—means of observation is mechanical rather than human. Video cameras, traffic counters, and other machines help observe and record behavior. Some unusual observation studies have used motion-picture cameras and time-lapse photography. An early application of this observation technique photographed train passengers and determined their levels of comfort by observing how they sat and moved in their seats. Another time-lapse study filmed traffic flows in an urban square and resulted in a redesign of the streets. Similar techniques may help managers determine how to better organize and arrange items in a warehouse or improve the design of store layouts to enhance traffic flow. Mechanical devices can also be utilized to observe employees and their actions when they cannot be observed in person as illustrated in the Research Snapshot "NeoTech's Mobile-Trak Observes Fleet Vehicles."

Television Monitoring

television monitoring
Computerized mechanical observation used to obtain television ratings.

Perhaps the best-known research project involving mechanical observation and computerized data collection is ACNielsen's **television monitoring** system for estimating national television audiences. Nielsen Media Research uses a consumer panel and a monitoring device called a PeopleMeter to obtain ratings for television programs nationwide.[6] The Nielsen PeopleMeter gathers data on what each television in a household is playing and who is watching it at the time. Researchers attach electronic boxes to television sets and remote controls to capture information on program choices and the length of viewing time. Nielsen matches the signals captured through these devices with its database of network broadcast and cable program schedules so that it can identify the specific programs being viewed.

When a television in the panel household is turned on, a red light on the PeopleMeter periodically flashes to remind viewers to indicate who is watching. The viewer then uses a remote control to record who is watching. One button on the control is assigned to each member of the household and a separate visitor button is used for potential guests. The household member presses his or her button to indicate the sex and age of the person who is watching. Knowing who in the family is watching allows executives to match television programs with demographic profiles.

Each night, Nielsen's computers automatically retrieve the data stored in the PeopleMeter's recording box. In this way, Nielsen gathers daily estimates of when televisions are in use, which

RESEARCH SNAPSHOT

NeoTech's Mobile-Trak Observes Fleet Vehicles

First incorporated in 1996, NeoTech has developed sophisticated monitoring and tracking devices for fleet vehicles. While managers cannot directly observe their driver's actions, the Mobile-Trak II modular vehicle tracking system provides detailed information about what is happening on the road. This electronic device can pinpoint the location of any equipped vehicle through its Global Positioning System (GPS), as well as record detailed trip information, including start and end times, distance traveled, average and top speed, idle time, off-hour usage, and the operator's driving habits.

NeoTech's Mobile-Trak II provides managers with the answers to important questions:

- Do my drivers report more hours than they should?
- Do my drivers stop too long at their stops?
- Are my drivers speeding?
- Do my drivers wear their seat belts?
- Are my drivers using our vehicles during off-hour periods?
- Are we getting accurate mileage readings?
- Have fault codes/malfunction indicators gone unreported?

© iStock

Not only is this observation technique useful to manage drivers, but it can assist fleet managers with many of their responsibilities. The service requirements for the vehicle can be carefully monitored, dispatchers know which driver is closest to the next service call, and the company can easily download data for route analysis, mileage reports, fuel tax reports, and state line crossings for tax purposes. The Mobile-Trak II even monitors g-loads so managers can be sure the vehicle is not operated in a dangerous manner or in a way that could damage delicate cargo.

An important issue for any manager is monitoring employees who are out in the field. The Mobile-Trak II is like having a manager riding with every driver.

Source: Based on NeoTech, Inc. PowerPoint presentation at http://www.neotech.com/view_presentation.htm, accessed February 22, 2009.

channels are used, and who is viewing each program. The panel includes more than five thousand households, selected to be representative of the U.S. population. For local programming, Nielsen uses additional panels equipped with recording devices but not PeopleMeters to record viewer demographics. (Nielsen uses surveys to record demographic data for local programming.)

Critics of the PeopleMeter argue that subjects in Nielsen's panel grow bored over time and do not always record when they begin or stop watching television. Arbitron, best known for measuring radio audiences, has attempted to answer this objection with its own measuring system, which it calls the Portable People Meter.[7] The Portable People Meter, which occupies about 4 cubic inches and weighs less than 3 ounces, reads inaudible codes embedded in audio signals to identify their source. Study participants wear or carry the meter throughout the day, and it automatically picks up codes embedded in whatever radio and television signals they encounter. At the end of the day, the participant inserts the meter into a "base station," which extracts the data collected, sends it to a household hub, and recharges the battery. The household hub then sends the data to Arbitron's computer over phone lines. To encourage cooperation, the meter has a motion sensor connected to a green light signaling that the meter senses it is being carried. Each participant is awarded points for the amount of time the meter is on. Total points are displayed in the base station and used to determine the size of the incentive paid to each participant. Arbitron's meter simplifies the participants' role and collects data on exposure to radio and

Traffic cameras that monitor speeding on major highways are becoming commonplace in Europe, Australia, and even in some parts of the United States. Would car companies learn anything from the observed behavior?

© AP PHOTO

television programming outside the home. However, the device records only signals that the radio or television system embeds using Arbitron's equipment.

Other devices gather data about the viewing of advertisements. The TiVo digital television recorder collects detailed viewing data, such as what commercials people skip by using fast-forward. The PreTesting Company sets up contrived observational studies in which viewers equipped with a remote control are invited to watch any of three prerecorded channels playing different programs and advertisements, including the client's ads to be tested.[8] The system records the precise points at which the viewer changes the channel. By combining the results from many participants, the company arrives at a Cumulative Zapping Score, that is, the percentage of viewers who had exited the client's advertisement by each point in the ad. So that viewing behavior will be more natural, subjects are told they are evaluating the programming, not the ads.

Monitoring Web Site Traffic

Computer technology makes gathering detailed data about online behavior easy and inexpensive. The greater challenges are to identify which measures are meaningful and to interpret the data correctly. For instance, most organizations record the number of hits at their Web sites—mouse clicks on a single page of a Web site. If the visitor clicks on many links, that page receives multiple hits. Similarly, they can track *page views,* or single, discrete clicks to load individual pages of a Web site. Page views more conservatively indicate how many users visit each individual page on the Web site and may also be used to track the path or sequence of pages that each visitor follows.

CLICK-THROUGH RATES

A **click-through rate** (CTR) is the percentage of people who are exposed to an advertisement who actually click on the corresponding hyperlink which takes them to the company's Web site. Counting hits or page views can suggest the amount of interest or attention a Web site is receiving, but these measures are flawed. First, hits do not differentiate between a lot of activity by a few visitors and a little activity by many visitors. In addition, the researcher lacks information about the meaning behind the numbers. If a user clicks on a site many times, is the person finding a lot of useful or enjoyable material, or is the user trying unsuccessfully to find something by looking in several places? Additionally, some hits are likely made by mistake. The consumers may have had no intention of clicking through the ad or may not have known what they were doing when they clicked on the ad.

click-through rate
Proportion of people who are exposed to an Internet ad who actually click on its hyperlink to enter the Web site; click-through rates are generally very low.

A more refined count is the number of *unique visitors* to a Web site. This measurement counts the initial access to the site but not multiple hits on the site by the same visitor during the same day or week. Operators of Web sites can collect the data by attaching small files, called *cookies,* to the computers of visitors to their sites and then tracking those cookies to see whether the same visitors return. Some research companies, notably Jupiter Research and Nielsen//NetRatings, specialize in monitoring this type of Internet activity. A typical approach is to install a special tracking program on the personal computers of a sample of Internet users who agree to participate in the research effort. Nielsen//NetRatings has its software installed in thirty thousand computers in homes and workplaces. Internet monitoring enables these companies to identify the popularity of Web sites. In recent years, accurate measurement of unique visitors has become more difficult, because over half of computer users have deleted cookies and many users block cookies to make themselves anonymous.[9]

As online advertising has become commonplace, business research has refined methods for measuring the effectiveness of the advertisements. The companies that place these ads can keep count of the click-through rate (CTR). Applying the CTR to the amount spent on the advertisement gives the advertiser a *cost per click.* These measures have been hailed as a practical way to evaluate advertising effectiveness. However, marketers have to consider that getting consumers to click on an ad is rarely the ad's objective. Companies are more often advertising to meet short- or long-term sales goals.

Google has benefited from CTR research indicating that the highest click-through rates tend to occur on pages displaying search results. (Not surprisingly, someone who searches for the term *kayaks* is more likely to be interested in an advertisement offering a good deal on kayaks.) The company showed Vanguard, for example, that its banner ads cost the financial firm less than 50 cents per click and generated a 14 percent click-through rate. That CTR is far above typical response rates for direct-mail advertising, but it does not indicate whether online clicks are as valuable in terms of sales.[10]

Scanner-Based Research

Lasers performing optical character recognition and barcode technology like the universal product code (UPC) have accelerated the use of mechanical observation in business research. Chapter 8 noted that a number of syndicated services offer secondary data about product category movement generated from retail stores using scanner technology.

This technology allows researchers to investigate questions that are demographically or promotionally specific. Scanner research has investigated the different ways consumers respond to price promotions and the effects of those differences on a promotion's profitability. One of the primary means of implementing this type of research is through the establishment of a **scanner-based consumer panel** to replace consumer purchase diaries. In a typical scanner panel, each household is assigned a bar-coded card, like a frequent-shopper card, which members present to the clerk at the register. The household's code number is coupled with the purchase information recorded by the scanner. In addition, as with other consumer panels, background information about the household obtained through answers to a battery of demographic and psychographic survey questions can also be coupled with the household code number.

scanner-based consumer panel

A type of consumer panel in which participants' purchasing habits are recorded with a laser scanner rather than a purchase diary.

Aggregate data, such as actual store sales as measured by scanners, are available to clients and industry groups. Data may also be aggregated by product category. To interpret the aggregated data, researchers can combine them with secondary research and panel demographics. For instance, data from Information Resources Inc. (IRI) have indicated a downward trend in sales of hair-coloring products. Demographic data suggest that an important reason is the aging of the population; many consumers who dye their hair reach an age at which they no longer wish to cover their gray hair. A smaller segment of the population is at an age where consumers typically begin using hair coloring.[11]

Data from scanner research parallel data provided by a standard mail diary panel, with some important improvements:

1. The data measure observed (actual) purchase behavior rather than reported behavior (recorded later in a diary).
2. Substituting mechanical for human record-keeping improves accuracy.
3. Measures are unobtrusive, eliminating interviewing and the possibility of social desirability or other bias on the part of respondents.
4. More extensive purchase data can be collected, because all UPC categories are measured. In a mail diary, respondents could not possibly reliably record all items they purchased. Because all UPC-coded items are measured in the panel, users can investigate many product categories to determine loyalty, switching rates, and so on for their own brands as well as for other companies' products and locate product categories for possible market entry.
5. The data collected from computerized checkout scanners can be combined with data about the timing of advertising, price changes, displays, and special sales promotions. Researchers can scrutinize them with powerful analytical software provided by the scanner data providers.

Scanner data can show a researcher week-by-week how a product is doing, even in a single store, and track sales in response to changes of sales personnel, local advertising, or price promotions. Also, several organizations have developed scanner panels, such as Information Resources Inc.'s Behavior Scan System, and expanded them into electronic test-market systems.

RESEARCH SNAPSHOT

Neuroco Peers into the Consumer's Brain

When Hewlett-Packard was developing advertisements for its digital photography products, the firm wanted to ensure its ad images would evoke the desired response. For guidance, the company turned to Neuroco and its high-tech research method, known as neuromarketing. Neuroco researchers showed subjects a pair of photos of the same woman, and about half of them preferred each picture. Then Neuroco measured the electrical activity in the brains of subjects looking at the same images, and the analysis showed a definite preference for one of the pictures in which the woman's smile was a little warmer.

Neuroco's approach uses a technology called *quantified electroencephalography* (*QEEG*). Subjects wear light and portable EEG equipment that records brain activity; software presents the data in computer maps that display activity levels in areas of the brain. Researchers can then evaluate whether the person is attentive and whether brain activity signifies emotional involvement or analytical thinking. QEEG is more flexible than the better-known use of functional magnetic resonance imaging (fMRI), which has provided many advances in brain research but requires all subjects to lie still in a large, noisy machine. With QEEG, the measuring equipment can travel with subjects as they walk around a store or watch advertisements.

© iStock

Consider a young woman demonstrating a Neuroco study by shopping with electrodes discreetly attached to her head. Neuroco chief scientist David Lewis observes a computer screen showing a map of her brain waves in red and green, with the colors signaling levels of alpha-wave activity. The zigzag pattern tells Lewis that this shopper is alert but not engaged in making purchase decisions. As the woman walks into a store's shoe department, however, the pattern changes when she picks up a pair of stiletto heels. An explosion of brain activity occurs, then the woman heads for the cash register, decision made.

As this example illustrates, observation can provide tremendous insight to businesses. Advances in observation technology are literally providing a view of what is happening inside the brain.

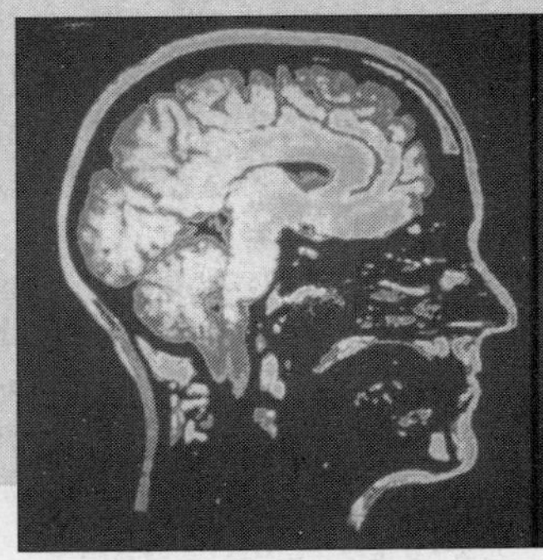

© HOWARD SOCHUREK/THE MEDICAL FILE/PETER ARNOLD, INC.

Source: Based on Mucha, Thomas, "This Is Your Brain on Advertising," *Business 2.0* (August 2005), downloaded from http://web2.infotrac.galegroup.com; and Laybourne, Peter, and David Lewis, "Neuromarketing: The Future of Consumer Research?" *Admap* (May 2005), 28–30.

Measuring Physiological Reactions

Researchers have used a number of mechanical devices to evaluate physical and physiological reactions to advertising copy, packaging, and other stimuli. Researchers use such means when they believe consumers are unaware of their own reactions to stimuli such as advertising or that consumers will not provide honest responses. Recent research approaches use devices to monitor and measure brain activity as described in the Research Snapshot "Neuroco Peers into the Consumer's Brain." Four major categories of mechanical devices are used to measure physiological reactions: (1) eye-tracking monitors, (2) pupilometers, (3) psychogalvanometers, and (4) voice-pitch analyzers.

A magazine or newspaper advertiser may wish to grab readers' attention with a visual scene and then direct it to a package or coupon. Or a television advertiser may wish to identify which selling points to emphasize. Eye-tracking equipment records how the subject reads a print ad or views a television commercial and how much time is spent looking at various parts of the stimulus. In physiological terms, the gaze movement of a viewer's eye is measured with an **eye-tracking monitor**, which measures unconscious eye movements. Originally developed to measure astronauts' eye fatigue, modern eye-tracking systems need not keep a viewer's head in a stationary position. The devices track eye movements with invisible infrared light beams that lock onto a subject's eyes. The light reflects off the eye, and eye-movement data are recorded while another tiny video camera monitors which magazine page is being perused. The data are analyzed by computer to determine which components in an ad (or other stimuli) were seen and which were overlooked. Eye-tracking monitors have recently been used to measure the way subjects view e-mail and Web messages. OgilvyOne has used this technology to learn that people often skip over more than half of the words in e-mail advertising, especially words on the right side of the message. Interestingly, consumers generally ignore the word *free*.[12]

eye-tracking monitor

A mechanical device used to observe eye movements; some eye monitors use infrared light beams to measure unconscious eye movements.

Other physiological observation techniques are based on a common principle that adrenaline is released when the body is aroused. This hormone causes the heart to enlarge and to beat

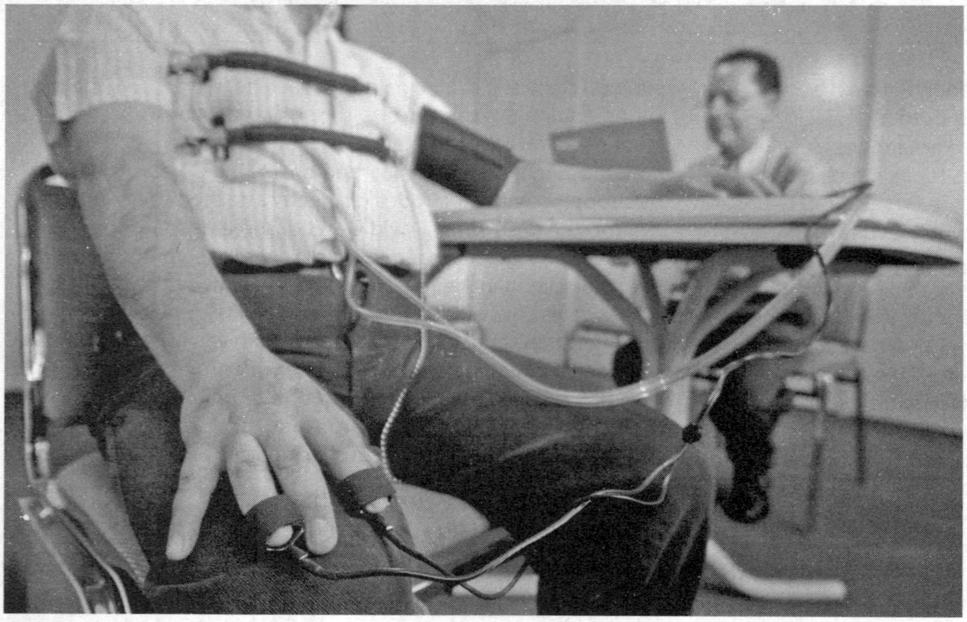

Physiological responses to advertising can be recorded with a device like this one.

pupilometer
A mechanical device used to observe and record changes in the diameter of a subject's pupils.

psychogalvanometer
A device that measures galvanic skin response, a measure of involuntary changes in the electrical resistance of the skin.

voice-pitch analysis
A physiological measurement technique that records abnormal frequencies in the voice that are supposed to reflect emotional reactions to various stimuli.

harder and faster. These changes increase the flow of blood to the fingers and toes. The blood vessels dilate, and perspiration increases, affecting the skin's electrical conductivity. Other physical changes following the release of adrenaline include dilation of the pupils, more frequent brain wave activity, higher skin temperature, and faster breathing. Methods that measure these and other changes associated with arousal can apply to a variety of business questions, such as subjects' reactions to advertising messages or product concepts.

A **pupilometer** observes and records changes in the diameter of a subject's pupils. A subject is instructed to look at a screen on which an advertisement or other stimulus is projected. When the brightness and distance of the stimulus from the subject's eyes are held constant, changes in pupil size may be interpreted as changes in cognitive activity that result from the stimulus, rather than from eye dilation and constriction in response to light intensity, distance from the object, or other physiological reactions to the conditions of observation. This method of research is based on the assumption that increased pupil size reflects positive attitudes toward and interest in advertisements.

A **psychogalvanometer** measures galvanic skin response (GSR), a measure of involuntary changes in the electrical resistance of the skin. This device is based on the assumption that physiological changes, such as increased perspiration, accompany emotional reactions to advertisements, packages, and slogans. Excitement increases the body's perspiration rate, which increases the electrical resistance of the skin. The test is an indicator of emotional arousal or tension.

Voice-pitch analysis is a relatively new physiological measurement technique that gauges emotional reactions as reflected in physiological changes in a person's voice. Abnormal frequencies in the voice caused by changes in the autonomic nervous system are measured with sophisticated, audio-adapted computer equipment. Computerized analysis compares the respondent's voice pitch during warm-up conversations (normal range) with verbal responses to questions about his or her evaluative reaction to television commercials or other stimuli. This technique, unlike other physiological devices, does not require the researcher to surround subjects with mazes of wires or equipment.

All of these devices assume that physiological reactions are associated with persuasiveness or predict some cognitive response. This assumption has not yet been clearly demonstrated. No strong theoretical evidence supports the argument that such a physiological change is a valid measure of future sales, attitude change, or emotional response. Another major problem with physiological research is the *calibration,* or sensitivity, of measuring devices. Identifying arousal is one thing, but precisely measuring *levels* of arousal is another. In addition, most of these devices are expensive. However, as a prominent researcher points out, physiological measurement is coincidental: "Physiological measurement isn't an exit interview. It's not dependent on what was remembered later on. It's a live blood, sweat, and tears, moment-by-moment response, synchronous with the stimulus."[13]

Each of these mechanical devices has another limitation: The subjects are usually placed in artificial settings, such as watching television in a laboratory rather than at home, and the participants know they are being observed.

TIPS OF THE TRADE

- While observation is a powerful and potentially useful research methodology, any insight is limited to the observable.
    - Observation may not be used for cognitive phenomena. Attitudes, motivations, expectations, intentions, and preferences are not observable; only overt behavior of short duration can be observed.
- Observation can eliminate some forms of bias.
    - Common survey bias from distortions, inaccuracies, or other response biases due to memory error, social desirability bias, and so forth are not present.
- Other forms of bias may be present.
    - Observer bias results from the cognitive or behavioral actions of the observer as they rely on their own interpretation.
- If researchers only record what they see, observation is one of the most unbiased methods for collecting data. If researchers go beyond what they see—offering personal interpretation of the events—observation can be an extremely biased research technique.

Summary

1. Discuss the role of observation as a business research method. Observation is a powerful tool for the business researcher. Scientific observation is the systematic process of recording the behavioral patterns of people, objects, and occurrences as they are witnessed. Questioning or otherwise communicating with subjects does not occur. A wide variety of information about the behavior of people and objects can be observed. Seven kinds of phenomena are observable: physical actions, verbal behavior, expressive behavior, spatial relations and locations, temporal patterns, physical objects, and verbal and pictorial records. Thus, both verbal and nonverbal behavior may be observed.

2. Describe the use of direct observation and contrived observation. Human observation, whether direct or contrived, is commonly used when the situation or behavior to be recorded is not easily predictable in advance of the research. It may be unobtrusive, and many types of data can be obtained more accurately through direct observation than by questioning respondents. Direct observation involves watching and recording what naturally occurs, without creating an artificial situation. For some data, observation is the most direct or the only method of collection. For example, researchers can measure response latency, the time it takes individuals to choose between alternatives. Observation can also be contrived by creating the situations to be observed, such as with a mystery shopper or a research laboratory. This can reduce the time and expense of obtaining reactions to certain circumstances.

3. Identify ethical issues in observation studies. Contrived observation, hidden observation, and other observation research designs have the potential to involve deception. For this reason, these methods often raise ethical concerns about subjects' right to privacy and right to be informed. We mentioned three questions to help determine the ethicality of observation: (1) is the behavior being observed commonly performed in public where others can observe it, (2) is anonymity of the subject assured, and (3) has the subject agreed to be observed? If the answers to 1 and 2 are "yes," or if the answer to 3 is "yes,' the observation is likely ethical.

4. Explain the observation of physical objects and message content. Physical-trace evidence serves as a visible record of past events. Researchers may examine whatever evidence provides such a record, including inventory levels, the contents of garbage cans, or the items in a consumer's pantry. Content analysis obtains data by observing and analyzing the contents of the messages in written or spoken communications.

5. Describe major types of mechanical observation. Mechanical observation uses a variety of devices to record behavior directly. It may be an efficient and accurate choice when the situation or behavior to be recorded is routine, repetitive, or programmatic. National television audience ratings are based on mechanical observation (for example, Nielsen's PeopleMeters) and computerized data collection. Web site traffic may be measured electronically. Scanner-based research provides product category sales data recorded by laser scanners in retail stores. Many syndicated services offer secondary data collected through scanner systems.

6. Summarize techniques for measuring physiological reactions. Physiological reactions, such as arousal or eye movement patterns, may be observed using a number of mechanical devices.

Eye-tracking monitors identify the direction of a person's gaze, and a pupilometer observes and records changes in the diameter of the pupils of subjects' eyes, based on the assumption that a larger pupil signifies a positive attitude. A psychogalvanometer measures galvanic skin response as a signal of a person's emotional reactions. Voice-pitch analysis measures changes in a person's voice and associates the changes with emotional response.

Key Terms and Concepts

click-through rate, *271*
content analysis, *268*
contrived observation, *265*
direct observation, *264*
eye-tracking monitor, *273*
hidden observation, *262*
observation, *261*
observer bias, *265*
psychogalvanometer, *274*
pupilometer, *274*
response latency, *265*
scanner-based consumer panel, *272*
television monitoring, *269*
visible observation, *262*
voice-pitch analysis, *274*

Questions for Review and Critical Thinking

1. Yogi Berra, former New York Yankee catcher, said, "You can observe a lot just by watching." How does this fit in with the definition of scientific observation?
2. What are the advantages and disadvantages of observation studies relative to surveys?
3. Under what conditions are observation studies most appropriate?
4. **ETHICS** The chapter showed a photograph of a traffic monitoring camera. Do you think the use of these cameras to issue speeding tickets is ethical? What types of behavior might cameras like these capture that would help automobile designers produce products that better match our needs as drivers?
5. A multinational fast-food corporation plans to locate a restaurant in La Paz, Bolivia. Secondary data for this city are sketchy and outdated. How might you determine the best location using observation?
6. Discuss how an observation study might be combined with a personal interview.
7. **'NET** Click-through rates for advertisements placed in Web sites are usually very, very low (less than 1 percent). What types of error might exist in using click-through rate data as a measure of an ad's success?
8. Outline a research design using observation for each of the following situations:
   a. A bank wishes to collect data on the number of customer services and the frequency of customer use of these services.
   b. A state government wishes to determine the driving public's use of seat belts.
   c. A researcher wishes to know how many women have been featured on *Time* covers over the years.
   d. A human resource manager wants to know what salaries their key competitors are offering for some common positions.
   e. A fast-food restaurant manger wishes to determine if they serve their customers as quickly as their competitors.
   f. A magazine publisher wishes to determine exactly what people look at and what they pass over while reading one of its magazines.
   g. An overnight package delivery service wishes to observe delivery workers beginning at the moment when they stop the truck, continuing through the delivery of the package, and ending when they return to the truck.
9. What is a scanner-based consumer panel?
10. What are the major types of mechanical observation?
11. **ETHICS** Comment on the ethics of the following situations:
    a. During the course of telephone calls to investors, a stockbroker records respondents' voices when they are answering sensitive investment questions and then conducts a voice pitch analysis. The respondents do not know that their voices are being recorded.
    b. A researcher plans to invite consumers to be test users in a simulated kitchen located in a shopping mall and then to videotape their reactions to a new microwave dinner from behind a two-way mirror (one that an observer behind the mirror can see through but the person looking into the mirror sees only the reflection).
    c. A researcher arranges to purchase the trash from the headquarters of a major competitor. The purpose is to sift through discarded documents to determine the company's strategic plans.
12. What is a psychogalvanometer?

Research Activities

1. **'NET** William Rathje, a researcher at the University of Arizona, Department of Anthropology, has become well-known for the "Garbage Project." The project involves observational research. Use **http://www.ask.com** to find information about the garbage project at the University of Arizona. What is the name of the book that describes some of the key findings of the Garbage Project? How do you think it involves observational research?
2. **'NET** The Internet is filled with Webcams. For example, Pebble Beach Golf Club has several Webcams (**http://www.pebblebeach.com**). How could a researcher use Webcams like these to collect behavioral data?

Case 11.1 Mazda and Syzygy

When Mazda Motor Europe set out to improve its Web site, the company wanted details about how consumers were using the site and whether finding information was easy. Mazda hired a research firm called Syzygy to answer those questions with observational research.[14] Syzygy's methods include the use of an eye-tracking device that uses infrared light rays to record what areas of a computer screen a user is viewing. For instance, the device measured the process computer users followed in order to look for a local dealer or arranging a test drive. Whenever a process seemed confusing or difficult, the company looked for ways to make the Web site easier to navigate.

To conduct this observational study, Syzygy arranged for 16 subjects in Germany and the United Kingdom to be observed as they used the Web site. The subjects in Germany were observed with the eye-tracking equipment. As the equipment measured each subject's gaze, software recorded the location on the screen and graphed the data. Syzygy's results included three-dimensional contour maps highlighting the "peak" areas where most of the computer users' attention was directed.

Questions

1. What could Mazda learn from eye-tracking software that would be difficult to learn from other observational methods?
2. What are the shortcomings of this method?
3. Along with the eye-tracking research, what other research methods could help Mazda assess the usability of its Web site? Summarize your advice for how Mazda could use complementary methods to obtain a complete understanding of its Web site usability.

Case 11.2 Texas Instruments and E-Lab

E-Lab, LLC is a business research and design firm in Chicago that specializes in observing people, identifying patterns in behavior, and developing an understanding of why these patterns exist.[15] The company then uses the knowledge that it gains as a framework in the product development process. Texas Instruments (TI) used E-Lab to investigate the mobility, connectivity, and communications needs of law enforcement officers, which led to ideas for a set of computing and communications products. As part of its product development research, TI's Advanced Integrated Systems Department and E-Lab researchers spent 320 hours shadowing police officers in three Texas police departments. Shadowing involves asking questions while observing. Researchers walked foot patrols, rode in patrol cars, and pedaled with bike patrols. They spent time with crowd control, narcotics, homicide, dispatch, and juvenile teams. They recorded their observations and interviews on paper, digital camera, and video.

A number of interesting findings emerged from all this research. First, police officers are very social, so it was important that any product TI developed should enhance socialization rather than detract from it. For example, an in-car computing and communications device should be able to access a database that lists names and numbers of experts on the force so officers can call or e-mail the experts directly. Second, police officers are not driven by procedure. That told TI that the procedures for an investigation should reside in the device and that the device should prompt the officer at each step in the process. And third, officers rely on informal information about people and activities on their beats. This information may be kept on scraps of paper, on a spreadsheet back in the office, or in the police officer's head. Business researchers concluded that any device that TI develops should have a place to compile and share informal information.

Questions

1. Identify the research design used by E-Lab.
2. Compare this research design with a survey research design. What advantages, if any, did this research design have over a survey?

CHAPTER 12
EXPERIMENTAL RESEARCH

LEARNING OUTCOMES

After studying this chapter, you should be able to

1. **Identify the independent variable, dependent variable, and construct a valid simple experiment to assess a cause and effect relationship**
2. **Understand and minimize systematic experimental error**
3. **Know ways of minimizing experimental demand characteristics**
4. **Avoid unethical experimental practices**
5. **Understand the advantages of a between-subjects experimental design**
6. **Weigh the trade-off between internal and external validity**
7. **Use manipulations to implement a completely randomized experimental design, a randomized-block design, and a factorial experimental design**

Chapter Vignette: Testing Web Protocols for Financial Markets

Technological advances have drastically changed the way we conduct banking and related financial services. ATMs, online banking, real-time stock trading, and other Web services have created a globally accessible 24-hour-a-day financial market. For most of us, how this happens is not that relevant. However, for information technology directors and financial managers, how this process occurs—and how to make it occur faster and cheaper—is vitally important. This vignette describes an experiment examining two protocols for transferring information over computer networks.

FIX (Financial Information eXchange) is the commonly used electronics communication protocol for global real-time information exchange for securities transactions and markets. With the annual volume of trade in trillions of dollars, financial service firms are constantly seeking ways to cost-effectively increase the speed of access to financial markets. SOAP (Simple Object Access Protocol) is a potential competitor for the FIX method of information exchange.

Researchers designed a laboratory experiment to compare the relative performance of FIX and SOAP in business computing scenarios.[1] By creating identical conditions—transferring the same information, using the same computers, over the same Ethernet connection—the performance of the two protocols was assessed. The researchers measured the time it took for a round-trip message from the client to the server and back. The results indicate that FIX remains a faster protocol for transferring financial market information. While most of us do not fully understand the difference between FIX and SOAP—and even fewer really care—it is not necessary for us to understand the purpose of the experiment. This experiment answers an important question to the financial world "How does the performance of these two approaches compare?" However, an understanding of the process of testing these two approaches is very important to business researchers. This chapter provides a basic understanding of experimental business research.

Introduction

Most students are familiar with scientific experiments from studying physical sciences like physics and chemistry. The term *experiment* typically conjures up an image of a chemist surrounded by bubbling test tubes and Bunsen burners. Behavioral and physical scientists have used experimentation far longer than have business researchers. Nevertheless, both social scientists and physical scientists use experiments for much the same purpose—to assess cause and effect relationships.

Causality

The concept of causality, as the name says, deals with cause-and-effect relationship. Although we use the word causality very often in our daily life, the scientific meaning of the concept of causality is more structured. For instance, when we say that A causes B, in the context of research we mean one of the many causes that might affect B. In other words, the meaning of causality in scientific sense is probabilistic, and not deterministic. It will be noted in this context that it is not possible to prove the cause-and-effect relationship, scientifically. This means that we cannot say that A causes B. At most we can only infer that A is one of the causes of B. This inference is driven by argument, which can be falsified. For instance, in some occasion we may have the support of data from which we can infer that A is one of the possible causes of B. However, if we do not get support of data in a different occasion, we may not be able to infer even for such relationship.

Conditions of Cause-and-Effect Relationship

To hypothesize a cause-and-effect relationship, the researcher must get satisfied with some of the conditions of causality. In the first instance, a researcher should know that both A and B vary together. This means the variation is concomitant (connected) or not. For example, suppose an automobile manufacturer believes that sales of new car is dependent on fuel efficiency of the car. Here fuel efficiency is the cause and sales of automobile is the effect. If this causal relationship supports concomitant variation, the researcher may infer that higher fuel efficiency would result in higher sales.

Secondly, the time of occurrence of the cause should not be after the effect. In other words, cause must occur either before or during the effect. In the above example, buyers need to have the proof of fuel efficiency of the car to generate high sales. Fuel efficiency of the car needs to occur before saies. It is possible that in a cause-and-effect relationship, a variable may be both cause and effect. For instance, higher the advertisement expenses, higher maybe the sales. In this relationship, advertisements expense acts as cause and sales acts as an effect. However, it may be said that if sales is high, management would increase the advertisement expense. In other words, higher the sales, higher would be the advertisement expense. In this relationship, both advertisement expense and sales act as cause as well as effect.

Finally, in a cause-and-effect relationship, it is important that all other possible causes are absent. This means that if the hypothesis wants to prove that advertisement expense effects sale, then all other causes that affect sale, i.e., product design, price, promotional expense, availability, etc., should be made constant.

Creating an Experiment

As described in an earlier chapter, experiments are widely used in causal research designs. Experimental research allows a researcher to control the research situation so that *causal* relationships among variables may be evaluated. The experimenter manipulates one or more independent variables and holds constant all other possible independent variables while observing effects on dependent variable(s). Events may be controlled in an experiment to a degree that is simply not possible in a survey.

Independent variables are expected to determine the outcomes of interest. In an experiment, they are controlled by the researcher through manipulations. Dependent variables are the outcomes of interest to the researcher and the decision makers. A simple example would be thinking about how changes in price would influence sales. Price would be an independent variable and sales would be a dependent variable. In our opening vignette, the protocol used (FIX or SOAP) would be an experimental manipulation—the independent variable—and the speed of data transmission is the important dependent variable.

The researcher's goal in conducting an experiment is to determine whether changing an experimental independent variable causes changes in the specified dependent variable. The assumption of the experiment described above is that the type of protocol used will affect the speed of financial data transfer. In other words, changing from FIX to SOAP will increase or decrease the time required for data transfer. If all the other conditions are the same, then a causal inference is supported.

A famous experiment in the marketing field investigated the influence of brand name on consumers' taste perceptions. An experimenter manipulated whether consumers preferred the taste of beer in labeled or unlabeled bottles. One week respondents were given a six-pack containing bottles labeled only with letters (A, B, C). The following week, respondents received another six-pack with brand labels (like Budweiser, Coors, Miller, and so forth). The experimenter measured reactions to the beers after each tasting. In every case, the beer itself was the same. So, every person involved in the experiment drank the very same beer. Therefore, the differences observed in taste, the key dependent variable, could only be attributable to the difference in labeling. When the consumers participating in the experiment expressed a preference for the branded beer, the conclusion is that brand name does influence consumers' taste perceptions.

An experiment can capture whether or not mangers can increase self-efficacy and enhance employee attitudes toward their job.

An Illustration: Can a Self-Efficacy Intervention Enhance Job Attitude?

©COMSTOCKIMAGES/JUPITERIMAGES

This chapter deals with business experiments, which can best be illustrated through examples like the opening vignette and the one which follows. We will refer back to these examples throughout the chapter.

Let's take a look at an experiment investigating how self-efficacy might influence an employee's attitude toward their job.[2] Self-efficacy is a person's confidence and belief in their own abilities to accomplish the tasks at hand. While the subjects of this particular research are accountants, and the results are highly relevant for those involved in fields like human resource management, it has implications for anyone in a managerial role. The key issue centers on a manager's ability to raise an employee's confidence in their ability to perform their job and the favorable outcomes of this increased confidence.

EXPERIMENTAL SUBJECTS

This experiment involved actual employees of an accounting firm. Seventy-one first and second year auditors of one major accounting firm participated in the study. Participants in experimental research are referred to as **subjects** rather than respondents. This is because the experimenter subjects them to some experimental treatment. In this experiment, 35 of the subjects were given positive feedback and encouragement from their supervisors as the experimental treatment. The other 36 subjects were not provided the positive feedback.

subjects

The sampling units for an experiment, usually human respondents who provide measures based on the experimental manipulation.

INDEPENDENT VARIABLES

The experiment involved one relevant independent variable, whether or not the employee received the positive feedback intended to enhance their self-efficacy. Employees receiving the experimental treatment participated in an interview and received three different pieces of written communication from their supervisors providing encouragement and expressing confidence that they would be successful in their positions.

While not a true independent variable, the length of time each employee had worked with the firm was also important to the researchers. Could new employees react differently to the positive feedback than employees who had already been with the firm? In this case, length of time cannot be manipulated by the researchers, but it can still be considered in the experiment. Variables such as this (another example would be the sex of the experimental subject) are referred to as **blocking variables**, which are discussed in more detail later in this chapter. Considering the independent variable (treatment or no treatment) and the

blocking variables

A categorical (less than interval) variable that is not manipulated as is an experimental variable but is included in the statistical analysis of experiments

EXHIBIT 12.1
Experimental Conditions in Self-Efficacy Experiment

Blocking Variable		Experimental Treatment: No Feedback	Experimental Treatment: Received Feedback
Employment	Newcomers (New Employees)	22 participants	22 participants
	Insiders (Current Employees)	14 participants	13 participants

blocking variable (new or current employee), four different experimental cells are possible. Exhibit 12.1 illustrates the four different experimental conditions for this experiment. An **experimental condition** refers to one of the possible levels of an experimental variable manipulation.

experimental condition
One of the possible levels of an experimental variable manipulation

Subjects were divided into "newcomers" (the new employees) and "insiders" (current employees) and then randomly assigned to either the treatment condition or the control group. By analyzing differences between the groups, the researcher can see what effects occur due to the independent and blocking variables.

EXPERIMENTAL OUTCOME

The key outcomes, or dependent variables, in this example are a subject's job satisfaction, organizational commitment, professional commitment, intent to quit the organization, and intent to quit the profession. In addition, the researchers followed up later to see if the subjects had actually left the firm. For simplicity, we will only look at the effect on one dependent variable, job satisfaction. In this case, subjects were asked to respond to a rating scale asking how much they agreed with a series of statements regarding their satisfaction with their job. The possible scores ranged from 1 to 7, where a higher score means higher job satisfaction.

EXHIBIT 12.2
Job Satisfaction Means in Self-Efficacy Experiment

Blocking Variable		Experimental Treatment: No Feedback	Experimental Treatment: Received Feedback	
Employment	Newcomers (New Employees)	5.80	5.93	5.87
	Insiders (Current Employees)	4.77	5.45	5.10
		5.38	5.68	

Exhibit 12.2 shows the average for each experimental condition. The results show that after receiving the positive feedback and encouragement, subjects that were already working for the firm reported an average job satisfaction score of 5.45, while the new employees that received the treatment reported an average score of 5.93. For those subjects that did not receive the treatment, the current employees' average scores was 4.77 and the new employee's average was 5.80.

Thus, the conclusion at this point seems to be that the difference in job satisfaction is primarily between the current and new employees. The self-efficacy treatment does not seem to have much impact. Or does it?

INDEPENDENT VARIABLE MAIN EFFECTS AND INTERACTION

The length of time that the employee works at the firm clearly appears to matter. But maybe the attempts to enhance self-efficacy shouldn't be dismissed so quickly. The researcher must examine both the effects of each experimental variable considered alone and the effects due to combinations of variables. A **main effect** refers to the experimental difference in means between the

main effect
The experimental difference in dependent variable means between the different levels of any single experimental variable.

interaction effect
Differences in dependent variable means due to a specific combination of independent variables.

different levels of any single experimental variable. In this case, there are potential main effects for the self-efficacy treatment and for the length of time as an employee, but only the differences associated with employment length are significant (at a .05 level).

An **interaction effect** is due to a specific combination of independent variables. In this case, it's possible that the combination of length of employment and the self-efficacy treatment creates effects that are not clearly represented in the main effects. Interaction results are often shown with a line graph as shown in Exhibit 12.3. Main effects are illustrated when the lines are at different heights as is the case here. Notice the line for new employees is higher than the line for current employees. When the lines have very different slopes, an interaction is likely present. In this case, the combination of length of employment and self-efficacy treatment is presenting an interaction leading to the following interpretation.

EXHIBIT 12.3
Experimental Graph Showing Results within Each Condition

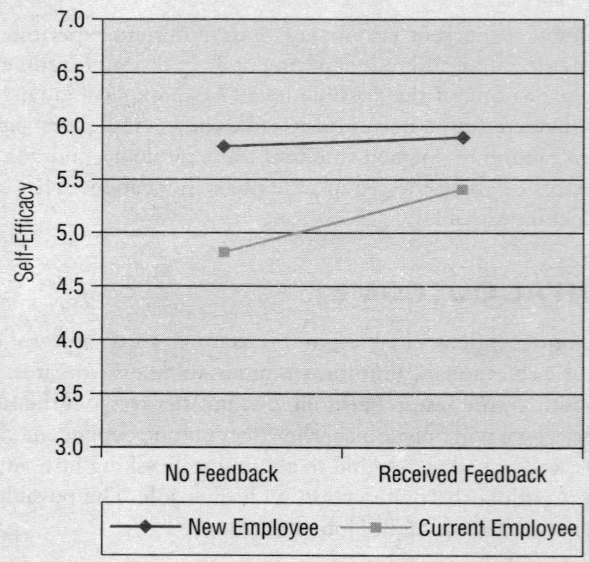

The worst situation is the current employees who do not receive positive feedback. Conversely, the best scenario regarding job satisfaction occurs when the treatment is given to new employees. It also appears that job satisfaction tends to decrease over time. The benefit of the self-efficacy treatment is greater for the employees that have been with the organization than for new employees. In other words, it appears that the self-efficacy treatment helps prevent the decline in job satisfaction.

Designing an Experiment to Minimize Experimental Error

Experimental design is a major research topic. In fact, there are courses and books devoted only to that topic.[3] Here, an introduction into experimental design is provided. A student should be able to design and implement basic experimental designs with this introduction. Fortunately, most experimental designs for business research are relatively simple.

Experimental designs involve no less than four important design elements. These issues include (1) manipulation of the independent variable(s); (2) selection and measurement of the dependent variable(s); (3) selection and assignment of experimental subjects; and (4) control over extraneous variables.[4] Each element can be implemented in a way that helps minimize error.

Manipulation of the Independent Variable

The thing that makes independent variables special in experimentation is that the researcher actually creates his or her values. This is how the researcher manipulates, and therefore controls,

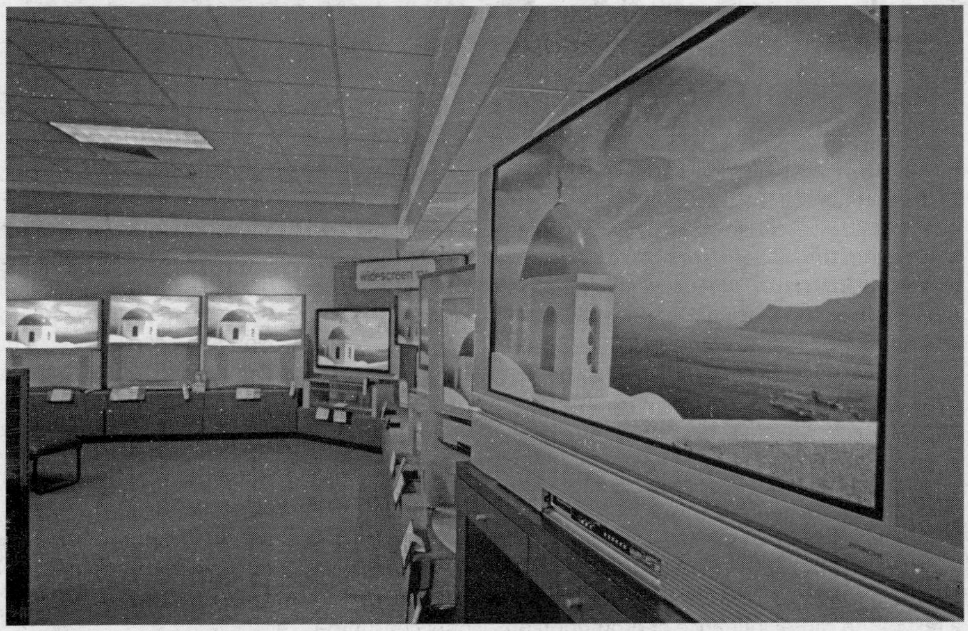

Business research involving retail stores often involves experiments that manipulate different elements of the physical environment.

independent variables. In the financial market protocol experiment, the researchers decided to test different protocols. In the self-efficacy example, the researchers chose to provide some employees with positive feedback and not give the same encouragement to others. Experimental independent variables are hypothesized to be causal influences. Therefore, experiments are very appropriate in causal designs.

An **experimental treatment** is the term referring to the way an experimental variable is manipulated. For example, the opening vignette manipulated the protocol by choosing FIX and SOAP for their test. In the self-efficacy study, the researchers had a personal interview with the employees and then had the supervisors send three encouraging letters to manipulate self-efficacy. Similarly, a medical researcher may manipulate an experimental variable by treating some subjects with one drug and the other subjects with a separate drug. Experimental variables often involve treatments with more than two levels. For instance, prices of \$1.29, \$1.69, and \$1.99 might represent treatments in a pricing experiment examining how price affects sales.

Experimental variables like these can not only be described as independent variables, but they also can be described as a *categorical variable* because they take on a value to represent some classifiable or qualitative aspect. Protocol, for example, is either FIX or SOAP. The employees either received the feedback or they did not. In other situations an independent variable may truly be a *continuous variable*. For example, the pricing experiment mentioned above could involve any price levels. The task for the researcher is to select appropriate levels of that variable as experimental treatments. For example, consumers might not perceive a difference between \$1.24 and \$1.29, but likely will notice the difference between \$1.29 and \$1.69. Before conducting the experiment, the researcher decides on levels that would be relevant to study. The levels should be noticeably different and realistic.

EXPERIMENTAL AND CONTROL GROUPS

In perhaps the simplest experiment, an independent variable is manipulated over two treatment levels resulting in two groups, an experimental group and a control group. An **experimental group** is one in which an experimental treatment is administered. A **control group** is one in which no experimental treatment is administered. In our self-efficacy example, the experimental group is comprised of the subjects that received the positive feedback. The control group did not receive the additional positive feedback designed to enhance self-efficacy. By holding conditions constant in the control group, the researcher controls for potential sources of error in the experiment. Job satisfaction (the dependent variable) in the two groups was compared at the end of the experiment to determine whether the encouragement (the independent variable) had any effect.

SEVERAL EXPERIMENTAL TREATMENT LEVELS

An experiment with one experimental and one control group may not tell a manager everything he or she wishes to know. If an advertiser wishes to understand the functional nature of the relationship between advertising and sales at several treatment levels, additional experimental groups

TOTHEPOINT

You never know what is enough unless you know what is more than enough.

—William Blake

We are neverd eceived; we deceive ourselves.

—Johann Wolfgang von Goethe

experimental treatment

The term referring to the way an experimental variable is manipulated.

experimental group

A group of subjects to whom an experimental treatment is administered.

control group

A group of subjects to whom no experimental treatment is administered.

RESEARCH SNAPSHOT

Does Promotion Cause Intoxication?

One of the most pressing issues on college campuses is over-indulgence in alcohol. What are all of the factors that lead to the abuse of alcohol among undergraduate college students? Cultural influences such as the rite of passage can be identified in qualitative research. However, when it comes to setting policies that govern the sale of alcohol on and near universities, decision makers need to know what controllable practices cause drunkenness among college students and what behaviors are caused by drunkenness.

If heavy price promotion leads to drunkenness, which leads to detrimental behaviors, bars may reconsider their use and policy makers may consider restricting the types of promotions allowable if they wish to maintain their license to sell alcoholic beverages. These questions have led to numerous experiments. For instance, the type of price promotion used by bars can be manipulated either in the field or in a lab experiment by exposing some subjects to an ad with one type of promotion and exposing others to a different type of promotion. This may allow a test of the causal influence of promotion on alcohol consumption. These studies show results like those shown in the chart titled "Mean Number of Drinks."

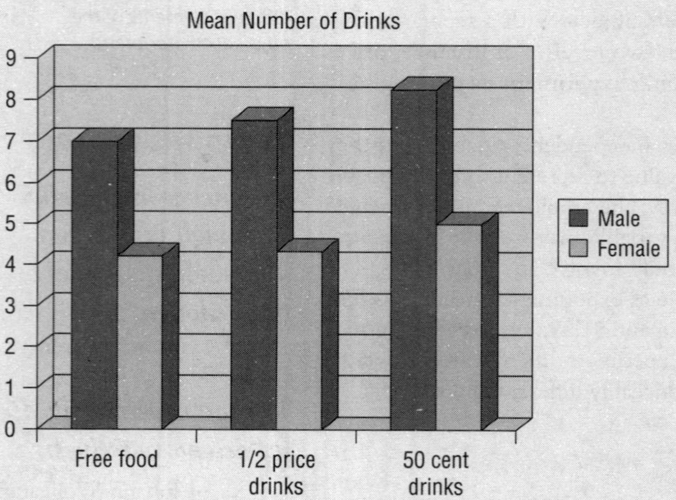

This experiment involves an experimental manipulation varying the promotion over three levels. One-third of the student-subjects were exposed to each condition. The results show that reduced price drinks do lead to an increase in the number of drinks that a student estimates he or she would drink. This effect looks to be slightly larger among men than among women, although women simply estimate they will drink less than men no matter what the experimental condition.

©JEFF GREENBERG/PHOTOEDIT

An experiment can also be used to show potentially negative results of too much drinking among college students. Researchers have designed simple experiments to examine how likely overdrinking is to lead a women to experience an unwanted sexual encounter. An experimental variable can be created that manipulates the amount of alcohol a student-subject actually consumes. This experiment can be performed in a lab environment, and one experimental condition could involve nonalcoholic drinking and another could involve heavy drinking and then asking subjects how likely they would be to consent to or actively resist unwanted sexual advances. A similar experiment showed results like those depicted in the chart titled "Reaction to Advances."

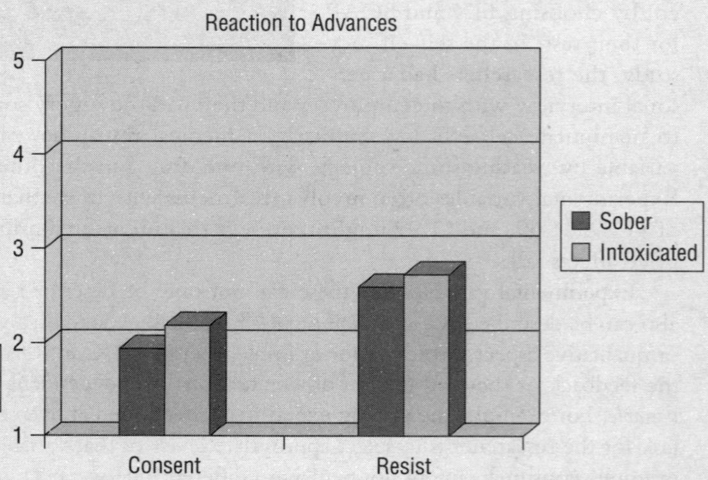

These results show that although self-reported consent is low in both cases (on a 1–5 scale with 5 indicating probable consent), it is slightly higher in the intoxicated case. There appears to be very little difference in self-reported aggressive resistance. Thus, the manipulation did not seem to affect the means on aggressive resistance. Other experiments looked at different interactions that have further implications for policy makers. Experimental manipulations like these are very helpful in implementing causal designs studying drinking related behaviors.

Sources: Christie, J., D. Fisher, J. Kozup, S. Smith, S. Burton, and E. Creyer, "The Effects of Bar-Sponsored Alcohol Beverage Promotions Across Binge and Nonbinge Drinkers," *Journal of Public Policy and Marketing* 20 (Fall 2001), 240–253; Davis, K. C., W. H. George, and J. Norris, "Women's Responses to Unwanted Sexual Advances: The Role of Alcohol and Inhibition Conflict," *Psychology of Women Quarterly* 28 (December 2004), 333–343.

© iStock

with annual advertising expenditures of \$250,000, \$500,000, \$750,000, and \$1 million might be studied. This experiment may still involve a control variable (keeping the advertising budget for a region at the current level of \$100,000). By analyzing more groups each with a different treatment level, a more precise result may be obtained than in a simple experimental group–control group experiment. This design, only manipulating the level of advertising, can produce only a main effect.

MORE THAN ONE INDEPENDENT VARIABLE

An experiment can also be made more complicated by including the effect of another experimental variable. Our extended example of the self-efficacy experiment would typify a still relatively simple two-variable experiment. Since there are two variables, each with two different levels, four experimental groups are obtained. Often, the term **cell** is used to refer to a treatment combination within an experiment. The number of cells involved in any experiment can be easily computed as follows:

cell
Refers to a specific treatment combination associated with an experimental group.

$$K = (T_1)(T_2)...(T_m)$$

where K = the number of cells, T_1 = the number of treatment levels for experimental group number one, T_2 = the number of treatment levels for experimental group number two, and so forth through the mth experimental group (T_m). In this case, since there are two variables each with two levels, the computation is quite simple:

$$K = 2 \times 2 = 4 \textit{ cells}$$

Including multiple variables allows a comparison of experimental treatments on the dependent variable. Since there are more than two experimental variables, this design involves both main effects and interactions.

REPEATED MEASURES

Experiments in which an individual subject is exposed to more than one level of an experimental treatment are referred to as **repeated measures** designs. Although this approach has advantages, including being more economical since the same subject provides more data than otherwise, it has several drawbacks that can limit its usefulness. We will discuss these in more detail later.

repeated measures
Experiments in which an individual subject is exposed to more than one level of an experimental treatment.

Selection and Measurement of the Dependent Variable

Selecting dependent variables is crucial in experimental design. Unless the dependent variables are relevant and truly represent an outcome of interest, the experiment will not be useful. Sometimes, the dependent variable is fairly obvious. In the protocol example, the speed of the data exchange is an important and logical dependent measure. Other dependent measures, such as number of errors in the data transmission, may also be of relevance. In the self-efficacy study, the researchers did consider several dependent measures in addition to job satisfaction (organizational commitment, professional commitment, intent to quit the profession, intent to quit the organization, and actual turnover). In some situations, however, clearly defining the dependent variable is not so easy. If researchers are experimenting with different forms of advertising copy appeals, defining the dependent variable may be more difficult. For example, measures of advertising awareness, recall, changes in brand preference, or sales might be possible dependent variables.

Choosing the right dependent variable is part of the problem definition process. Like the problem definition process in general, it sometimes is considered less carefully than it should be. The experimenter's choice of a dependent variable determines what type of answer is given to assist managers in decision making.

Consider how difficult one might find selecting the right dependent variable in an advertising experiment. While sales are almost certainly important, when should sales be measured? What about brand image or recognition? The amount of time needed for effects to become evident should be considered in choosing the dependent variable. Sales may be measured several months after the changes in advertising to determine if there were any carryover effects. Changes that are relatively permanent or longer lasting than changes generated only during the period of the experiment should be considered. Repeat purchase behavior may be important too, since the advertising may motivate some consumers to try a product once, but then never choose that product again. Consumers often try a "loser" once, but they do not buy a "loser" again and again.

The introduction of the original Crystal Pepsi illustrates the need to think beyond consumers' initial reactions. When Crystal Pepsi, a clear cola, was introduced, the initial trial rate was high, but only a small percentage of customers made repeat purchases. The brand never achieved high repeat sales within a sufficiently large market segment. Brand awareness, trial purchase, and repeat purchase are all possible dependent variables in an experiment. The dependent variable therefore should be considered carefully. Thorough problem definition will help the researcher select the most important dependent variable or variables.

Selection and Assignment of Test Units

test units

The subjects or entities whose responses to the experimental treatment are measured or observed.

Test units are the subjects or entities whose responses to the experimental treatment are measured or observed. Individual consumers, employees, organizational units, sales territories, market segments, or other entities may be the test units. People, whether as customers or employees, are the most common test units in most organizational behavior, human resources, and marketing experiments.

SAMPLE SELECTION AND RANDOM SAMPLING ERRORS

Although experiments are often administered in groups, if all groups are not the same, then systematic error is introduced.

As in other forms of business research, random sampling errors and sample selection errors may occur in experimentation. For example, experiments sometimes go awry even when a geographic area is specially chosen for a particular investigation. A case in point was the experimental testing of a new lubricant for outboard boat motors by Dow Chemical Company. The lubricant was tested in Florida. Florida was chosen because researchers thought the hot, muggy climate would provide the most demanding test. In Florida the lubricant was a success. However, the story was quite different when the product was sold in Michigan. Although the lubricant sold well and worked well during the summer, the following spring Dow discovered the oil had congealed, allowing the outboard motors, idle all winter, to rust. The rusting problem never came to light in Florida, where the motors were in year-round use. Thus, sample selection error occurs because of flaws in procedures used to assign experimental test units. Florida conditions made the experiment irrelevant in Michigan.

©BILL LYONS/ALAMY

©DAVIS BARBER/PHOTOEDIT

systematic or nonsampling error

Occurs if the sampling units in an experimental cell are somehow different than the units in another cell, and this difference affects the dependent variable.

Systematic or nonsampling error may occur if the sampling units in an experimental cell are somehow different than the units in another cell, and this difference affects the dependent variable. For example, suppose some professors are interested in testing the effect of providing snacks during exams on student's scores. The experimental variable is snacks, manipulated over three levels: (1) fruit, (2) cookies, and (3) chocolate. The test units in this case are individual students. When the professors conduct the experiment, for convenience, they decide to give all of the 8:00 a.m. classes chocolate for a snack, all of the 1:00 p.m. classes get fruit, and all of the 7:00 p.m. classes get cookies. While this type of procedure is often followed, if our tastes and digestive systems react differently to different foods at different times of the day, systematic error is introduced into the experiment. Furthermore, because the night classes contain students who are older on average, the professors may reach the conclusion that students perform better when they eat cookies, when it may really be due to the fact that students who are older perform better no matter what they are fed.

randomization

The random assignment of subject and treatments to groups; it is one device for equally distributing the effects of extraneous variables to all conditions.

RANDOMIZATION

nuisance variables

Items that may affect the dependent measure but are not of primary interest.

Randomization—the random assignment of subject and treatments to groups—is one device for equally distributing the effects of extraneous variables to all conditions. These **nuisance variables**, items that may affect the dependent measure but are not of primary interest, often cannot be eliminated. However, they will be controlled because they are likely to exist to the same degree in every experimental cell if subjects are randomly assigned. In our self-efficacy experiment, it is likely that some subjects are happier with their positions to start with, have greater or lesser ability, and so forth. By randomly assigning employees to the control and experimental group, all these factors should balance out. Thus, all cells would be expected to yield similar average scores on the dependent variables if it were not for the experimental treatment administered. In other words, the researcher would like to set up a situation where everything in every cell is the same except for the experimental treatment. Random assignment of subjects allows the researcher to make this assumption.

MATCHING

Random assignment of subjects to the various experimental groups is the most common technique used to prevent test units from differing from each other on key variables; it assumes that all characteristics of the subjects have been likewise randomized. Matching the respondents on the basis of pertinent background information is another technique for controlling systematic error by assigning subjects in a way that their characteristics are the same in each group. This is best thought of in terms of demographic characteristics. If a subject's sex is expected to influence dependent variable responses, as in a taste test, then the researcher may make sure that there are equal numbers of men and women in each experimental cell. In general, if a researcher believes that certain extraneous variables may affect the dependent variable, he or she can make sure that the subjects in each group are the same on these characteristics.

For example, in an experiment examining three different training programs designed to develop leadership skills, it might be important to match the subjects on the basis of sex. That way, the same number of men and women will be exposed to Program A, Program B, and Program C. While matching can be a useful approach for a handful of key factors, the researcher can never be sure that sampling units are matched on all characteristics. Here, for example, perhaps the subjects in the leadership experiment need to be matched on education, intelligence, and work experience in addition to sex. It is easy to see the increasing complexity of trying to match the subjects on these four factors. However, even if this is accomplished, the researcher can still not know about other factors, such as interest in leadership, family influences, and various personality issues. As a result, random assignment is a more common approach to balancing subject characteristics than matching.

CONTROL OVER EXTRANEOUS VARIABLES

The fourth decision about the basic elements of an experiment concerns control over extraneous variables. This is related to the various types of experimental error. In an earlier chapter, we classified total survey error into two basic categories: random sampling error and systematic error. The same dichotomy applies to all research designs, but the terms *random (sampling) error* and *systematic error* are more frequently used when discussing experiments.

EXPERIMENTAL CONFOUNDS

We have already discussed how systematic error can occur when the extraneous variables or the conditions of administering the experiment are allowed to influence the dependent variables. When this occurs, the results will be confounded because the extraneous variables have not been controlled or eliminated. A **confound** means that there is an alternative explanation beyond the experimental variables for any observed differences in the dependent variable. Once a potential confound is identified, the validity of the experiment is severely questioned.

confound

A confound means that there is an alternative explanation beyond the experimental variables for any observed differences in the dependent variable.

Recall from the opening vignette the experimental procedures involved in the protocol test. The same data was sent over the two protocols in the experiment. What if the FIX protocol was better suited to handling small files, while the SOAP protocol was better suited for large files? If only small files were tested, the experiment has a confound. The size of the file is confounding the explanation that the FIX protocol is faster for sending financial data. In fact, it may depend on the size of the data file which protocol is faster. If large data sets had been used, the results may have indicated that SOAP was the faster protocol.

In a simple experimental group–control group experiment, if subjects in the experimental group are always administered treatment in the morning and subjects in the control group always receive the treatment in the afternoon, a systematic error occurs. In such a situation, time of day represents a confound. In a training experiment the sources of constant error might be the persons who do the training (line or external specialists) or whether the training is conducted on the employees' own time or on company time. These and other characteristics of the training may have an impact on the dependent variable and will have to be taken into account:

> *The effect of a constant error is to distort the results in a particular direction, so that an erroneous difference masks the true state of affairs. The effect of a random error is not to distort the results in any particular direction, but to obscure them. Constant error is like a distorting mirror in a fun house; it produces a picture that is clear but incorrect. Random error is like a mirror that has become cloudy with age; it produces a picture that is essentially correct but unclear.*[5]

EXTRANEOUS VARIABLES

Most business students realize that the marketing mix variables—price, product, promotion, and distribution—interact with uncontrollable forces in the market, such as economic variables, competitor activities, and consumer trends. Thus, many marketing experiments are subject to the effect of **extraneous variables**. Since extraneous variables can produce confounded results, they must be identified before the experiment if at all possible.

extraneous variables
Variables that naturally exist in the environment that may have some systematic effect on the dependent variable.

One issue with significant business and public policy implications is cigarette smoking. Does cigarette advertising cause young people to smoke? Although this is an often asked question, it is far from settled. One of the primary reasons for the inconclusiveness of this debate is the failure for most of the research to control for extraneous variables.[6] For instance, consider a study in which two groups of U.S. high school students are studied over the course of a year. One is exposed to foreign television media in which American cigarettes are more often shown in a flattering and glamorous light. In fact, the programming includes cigarette commercials. The other group is a control group in which their exposure to media is not controlled. At the end of the year, the experimental group reports a greater frequency and incidence of cigarette smoking. Did the increased media exposure involving cigarettes cause smoking behavior?

While the result seems plausible at first, the careful researcher may ask the following questions:

- Was the demographic makeup of the two groups the same? While it is clear that the ages of the two groups are likely the same, it is well known that different ethnic groups have different smoking rates. Approximately 28 percent of all high school students report smoking, but the rate is higher among Hispanic teens, for example.[7] Therefore, if one group contained more Hispanics, we might expect it to report different smoking rates than otherwise. Similarly, smoking varies with social class. Were the two groups comprised of individuals from comparable social classes?
- How did the control group fill the time consumed by the experimental group in being exposed to the experimental treatment? Could it be that it somehow dissuaded them from smoking? Perhaps they were exposed to media with more anti-smoking messages?
- Were the two groups of the same general achievement profiles? Those who are high in the need for achievement may be less prone to smoke than are other students.
- Although it is a difficult task to list all possible extraneous factors, some that even sound unusual can sometimes have an effect. For example, did the students have equally dispersed birthdays? Researchers have shown that smoking rates correspond to one's birthday, meaning that different astrological groups have different smoking rates.[8]

Because an experimenter does not want extraneous variables to affect the results, he or she must eliminate or control such variables. It is always better to spend time thinking about how to control for possible extraneous variables before the experiment, since often there is nothing that can be done to salvage results if a confounding effect is identified after the experiment is conducted.

Demand Characteristics

What Are Demand Characteristics?

The term **demand characteristic** refers to an experimental design element that unintentionally provides subjects with hints about the research hypothesis. Researchers cannot reveal the research hypotheses to subjects before the experiment or else they can create a confounding effect. Think about the self-efficacy experiment. If the subjects learned that they were being intentionally given positive feedback to enhance their confidence and attitudes toward their job, the researcher would never be sure if their responses to the dependent variable were really due to the differences in the experimental stimuli or due to the fact that the subjects were trying to provide a "correct" response. Once subjects know the hypotheses, there is little hope that they will respond naturally.

demand characteristic
Experimental design element or procedure that unintentionally provides subjects with hints about the research hypothesis.

A confound may be created by knowledge of the experimental hypothesis. This particular type of confound is known as a **demand effect**. Demand characteristics make demand effects very likely.

demand effect
Occurs when demand characteristics actually affect the dependent variable.

Experimenter Bias and Demand Effects

Demand characteristics are aspects of an experiment that *demand* (encourage) that the subjects respond in a particular way. Hence, they are a source of systematic error (see Exhibit 12.4). If participants recognize the experimenter's expectation or demand, they are likely to act in a manner consistent with the experimental treatment. Even slight nonverbal cues may influence their reactions.

Prominent demand characteristics are often presented by the person administering experimental procedures. If an experimenter's presence, actions, or comments influence the subjects' behavior or sway the subjects to slant their answers to cooperate with the experimenter, the experiment has introduced *experimenter bias*. When subjects slant their answers to cooperate with the experimenter, they are exhibiting behaviors that might not represent their behavior in the marketplace. For example, if subjects in an advertising experiment understand that the experimenter is interested in whether they changed their attitudes in accord with a given advertisement, they may answer in the desired direction. Acting in this manner reflects a demand effect rather than a true experimental treatment effect.

The experimenter unintentionally can create a demand effect by smiling, nodding, or frowning at the wrong time.

EXHIBIT 12.4
By Smiling or Looking Solemn, Experimenters Can Modify Subject's Behavior

Hawthorne Effect

A famous management experiment illustrates a common demand characteristic. Researchers were attempting to study the effects on productivity of various working conditions, such as hours of work, rest periods, lighting, and methods of pay, at the Western Electric Hawthorne plant in Cicero, Illinois. The researchers found that workers' productivity increased whether the work hours were lengthened or shortened, whether lighting was very bright or very dim, and so on. The surprised investigators realized that the workers' morale was higher because they were aware of being part of a special experimental group. This totally unintended effect is now known as the **Hawthorne effect** because researchers realize that people will perform differently when they know they are experimental subjects.[9]

Hawthorne effect
People will perform differently from normal when they know they are experimental subjects.

If subjects in a laboratory experiment interact (i.e., are not relatively isolated), their conversations may produce joint decisions rather than a desired individual decision. For this reason, social interaction generally is restricted in laboratory experiments.

Reducing Demand Characteristics

Although it is practically impossible to eliminate demand characteristics from experiments, there are steps that can be taken to reduce them. Many of these steps make it difficult for subjects to know what the researcher is trying to find out. Some or all of these may be appropriate in a given experiment.

1. Use an experimental disguise.
2. Isolate experimental subjects.
3. Use a "blind" experimental administrator.
4. Administer only one experimental treatment level to each subject.

EXPERIMENTAL DISGUISE

Subjects participating in the experiment can be told that the purpose of the experiment is somewhat different than the actual purpose. Most often, they are simply told less than the complete "truth" about what is going to happen. In other cases, more deceit may be needed. For example, psychologists studying how much pain one person may be willing to inflict on another might use a ruse telling the subject that they are actually interested in the effect of pain on human performance. The researcher tells the subject to administer a series of questions to another person (who is actually a research assistant) and to provide them with an increasingly strong electric shock each time an incorrect answer is given. In reality, the real dependent variable has something to do with how long the actual subject will continue to administer shocks before stopping.

A **placebo** is an experimental deception involving a false treatment. A **placebo effect** refers to the corresponding effect in a dependent variable that is due to the psychological impact that goes along with knowledge of the treatment. A placebo is particularly important when the experimental variable involves physical consumption of some product. The placebo should not be different in any observable manner from the true treatment that is actually noticeable by the research subject. Assume a researcher is examining the ability of a special food additive to suppress appetite. The additive is a product that is supposed to be sprinkled on food before it is eaten. The experimental group would be given the actual product to test, while the control group would be given a placebo that looks exactly like the actual food additive but is actually an inert compound. Both groups are likely to show some difference in consumption compared to someone undergoing no effect. The difference in the actual experimental group and the placebo group would represent the true effect of the additive.

placebo

A false experimental condition aimed at creating the impression of an effect.

placebo effect

The effect in a dependent variable associated with the psychological impact that goes along with knowledge of some treatment being administered.

Placebo effects exist in marketing research. For example, when subjects are told that an energy drink is sold at a discount price, they believe it is significantly less effective than when it is sold at the regular, non-discounted price.[10] Later, we will return to the ethical issues involved in experimental deception.

ISOLATE EXPERIMENTAL SUBJECTS

Researchers should minimize the extent to which subjects are able to talk about the experimental procedures with each other. Although it may be unintentional, discussion among subjects may lead them to guess the experimental hypotheses. For instance, it could be that different subjects received different treatments, which the subjects could discover if they talked to one another. The experimental integrity will be higher when each subject only knows enough to participate in the experiment.

USE A "BLIND" EXPERIMENTAL ADMINISTRATOR

When possible, the people actually administering the experiment may not be told the experimental hypotheses. The advantage is that if they do not know what exactly is being studied, then they are less likely to give off clues that result in demand effects. Like the subjects, when there is some reason to expect that their knowledge may constitute a demand characteristic, administrators best know only enough to do their job.

ADMINISTER ONLY ONE EXPERIMENTAL CONDITION PER SUBJECT

When subjects know more than one experimental treatment condition, they are much more likely to guess the experimental hypothesis. So, even though there are cost advantages to administering multiple treatment levels to the same subject, it should be avoided when possible. For example, in the self-efficacy experiment, if the subjects were asked to complete a questionnaire regarding their self-confidence in doing their job and their job satisfaction, then again asked to respond to the same questions after the personal interview, and then again after each of the three letters giving them positive feedback, they are very likely to guess that they are intentionally being given the feedback to enhance their self-efficacy.

Establishing Control

The major difference between experimental research and descriptive research is an experimenter's ability to control variables by either holding conditions constant or manipulating the experimental variable. If the color of beer causes preference, a brewery experimenting with a new clear beer must determine the possible extraneous variables other than color that may affect an experiment's results and attempt to eliminate or control those variables. Marketing theory tell us that brand image and packaging design are important factors in beer drinkers' reactions. Therefore, the researcher may wish to control the influence of these variables. He or she may eliminate these two extraneous variables by packaging the test beers in plain brown packages without any brand identification.

constancy of conditions

Means that subjects in all experimental groups are exposed to identical conditions except for the differing experimental treatments.

When extraneous variables cannot be eliminated, experimenters may strive for **constancy of conditions**. This means that subjects in all experimental groups are exposed to identical conditions except for the differing experimental treatments. Random assignment and the principle of matching discussed earlier help make sure that constancy is achieved.

A supermarket experiment involving shelf space shows the care that must be taken to hold all factors constant. The experiment required that all factors other than shelf space be kept constant throughout the testing period. In all stores, the shelf level that had existed before the test began was to be maintained throughout the test period. Only the *amount* of shelf space (the treatment) was changed. One problem involved store personnel accidentally changing shelf level when stocking the test products. This deviation from the constancy of conditions was minimized by auditing each store four times a week. In this way, any change could be detected in a minimum amount of time. The experimenter personally stocked as many of the products as possible, and the cooperation of stock clerks also helped reduce treatment deviations.

If an experimental method requires that the same subjects be exposed to two or more experimental treatments, an error may occur due to the *order of presentation*. For instance, if subjects are examining the effects of different levels of graphical interface on video game enjoyment, and they are asked to view each of four different levels, the order in which they are presented may influence enjoyment. Subjects might prefer one level simply because it follows a very poor level.

counterbalancing

Attempts to eliminate the confounding effects of order of presentation by requiring that one-fourth of the subjects be exposed to treatment A first, one-fourth to treatment B first, one-fourth to treatment C first, and finally one-fourth to treatment D first.

Counterbalancing attempts to eliminate the confounding effects of order of presentation by requiring that one-fourth of the subjects be exposed to treatment A first, one-fourth to treatment B first, one-fourth to treatment C first, and finally one-fourth to treatment D first. Likewise, the other levels are counterbalanced so that the order of presentation is rotated among subjects. It is easy to see where counterbalancing is particularly important for experiments such as taste tests, where the order of presentation may have significant effects on consumer preference.

Problems Controlling Extraneous Variables

In many experiments it is not always possible to control every potential extraneous variable. For example, competitors may bring out a product during the course of a test-market. This form of competitive interference occurred in a Boston test-market for Anheuser-Busch's import beer, Wurzburger Hofbrau. During the test, Miller Brewing Company introduced its own brand, Munich Oktoberfest, and sent eight salespeople out to blitz the Boston market. A competitor who learns of a test-market experiment may knowingly change its prices or increase advertising to confound the test results. This brings us to ethical issues in experimentation.

Ethical Issues in Experimentation

Ethical issues with business research were discussed in Chapter 5. There, the question of deception was raised. Although deception is necessary in most experiments, when subjects can be returned to their prior condition through debriefing, then the experiment is probably consistent with high moral standards. If subjects might be injured significantly or truly psychologically harmed, debriefing will not return them to their formal condition and the experiment should not be undertaken. Therefore, some additional commentary on debriefing is warranted.

Debriefing experimental subjects by communicating the purpose of the experiment and the researcher's hypotheses is expected to counteract negative effects of deception, relieve stress, and provide an educational experience for the subject.

> *Proper debriefing allows the subject to save face by uncovering the truth for himself. The experimenter should begin by asking the subject if he has any questions or if he found any part of the experiment odd, confusing, or disturbing. This question provides a check on the subject's suspiciousness and effectiveness of*

manipulations. The experimenter continues to provide the subject cues to the deception until the subject states that he believes there was more to the experiment than met the eye. At this time the purpose and procedure of the experiment [are] revealed.[11]

Additionally, there is the issue of test-markets and efforts extended toward interfering with a competitor's test-market. The Research Snapshot dealing with Hidden Valley Ranch salad dressings describes just such a situation. When a company puts a product out for public consumption, they should be aware that competitors may also now freely consume the product. When attempts to interfere with a test-market are aimed solely at invalidating test results or they are aimed at infringing on some copyright protection, those acts are ethically questionable.

Practical Experimental Design Issues

Basic versus Factorial Experimental Designs

In *basic experimental designs* a single independent variable is manipulated to observe its effect on a single dependent variable. Our example of the computer communication protocols falls into this category—one independent variable (the two protocols) was examined and one dependent measure (speed of the data transfer) was assessed. However, we know that most business situations are much more complex and multiple independent and dependent variables are possible. Our self-efficacy experiment illustrated this as both the treatment and the length of time as an employee were independent variables and multiple dependent variables were examined. In a complex marketing experiment, multiple dependent variables such as sales, product usage, and preference are influenced by several factors. The simultaneous change in independent variables such as price and advertising may have a greater influence on sales than if either variable is changed alone. In job satisfaction studies, we know that no one thing totally determines job satisfaction. Salary, opportunities for advancement, the pleasantness of the workplace, interactions with colleagues, and many more factors all combine and interact to determine how satisfied employees are with their job. *Factorial experimental designs* are more sophisticated than basic experimental designs and allow for an investigation of the interaction of two or more independent variables.

Laboratory Experiments

A business experiment can be conducted in a natural setting (a field experiment) or in an artificial setting (a laboratory experiment). In social sciences, the actual laboratory may be a behavioral lab, which is somewhat like a focus group facility. However, it may simply be a room or classroom dedicated to collecting data, or it can even take place in one's home.

In a **laboratory experiment** the researcher has more complete control over the research setting and extraneous variables. Our example of the financial protocol experiment illustrates the benefits of a laboratory setting. The researchers were able to control for many factors, such as the size of the data file, the models of the computers, the Internet line, and so forth. This enhanced their confidence in establishing that the differences noted in speed were due to the different protocols. However, the researchers were not able to determine how the protocols compared when used in the field, on various computers, with a variety of file sizes, and under differing "real-world" circumstances.

laboratory experiment
The researcher has more complete control over the research setting and extraneous variables.

In testing the effectiveness of a television commercial, subjects can be recruited and brought to an advertising agency's office, a research agency's office, or perhaps a mobile unit designed for research purposes. They are exposed to a television commercial within the context of a program that includes competitors' ads among the commercials shown. As compensation for their time, they are then allowed to purchase either the advertised product or one of several competing products in a simulated store environment. Trial purchase measures are thus obtained. A few weeks later, subjects are contacted again to measure their satisfaction and determine repeat purchasing intention.

This laboratory experiment gives the consumer an opportunity to "buy" and "invest." In a short time span, the marketer is able to collect information on decision making. In this example, many of the outside influences can be controlled.

Other laboratory experiments may be more controlled or artificial. For example, a **tachistoscope** allows a researcher to experiment with the visual impact of advertising, packaging, and so on by controlling the amount of time a subject is exposed to a visual image. Each stimulus (for example, package design) is projected from a slide to the tachistoscope at varying exposure lengths (1/10 of a second, 2/10, 3/10, and so on). The tachistoscope simulates the split-second duration of a customer's attention to a package in a mass display.

Field Experiments

Facilities like this one can break down the food that companies sell and tell them exactly what it should taste like. Is this a good way to test the taste of new products?

Field experiments are research projects involving experimental manipulations that are implemented in a natural environment. They can be useful in fine-tuning managerial strategies and tactical decisions. Our self-efficacy study is an example of a field experiment. Rather than bring subjects into an artificial setting and trying to manipulate their self-efficacy and then measure their perceptions of job satisfaction, the researchers took their experiment to the field and used actual employees, which were provided feedback from their supervisors. In the marketing discipline, test-markets are good examples of field experiments. Betty Crocker's Squeezit (a 10 percent fruit juice drink in a squeeze bottle) was so successful in a test-market that production could not keep up with demand. As a result, the product's national introduction was postponed until production capacity could be increased.

tachistoscope
Device that controls the amount of time a subject is exposed to a visual image.

field experiments
Research projects involving experimental manipulations that are implemented in a natural environment.

McDonald's conducted a field experiment testing the Triple Ripple, a three-flavor ice cream product. The product was dropped because the experiment revealed distribution problems reduced product quality and limited customer acceptance. In the distribution system the product would freeze, defrost, and refreeze. Solving the problem would have required each McDonald's city to have a local ice cream plant with special equipment to roll the three flavors into one. While a laboratory experiment might have shown tremendous interest, a naturalistic setting for the experiment helped McDonald's executives realize the product was impractical.

The naturally occurring noise that exists in the field can interfere with experimental manipulations.

Experiments vary in their degree of artificiality and control. Exhibit 12.5 shows that as experiments increase in naturalism, they begin to approach a pure field experiment. As they become more artificial, they approach a pure laboratory experiment.

©MIKE MCQUEEN/CORBIS

In field experiments, a researcher manipulates experimental variables but cannot possibly control all the extraneous variables. An example is NBC's research on new television programs. Viewers who subscribe to a cable television service are asked to watch a cable preview on their home television sets at a certain time on a certain cable channel. While the program is being aired, telephone calls from the viewers' friends cannot be controlled. In contrast, an advertising professor may test some advertising effect by showing subjects advertising in a classroom setting. Here, there are no phone calls and little to distract the subject. Which produces a better experiment?

RESEARCH SNAPSHOT

The Hidden in Hidden Valley Ranch

A few years ago, Hidden Valley Ranch (HVR) conducted a field market experiment to examine how effective three new flavors of salad dressings would be in the marketplace. Thus, there were three levels of the experimental variable, each representing a different flavor. Tests like this can be costly. HVR had to produce small batches of each flavor, get them bottled, and ship them to their sales representatives, who then had to stock the dressings in the participating retail stores. All of this is very expensive.

The first day of the test was consumed with sales reps placing the products in the salad dressing sections of retail stores. The second day, each rep went back to each store to record the number of sales for each flavor. By the third day, all of the bottles of all flavors had sold! Amazing! Was every flavor a huge success? Actually, one of HVR's competitors had noticed the test and sent its sales reps around beginning on the second day to buy every bottle of the new HVR dressings in every store it had been placed in. Thus, HVR was unable to produce any valid sales data (the dependent variable) and the competitor was able to break down the dressing in its labs and determine the recipe.

This illustrates one risk that comes along with field tests. Once a product is available for sale, there are no secrets. Also, you risk espionage of this type that can render the experiment invalid.

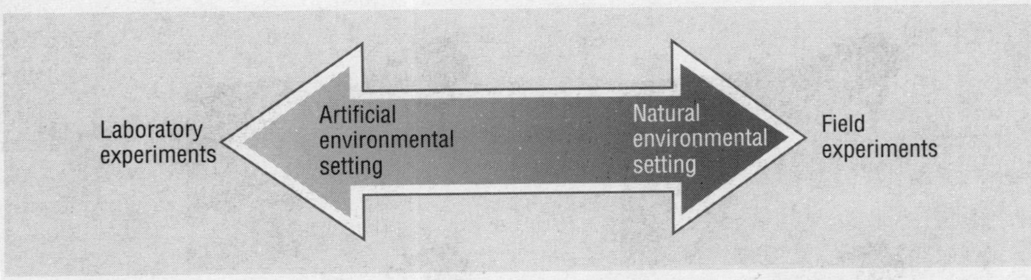

EXHIBIT 12.5
The Artificiality of Laboratory versus Field Experiments

Generally, subjects know when they are participating in a laboratory experiment. Performance of certain tasks, responses to questions, or some other form of active involvement is characteristic of laboratory experiments. In field experiments, such as test-markets or the self-efficacy experiment, subjects do not even know they are taking part in an experiment. Ethically, consent should be sought before having someone participate in an experiment. However, with field experiments the consent is implied since subjects are not asked to do anything departing from their normal behavior to participate in the experiment. All precautions with respect to safety and confidentiality should be maintained.

Field experiments involving new products or promotions are often conducted in a retail store. These are known as controlled store tests. The products are put into stores in a number of small cities or into selected supermarket chains. Product deliveries are made not through the traditional warehouse but by the research agency, so product information remains confidential. The Research Snapshot "The Hidden in Hidden Valley Ranch" describes such a test. While they can be less expensive than a full-blown market test, they also have drawbacks because of the relatively small sample of stores and the limitations on the type of outlet where the product is tested. Thus, their results may not generalize to all consumers in a population.

Experiments Conducted in Laboratory and Infield

Experiments can be conducted in laboratory as well as in the field. Experiments conducted in laboratory are done in a simulated environment. Simulated environment is created by the researchers to suit their research questions and the hypothesis they form. Such environments are created to conduct a specific experiment. Field experiments, on the other hand, are conducted in actual market scenario. For example, effectiveness of a commercial can be tested through an experiment in laboratory setting.[12] Purchase intention of the respondents for a particular product is measured before exposing them to the commercial. Then they are exposed to the commercial inside a laboratory under control condition. Purchase intention is again measured after they have watched the commercial. Data is then analyzed to see if there is significant difference in purchase intention after seeing the commercial. On the other hand, if the same experiment is conducted through a panel of respondents at their home during the time they watch television, and similar way the purchase intention is measured, then we can say that experiment is conducted in field environment.

Both types of experiments—field and laboratory—have their own advantages and disadvantages. Library environment are controlled and the experiments are conducted inside a well monitored environmental setting by the researcher. Hence, extraneous variable like history can be minimized to a great extent. Since repeated experiment conducted in a laboratory setting may give more or less the same result, it has high internal validity, however, it lacks on generalizability or the external validity of experiment. Since laboratory experiments are conducted in a controlled atmosphere they are often unrealistic in actual scenario, for instance in the above example the viewer may have several disturbances and engagements when they watch TV. Their measurement of purchase intention may be exaggerated if the experiment is conducted in a laboratory setting. Similarly, a field experiment has very high external validity, however, has very low internal validity.

EXHIBIT 12.6
Within- and Between-Subjects Designs

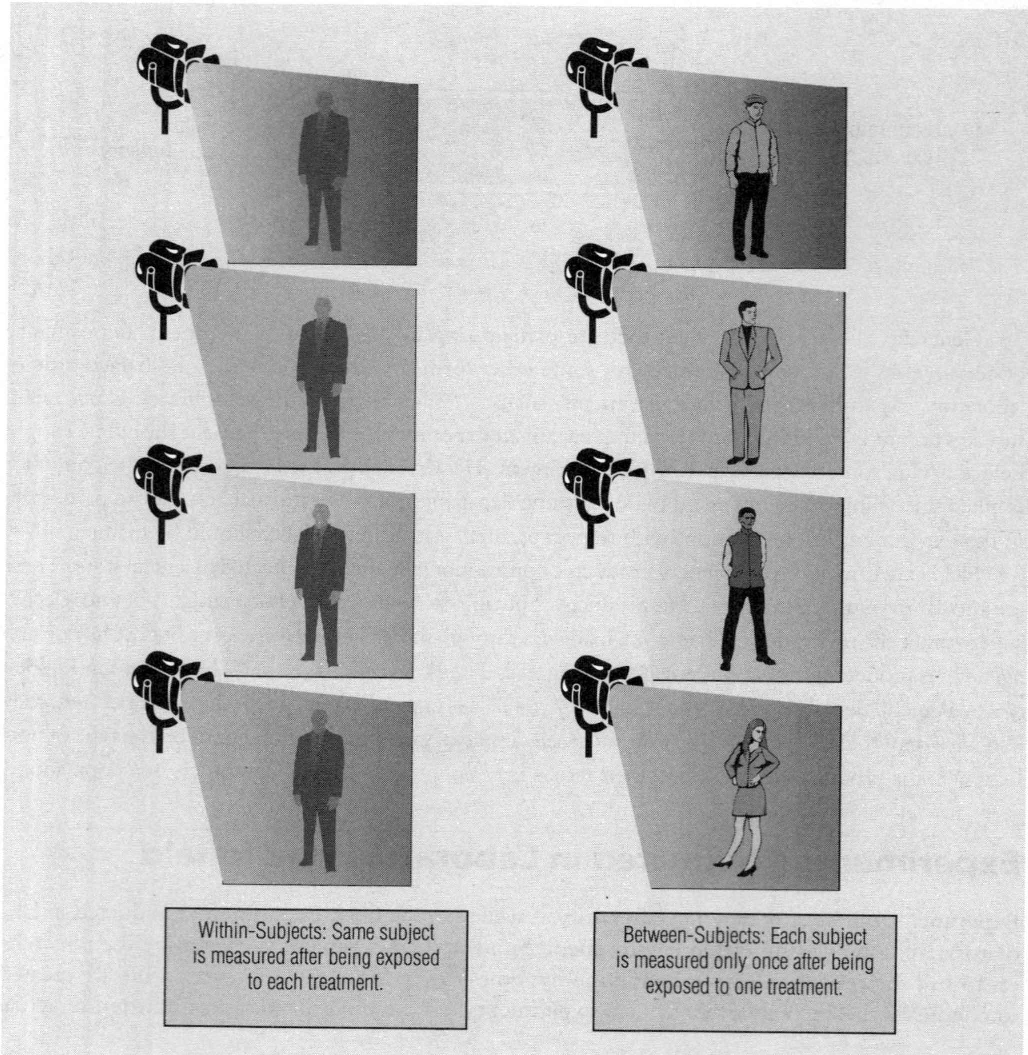

Within-Subjects and Between-Subjects Designs

A basic question faced by the researchers involves how many treatments a subject should receive. For economical reasons, the researcher may wish to apply multiple treatments to the same subject. Thus, multiple observations on the dependent variable can be obtained from a single subject. Such a design is called a **within-subjects design**. Within-subjects designs involve repeated measures because with each treatment the same subject is measured.

within-subjects design

Involves repeated measures because with each treatment the same subject is measured.

In contrast, the researcher could decide that each person will receive only one treatment combination. This is referred to as a **between-subjects design**. Each dependent variable is measured only once for every subject. Exhibit 12.6 illustrates this point.

between-subjects design

Each subject receives only one treatment combination.

Between-subjects designs are usually advantageous even though they are typically more costly. The validity of between-subjects designs is usually higher since applying only one treatment combination to each subject greatly reduces the possibility of demand characteristics. In addition, as we will see later, statistical analysis of between-subjects designs are simpler than within-subjects designs. This also means the results are easier to report and explain to management.

Issues of Experimental Validity

An experiment's quality is judged by two types of validity. These are known as internal and external validity.

Internal Validity

Internal validity exists to the extent that an experimental variable is truly responsible for any variance in the dependent variable. In other words, does the experimental manipulation truly cause changes in the specific outcome of interest? If the observed results were influenced or confounded by extraneous factors, the researcher will have problems making valid conclusions about the relationship between the experimental treatment and the dependent variable.

internal validity

Exists to the extent that an experimental variable is truly responsible for any variance in the dependent variable.

Thus, a lab experiment enhances internal validity because it maximizes control of outside forces. If we wish to know whether certain music causes increased productivity among workers, we may set up a task in a room with different music piped in (our experimental manipulation), but with the temperature, lighting, density, other sounds, and any other factors all controlled, which would be difficult or impossible to control outside of a lab environment. If the only thing that varies from subject to subject is the music, then we can safely say that any differences in performance must be attributable to human reactions to the music. Our opening example of the protocol experiment focused on maximizing internal validity. By testing the protocols in a lab setting, the researchers were able to control extraneous variables such as differences in computing hardware, network issues, and so forth.

MANIPULATION CHECKS

Internal validity depends in large part on successful manipulations. Manipulations should be carried out in a way that the independent variable differs over meaningful levels. If the levels are too close together, the experiment may lack the power necessary to observe differences in the dependent variable. In a pricing experiment, it may be that manipulating the price of an automobile over two levels, \$24,600 and \$24,800, would not be successful in creating truly different price categories. Respondents might not perceive the differences or experience any reaction to such a slight deviation.

The validity of manipulations can often be determined with a **manipulation check**. If a drug is administered in different dosages that should affect blood sugar levels, the researcher could actually measure blood sugar level after administering the drug to make sure that the dosages were different enough to produce a change in blood sugar. In business research, the manipulation check is often conducted by asking a survey question or two. In the pricing example above, subjects may be asked a question about how low they believe the price of the car to be. A valid manipulation

manipulation check

A validity test of an experimental manipulation to make sure that the manipulation does produce differences in the independent variable.

would produce substantially different average responses to that question in a "high" and "low" price group. In our self-efficacy example, the researchers were interested in the impact increased self-efficacy (the independent variables) had on job satisfaction (the dependent variable). The experimental manipulation was the positive feedback the subjects were given. The manipulation check was a series of questions assessing the subject's self-efficacy. Did the positive feedback actually increase self-efficacy? If it did, then the researchers could examine the other relationships of interest. However, if self-efficacy did not increase, then the researchers would have to reconsider their manipulation and find another way to enhance self-efficacy to carry out the study. Manipulation checks should always be administered after dependent variables in self-response format experiments. This keeps the manipulation check item from becoming a troublesome demand characteristic.

Extraneous variables can jeopardize internal validity. The six major ones are *history, maturation, testing, instrumentation, selection,* and *mortality*.

HISTORY

history effect

Occurs when some change other than the experimental treatment occurs during the course of an experiment that affects the dependent variable.

A **history effect** occurs when some change other than the experimental treatment occurs during the course of an experiment that affects the dependent variable. A common history effect occurs when competitors change their marketing strategies during a test marketing experiment. Another example would be if some of our subjects in the self-efficacy exam are offered a position by another firm. A different job offer may affect several of the dependent measures in the study. History effects are particularly prevalent in repeated measures experiments that take place over an extended time. If we wanted to assess how much a change in recipe improves individual subjects' consumption of a food product, we would first measure their consumption and then compare it with consumption after the change. Since several weeks may pass between the first and second measurement, there are many things that could occur that would also influence subjects' diets.

Although it would be extreme, examining the effect of a dietary supplement on various health-related outcomes may require that a subject be confined during the experiment's course. This may take several weeks. Without confining the subject in something like a hospital setting, there would be little way of controlling food and drink consumption, exercise activities, and other factors that may also affect the dependent variables.

cohort effect

Refers to a change in the dependent variable that occurs because members of one experimental group experienced different historical situations than members of other experimental groups.

A special case of the history effect is the **cohort effect**, which refers to a change in the dependent variable that occurs because members of one experimental group experienced different historical situations than members of other experimental groups. For example, groups of managers used as subjects may be in different cohorts because one group encountered different experiences over the course of an experiment. Let's assume the experimental manipulation involves different levels of financial incentives and performance is the dependent variable. The experiment is being conducted in waves; as the managers come to the home office for training they are told about the financial incentives that are being implemented. During this period, however, a financial crisis occurs. Since the first group participated prior to this development, they would not be affected by it. However, subsequent groups might have different attitudes and increased performance due to the environmental change. The possibility exists that the financial crisis rather than the change in incentive is truly causing differences in performance.

MATURATION

maturation effects

Effects that are a function of time and the naturally occurring events that coincide with growth and experience.

Maturation effects are effects that are a function of time and the naturally occurring events that coincide with growth and experience. Experiments taking place over longer time spans may see lower internal validity as subjects simply grow older or more experienced. For example, our self-efficacy study shows that job satisfaction seems to decline with time (note in Figure 12.2 that the control group subjects that are new employees report a mean of 5.80 while the current employees mean is 4.77). Conversely, job skill tends to increase over time. Suppose an experiment were designed to test the impact of a new compensation program on sales productivity. If this program were tested over a year's time, some of the salespeople probably would mature as a result of more selling experience and gain increased knowledge and skill. Their sales productivity might improve because of their knowledge and experience rather than the compensation program.

TESTING

Testing effects are also called *pretesting effects* because the initial measurement or test alerts or primes subjects in a way that affects their response to the experimental treatments. Testing effects only occur in a before-and-after study. A before-and-after study is one requiring an initial baseline measure be taken before an experimental treatment is administered. So, before-and-after experiments are a special case of a repeated measures design. For example, students taking standardized achievement and intelligence tests for the second time usually do better than those taking the tests for the first time. The effect of testing may increase awareness of socially appropriate answers, increase attention to experimental conditions (that is, the subject may watch more closely), or make the subject more conscious than usual of the dimensions of a problem.

testing effects
A nuisance effect occurring when the initial measurement or test alerts or primes subjects in a way that affects their response to the experimental treatments.

INSTRUMENTATION

A change in the wording of questions, a change in interviewers, or a change in other procedures used to measure the dependent variable causes an **instrumentation effect**, which may jeopardize internal validity. Sometimes instrumentation effects are difficult to control. For example, if the same interviewers are used to ask questions for both before and after measurement, some problems may arise. With practice, interviewers may acquire increased skill in interviewing, or they may become bored and decide to reword the questionnaire in their own terms. To avoid this problem, new interviewers could be hired. But this introduces another set of issues as different individuals are also a source of extraneous variation. There are numerous other sources of instrument decay or variation. Again, instrumentation effects are problematic with any type of repeated measures design.

instrumentation effect
A nuisance that occurs when a change in the wording of questions, a change in interviewers, or a change in other procedures causes a change in the dependent variable.

SELECTION

The **selection effect** is a sample bias that results from differential selection of respondents for the comparison groups, or sample selection error, discussed earlier. Researchers must make sure the characteristics of the research subjects accurately reflect the population of relevance. Furthermore, the key characteristics of the subjects must be distributed in such a way to create equal groups. That is, the subjects in the experimental and control groups, or in different experimental cells, must be equal across all variables of interest and those that could affect the dependent measure.

selection effect
Sample bias from differential selection of respondents for experimental groups.

MORTALITY

If an experiment is conducted over a period of a few weeks or more, some sample bias may occur due to the **mortality effect (sample attrition)**. Sample attrition occurs when some subjects withdraw from the experiment before it is completed. Mortality effects may occur if subjects drop from one experimental treatment group disproportionately than from other groups. Consider a sales training experiment investigating the effects of close supervision of salespeople (high pressure) versus low supervision (low pressure). The high-pressure condition may misleadingly appear superior if those subjects who completed the experiment did very well. If, however, the high-pressure condition caused more subjects to drop out than the other conditions, this apparent superiority may be due to the fact that only very determined and/or talented salespeople stuck with the program. Similarly, in the self-efficacy study, accountants that did not feel commitment to the organization and maintain a high level of job satisfaction may have left the organization before the final measures.

mortality effect (sample attrition)
Occurs when some subjects withdraw from the experiment before it is completed.

External Validity

external validity
Is the accuracy with which experimental results can be generalized beyond the experimental subjects.

External validity is the accuracy with which experimental results can be generalized beyond the experimental subjects. External validity is increased when the subjects comprising the sample truly represent the population of interest and when the results extend to other market segments or groups of people. The higher the external validity, the more researchers and managers can count on the fact that any results observed in an experiment will also be seen in the "real world" (financial market, workplace, sales floor, and so on).

For instance, to what extent would results from our protocol experiment, which represents a simulated financial market data exchange, transfer to a real-world trading situation? Would the FIX protocol prove to be faster across computer systems, Internet line transfer speeds, and different traders? Would increases in self-efficacy enhance the job satisfaction of retail store workers, salespeople, or human resource managers as it did for accountants? Can one extrapolate the results from a tachistoscope to an in-store shopping situation? Lab experiments, such as the protocol experiment, are associated with low external validity because the limited set of experimental conditions, holding all else constant, do not adequately represent all the influences existing in the real world. In other words, the experimental situation may be too artificial. When a study lacks external validity, the researcher will have difficulty repeating the experiment with any change in subjects, settings, or time.

STUDENT SUBJECTS

Basic researchers often use college students as experimental subjects.[13] Convenience, time, money, and a host of other practical considerations often result in students being used as research subjects. This practice is widespread in academic studies. Some evidence shows that students are quite similar to household consumers, but other evidence indicates that they do not provide sufficient external validity to represent most consumer or employee groups. This is particularly true when students are used as substitutes or surrogates for businesspeople.

The issue of external validity should be seriously considered because the student population is likely to be atypical. Students are easily accessible, but they often are not representative of the total population. This is not always the case, however, and when behaviors are studied for which students have some particular expertise (the purchase of relevant products such as MP3 players or job search skills), then they are certainly appropriate. For instance, the Research Snapshot "Does Promotion Cause Intoxication?" is an example where students are very appropriate research subjects.

Trade-Offs Between Internal and External Validity

Naturalistic field experiments tend to have greater external validity than artificial laboratory experiments. Researchers often must trade internal validity for external validity. A researcher who wishes to test advertising effectiveness by manipulating treatments via a split-cable experiment has the assurance that the advertisement will be viewed in an externally valid situation, the subjects' homes. However, the researcher has no assurance that some interruption (for example, the telephone ringing, a child calling, or a pot boiling over on the stove) will not have some influence that will reduce the internal validity of the experiment. Laboratory experiments with many controlled factors usually are high in internal validity, while field experiments generally have less internal validity but greater external validity. Typically, it is best to establish internal validity first, and then focus on external validity. Thus, results from lab experiments would be followed up with some type of field test.

Classification of Experimental Designs

An experimental design may be compared to an architect's plans for a building. The basic requirements for the structure are given to the architect by the prospective owner. Several different plans may be drawn up as options for meeting the basic requirements. Some may be more costly than others. One may offer potential advantages that another does not.

There are various types of experimental designs. If only one variable is manipulated, the experiment has a **basic experimental design**. If the experimenter wishes to investigate several levels of the independent variable (for example, four different employee salary levels) or to investigate the interaction effects of two or more independent variables (salary level and retirement package), the experiment requires a *complex*, or *statistical*, experimental design.

basic experimental design
An experimental design in which only one variable is manipulated.

Symbolism for Diagramming Experimental Designs

The work of Campbell and Stanley has helped many students master the subject of basic experimental designs.[14] The following symbols will be used in describing the various experimental designs:

X = *exposure of a group to an experimental treatment*

O = *observation or measurement of the dependent variable; if more than one observation or measurement is taken, subscripts (that is,* O_1, O_2, *etc.) indicate temporal order*

R = *random assignment of test units; R symbolizes that individuals selected as subjects for the experiment are randomly assigned to the experimental groups*

The diagrams of experimental designs that follow assume a time flow from left to right. Our first example will make this clearer.

Three Examples of Quasi-Experimental Designs

Quasi-experimental designs do not involve random allocation of subjects to treatment combinations. In this sense, they do not qualify as true experimental designs because they do not adequately control for the problems associated with loss of internal validity. However, sometimes quasi-experimental designs are the only way to implement a study.

quasi-experimental designs
Experimental designs that do not involve random allocation of subjects to treatment combinations.

ONE-SHOT DESIGN

The one-shot design, or *after-only design*, is diagrammed as follows:

$$X \quad O_1$$

Suppose that during a very cold winter an automobile dealer finds herself with a large inventory of cars. She decides to experiment for the month of January with a promotional scheme. She offers a free trip to New Orleans with every car sold. She experiments with the promotion (X = experimental treatment) and measures sales (O_1 = measurement of sales after the treatment is administered).

This one-shot design is a case study of a research project fraught with problems. Subjects or test units participate because of voluntary self-selection or arbitrary assignment, not because of random assignment. The study lacks any kind of comparison or any means of controlling extraneous influences. There should be a measure of what will happen when the test units have not been exposed to X to compare with the measures of when subjects have been exposed to X. The one-shot experimental design commonly suffers from most of the threats to internal validity discussed above. Nevertheless, under certain circumstances, it is the only viable choice.

ONE-GROUP PRETEST–POSTTEST DESIGN

Suppose a real estate franchiser wishes to provide a training program for franchisees. If the franchiser measures subjects' knowledge of real estate selling before (O_1) they are exposed to the experimental treatment (X) and then measures real estate selling knowledge after (O_2) they are exposed to the treatment, the design will be as follows:

$$O_1 \quad X \quad O_2$$

In this example the trainer is likely to conclude that the difference between O_2 and O_1 ($O_2 - O_1$) is the measure of the influence of the experimental treatment. This one-group pretest–posttest design offers a comparison of the same individuals before and after training. Although this is an improvement over the one-shot design, this research still has several weaknesses that may jeopardize internal validity. For example, if the time lapse between O_1 and O_2 was a period of several months, the trainees may have matured as a result of experience on the job (maturation effect). History effects—such as a change in interest rates—may also influence the dependent measure in this design. Perhaps some subjects dropped out of the training program (mortality effect). The effect of testing may also have confounded the experiment.

Although this design has a number of weaknesses, it is commonly used in business research. Remember, the cost of the research is a consideration in most business situations. While there will be some problems of internal validity, the researcher must always take into account questions of time and cost.

STATIC GROUP DESIGN

In a static group design, each subject is identified as a member of either an experimental group or a control group (for example, exposed or not exposed to a training program). The experimental group is measured after being exposed to an experimental treatment and the control group is measured without having been exposed to this experimental treatment:

Experimental group:	X	O_1
Control group:		O_2

The results of the static group design are computed by subtracting the observed results in the control group from those in the experimental group ($O_1 - O_2$). A major weakness of this design is its lack of assurance that the groups were equal on variables of interest before the experimental group received the treatment. If entry into either group was voluntary, systematic differences between the groups could invalidate the conclusions about the effect of the treatment. For example, if the real estate franchisor mentioned above asked her franchisees who would like to attend the training program, we have no way of knowing if those who chose to attend are the same as those who did not. Random assignment of subjects may eliminate problems with group differences. If groups are established by the experimenter rather than existing as a function of some other causation, the static group design is referred to as an *after-only design with control group*.

On many occasions, an after-only design is the only possible option. This is particularly true when conducting use tests for new products or brands. Cautious interpretation and recognition of the design's shortcomings may enhance the value of this design.

Three Alternative Experimental Designs

In a formal scientific sense, the three designs just discussed are not pure experimental designs. Subjects for the experiments were not selected from a common pool of subjects and randomly assigned to one group or another. In the following discussion of three basic experimental designs, the symbol to the left of the diagram indicates that the first step in a true experimental design is the random assignment of subjects.

PRETEST–POSTTEST CONTROL GROUP DESIGN (BEFORE–AFTER WITH CONTROL)

A pretest–posttest control group design, or *before–after with control group design*, is the classic experimental design:

Experimental group:	R	O_1	X	O_2
Control group:	R	O_3		O_4

As the diagram indicates, the subjects in the experimental group are tested before and after being exposed to the treatment. The control group is tested at the same two times as the experimental group, but subjects are not exposed to the experimental treatment. This design has the advantages of the before–after design with the additional advantages gained by its having a control group. The effect of the experimental treatment equals:

$$(O_2 - O_1) - (O_4 - O_3)$$

It is important to note that we expect $O_1 = O_3$. One of the threats we discussed to internal validity was selection and the assumption of equal groups. If the two groups are not equal at the beginning of the experiment, the study has a fatal flaw and the researchers should start over. Let's assume there is brand awareness among 20 percent of the subjects (O_1 = 20 percent, O_3 = 20 percent) before an advertising treatment and then 35 percent awareness in the experimental group (O_2 = 35 percent) and 22 percent awareness in the control group (O_4 = 22 percent) after exposure to the treatment, the treatment effect equals 13 percent:

$$(0.35 - 0.20) - (0.22 - 0.20) = (0.15) - (0.02) = 0.13 \text{ or } 13\%$$

Not only are the groups assumed to be equal at the beginning, but the effect of all extraneous variables is assumed to be the same on both the experimental and the control groups. For instance, since both groups receive the pretest, no difference between them is expected for the pretest effect. This assumption is also made for effects of other events between the before and after measurements (history), changes within the subjects that occur with the passage of time (maturation), testing effects, and instrumentation effects. In reality there may be some differences in the sources of extraneous variation. Nevertheless, in most cases assuming that the effect is approximately equal for both groups is reasonable.

However, a testing effect is possible when subjects are sensitized to the subject of the research. This is analogous to what occurs when people learn a new vocabulary word. Soon they discover that they notice it much more frequently in their reading. In an experiment the combination of being interviewed on a subject and receiving the experimental treatment might be a potential source of error. For example, a subject exposed to a certain advertising message in a split-cable experiment might say, "Ah, there is an ad about the product I was interviewed about yesterday!" The subject may pay more attention than normal to the advertisement and be more prone to change his or her attitude than in a situation with no interactive testing effects. This weakness in the before–after with control group design can be corrected (see the next two designs).

Testing the effectiveness of television commercials in movie theaters provides an example of the before–after with control group design. Subjects are selected for the experiments by being told that they are going to preview several new television shows. When they enter the theater, they learn that a drawing for several types of products will be held, and they are asked to complete a product preference questionnaire (see Exhibit 12.7). Then a first drawing is held. Next,

EXHIBIT 12.7 **Product Preference Measure in an Experiment**

We are going to give away a series of prizes. If you are selected as one of the winners, which brand from each of the groups listed below would you truly want to win?

Special arrangements will be made for any product for which bulk, or one-time, delivery is not appropriate.

Indicate your answers by filling in the box like this: ■

Do not "X," check, or circle the boxes please.

Cookies

(A 3-month supply, pick ONE.)

NABISCO OREO	☐	(1)
NABISCO OREO DOUBLE STUFF	☐	(2)
NABISCO NUTTER BUTTER	☐	(3)
NABISCO VANILLA CREMES	☐	(4)
HYDROX CHOCOLATE	☐	(5)
HYDROX DOUBLES	☐	(6)
NABISCO COOKIE BREAK	☐	(7)
NABISCO CHIPS AHOY	☐	(8)
KEEBLER E.L. FUDGE	☐	(9)
KEEBLER FUDGE CREMES	☐	(10)
KEEBLER FRENCH VANILLA CREMES	☐	(11)

Allergy Relief Products

(A year's supply, pick ONE.)

ALLEREST	☐	(1)
BENADRYL	☐	(2)
CONTAC	☐	(3)
TAVIST-D	☐	(4)
DRISTAN	☐	(5)
SUDAFED	☐	(6)
CHLOR-TRIMETON	☐	(7)

the television pilots and commercials are shown. Then the emcee announces additional prizes and a second drawing. Finally, subjects fill out the same questionnaire about prizes. The information from the first questionnaire is the before measurement, and that from the second questionnaire is the after measurement. The control group receives similar treatment except that on the day they view the pilot television shows, different (or no) television commercials are substituted for the experimental commercials.

POSTTEST-ONLY CONTROL GROUP DESIGN (AFTER-ONLY WITH CONTROL)

In some situations pretest measurements are impossible. In other situations selection error is not anticipated to be a problem because the groups are known to be equal. The posttest-only control group design, or *after-only with control group design,* is diagrammed as follows:

Experimental group:	R	X	O_1
Control group:	R		O_2

The effect of the experimental treatment is equal to $O_1 - O_2$.

Suppose the manufacturer of an athlete's-foot remedy wishes to demonstrate by experimentation that its product is better than a competing brand. No pretest measure about the effectiveness of the remedy is possible. The design is to randomly select subjects, perhaps students, who have contracted athlete's foot and randomly assign them to the experimental or the control group. With only the posttest measurement, the effects of testing and instrument variation are eliminated. Furthermore, researchers make the same assumptions about extraneous variables described above—that is, that they operate equally on both groups, as in the before–after with control group design.

COMPROMISE DESIGNS

True experimentation is often simply not possible. The researcher may compromise by approximating an experimental design. A compromise design is one that falls short of assigning subjects or treatments randomly to experimental groups.

Consider a situation in which a researcher would ideally implement a pretest–posttest control group design to study the effect of training on employee performance. In this case, subjects may not be able to be assigned randomly to the experimental and control group because the researcher cannot take workers away from their work groups. Thus, one entire work group is used as the experimental group and a separate work group is used as a control group. The researcher has no assurance that the groups are equivalent. The situation has forced a compromise to experimental integrity.

The alternative to the compromise design when random assignment of subjects is not possible is to conduct the experiment *without* a control group. Generally this is considered a greater weakness than using groups that have already been established. When the experiment involves a longitudinal study, circumstances usually dictate a compromise with true experimentation.

Time Series Designs

Many experiments may be conducted in a short period of time (a few hours, a week, or a month). However, a business experiment investigating long-term strategic and/or structural changes may require a **time series design**. Time series designs are quasi-experimental because they generally do not allow the researcher full control over the treatment exposure or influence of extraneous variables. When experiments are conducted over long periods of time, they are most vulnerable to history effects due to changes in population, attitudes, economic patterns, and the like. Although seasonal patterns and other exogenous influences may be noted, the experimenter can do little about them when time is a major factor in the design.

time series design
Used for an experiment investigating long-term structural changes.

EXHIBIT 12.8
Selected Time Series Outcomes

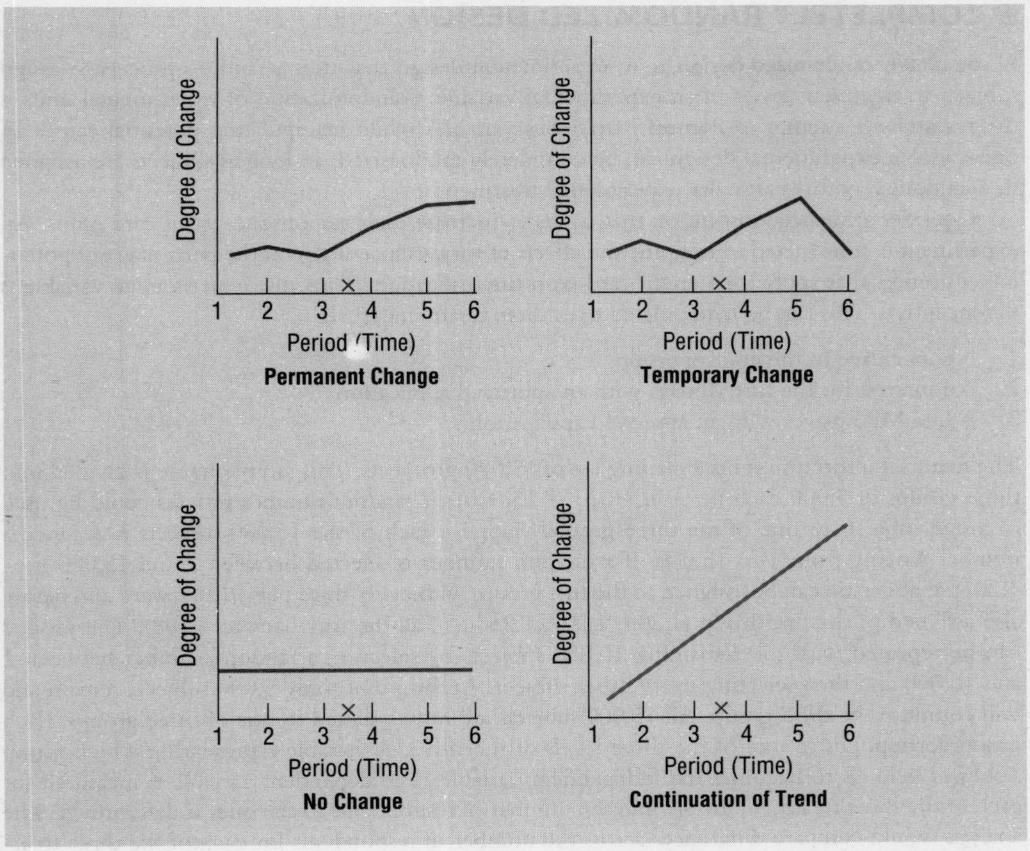

Political tracking polls provide an example. A pollster normally uses a series of surveys to track candidates' popularity. Consider the candidate who plans a major speech (the experimental treatment) to refocus the political campaign. The simple time series design can be diagrammed as follows:

$$O_1 \quad O_2 \quad O_3 \quad X \quad O_4 \quad O_5 \quad O_6$$

Several observations have been taken to identify trends before the speech (X) is given. After the treatment has been administered, several observations are made to determine if the patterns *after* the treatment are similar to those *before*. If the longitudinal pattern shifts after the political speech, the researcher may conclude that the treatment had a positive impact on the pattern. Of course, this time series design cannot give the researcher complete assurance that the treatment caused the change in the trend, rather than some external event. Problems of internal validity are greater than in more tightly controlled before-and-after designs for experiments of shorter duration.

One unique advantage of the time series design is its ability to distinguish temporary from permanent changes. Exhibit 12.8 shows some possible outcomes in a time series experiment.

Complex Experimental Designs

The previous discussion focused on simple experimental designs—experiments manipulating a single variable. Here, the focus shifts to more complex experimental designs involving multiple experimental variables. Complex experimental designs are statistical designs that isolate the effects of confounding extraneous variables or allow for manipulation of more than one independent variable in the experiment. *Completely randomized designs, randomized block designs, and factorial designs* are covered in the following section.

COMPLETELY RANDOMIZED DESIGN

completely randomized design

An experimental design that uses a random process to assign subjects to treatment levels of an experimental variable.

A **completely randomized design** is an experimental design that uses a random process to assign subjects to treatment levels of an experimental variable. Randomization of experimental units is the researcher's attempt to control extraneous variables while manipulating potential causes. A one-variable experimental design can be completely randomized, so long as subjects are assigned in a random way to a particular experimental treatment level.

Consider a financial institution that wants to increase their response to credit card offers. An experiment is constructed to examine the effects of various incentives on the percentage of potential customers that apply for a credit card with the institution. Thus, the experimental variable is the incentive. This can be manipulated over three treatment levels:

1. No incentive to the control group
2. No interest for the first 90 days with an approved application
3. A free MP3 player with an approved application

The financial institution rents a mailing list of 15,000 prospects. This sample frame is divided into three groups of 5,000 each ($n_1 + n_2 + n_3 = 15{,}000$). A random number process could be used to assign subjects to one of the three groups. Suppose each of the 15,000 subjects is assigned a number ranging from 1 to 15,000. If a random number is selected between 1 and 15,000 (i.e., 1,201), that person can be assigned to the first group, with every third person afterward and before also assigned to the first group (1,204, 1,207, 1,210 . . . all the way back to 1,198). The process can be repeated with the remaining 10,000 subjects by selecting a random number between 1 and 10,000 and then selecting every other subject. At this point, only 5,000 subjects remain and will comprise the third group. All 15,000 subjects are now assigned to one of three groups. Each group corresponds to one of the three levels of incentive. A variable representing which group a subject belongs to becomes the independent variable. The dependent variable is measured for each of the three treatment groups and the number of respondents to the offer is determined. The analysis would compare differences across the number of respondents for each of the three treatment levels.

RANDOMIZED-BLOCK DESIGN

randomized-block design

A design that attempts to isolate the effects of a single extraneous variable by blocking out its effects on the dependent variable

The **randomized-block design** is an extension of the completely randomized design. A form of randomization is used to control for *most* extraneous variation; however, the researcher has identified a single extraneous variable that might affect subjects' responses systematically. The researcher will attempt to isolate the effects of this single variable by blocking out its effects.

A blocking variable is a categorical variable that is expected to be associated with different values of a dependent variable for each group. Sex is a common blocking variable. Many potential dependent variables are expected to be different for men and women. For instance, work-family conflict—conflict between the obligations a person has to their family and with their work commitments—has been found to differ between women and men. So, if a researcher is studying how salary and length of vacation time affects employee job satisfaction, they may want to also record a person's sex and include it as an extra explanatory variable over and above the experimental variable's salary and vacation time. The concept of a blocking variable was introduced in the self-efficacy study where the researchers "blocked" on length of time the subjects had been an employee (new versus current).

EXHIBIT 12.9 **Randomized Block Design**

	Percentage Who Purchase Product			
Treatment	**Southwest**	**Midwest**	**Atlantic Coast**	**Mean for Treatments**
Package A	14.0% (Phoenix)	12.0% (St. Louis)	7.0% (Boston)	11.0%
Package B	16.0% (Albuquerque)	15.0% (Peoria)	10.0% (New York)	13.6%
Mean for cities	15.0%	13.5%	8.5%	

The term *randomized block* originated in agricultural research that applied several levels of a treatment variable to each of several blocks of land. Systematic differences in agricultural yields due to the quality of the blocks of land may be controlled in the randomized-block design. In business research, the researcher may wish to isolate block effects such as bank branch territories, job work units, or employee tenure, and so on. Suppose that a manufacturer of Mexican food is considering two packaging alternatives. Marketers suspect that geographic region might confound the experiment. They have identified three regions where attitudes toward Mexican food may differ (the Southwest, the Midwest, and the Atlantic Coast). In a randomized-block design, each block must receive every treatment level. Assigning treatments to each block is a random process. In this example the two treatments will be randomly assigned to different cities within each region.

Sales results such as those in Exhibit 12.9 might be observed. The logic behind the randomized-block design is similar to that underlying the selection of a stratified sample rather than a simple random one. By isolating the block effects, one type of extraneous variation is partitioned out and a more efficient experimental design therefore results. This is because experimental error is reduced with a given sample size.

FACTORIAL DESIGNS

Factorial design is one type of statistical experimental design that can accommodate two or more independent variables which take different level of values and also allow interaction between the variables. Unlike other statistical experimental design, factorial design has the advantage of estimated interaction between two or more independent variables. It can be said that two variables have interaction effects when the effect of simultaneous change of two variables is significantly different from some of their individual effects. For example, a manufacturer believes that if it increases advertisement expense the sales might increase. At the same time, if the manufacturer increases the number of retail outlets to sell the product, then also the sales will increase. In this case, each of the advertisement expenses as well as number of retail outlets has varied individual effect on sales. However, if the manufacturer changes both the variables, meaning, if it increases the advertisement expense as well as the number of outlets, the combined sales may be more than the sum of the individual increase of sales due to change in advertisement expense and number of retail outlets. The incremental change about this sum is the amount of sales increased due to interaction between the two variables, that is, advertisement expense and number of retail outlets.

A 2×2 factorial design can be represented by a table having one variable in row and another variable in column. A 2×2 factorial design means that there are two variables that have two levels in each variable. Similarly, factorial design can be prepared for three or more factors. However, in this case the researcher Nick has three or more dimensional tables to represent the design. While it is not possible to draw a table in more than three-dimensions, computing can calculate the main effect and the interaction effect by using algorithms.

Suppose a human resource manager believes that an experiment that manipulates the level of salary offered is useful, but too limited. The recruiters for the firm have been visiting college campuses and know that graduates seeking jobs are concerned about salary, but they are also concerned about the number of vacation days they will receive. However, the level of salary and actual number of vacation days needs to determined. Thus, an experiment to assess this requires more than one independent variable be incorporated into the research design. Even though the single-factor experiments considered so far may have one specific variable blocked and other confounding sources controlled, they are still limited. A **factorial design** allows for the testing of the effects of two or more treatments (factors) at various levels.

factorial design

A design that allows for the testing of the effects of two or more treatments (experimental variables) at various levels

EXHIBIT 12.10

Factorial Design—Salary and Vacation

	Vacation Days	
Salary	**10 Days**	**14 Days**
$37,500	Cell 1	Cell 4
$40,000	Cell 2	Cell 5
$42,500	Cell 3	Cell 6

We discussed earlier in this chapter that experiments produce main effects and interactions. Main effects are differences (in the dependent variable) between treatment levels. Interactions produce differences (in the dependent variable) between experimental cells based on combinations of variables. In the self-efficacy example, we learned that the experimental treatment had a stronger effect on the current employees than the new employees (see Exhibit 12.3).

To further explain the terminology of experimental designs, let us develop the recruiting experiment more fully. The human resource manager wants to measure the effect of the salary and vacation days on the percentage of job offers accepted. Exhibit 12.10 indicates three treatment levels of salary offered ($37,500, $40,000, and $42,500) and two levels of vacation time (10 days and 14 days). The table shows that every combination of treatment level requires a separate experimental group. In this experiment, with three levels of salary and two levels of vacation, we have a 3 × 2 (read "three by two") factorial design because the first factor (the salary variable) is varied in three ways and the second factor (the location variable) is varied in two ways. A 3 × 2 design requires six cells, or six experimental groups (3 × 2 = 6). If the subjects each receive only one combination of experimental variables, then we use the term 3 × 2 between-subjects design to describe the experiment.

The number of treatments (factors) and the number of levels of each treatment identify the factorial design. A 3 × 3 design means there are two factors, each having three levels; a 2 × 2 × 2 design has three factors, each having two levels. The treatments need not have the same number of levels; for example, a 3 × 2 × 4 factorial design is possible. The important idea is that in a factorial experiment, each treatment level is combined with every other treatment level.

In addition to the advantage of investigating two or more independent variables simultaneously, factorial designs allow researchers to measure interaction effects. In a 2 × 2 experiment the interaction is the effect produced by treatments A and B combined. If the effect of one treatment differs at various levels of the other treatment, interaction occurs.

To illustrate the value of a factorial design, suppose a researcher is comparing two magazine ads. The researcher is investigating the believability of ads on a scale from 0 to 100 and wishes to consider the sex of the reader as a blocking factor. The experiment has two independent variables: sex and ads. This 2 × 2 factorial experiment permits the experimenter to test three hypotheses. Two hypotheses examine the main effects:

- Advertisement A is more believable than ad B.
- Men believe advertisements more than women.

However, the primary research question may deal with the interaction hypothesis:

- Advertisement A is more believable than ad B among women, but ad B is more believable than ad A among men.

A high score indicates a more believable ad. Exhibit 12.11 shows that the mean believability score for both sex is 65. This suggests that there is no main sex effect. Men and women evaluate believability of the advertisements equally. The main effect for ads indicates that ad A is more believable than ad B (70 versus 60), supporting the first hypothesis. However, if we inspect the data and look within the levels of the factors, we find that men find ad B more believable and women find ad A more believable. This is an interaction effect because the believability score of the advertising factor differs at different values of the other independent variable, sex. Thus, the interaction hypothesis is supported.

Exhibit 12.12 graphs the results of the believability experiment. The line for men represents the two mean believability scores for ads A and B. The other line represents the same relationship for women. Notice the difference between the slopes of the two lines. This also illustrates support for the interaction of the ad copy with biological sex. The difference in the slopes means that the believability of the advertising copy depends on whether a man or a woman is reading the advertisement. We witnessed a similar effect in our self-efficacy example.

TIPS OF THE TRADE

© iStock

- Survey research cannot determine cause and effect; experiments are the only method available to a business researcher to establish causality.
- Sample size and random assignment are the experimental researcher's friends.
  - For experiments to be valid, we need to know the subjects in the different experimental groups are equal. It is virtually impossible to identify and assess all the characteristics that could affect an experiment. However, if we have a large enough sample size (cell count) and randomly assign subjects to the experimental groups, all characteristics should balance out.
- We must establish both internal and external validity of our experiments.
  - Establishing internal validity first makes sense—if we cannot show that our independent variable is the cause of the observed change in our dependent variable, there is no reason to consider external validity.
  - Laboratory experiments are better suited to establishing internal validity, while field experiments are more effective at establishing external validity. Thus, we typically move from the laboratory to the field.

EXHIBIT 12.11 A 2×2 Factorial Design That Illustrates the Effects of Sex and Ad Content on Believability

	Ad A	Ad B		
Men	60	70	65	Main effects of sex
Women	80	50	65	
	70	60		
	Main effects of ad			

EXHIBIT 12.12 Graphic Illustration of Interaction Between Sex and Advertising Copy

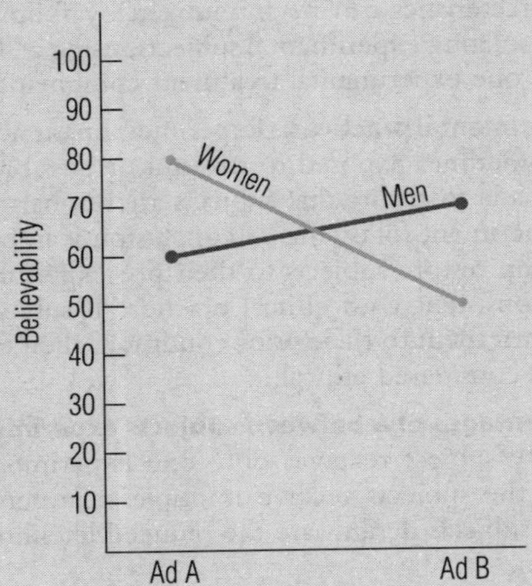

FRACTIONAL FACTORIAL DESIGN

While the number of factors is more and the number of levels in each factor is large, a very large number of combinations are generated. For example, if a desktop computer manufacturer wants to know consumers' preference of different types of desktop computers, it must elect five factors, namely, brand, processor speed, hard disk capacity, monitor type, and price. Each of these factors may have three or more levels in each. For instance, there could be different sizes of hard disk capacity like 200 GB, 300 GB, 500 GB, 1TB. Similarly, if we show that each of the above factors has four levels then the number of combinations of desktop computers that can be made is equal to $4 \times 4 \times 4 \times 4 \times 4 = 4^5 = 1024$. It is often difficult for the researcher to handle such a large number of combinations to estimate preference of the consumer. In such cases, a manageable number of combinations are derived from the original combination. This procedure is called fractional factorial design. One of the statistical methods used to calculate the number of profiles is known as orthogonal design. SPSS and other statistical software can generate orthogonal design quite easily.

Summary

1. Identify the independent variable, dependent variable, and construct a valid simple experiment to assess a cause and effect relationship. Independent variables are created through manipulation in experiments rather than through measurement. The researcher creates unique experimental conditions that represent unique levels of an independent variable. In our protocol example, the researcher manipulated the type of protocol used for the transmission of financial data. In the self-efficacy study, the subjects were either given or not given the treatment. Levels of an independent variable should be different enough to represent meaningful categories. The dependent variable(s) must be outcome measures that are anticipated to change based on the differing levels of the independent variable. The researchers expected the speed of data transmission to differ based on the protocol used. In the self-efficacy study, job satisfaction (and other key dependent variables) was expected to change if self-efficacy was enhanced.

2. Understand and minimize systematic experimental error. Systematic experimental error occurs because sampling units (research subjects) in one experimental cell are different from those in another cell in a way that affects the dependent variable. In the self-efficacy study, it is important to have employees randomly assigned to the experiment or control group, rather than choosing those employees that appear to most need their self confidence enhanced to be exposed to the treatment. Randomization is an important way of minimizing systematic experimental error. If research subjects are randomly assigned to different treatment combinations, then the differences among people that exist naturally within a population should also exist within each experimental cell.

3. Know ways of minimizing experimental demand characteristics. Demand characteristics are experimental procedures that somehow inform the subject about the actual research purpose. Demand effects can result from demand characteristics. When this happens, the results are confounded. Demand characteristics can be minimized by following these simple rules: using an experimental disguise, isolating experimental subjects, using a "blind" experimental administrator, and administering only one experimental treatment combination to each subject.

4. Avoid unethical experimental practices. Experiments naturally involve deception. Additionally, research subjects are sometimes exposed to stressful or possibly dangerous manipulations. Every precaution should be made to ensure that subjects are not harmed. Debriefing subjects about the true purpose of the experiment following its conclusion is important for the ethical treatment of subjects. If debriefing can restore subjects to their pre-experimental condition, the experimental procedures are likely consistent with ethical practice. If subjects are affected in some way that makes it difficult to return them to their prior condition, then the experimental procedures probably go beyond what is considered ethical.

5. Understand the advantages of a between-subjects experimental design. A between-subjects design means that every subject receives only one experimental treatment combination. In a within-subjects design the subjects receive multiple treatments and measurements. The main advantages of between-subjects designs are the reduced likelihood of demand effects and simpler analysis and presentation.

6. Weigh the trade-off between internal and external validity. Lab experiments, such as the protocol example, offer higher internal validity because they maximize control of extraneous variables. High internal validity is a good thing because we can be more certain that the experimental variable is truly the cause of any variance in the dependent variable. Field experiments, such as the self-efficacy study, maximize external validity because they are conducted in a more natural setting meaning that the results are more likely to generalize to the actual business situation. The increased external validity comes at the expense of internal validity.

7. Use manipulations to implement a completely randomized experimental design, a randomized-block design, and a factorial experimental design. The key to randomization is to assign subjects to experimental cells in a way that spreads extraneous variables out evenly across every condition. Blocking variables can be added to simple randomized experimental designs to control for categorical variables that are expected to be related to the dependent variable. Finally, a factorial design results when multiple experimental and/or blocking variables are included in a single model. Both main effects and interactions result.

Key Terms and Concepts

basic experimental design, *301*
between-subjects design, *297*
blocking variables, *280*
cell, *285*
cohort effect, *298*
completely randomized design, *306*
confound, *287*
constancy of conditions, *292*
control group, *283*
counterbalancing, *292*
demand characteristic, *289*
demand effect, *289*
experimental condition, *281*
experimental group, *283*
experimental treatment, *283*
external validity, *300*
extraneous variables, *288*
factorial design, *307*
field experiments, *294*
Hawthorne effect, *290*
history effect, *298*
instrumentation effect, *299*
interaction effect, *282*
internal validity, *297*
laboratory experiment, *293*
main effect, *281*
manipulation check, *297*
maturation effects, *298*
mortality effect (sample attrition), *299*
nuisance variables, *286*
placebo, *291*
placebo effect, *291*
quasi-experimental designs, *301*
randomization, *286*
randomized-block design, *306*
repeated measures, *285*
selection effect, *299*
subjects, *280*
systematic or nonsampling error, *286*
tachistoscope, *294*
test units, *286*
testing effects, *299*
time series design, *304*
within-subjects design, *297*

Questions for Review and Critical Thinking

1. Define *experimental condition, experimental treatment,* and *experimental group.* How are these related to the implementation of a valid manipulation?
2. A tissue manufacturer that has the fourth-largest market share plans to experiment with a 50¢ off coupon during November and a buy one, get one free coupon during December. The experiment will take place at Target stores in St. Louis and Kansas City. Sales will be recorded by scanners from which mean tissue sales for each store for each month can be computed and interpreted.
   a. What are the independent variable and the dependent variable?
   b. Prepare a "dummy" table that would describe what the results of the experiment would look like.
3. What is the difference between a *main effect* and an *interaction* in an experiment? In question 2, what will create a main effect? Is an interaction possible?
4. In what ways might the design in question 2 yield systematic or nonsampling error?
5. What purpose does the random assignment of subjects serve?
6. Why is an experimental confound so damaging to the conclusions drawn from an experiment?
7. What are demand characteristics? How can they be minimized?
8. **ETHICS** Suppose researchers were experimenting with how much more satisfied consumers are with a "new and improved" version of some existing product. How might the researchers design a placebo within an experiment testing this research question? Is using such a placebo ethical or not?
9. If a company wanted to know whether to implement a new management training program based on how much it would improve ROI in its southwest division, would you recommend a field or lab experiment?
10. **'NET** Suppose you wanted to test the effect of three different e-mail requests inviting people to participate in a survey posted on the Internet. One simply contained a hyperlink with no explanation, the other said if someone participated $10 would be donated to charity, and the other said if someone participated he or she would have a chance to win $1,000. How would this experiment be conducted differently based on whether it was a between-subjects or within-subjects design? What are the advantages of a between-subjects design?
11. What is a manipulation check? How does it relate to internal validity?
12. **ETHICS** What role does debriefing play in ensuring that experimental procedures are consistent with good ethical practice?

Research Activities

1. Consider the following scenario:
   Sea Snapper brand gourmet frozen fish products claimed in advertising that their fish sticks are preferred more than two to one over the most popular brand, Captain John's. The advertisements all include a definitive statement indicating that research existed which substantiated this claim.

   Captain John's reaction was *war;* or at least legal war. They decided to sue Sea Snapper claiming that the advertisements include false claims based on faulty research. In court, the research is described in great detail. Sea Snapper conducted taste tests involving four hundred consumers who indicated that they regularly ate frozen food products. Two hundred tasted Sea Snapper premium fish sticks and the other two hundred tasted Captain John's premium fish sticks. Consumer preference was measured with a 100-point rating scale. The results showed the average preference score for Sea Snapper was 78.2 compared to 39.0 for Captain John's.

   Captain John's attorney hires a research firm to assist in the lawsuit. They claim that the research is faulty because the procedures were improperly conducted. First, it turns out that

Sea Snapper fish sticks were always presented to consumers on a blue plate while Captain John's were always presented to consumers on an orange plate. Second, the Sea Snapper products used in the experiment were taken directly from the Sea Snapper kitchens to the testing facility, while the Captain John's products were purchased at a local warehouse store.

a. Provide a critique of the procedures used to support the claim that Sea Snapper's product is superior. Prepare it in a way that it could be presented as evidence in court.
b. Design an experiment that would provide a more valid test of the research question, "Do consumers prefer Sea Snapper fish sticks compared to Captain John's fish sticks?"

2. Conduct a taste test involving some soft drinks with a group of friends. Pour them several ounces of three popular soft drinks and simply label the cups A, B, and C. Make sure they are blind to the actual brands. Then, let them drink as much as they want and record how much of each they drink. You may also ask them some questions about the drinks. Then, allow other subjects to participate in the same test, but this time, let them know what the three brands are. Record the same data and draw conclusions. Does brand knowledge affect behavior and attitudes about soft drinks?

Case 12.1 Tooheys

Sixty-six willing Australian drinkers helped a Federal Court judge decide that Tooheys didn't engage in misleading or deceptive advertising for its 2.2 beer. The beer contains 2.2 percent alcohol, compared to 6 percent for other beers, leading to a claim that could be interpreted as implying it was non-alcoholic.

Volunteers were invited to a marathon drinking session after the Aboriginal Legal Service claimed Tooheys' advertising implied beer drinkers could imbibe as much 2.2 as desired without becoming legally intoxicated. Drunken driving laws prohibit anyone with a blood-alcohol level above 0.05 from getting behind the wheel in Australia.

So, an experiment was conducted to see what happens when a lot of 2.2 is consumed. But the task wasn't easy or that much fun. Some subjects couldn't manage to drink the required 10 "middies," an Aussie term for a beer glass of 10 fluid ounces, over the course of an hour.

Thirty-six participants could manage only nine glasses. Four threw up and were excluded. Two more couldn't manage the "minimum" nine glasses and had to be replaced.

Justice J. Beaumont observed that consuming enough 2.2 in an hour to reach the 0.05 level was "uncomfortable and therefore an unlikely process." Because none of the ads mentioned such extreme quantities, he ruled they couldn't be found misleading or deceptive.[15]

Questions

1. Would a lab experiment or a field experiment be more "valid" in determining whether Tooheys could cause a normal beer consumer to become intoxicated? Explain.
2. Describe an alternate research design that would have higher validity.
3. Is the experiment described in this story consistent with good ethical practice? Likewise, comment on how the design described in part 2 would be made consistent with good ethical practices.
4. Is validity or ethics more important?

Part 4
Measurement Concepts

© BRAND X PICTURES/JUPITER IMAGES

CHAPTER 13
MEASUREMENT AND SCALING CONCEPTS

LEARNING OUTCOMES

After studying this chapter, you should be able to

1. **Determine what needs to be measured to address a research question or hypothesis**
2. **Distinguish levels of scale measurement**
3. **Know how to form an index or composite measure**
4. **List the three criteria for good measurement**
5. **Perform a basic assessment of scale reliability and validity**

Chapter Vignette—Money Matters?

Griff Mitchell is the vice president of customer relationship management (CRM) for one of the world's largest suppliers of industrial heavy equipment. In this role, he oversees all sales and service operations. This year, for the first time, the company has decided to perform a CRM employee evaluation process that will allow an overall ranking of all CRM employees. Griff knows this will be a difficult task for many reasons, not the least of which is that he oversees over a thousand employees worldwide.

The ranking will be used to single out the best performers. These employees will be recognized at the company's annual CRM conference. The rankings will also be used to identify the lowest 20 percent of performers. These employees will be put on a probationary list with specific targeted improvement goals that will have to be met within 12 months or they will be fired. Griff is becoming really stressed out trying to define the performance ranking process.

Griff's key question is, "What is performance?" Although these employees are now often referred to as CRM employees, they have traditionally performed the sales function. Griff calls a meeting of senior CRM managers to discuss how ranking decisions should be made.

© AP PHOTO/FAIRMONT SENTINEL, CHIP PEARSON

One manager simply argues that sales volume should be the sole criteria. She believes that "sales figures provide an objective performance measure that will make the task easy and difficult to refute." Another counters that for the past 22 years, he has simply used his opinion of each employee's performance to place each of them into one of three groups: top performers, good performers, and underperformers. "I think about who is easy to work with and doesn't cause much trouble. It has worked for 22 years, why won't it work now?" Another responds curtly, "It's margin! It's margin! I don't care about sales volume; I want my guys selling things that improve my division's profit!" One of the newer managers sits silently through most of the meeting and finally summons up the courage to speak. "Aren't we CRM? That means performance should not be tied to sales, profits, or convenience, it should be based on how well a salesperson builds and maintains relationships with customers. So, we should see how satisfied the customers assigned to the employee are and use this in the evaluation process!" After this, the meeting disintegrates into a shouting match with each manager believing the others' ideas are flawed.

Griff feels like he is back to square one. "How do I make sure I have a valid performance measure so that all of our people are treated fairly?" He decides to seek out an opinion from a long-time friend in the research business, Robin Donald. Robin suggests that a research project may be needed to define a reliable and valid measure. She also brings up the fact that because employees from all over the world will be considered, the measure will have to maintain its reliability and validity anywhere it is used! Griff agrees to the project. He also feels good about letting someone outside the company develop the measure, because he certainly realizes the tremendous challenges that are present.

Griff's situation in this vignette illustrates how difficult it can be to define, let alone measure, important business phenomena. While some items can be measured quite easily, others present tremendous challenges to the business researcher. This is the first of two chapters that deal with measurement in business research.

Introduction

Not every cook or chef needs to follow a recipe to create a great dish, but most amateur chefs find one very useful. Look at Exhibit 13.1. The recipe shows ingredients that can produce a tasty chicken dish. However, many readers, even those with some cooking ability, may have a difficult time following this recipe. Why? First, many may have difficulty translating all the French terms. Second, even when this is done, many will have difficulty knowing just what amounts of what ingredients should be included. How many could easily deal with the different measures listed by the ingredients? "How much is 50 ml?" "What is 454 g?" "How much is a pinch?" "Can I use my normal measuring utensils (scales)?"

Likewise, the chapter vignette describes a situation in which Griff must develop a "recipe" for distinguishing employees based on job performance. Before the measurement process can be defined, he will have to decide exactly what it is that needs to be produced. In this case, the outcome should be a valid job performance measure.

EXHIBIT 13.1 More Ways Than One to Measure Ingredients

(a) Recette de la Jour

454 g	Poitrine de Poulet
50 ml	Farine Tout Usage
2 ml	De Poudre d'Ail
2 ml	De Poudre d'Oignon
1 ml	De Sel
2	Blancs d'Oeuf
50 ml	De Lait Écrémé
Pincée	De le Poivre Rouge
36	Crackers (Tout Crounche)

(b) Dogtes de Poulet Faibles avec Crackers

© FOOD PIX/JUPITER IMAGES

What Do I Measure?

measurement
The process of describing some property of a phenomenon of interest, usually by assigning numbers in a reliable and valid way.

The decision statement, corresponding research questions, and research hypotheses can be used to decide what concepts need to be measured in a given project. **Measurement** is the process of describing some property of a phenomenon of interest, usually by assigning numbers in a reliable and valid way. The numbers convey information about the property being measured. When numbers are used, the researcher must have a rule for assigning a number to an observation in a way that provides an accurate description.

We measure attributes of objects. We do not measure objects. For example, we may share information of people, here it is the attribute of the object, people. Hence, we do not measure the object but a major attribute of the object. Similarly, we measure sales of the company. Sales is the attribute of the object, company. We measure perception of consumers. Perception is the attribute of the object, consumer.

Measurement can be illustrated by thinking about the way instructors assign students' grades. A grade represents a student's performance in a class. Students with higher performance should receive a different grade than students with lower performance. Even the apparently simple concept of student performance is measured in many different ways. Consider the following options:

1. A student can be assigned a letter corresponding to his/her performance.
   a. A — Represents excellent performance
   b. B — Represents good performance
   c. C — Represents average performance
   d. D — Represents poor performance
   e. F — Represents failing performance
2. A student can be assigned a number from 1 to 20.
   a. 20 — Represents outstanding performance
   b. 11–20 — Represents differing degrees of passing performance
   c. Below 11 — Represents failing performance
3. A student can be assigned a number corresponding to a percentage performance scale.
   a. 100 percent — Represents a perfect score. All assignments are performed correctly.
   b. 60–99 percent — Represents differing degrees of passing performance, each number representing the proportion of correct work.
   c. 0–59 percent — Represents failing performance but still captures proportion of correct work.
4. A student can be assigned one of two letters corresponding to performance.
   a. P — Represents a passing mark
   b. F — Represents a failing mark

Actually, this is not terribly different than a manager who must assign performance scores to employees. In each case, students with different marks are distinguished in some way. However, some scales may better distinguish students. Each scale also has the potential of producing error or some lack of validity. Exhibit 13.2 illustrates a common measurement application.

Often, instructors may use a percentage scale all semester long and then be required to assign a letter grade for a student's overall performance. Does this produce any measurement problems? Consider two students who have percentage scores of 79.4 and 70.0, respectively. The most likely outcome when these scores are translated into "letter grades" is that each receives a C (the common 10-point spread would yield a 70–80 percent range for a C). Consider a third student who finishes with a 69.0 percent average and a fourth student who finishes with a 79.9 percent average.

Which students are happiest with this arrangement? The first two students receive the same grade, even though their scores are 9.4 percent apart. The third student gets a grade lower (D) performance than the second student, even though their percentage scores are only 1.0 percentage point different. The fourth student, who has a score only 0.5 percent higher than the first student, would receive a B. Thus, the measuring system (final grade) suggests that the fourth student outperformed the first (assuming that 79.9 is rounded up to 80) student (B versus C), but the first

EXHIBIT 13.2
Are There Any Validity Issues with This Measurement?

Student	Percentage Grade	Difference from Next Highest Student	Letter Grade
1	79.4%	0.5%	C
2	70.0%	9.4%	C
3	69.0%	1.0%	D
4	79.9%	NA	B

student did not outperform the second (each gets a C), even though the first and second students have the greatest difference in percentage scores.

A strong case can be made that error exists in this measurement system. All measurements, particularly in the social sciences, contain error. Researchers, if we are to represent concepts truthfully, must make sure that the measures used, if not perfect, are accurate enough to yield correct conclusions. Ultimately, research and measurement are tied closely together.

Concepts

A researcher has to know what to measure before knowing how to measure something. The problem definition process should suggest the concepts that must be measured. A **concept** can be thought of as a generalized idea that represents something of meaning. Concepts such as *age, sex, education,* and *number of children* are relatively concrete properties. They present few problems in either definition or measurement. Other concepts are more abstract. Concepts such as *loyalty, personality, channel power, trust, corporate culture, customer satisfaction, value,* and so on are more difficult to both define and measure. For example, *loyalty* has been measured as a combination of *customer share* (the relative proportion of a person's purchases going to one competing brand/store) and *commitment* (the degree to which a customer will sacrifice to do business with a brand/store).[1] Thus, we can see that loyalty consists of two components, the first is behavioral and the second is attitudinal.

concept
A generalized idea that represents something of meaning.

Operational Definitions

Researchers measure concepts through a process known as **operationalization**. This process involves identifying scales that correspond to variance in the concept. **Scales**, just as a scale you may use to check your weight, provide a range of values that correspond to different values in the concept being measured. In other words, scales provide **correspondence rules** that indicate that a

operationalization
The process of identifying scales that correspond to variance in a concept to be involved in a research process.

scales
A device providing a range of values that correspond to different values in a concept being measured.

correspondence rules
Indicate the way that a certain value on a scale corresponds to some true value of a concept.

certain value on a scale corresponds to some true value of a concept. Hopefully, they do this in a truthful way.

Here is an example of a correspondence rule: "Assign the numbers 1 through 7 according to how much trust you have in your sales representative. If the sales representative is perceived as completely untrustworthy, assign the numeral 1, if the sales rep is completely trustworthy, assign a 7."

VARIABLES

Researchers use variance in concepts to make diagnoses. Therefore, when we defined variables in an earlier chapter, we really were suggesting that variables capture different concept values. Scales capture variance in concepts and, as such, the scales provide the researcher's variables. Thus, for practical purposes, once a research project is underway, there is little difference between a concept and a variable. Consider the following hypothesis:

H1: Experience *is positively related to* job performance.

The hypothesis implies a relationship between two variables, experience and job performance. The variables capture variance in the experience and performance concepts. One employee may have 15 years of experience and be a top performer. A second may have 10 years experience and be a good performer. The scale used to measure experience is quite straightforward in this case and would involve simply providing the number of years an employee has been with the company. Job performance, on the other hand, can be quite complex, as described in the opening vignette.

CONSTRUCTS

Sometimes, a single variable cannot capture a concept alone. Using multiple variables to measure one concept can often provide a more complete account of some concept than could any single variable. Even in the physical sciences, multiple measurements are often used to make sure an accurate representation is obtained. In social science, many concepts are measured with multiple measurements.

construct
A term used to refer to concepts measured with multiple variables.

A **construct** is a term used for concepts that are measured with multiple variables. For instance, when a business researcher wishes to measure the customer orientation of a salesperson, several variables like these may be used, each captured on a 1–5 scale:

1. I offer the product that is best suited to a customer's problem.
2. A good employee has to have the customer's best interests in mind.
3. I try to find out what kind of products will be most helpful to a customer.[2]

TOTHEPOINT

Not everything that can be counted counts, and not everything that counts can be counted.

—Albert Einstein

Constructs are underlying dimensions which are subjective in nature and are complex abstractions. They represent implicit dimensions of concepts. Constructs are not directly measured. Constructs are usually measured through indicator variables.These indicator variables can be directly measured and the respondents can give response to these indicator variables without much random error. For example, loyalty is a construct. If we try to measure loyalty directly, different respondents will mean loyalty in different ways and the response will have random errors. However, if we measure loyalty to three indicator variables, (1) number of times the respondent visited a particular store, (2) amount purchased from a particular store, and (3) number of people the respondent recommended to the particular store, the respond to these three variables will be consistent across the respondents and there will be less random error.

Relationship Between Measurement Error and Scaling Concepts

Relationship between measurement error and scaling is given as

$X_O = X_T + X_S + X_R$

where

Xo is observed score or measurement
XT is true score of the characteristic
XS is systematic error
XR is random error
Examples of systematic error are:

1. Social desirability
2. Cross cultural differences
3. Personality differences
4. Seasonality

Examples of random error are:

1. Person's mood
2. Question ambiguity
3. Fatigue

Constructs can be very helpful in operationalizing a concept.

An operational definition is like a manual of instructions or a recipe: even the truth of a statement like "Gaston Gourmet likes key lime pie" depends on the recipe. Different instructions lead to different results. In other words, how we define the construct will affect the way we measure it.[3]

An operational definition tells the investigator, "Do such-and-such in so-and-so manner."[4] Exhibit 13.3 presents a concept definition and an operational definition from a study on a construct called *susceptibility to interpersonal influence*.

Levels of Scale Measurement

Business researchers use many scales or number systems. Not all scales capture the same richness in a measure. Not all concepts require a rich measure. Traditionally, the level of scale measurement is seen as important because it determines the mathematical comparisons that are allowable. The four levels or types of scale measurement are *nominal*, *ordinal*, *interval*, and *ratio* level scales. Each type offers the researcher progressively more power in analyzing and testing the validity of a scale.

EXHIBIT 13.3 Susceptibility to Interpersonal Influence: An Operational Definition

Concept	Conceptual Definition	Operational Definition
Susceptibility to interpersonal influence	Susceptibility to interpersonal influence is "the need to identify with or enhance one's image in the opinion of significant others through the acquisition and use of products and brands, the willingness to conform to the expectations of others regarding purchase decisions, and/or the tendency to learn about products and services by observing others or seeking information from others." Susceptibility to interpersonal influence is a general trait that varies across individuals.	Please tell me how much you agree or disagree with each of the following statements: 1. I frequently gather information about stocks from friends or family before I invest in them. 2. To make sure I buy the right stock, I often observe what other investors invest in. 3. I often consult other people to help choose the best stock to invest in. 4. If I have little experience with a (type of) stock, I often ask my friends and acquaintances about the stock. 5. I like to know what investment decisions make good impressions on others. 6. I generally purchase those stocks that I think others will approve of. 7. I often identify with other people by purchasing or selling the same stocks they sell or purchase. 8. I achieve a sense of belonging by purchasing or selling the same stocks that others purchase or sell. 9. If others can see in which stocks I invest, I often invest in stocks that they invest in.

Sources: Bearden, W. O., R. G. Netemeyer, and M. F. Mobley, *Handbook of Marketing Scales: Multi Item Measures for Marketing and Consumer Behavior Research*, 2nd ed. (Newbury Park, Calif: Sage Publications, 1999); Hoffmann, A. O. I. and T. L. J. Broekhuizen, "Susceptibility to and Impact of Interpersonal Influence in an Investment Context," *Journal of the Academy of Marketing Science* doi 10.1007/s11747-008-0128-7 (forthcoming), published with open access at http://springerlink.com.

Scale Characteristics

All the scales, which we use for business research, are constructed based on three characteristics. These three characteristics, whether they are present in a particular scale or not, define the scale. These three characteristics are order, distance, and origin.

Order. It denotes the relative size, position, or importance associated with the characteristics of an object. Order represents the relative position and does not say anything about the absolute value of the characteristics of an object. For instance, characteristics of an object may assume value: good, better, best. It may be seen that good, better, and best are based on the description of the characteristics of an object. These three descriptions have an order among them. This means that *better* is better than *good* and *best* is better than *better.*

For example, a list of movies may be provided to the consumer who is then required to rate them in order of preference. All scales do not possess the order characteristic. For example, in a yes/no scale neither of them can be said to be greater than or less than the other, though numerical values are assigned to both these options. Similarly, gender scale is another example which does not possess any order.

Distance. It indicates that there are clearly known and measurable differences between the scale descriptors. Consider the number of customers visiting the shop in a specific time period. For different times, the numbers measured have a clearly defined difference between them. Clearly a scale that has distance also has order. In the above example, we have certain intervals which have higher number of people visiting and, hence, are higher up in the order, as compared to others.

nominal scales
Represent the most elementary level of measurement in which values are assigned to an object for identification or classification purposes only.

Origin. It implies that the scale has a unique or fixed beginning point, also called a zero point. Again the example of number of customers visiting in a specific interval is an example of a scale with origin as we have zero point for the case when we have no customer visiting in the interval. While perception scales and gender scales are generally devoid of origin.

Nominal Scale

Nominal scales represent the most elementary level of measurement. A nominal scale assigns a value to an object for identification or classification purposes only. The value can be, but does not have to be, a number because no quantities are being represented. In this sense, a nominal scale is truly a qualitative scale. Nominal scales are extremely useful, and are sometimes the only appropriate measure, even though they can be considered elementary.

Athletes wear nominal numbers on their jerseys. Ben Roethlisberger wears number 7 for the Pittsburgh Steelers, while Marvel Smith wears number 77. This does not mean that Marvel is 11 times better than Ben, or bigger than Ben, or faster than Ben, or anything else.

© MIKE LONGO/AI WIRE/LANDOV

Business researchers use nominal scales quite often. Suppose Barq's Root Beer was experimenting with three different types of sweeteners (cane sugar, corn syrup, or fruit extract). The researchers would like the experiment to be blind, so when subjects are asked to taste one of the three root beers, the drinks are labeled A, B, or C, not cane sugar, corn syrup, or fruit extract. Or, a researcher interested in examining the production efficiency of a company's different plants might refer to them as "Plant 1," "Plant 2," and so forth.

Nominal scaling is arbitrary. What we mean is that each label can be assigned to any of the categories without introducing error. For instance, in the root beer example above, the researcher can assign the letter C to any of the three options without damaging scale validity. The researcher could just as easily use numbers instead of letters, as in the plant efficiency example, and vice versa. If so, cane sugar, corn syrup, and fruit extract might be identified with the numbers 1, 2, and 3, respectively, or even 543, 26, and 2010, respectively. The important thing to note is the numbers are not representing different quantities or the value of the object. Thus any set of numbers, letters, or any other identification is equally valid.

We encounter nominal numbering systems all the time. Sports uniform numbers are nominal numbers. Ben Roethlisberger is identified on the football field by his jersey number. School bus numbers are nominal in that they simply identify a bus. Elementary school buses sometimes use both a number and an animal designation to help small children get on the right bus. So, bus number "8" may also be the "tiger" bus, but it could just as easily be the "horse" bus or the "cardinal" bus.

The first drawing in Exhibit 13.4 depicts the number 7 on a horse's colors. This is merely a label to allow bettors and racing enthusiasts to identify the horse. The assignment of a 7 to this horse does not mean that it is the seventh fastest horse or that it is the seventh biggest, or anything else meaningful. But the 7 does let you know when you have won or lost your bet!

In sum, nominal scale properties mean the numbering system simply identifies things. Exhibit 13.5 lists some nominal scales commonly used by business researchers.

Ordinal Scale

ordinal scales
Ranking scales allowing things to be arranged based on how much of some concept they possess.

Ordinal scales allow things to be arranged in order based on how much of some concept they possess. In other words, an ordinal scale is a ranking scale. In fact, we often use the term *rank order* to describe an ordinal scale. When class rank for high school students is determined, we have used an ordinal scale. We know that the student ranked seventh finished ahead of the student ranked eighth, who finished ahead of the ninth ranked student. However, we do not really know what the actual GPA was or how close these three students are to each other in overall grade point average.

Research participants often are asked to *rank* things based on preference. So, preference is the concept, and the ordinal scale lists the options from most to least preferred, or vice versa. Five objects can be ranked from 1–5 (least preferred to most preferred) or 1–5 (most preferred to least preferred) with no loss of meaning. In this sense, ordinal scales are somewhat arbitrary, but not nearly as arbitrary as a nominal scale.

When business professors take some time off and go to the race track, even they know that a horse finishing in the "show" position has finished after the "win" and "place" horses (see the

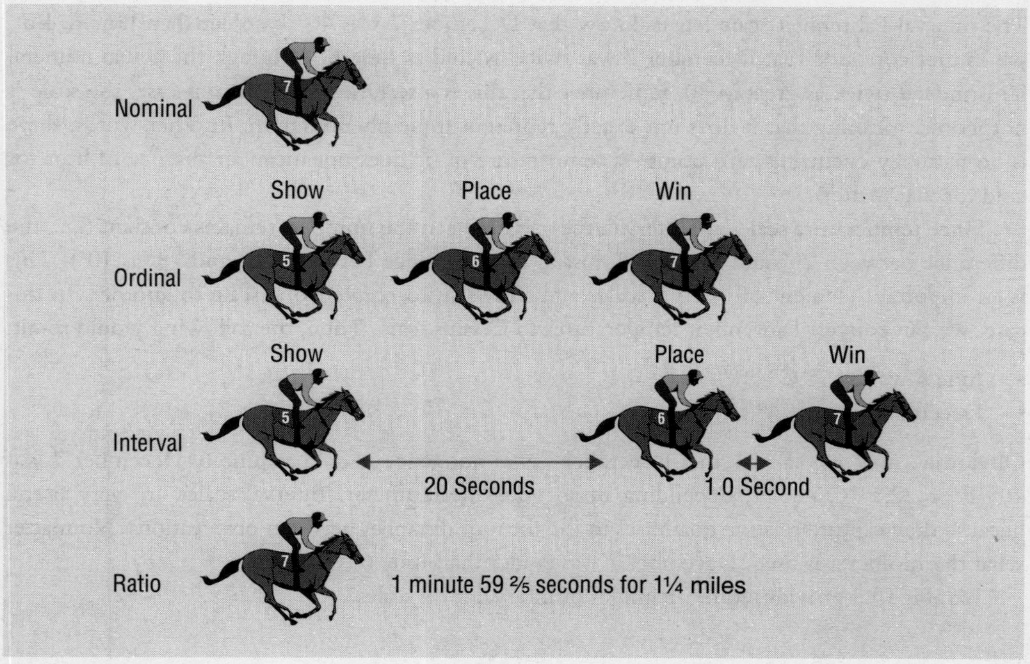

EXHIBIT 13.4
Nominal, Ordinal, Interval, and Ratio Scales Provide Different Information

second drawing in Exhibit 13.4). The order of finish can be accurately represented by an ordinal scale using an ordered number rule:

- Assign 1 to the "win" position
- Assign 2 to the "place" position
- Assign 3 to the "show" position

Perhaps the winning horse defeated the place horse by a nose, but the place horse defeated the show horse by 20 seconds. The ordinal scale does not tell how far apart the horses were, but it is good enough to let someone know the result of a wager. Typical ordinal scales in business research ask respondents to rank their three favorite brands, have personnel managers rank potential employees after job interviews, or judge investments as "buy," "hold," or "sell." Researchers know how each item, person, or stock is judged relative to others, but they do not know by how much.

Interval Scale

interval scales

Scales that have both nominal and ordinal properties, but that also capture information about differences in quantities of a concept from one observation to the next.

Interval scales have both nominal and ordinal properties, but they also capture information about differences in quantities of a concept. So, not only would a sales manager know that a particular salesperson outperformed a colleague, information that would be available with an ordinal measure, but the manager would know by how much. If a professor assigns grades to term papers using a numbering system ranging from 1.0–20.0, not only does the scale represent the fact that a student with a 16.0 outperformed a student with 12.0, but the scale would show by how much (4.0).

The third drawing in Exhibit 13.4 depicts a horse race in which the win horse is one second ahead of the place horse, which is 20 seconds ahead of the show horse. Not only are the horses identified by the order of finish, but the difference between each horse's performance is known. So, horse number 7 and horse number 6 performed similarly (1 second apart), but horse number 5 performed not nearly as well (20 seconds slower).

The classic example of an interval scale is temperature. Consider the following weather:

- June 6 was 80° F
- December 7 was 40° F

The interval Fahrenheit scale lets us know that December 7 was 40° F colder than June 6. But, we cannot conclude that December 7 was twice as cold as June 6. Although the actual numeral 80 is indeed twice as great as 40, remember that this is a scaling system. In this case, the scale is not iconic, meaning that it does not exactly represent some phenomenon. In other words, there is no naturally occurring zero point—a temperature of 0° does not mean an absence of heat (or cold for that matter).

Since temperature scales are interval, the gap between the numbers remains constant (i.e., the difference between 20° and 30° is 10°, just as the difference between 68° and 78° is 10°). This is an important element of interval scales and allows us to convert one scale to another. In this case, we can convert Fahrenheit temperatures to Celsius scale. Then, the following would result:

- June 6 was 26.7° C
- December 7 was 4.4° C

Obviously, now we can see that December 7 was not twice as cold as June 6. December 7 was 40° F or 22.3° C cooler, depending upon your thermometer. Interval scales are very useful because they capture relative quantities in the form of distances between observations. No matter what thermometer is used, December 7 was colder than June 6.

Exhibit 13.5 provides some examples of interval level scales.

EXHIBIT 13.5 Facts About the Four Levels of Scales

Level	Examples	Numerical Operations	Descriptive Statistics
Nominal	Student ID number	Counting	• Frequencies
	Yes – No		• Mode
	Male – Female		
	Buy – Did Not Buy		
	East region		
	Central region		
	West region		
Ordinal	Student class rank	Counting	• Frequencies
	Please rank your three favorite movies.	Ordering	• Mode
	Choose from the following:		• Median
	• Dissatisfied		• Range
	• Satisfied		
	• Very satisfied		
	• Delighted		
	Indicate your level of education:		
	• Some high school		
	• High school diploma		
	• Some college		
	• College degree		
	• Graduate degree		
Interval	Student grade point average (GPA)	Common	• Frequencies
	Temperature (Celsius and Fahrenheit)	arithmetic	• Mode
	Points given on an essay question	operations	• Median
	100-point job performance rating provided by supervisor		• Range
			• Mean
			• Variance
			• Standard deviation
Ratio	Amount spent on last purchase	All	• Frequencies
	Salesperson sales volume	arithmetic	• Mode
	Number of stores visited on a shopping trip	operations	• Median
	Annual family income		• Range
	Time spent viewing a Web page		• Mean
			• Variance
			• Standard deviation

Ratio Scale

ratio scales
Represent the highest form of measurement in that they have all the properties of interval scales with the additional attribute of representing absolute quantities; characterized by a meaningful absolute zero.

Ratio scales represent the highest form of measurement in that they have all the properties of interval scales with the additional attribute of representing absolute quantities. Interval scales possess only relative meaning, whereas ratio scales represent absolute meaning. In other words, ratio scales provide iconic measurement.

Zero, therefore, has meaning in that it represents an absence of some concept. An absolute zero is the defining characteristic differentiating between ratio and interval scales. For example, money is a way to measure economic value. Consider the following items offered for sale in an online auction:

- "Antique" 1970s digital watch—did not sell and there were no takers for free
- Gold-filled Elgin wristwatch circa 1950—sold for $100
- Vintage stainless steel Omega wristwatch—sold for $1,000
- Antique rose gold Patek Philippe "Top Hat" wristwatch—sold for $9,000

We can make the ordinal conclusions that the Patek was worth more than the Omega, and the Omega was worth more than the Elgin. All three of these were worth more than the 1970s digital watch. We can make interval conclusions such as that the Omega was worth $900 more than the Elgin. We can also conclude that the Patek was worth nine times as much as the Omega and that the 1970s watch was worthless (selling price = $0.00). The latter two conclusions are possible because price represents a ratio scale.

The fourth drawing in Exhibit 13.4 shows the time it took horse 7 to complete the race. If we know that horse 7 took 1 minute 59 2/5 seconds to finish the race, and we know the time it took for all the other horses, we can determine the time difference between horses 7, 6, and 5. In other words, if we knew the ratio information regarding the performance of each horse—the time to complete the race—we could determine the interval level information and the ordinal level information. However, if we only knew the ordinal level information, we could not create the interval or ratio information. Similarly, with only the interval level data we cannot create the ratio level information.

Using our opening vignette as an example, Griff could decide to use a ratio measure—salesperson annual sales volume—as the indicator of performance for the CRM division. If he did this, he could create interval level data (groups of salespeople) or ordinal level data (the rank of each salesperson). However, this would be valid only if performance was truly equal to sales.

Mathematical and Statistical Analysis of Scales

TOTHEPOINT

When you can measure what you are talking about and express it in numbers, you know something about it.

—William Thompson, Lord Kelvin

While it is true that mathematical operations can be performed with numbers from nominal scales, the result may not have a great deal of meaning. For instance, a school district may perform mathematical operations on the nominal school bus numbers. With this, they may find that the average school bus number is 77.7 with a standard deviation of 20.5. Will this help them use the buses more efficiently or better assign bus routes? Probably not. Can a professor judge the quality of her classes by the average ID number? While it could be calculated, the result is meaningless. Thus, although you can put numbers into formulas and perform calculations with almost any numbers, the researcher has to know the meaning behind the numbers before meaningful conclusions can be drawn.[5]

DISCRETE MEASURES

discrete measures

Measures that take on only one of a finite number of values.

Discrete measures are those that take on only one of a finite number of values. A discrete scale is most often used to represent a classification variable. Therefore, discrete scales do not represent intensity of measures, only membership. Common discrete scales include any yes-or-no response, matching, color choices, or practically any scale that involves selecting from among a small number of categories. Thus, when someone is asked to choose from the following responses

- Disagree
- Neutral
- Agree

RESEARCH SNAPSHOT

Football Follies

The subject of whether or not certain mathematical properties can be conducted with certain types of scales has been debated in the social science literature for decades. One famous statistician used a funny parable about a football folly to make a point about this very well. The story goes something like this:

A football coach purchased a vending machine that would assign numbers (0 to 99) to the school's football players randomly. Over the years, then, all numbers should be equally used. By randomly assigning the numbers in this way, no players were treated unequally because no one could choose one of their favorite numbers. Everybody simply got the number the machine spit out.

Professor Aaron Urd, naturally curious about anything having to do with numbers, became suspicious that the football players had secretly been breaking into the machine to select more preferred numbers. Professor Urd believed that football had no place in college and would have loved to show how unscrupulous the football players really are—stealing numbers no less! However, Professor Urd had a problem. Football numbers are nominal numbers; all they do is identify! Therefore, as all good statisticians knew, you cannot compute averages with nominal numbers. In fact, all you can do is count nominal numbers. This problem tormented Professor Urd for years. He desperately wanted to test his hypothesis about the football number theft. Many times he entered the football numbers into a spreadsheet but could not bring himself to add, multiply, or divide them. It just wouldn't be right!

One fall, Aleck Smart, a star defensive tackle on the football team, wrote a term paper for Professor Aaron Urd entitled "A Statistical Treatment of the Football Team Numbering System." Aleck, not being the brightest student, missed the day when Professor Urd taught students that you could not do arithmetic with nominal numbers. So, Aleck Smart computed all manner of statistics with data consisting of the last ten years of football numbers worn by the team. Among these, he showed that the average football number over those years was 40.1. Professor Aaron Urd was conflicted with this result. How can this be? If the numbers were assigned randomly, then shouldn't the average be 50? This must confirm his suspicion about the football number theft. But even to think this troubled him because it meant his brain was unintentionally computing the average of nominal numbers!

A few days later, Aleck dropped by Professor Aaron Urd's office to pick up his paper (after office hours of course). Professor Urd lit into Aleck: "I have given you a failing grade, Mr. Smart. Numbers from football jerseys are nominal numbers! Don't you know that you cannot take the average of nominal numbers?"

Aleck thought about that a while and answered, "Professor Urd, the numbers don't know where they came from."

Professor Urd decided to change Aleck's grade to a B–. He then used Aleck's calculations to try and show the faculty senate that the football team was indeed breaking into the machine.

Sources: Lord, F. M., "On the Statistical Treatment of Football Numbers," *American Psychologist* 8 (1953), 750–751; Cohen, Jacob, "Things I Have Learned (So Far)," *American Psychologist* 45 (December 1990), 1304–1312.

the result is a discrete value that can be coded 1, 2, or 3, respectively. This is also an ordinal scale to the extent that it represents an ordered arrangement of agreement. Nominal and ordinal scales are discrete measures.

Certain statistics are most appropriate for discrete measures. Exhibit 13.5 shows statistics for each scale level. The largest distinction is between statistics used for discrete versus continuous measures. For instance, the central tendency of discrete measures is best captured by the mode. When a student wants to know what the most likely grade is for MGT 341, the mode will be very useful. Observe the results below from the previous semester:

A	3 Students	D	3 Students
B	9 Students	F	1 Student
C	6 Students		

The mode is a "B" since more students obtained that value than any other value. Therefore, the "average" student would expect a B in MGT 341.

continuous measures

Measures that reflect the intensity of a concept by assigning values that can take on any value along some scale range.

CONTINUOUS MEASURES

Continuous measures are those assigning values anywhere along some scale range in a place that corresponds to the intensity of some concept. Ratio measures are continuous measures. Thus, when Griff measures sales for each salesperson using the dollar amount sold, he is assigning a continuous measure. A number line could be constructed ranging from the least amount sold to the most, and a spot on the line would correspond exactly to a salesperson's performance.

Strictly speaking, interval scales are not necessarily continuous. Consider the following common type of survey question:

	Strongly Disagree	Disagree	Neutral	Agree	Strongly Agree
I enjoy participating in online auctions	1	2	3	4	5

This is a discrete scale because only the values 1, 2, 3, 4, or 5 can be assigned. Furthermore, it is an ordinal scale because it only orders based on agreement. We really have no way of knowing that the difference in agreement of somebody marking a 5 instead of a 4 is the same as the difference in agreement of somebody marking a 2 instead of a 1. Therefore, the mean is not an appropriate way of stating central tendency and, technically, we really shouldn't use many common statistics on these responses.

However, as a scaled response of this type takes on more values, the error introduced by assuming that the differences between the discrete points are equal becomes smaller. This may be seen by imagining a *Likert scale* (the traditional business research agreement scale shown above) with a thousand levels of agreement rather than three. The differences between the different levels become so small with a thousand levels that only tiny errors could be introduced by assuming each interval is the same. Therefore, business researchers generally treat interval scales containing five or more categories of response as interval. When fewer than five categories are used, this assumption is inappropriate.

The researcher should keep in mind, however, the distinction between ratio and interval measures. Errors in judgment can be made when interval measures are treated as ratio. For example, attitude is usually measured with an interval scale. An attitude of zero means nothing. In fact, attitude would only have meaning in a relative sense. In other words, attitude takes on meaning when one person's response is compared to another or through some other comparison. A single attitude score alone contains little useful information.

The mean and standard deviation may be calculated from continuous data. Using the actual quantities for arithmetic operations is permissible with ratio scales. Thus, the ratios of scale values are meaningful. A ratio scale has all the properties of nominal, ordinal, and interval scales. However, the same cannot be said in reverse. An interval scale, for example, has ordinal and nominal properties, but it does not have ratio properties (see Exhibit 13.5).

Chapters 19 through 23 further explore the limitations scales impose on the mathematical analysis of data.

Index Measures

attribute

A single characteristic or fundamental feature of an object, person, situation, or issue.

Earlier, we distinguished constructs as concepts that require multiple variables to measure them adequately. Looking back to the chapter vignette, could it be that multiple items will be required to adequately represent job performance? Likewise, a consumer's attitude toward some product is usually a function of multiple attributes. An **attribute** is a single characteristic or fundamental feature of an object, person, situation, or issue.

RESEARCH SNAPSHOT

Recoding Made Easy

Most computer statistical software makes scale recoding easy. The screenshot shown here is from SPSS (Statistical Package for the Social Sciences), perhaps the most widely used statistical software in business-related research. All that needs to be done to reverse code a scale is to go through the right click-through sequence described below:

1. Click on transform.
2. Click on recode.
3. Choose to recode into the same variable.
4. Select the variable(s) to be recoded.
5. Click on old and new values.
6. Use the menu that appears to enter the old values and the matching new values. Click add after entering each pair.
7. Click continue.

This process would successfully recode a variable that needed to be reverse coded.

© iStock

© ROYALTY-FREE/CORBIS

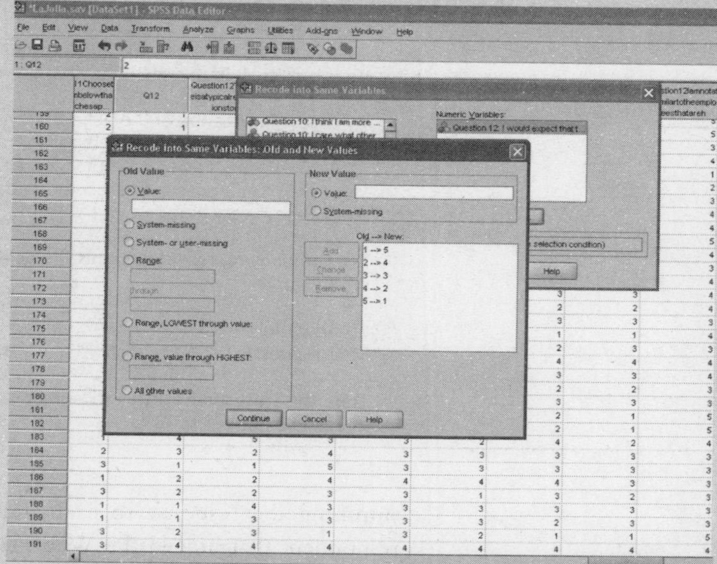

COURTESY OF SPSS STATISTICS 17.0.

Indexes and Composites

Multi-item instruments for measuring a construct are called *index measures*, or *composite measures*. An **index measure** assigns a value based on how much of the concept being measured is associated with an observation. Indexes often are formed by putting several variables together. For example, a social class index might be based on three weighted variables: occupation, education, and area of residence. Usually, occupation is seen as the single best indicator and would be weighted highest. With an index, the different attributes may not be strongly correlated with each other. A person's education does not always relate strongly to their area of residence. The American Consumer Satisfaction Index shows how satisfied American consumers are based on an index of satisfaction scores. Readers are likely not surprised to know that Americans appear more satisfied with soft drinks than they are with cable TV companies based on this index.[6]

index measure
An index assigns a value based on how much of the concept being measured is associated with an observation. Indexes often are formed by putting several variables together.

Composite measures also assign a value based on a mathematical derivation of multiple variables. For example, salesperson satisfaction may be measured by combining questions such as "How satisfied are you with your job? How satisfied are you with your territory? How satisfied are you with the opportunity your job offers?" For most practical applications, composite measures and indexes are computed in the same way.[7]

composite measures
Assign a value to an observation based on a mathematical derivation of multiple variables.

Computing Scale Values

Exhibit 13.6 demonstrates how a composite measure can be created from common rating scales. This scale was developed to assess how much a consumer trusts a Web site.[8] This particular composite represents a **summated scale.** A summated scale is created by simply

summated scale
A scale created by simply summing (adding together) the response to each item making up the composite measure.

EXHIBIT 13.6
Computing a Composite Scale

Item	Strongly Disagree (SD) → Strongly Agree (SA)				
This site appears to be more trustworthy than other sites I have visited.	SD	(D)	N	A	SA
My overall trust in this site is very high.	SD	D	(N)	A	SA
My overall impression of the believability of the information on this site is very high.	SD	(D)	N	A	SA
My overall confidence in the recommendations on this site is very high.	SD	(D)	N	A	SA
The company represented in this site delivers on its promises.	SD	D	N	(A)	SA

Computation:
Scale Values: SD = 1, D = 2, N = 3, A = 4, SA = 5

Thus, the Trust score for this consumer is
2 + 3 + 2 + 2 + 4 = 13

summing the response to each item making up the composite measure. For this scale, a respondent that judged the Web site as extremely trustworthy would choose *SA* (value of 5) for each question. Across the five questions, this respondent's score would be 25. Conversely, a respondent that thought the Web site was very untrustworthy would chose *SD* (value of 1) for each question; a total of 5. Most respondents would likely be somewhere between these extremes. For the example respondent in Exhibit 13.6, the summated scale score would be 13 based on his responses to the five items (2 + 3 + 2 + 2 + 4 = 13). A researcher may sometimes choose to average the scores rather than summing them. The advantage to this is that the composite measure is expressed on the same scale (1–5 rather than 5–25) as the original items. So, instead of a 13, the consumer would have a score of 2.6. While this approach might be more easily understood, the information contained in either situation (13 versus 2.6) is the same.

reverse coding
Means that the value assigned for a response is treated oppositely from the other items.

Sometimes, a response may need to be reverse-coded before computing a summated or averaged scale value. **Reverse coding** means that the value assigned for a response is treated oppositely from the other items. If a sixth item was included on the Web site trust scale that said, "I do not trust this Web site," reverse coding would be necessary to make sure the composite made sense. For example, the respondent that judged the Web site is extremely trustworthy would choose *SA* for the first five items, then *SD* for the sixth. We can see that we would not want to just add these up, as this score of 21 would not really reflect someone that felt very positive about the trustworthiness of the site. Since the content of the sixth item is the reverse of trust (distrust), so the scale itself should be reversed. Thus, on a 5-point scale, the values are reversed as follows:

- 5 becomes 1
- 4 becomes 2
- 3 stays 3
- 2 becomes 4
- 1 becomes 5

After the reverse coding, our respondent that felt the Web site was trustworthy would have a summated score of 25, which does correctly reflect a very positive attitude. If the respondent described in Exhibit 13.6 responded to this new item with an *SA* (5), it would be reverse coded as a 1 before computing the summated scale. Thus, the summated scale value for the six items would become 14. The process of reverse coding is discussed in the Research Snapshot titled "Recoding Made Easy."

Three Criteria for Good Measurement

The three major criteria for evaluating measurements are reliability, validity, and sensitivity.

Reliability

Reliability is an indicator of a measure's internal consistency. Consistency is the key to understanding reliability. A measure is reliable when different attempts at measuring something converge on the same result. For example, consider an exam that has three parts: 25 multiple-choice questions, 2 essay questions, and a short case. If a student gets 20 of the 25 (80 percent) multiple-choice questions correct, we would expect she would also score about 80 percent on the essay and case portions of the exam. Further, if a professor's research tests are reliable, a student should tend toward consistent scores on all tests. In other words, a student who makes an 80 percent on the first test should make scores close to 80 percent on all subsequent tests. Another way to look at this is that the student who makes the best score on one test will exhibit scores close to the best score in the class on the other tests. If it is difficult to predict what students would make on a test by examining their previous test scores, the tests probably lack reliability or the students are not preparing the same each time.

reliability
An indicator of a measure's internal consistency.

So, the concept of reliability revolves around consistency. Think of a scale to measure weight. You would expect this scale to be consistent from one time to the next. If you stepped on the scale and it read 140 pounds, then got off and back on, you would expect it to again read 140. If it read 110 the second time, while you may be happier, the scale would not be reliable.

INTERNAL CONSISTENCY

Internal consistency represents a measure's homogeneity. An attempt to measure trustworthiness may require asking several similar but not identical questions, as shown in Exhibit 13.6. The set of items that make up a measure are referred to as a *battery* of scale items. *Internal consistency* of a multiple-item measure can be measured by correlating scores on subsets of items making up a scale.

internal consistency
Represents a measure's homogeneity or the extent to which each indicator of a concept converges on some common meaning.

The **split-half method** of checking reliability is performed by taking half the items from a scale (for example, odd-numbered items) and checking them against the results from the other half (even-numbered items). The two scale *halves* should produce similar scores and correlate highly. The problem with split-half method is determining the two halves. Should it be even- and odd-numbered questions? Questions 1–3 compared to 4–6? Coefficient alpha provides a solution to this dilemma.

split-half method
A method for assessing internal consistency by checking the results of one-half of a set of scaled items against the results from the other half.

Coefficient alpha (α) is the most commonly applied estimate of a multiple-item scale's reliability.[9] Coefficient α represents internal consistency by computing the average of all possible split-half reliabilities for a multiple-item scale. The coefficient demonstrates whether or not the different items converge. Although coefficient α does not address validity, many researchers use α as the sole indicator of a scale's quality. Coefficient alpha ranges in value from 0, meaning no consistency, to 1, meaning complete consistency (all items yield corresponding values). Generally speaking, scales with a coefficient α between 0.80 and 0.95 are considered to have very good reliability. Scales with a coefficient α between 0.70 and 0.80 are considered to have good reliability, and an α value between 0.60 and 0.70 indicates fair reliability. When the coefficient α is below 0.6, the scale has poor reliability.[10] Most statistical software packages, such as SPSS, will easily compute coefficient α.

coefficient alpha (α)
The most commonly applied estimate of a multiple-item scale's reliability. It represents the average of all possible split-half reliabilities for a construct.

TEST-RETEST RELIABILITY

The **test-retest method** of determining reliability involves administering the same scale or measure to the same respondents at two separate times to test for stability. If the measure is stable over time, the test, administered under the same conditions each time, should obtain similar results. Test-retest reliability represents a measure's repeatability.

test-retest method
Administering the same scale or measure to the same respondents at two separate points in time to test for stability.

Suppose a researcher at one time attempts to measure buying intentions and finds that 12 percent of the population is willing to purchase a product. If the study is repeated a few weeks later under similar conditions, and the researcher again finds that 12 percent of the population is willing to purchase the product, the measure appears to be reliable. High stability correlation or consistency between two measures at time 1 and time 2 indicates high reliability.

Let's assume that a person does not change his or her attitude about dark beer. Attitude might be measured with an item like the one shown below:

I prefer dark beer to all other types of beer.

If repeated measurements of that individual's attitude toward dark beer are taken with the same scale, a reliable instrument will produce the same results each time the scale is measured. Thus one's attitude in October of 2009 should tend to be the same as one's attitude in May 2010. When a measuring instrument produces unpredictable results from one testing to the next, the results are said to be unreliable because of error in measurement.

As another example, consider these remarks by a Gillette executive made about the reliability problems in measuring reactions to razor blades:

> *There is a high degree of noise in our data, a considerable variability in results. It's a big mish-mash, what we call the night sky in August. There are points all over the place. A man will give a blade a high score one day, but the next day he'll cut himself a lot and give the blade a terrible score. But on the third day, he'll give the same blade a good score. What you have to do is try to see some pattern in all this. There are some gaps in our knowledge.*[11]

Measures of test-retest reliability pose two problems that are common to all longitudinal studies. First, the pre-measure, or first measure, may sensitize the respondents to their participation in a research project and subsequently influence the results of the second measure (you may recall we referred to this as "demand characteristics" in Chapter 12). Furthermore, if the time between measures is long, there may be an attitude change or other maturation of the subjects. Thus, a reliable measure can indicate a low or a moderate correlation between the first and second administration, but this low correlation may be due to an attitude change over time rather than to a lack of reliability in the measure itself.

Validity

Good measures should be both consistent and accurate. Reliability represents how consistent a measure is, in that the different attempts at measuring the same thing converge on the same point. Accuracy deals more with how a measure assesses the intended concept. **Validity** is the accuracy of a measure or the extent to which a score truthfully represents a concept. In other words, are we accurately measuring what we think we are measuring?

validity
The accuracy of a measure or the extent to which a score truthfully represents a concept.

Achieving validity is not a simple matter. The opening vignette describes this point. The job performance measure should truly reflect job performance. If a supervisor's friendship affects the performance measure, then the scale's validity is diminished. Likewise, if the performance scale is defined as effort, the result may well be a reliable scale but not one that actually reflects performance. Effort may well lead to performance but effort probably does not equal performance.

Students should be able to empathize with the following validity problem. Consider the controversy about highway patrol officers using radar guns to clock speeders. A driver is clocked at 83 mph in a 55 mph zone, but the same radar gun aimed at a house registers 28 mph. The error occurred because the radar gun had picked up impulses from the electrical system of the squad car's idling engine. Obviously, the house was not moving, thus how can we be sure the car was speeding? In this case, we would certainly question if the accusation that the car was actually going 83 mph is completely valid.

ESTABLISHING VALIDITY

Researchers have attempted to assess validity in many ways. They attempt to provide some evidence of a measure's degree of validity by answering a variety of questions. Is there a consensus among other researchers that my attitude scale measures what it is supposed to measure? Does my measure cover everything that it should? Does my measure correlate with other measures of the same concept? Does the behavior expected from my measure predict actual observed behavior? The four basic approaches to establishing validity are *face validity, content validity, criterion validity,* and *construct validity.*

© BRAND X PICTURES/JUPITER IMAGES

A golfer can hit reliable but not valid putts. This fellow misses all his putts to the left.

face validity

A scale's content logically appears to reflect what was intended to be measured.

Face validity refers to the subjective agreement among professionals that a scale logically reflects the concept being measured. Do the test items look like they make sense given a concept's definition? When an inspection of the test items convinces experts that the items match the definition, the scale is said to have face validity.

Clear, understandable questions such as "How many children do you have?" generally are agreed to have face validity. But it becomes more difficult to assess face validity in regard to more complicated business phenomena. For instance, consider the concept of *customer loyalty.* Does the statement "I prefer to purchase my groceries at Delavan Fine Foods" appear to capture loyalty? How about "I am very satisfied with my purchases from Delavan Fine Foods"? What about "Delavan Fine Foods offers very good value"? While the first statement appears to capture loyalty, it can be argued the second question is not loyalty but rather satisfaction. What does the third statement reflect? Do you think it looks like a loyalty statement?

In scientific studies, face validity might be considered a first hurdle. In comparison to other forms of validity, face validity is relatively easy to assess. However, researchers are generally not satisfied with simply establishing face validity. Because of the elusive nature of attitudes and other business phenomena, additional forms of validity are sought.

content validity

The degree that a measure covers the breadth of the domain of interest.

Content validity refers to the degree that a measure covers the domain of interest. Do the items capture the entire scope, but not go beyond, the concept we are measuring? If an exam is supposed to cover chapters 1–5, it is fair for students to expect that questions should come from all five chapters, rather than just one or two. It is also fair to assume that the questions will not come from chapter 6. Thus, when students complain about the material on an exam, they are often claiming it lacks content validity. Similarly, an evaluation of an employee's job performance should cover all important aspects of the job, but not something outside of the employee's specified duties.

It has been argued that shoppers receive value from two primary elements.[12] Hedonic shopping value refers to the pleasure and enjoyment one gets from the shopping experience, while utilitarian shopping value refers to value received from the actual acquisition of the product desired. If a researcher assessing shopping value only asked questions regarding the utilitarian aspects of shopping, we could argue the measure lacks content validity since part of the domain (hedonic value) is ignored.

criterion validity

The ability of a measure to correlate with other standard measures of similar constructs or established criteria.

Criterion validity addresses the question, "How well does my measure work in practice?" Because of this, criterion validity is sometimes referred to as *pragmatic validity.* In other words, is my measure practical? Criterion validity may be classified as either *concurrent validity* or *predictive validity* depending on the time sequence in which the new measurement scale and the criterion measure are correlated. If the new measure is taken at the same time as the criterion measure and is shown to be valid, then it has concurrent validity. Predictive validity is established when a new measure predicts a future event. The two measures differ only on the basis of a time dimension—that is, the criterion measure is separated in time from the predictor measure.

For instance, a home pregnancy test is designed to have concurrent validity—to accurately determine if a person is pregnant at the time of the test. Fertility tests, on the other hand, are designed for predictive validity—to determine if a person can become pregnant in the future. In a business setting, participants in a training seminar might be given a test to assess their knowledge of the concepts covered, establishing concurrent validity. Personnel managers may give potential employees an exam to predict if they will be effective salespeople (predictive validity). While face validity is a subjective evaluation, criterion validity provides a more rigorous empirical test.

construct validity
Exists when a measure reliably measures and truthfully represents a unique concept; consists of several components including face validity, content validty, criterion validity, convergent validity, and discriminant validity.

convergent validity
Concepts that should be related to one another are in fact related; highly reliable scales contain convergent validity.

discriminant validity
Represents how unique or distinct is a measure; a scale should not correlate too highly with a measure of a different construct.

Construct validity exists when a measure reliably measures and truthfully represents a unique concept. Construct validity consists of several components, including

- Face validity
- Content validity
- Criterion validity
- Convergent validity
- Discriminant validity

We have discussed face validity, content validity, and criterion validity. Before we move further, we must be sure our measures look like they are measuring what they are intended to measure (face validity) and adequately cover the domain of interest (content validity). If so, we can assess **convergent validity** and **discriminant validity**.

These forms of validity represent how unique or distinct a measure is. Convergent validity requires that concepts that should be related are indeed related. For example, in business we believe customer satisfaction and customer loyalty are related. If we have measures of both, we would expect them to be positively correlated. If we found no significant correlation between our measures of satisfaction and our measures of loyalty, it would bring into question the convergent validity of these measures. On the other hand, our customer satisfaction measure should not correlate too highly with the loyalty measure if the two concepts are truly different. If the correlation is too high, we have to ask if we are measuring two different things, or if satisfaction and loyalty are actually one concept. As a rough rule of thumb, when two scales are correlated above 0.75, discriminant validity may be questioned. So, we expect related concepts to display a significant correlation (convergent validity), but not to be so highly correlated that they are not independent concepts (discriminant validity).

Multivariate procedures like factor analysis can be useful in establishing construct validity. The reader is referred to other sources for a more detailed discussion.[13]

Reliability versus Validity

Reliability is a necessary but not sufficient condition for validity. A reliable scale may not be valid. For example, a purchase intention measurement technique may consistently indicate that 20 percent of those sampled are willing to purchase a new product. Whether the measure is valid depends on whether 20 percent of the population indeed purchases the product. A reliable but invalid instrument will yield consistently inaccurate results.

The differences between reliability and validity can be illustrated by the rifle targets in Exhibit 13.7. Suppose an expert sharpshooter fires an equal number of rounds with a century-old rifle and a modern rifle.[14] The shots from the older gun are considerably scattered, but those from the newer gun are closely clustered. The variability of the old rifle compared with that of the new one indicates it is less reliable. The target on the right illustrates the concept of a systematic bias influencing validity. The new rifle is reliable (because it has little variance), but the sharpshooter's vision is hampered by glare. Although shots are consistent, the sharpshooter is unable to hit the bull's-eye.

TIPS OF THE TRADE

- When determining which level of scale measurement to use, a researcher is usually best served by collecting the highest quality of data possible. If you have ratio level data, you can create interval or ordinal level data. For instance, if you collect the actual sales figures for each salesperson, the rank (ordinal) of each salesperson can be determined, or interval level categories can be established. You cannot move the other direction. However, there are exceptions to this rule.
  - First, when you anticipate that ranking will result in greater variance than rating the items independently, it might be better to collect ordinal data rather than interval. For example, if an employee is asked rate the importance of (1) salary, (2) opportunities for advancement, and (3) enjoyable work environment on a five-point interval scale, he could very well give a 5 to each. If asked to rank these three, the respondent could likely assign them a 1, 2, and 3, which would provide greater variance and more information.
  - A second situation involves sensitive information. While we could collect ratio level data regarding annual income by asking for an actual number, we typically collect interval level data by creating multiple ranges as this is not as intrusive to the respondent.
- We can think of internal consistency of asking multiple questions at one point in time to assess reliability; we can think of test-retest of asking the same question(s) to the same respondents at different points in time. Since we typically prefer to collect data once instead of twice, internal consistency is the most common method of establishing reliability in business research.
- Reliability is necessary, but not sufficient, to establish validity. A measure can be reliable, but not valid. However, a valid measure is reliable. Since validity is our true goal, why do we even deal with validity?
  - The issue here revolves around our ability to establish reliability and validity. Reliability is relatively easy to assess, while validity is much more difficult. In fact, it is fair to say we can never unequivocally establish validity; validity must be inferred. So, if our measure is not reliable, we have no reason to try the more difficult task of establishing validity.

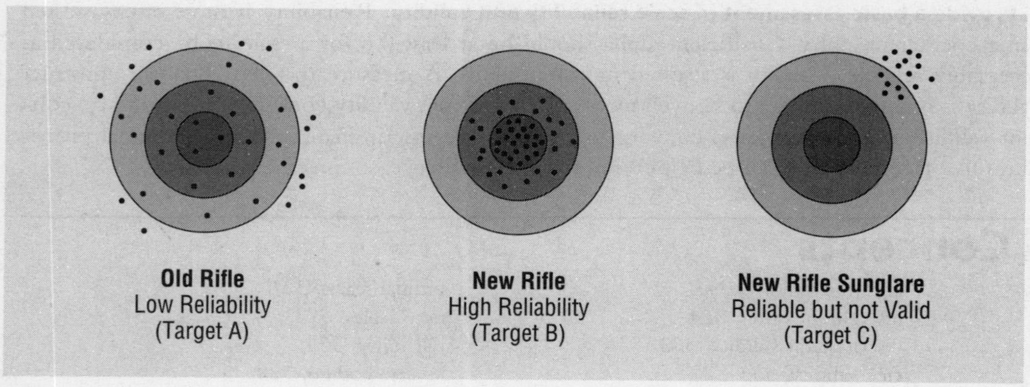

EXHIBIT 13.7
Reliability and Validity on Target

Sensitivity

The sensitivity of a scale is an important measurement concept, particularly when *changes* in attitudes or other hypothetical constructs are under investigation. **Sensitivity** refers to an instrument's ability to accurately measure variability in a concept. A dichotomous response category, such as "agree or disagree," does not allow the recording of subtle attitude changes. A more sensitive measure with numerous categories on the scale may be needed. For example, adding "strongly agree," "mildly agree," "neither agree nor disagree," "mildly disagree," and "strongly disagree" will increase the scale's sensitivity.

sensitivity
A measurement instrument's ability to accurately measure variability in stimuli or responses.

The sensitivity of a scale based on a single question or single item can also be increased by adding questions or items. In other words, because composite measures allow for a greater range of possible scores, they are more sensitive than single-item scales. Thus, sensitivity is generally increased by adding more response points or adding scale items.

Summary

1. Determine what needs to be measured to address a research question or hypothesis. Researchers can determine what concepts must be measured by examining research questions and hypotheses. A hypothesis often states that one concept is related to another. Therefore, the concepts listed in the hypotheses must have operational measures if the research is to be performed.

2. Distinguish levels of scale measurement. Four levels of scale measurement can be identified. Each level is associated with increasingly more complex properties. Nominal scales assign numbers or letters to objects for identification or classification. Ordinal scales arrange objects based on relative magnitude of a concept. Thus, ordinal scales represent rankings. Interval scales also represent an ordering based on relative amounts of a concept, but they also capture the differences between scale values. Thus, interval scales allow stimuli to be compared to each other based on the difference in their scale scores. Ratio scales are absolute scales, starting with absolute zeros at which there is a total absence of the attribute. Nominal and ordinal scales are discrete. The mode is the best way to represent central tendency for discrete measures. Ratio measures are continuous and interval scales are generally treated as continuous. For continuous measures, the mean represents a valid representation of central tendency.

3. Know how to form an index or composite measure. Indexes and composite measures are formed by combining scores from multiple items. For instance, a composite score can be formed by adding the scores to multiple items, each intended to represent the same concept.

4. List the three criteria for good measurement. Good measurement exists when a measure is reliable, valid, and sensitive. Thus, reliability, validity, and sensitivity are characteristics of good measurement. Reliability represents the consistency and repeatability of a measure. Validity refers to the degree to which the instrument measures the concept the researcher wants to measure. Sensitivity is the instrument's ability to accurately measure variability in stimuli or responses.

5. Provide a basic assessment of scale reliability and validity. Reliability is most often assessed using coefficient alpha. Coefficient alpha should be at least 0.6 for a scale to be considered as acceptably reliable. Validity is assessed in components. A measure that has adequate construct validity is one that is likely to be well measured. Construct validity consists of face validity, content validity, criterion validity, convergent validity, and discriminant validity. Statistical procedures like factor analysis can be helpful in providing evidence of construct validity.

Key Terms and Concepts

attribute, *326*
coefficient alpha (α), *329*
composite measures, *327*
concept, *318*
construct, *318*
construct validity, *332*
content validity, *331*
continuous measures, *326*
convergent validity, *332*
correspondence rules, *318*
criterion validity, *331*
discrete measures, *324*
discriminant validity, *332*
face validity, *331*
index measure, *327*
internal consistency, *329*
interval scales, *322*
measurement, *316*
nominal scales, *320*
operationalization, *318*
ordinal scales, *321*
ratio scales, *323*
reliability, *329*
reverse coding, *328*
scales, *318*
sensitivity, *333*
split-half method, *329*
summated scale, *327*
test-retest method, *329*
validity, *330*

Questions for Review and Critical Thinking

1. Define *measurement*. How is your performance in your research class being measured?
2. What is the difference between a *concept* and a *construct?*
3. Suppose a researcher takes over a project only after a proposal has been written by another researcher. Where will the researcher find the things that need to be measured?
4. Describe, compare, and contrast the four different levels of scale measurement.
5. Consider the different grading measuring scales described at the beginning of the chapter. Describe what level of measurement is represented by each. Which method do you think contains the least opportunity for error?
6. Look at the responses to the following survey items that describe how stressful consumers believed a Christmas shopping trip was using a ten-point scale ranging from 1 (= no stress at all) to 10 (= extremely stressful):
   a. How stressful was finding a place to park? 7
   b. How stressful was the checkout procedure? 5
   c. How stressful was trying to find exactly the right product? 8
   d. How stressful was finding a store employee? 6

i. What would be the stress score for this respondent based on a summated scale score?
ii. What would be the stress score for this respondent based on an average composite scale score?
iii. Do any items need to be reverse-coded? Why or why not?

7. How is it that business researchers can justify treating a seven-point Likert scale as interval?
8. What are the components of construct validity? Describe each.
9. Why might a researcher wish to use more than one question to measure satisfaction with a particular aspect of retail shopping?
10. How can a researcher assess the reliability and validity of a multi-item composite scale?
11. Comment on the validity and reliability of the following:
    a. A respondent's report of an intention to subscribe to *Consumer Reports* is highly reliable. A researcher believes this constitutes a valid measurement of dissatisfaction with the economic system and alienation from big business.
    b. A general-interest magazine claimed that it was a better advertising medium than television programs with similar content. Research had indicated that for a soft drink and other test products, recall scores were higher for the magazine ads than for 30-second commercials.
    c. A respondent's report of frequency of magazine reading consistently indicates that she regularly reads *Good Housekeeping* and *Gourmet* and never reads *Cosmopolitan*.
12. Indicate whether the following measures use a nominal, ordinal, interval, or ratio scale:
    a. Prices on the stock market
    b. Marital status, classified as "married" or "never married"
    c. A yes/no question asking whether a respondent has ever been unemployed
    d. Professorial rank: assistant professor, associate professor, or professor
    e. Grades: A, B, C, D, or F

Research Activities

1. Go to the library and find out how *Sales and Marketing Management* magazine constructs its buying-power index.
2. Define each of the following concepts, and then operationally define each one by providing correspondence rules between the definition and the scale:
    a. A good bowler
    b. The television audience for *The Tonight Show*
    c. Purchasing intention for an iPhone
    d. Consumer involvement with cars
    e. A workaholic
    f. Outstanding supervisory skills
    g. A risk averse investor
3. **'NET** Use the ACSI scores found at **http://www.theacsi.org** to respond to this question. Using the most recent two years of data, test the following two hypotheses:
    a. American consumers are more satisfied with breweries than they are with wireless telephone services.
    b. **'NET** American consumers are more satisfied with discount and department stores than they are with automobile companies.
4. Refer back to the opening vignette. Use a search engine to find stories dealing with job performance. In particular, pay attention to stories that may be related to CRM. Make a recommendation to Griff concerning a way that job performance should be measured. Would your scale be nominal, ordinal, interval, or ratio?
5. **'NET** Go to **http://www.queendom.com/tests**. Click on the lists of personality tests. Take the hostility test. Do you think this is a reliable and valid measure of how prone someone is to generally act in a hostile manner?

Case 13.1 FlyAway Airways

© GETTY IMAGES/ PHOTODISC GREEN

Wesley Shocker, research analyst for FlyAway Airways, was asked by the director of research to make recommendations regarding the best approach for monitoring the quality of service provided by the airline.[15] FlyAway Airways is a national air carrier that has a comprehensive route structure consisting of long-haul, coast-to-coast routes and direct, nonstop routes between short-haul metropolitan areas. Current competitors include Midway and Alaska Airlines. FlyAway Airlines is poised to surpass the billion-dollar revenue level required to be designated as a major airline. This change in status brings a new set of competitors. To prepare for this move up in competitive status, Shocker was asked to review the options available for monitoring the quality of FlyAway Airways service and the service of its competitors. Such monitoring would involve better understanding the nature of service quality and the ways in which quality can be tracked for airlines.

After some investigation, Shocker discovered two basic approaches to measuring quality of airline service that can produce similar ranking results. His report must outline the important aspects to consider in measuring quality as well as the critical points of difference and similarity between the two approaches to measuring quality.

Some Background on Quality

In today's competitive airline industry, it's crucial that an airline do all it can do to attract and retain customers. One of the best ways to do this is by offering quality service to consumers. Perceptions of service quality vary from person to person, but an enduring element of service quality is the consistent achievement of customer satisfaction. For customers to perceive an airline as offering quality service, they must be satisfied, and that usually means receiving a service outcome that is equal to or greater than what they expected.

An airline consumer usually is concerned most with issues of schedule, destination, and price when choosing an airline. Given that most airlines have competition in each of these areas, other factors that relate to quality become important to the customer when making a choice between airlines. Both subjective aspects of quality (that is, food, pleasant employees, and so forth) and objective aspects (that is, on-time performance, safety, lost baggage, and so forth) have real meaning to consumers. These secondary factors may not be as critical as schedule, destination, and price, but they do affect quality judgments of the customer.

There are many possible combinations of subjective and objective aspects that could influence a customer's perception of quality at different times. Fortunately, since 1988, consumers of airline services have had access to objective information from the Department of Transportation regarding service performance in some basic categories. Unfortunately, the average consumer is most likely unaware of or uninterested in these data on performance; instead, consumers rely on personal experience and subjective opinion to judge quality of service. Periodic surveys of subjective consumer opinion regarding airline service experience are available through several sources. These efforts rely on contact with a sample of consumers who may or may not have informed opinions regarding the quality of airline service for all airlines being compared.

A Consumer Survey Approach

In his research, Shocker discovered a recent study conducted to identify favorite airlines of frequent fliers. This study is typical of the survey-based, infrequent (usually only annually), subjective efforts conducted to assess airline quality. A New York firm, Research & Forecasts, Inc., published results of a consumer survey of frequent fliers that used several criteria to rate domestic and international airlines. Criteria included comfort, service, reliability, food quality, cost, delays, routes served, safety, and frequent-flier plans. The questionnaire was sent to 25,000 frequent fliers.

The 4,462 people who responded were characterized as predominantly male (59 percent) professional managers (66 percent) whose average age was 45 and who traveled an average of at least 43 nights a year for both business and pleasure. This group indicated that the most important factors in choosing an airline were 1) route structure (46 percent), 2) price (42 percent), 3) reliability (41 percent), 4) service (33 percent), 5) safety (33 percent), 6) frequent-flier plans (33 percent), and 7) food (12 percent). When asked to rate twenty different airlines, respondents provided the rankings in Case Exhibit 13.1–1.

A Weighted Average Approach

Shocker also discovered a newer, more objective approach to measuring airline quality in a study recently published by the National Institute for Aviation Research at the Wichita State University in Wichita, Kansas. The Airline Quality Rating (AQR) is a weighted average of 19 factors that have relevance when judging the quality of airline services (see Case Exhibit 13.2–2). The AQR is based on data that are readily obtainable (most of the data are updated monthly) from published sources for each major airline operating in the United States. Regularly published data on such factors as consumer complaints, on-time performance, accidents, number of aircraft, and financial performance are available from the Department of Transportation, the National Transportation Safety Board, Moody's Bond Record, industry trade publications, and annual reports of individual airlines.

To establish the 19 weighted factors, an opinion survey was conducted with a group of 65 experts in the aviation field. These experts included representatives of most major airlines, air travel experts, Federal Aviation Administration (FAA) representatives, academic researchers, airline manufacturing and support firms, and individual consumers. Each expert was asked to rate the importance that each individual factor might have to a consumer of airline services using a scale of 0 (no importance) to 10 (great importance). The average importance ratings for each of the 19 factors were then used as the weights for those factors in the AQR. Case Exhibit 13.1–2 shows the factors included in the Airline Quality Rating, the weight associated with each factor, and whether the factor has a positive or negative impact on quality from the consumer's perspective.

Using the Airline Quality Rating formula and recent data, produce AQR scores and rankings for the 10 major U.S. airlines shown in Case Exhibit 13.1–3.

CASE EXHIBIT 13.1–1 **Ranking of Major Airlines: Consumer Survey Approach**

1. American	11. Lufthansa
2. United	12. USAir
3. Delta	13. KLM
4. TWA	14. America West
5. SwissAir	15. JAL
6. Singapore	16. Alaska
7. British Airways	17. Qantas
8. Continental	18. Midway
9. Air France	19. Southwest
10. Pan Am	20. SAS

CASE EXHIBIT 13.1–2 **Factors Included in the Airline Quality Rating (AQR)[a]**

Factor	Weight
1. Average age of fleet	25.85
2. Number of aircraft	14.54
3. On-time performance	18.63
4. Load factor	26.98
5. Pilot deviations	28.03
6. Number of accidents	28.38
7. Frequent-flier awards	27.35
8. Flight problems[b]	28.05
9. Denied boardings[b]	28.03
10. Mishandled baggage[b]	27.92
11. Fares[b]	27.60
12. Customer service[b]	27.20
13. Refunds	27.32
14. Ticketing/boarding[b]	−7.08
15. Advertising[b]	−6.82
16. Credit[b]	25.94
17. Other[b]	27.34
18. Financial stability	26.52
19. Average seat-mile cost	24.49

$$AQR = \frac{w_1F_1 - w_2F_2 + w_3F_3 + \cdots - w_{19}F_{19}}{w_1 + w_2 + w_3 + \cdots + w_{19}}$$

a. The 19-item rating has a reliability coefficient (Cronbach's Alpha) of 0.87.
b. Data for these factors come from consumer complaints registered with the Department of Transportation.

CASE EXHIBIT 13.1–3 **Airline Rankings**

Rank	Airline	AQR Score
1	American	10.328
2	Southwest	10.254
3	Delta	10.209
4	United	10.119
5	USAir	10.054
6	Pan Am	10.003
7	Northwest	20.063
8	Continental	20.346
9	America West	20.377
10	TWA	20.439

What Course to Chart?

Shocker has discovered what appear to be two different approaches to measuring quality of airlines. One relies on direct consumer opinion and is mostly subjective in its approach to quality and the elements considered. The other relies on performance data that are available through public sources and appear to be more objective. Both approaches incorporate pertinent elements that could be used by consumers to judge the quality of an airline. Shocker's recommendation must consider the comprehensiveness and usefulness of these approaches for FlyAway Airways as it moves into a more competitive environment. What course of action should he recommend?

Questions

1. How comparable are the two different methods? In what ways are they similar? In what ways are they different?
2. What are the positive and negative aspects of each approach that Shocker should consider before recommending a course of action for FlyAway Airways?
3. What aspects of service quality does each approach address well and not so well?
4. Considering the two methods outlined, what types of validity would you consider to be demonstrated by the two approaches to measuring quality? Defend your position.
5. Which of the methods should Shocker recommend? Why?

CHAPTER 14
ATTITUDE MEASUREMENT

LEARNING OUTCOMES

After studying this chapter, you should be able to

1. **Describe how business researchers think of attitudes**
2. **Identify basic approaches to measuring attitudes**
3. **Discuss the use of rating scales for measuring attitudes**
4. **Represent a latent construct by constructing a summated scale**
5. **Summarize ways to measure attitudes with ranking and sorting techniques**
6. **Discuss major issues involved in the selection of a measurement scale**

Chapter Vignette: Heat and Smoke—What Keeps Them Happy?

The history of steel factories and the challenges of the furnace workers who work in those factories is well documented. While many people are familiar with the stories of the great steel industrialists such as Carnegie and Frick of the nineteenth century, few people realize that the work of the furnace worker continues to this day. It is hard and difficult work—despite the great advances in technology and an ever-increasing focus on safety, furnace workers still face dangerous work environments filled with heat and smoke. The molten metal must be carefully managed within the furnace, with temperatures in the vessel exceeding thousands of degrees. The possibility of critical injury or death is ever-present, either through the long-term exposure to metallic fumes or from the immediate effects of a furnace explosion.

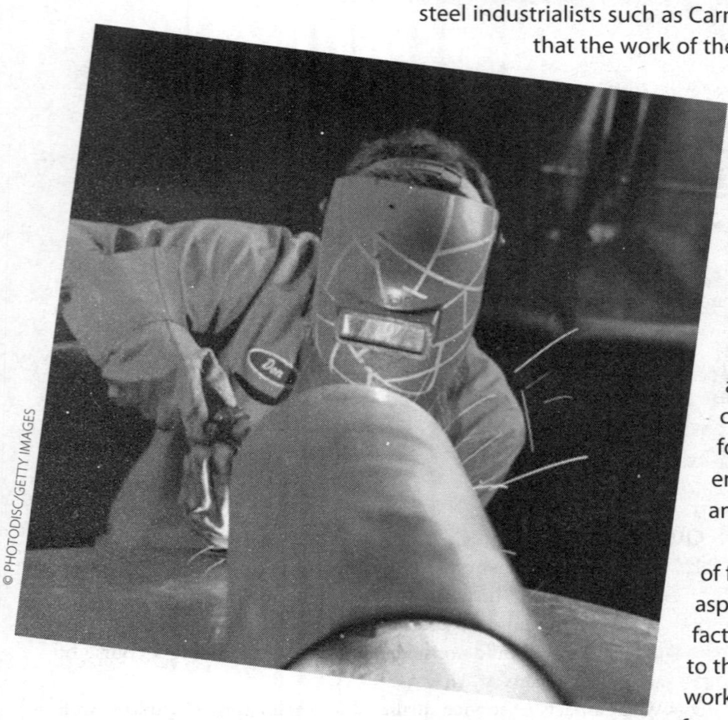

A company which specializes in making high-grade metals knew how important these furnace workers were to their success, and was keenly interested in what kept them satisfied with their company. Several of their furnace employees had been with them for over 20 years, and the skills and expertise of these experienced employees were invaluable to the training of new furnace workers, and the manufacturing process itself.

A team of business researchers was asked to do an assessment of furnace employee attitudes, with the goal of identifying what aspects of their work environment contributed to their overall satisfaction. Using a survey questionnaire, a series of statements related to the company's benefits, supervisory relationships, and general work-related conditions was developed. These researchers asked the furnace workers to indicate their level of agreement, on a scale which ranged from strongly disagree to strongly agree, to these statements. Examples of these statements included:

1. Our company has a health plan that addresses the needs of my family.
2. My experiences with the health plan coordinator have been good.
3. My supervisor sees me as an asset to the company.
4. My supervisor encourages me to contribute ways that can make our work space better.
5. My company puts safety as a top priority.

For each of the statements, the researchers compiled responses from the furnace workers to see if these areas were positively related to the overall work satisfaction of the furnace employees. Results showed some interesting outcomes. While the furnace workers viewed company health benefits and the company's safety program as important to overall work satisfaction, the opportunity to have a supervisor who they perceived as valuing their input and who saw them as important assets to the company was a very important factor related to their satisfaction.

In a nutshell, the very dangerous work environment of the furnace floor did require a focus on safety and health benefits in their minds. But not unlike workers in safer environments, it was the positive and supportive relationship with their immediate supervisor that really made the difference.

Measurement of attitudes is a common objective in business research. Just as a company can apply this study's results to craft practical responses—for example, hiring and training supervisors who are oriented towards positively supporting their employees—other business researchers explore attitudes to answer questions that range from identifying needs to evaluating satisfaction with other aspects of a company's work processes. This chapter describes various methods of attitude measurement.

Introduction

For social scientists, an **attitude** is as an enduring disposition to respond consistently to specific aspects of the world, including actions, people, or objects. One way to understand an attitude is to break it down into its components. Consider this brief statement: "Sally likes shopping at Wal-Mart. She believes the store is *clean,* conveniently *located,* and has low *prices*. She intends to shop there every Thursday." This simple example demonstrates attitude's three components: affective, cognitive, and behavioral. The affective component refers to an individual's general feelings or emotions toward an object. Statements such as "I really like my Corvette," "I enjoy reading new Harry Potter books," and "I hate cranberry juice" reflect an emotional character of attitudes. A person's attitudinal feelings are driven directly by his/her *beliefs* or *cognitions*. This cognitive component represents an individual's knowledge about attributes and their consequences. One person might feel happy about the purchase of an automobile because she believes the car "gets great gas mileage" or knows that the dealer is "the best in New Jersey." The behavioral component of an attitude reflects a predisposition to action by reflecting an individual's intentions.

attitude
An enduring disposition to consistently respond in a given manner to various aspects of the world, composed of affective, cognitive, and behavioral components.

Attitude is measurement done by scaling whose basics have been discussed earlier. Defining a zero for the attitude measurement is a challenge and the common practice is to have a neutral point and measure positive or negative deviation from it.

We have various methods for collecting data related to attitude measurement. These include questionnaires and observation methods. There are certain specific methods of measuring attitude which may be *disguised* and *undisguised*, and also *structured* or *unstructured*. Undisguised and unstructured techniques include depth interviews and focus group interviews. Unstructured techniques which are disguised are methods like word association and sentence completion. Term disguised refers to whether the respondent is aware of the purpose of the process being conducted. Going further we have undisguised and structured techniques like graphic rating scales and the multi-item scales. Finally, structured and disguised tests are used where the extent and direction of guessing errors is used to measure the consumer attitude. This is driven by the thought that individuals tend to gather information that support their attitude and hence the information they have can serve as an indicator of the attitude. Each of the techniques has its own positives and negatives and depending upon the application one needs to choose the right tool to be used.

Attitudes as Hypothetical Constructs

Business researchers often pose questions involving psychological variables that cannot directly be observed. For example, someone may have an attitude toward working on a commission basis. We cannot actually see this attitude. Rather, we can measure an attitude by making an inference

While cats' attitudes may be difficult to measure, we can easily measure how consumers feel about different types of cat food.

© BRENDA CARSON/SHUTTERSTOCK

based on the way an individual responds to multiple scale indicators. Because we can't directly see these phenomena, they are known as latent constructs, **hypothetical constructs**, or just simply constructs. Common constructs include job satisfaction, organizational commitment, personal values, feelings, role stress, perceived value, and many more. The Research Snapshot "Is It Positive Emotionality, or Is It Love?" talks about measuring love. Is love a hypothetical construct?

Importance of Measuring Attitudes

Most managers hold the intuitive belief that changing consumers' or employees' attitudes toward their company or their company's products or services is a major goal. Because modifying attitudes plays a pervasive role in developing strategies to address these goals, the measurement of attitudes is an important task. For example, after Whiskas cat food had been sold in Europe for decades, the brand faced increased competition from new premium brands, and consumers had difficulty identifying with the brand. The company conducted attitude research to determine how people felt about their cats and their food alternatives. The study revealed that cat owners see their pets both as independent and as dependent fragile beings.[1] Cat owners held the attitude that cats wanted to enjoy their food but needed nutrition. This attitude research was directly channeled into managerial action. Whiskas marketers begin positioning the product as having "Catisfaction," using advertisements that featured a purring silver tabby—a pedigreed cat—which symbolizes premium quality but also presents the image of a sweet cat. The message: "Give cats what they like with the nutrition they need. If you do, they'll be so happy that they'll purr for you." This effort reversed the sales decline the brand had been experiencing.

hypothetical constructs
Variables that are not directly observable but are measurable through indirect indicators, such as verbal expression or overt behavior.

Techniques for Measuring Attitudes

A remarkable variety of techniques has been devised to measure attitudes. This variety stems in part from lack of consensus about the exact definition of the concept. In addition, the affective, cognitive, and behavioral components of an attitude may be measured by different means. For example, sympathetic nervous system responses may be recorded using physiological measures to quantify affect, but they are not good measures of behavioral intentions. Direct verbal statements concerning affect, belief, or behavior are used to measure behavioral intent. However, attitudes may also be interpreted using qualitative techniques like those discussed in Chapter 7.

Research may assess the affective (emotional) components of attitudes through physiological measures such as galvanic skin response (GSR), blood pressure, and pupil dilation. These measures provide a means of assessing attitudes without verbally questioning the respondent. In general, they can provide a gross measure of likes or dislikes, but they are not extremely sensitive to the different gradients of an attitude.

Obtaining verbal statements from respondents generally requires that the respondents perform a task such as ranking, rating, sorting, or making choices. A **ranking** task requires the respondent to rank order a small number of stores, brands, feelings, or objects on the basis of overall preference or some characteristic of the stimulus. **Rating** asks the respondent to estimate the magnitude or the extent to which some characteristic exists. A quantitative score results. The rating task involves marking a response indicating one's position using one or more attitudinal or cognitive scales. A **sorting** task might present the respondent with several different concepts printed on cards and require the respondent to classify the concepts by placing the cards into groups (stacks of cards). Another type of attitude measurement is **choice** between two or more alternatives. If a respondent chooses one object over another, the researcher assumes that the respondent prefers the chosen object, at least in this setting. The following sections describe the most popular techniques for measuring attitudes.

ranking
A measurement task that requires respondents to rank order a small number of stores, brands, or objects on the basis of overall preference or some characteristic of the stimulus.

rating
A measurement task that requires respondents to estimate the magnitude of a characteristic or quality that a brand, store, or object possesses.

sorting
A measurement task that presents a respondent with several objects or product concepts and requires the respondent to arrange the objects into piles or classify the product concepts.

choice
A measurement task that identifies preferences by requiring respondents to choose between two or more alternatives

RESEARCH SNAPSHOT

Is It Positive Emotionality, or Is It LOVE?

Love is a four-letter word. Or is it more than that? Psychologists and cognitive scientists view love as just one example of positive emotionality, and have developed numerous definitions to describe what love is and how it works. In fact, a recent study found there are nine different ways love can be defined and/or measured! The concept of love is a hypothetical construct—that is, a term that psychologists use to describe or explain a particular pattern of human behavior. Love, hate, thirst, learning, intelligence—all of these are hypothetical constructs. They are hypothetical in that they do not exist as physical entities; therefore, they cannot be seen, heard, felt, or measured directly. There is no love center in the brain that, if removed, would leave a person incapable of responding positively and affectionately toward other people and things. Love and hate are constructs in that we invent these terms to explain why, for instance, a young man spends all his time with one young woman while completely avoiding another. From a scientific point of view, we might be better off if we said that this young man's behavior suggested that he had a relatively enduring, positive-approach attitude toward the first woman and a negative avoidance attitude toward the second.

Source: Based on Myers, Jane and Matthew Shurts, "Measuring Positive Emotionality: A Review of Instruments Assessing Love," *Measurement and Evaluation in Counseling and Development* 34 (2002), 238–254.

Attitude Rating Scales

Perhaps the most common practice in business research is using rating scales to measure attitudes. This section discusses many rating scales designed to enable respondents to report the intensity of their attitudes.

Simple Attitude Scales

In its most basic form, attitude scaling requires that an individual agree or disagree with a statement or respond to a single question. For example, respondents in a political poll may be asked whether they agree or disagree with the statement "The president should run for re-election." Or, an individual might indicate whether he or she likes or dislikes jalapeño bean dip. This type of self-rating scale merely classifies respondents into one of two categories, thus having only the properties of a nominal scale, and the types of mathematical analysis that may be used with this basic scale are limited.

Despite the disadvantages, simple attitude scaling may be used when questionnaires are extremely long, when respondents have little education, or for other specific reasons. A number of simplified scales are merely checklists: A respondent indicates past experience, preference, and the like merely by checking an item. In many cases the items are adjectives that describe a particular object. In a survey of small-business owners and managers, respondents indicated whether they found working in a small firm more rewarding than working in a large firm, as well as whether they agreed with a series of attitude statements about small businesses. For example, 77 percent said small and mid-sized businesses "have less bureaucracy," and 76 percent said smaller companies "have more flexibility" than large ones.[2]

Most attitude theorists believe that attitudes vary along continua. Early attitude researchers pioneered the view that the task of attitude scaling is to measure the distance from "good" to "bad," "low" to "high," "like" to "dislike," and so on. Thus, the purpose of an attitude scale is to find an individual's position on the continuum. However, simple scales do not allow for fine distinctions between attitudes. Several other scales have been developed for making more precise measurements.

RESEARCH SNAPSHOT

Students Ask—Are You Responsible?

Businesses today face an increasing need to be perceived as having an interest in social responsibility. In many instances, products and services have been promoted based upon the fact that the product or service is environmentally friendly, or has a tie to improving the social environment. Companies such as Toyota (with an emphasis on hybrid vehicles) and Yoplait (with its contributions to breast cancer research) highlight a trend that showing interest in improving the world can also have bottom line implications. The Alloy Eighth Annual College Explorer study, conducted with the assistance of the Harris Group, recently surveyed 1,554 college students to determine their opinions about corporate social responsibility. Results indicate that 41 percent of college students consciously prefer products and services from companies they *perceive* as having a social role. Large companies such as Toyota and smaller companies like Burt's Bees were ranked as highly socially responsible brands.

The implications for business leaders are quite interesting. Increasingly, perceptions of the company itself, and not just its products, drive purchasing decisions among this important demographic.

Source: Based on Bush, Michael, "Students Rank Social Responsibility," *Advertising Age* 79 (August 4, 2008), 11.

© iStock

Category Scales

The simplest rating scale contains only two response categories: agree/disagree. Expanding the response categories provides the respondent with more flexibility in the rating task. Even more information is provided if the categories are ordered according to a particular descriptive or evaluative dimension. Consider the following question:

How often do you disagree with your spouse about how much to spend on vacation?				
Never	Rarely	Sometimes	Often	Very often
☐	☐	☐	☐	☐

category scale
A rating scale that consists of several response categories, often providing respondents with alternatives to indicate positions on a continuum.

This **category scale** is a more sensitive measure than a scale that has only two response categories. By having more choices for a respondent, the potential exists to provide more information. However, if the researcher tries to represent something that is truly bipolar (yes/no, female/male, member/nonmember, and so on) with more than two categories, error may be introduced.

Question wording is an extremely important factor in the usefulness of these scales. Exhibit 14.1 shows some common wordings used in category scales. The issue of question wording is discussed in Chapter 15.

In statistical analysis, unless otherwise specifically mentioned, the levels of measurements are metric. Consequently, mean and standard deviation calculated from a set of data would essentially mean the central tendency and dispersion of the data. However, such statistics are not meaningful in the context of categorical data. For example, it would not make sense to compute an average hair color. An average of a categorical variable does not make much sense because there is no intrinsic ordering of the levels of the categories, and if such ordering exists, since the distance between the categories are not equal, it is not possible to calculate exact central point or the dispersion from a dataset that is measured in categorical scale. Moreover, if you tried to compute the average of educational experience which is ordinal in nature, the result may not make any sense. This is because the distance between different levels of educational qualification are not the same implying that the average value of the variable is not correct. It is important to know that to calculate average and standard deviation one has two major variables in metric scale (either interval or in ratio scale).

Sometimes we need to deal with variables that are neither ordinal nor interval. For instance, a five-point Likert scale will have values ranging from strongly agree to strongly disagree, that is, "strongly agree," "agree," "neutral," "disagree," and "strongly disagree." We may not be able to say that a Likert scale is an interval scale unless we are sure that the distance between the categories are the same. However, in order to carry out statistical analysis using software we assume that

EXHIBIT 14.1 **Selected Category Scales**

		Quality		
Excellent	Good	Fair	Poor	
Very good	Fairly good	Neither good nor bad	Not very good	Not good at all
Well above average	Above average	Average	Below average	Well below average
		Importance		
Very important	Fairly important	Neutral	Not so important	Not at all important
		Interest		
Very interested		Somewhat interested		Not very interested
		Satisfaction		
Completely satisfied	Somewhat satisfied	Neither satisfied nor dissatisfied	Somewhat dissatisfied	Completely dissatisfied
Very satisfied	Quite satisfied	Somewhat satisfied	Not at all satisfied	
		Frequency		
All of the time	Very often	Often	Sometimes	Hardly ever
Very often	Often	Sometimes	Rarely	Never
All of the time	Most of the time	Some of the time	Just now and then	
		Truth		
Very true	Somewhat true	Not very true	Not at all true	
Definitely yes	Probably yes	Probably no	Definitely no	
		Uniqueness		
Very different	Somewhat different	Slightly different	Not at all different	
Extremely unique	Very unique	Somewhat unique	Slightly unique	Not at all unique

each of the above five categories are equally spaced meaning that the distance between the two consecutive categories are the same.

Discrete choice measurement in business research involves selection of a particular alternative from a set of two or more alternatives. For example, a computer purchaser may select to buy the brand Apple from a set of brands, namely, Sony, Apple, Dell, HP. Similarly, an HR manager will have to decide whether to promote an employee or not, promoting an employee depending upon his/her performance. In other words, discrete choice is categorical nature and cannot be dealt the same way we handle a metric variable since the outcome in the discrete choice is not continuous.

Discrete choice models are used in business research in consumer buying decision, organizational strategy, human resource management, finance management, etc. Discrete choice models are also used by government and non-government agencies. The theoretical basis of discrete choice was developed by Daniel McFadden who received Nobel Prize for this work in the year 2000.

Discrete choice model considers relation between individual specific attributes and the attributes of the alternatives he/she selects. For instance, which brand of car a consumer would buy would depend on that person's individual specific attributes like age, educational qualification, income level, social status, taste and preference, previous information on the product, his/her risk adversity, etc., as well as several other product related variables like fuel efficiency of the car, brand of the car, etc.

Method of Summated Ratings: The Likert Scale

Likert scale

A measure of attitudes designed to allow respondents to rate how strongly they agree or disagree with carefully constructed statements, ranging from very positive to very negative attitudes toward some object.

A method that is simple to administer and therefore extremely popular is business researchers' adaptation of the method of summated ratings, developed by Rensis Likert.[3] With the **Likert scale**, respondents indicate their attitudes by checking how strongly they agree or disagree with carefully constructed statements, ranging from very positive to very negative attitudes toward some object. Individuals generally choose from approximately five response alternatives—strongly agree, agree, uncertain, disagree, and strongly disagree—although the number of alternatives may range from three to nine. In the following example, from a study of food-shopping behavior, there are five alternatives:

In buying food for my family, price is no object.				
Strongly Disagree	Disagree	Uncertain	Agree	Strongly Agree
☐	☐	☐	☐	☐
(1)	(2)	(3)	(4)	(5)

Researchers assign scores, or weights, to each possible response. In this example, numerical scores of 1, 2, 3, 4, and 5 are assigned to each level of agreement, respectively. The numerical scores, shown in parentheses, may not be printed on the questionnaire or computer screen. Strong agreement indicates the most favorable attitude on the statement, and a numerical score of 5 is assigned to this response.

REVERSE RECODING

reverse recoding

A method of making sure all the items forming a composite scale are scored in the same direction. Negative items can be recoded into the equivalent responses for a non-reverse coded item.

The statement given in this example is positively framed. If a statement is framed negatively (such as "I carefully budget my food expenditures"), the numerical scores would need to be reversed. This is done by **reverse recoding** the negative item so that a strong agreement really indicates an unfavorable response rather than a favorable attitude. In the case of a five-point scale, the recoding is done as follows:

Old Value	New Value
1	5
2	4
3	3
4	2
5	1

Recoding in this fashion turns agreement with a negatively worded item into a mirror image, meaning the result is the same as disagreement with a positively worded item. SPSS has a recode function that allows simple recoding to be done by entering "old" and "new" scale values. Alternatively, a simple mathematical formula can be entered. For a typical 1–5 scale, the formula

$$X_{new\ value} = 6 - X_{old\ value}$$

would result in the same recoding.

COMPOSITE SCALES

composite scale

A way of representing a latent construct by summing or averaging respondents' reactions to multiple items each assumed to indicate the latent construct.

A Likert scale may include several scale items to form a **composite scale**. Each statement is assumed to represent an aspect of a common attitudinal domain.

In Likert's original procedure, a large number of statements are generated, and an *item analysis* is performed. The purpose of the item analysis is to ensure that final items evoke a wide response and discriminate among those with positive and negative attitudes. Items that are poor because they lack clarity or elicit mixed response patterns are eliminated from the final statement list. Scales that use multiple items can be analyzed for reliability and validity. Only a set of items that demonstrates good reliability and validity should be summed or averaged to form a composite scale representing a hypothetical construct. Unfortunately, not all researchers are willing or able to thoroughly assess reliability and validity. Without this test, the use of Likert scales can be disadvantageous because there is no way of knowing exactly what the items represent or how well they represent anything of interest. Without valid and reliable measures, researchers cannot guarantee they are measuring what they say they are measuring.

Semantic Differential

semantic differential
A measure of attitudes that consists of a series of seven-point rating scales that use bipolar adjectives to anchor the beginning and end of each scale.

The **semantic differential** is actually a series of attitude scales. This popular attitude measurement technique consists of getting respondents to react to some concept using a series of seven-point bipolar rating scales. Bipolar adjectives—such as "good" and "bad," "modern" and "old-fashioned," or "clean" and "dirty"—anchor the beginning and the end (or poles) of the scale. The subject makes repeated judgments about the concept under investigation on each of the scales. Exhibit 14.2 shows seven of eighteen scales used in a research project that measured attitudes toward supermarkets.

The scoring of the semantic differential can be illustrated using the scale bounded by the anchors "modern" and "old-fashioned." Respondents are instructed to check the place that indicates the nearest appropriate adjective. From left to right, the scale intervals are interpreted as "extremely modern," "very modern," "slightly modern," "both modern and old-fashioned," "slightly old-fashioned," "very old-fashioned," and "extremely old-fashioned":

Modern ___ ___ ___ ___ ___ ___ ___ *Old-fashioned*

The semantic differential technique originally was developed as a method for measuring the meanings of objects or the "semantic space" of interpersonal experience.[4] Researchers have found the semantic differential versatile and useful in business applications. The validity of the semantic differential depends on finding scale anchors that are semantic opposites. This can sometimes prove difficult. However, in attitude or image studies simple anchors such as very unfavorable and very favorable work well.

For scoring purposes, a numerical score is assigned to each position on the rating scale. Traditionally, score ranges such as 1, 2, 3, 4, 5, 6, 7 or −3, −2, −1, 0, +1, +2, +3 are used. Many business researchers find it desirable to assume that the semantic differential provides interval data. This

EXHIBIT 14.2
Semantic Differential Scales for Measuring Attitudes toward Supermarkets

Inconvenient location __ __ __ __ __ __ __ Convenient location

Low prices __ __ __ __ __ __ __ High prices

Pleasant atmosphere __ __ __ __ __ __ __ Unpleasant atmosphere

Modern __ __ __ __ __ __ __ Old-fashioned

Cluttered __ __ __ __ __ __ __ Spacious

Fast checkout __ __ __ __ __ __ __ Slow checkout

Dull __ __ __ __ __ __ __ Exciting

Source: Yu, Julie H., Gerald Albaum, and Michael Swenson, "Is a Central Tendency Error Inherent in the Use of Semantic Differential Scales in Different Cultures?" *International Journal of Market Research*, Summer 2003, downloaded from Business & Company Resource Center, http://galenet.galegroup.com.

assumption, although widely accepted, has its critics, who argue that the data have only ordinal properties because the numerical scores are arbitrary. Practically speaking, most researchers will treat semantic differential scales as metric (at least interval). This is because the amount of error introduced by assuming the intervals between choices are equal (even though this is uncertain) is fairly small.

Because the data are assumed to be interval, either the arithmetic mean or the median will be used to compare the profile of one product, brand, or store with that of a competing product, brand, or store.

Numerical Scales

numerical scale
An attitude rating scale similar to a semantic differential except that it uses numbers, instead of verbal descriptions, as response options to identify response positions.

A **numerical scale** simply provides numbers rather than a semantic space or verbal descriptions to identify response options or categories (response positions). For example, a scale using five response positions is called a five-point numerical scale. A six-point scale has six positions and a seven-point scale seven positions, and so on. Consider the following numerical scale:

Now that you've had your automobile for about one year, please tell us how satisfied you are with your Ford Taurus.

Extremely Dissatisfied 1 2 3 4 5 6 7 *Extremely Satisfied*

This numerical scale uses bipolar adjectives in the same manner as the semantic differential.

In practice, researchers have found that a scale with numerical labels for intermediate points on the scale is as effective a measure as the true semantic differential. The Research Snapshot "A Measuring Stick for Web Site Usability" demonstrates how numerical scales can be helpful in assessing Web site effectiveness.

Stapel Scale

Stapel scale
A measure of attitudes that consists of a single adjective in the center of an even number of numerical values.

The **Stapel scale**, named after Jan Stapel, was originally developed in the 1950s to measure simultaneously the direction and intensity of an attitude. Modern versions of the scale, with a single adjective, are used as a substitute for the semantic differential when it is difficult to create pairs of bipolar adjectives. The modified Stapel scale places a single adjective in the center of an even number of numerical values (ranging, perhaps, from +3 to −3). The scale measures how close to or distant from the adjective a given stimulus is perceived to be.

The advantages and disadvantages of the Stapel scale are very similar to those of the semantic differential. However, the Stapel scale is markedly easier to administer, especially over the telephone. Because the Stapel scale does not require bipolar adjectives, it is easier to construct than the semantic differential. Research comparing the semantic differential with the Stapel scale indicates that results from the two techniques are largely the same.[5]

Constant-Sum Scale

constant-sum scale
A measure of attitudes in which respondents are asked to divide a constant sum to indicate the relative importance of attributes; respondents often sort cards, but the task may also be a rating task.

A **constant-sum scale** requires respondents to divide a fixed number of points among several attributes corresponding to their relative importance or weight. Suppose United Parcel Service (UPS) wishes to determine the importance of the attributes of accurate invoicing, delivery as promised, and price to organizations that use its service in business-to-business settings. Respondents might be asked to divide a constant sum of 100 points to indicate the relative importance of those attributes:

Divide 100 points among the following characteristics of a delivery service according to how important each characteristic is to you when selecting a delivery company.

RESEARCH SNAPSHOT

A Measuring Stick for Web Site Usability

Two technology experts looking for a standard way to measure Web sites' usability developed metrics emphasizing attitudes. Rather than, say, measuring how long it took users to accomplish a particular task, they asked users to rate their experiences using each site. Each rater evaluated the site's content (information and transactions), ease of use, promotion (advertising on the site), "made for the medium" (features that make the site fit the user's particular needs), and emotions (sense of accomplishment, interest in the site's content, credibility, and control over the flow of content).

Of course, what is very important on one site may be minor on another. A prospective investor looking for information about an airline would likely seek a different online experience than a consumer visiting the same site to plan a vacation, and they both would have still different expectations for an online bookstore. As a result, the usability assessment begins by asking respondents to rate each category being evaluated in terms of how important it is for a particular kind of company, assuming the rater is either a consumer or an investor. For example, a user might rate an airline Web site's content, ease of use, and so on for a consumer. These ratings use a 100-point constant-sum scale. Each rater divides 100 points among the five categories. The rater then evaluates, on a scale of 1 to 10, how well the site performs in each category. The importance ratings weight those scores. So, if a rater assigns 5 points to the emotion category and thinks the site performs at a 6 on the 1-to-10 scale, the weighted score is 30. By combining all the ratings for a Web site, a site can earn between 0 and 1,000 points. In the researchers' test of this rating system, it delivered helpful insights.

© PHOTODISC/GETTY IMAGES

Source: Based on Ritu Agarwal and Viswanath Venkatesh, "Assessing a Firm's Web Presence: A Heuristic Evaluation Procedure for the Measurement of Usability," *Information Systems Research* (June 2002), http://galenet.galegroup.com; Buchholz, G. A., "Losability vs. Usability," *Digital Web* (July 11, 2005), http://www.digital-web.com.

© iStock

____ *Accurate invoicing*
____ *Package not damaged*
____ *Delivery as promised*
____ *Lower price*
____ *100 points*

The constant-sum scale works best with respondents who have high educational levels. If respondents follow the instructions correctly, the results will approximate interval measures. As the number of stimuli increases, this technique becomes increasingly complex.

This technique may be used for measuring brand preference. The approach, which is similar to the paired-comparison method, is as follows:

Divide 100 points among the following brands according to your preference for each brand:
____ *Brand A*
____ *Brand B*
____ *Brand C*
____ *100 points*

In this case, the constant-sum scale is a rating technique. However, with minor modifications, it can be classified as a sorting technique. Although the constant-sum scale is widely used, strictly speaking, the scale is flawed because the last response is completely determined by the way the respondent has scored the other choices. Although this is probably somewhat complex to understand, the fact is that practical reasons often outweigh this concern.

Graphic Rating Scales

graphic rating scale
A measure of attitude that allows respondents to rate an object by choosing any point along a graphic continuum.

A **graphic rating scale** presents respondents with a graphic continuum. The respondents are allowed to choose any point on the continuum to indicate their attitude. Exhibit 14.3 shows a traditional

EXHIBIT 14.3
Graphic Rating Scale

Please evaluate each attribute in terms of how important it is to you by placing an X at the position on the horizontal line that most reflects your feelings.

Seating comfort Not important ______________________ Very important

In-flight meals Not important ______________________ Very important

Airfare Not important ______________________ Very important

graphic scale, ranging from one extreme position to the opposite position. Typically a respondent's score is determined by measuring the length (in millimeters) from one end of the graphic continuum to the point marked by the respondent. Many researchers believe that scoring in this manner strengthens the assumption that graphic rating scales of this type are interval scales. Alternatively, the researcher may divide the line into predetermined scoring categories (lengths) and record respondents' marks accordingly. In other words, the graphic rating scale has the advantage of allowing the researcher to choose any interval desired for scoring purposes. The disadvantage of the graphic rating scale is that there are no standard answers.

Graphic rating scales are not limited to straight lines as sources of visual communication. Picture response options or another type of graphic continuum may be used to enhance communication with respondents. A variation of the graphic ratings scale is the ladder scale. This scale also includes numerical options:

> *Here is a ladder scale (response scale is shown in Exhibit 14.4). It represents the "ladder of life." As you see, it is a ladder with eleven rungs numbered 0 to 10. Let's suppose the top of the ladder represents the best possible life for you as you describe it, and the bottom rung represents the worst possible life for you as you describe it.*
>
> *On which rung of the ladder do you feel your life is today?*
> *0 1 2 3 4 5 6 7 8 9 10*

EXHIBIT 14.4
A Ladder Scale

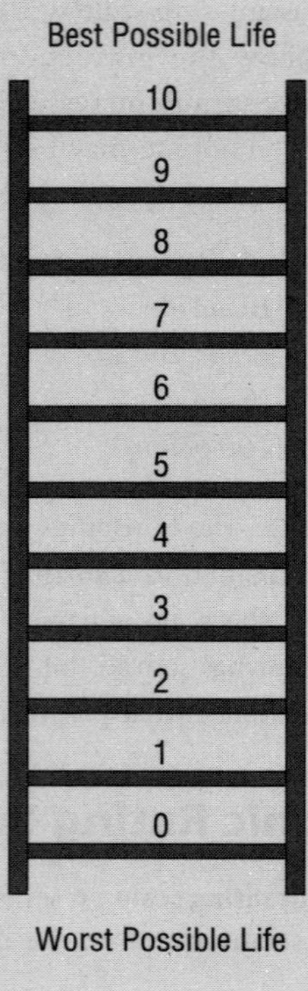

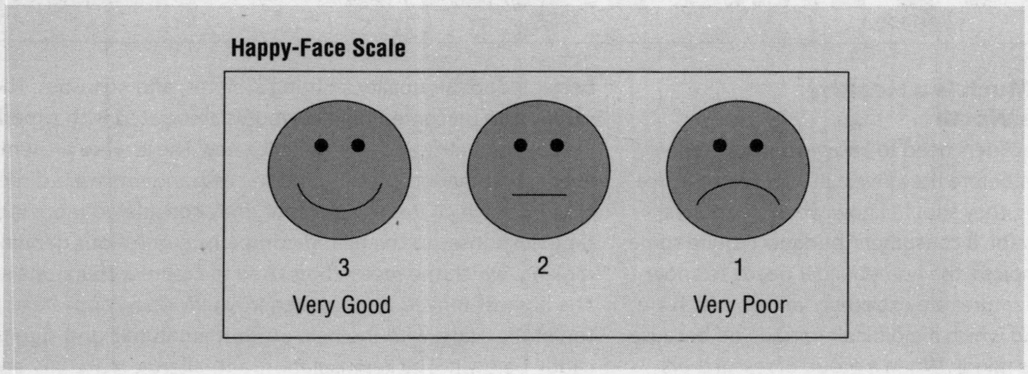

EXHIBIT 14.5
Graphic Rating Scale with Picture Response Categories Stressing Visual Communication

Research to investigate children's attitudes has used happy-face scales (see Exhibit 14.5). The children are asked to indicate which face shows how they feel about candy, a toy, or some other concept. Research with the happy-face scale indicates that children tend to choose the faces at the ends of the scale. Although this may be because children's attitudes fluctuate more widely than adults' or because they have stronger feelings both positively and negatively, the tendency to select the extremes is a disadvantage of the scale.

Thurstone Interval Scale

In 1927 attitude research pioneer Louis Thurstone developed the concept that attitudes vary along continua and should be measured accordingly. The construction of a **Thurstone scale** is a fairly complex process that requires two stages. The first stage is a ranking operation, performed by judges who assign scale values to attitudinal statements. The second stage consists of asking subjects to respond to the attitudinal statements.

Thurstone scale
An attitude scale in which judges assign scale values to attitudinal statements and subjects are asked to respond to these statements.

The Thurstone method is time-consuming and costly. From a historical perspective, it is valuable, but its current popularity is low. This method is rarely used in applied research settings. Exhibit 14.6 summarizes the attitude-rating techniques discussed in this section.

EXHIBIT 14.6 **Summary of Advantages and Disadvantages of Rating Scales**

Rating Measure	Subject Must	Advantages	Disadvantages
Category scale	Indicate a response category	Flexible, easy to respond to	Items may be ambiguous; with few categories, only gross distinctions can be made
Likert scale	Evaluate statements on a scale of agreement	Easiest scale to construct	Hard to judge what a single score means
Semantic differential and numerical scales	Choose points between bipolar adjectives on relevant dimensions	Easy to construct; norms exist for comparison, such as profile analysis	Bipolar adjectives must be found; data may be ordinal, not interval
Stapel scale	Choose points on a scale with a single adjective in the center	Easier to construct than semantic differential, easy to administer	Endpoints are numerical, not verbal, labels
Constant-sum scale	Divide a constant sum among response alternatives	Approximates an interval measure	Difficult for respondents with low education levels
Graphic scale	Choose a point on a continuum	Visual impact, unlimited scale points	No standard answers
Graphic scale with picture response categories	Choose a visual picture	Visual impact, easy for poor readers	Hard to attach a verbal explanation to a response

RESEARCH SNAPSHOT

How Much Is a Healthy Home Worth?

Homebuilders need to know what consumers like, but before they invest in a lot of expensive features, they should know what consumers will pay for. If consumers' budgets require some hard choices, the homebuilder needs to know which features are extremely valued, which are nice but not important, and which are difficult to trade off because they are so close in buyer's minds. When a group of researchers at the University of British Columbia wanted to measure attitudes toward features of "healthy houses," they compared the scores with a Thurstone scale.

A *healthy house* refers to one built with materials and a design affording superior indoor air quality, lighting, and acoustics. The researchers mailed a survey asking respondents whether they would be willing to pay extra if the builder could guarantee better indoor air quality, lighting systems, and acoustics. The survey also presented nine attributes associated with superior indoor air quality and energy efficiency. These were presented i every combination of pairs, and the respondents were directed to choose which item in each pair they considered more impor- tant. Responses to the paired-comparison questions generated ranking, which the researchers used to create a Thurstone scale The highest-ranked attribute (energy efficiency) appears at the top of the scale, with the next attribute (natural light) significantly below it. Thicker insulation, anti-allergic materials, and airtightness are grouped close together below natural light, anc artificial light falls noticeably below the other features.

Source: Spetic, Wellington, Robert Kozak, and David Cohen, "Willingness to Pay and Preferences for Healthy Home Attributes in Canada," *Forest Products Journal* 5 (October 2005), 19–24; Bower, John, *Healthy House Building for the New Millennium* (Bloomington, IN: Healthy House Institute, 1999).

Measuring Behavioral Intention

The behavioral component of an attitude involves the behavioral expectations of an individual toward an attitudinal object. The component of interest to researchers may be turnover intentions, a tendency to make business decisions in a certain way, or plans to expand operations or product offerings. For example, category scales for measuring the behavioral component of an attitude ask about a respondent's likelihood of purchase or intention to perform some future action, using questions such as the following:

How likely is it that you will purchase an MP3 player such as an iPod?

- *I definitely will buy.*
- *I probably will buy.*
- *I might buy.*
- *I probably will not buy.*
- *I definitely will not buy.*

How likely am I to write a letter to my representative in Congress or other government official in support of this company if it were in a dispute with government?

- *Extremely Likely*
- *Very Likely*
- *Somewhat Likely*
- *Likely, about a 50–50 chance*
- *Somewhat Unlikely*
- *Very Unlikely*
- *Absolutely Unlikely*

The wording of statements used in these scales often includes phrases such as "I would recommend," "I would write," or "I would buy" to indicate action tendencies.

Expectations also may be measured using a scale of subjective probabilities, ranging from 100 for "absolutely certain" to 0 for "absolutely no chance." Researchers have used the following subjective probability scale to estimate the chance that a job candidate will accept a position within a company:

100%	*(Absolutely certain) I will accept*
90%	*(Almost sure) I will accept*
80%	*(Very big chance) I will accept*
70%	*(Big chance) I will accept*
60%	*(Not so big a chance) I will accept*
50%	*(About even) I will accept*
40%	*(Smaller chance) I will accept*
30%	*(Small chance) I will accept*
20%	*(Very small chance) I will accept*
10%	*(Almost certainly not) I will accept*
0%	*(Certainly not) I will accept*

Behavioral Differential

A general instrument, the **behavioral differential**, is used to measure the behavioral intentions of subjects toward an object or category of objects. As in the semantic differential, a description of the object to be judged is followed by a series of scales on which subjects indicate their behavioral intentions toward this object. For example, one item might be something like this:

behavioral differential

A rating scale instrument similar to a semantic differential, developed to measure the behavioral intentions of subjects toward future actions.

A 25-year-old female sales representative

Would ___ ___ ___ ___ ___ *Would not*

ask this person for advice.

Ranking

Consumers often *rank order* their preferences. An ordinal scale may be developed by asking respondents to rank order (from most preferred to least preferred) a set of objects or attributes. Respondents easily understand the task of rank ordering the importance of product attributes or arranging a set of brand names according to preference. Like the constant-sum scale, technically the ranking scale also suffers from inflexibility in that if we know how some ranked five out of six alternatives, we know the answer to the sixth.

Paired Comparisons

Consider a situation in which a chainsaw manufacturer learned that a competitor had introduced a new lightweight (6-pound) chainsaw. The manufacturer's lightest chainsaw weighed 9 pounds. Executives wondered if they needed to introduce a 6-pound chainsaw into the product line. The research design chosen was a **paired comparison**. A 6-pound chainsaw was designed, and a prototype built. To control for color preferences, the competitor's chainsaw was painted the same color as the 9- and 6-pound chainsaws. Respondents were presented with two chainsaws at a time and asked to pick the one they preferred. Three pairs of comparisons were required to determine the most preferred chainsaw.

paired comparison

A measurement technique that involves presenting the respondent with two objects and asking the respondent to pick the preferred object; more than two objects may be presented, but comparisons are made in pairs.

The following question illustrates the typical format for asking about paired comparisons.

I would like to know your overall opinion of two brands of adhesive bandages. They are Curad and Band-Aid. Overall, which of these two brands—Curad or Band-Aid—do you think is the better one? Or are both the same?

Curad is better.
Band-Aid is better.
They are the same.

If researchers wish to compare four brands of pens on the basis of attractiveness or writing quality, six comparisons $[(n)(n-1)/2]$ will be necessary.

When comparing only a few items, ranking objects with respect to one attribute is not difficult. As the number of items increases, the number of comparisons increases geometrically. If the number of comparisons is too large, respondents may become fatigued and no longer carefully discriminate among them.

Sorting

TOTHEPOINT

My tastes are very simple. I only want the best.

—Oscar Wilde

Sorting tasks ask respondents to indicate their attitudes or beliefs by arranging items on the basis of perceived similarity or some other attribute. One advertising agency has had consumers sort photographs of people to measure their perceptions of a brand's typical user. Another agency used a sorting technique in which consumers used a deck of 52 cards illustrating elements from advertising for the brand name being studied. The study participants created a stack of cards showing elements they recalled seeing or hearing, and the interviewer then asked the respondent to identify the item on each of those cards. National City Corporation, a banking company, has used sorting as part of its research into the design of its Web site. Consumers participating in the research were given a set of cards describing various parts of processes that they might engage in when they are banking online. The participants were asked to arrange the cards to show their idea of a logical way to complete these processes. This research method shows the Web site designers how consumers go about doing something—sometimes very differently from the way bankers expect.[6]

A variant of the constant-sum technique uses physical counters (for example, poker chips or coins), to be divided among the items being tested. In an airline study of customer preferences, the following sorting technique could be used:

Here is a sheet that lists several airlines. Next to the name of each airline is a pocket. Here are ten cards. I would like you to put these cards in the pockets next to the airlines you would prefer to fly on your next trip. Assume that all of the airlines fly to wherever you would choose to travel. You can put as many cards as you want next to an airline, or you can put no cards next to an airline.

	Cards
American Airlines	___
Delta Airlines	___
United Airlines	___
Southwest Airlines	___
Northwest Airlines	___

Other Methods of Attitude Measurement

Attitudes, as hypothetical constructs, cannot be observed directly. We can, however, infer one's attitude by the way he or she responds to multiple attitude indicators. A summated rating scale can be made up of three indicators of attitude. Consider the following three semantic differential items that may capture a person's attitude towards their immediate supervisor:

very good	___ ___ ___ ___ ___ ___ ___	*very bad*
very unfavorable	___ ___ ___ ___ ___ ___ ___	*very favorable*
very positive	___ ___ ___ ___ ___ ___ ___	*very negative*

The terminology is such that now attitude would be represented as a latent (unobservable) construct indicated by the person's response to these items.

Selecting a Measurement Scale: Some Practical Decisions

Now that we have looked at a number of attitude measurement scales, a natural question arises: "Which is most appropriate?" As in the selection of a basic research design, there is no single best answer for all research projects. The answer to this question is relative, and the choice of scale will depend on the nature of the attitudinal object to be measured, the manager's problem definition, and the backward and forward linkages to choices already made (for example, telephone survey versus mail survey). However, several questions will help focus the choice of a measurement scale:

1. Is a ranking, sorting, rating, or choice technique best?
2. Should a monadic or a comparative scale be used?
3. What type of category labels, if any, will be used for the rating scale?
4. How many scale categories or response positions are needed to accurately measure an attitude?
5. Should a balanced or unbalanced rating scale be chosen?
6. Should a scale that forces a choice among predetermined options be used?
7. Should a single measure or an index measure be used?

We will discuss each of these issues.

Ranking, Sorting, Rating, or Choice Technique?

The decision whether to use ranking, sorting, rating, or a choice technique is determined largely by the problem definition and especially by the type of statistical analysis desired. For example, ranking provides only ordinal data, limiting the statistical techniques that may be used.

Monadic or Comparative Scale?

If the scale to be used is not a ratio scale, the researcher must decide whether to include a standard of comparison in the verbal portion of the scale. Consider the following rating scale:

Now that you've had your automobile for about one year, please tell us how satisfied you are with its engine power and pickup.

Completely Dissatisfied	Dissatisfied	Somewhat Satisfied	Satisfied	Completely Satisfied
☐	☐	☐	☐	☐

This is a **monadic rating scale**, because it asks about a single concept (the brand of automobile the individual actually purchased) in isolation. The respondent is not given a specific frame of reference. A **comparative rating scale** asks a respondent to rate a concept, such as a specific amount of responsibility or authority, in comparison with a benchmark—perhaps another similar concept—explicitly used as a frame of reference. In many cases, the comparative rating scale presents an ideal situation as a reference point for comparison with the actual situation. For example:

monadic rating scale
Any measure of attitudes that asks respondents about a single concept in isolation.

comparative rating scale
Any measure of attitudes that asks respondents to rate a concept in comparison with a benchmark explicitly used as a frame of reference.

Please indicate how the amount of authority in your present position compares with the amount of authority that would be ideal for this position.

Too much ☐ *About right* ☐ *Too little* ☐

What Type of Category Labels, If Any?

We have discussed verbal labels, numerical labels, and unlisted choices. Many rating scales have verbal labels for response categories because researchers believe they help respondents better understand the response positions. The maturity and educational levels of the respondents will influence this decision. The semantic differential, with unlabeled response categories between two bipolar adjectives, and the numerical scale, with numbers to indicate scale positions, often are selected because the researcher wishes to assume interval-scale data.

How Many Scale Categories or Response Positions?

Should a category scale have four, five, or seven response positions or categories? Or should the researcher use a graphic scale with an infinite number of positions? The original developmental research on the semantic differential indicated that five to eight points is optimal. However, the researcher must determine the number of meaningful positions that is best for the specific project. This issue of identifying how many meaningful distinctions respondents can practically make is basically a matter of sensitivity, but at the operational rather than the conceptual level.

Balanced or Unbalanced Rating Scale?

The fixed-alternative format may be balanced or unbalanced. For example, the following question, which asks about parent-child decisions relating to television program watching, is a **balanced rating scale**:

balanced rating scale
A fixed-alternative rating scale with an equal number of positive and negative categories; a neutral point or point of indifference is at the center of the scale.

Who decides which television programs your children watch?

Child decides all of the time. ☐
Child decides most of the time. ☐
Child and parent decide together. ☐
Parent decides most of the time. ☐
Parent decides all of the time. ☐

unbalanced rating scale
A fixed-alternative rating scale that has more response categories at one end than the other, resulting in an unequal number of positive and negative categories.

This scale is balanced because a neutral point, or point of indifference, is at the center of the scale.

Unbalanced rating scales may be used when responses are expected to be distributed at one end of the scale. Unbalanced scales, such as the following one, may eliminate this type of "end piling":

Completely Dissatisfied	Dissatisfied	Somewhat Satisfied	Satisfied	Completely Satisfied
☐	☐	☐	☐	☐

Notice that there are three "satisfied" responses and only two "dissatisfied" responses above. The choice of a balanced or unbalanced scale generally depends on the nature of the concept or the researcher's knowledge about attitudes toward the stimulus to be measured.

Use a Scale That Forces a Choice among Predetermined Options?

forced-choice rating scale
A fixed-alternative rating scale that requires respondents to choose one of the fixed alternatives.

In many situations, a respondent has not formed an attitude toward the concept being studied and simply cannot provide an answer. If a **forced-choice rating scale** compels the respondent to answer, the response is merely a function of the question. If answers are not forced, the midpoint of the scale may be used by the respondent to indicate unawareness as well as indifference. If many respondents in the sample are expected to be unaware of the attitudinal object under investigation, this problem may be eliminated by using a non-forced-choice scale that provides a "no opinion" category, as in the following example:

How does the Bank of Commerce compare with the First National Bank?

☐ *Bank of Commerce is better than First National Bank.*
☐ *Bank of Commerce is about the same as First National Bank.*
☐ *Bank of Commerce is worse than First National Bank.*
☐ *Can't say.*

TOTHEPOINT

Refusing to have an opinion is a way of having one, isn't it?
—Luigi Pirandello

Asking this type of question allows the investigator to separate respondents who cannot make an honest comparison from respondents who have had experience with both banks. The

TIPS OF THE TRADE

- Attitudes are widely used in research because they are very diagnostic—meaning that weaknesses in firm performance can be easily linked to a lower attitude score.
- Rating scales are preferable to ranking scales in most situations.
- Ranking scales have a problem in that the last category ranked is determined by the ranking of the other categories.
- Single items can be used when concepts are very simple. In these cases, the meaning of the concept should be indisputable. As meanings become less simple, multiple item measures should be used.
- Most often, psychological concepts involve multiple item measurement.

argument for forced choice is that people really do have attitudes, even if they are unfamiliar with the banks, and should be required to answer the question. Still, the use of forced-choice questions is associated with higher incidences of "no answer." Internet surveys make forced-choice questions easy to implement because the delivery can be set up so that a respondent cannot go to the next question until the previous question is answered. Realize, however, if a respondent truly has no opinion, and the no opinion option is not included, he or she may simply quit responding to the questionnaire.

Single Measure or an Index Measure?

Whether to use a single measure or an index measure depends on the complexity of the issue to be investigated, the number of dimensions the issue contains, and whether individual attributes of the stimulus are part of a holistic attitude or are seen as separate items. Very simple concepts that do not vary from context to context can be measured by single items. However, most psychological concepts are more complex and require multiple-item measurement. Additionally, multiple-item measures are easier to test for construct validity (discussed in later chapters). The researcher's conceptual definition will be helpful in making this choice.

The researcher has many scaling options. Generally, the choice is influenced by plans for the later stages of the research project. Again, problem definition becomes a determining factor influencing the research design.

Summary

1. Describe how business researchers think of attitudes. Attitudes are enduring dispositions to consistently respond in a given manner to various aspects of the world, including persons, events, and objects. Attitudes consist of three components: the affective, or the emotions or feelings involved; the cognitive, or awareness or knowledge; and the behavioral, or the predisposition to action. Attitudes are latent constructs and because of this, they are not directly observable.

2. Identify basic approaches to measuring attitudes. Many methods for measuring attitudes have been developed for attitude measurement. Most fall into the categories of ranking, rating, sorting, and choice techniques.

3. Discuss the use of rating scales for measuring attitudes. One class of rating scales, category scales, provides several response categories to allow respondents to indicate the intensity of their attitudes. The Likert scale uses a series of statements with which subjects indicate agreement or disagreement. The levels of agreement with some statement are assigned numerical scores. A semantic differential uses a series of attitude scales anchored by bipolar adjectives. The respondent indicates where his or her attitude falls between the polar attitudes. Variations on this method, such as numerical scales and the Stapel scale, are also used. The Stapel scale puts a single adjective in the center of a range of numerical values from +3 to –3. Constant-sum scales require the respondent to divide a constant sum into parts, indicating the weights to be given to various attributes of the item being studied.

4. Represent a latent construct by constructing a summated scale. Researchers use composite scales to represent latent constructs. An easy way to create a composite scale is to add the responses to multiple items together to form a total. Thus, a respondent's scores to four items can be simply added together to form a summated scale. The researcher must check to make sure that each scale item is worded positively, or at least all in the same direction. For example, if multiple items are used to form a satisfaction construct, a higher score for each item should lead to higher satisfaction. If one of the items represents dissatisfaction, such that a higher score represents lower satisfaction, this item must be reverse recoded prior to creating the composite scale.

5. Summarize ways to measure attitudes with ranking and sorting techniques. People often rank order their preferences. Thus, ordinal scales that ask respondents to rank order a set of objects or attributes may be developed. In the paired-comparison technique, two alternatives are paired and respondents are asked to pick the preferred one. Sorting requires respondents to indicate their attitudes by arranging items into piles or categories.

6. Discuss major issues involved in the selection of a measurement scale. The researcher can choose among a number of attitude scales. Choosing among the alternatives requires considering several questions, each of which is generally answered by comparing the advantages of each alternative to the problem definition. A monadic rating scale asks about a single concept. A comparative rating scale asks a respondent to rate a concept in comparison with a benchmark used as a frame of reference. Scales may be balanced or unbalanced. Unbalanced scales may prevent responses from piling up at one end. Forced-choice scales require the respondent to select an alternative; non-forced-choice scales allow the respondent to indicate an inability to select an alternative.

Key Terms and Concepts

attitude, *339*
balanced rating scale, *355*
behavioral differential, *352*
category scale, *342*
choice, *340*
comparative rating scale, *354*
composite scale, *344*
constant-sum scale, *348*
forced-choice rating scale, *355*
graphic rating scale, *348*
hypothetical constructs, *315*
image profile, *346*
Likert scale, *344*
monadic rating scale, *354*
numerical scale, *346*
paired comparison, *352*
ranking, *340*
rating, *340*
reverse recoding, *344*
semantic differential, *345*
sorting, *340*
Stapel scale, *347*
Thurstone scale, *350*
unbalanced rating scale, *355*

Questions for Review and Critical Thinking

1. What is an *attitude*? Is there a consensus concerning its definition?
2. Distinguish between *rating* and *ranking*. Which is a better attitude measurement technique? Why?
3. Assume the researcher wanted to create a summated scale indicating a respondent's attitude toward the trucking industry. What would the result be for the respondent whose response is as indicated below?
4. How would you perform reverse recoding using statistical software like SAS or SPSS?
5. What advantages do numerical scales have over semantic differential scales?
6. Identify the issues a researcher should consider when choosing a measurement scale.
7. Should a Likert scale ever be treated as though it had ordinal properties?
8. In each of the following, identify the type of scale and evaluate it:
   a. A U.S. representative's questionnaire sent to constituents:

   Do you favor or oppose the Fair Tax Proposal?

In Favor	*Opposed*	*No Opinion*
☐	☐	☐

   b. How favorable are you toward the Fair Tax Proposal?

   Very Unfavorable ☐ ☐ ☐ ☐ ☐ *Very Favorable*

   c. A psychographic statement asking the respondent to circle the appropriate response:
   I shop a lot for specials.

Strongly Disagree	*Disagree*	*Neutral*	*Agree*	*Strongly Agree*
1	2	3	4	5

9. What is the difference between a measured variable and a latent construct?
10. If a Likert summated scale has ten scale items, do all ten items have to be phrased as either positive or negative statements, or can the scale contain a mix of positive and negative statements?
11. If a semantic differential has ten scale items, should all the positive adjectives be on the right and all the negative adjectives on the left?
12. **ETHICS** A researcher thinks many respondents will answer "don't know" or "can't say" if these options are printed on an attitude scale along with categories indicating level of agreement. The researcher does not print either "don't know" or "can't say" on the questionnaire because the resulting data would be more complicated to analyze and report. Is this proper?
13. **'NET** SRI International investigates U.S. consumers by asking questions about their attitudes and values. It has a Web site so people can VALS-type themselves. To find out your VALS type, go to **http://www.sric-bi.com/VALS/presurvey.shtml**.

Research Activity

1. A researcher wishes to compare two hotels on the following attributes:
   Convenience of location
   Friendly personnel
   Value for money
   a. Design a Likert scale to accomplish this task.
   b. Design a semantic differential scale to accomplish this task.
   c. Design a graphic rating scale to accomplish this task.

Case 14.1 Measurement and Scaling

The service sector in India accounts for 55% of the gross domestic product (GDP), and employs around 30 percent of its workforce. The service sector is responsible for more than 45% of the nation's consumer spending. IT and ITES form the significant chunk of service industry. Recent survey of Business Today invited major customers of these companies to answer the questionnaire, online as well as on paper, regarding the quality of the service; a total of 2560 readers responded to the survey. The results of the specified survey are as follows:

Company	Good (%)	Bad (%)	No Response (%)
TCS	87	4	9
Infosys	85	7	8
Wipro	72	18	10
Mahindra Satyam	47	48	5
Patni	64	31	5
Mind Tree	50	27	33
Cognizant	84	15	1
Mastek	47	19	34
I-Flex Solutions Limited	48	20	32
CMC Limited	42	18	40
MphasiS BFL Limited	44	14	42
Tata Infotech Limited	67	17	16

Questions

1. What are the constructs? What are the constitutive definitions present in the case? Do you think they are sufficient? If no, what are the implications?
2. Which scale probably was used? What highest level of scaling could have been used? State examples.
3. Describe possible sources of error which can be in data.
4. Do you think the scale is reliable? State the reason to support your answer. What could be done to have a test for reliability?
5. In your opinion is this scale valid? Give the reason. How may you determine the validity?

Case 14.2 Roeder-Johnson Corporation

A decade ago, the talk in business circles was all about the central role of technology, especially the Internet, in the success of new businesses. Some investors seemed eager to back almost any start-up with "dot-com" in its name or its business plan. Although the go-go investment climate of the 1990s seems far away, entrepreneurs still start companies every year, and they are still making their case to the investment community. What business ideas do investors like? Is high-tech still important? Public relations firm Roeder-Johnson Corporation, which specializes in start-up companies and those involved in technology innovation, conducted an online survey into the attitudes of 70 subjects, including venture capitalists, entrepreneurs, journalists, and company analysts.[7] The central question was this:

Do you believe that unique technology is crucial to the success of startup companies today?

1. *Rarely*
2. *Occasionally*
3. *Frequently*
4. *Usually*

5. *Always*

The remainder of the survey asked for reasons why technology is important to start-ups and invited comments from the respondents.

In its news release, Roeder-Johnson reported that 91 percent of respondents consider technology to be important at least frequently. The breakdown was 39 percent frequently, 39 percent usually, and 13 percent always. The remaining 9 percent of respondents cited technology as important only occasionally, and none said it is rarely important.

Questions

1. Evaluate the rating scale used for the question in this survey. Is it balanced? Are the category labels clear? Is the number of categories appropriate?
2. Suggest three ways that Roeder-Johnson could improve this survey without a major cost increase.
3. Based on the information given here, what do you think the research objectives for this survey might have been? Do you think the survey met its objectives? Explain.

Case 14.3 Attitudes toward Technology and Lifestyle

A marketing research company sent the attitude scales in Case Exhibit 14.3–1 to members of its consumer panel. Other questions on the questionnaire were about ownership and/or use of computers, consumer electronic devices, satellite TV ownership, cellular phones, and Internet activity.

Questions

1. What type of attitude scale appears in the case study?
2. Evaluate the list of statements. Do the statements appear to measure a single concept?
3. What do they appear to be measuring?

CASE EXHIBIT 14.3–1 **Attitude Scale**

Below is a list of statements that may or may not be used to describe your attitudes toward technology and your lifestyle. Please indicate to what extent each statement describes your attitudes by placing an X in a box from 1 to 10, where 10 means that statement "Describes your attitudes completely" and a 1 means that statement "Does not describe your attitudes at all." (X ONE BOX ACROSS FOR EACH STATEMENT.)

	Does Not Describe Your Attitudes At All									Describes Your Attitudes Completely
	1	2	3	4	5	6	7	8	9	10
I like to impress people with my lifestyle.	☐	☐	☐	☐	☐	☐	☐	☐	☐	☐
Technology is important to me.	☐	☐	☐	☐	☐	☐	☐	☐	☐	☐
I am very competitive when it comes to my career.	☐	☐	☐	☐	☐	☐	☐	☐	☐	☐
Having fun is the whole point of life.	☐	☐	☐	☐	☐	☐	☐	☐	☐	☐
Family is important, but I have other interests that are just as important to me.	☐	☐	☐	☐	☐	☐	☐	☐	☐	☐
I am constantly looking for new ways to entertain myself.	☐	☐	☐	☐	☐	☐	☐	☐	☐	☐
Making a lot of money is important to me.	☐	☐	☐	☐	☐	☐	☐	☐	☐	☐
I spend most of my free time doing fun stuff with my friends.	☐	☐	☐	☐	☐	☐	☐	☐	☐	☐
I like to spend time learning about new technology products.	☐	☐	☐	☐	☐	☐	☐	☐	☐	☐
I like to show off my taste and style.	☐	☐	☐	☐	☐	☐	☐	☐	☐	☐
I like technology.	☐	☐	☐	☐	☐	☐	☐	☐	☐	☐
My family is by far the most important thing in my life.	☐	☐	☐	☐	☐	☐	☐	☐	☐	☐
I put a lot of time and energy into my career.	☐	☐	☐	☐	☐	☐	☐	☐	☐	☐
I am very likely to purchase new technology products or services.	☐	☐	☐	☐	☐	☐	☐	☐	☐	☐
I spend most of my free time working on improving myself.	☐	☐	☐	☐	☐	☐	☐	☐	☐	☐

CHAPTER 15
QUESTIONNAIRE DESIGN

LEARNING OUTCOMES

After studying this chapter, you should be able to

1. **Explain the significance of decisions about questionnaire design and wording**
2. **Define alternatives for wording open-ended and fixed-alternative questions**
3. **Summarize guidelines for questions that avoid mistakes in questionnaire design**
4. **Describe how the proper sequence of questions may improve a questionnaire**
5. **Discuss how to design a questionnaire layout**
6. **Describe criteria for pretesting and revising a questionnaire and for adapting it to global markets**

Chapter Vignette: J.D. Power Asks Consumers to Get Real

Are you driving your dream car? Most of us can't, because we bump up against the practical reality that we can't pay for every great new feature. As car makers consider adding new features, they have to evaluate not only which ones appeal to consumers but also which ones will actually sell, considering their likely cost. J.D. Power and Associates recently addressed this issue in a survey of about seventeen thousand consumers.[1]

© ROYALTY FREE/CORBIS

In the J.D. Power survey, consumers were asked whether they were familiar with twenty-two different emerging technologies. Then they were asked about their interest in each technology, rating their interest using a scale ("definitely interested," "probably interested," and so on). Next, the study indicated the likely price of each technology, and consumers were again asked their interest, given the price. The results ranked the features according to interest level, based on the percentage who indicated they were either definitely or probably interested in the feature.

Learning price information often changed consumers' interest levels. Night vision systems appealed to 72 percent of consumers, placing it in second place in the rankings. But when consumers learned the systems would likely add $1,500 to the price of a car, this technology dropped to a rank of 17, near the bottom. In contrast, HD radio ranked in sixteenth place until consumers saw a price tag of just $150. That price pushed the feature up to third place. Still, two features remained in the top five even with pricing information: run-flat tires and stability control. And three of the bottom-five features—a reconfigurable cabin, lane departure warning system, and smart sensing power-swing front doors—stayed in the bottom rankings. Automakers can use findings such as these to determine which features are price-sensitive and which might be appealing even at a higher price.

The J.D. Power survey shows how extremely useful information can be gathered with a questionnaire. It also shows how results can differ by exactly what question is asked and the amount of information provided. This chapter outlines a procedure for questionnaire design, which addresses concerns such as the wording and order of questions and the layout of the questionnaire.

Introduction

Each stage in the business research process is important and interdependent. The research questionnaire development stage is critically important as the information provided is only as good as the questions asked. However, the importance of question wording is easily, and far too often, overlooked.

Businesspeople who are inexperienced at research frequently believe that constructing a questionnaire is a simple task. Amateur researchers think a short questionnaire can be written in minutes. Unfortunately, newcomers who naively believe that good grammar is all a person needs to construct a questionnaire generally end up with useless results. Ask a bad question, get bad results.

Good questionnaire design requires far more than correct grammar. People don't understand questions just because they are grammatically correct. Respondents simply may not know what is being asked. They may be unaware of the business issue or topic of interest. They may confuse the subject with something else. The question may not mean the same thing to everyone interviewed. Finally, people may refuse to answer personal questions. Most of these problems can be minimized, however, if a skilled researcher composes the questionnaire.

Questionnaire Quality and Design: Basic Considerations

For a questionnaire to fulfill a researcher's purposes, the questions must meet the basic criteria of *relevance* and *accuracy*. To achieve these ends, a researcher who is systematically planning a questionnaire's design will be required to make several decisions—typically, but not necessarily, in the following order:

1. What should be asked?
2. How should questions be phrased?
3. In what sequence should the questions be arranged?
4. What questionnaire layout will best serve the research objectives?
5. How should the questionnaire be pretested? Does the questionnaire need to be revised?

This chapter provides guidelines for answering each question.

What Should Be Asked?

Certain decisions made during the early stages of the research process will influence the questionnaire design. The preceding chapters stressed good problem definition and clear research questions. This leads to specific research hypotheses that, in turn, clearly indicate what must be measured. Different types of questions may be better at measuring certain things than are others. In addition, the communication medium used for data collection—that is, telephone interview, personal interview, or self-administered questionnaire—must be determined. This decision is another forward linkage that influences the structure and content of the questionnaire. Therefore, the specific questions to be asked will be a function of previous decisions made in the research process. At the same time, the latter stages of the research process will also have an important impact on questionnaire wording and measurement. For example, when designing the questionnaire, the researcher should consider the types of statistical analysis that will be conducted.

TOTHEPOINT

How often misused words generate misleading thoughts.

—Herbert Spencer

Questionnaire Relevancy

A questionnaire is *relevant* to the extent that all information collected addresses a research question that will help the decision maker address the current business problem. Asking a wrong question or an irrelevant question is a common pitfall. If the task is to pinpoint store image problems, questions asking for political opinions are likely irrelevant. The researcher should be specific about data needs and have a rationale for each item requesting information. Irrelevant questions are more than a nuisance because they make the survey needlessly long. In a study where two samples of the same group of businesses received either a one-page or a three-page questionnaire, the response rate was nearly twice as high for the one-page survey.[2]

Conversely, many researchers, after conducting surveys, find that they omitted some important questions. Therefore, when planning the questionnaire design, researchers must think about possible omissions. Is information on the relevant demographic and psychographic variables being collected? Would certain questions help clarify the answers to other questions? Will the results of the study provide the answer to the manager's problem?

Questionnaire Accuracy

Once a researcher decides what should be asked, the criterion of accuracy becomes the primary concern. *Accuracy* means that the information is reliable and valid. While experienced researchers generally believe that questionnaires should use simple, understandable, unbiased, unambiguous, and nonirritating words, no step-by-step procedure for ensuring accuracy in question writing can be generalized across projects. Obtaining accurate answers from respondents depends strongly on the researcher's ability to design a questionnaire that will facilitate recall and motivate respondents to cooperate. Respondents tend to be more cooperative when the subject of the research interests them. When questions are not lengthy, difficult to answer, or ego threatening, there is a higher probability of obtaining unbiased answers.

Question wording and sequence also substantially influence accuracy, which can be particularly challenging when designing a survey for technical audiences. The Department of Treasury commissioned a survey of insurance companies to evaluate their offering of terrorism insurance as required by the government's terrorism reinsurance program. But industry members complained that the survey misused terms such as "contract" and "high risk," which have precise meanings for insurers, and asked for policy information "to date," without specifying which date. These questions caused confusion and left room for interpretation, calling the survey results into question.[3]

Wording Questions

There are many ways to phrase questions, and many standard question formats have been developed in previous research studies. This section presents a classification of question types and provides some helpful guidelines for writing questions.

Open-Ended Response versus Fixed-Alternative Questions

The first decision in questionnaire design is based on the amount of freedom respondents have in answering. Should the question be open-ended, allowing the participants freedom to choose their manner of response, or closed, where the participants choose their response from an already determined fixed set of choices?

open-ended response questions
Questions that pose some problem and ask respondents to answer in their own words.

Open-ended response questions pose some problem or topic and ask respondents to answer in their own words. If the question is asked in a personal interview, the interviewer may probe for more information, as in the following examples:

What names of local banks can you think of?
What comes to mind when you look at this advertisement?
In what way, if any, could this product be changed or improved? I'd like you to tell me anything you can think of, no matter how minor it seems.
What things do you like most about working for Federal Express? What do you like least?
Why do you buy more of your clothing in Nordstrom than in other stores?
How would you describe your supervisor's management style?
Please tell us how our stores can better serve your needs.

Open-ended response questions are free-answer questions. They may be contrasted with **fixed-alternative questions**—sometimes called *closed-ended questions*—which give respondents specific limited-alternative responses and ask them to choose the one closest to their own viewpoints. For example:

fixed-alternative questions
Questions in which respondents are given specific, limited-alternative responses and asked to choose the one closest to their own viewpoint.

Did you use any commercial feed or supplement for livestock or poultry in 2010?

☐ *Yes* ☐ *No*

Would you say that the labor quality in Japan is higher, about the same, or not as good as it was 10 years ago?

☐ *Higher*
☐ *About the same*
☐ *Not as good*

Do you think the Renewable Energy Partnership Program has affected your business?

☐ *Yes, for the better*
☐ *Not especially*
☐ *Yes, for the worse*

How much of your welding supplies do you purchase from our Tier One *suppliers?*

☐ *All of it*
☐ *Most of it*
☐ *About one-half of it*
☐ *About one-quarter of it*
☐ *Less than one-quarter of it*

The Research Snapshot " Corporate Reputations: Consumers Put Johnson & Johnson, Microsoft, and Google on Top" illustrates the use of a multifaceted survey to assess corporate reputation.

USING OPEN-ENDED RESPONSE QUESTIONS

Open-ended response questions are most beneficial when the researcher is conducting exploratory research, especially when the range of responses is not yet known. Respondents are free to answer with whatever is foremost in their minds. Such questions can be used to learn which words and phrases people spontaneously give to the free-response question. Such responses will reflect the flavor of the language that people use in talking about the issue and thus may provide guidance in the wording of questions and responses for follow up surveys.

Also, open-ended response questions are valuable at the beginning of an interview. They are good first questions because they allow respondents to warm up to the questioning process. They are also good last questions for a fixed-alternative questionnaire, when a researcher can ask the respondent to expand in a manner that provides greater richness to the data. For example, an employee satisfaction survey may collect data with a series of fixed-alternative questions, then conclude with "Can you provide one suggestion on how our organization can enhance employee satisfaction?"

The cost of administering open-ended response questions is substantially higher than that of administering fixed-alternative questions because the job of editing, coding, and analyzing the data is quite extensive. As each respondent's answer is somewhat unique, there is some difficulty in categorizing and summarizing the answers. The process requires that an editor go over a sample of questions to develop a classification scheme. This scheme is then used to code all answers according to the classification scheme.

Another potential disadvantage of the open-ended response question is the possibility that interviewer bias will influence the answer. While most interviewer instructions state that answers are to be recorded verbatim, rarely does even the best interviewer get every word spoken by the respondent. Interviewers have a tendency to take shortcuts. When this occurs, the interviewer may well introduce error because the final answer may reflect a combination of the respondent's and interviewer's ideas.

RESEARCH SNAPSHOT

Corporate Reputations: Consumers Put Johnson & Johnson, Microsoft, and Google on Top

To report the reputations of well-known companies, the *Wall Street Journal* sponsors an annual research project. Harris Interactive has used the Harris Reputation Quotient (RQ) to assess the reputations of the 60 most visible companies in the U.S. since 1999. The Corporate Reputation Survey allows U.S. adults to provide their perceptions of corporations.

The study has two phases. In the first phase, the researchers identified the companies that were most "visible," meaning companies that people were most likely to think about—and therefore have an attitude toward. This phase avoided the problem of asking individuals to rate the qualities of a company they have never heard of. This research used open-ended questions asking respondents to name two companies they felt had the best reputation and two that had the worst. The researchers determined the number of times each company was mentioned and selected the 60 named most often for the second phase of the study.

The second phase was aimed at generating rankings of the corporations, so questions and answer choices needed to be more specific. The researchers identified six dimensions of a corporate reputation: products and services, financial performance, workplace environment, social responsibility, vision and leadership, and emotional appeal. Within these categories, they identified 20 attributes, such as whether respondents would trust the company if they had a problem with its goods or services, and how sincere its corporate communications were. In an online survey, each respondent was asked to rate one company on all 20 attributes. Then the respondent was invited (not required) to rate a second company. Each year, about 20,000 people participated in the study and more than 250 ratings were generated for each company. These responses were combined to create an overall rating for the company.

The top-ranked company for each of the first seven years of the survey was Johnson & Johnson. On the six dimensions of reputation, J&J was top in emotional appeal and its goods and services, and it made the top five on the other dimensions. This honor is more than just good publicity; J&J also was the firm from which the largest share of people said they would "definitely purchase" products. However, Microsoft was named the top company in the 2006 study, followed by Google in 2007. In both years, Johnson & Johnson remained number two on the list of the reputations of the 60 most visible companies.

Source: Based on Alsop, Ronald, "Ranking Corporation Reputations," *Wall Street Journal* (December 6, 2005), http://online.wsj.com; "The Annual RQ 2007: The Reputations of the Most Visible Companies," Harris Interactive, Inc. (2008), http://www.harrisinteractive.com/services/pubs/HI_BSC_REPORT_AnnualRQ2007_Rankings.pdf; "The Annual RQ 2007: Methodological Overview," Harris Interactive, Inc. (2008), http://www.harrisinteractive.com/services/pubs/HI_BSC_REPORT_AnnualRQ2007_Methodology.pdf; "The 9th Annual RQ: Reputations of the 60 Most Visible Companies," Harris Interactive, Inc. (2008), http://www.harrisinteractive.com/News/MediaAccess/2008/HI_BSC_REPORT_AnnualRQ_USASummary07-08.pdf.

In addition, articulate individuals tend to give longer answers to open-ended response questions. Such respondents often are better educated and from higher income groups and therefore may not be good representatives of the entire population. Yet, they may provide the most information.

USING FIXED-ALTERNATIVE QUESTIONS

In contrast, fixed-alternative questions require less interviewer skill, take less time, and are easier for the respondent to answer. This is because answers to closed questions are classified into standardized groupings prior to data collection. Standardizing alternative responses to a question provides comparability of answers, which facilitates coding, tabulating, and ultimately interpreting the data.

However, when a researcher is unaware of the potential responses to a question, fixed-alternative questions obviously cannot be used. If the researcher assumes what the responses will be, but is in fact wrong, he or she will have no way of knowing the extent to which the assumption was incorrect. Sometimes this type of error comes to light after the questionnaire has been used. Researchers found cross-cultural misunderstandings in a survey of mothers called the Preschooler Feeding Questionnaire. By talking to a group of African-American mothers, a researcher at the University of Chicago determined that they had experiences with encouraging children to eat more and using food to calm children, but they used different language for these situations than the questionnaire used, so they misinterpreted some questions.[4]

Unanticipated alternatives emerge when respondents believe that closed answers do not adequately reflect their feelings. They may make comments to the interviewer or write additional answers on the questionnaire indicating that the exploratory research did not yield a complete array of responses. After the fact, little can be done to correct a closed question that does not provide the correct responses or enough alternatives. Therefore, a researcher may find exploratory research with open-ended responses valuable before writing a descriptive questionnaire. The researcher should strive to ensure that there are sufficient response choices to include almost all possible answers.

Respondents may check off obvious alternatives, such as *salary* or *health benefits* in an employee survey, if they do not see *opportunities for advancement,* the choice they would prefer. Also, a fixed-alternative question may tempt respondents to check an answer that is more prestigious or socially acceptable than the true answer. Rather than stating that they do not know why they chose a given product, they may select an alternative among those presented, or as a matter of convenience, they may select a given alternative rather than think of the most correct response.

Most questionnaires mix open-ended and closed questions. As we have discussed, each form has unique benefits. In addition, a change of pace can eliminate respondent boredom and fatigue.

Types of Fixed-Alternative Questions

Earlier in the chapter a variety of fixed-alternative questions were presented. Here we identify and categorize the various types.

The **simple-dichotomy (dichotomous) question** requires the respondent to choose one of two alternatives. The answer can be a simple "yes" or "no" or a choice between "this" and "that." For example:

simple-dichotomy (dichotomous) question
A fixed-alternative question that requires the respondent to choose one of two alternatives.

Did you have any overnight travel for work-related activities last month?

☐ *Yes* ☐ *No*

Several types of questions provide the respondent with *multiple-choice alternatives.* The **determinant-choice question** requires the respondent to choose one—and only one—response from among several possible alternatives. For example:

determinant-choice question
A fixed-alternative question that requires the respondent to choose one response from among multiple alternatives.

Please give us some information about your flight. In which section of the aircraft did you sit?

☐ *First class*
☐ *Business class*
☐ *Coach class*

The **frequency-determination question** is a determinant-choice question that asks for an answer about the general frequency of occurrence. For example:

frequency-determination question
A fixed-alternative question that asks for an answer about general frequency of occurrence.

How frequently do you watch MTV?

☐ *Every day*
☐ *5–6 times a week*
☐ *2–4 times a week*
☐ *Once a week*
☐ *Less than once a week*
☐ *Never*

Attitude rating scales, such as the Likert scale, semantic differential, Stapel scale, and so on, are also fixed-alternative questions. These scales were discussed in Chapter 14.

The **checklist question** allows the respondent to provide multiple answers to a single question. The respondent indicates past experience, preference, and the like merely by checking off items. In many cases the choices are adjectives that describe a particular object. A typical checklist question might ask the following:

checklist question
A fixed-alternative question that allows the respondent to provide multiple answers to a single question by checking off items.

Please check which, if any, of the following sources of information about investments you regularly use.

- ☐ *Personal advice of your broker(s)*
- ☐ *Brokerage newsletters*
- ☐ *Brokerage research reports*
- ☐ *Investment advisory service(s)*
- ☐ *Conversations with other investors*
- ☐ *Web page(s)*
- ☐ *None of these*
- ☐ *Other (please specify)* ______

totally exhaustive
A category exists for every respondent in among the fixed-alternative categories

mutually exclusive
No overlap exists among the fixed-alternative categories

A major problem in developing dichotomous or multiple-choice alternatives is establishing the response alternatives. Alternatives should be **totally exhaustive**, meaning that all the response options are covered and that every respondent has an alternative to check. The alternatives should also be **mutually exclusive**, meaning there should be no overlap among categories and only one dimension of an issue should be related to each alternative. So, there is a response category for everyone, but only a single response category for each individual. In other words, a place for everything and everything in its place! The following listing of income groups illustrates common errors:

- ☐ *$10,000–$30,000*
- ☐ *$30,000–$50,000*
- ☐ *$50,000–$70,000*
- ☐ *$70,000–$90,000*
- ☐ *$90,000–$110,000*
- ☐ *Over $110,000*

Which category would a respondent with an annual income of $30,000 check? How many people with incomes of $30,000 will be in the second group, and how many will be in the third group? Researchers have no way to determine the answer. This is an example of failing to have mutually exclusive response categories. The question also is not totally exhaustive, as there is no category for those earning less than $10,000 to check. Also, few people relish being in the lowest category. To negate the potential bias caused by respondents' tendency to avoid an extreme category, researchers often include a category lower than the lowest expected answers. The following response categories address the totally exhaustive and mutually exclusive issues.

- ☐ *Less than $10,000*
- ☐ *$10,000–$29,999*
- ☐ *$30,000–$49,999*
- ☐ *$50,000–$69,999*
- ☐ *$70,000–$89,999*
- ☐ *$90,000–$109,999*
- ☐ *Over $110,000*

While this example makes the totally exhaustive and mutually exclusive categories rather clear, it can actually become quite challenging. Consider the preceding frequency-determination question regarding MTV. With a question such as this, it can become difficult to establish response categories that meet these rules.

Phrasing Questions for Self-Administered, Telephone, and Personal Interview Surveys

The means of data collection—telephone interview, personal interview, self-administered questionnaire—will influence the question format and question phrasing. In general, questions for telephone in particular, as well as Internet and mail surveys, must be less complex than those used in personal interviews. Questionnaires for telephone and personal interviews should be written

Mail Form:

How willing are you to buy 'Maggi'?

1 Extremely willing
2 Quite willing
3 Somewhat willing
4 Slightly willing
5 Neither willing nor unwilling
6 Slightly unwilling
7 Somewhat unwilling
8 Quite unwilling
9 Extremely unwilling

Revised for Telephone:

How willing are you to buy Maggi? Would you say you are extremely willing, somewhat willing, neither willing nor unwilling, somewhat unwilling, or extremely unwilling?

Extremely willing	1
Somewhat willing	2
Neither willing nor unwilling	3
Somewhat unwilling	4
Extremely unwilling	5

EXHIBIT 15.1
Reducing Question Complexity by Providing Fewer Responses for Telephone Interviews

in a conversational style. It is particularly important that telephone surveys use easy to understand response categories. Exhibit 15.1 illustrates how a question may be revised for a different medium.

In a telephone survey about attitudes toward police services, the questionnaire not only asked about general attitudes such as how much respondents trust their local police officers and whether the police are "approachable," "dedicated," and so on, but also provided basic scenarios to help respondents put their expectations into words. For example, the interviewer asked respondents to imagine that someone had broken into their home and stolen items, and that the respondent called the police to report the crime. The interviewer asked how quickly or slowly the respondent expected the police to arrive.[5]

When a question is read aloud, remembering the alternative choices can be difficult. Consider the following question from a personal interview:

There has been a lot of discussion about the potential health risks to nonsmokers from tobacco smoke in public buildings, restaurants, and business offices. How serious a health threat to you personally is the inhaling of this secondhand smoke, often called passive smoking: *Is it a very serious health threat, somewhat serious, not too serious, or not serious at all?*

1. *Very serious*
2. *Somewhat serious*
3. *Not too serious*
4. *Not serious at all*
5. *(Don't know)*

The last portion of the question was a listing of the four alternatives that serve as answers. This listing at the end is often used in interviews to remind the respondent of the alternatives, since they are not presented visually. The fifth alternative, "Don't know," is in parentheses because, although the interviewer knows it is an acceptable answer, it is not read. The researcher only uses this response when the respondent truly cannot provide an answer.

The data collection technique also influences the layout of the questionnaire. Layout will be discussed later in the chapter.

RESEARCH SNAPSHOT

What to Do with the Clubhouse?

Mathematician Jennifer Lewis Priestley helps the managers of golf and country clubs collect and interpret data. One club showed her a member survey containing the following question:

We need to make some decisions about our clubhouse. The clubhouse itself is too small and requires substantial physical improvement, and it's been a long time since we undertook a major redecorating project. Do you favor

a. remodeling the current clubhouse?
b. building a new clubhouse?
c. doing nothing?

The wording of the question and the answer choices are biased in favor of action. The question criticizes the current clubhouse and places the question in the context of "a long time since we undertook a major redecorating project." To select choice *c*, the respondent would have to disregard the premise of the question.

© iStock

To eliminate the bias and include neutral wording so that the responses could more accurately represent the members' opinions, Priestley recommended some changes:

Considering the current clubhouse, which of the following statements most closely reflects your views?

a. The current clubhouse should remain the same.
b. The current clubhouse should be remodeled (size will remain the same).
c. The current clubhouse should be remodeled and expanded.
d. The club needs a new clubhouse (current clubhouse torn down).

Source: Based on Priestley, Jennifer Lewis, "Determining What Your Marketing Members Want," *Club Management* (October 2004), http://infotrac.galegroup.com.

© TODD HACKWELDER/SHUTTERSTOCK

Guidelines for Constructing Questions

Developing good business research questionnaires is a combination of art and science. Few hard-and-fast rules exist in guiding the development of a questionnaire. Fortunately, research experience has yielded some guidelines that help prevent the most common mistakes. The Research Snapshot "What to Do with the Clubhouse?" illustrates problems with question wording in a simple descriptive research project.

Avoid Complexity: Use Simple, Conversational Language

TOTHEPOINT

I don't know the rules of grammar. . . . If you're trying to persuade people to do something, or buy something, it seems to me you should use their language, the language they use every day, the language in which they think. We try to write in the vernacular.

—David Ogilvy

Words used in questionnaires should be readily understandable to all respondents. The researcher usually has the difficult task of adopting the conversational language of people at the lower education levels without talking down to better-educated respondents. Remember, not all people have the vocabulary of a college graduate. In fact, in the U.S., less than 25 percent of the population has a bachelor's degree.

Respondents can probably tell an interviewer whether they are married, single, divorced, separated, or widowed, but providing their *marital status* may present a problem. The technical jargon of top corporate executives should be avoided when surveying retailers or industrial users. "Brand image," "positioning," "marginal analysis," and other corporate language may not have the same meaning for, or even be understood by, a store owner-operator in a retail survey. The vocabulary used in the following question from an attitude survey on social problems probably would confuse many respondents:

> *When effluents from a paper mill can be drunk and exhaust from factory smokestacks can be breathed, then humankind will have done a good job in saving the environment. . . . Don't you agree that what we want is zero toxicity: no effluents?*

Besides being too long and confusing, this question is leading. Survey questions should be short and to the point. Like this:

> *The stock market is too risky to invest in these days.*

Avoid Leading and Loaded Questions

Leading and loaded questions are a major source of bias in question wording. A **leading question** suggests or implies certain answers. A study of the dry cleaning industry asked this question:

leading question
A question that suggests or implies certain answers.

Many people are using dry cleaning less because of improved wash-and-wear clothes. How do you feel wash-and-wear clothes have affected your use of dry cleaning facilities in the past 4 years?

☐ *Use less* ☐ *No change* ☐ *Use more*

It should be clear that this question leads the respondent to report lower usage of dry cleaning. The potential "bandwagon effect" implied in this question threatens the study's validity. *Partial mention of alternatives* is a variation of this phenomenon:

Do accounting graduates who attended state universities, such as Washington State University, make better auditors?

A **loaded question** suggests a socially desirable answer or is emotionally charged. Consider the following question from a survey about media influence on politics:[6]

loaded question
A question that suggests a socially desirable answer or is emotionally charged.

What most influences your vote in major elections?

☐ *My own informed opinion*
☐ *Major media outlets such as CNN*
☐ *Newspaper endorsements*
☐ *Popular celebrity opinions*
☐ *Candidate's physical attractiveness*
☐ *Family or friends*
☐ *Video advertising (television or Web video)*
☐ *Other*

The vast majority of respondents chose the first alternative. Although this question is not overly emotionally loaded, many people could be reluctant to say they are swayed by the media or advertising as opposed to their independent mindset. In fact, a research question dealing with what influences decisions like these may best be done by drawing some inference based on less direct questioning.

Certain answers to questions are more socially desirable than others. For example, a truthful answer to the following classification question might be painful:

Where did you rank academically in your high school graduating class?

☐ *Top quarter*
☐ *2nd quarter*
☐ *3rd quarter*
☐ *4th quarter*

When taking personality or psychographic tests, respondents frequently can interpret which answers are most socially acceptable even if those answers do not portray their true feelings. For example, which are the socially desirable answers to the following questions on a self-confidence scale?

I feel capable of handling myself in most social situations.

☐ *Agree* ☐ *Disagree*

I fear my actions will cause others to have low opinions of me.

☐ *Agree* ☐ *Disagree*

Invoking the status quo is a form of loading that results in bias because most people tend to resist change.[7] An experiment conducted in the early days of polling illustrates the unpopularity of change.[8] Comparable samples of respondents were simultaneously asked two questions about presidential succession. One sample was asked:

Would you favor or oppose adding a law to the Constitution preventing a president from succeeding himself more than once?

The other sample was asked:

Would you favor or oppose changing the Constitution in order to prevent a president from succeeding himself more than once?

About half of respondents answered negatively to the first question. For the second question, about two out of three respondents answered negatively. Thus, the public would rather add to than change the Constitution.

The field of political research is fraught with bias. Consider the question asked by the National Republican Senatorial Committee (**www.nrsc.org**) on a survey:

Should foreign terrorists caught in the future or currently being held in U.S. detainment facilities be given the same legal rights and privileges as U.S. Citizens?

Clearly, the authors are asking for a "No" response. A pro-Democrat pollster might word the question something like this:[9]

Do you believe it is acceptable for the United States to detain potentially innocent battlefield detainees without legal representation and to inhumanely interrogate them by means that violate the Geneva Convention and the United Nations Convention against torture?

Obviously, this question is likewise biased toward a no response.

A more straightforward question might ask:

Does the presumption of innocence apply to suspected enemy combatants?

Asking respondents "how often" they use a product or visit a store leads them to generalize about their habits, because there usually is some variance in their behavior. In generalizing, a person is likely to portray an *ideal* behavior rather than an *average* behavior. For instance, brushing your teeth after each meal may be ideal, but busy people may skip a brushing or two. An introductory **counterbiasing statement** or preamble to a question that reassures respondents that their "embarrassing" behavior is not abnormal may yield truthful responses:

counterbiasing statement
An introductory statement or preamble to a potentially embarrassing question that reduces a respondent's reluctance to answer by suggesting that certain behavior is not unusual.

Some people have time to brush three times daily but others do not. How often did you brush your teeth yesterday?

If a question embarrasses the respondent, it may elicit no answer or a biased response. This is particularly true with respect to personal or classification data such as income or education. The problem may be mitigated by introducing the section of the questionnaire with a statement such as this:

To help classify your answers, we'd like to ask you a few questions. Again, your answers will be kept in strict confidence.

A question statement may be leading because it is phrased to reflect either the negative or the positive aspects of an issue. To control for this bias, the wording of attitudinal questions may be reversed for 50 percent of the sample. This **split-ballot technique** is used with the expectation that two alternative phrasings of the same question will yield a more accurate total response than will a single phrasing. For example, in a study on small-car buying behavior, one-half of a sample of imported-car purchasers received a questionnaire in which they were asked to agree or disagree with the statement "Small U.S. cars are cheaper to maintain than small imported cars." The other half of the import-car owners received a questionnaire in which the statement read "Small imported cars are cheaper to maintain than small U.S. cars."

split-ballot technique
Using two alternative phrasings of the same question for respective halves of a sample to elicit a more accurate total response than would a single phrasing.

All of these illustrations are meant as examples of one questionnaire flaw, writing questions in a manner that leads participants to respond in a way that does not accurately reflect their feelings, attitudes, or behaviors. The business researcher should read all the questions and ensure that each does not contain bias.

Avoid Ambiguity: Be as Specific as Possible

Items on questionnaires often are ambiguous because they are too general. Consider such indefinite words as *often, occasionally, regularly, frequently, many, good,* and *poor.* Each of these words has many different meanings. For one consumer, *frequent* reading of *Fortune* magazine may be reading all 25 issues in a year, while another might think 12, or even 6 issues a year is frequent. Earlier, we used the following question as an example of a checklist question:

Please check which, if any, of the following sources of information about investments you regularly use.

What exactly does *regularly* mean? It can certainly vary from respondent to respondent. How exactly does *hardly any* differ from *occasionally*? Where is the cutoff? It is much better to use specific time periods whenever possible.

A brewing industry study on point-of-purchase advertising (store displays) asked their distributors:

How often does the company shut down production for sanitary maintenance?

- ☐ *Annually (once a year)*
- ☐ *Semiannually (once every six months)*
- ☐ *Quarterly (about every three months)*
- ☐ *At least once monthly*
- ☐ *Less frequently (less often than once a year)*

Here the researchers clarified the terms *permanent, semipermanent,* and *temporary* by defining them for the respondent. However, the question remained somewhat ambiguous. Beer marketers often use a variety of point-of-purchase devices to serve different purposes—in this case, what is the purpose? In addition, analysis was difficult because respondents were merely asked to indicate a preference rather than a *degree* of preference. Thus, the meaning of a question may not be clear because the frame of reference is inadequate for interpreting the context of the question.

A student research group asked this question:

What media do you rely on most?

- ☐ *Television*
- ☐ *Radio*
- ☐ *Internet*
- ☐ *Newspapers*

This question is ambiguous because it does not provide information about the context. "Rely on most" for what—news, sports, entertainment? When—while getting dressed in the morning, driving to work, at home in the evening? Knowing the specific circumstance can affect the choice made.

Each of these examples shows how a question can be ambiguous and interpreted differently by different individuals. While we might not be able to completely eliminate ambiguity, by using words or descriptions that have universal meaning, replacing terms with specific response categories, and defining the situation surrounding the question, we can improve our business research questionnaires.

Avoid Double-Barreled Items

A question covering several issues at once is referred to as a **double-barreled question** and should always be avoided. Making the mistake of asking two questions rather than one is easy—for example, "Do you feel our hospital emergency room waiting area is clean and comfortable?" What do we learn from this question? If the respondent responds positively, we could likely infer that our waiting area is clean and comfortable. However, if the response is negative, is it because the room is not clean, or not comfortable? Or both? Certainly for a manager to make improvements

double-barreled question

A question that may induce bias because it covers two issues at once.

it is important to know which element needs attention. When multiple questions are asked in one question, the results may be exceedingly difficult to interpret.

One of the questions we presented earlier when discussing fixed-alternative questions provides a good example of a double-barreled question:

Did your plant use any commercial feed or supplement for livestock or poultry in 2010?

☐ *Yes* ☐ *No*

Here, the question could actually be thought of as a "double-double-barreled" question. Both *commercial feed or supplement* and *livestock or poultry* are double barreled. Interpreting the answer to this question would be challenging.

The following comment offers good advice regarding double-barreled questions:

> *Generally speaking, it is hard enough to get answers to one idea at a time without complicating the problem by asking what amounts to two questions at once. If two ideas are to be explored, they deserve at least two questions. Since question marks are not rationed, there is little excuse for the needless confusion that results [from] the double-barreled question.*[10]

A researcher is well served to carefully examine any survey question that includes the words *and* or *or*. While sometimes words such as these may be used to reinforce or clarify a question, they are often a sign of a double-barreled question. If you have two (or three) questions, ask them separately, not all together.

TOTHEPOINT

"How am I to get in?" asked Alice again, in a louder tone.
"Are you to get in at all?" said the Footman, "That's the first question, you know."

—Lewis Carroll, *Alice's Adventures in Wonderland*

Avoid Making Assumptions

Consider the following question:

Should General Electric continue to pay its outstanding quarterly dividends?

☐ *Yes* ☐ *No*

This question has a built-in assumption: that people believe the dividends paid by General Electric are outstanding. By answering "yes," the respondent implies that the program is, in fact, outstanding and that things are fine just as they are. When a respondent answers "no," he or she implies that GE should discontinue the dividends. The researchers should not place the respondent in that sort of bind by including an implicit assumption in the question.

Another frequent mistake is assuming that the respondent had previously thought about an issue. For example, the following question appeared in a survey concerning Jack-in-the-Box: "Do you think Jack-in-the-Box restaurants should consider changing their name?" Respondents have not likely thought about this question beforehand. Most respondents answered the question even though they had no prior opinion concerning the name change. Research that induces people to express attitudes on subjects they do not ordinarily think about is rather meaningless.

Avoid Burdensome Questions That May Tax the Respondent's Memory

A simple fact of human life is that people forget. Researchers writing questions about past behavior or events should recognize that certain questions may make serious demands on the respondent's memory. Writing questions about prior events requires a conscientious attempt to minimize the problems associated with forgetting.

In many situations, respondents cannot recall the answer to a question. For example, a telephone survey conducted during the 24-hour period following the airing of the Super Bowl might establish whether the respondent watched the Super Bowl and then ask, "Do you recall any commercials on that program?" If the answer is positive, the interviewer might ask, "What brands were advertised?" These two questions measure *unaided recall,* because they give the respondent no clue as to the brand of interest.

If the researcher suspects that the respondent may have forgotten the answer to a question, he or she may rewrite the question in an *aided-recall* format—that is, in a format that provides a clue to help jog the respondent's memory. For instance, the question about an advertised beer in an aided-recall format might be "Do you recall whether there was a brand of beer advertised on that program?" or "I am going to read you a list of beer brand names. Can you pick out the name of the beer that was advertised on the program?" While aided recall is not as strong a test of attention or memory as unaided recall, it is less taxing to the respondent's memory.

Telescoping and squishing are two additional consequences of respondents' forgetting the exact details of their behavior. *Telescoping error* occurs when respondents believe that past events happened more recently than they actually did. For instance, most people will estimate that they have changed the oil in their car more recently than they actually have. The opposite effect, *squishing error,* occurs when respondents think that recent events took place longer ago than they really did. A solution to this problem may be to refer to a specific event that is memorable—for example, "How often have you gone to a sporting event since the World Series?" Because forgetting tends to increase over time, the question may concern a recent period: "How often did you watch HBO on cable television last week?" During pretesting or the questionnaire editing stage, the most appropriate time period can be determined.

In situations in which "I don't know" or "I can't recall" is a meaningful answer, simply including a "don't know" response category may solve the question writer's problem.

Make Certain Questions Generate Variance

We want our variables to vary! It is important that the response categories provided cover the breadth of possibilities (totally exhaustive), but also critical that they yield variance across respondents. In many ways, if all of the respondents check the same box, we have not generated usable information.

For example, the U.S. census uses the following age categories:

Under 5 years
5 to 9 years
10 to 14 years
15 to 19 years
20 to 24 years
25 to 29 years
. . . .
. . . .
. . . .
95 to 99 years
100 years and over

While these five-year age categories do capture the range of ages and provide rather detailed census information regarding the general population, what would happen if they were used for a survey of undergraduate students? In many institutions, 95 percent or more of the respondents would fall into two groups. What might be more appropriate and provide better information in a study of undergraduates?

When we discussed measurement issues in Chapter 13, we noted that there were benefits from constructing scaled responses with a larger number of response categories rather than fewer. In general, this is a good rule, with seven- or ten-point scales likely providing greater variance than three- or four-point scales. In practice, it is also often better to use a scaled response than a dichotomous response form. For example, our earlier example of a simple-dichotomy (dichotomous) question asked:

Did you have any overnight travel for work-related activities last month?

☐ *Yes* ☐ *No*

While the respondent could likely answer this question and we may simply desire to place respondents into either the "did travel" or "did not travel" category, we really do not gain much information from this question. It fails to discriminate at all between employees that travel once a month, twice a month, or were gone for 25 days last month. It is likely that these employees have different attitudes and needs regarding business travel. A better approach might be to create multiple categories (0, 1–5, 6–10, 11–15, 16–20, 21–25, 26+ nights) or ask for a specific number of nights away on business travel. From this, we could always recode the respondents into the nominal data categories of yes/no if needed. However, if we collect yes/do data to begin with, we cannot make more detailed distinctions later.

In other situations, we might need to change the wording of a question to increase variance. If we were using a Likert scale (Strongly Disagree to Strongly Agree), it might be better to ask the customer to respond to the statement "Edward Jones provides *excellent* advice for investors" rather than "Edward Jones provides *good* advice for investors." The point is not to generate a specific score, but to create variance which allows us to examine investors with different attitudes.

It is important for our questions to generate variance. In a perfect world, our questions would result in something close to a normal distribution.

Interactive and Adaptive Questions

Adaptive and interactive questions usually require electronic media. Several software are available nowadays that can easily create interactive and adaptive questions. An adaptive question adapts its appearance, its scoring pattern, and also the response to each of the candidate's attempts. For example, a question has free box for answering but the candidate doesn't give a satisfactory answer. On receiving an unsatisfactory answer, the adaptive questionnaire presents a simple choice to the candidate. In adapting conjoint analysis questionnaire, next choice options appear on the basis of the response given by the respondent in previous choice option.

Adaptive questions, in reality, create questions that are used in formative situations. They guide candidates through a given questionnaire while providing an outcome that takes into consideration their path. Some certification exams have evolved into adaptive format in which the exam pattern and number of questions adapt themselves to the responses of the candidate. In the same manner, an adaptive questionnaire, depending on the speed and accuracy of the candidate, modifies the upcoming questions to best suit that candidate. So, we see that interactive questions actually interact with the candidate. The candidate has to select the option and accordingly the questionnaire guides him to the next questions.

What Is the Best Question Sequence?

The order of questions, or the question sequence, may serve several functions for the researcher. If the opening questions are interesting, simple to comprehend and easy to answer, respondents' cooperation and involvement can be maintained throughout the questionnaire. Asking easy-to-answer questions teaches respondents their role and builds their confidence.

A mail survey among department store buyers drew an extremely poor return rate. A substantial improvement in response rate occurred, however, when researchers added some introductory questions seeking opinions on pending legislation of great importance to these buyers. Respondents continued on to complete all the questions, not only those in the opening section.

In their attempt to "warm up" respondents toward the questionnaire, student researchers frequently ask demographic or classification questions at the beginning of the survey. This generally is not advisable, because asking for personal information such as income level or education may embarrass or threaten respondents. Asking these questions at the end of the questionnaire usually is better, after rapport has been established between respondent and interviewer.

order bias
Bias caused by the influence of earlier questions in a questionnaire or by an answer's position in a set of answers.

Order bias can result from a particular answer's position in a set of answers or from the sequencing of questions. In political elections in which candidates lack high visibility, such as elections for county commissioners and judges, the first name listed on the ballot often receives the highest percentage of votes. For this reason, many election boards print several ballots so that each candidate's name appears in every possible position on the ballot.

RESEARCH SNAPSHOT

What Citizens (Don't) Know about Climate Change

Climate change as a result of global warming has frequently been featured in the news, especially in stories related to science and technology. Scientists at the Massachusetts Institute of Technology's Laboratory for Energy and the Environment (LFEE) have dedicated themselves to researching a variety of approaches to slow down climate change. The scientists recognize, however, that these innovations have a cost, so their use will depend partly on public interest in the problem and demand for solutions. As a result, LFEE conducted an online survey, which it sent to a national panel.

One challenge for the study was that before researchers could gauge citizens' willingness to pay for new technologies, they needed to know whether most people were even aware of the energy alternatives. They asked, "Have you heard of or read about any of the following in the past year? Check all that apply," followed by a list of ten technologies for mitigating climate change. Only three technologies—more efficient cars, solar energy, and nuclear energy—were checked by a majority of respondents. Seventeen percent admitted to not hearing about any of the technologies, a number that the researchers acknowledge may be too low, because some people might want to appear better informed than they are.

Perhaps lack of interest is a factor as well. Another question gave respondents a list of 22 issues and asked them to choose the most important. The environment was ranked thirteenth. In a question asking respondents to rank the importance of specific environmental problems however, "global warming" was in sixth place, trailing water pollution, destruction of ecosystems, and toxic waste.

All of these questions presented respondents with a list of alternatives to check. What precautions should the survey have taken to minimize the chance that the order of alternatives influenced respondents' opinions that some items were familiar or important?

Source: Based on "U.S. Public in the Dark on Climate Change Issues," *Bulletin of the American Meteorological Society* 86, no. 6 (June 2005), http://firstsearch.oclc.org; Herzog, Howard J., Thomas E. Curry, David M. Reiner, and Stephen Ansolabehere, "Climate Change Poorly Understood, Not a High Priority, Shows MIT Public Survey," *Energy and Environment*, (December 2004), 7–8, accessed at http://lfee.mit.edu.

Order bias can also distort survey results. For example, suppose a questionnaire's purpose is to measure levels of awareness of several charitable organizations. If Big Brothers and Big Sisters is always mentioned first, the American Red Cross second, and the American Cancer Society third, Big Brothers and Big Sisters may receive an artificially high awareness rating because respondents are prone to yea-saying (by indicating awareness of the first item in the list).

Asking specific questions before asking about broader issues is a common cause of order bias. For example, people who are first asked, "Are you satisfied with your marriage?" will respond differently to a follow-up question that asks, "Are you satisfied with your life?" than if the questions are asked in the reverse order. Generally, researchers should ask general questions before specific questions. This procedure, known as the **funnel technique**, allows the researcher to understand the respondent's frame of reference before asking more specific questions about the level of the respondent's information and the intensity of his or her opinions.

funnel technique
Asking general questions before specific questions in order to obtain unbiased responses.

Consider how later answers might be biased by previous questions in this questionnaire on environmental pollution:

Please consider each of the following issues. Circle the number for each that best indicates your feelings about the severity of that issue as an environmental problem:

Issue	*Not At All A Problem*				*Very Severe Problem*
Air pollution from automobile exhausts	1	2	3	4	5
Air pollution from open burning	1	2	3	4	5
Air pollution from industrial smoke	1	2	3	4	5
Air pollution from foul odors	1	2	3	4	5
Noise pollution from airplanes	1	2	3	4	5
Noise pollution from cars, trucks, motorcycles	1	2	3	4	5
Noise pollution from industry	1	2	3	4	5

Not surprisingly, researchers found that the responses to the air pollution questions were highly correlated—in fact, almost identical. What if the first issue was *foul odors* instead of *automobile exhaust*? Do you think it would affect the remaining responses?

With attitude scales, there also may be an *anchoring effect*. The first concept measured tends to become a comparison point from which subsequent evaluations are made. Randomization of items on a questionnaire susceptible to the anchoring effect helps minimize order bias.

A related problem is bias caused by the order of alternatives on closed questions. To avoid this problem, the order of these choices should be rotated if producing alternative forms of the questionnaire is possible. Unfortunately, business researchers rarely print alternative questionnaires to eliminate problems resulting from order bias. With Internet surveys, however, reducing order bias by having the computer randomly order questions and/or response alternatives is quite easy. With complete randomization, question order is random and respondents see response alternatives in different positions.

filter question
A question that screens out respondents who are not qualified to answer a second question.

Asking a question that does not apply to the respondent or that the respondent is not qualified to answer may be irritating or cause a biased response because the respondent wishes to please the interviewer or to avoid embarrassment. Including a **filter question** minimizes the chance of asking questions that are inapplicable. Asking a human resource manager "How would you rate the third party administrator (TPA) of your employee health plan?" may elicit a response even though the organization does not utilize a TPA. The respondent may wish to please the interviewer with an answer. A filter question such as "Does your organization use a third party administrator (TPA) for your employee health plan?" followed by "If you answered *Yes* to the previous question, how would you rate your TPA on . . . ?" would screen out the people who are not qualified to answer. If embedded in the questionnaire, this would create the need for a *skip question* for those that did not use a TPA as discussed below.

pivot question
A filter question used to determine which version of a second question will be asked.

Another form of filter question, the **pivot question**, can be used to obtain income information and other data that respondents may be reluctant to provide. For example,

"Is your total family income over or under $50,000?" IF UNDER, ASK, "Is it over or under $25,000?" IF OVER, ASK, "Is it over or under $75,000?"

—Under $25,000	*—$50,001–$75,000*
—$25,001–$50,000	*—Over $75,000*

Exhibit 15.2 gives an example of a flowchart plan for a questionnaire. Structuring the order of the questions so that they are logical will help to ensure the respondent's cooperation and eliminate confusion or indecision. The researcher maintains legitimacy by making sure that the respondent can comprehend the relationship between a given question (or section of the questionnaire) and the overall purpose of the study. Furthermore, a logical order may aid the individual's memory. Informational and transitional comments explaining the logic of the questionnaire may ensure that the respondent continues. Here are two examples:

We have been talking so far about general shopping habits in this city. Now I'd like you to compare two types of grocery stores—regular supermarkets and grocery departments in wholesale club stores.

So that I can combine your answers with those of other plant managers who are similar to you, I need some personal information about you. Your answers to these questions—just as all of the others you've answered—are confidential, and you will never be identified individually. Thanks for your help so far. If you'll answer the remaining questions, it will help me analyze all your answers.

EXHIBIT 15.2 Aided and unaided recall study-Sequence of questions in questionnaire design

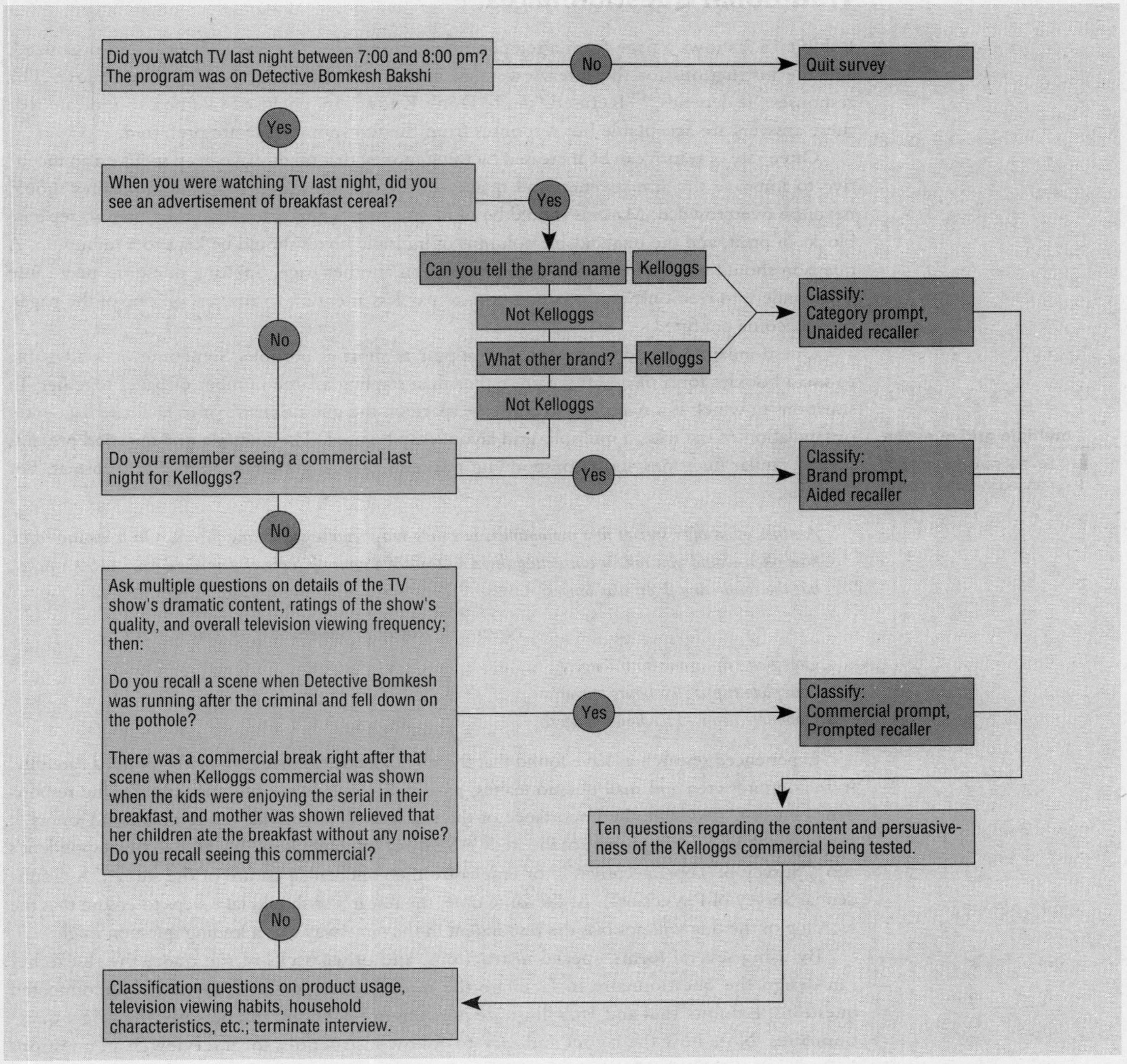

What Is the Best Layout?

Good layout and physical attractiveness are crucial in mail, Internet, and other self-administered questionnaires. For different reasons, a good layout in questionnaires designed for personal and telephone interviews is also important.

Traditional Questionnaires

Exhibit 15.3 shows a page from a telephone questionnaire. The layout is neat and organized, and the instructions for the interviewer (all boldface capital letters) are easy to follow. The responses "It depends," "Refused," and "Don't Know" are enclosed in a box to indicate that these answers are acceptable but responses from the five-point scale are preferred.

Often rate of return can be increased by using money that might have been spent on an incentive to improve the attractiveness and quality of the questionnaire. Mail questionnaires should never be overcrowded. Margins should be of decent size, white space should be used to separate blocks of print, and the unavoidable columns of multiple boxes should be kept to a minimum. A question should not begin on one page and end on another page. Splitting questions may cause a respondent to read only part of a question, to pay less attention to answers on one of the pages, or to become confused.

multiple-grid question
Several similar questions arranged in a grid format.

Questionnaires should be designed to appear as short as possible. Sometimes it is advisable to use a booklet form of questionnaire rather than stapling a large number of pages together. In situations in which it is necessary to conserve space on the questionnaire or to facilitate data entry or tabulation of the data, a multiple-grid layout may be used. The **multiple-grid question** presents several similar questions and corresponding response alternatives arranged in a grid format. For example,

Airlines often offer special fare promotions, but they may require connecting flights. On a vacation trip, how often would you take a connecting flight instead of a nonstop flight if you could save $100 a ticket, but the connecting flight was longer?

	Never	*Rarely*	*Sometimes*	*Often*	*Always*
Complete trip is one hour longer?	□	□	□	□	□
Complete trip is two hours longer?	□	□	□	□	□
Complete trip is three hours longer?	□	□	□	□	□

Experienced researchers have found that the title of a questionnaire should be phrased carefully. In self-administered and mail questionnaires, a carefully constructed title may capture the respondent's interest, underline the importance of the research ("Nationwide Study of Blood Donors"), emphasize the interesting nature of the study ("Study of Internet Usage"), appeal to the respondent's ego ("Survey of Top Executives"), or emphasize the confidential nature of the study ("A Confidential Survey of Physicians"). At the same time, the researcher should take steps to ensure that the wording of the title will not bias the respondent in the same way that a leading question might.

By using several forms, special instructions, and other tricks of the trade, the researcher can design the questionnaire to facilitate the interviewer's job of following interconnected questions. Exhibits 15.4 and 15.5 illustrate portions of telephone and personal interview questionnaires. Note how the layout and easy-to-follow instructions for interviewers in questions 1, 2, and 3 of Exhibit 15.4 help the interviewer follow the question sequence.

Instructions are often capitalized or printed in bold to alert the interviewer that it may be necessary to proceed in a certain way. For example, if a particular answer is given, the interviewer or respondent may be instructed to skip certain questions or go to a special sequence of questions. To facilitate coding, question responses should be precoded when possible, as in Exhibit 15.4.

Exhibit 15.5 illustrates some other useful techniques that are possible with personal interviews. Questions 3 and 6 instruct the interviewer to hand the respondent a card bearing a list of alternatives. Cards may help respondents grasp the intended meaning of the question and remember all the brand names or other items they are being asked about. Also, questions 2, 3, and 6 instruct the interviewer that rating of the banks will start with the bank that has been checked in red pencil on the printed questionnaire. The name of the red-checked bank is not the same on every

EXHIBIT 15.3 **Layout of a Page from a Telephone Questionnaire**

I shall now read out the names of different streams of undergraduate students. For each of them, please tell me how easy you think one would get financial assistance in post graduate programs given that a student has scored A grade. Your responses should be in 'very easy to get', 'somewhat easy to get', 'somewhat difficult to get', 'very difficult to get', and 'assistance is not available'. First . . . **(START AT X'D ITEM. CONTINUE DOWN AND UP THE LIST UNTIL ALL ITEMS HAVE BEEN READ AND RATED.)**

						(DO NOT READ)		
START HERE:	**Very Easy to Get**	**Some-what Easy to Get**	**Some-what Difficult to Get**	**Very Difficult to Get**	**Assistance is not Available**	**It Depends**	**Refused**	**Don't Know**
[ ] Physics	1	2	3	4	5	0	X	Y (24)
[X] Chemistry	1	2	3	4	5	0	X	Y (25)
[ ] Biology	1	2	3	4	5	0	X	Y (26)
[ ] Mathematics	1	2	3	4	5	0	X	Y (27)
[ ] Political Science	1	2	3	4	5	0	X	Y (28)
[ ] Engineering	1	2	3	4	5	0	X	Y (29)
[ ] Humanity	1	2	3	4	5	0	X	Y (30)
[ ] Social Science	1	2	3	4	5	0	X	Y (31)
[ ] Management	1	2	3	4	5	0	X	Y (32)
[ ] Commercial Studies	1	2	3	4	5	0	X	Y (33)
[ ] Economics	1	2	3	4	5	0	X	Y (34)
[ ] Information Technology	1	2	3	4	5	0	X	Y (35)
[ ] Medicine	1	2	3	4	5	0	X	Y (36)
[ ] Astronomy	1	2	3	4	5	0	X	Y (37)

questionnaire. By rotating the order of the check marks, the researchers attempted to reduce order bias caused by respondents' tendency to react more favorably to the first set of questions.

Exhibit 15.6 illustrates a series of questions that includes a *skip question*. Either skip instructions or an arrow drawn pointing to the next question informs the respondent which question comes next.

Layout is extremely important when questionnaires are long or require the respondent to fill in a large amount of information. In many circumstances, using headings or subtitles to indicate groups of questions will help the respondent grasp the scope or nature of the questions to be asked. Thus, at a glance, the respondent can follow the logic of the questionnaire.

Internet Questionnaires

Layout is also an important issue for questionnaires appearing on the Internet. A questionnaire on a Web site should be easy to use, flow logically, and have a clean look and overall feel that motivate the respondent to cooperate from start to finish. Many of the guidelines for layout of paper questionnaires apply to Internet questionnaires. There are, however, some important differences.

EXHIBIT 15.4 Telephone Questionnaire with Skip Questions

1. Did you take the two wheeler you had checked to the Indian Automobiles for repairs?

   −1 Yes **(SKIP TO Q. 3)** −2 No

2. **(IF NO, ASK:)** Did you have the repair work done?

   −1 Yes ↓

   1. Where was the repair work done? ______________________

   2. Why didn't you have the repair work done at the Indian Automobiles? ______________________

   −2 No ↓

   1. Why didn't you have the two wheeler repaired? ______________________

3. **(IF YES TO Q. 1, ASK:)** How satisfied were you with the repair work? Were you . . .

   −1 Very satisfied

   −2 Somewhat satisfied

   −3 Somewhat dissatisfied

   −4 Very dissatisfied

   (IF SOMEWHAT OR VERY DISSATISFIED:) In what way were you dissatisfied? ______________________

4. **(ASK EVERYONE:)** Do you ever buy Servo Engine Oil?

   −1 Yes −2 No **(SKIP TO Q. 6)**

5. **(IF YES, ASK:)** How often do you buy Servo?

   −1 Always

   −2 Almost always

   −3 Most of the time

   −4 Part of the time

   −5 Hardly ever

6. Have you ever had your two wheeler serviced at Indian Automobiles?

   −1 Yes −2 No

7. Have you ever had an oil change or lubrication done there?

   −1 Yes −2 No

With *graphical user interface* (GUI) software, the researcher can exercise control over the background, colors, fonts, and other visual features displayed on the computer screen so as to create an attractive and easy-to-use interface between the computer user and the Internet survey. GUI software allows the researcher to design questionnaires in which respondents click on the appropriate answer rather than having to type answers or codes.

There are a large number of Web publishing software packages (e.g., WebSurveyor, FrontPage, etc.) and Web survey host sites (such as **www.zoomerang.com** and **www.surveymonkey.com**) to assist

EXHIBIT 15.5 Personal Interview Questionnaire

Good Morning! I am Prashant. I am doing this research for academic purpose. This is an opinion survey about organized retail outlets for purchasing food items for monthly consumption at your household.

1. What are the names of retail outlets you can think of offhand? (INTERVIEWER: List names in order mentioned.)
   a. ______
   b. ______
   c. ______
   d. ______
   e. ______
   f. ______
   g. ______

2. Thinking now about the experiences you have had with the different retail outlets here in Kolkata, have you ever talked to or done business with . . . (INTERVIEWER: Insert name of bank checked in red below.)
   a. Are you personally acquainted with any of the employees or officers at ______?
   b. (If YES) Who is that? ______
   c. How long has it been since you have been inside ______?

   (INTERVIEWER: Now go back and repeat 2–2c for all other retail outlets listed.)

	(2) Talked		(2a and 2b) Know Employee Or Officer		(2c) Been in Store in:				
	Yes	No	No	Name	Last Month	1–5	5-Plus	No	DK
Local Kirana Store	1	2	1	______	1	2	3	4	5
Big Bazaar	1	2	1	______	1	2	3	4	5
Spencer's	1	2	1	______	1	2	3	4	5
Food World	1	2	1	______	1	2	3	4	5
Arambagh's	1	2	1	______	1	2	3	4	5

3. (HAND RETAIL OUTLET RATING CARD) On this card there are a number of contrasting phrases or statements—for example, "Large" and "Small." We'd like to know how you rate (NAME OF RETAIL OUTLET CHECKED IN RED BELOW) in terms of these statements or phrases. Just for example, let's use the terms "fast service" and "slow service." If you were to rate a retail outlet #1 on this scale, it would mean you find their service "very fast." On the other hand, a 7 rating would indicate you feel their service is "very slow," whereas a 4 rating means you don't think of them as being either "very fast" or "very slow." Are you ready to go ahead? Good! Tell me then how you would rate (NAME OF RETAIL OUTLET CHECKED IN RED) in terms of each of the phrases or statements on that card. How about (READ NEXT RETAIL OUTLET NAME)? . . . (INTERVIEWER: Continue on until respondent has evaluated all six banks.)

	Local Kirana Store	Big Bazaar	Spencer's	Food World	Arambagh's
a. Service	______	______	______	______	______
b. Size	______	______	______	______	______
c. Business vs. Family	______	______	______	______	______
d. Friendliness	______	______	______	______	______
e. Big/Small Business	______	______	______	______	______
f. Rate of Growth	______	______	______	______	______
g. Modernness	______	______	______	______	______
h. Leadership	______	______	______	______	______
i. Delivery Ease	______	______	______	______	______
j. Location	______	______	______	______	______
k. Hours	______	______	______	______	______
l. Ownership	______	______	______	______	______
m. Community Involvement	______	______	______	______	______

Organized Retail 6
Other (Specify) ______
DK/Wouldn't 9

(continued)

EXHIBIT 15.5 Personal Interview Questionnaire *(continued)*

4. Suppose a friend of yours who has just moved to Kolkata asked you to recommend a retail outlet. Which one would you recommend? Why would you recommend that particular retail outlet?

Local Kirana Store	1
Big Bazaar	2
Spencer's	3
Food World	4
Arambagh's	5
Other (Specify) ________	
DK/Wouldn't	9

5. Which of the retail outlets do you think of as: (INTERVIEWER: Read red-checked item first, then read each of the other five.)

Woman friendly? ________

Express check out? ________

Fair price? ________

Fresh products? ________

Deals? ________

Quality products? ________

6. If a friend asked you to recommend a place where he or she could shop, which retail outlet would you probably recommend? (INTERVIEWER: Probe for specific name.) Why would you recommend (RETAIL OUTLET NAMED)?
Would Recommend: ________

____

Wouldn't	0
DK/Not Sure	9

EXHIBIT 15.6
Example of a Skip Question

1. If you had to buy a mobile phone tomorrow, which of the following three types of computers do you think you would buy?

   1 Smart phone—Go to Q. 3
   2 Feature phone—Go to Q. 2

2. (If "smartphone" on Q. 1, ask): What brand do you think you would buy?

3. What is your age?

a researcher with Internet data collection. However, several features of a respondent's computer may influence the appearance of an Internet questionnaire. For example, discrepancies between the designer's and the respondent's computer settings for screen configuration (e.g., 1,024 × 768 pixels versus 1,280 × 800 pixels) may result in questions not being fully visible on the respondent's screen, misaligned text, or other visual problems. The possibility that the questionnaire the researcher/designer constructs on his or her computer may look different from the questionnaire that appears on the respondent's computer should always be considered when designing Internet surveys. One sophisticated remedy is to use the first few questions on an Internet survey to ask about operating system, browser software, and other computer configuration issues so that the questionnaire that is delivered is as compatible as possible with the respondent's computer. A simpler solution is to limit the horizontal width of the questions to 70 characters or less, to decrease the likelihood of wrap-around text.

LAYOUT ISSUES

Even if the questionnaire designer's computer and the respondents' computers are compatible, a Web questionnaire designer should consider several layout issues. The first decision is whether the questionnaire will appear page by page, with individual questions or groups of questions on separate screens (Web pages), or on a scrolling basis, with the entire questionnaire appearing on a single Web page that the respondent scrolls from top to bottom. The *paging layout* (going from screen to screen) greatly facilitates skip patterns. Based on a respondent's answers to filter questions, the computer can automatically insert relevant questions on subsequent pages. If the entire questionnaire appears on one page (the *scrolling layout*), the display should advance smoothly, as if it were a piece of paper being moved up or down. The scrolling layout gives the respondent the ability to read any portion of the questionnaire at any time, but the absence of page boundaries can cause problems. For example, suppose a Likert scale consists of 15 statements in a grid-format layout, with the response categories Strongly Disagree, Disagree, Neutral, Agree, and Strongly Agree at the beginning of the questionnaire. Once the respondent has scrolled down beyond the first few statements, he or she may not be able to see both the statements at the end of the list and the response categories at the top of the grid simultaneously. Thus, avoiding the problems associated with splitting questions and response categories may be difficult with scrolling questionnaires.

When a scrolling questionnaire is long, category or section headings are helpful to respondents. It is also a good idea to provide links to the top and bottom parts of each section, so that users can navigate through the questionnaire without having to scroll through the entire document.[11]

Whether a Web survey is page-by-page or scrolling format a **push button** with a label should clearly describe the actions to be taken. For example, if the respondent is to go to the next page, a large arrow labeled "NEXT" might appear in color at the bottom of the screen.

push button

In a dialog box on an Internet questionnaire, a small outlined area, such as a rectangle or an arrow, that the respondent clicks on to select an option or perform a function, such as submit.

Decisions must be made about the use of color, graphics, animation, sound, and other special features that the Internet makes possible. One point to remember is that, although sophisticated graphics are not a problem for most people with powerful computers and high speed Internet, many respondents' computers and/or Internet connections are not powerful enough to deliver complex graphics at a satisfactory speed.

With a paper questionnaire, the respondent knows how many questions he or she must answer. Because many Internet surveys offer no visual clues about the number of questions to be asked, it is important to provide a **status bar** or some other visual indicator of questionnaire length. For example, including a partially filled rectangular box as a visual symbol and a statement such as "The status bar at top right indicates approximately what portion of the survey you have completed" increases the likelihood that the respondent will finish the entire sequence of questions. Exhibit 15.7 shows a question from an online survey that uses a simple and motivating design. The survey presents one question at a time for simplicity. So that respondents can see their progress toward the end of the questionnaire, a gauge in the upper right corner fills from left to right as the respondent proceeds from Start to Finish.

status bar

In an Internet questionnaire, a visual indicator that tells the respondent what portion of the survey he or she has completed.

An Internet questionnaire uses dialog boxes to display questions and record answers. Exhibit 15.8 portrays four common ways of displaying questions on a computer screen. Many Internet questionnaires require the respondent to activate his or her answer by clicking on the **radio button** for a response. Radio buttons work like push buttons on automobile radios: Clicking on an alternative response deactivates the first choice and replaces it with the new response. A **drop-down box**, such as the one shown in Exhibit 15.8, is a space-saving device that allows the researcher to provide a list of responses that are hidden from view until they are needed. A general statement, such as "Please select" or "Click here," is shown initially. Clicking on the downward-facing arrow makes the full range of choices appear.

radio button

In an Internet questionnaire, a circular icon, resembling a button, that activates one response choice and deactivates others when a respondent clicks on it.

Checklist questions may be followed by **check boxes**, several, none, or all of which may be checked by the respondent. **Open-ended boxes** are boxes in which respondents type their answers to open-ended questions. Open-ended boxes may be designed as *one-line text boxes* or *scrolling text*

EXHIBIT 15.7

Question in an Online Screening Survey for Joining a Consumer Panel

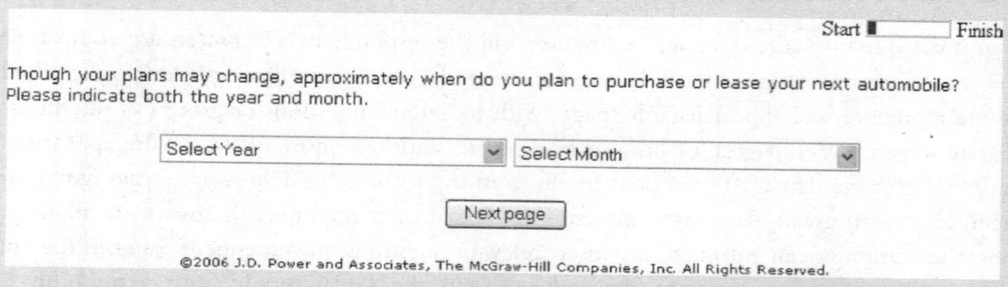

Source: J.D. Power and Associates, "JDPowerPanel," https://ia.jdpa.com/20/survey/onsurvey.phtml, accessed March 9, 2006.

boxes, depending on the breadth of the expected answer. Of course, open-ended questions require that respondents have both the skill and the willingness to keyboard lengthy answers on the computer. Some open-ended boxes are designed so that respondents can enter numbers for frequency response, ranking, or rating questions. For example,

Below you will see a series of statements that might or might not describe how you feel about your career. Please rate each statement using a scale from 1 to 5, where 1 means "Totally Disagree," 2 means "Somewhat Disagree," 3 means "Neither Agree nor Disagree," 4 means "Somewhat Agree," and 5 means "Totally Agree." Please enter your numeric answer in the box provided next to each statement. Would you say that . . .

A lack of business knowledge relevant to my field/career could hurt my career advancement.

My career life is an important part of how I define myself.

I am seriously considering a change in careers.

drop-down box

In an Internet questionnaire, a space-saving device that reveals responses when they are needed but otherwise hides them from view.

check boxes

In an Internet questionnaire, small graphic boxes, next to answers, that a respondent clicks on to choose an answer; typically, a check mark or an **X** appears in the box when the respondent clicks on it.

Pop-up boxes are message boxes that can be used to highlight important information. For example, pop-up boxes may be used to provide a privacy statement, such as the following:

IBM would like your help in making our Web site easier to use and more effective. Choose to complete the survey now or not at all.

Clicking on Privacy Statement opens the following pop-up box:

Survey Privacy Statement

This overall Privacy Statement verifies that IBM is a member of the TRUSTe program and is in compliance with TRUSTe principles. This survey is strictly for market research purposes. The information you provide will be used only to improve the overall content, navigation, and usability of ibm.com.

open-ended boxes

In an Internet questionnaire, boxes where respondents can type in their own answers to open-ended questions.

pop-up boxes

In an Internet questionnaire, boxes that appear at selected points and contain information or instructions for respondents.

In some cases, respondents can learn more about how to use a particular scale or get a definition of a term by clicking on a link, which generates a pop-up box. One of the most common reasons for using pop-up boxes is *error trapping*, a topic discussed in the next section.

Chapter 14 described graphic rating scales, which present respondents with a graphic continuum. On the Internet, researchers can take advantage of scroll bars or other GUI software features to make these scales easy to use. For example, the graphic continuum may be drawn as a measuring rod with a plus sign on one end and a minus sign on the other. The respondent then moves a small rectangle back and forth between the two ends of the scale to scroll to any point on the continuum. Scoring, as discussed in Chapter 14, is in terms of some measure of the length (millimeters) from one end of the graphic continuum to the point marked by the respondent.

Finally, researchers should include a customized thank-you page at the end of an Internet questionnaire, so that a brief thank-you note pops onto respondents' screens when they click on the Submit push button.[12]

EXHIBIT 15.8
Alternative Ways of Displaying Internet Questions

Radio button

Last month, did you purchase products or services over the Internet?

○ **Yes**

○ **No**

How familiar are you with Microsoft's Xbox video game player?

Know Extremely Well	Know Fairly Well	Know a Little	Know Just Name	Never Heard of
○	○	○	○	○

Drop-down box, closed position

In which country or region do you currently reside?

Click Here ▼

Drop-down box, open position

In which country or region do you currently reside?

Click Here ▼

Click Here
United States
Asia/Pacific (excluding Hawaii)
Africa
Australia or New Zealand
Canada
Europe
Latin America, South America, or Mexico
Middle East
Other

Check box

From which location(s) do you access the Internet? Select all that apply.

- ☐ Home
- ☐ Work
- ☐ Other Location

Please indicate which of the following Web sites you have ever visited or used. (CHOOSE ALL THAT APPLY.)

- ☐ E*Trade's Web site
- ☐ Waterhouse's Web site
- ☐ Merrill Lynch's Web site
- ☐ Fidelity's Web site
- ☐ Schwab's Web site
- ☐ Powerstreet
- ☐ Yahoo! Finance
- ☐ Quicken.com
- ☐ Lycos Investing
- ☐ AOL's Personal Finance
- ☐ None of the above

Open-ended, one-line box

What company do you think is the most visible sponsor of sports?

Open-ended, scrolling text box

What can we do to improve our textbook?

SOFTWARE THAT MAKES QUESTIONNAIRES INTERACTIVE

Computer code can be written to make Internet questionnaires interactive and less prone to errors. The writing of software programs is beyond the scope of this discussion. However, several of the interactive functions that software makes possible should be mentioned here.

Internet software allows the branching off of questioning into two or more different lines, depending on a particular respondent's answer, and the skipping or filtering of questions. Questionnaire-writing software with skip and branching logic are readily available. Most of these programs have *hidden skip logic* so that respondents never see any evidence of skips. It is best if the questions the respondent sees flow in numerical sequence. However, some programs number all potential questions in numerical order, and the respondent sees only the numbers on the questions he or she answers. Thus, a respondent may answer questions 1 through 11 and then next see a question numbered 15 because of the skip logic.

variable piping software
Software that allows variables to be inserted into an Internet questionnaire as a respondent is completing it.

error trapping
Using software to control the flow of an Internet questionnaire—for example, to prevent respondents from backing up or failing to answer a question.

forced answering software
Software that prevents respondents from continuing with an Internet questionnaire if they fail to answer a question.

interactive help desk
In an Internet questionnaire, a live, real-time support feature that solves problems or answers questions respondents may encounter in completing the questionnaire.

Software can systematically or randomly manipulate the questions a respondent sees. **Variable piping software** allows variables, such as answers from previous questions, to be inserted into unfolding questions. Other software can randomly rotate the order of questions, blocks of questions, and response alternatives from respondent to respondent.

Researchers can also use software to control the flow of a questionnaire. Respondents can be blocked from backing up, or they can be allowed to stop in mid-questionnaire and come back later to finish. A questionnaire can be designed so that if the respondent fails to answer a question or answers it with an incorrect type of response, an immediate error message appears. This is called **error trapping.** With **forced answering software**, respondents cannot skip over questions as they do in mail surveys. The program will not let them continue if they fail to answer a question. The software may insert a boldfaced error message on the question screen or insert a pop-up box instructing the respondent how to continue. For example, if a respondent does not answer a question and tries to proceed to another screen, a pop-up box might present the following message:

> *You cannot leave a question blank. On questions without a "Not sure" or "Decline to answer" option, please choose the response that best represents your opinions or experiences.*

The respondent must close the pop-up box and answer the question in order to proceed to the next screen.

Some designers include an **interactive help desk** in their Web questionnaire so that respondents can solve problems they encounter in completing a questionnaire. A respondent might e-mail questions to the survey help desk or get live, interactive, real-time support via an online help desk.

Some respondents will leave the questionnaire Web site, prematurely terminating the survey. In many cases sending an e-mail message to these respondents at a later date, encouraging them to revisit the Web site, will persuade them to complete the questionnaire. Through the use of software and cookies, researchers can make sure that the respondent who revisits the Web site will be able to pick up at the point where he or she left off.

Once an Internet questionnaire has been designed, it is important to pretest it to ensure that it works with Internet Explorer, Mozilla Firefox, Safari, Opera, Maxthon, and other browsers. Some general-purpose programming languages, such as Java, do not always work with all browsers. While more compatible then ever, different browsers still have different peculiarities, thus a survey that works perfectly well with one may not function at all with another.[13]

How Much Pretesting and Revising Are Necessary?

Many novelists write, rewrite, revise, and rewrite again certain chapters, paragraphs, or even sentences. The researcher works in a similar world. Rarely—if ever—does he or she write only

RESEARCH SNAPSHOT

Pretesting the CAHPS Hospital Survey

The federal government's Centers for Medicare and Medicaid Services (CMS) is supposed to make information about hospital performance available to the public so that patients can compare hospitals and make informed choices about health-care services. An important aspect of hospital performance is whether patients feel satisfied with the care they receive. Many hospitals have used surveys to measure patient satisfaction, but comparing hospitals requires that all facilities use the same survey. So, CMS has spent several years creating and modifying a questionnaire, the Consumer Assessment of Health Providers and Systems (CAHPS) Hospital Survey, and similar questionnaires for other health-care providers.

Considering that the CAHPS Hospital Survey is being made available to all U.S. hospitals and the data will be made public, the researchers developing the survey have put it through extensive pretesting, with public comment invited at each stage of the process. The first version of the survey, consisting of 68 questions, was given to a sample of 18 individuals drawn from the general population, who were then interviewed to discuss how they interpreted the questions. Based on their reactions, the researchers modified the survey to make it clearer and then tested it on 13 more people. Almost half the interviews were conducted in Spanish. This process resulted in a draft survey with 66 items.

Next, the 66-item survey underwent pilot testing with almost 50,000 patients at hospitals in three states. Hospitals were selected to represent a cross-section of hospital types in those states. The researchers verified that a representative sample of the population completed the survey, and they analyzed the data to assess which questions best predicted satisfaction levels. Based on these analyses, the questionnaire was reduced to 32 items. That questionnaire was tested at several more hospitals and reviewed by the National Quality Forum. Based on this feedback, seven items were deleted and then two items were restored to the questionnaire. Finally, the resulting 27-item survey was ready for use nationwide.

Source: Goldstein, Elizabeth, Marybeth Farquhar, Christine Crofton, Charles Darby, and Steven Garfinkel, "Measuring Hospital Care from the Patients' Perspective: An Overview of the CAHPS Hospital Survey Development Process," *Health Services Research* (December 2005), http://galenet.galegroup.com; "CAHPS Surveys and Tools to Advance Patient-Centered Care," U.S. Department of Health and Human Services, Agency for Healthcare Research and Quality (AHRQ), http://www.cahps.ahrq.gov, last updated February 28, 2006; "CAHPS Survey Products," AHRQ, http://www.cahps.ahrq.gov, last updated March 6, 2006; Hays, Ron D. and Julie Brown, "Field Testing: What It Is and How We Do It," *CAHPS Connection* (December 2005), http://www.cahps.ahrq.gov.

a first draft of a questionnaire. Usually the questionnaire is written, revised, shared with others for feedback, then revised again. After that, it is tried out on a group, selected on a convenience basis, that is similar in makeup to the one that ultimately will be sampled. Although the researcher should not select a group too divergent from the target market—for example, selecting business students as surrogates for businesspeople—pretesting does not require a statistical sample. The pretesting process allows the researcher to determine whether respondents have any difficulty understanding the questionnaire and whether there are any ambiguous or biased questions. This process is exceedingly beneficial. Making a mistake with 25 or 50 subjects can avoid the potential disaster of administering an invalid questionnaire to several hundred individuals. For a questionnaire investigating teaching-students' experience with Web-based instruction, the researcher had the questionnaire reviewed first by university faculty members to ensure the questions were valid, then asked 20 teaching students to try answering the questions and indicate any ambiguities they noticed. Their feedback prompted changes in the format and wording. Pretesting was especially helpful because the English-language questionnaire was used in a school in the United Arab Emirates, where English is spoken but is not the primary language.[14]

Tabulating the results of a pretest helps determine whether the questionnaire will meet the objectives of the research. A **preliminary tabulation** often illustrates that, although respondents can easily comprehend and answer a given question, that question is inappropriate because it does not provide relevant information to help solve the business problem. Consider the following example from a survey among distributors of power-actuated tools such as stud drivers concerning the percentage of sales to given industries:

preliminary tabulation

A tabulation of the results of a pretest to help determine whether the questionnaire will meet the objectives of the research.

Please estimate what percentage of your fastener and load sales go to the following industries:

— *% heating, plumbing, and air conditioning*
— *% carpentry*
— *% electrical*
— *% maintenance*
— *% other (please specify)*

The researchers were fortunate to learn that asking the question in this manner made it virtually impossible to obtain the information actually desired. The categories are rather vague, a high percentage may fall into the *Other* category, and most respondents' answers did not total 100 percent. As a result, the question had to be revised. In general, getting respondents to add everything correctly is a difficult task, and virtually impossible if they cannot see all the categories (not a good idea for a telephone survey!). Pretesting difficult questions such as these is essential.

What administrative procedures should be implemented to maximize the value of a pretest? Administering a questionnaire exactly as planned in the actual study often is not possible. For example, mailing out a questionnaire is quite expensive and might require several weeks that simply cannot be spared. Pretesting a questionnaire in this manner would provide important information on response rate, but may not point out why questions were skipped or what questions are ambiguous or confusing. Personal interviewers can record requests for additional explanation or comments that indicate respondents' difficulty with question sequence or other factors. This is the primary reason why interviewers are often used for pretest work. Self-administered questionnaires are not reworded to be personal interviews, but interviewers are instructed to observe respondents and ask for their comments after they complete the questionnaire. When pretesting personal or telephone interviews, interviewers may test alternative wordings and question sequences to determine which format best suits the intended respondents.

No matter how the pretest is conducted, the researcher should remember that its purpose is to uncover any problems that the questionnaire may cause. Thus, pretests typically are conducted to answer questions about the questionnaire such as the following:

- Can the questionnaire format be followed by the interviewer?
- Does the questionnaire flow naturally and conversationally?
- Are the questions clear and easy to understand?
- Can respondents answer the questions easily?
- Which alternative forms of questions work best?

Pretests also provide means for testing the sampling procedure—to determine, for example, whether interviewers are following the sampling instructions properly and whether the procedure is efficient. Pretests also provide estimates of the response rates for mail surveys and the completion rates for telephone surveys.

Usually a questionnaire goes through several revisions. The exact number of revisions depends on the researcher's and client's judgment. The revision process usually ends when both agree that the desired information is being collected in an unbiased manner.

How to Administer a Questionnaire?

While administering the questionnaire there are different factors one need to consider. Some of them are listed below:

a. The objectives of the study
b. The target group and its distribution definition
c. Types of questions (while a 9 point scale ranking will be inducing stress a yes or no type or pictorial will be easy for one who is not a graduate)
d. The availability of resource (if enough resources are present they can be privately given to each responder and the response may be received; if it should be cost effective then mail can be used)
e. Cultural hindrance - when doing surveys across different cultures, the cultural factors should be considered. What is acceptable? What should be properly understood?

There are different ways to administer a questionnaire:

1. Interview
2. Through telephone
3. Through e-mail
4. Through post
5. Through the Internet

The first two means are interviewer stimulated. These types don't require any structured questionnaire as the questions can be modified to get proper response. The interviewer should be skilled enough to administer these types of questionnaire

Means	Advantages	Disadvantages
Interview	Lesser burden on the respondent because there is no writing required	Interaction and interviewers may bias responses. Costly as it requires a lot of time and an interviewer
	Higher response rate	If the respondents are widespread this proves to be useless
	Respondents can be observed	
	It is good for any visual ad response	
Telephone	Good for consequential questions	Most of the users feel that their personal space is encroached
	Easy to interview, anonymity can be more than personal interview	It can be difficult if there are large numbers of alternatives to choose from
	Less costly than interview	Not suitable for long answers

The other three means are self administered where the control over the response is very limited but the number of responses can be enormous with less cost. These questionnaires should be properly structured.

Means	Advantages	Disadvantages
By mail	Easy to administer, control over visual instrument is possible, not costly, greater degree of anonymity	Inability to control the returning of the response by the respondent or filling the questionnaire in a sensible manner; literacy is required; can't observe the respondent
By e-mail	Easier to administer and less costly than mail surveys	Anonymity may not be possible
	People more likely to return the response than through mail	
By Internet	Can be very good means if the sample is specific	Requires IT literacy from the respondent
		Difficult for complex questionnaire
	Easier to show visual material than mail and e-mail	
	Not very costly	

To increase the completion and response rate for self-administered surveys, one needs to adopt certain things which are as follows:

1. Providing an incentive will improve the response rate (may be a gift or a lucky draw).
2. The survey should be easy and simple. The survey should not take more than 10 minutes.
3. The questionnaire should look professional to increase the authenticity.
4. Contacting personally will help. Sending reminder mails will also increase the questionnaire filling rate.
5. The purpose of the questionnaire should be stated properly.
6. The assurance of confidentiality should be provided.
7. Thanking the response with a mail will also help in future response.

Analyzing the Respondent

The objective of a structured questionnaire with prefixed option enables the respondent to answer quickly and without much stress. Respondents' task overload increases if the questionnaire is not properly framed and the options are not arranged in a scientific manner. A well-designed questionnaire encourages the respondent to complete the survey with adequate involvement and interest.

It is important for the researcher to understand that the respondents may have diverse economy as well as educational background. Such diversity often causes constraint in collecting data through structured questionnaire. For instance, if a questionnaire is designed to capture consumers' perception about using low-cost detergent powder, prospective consumers may belong to any economy, education, and geographic background. In such a condition, it is necessary for researcher to design a questionnaire that is understandable to such diverse respondents. Following are some of the points important for the researcher to consider before conducting survey through a structured questionnaire:

1. **Describing project topics and the purpose of survey in the beginning of the questionnaire.** It is necessary for the researcher to indicate the research topic as well as the purpose of the research in a clear manner in the beginning of the survey questionnaire. This helps the respondent to understand the circumstances and the objective of the survey. This in turn helps him/her to provide response more accurately.
2. **Asking questions that do not require respondent to remember long-term information.** Often respondents are asked to provide data on their consumption in long past. Consider the following example for clarifying this concept:
   How many times have you visited Reliance Fresh in the last six months?
   How much did you spend on soft drink in the last three months?
   As you follow, these questions asked respondents to remember information which is difficult for a human brain to process and store. In such operations respondents predominantly provide a random response which may not be his actual consumption or usage. Instead of the above questions if the researchers ask the following questions, accurate response can be expected:
   How many times have you visited Reliance Fresh in the last month?
   How much did you spend on soft drink in the last week?
   It is possible for the respondent to remember his usage in such small time and provide accurate information.
   Researchers opined that it is necessary to provide sufficient used cues to the respondent about the event researcher want information so that the respondent can understand the situation through aided or unaided recall. Cue provided for aided recall increases respondents' interest to provide accurate information. However, the researcher must be careful in providing cues so that the respondent is not biased while providing his frequency.
3. **Asking respondents to describe a phenomenon.** Sometimes researchers ask the respondents to describe what they like/dislike about a particular brand, product, store, or the shop. It is important to note that most respondents may not be able to articulate in a proper language what researchers ask. To eliminate bias caused due to inability of the respondents to provide proper information researchers must provide the alternative descriptions so that the respondents may be able to indicate the best description that they feel appropriate for their perception. Sometimes aids like picture and description about the question asked can be helpful for the respondent to understand the question and provide the response.

Overcoming Unwillingness to Answer

1. It is common in all primary surveys that the respondents do not devote extraordinary effort to provide information to the questions of the researchers. The response rate decreases significantly as the respondents become unwilling to answer the questions that might require additional effort. Following are some of the areas where researchers may reduce respondents' effort to increase the response rate:
   a. **Providing options instead of asking for the options.** Some researchers ask the respondents to write about their opinion or response to the question asked. This increases task overload of the respondents and the respondents may often avoid replying to such questions. Instead of that researchers could provide options so that the respondent may check the closest option that he might find suitable.
   b. **Organizing the questions in proper structure.** Researchers may organize questions in tabular form which might help the respondents to understand the question quickly and provide the answers. Many times researchers tabulate perception questions by writing the questions in the left-hand side and the skills in the right-hand side which respondents may find convenient to answer. This reduces respondent's task overload and increases the response rate.

2. Respondents may be unwilling to respond to questions that they feel inappropriate in the context of the study. For example, a survey on consumers' perception about fast food restaurants asking respondents' personal expenditure on entertainment might cause respondents' inhibition to respond to such questions. Respondents may feel that information on personal expenditure on entertainment may not have any relevance in the context of the study. Consequently they may not be willing to answer such questions. In such situation, researchers may modify the question to make it relevant in the context of the study. In the above example, researcher may ask information on expenditure on fast food.
3. Respondents are often reluctant to disclose personal sensitive information in survey questionnaire. If such questions are asked in the survey, respondents often give biased responses which are not actual. Such biased response might contaminate the data resulting in wrong findings. Surveys related to alcohol/tobacco consumption behavior, usage of contraceptives, etc., require careful designing of questionnaire to ensure responses to such information. It is advisable to ask opinion of the respondent in case of sensitive information. Research has found that consumers provide the opinion the way they behave and believe.

Providing All Possible Alternatives and Avoiding Generalization

Questionnaire should include all possible alternatives in order to avoid implicit alternatives and implicit assumptions.

- **Implicit alternatives.** Alternative that is not explicitly expressed in the opinion

  Do you like to shop from Reliance Fresh? (Wrong)

  In this question, alternative is implicit so the person can compare it with any mode of shopping which will lead to confusion and biased answering.

  Do you like to shop from Reliance Fresh, or would you rather prefer kirana stores? (Correct)

  In this question, it has been made clear that we want the person to compare the Reliance Fresh with kirana stores, this will avoid the implicit assumption and can provide consistent response.

  In the first question, the person may like to yield a greater preference for Reliance Fresh than the second question.

- **Implicit assumptions.** Questions should not be formed in such a way that the answer is dependent upon implicit assumptions about what will happen as a consequence.

  Are you in favor of voting for UPA? (Wrong)

  Are you in favor of voting for UPA if it would result in an increase in the inflation? (Correct)

  In the first question, the implicit assumption was the situation arises from the question which could be different from person to person.

  In the second question, the outcome of the question has been made clear so the person can take the informed decision.

- **Selection of no-opinion response option.**

  When asking about subjective phenomenon, sometimes we presume that respondents' answers reflect information or opinions that they previously had stored in memory.

  In some cases, respondents may not have adequate information or depending on the question they form an assumption at the moment.

  Arbitrary answering increases if the question's wording suggests that the respondents should have an opinion and they do not wish to appear uninformed.

  In this case, we can offer an option "don't know" and we can conclude that people who select no responses have characteristics suggesting that they are least likely to have formed real opinions.

  This option also has a disadvantage that if it comes at the end where motivation of the respondent is waning, they are prone to select this option in order to finish it fast.

- **Generalization.**

  Questions should be specific and should be worded so that the respondent does not have to make generalizations or compute estimates.

  Generalizing the results to the population involves thorough understanding of the population, taking representative samples from the population, deciding whether to provide no-opinion option, and the effect of the opinion on generalizing the result to the population.

Peer Review of Questionnaire

Peer review of questionnaire is very important as it will give the following data:

- Time required to complete the questionnaire
- To check the questions if they are ambiguous
- To check if the instructions are clear
- To allow you to eliminate questions that do not yield usable data

Peer reviewing involves asking a number of people who are involved during the designing of questionnaire. A peer review can range from sending the questionnaire informally to colleagues to asking a panel of experts to review it.

The purpose of peer reviewing the questionnaire is to determine:

- whether the questions as they are worded will achieve the desired results.
- whether the questions have been placed in the best order.
- whether the questions are understood by all classes of respondents.
- whether additional or specifying questions are needed or whether some questions should be eliminated.
- whether the instructions to interviewers are adequate.

ADVANTAGES

- Helps the researchers identify the areas and functions in which they need to enhance their capacities
- Helps the researchers make informed decisions about how to improve the design
- Provides the researcher an independent opinion on the design and interpretation
- Provides the researcher assurance as to the appropriateness of the questionnaire design
- Cost effective and gives better solution before actual survey

DISADVANTAGES

- Testing is done on the people who may not be from the population on which the survey is intended.
- Decision depending on personal bias will lead to wrong conclusion.
- Selection of peer review team is important; underqualified team could lead to false interpretation which affects the final survey.

Designing Questionnaires for Global Markets

Now that business research is being conducted around the globe, researchers must take cultural factors into account when designing questionnaires. The most common problem involves translating

© iStock

TIPS OF THE TRADE

- There must be a very close correspondence between the research objectives and the questions on the survey:
  - Match up each research objective or hypothesis with a question or questions on the survey. Similarly, match up each survey question with a research objective. Are you sure you will have the information to address the research objective and/or test the research hypothesis? If not, you need more questions. If you have questions that do not link directly with a research objective or hypothesis, why are they included? Shorter surveys enhance response rates, but there is no benefit if you do not gather all the important information.
- Think of open-ended response questions as an essay exam; think of fixed-alternative questions as a multiple-choice exam. An essay exam can be developed in much less time than a multiple-choice exam, but takes much longer to grade. Similarly, an open-ended questionnaire is faster to develop, but takes much longer to edit, code, and interpret.
- It is important to minimize the cognitive complexity of questions, particularly for telephone surveys. Keep the response categories consistent and straightforward, as it is very difficult for the respondent to understand and remember the response choices when they are hearing them on the phone. A ten-point scale works very well in this situation.
- More sensitive or potentially embarrassing questions and the collection of demographic information should be at the end of the questionnaire. Asking these questions at the end of the questionnaire, after rapport has been established, enhances the probability of the participant responding. Do not start the survey with these questions.
- Always evaluate your questionnaire in regard to these issues:
  - Make certain you have totally exhaustive and mutually exclusive response categories.
  - Avoid technical terminology and jargon; use simple language.
  - Avoid leading questions.
  - Avoid ambiguity.
  - Avoid double-barreled questions; if you have two questions, ask two separate questions, rather than roll them into one.
  - Avoid making assumptions of the respondents.
  - Minimize respondent cognitive load; use consistent measurement scales and specify time frames that are easy to recall.
  - Make sure variables vary; questions and response categories should ensure that there will be a reasonable distribution of responses. An increased number of scale points often helps achieve this.

a questionnaire into other languages. A questionnaire developed in one country may be difficult to translate because equivalent language concepts do not exist or because of differences in idiom and vernacular. Although Spanish is spoken in both Mexico and Venezuela, one researcher found out that the Spanish translation of the English term *retail outlet* works in Mexico but not in Venezuela. Venezuelans interpreted the translation to refer to an electrical outlet, an outlet of a river into an ocean, or the passageway onto a patio.

Counting on an international audience to speak a common language such as English does not necessarily bridge these gaps, even when the respondents actually do speak more than one language. Cultural differences incorporate many shades of meaning that may not be captured by a survey delivered in a language used primarily for, say, business transactions. In a test of this idea, undergraduate students in 24 countries completed questionnaires about attitudes toward school and career. Half received the questionnaire in English, and half in their native language. The results varied, with country-to-country differences being smaller when students completed the questionnaire in English.[15]

International researchers often have questionnaires back translated. **Back translation** is the process of taking a questionnaire that has previously been translated from one language to another and having it translated back again by a second, independent translator. The back translator is often a person whose native tongue is the language that will be used for the questionnaire. This process can reveal inconsistencies between the English version and the translation. For example, when a soft-drink company translated its slogan "Baby, it's cold inside" into Cantonese for research in Hong Kong, the result read "Small Mosquito, on the inside, it is very cold." In Hong Kong, *small mosquito* is a colloquial expression for a small child. Obviously the intended meaning of the advertising message had been lost in the translated questionnaire.[16]

back translation

Taking a questionnaire that has previously been translated into another language and having a second, independent translator translate it back to the original language.

Literacy rates also influence the designs of self-administered questionnaires and interviews. Knowledge of the literacy rates in foreign countries, especially those that are just developing modern economies, is vital.

Summary

1. Explain the significance of decisions about questionnaire design and wording. Good questionnaire design is a key to obtaining accurate survey results. The specific questions to be asked will be a function of the type of information needed to answer the manager's questions and the communication medium of data collection. Relevance and accuracy are the basic criteria for judging questionnaire results. A questionnaire is *relevant* if no unnecessary information is collected and the information needed for solving the business problem is obtained. *Accuracy* means that the information is reliable and valid.

2. Define alternatives for wording open-ended and fixed-alternative questions. Knowing how each question should be phrased requires some knowledge of the different types of questions possible. Open-ended response questions pose some problem or question and ask the respondent to answer in his or her own words. Fixed-alternative questions require less interviewer skill, take less time to complete, and are easier to answer. In fixed-alternative questions the respondent is given specific limited alternative responses and asked to choose the one closest to his or her own viewpoint. Standardized responses are easier to code, tabulate, and interpret. Care must be taken to formulate the responses so that they do not overlap and cover all the possibilities. Respondents whose answers do not fit any of the fixed alternatives may be forced to select alternatives that do not communicate what they really mean. Open-ended response questions are especially useful in exploratory research or at the beginning or end of a questionnaire. They make a questionnaire more expensive to analyze because of the uniqueness of the answers. Also, interviewer bias can influence the responses to such questions.

3. Summarize guidelines for questions that avoid mistakes in questionnaire design. Some guidelines for questionnaire construction have emerged from research experience. The language should be simple to allow for variations in educational level. Researchers should avoid leading or loaded questions, which suggest answers to the respondents, as well as questions that induce them to give socially desirable answers. Respondents have a bias against questions that suggest changes in the status quo. Their reluctance to answer personal questions can be reduced by explaining the need for the questions and by assuring respondents of the confidentiality of their replies. The researcher should carefully avoid ambiguity in questions. Another common problem is the double-barreled question, which asks two questions at once. Finally, researchers need to examine the question to ensure that it will provide variance in responses.

4. Describe how the proper sequence of questions may improve a questionnaire. Question sequence can be very important to the success of a survey. The opening questions should be designed to capture respondents' interest and keep them involved. General questions should precede specific ones. In a series of attitude scales the first response may be used as an anchor for comparison with the other responses. The order of alternatives on closed questions can affect the results. Filter questions are useful for avoiding unnecessary questions that do not apply to a particular respondent. Such questions may be put into a flowchart for personal or telephone interviewing. Personal questions, demographics, and categorical questions should be placed at the end of the questionnaire.

5. Discuss how to design a questionnaire layout. The layout of a mail or other self-administered questionnaire can affect its response rate. An attractive questionnaire encourages a response, as does a carefully phrased title. Internet questionnaires present unique design issues. Decisions must be made about the use of color, graphics, animation, sound, and other special layout effects that the Internet makes possible.

6. Describe criteria for pretesting and revising a questionnaire and for adapting it to global markets. Pretesting helps reveal errors while they can still be corrected easily. A preliminary tabulation may show that, even if respondents understand questions, the responses are not relevant to the business problem. Often, the most efficient way to conduct a pretest is with interviewers to generate quick feedback. International business researchers must take cultural factors into account when designing questionnaires. The most widespread problem involves translation into another language. International questionnaires are often back translated to ensure the original concepts are correctly translated.

Key Terms and Concepts

back translation, *393*
check boxes, *384*
checklist question, *365*
counterbiasing statement, *370*
determinant-choice question, *365*
double-barreled question, *371*
drop-down box, *384*
error trapping, *386*
filter question, *376*
fixed-alternative questions, *363*
forced answering software, *386*
frequency-determination question, *365*
funnel technique, *375*
interactive help desk, *386*
leading question, *369*
loaded question, *369*
multiple-grid question, *378*
mutually exclusive, *366*
open-ended boxes, *384*
open-ended response questions, *362*
order bias, *374*
pivot question, *376*
pop-up boxes, *384*
preliminary tabulation, *387*
push button, *383*
radio button, *383*
simple-dichotomy (dichotomous) question, *365*
split-ballot technique, *370*
status bar, *383*
totally exhaustive, *366*
variable piping software, *386*

Questions for Review and Critical Thinking

1. Evaluate and comment on the following questions, taken from several questionnaires. Do they follow the rules discussed in this chapter?

   a. A university computer center survey on SPSS usage:

   How often do you use SPSS statistical software? Please check one.

   ☐ *Infrequently (once a semester)*
   ☐ *Occasionally (once a month)*
   ☐ *Frequently (once a week)*
   ☐ *All the time (daily)*

   b. A survey of advertising agencies:

   Do you understand and like the Federal Trade Commission's new corrective advertising policy?

   ____*Yes* ____*No*

   c. A survey on a new, small electric car:

   Assuming 90 percent of your driving is in town, would you buy this type of car?

   ____*Yes* ____*No*

   If this type of electric car had the same initial cost as a current "Big 3" full-size, fully equipped car, but operated at one-half the cost over a five-year period, would you buy one?

   ____*Yes* ____*No*

   d. A student survey:

   Since the beginning of this semester, approximately what percentage of the time do you get to campus using each of the forms of transportation available to you per week?

   ___*% Walk* ___*% Bicycle* ___*% Public transportation*
   ___*% Motor vehicle*

   e. A survey of motorcycle dealers:

   Should the company continue its generous cooperative advertising program?

   f. A government survey of gasoline retailers:

   Suppose the full-service pump selling price for regular gasoline is 232.8 cents per gallon on the first day of the month. Suppose on the 10th of the month the price is raised to 234.9 cents per gallon, and on the 25th of the month it is reduced to 230.9 cents per gallon. In order to provide the required data you should list the accumulator reading on the full-service regular gasoline pump when the station opens on the 1st day, the 10th day, and the 25th day of the month and when the station closes on the last day of the month.

   g. An anti-gun-control group's survey:

   Do you believe that private citizens should have the right to own firearms to defend themselves, their families, and their property from violent criminal attack?

   ____*Yes* ____*No*

   h. A survey of the general public:

   In the next year, after accounting for inflation, do you think your real personal income will go up or down?

   1. Up
   2. (Stay the same)
   3. Down
   4. (Don't know)

   i. **ETHICS** A survey of the general public:

   Some people say that companies should be required by law to label all chemicals and substances that the government states are potentially harmful. The label would tell what the chemical or substance is, what dangers it might pose, and what safety procedures should be used in handling the substance. Other people say that such laws would be too strict. They say the law should require labels on only those chemicals and substances that the companies themselves decide are potentially harmful. Such a law, they say, would be less costly for the companies and would permit them to exclude those chemicals and substances they consider to be trade secrets. Which of these views is closest to your own?

   1. Require labels on all chemicals and substances that the government states are potentially harmful.
   2. (Don't know)
   3. Require labels on only those chemicals and substances that companies decide are potentially harmful.

2. The following question was asked of a sample of television viewers:

   We are going to ask you to classify the type of fan you consider yourself to be for different sports and sports programs.

- *Diehard Fan: Watch games, follow up on scores and sports news multiple times a day*
- *Avid Fan: Watch games, follow up on scores and sports news once a day*
- *Casual Fan: Watch games, follow up on scores and sports news occasionally*
- *Championship Fan: Watch games, follow up on scores and sports news only during championships or playoffs*
- *Non-Fan: Never watch games or follow up on scores*
- *Anti-Fan: Dislike, oppose, or object to a certain sport*

Does this question do a good job of avoiding ambiguity?

3. How might the wording of a question about income influence respondents' answers?
4. What is the difference between a *leading question* and a *loaded question?*
5. Design one or more open-ended response questions to measure reactions to a magazine ad for a Xerox photocopier.
6. Evaluate the layout of the filter question that follows:

> Are you employed either full time or part time?
> *Mark (x) one.* ☐ Yes ☐ No
>
> If yes: How many hours per week are you usually employed? *Mark (x) one.*
> ☐ Less than 35 ☐ 35 or more
>
> What is the zip code at your usual place of work?
>
> ------------------

7. Develop a checklist of things to consider in questionnaire construction.
8. It has been said that surveys show that consumers hate advertising, but like specific ads. Comment.
9. Design a complete questionnaire:
   a. To evaluate a new fast-food fried chicken restaurant.
   b. To measure consumer satisfaction with an airline.
   c. For your local Big Brothers and Big Sisters organization to investigate awareness of and willingness to volunteer time to this organization.
   d. For a bank located in a college town to investigate the potential for attracting college students as checking account customers.
10. The Apple Assistance Center is a hotline to solve problems for users of Macintosh computers and other Apple products. Design a short (postcard-size) consumer satisfaction/service quality questionnaire for the Apple Assistance Center.
11. **'NET** Visit the following Web site: **http://www.history.org**. What type of questions might be asked in a survey to evaluate the effectiveness of this Web site in terms of being informative and in terms of being an effective sales medium?
12. A client tells a researcher that she wants a questionnaire that evaluates the importance of 30 product characteristics and rates her brand and 10 competing brands on these characteristics. The researcher believes that this questionnaire will induce respondent fatigue because it will be far too long. Should the researcher do exactly what the client says or risk losing the business by suggesting a different approach?
13. **ETHICS** Go to **http://www.nrsc.org** and look at one of the available surveys. Usually, these involve a short questionnaire about its political position. It also includes a "Support Reply Form," a solicitation for donations. Is this approach ethical?
14. **'NET** Visit Mister Poll at **http://www.misterpoll.com**, where you will find thousands of user-contributed polls on every imaginable topic from the controversial to the downright zany. What you find will depend on when you visit the site. However, you might find something such as a movie poll, where you pick your favorite film of the season. Evaluate the questions in the poll.
15. Try to find two friends that know the same foreign language. Write 10 Likert questions that measure how exciting a retail store environment is to shop in. Have one of your friends interpret the question into the foreign language. Have the other take the translation and state each question in English. How similar is the translated English to the original English? Comment.

Research Activity

1. Design eight questions that assess how effective an undergraduate college business course has been.

Case 15.1 Agency for Health Care Research and Quality

© GETTY IMAGES/ PHOTODISC GREEN

At the U.S. Department of Health and Human Services, the Agency for Healthcare Research and Quality (AHRQ) developed a survey to measure hospital employees' attitudes about patient safety in their facilities.[17] The survey is designed to help hospitals ensure safety by creating an environment in which employees share information, improve safety when problems are identified, and if necessary, change the way employees deliver care. The AHRQ suggests that hospitals use the survey to identify areas needing improvement and repeat its use to track changes over time.

The survey is shown in Case Exhibit 15.1–1.

Questions

1. Evaluate the questionnaire. Can you suggest any improvements?
2. Will this survey meet its objectives? Explain.

CASE EXHIBIT 15.1–1 **AHRQ Hospital Questionnaire**

HOSPITAL SURVEY ON PATIENT SAFETY CULTURE

INSTRUCTIONS

This survey asks for your opinions about patient safety issues, medical error, and event reporting in your hospital and will take about 10 to 15 minutes to complete.

- *An "event" is defined as any type of error, mistake, incident, accident, or deviation, regardless of whether or not it results in patient harm.*
- *"Patient safety" is defined as the avoidance and prevention of patient injuries or adverse events resulting from the processes of health care delivery.*

SECTION A: Your Work Area/Unit

In this survey, think of your "unit" as the work area, department, or clinical area of the hospital where you spend *most* of your work time or provide *most* of your clinical services.

What is your primary work area or unit in this hospital? Mark ONE answer by filling in the circle.

○ a. Many different hospital units/No specific unit

○ b. Medicine (non-surgical)
○ c. Surgery
○ d. Obstetrics
○ e. Pediatrics
○ f. Emergency department
○ g. Intensive care unit (any type)
○ h. Psychiatry/mental health
○ i. Rehabilitation
○ j. Pharmacy
○ k. Laboratory
○ l. Radiology
○ m. Anesthesiology
○ n. Other, please specify:

Please indicate your agreement or disagreement with the following statements about your work area/unit. Mark your answer by filling in the circle.

Think about your hospital work area/unit...	Strongly Disagree ▼	Disagree ▼	Neither ▼	Agree ▼	Strongly Agree ▼
1. People support one another in this unit	①	②	③	④	⑤
2. We have enough staff to handle the workload	①	②	③	④	⑤
3. When a lot of work needs to be done quickly, we work together as a team to get the work done	①	②	③	④	⑤
4. In this unit, people treat each other with respect	①	②	③	④	⑤
5. Staff in this unit work longer hours than is best for patient care	①	②	③	④	⑤
6. We are actively doing things to improve patient safety	①	②	③	④	⑤
7. We use more agency/temporary staff than is best for patient care	①	②	③	④	⑤
8. Staff feel like their mistakes are held against them	①	②	③	④	⑤
9. Mistakes have led to positive changes here	①	②	③	④	⑤
10. It is just by chance that more serious mistakes don't happen around here	①	②	③	④	⑤
11. When one area in this unit gets really busy, others help out	①	②	③	④	⑤
12. When an event is reported, it feels like the person is being written up, not the problem	①	②	③	④	⑤

(continued)

CASE EXHIBIT 15.1–1 **AHRQ Hospital Questionnaire** *(continued)*

SECTION A: Your Work Area/Unit (continued)

Think about your hospital work area/unit...	Strongly Disagree ▼	Disagree ▼	Neither ▼	Agree ▼	Strongly Agree ▼
13. After we make changes to improve patient safety, we evaluate their effectiveness	①	②	③	④	⑤
14. We work in "crisis mode" trying to do too much, too quickly	①	②	③	④	⑤
15. Patient safety is never sacrificed to get more work done	①	②	③	④	⑤
16. Staff worry that mistakes they make are kept in their personnel file	①	②	③	④	⑤
17. We have patient safety problems in this unit	①	②	③	④	⑤
18. Our procedures and systems are good at preventing errors from happening	①	②	③	④	⑤

SECTION B: Your Supervisor/Manager

Please indicate your agreement or disagreement with the following statements about your immediate supervisor/manager or person to whom you directly report. Mark your answer by filling in the circle.

	Strongly Disagree ▼	Disagree ▼	Neither ▼	Agree ▼	Strongly Agree ▼
1. My supervisor/manager says a good word when he/she sees a job done according to established patient safety procedures	①	②	③	④	⑤
2. My supervisor/manager seriously considers staff suggestions for improving patient safety	①	②	③	④	⑤
3. Whenever pressure builds up, my supervisor/manager wants us to work faster, even if it means taking shortcuts	①	②	③	④	⑤
4. My supervisor/manager overlooks patient safety problems that happen over and over	①	②	③	④	⑤

SECTION C: Communications

How often do the following things happen in your work area/unit? Mark your answer by filling in the circle.

Think about your hospital work area/unit...	Never ▼	Rarely ▼	Some-times ▼	Most of the time ▼	Always ▼
1. We are given feedback about changes put into place based on event reports	①	②	③	④	⑤
2. Staff will freely speak up if they see something that may negatively affect patient care	①	②	③	④	⑤
3. We are informed about errors that happen in this unit	①	②	③	④	⑤
4. Staff feel free to question the decisions or actions of those with more authority	①	②	③	④	⑤
5. In this unit, we discuss ways to prevent errors from happening again	①	②	③	④	⑤
6. Staff are afraid to ask questions when something does not seem right	①	②	③	④	⑤

(continued)

CASE EXHIBIT 15.1–1 **AHRQ Hospital Questionnaire** *(continued)*

SECTION D: Frequency of Events Reported

In your hospital work area/unit, when the following mistakes happen, *how often are they reported?* Mark your answer by filling in the circle.

	Never	Rarely	Sometimes	Most of the time	Always
1. When a mistake is made, but is *caught and corrected before affecting the patient*, how often is this reported?	①	②	③	④	⑤
2. When a mistake is made, but has *no potential to harm the patient*, how often is this reported?	①	②	③	④	⑤
3. When a mistake is made that *could harm the patient*, but does not, how often is this reported?	①	②	③	④	⑤

SECTION E: Patient Safety Grade

Please give your work area/unit in this hospital an overall grade on patient safety. Mark ONE answer.

○ A Excellent	○ B Very Good	○ C Acceptable	○ D Poor	○ E Failing

SECTION F: Your Hospital

Please indicate your agreement or disagreement with the following statements about your hospital. Mark your answer by filling in the circle.

Think about your hospital...	Strongly Disagree	Disagree	Neither	Agree	Strongly Agree
1. Hospital management provides a work climate that promotes patient safety	①	②	③	④	⑤
2. Hospital units do not coordinate well with each other	①	②	③	④	⑤
3. Things "fall between the cracks" when transferring patients from one unit to another	①	②	③	④	⑤
4. There is good cooperation among hospital units that need to work together	①	②	③	④	⑤
5. Important patient care information is often lost during shift changes	①	②	③	④	⑤
6. It is often unpleasant to work with staff from other hospital units	①	②	③	④	⑤
7. Problems often occur in the exchange of information across hospital units	①	②	③	④	⑤
8. The actions of hospital management show that patient safety is a top priority	①	②	③	④	⑤
9. Hospital management seems interested in patient safety only after an adverse event happens	①	②	③	④	⑤
10. Hospital units work well together to provide the best care for patients	①	②	③	④	⑤
11. Shift changes are problematic for patients in this hospital	①	②	③	④	⑤

SECTION G: Number of Events Reported

In the past 12 months, how many event reports have you filled out and submitted? Mark ONE answer.

- ○ a. No event reports
- ○ b. 1 to 2 event reports
- ○ c. 3 to 5 event reports
- ○ d. 6 to 10 event reports
- ○ e. 11 to 20 event reports
- ○ f. 21 event reports or more

(continued)

CASE EXHIBIT 15.1–1 **AHRQ Hospital Questionnaire** *(continued)*

SECTION H: Background Information

This information will help in the analysis of the survey results. Mark ONE answer by filling in the circle.

1. How long have you worked in this hospital?
   - O a. Less than 1 year
   - O b. 1 to 5 years
   - O c. 6 to 10 years
   - O d. 11 to 15 years
   - O e. 16 to 20 years
   - O f. 21 years or more

2. How long have you worked in your current hospital work area/unit?
   - O a. Less than 1 year
   - O b. 1 to 5 years
   - O c. 6 to 10 years
   - O d. 11 to 15 years
   - O e. 16 to 20 years
   - O f. 21 years or more

3. Typically, how many hours per week do you work in this hospital?
   - O a. Less than 20 hours per week
   - O b. 20 to 39 hours per week
   - O c. 40 to 59 hours per week
   - O d. 60 to 79 hours per week
   - O e. 80 to 99 hours per week
   - O f. 100 hours per week or more

4. What is your staff position in this hospital? Mark ONE answer that best describes your staff position.
   - O a. Registered Nurse
   - O b. Physician Assistant/Nurse Practitioner
   - O c. LVN/LPN
   - O d. Patient Care Assistant/Hospital Aide/Care Partner
   - O e. Attending/Staff Physician
   - O f. Resident Physician/Physician in Training
   - O g. Pharmacist
   - O h. Dietician
   - O i. Unit Assistant/Clerk/Secretary
   - O j. Respiratory Therapist
   - O k. Physical, Occupational, or Speech Therapist
   - O l. Technician (e.g., EKG, Lab, Radiology)
   - O m. Administration/Management
   - O n. Other, please specify:

5. In your staff position, do you typically have direct interaction or contact with patients?
   - O a. YES, I typically have direct interaction or contact with patients.
   - O b. NO, I typically do NOT have direct interaction or contact with patients.

6. How long have you worked in your current specialty or profession?
   - O a. Less than 1 year
   - O b. 1 to 5 years
   - O c. 6 to 10 years
   - O d. 11 to 15 years
   - O e. 16 to 20 years
   - O f. 21 years or more

SECTION I: Your Comments

Please feel free to write any comments about patient safety, error, or event reporting in your hospital.

THANK YOU FOR COMPLETING THIS SURVEY.

Source: Agency for Healthcare Research and Quality, "Hospital Survey on Patient Safety Culture," http://www.ahrq.gov/qual/hospculture/.

Case 15.2 Canterbury Travels

© GETTY IMAGES/ PHOTODISC GREEN

Hometown, located in the north central United States, had a population of about fifty thousand. There were two travel agencies in Hometown before Canterbury Travels opened its doors.

Canterbury Travels was in its second month of operations. Owner Roxanne Freeman had expected to have more business than she actually had. She decided that she needed to conduct a survey to determine how much business Hometown offered. She also wanted to learn whether people were aware of Canterbury Travels. She thought that this survey would determine the effectiveness of her advertising.

The questionnaire that Roxanne Freeman designed is shown in Case Exhibit 15.2–1.

Questions

1. Critically evaluate the questionnaire.
2. Will Canterbury Travels gain the information it needs from this survey?
3. Design a questionnaire to satisfy Roxanne Freeman's information needs.

CASE EXHIBIT 15.2–1 **Travel Questionnaire**

The following questionnaire pertains to a project being conducted by a local travel agency. The intent of the study is to better understand the needs and attitudes of Hometown residents toward travel agencies. The questionnaire will take only 10 to 15 minutes to fill out at your convenience. Your name will in no way be connected with the questionnaire.

1. Have you traveled out of state? _____Yes _____No
2. If yes, do you travel for:
   Business Both
   Pleasure
3. How often do you travel for the above?
   0–1 times per month 0–1 times per year
   2–3 times per month 2–3 times per year
   4–5 times per month 4–5 times per year
   6 or more times per month 6 or more times per year
4. How do you make your travel arrangements?
   Airline Travel agency
   Other (please specify) ______________________________
5. Did you know that travel agencies do not charge the customer for their services?
   _____Yes _____No
6. Please rate the following qualities that would be most important to you in the selection of a travel agency:

	Good				Bad
Free services (reservations, advice, and delivery of tickets and literature)	____	____	____	____	____
Convenient location	____	____	____	____	____
Knowledgeable personnel	____	____	____	____	____
Friendly personnel	____	____	____	____	____
Casual atmosphere	____	____	____	____	____
Revolving charge account	____	____	____	____	____
Reputation	____	____	____	____	____
Personal sales calls	____	____	____	____	____

7. Are you satisfied with your present travel agency?

	Very satisfied				Very dissatisfied
Holiday Travel	____	____	____	____	____
Leisure Tours	____	____	____	____	____
Canterbury Travels	____	____	____	____	____
Other ______________	____	____	____	____	____

8. If not, what are you dissatisfied with about your travel agency?

	Good				Bad
Free services (reservations, advice, and delivery of tickets and literature)	____	____	____	____	____
Convenient location	____	____	____	____	____
Knowledgeable personnel	____	____	____	____	____
Friendly personnel	____	____	____	____	____
Casual atmosphere	____	____	____	____	____
Revolving charge account	____	____	____	____	____
Reputation	____	____	____	____	____
Personal sales calls	____	____	____	____	____

(continued)

CASE EXHIBIT 15.2–1 Travel Questionnaire *(continued)*

9. Did you know that there is a new travel agency in Hometown?
 ________Yes ________No

10. Can you list the travel agencies in Hometown and their locations?
____
____
____

11. Do you use the same travel agency repeatedly?

	0–1 times per month	2–3 times per month	4–5 times per month	6 or more times per month	0–1 times per year	2–3 times per year	4–5 times per year	6 or more times per year
Holiday Travel								
Leisure Tours								
Canterbury Travels								
Other (please specify)								

12. Have you visited the new travel agency in Hometown?
 ______Yes ______No
13. If yes, what is its name? ____
14. How do you pay for your travel expenses?
 Cash Company charge
 Check Personal charge
 Credit card Other ________________________
15. Which of these have you seen advertising for?
 Holiday Travel
 Canterbury Travels
 Other ________________________
16. Where have you seen or heard the advertisement you described above?
17. Would you consider changing travel agencies?
 ______Yes ______No

The following are some personal questions about you that will be used for statistical purposes only. Your answers will be held in the strictest confidence.

18. What is your age?
 19–25 46–55
 26–35 56–65
 36–45 Over 65
19. What is your sex?
 Male Female
20. What is your marital status?
 Single Divorced
 Married Widowed
21. How long have you lived in Hometown?
 0–6 months 5–10 years
 7–12 months 11–15 years
 1–4 years Over 15 years
22. What is your present occupation?
 Business and professional Laborer
 Salaried and semiprofessional Student
 Skilled worker
23. What is the highest level of education you have completed?
 Elementary school 1–2 years of college
 Junior high school 3–4 years of college
 Senior high school More than 4 years of college
 Trade or vocational school
24. What is your yearly household income?
 $0–$5,000 $25,001–$40,000
 $5,001–$10,000 $40,001–$60,000
 $10,001–$15,000 $60,000 and above
 $15,001–$25,000

Case 15.3 McDonald's Spanish Language Questionnaire

© GETTY IMAGES/ PHOTODISC GREEN

The questions in Case Exhibit 15.3–1, about a visit to McDonald's, originally appeared in Spanish and were translated into English.

Questions

1. What is the typical process for developing questionnaires for markets where consumers speak a language other than English?
2. Find someone who speaks Spanish and have him or her back translate the questions that appear in Case Exhibit 15.3–1. Are these Spanish-language questions adequate?

CASE EXHIBIT 15.3–1 **McDonald's Questionnaire**

AQUI SE EMPIEZA → **1. En general, ¿qué tan satisfecho/a quedó con su visita a este McDonald's hoy?** ....

☹ Nada Satisfecho/a				Muy Satisfecho/a ☺
1	2	3	4	5

2. Su visita fue....... Adentro (**A**) o en el Drive-thru (**DT**) — [A] Adentro [DT] Drive-thru

3. Su visita fue....... Durante el Desayuno (**D**), Almuerzo (**A**), Cena (**C**) — [D] Desayuno [A] Almuerzo [A] Cena

4. Su visita fue....... Entre semana (**E**) o Fin de semana (**F**) — [E] Entre semana [F] Fin de semana

COMIDA

5. ¿Quedó satisfecho/a con la comida que recibio hoy? [S] Sí [N] No

Si NO, ¿cuál fue el problema?
Favor de rellenar el(los) círculo(s) apropiado(s).

- Sandwich / platillo frío ☐
- Apariencia desagradable ☐
- Mal sabor de la comida ☐
- Pocas papas en la bolsa / caja ☐
- Papas / tortitas de papa frías ☐
- Papas no bien saladas ☐
- Bebida aguada / de mal sabor ☐

Case 15.4 Schönbrunn Palace in Vienna

© GETTY IMAGES/ PHOTODISC GREEN

The Schönbrunn Palace in Vienna was constructed in the eighteenth century during the reign of the Hapsburgs. Today this former summer residence of the imperial family is one of Austria's top tourist attractions.

The questions in Case Exhibit 15.4–1, about a visit to the Schönbrunn Palace, originally appeared in German and were translated into English.

Questions

1. What is the typical process for developing questionnaires for markets where consumers speak a different language?
2. Find someone who speaks German and have him or her back translate the questions that appear in Case Exhibit 15.4–1. Are these German questions adequate?

CASE EXHIBIT 15.4-1 **Schönbrunn Palace Questionnaire**

Befragung der Besucher **Schloß Schönbrunn**

Land/Staat ________ **Bundesland (nur für Ö)** ________

Alter ______ Jahre **Geschlecht** ◻ männlich ◻ weiblich

Heutiges Datum ___ . ___ . 199__ **Uhrzeit** ________

- **Waren Sie heute zum ersten Mal im Schloß Schönbrunn?**
  ◻ ja ◻ nein, zum ___. Mal

- **Welche Tour haben Sie gemacht?**
  ◻ *Grand Tour* (40 Räume)
  ◻ *Imperial Tour* (22 Räume)

- **Welche Art von Führung haben Sie gewählt?**
  ◻ *Schönbrunn Führung (Angebot des Schlosses)*
  ◻ *eigener Reiseführer (Reisegruppe, Fremdenführer)*
  ◻ *Tonbandführer (Audioguide) in* ________ *Sprache*
  ◻ *keinerlei Führung*

- **Falls Sie an einer Führung teilgenommen haben:**
  Wie finden Sie Ihren Führer bzw. Ihre Führerin?
  ◻ sehr freundlich ◻ eher freundlich ◻ eher unfreundlich ◻ sehr unfreundlich
  weil ... ________

- **Bei Verwendung eines Tonbandführers (Audioguide):**
  Wie finden Sie die angebotenen Audioguides?
  ◻ sehr gut ◻ eher gut ◻ eher schlecht ◻ sehr schlecht
  weil ... ________

- **Wie ist Ihr Gesamteindruck vom Schloß Schönbrunn alles in allem?**
  ◻ sehr gut ◻ eher gut ◻ eher schlecht ◻ sehr schlecht
  weil ... ________

- **Wie ist Ihr Eindruck vom Personal im Schloß?**
  ◻ sehr gut ◻ eher gut ◻ eher schlecht ◻ sehr schlecht
  weil ... ________

- **Wie gut finden Sie sich im Schloß Schönbrunn/Park zurecht (Hinweisschilder, kennt man sich gut aus, findet man die Kassen, Toiletten, den Ausgang, etc.)?**
  ◻ sehr gut ◻ eher gut ◻ eher schlecht ◻ sehr schlecht
  weil ... ________

- **Fühlten Sie sich nach dem Besuch gut informiert über das Schloß und seine Geschichte?**
  ◻ sehr gut ◻ eher gut ◻ eher schlecht ◻ sehr schlecht

- **Wurden Sie bei der Besichtigung gestört?**
  durch (andere) Gruppen:
  ◻ sehr stark ◻ etwas ◻ kaum ◻ gar nicht
  durch Einzelbesucher:
  ◻ sehr stark ◻ etwas ◻ kaum ◻ gar nicht

- **Wie finden Sie die Art, wie die Räume dargestellt werden (Einrichtung, Möblierung, Beleuchtung, Dekoration, etc.)?**
  ◻ sehr gut ◻ eher gut ◻ eher schlecht ◻ sehr schlecht
  weil ... ________

- **Haben Sie nach dem Besuch im Schloß Schönbrunn eine lebendige Vorstellung vom einstigen Leben bei Hof?**
  ◻ ja ◻ etwas ◻ kaum ◻ nein
  weil ... ________

- **Was würden Sie noch gerne über das Schloß erfahren?**
  ____

- **Wie finden Sie die Eintrittspreise?**
  ◻ viel zu teuer ◻ etwas zu teuer ◻ angemessen ◻ günstig

- **Wie finden Sie das Angebot im Museumshop?**
  ◻ sehr gut ◻ eher gut ◻ eher schlecht ◻ sehr schlecht
  weil ... ________

- **Was könnte Ihrer Meinung nach noch verbessert werden?**
  ____
  ____
  ____
  ____

Vielen Dank für Ihren Besuch und Ihre Anregungen!

APPENDIX 15A QUESTION WORDING AND MEASUREMENT SCALES FOR COMMONLY RESEARCHED TOPICS

As Chapters 13, 14, and 15 explain, problem definitions and research objectives determine the nature of the questions to be asked. In most cases researchers construct custom questions for their specific projects. However, in many instances different research projects have some common research objectives. This appendix compiles question wordings and measurement scales frequently used by business researchers. It is by no means exhaustive. It does not repeat every question already discussed in the text. For example, it does not include the hundreds of possible semantic differential items or Likert scale items discussed in Chapter 14.

The purpose of this appendix is to provide a bank of questions and scales for easy reference. It can be used when business research objectives dictate investigation of commonly researched issues.

Questions about Advertising

Awareness

Have you ever seen any advertising for (brand name)?

☐ *Yes* ☐ *No*

Are you aware of (brand name)?

☐ *Yes* ☐ *No*

If yes, how did you first become aware of (brand name)?

- *In-flight airline magazine*
- *Poster or billboard at airport*
- *Television at airport*
- *Card in the seatback pocket*
- *Other (please specify)* __________

Unaided Recall/Top of the Mind Recall

Can you tell me the names of any brands of (product category) for which you have seen or heard any advertising recently?

____

____

____

(After reading a magazine or viewing a TV program with commercials) Please try to recall all the brands you saw advertised on/in (name of program or magazine). (DO NOT PROBE. WRITE BRAND NAMES IN ORDER MENTIONED BY RESPONDENT.)

(After establishing that the respondent watched a certain television program) Do you recall seeing a commercial for any (product category)? (IF YES) What brand of (product category) was advertised?

Aided Recall

(After establishing that the respondent watched a certain television program or read a certain magazine) Now, I'm going to read you a list of brands. Some of them were advertised on/in (name of program or magazine); others were not. Please tell me which ones you remember seeing, even if you mentioned them before.

Brand A (Advertised)
Brand B (Not advertised)
Brand C (Advertised)

Do you remember seeing a commercial for (specific brand name)?

☐ *Yes* ☐ *No*

Recognition

(Show advertisement to respondent) Did you see or read any part of this advertisement?

☐ *Yes* ☐ *No*

Message Communication/Playback (Sales Point Playback)

These questions require that the researcher first qualify awareness with a question such as "Have you ever seen any advertising for (brand name)?" The interviewer then asks message playback questions.

(If yes) What did the advertising tell you about (brand name or product category)?

____

____

Other than trying to sell you the product, what do you think was the main idea in the description you just read (commercial you just saw)?

____

____

What was the main thing it was trying to communicate about the product?
What did the advertising for (brand name) say about the product?

____

____

What did you learn about (brand name) from this advertisement?

____

____

Attitude Toward the Advertisement

Please choose the statement below that best describes your feelings about the commercial you just saw.

☐ *I liked it very much.*
☐ *I liked it.*
☐ *I neither liked nor disliked it.*
☐ *I disliked it.*
☐ *I disliked it very much.*

Was there anything in the commercial you just saw that you found hard to believe?

☐ *Yes* ☐ *No*

What thoughts or feelings went through your mind as you watched the advertisement?

Attitude Toward Advertised Brand (Persuasion)

Based on what you've seen in this commercial, how interested would you be in trying the product?

☐ *Extremely interested*
☐ *Very interested*
☐ *Somewhat interested*
☐ *Not very interested*
☐ *Not at all interested*

The advertisement tried to increase your interest in (brand). How was your buying interest affected?

☐ *Increased considerably*
☐ *Increased somewhat*
☐ *Not affected*
☐ *Decreased somewhat*
☐ *Decreased considerably*

Based on what you've just seen in this commercial, how do you think (brand name) might compare to other brands you've seen or heard about?

☐ *Better*
☐ *As good as*
☐ *Not as good as*

Readership/Viewership

Have you ever read (seen) a copy of (advertising medium)?

☐ *Yes* ☐ *No*

How frequently do you (watch the evening news on channel X)?

☐ *Every day*
☐ *5–6 times a week*
☐ *2–4 times a week*
☐ *Once a week*
☐ *Less than once a week*
☐ *Never*

Several of the questions about products or brands in the following section are also used to assess attitudes toward advertised brands.

Questions about Ownership and Product Usage

Ownership

Do you own a (product category)?

☐ *Yes* ☐ *No*

Purchase Behavior

Have you ever purchased a (product category or brand name)?

☐ *Yes* ☐ *No*

Regular Usage

Which brands of (product category) do you regularly use?

☐ *Brand A*
☐ *Brand B*
☐ *Brand C*
☐ *Do not use* ___________

Which brands of (product category) have you used in the past month?

☐ *Brand A*
☐ *Brand B*
☐ *Brand C*
☐ *Do not use* ___________

In an average month, how often do you buy (product category or brand name)?

Record Number of Times per Month ___________

How frequently do you buy (product category or brand name)?

☐ *Every day*
☐ *5–6 times a week*
☐ *2–4 times a week*
☐ *Once a week*
☐ *Less than once a week*
☐ *Never*

Would you say you purchase (product category or brand name) more often than you did a year ago, abo same as a year ago, or less than a year ago?

☐ *More often than a year ago*
☐ *About the same as a year ago*
☐ *Less than a year ago*

Questions about Goods and Services

Ease of Use

How easy do you find using (brand name)?

☐ *Very easy*
☐ *Easy*
☐ *Neither easy nor difficult*
☐ *Difficult*
☐ *Very difficult*

Uniqueness

How different is this brand from other brands of (product category)?

☐ *Very different*
☐ *Somewhat different*

☐ *Slightly different*
☐ *Not at all different*

How would you rate this product (brand name) on uniqueness?

☐ *Extremely unique*
☐ *Very unique*
☐ *Somewhat unique*
☐ *Slightly unique*
☐ *Not at all unique*

Please form several piles of cards so that statements that are similar to each other or say similar things are in the same pile. You may form as many piles as you like, and you may put as many or as few cards as you want in a pile. You can set aside any statements that you feel are unique or different and are not similar to any of the other statements.

Attribute Ratings/Importance of Characteristics

Measurement scales such as the semantic differential and Likert scales are frequently used to assess product attributes, especially when measuring brand image or store image. See Chapter 15.

How important is (specific attribute), as far as you are concerned?

☐ *Very important*
☐ *Of some importance*
☐ *Of little importance*
☐ *Of absolutely no importance*

We would like you to rate (brand name or product category) on several different characteristics. (For concept tests, add: Since you may not have used this product before, please base your answers on your impressions from what you've just read.)

Characteristic A

☐ *Excellent*
☐ *Good*
☐ *Fair*
☐ *Poor*

Interest

In general, how interested are you in trying a new brand of (product category)?

☐ *Very interested*
☐ *Somewhat interested*
☐ *Not too interested*
☐ *Not at all interested*

Like/Dislike

What do you like about (brand name)?

____

____

What do you dislike about (brand name)?

____

____

How do you like the taste of (brand name)?

- ☐ *Like it very much*
- ☐ *Like it*
- ☐ *Neither like nor dislike it*
- ☐ *Dislike it*
- ☐ *Strongly dislike it*

Preference

Which credit card do you prefer to use?

- ☐ *American Express*
- ☐ *MasterCard*
- ☐ *Visa*
- ☐ *No preference*

Expectations

How would you compare the way (company's) service was actually delivered with the way you had anticipated that (company) would provide the service?

- ☐ *Much better than expected*
- ☐ *Somewhat better than expected*
- ☐ *About the same as expected*
- ☐ *Somewhat worse than expected*
- ☐ *Much worse than expected*

Satisfaction

How satisfied were you with (brand name)?

- ☐ *Very satisfied*
- ☐ *Somewhat satisfied*
- ☐ *Very dissatisfied*

How satisfied were you with (brand name)?

- ☐ *Very satisfied*
- ☐ *Very dissatisfied*
- ☐ *Somewhere in between*

(If somewhere in between) On balance, would you describe yourself as leaning toward being more satisfied or more dissatisfied with (brand name) than with the brand you normally use?

- ☐ *Satisfied*
- ☐ *Dissatisfied*

Now that you have owned (brand name) for 6 months, please tell us how satisfied you are with it.

- ☐ *Completely satisfied*
- ☐ *Very satisfied*
- ☐ *Fairly well satisfied*
- ☐ *Somewhat dissatisfied*
- ☐ *Very dissatisfied*

Quality

How would you rate the quality of (brand name)?

- ☐ *Excellent*
- ☐ *Good*
- ☐ *Fair*
- ☐ *Poor*

Please indicate how the quality of (Brand A) compares with the quality of (Brand B).

- ☐ *Better*
- ☐ *About the same*
- ☐ *Worse*

Problems

Have you experienced problems with (company's) service?

☐ *Yes* ☐ *No*

When attempting to contact (company's) representative, how much of a problem, if any, was each of the following:

Phones busy

☐ *No problem at all* ☐ *Slight problem* ☐ *Somewhat of a problem* ☐ *Major problem*

Put on hold too long or too often

☐ *No problem at all* ☐ *Slight problem* ☐ *Somewhat of a problem* ☐ *Major problem*

What are the major shortcomings of (brand name)? (PROBE: What other shortcomings are there?)

Benefits

Do you think (product concept) would have major benefits, minor benefits, or no benefits at all?

- ☐ *Major benefits*
- ☐ *Minor benefits*
- ☐ *No benefits at all*

Improvements

In what ways, if any, could (brand name) be changed or improved? We would like you to tell us anything you can think of, no matter how minor it seems.

Buying Intentions for Existing Products

Do you intend to buy a (brand name or product category) in the next month (3 months, year, etc.)?

☐ *Yes* ☐ *No*

If a free (product category) were offered to you, which would you select?

- ☐ *Brand A*
- ☐ *Brand B*
- ☐ *Brand C*
- ☐ *Do not use*

Buying Intentions Based on Product Concept

(Respondent is shown a prototype or asked to read a concept statement.) Now that you have read about (product concept), if this product were available at your local store, how likely would you be to buy it?

- ☐ *Would definitely buy it*
- ☐ *Would probably buy it*
- ☐ *Might or might not buy it*
- ☐ *Would probably not buy it*

☐ *Would definitely not buy it*

(Hand response card to respondent.) Which phrase on this card indicates how likely you would be to buy this product the next time you go shopping for a product of this type?

☐ *Would definitely buy it*
☐ *Would probably buy it*
☐ *Might or might not buy it*
☐ *Would probably not buy it*
☐ *Would definitely not buy it*

Now that you have read about (product concept), if this product were available at your local store for (price), how likely would you be to buy it?

☐ *Would definitely buy it*
☐ *Would probably buy it*
☐ *Might or might not buy it*
☐ *Would probably not buy it*
☐ *Would definitely not buy it*

How often, if ever, would you buy (product concept)?

☐ *Once a week or more*
☐ *Once every 2 to 3 weeks*
☐ *Once a month/every 4 weeks*
☐ *Once every 2 to 3 months*
☐ *Once every 4 to 6 months*
☐ *Less than once a year*
☐ *Never*

Based on your experience, would you recommend (company) to a friend who wanted to purchase (product concept)?

☐ *Recommend that the friend buy from (company)*
☐ *Recommend that the friend not buy from (company)*
☐ *Offer no opinion either way*

Reason for Buying Intention

Why do you say that you would (would not) buy (brand name)? (PROBE: What other reason do you have for feeling this way?)

Questions about Demographics

Age

What is your age, please?

What year were you born?

Education

What is your level of education?

☐ *Some high school or less*
☐ *Completed high school*
☐ *Some college*

☐ *Completed college*
☐ *Some graduate school*
☐ *Completed graduate school*

What is the highest level of education you have obtained?

☐ *Some high school or less*
☐ *High school graduate*
☐ *Some college*
☐ *College graduate*
☐ *Postgraduate school*
☐ *Completed graduate school*

Marital Status

What is your marital status?'

☐ *Married*
☐ *Divorced/separated*
☐ *Widowed*
☐ *Never married/single*

Children

Are there any children under the age of 6 living in your household?

☐ *Yes* ☐ *No*

If yes, how many?

Income

Which group describes your annual family income?

☐ *Under $20,000*
☐ *$20,000–$39,999*
☐ *$40,000–$59,999*
☐ *$60,000–$79,999*
☐ *$80,000–$99,999*
☐ *$100,000–$149,999*
☐ *$150,000 or more*

Please check the box that describes your total household income before taxes in (year). Include income for yourself as well as for all other persons who live in your household.

☐ *Less than $10,000*
☐ *$10,000–$14,999*
☐ *$15,000–$19,999*
☐ *$20,000–$24,999*
☐ *$25,000–$29,999*
☐ *$30,000–$34,999*
☐ *$35,000–$39,999*
☐ *$40,000–$49,999*
☐ *$50,000–$59,999*
☐ *$60,000–$74,999*
☐ *$75,000 or more*

Occupation

What is your occupation?

☐ *Professional* ☐ *Technical*

☐ *Executive*	☐ *Labor*
☐ *Managerial*	☐ *Secretarial*
☐ *Administrative*	☐ *Clerical*
☐ *Sales*	☐ *Other*

What is your occupation?

☐ *Homemaker*	☐ *Clerical or service worker*
☐ *Professional/technical*	☐ *Tradesperson/machine operator*
☐ *Upper management/executive*	☐ *Laborer*
☐ *Middle management*	☐ *Retired*
☐ *Sales/marketing*	☐ *Student*

Part 5
Sampling and Fieldwork

© ISTOCKPHOTO/THINKSTOCK

CHAPTER 16
SAMPLING DESIGNS AND SAMPLING PROCEDURES

LEARNING OUTCOMES

After studying this chapter, you should be able to

1. Explain reasons for taking a sample rather than a complete census
2. Describe the process of identifying a target population and selecting a sampling frame
3. Compare random sampling and systematic (nonsampling) errors
4. Identify the types of nonprobability sampling, including their advantages and disadvantages
5. Summarize the advantages and disadvantages of the various types of probability samples
6. Discuss how to choose an appropriate sample design, as well as challenges for Internet sampling

Chapter Vignette: Changing Pocketbook Problems for Today's Families

It is easy to ask people what they consider to be the most pressing financial problems they face. From low wages, to rising health care and housing costs, to a concern for too much debt, these problems are constantly on the minds of many families today. When pressed about which financial problem is *most* important, some interesting trends occur. These trends could not have been captured if not for the work of large-scale sampling of populations.

Each quarter, the Gallup Corporation develops a representative sample of approximately 1,000 U.S. adults, aged 18 and older, to capture public perceptions on a variety of relevant topics, to include financial concerns of the family. Since the sample is developed and obtained carefully, it serves as a representation of the population of adults in the U.S. who are 18 years or older. As a result of this sampling technique, researchers can be 95 percent confident that the responses of the sample are reflective of this national population, with a sampling error of less than 3 percent. Using telephone based interviews, the Gallup Corporation asks the respondent to describe "the most important financial problem facing your family today." Responses are open-ended, and are then coded based upon the theme of the response.

Interestingly, trends suggest that the most important financial problem facing families can often change over time, and may be reflective of the respondent's current awareness of the financial challenges of the day. For example, when energy and gas prices were at their highest during the summer of 2008, almost one-third (29 percent) of the July 2008 Gallup respondents listed energy and gas prices as their most important problem. However, in less than six months (January 2009), energy and gas prices were mentioned by only 3 percent. While health care costs were mentioned by 19 percent of families in October 2007, only 9 mentioned health care a year later.

The implication of these types of changing trends suggests that financial problems facing families evolve over time. And, families often look no further than their own pocketbook (or credit card statement) when they consider their greatest financial challenges. The use of large-scale representative samples by the Gallup Corporation helped reveal these interesting trends.[1]

Introduction

Sampling is a familiar part of daily life. A customer in a bookstore picks up a book, looks at the cover, and skims a few pages to get a sense of the writing style and content before deciding whether to buy. A high school student visits a college classroom to listen to a professor's lecture. Selecting a university on the basis of one classroom visit may not be scientific sampling, but in a personal situation, it may be a practical sampling experience. When measuring every item in a population is impossible, inconvenient, or too expensive, we intuitively take a sample.

Although sampling is commonplace in daily activities, these familiar samples are seldom scientific. For researchers, the process of sampling can be quite complex. Sampling is a central aspect of business research, requiring in-depth examination. This chapter explains the nature of sampling and ways to determine the appropriate sample design.

Sampling Terminology

As seen in the chapter vignette above, the process of sampling involves using a portion of a population to make conclusions about the whole population. A **sample** is a subset, or some part, of a larger population. The purpose of sampling is to estimate an unknown characteristic of a population.

Sampling is defined in terms of the population being studied. A **population (universe)** is any complete group—for example, of people, sales territories, stores, or college students—that shares some common set of characteristics. The term **population element** refers to an individual member of the population.

Researchers could study every element of a population to draw some conclusion. A **census** is an investigation of all the individual elements that make up the population—a total enumeration rather than a sample. Thus, if we wished to know whether more adult Texans drive pickup trucks than sedans, we could contact every adult Texan and find out whether or not they drive a pickup truck or a sedan. We would then know the answer to this question definitively.

sample
A subset, or some part, of a larger population.

population (universe)
Any complete group of entities that share some common set of characteristics.

population element
An individual member of a population.

census
An investigation of all the individual elements that make up a population.

Why Sample?

At a wine tasting, guests sample wine by having a small taste from each of a number of different wines. From this, the taster decides if he or she likes a particular wine and if it is judged to be of low or high quality. If an entire bottle were consumed to decide, the taster may end up not caring care about the next bottle. However, in a scientific study in which the objective is to determine an unknown population value, why should a sample rather than a complete census be taken?

Pragmatic Reasons

Applied business research projects usually have budget and time constraints. If Ford Motor Corporation wished to take a census of past purchasers' reactions to the company's recalls of defective models, the researchers would have to contact millions of automobile buyers. Some of them would be inaccessible (for example, out of the country), and it would be impossible to contact all these people within a short time period.

A researcher who wants to investigate a population with an extremely small number of population elements may elect to conduct a census rather than a sample because the cost, labor, and time drawbacks would be relatively insignificant. For a company that wants to assess salespersons' satisfaction with its computer networking system, circulating a questionnaire to all 25 of its employees is practical. In most situations, however, many practical reasons favor sampling. Sampling cuts costs, reduces labor requirements, and gathers vital information quickly. These advantages may be sufficient in themselves for using a sample rather than a census, but there are other reasons.

Accurate and Reliable Results

As seen in the Research Snapshot titled "Finding Out about Work Is a Lot of Work," another major reason for sampling is that most properly selected samples give results that are reasonably accurate. If the elements of a population are quite similar, only a small sample is necessary to accurately portray the characteristic of interest. Thus, a population consisting of 10,000 eleventh grade students in all-boys Catholic high schools will require a smaller sample than a broader population consisting of 10,000 high school students from coeducational secondary schools.

A visual example of how different-sized samples produce generalizable conclusions can be thought as number of dots in producing photograph in JPEG images that contain different numbers of "dots." More dots mean more memory is required to store the photo. In this case, the dots can be thought of as sampling units representing the population which can be thought of as all the little pieces of detail that form the actual image.

A photograph is comprised of several thousands of dots resulting in a very detailed photograph. Very little detail is lost and the face can be confidently recognized. However, if the number of dots per area is reduced to say 2000 dots, the photographs would provide less detail, but the face would be still very recognizable, but less detail is retained as compared to the first photograph. Similarly, if a photograph is made up of 1,000 dots, constituting a sample that is only half as large as that in previous photograph, the sample would provide an image that can still be recognized but with very less detail. However, if a photograph consists of only 250 dots, the photograph may not be recognizable and it may be of no use for the user. Hence, we can see from this illustration that as you reduce the sample, one can have a proper representation of the phenomena with lesser but workable detail, however, if the sample size is reduced after certain level, the result of the research may not be of much use. Interpretation from such research may lead to wrong conclusion.

A sample may on occasion be more accurate than a census. Interviewer mistakes, tabulation errors, and other nonsampling errors may increase during a census because of the increased volume of work. In a sample, increased accuracy may sometimes be possible because the fieldwork and tabulation of data can be more closely supervised. In a field survey, a small, well-trained, closely supervised group may do a more careful and accurate job of collecting information than a large group of nonprofessional interviewers who try to contact everyone. An interesting case in point is the use of samples by the Bureau of the Census to check the accuracy of the U.S. Census. If the sample indicates a possible source of error, the census is redone.

Destruction of Test Units

Many research projects, especially those in quality-control testing, require the destruction of the items being tested. If a manufacturer of firecrackers wished to find out whether each unit met a specific production standard, no product would be left after the testing. This is the exact situation in many research strategy experiments. For example, if an experimental sales presentation were presented to every potential customer, no prospects would remain to be contacted after the experiment. In other words, if there is a finite population and everyone in the population participates in the research and cannot be replaced, no population elements remain to be selected as sampling units. The test units have been destroyed or ruined for the purpose of the research project.

Practical Sampling Concepts

Before taking a sample, researchers must make several decisions. Exhibit 16.1 presents these decisions as a series of sequential stages, but the order of the decisions does not always follow this sequence. These decisions are highly interrelated. The issues associated with each of these stages, except for fieldwork, are discussed in this chapter and Chapter 17. Fieldwork is examined in Chapter 18.

Defining the Target Population

Once the decision to sample has been made, the first question concerns identifying the target population. What is the relevant population? In many cases this question is easy to answer. Registered voters may be clearly identifiable. Likewise, if a company's 106-person sales force is the population of concern, there are few definitional problems. In other cases the decision may be difficult. One survey concerning organizational buyer behavior incorrectly defined the population as purchasing agents whom sales representatives regularly contacted. After the survey, investigators discovered that industrial engineers within the customer companies rarely talked with the salespeople but substantially affected buying decisions. For consumer-related research, the appropriate population element frequently is the household rather than an individual member of the household. This presents some problems if household lists are not available.

At the outset of the sampling process, the target population must be carefully defined so that the proper sources from which the data are to be collected can be identified. The usual technique for defining the target population is to answer questions about the crucial characteristics of the population. Does the term *comic book reader* include children under six years of age who do not actually read the words? Does *all persons west of the Mississippi* include people in east bank towns that border the river, such as East St. Louis, Illinois? The question to answer is, "Whom do we want to talk to?" The answer may be users, nonusers, recent adopters, or brand switchers.

To implement the sample in the field, tangible characteristics should be used to define the population. A baby food manufacturer might define the population as all women still capable of bearing children. However, a more specific *operational definition* would be women between the ages of 12 and 50. While this definition by age may exclude a few women who are capable of childbearing and include some who are not, it is still more explicit and provides a manageable basis for the sample design.

The Sampling Frame

In practice, the sample will be drawn from a list of population elements that often differs somewhat from the defined target population. A list of elements from which the sample may be drawn is called a **sampling frame**. The sampling frame is also called the *working population* because these

sampling frame
A list of elements from which a sample may be drawn; also called working population.

RESEARCH SNAPSHOT

Finding Out about Work Is a Lot of Work!

What do people do for work? How long does it take them to get there? What do they earn? These and many other questions are critically important for United States economists and social scientists. The U.S. Census Bureau and the Bureau of Labor Statistics have jointly asked these questions, every month, for almost 70 years.

The work of these two Bureaus is captured by the Current Population Survey (CPS). The CPS uses a scientifically derived panel sample of 60,000 households. The participating households are surveyed for four months out of the sample of eight months, and then are sampled again for four more months before they are removed from the panel. Moreover, the sample is surveyed for each month on a week that contains the 19th of that month. Not surprisingly, the cost of conducting the CPS is measured in the millions of dollars.

The sophistication and detail of the CPS is required to ensure that accurate national statistics are captured on a monthly basis. As a result, the CPS is considered one of the standards by which other household surveys are conducted. The cost of the CPS, as well as the need for extensive telephone and field staff, really does represent a lot of "work"!

Source: U.S. Department of Labor, Bureau of Labor Statistics, and U.S Department of Commerce, U.S. Census Bureau, *Current Population Survey: Design and Methodology*, Technical Paper 63RV (2002).

EXHIBIT 16.1
Stages in the Selection of a Sample

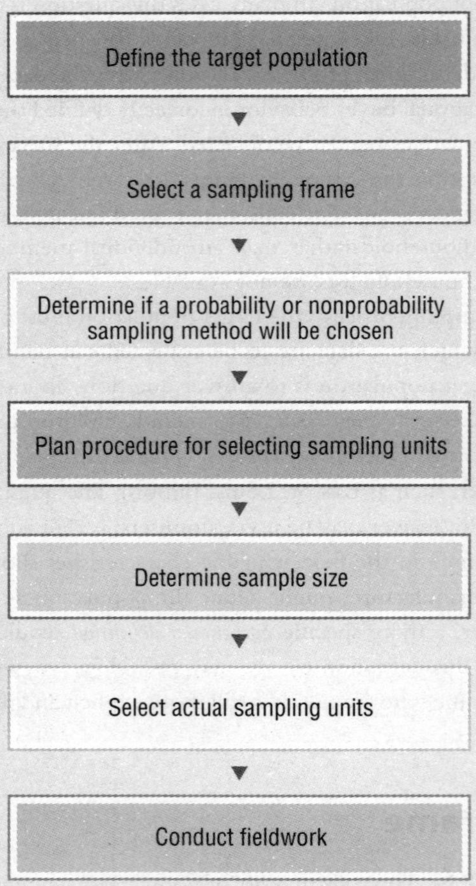

RESEARCH SNAPSHOT

How Much Does Your Prescription Cost? It Depends on Who You Buy It from

Many people are sensitive to the costs of their prescription drugs. For some drugs, these costs can make up a significant part of a person's monthly or yearly budget. Generally speaking, however, most people would expect that their prescriptions would cost about the same, no matter where they buy them. After a number of complaints to the contrary, the state of Michigan sought to answer that very question.

The attorney general of the state of Michigan commissioned a targeted survey of 200 pharmacies to capture drug prescription costs for 11 common drugs used by people within the state. The survey was further focused on 10 specific communities, to include Detroit and Grand Rapids, as well as the Upper Peninsula of the State of Michigan.

Since the sample was drawn purposely, there was confidence that the survey would lead to some fruitful insights. Not surprisingly, the results confirmed the complaints of customers to the attorney general. Prices for the same prescription could vary as much as $100, and the variation may exist even though pharmacies were quite literally "down the block." Long term, the use of a carefully drawn sample led to a consumer alert from the attorney general's office—encouraging customers to shop carefully for their prescription drugs in the state.

Source: May 2007 Prescription Drug Survey Summary, Office of the Attorney General, State of Michigan (May 2007).

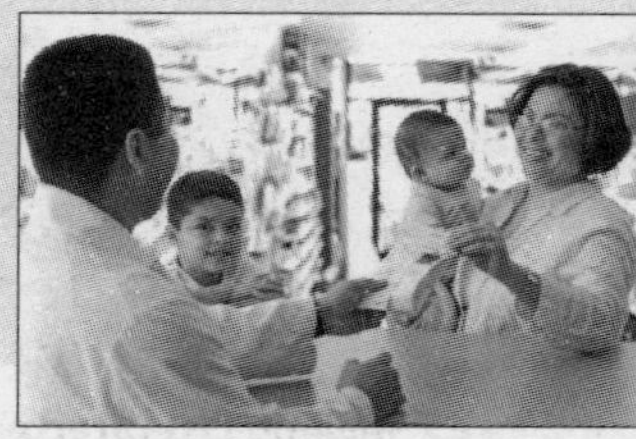

units will eventually provide units involved in analysis. A simple example of a sampling frame would be a list of all members of the American Medical Association.

In practice, almost every list excludes some members of the population. For example, would a university e-mail directory provide an accurate sampling frame for a given university's student population? Perhaps the sampling frame excludes students who registered late and includes students who have resigned from the university. The e-mail directory also will likely list only the student's official university e-mail address. However, many students may not ever use this address, opting to use a private e-mail account instead. Thus, the university e-mail directory could not be expected to perfectly represent the student population. However, a perfect representation isn't always possible or needed.

Some firms, called *sampling services* or *list brokers*, specialize in providing lists or databases that include the names, addresses, phone numbers, and e-mail addresses of specific populations. Exhibit 16.2 shows a page from a mailing list company's offerings. Lists offered by companies such as this are compiled from subscriptions to professional journals, credit card applications, warranty card registrations, and a variety of other sources. One sampling service obtained its listing of households with children from an ice cream retailer who gave away free ice cream cones on children's birthdays. The children filled out cards with their names, addresses, and birthdays, which the retailer then sold to the mailing list company.

A valuable source of names is Equifax's series of city directories. Equifax City Directory provides complete, comprehensive, and accurate business and residential information. The city directory records the name of each resident over 18 years of age and lists pertinent information about each household. The reverse directory pages offer a unique benefit. A **reverse directory** provides, in a different format, the same information contained in a telephone directory. Listings may be by city and street address or by phone number, rather than alphabetical by last name. Such a directory is particularly useful when a research wishes to survey only a certain geographical area of a city or when census tracts are to be selected on the basis of income or another demographic criterion.

reverse directory
A directory similar to a telephone directory except that listings are by city and street address or by phone number rather than alphabetical by last name.

sampling frame error

An error that occurs when certain sample elements are not listed or are not accurately represented in a sampling frame.

A **sampling frame error** occurs when certain sample elements are excluded or when the entire population is not accurately represented in the sampling frame. Election polling that used a telephone directory as a sampling frame would be contacting households with listed phone numbers, not households whose members are likely to vote. A better sampling frame might be voter registration records. Another potential sampling frame error involving phone records is the possibility that a phone survey could underrepresent people with disabilities. Some disabilities, such as hearing and speech impairments, might make telephone use impossible. However, when researchers in Washington State tested for this possible sampling frame error by comparing Census Bureau data on the prevalence of disability with the responses to a telephone survey, they found the opposite effect. The reported prevalence of a disability was actually higher in the phone survey.[2] These findings could be relevant for research into a community's health status or the level of demand for services for disabled persons.

As in this example, population elements can be either under- or overrepresented in a sampling frame. A savings and loan defined its population as all individuals who had savings accounts. However, when it drew a sample from the list of accounts rather than from the list

EXHIBIT 16.2 **Mailing List Directory Page**

Lists Available - Alphabetical

S.I.C. Code	List Title	United States Total Count	United States State Count Page	Canadian Count
	A			
5122-02	Abdominal Supports	201	‡	28
8399-03	Abortion Alternatives Organizations`	946	‡	*
8093-04	Abortion Information & Services	551	‡	*
5085-23	Abrasives	1811	‡	277
5169-04	Absorbents	145	‡	*
6541-03	Abstracters	4057	58	*
6411-06	Accident & Health Insurance	2113	‡	9
8748-52	Accident Reconstruction Service	125	‡	*
8721-01	Accountants	127392	64	6933
8721-02	Accounting & Bookkeeping General Svc	27996	64	2072
5044-08	Accounting & Bookkeeping Machines/Supls	889	‡	50
5044-01	Accounting & Bookkeeping Systems	624	‡	1230
8711-02	Acoustical Consultants	381	‡	91
1742-02	Acoustical Contractors	3063	47	433
1742-01	Acoustical Materials	878	‡	210
8999-10	Actuaries	1185	‡	*
8049-13	Acupuncture (Acupuncturists)	2921	62	493
5044-02	Adding & Calculating Machines/Supplies	5524	49	648
5044-09	Addressing Machines & Supplies	345	‡	29
5169-12	Adhesives & Glues	1187	‡	4
3579-02	Adhesives & Gluing Equipment	170	‡	204
6411-02	Adjusters	6164	57	8357
6411-01	Adjusters-Public	161	‡	*
8322-07	Adoption Agencies	1621	‡	32
8059-03	Adult Care Facilities	596	‡	*
8361-08	Adult Congregate Living Facilities	170	‡	*
7319-03	Advertising-Aerial	337	‡	26
7311-01	Advertising-Agencies & Counselors	27753	59	2552
7336-05	Advertising-Art Layout & Production Svc	457	‡	101
7331-05	Advertising-Direct Mail	6347	59	540
7311-03	Advertising-Directory & Guide	2465	‡	124
7319-01	Advertising-Displays	3441	59	571
7319-11	Advertising-Indoor	209	‡	63
7311-05	Advertising-Motion Picture	143	‡	11
7311-06	Advertising-Newspaper	4274	59	404
7312-01	Advertising-Outdoor	3052	59	297
7311-08	Advertising-Periodical	817	‡	78

S.I.C. Code	List Title	United States Total Count	United States State Count Page	Canadian Count
7313-03	Advertising-Radio	2866	59	247
7311-07	Advertising-Shoppers' Guides	392	‡	4
5199-17	Advertising-Specialties	12827	52	1648
7389-12	Advertising-Telephone	120	‡	*
7313-05	Advertising-Television	1746	‡	102
7319-02	Advertising-Transit & Transportation	179	‡	38
0721-03	Aerial Applicators (Service)	1479	‡	61
3999-01	Aerosols	158	‡	*
3812-01	Aerospace Industries	426	‡	*
	Affluent Americans		73	
5191-04	Agricultural Chemicals	549	‡	210
8748-20	Agricultural Consultants	1047	‡	474
9999-32	Air Balancing	353	‡	*
5084-64	Air Brushes	219	‡	*
4512-02	Air Cargo Service	6005	48	*
5075-01	Air Cleaning & Purifying Equipment	2055	‡	342
5084-02	Air Compressors	4358	50	717
	(See Compressors Air & Gas)			
1711-17	Air Conditioning Contractors & Systems	50951	47	2667
	Available By Brands Sold			
	Airtemp (A)	187		
	Amana (B)	1450		
	Arco Aire (2)	673		
	Armstrong/Magic Chef (C)	395		
	Arvin (4)	106		
	Bryant (D)	2223		
	Carrier (E)	5927		
	Coleman (5)	1176		
	Comfortmaker/Singer (O)	989		
	Day & Night (Z)	749		
	Fedders (H)	318		
	Heli/Quaker (3)	1977		
	Janitrol (7)	587		
	Kero-Sun (W)	2		
	Lennox (K)	4390		
	Luxaire (L)	510		
	Payne (M)	553		

of names of individuals, individuals who had multiple accounts were overrepresented in the sample.

SAMPLING FRAMES FOR INTERNATIONAL RESEARCH

The availability of sampling frames around the globe varies dramatically. Not every country's government conducts a census of population. In some countries telephone directories are incomplete, no voter registration lists exist, and accurate maps of urban areas are unobtainable. However, in Taiwan, Japan, and other Asian countries, a researcher can build a sampling frame relatively easily because those governments release some census information. If a family changes households, updated census information must be reported to a centralized government agency before communal services (water, gas, electricity, education, and so on) are made available.[3] This information is then easily accessible in the local *Inhabitants' Register.*

Sampling Units

During the actual sampling process, the elements of the population must be selected according to a certain procedure. The **sampling unit** is a single element or group of elements subject to selection in the sample. For example, if an airline wishes to sample passengers, it may take every 25th name on a complete list of passengers. In this case the sampling unit would be the same as the element. Alternatively, the airline could first select certain flights as the sampling unit and then select certain passengers on each flight. In this case the sampling unit would contain many elements.

If the target population has first been divided into units, such as airline flights, additional terminology must be used. A unit selected in the first stage of sampling is called a **primary sampling unit (PSU)**. A unit selected in a successive stages of sampling is called a **secondary sampling unit** or (if three stages are necessary) **tertiary sampling unit**. When there is no list of population elements, the sampling unit generally is something other than the population element. In a random-digit dialing study, the sampling unit will be telephone numbers.

sampling unit
A single element or group of elements subject to selection in the sample.

primary sampling unit (PSU)
A term used to designate a unit selected in the first stage of sampling.

secondary sampling unit
A term used to designate a unit selected in the second stage of sampling.

tertiary sampling unit
A term used to designate a unit selected in the third stage of sampling.

random sampling error
The difference between the sample result and the result of a census conducted using identical procedures.

Random Sampling and Nonsampling Errors

An advertising agency sampled a small number of shoppers in grocery stores that used Shopper's Video, an in-store advertising network. The agency hoped to measure brand awareness and purchase intentions. Investigators expected this sample to be representative of the grocery-shopping population. However, if a difference exists between the value of a sample statistic of interest (for example, the sample group's average willingness to buy the advertised brand) and the value of the corresponding population parameter (the population's average willingness to buy), a *statistical error* has occurred. Two basic causes of differences between statistics and parameters were introduced in an earlier chapter and are described below:

1. random sampling errors
2. systematic (nonsampling) error

An estimation made from a sample is not the same as a census count. **Random sampling error** is the difference between the sample result and the result of a census conducted using identical procedures. Of course, the result of a census is unknown unless one is taken, which is rarely done. Other sources of error also can be present. Random sampling error occurs because of chance variation in the scientific selection of sampling units. The sampling units, even if properly selected according to sampling theory, may not perfectly represent the population, but generally they are reliable estimates. Our discussion on the process of randomization (a procedure designed to give everyone in the population an equal chance of being selected as a sample member) will show that, because random sampling errors follow chance variations, they tend to cancel one another out when averaged. This means that properly selected samples generally are good approximations of the population. Still, the true population value almost always differs slightly from the sample value, causing a small random sampling error. Every once in a while, an unusual sample is selected because too many atypical people were included in the sample and a large random sampling error occurred.

Random Sampling Error

Random sampling error is a function of sample size. As sample size increases, random sampling error decreases. Of course, the resources available will influence how large a sample may be taken. It is possible to estimate the random sampling error that may be expected with various sample sizes. Suppose a survey of approximately 1,000 people has been taken in Fresno to determine the feasibility of a new soccer franchise. Assume that 30 percent of the respondents favor the idea of a new professional sport in town. The researcher will know, based on the laws of probability, that 95 percent of the time a survey of slightly fewer than 900 people will produce results with an error of approximately plus or minus 3 percent. If the survey were conducted with only 325 people, the margin of error would increase to approximately plus or minus 5 percentage points. This example illustrates random sampling errors.

Systematic Sampling Error

Systematic (nonsampling) errors result from nonsampling factors, primarily the nature of a study's design and the correctness of execution. These errors are *not* due to chance fluctuations. For example, highly educated respondents are more likely to cooperate with mail surveys than poorly educated ones, for whom filling out forms is more difficult and intimidating. Sample biases such as these account for a large portion of errors in marketing research. The term *sample bias* is somewhat unfortunate, because many forms of bias are not related to the selection of the sample.

We discussed nonsampling errors in Chapter 8. Errors due to sample selection problems, such as sampling frame errors, are systematic (nonsampling) errors and should not be classified as random sampling errors.

Less Than Perfectly Representative Samples

Random sampling errors and systematic errors associated with the sampling process may combine to yield a sample that is less than perfectly representative of the population. Exhibit 16.4 illustrates two nonsampling errors (sampling frame error and nonresponse error) related to sample design. The total population is represented by the area of the largest square. Sampling frame errors eliminate some potential respondents. Random sampling error (due exclusively to random, chance fluctuation) may cause an imbalance in the representativeness of the group. Additional errors will occur if individuals refuse to be interviewed or cannot be contacted. Such nonresponse error may also cause the sample to be less than perfectly

EXHIBIT 16.4 **Errors Associated with Sampling**

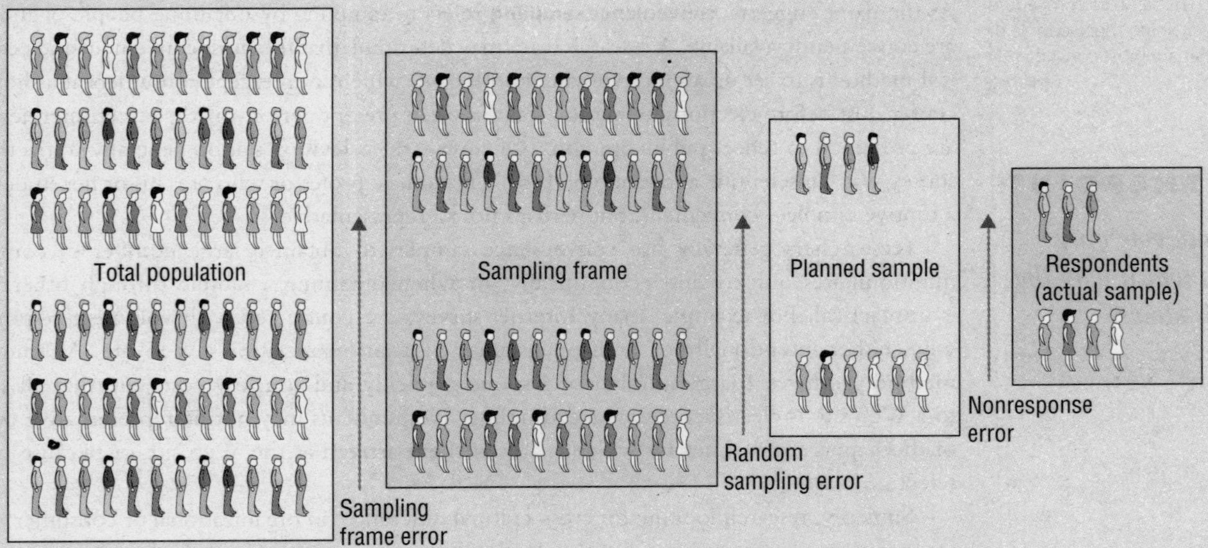

Source: Adapted from Cox, Keith K. and Ben M. Enis, *The Marketing Research Process* (Pacific Palisades, CA: Goodyear, 1972); and Bellenger, Danny N. and Barnet A. Greenberg, *Marketing Research: A Management Information Approach* (Homewood, IL: Richard D. Irwin, 1978), pp. 154–155.

representative. Thus, the actual sample is drawn from a population different from (or smaller than) the ideal.

Probability versus Nonprobability Sampling

Several alternative ways to take a sample are available. The main alternative sampling plans may be grouped into two categories: probability techniques and nonprobability techniques.

In **probability sampling**, every element in the population has a *known, nonzero probability* of selection. The simple random sample, in which each member of the population has an equal probability of being selected, is the best-known probability sample.

probability sampling
A sampling technique in which every member of the population has a known, nonzero probability of selection.

In **nonprobability sampling**, the probability of any particular member of the population being chosen is unknown. The selection of sampling units in nonprobability sampling is quite arbitrary, as researchers rely heavily on personal judgment. Technically, no appropriate statistical techniques exist for measuring random sampling error from a nonprobability sample. Therefore, projecting the data beyond the sample is, technically speaking, statistically inappropriate. Nevertheless, as the Research Snapshot on prescription drug costs shows, researchers sometimes find nonprobability samples best suited for a specific research purpose. As a result, nonprobability samples are pragmatic and are used in market research.

nonprobability sampling
A sampling technique in which units of the sample are selected on the basis of personal judgment or convenience; the probability of any particular member of the population being chosen is unknown.

Nonprobability Sampling

Although probability sampling is preferred, we will discuss nonprobability sampling first to illustrate some potential sources of error and other weaknesses in sampling.

Convenience Sampling

convenience sampling
The sampling procedure of obtaining those people or units that are most conveniently available.

As the name suggests, **convenience sampling** refers to sampling by obtaining people or units that are conveniently available. A research team may determine that the most convenient and economical method is to set up an interviewing booth from which to intercept consumers at a shopping center. Just before elections, television stations often present person-on-the-street interviews that are presumed to reflect public opinion. (Of course, the television station generally warns that the survey was "unscientific and random" [*sic*].) The college professor who uses his or her students has a captive sample—convenient, but perhaps not so representative.

TOTHEPOINT

A straw vote only shows which way the hot air blows.

—O. Henry

Researchers generally use convenience samples to obtain a large number of completed questionnaires quickly and economically, or when obtaining a sample through other means is impractical. For example, many Internet surveys are conducted with volunteer respondents who, either intentionally or by happenstance, visit an organization's Web site. Although this method produces a large number of responses quickly and at a low cost, selecting all visitors to a Web site is clearly convenience sampling. Respondents may not be representative because of the haphazard manner by which many of them arrived at the Web site or because of self-selection bias.

Similarly, research looking for cross-cultural differences in organizational or consumer behavior typically uses convenience samples. Rather than selecting cultures with characteristics relevant to the hypothesis being tested, the researchers conducting these studies often choose cultures to which they have access (for example, because they speak the language or have contacts in that culture's organizations). Further adding to the convenience, cross-cultural research often defines "culture" in terms of nations, which are easier to identify and obtain statistics for, even though many nations include several cultures and some people in a given nation may be more involved with the international business or academic community than with a particular ethnic culture.[4] Here again, the use of convenience sampling limits how well the research represents the intended population.

The user of research based on a convenience sample should remember that projecting the results beyond the specific sample is inappropriate. Convenience samples are best used for exploratory research when additional research will subsequently be conducted with a probability sample.

Judgment Sampling

judgment (purposive) sampling
A nonprobability sampling technique in which an experienced individual selects the sample based on personal judgment about some appropriate characteristic of the sample member.

Judgment (purposive) sampling is a nonprobability sampling technique in which an experienced individual selects the sample based on his or her judgment about some appropriate characteristics required of the sample member. Researchers select samples that satisfy their specific purposes, even if they are not fully representative. The consumer price index (CPI) is based on a judgment sample of market-basket items, housing costs, and other selected goods and services expected to reflect a representative sample of items consumed by most Americans. Test-market cities often are selected because they are viewed as typical cities whose demographic profiles closely match the national profile. A fashion manufacturer regularly selects a sample of key accounts that it believes are capable of providing information needed to predict what may sell in the fall. Thus, the sample is selected to achieve this specific objective.

Judgment sampling often is used in attempts to forecast election results. People frequently wonder how a television network can predict the results of an election with only 2 percent of the votes reported. Political and sampling experts judge which small voting districts approximate overall state returns from previous election years; then these *bellwether precincts* are selected as the sampling units. Of course, the assumption is that the past voting records of these districts are still representative of the political behavior of the state's population.

RESEARCH SNAPSHOT

American Kennel Club Tries to Keep Pet Owners out of the Doghouse

The American Kennel Club (AKC) is an organization dedicated to promoting purebred dogs and their health and well-being as family companions. So the organization commissioned a study to investigate dog ownership and the acceptance of dogs in their neighborhoods. The AKC used quota sampling in its recent Dog Ownership Study, which set out to compare attitudes of dog owners and nonowners, based on a sample of one thousand people. In such a small sample of the U.S. population, some groups might not be represented, so the study design set quotas for completed interviews in age, sex, and geographic categories. The primary sampling units for this phone survey were selected with random-digit dialing. In the next phase of selection, the researchers ensured that respondents filled the quotas for each group. They further screened respondents so that half owned dogs and half did not.

© iStock

An objective of the survey was to help dog owners understand concerns of their neighbors so that the AKC can provide better education in responsible dog ownership, contributing to greater community harmony. The study found that people without dogs tended to be most concerned about dogs jumping and barking and owners not "picking up after their dogs." Lisa Peterson, director of club communications for AKC, commented, "Anyone considering bringing a dog home should realize that it's a 10- to 15-year commitment of time, money, and love that should not be taken lightly."

The study addressed the pleasures of a pet's companionship, as well as the duties. A benefit of ownership was that dog owners were somewhat more likely than nonowners to describe themselves as laid-back and happy.

Source: "AKC Mission Statement" and "History of the American Kennel Club," American Kennel Club, http://www.akc.org, accessed March 20, 2006; "AKC Responsible Dog Ownership Day Survey Reveals Rift between Dog and Non-Dog Owners," American Kennel Club news release, http://www.akc.org, accessed March 20, 2006.

© IMAGE SOURCE PINK/JUPITER IMAGES

Quota Sampling

Suppose a firm wishes to investigate consumers who currently subscribe to an HDTV (high definition television) service. The researchers may wish to ensure that each brand of HDTV televisions is included proportionately in the sample. Strict probability sampling procedures would likely underrepresent certain brands and overrepresent other brands. If the selection process were left strictly to chance, some variation would be expected.

As seen in the Research Snapshot "American Kennel Club Tries to Keep Pet Owners out of the Doghouse," the purpose of **quota sampling** is to ensure that the various subgroups in a population are represented on pertinent sample characteristics to the exact extent that the investigators desire. Stratified sampling, a probability sampling procedure described in the next section, also has this objective, but it should not be confused with quota sampling. In quota sampling, the interviewer has a quota to achieve. For example, an interviewer in a particular city may be assigned 100 interviews, 35 with owners of Sony TVs, 30 with owners of Samsung TVs, 18 with owners of Panasonic TVs, and the rest with owners of other brands. The interviewer is responsible for finding enough people to meet the quota. Aggregating the various interview quotas yields a sample that represents the desired proportion of each subgroup.

quota sampling
A nonprobability sampling procedure that ensures that various subgroups of a population will be represented on pertinent characteristics to the exact extent that the investigator desires.

POSSIBLE SOURCES OF BIAS

The logic of classifying the population by pertinent subgroups is essentially sound. However, because respondents are selected according to a convenience sampling procedure rather than on a probability basis (as in stratified sampling), the haphazard selection of subjects may introduce bias. For example, a college professor hired some of his students to conduct a quota sample based on age. When analyzing the data, the professor discovered that almost all the people in the "under 25 years" category were college-educated. Interviewers, being human, tend to prefer to interview people who are similar to themselves.

Quota samples tend to include people who are easily found, willing to be interviewed, and middle class. Fieldworkers are given considerable leeway to exercise their judgment concerning selection of actual respondents. Interviewers often concentrate their interviewing in areas with heavy pedestrian traffic such as downtowns, shopping malls, and college campuses. Those who interview door-to-door learn quickly that quota requirements are difficult to meet by interviewing whoever happens to appear at the door. People who are more likely to stay at home generally share a less active lifestyle and are less likely to be meaningfully employed. One interviewer related a story of working in an upper-middle-class neighborhood. After a few blocks, he arrived in a neighborhood of mansions. Feeling that most of the would-be respondents were above his station, the interviewer skipped these houses because he felt uncomfortable knocking on doors that would be answered by these people or their hired help.

ADVANTAGES OF QUOTA SAMPLING

The major advantages of quota sampling over probability sampling are speed of data collection, lower costs, and convenience. Although quota sampling has many problems, carefully supervised data collection may provide a representative sample of the various subgroups within a population. Quota sampling may be appropriate when the researcher knows that a certain demographic group is more likely to refuse to cooperate with a survey. For instance, if older men are more likely to refuse, a higher quota can be set for this group so that the proportion of each demographic category will be similar to the proportions in the population. A number of laboratory experiments also rely on quota sampling because it is difficult to find a sample of the general population willing to visit a laboratory to participate in an experiment.

Snowball Sampling

snowball sampling

A sampling procedure in which initial respondents are selected by probability methods and additional respondents are obtained from information provided by the initial respondents.

A variety of procedures known as **snowball sampling** involve using probability methods for an initial selection of respondents and then obtaining additional respondents through information provided by the initial respondents. This technique is used to locate members of rare populations by referrals. Suppose a manufacturer of sports equipment is considering marketing a mahogany croquet set for serious adult players. This market is certainly small. An extremely large sample would be necessary to find 100 serious adult croquet players. It would be much more economical to survey, say, 300 people, find 15 croquet players, and ask them for the names of other players.

TOTHEPOINT

Make everything as simple as possible, but not simpler.

—Albert Einstein

Reduced sample sizes and costs are clear-cut advantages of snowball sampling. However, bias is likely to enter into the study because a person suggested by someone also in the sample has a higher probability of being similar to the first person. If there are major differences between those who are widely known by others and those who are not, this technique may present some serious problems. However, snowball sampling may be used to locate and recruit heavy users, such as consumers who buy more than 50 compact discs per year, for focus groups. As the focus group is not expected to be a generalized sample, snowball sampling may be appropriate.

Probability Sampling

All probability sampling techniques are based on chance selection procedures. Because the probability sampling process is random, the bias inherent in nonprobability sampling procedures is eliminated. Note that the term *random* refers to the procedure for selecting the sample; it does not describe the data in the sample. *Randomness* characterizes a procedure whose outcome cannot be predicted because it depends on chance. Randomness should not be thought of as unplanned or unscientific—it is the basis of all probability sampling techniques. This section will examine the various probability sampling methods.

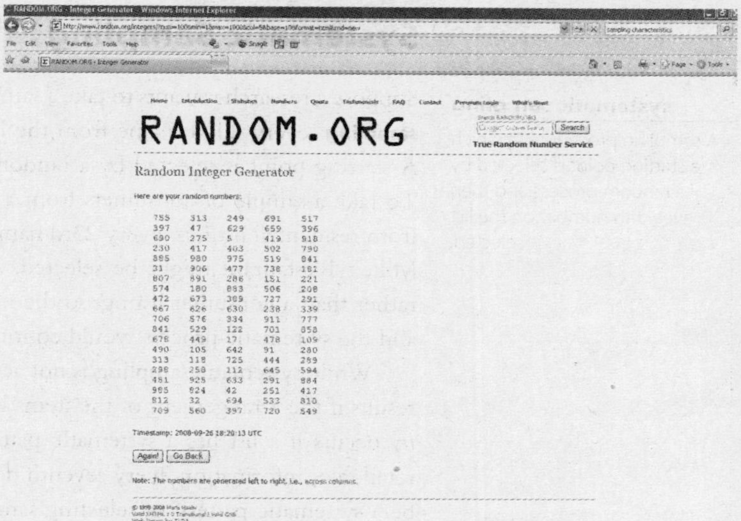

COURTESY OF © 1998–2008 MADS HAAHR

Random number tables are also found on the Internet. This is just one example.

Simple Random Sampling

The sampling procedure that ensures each element in the population will have an equal chance of being included in the sample is called **simple random sampling**. Examples include drawing names from a hat and selecting the winning raffle ticket from a large drum. If the names or raffle tickets are thoroughly stirred, each person or ticket should have an equal chance of being selected. In contrast to other, more complex types of probability sampling, this process is simple because it requires only one stage of sample selection.

Although drawing names or numbers out of a fishbowl, using a spinner, rolling dice, or turning a roulette wheel may be an appropriate way to draw a sample from a small population, when populations consist of large numbers of elements, sample selection is based on tables of random numbers or computer-generated random numbers.

Suppose a researcher is interested in selecting a simple random sample of all the Honda dealers in California, New Mexico, Arizona, and Nevada. Each dealer's name is assigned a number from 1 to 105. The numbers can be written on paper slips, and all the slips can be placed in a bowl. After the slips of paper have been thoroughly mixed, one is selected for each sampling unit. Thus, if the sample size is 35, the selection procedure must be repeated 34 times after the first slip has been selected. Mixing the slips after each selection will ensure that those at the bottom of the bowl will continue to have an equal chance of being selected in the sample.

simple random sampling
A sampling procedure that assures each element in the population of an equal chance of being included in the sample.

To use a table of random numbers, a serial number is first assigned to each element of the population. Assuming the population is 99,999 or fewer, five-digit numbers may be selected from the table of random numbers merely by reading the numbers in any column or row, moving up, down, left, or right. A random starting point should be selected at the outset.

The random-digit dialing technique of sample selection requires that the researcher identify the exchange or exchanges of interest (the first three numbers) and then use a table of numbers to select the next four numbers. In practice, the exchanges are not always selected randomly. Researchers who wanted to find out whether Americans of African descent prefer being called "black" or "African-American" narrowed their sampling frame by selecting exchanges associated with geographic areas where the proportion of the population (African-Americans/blacks) was at least 30 percent. The reasoning was that this made the survey procedure far more efficient, considering that the researchers were trying to contact a group representing less than 15 percent of U.S. households. This initial judgment sampling raises the same issues we discussed regarding nonprobability sampling. In this study, the researchers found that respondents were most likely to prefer the term *black* if they had attended schools that were about half black and half white.[5] If such experiences influence the answers to the question of interest to the researchers, the fact that blacks who live in predominantly white communities are underrepresented may introduce bias into the results.

Systematic Sampling

systematic sampling

A sampling procedure in which a starting point is selected by a random process and then every *n*th number on the list is selected.

Suppose a researcher wants to take a sample of 1,000 from a list of 200,000 names. With **systematic sampling**, every 200th name from the list would be drawn. The procedure is extremely simple. A starting point is selected by a random process; then every *n*th number on the list is selected. To take a sample of consumers from a rural telephone directory that does not separate business from residential listings, every 23rd name might be selected as the *sampling interval.* In the process, Mike's Restaurant might be selected. This unit is inappropriate because it is a business listing rather than a consumer listing, so the next eligible name would be selected as the sampling unit, and the systematic process would continue.

While systematic sampling is not actually a random selection procedure, it does yield random results if the arrangement of the items in the list is random in character. The problem of *periodicity* occurs if a list has a systematic pattern—that is, if it is not random in character. Collecting retail sales information every seventh day would result in a distorted sample because there would be a systematic pattern of selecting sampling units—sales for only one day of the week (perhaps Monday) would be sampled. If the first 50 names on a list of contributors to a charity were extremely large donors, periodicity bias might occur in sampling every 200th name. Periodicity is rarely a problem for most sampling in marketing research, but researchers should be aware of the possibility.

Stratified Sampling

The usefulness of dividing the population into subgroups, or *strata,* whose members are more or less equal with respect to some characteristic was illustrated in our discussion of quota sampling. The first step is the same for both stratified and quota sampling: choosing strata on the basis of existing information—for example, classifying retail outlets based on annual sales volume. However, the process of selecting sampling units within the strata differs substantially. In **stratified sampling**, a subsample is drawn using simple random sampling within each stratum. This is not true of quota sampling.

stratified sampling

A probability sampling procedure in which simple random subsamples that are more or less equal on some characteristic are drawn from within each stratum of the population.

The reason for taking a stratified sample is to obtain a more efficient sample than would be possible with simple random sampling. Suppose, for example, that urban and rural groups have widely different attitudes toward energy conservation, but members within each group hold very similar attitudes. Random sampling error will be reduced with the use of stratified sampling, because each group is internally homogeneous but there are comparative differences between groups. More technically, a smaller standard error may result from this stratified sampling because the groups will be adequately represented when strata are combined.

Another reason for selecting a stratified sample is to ensure that the sample will accurately reflect the population on the basis of the criterion or criteria used for stratification. This is a concern because occasionally simple random sampling yields a disproportionate number of one group or another and the sample ends up being less representative than it could be.

A researcher can select a stratified sample as follows. First, a variable (sometimes several variables) is identified as an efficient basis for stratification. A stratification variable must be a characteristic of the population elements known to be related to the dependent variable or other variables of interest. The variable chosen should increase homogeneity within each stratum and increase heterogeneity between strata. The stratification variable usually is a categorical variable or one easily converted into categories (that is, subgroups). For example, a pharmaceutical company interested in measuring how often physicians prescribe a certain drug might choose physicians' training as a basis for stratification. In this example the mutually exclusive strata are MDs (medical doctors) and ODs (osteopathic doctors).

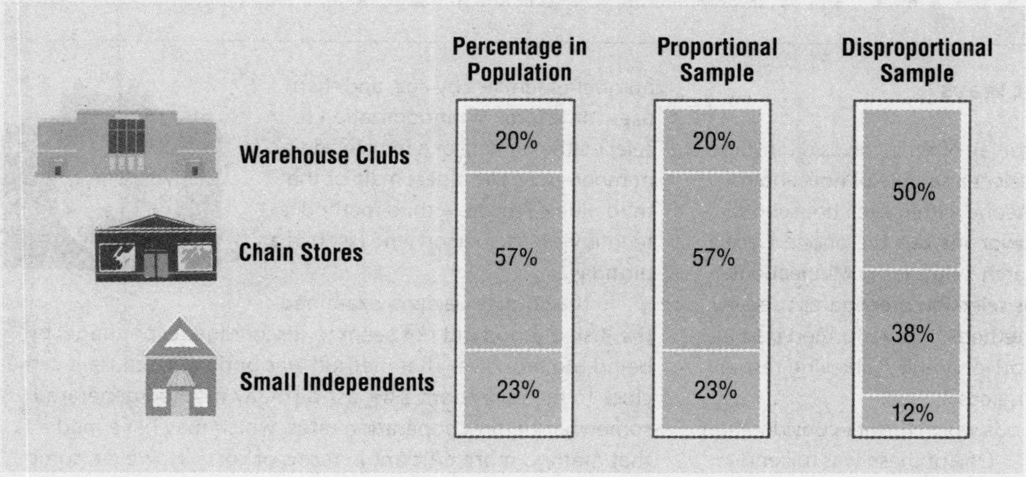

EXHIBIT 16.5
Disproportional Sampling: Hypothetical Example

Next, for each separate subgroup or stratum, a list of population elements must be obtained. (If such lists are not available, they can be costly to prepare, and if a complete listing is not available, a true stratified probability sample cannot be selected.) Using a table of random numbers or some other device, a *separate* simple random sample is then taken within each stratum. Of course, the researcher must determine how large a sample to draw for each stratum. This issue is discussed in the following section.

Proportional versus Disproportional Sampling

If the number of sampling units drawn from each stratum is in proportion to the relative population size of the stratum, the sample is a **proportional stratified sample**. Sometimes, however, a disproportional stratified sample will be selected to ensure an adequate number of sampling units in every stratum. Sampling more heavily in a given stratum than its relative population size warrants is not a problem if the primary purpose of the research is to estimate some characteristic separately for each stratum and if researchers are concerned about assessing the differences among strata. Consider, however, the percentages of retail outlets presented in Exhibit 16.5. A proportional sample would have the same percentages as in the population. Although there is a small percentage of warehouse club stores, the average dollar sales volume for the warehouse club store stratum is quite large and varies substantially from the average store size for the smaller independent stores. To avoid overrepresenting the chain stores and independent stores (with smaller sales volume) in the sample, a disproportional sample is taken.

proportional stratified sample
A stratified sample in which the number of sampling units drawn from each stratum is in proportion to the population size of that stratum.

In a **disproportional stratified sample** the sample size for each stratum is not allocated in proportion to the population size but is dictated by analytical considerations, such as variability in store sales volume. The logic behind this procedure relates to the general argument for sample size: As variability increases, sample size must increase to provide accurate estimates. Thus, the strata that exhibit the greatest variability are sampled more heavily to increase sample efficiency—that is, produce smaller random sampling error. Complex formulas (beyond the scope of an introductory course in business research) have been developed to determine sample size for each stratum. A simplified rule of thumb for understanding the concept of optimal allocation is that the stratum sample size increases for strata of larger sizes with the greatest relative variability. Other complexities arise in determining population estimates. For example, when disproportional stratified sampling is used, the estimated mean for each stratum has to be weighed according to the number of elements in each stratum in order to calculate the total population mean.

disproportional stratified sample
A stratified sample in which the sample size for each stratum is allocated according to analytical considerations.

RESEARCH SNAPSHOT

Who's at Home? Different Ways to Select Respondents

A carefully planned telephone survey often involves multistage sampling. First the researchers select a sample of households to call, and then they select someone within each household to interview—not necessarily whoever answers the phone. Cecilie Gaziano, a researcher with Research Solutions in Minneapolis, conducted an analysis of various selection procedures used in prior research, looking for the methods that performed best in terms of generating a representative sample, achieving respondent cooperation, and minimizing costs.

Gaziano found several methods worth further consideration. One of these was full enumeration, in which the interviewer requests a list of all the adults living in the household, generates a random number, uses the number to select a name from that list, and asks to speak with that person. In a variation of this approach, called the *Kish method,* the interviewer requests the number of males by age and the number of females by age, and then uses some form of randomization to select either a male or a female and a number—say, the oldest male or the third oldest female. A third method is to interview the person who last had a birthday.

© STONE/GETTY IMAGES

In the studies Gaziano examined, the Kish method did not seem to discourage respondents by being too intrusive. That method was popular because it came close to being random. The last-birthday method generated somewhat better cooperation rates, which may have made that method more efficient in terms of costs. However, some question whether the person on the phone accurately knows the birthdays of every household member, especially in households with several adults. Methods that request the gender of household members also address a challenge of getting a representative phone survey sample: females tend to answer the phone more often than males.

Source: Gaziano, Cecilie, "Comparative Analysis of Within-Household Respondent Selection Techniques," *Public Opinion Quarterly* 69 (Spring 2005), 124–157; "Communication Researchers and Policy-Making," *Journal of Broadcasting & Electronic Media* (March 2004), http://www.allbusiness.com, accessed March 19, 2006.

© iStock

Cluster Sampling

cluster sampling
An economically efficient sampling technique in which the primary sampling unit is not the individual element in the population but a large cluster of elements; clusters are selected randomly.

The purpose of **cluster sampling** is to sample economically while retaining the characteristics of a probability sample. Consider a researcher who must conduct five hundred personal interviews with consumers scattered throughout the United States. Travel costs are likely to be enormous because the amount of time spent traveling will be substantially greater than the time spent in the interviewing process. If an aspirin marketer can assume the product will be equally successful in Phoenix and Baltimore, or if a frozen pizza manufacturer assumes its product will suit the tastes of Texans equally as well as Oregonians, cluster sampling may be used to represent the United States.

In a cluster sample, the primary sampling unit is no longer the individual element in the population (for example, grocery stores) but a larger cluster of elements located in proximity to one another (for example, cities). The *area sample* is the most popular type of cluster sample. A grocery store researcher, for example, may randomly choose several geographic areas as primary sampling units and then interview all or a sample of grocery stores within the geographic clusters. Interviews are confined to these clusters only. No interviews occur in other clusters. Cluster sampling is classified as a probability sampling technique because of either the random selection of clusters or the random selection of elements within each cluster. Some examples of clusters appear in Exhibit 16.6

Cluster samples frequently are used when lists of the sample population are not available. For example, when researchers investigating employees and self-employed workers for a downtown revitalization project found that a comprehensive list of these people was not available, they decided

EXHIBIT 16.6
Examples of Clusters

Population Element	Possible Clusters in the United States
U.S. adult population	States
	Counties
	Metropolitan Statistical Areas
	Census Tracts
	Blocks
	Households
College seniors	Colleges
Manufacturing firms	Counties
	Metropolitan Statistical Areas
	Localities
	Plants
Airline travelers	Airports
	Planes
Sports fans	Football Stadiums
	Basketball Arenas
	Baseball Parks

to take a cluster sample, selecting organizations (business and government) as the clusters. A sample of firms within the central business district was developed, using stratified probability sampling, to identify clusters. Next, individual workers within the firms (clusters) were randomly selected and interviewed concerning the central business district.

Ideally a cluster should be as heterogeneous as the population itself—a mirror image of the population. A problem may arise with cluster sampling if the characteristics and attitudes of the elements within the cluster are too similar. For example, geographic neighborhoods tend to have residents of the same socioeconomic status. Students at a university tend to share similar beliefs. This problem may be mitigated by constructing clusters composed of diverse elements and by selecting a large number of sampled clusters.

Multistage Area Sampling

multistage area sampling
Sampling that involves using a combination of two or more probability sampling techniques.

So far we have described two-stage cluster sampling. **Multistage area sampling** involves two or more steps that combine some of the probability techniques already described. Typically, geographic areas are randomly selected in progressively smaller (lower-population) units. For example, a political pollster investigating an election in Arizona might first choose counties within the state to ensure that the different areas are represented in the sample. In the second step, precincts within the selected counties may be chosen. As a final step, the pollster may select blocks (or households) within the precincts, then interview all the blocks (or households) within the geographic area. Researchers may take as many steps as necessary to achieve a representative sample.

The Bureau of the Census provides maps, population information, demographic characteristics for population statistics, and so on, by several small geographical areas; these may be useful in sampling. Census classifications of small geographical areas vary, depending on the extent of urbanization within Metropolitan Statistical Areas (MSAs) or counties. Exhibit 16.7 illustrates the geographic hierarchy inside urbanized areas.

EXHIBIT 16.7
Geographic Hierarchy inside Urbanized Areas

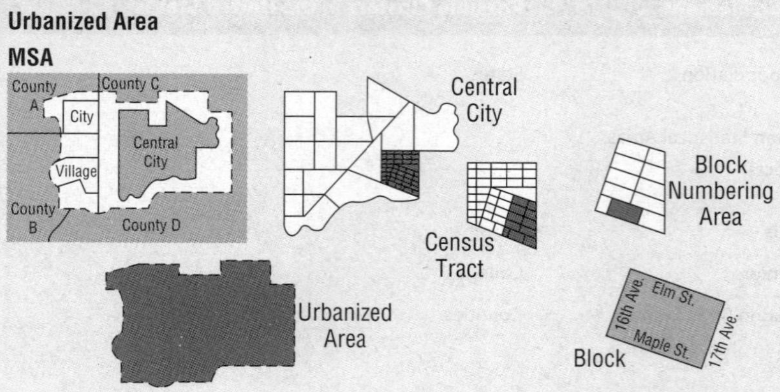

Source: From U.S. Bureau of the Census, "Geography—Concepts and Products," Washington, DC, August 1985, p. 3.

Concepts of Accuracy and Diversity in Sampling

The accuracy and diversity of sample can be understood through the concept of sampling distribution. To understand these concepts, consider that there is a population of sesame plant that has a population mean of fatty acid content in sesame seed which can be denoted by population characteristic M (termed as parameter). M is defined as the average amount of fatty acid content in sesame seeds variety grown on a plot, having a total of say $N = 100$ plants. Under the given set of Agro climatic condition, the sesame variety will have an inherent value of population mean of fatty acid content.

If we take a sample of size $n = 10$ plants from the plot using some suitable random sampling design, we shall get a sample average of the seeds of 10 plants. If we calculate the sample average which is denoted as m based on the 10 plants in the sample we shall get one value. The sample, thus, provides us with an estimate m for the inherent true population value M.

It is quite natural that the value of sample average m will rarely, if ever, match exactly the value of population mean M. One obvious reason for this difference is the fact that the sample contains only a small subset of the total population which may be representative of the population but not exactly equal to the population parameter value. Hence, there will be some amount of error in the estimate, and the estimated sample average will be different from the actual population mean.

However, we may be able to take ${}^{100}C_{10}$ number of samples, each of size $n = 10$, from a population of $N = 100$ plants. Each of the ${}^{N}C_{n}$ possible samples will have the same chance of being the sample that is actually used. Each such sample will produce a different sample mean m. If we plot frequency distribution of all these ${}^{N}C_{n}$ values of m, the distribution will have an expected value of average fatty acid content in the sample which can be denoted as $E(m)$ and read as expected value of m. The distribution will also have a standard deviation, and the value of the standard deviation will be $\sigma/\sqrt{n}$, where σ is population standard deviation. In such case, the sample mean $E(m)$ is said to be an unbiased estimate of the population mean M.

The three quantities M, $E(m)$, and $\sigma/\sqrt{n}$ would provide a basis to define the concepts of accuracy of any sample statistic m as an estimate of the population parameter M. We may also be able to calculate the bias in the estimate from the expected value of sample average m, and actual population mean value M. The expression of *bias*, $B(m)$, of an estimate m is defined as:

$$B(m) = E(m) - M$$

We can also calculate the amount of sampling error in the estimate of m. The expression of sampling error, $S(m)$, in an estimate m is:

$$S(m) = m - E(m)$$

We can also calculate through this procedure the estimated error and mean square error (MSE) of an estimate m. The *estimation error*, $ES(m)$, of an estimate m is defined as:

$$ES(m) = m - M = [\{m - E(m)\} + \{E(m) - M\}]$$

Similarly, the *mean square error* (MSE) of an estimate *m* is defined as:

$$\text{MSE}(m) = E[\{m - M\}^2] = E[\{m - E(m)\}^2] + \{E(m) - M\}^2$$

(Covariance term is zero due to independence.)

$$= \text{var}(m) + [B(m)]^2$$

= sampling variance + $(\text{Bias})^2$

From the above equation of MSE we can see that the first term is the expected value of square of the sampling errors. This value is called sampling variance of estimate *m*. The second term of the equation is square of the bias of estimate *m*. Hence, it can be said that the total amount of uncertainty involved in estimate of *m* measured by MSE (*m*) is due to sampling error and bias.

We can also calculate the total error of estimate *m*. The *total error*, $TE(m)$ is equal to:

$$TE(m) = [\text{MSE}(m)]^{1/2} = \{\text{var}(m) + [B(m)]^2\}^{1/2}$$

Hence, we can infer that for an unbiased estimate, $TE(m) = [\text{var}(m)]^{1/2}$ since bias is absent.

In view of above we may conclude that the accuracy of an estimate *m* is a function of the bias in the estimate. Less is the bias, more accurate is the estimate.

Effect of Diversity on Precision

Confidence interval of sampling is given by the equation

$$CI_x = x \pm Z_{95\%} \times \sigma / \sqrt{n}$$

This shows that for a given sample size *n* and confidence interval, the factor that can change accuracy is variation. Confidence interval is inversely proportional to diversity. As diversity increases, the variance of the sample also increases. This leads to increase in confidence interval. This results in reduction in precision of sampling. Thus, precision of sampling can be improved by reducing the diversity with the sampling units.

What Is the Appropriate Sample Design?

A researcher who must decide on the most appropriate sample design for a specific project will identify a number of sampling criteria and evaluate the relative importance of each criterion before selecting a sampling design. This section outlines and briefly discusses the most common criteria. Exhibit 16.9 summarizes the advantages and disadvantages of each nonprobability sampling technique, and Exhibit 16.10 does the same for the probability sampling techniques.

Degree of Accuracy

Selecting a representative sample is important to all researchers. However, the degree of accuracy required or the researcher's tolerance for sampling and nonsampling error may vary from project to project, especially when cost savings or another benefit may be a trade-off for a reduction in accuracy.

For example, when the sample is being selected for an exploratory research project, a high priority may not be placed on accuracy because a highly representative sample may not be necessary. For other, more conclusive projects, the sample result must precisely represent a population's characteristics, and the researcher must be willing to spend the time and money needed to achieve accuracy.

EXHIBIT 16.8 **Comparison of Sampling Techniques: Nonprobability Samples**

Nonprobability Samples			
Description	**Cost and Degree of Use**	**Advantages**	**Disadvantages**
1. *Convenience:* The researcher uses the most convenient sample or economical sample units.	Very low cost, extensively used	No need for list of population	Unrepresentative samples likely; random sampling error estimates cannot be made; projecting data beyond sample is relatively risky
2. *Judgment:* An expert or experienced researcher selects the sample to fulfill a purpose, such as ensuring that all members have a certain characteristic.	Moderate cost, average use	Useful for certain types of forecasting; sample guaranteed to meet a specific objective	Bias due to expert's beliefs may make sample unrepresentative; projecting data beyond sample is risky
3. *Quota:* The researcher classifies the population by pertinent properties, determines the desired proportion to sample from each class, and fixes quotas for each interviewer.	Moderate cost, very extensively used	Introduces some stratification of population; requires no list of population	Introduces bias in researcher's classification of subjects; nonrandom selection within classes means error from population cannot be estimated; projecting data beyond sample is risky
4. *Snowball:* Initial respondents are selected by probability samples; additional respondents are obtained by referral from initial respondents.	Low cost, used in special situations	Useful in locating members of rare populations	High bias because sample units are not independent; projecting data beyond sample is risky

EXHIBIT 16.9 **Comparison of Sampling Techniques: Probability Samples**

Probability Samples			
Description	**Cost and Degree of Use**	**Advantages**	**Disadvantages**
1. *Simple random:* The researcher assigns each member of the sampling frame a number, then selects sample units by random method.	High cost, moderately used in practice (most common in random digit dialing and with computerized sampling frames)	Only minimal advance knowledge of population needed; easy to analyze data and compute error	Requires sampling frame to work from; does not use knowledge of population that researcher may have; larger errors for same sampling size than in stratified sampling; respondents may be widely dispersed, hence cost may be higher
2. *Systematic:* The researcher uses natural ordering or the order of the sampling frame, selects an arbitrary starting point, then selects items at a preselected interval.	Moderate cost, moderately used	Simple to draw sample; easy to check	If sampling interval is related to periodic ordering of the population, may introduce increased variability
3. *Stratified:* The researcher divides the population into groups and randomly selects subsamples from each group. Variations include proportional, disproportional, and optimal allocation of subsample sizes.	High cost, moderately used	Ensures representation of all groups in sample; characteristics of each stratum can be estimated and comparisons made; reduces variability for same sample size	Requires accurate information on proportion in each stratum; if stratified lists are not already available, they can be costly to prepare
4. *Cluster:* The researcher selects sampling units at random, then does a complete observation of all units or draws a probability sample in the group.	Low cost, frequently used	If clusters geographically defined, yields lowest field cost; requires listing of all clusters, but of individuals only within clusters; can estimate characteristics of clusters as well as of population	Larger error for comparable size than with other probability samples; researcher must be able to assign population members to unique cluster or else duplication or omission of individuals will result
5. *Multistage:* Progressively smaller areas are selected in each stage by some combination of the first four techniques.	High cost, frequently used, especially in nationwide surveys	Depends on techniques combined	Depends on techniques combined

RESEARCH SNAPSHOT

New on Campus: Student Adjustment to College Life

Transitions to new jobs, new cities, or new work environments can create physical and emotional stress on people. Stress and tension can also impact students when they first arrive at a college and university. The new environment, new classroom experience, and a lack of friends can create psychological distress that can lead to alcohol or substance abuse, physical health concerns, and mental stresses or strains. The question is how students adjust to this new environment. To answer this question, researchers had to conduct a panel study, where incoming students were assessed on their psychological traits and coping behaviors upon entry, and were then resurveyed at the end of their first year.

The results indicate that those students who engaged in negative coping behaviors or who had perfectionist tendencies would more likely have poor adjustment outcomes after the first year. However, for those students who were optimistic and socially oriented, these students were much more likely to adjust to the new college environment.

The use of a panel approach was necessary, since the researchers were interested in the change that occurred within a sample of students over time. These results can be used by college administrators to develop newcomer programs or experiences that students can use to adjust to their new college environment. College is stressful enough—it is critical that new students understand that help and support are there if they need it!

Source: Pritchard, M.E., G. S. Wilson, and B. Yamnitz, "What Predicts Adjustment Among College Students? A Longitudinal Study," *Journal of American College Health* 56, no. 1 (2007), 15–21.

© iStock

Resources

The cost associated with the different sampling techniques varies tremendously. If the researcher's financial and human resources are restricted, certain options will have to be eliminated. For a graduate student working on a master's thesis, conducting a national survey is almost always out of the question because of limited resources. Managers concerned with the cost of the research versus the value of the information often will opt to save money by using a nonprobability sampling design rather than make the decision to conduct no research at all.

Time

A researcher who needs to meet a deadline or complete a project quickly will be more likely to select a simple, less time-consuming sample design. As seen in the Research Snapshot "Who's at Home? Different Ways to Select Respondents," a telephone survey that uses a sample based on random-digit dialing, when conducted carefully, takes considerably less time than a survey that uses an elaborate disproportional stratified sample.

Advance Knowledge of the Population

Advance knowledge of population characteristics, such as the availability of lists of population members, is an important criterion. In many cases, however, no list of population elements will be available to the researcher. This is especially true when the population element is defined by ownership of a particular product or brand, by experience in performing a specific job task, or on a qualitative dimension. A lack of adequate lists may automatically rule out systematic sampling, stratified sampling, or other sampling designs, or it may dictate that a preliminary study, such as a short telephone survey using random digit dialing, be conducted to generate information to build a sampling frame for the primary study. In many developing countries, things like reverse directories are rare. Thus, researchers planning sample designs have to work around this limitation.

National versus Local Project

Geographic proximity of population elements will influence sample design. When population elements are unequally distributed geographically, a cluster sample may become much more attractive.

Internet Sampling Is Unique

Internet surveys allow researchers to reach a large sample rapidly—both an advantage and a disadvantage. Sample size requirements can be met overnight or in some cases almost instantaneously. A researcher can, for instance, release a survey during the morning in the Eastern Standard Time zone and have all sample size requirements met before anyone on the West Coast wakes up. If rapid response rates are expected, the sample for an Internet survey should be metered out across all time zones. In addition, people in some populations are more likely to go online during the weekend than on a weekday. If the researcher can anticipate a day-of-the-week effect, the survey should be kept open long enough so that all sample units have the opportunity to participate in the research project.

The ease and low cost of an Internet survey also has contributed to a flood of online questionnaires, some more formal than others. As a result, frequent Internet users may be more selective about which surveys they bother answering. Researchers investigating college students' attitudes toward environmental issues found that those who responded to an e-mail request that had been sent to all students tended to be more concerned about the environment than students who were contacted individually through systematic sampling. The researchers concluded that students who cared about the issues were more likely to respond to the online survey.[6]

Another disadvantage of Internet surveys is the lack of computer ownership and Internet access among certain segments of the population. A sample of Internet users is representative only of Internet users, who tend to be younger, better educated, and more affluent than the general population. This is not to say that all Internet samples are unrepresentative of all target populations. Nevertheless, when using Internet surveys, researchers should be keenly aware of potential sampling problems that can arise due to systematic characteristics of heavy computer users.

Web Site Visitors

As noted earlier, many Internet surveys are conducted with volunteer respondents who visit an organization's Web site intentionally or by happenstance. These *unrestricted samples* are clearly convenience samples. They may not be representative because of the haphazard manner by which many respondents arrived at a particular Web site or because of self-selection bias.

A better technique for sampling Web site visitors is to randomly select sampling units. SurveySite, a company that specializes in conducting Internet surveys, collects data by using its "pop-up survey" software. The software selects Web visitors at random and "pops up" a small JavaScript window asking the person if he or she wants to participate in an evaluation survey. If the person clicks yes, a new window containing the online survey opens up. The person can then browse the site at his or her own pace and switch to the survey at any time to express an opinion.[7]

Randomly selecting Web site visitors can cause a problem. It is possible to overrepresent frequent visitors to the site and thus represent site visits rather than visitors. Several programming techniques and technologies (using cookies, registration data, or prescreening) are available to help accomplish more representative sampling based on site traffic.[8] Details of these techniques are beyond the scope of this discussion.

This type of random sampling is most valuable if the target population is defined as visitors to a particular Web site. Evaluation and analysis of visitors' perceptions and experiences of the Web site would be a typical survey objective with this type of sample. Researchers who have broader interests may obtain Internet samples in a variety of other ways.

In Internet sampling, sampling procedure is conducted through the Internet. While in most cases the responses are collected through e-mails, there are several Web sites which also help collecting responses. There are several advantages and disadvantages of e-mail sampling. Some of the advantages are (1) convenience of the respondents; (2) it can be conducted very fast; (3) reminders can be sent at a regular basis; and (4) the cost of getting responses is low. However, Internet sampling does have some serious disadvantages like (1) it may not be representative of the population since access to the Internet is very limited in India and other developing countries and (2) personal persuasion cannot be made and hence response rate is very low. For example, if HUL wanted to conduct a survey of housewives to determine their preference of liquid detergents, an Internet survey would be a bad choice as this would not be a representation of the target population.

Internet sampling is authentic when the target population lives in cities. In such a case, the sample will be a good representative of the target population. As the Internet penetration increases, Internet sampling also becomes more relevant for research. Internet sampling may also be useful for the products that are sold through Web sites. For example, Internet sampling would be a good choice for a company like eBay to find out the preferences of its target customers.

Chance of sampling error is also high in Internet sampling and the sample may not be representative of the population. Another difficulty associated with Internet sampling is that one respondent may give more than one response. This is called "stuffing the ballot."

There are two types of Internet sampling techniques: (1) online intercepted method and (2) online recruited method.

Online intercepted method. In this method, visitors to a web site are intercepted and showed a pop to participate in a survey. Online intercepted method can be used both to random as well as non-random interception. Random interception online sampling ensures that respondents are selected without any bias and improves representativeness than a nonrandom interception method.

Online recruited method. Internet sampling is also done through panel and non-panel sampling. Several market research companies maintain an online panel to ensure steady source of data. These companies recruit panel members based on certain criteria of the consumers and offer rewards points to these members for being part of the panel. To maintain reliability and validity of the survey the panel members are given individual identification number as well as password.

Panel Samples

Drawing a probability sample from an established consumer panel or other prerecruited membership panel is a popular, scientific, and effective method for creating a sample of Internet users. Typically, sampling from a panel yields a high response rate because panel members have already agreed to cooperate with the research organization's e-mail or Internet surveys. Often panel members are compensated for their time with a sweepstakes, a small cash incentive, or redeemable points. Further, because the panel has already supplied demographic characteristics and other information from previous questionnaires, researchers are able to select panelists based on product ownership, lifestyle, or other characteristics. As seen in the Research Snapshots on the Current Population Survey and student adjustment, a variety of sampling methods and data transformation techniques can be applied to ensure that sample results are representative of the general public or a targeted population.

Consider Harris Interactive Inc., an Internet survey research organization that maintains a panel of more than 6.5 million individuals in the United States. In the early twenty-first century, Harris plans to expand this panel to between 10 million and 15 million and to include an additional 10 million people internationally.[9] A database this large allows the company to draw simple random samples, stratified samples, and quota samples from its panel members.

Harris Interactive finds that two demographic groups are not fully accessible via Internet sampling: people of ages 65 and older—a group that is rapidly growing—and those with annual incomes of less than $15,000. In contrast, 18- to 25-year-olds—a group that historically has been very hard to reach by traditional research methods—are now extremely easy to reach over the Internet.[10]

TIPS OF THE TRADE

- Business research rarely requires a census.
- Accurately defining the target population is critical in research involving forecasts of how that population will react to some event. Consider the following in defining the population.
    - Who are we not interested in?
    - What are the relevant market segment characteristics involved?
    - Is region important in defining the target population?
    - Is the issue being studied relevant to multiple populations?
    - Is a list available that contains all members of the population?
- Online panels are a practical reality in survey research. A sample can be quickly measured that matches the demographic profiles of the target population.
- As with all panels, the researcher faces a risk that systematic error is introduced in some way. For example, this sample may be higher in willingness to give opinions or may be responding only for an incentive.
    - The researcher should take extra steps such as including more screening questions to make sure the responses are representative of the target population.
- Convenience samples do have appropriate uses in behavioral research.

Convenience samples are particularly appropriate when:

- Exploratory research is conducted.
- The researcher is primarily interested in internal validity (testing a hypothesis under any condition) rather than external validity (understanding how much the sample results project to a target population).
- When cost and time constraints only allow a convenience sample:
    - Researchers can think backwards and project the population for whom the results apply to based on the nature of the convenience sample.
- Researchers seldom have a perfectly representative sample. Thus, the report should qualify the generalizability of the results based on sample limitations.

To ensure that survey results are representative, Harris Interactive uses a *propensity-weighting* scheme. The research company does parallel studies—by phone as well as over the Internet—to test the accuracy of its Internet data-gathering capabilities. Researchers look at the results of the telephone surveys and match those against the Internet-only survey results. Next, they use propensity weighting to adjust the results, taking into account the motivational and behavioral differences between the online and offline populations. (How propensity weighting adjusts for the difference between the Internet population and the general population is beyond the scope of this discussion.)

Panel sample or panel data contain observations of indicator variables of individual consumer or companies over a period of time across several variables on various respondents. In other words, panel sample of two or more dimensions. A two-dimensional panel sample typically has cross-sectional data over a period of time. However there could be more than two-dimensional panel data. An example of a multi dimensional panel data could be data of individual brands (first dimension) in different countries (second dimension) for several years (third dimension).

Recruited Ad Hoc Samples

Another means of obtaining an Internet sample is to obtain or create a sampling frame of e-mail addresses on an *ad hoc* basis. Researchers may create the sampling frame offline or online. Databases containing e-mail addresses can be compiled from many sources, including customer/client lists, advertising banners on pop-up windows that recruit survey participants, online sweepstakes, and registration forms that must be filled out in order to gain access to a particular Web site. Researchers may contact respondents by "snail mail" or by telephone to ask for their e-mail addresses and obtain permission for an Internet survey. Using offline techniques, such as random-digit dialing and short telephone screening interviews, to recruit respondents can be a very practical way to get a representative sample for an Internet survey. Companies anticipating future Internet research can develop a valuable database for sample recruitment by including e-mail addresses in their customer relationship databases (by inviting customers to provide that information on product registration cards, in telephone interactions, through on-site registration, etc.).[11]

Opt-in Lists

Survey Sampling International specializes in providing sampling frames and scientifically drawn samples. The company offers more than 3,500 lists of high-quality, targeted e-mail addresses of individuals who have given permission to receive e-mail messages related to a particular topic of interest. Survey Sampling International's database contains millions of Internet users who **opt in** for limited participation. An important feature of Survey Sampling International's database is that the company has each individual confirm and reconfirm interest in communicating about a topic before the person's e-mail address is added to the company's database.[12]

opt in

To give permission to receive selected e-mail, such as questionnaires, from a company with an Internet presence.

By whatever technique the sampling frame is compiled, it is important *not* to send unauthorized e-mail to respondents. If individuals do not *opt in* to receive e-mail from a particular organization, they may consider unsolicited survey requests to be spam. A researcher cannot expect high response rates from individuals who have not agreed to be surveyed. Spamming is not tolerated by experienced Internet users and can easily backfire, creating a host of problems—the most extreme being complaints to the Internet service provider (ISP), which may shut down the survey site.

Summary

1. Explain reasons for taking a sample rather than a complete census. Sampling is a procedure that uses a small number of units of a given population as a basis for drawing conclusions about the whole population. Sampling often is necessary because it would be practically impossible to conduct a census to measure characteristics of all units of a population. Samples also are needed in cases where measurement involves destruction of the measured unit.

2. Describe the process of identifying a target population and selecting a sampling frame. The first problem in sampling is to define the target population. Incorrect or vague definition of this population is likely to produce misleading results. A sampling frame is a list of elements, or individual members, of the overall population from which the sample is drawn. A sampling unit is a single element or group of elements subject to selection in the sample.

3. Compare random sampling and systematic (nonsampling) errors. There are two sources of discrepancy between the sample results and the population parameters. One, random sampling error, arises from chance variations of the sample from the population. Random sampling error is a function of sample size and may be estimated using the central-limit theorem, discussed in Chapter 17. Systematic, or nonsampling, error comes from sources such as sampling frame error, mistakes in recording responses, or nonresponses from persons who are not contacted or who refuse to participate.

4. Identify the types of nonprobability sampling, including their advantages and disadvantages. The two major classes of sampling methods are probability and nonprobability techniques. Nonprobability techniques include convenience sampling, judgment sampling, quota sampling, and snowball sampling. They are convenient to use, but there are no statistical techniques with which to measure their random sampling error.

5. Summarize the advantages and disadvantages of the various types of probability samples. Probability samples are based on chance selection procedures. These include simple random sampling, systematic sampling, stratified sampling, and cluster sampling. With these techniques, random sampling error can be accurately predicted.

6. Discuss how to choose an appropriate sample design, as well as challenges for Internet sampling. A researcher who must determine the most appropriate sampling design for a specific project will identify a number of sampling criteria and evaluate the relative importance of each criterion before selecting a design. The most common criteria concern accuracy requirements, available resources, time constraints, knowledge availability, and analytical requirements. Internet sampling presents some unique issues. Researchers must be aware that samples may be unrepresentative because not everyone has a computer or access to the Internet. Convenience samples drawn from Web site visitors can create problems. Drawing a probability sample from an established consumer panel or an ad hoc sampling frame whose members opt in can be effective.

Key Terms and Concepts

census, *417*
cluster sampling, *431*
convenience sampling, *425*
disproportional stratified sample, *430*
judgment (purposive) sampling, *426*
multistage area sampling, *432*
nonprobability sampling, *425*
opt in, *441*
population (universe), *417*
population element, *417*
primary sampling unit (PSU), *423*
probability sampling, *425*
proportional stratified sample, *430*
quota sampling, *427*
random sampling error, *424*
reverse directory, *422*
sample, *417*
sampling frame, *420*
sampling frame error, *422*
sampling unit, *423*
secondary sampling unit, *423*
simple random sampling, *428*
snowball sampling, *428*
stratified sampling, *430*
systematic sampling, *429*
tertiary sampling unit, *423*

Questions for Review and Critical Thinking

1. If you decide whether you want to see a new movie or television program on the basis of the "coming attractions" or television commercial previews, are you using a sampling technique or a scientific sampling technique?
2. Name some possible sampling frames for the following:
   a. Electrical contractors
   b. Tennis players
   c. Dog owners
   d. Foreign-car owners
   e. Wig and hair goods retailers
   f. Minority-owned businesses
   g. Men over six feet tall
3. Describe the difference between a probability sample and a nonprobability sample.
4. In what types of situations is conducting a census more appropriate than sampling? When is sampling more appropriate than taking a census?
5. Comment on the following sampling designs:
   a. A citizen's group interested in generating public and financial support for a new university basketball arena prints a questionnaire in area newspapers. Readers return the questionnaires by mail.
   b. A department store that wishes to examine whether it is losing or gaining customers draws a sample from its list of credit card holders by selecting every tenth name.
   c. A motorcycle manufacturer decides to research consumer characteristics by sending one hundred questionnaires to each of its dealers. The dealers will then use their sales records to track down buyers of this brand of motorcycle and distribute the questionnaires.
   d. An advertising executive suggests that advertising effectiveness be tested in the real world. A one-page ad is placed in a magazine. One-half of the space is used for the ad itself. On the other half, a short questionnaire requests that readers comment on the ad. An incentive will be given for the first thousand responses.
   e. A research company obtains a sample for a focus group through organized groups such as church groups, clubs, and schools. The organizations are paid for securing respondents; no individual is directly compensated.
   f. A researcher suggests replacing a consumer diary panel with a sample of customers who regularly shop at a supermarket that uses optical scanning equipment. The burden of recording purchases by humans will be replaced by computerized longitudinal data.
   g. A banner ad on a business-oriented Web site reads, "Are you a large company Sr. Executive? Qualified execs receive $50 for less than 10 minutes of time. Take the survey now!" Is this an appropriate way to select a sample of business executives?
6. When would a researcher use a judgment, or purposive, sample?
7. A telephone interviewer asks, "I would like to ask you about race. Are you Native American, Hispanic, African-American, Asian, or White?" After the respondent replies, the interviewer says, "We have conducted a large number of surveys with people of your background, and we do not need to question you further. Thank you for your cooperation." What type of sampling is likely being used?
8. If researchers know that consumers in various geographic regions respond quite differently to a product category, such as tomato sauce, is area sampling appropriate? Why or why not?
9. What are the benefits of stratified sampling?
10. What geographic units within a metropolitan area are useful for sampling?
11. Researchers often are particularly interested in the subset of a market that contributes most to sales (for example, heavy beer drinkers or large-volume retailers). What type of sampling might be best to use with such a subset? Why?
12. Outline the step-by-step procedure you would use to select the following:
    a. A simple random sample of 150 students at your university
    b. A quota sample of 50 light users and 50 heavy users of beer in a shopping mall intercept study
    c. A stratified sample of 50 mechanical engineers, 40 electrical engineers, and 40 civil engineers from the subscriber list of an engineering journal
13. Selection for jury duty is supposed to be a totally random process. Comment on the following computer selection procedures, and determine if they are indeed random:
    a. A program instructs the computer to scan the list of names and pick names that were next to those from the last scan.
    b. Three-digit numbers are randomly generated to select jurors from a list of licensed drivers. If the weight information listed on the license matches the random number, the person is selected.
    c. The juror source list is obtained by merging a list of registered voters with a list of licensed drivers.
14. **ETHICS** To ensure a good session, a company selects focus group members from a list of articulate participants instead of conducting random sampling. The client did not inquire about sample selection when it accepted the proposal. Is this ethical?

Research Activities

1. Phone directories are sometimes used for sampling frames. Go to **www.reversephonedirectory.com** and put in a phone number of someone you know in the reverse phone search (the number must be a listed number to get results). Comment on the the "Quick Facts" or "Population Finder" helpful) from this Web site. Find the data for Louisiana. Suppose a representative sample of the state of Louisiana is used to represent the current U.S. population. How well does Louisiana represent the United accuracy of the information and the appropriateness of phone directories as a representative sample.
2. **'NET** Go to the U.S. Census Bureau's home page at **http://www.census.gov**. Profiles of every state are available (you may find States overall? How well does Louisiana represent California or Maine? Use the profiles of the states and of the country to form your opinion.

Case 16.1 Who's Fishing?

© GETTY IMAGES/PHOTODISC GREEN

Washington Times columnist Gene Mueller writes about fishing and other outdoor sporting activities.[13] Mueller commented recently that although interest groups express concerns about the impact of saltwater fishers on the fish population, no one really knows how many people fish for recreation or how many fish they catch. This situation would challenge marketers interested in the population of anglers.

How could a researcher get an accurate sample? One idea would be to contact residents of coastal counties using random-digit dialing. This sampling frame would include many, if not all, of the people who fish in the ocean, but it would also include many people who do not fish—or who fish for business rather than recreation. A regional agency seeking to gather statistics on anglers, the Atlantic Coastal Cooperative Statistics Program, prefers to develop a sampling frame more related to people who fish.

Another idea would be to use state fishing license records. Privacy would be a drawback, however. Some people might not want their records shared, and they might withhold phone numbers. Further complicating this issue for Atlantic fishing is that most states in the Northeast do not require a license for saltwater fishing. Also exempt in some states are people who fish from the shore and from piers.

A political action group called the Recreational Fishing Alliance suggests that charter fishing businesses collect data.

Questions

1. Imagine that an agency or business has asked for help in gathering data about the number of sports anglers who fish off the coast of Georgia. What advice would you give about sampling? What method or combination of methods would generate the best results?
2. What other criteria besides accuracy would you expect to consider? What sampling methods could help you meet those criteria?

Case 16.2 Scientific Telephone Samples

© GETTY IMAGES/PHOTODISC GREEN

Scientific Telephone Samples (STS), located in Santa Ana, California, specializes in selling sampling frames for marketing research.[14] The STS sampling frame is based on a database of all working residential telephone exchanges in the United States. Thus, STS can draw from any part of the country—no matter how large or how small. The information is updated several times per year and cross-checked against area code and assigned exchange lists furnished by telephone companies. Exchange and/or working blocks designated for business or governmental telephones, mobile phones, and other commercial services are screened out.

STS can furnish almost any type of random-digit sample desired, including

- National samples (continental United States only, or with Alaska and Hawaii)
- Stratified national samples (by census region or division)
- Census region or division samples
- State samples
- Samples by MSA
- County samples
- Samples by zip code
- City samples by zip code
- Exchange samples generated from lists of three-digit exchanges
- Targeted random-digit dialing samples (including over 40 variables and special databases for high-income areas, Hispanics, African-Americans, and Asians)

STS offers two different methods for pulling working blocks. Either method can be used regardless of the geographic sampling unit (for example, state, county, zip). The two versions are Type A (unweighted) and Type B (weighted/efficient).

Type A samples are pulled using a strict definition of randomness. They are called "unweighted" samples because each working block has an equal chance of being selected to generate a random-digit number. Completed interviews from a Type A sample that has been dialed to exhaustion should be highly representative of the population under study.

Type B, or "efficient," samples are preweighted, so random-digit dialing numbers are created from telephone working blocks in proportion to the number of estimated household listings in each working block. Working blocks that are more filled with numbers will be more prevalent in a sample. For example, a working block that had 50 known numbers in existence would have twice the probability of being included as one that had just 25 numbers.

Type B samples are most useful when a researcher is willing to overlook a strict definition of randomness in favor of slightly more calling efficiency because of fewer "disconnects." In theory, completed interviews from Type B samples may tend to overrepresent certain types of working blocks, but many researchers feel there is not much difference in representativeness.

Questions

1. Evaluate the geographic options offered by STS. Do they seem to cover all the bases?
2. Evaluate the STS method of random-digit dialing.

CHAPTER 17
DETERMINATION OF SAMPLE SIZE: A REVIEW OF STATISTICAL THEORY

LEARNING OUTCOMES

After studying this chapter, you should be able to

1. Understand basic statistical terminology
2. Interpret frequency distributions, proportions, and measures of central tendency and dispersion
3. Distinguish among population, sample, and sampling distributions
4. Explain the central-limit theorem
5. Summarize the use of confidence interval estimates
6. Discuss major issues in specifying sample size

Chapter Vignette: Federal Reserve Finds Cards Are Replacing Cash

Payment options have gone high-tech. Businesses that sell to consumers—and even charities that seek donations from individuals—need to plan for a wide range of choices beyond traditional cash or checks. Today's spenders are more likely to pay with a debit or credit card or through a variety of methods for electronic transfer of funds. To measure this trend in more detail, researchers at the Federal Reserve conducted surveys of depository institutions (banks, savings and loan institutions, and credit unions), asking them to report the number of each type of payment the institutions processed.[1]

© THINKSTOCK IMAGES/JUPITER IMAGES

In planning this survey, the Fed's researchers carefully designed the sample, including the number of institutions to contact. The total number of depository institutions in the United States was already known: 14,117. The researchers had to select enough institutions from this population to be confident that the answers would be representative of transactions nationwide. A stratified random sample was used so that each type of institution would be included. The researchers had conducted a similar survey three years earlier and obtained a 54 percent response rate, so they assumed the rate would be similar. Using techniques such as those described in this chapter, the researchers determined that, given the total number of institutions and the response rate, they would need to sample 2,700 depository institutions to obtain results that they could say, with 95 percent confidence, were accurate to within ±5 percent.

With a response rate just above that of the prior survey, 1,500 institutions responded, giving data on the number of transactions processed in each payment category. Their responses confirmed earlier analysis showing that the number of checks paid in the United States is declining while the number of electronic payments is increasing. Because this survey measured institutional transactions, it could not count the number of purchases made with cash.

Formally identifying the proper sample size requires applied statistical theory. We understand that the word *statistics* often inspires dread among students. However, when a would-be researcher learns a few tricks of the trade, using statistics can become second nature. Many of these "tricks" involve simply learning the specialized language of statisticians. If you do not understand the basics of the language, you will have problems in conversation. Statistics is the language of the researcher. This chapter reviews some of the basic terminology of statistical analysis and applies statistical principles to the process of determining a sample size.

Introduction

The first six sections of this chapter summarize key statistical concepts necessary for understanding the theory that underlies the calculation of sample size. These sections are intended for students who need to review the basic aspects of statistics theory. Even those students who received good grades in their elementary statistics classes probably will benefit from a quick review of the basic statistical concepts. Some students will prefer to just skim this material and proceed to the section "Sample Size," where the discussion of the actual determination of sample size begins. Others need to study these sections carefully to acquire an understanding of statistics.

Descriptive and Inferential Statistics

The *Statistical Abstract of the United States* presents table after table of figures associated with numbers of births, number of employees in each county of the United States, and other data that the average person calls "statistics." Technically, these are **descriptive statistics**, which describe basic characteristics and summarize the data in a straightforward and understandable manner. Another type of statistics, **inferential statistics**, is used to make inferences or to project from a sample to an entire population. For example, when a firm test-markets a new product in Peoria and Fort Worth, it is not only concerned about how customers in these two cities feel, but they want to make an inference from these sample markets to predict what will happen throughout the United States. So, two applications of statistics exist: (1) descriptive statistics which describe characteristics of the population or sample and (2) inferential statistics which are used to generalize from a sample to a population.

descriptive statistics
Statistics which summarize and describe the data in a simple and understandable manner.

inferential statistics
Using statistics to project characteristics from a sample to an entire population.

Sample Statistics and Population Parameters

A sample is a subset or relatively small portion of the total number of elements in a given population. **Sample statistics** are measures computed from sample data. Since business researchers typically deal with samples—we rarely talk to every consumer, manager, or organization—we normally base our decisions off of sample data. The primary purpose of inferential statistics is to make a judgment about a population, or the total collection of all elements about which a researcher seeks information, based from a subset of that population.

Population parameters are measured characteristics of a specific population. In other words, information about the entire universe of interest. Sample statistics are used to make inferences (guesses) about population parameters based on sample data.[2] In our notation, we will generally represent population parameters with Greek lowercase letters—for example, μ or α—and sample statistics with English letters, such as X or S.

sample statistics
Variables in a sample or measures computed from sample data.

population parameters
Variables in a population or measured characteristics of the population.

Making Data Usable

Suppose a telephone survey has been conducted for a savings and loan association. The data have been recorded on a large number of questionnaires. To make the data usable, this information must be organized and summarized. Methods for doing this include frequency distributions, proportions, measures of central tendency, and measures of dispersion.

Frequency Distributions

One of the most common ways to summarize a set of data is to construct a *frequency table,* or **frequency distribution.** The process begins with recording the number of times a particular value of a variable occurs. This is the frequency of that value. Using an example of a telephone survey for a savings and loan association, Exhibit 17.1 represents a frequency distribution of respondents'

frequency distribution
A set of data organized by summarizing the number of times a particular value of a variable occurs.

answers to a question that asked how much money customers had deposited in the institution. In this case, we can see that more respondents (811) checked the highest box of $12,000 or more.

percentage distribution

A frequency distribution organized into a table (or graph) that summarizes percentage values associated with particular values of a variable.

A similar method of describing the data is to construct a distribution of relative frequency, or a **percentage distribution**. To develop a frequency distribution of percentages, divide the frequency of each value by the total number of observations, and multiply the result by 100. Based on the data in Exhibit 17.1, Exhibit 17.2 shows the percentage distribution of deposits; that is, the percentage of people holding deposits within each range of values. The highest percentage is in the top range, with 26% of all of the respondents.

probability

The long-run relative frequency with which an event will occur.

Probability is the long-run relative frequency with which an event will occur. Inferential statistics uses the concept of a probability distribution, which is conceptually the same as a percentage distribution except that the data are converted into probabilities. Exhibit 17.3 shows the probability distribution of the savings and loan deposits. We know that the probability of a respondent falling into the top category of $12,000 or more is the highest, 0.26.

EXHIBIT 17.1
Frequency Distribution of Deposits

Amount	Frequency (Number of People Who Hold Deposits in Each Range)
Under $3,000	499
$3,000–$5,999	530
$6,000–$8,999	562
$9,000–$11,999	718
$12,000 or more	811
	3,120

EXHIBIT 17.2
Percentage Distribution of Deposits

Amount	Percent (Percentage of People Who Hold Amount Deposits in Each Range)
Under $3,000	16%
$3,000–$5,999	17%
$6,000–$8,999	18%
$9,000–$11,999	23%
$12,000 or more	26%
	100%

EXHIBIT 17.3
Probability Distribution of Deposits

Amount	Probability
Under $3,000	0.16
$3,000–$5,999	0.17
$6,000–$8,999	0.18
$9,000–$11,999	0.23
$12,000 or more	0.26
	1.00

Proportions

When a frequency distribution portrays only a single characteristic in terms of a percentage of the total, it defines the **proportion** of occurrence. A proportion, such as the proportion of CPAs at an accounting firm, indicates the percentage of population elements that successfully meet some standard concerning the particular characteristic. A proportion may be expressed as a percentage (25%), a fraction (1/4), or a decimal value (0.25).

proportion
The percentage of elements that meet some criterion.

Measures of Central Tendency

On a typical day, a sales manager counts the number of sales calls each sales representative makes. She may want to inspect the data to find the average, center, or middle area, of the frequency distribution. Central tendency can be measured in three ways—the mean, median, or mode—each of which has a different meaning. The Research Snapshot "The Well-Chosen Average" illustrates how these measures may differ.

THE MEAN

We all have been exposed to the average known as the **mean**. The mean is simply the arithmetic average, and it is perhaps the most common measure of central tendency. More likely than not, you already know how to calculate a mean. However, knowing how to distinguish among the symbols Σ, μ, and X is helpful to understand statistics.

mean
A measure of central tendency; the arithmetic average.

To express the mean mathematically, we use the summation symbol, the capital Greek letter *sigma* (Σ). A typical use might look like this:

$$\sum_{i=1}^{n} X_i$$

which is a shorthand way to write the sum

$$X_1 + X_2 + X_3 + X_4 + X_5 + \cdots + X_n$$

Below the Σ is the initial value of an index, usually, *i*, *j*, or *k*, and above it is the final value, in this case *n*, the number of observations. The shorthand expression says to replace *i* in the formula with the values from 1 to 8 and total the observations obtained. Without changing the basic formula, the initial and final index values may be replaced by other values to indicate different starting and stopping points.

Suppose our sales manager supervises the eight salespeople listed in Exhibit 17.4. To express the sum of the salespeople's calls in Σ notation, we just number the salespeople (this number becomes the index number) and associate subscripted variables with their numbers of calls:

Index		Salesperson	Variable		Number of Calls
1	=	Mike	X_1	=	4
2	=	Patty	X_2	=	3
3	=	Billie	X_3	=	2
4	=	Bob	X_4	=	5
5	=	John	X_5	=	3
6	=	Frank	X_6	=	3
7	=	Chuck	X_7	=	1
8	=	Samantha	X_8	=	5

RESEARCH SNAPSHOT

The Well-Chosen Average

When you read an announcement by a corporate executive or a business proprietor that the average pay of the people who work in his or her establishment is so much, the figure may mean something or it may not. If the average is a median, you can learn something significant from it: Half of the employees make more than that; half make less. But if it is a mean (and believe me, it may be, if its nature is unspecified), you may be getting nothing more revealing than the average of one $450,000 income—the proprietor's—and the salaries of a crew of lower wage workers. "Average annual pay of $57,000" may conceal both the $20,000 salaries and the owner's profits taken in the form of a whopping salary.

Number of People	Title	Salary	
1	Proprietor	$450,000	
1	President	150,000	
2	Vice presidents	100,000	
1	Controller	57,000	• Mean (arithmetical average)
3	Directors	50,000	
4	Managers	37,000	
1	Supervisor	30,000	• Median *(the one in the middle; 12 above, 12 below)*
12	Workers	20,000	• Mode *(occurs most frequently)*

Let's take a longer look at this scenario. This table shows how many people get how much. The boss might like to express the situation as "average wage $57,000," using that deceptive mean. The mode, however, is more revealing: The most common rate of pay in this business is $20,000 a year. As usual, the median tells more about the situation than any other single figure. Half of the people get more than $30,000 and half get less.

Imagine what would happen to your hometown's average income if Ross Perot and Bill Gates moved into town! Or, perhaps your university had an NBA lottery pick or a first round NFL football player. Adding in their multimillion dollar first-year salaries would certainly raise the "mean starting salary" for students. However, the median and mode would likely not change at all with these "outliers" included.

Do politicians use statistics to lie or do the statistics lie? Politicians sometimes try to play one class of people against another in trying to get elected. One political claim is that the "rich do not pay taxes" or the "rich do not pay their fair share of taxes." If you are curious about this, some facts are available at **http://www.taxfoundation.org** or **http://www.irs.gov/pub/irs-soi/disindin.pdf**. Do the top 1 percent of wage earners pay taxes? Do the top 5 percent of wage earners pay taxes?

Sources: Huff, Darrell and Irving Geis, *How to Lie with Statistics* (New York: W. W. Norton, 1954), 33; Jackson, Brooks and Kathleen H. Jamieson, "Finding Fact in Political Debate," *American Behavioral Scientist* 48 (October 1, 2004), 233–247.

We then write an appropriate Σ formula and evaluate it:

$$\sum_{i=1}^{8} X_i = X_1 + X_2 + X_3 + X_4 + X_5 + X_6 + X_7 + X_8$$
$$= 4 + 3 + 2 + 5 + 3 + 3 + 1 + 5$$
$$= 26$$

EXHIBIT 17.4

Number of Sales Calls per Day by Salesperson

Salesperson	Number of Sales Calls
Mike	4
Patty	3
Billie	2
Bob	5
John	3
Frank	3
Chuck	1
Samantha	5
Total	26

This notation is the numerator in the formula for the arithmetic mean:

$$\text{Mean} = \frac{\sum_{i=1}^{n} X_i}{n} = \frac{26}{8} = 3.25$$

The sum $\sum_{i=1}^{n} X_i$ tells us to add all the Xs whose subscripts are between 1 and n inclusive, where n equals the number of observations. The formula shows that the mean number of sales calls in this example is 3.25.

Researchers generally wish to know the population mean, μ (lowercase Greek letter *mu*), which is calculated as follows:

$$\mu = \frac{\sum_{i=1}^{n} X_i}{N}$$

where

N = number of all observations in the population

Often we will not have the data to calculate the population mean, μ, so we will calculate a sample mean, $\overline{X}$ (read "X bar"), with the following formula:

$$\overline{X} = \frac{\sum_{i=1}^{n} X_i}{n}$$

where

n = number of observations made in the sample

In this introductory discussion of the summation sign (Σ), we have used very detailed notation that includes the subscript for the initial index value (i) and the final index value (n). However, from this point on, references to Σ will sometimes omit the subscript for the initial index value (i) and the final index value (n).

THE MEDIAN

The next measure of central tendency, the **median**, is the midpoint of the distribution, or the 50th percentile. In other words, the median is the value below which half the values in the sample fall, and above which half of the values fall. In the sales manager example, 3 is the median because half the observations are greater than 3 and half are less than 3.

median
A measure of central tendency that is the midpoint; the value below which half the values in a distribution fall.

THE MODE

In apparel, *mode* refers to the most popular fashion. In statistics the **mode** is the measure of central tendency that identifies the value that occurs most often. In our example of sales calls, Patty, John, and Frank each made three sales calls. The value 3 occurs most often, so 3 is the mode. The mode is determined by listing each possible value and noting the number of times each value occurs.

mode
A measure of central tendency; the value that occurs most often.

Measures of Dispersion

The mean, median, and mode summarize the central tendency of frequency distributions. Accurate analysis of data also requires knowing the tendency of observations to depart from the central tendency. What is the spread across the observations? Thus, another way to summarize the data is to calculate the dispersion of the data, or how the observations vary from the mean. Consider, for instance, the 12-month sales patterns of the two products shown in Exhibit 17.5. Both have a mean monthly

EXHIBIT 17.5
Sales Levels for Two Products with Identical Average Sales

	Units Product A	Units Product B
January	196	150
February	198	160
March	199	175
April	200	181
May	200	192
June	200	200
July	200	200
August	201	202
September	201	213
October	201	224
November	202	240
December	202	261
Average	**200**	**200**

sales volume of 200 units, as well as a median and mode of 200, but the dispersion of observations for product B is much greater than that for product A. There are several measures of dispersion.

THE RANGE

The simplest measure of dispersion is the range. It is the distance between the smallest and the largest values of a frequency distribution. In Exhibit 17.5, the range for product A is between 196 units and 202 units (6 units), whereas for product B the range is between 150 units and 261 units (111 units). The range does not take into account all the observations; it merely tells us about the extreme values of the distribution.

Just as people may be fat or skinny, distributions may be fat or skinny. While we do not expect all observations to be exactly like the mean, in a skinny distribution they will lie a short distance from the mean. Product A is an example; the observations are close together and reasonably close to the mean. In a fat distribution, such as the one for Product B, they will be spread out. Exhibit 17.6 illustrates this concept graphically with two frequency distributions on a seven-point scale that have identical modes, medians, and means but different degrees of dispersion.

EXHIBIT 17.6
Low Dispersion versus High Dispersion

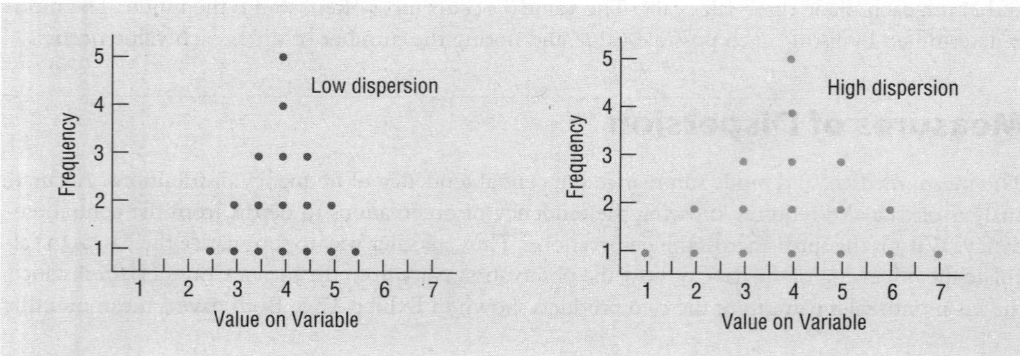

The interquartile range is the range that encompasses the middle 50 percent of the observations—in other words, the range between the bottom quartile (lowest 25 percent) and the top quartile (highest 25 percent).

WHY USE THE STANDARD DEVIATION?

Statisticians have derived several quantitative indexes to reflect a distribution's spread, or variability. The *standard deviation* is perhaps the most valuable index of spread, or dispersion. Students often have difficulty understanding it. Learning about the standard deviation will be easier if we first look at several other measures of dispersion that may be used. Each of these has certain limitations that the standard deviation does not.

First is the *deviation*. Deviation is a method of calculating how far any observation is from the mean. To calculate a deviation from the mean, use the following formula:

$$d_{i_i} = X_i - \overline{X}$$

For the value of 150 units for product B for the month of January, the deviation score is −50; that is, 150 − 200 = −50. If the deviation scores are large, we will have a fat distribution because the distribution exhibits a broad spread.

Next is the *average deviation*. We compute the average deviation by calculating the deviation score of each observation value (that is, its difference from the mean), summing these scores, and then dividing by the sample size (n):

$$\text{Average deviation} = \frac{\Sigma(X_i - \overline{X})}{n}$$

While this measure of spread may seem initially interesting, it is never used. Positive deviation scores are canceled out by negative scores with this formula, leaving an average deviation value of zero no matter how wide the spread may be. Hence, the average deviation is a useless spread measure.

One might correct for the disadvantage of the average deviation by computing the absolute values of the deviations, termed *mean absolute deviation*. In other words, we ignore all the positive and negative signs and use only the absolute value of each deviation. The formula for the mean absolute deviation is

$$\text{Mean absolute deviation} = \frac{\Sigma\,|X_i - \overline{X}|}{n}$$

While this procedure eliminates the problem of always having a zero score for the deviation measure, some technical mathematical problems make it less valuable than some other measures.

The *mean squared deviation* provides another method of eliminating the positive/negative sign problem. In this case, the deviation is squared, which eliminates the negative values. The mean squared deviation is calculated by the following formula:

$$\text{Mean squared deviation} = \frac{\Sigma(X_i - \overline{X})^2}{n}$$

This measure is quite useful for describing the sample variability.

Variance

However, we typically wish to make an inference about a population from a sample, and so the divisor $n - 1$ is used rather than n in most pragmatic marketing research problems.[3] This new measure of spread, called **variance**, has the following formula:

variance

A measure of variability or dispersion. Its square root is the standard deviation.

$$\text{Variance} = S^2 = \frac{\Sigma(X_i - \overline{X})^2}{n - 1}$$

Variance is a very good index of dispersion. The variance, S^2, will equal zero if and only if each and every observation in the distribution is the same as the mean. The variance will grow larger as the observations tend to differ increasingly from one another and from the mean.

Standard Deviation

While the variance is frequently used in statistics, it has one major drawback. The variance reflects a unit of measurement that has been squared. For instance, if measures of sales in a territory are made in dollars, the mean number will be reflected in dollars, but the variance will be in squared dollars. Because of this, statisticians often take the square root of the variance. Using the square root of the variance for a distribution, called the **standard deviation**, eliminates the drawback of having the measure of dispersion in squared units rather than in the original measurement units. The formula for the standard deviation is

standard deviation

A quantitative index of a distribution's spread, or variability; the square root of the variance for a distribution.

$$S = \sqrt{S^2} = \sqrt{\frac{\Sigma(X_i - \overline{X})^2}{n - 1}}$$

Exhibit 17.7 illustrates that the calculation of a standard deviation requires the researcher to first calculate the sample mean. In the example with eight salespeople's sales calls (Exhibit 17.4), we calculated the sample mean as 3.25. Exhibit 17.7 illustrates how to calculate the standard deviation for these data.

EXHIBIT 17.7
Calculating a Standard Deviation: Number of Sales Calls per Day for Eight Salespeople

X	$(X - \overline{X})$	$(X - \overline{X})^2$
4	(4 − 3.25) = .75	.5625
3	(3 − 3.25) = −.25	.0625
2	(2 − 3.25) = −1.25	1.5625
5	(5 − 3.25) = 1.75	3.0625
3	(3 − 3.25) = −.25	.0625
3	(3 − 3.25) = −.25	.0625
1	(1 − 3.25) = −2.25	5.0625
5	(5 − 3.25) = 1.75	3.0625
Σ[a]	0	13.5000

$n = 8 \quad \overline{X} = 3.25$

$$S = \sqrt{\frac{\Sigma(X - \overline{X})^2}{n - 1}} = \sqrt{\frac{13.5}{8 - 1}} = \sqrt{\frac{13.5}{7}} = \sqrt{1.9286} = 1.3887$$

[a]The summation of this column is not used in the calculation of the standard deviation.

At this point we can return to thinking about the original purpose for measures of dispersion. We want to summarize the data from survey research and other forms of business research. Indexes of central tendency, such as the mean, help us interpret the data. In addition, we wish to calculate a measure of variability that will give us a quantitative index of the dispersion of the distribution. We have looked at several measures of dispersion to arrive at two very adequate means of measuring dispersion: the variance and the standard deviation. The formula given is for the sample standard deviation, S.

The formula for the population standard deviation, σ, which is conceptually very similar, has not been given. Nevertheless, you should understand that σ measures the dispersion in the population and S measures the dispersion in the sample. These concepts are crucial to understanding statistics. Remember, a business researcher must know the language of statistics to use it in a research project. If you do not understand the language at this point, your should review this material now.

The Normal Distribution

One of the most common probability distributions in statistics is the **normal distribution**, commonly represented by the *normal curve*. This mathematical and theoretical distribution describes the expected distribution of sample means and many other chance occurrences. The normal curve is bell shaped, and almost all (99 percent) of its values are within ±3 standard deviations from its mean. An example of a normal curve, the distribution of IQ scores, appears in Exhibit 17.8. In this example, 1 standard deviation for IQ equals 15. We can identify the proportion of the curve by measuring a score's distance (in this case, standard deviation) from the mean (100).

normal distribution
A symmetrical, bell-shaped distribution that describes the expected probability distribution of many chance occurrences.

The **standardized normal distribution** is a specific normal curve that has several characteristics:

standardized normal distribution
A purely theoretical probability distribution that reflects a specific normal curve for the standardized value, *z*.

1. It is symmetrical about its mean; the tails on both sides are equal.
2. The mode identifies the normal curve's highest point, which is also the mean and median, and the vertical line about which this normal curve is symmetrical.
3. The normal curve has an infinite number of cases (it is a continuous distribution), and the area under the curve has a probability density equal to 1.0.
4. The standardized normal distribution has a mean of 0 and a standard deviation of 1.

Exhibit 17.9 illustrates these properties. Exhibit 17.10 is a summary version of the typical standardized normal table found at the end of most statistics textbooks. A more complex table of areas under the standardized normal distribution appears in Table A.2 in the appendix.

The standardized normal distribution is a purely theoretical probability distribution, but it is the most useful distribution in inferential statistics. Statisticians have spent a great deal of time and effort making it convenient for researchers to find the probability of any portion of the area under the standardized normal distribution. All we have to do is transform, or convert, the data from other observed normal distributions to the standardized normal curve. In other words, the standardized normal distribution is extremely valuable because we can translate, or transform, any normal variable, X, into the standardized value, Z. Exhibit 17.11 illustrates how either a skinny distribution or a fat distribution can be converted into the standardized normal distribution. This ability to transform normal variables has many pragmatic implications for the business researcher. The standardized normal table in the back of most statistics and research books allows us to evaluate the probability of the occurrence of many events without any difficulty.

Computing the standardized value, Z, of any measurement expressed in original units is simple: Subtract the mean from the value to be transformed, and divide by the standard deviation (all expressed in original units).

By recording the results of spins of the roulette wheel, one might find a pattern or distribution of the results.

© NUK NENZIC/SHUTTERSTOCK

EXHIBIT 17.8
Normal Distribution: Distribution of Intelligence Quotient (IQ) Scores

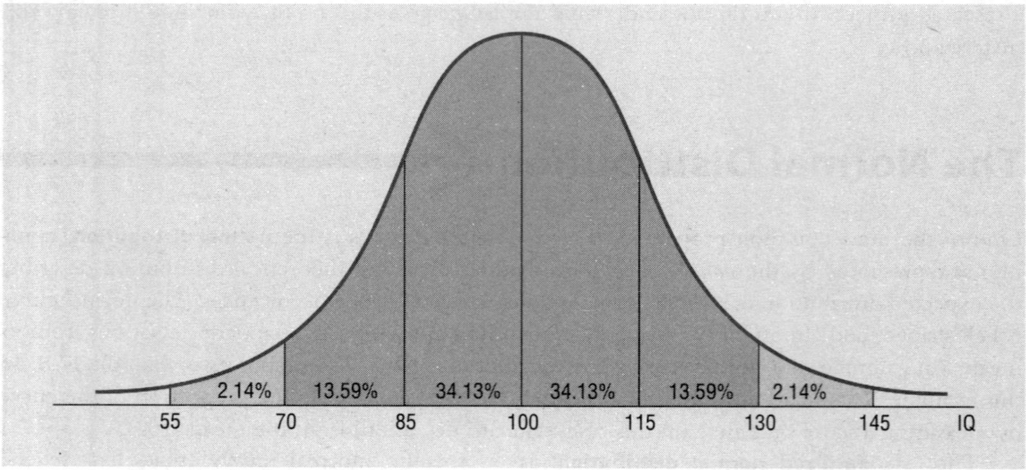

EXHIBIT 17.9
Standardized Normal Distribution

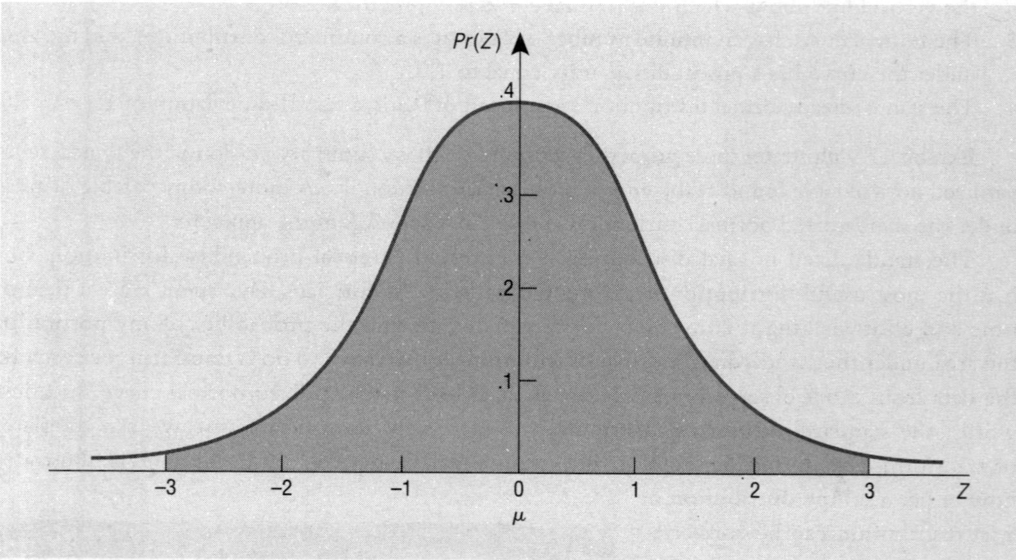

EXHIBIT 17.10 Standardized Normal Table: Area under Half of the Normal Curve[a]

Z Standard Deviations from the Mean (Units)	Z Standard Deviations from the Mean (Tenths of Units) .0	.1	.2	.3	.4	.5	.6	.7	.8	.9
0.0	.000	.040	.080	.118	.155	.192	.226	.258	.288	.315
1.0	.341	.364	.385	.403	.419	.433	.445	.455	.464	.471
2.0	.477	.482	.486	.489	.492	.494	.495	.496	.497	.498
3.0	.499	.499	.499	.499	.499	.499	.499	.499	.499	.499

[a]Area under the segment of the normal curve extending (in one direction) from the mean to the point indicated by each row–column combination. For example, about 68 percent of normally distributed events can be expected to fall within 1.0 standard deviation on either side of the mean (0.341 × 2). An interval of almost 2.0 standard deviations around the mean will include 95 percent of all cases.

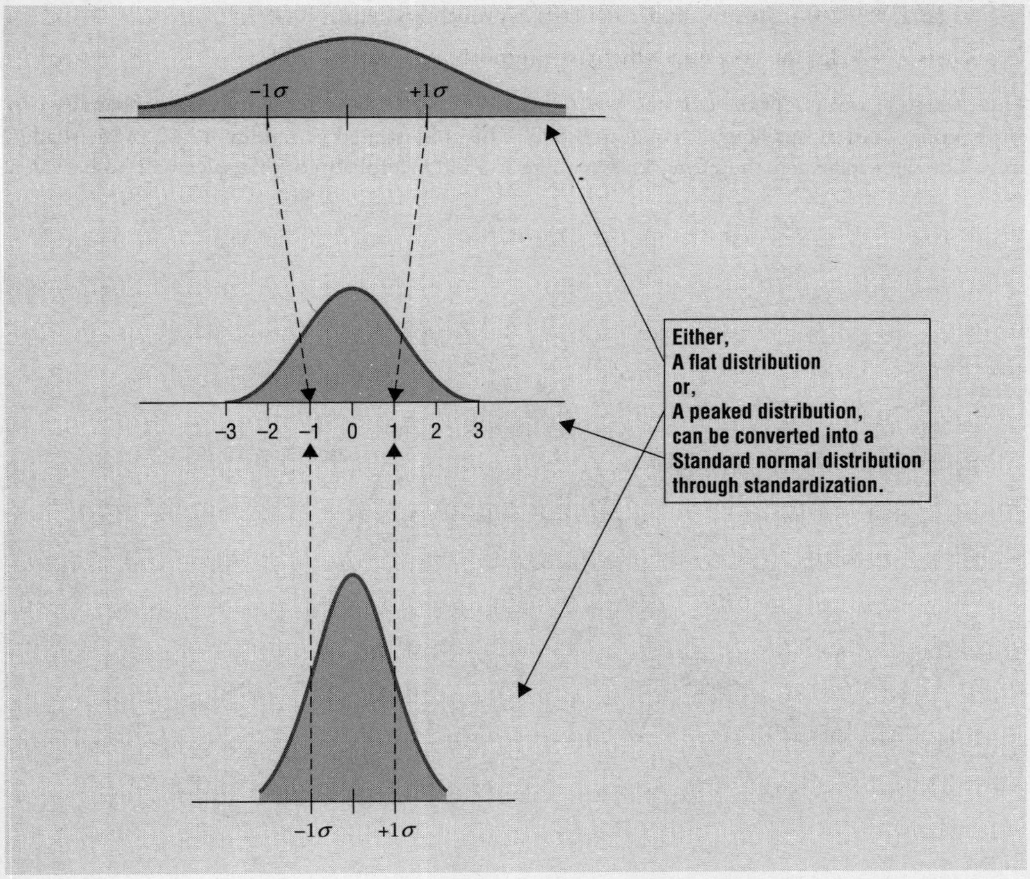

EXHIBIT 17.11
Standardized Values Can Be Computed from Flat or Peaked Distributions Resulting in a Standardized Normal Curve

The formula for this procedure and its verbal statement follow. In the formula, note that σ, the population standard deviation, is used for calculation.[4] Also note that we do not use an absolute value, but rather allow the Z value to be either negative (below the mean) or positive (above the mean).

$$\text{Standardized value} = \frac{\text{Value to be transformed} - \text{Mean}}{\text{Standard deviation}}$$

$$Z = \frac{X - \mu}{\sigma}$$

where

μ = hypothesized or expected value of the mean

Suppose that in the past a toy manufacturer has experienced mean sales, μ, of 9,000 units and a standard deviation, σ, of 500 units during September. The production manager wishes to know whether wholesalers will demand between 7,500 and 9,625 units during September of the upcoming year. Because no tables are available showing the distribution for a mean of 9,000 and a standard deviation of 500, we must transform our distribution of toy sales, X, into the standardized form using our simple formula:

$$Z = \frac{X - \mu}{\sigma} = \frac{7500 - 9000}{500} = -3.00$$

$$Z = \frac{X - \mu}{\sigma} = \frac{9625 - 9000}{500} = 1.25$$

The −3.00 indicates the standardized Z for sales of 7,500, while the 1.25 is the Z score for 9,625. Using Exhibit 17.10 (or Table A.2 in the appendix), we find that

When $Z = -3.00$, the area under the curve (probability) equals 0.499.

When $Z = 1.25$, the area under the curve (probability) equals 0.394.

Thus, the total area under the curve is $0.499 + 0.394 = 0.893$. In other words, the probability (*Pr*) of obtaining sales in this range is equal to 0.893. This is illustrated in Exhibit 17.12 in the shaded area. The sales manager, therefore, knows there is a 0.893 probability that sales will be between

EXHIBIT 17.12
Standardized Distribution Curve

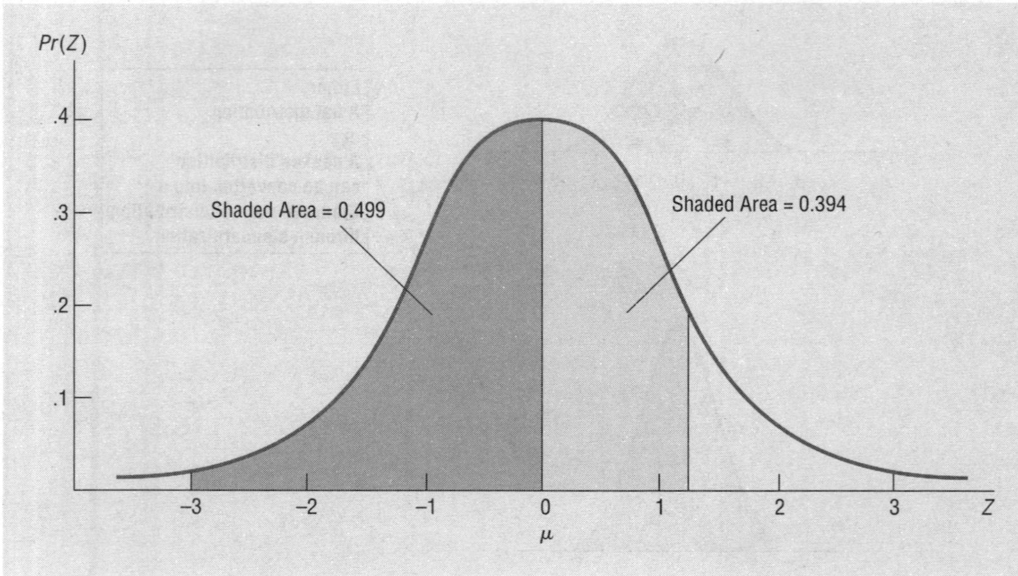

TOTHEPOINT

Order is heaven's law.

—Alexander Pope

7,500 and 9,625. We can go a step further here by comparing the area under the curve to the total. Since the distribution is symmetrical, 0.500 of the distribution is on either side of the center line. For the 7,500 figure the area under our curve is 0.499, so the probability of sales being *less* than 7,500 is 0.001 (0.500 − 0.499). Similarly, the probability of sales being *more* than 9,625 is 0.106 (0.500 − 0.394).

At this point, it is appropriate to repeat that understanding statistics requires an understanding of the language that statisticians use. Each concept discussed so far is relatively simple, but a clear-cut command of this terminology is essential for understanding what we will discuss later on.

Population Distribution, Sample Distribution, and Sampling Distribution

Before we outline the technique of statistical inference, three additional types of distributions must be defined: population distribution, sample distribution, and sampling distribution. When conducting a research project or survey, the researcher's purpose is typically not to describe only the sample of respondents, but to make an inference about the population. As defined previously, a population, or universe, is the total set, or collection, of potential units for observation. The sample is a smaller subset of this population.

population distribution
A frequency distribution of the elements of a population.

sample distribution
A frequency distribution of a sample.

A frequency distribution of the population elements is called a **population distribution**. The mean and standard deviation of the population distribution are represented by the Greek letters μ and σ. A frequency distribution of a sample is called a **sample distribution**. The sample mean is designated $\overline{X}$, and the sample standard deviation is designated S.

The concepts of population distribution and sample distribution are relatively simple. However, we must now introduce another distribution, which is the crux of understanding statistics:

the *sampling distribution of the sample mean.* The sampling distribution is a theoretical probability distribution that in actual practice would never be calculated. Hence, practical, business-oriented students have difficulty understanding why the notion of the sampling distribution is important. Statisticians, with their mathematical curiosity, have asked themselves, "What would happen if we were to draw a large number of samples (say, 50,000), each having n elements, from a specified population?" Assuming that the samples were randomly selected, the sample means, $\overline{X}$s, could be arranged in a frequency distribution. Because different people or sample units would be selected in the different samples, the sample means would not be exactly equal. The shape of the sampling distribution is of considerable importance to statisticians. If the sample size is sufficiently large and if the samples are randomly drawn, we know from the central-limit theorem (discussed below) that the sampling distribution of the mean will be approximately normally distributed.

A formal definition of the sampling distribution is as follows:

A ***sampling distribution*** *is a theoretical probability distribution that shows the functional relation between the possible values of some summary characteristic of* n *cases drawn at random and the probability (density) associated with each value over all possible samples of size* n *from a particular population.*[5]

sampling distribution

A theoretical probability distribution of sample means for all possible samples of a certain size drawn from a particular population.

The sampling distribution's mean is called the *expected value* of the statistic. The expected value of the mean of the sampling distribution is equal to μ. The standard deviation of a sampling distribution of $\overline{X}$ is called **standard error of the mean** ($S_{\overline{X}}$) and is approximately equal to

standard error of the mean

The standard deviation of the sampling distribution.

$$S_{\overline{X}} = \frac{\sigma}{\sqrt{n}}$$

To review, for us to make an inference about a population from a sample, we must know about three important distributions: the population distribution, the sample distribution, and the sampling distribution. They have the following characteristics:

	Mean	Standard Deviation
Population distribution	μ	σ
Sample distribution	$\overline{X}$	S
Sampling distribution	$\mu_x = \mu$	$S_{\overline{X}}$

We now have much of the information we need to understand the concept of statistical inference. To clarify why the sampling distribution has the characteristic just described, we will elaborate on two concepts: the standard error of the mean and the central-limit theorem. You may be wondering why the standard error of the mean, $S_{\overline{X}}$, is defined as $S_{\overline{X}} = \sigma/\sqrt{n}$. The reason is based on the notion that the variance or dispersion within the sampling distribution of the mean will be less if we have a larger sample size for independent samples. It should make intuitive sense that a larger sample size allows the researcher to be more confident that the sample mean is closer to the population mean. In actual practice, the standard error of the mean is estimated using the sample's standard deviation. Thus, $S_{\overline{X}}$ is estimated using $S/\sqrt{n}$.

Exhibit 17.13 shows the relationship among a population distribution, the sample distribution, and three sampling distributions for varying sample sizes. In part (a) the population distribution is not a normal distribution. In part (b) the first sample distribution resembles the distribution of the population; however, there may be other distributions as shown in the second and third sample distributions. In part (c) each sampling distribution is normally distributed and has the same mean. However, as sample size increases, the spread of the sample means around μ decreases. Thus, with a larger sample size we will have a more narrow sampling distribution.

Central-Limit Theorem

Finding that the means of random samples of a sufficiently large size will be approximately normal in form and that the mean of the sampling distribution will approach the population mean is very

EXHIBIT 17.13
Fundamental Types of Distributions

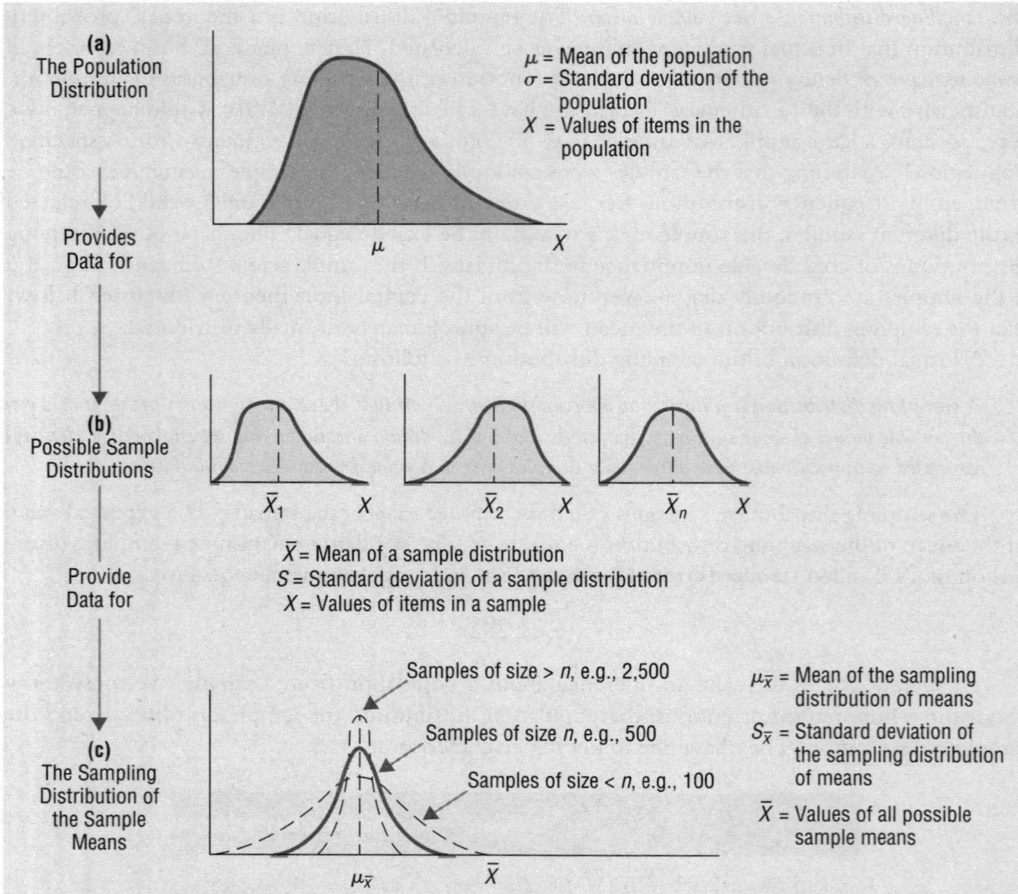

Source: Adapted from Sanders, D. H., A. F. Murphy, and R. J. Eng, *Statistics: A Fresh Approach* (New York: McGraw-Hill, 1980), 123.

central-limit theorem
The theory that, as sample size increases, the distribution of sample means of size *n*, randomly selected, approaches a normal distribution.

useful. Mathematically, this is the assertion of the **central-limit theorem**, which states, as the sample size, n, increases, the distribution of the mean, $\overline{X}$, of a random sample taken from practically any population approaches a normal distribution (with a mean μ and a standard deviation $\sigma/\sqrt{n}$).[6] The central-limit theorem works regardless of the shape of the original population distribution (see Exhibit 17.14).

A simple example will demonstrate the central-limit theorem. Assume that a quality control specialist is examining the number of defects in the products produced by assembly line workers. Assume further that the population the researcher is investigating consists of six different workers in the same plant. Thus, in this example, the population consists of only six individuals. Exhibit 17.15 shows the population distribution of defects in a week. Donna, a dedicated and experienced worker, only has one defect in the entire week's production. On the other hand, Eddie, a sloppy worker with little regard for quality, has six defects a week. The average number of defects each week is 3.5, so the population mean, μ, equals 3.5 (see Exhibit 17.16).

Now assume that we do not know everything about the population, and we wish to take a sample with two observations, to be drawn randomly from the population of the six individuals. How many possible samples are there? The answer is 15, as follows:

1, 2				
1, 3	*2, 3*			
1, 4	*2, 4*	*3, 4*		
1, 5	*2, 5*	*3, 5*	*4, 5*	
1, 6	*2, 6*	*3, 6*	*4, 6*	*5, 6*

Exhibit 17.17 lists the sample mean for each of the possible 15 samples and the frequency distribution of these sample means with their appropriate probabilities. These sample means comprise a sampling distribution of the mean, and the distribution is *approximately* normal. If we increased the sample size to three, four, or more, the distribution of sample means would more closely approximate a normal distribution. While this simple example is not a proof of the central-limit theorem, it should give you a better understanding of the nature of the sampling distribution of the mean.

This theoretical knowledge about distributions can be used to solve two practical business research problems: estimating parameters and determining sample size.

Estimation of Parameters

A catalog retailer, such as dELiA★s, may rely on sampling and statistical estimation to prepare for Christmas orders. The company can expect that 28 days after mailing a catalog, it will have

EXHIBIT 17.14
Distribution of Sample Means for Samples of Various Sizes and Population Distributions

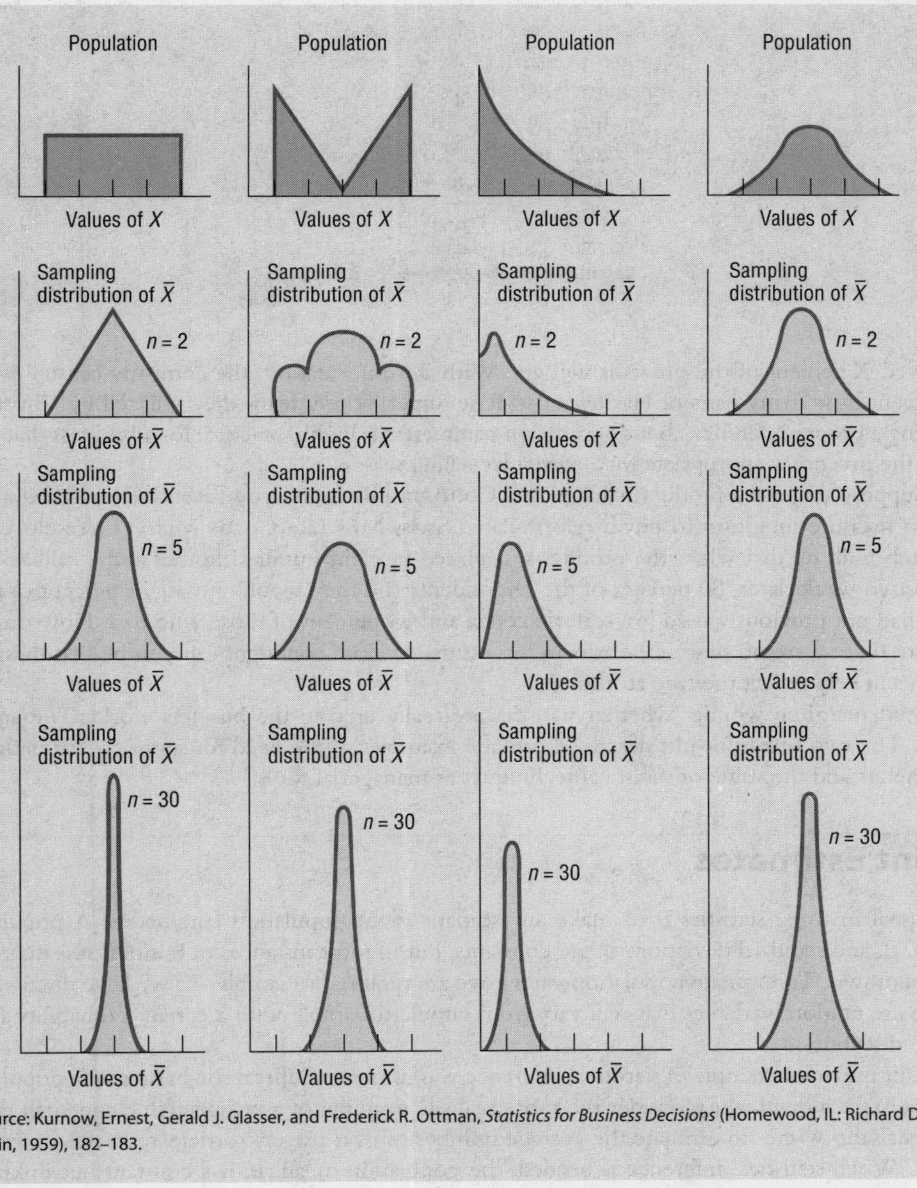

Source: Kurnow, Ernest, Gerald J. Glasser, and Frederick R. Ottman, *Statistics for Business Decisions* (Homewood, IL: Richard D. Irwin, 1959), 182–183.

EXHIBIT 17.15
Population Distribution: Hypothetical Product Defect

Employee	Defects
Donna	1
Heidi	2
Jason	3
Jennifer	4
Mark	5
Eddie	6

EXHIBIT 17.16
Calculation of Population Mean

X
1
2
3
4
5
6
$\Sigma 21$

Calculations: $\mu = \frac{\Sigma X}{n} = \frac{21}{6} = 3.5 = \mu_{\bar{X}}$

received X percent of the orders it will get. With this information, the company can tell within 5 percent how many pairs of Harlow Low-Rise Super Skinny Jeans they will sell by Christmas. Making a proper inference about population parameters is highly practical for a business that must have the inventory appropriate for a particular selling season.

Suppose you are a product manager for ConAgra Foods and you recently conducted a taste test to measure intention to buy a reformulated Swiss Miss Lite Cocoa Mix. The results of the research indicate that when the product was placed in eight hundred homes and a callback was made two weeks later, 80 percent of the respondents said they would buy it: 76 percent of those who had not previously used low-calorie cocoa and 84 percent of those who had. How can you be sure there were no statistical errors in this estimate? How confident can you be that these figures accurately reflect the true attitudes?

Students often wonder whether statistics are really used in the business world. The answer is *yes*. The two situations just described provide examples of the need for statistical estimation of parameters and the value of statistical techniques as managerial tools.

Point Estimates

Our goal in using statistics is to make an estimate about population parameters. A population mean, μ, and standard deviation, σ, are constants, but in most instances of business research, they are unknown. To estimate population values, we are required to sample. As we have discussed, $\bar{X}$ and S are random variables that will vary from sample to sample with a certain probability (sampling) distribution.

Our previous example of statistical inference was somewhat unrealistic because the population had only six individuals. Consider the more realistic example of a prospective racquetball entrepreneur who wishes to estimate the average number of days players participate in this sport each week. When statistical inference is needed, the population mean, μ, is a constant but unknown

EXHIBIT 17.17
Arithmetic Means of Samples and Frequency Distribution of Sample Means

Sample Means			
Sample	ΣX	$\overline{X}$	Probability
1, 2	3.00	1.50	1/15
1, 3	4.00	2.00	1/15
1, 4	5.00	2.50	1/15
1, 5	6.00	3.00	1/15
1, 6	7.00	3.50	1/15
2, 3	5.00	2.50	1/15
2, 4	6.00	3.00	1/15
2, 5	7.00	3.50	1/15
2, 6	8.00	4.00	1/15
3, 4	7.00	3.50	1/15
3, 5	8.00	4.00	1/15
3, 6	9.00	4.50	1/15
4, 5	9.00	4.50	1/15
4, 6	10.00	5.00	1/15
5, 6	11.00	5.50	1/15

Frequency Distribution		
Sample Mean	Frequency	Probability
1.50	1	1/15
2.00	1	1/15
2.50	2	2/15
3.00	2	2/15
3.50	3	3/15
4.00	2	2/15
4.50	2	2/15
5.00	1	1/15
5.50	1	1/15

parameter. To estimate the average number of playing days, we could take a sample of three hundred racquetball players throughout the area where our entrepreneur is thinking of building club facilities. If the sample mean, $\overline{X}$, equals 2.6 days per week, we might use this figure as a **point estimate**. This single value, 2.6, would be the best estimate of the population mean. However, we would be extremely lucky if the sample estimate were exactly the same as the population value. A less risky alternative would be to calculate a confidence interval. An example of a point estimate and confidence interval is provided in the Research Snapshot "Accuracy of Political Polls."

point estimate
An estimate of the population mean in the form of a single value, usually the sample mean.

confidence interval estimate
A specified range of numbers within which a population mean is expected to lie; an estimate of the population mean based on the knowledge that it will be equal to the sample mean plus or minus a small sampling error.

Confidence Intervals

If we specify a range of numbers, or interval, within which the population mean should lie, we can be more confident that our inference is correct. A **confidence interval estimate** is based on the knowledge that $\mu = \overline{X} \pm$ a small sampling error. After calculating an interval estimate, we

RESEARCH SNAPSHOT

Accuracy of Political Polls

Over 20 organizations conduct national political polls. For the candidates, these polls are great sources of information. Results of these polls can illustrate trends, identify messages to use in their promotional efforts, and target areas for special campaign emphasis. While many surveys are used in the business world to predict outcomes, we often have difficulty determining how accurate the surveys were. Political polls are quite different, as we get specific results and can analyze how accurate the polls were after the fact.

Zogby International (**http://www.zogby.com**) is one of these polling organizations. Zogby International is an independent and nonpartisan polling organization that conducts political polls in the United States, as well as far reaching parts of the world, including the Middle East, Latin America, and the 2009 Albanian elections. Zogby has a reputation as a highly accurate polling organization.

In the 2008 U.S. Presidential election, Zogby's final poll consisted of 1,205 likely voters. This poll indicated that 50.9 percent of voters would vote for Barak Obama and 43.8 percent for John McCain. According to the researchers, the confidence level was 95 percent that the sampling error was not greater than ± 3 percentage points. So, Zogby was 95 percent sure that Obama would receive between 53.9 percent and 47.9 percent of the overall vote, while McCain would receive between 46.8 percent and 40.8 percent.

© iStock

The final vote tally totals show that out of over 125 million votes cast, Barak Obama received 53 percent of the popular vote while John McCain received 46 percent. Indeed, Zogby was quite accurate in their ability to predict the overall vote from a sample that represented less than 0.001% of the vote.

Sources: Based on "Final Presidential Polls," *The Huffington Post* November 2, 2008, http://www.huffingtonpost.com/2008/11/02/latest-presidential-polls_n_140177.html; "Reuters/C-SPAN/Zogby Poll: Final: Obama in Double-Digit Lead, 54% to 43%," Zoby International, http://www.zogby.com/search/ReadNews.cfm?ID=1633, accessed March 18, 2009.

---

can determine how probable it is that the population mean will fall within this range of statistical values. In the racquetball project, the researcher, after setting up a confidence interval, would be able to make a statement such as "With 95 percent confidence, I think that the average number of days played per week is between 2.3 and 2.9." This information can be used to estimate market demand because the researcher has a certain confidence that the interval contains the value of the true population mean.

The crux of the problem for a researcher is to determine how much random sampling error to tolerate. In other words, what should the confidence interval be? How much of a gamble should be taken that μ will be included in the range? Do we need to be 80 percent, 90 percent, 95 percent, or 99 percent sure? The **confidence level** is a percentage or decimal that indicates the long-run probability that the results will be correct. Traditionally, researchers have used the 95 percent confidence level. While there is nothing magical about the 95 percent confidence level, it is useful to select this confidence level in our examples.

confidence level
A percentage or decimal value that tells how confident a researcher can be about being correct; it states the long-run percentage of confidence intervals that will include the true population mean.

As mentioned, the point estimate gives no information about the possible magnitude of random sampling error. The confidence interval gives the estimated value of the population parameter, plus or minus an estimate of the error. We can express the idea of the confidence interval as follows:

$$\mu = \bar{X} \pm \text{a small sampling error}$$

More formally, assuming that the researchers select a large sample (more than 30 observations), the small sampling error is given by

$$\text{Small sampling error} = Z_{c.l.} S_{\bar{X}}$$

where

$Z_{c.l.}$ = value of Z, or standardized normal variable, at a specified confidence level (*c.l.*)

$S_{\bar{X}}$ = standard error of the mean

The precision of our estimate is indicated by the value of $Z_{c.l.} S_{\bar{X}}$. It is useful to define the range of possible error, E, as follows:

$$E = Z_{c.l.} S_{\bar{X}}$$

Thus,

$$\mu = \overline{X} \pm E$$

where

$\overline{X}$ = sample mean

E = range of sampling error

or

$$\mu = \overline{X} \pm Z_{c.l.} S_{\overline{X}}$$

The confidence interval $\pm E$ is always stated as one-half (thus the plus or minus) of the total confidence interval.

The following step-by-step procedure can be used to calculate confidence intervals:

1. Calculate $\overline{X}$ from the sample.
2. Assuming σ is unknown, estimate the population standard deviation by finding S, the sample standard deviation.
3. Estimate the standard error of the mean, using the following formula:
$$S_{\overline{X}} = \frac{S}{\sqrt{n}}$$
4. Determine the Z-value associated with the desired confidence level. The confidence level should be divided by 2 to determine what percentage of the area under the curve to include on each side of the mean.
5. Calculate the confidence interval.

The following shows how a confidence interval can be calculated. Suppose you are a financial planner and are interested in knowing how long investors tend to own individual stocks. In a survey of 100 investors, you find that the mean length of time a stock is held ($\overline{X}$) is 37.5 months, with a standard deviation (S) of 12.0 months. Even though 37.5 months is the "expected value" and the best guess for the true mean in the population (μ), the likelihood is that the mean is not exactly 37.5. Thus, a confidence interval around the sample mean computed using the steps just given will be useful:

1. $\overline{X}$ = 37.5 months
2. S = 12.0 months
3. $S_{\overline{X}} = \dfrac{12.0}{\sqrt{100}} = 1.2$
4. Suppose you wish to be 95 percent confident—that is, assured that 95 times out of 100, the estimates from your sample will include the population parameter. Including 95 percent of the area requires that 47.5 percent (one-half of 95 percent) of the distribution on each side be included. From the Z-table (Table A.2 in the appendix), you find that 0.475 corresponds to the Z-value 1.96.
5. Substitute the values for $Z_{c.l.}$ and $S_{\overline{X}}$ into the confidence interval formula:
$$\begin{aligned}\mu &= 37.5 \pm (1.96)(1.2)\\ &= 37.5 \pm 2.352\end{aligned}$$

You can thus expect that μ is contained in the range from 35.148 to 39.852 months. Intervals constructed in this manner will contain the true value of μ 95 percent of the time.

Step 3 can be eliminated by entering S and n directly in the confidence interval formula:

$$\mu = \overline{X} \pm Z_{c.l.} \frac{S}{\sqrt{n}}$$

Remember that $S/\sqrt{n}$ represents the standard error of the mean. Its use is based on the central-limit theorem.

If you wanted to increase the probability that the population mean will lie within the confidence interval, you could use the 99 percent confidence level, with a Z-value of 2.57. You may want to calculate the 99 percent confidence interval for the preceding example; you can expect that μ will be in the range between 34.416 and 40.584 months. It should make intuitive sense that if we are 99 percent confident that the spread will be larger than if we are only 95 percent confident. If we want to be more confident, we need a broader range.

We have now examined the basic concepts of inferential statistics. You should understand that sample statistics such as the sample means, $\overline{X}$s, can provide good estimates of population parameters such as μ. You should also realize that there is a certain probability of being in error when you estimate a population parameter from sample statistics. In other words, there will be a random sampling error, which is the difference between the results of a survey of a sample and the results of surveying the entire population. If you have a firm understanding of these basic terms and ideas, which are the essence of statistics, the remaining statistics concepts will be relatively simple for you. Several ramifications of the simple ideas presented so far will permit you to make better decisions about populations based on surveys or experiments.

Sample Size

Random Error and Sample Size

When asked to evaluate a business research project, most people, even those with little research training, begin by asking, "How big was the sample?" Intuitively we know that the larger the sample, the more accurate the research. This is in fact a statistical truth; random sampling error varies with samples of different sizes. In statistical terms, increasing the sample size decreases the width of the confidence interval at a given confidence level. Obviously if we collect information from every member of the population, we know the population parameters, so there would be no interval. When the standard deviation of the population is unknown, a confidence interval is calculated using the following formula:

$$\text{Confidence interval} = \overline{X} \pm Z\frac{S}{\sqrt{n}}$$

Observe that the equation for the plus or minus error factor in the confidence interval includes n, the sample size:

$$E = Z\frac{S}{\sqrt{n}}$$

If n increases, E is reduced. Exhibit 17.18 illustrates that the confidence interval (or magnitude of error) decreases as the sample size, n, increases.

EXHIBIT 17.18

Relationship between Sample Size and Error

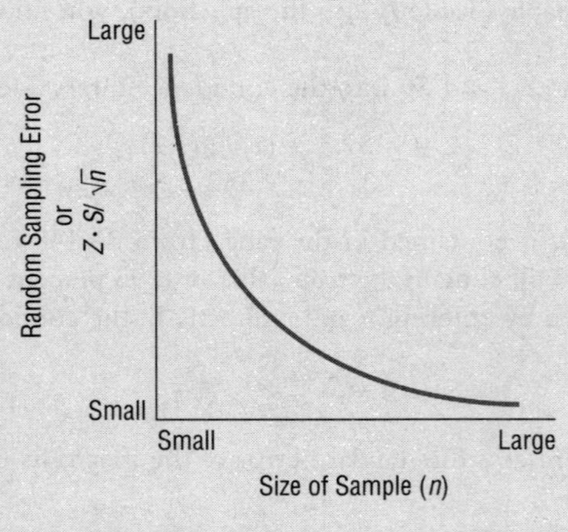

Source: From *Foundations of Behavioral Research*, 3rd edition, by Fred N. Kerlinger. © 1986. Reprinted with permission of Wadsworth, a division of Cengage Learning, http://www.cengage.com/permissions/. Fax 800-730-2215.

We already noted that it is not necessary to take a census of all elements of the population to conduct an accurate study. The laws of probability give investigators sufficient confidence regarding the accuracy of data collected from a sample. Knowledge of the characteristics of the sampling distribution helps researchers make reasonably precise estimates.

Increasing the sample size reduces the sampling error. However, those familiar with the law of diminishing returns in economics will easily grasp the concept that increases in sample size reduce sampling error at a *decreasing rate*. For example, doubling a sample of 1,000 will reduce random sampling error by 1 percentage point, but doubling the sample from 2,000 to 4,000 will reduce random sampling error by only another half percentage point. More technically, random sampling error is inversely proportional to the square root of n. (Exhibit 17.18 gives an approximation of the relationship between sample size and error.) Thus, the main issue becomes one of determining the optimal sample size. The Research Snapshot "Target and Wal-Mart Shoppers Really Are Different" discusses sample size and shows that some samples are extremely large.

Factors in Determining Sample Size for Questions Involving Means

Three factors are required to specify sample size: (1) the heterogeneity (i.e., variance) of the population; (2) the magnitude of acceptable error (i.e., ± some amount); and (3) the confidence level (i.e., 90 percent, 95 percent, 99 percent).

The determination of sample size heavily depends on the variability within the sample. The *variance*, or *heterogeneity*, of the population is the first necessary bit of information. In statistical terms, this refers to the *standard deviation* of the population. Only a small sample is required if the population is homogeneous. For example, predicting the average age of college students requires a smaller sample than predicting the average age of people who visit the zoo on a given Sunday afternoon. As *heterogeneity* increases, so must sample size. Thus, to test the effectiveness of an employee training program, the sample must be large enough to cover the range of employee work experience (for example).

The *magnitude of error*, or the confidence interval, is the second necessary bit of information. Defined in statistical terms as E, the magnitude of error indicates how precise the estimate must be. It indicates a certain precision level. From a managerial perspective, the importance of the decision in terms of profitability will influence the researcher's specifications of the range of error. If, for example, favorable results from a test-market sample will result in the construction of a new plant and unfavorable results will dictate not marketing the product, the acceptable range of error probably will be small; the cost of an error would be too great to allow much room for random sampling errors. In other cases, the estimate need not be extremely precise. Allowing an error of ±\$1,000 in total family income instead of $E = \pm 50$ may be acceptable in most market segmentation studies.

The third factor of concern is the *confidence level*. In our examples, as in most business research, we will typically use the 95 percent confidence level. This, however, is an arbitrary decision based on convention; there is nothing sacred about the 0.05 chance level (that is, the probability of 0.05 of the true population parameter being incorrectly estimated). Exhibit 17.19 summarizes the information required to determine sample size.

Variable	Symbol	Typical Source of Information
Standard deviation	S	Pilot study or rule of thumb
Magnitude of error	E	Managerial judgment or calculation ($Z S_{\bar{X}}$)
Confidence level	$Z_{c.l.}$	Managerial judgment

EXHIBIT 17.19
Statistical Information Needed to Determine Sample Size for Questions Involving Means

RESEARCH SNAPSHOT

Target and Wal-Mart Shoppers Really Are Different

Scarborough Research conducts ongoing consumer research that combines a telephone interview on media behavior with a mail survey about shopping habits and lifestyle and a television diary for detailed data about television viewing. Scarborough recognizes the importance of sample size for minimizing errors. Its sample includes over 200,000 adults so that it can make estimates of the U.S. population.

An example is a recent comparison of consumers who shop exclusively at either Target or Wal-Mart. When respondents were asked to identify the stores at which they had shopped during the preceding three months, the largest share (40 percent) named both Target and Wal-Mart. However, 31 percent shopped at Wal-Mart but not Target, and 12 percent shopped at Target but not Wal-Mart. Scarborough compared the consumer behavior of the latter two groups.

Target shoppers who shunned Wal-Mart were more likely to shop at more upscale stores, including Macy's and Nordstrom. They also were more likely than the average shopper to visit many different stores. Wal-Mart shoppers who stayed away from Target were more likely to shop at discounters such as Dollar General and Kmart, and they were more likely to be at least 50 years old. Target-only shoppers tended to be younger and were more likely to have a high household income.

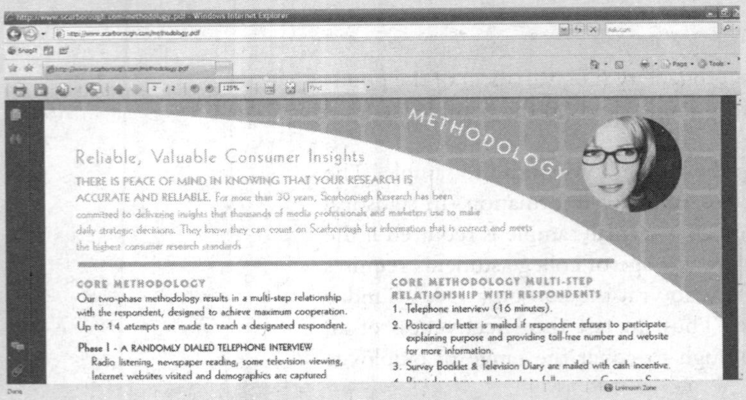

Given a U.S. adult population of approximately 220 million, do you think the sample size was adequate to make these comparisons?

Source: Based on "In the Battle for Discount Shoppers, Target and Wal-Mart Find Brand Loyalty in Different Customer Groups," Scarborough Research news release (September 19, 2005), http://www.scarborough.com; "About Scarborough: Methodology," Scarborough Research, http://www.scarborough.com, accessed March 16, 2006; U.S. Census Bureau, *Statistical Abstract of the United States* (2006), table 11, p. 13.

Estimating Sample Size for Questions Involving Means

Once the preceding concepts are understood, determining the actual size for a simple random sample is quite easy. The researcher must follow three steps:

1. Estimate the standard deviation of the population.
2. Make a judgment about the allowable magnitude of error.
3. Determine a confidence level.

The judgment about the allowable error and the confidence level are the manager's decision to make. Thus, the only problem is estimating the standard deviation of the population. Ideally, similar studies conducted in the past will give a basis for judging the standard deviation. In practice, researchers who lack prior information may conduct a pilot study to estimate the population parameters so that another, larger sample of the appropriate sample size may be drawn. This procedure is called *sequential sampling* because researchers take an initial look at the pilot study results before deciding on a larger sample to provide more precise information.

A rule of thumb for estimating the value of the standard deviation is to expect it to be about one-sixth of the range. If researchers conducting a study on television purchases expected the price paid to range from \$100 to \$700, a rule-of-thumb estimate for the standard deviation would be \$100. This is also useful when the question is a scaled response on a questionnaire. For example, if we plan on using a 10-point purchase intention scale, we can use our rule to determine the estimate for the standard deviation (10/6 = 1.67).

For the moment, assume that the standard deviation has been estimated in some preliminary work. If our concern is to estimate the mean of a particular population, the formula for sample size is

$$n = \left(\frac{ZS}{E}\right)^2$$

where

Z = standardized value that corresponds to the confidence level

S = sample standard deviation or estimate of the population standard deviation

E = acceptable magnitude of error, plus or minus error factor (range is one-half of the total confidence interval)[7]

Suppose a survey researcher studying annual expenditures on lipstick wishes to have a 95 percent confidence level ($Z = 1.96$) and a range of error (E) of less than \$2. If the estimate of the standard deviation is \$29, the sample size can be calculated as follows:

$$n = \left(\frac{ZS}{E}\right)^2 = \left(\frac{(1.96)(29)}{2}\right)^2 = \left(\frac{56.84}{2}\right)^2 = 28.42^2 = 808$$

If a range of error (E) of \$4 is acceptable, the necessary sample size will be reduced:

$$n = \left(\frac{ZS}{E}\right)^2 = \left(\frac{(1.96)(29)}{4}\right)^2 = \left(\frac{56.84}{4}\right)^2 = 14.21^2 = 202$$

Thus, doubling the range of acceptable error reduces sample size to approximately one-quarter of its original size. Stated conversely in a general sense, doubling sample size will reduce error by only approximately one-quarter.

The Influence of Population Size on Sample Size

The ACNielsen Company estimates television ratings. Throughout the years, it has been plagued with questions about how it is possible to rate 98 million or more television homes with such a small sample (approximately 5,000 households). The answer to that question is that in most cases the size of the population does not have an effect on the sample size. As we have indicated, the variance of the population has the largest effect on sample size. However, a finite correction factor may be needed to adjust a sample size that is more than 5 percent of a finite population. If the sample is large relative to the population, the foregoing procedures may overestimate sample size, and the researcher may need to adjust sample size. The finite correction factor is

$$\sqrt{\frac{(N-n)}{(N-1)}}$$

where

N = population size and n = sample size.

Factors in Determining Sample Size for Proportions

Researchers frequently are concerned with determining sample size for problems that involve estimating population proportions or percentages. When the question involves the estimation of a proportion, the researcher requires some knowledge of the logic for determining a confidence interval around a sample proportion estimation (p) of the population proportion (π). For a confidence interval to be constructed around the sample proportion (p), an estimate of the standard error of the proportion (S_p) must be calculated and a confidence level specified.

The precision of the estimate is indicated by the value $Z_{c.l.}S_p$. Thus, the plus-or-minus estimate of the population proportion is

$$\text{Confidence interval} = p \pm Z_{c.l.}S_p$$

If the researcher selects a 95 percent probability for the confidence interval, $Z_{c.l.}$ will equal 1.96 (see Table A.2 in the appendix). The formula for S_p is

$$S_p = \sqrt{\frac{pq}{n}} \text{ or } S_p = \sqrt{\frac{p(1-p)}{n}}$$

where

S_p = estimate of the standard error of the proportion

p = proportion of successes

$q = 1 - p$, or proportion of failures

Suppose that 20 percent of a sample of 1,200 television viewers recall seeing an advertisement. The proportion of successes (p) equals 0.2, and the proportion of failures (q) equals 0.8. We estimate the 95 percent confidence interval as follows:

$$\begin{aligned}\text{Confidence Interval} &= p \pm Z_{c.l.} S_p \\ &= 0.2 \pm 1.96 S_p \\ &= 0.2 \pm 1.96\sqrt{\frac{p(1-p)}{n}} \\ &= 0.2 \pm 1.96\sqrt{\frac{0.2(1-0.2)}{1{,}200}} \\ &= 0.2 \pm 1.96\sqrt{\frac{0.16}{1{,}200}} = 0.2 \pm 1.96(0.0115) \\ &= 0.2 \pm 0.022\end{aligned}$$

Thus, the population proportion who see an advertisement is estimated to be included in the interval between 0.178 and 0.222, or roughly between 18 and 22 percent, with a 95 percent confidence coefficient.

To determine *sample size* for a proportion, the researcher must make a judgment about confidence level and the maximum allowance for random sampling error. Furthermore, the size of the proportion influences random sampling error, so an estimate of the expected proportion of successes must be made, based on intuition or prior information. The formula is

$$n = \frac{Z_{c.l.}^2 pq}{E^2}$$

where

n = number of items in sample

$Z_{c.l.}^2$ = square of the confidence level in standard error units

p = estimated proportion of successes

$q = 1 - p$, or estimated proportion of failures

E^2 = square of the maximum allowance for error between the true proportion and the sample proportion, or $Z_{c.l.} S_p$ squared

Suppose a researcher believes that a simple random sample will show that 60 percent of the population (p) recognizes the name of an automobile dealership. The researcher wishes to estimate with 95 percent confidence ($Z_{c.l.} = 1.96$) that the allowance for sampling error is not greater than 3.5 percentage points (E). Substituting these values into the formula gives

$$\begin{aligned}n &= \frac{(1.96)^2(0.6)(0.4)}{0.035^2} \\ &= \frac{(3.8416)(0.24)}{0.001225} \\ &= \frac{0.922}{0.001225} = 753\end{aligned}$$

Calculating Sample Size for Sample Proportions

In practice, a number of tables have been constructed for determining sample size.

The theoretical principles underlying calculation of sample sizes of proportions are similar to the concepts discussed in this chapter. Suppose we wish to take samples in two large cities, New Orleans and Miami. We wish no more than 2 percentage points of error, and we will be satisfied with a 95 percent confidence level. If we assume all other things are equal, then in the New Orleans market, where 15 percent of the consumers favor our product and 85 percent prefer competitors' brands, we need a sample of 1,222 to get results with only 2 percentage points of error. In the Miami market, however, where 30 percent of the consumers favor our brand and 70 percent prefer other brands (a less heterogeneous market), we need a sample size of 2,009 to get the same sample reliability.

Determining Sample Size on the Basis of Judgment

Just as sample units may be selected to suit the convenience or judgment of the researcher, sample size may also be determined on the basis of managerial judgments. Using a sample size similar to those used in previous studies provides the inexperienced researcher with a comparison with other researchers' judgments.

Another judgmental factor that affects the determination of sample size is the selection of the appropriate item, question, or characteristic to be used for the sample size calculations. Several different characteristics affect most studies, and the desired degree of precision may vary for these items. The researcher must exercise some judgment to determine which item will be used. Often the item that will produce the largest sample size will be used to determine the ultimate sample size. However, the cost of data collection becomes a major consideration, and judgment must be exercised regarding the importance of such information.

Another consideration stems from most researchers' need to analyze various subgroups within the sample. For example, suppose a researcher wants to look at employee attitudes, but is particularly interested in differences across genders and age groups. The analyst will want to make sure to sample an adequate number of men and women, as well as across the various age groups to ensure that subgroup comparisons are reliable. There is a judgmental rule of thumb for selecting minimum subgroup sample size: Each subgroup to be separately analyzed should have a minimum of 100 units in each category of the major breakdowns. With this procedure, the total sample size is computed by totaling the sample sizes necessary for these subgroups.

Determining Sample Size for Stratified and Other Probability Samples

Stratified sampling involves drawing separate probability samples within the subgroups to make the sample more efficient. With a stratified sample, the sample variances are expected to differ by strata. This makes the determination of sample size more complex. Increased complexity may also characterize the determination of sample size for cluster sampling and other probability sampling methods. The formulas are beyond the scope of this book. Students interested in these advanced sampling techniques should investigate advanced sampling textbooks.

Determining Level of Precision after Data Collection

Up to this point, we have discussed the process for determining how large of a sample we need to collect given the estimated variance among the responses and our desired level of precision and acceptable error. This is a very important consideration for researchers. However, after we have collected the data, we also want to determine our level of precision, given the size of the sample, the variance, and the confidence level. In this case, we can rewrite our equation for determining sample size:

$$n = \left(\frac{ZS}{E}\right)^2$$

Rather than solving for n, we now know n and instead want to solve for E, the magnitude of error. Our new equation would be:

$$E^2 = \frac{(ZS)^2}{n}$$

So, we could solve for E^2, and then take the square root of this to determine our level of precision. This is a useful approach to use after-the-fact to show our final level of precision. In our earlier example of sample size regarding lipstick expenditures, we found that if we wanted to be 95% confident (Z value of 1.96) that our estimate of expenditures was within \$2.00 and we had a standard deviation of \$29.00, we would need a sample size of 808. Using the same situation, let's assume we had already collected the data, but were not certain of our level of precision. Our formula above would show:

$$(1.96 \times 29)^2/808 = 4$$

The square root of 4 is 2.

When completing a research project it is often a good idea to provide managers with the level of precision for key measures. This formula will allow you to do so.

Determination of Sample Size

Sample size refers to the number of elements to be included in the research study. There are a lot of important qualitative factors that should be considered while determining the sample size. These include

1. The importance of the decision
2. The nature of the research
3. The number of variables
4. The nature of the analysis
5. Sample sizes used in similar studies
6. Incidence rates
7. Completion rates
8. Resource constraints

More information is necessary for more important decisions and this should be obtained more precisely. This requires larger sample size, but as the sample size increases, each extra unit of information is obtained at higher cost. The degree of precision can be measured in terms of standard deviation of the mean. This standard deviation is inversely proportional to the square root of the sample size.

The sample size is usually small for exploratory research designs whereas larger samples are required for conclusive research. Large samples are required if data is being collected about a number of variables.

The sample size should be large if we intend to do sophisticated analysis of the data using multivariate techniques. The same applies if the data are to be scrutinized in great detail. Thus, a larger sample would be required if data is being evaluated at the subgroup or segment level than if the evaluation is limited to the total sample.

Resource constraints should also be taken into consideration while deciding on the sample size. In any marketing research project, money and time are limited. Some of the other constraints can be the availability of competent personnel for data collection.

Confidence interval method to determine sample size:

1. Using means:

$$n = \frac{\sigma^2 z^2}{D^2}$$

where

n = sample size

z = the number of standard errors a point is away from the mean or proportion,

$$z = \frac{(x - \mu)}{s/\sqrt{n}}$$

x = sample mean

σ = sample standard deviation

D = deviation of x from μ

Type of Study	Min Size	Typical Range
Problem identification research	500 or 15 times of the number of variables whichever is more.	1000–2500
Problem-solving research	200 or 10 times of the number of variables whichever is more.	300–500
Product tests	200 or 10 times of the number of variables whichever is more.	300–500
Test-marketing studies	200 or 10 times of the number of variables whichever is more.	300–500
TV/Radio/Print advertising	150 or 7 times of the number of variables whichever is more.	200–300
Test-market audits	10 stores	10–20 stores
Focus groups	3 groups	6–15 groups

With finite population correction,

$$n_c = \frac{nN}{(N + n - 1)}$$

2. Using proportions:

$$n = \frac{\pi(1-\pi)z^2}{D^2}$$

where

π = population proportion

D = deviation of sample proportion from population proportion, $D = p - \pi$

p = sample proportion

Non-Response and Handling of Non-Responses

Non-response error happens when some of the respondents included in the sample do not respond to it. The two major non-response issues involved in sampling are improving response rates and making adjustments for non-response. Non-respondents may differ from respondents in terms of psychographic, demographic, attitudinal, personality, motivational, and behavioral variables. The sample estimates are seriously biased in such cases. Higher response rates usually imply lower rates of non-response bias but response rates do not always indicate whether the respondents are demonstrative of the original sample.

TIPS OF THE TRADE

- Population parameters are the numerical characteristics of a population. Statistics are the numerical characteristics of a sample.
  - Thus, a parameter represents for a population what a statistic represents for a sample.
- When we know all the information from all members of the population, we don't need inferential statistics. For example, if we find that the average grade on the business research exam for our class is 86 for women and 84 for men, we can conclude that—on average—women in our class scored higher than men in our class. In this case, the population of interest is our class. We do not need to do any statistical test. However, if we want to project these results onto all women and men taking the business research class at all universities, then we would need to use inferential statistics. The exact statistical test we would use is discussed in Chapter 21.
- The three measures of central tendency discussed in this chapter each have their own strengths and weaknesses. The mean is very commonly used as it represents the arithmetic average of all the observations. However, the mean can be misleading, especially when there are *outliers* in the data. In this case, the median is usually a better indicator of the "average" value. This is common in situations such as income or real estate prices.
- The formula for calculating sample size is based on three factors—the level of confidence, the acceptable error, and the variance in the population. For all practical purposes, the size of the population does not matter. Consider an employee satisfaction study. If we have 100,000 employees and they all feel exactly the same (no variance), we would only have to talk to one employee to know how satisfied they were. However, if we have 10 employees, but they all have very different attitudes, we might need to talk to all 10. The variance in the population is the key issue, not the size of the population.

Handling Non-Responses

1. Sub-sampling of non-respondents: This can be effective in case of mail surveys. In this method, the researcher contacts a sub-sample of the non-respondents by means of personal interviews or telephone. This results in a high response rate within the sub-sample.
2. Replacement: In this method, the non-respondents in the survey are replaced with non-respondents from an earlier, similar survey. The researcher attempts to contact these non-respondents from the earlier survey and sends the current survey questionnaire to them. This can only be possibly by offering a suitable incentive to fill out the survey.
3. Substitution: Here, the researcher substitutes for non-respondents from the sampling frame that is expected to respond. For this initially the sampling frame is divided into subgroups which are internally homogenous in terms of respondent features, but heterogeneous in terms of their response rates. These subgroups are used to identify substitutes similar to particular non-respondents but dissimilar to respondents in the sample.
4. Subjective estimates: When it is no longer possible to increase the response rate by sub-sampling, substitution, or replacement, it may be feasible to arrive at subjective estimates of the nature and effect of non-response bias. This method involves evaluating the likely effects of non-response based on available information and experience.
5. Trend analysis: It is an attempt to detect a trend between early and late respondents. This trend is anticipated for non-respondents to estimate where they stand on the particular characteristic of interest. Each successive wave of respondents becomes closer to the non-respondents.
6. Weighting: It tries to account for non-responses by assigning differential weights to the data contingent on the response rates. In examining the data, the subgroups are given weights inversely proportional to their response rates. Although this method can correct for differential effects of non-response, it also leads to destruction of the self-weighing nature of the sampling design and hence leads to other complications.
7. Imputation: This involves assigning the characteristic of the non-respondents based on similarity of variables available for both respondents and non-respondents. For example, a

respondent who did not report brand usage can be imputed from the usage of a respondent with comparable demographic characteristics. Often there is a strong correlation between the characteristic of our interest and some other variables. In these cases, this correlation can be used to forecast the value of the characteristic for non-respondents.

A Reminder about Statistics

Learning the terms and symbols defined in this chapter will provide you with the basics of the language of statisticians and researchers. As you learn more about the pragmatic use of statistics in marketing research, do not forget these concepts. Rules are important in learning a foreign language and when the rules are forgotten, being understood becomes very difficult. The same is true for the student who forgets the basics of the "foreign language" of statistics.

Summary

1. Understand basic statistical terminology. Determination of sample size requires a knowledge of statistics. Statistics is the language of the researcher, and this chapter introduced its vocabulary. Descriptive statistics describe characteristics of a population or sample. Thus, calculating a mean and a standard deviation to "describe" or profile a sample is a commonly applied descriptive statistical approach. Inferential statistics investigate samples to draw conclusions about entire populations. If a mean is computed and then compared to some preconceived standard, then inferential statistics are being implemented.

2. Interpret frequency distributions, proportions, and measures of central tendency and dispersion. A frequency distribution shows how frequently each response or classification occurs. A simple tally count illustrates a frequency distribution. A proportion indicates the percentage of group members that have a particular characteristic. Three measures of central tendency are commonly used: the mean, or arithmetic average; the median, or halfway value; and the mode, or most frequently observed value. These three values may be either the same or they may differ, and care must be taken to understand distortions that may arise from using the wrong measure of central tendency. Measures of dispersion further describe a distribution. The range is the difference between the largest and smallest values observed. The most useful measures of dispersion are the variance (the summation of each observation's deviation from the mean, divided by one less than the number of observations) and standard deviation, which is the square root of the variance.

3. Distinguish among population, sample, and sampling distributions. The techniques of statistical inference are based on the relationship among the population distribution, the sample distribution, and the sampling distribution. The population distribution is a frequency distribution of the elements of a population. The sample distribution is a frequency distribution of a sample. A sampling distribution is a theoretical probability distribution of sample means for all possible samples of a certain size drawn from a particular population. The sampling distribution's mean is the expected value of the mean, which equals the population's mean. The standard deviation of the sampling distribution is the standard error of the mean, approximately equal to the standard deviation of the population, divided by the square root of the sample size.

4. Explain the central-limit theorem. The central-limit theorem states that as sample size increases, the distribution of sample means of size n, randomly selected, approaches a normal distribution. This theoretical knowledge can be used to estimate parameters and determine sample size.

5. Summarize the use of confidence interval estimates. Estimating a population mean with a single value gives a point estimate. The confidence interval estimate is a range of numbers within which the researcher is confident that the population mean will lie. The confidence level is a percentage that indicates the long-run probability that the confidence interval estimate will be correct. Many research problems involve the estimation of proportions. Statistical techniques may be used to determine a confidence interval around a sample proportion.

6. Discuss the major issues in specifying sample size. The statistical determination of sample size requires knowledge of (1) the variance of the population, (2) the magnitude of acceptable error, and (3) the confidence level. Several computational formulas are available for determining sample size. Furthermore, a number of easy-to-use tables have been compiled to help researchers calculate sample size. The main reason a large sample size is desirable is that sample size is related to random sampling error. A smaller sample makes a larger error in estimates more likely. Calculation of sample size for a sample proportion is not difficult. However, most researchers use tables that indicate predetermined sample sizes.

Key Terms and Concepts

Questions for Review and Critical Thinking

1. What is the difference between descriptive and inferential statistics?
2. Suppose the speed limits in 13 countries in miles per hour are as follows:

Country	Highway Miles per Hour
Italy	87
France	81
Hungary	75
Belgium	75
Portugal	75
Great Britain	70
Spain	62
Denmark	62
Netherlands	62
Greece	62
Japan	62
Norway	56
Turkey	56

What is the mean, median, and mode for these data? Feel free to use your computer (statistical software or spreadsheet) to get the answer.

3. Prepare a frequency distribution for the data in question 2.
4. Why is the standard deviation rather than the average deviation typically used?
5. Calculate the standard deviation for the data in question 2.
6. Draw three distributions that have the same mean value but different standard deviation values. Draw three distributions that have the same standard deviation value but different mean values.
7. A manufacturer of MP3 players surveyed one hundred retail stores in each of the firm's sales regions. An analyst noticed that in the South Atlantic region the average retail price was $165 (mean) and the standard deviation was $30. However, in the Mid-Atlantic region the mean price was $170, with a standard deviation of $15. What do these statistics tell us about these two sales regions?
8. What is the sampling distribution? How does it differ from the sample distribution?
9. What would happen to the sampling distribution of the mean if we increased sample size from 5 to 25?
10. Suppose a fast-food restaurant wishes to estimate average sales volume for a new menu item. The restaurant has analyzed the sales of the item at a similar outlet and observed the following results:

$\overline{X}$ = 500 (mean daily sales)
s = 100 (standard deviation of sample)
n = 25 (sample size)

The restaurant manager wants to know into what range the mean daily sales should fall 95 percent of the time. Perform this calculation.

11. In our example of research on lipstick, where E = $2 and S = $29, what sample size would we require if we desired a 99 percent confidence level? What about if we keep the 95% confidence level, but decide that our acceptable error is $4?
12. Suppose you are planning to sample cat owners to determine the average number of cans of cat food they purchase monthly. The following standards have been set: a confidence level of 99 percent and an error of less than five units. Past research has indicated that the standard deviation should be 6 units. What is the required sample size?
13. In a survey of 500 people, 60 percent responded with agreement to an attitude question. Calculate a confidence interval at 95 percent to get an interval estimate for a proportion.
14. What is a standardized normal curve?
15. A researcher expects the population proportion of Cubs fans in Chicago to be 80 percent. The researcher wishes to have an error of less than 5 percent and to be 95 percent confident of an estimate to be made from a mail survey. What sample size is required?

16. **ETHICS** Using the formula in this chapter, a researcher determines that at the 95 percent confidence level, a sample of 2,500 is required to satisfy a client's requirements. The researcher actually uses a sample of 1,200, however, because the client has specified a budget cap for the survey. What are the ethical considerations in this situation?
17. **'NET** Go to **http://www.dartmouth.edu/~chance/** to visit the Chance course. The Chance course is an innovative program to creatively teach introductory materials about probability and statistics. The Chance course is designed to enhance quantitative literacy. Numerous videos can be played online.
18. **'NET** Go to **http://www.researchinfo.com**. Click on "Marketing Research Calculators." Which of the calculators can be used to help find the sample size required? How big of a sample is needed to make an inference about the U.S. population ±5 percent? How large a sample is needed to make an inference about the population of Norway ±5 percent? Remember, population statistics can be found in the *CIA World Factbook* online. Comment.
19. **'NET** A random number generator and other statistical information can be found at **http://www.random.org**. Flip some virtual coins. Perform 20 flips with an Aurelian coin. Perform 20 flips with a Constatius coin. Perform frequency tables for each result. What conclusion might you draw? Would the result change if you flipped the coins 200 times or 2,000 times?

Research Activities

1. **'NET** Go to **http://www.surveypro.com**. Click on pricing. Write a brief report that describes how prices are charged to someone wishing to use this service to host a survey. What happens as the desired sample size increases? Why is this?
2. **'NET** Use an online library service to find basic business research studies that report a "response rate" or number of respondents compared to number of contacts. You may wish to consult journals such as the *Journal of Business Research,* the *Journal of Marketing,* or the *Journal of Management.* Find at least 25 such studies. What is the average response rate across all of these studies? Do there appear to be any trends or factors that are associated with lower response rates? Write a brief report on your findings.

Case 17.1 Pointsec Mobile Technologies

© GETTY IMAGES/ PHOTODISC GREEN

When salespeople, construction supervisors, managers, and other employees are away from the workplace, many of them carry mobile devices such as laptop computers and PDAs, often containing valuable, private data related to their jobs. Pointsec (**http://www.checkpoint.com/pointsec**) provides security systems to protect such data. To bring home the vulnerability of mobile devices, Pointsec decided to share information about the number of such devices left behind in taxis.[8]

The research involved conducting a survey of taxi drivers. Staff members at Pointsec's public relations firm called major taxi companies in nine cities in Australia, Denmark, Finland, France, Germany, Norway, Sweden, Great Britain, and the United States. Each of the cooperating companies put these interviewers in touch with about one hundred drivers. Drivers were asked how many devices of each type—cell phones, PDAs, computers, and so on—had been left in their cab over the preceding six months. From these numbers, they came up with the rate of items left behind. Multiplying by the size of taxi fleets in each city, the researchers came up with city-by-city numbers: 3.42 cell phones per cab yielded 85,619 cell phones left behind in Chicago, for example. In London, the researchers concluded 63,135 cell phones were left in cabs, a startling increase of 71 percent compared to four years earlier.

Questions

1. Discuss why the sampling method and sample size make these results questionable, even though the numbers were reported as if they were precise.
2. The simple survey method described in the case may have been sufficient as a way to draw attention to the issue of data security. However, if the company were using data on lost mobile devices to predict demand for a product, accuracy might be more significant. Imagine that you have been asked to collect data on mobile devices left in cabs, and you wish to be able to report results with a 95 percent confidence level. How can you improve the sample design and select an appropriate sample size?

CHAPTER 18
FIELDWORK

LEARNING OUTCOMES

After studying this chapter, you should be able to

1. **Describe the role and job requirements of fieldworkers**
2. **Summarize the skills to cover when training inexperienced interviewers**
3. **List principles of good interviewing**
4. **Describe the activities involved in the management of fieldworkers**
5. **Discuss how supervisors can minimize errors in the field**

Chapter Vignette: Software for Fieldwork? Ask Askia

Fieldwork is difficult to quantify, but it can best be described as collecting data "out there." Whether it is in a mall or customer service location or even in remote towns and villages, fieldwork requires a researcher to oftentimes directly interact with consumers and households to gather specialized or detailed data. In the past, fieldworkers used notebooks and clipboards to gather data, capturing information by hand as they interacted with the respondent. Once the information was collected, the fieldworker often would return to the research organization and arduously code the handwritten notes into a database or statistical package. Fortunately, technology has made this process significantly easier.

One example of a company that has specialized in face-to-face fieldwork software is Askia. Askia has developed a fully functioning software application that works with tablet PCs and PDAs for field researchers. Their system (Askia Face) represents an important advantage to field research, since their interface provides seamless integration with telephone-assisted survey databases and an ability to directly download data into an analysis program. The Askia Face system fieldworkers can have their survey applications updated on-the-fly, without having to return to their research base to update materials. Users can even use multimedia to present products or services, or provide illustrations for the respondent. Askia has developed client relationships with companies around the world, and has seen the number of their customers triple each year.

© STEPHEN COBURN/SHUTTERSTOCK

Conducting field research is hard enough, without having the proper quality control and information turnaround that is so critical these days. The ability to capture and integrate field notes and information through Askia Face is one example of how technology has assisted fieldwork research. So, if you are challenged by your own fieldwork data needs, perhaps you too should "Ask Askia!"[1]

Introduction

Much of the work of a business researcher involves interacting with stakeholders within the organization. But when it is required, the researcher must conduct data collections with potential clients or customers outside of the firm. Similar to the term used for anthropologists or biologists who must go into far-away countries or into local fields and forests; this is referred to as working "in the field," or fieldwork. This chapter highlights this critical activity for business researchers.

The Nature of Fieldwork

A personal interviewer administering a questionnaire door to door, a telephone interviewer calling from a central location, an observer counting pedestrians in a shopping mall, and others involved in the collection of data and the supervision of that process—each of these people is a **fieldworker**. The activities they perform vary substantially. The supervision of data collection for a mail survey differs from that for an observation study as much as the factory production process for cereal differs from that for a pair of ski boots. Yet, just as quality control is basic to each production operation, the same basic issues arise in the various types of fieldwork. For ease of presentation, this chapter focuses on the interviewing process conducted by personal interviewers. However, many of the issues apply to all fieldworkers, no matter what their specific settings.

fieldworker
An individual who is responsible for gathering data in the field.

Who Conducts the Fieldwork?

The actual data collection process is rarely carried out by the person who designs the research. However, the data-collecting stage is crucial, because the research project is no better than the data collected in the field. So, the research director must select capable people and trust them to gather the data. An irony of business research is that highly educated and trained individuals design the research, but when typical surveys are conducted, the people who gather the data usually have little research training or experience. Knowing that research is no better than the data collected in the field, research administrators must concentrate on carefully selecting fieldworkers.

Much fieldwork is conducted by research suppliers that specialize in data collection. When a second party is subcontracted, the job of the study designer at the parent firm is not only to hire a research supplier but also to build in supervisory controls over the field service. In some cases a third-party firm is employed. For example, a company may contact a research firm that in turn subcontracts the fieldwork to a **field interviewing service**.

field interviewing service
A research supplier that specializes in gathering data.

As seen in the Research Snapshot "Interviewing for Horizon Research Services," various field interviewing services and full-service research agencies perform all manner of personal surveys including central location telephone interviewing, mall-intercepts, and other forms of fieldwork for a fee. These agencies typically employ field supervisors who supervise and train interviewers, edit completed questionnaires in the field, and telephone or recontact respondents to confirm that interviews have been conducted.

Whether the research administrator hires an **in-house interviewer** or selects a field interviewing service, fieldworkers should ideally meet certain job requirements. Although the job requirements for different types of surveys vary, normally interviewers should be healthy, outgoing, and of pleasing appearance—that is, well-groomed and tailored. People who enjoy talking with strangers usually make better interviewers. An essential part of the interviewing process is establishing rapport with the respondent. An outgoing nature may help interviewers ensure respondents' full cooperation. Interviewer bias may occur if the fieldworker's clothing or physical appearance is unattractive or unusual. One exception to this would be ethnographic research. In ethnographic research, the interviewer should dress to blend in with the group being studied. So, if holey jeans and a dirty T-shirt are the dress *du jour,* then the interviewer should dress likewise.

in-house interviewer
A fieldworker who is employed by the company conducting the research.

TOTHEPOINT

The knowledge of the world is only to be acquired in the world and not in the closet.

—Lord Chesterfield

Survey interviewers generally are paid hourly rates or per-interview fees. Often interviewers are part-time workers from a variety of backgrounds—homemakers, graduate students, schoolteachers, and others. Some research projects require special knowledge or skills, such as familiarity with the topic they are asking about. In a survey investigating whether health education improves the likelihood that people who have suffered a stroke will quit smoking, the researchers used trained nurses to administer questionnaires that included each patient's medical history.[2] Taking an accurate medical history is a skill that requires more training than most interviewers would likely have.

In-House Training for Inexperienced Interviewers

After personnel are recruited and selected, they must be trained.[3] Suppose a woman who has just sent her youngest child off to first grade is hired by a research interviewing firm. She has decided to become a professional interviewer. The training she will receive after being hired may vary from virtually no training to an extensive, three-day program if she is selected by one of the larger research companies. Almost always, trainees will receive a **briefing session** on the particular project.

briefing session
A training session to ensure that each interviewer is provided with common information.

The objective of training is to ensure that the data collection instrument will be administered in a uniform fashion by all fieldworkers. The goal of training sessions is to ensure that each respondent is provided with common information. If the data are collected in a uniform manner from all respondents, the training session will have succeeded.

More extensive training programs are likely to cover the following topics:

- How to make initial contact with the respondent and secure the interview
- How to ask survey questions
- How to probe
- How to record responses
- How to terminate the interview

Typically, recruits record answers on a practice questionnaire during a simulated training interview.

Making Initial Contact and Securing the Interview

PERSONAL INTERVIEWS

Personal interviewers may carry a letter of identification or an ID card to indicate that the study is a *bona fide* research project and not a sales pitch. Interviewers are trained to make appropriate opening remarks that will convince the respondent that his or her cooperation is important, as in this example:

> *Good afternoon, my name is ____________, and I'm with [insert name of firm], an international research company. We are conducting a survey concerning ____________. I would like to get a few of your ideas. It will take [insert accurate time estimate] minutes.*

TELEPHONE INTERVIEWS

For the initial contact in a telephone interview, the introduction might be something like this:

> *Good evening, my name is ____________. I am not trying to sell anything. I'm calling from [insert name of firm] in Mason, Ohio. We are seeking your opinions on some important matters and it will only take [insert accurate time estimate] minutes of your time.*

Giving the interviewer's name personalizes the call. The name of the research agency is used to imply that the caller is trustworthy. The respondent must be given an accurate estimate of the time

RESEARCH SNAPSHOT

Interviewing for Horizon Research Services

Along with the big-name national and international research firms like Yankelovich, Nielsen, and Gallup, many smaller research companies offer interviewing and other services to clients in their city or region. An example is Horizon Research Services (**http://www.horizonresearch.com**), located in Columbia, Missouri. Founded by Kathleen Anger, a psychologist with a deep sense of curiosity, Horizon has served local organizations including Columbia's banks and hospitals. The company conducts focus groups, telephone surveys, and other research projects.

One of the most significant challenges of the interviewer's job is simply to keep the respondent from hanging up. In the first few seconds of the phone call, fieldworkers quickly reassure the person that the call is for research, not to sell them something. After that, retaining respondents becomes a matter of reinforcing that they are "doing a good service [because] it's for research."

Horizon's telephone interviewers also recruit people to participate in focus groups. Typically, the company needs four interviewers to spend about three hours just to fill a twelve-person focus group. The reason is that finding willing individuals who meet the project's specifications may require up to six hundred phone calls!

Horizon has recently formed partnerships with World Marketing and Fusion Marketing & Design. As a result, a researcher can get both consulting services and creative design to go along with the field research. In the end, they can get the total package by using all three partners together.

Source: Based on Coleman, Kevin, "Research Firm Reflects Consumer Trends," Columbia (Missouri) *Daily Tribune* (May 21, 2005), downloaded from http://www.columbiatribune.com; and Horizon Research Services Web site, http://www.horizonresearch.com, accessed March 27, 2006.

it will take to participate in the interview. If someone is told that only three minutes will be required for participation, and the interview proceeds to five minutes or more, the respondent will tend to quit before completing the interview. Providing an accurate estimate of the time not only helps gain cooperation, but it is also the ethically correct thing to do.

Fieldworkers need training both in the basics and required practices or good interviewing principles.

INTERNET SURVEYS

A similar approach may be used to an Internet survey. The potential respondent may receive an e-mail requesting assistance, as in the following example:

> *We are contacting you because of your interest in [subject matter inserted here]. We would like to invite you to participate in a survey that asks your opinion on matters related to [subject matter inserted here]. In return for your participation, we will [insert incentive here]. To participate, click on this URL: http:/lwww.clickhere.com.*

GAINING PARTICIPATION

The Interviewer's Manual from the Survey Research Center at the University of Michigan recommends avoiding questions that ask permission for the interview, such as "May I come in?" and "Would you mind answering some questions?" Some people will refuse to participate or object to being interviewed. Interviewers should be instructed on handling objections. For example, if the respondent says, "I'm too busy right now," the interviewer might be instructed to respond, "Will you be in at four o'clock this afternoon? I would be happy to schedule a time with you." In other cases, client companies will not wish to offend any individual. In this case, the interviewer will be instructed to merely say, "Thank you for your time."

foot-in-the-door compliance technique

A technique for obtaining a high response rate, in which compliance with a large or difficult task is induced by first obtaining the respondent's compliance with a smaller request.

door-in-the-face compliance technique

A two-step process for securing a high response rate. In step 1 an initial request, so large that nearly everyone refuses it, is made. Next, a second request is made for a smaller favor; respondents are expected to comply with this more reasonable request.

The **foot-in-the-door compliance technique** and the **door-in-the-face compliance technique** are useful in securing interviews. Foot-in-the-door theory attempts to explain compliance with a large or difficult task on the basis of respondents' earlier compliance with a smaller initial request. One experiment has shown that compliance with a minor telephone interview (that is, a small request that few people refuse) will lead to greater compliance with a second, larger request to fill out a long mail questionnaire. An interviewer employing door-in-the-face technique begins by making an initial request so large that nearly everyone will react negatively (that is, slam the door in his or her face). When this happens, the interviewer can then request a smaller favor, such as asking a respondent to participate in a "short" survey. However, this technique presents an ethical issue if the respondent is deceived. Thus, the initial request should also be a legitimate request.

Asking the Questions

The purpose of an interview is, of course, to record a respondent's answers. Training in the art of asking questions can be extremely beneficial, because interviewer bias can be a source of considerable error in survey research.

There are five major rules for asking questions:

1. Ask questions exactly as they are worded in the questionnaire.
2. Read each question very carefully and clearly.
3. Ask the questions in the specified order.
4. Ask every question specified in the questionnaire.
5. Repeat questions that are misunderstood or misinterpreted.[4]

Interviewers are generally trained to know these rules, but when working in the field, many do not follow these procedures exactly. Inexperienced interviewers may not understand the importance of strict adherence to the instructions. Even professional interviewers take shortcuts when the task becomes monotonous. Interviewers may shorten questions or rephrase unconsciously when they rely on their memory of the question rather than reading the question as it is worded. Even the slightest change in wording may inject some bias into a study. By reading the question, the interviewer may be reminded to concentrate on avoiding slight variations in tone of voice on particular words or phrases.

If respondents do not understand a question, they usually will ask for some clarification. The recommended procedure is to repeat the question. If the person does not understand a word such as HDTV (high definition television) in the question "Do you feel HDTV should be the standard delivery for television networks?" the interviewer should respond with the full name of the acronym. If the respondent still doesn't understand, then the interviewer may say, "Just whatever it means to you." However, interviewers often supply their own personal definitions and ad lib clarifications, and they may include words that are not free from bias. One reason interviewers do this is that field supervisors tend to reward people for submitting completed questionnaires and to be less tolerant of interviewers who leave questions blank because of alleged misunderstandings.

Often respondents volunteer information relevant to a question that is supposed to be asked at a later point in the interview. In this situation the response should be recorded under the question that deals specifically with that subject. Then, rather than skip the question that was answered out of sequence, the interviewer should be trained to say something like "We have briefly discussed this, but let me ask you. . . ." By asking every question, the interviewer can be sure that complete answers are recorded. If the partial answer to a question answered out of sequence is recorded on the space reserved for the earlier question and the subsequent question is skipped, an omission error will occur when the data are tabulated.

Probing When No Response Is Given

Similar to the approach discussed for qualitative interviews, interviewers should be provided instructions on how to probe when respondents give no answer, incomplete answers, or answers

RESEARCH SNAPSHOT

Why Is "Why" Important?

The use of field interviews to answer specific research questions has many logistic and quality management challenges, but in many ways field interviews are unique in the ability to really capture what a respondent is thinking about. This is due to the very nature of the field interview—the ability to follow up and probe deeper on a respondent's initial response. A key way that interviewers can capture this is through asking "why" follow-up questions.

Calo Research Services makes asking "why" their business. Whether it is for consumer research or for managerial strategy, Calo Research Services has adopted a philosophy from the top down that stresses the importance of asking why. For example, a company that was a participant in a professional trade show determined that capturing the number of visitors to their booth would help them evaluate the success of their presentation. However, it became clear that counting visitors does not really determine success—visitors can stop by for any number of reasons—the real question is why they stopped by the booth.

© XINHUA/LANDOV

Calo assisted the company by conducting a short interview that asked why the visitor to the booth was there, and what got their attention when they first appeared. This allowed the company to understand what was really connecting visitors to their booth, and allowed them to build on what was successful for their other presentations around the country.

Field interviewers that can probe deeper into the question of interest will recognize the value of this approach. Because the face-to-face interview can help tease out this kind of information—why not take advantage of this approach?

Source: Calo Research Services, Inc., http://www.caloresearch.com, accessed April 8, 2009.

© iStock

that require clarification. As demonstrated in the two preceding snapshots, probing questions can help in the clarification of a question within the interview process. By asking "why" carefully, the researcher can gain additional insight into the thoughts, attitudes, and behaviors of the respondent. First, probing is necessary when a respondent must be motivated to expand on, clarify, explain, or complete his or her answer. Interviewers must encourage respondents to clarify or expand on answers by providing a stimulus that will not suggest their own ideas or attitudes. An ability to probe with neutral stimuli is a mark of an experienced and effective interviewer. Second, probing may be necessary when a respondent begins to ramble or lose track. In such cases, a respondent must be led to focus on the specific content of the interview and to avoid irrelevant and unnecessary information.

Interviewers have several possible probing tactics to choose from, depending on the situation:

- *Repeating the question.* When the respondent remains completely silent, he or she may not have understood the question or decided how to answer it. Mere repetition may encourage the respondent to answer in such cases. For example, if the question is "What do you not like about Guinness?" and the respondent does not answer, the interviewer may probe: "Just to check, is there anything that you do not like about Guinness?"
- *Using a silent probe.* If the interviewer believes that the respondent has more to say, a silent probe—that is, an expectant pause or look—may motivate the respondent to gather his or her thoughts and give a complete response.
- *Repeating the respondent's reply.* As the interviewer records the response, he or she may repeat the respondent's reply verbatim. This may stimulate the respondent to expand on the answer.
- *Asking a neutral question.* Asking a neutral question may specifically indicate the type of information that the interviewer is seeking. For example, if the interviewer believes that the respondent's motives should be clarified, he or she might ask, "Tell me about this feeling." If the interviewer feels that there is a need to clarify a word or phrase, he or she might say, "What do you mean by ______________?"

The purpose of asking questions as probes is to encourage responses. Such probes should be neutral and not leading. Probes may be general (such as "Anything else?") or they may be questions specifically designed by the interviewer to clarify a particular statement by the respondent.

RESEARCH SNAPSHOT

Probing for Deeper Meaning at Olson Zaltman Associates

At Olson Zaltman Associates, highly trained interviewers probe for the deeper thinking that underlies attitudes toward brands or product categories. The research firm's method, called ZMET (for Zaltman Metaphor Elicitation Technique), begins by asking each respondent to come to a one-on-one interview, bringing along a set of eight to ten photographs related to their thoughts and feelings about the interview's topic. The interviewer uses the photos as nonverbal clues about the associations the person makes with the product or brand.

A typical interview lasts two hours. The interviewer's challenge is to ask questions that reveal what is behind the selection of the photographs without actually suggesting the interviewer's own ideas. The interviewer begins by asking the respondent to describe the topic-related thoughts and feelings that each picture illustrates. The interviewer then probes to uncover a deeper meaning by asking the respondent to elaborate on the initial statements. This process requires skill based on training in fields such as psychotherapy and sociology. Finally, the respondent works with an associate to create a computerized collage that illustrates the respondent's thoughts and feelings about the topic.

Researchers then use computer software to identify response patterns that suggest "metaphors" for the product—a general theme that describes respondents' attitudes. In a study of air fresheners, people want to avoid having odors in their home that alienate them from visitors (an underlying desire for connection with others); they also want an air freshener to seem natural, rather than masking something (an underlying desire to evoke nature). Based on these ideas, the client developed Breeze air freshener. In another project, Motorola hired Olson Zaltman to help it market a high-tech security system. Many research participants brought in images of dogs, signifying the protection that dogs give their owners. As a result, Motorola avoided brand names emphasizing technology, instead calling the new system the Watchdog.

Source: Based on Wielaard, Robert, "What People Don't Know They Know," *America's Intelligence Wire* (December 8, 2005), downloaded from http://www.accessmylibrary.com; Olson Zaltman Associates, home page and "What We Do," http://www.olsonzaltman.com, accessed March 23, 2006; Christensen, Glenn L. and Jerry C. Olson, "Mapping Consumers' Mental Models with ZMET," *Psychology & Marketing* 19, no. 6 (June 2002): 477–502.

Recording the Responses

An analyst who fails to instruct fieldworkers in the techniques of properly recording survey answers rarely forgets to do so a second time. Although recording an answer seems extremely simple, mistakes can occur in this phase of the research. Each fieldworker should use the same recording process. The opening chapter vignette demonstrates how one company is harnessing technology to help with this recording process.

Rules for recording responses to fixed-alternative questions vary with the specific questionnaire. A general rule, however, is to place a check mark in the box that correctly reflects the respondent's answer. All too often interviewers don't bother recording the answer to a filter question because they believe the subsequent answer will make the answer to the filter question obvious. However, editors and coders do not know how the respondent actually answered a question.

The general instruction for recording open-ended questions is to record the response verbatim, a task that is difficult for most people. Inexperienced interviewers should be given an opportunity to practice verbatim recording of answers before being sent into the field. Some suggestions for recording open-ended answers include

- Record responses during the interview.
- Use the respondent's own words.
- Do not summarize or paraphrase the respondent's answer.
- Include everything that pertains to the question objectives.
- Include all of your probes.[5]

Especially for sensitive topics, decisions about how to record responses may be more difficult than these guidelines suggest. For a survey that included open-ended questions about sexual behavior, researchers found that some decisions about how to record answers affected the way responses were later interpreted. For example, they defined notation that would indicate pauses and vocal emphasis, which helped researchers identify answers that involved confusion or strong emotions. However, recording every nonverbal behavior led researchers to speculate about whether one respondent was crying or using drugs (he had a cold). Likewise, when transcriptions recorded the respondent's exact words and pronunciation, including dialects and mistakes in grammar and word usage, researchers were tempted to speculate about demographic characteristics, such as a speaker's race or educational level. As the researchers evaluated the effects of these decisions about how to record answers, they concluded that such decisions should be made carefully in light of the research objectives.[6]

Terminating the Interview

The final aspect of training is to instruct interviewers on how to close the interview. Fieldworkers should wait to close the interview until they have secured all pertinent information. The interviewer who departs hastily will be unable to record the spontaneous comments respondents sometimes offer after all formal questions have been asked. Merely recording one of these comments may result in a new idea or creative interpretation of the results. Avoiding hasty departures is also a matter of courtesy. The fieldworker should also answer any respondent questions concerning the nature and purpose of the study to the best of his or her ability.

Finally, it is extremely important to thank the respondent for his or her time and cooperation. The fieldworker may be required to reinterview the respondent at some future time. So, the respondent should be left with a positive feeling about having cooperated in a worthwhile operation.

Principles of Good Interviewing

Yankelovich Partners is one of USA's top research organizations.[7] One reason for its success is its careful attention to fieldwork. This section presents this organization's principles of good interviewing. These principles apply no matter what the nature of the specific assignment; they are universal and represent the essence of sound data collection for business research purposes. For clarity, they have been divided into two categories: *the basics* (the interviewing point of view) and *required practices* (standard inquiry premises and procedures).

The Basics

Interviewing is a skilled occupation so not everyone can do it, and even fewer can do it extremely well. A good interviewer observes the following basic principles:

1. *Have integrity, and be honest.* This is the cornerstone of all professional inquiry, regardless of its purpose.
2. *Have patience and tact.* Interviewers ask for information from people they do not know. Thus, all the rules of human relations that apply to inquiry situations—patience, tact, and courtesy—apply even more to interviewing. You should at all times follow the standard business conventions that control communications and contact.
3. *Pay attention to accuracy and detail.* Among the greatest interviewing "sins" are inaccuracy and superficiality, for the professional analyst can misunderstand, and in turn mislead, a client. A good rule to follow is not to record a response unless you fully understand it yourself. Probe for clarification and rich, full answers. Record responses verbatim: Never assume you know what a respondent is thinking or jump to conclusions as to what he or she might have said but did not.
4. *Exhibit a real interest in the inquiry at hand, but keep your own opinions to yourself.* Impartiality is imperative—if your opinions were wanted, you would be asked, not your respondent. You are an asker and a recorder of other people's opinions, not a contributor to the study data.

5. *Be a good listener.* Too many interviewers talk too much, wasting time when respondents could be supplying more pertinent facts or opinions on the study topic.
6. *Keep the inquiry and respondents' responses confidential.* Do not discuss the studies you are doing with relatives, friends, or associates; it is unacceptable to both the research agency and its clients. Above all, *never* quote one respondent's opinion to another—that is the greatest violation of privacy.
7. *Respect others' rights.* Business research depends on people's willingness to provide information. In obtaining this information, you must follow a happy medium path. Between the undesirable extremes of failure to get it all and unnecessary coercion, this middle road is one of clear explanation, friendliness, and courtesy, offered in an interested and persuasive tone. Impress upon prospective respondents that their cooperation is important and valuable.

Required Practices

Here are practical rules of research inquiry that should be followed and used without exception:

1. *Complete the number of interviews according to the sampling plan assigned to you.* Both are calculated with the utmost precision so that when assignments are returned, the study will benefit from having available the amount and type of information originally specified.
2. *Follow the directions provided.* Remember that many other interviewers are working on the same study in other places. Lack of uniformity in procedure can only spell disaster for later analysis. Each direction has a purpose, even though it may not be completely evident to you.
3. *Make every effort to keep schedules.* Schedules range from "hurry up" to "there should be plenty of time," but there is always a good reason, and you should be as responsive as possible. If you foresee problems, call and explain.
4. *Keep control of each interview you do.* It is up to you to determine the pace of a particular interview, keeping several points in mind:
   a. There is an established *average* length of an interview from the time you start to talk to the respondent to the time you finish. It represents a *guideline*, but some interviews will be shorter and some longer.
   b. Always get the whole story from a respondent, and write it all down in the respondent's own words. Also, remember to keep the interview focused on the subject at hand and prevent it from wandering off into unnecessary small talk.
   c. Avoid offending the respondent by being too talkative yourself.
5. *Complete the questionnaires meticulously.*
   a. Follow exactly all instructions that appear directly on the questionnaire. Before you start interviewing, learn what these instructions direct you to do.
   b. Ask the questions from the first to the last in the exact numerical order (unless directed to do otherwise in some particular instances). Much thought and effort go into determining the order of the questioning to avoid bias or to set the stage for subsequent questions.
   c. Ask each question exactly as it is written. The cost of doing so is lack of uniformity; the research agency would never know whether all respondents were replying to the same question or replying to 50 different interviewers' interpretations of the question.
   d. Never leave a question blank. It will be difficult to tell whether you failed to ask it, whether the respondent could not answer it because of lack of knowledge or certainty, or whether the respondent refused to answer it for personal reasons. If none of the answer categories provided prove suitable, write in what the respondent said, in his or her own words.

e. Use all the props provided to aid both interviewers and respondents: show cards, pictures, descriptions, sheets of questions for the respondents to answer themselves, and so on. All have a specific interview purpose. Keys to when and how to use them appear on the questionnaire at the point at which they are to be used.

6. *Check over each questionnaire you have completed.* This is best done directly after it has been completed. If you find something you did wrong or omitted, correct it. Often you can call a respondent back, admit you missed something (or are unclear about a particular response), and then straighten out the difficulty.
7. *Compare your sample execution and assigned quota with the total number of questionnaires you have completed.* Do not consider your assignment finished until you have done this.
8. *Clear up any questions with the research agency.* At the start of an assignment or after you have begun, if you have questions for which you can find no explanatory instructions, call the agency to get the matter clarified.

Fieldwork Management

Research managers preparing for the fieldwork stage should consider the meaning of the following stanza from Robert Burns's poem "To a Mouse":

The best laid schemes o' mice and men
Gang aft a-gley;
An' lea'e us nought but grief and pain,
For promis'd joy.

The best plans of mice, men, and researchers may go astray. An excellent research plan may go astray if the field operations are performed incorrectly. A proper research design will eliminate numerous sources of error, but careful execution of the fieldwork is necessary to produce results without substantial error. For these reasons fieldwork management is an essential part of the research process.

Managers of field operations select, train, supervise, and control fieldworkers. Our discussion of fieldwork principles mentioned selection and training. This section investigates the tasks of the fieldwork managers in greater detail.

Briefing Session for Experienced Interviewers

Whether interviewers have just completed their training in fundamentals or are already experienced, they always need to be informed about the individual project. Both experienced and inexperienced fieldworkers must be briefed on the background of the sponsoring organization, sampling techniques, asking of questions, callback procedures, and other matters specific to the particular project.

If there are any special instructions—for example, about using show cards or video equipment or restricted interviewing times—they should also be covered during the training session. Instructions for handling certain key questions are always important. For example, the following fieldworker instructions appeared in a survey of institutional investors who make buy-and-sell decisions about stocks for banks, pension funds, and so on:

Questions 13a, 13b

These questions will provide verbatim comments for the report to the client. Probe for more than one- or two-word answers and record verbatim. Particularly, probe for more information when respondent gives a general answer—e.g., "Poor management," "It's in a good industry." Ask, "In what ways is management poor?" "What's good about the industry?" And so on.

A training session for experienced interviewers might go something like this: All interviewers report to the central office, where they receive a brief explanation of the firm's background and the general aims of the study. Interviewers are provided with minimal information about the purpose of the study to ensure that they will not transmit any preconceived notions to respondents. For example, in a survey about the banks in a community, the interviewers would be told that the research is a banking study but not the name of the sponsoring bank. To train the interviewers about the questionnaire, a field supervisor conducts an interview with another field supervisor who acts as a respondent. The trainees observe the interviewing process, after which they each interview and record the responses of another field supervisor who acts as a respondent. After the practice interview, the trainees receive additional instructions.

Training to Avoid Procedural Errors in Sample Selection

The briefing session also covers the sampling procedure. A number of research projects allow the interviewer to be at least partially responsible for selecting the sample. These sampling methods offer the potential for selection bias. This potential for bias is obvious in the case of quota sampling but less obvious in other cases. For example, in probability sampling in which every *n*th house is selected, the fieldworker uses his or her discretion in identifying housing units. Avoiding selection bias may be more difficult than it sounds. For example, in an old, exclusive neighborhood, a mansion's coach house or servants' quarters may have been converted into an apartment that should be identified as a housing unit. This type of dwelling and other unusual housing units (apartments with alley entrances only, lake cottages, or rooming houses) may be overlooked, giving rise to selection error. Errors may also occur in the selection of random-digit dialing samples. Considerable effort should be expended in training and supervisory control to minimize these errors.

Another selection problem is the practice of contacting a respondent when and where it is convenient for both parties. Consider the following anecdote from an industrial research interviewer:

> *Occasionally getting to the interview is half the challenge and tests the interviewer's ingenuity. Finding your way around a huge steel mill is not easy. Even worse is trying to find a correct turn-off to gravel pit D when it's snowing so hard that most direction signs are obliterated. In arranging an appointment with an executive at a rock quarry outside Kansas City, he told me his office was in "Cave Number 3." It was no joke. To my surprise, I found a luxurious executive office in a cave, which had long ago been hollowed by digging for raw material.*[8]

In that case, finding the sample unit was half the battle.

Supervision of Fieldworkers

Although briefing and training interviewers will minimize the probability of their interviewing the wrong households or asking biased questions, there is still considerable potential for errors in the field. Direct supervision of personal interviewers, telephone interviewers, and other fieldworkers is necessary to ensure that the techniques communicated in the training sessions are implemented in the field.

Supervision of interviewers, like other forms of supervision, refers to controlling the efforts of workers. Field supervision of interviewers requires checking to see that field procedures are being properly followed. A supervisor checks field operations to ensure that the interviewing schedule is being met. Supervisors collect the questionnaires or other instruments daily and edit them for completeness and legibility. (See Chapter 19 for more details on editing.) If problems arise, supervisors discuss them with the fieldworkers, providing training when necessary.

As seen in the Research Snapshot "Total Quality Management for Interviewing," the importance of quality control cannot be underestimated. In addition to quality control, continual training may be provided. For example, if a telephone supervisor notices that interviewers are allowing the

RESEARCH SNAPSHOT

Total Quality Management for Interviewing

Interviewers and their supervisors can improve the process of data collection to minimize errors. One popular method, total quality management (TQM), seeks continuous improvement by getting everyone involved in measuring performance and looking for ways to improve processes:

- *Measure response rates, and improve interviewer training to improve response rates.* To do this, researchers must describe the procedure for contacting subjects and consider alternatives, such as letters of introduction, the timing of contacts, and the number of attempts to make before a subject is classified as a nonrespondent. Interviewers should be taught about the impact on research quality of interviewing only the people who are easiest to contact, and they should be trained to persuade people to participate.
- *Measure defects in terms of measurement errors and improve interviewer techniques and respondent behavior.* Researchers should measure the pattern of response rates by interviewer, looking for interviewer variance (a tendency for different interviewers to obtain different answers). To measure respondent behavior, researchers can ask interviewers for objective information such as the presence of a third person, as well as for an evaluation of each interview's success; the data may signal respondent behaviors with a potential to bias responses from certain segments.
- *Measure the interview process, including the training provided, the application of principles from training, and feedback about the interviewer.* The training should be aimed at specific, measurable objectives, with a plan for measuring whether the interviewers' performance shows that training objectives were met. For a standardized interview, one way to tell whether the interviews are following the guidelines is to measure whether they all last about the same amount of time. Verification by reinterviewing a subsample provides insight into the accuracy of recording responses. Where variances occur, the supervisor and interviewers should investigate the cause, looking for ways to improve training and interviewing.

Source: Based on Loosveldt, Geert, Ann Carton, and Jaak Billiet, "Assessment of Survey Data Quality: A Pragmatic Approach Focused on Interviewer Tasks," *International Journal of Market Research* (Spring 2004), pp. 65–82)

© IMAGE 100/JUPITER IMAGES

© iStock

phone to ring more than eight times before considering the call a "no answer," the supervisor can instruct interviewers not to do so, as the person who eventually answers is likely to be annoyed.

Sampling Verification

Another important job of a supervisor is to verify that interviews are being conducted according to the sampling plan rather than with the sampling units most accessible to the interviewer. An interviewer might be tempted to go to the household next door for an interview rather than record the sampling unit as not at home, which would require a callback. Carefully recording the number of completed interviews will help ensure that the sampling procedure is being properly conducted. Supervisors are responsible for motivating interviewers to follow the sampling plan carefully.

Closer supervision of the interviewing procedure can occur in central-location telephone interviewing. Supervisors may be able to listen to the actual interview by switching onto the interviewer's line. Of course, this is harder to do when interviewers call from their own homes.

Supervisors must also make sure that the right people within the household or sampling unit are being contacted. One research project for a children's cereal required that several products be placed in the home and that children record their daily consumption and reactions to each cereal in a diary. Although the interviewers were supposed to contact the children to remind them to fill out the diaries, a field supervisor observed that in almost half the cases the mothers were filling out the diaries after the children left for school because their children had not done so. The novelty of the research project had worn off after a few days; eating a specific cereal each day was no longer fun after the first few times, and the children had stopped keeping the diaries. Similar situations may occur with physicians, executives, and other busy people. The interviewer may find it easier to interview a nurse, secretary, or other assistant rather than wait to speak with the right person.

Interviewer Cheating

interviewer cheating
The practice by fieldworkers of filling in fake answers or falsifying interviews.

curb-stoning
A form of interviewer cheating in which an interviewer makes up the responses instead of conducting an actual interview.

The most blatant form of **interviewer cheating** occurs when an interviewer falsifies interviews, merely filling in fake answers rather than contacting respondents. This is sometimes referred to as **curb-stoning**. Although this situation does occur, it is not common if the job of selection has been properly accomplished. However, less obvious forms of interviewer cheating occur with greater frequency. Interviewers often consider quota sampling to be time consuming, so an interviewer may stretch the requirements a bit to obtain seemingly qualified respondents. In the interviewer's eyes, a young-looking 36-year-old may be the same as a 30-year-old who fits the quota requirement; checking off the under-30 category thus isn't really cheating. Consider the fieldworker who must select only heavy users of a certain brand of hand lotion that the client says is used by 15 percent of the population. If the fieldworker finds that only 3 percent qualify as heavy users, he or she may be tempted to interview an occasional user to stretch the quota somewhat. All of these approaches are unethical.

An interviewer may fake part of a questionnaire to make it acceptable to the field supervisor. In a survey on automobile satellite radio systems, suppose an interviewer is requested to ask for five reasons why consumers have purchased this product. If he or she finds that people typically give two or perhaps three reasons and even with extensive probing cannot think of five reasons, the interviewer might be tempted to cheat. Rather than have the supervisor think he or she was goofing off on the probing, the interviewer may fill in five reasons based on past interviews. In other cases, the interviewer may cut corners to save time and energy.

Interviewers may fake answers when they find questions embarrassing or troublesome to ask because of sensitive subjects. Thus, the interviewer may complete most of the questionnaire but leave out a question or two because he or she found it troublesome or time-consuming. For example, in a survey among physicians, an interviewer might find questions about artificial-insemination donor programs embarrassing, skip these questions, and fill in the gaps later.

What appears to be interviewer cheating often is caused by improper training or fieldworkers' inexperience. A fieldworker who does not understand the instructions may skip or miss a portion of the questionnaire.

Interviewers may be reluctant to interview sampling units who they feel may be difficult or undesirable to interview. Sometimes fieldworkers are instructed to say at the conclusion of each interview, "Thank you for your time—and by the way, my supervisor may call you to ask about my work. Please say whatever you wish." This or a similar statement not only increases the number of respondents willing to cooperate with the verification process but also improves the quality of fieldwork.

Verification by Reinterviewing

verification
Quality-control procedures in fieldwork intended to ensure that interviewers are following the sampling procedures and to determine whether interviewers are cheating.

Supervision for quality control attempts to ensure that interviewers are following the sampling procedure and to detect falsification of interviews. Supervisors verify approximately 15 percent of the interviews by reinterviewing. Normally the interview is not repeated; rather, supervisors recontact respondents and ask about the length of the interview and their reactions to the interviewer; then they collect basic demographic data to check for interviewer cheating. Such **verification** does not detect the more subtle form of cheating in which only portions of the interview have been falsified. A validation check may simply point out that an interviewer contacted the proper household but interviewed the wrong individual in that household—which, of course, can be a serious error.

Fieldworkers should be aware of supervisory verification practices. Knowing that there may be a telephone or postcard validation check often reminds interviewers to be conscientious in their

TIPS OF THE TRADE

- Fieldworkers are a potential source of error in gathering information. Investing resources into making sure fieldworkers are competent in carrying out their assigned tasks is money and time well spent.
- Fieldworkers should wear name badges and/or clearly introduce themselves and their employer (the research firm) to the potential respondent.
- Avoid incentives that strongly encourage (coerce) fieldworkers to submit a large amount of completed interviews. This motivates the fieldworkers to be sloppy or dishonest.
- Unusual responses need to be followed up with probing questions that attempt to verify the initial response.
- Respondents in online panels or chat rooms should routinely be asked follow-up questions for the purpose of validating the reported behavior.

work. The interviewer who is conducting quota sampling and needs an upper-income Hispanic male will be less tempted to interview a middle-income Hispanic man and falsify the income data in this situation.

Certain information may allow for partial verification without recontacting the respondent. Computer-assisted telephone interviewers often do not know the phone number dialed by the computer or other basic information about the respondent. Thus, answers to questions added to the end of the telephone interview to identify a respondent's area code, phone number, city, zip code, and so on may be used to verify the interview. The computer can also record every attempted call, the time intervals between calls, and the time required to conduct each completed interview—data that may help in identifying patterns related to cheating by interviewers.

Summary

1. Describe the role and job requirements of fieldworkers. Fieldworkers are responsible for gathering data in the field. These activities may be performed by the organization that needs the information, by research suppliers, or by third-party field service organizations. Proper execution of fieldwork is essential to produce research results without substantial error. Proper control of fieldwork begins with interviewer selection. Fieldworkers generally should be healthy, outgoing, and well groomed.

2. Summarize the skills to cover when training inexperienced interviewers. New fieldworkers must be trained in opening the interview, asking the questions, probing for additional information, recording the responses, and terminating the interview.

3. List principles of good interviewing. Good interviewers have integrity, patience, and tact. They are attentive to detail and interested in the inquiry at hand. They behave impartially, listen carefully, and maintain confidentiality. They respect the rights of others. Interviewing should adhere to several required practices. Interviewers should complete all interviews according to the sample plan and follow the directions provided. They should try to meet schedules and maintain control of the interview. They should fill in answers meticulously and then check over the questionnaire to make sure it is complete. Before finishing an assignment, they should verify that the number of completed questionnaires matches the sampling plan and assigned quotas. If they have questions, they should check with the agency conducting the research.

4. Describe the activities involved in the management of fieldworkers. Experienced fieldworkers are briefed for each new project to familiarize them with its specific requirements. A particular concern of the briefing session is reminding fieldworkers to adhere closely to the prescribed sampling procedures.

5. Discuss how supervisors can minimize errors in the field. Careful supervision of fieldworkers also is necessary. Supervisors gather and edit questionnaires each day. They check to see that field procedures are being properly followed and that interviews are on schedule. They also check to ensure that the correct sampling units are being used and that the proper people are responding in the study. Finally, supervisors check for interviewer cheating and verify portions of the interviews by reinterviewing a certain percentage of each fieldworker's respondents.

Key Terms and Concepts

briefing session, *480*
curb-stoning, *491*
door-in-the-face compliance technique, *482*
field interviewing service, *479*
fieldworker, *479*
foot-in-the-door compliance technique, *482*
in-house interviewer, *479*
interviewer cheating, *491*
verification, *491*

Questions for Review and Critical Thinking

1. What qualities should fieldworkers possess?
2. **ETHICS** An interviewer has a rather long telephone interview. The estimate suggests that fully completing the survey will take 30 minutes. However, what do you think the response rate will be if people are told ahead of time that it will take 30 minutes to finish participating in the survey? Should the interviewer fudge a little and state that the survey will take only 15 minutes? Explain.
3. What should the interviewer do if a question is misunderstood or if a respondent answers a question before encountering it in the questionnaire?
4. When should interviewers probe? Give some examples of how probing should be done.
5. How should respondents' answers to open-ended questions be recorded?
6. How should the fieldworker terminate the interview?
7. Why is it important to ensure that fieldworkers adhere to the sampling procedure specified for a project?
8. **ETHICS** What forms does interviewer cheating take? How can such cheating be prevented or detected?
9. **ETHICS** Two interviewers are accused of curb-stoning. What have they done?
10. Comment on the following field situations.
    a. After conducting a survey with 10 people, an interviewer noticed that many of the respondents were saying "Was I right?" after a particular question.
    b. A questionnaire asking about a new easy-opening can has the following instructions to interviewers:

       (Hand respondent can and matching instruction card.)

       "Would you please read the instructions on this card and then open this can for me?" *(Interviewer: Note any comments respondent makes. Do not under any circumstances help him or her to open the can or offer any explanation as to how to open it. If respondent asks for help, tell him that the instructions are on the card. Do not discuss the can or its contents.)*
    c. A researcher gives balloons to children of respondents to keep the children occupied during the interview.
    d. An interviewer tells the supervisor, "With the price of gas, this job isn't paying as well as before!"
    e. When a respondent asks how much time the survey will take, the interviewer responds, "15 to 20 minutes." The respondent says, "I'm sorry, I have to refuse. I can't give you that much time right now."
11. Write some interviewer instructions for a telephone survey.
12. A fieldworker conducting a political poll is instructed to interview registered voters. The fieldworker interviews all willing participants who are eligible to vote (those who may register in the future) because allowing their opinions to be recorded is part of her patriotic duty. Is she doing the right thing?
13. An interviewer finds that when potential respondents ask how much time the survey will take, most refuse if they are told 15 minutes. The interviewer now says 10 minutes and finds that most respondents enjoy answering the questions. Is this the right thing to do?
14. A fieldworker asks respondents whether they will answer a few questions. However, the interviewer also observes the respondent's race and approximate age. Is this ethical?

Research Activity

1. **'NET** Go to http://www.quirks.com/directory/telephone/index.aspx. Using the search window, investigate the following.

   Suppose you were interested in conducting telephone interviews in a number of places. List telephone facilities in Denmark, Mexico, South Korea, and Alabama (United States). Is CATI available in every county of Alabama?

Case 18.1 Thomas and Dorothy Leavey Library

The Thomas and Dorothy Leavey Library serves the students and faculty of the University of Southern California. Staff at the busy library wanted to know more about its patrons, what library resources they find helpful, and whether they are satisfied with the library's services. However, like many libraries, this organization had a tiny budget for business research. As a result, the goal was to conduct exploratory research while spending less than $250.[9]

Staff members studied surveys conducted by other libraries to get ideas for a one-page printed questionnaire. Colleagues on the library staff provided suggestions, and a few undergraduates tested the survey for clarity. Next, the survey schedule was chosen: 36 continuous hours that did not conflict with any holidays or exams.

The fieldwork involved setting up and staffing a table offering the survey and then inviting library patrons to stop and fill out a questionnaire. Possible locations included space near an elevator, stairs, or computers, but the lobby area offered the greatest opportunity, because everyone passed through the lobby when using the facility's only entrance. The survey's planners divided the time into 60 slots and recruited students with jobs at the library to serve as the fieldworkers. Other members of the library staff also volunteered to fill time slots. The students in particular were enthusiastic about inviting library patrons to complete questionnaires. A bowl of candy for participants was a small incentive, combined with a raffle for donated prizes.

Questions

1. Imagine that you were asked to help prepare for this survey. What fieldwork challenges would you expect to arise in a survey such as this, to be carried out by inexperienced fieldworkers?
2. What training would you recommend for the students and other library staffers conducting this survey? Suggest topics to cover and advice to give these fieldworkers.

Case 18.2 Margaret Murphy O'Hara

Margaret Murphy O'Hara was fatigued. As she wiped the perspiration from her brow, she felt that the Massachusetts summer sun was playing a trick on her. It was her first day at work, and the weather was hot. She had no idea that being a field interviewer required so much stamina. Even though she was tired, she was happy with her new job. She didn't yet have the knack of holding her purse, questionnaires, and clipboard while administering the show cards, but she knew she'd get the hang of it. The balancing act can be learned, she thought.

When she met her supervisor, Mary Zagorski, at the end of her first day, Margaret described her day. Margaret said she thought the questionnaire was a bit too long. She laughed, saying that an elderly lady had fallen asleep after about 20 minutes of interviewing.

Margaret mentioned that a number of people had asked why they were selected. Margaret said she did not know exactly what to say when somebody asked, "Why did you pick me?"

She said that the nicest person she had interviewed was a man whose wife wasn't home to be surveyed. He was very friendly and didn't balk at being asked about his income and age like some of the other people she had interviewed.

She said she had one problem that she needed some help with resolving. Four or five people refused to grant the interview. Margaret explained that one woman answered the door and said she was too busy because her son, an army private, was leaving the country. The woman was throwing a little party for him before he went off to the airport. Margaret didn't want to spoil their fun with the survey. Another lady said that she was too busy and really didn't know anything about the subject anyway. However, she did suggest her next-door neighbor, who was very interested in the subject. Margaret was able to interview this person to make up for the lost interview. It actually went quite well.

Margaret said another woman wouldn't be interviewed because she didn't know anything about the Zagorski interviewing service, and Margaret didn't know quite what to tell her. Finally, she couldn't make one interview because she didn't understand the address: 9615 South Francisco Rear. Margaret told Mary it was quite a day, and she looked forward to tomorrow.

Questions

1. Is Margaret going to be a good professional interviewer?
2. What should Mary Zagorski tell Margaret?

Part 6
Data Analysis and Presentation

© NONSTOCK/JUPITER IMAGES

CHAPTER 19
EDITING AND CODING: TRANSFORMING RAW DATA INTO INFORMATION

LEARNING OUTCOMES

After studying this chapter, you should be able to

1. Know when a response is really an error and should be edited
2. Appreciate coding of pure qualitative research
3. Understand the way data are represented in a data file
4. Understand the coding of structured responses including a dummy variable approach
5. Appreciate the ways that technological advances have simplified the coding process

Chapter Vignette: Coding What a Person's Face "Says"

Understanding what respondents say, or coding the data gathered from a survey represents a challenge that all business researchers face. But technological advances have now allowed business researchers a chance to collect and code data not based upon what people say, but what their face "says." Welcome to the new world of Sensory Logic, and the Tobii Eye Tracker and Studio.

Body language is a key way that people communicate their thoughts and emotional states. Researchers have long known the power of non-verbal cues and response states, and have sought to understand and capture how non-verbal communication unfolds. Sensor Logic's Tobii system is one example of how research in eye movement and facial coding has advanced to a point where respondent physical data can be captured in real time for research purposes. Facial coding reveals a person's engagement, their positive and negative emotional states given a particular stimuli, and the impact or appeal of what they are responding to. Eye tracking can tell researchers exactly what a person is looking at, and based upon the almost imperceptible muscle changes in their facial expressions, code their emotional state.

The Tobii system is used in a number of consumer and market research environments. For example, a company may develop a Web page designed to showcase their product line. Using the Tobii system, focus group members can have their nonverbal responses and eye tracking analyzed, to see which aspects of the product are being examined, and what immediate emotional response is generated. The objective data can then be paired with other data, and analyzed for business purposes.

In the future, the ability to capture and code physical data will become more and more commonplace. Perhaps you too will have a chance to participate in a product or service research study using the Tobii system, and be given an opportunity to "speak" without ever saying a word.[1]

This chapter deals with coding and editing raw data. Researchers must pay careful attention to their coding because poor coding leads directly to nonresponse error.[2]

Introduction

A very common phrase that is used by researchers is "garbage in, garbage out." This refers to the idea that if data is collected improperly, or coded incorrectly, your results are "garbage," because that is what was entered into the data set to begin with. This chapter focuses on the critical key step of data entry and coding. Like any part of the business research process, care and attention to detail are important requirements for data editing and coding.

Stages of Data Analysis

Practically all researchers will be very anxious to begin data analysis once the field work is complete. Now, the raw data can be transformed into intelligence. However, **raw data** may not be in a form that lends itself well to analysis. Raw data are recorded just as the respondent indicated. For an oral response, the raw data are in the words of the respondent, whereas for a questionnaire response, the actual number checked is the number stored. Raw data will often also contain errors both in the form of respondent errors and nonrespondent errors. Whereas a respondent error is a mistake made by the respondent, a **nonrespondent error** is a mistake made by an interviewer or by a person responsible for creating an electronic data file representing the responses.

raw data

The unedited responses from a respondent exactly as indicated by that respondent.

nonrespondent error

Error that the respondent is not responsible for creating, such as when the interviewer marks a response incorrectly.

Exhibit 19.1 provides an overview of data analysis. The first two stages result in an electronic file suitable for data analysis. This file can then be used in the application of various statistical routines including those associated with descriptive, univariate, bivariate, or multivariate analysis. Each of these data analysis approaches will be discussed in the subsequent chapters. An important part of the editing, coding, and filing stages is checking for errors. As long as error remains in the data, the process of transformation from raw data to intelligence will be made more risky and more difficult. Editing and coding are the first two stages in the data analysis process.

EXHIBIT 19.1
Overview of the Stages of Data Analysis

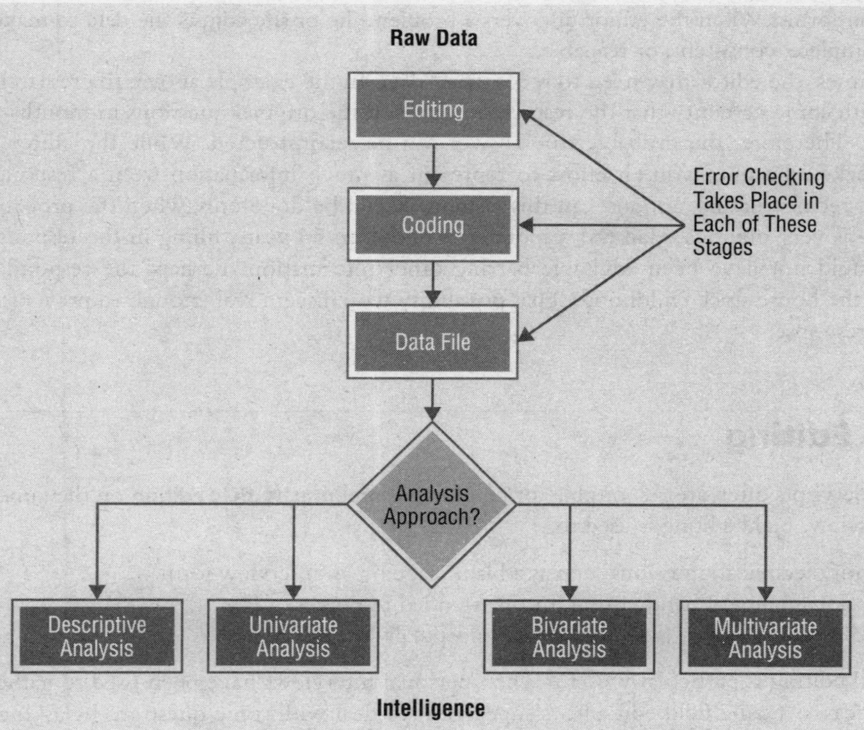

Source: *Survey and Opinion Research: Procedures for Processing and Analysis*, Sonquist, J.A. & Dunkelberg, W.C. (1977). Englewood Cliffs, NJ: Prentice-Hall. Reprinted by permission of Pearson Education, Inc., Upper Saddle River, NJ.

data integrity
The notion that the data file actually contains the information that the researcher promised the decision maker he or she would obtain, meaning in part that the data have been edited and properly coded so that they are useful to the decision maker.

Data integrity refers to the notion that the data file actually contains the information that the researcher promised the decision maker he or she would obtain. Additionally, data integrity extends to the fact that the data have been edited and properly coded so that they are useful to the decision maker. Any errors in this process, just as with errors or shortcuts in the interview process itself, harm the integrity of the data.

Editing

Fieldwork often produces data containing mistakes. For example, consider the following simple questionnaire item and response:

How long have you lived at your current address? 48

The researcher had intended the response to be in years. Perhaps the respondent has indicated the number of months rather than years he or she has lived at this address? Alternatively, if this was an interviewer's form, he or she may have marked the response in months without indicating this on the form. How should this be treated? Sometimes, responses may be contradictory. What if the same respondent above gives this response?

What is your age? *32 years*

This answer contradicts the earlier response. If the respondent is 32 years of age, then how could he or she have lived at the same address for 48 years? Therefore, an adjustment should be made to accommodate this information. The most likely case is that this respondent has lived at the current address for four years.

editing
The process of checking the completeness, consistency, and legibility of data and making the data ready for coding and transfer to storage.

This example illustrates data **editing**. Editing is the process of checking and adjusting data for omissions, consistency, and legibility. In this way, the data become ready for analysis by a computer. So, the editor's task is to check for errors and omissions on questionnaires or other data collection forms. When the editor discovers a problem, he or she adjusts the data to make them more complete, consistent, or readable.

At times, the editor may need to reconstruct data. In the example above, the researcher can guess with some certainty that the respondent entered the original questions in months instead of years. Therefore, the probable true answer can be reconstructed. While the editor should try to make adjustments in an effort to represent as much information from a respondent as possible, reconstructing responses in this fashion should be done only when the probable true response is very obvious. Had the respondent's age been 55 years, filling in the response with years would not have been advisable barring other information. Perhaps the respondent has lived in the house since childhood? That possibility would seem real enough to prevent changing the response.

field editing
Preliminary editing by a field supervisor on the same day as the interview to catch technical omissions, check legibility of handwriting, and clarify responses that are logically or conceptually inconsistent.

Field Editing

Field supervisors often are responsible for conducting preliminary **field editing** on the same day as the interview. Field editing is used to

1. Identify technical omissions such as a blank page on an interview form
2. Check legibility of handwriting for open-ended responses
3. Clarify responses that are logically or conceptually inconsistent

Field editing is particularly useful when personal interviews have been used to gather data. In these cases, a daily field edit allows supervisors to deal with some questions by asking interviewers, who may still be able to remember the interviews, about facts that may allow errors to be identified and perhaps corrected. In addition, the number of unanswered questions or incomplete responses can be reduced with rapid follow up. A daily field edit allows fieldworkers to identify respondents who should be recontacted to fill in omissions in a timely fashion.

The supervisor may also use field edits to spot the need for further interviewer training or to correct faulty procedures. For example, if an interviewer did not correctly follow skip patterns, training may be indicated. The supervisor may also notice that an interviewer is not properly probing some open-ended responses.

© CREATAS IMAGES/JUPITER IMAGES

Field edits allow supervisors to spot errors before the data file is created.

In-House Editing

Although simultaneous field editing is highly desirable, in many situations (particularly with mail questionnaires) early reviewing of the data is not always possible. **In-house editing** rigorously investigates the results of data collection. The research supplier or research department normally has a centralized office staff perform the editing and coding function.

For example, Arbitron measures radio audiences by having respondents record their listening behavior—time, station, and place (home or car)—in diaries. After the diaries are returned by mail, in-house editors perform usability edits in which they check that the postmark is after the last day of the survey week, verify the legibility of station call letters (station WKXY could look like KWXY), look for completeness of entries on each day of the week, and perform other editing activities. If the respondent's age or sex is not indicated, the respondent is called to ensure that this information is included.

in-house editing

A rigorous editing job performed by a centralized office staff.

ILLUSTRATING INCONSISTENCY—FACT OR FICTION?

Consider a situation in which a telephone interviewer has been instructed to interview only registered voters in a state that requires voters to be at least 18 years old. If the editor's review of a questionnaire indicates that the respondent was only 17 years old, the editor's task is to correct this mistake by deleting this response because this respondent should never have been considered as a sampling unit. The sampling units (respondents) should all be consistent with the defined population.

The editor also should check for consistency within the data collection framework. For example, a survey on out-shopping behavior (shopping in towns other than the one in which the person resides) might have a question such as the following:

In which of the following cities have you shopped for clothing during the last year?

- *San Francisco*
- *Sacramento*
- *San José*
- *Los Angeles*
- *Other* __________

Please list the clothing stores where you have shopped during the last two months.

Suppose a respondent checks Sacramento and San Francisco to the first question. If the same respondent lists a store that has a location only in Los Angeles in the second question, an error is indicated. Either the respondent failed to list Los Angeles in the first question or listed an erroneous store in the second question. These answers are obviously inconsistent.

TOTHEPOINT

Excellence is to do a common thing in an uncommon way.

—Booker T. Washington

TAKING ACTION WHEN RESPONSE IS OBVIOUSLY AN ERROR

What should the editor do? If solid evidence exists that points to the fact that the respondent simply failed to check Los Angeles, then the response to the first question can be changed to indicate

RESEARCH SNAPSHOT

Do You Have Integrity?

Data integrity is essential to successful research and decision making. Sometimes, this is a question of ethics. Whereas data integrity can suffer when an interviewer or coder simply makes up data, other things can occur that limit data integrity. For instance, data with a large portion of nonresponse has lower integrity than data without so much missing data. However, if respondents have truly left questions blank, the editor should not feel compelled to just "make up" responses.

Data integrity can also suffer simply because the data are edited or coded poorly. For example, the data coder should be aware that data may be used by other downstream users. Therefore, consistent coding should exist. For example, if a coder sometimes uses 1 for women and 2 for men, while on another data set uses 0 for men and 1 for women, the possibility exists that analyses using these categories will be confused. Who exactly are the men and who are the women? This is particularly true if the coder does not enter value labels for the variable.

Consider how important consistent coding is for companies that share or sell secondary data. Occupations need a common coding just as do product classes, industries, and numerous other potential data values. Fortunately, industries have standard codes such as NAICS (North American Industrial Classification System) and SIC (Standardized Industrial Classification) codes. Some professional coders have adopted postal service guidelines for coding things like states and addresses. A search of the U.S. Post Office Web site should come to a page with these guidelines (**http://pe.usps.gov**). Without a standardized approach, analysts may never be quite sure what they are looking at from one data set to another. Thus, research firms need to carefully maintain information coding systems that help maximize data integrity.

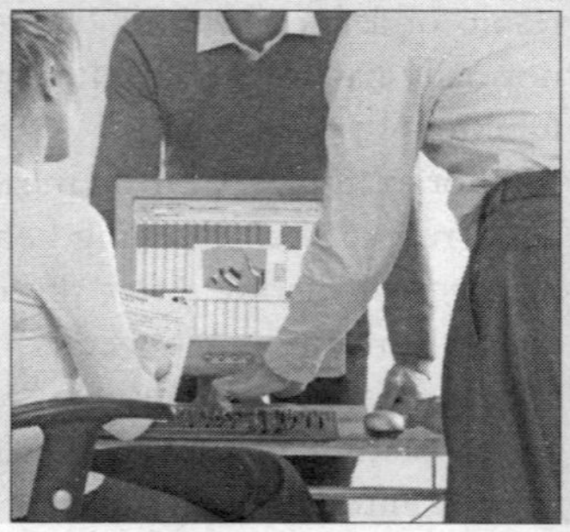

Sources: Dubberly, Hugh, "The Information Loop," *CIOInsight* 43 (September 2004), 55–61; Shonerd, René, "Data Integrity Rules," *Association Management* 55, no. 9 (2003), 14.

that the person shopped in that city as well. Since Los Angeles is not listed next to Sacramento or San Francisco, it is unlikely that the respondent checked the wrong city inadvertently. Perhaps the question about the stores triggered a memory that did not come to the respondent when checking off the cities. This seems quite possible, and if another question can also point strongly to the fact that the respondent actually shopped at the store in Los Angeles, then the change should be made.

However, perhaps the respondent placed a mail order with the store in Los Angeles and simply did not physically shop in the store. If other evidence suggests this possibility, then the researcher should not make an adjustment to the first question. For example, a later question may have the respondent list any clothing orders placed via mail order (or by telephone or Internet order).

Responses should be logically consistent, but the researcher should not jump to the conclusion that a change should be made at the first site of an inconsistency. In all but the most obvious situations, a change should only be made when multiple pieces of evidence exist that some response is in error and when the likely true response is obvious.

Many surveys use filter or "skip" questions that direct a respondent to a specific set of questions depending on how the filter question is answered according to the respondent's answers. Common filter questions involve age, sex, home ownership, or product usage. A survey might involve different questions for a home owner than for someone who does not own a home. A data record may sometimes contain data on variables that the respondent should never have been asked. For example, if someone indicated that he or she did not own a home, yet responses for the home questions are provided, a problem is indicated. The editor may check other responses to make sure that the screening question was answered accurately. For instance, if the respondent left the question about home value unanswered, then the editor will be confident that the person truly does not own a home. In cases like this, the editor should adjust these answers by considering all answers to the irrelevant questions as "no response" or "not applicable."

EDITING TECHNOLOGY

Today, computer routines can check for inconsistencies automatically. Thus, for electronic questionnaires, rules can be entered which prevent inconsistent responses from ever being stored in the file used for data analysis. These rules should represent the conservative judgment of a trained data analyst. Some online survey services can assist in providing this service. In fact, the rules can even be preprogrammed to prevent many inconsistent responses. Thus, if a person who is 25 indicates that he or she has lived in the same house for 48 years, a pop-up window can appear requiring the respondent to go back and fix an earlier incorrect response. Electronic questionnaires can also prevent a respondent from being directed to the wrong set of questions based on a screening question response.

Editing for Completeness

In some cases the respondent may have answered only the second portion of a two-part question. The following question creates a situation in which an in-house editor may have to adjust answers for completeness:

Does your organization have more than one computer network server?

☐ *Yes* ☐ *No*

If yes, how many? ____

If the respondent checked neither yes nor no but indicated three computer installations, the editor should change the first response to a "Yes" as long as other information doesn't indicate otherwise. Here again, a computerized questionnaire may either not allow a response to the "how many" question if someone checked yes or require the respondent to go back to the previous question once he or she tries to enter a number for the "how many" question.

item nonresponse
The technical term for an unanswered question on an otherwise complete questionnaire resulting in missing data.

Item nonresponse is the technical term for an unanswered question on an otherwise complete questionnaire. Missing data results from item nonresponse. Specific decision rules for handling this problem should be meticulously outlined in the editor's instructions. In many situations the decision rule is to do nothing with the missing data and simply leave the item blank. However, when the relationship between two questions is important, such as that between a question about job satisfaction and one's pay, the editor may be tempted to insert a **plug value**. The decision rule may be to plug in an average or neutral value in each instance of missing data. Several choices are available:

plug value
An answer that an editor "plugs in" to replace blanks or missing values so as to permit data analysis; choice of value is based on a predetermined decision rule.

impute
To fill in a missing data point through the use of a statistical algorithm that provides a best guess for the missing response based on available information.

1. Leave the response blank. Because the question is so important, the risk of creating error by plugging a value is too great.
2. Plug in alternate choices for missing data ("yes" the first time, "no" the second time, "yes" the third time, and so forth).
3. Randomly select an answer. The editor may flip a coin with heads for "yes" and tails for "no."
4. The editor can **impute** a missing value based on the respondent's choices to other questions. Many different techniques exist for imputing data. Some involve complex statistical estimation approaches that use the available information to forecast a best guess for the missing response.[3]

This issue used to be a bigger concern when many statistical software programs required complete data for an analysis to take place. Other routines may require that an entire sampling unit be eliminated from analysis if even a single response is missing (list-wise deletion). Today, most statistical programs can accommodate an occasional missing response through the use of pair-wise deletion. Pair-wise deletion means the data that the respondent did provide can still be used in statistical analysis. As a result, pair-wise deletion produces a larger effective sample size than list-wise deletion.

Option one above is not a bad option unless a response for that particular respondent is crucial, which would rarely be the case. Option four could also be a good option if the response is important or if the effective sample size would be too small if all missing responses are deleted. As long as the researcher is confident that the imputation methods are providing good guesses, this method may allow a response to this item to be salvaged.

The editor must decide whether an entire questionnaire is usable. When a questionnaire has too many missing answers, it may not be suitable for the planned data analysis. While no exact answer exists for this question, a questionnaire with a quarter of the responses or more missing is suspect. In such a situation the editor can record that a particular incomplete questionnaire has been dropped from the sample.

Editing Questions Answered Out of Order

Another task an editor may face is rearranging the answers given to open-ended questions such as may occur in a focus group interview. The respondent may have provided the answer to a subsequent question in his or her comments to an earlier open-ended question. Because the respondent already had clearly identified the answer, the interviewer may not have asked the subsequent question, wishing to avoid hearing "I already answered that earlier" and to maintain interview rapport. If the editor is asked to list answers to all questions in a specific order, the editor may move certain answers to the section related to the skipped question.

Facilitating the Coding Process

While all of the previously described editing activities will help coders, several editing procedures are designed specifically to simplify the coding process. For example, the editor should check written responses for any stray marks. Respondents are often asked to circle responses. Sometimes, a respondent may accidentally draw a circle that overlaps two numbers. For example, the circle may include both 3 and 4. The editor may be able to decide which number is the most accurate response and indicate that on the form. Occasionally, a respondent may do this to indicate indecision between the 3 and the 4. Again, if the editor sees that the circle is carefully drawn to include both responses, he or she may indicate a 3.5 on the form. Such ambiguity is impossible with an electronic questionnaire.

EDITING AND TABULATING "DON'T KNOW" ANSWERS

In many situations, respondents answer "don't know." On the surface, this response seems to indicate unfamiliarity with the subject matter at question. A *legitimate* "don't know" response is the same as "no opinion." However, there may be reasons for this response other than the legitimate "don't know." A *reluctant* "don't know" is given when the respondent simply does not want to answer a question. For example, asking an individual who is not the head of the household about family income may elicit a "don't know" answer meaning, "This is personal, and I really do not want to answer the question." If the individual does not understand the question, he or she may give a *confused* "I don't know" answer.

In some situations the editor can separate the legitimate "don't knows" ("no opinion") from the other "don't knows." The editor may try to identify the meaning of the "don't know" answer from other data provided on the questionnaire. For instance, the value of a home could be derived from knowledge of the zip code and the average value of homes within that area.

In structured questionnaires, the researcher has to decide whether to provide the respondent with a "don't know" or "no opinion" option. If neither of these is offered, the respondents may simply choose not to answer when they honestly don't know how or don't want to respond to a question. A computerized questionnaire can be set up to require a response to every question. Here, if a "no opinion" or "don't know" opinion is not made available, the result is a forced choice design. The advantages and disadvantages of forced choice questioning were discussed in Chapter 14.

Pitfalls of Editing

Subjectivity can enter into the editing process. Data editors should be intelligent, experienced, and *objective*. A *systematic procedure* for assessing the questionnaires should be developed by the research analyst so that the editor has clearly defined decision rules to follow. Any inferences such as imputing missing values should be done in a manner that limits the chance for the data editor's subjectivity to influence the response.

Pretesting Edit

Editing questionnaires during the pretest stage can prove very valuable. For example, if respondents' answers to open-ended questions were longer than anticipated, the fieldworkers, respondents, and analysts would benefit from a change to larger spaces for the answers. Answers will be more legible because the writers have enough space, answers will be more complete, and answers will be verbatim rather than summarized. Examining answers to pretests may identify poor instructions or inappropriate question wording on the questionnaire.

Coding

Editing may be differentiated from **coding**, which is the assignment of numerical scores or classifying symbols to previously edited data. Careful editing makes the coding job easier. Codes are meant to represent the meaning in the data.

Assigning numerical symbols permits the transfer of data from questionnaires or interview forms to a computer. **Codes** often, but not always, are numerical symbols. However, they are more broadly defined as rules for interpreting, classifying, and recording data. In qualitative research, numbers are seldom used for codes.

coding
The process of assigning a numerical score or other character symbol to previously edited data.

codes
Rules for interpreting, classifying, and recording data in the coding process; also, the actual numerical or other character symbols assigned to raw data.

Coding Qualitative Responses

UNSTRUCTURED QUALITATIVE RESPONSES (LONG INTERVIEWS)

Qualitative coding was introduced in Chapter 7. In qualitative research, the codes are usually words or phrases that represent themes. Exhibit 19.2 shows a hermeneutic unit in which a qualitative researcher is applying a code to a text describing in detail a respondent's reactions to several different glasses of wine. The researcher is trying to understand in detail what defines the wine drinking experience. In this case, coding is facilitated by the use of qualitative software.

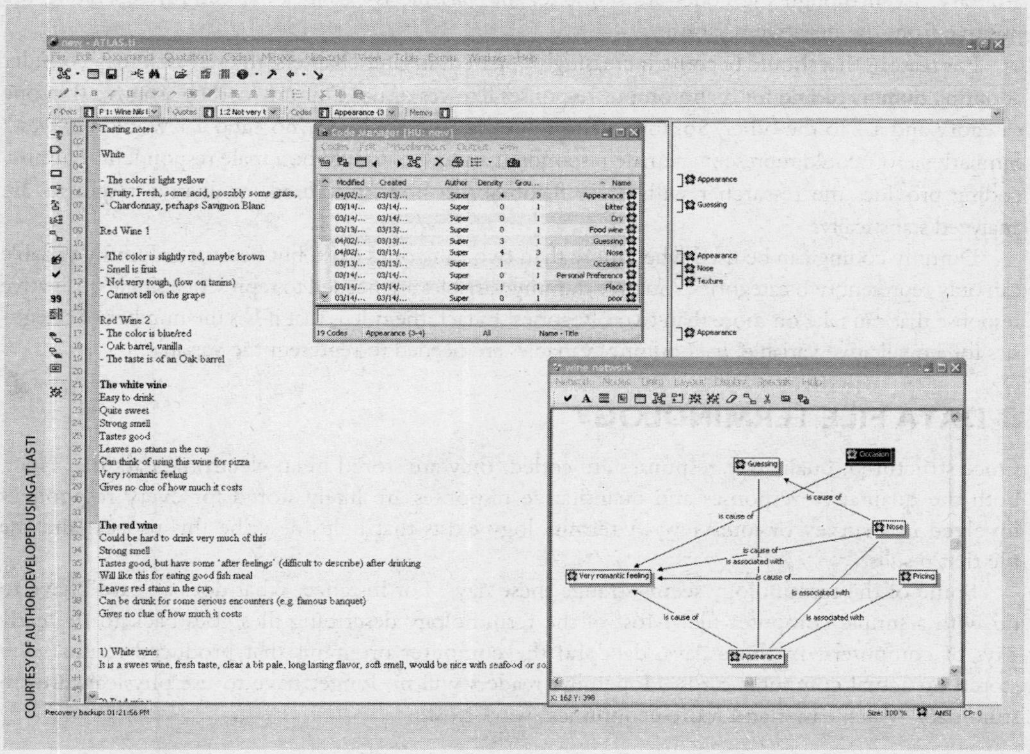

COURTESY OF AUTHOR DEVELOPED USING ATLAS.TI

EXHIBIT 19.2
Coding Qualitative Data with Words

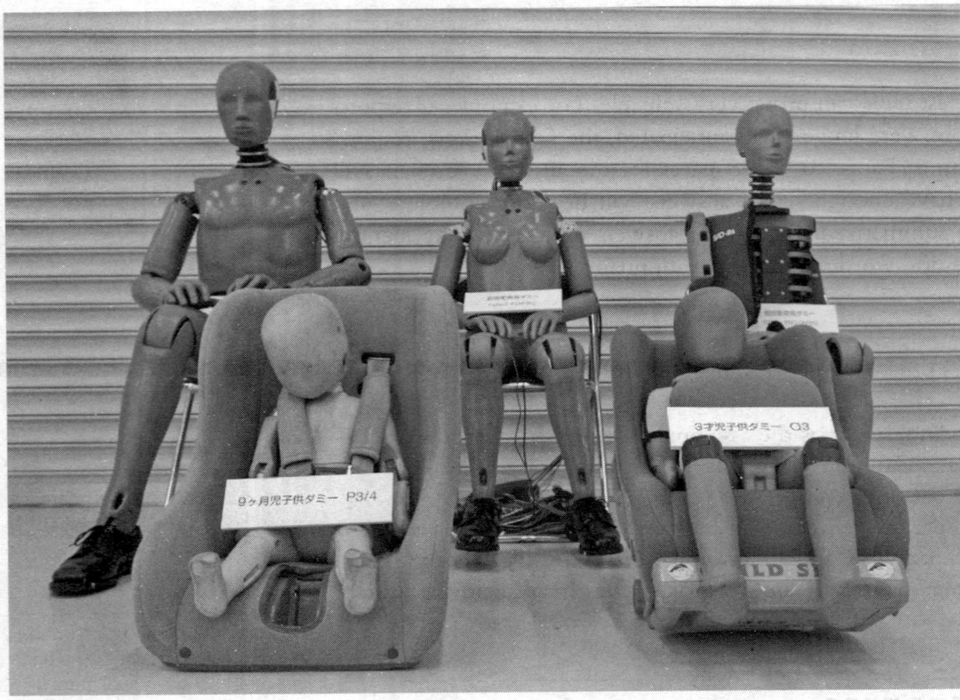

After reading through the text several times, and applying a word-counting routine, the researcher realizes that appearance, the nose (aroma), and guessing (trying to guess what the wine will be like or what type of wine is in the glass) are important themes. A code is assigned to these categories. Similarly, other codes are assigned as shown in the *code manager window*. The density column shows how often a code is applied. After considerable thought and questioning of the experience, the researcher builds a network, or grounded theory, that suggests how a wine may come to be associated with feelings of romance. This theory is shown in the network view. The reader interested in learning more about using software to help with qualitative coding should refer to the software sources provided in Chapter 7.

Dummy coding is a simple (dummy-proof) way to represent classification variables.

STRUCTURED QUALITATIVE RESPONSES

dummy coding

Numeric "1" or "0" coding where each number represents an alternate response such as "female" or "male."

Qualitative responses to structured questions such as "yes" or "no" can be stored in a data file with letters such as "Y" or "N." Alternatively, they can be represented with numbers, one each to represent the respective category. So, the number 1 can be used to represent "yes" and 2 can be used to represent "no." Since this represents a nominal numbering system, the actual numbers used are arbitrary. Even though the codes are numeric, the variable is classificatory, simply separating the positive from the negative responses.

For reasons that should become increasingly apparent in later chapters, the research may consider adopting **dummy coding** for dichotomous responses like yes or no. Dummy coding assigns a 0 to one category and a 1 to the other. So, for yes/no responses, a 0 could be "no" and a 1 would be "yes." Similarly, a "1" could represent a female respondent and a "0" would be a male respondent. Dummy coding provides the researcher with more flexibility in how structured, qualitative responses are analyzed statistically.

Dummy coding can be used when more than two categories exist, but because a dummy variable can only represent two categories, multiple dummy variables are needed to represent a single qualitative response that can take on more than two categories. In fact, the rule is that if k is the number of categories for a qualitative variable, $k-1$ dummy variables are needed to represent the variable.

DATA FILE TERMINOLOGY

Once structured, qualitative responses are coded, they are stored in an electronic data file. Here, both the qualitative responses and quantitative responses are likely stored for every respondent involved in a survey or interview. A terminology exists that helps describe this process and the file that results.

Some of the terminology seems strange these days. For instance, what does a "card" have to do with a simple computer file? Most of the terminology describing files goes back to the early days of computers. In those days, data and the computer programs that produced results were stored on actual computer cards. Hopefully, readers will no longer have to use physical cards to store data. Much easier and more economical ways exist.

Researchers organize coded data into cards, fields, records, and files. Cards are the collection of records that make up a file. A **field** is a collection of characters (a *character* is a single number, letter, or special symbol such as a question mark) that represents a single piece of data, usually a variable. Some variables may require a large field, particularly for text data; other variables may require a field of only one character. Text variables are represented by **string characters**, which is computer terminology for a series of alphabetic characters (non-numeric characters) that may form a word. String characters often contain long fields of eight or more characters. In contrast, a dummy variable is a numeric variable that needs only one character to form a field.

A **record** is a collection of related fields. A record was the way a single, complete computer card was represented. Researchers may use the term *record* to refer to one respondent's data. A **data file** is a collection of related records that make up a data set.

Exhibit 19.3 shows the SPSS variable view used to describe the data in a file. Most of the headings are straightforward, beginning with the name of the variable, the type of variable (numeric or string), the size, the label, and so forth. Notice toward the bottom that the variable *country* is a string variable. The values for this variable are words that correspond to the country from which the specific record originates (United States, United Kingdom, Canada, or Australia). All of the remaining variables are numeric.

The coder will sometimes like to associate a label with specific values of a numeric variable. Exhibit 19.3 shows the value labels dialog box that opens when the "Values" column is clicked. Notice that the variable *dummy* contains an entry in this column. **Value labels** are extremely useful and allow a word or short phrase to be associated with a numeric coding. In this case, the value label helps describe whether or not someone has an MBA degree. The labels are matched to the numeric code as follows:

- If dummy = 0, the value label is "no degree"
- If dummy = 1, the value label is "MBA"

The analysts will no doubt appreciate the coder's value labeling. Now, when frequencies or other statistical output is created for this variable, the value label will appear instead of simply a number. The advantage is that the analyst will not have to remember what coding was used. In other words, he or she won't have to remember that a "1" meant an MBA. Other statistical programs accommodate value labels in similarly easy fashions. With SAS, the coder could create a format statement as follows:

```
proc format;
value labels
```

field

A collection of characters that represents a single type of data—usually a variable.

string characters

Computer terminology to represent formatting a variable using a series of alphabetic characters (nonnumeric characters) that may form a word.

record

A collection of related fields that represents the responses from one sampling unit.

data file

The way a data set is stored electronically in spreadsheet-like form in which the rows represent sampling units and the columns represent variables.

value labels

Unique labels assigned to each possible numeric code for a response.

EXHIBIT 19.3 **Data Storage Terminology in SPSS**

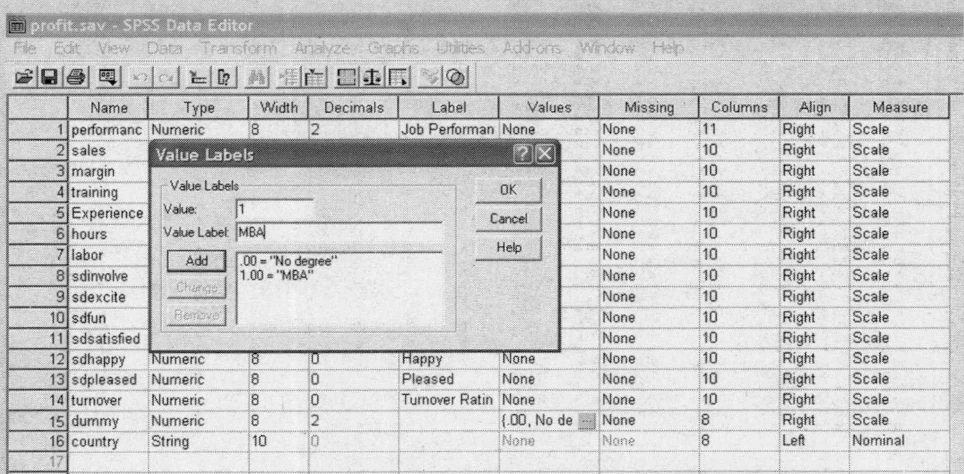

COURTESY OF SPSS STATISTICS 17.0.

By clicking in the country row and values column, the value labels dialog box appears, which allows one to set each value to a text label as shown.

```
    0 = 'none'
    1 = 'mba';
data chap19;
input dummy perf sales;
format dummy labels.;
```

This sequence reads three variables: dummy, perf (performance), and sales. Just as in the SPSS example, the sequence assigns the label "none" to a value of 0 for dummy and a label of "mba" to a value of 1 for dummy.

The Data File

Data are generally stored in a matrix that resembles a common spreadsheet file. A data file stores the data from a research project and is typically represented in a rectangular arrangement (matrix) of data in rows and columns. Typically, each row represents a respondent's scores on each variable and each row represents a variable for which there is a value for every respondent. Exhibit 19.4 illustrates a data matrix corresponding to the variable view in Exhibit 19.3. In this case, data exist for 40 respondents. No doubt, the data file appears to be a spreadsheet. A spreadsheet like Excel is an acceptable way to store a data file, and increasingly, statistical programs like SPSS, SAS, and others can work easily with an Excel spreadsheet. The careful construction of data files is critical to business research. For some businesses, their data is coded and stored in data warehouses. These data warehouses, where customer, supplier, and organization level data are coded, stored, and analyzed, are often the lifeblood of the company. The Research Snapshot "Building a Multi-Petabyte Data System" highlights the size and investment companies have in such data storage systems.

Each column in Exhibit 19.4 represents a particular variable. The first two columns are ratio variables representing hours worked and labor costs, respectively. The next seven columns are variables taken from survey questions. Six of these are semantic differential scales that are scored from 1 to 10 based on the respondent's opinion. The next variable is a variable indicating likelihood of quitting, also using a 10-point scale. Finally, the last two variables, dummy and country, represent whether or not the respondent has an MBA and in which country he or she works, respectively.

EXHIBIT 19.4 A Data File Stored in SPSS

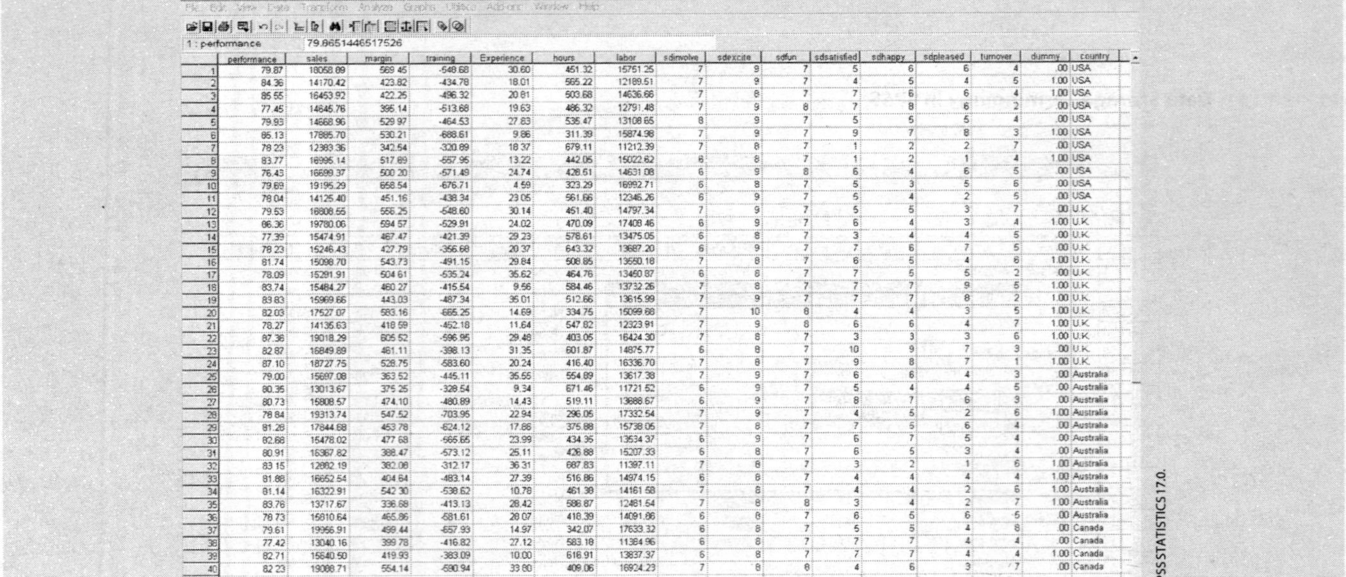

	performance	sales	margin	training	Experience	hours	labor	sdinvolve	sdexcite	sdfun	sdsatisfied	sdhappy	sdpleased	turnover	dummy	country
1	79.87	18058.89	569.45	-548.68	30.60	451.32	15751.25	7	9	7	5	6	6	4	.00	USA
2	84.36	14170.42	423.82	-434.78	18.01	565.22	12189.51	7	9	7	4	5	4	5	1.00	USA
3	85.55	16453.92	422.25	-496.32	20.81	503.68	14636.66	7	8	7	7	6	6	4	1.00	USA
4	77.45	14645.76	395.14	-513.68	19.63	486.32	12791.48	7	9	8	7	8	6	2	.00	USA
5	79.93	14668.96	529.97	-464.53	27.83	535.47	13108.65	8	9	7	5	5	5	4	.00	USA
6	85.13	17885.70	530.21	-688.61	9.86	311.39	15874.38	7	9	7	9	7	8	3	1.00	USA
7	78.23	12383.36	342.54	-320.89	18.37	679.11	11212.39	7	8	7	1	2	2	7	.00	USA
8	83.77	16995.14	517.89	-557.95	13.22	442.05	15022.62	6	8	7	1	2	1	4	1.00	USA
9	76.43	16699.37	500.20	-571.49	24.74	428.51	14631.08	6	9	8	6	4	6	5	.00	USA
10	79.69	19195.29	658.54	-676.71	4.59	323.29	16992.71	6	8	7	5	3	5	6	.00	USA
11	78.04	14125.40	451.16	-438.34	23.05	561.66	12346.26	6	9	7	5	4	2	5	.00	USA
12	79.53	16808.55	556.25	-548.60	30.14	451.40	14797.34	7	9	7	5	5	3	7	.00	U.K.
13	86.36	19780.06	594.57	-529.91	24.02	470.09	17408.46	6	9	7	6	4	3	4	1.00	U.K.
14	77.39	15474.91	467.47	-421.39	29.23	578.61	13475.05	6	8	7	3	4	4	5	.00	U.K.
15	78.23	15246.43	427.79	-356.68	20.37	643.32	13687.20	6	9	7	7	6	7	5	.00	U.K.
16	81.74	15098.70	543.73	-491.15	29.84	508.85	13550.18	7	8	7	6	5	4	6	1.00	U.K.
17	78.09	15291.91	504.61	-535.24	35.62	464.76	13450.87	6	8	7	7	5	5	2	.00	U.K.
18	83.74	15484.27	460.27	-415.54	9.56	584.46	13732.26	7	8	7	7	7	9	5	1.00	U.K.
19	83.83	15969.66	443.03	-487.34	35.01	512.66	13615.99	7	9	7	7	7	8	2	1.00	U.K.
20	82.03	17527.07	583.16	-665.25	14.69	334.75	15099.68	7	10	8	4	4	3	5	1.00	U.K.
21	78.27	14135.63	418.59	-452.18	11.64	547.82	12323.91	7	9	8	6	6	4	7	1.00	U.K.
22	87.36	19018.29	605.52	-596.95	29.48	403.05	16424.30	7	8	7	3	3	3	6	1.00	U.K.
23	82.87	16849.89	461.11	-398.13	31.35	601.87	14875.77	6	8	7	10	9	7	3	.00	U.K.
24	87.10	18727.75	528.75	-583.60	20.24	416.40	16336.70	7	8	7	9	8	7	1	1.00	U.K.
25	79.00	15697.08	363.52	-445.11	35.55	554.89	13617.38	7	9	7	6	6	4	3	.00	Australia
26	80.35	13013.67	375.25	-328.54	9.34	671.46	11721.52	6	9	7	5	4	4	5	.00	Australia
27	80.73	15808.57	474.10	-480.89	14.43	519.11	13688.67	6	9	7	8	7	6	3	.00	Australia
28	78.84	19313.74	547.52	-703.95	22.94	296.05	17332.54	7	9	7	4	5	2	6	1.00	Australia
29	81.28	17844.68	453.78	-624.12	17.86	375.88	15738.05	7	8	7	7	5	6	4	.00	Australia
30	82.66	15478.02	477.68	-565.65	23.99	434.35	13534.37	6	9	7	6	7	5	4	.00	Australia
31	80.91	16367.82	388.47	-573.12	25.11	426.88	15207.33	6	8	7	6	5	3	4	.00	Australia
32	83.15	12882.19	382.08	-312.17	36.31	687.83	11397.11	7	8	7	3	2	1	6	1.00	Australia
33	81.88	16652.54	404.64	-483.14	27.39	516.86	14974.15	6	8	7	4	4	4	4	1.00	Australia
34	81.14	16322.91	542.30	-538.62	10.78	461.38	14161.58	7	8	7	4	4	2	6	1.00	Australia
35	83.76	13717.67	336.68	-413.13	28.42	586.87	12481.54	7	8	8	3	4	2	7	1.00	Australia
36	78.73	15810.64	465.86	-581.61	28.07	418.39	14091.86	6	8	7	6	5	6	5	.00	Australia
37	79.61	19956.91	499.44	-657.93	14.97	342.07	17633.32	6	8	7	5	5	4	8	.00	Canada
38	77.42	13040.16	399.78	-416.82	27.12	583.18	11384.96	6	8	7	7	7	4	4	.00	Canada
39	82.71	15640.50	419.93	-383.09	10.00	616.91	13837.37	6	8	7	7	7	4	4	1.00	Canada
40	82.23	19088.71	554.14	-580.94	33.80	409.06	16924.23	7	8	8	4	6	3	7	.00	Canada

RESEARCH SNAPSHOT

Building a Multi-Petabyte Data System

What is a petabyte? For those of you familiar with disk storage measured in gigabytes (GB), a petabyte is 1,000,000 GBs. Who could possibly need such a large data system? Not surprisingly, the largest retailer in the world—Wal-Mart. With over 800 million transactions tied to over 30 million customers each day, the data coding and analysis needs for such a system are clear.

The design of the data system is a critical need for Wal-Mart. Whether it is suppliers who wish to view product movement and sales in real time, or executives who are interested in business intelligence or scenario planning, the data design aspect of Wal-Mart's data warehouse is the key to its success. Because virtually all of the transactions are processed in real time, data integrity and error checking are success factors valued by Wal-Mart executives.

Over time, as the demands for richer, more robust, and timely data analyses increase, Wal-Mart appears to have made the investments needed to grow their data warehouse into the future. In the future, there are even plans to have data marts—smaller, subject-specific data systems that can handle the needs of a particular business area.

© iStock

Source: Hayes Weier, Mary, "Hewlett-Packard Data Warehouse Lands in Wal-Mart's Shopping Cart," *Intelligent Enterprise* (August 4, 2007), http://www.intelligententerprise.com/showArticle.jhtml?articleID=201203079, accessed April 20, 2009.

Code Construction

There are two basic rules for code construction. First, the coding categories should be *exhaustive,* meaning that a coding category should exist for all possible responses. With a categorical variable such as sex, making categories exhaustive is not a problem. However, trouble may arise when the response represents a small number of subjects or when responses might be categorized into a class not typically found. For example, when questioned about automobile ownership, an antique car collector might mention that he drives a Packard Clipper. This may present a problem if separate categories have been developed for all possible makes of cars. Solving this problem frequently requires inclusion of an "other" code category to ensure that the categories are all-inclusive. For example, household size might be coded 1, 2, 3, 4, and 5 or more. The "5 or more" category assures all subjects of a place in a category.

Missing data should also be represented with a code. In the "good old days" of computer cards, a numeric value such as 9 or 99 was used to represent missing data. Today, most software will understand that either a period or a blank response represents missing data.

Second, the coding categories should be *mutually exclusive* and *independent.* This means that there should be no overlap among the categories to ensure that a subject or response can be placed in only one category.

Precoding Fixed-Alternative Questions

When a questionnaire is highly structured, the categories may be precoded before the data are collected. Exhibit 19.5 presents a questionnaire for which the precoded response categories were determined before the start of data collection. The codes in the data file will correspond to the small numbers beside each choice option. In most instances, the codes will not actually appear on the questionnaire.

The questionnaire in Exhibit 19.5 shows several demographic questions classifying individuals' scores. Question 29 has three possible answers, and they are precoded 1, 2, 3. Question 30 asks a person to respond "yes" (1) or "no" (2) to the question "Are you the male or female head of the household?" Once again, technology is making things easier and much of this type of coding is automated. For users of Web-based survey services, all that one need do is submit a questionnaire and in return he or she will receive a coded data file in the software of his or her choice.

Telephone interviews are still widely used. The partial questionnaire in Exhibit 19.6 shows a precoded format for a telephone interview. In this situation the interviewer circles the coded numerical score as the answer to the question.

Precoding can be used if the researcher knows what answer categories exist before data collection occurs. Once the questionnaire has been designed and the structured (or closed-form) answers

EXHIBIT 19.5 Precoding Fixed-Alternative Responses

29. Do you—or does anyone else in your immediate household—belong to a labor union?

[1]☐ Yes, I personally belong to a labor union.
[2]☐ Yes, another member of my household belongs to a labor union.
[3]☐ No, no one in my household belongs to a labor union.

30. Are you the male or female head of the household—that is, the person whose income is the chief source of support of the household?

[1]☐ Yes [2]☐ No

31. Would you please check the appropriate combined yearly income *(before income taxes and any other payroll deductions)* from all sources of all those in your immediate household? *(Please include income from salaries, investments, dividends, rents, royalties, bonuses, commissions, etc.)* Please remember that your individual answers will not be divulged.

[1]☐ Less than $4,000
[2]☐ $4,000–$4,999
[3]☐ $5,000–$5,999
[4]☐ $6,000–$6,999
[5]☐ $7,000–$7,499
[6]☐ $7,500–$7,999
[7]☐ $8,000–$8,999
[8]☐ $9,000–$9,999
[9]☐ $10,000–$12,499
[10]☐ $12,500–$14,999
[11]☐ $15,000–$19,999
[12]☐ $20,000–$24,999
[13]☐ $25,000–$29,999
[14]☐ $30,000–$39,999
[15]☐ $40,000–$49,999
[16]☐ $50,000–$74,999
[17]☐ $75,000–$99,999
[18]☐ $100,000 or more

32. a. Do you personally own corporate stocks? [1]☐ Yes [2]☐ No

b. Do you own stocks in the corporation for which you work? Do you own them in a corporation for which you do not work? *(Please check as many as apply.)*

Own STOCK in:
[1]☐ Company for which I work [2]☐ Other company

THANK YOU VERY MUCH FOR YOUR COOPERATION

If you would like to make any comments on any of the subjects covered in this study, please use the space below:

____

____

identified, coding then becomes routine. In some cases, predetermined responses are based on standardized classification schemes. A coding framework that standardizes occupation follows:

What is your occupation? (PROBE: *What kind of work is that?*)

01 *Professional, technical, and kindred workers*
02 *Farmers*
03 *Managers, officials, and proprietors*
04 *Clerical*
05 *Sales workers*
06 *Craftsmen, foremen, and kindred workers*
07 *Operatives and kindred workers*
08 *Service workers*
09 *Laborers, except farm and mine*
10 *Retired, widow, widower*
11 *Student*
12 *Unemployed, on relief, laid off*
13 *Homemaker*
14 *Other (specify)*
99 *No occupation given*

Computer-assisted telephone interviewing (CATI) requires precoding. Changing the coding framework after the interviewing process has begun is extremely difficult because it requires changes in the computer programs. In any event, coding closed-ended structured responses is a straightforward process of entering the code into the data file.

More on Coding Open-Ended Questions

Surveys that are largely structured will sometimes contain some semi-structured open-ended questions. These questions may be exploratory or they may be potential follow-ups to structured questions. The purpose of coding such questions is to reduce the large number of individual responses to a few general categories of answers that can be assigned numerical codes.

EXHIBIT 19.6 Precoded Format for Telephone Interview

Study #45641 — For office use only
Travel (Telephone Screening) — Respondent #______

City:
Chicago
Gary
Ft. Wayne
Bloomington

Hello, I'm ______________ from __________, a national survey research company. We are conducting a study and would like to ask you a few questions.

A. Before we begin, do you—or any member of your family—work for . . .
   1 A travel agency   2 An advertising agency   3 A marketing research company
   (If "yes" to any of the above, terminate and tally on contact sheet)

B. By the way, have you been interviewed as part of a survey research study within the past month?
   1 Yes—(Terminate and tally on contact sheet)
   2 No—(Continue)

1. Have you yourself made any trips of over 100 miles within the continental 48 states in the past 3 months?
   1 Yes
   2 No—(Skip to Question 10)

2. Was the trip for business reasons (paid for by your firm), vacation, or personal reasons?

	Last Trip	**Second Last Trip**	**Other Trips**
Business	1	1	1
Vacation	2	2	2
Personal (excluding a vacation)	3	3	3

Similar answers should be placed in a general category and assigned the same code much as the codes are assigned in the qualitative sample involving wine consumption above, except in this case, a small amount of data may be obtained from a large number of respondents, whereas in the hermeneutic unit above, a large amount of data is obtained from one or a small number of respondents. For example, a consumer survey about frozen food also asked why a new microwaveable product would not be purchased:

- We don't buy frozen food very often.
- I like to prepare fresh food.
- Frozen foods are not as tasty as fresh foods.
- I don't like that freezer taste.

All of these answers could be categorized under "dislike frozen foods" and assigned the code 1. Code construction in these situations reflects the judgment of the researcher.

A major objective in the code-building process is to accurately transfer the meanings from written responses to numeric codes. Experienced researchers recognize that the key idea in this process is that code building is based on thoughts, not just words. The end result of code building should be a list, in an abbreviated and orderly form, of all comments and thoughts given in answers to the questions.

Developing an appropriate code from the respondent's exact comments is somewhat of an art. Researchers generally perform a test tabulation to identify verbatim responses from approximately 20 percent of the completed questionnaires and then establish coding categories reflecting the judgment of the person constructing the codes. **Test tabulation** is the tallying of a small sample of the total number of replies to a particular question. The purpose is to preliminarily identify the stability and distribution of answers that will determine a coding scheme. Exhibit 19.7 illustrates open-ended responses and preliminary open-ended codes generated for the question "Why does the chili you just tasted taste closer to homemade?" During the coding procedure, the respondent's opinions are divided into mutually exclusive thought patterns. These separate divisions may

test tabulation
Tallying of a small sample of the total number of replies to a particular question in order to construct coding categories.

EXHIBIT 19.7 **Coding Open-Ended Questions about Chili**

Responses	Codes
You don't get that much meat in a can. The beans are cooked just right.	1. Don't get that much meat in a can 2. Beans are cooked just right
It just (doesn't look) like any canned chili I've had. I can see spices; I've never seen it in any canned chili. It is not too spicy, but it is tasty—savory. It's not (loaded with beans)—just enough beans. It's moist—not too chewy.	3. I can see spices 4. Not too spicy 5. It is tasty 6. Has just enough beans 7. Moist 8. Not too chewy
Tastes (fresh). The canned stuff is too (soft). Too overcooked usually. It doesn't have a lot of filler and not too many beans.	9. Fresh taste 10. Canned is usually overcooked 11. Not a lot of filler 12. Not too many beans
It's not too spicy. It's not too hot, it's mild. Has enough spice to make it tastier. It seems to have a pretty good gravy. Some are watery.	13. Not too hot, it's mild 14. Has enough spice 15. Gravy not watery

Walker Research, "Coding Open Ends Based on Thoughts," *The Marketing Researcher*, December 1979, pp. 1–3.

consist of a single word, a phrase, or a number of phrases, but in each case represent only one thought. Each separate thought is coded once. When a thought is composed of more than one word or phrase, only the most specific word or phrase is coded.

After tabulating the basic responses, the researcher must determine how many answer categories will be acceptable. This will be influenced by the purpose of the study and the limitations of the computer program or plan for data entry. For example, if only one single-digit field is assigned to a particular survey question, the number of possible categories is limited. If an "other" or "miscellaneous" code category appears along with a "don't know/no answer" category, the code construction will be further limited.

Devising the Coding Scheme

The coder will try to classify all of the comments from the interviewer in a code that facilitates analysis.

© CREATAS IMAGES/JUPITER IMAGES

A coding scheme should not be too elaborate. The coder's task is only to summarize the data. Exhibit 19.8 shows a test tabulation of airport visitors' responses to a question that asked for comments about the Honolulu Airport. After the first pass at devising the coding scheme, the researcher must decide whether to revise it and whether the codes are appropriate for answering management's questions. A preliminary scheme with too many categories can always be collapsed or reduced later in the analysis. If initial coding is too abstract and only a few categories are established, revising the codes to more concrete statements will be difficult unless the raw data were recorded.

EXHIBIT 19.8
Open-Ended Responses to a Survey about the Honolulu Airport

	Number
Prices high: restaurant/coffee shop/snack bar	90
Dirty—filthy—smelly restrooms/airport	65
Very good/good/excellent/great	59
Need air-conditioning	52
Nice/beautiful	45
Gift shops expensive	32
Too warm/too hot	31
Friendly staff/people	25
Airport is awful/bad	23
Long walk between terminal/gates	21
Clean airport	17
Employees rude/unfriendly/poor attitude	16
More signs/maps in lobby/streets	16
Like it	15
Love gardens	11
Need video games/arcade	10
More change machines/different locations	8
More padded benches/comfortable waiting area	8
More security personnel including HPD	8
Replace shuttle with moving walkways	8
Complaint: flight delay	7
Cool place	7
Crowded	7
Provide free carts for carry-on bags	7
Baggage storage inconvenient/need in different locations	6
Floor plan confusing	6
Mailbox locations not clear/more needed	6
More restaurants and coffee shops/more variety	6
Need a place to nap	6
Polite VIP/friendly/helpful	6
Poor help in gift shops/rude/unfriendly	6
Slow baggage delivery/service	6
Very efficient/organized	6
Excellent food	5
Install chilled water drinking fountains	5
Love Hawaii	5
More TV sets	5
Noisy	5
People at sundries/camera rude	5
Shuttle drivers rude	5
Something to do for passengers with long waits	5
Airport too spread out	4
Better information for departing/arriving flights	4
Better parking for employees	4
Better shuttle service needed	4
Cute VIP	4

In the Honolulu Airport example, the preliminary tabulation contained too many codes, but it could be reduced to a smaller number of categories. For example, the heading "Friendly/attractive personnel" could include the responses "Friendly staff/people," "Polite VIP/friendly/helpful," and "Cute VIP." Experienced coders group answers under generalized headings that are pertinent to the research question. Individual coders should give the same code to similar responses. The categories should be sufficiently unambiguous that coders will not classify items in different ways.

Coding open-ended questions is a very complex issue. Certainly, this task cannot be mastered simply from reading this chapter. However, the reader should have a feel for the art of coding responses into similar categories. With practice, and by using multiple coders so that consistency can be examined, one can become skilled at this task.

RESEARCH SNAPSHOT

Coding Data "On-the-Go"

Collecting business-critical data takes time. Often data collection specialists and researchers must stop their other organizational responsibilities to code a data value into a spreadsheet or business database. This can take valuable and productive time away from their other responsibilities. For example, a warehouse worker operating a forklift might need to code where a particular pallet of product is in a warehouse, after they have moved it from one section to another. This would require that they stop and code into a computer the new pallet location. Vangard Voice Systems aims to change this in a big way.

© iStock

Vangard's AccuSpeech and Mobile Voice Platform (MVP) is a mobile enterprising system that uses cellular phone technology and proprietary voice recognition software to execute voice commands to store, code, or recode data hands-free. For the forklift driver, data can be entered through voice commands, thus allowing them to continue to work within their warehouse without any productivity downtime. In many ways, taking advantage of the portability of cellular technology is a natural fit for supply chain companies. Using Vangard Voice's AccuSpeech, data can truly be collected and coded "on-the-go"!

© THINKSTOCK (RF) JUPITER IMAGES

Source: http://www.vangardvoice.com, Vangard Voice Systems, accessed April 19, 2009.

Code Book

code book
A book that identifies each variable in a study and gives the variable's description, code name, and position in the data matrix.

A **code book** gives each variable in the study and its location in the data matrix. In essence, the code book provides a quick summary that is particularly useful when a data file becomes very large. Exhibit 19.9 illustrates a portion of a code book from the telephone interview illustrated in Exhibit 19.6. Notice that the first few fields record the study number, city, and other information used for identification purposes. Researchers commonly identify individual respondents by giving each an identification number or questionnaire number. When each interview is identified with a number entered into each computer record, errors discovered in the tabulation process can be checked on the questionnaire to verify the answer.

Editing and Coding Combined

Frequently the person coding the questionnaire performs certain editing functions, such as translating an occupational title provided by the respondent into a code for socioeconomic status. A question that asks for a description of the job or business often is used to ensure that there will be no problem in classifying the responses. For example, respondents who indicate "salesperson" as their occupation might write their job description as "selling shoes in a shoe store" or "selling IBM supercomputers to the defense department." Generally, coders are instructed to perform this type of editing function, seeking the help of a tabulation supervisor if questions arise.

Computerized Survey Data Processing

data entry
The activity of transferring data from a research project to computers.

optical scanning system
A data processing input device that reads material directly from mark-sensed questionnaires.

In most studies with large sample sizes, a computer is used for data processing. The process of transferring data from a research project, such as answers to a survey questionnaire, to computers is referred to as **data entry**. Several alternative means exist for entering data into a computer. In studies involving highly structured paper and pencil questionnaires, an **optical scanning system** may be used to read material directly into the computer's memory from *mark-sensed questionnaires*. The form may look similar to the type a student uses to take a multiple-choice test. As seen in the Research Snapshot titled "Coding Data On-the-Go," even mobile phone technology is now being used to aid data processing.

In a research study using computer-assisted telephone interviewing or a self-administered Internet questionnaire, responses are automatically stored and tabulated as they are collected.

EXHIBIT 19.9
Portion of a Code Book from a Travel Study

		Study #45641 January 20__ N = 743
Question Number	**Field or Column Number**	**Description and Meaning of Code Values**
—	1–5	Study number (45641)
—	6	City 1. Chicago 2. Gary 3. Ft. Wayne 4. Bloomington
—	7–9	Interview number (3 digits on upper left-hand corner of questionnaire)
A	Not entered	Family, work for 1. Travel agency 2. Advertising agency 3. Marketing research company
B	Not entered	Interviewed past month 1. Yes 2. No
1.	10	Traveled in past 3 months 1. Yes 2. No
2.	11	Purpose last trip 1. Business 2. Vacation 3. Personal
	12	Purpose second last trip 1. Business 2. Vacation 3. Personal
	13	Purpose other trips 1. Business 2. Vacation 3. Personal

Direct data capture substantially reduces clerical errors that occur during the editing and coding process. If researchers have security concerns, the data collected in an Internet survey should be encrypted and protected behind a firewall.

As the opening vignette shows, collecting data using computer technology is an ever-growing phenomenon in business research. When data are not optically scanned or directly entered into the computer the moment they are collected, data processing begins with keyboarding. A data entry process transfers coded data from the questionnaires or coding sheets onto a hard drive. As in every stage of the research process, there is some concern about whether the data entry job has been done correctly. Data entry workers, like anyone else, may make errors. To ensure 100 percent accuracy in transferring the codes, the job should be *verified* by a second data entry worker. If an error has been made, the verifier corrects the data entry. This process of verifying the data is never performed by the same person who entered the original data. A person who misread the coded questionnaire during the keyboarding operation might make the same mistake during the verifying process, and the mistake might go undetected.

Error Checking

The final stage in the coding process is error checking and verification, or *data cleaning,* to ensure that all codes are legitimate. For example, computer software can examine the entered data and

TIPS OF THE TRADE

- Check responses for inconsistent answers.
- Remove any specific piece of data that is indicated by inconsistent responses.
- Include check questions—particularly on lengthy questionnaires or any time when respondents may have very low involvement.

- Missing data can be a problem, particularly when the missing data is not missing randomly. Several options for dealing with missing data exist.
  - Replace missing responses with some actual value imputed to minimize chance error.
    - Imputation should be done with great care as it is at best a sophisticated guess.
  - Pair-wise deletion is a good way to handle missing data in most applications.
- Take advantage of technology. When possible, use a computerized survey tool.

© iStock

identify coded values that lie outside the range of acceptable answers. For example, if "sex" is coded 1 for "male" and 2 for "female" and a 3 code is found, a mistake obviously has occurred and an adjustment must be made.

Summary

1. Know when a response is really an error and should be edited. Data editing is necessary before coding and storing the data file. The data editor must sometimes alter a respondent's answer. Often, this situation arises because of inconsistent responses; that is, responses to different questions that contradict each other. The editor should be cautious in altering a respondent's answer. Only when a certain response is obviously wrong and the true response is easily determined should the coder substitute a new value for the original response. Ideally, multiple pieces of evidence would suggest the original response as inaccurate and also suggest the accurate response before the respondent takes such a step. Missing data should generally be left as missing, although imputation methods exist to provide an educated guess for missing values. These imputation methods can be used when the sample size is small and the researcher needs to retain as many responses as possible.

2. Appreciate coding of pure qualitative research. Qualitative research such as typified by depth interviews, conversations, or other responses is coded by identifying the themes underlying some interview. The codes become a key component of a hermeneutic unit that ultimately can be linked to one another to form a grounded theory. The frequency with which some thought is expressed helps to identify appropriate coding for unstructured qualitative data.

3. Understand the way data are represented in a data file. A survey provides an overview of respondents based on their answers to questions. These answers are edited, coded, and then stored in a data file. The data file is structured as a data matrix in which the rows represent respondents and the columns represent variables. Thus, a survey in which 200 respondents are asked 50 structured questions would result in a data matrix consisting of 200 rows and 50 columns.

4. Understand the coding of structured responses including a dummy variable approach. Quantitative structured responses are generally coded simply by marking the number corresponding to the choice selected by the respondent. Qualitative structured responses must also be coded. Dichotomous variables lend themselves well to dummy coding. With dummy coding, the two possible choices to a question are coded with a "1" for one response and a "0" for the other. Short-answer or list questions are coded by assigning a number to all responses that seem to suggest the same theme even if different words are used.

5. Appreciate the ways that technological advances have simplified the coding process. Throughout the chapter, technological advances in data collection were mentioned. These advances have automated a great deal of data coding and reduced the chances of respondent error. For instance, some inconsistent responses can be automatically screened and the respondent can be prompted to go back and correct a response that seems inconsistent. Also, if a respondent fails to answer a question, a pop-up window can take that respondent back to the question and force him or her to respond in order to continue through the rest of the questionnaire.

Key Terms and Concepts

code book, *512*
codes, *503*
coding, *503*
data entry, *512*
data file, *505*
data integrity, *498*
dummy coding, *504*
editing, *498*
field, *505*
field editing, *498*
impute, *501*
in-house editing, *499*
item nonresponse, *501*
nonrespondent error, *497*
optical scanning system, *512*
plug value, *501*
raw data, *497*
record, *505*
string characters, *505*
test tabulation, *509*
value labels, *505*

Questions for Review and Critical Thinking

1. What is the purpose of editing? Provide some examples of questions that might need editing.
2. When should the raw data from a respondent be altered by a data editor?
3. How is data coding different from data editing?
4. A 25-year-old respondent indicates that she owns her own house in Springfield, Illinois, and it is valued at $990 million. Later in the interview, she indicates that she didn't finish high school and that she drives a 1993 Buick Century. Should the editor consider altering any of these responses? If so, how?
5. What role might a word counter play in coding qualitative research results?
6. A survey respondent from Florida has been asked to respond as to whether or not he or she owns a boat, and if so, whether he or she stores the boat at a marina. Over two hundred respondents are included in this sample. What suggestions do you have for coding the information provided?
7. How would a dummy variable be used to represent whether or not a respondent in a restaurant ordered dessert after their meal?
8. List at least three ways in which recent technological advances (within the last 15 years) have changed the way data are coded.
9. **ETHICS** A large retail company implements an employee survey that ostensibly is aimed at customer satisfaction. The survey includes a yes or no question that asks whether or not the employee has ever stolen something from the workplace. How could this data be coded? What steps could be attempted to try and ensure that the employee's response is honest? Do you believe it is fair to ask this question? Should the employee take action against employees who have indicated that they have stolen something?
10. A researcher asks, "What do you remember about advertising for Gillette Turbo razors?" A box with enough room for 100 words is provided in which the respondent can answer the question. The survey involves responses from 250 consumers. How should the code book for this question be structured? What problems might it present?
11. **'NET** Use **http://www.naicscode.com** to help with this response. What is the NAICS code for golf (country) clubs? What is the NAICS code for health clubs? How can these codes be useful in creating data files?
12. **'NET** Explore the advantages of computerized software such as ATLAS.ti. The Web site is at **http://www.atlasti.com**. How do you think it might assist in coding something like a depth interview or a collage created by a respondent?

Research Activities

1. Design a short questionnaire with fewer than five fixed-alternative questions to measure student satisfaction with your college bookstore. Interview five classmates and then arrange the database into a data matrix.
2. **'NET** The Web page of the Research Triangle Institute (**http://www.rti.org**) describes its research tools and methods in some detail. Click on *tools and methods* and explore the surveys and survey tools described there. How might these methods assist in coding?

Case 19.1 U.S. Department of the Interior Heritage Conservation and Recreation Service

© GETTY IMAGES/ PHOTODISC GREEN

Some years ago the U.S. Department of the Interior conducted a telephone survey to help plan for future outdoor recreation. A nine-page questionnaire concerning participation in outdoor recreational activities and satisfaction with local facilities was administered by the Opinion Research Corporation of Princeton, New Jersey, to 4,029 respondents. The last two pages of the questionnaire appear in Case Exhibit 19.1–1. Assume the data will be entered into a data file in which each data entry should include the following information:

- Respondent number
- State code (all 50 states)

Question

Design the coding for this portion of the questionnaire. Assume that the data from previous pages of the questionnaire will follow these data.

CASE EXHIBIT 19.1–1 Sample Page from Questionnaire

The following questions are for background purposes.

32. Do you live in an . . .
    - ☐ Urban location
    - ☐ Suburban location
    - ☐ Rural location

33. Counting yourself, how many members of your family live here? (If "1" on Q.33, go to Q.35)

34. How many family members are . . .
    - Over 65 years ______
    - 40 to 65 years ______
    - 21 to 39 years ______
    - 12 to 20 years ______
    - 5 to 11 years ______
    - Under 5 years ______

35. What is your age? (Years)

36. In school, what is the highest grade (or year) you have completed? (Circle response)

Elementary school	01	02	03	04	05	06
Junior high school	07	08				
High school	09	10	11	12		
College	13	14	15	16		
Graduate school	17	18	19	20	21	

37. What is your occupation? What kind of work is that?
    - ☐ Professional, technical, and kindred workers
    - ☐ Farmers
    - ☐ Managers, officials, and proprietors
    - ☐ Clerical and kindred workers
    - ☐ Sales workers
    - ☐ Craftspersons, forepersons, and kindred workers
    - ☐ Operatives and kindred workers
    - ☐ Service workers
    - ☐ Laborers, except farm and mine
    - ☐ Retired, widow, widower
    - ☐ Student
    - ☐ Unemployed, on relief, laid off → Go to Q.43
    - ☐ Housewife
    - ☐ Other (specify)

38. How many hours a week do you work at your place of employment? ___ (hours)

39. How many days of vacation do you get in a year? ___ (days)

40. Please tell me which of the following income categories most closely describe the total family income for the year before taxes, including wages and all other income. Is it . . .
    - ☐ Under $12,000
    - ☐ $12,000–$20,000
    - ☐ $20,001–$30,000
    - ☐ $30,001–$50,000
    - ☐ $50,001–$100,000
    - ☐ Over $100,001

41. Sex of respondent . . .
    - ☐ Male
    - ☐ Female

42. What is the zip code at your place of employment?

This concludes the interview; thank you very much for your cooperation and time.

Case 19.2 Shampoo 9–10

© GETTY IMAGES/ PHOTODISC GREEN

A shampoo, code named "9–10" was given to women for trial use.[4] The respondents were asked what they liked and disliked about the product. Some sample codes are given in Case Exhibits 19.2–1 and 19.2–2.

There were two separate sets of codes: the codes in Case Exhibit 19.2–1 were for coding the respondents' likes, and the codes in Case Exhibit 19.2–2 were for coding their dislikes. The headings identify fields in the data matrix and the different attributes of shampoo. The specific codes are listed under each attribute. The coding instructions were first to look for the correct heading, and then to locate the correct comment under that heading and use that number as the code.

For example, if, in response to a "like" question, a respondent had said, "The shampoo was gentle and mild," a coder would look in field 10, the "gentleness" field, and find the comment

"Gentle/mild/not harsh"; then the coder would write "11" next to the comment. If, under "dislikes," someone had said, "I would rather have a shampoo with a crême rinse," the coder would look in field 16 for comparison to other shampoos and write "74" ("Prefer one with a crême rinse") beside that response.

The sample questionnaires appear in Case Exhibit 19.2–3.

Questions

1. Code each of the three questionnaires.
2. Evaluate this coding scheme.

CASE EXHIBIT 19.2–1 Sample Codes for "Like" Questions

Test No. Shampoo
Question: Likes

Field 10 Gentleness		**Field 11 Result on Hair**	
11	Gentle/mild/not harsh	21	Good for hair/helps hair
12	Wouldn't strip hair of natural oils	22	Leaves hair manageable/no tangles/no need for crême rinse
13	Doesn't cause/helps flyaway hair	23	Gives hair body
14	Wouldn't dry out hair	24	Mends split ends
15	Wouldn't make skin/scalp break out	25	Leaves hair not flyaway
16	Organic/natural	26	Leaves hair silky/smooth
17		27	Leaves hair soft
18		28	Leaves hair shiny
19		29	Hair looks/feels/good/clean
20		30	
1−		2−	
1+	Other gentleness	2+	Other results on hair
Field 12 Cleaning		**Field 13 Miscellaneous**	
31	Leaves no oil/keeps hair dry	41	Cheaper/economical/good price
32	It cleans well	42	Smells good/nice/clean
33	Lifts out oil/dirt/artificial conditioners	43	Hairdresser recommended
34	Don't have to scrub as much	44	Comes in different formulas
35	No need to wash as often/keeps hair cleaner longer	45	Concentrated/use only a small amount
36	Doesn't leave a residue on scalp	46	Good for whole family (unspecified)
37	Good lather	47	
38	Good for oily hair	48	
39		49	
40		50	
3−		4−	Other miscellaneous
3+	Other cleaning	4+	Don't know/nothing

CASE EXHIBIT 19.2-2 **Sample Codes for "Dislike" Questions**

Test No. Shampoo
Question: Dislikes

Field 14 Harshness		**Field 15 Cleaning**	
51	Too strong	61	Doesn't clean well
52	Strips hair/takes too much oil out	62	Leaves a residue on scalp
53	Dries hair out	63	Poor lather
54	Skin reacts badly to it	64	Not good for oily hair
55		65	
56		66	
57		67	
58		68	
59		69	
60		70	
5−		6−	
5+	Other harshness	6+	Other cleaning
Field 16 Comparison to Others		**Field 17 Miscellaneous**	
71	Prefer herbal/organic shampoo	81	Don't like the name
72	Prefer medicated/dandruff shampoo	82	Too expensive
73	Same as other shampoos—doesn't work any differently	83	Not economical for long hair
74	Prefer one with a crême rinse	84	Use what hairdresser recommends
75	Prefer another brand (unspecified)	85	
76		86	
77		87	
78		88	
79		89	
80		90	
7−		8−	Other miscellaneous
7+	Other comparison to others	8+	Don't know what/disliked/nothing

CASE EXHIBIT 19.2–3 **Sample Questionnaires for Shampoo 9–10 Survey**

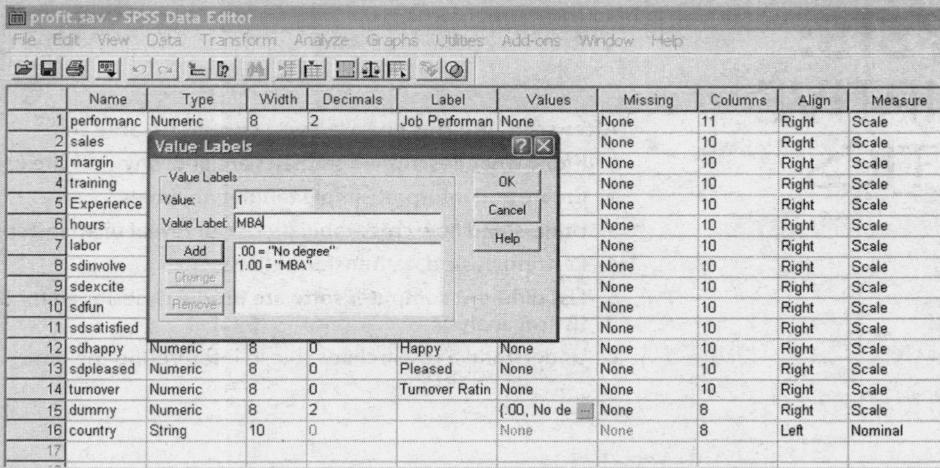

1. **What, if anything, did you particularly like about this shampoo?**

There are different kinds for different types of hair. I use the one for dry hair. It doesn't dry out my hair. It leaves it soft & shiny. It works so well I only have to use a little bit for each shampoo.

2. **What, if anything, did you particularly dislike about this shampoo?**

Nothing. I liked it.

---

1. What, if anything, did you particularly like about this shampoo?

I have limp, oily hair and have to wash it real often. With this shampoo I found it stayed cleaner longer, so I don't have to shampoo as often and my hair has more body.

2. What, if anything, did you particularly dislike about this shampoo?

I like the shampoo but I don't think the name is very appealing.

CHAPTER 20
BASIC DATA ANALYSIS: DESCRIPTIVE STATISTICS

LEARNING OUTCOMES

After studying this chapter, you should be able to

1. **Know what descriptive statistics are and why they are used**
2. **Create and interpret simple tabulation tables**
3. **Understand how cross-tabulations can reveal relationships**
4. **Perform basic data transformations**
5. **List different computer software products designed for descriptive statistical analysis**
6. **Understand a researcher's role in interpreting the data**

Chapter Vignette: Choose Your "Poison"

Most Americans enjoy an adult beverage occasionally. But not all Americans like the same drink. Many decision makers are interested in what Americans like to drink. Retailers need to have the correct product mix for their particular customers if profits are to be increased and customers made more satisfied. Restaurants need to know what their customers like to have with the types of food they serve. Policy makers need to know what types of restrictions should be placed on what types of products to prevent underage drinking and alcohol abuse. Researchers could apply sophisticated statistics to address questions related to Americans' drinking preferences, but a lot can be learned from just counting what people are buying.

© STEPHEN OLIVER/DORLING KINDERSLEY/GETTY IMAGES

A grocery store built in 1975 in Chicago allocates 15 percent of their floor space to adult beverage products. Out of this 15 percent, 60 percent is allocated to beer, 25 percent to spirits, and 15 percent to wine. Since the products are not merchandised the same way (different types of shelving, aisles, and racking are needed), adjusting the floor space to change these percentages is not an easy task. Over the three-decade history of the store, the customer base has changed. Originally, stay-at-home moms buying groceries for the family best characterized the customer base. During the 1990s, empty-nesters, including retirees with high disposable incomes, characterized the customer base. More recently, younger singles just starting careers have moved into the nearby neighborhoods. Should the store reconsider its adult beverage merchandising?

In 1992, American consumers showed a heavy preference toward beer. Among American adults who drank adult beverages,[1]

- 47 percent drank beer
- 21 percent drank spirits
- 27 percent drank wine

By 2005, Americans had changed their drinking preferences. Now,

- 36 percent drink beer
- 21 percent drink spirits
- 39 percent drink wine

A couple of other facts have become clear. A count of the preferred beverages among American adult consumers 29 and younger shows the following preferences in 2005:

- 48 percent drink beer
- 32 percent drink liquor
- 17 percent drink wine

Perhaps due to the emergence of this younger group, a 2008 study shows beer has regained the position as America's favorite adult beverage:[2]

- 42 percent drink beer
- 23 percent drink spirits
- 31 percent drink wine

Across America, grocers account for 35 percent of all beer sales, but convenience stores, where younger consumers tend to shop, account for 45 percent.[3] If the grocery store is converting more to a convenience store, maybe a continued emphasis on beer is wise. However, wine consumers are more *attractive* from several perspectives. Wine now ranks among the top 10 food categories in America, based on grocery store dollar sales volume. Forty-five percent of all wine is sold in grocery stores. What we find is that the consumer who buys wine is also more likely to buy products like prime or choice beef and imported cheeses, instead of lower quality and lower priced meat and cheese products. As a result, the average $13.44 spent on wine in a grocery store (as opposed to $11.94 on beer) is only part of the story in explaining why wine customers may be *grape* customers![4]

What should the grocer emphasize in marketing adult beverages? Perhaps the research based on counting can address this decision.

Introduction

Perhaps the most basic statistical analysis is descriptive analysis. Descriptive statistics can summarize responses from large numbers of respondents in a few simple statistics. When a sample is obtained, the sample descriptive statistics are used to make inferences about characteristics of the entire population of interest. This chapter introduces basic descriptive statistics, which are simple but powerful. This chapter also provides the foundation for Chapter 21, which will extend basic statistics into the area of univariate statistical analysis.

The Nature of Descriptive Analysis

Descriptive analysis is the elementary transformation of data in a way that describes the basic characteristics such as central tendency, distribution, and variability. For example, consider the business researcher who takes responses from 1,000 American consumers and tabulates their favorite soft drink brand and the price they expect to pay for a six-pack of that product. The mean, median, and mode for favorite soft drink and the average price across all 1,000 consumers would be descriptive statistics that describe central tendency in three different ways. Means, medians, modes, variance, range, and standard deviation typify widely applied descriptive statistics.

descriptive analysis
The elementary transformation of raw data in a way that describes the basic characteristics such as central tendency, distribution, and variability.

Chapter 13 indicated that the level of scale measurement helps the researcher choose the most appropriate form of statistical analysis. Exhibit 20.1 shows how the level of scale measurement influences the choice of descriptive statistics. Remember that all statistics appropriate for lower-order scales (nominal and ordinal) are suitable for higher-order scales (interval and ratio), but the reverse is not true.

Consider the following data. Sample consumers were asked where they most often purchased beer. The result is a nominal variable which can be described with a frequency distribution (see the bar chart in Exhibit 20.1). Ten percent indicated they most often purchased beer in a drug store, 45 percent indicated a convenience store, 35 percent indicated a grocery store, and 7 percent indicated a specialty store. Three percent listed some "other" outlet (not shown in the bar chart). The mode is convenience store since more respondents chose this than any other category. A similar distribution may have been obtained if the chart plotted the number of respondents ranking each store as their favorite type of place to purchase beer.

histogram
A graphical way of showing a frequency distribution in which the height of a bar corresponds to the observed frequency of the category.

The bottom part of Exhibit 20.1 displays example descriptive statistics for interval and ratio variables. In this case, the chart displays results of a question asking respondents how much they typically spend on a bottle of wine purchased in a store. The mean and standard deviation are displayed beside the chart as 11.7 and 4.5, respectively. Additionally, a frequency distribution is shown with a histogram. A **histogram** is a graphical way of showing a frequency distribution in which the height of a bar corresponds to the frequency of a category. Histograms are useful for any type of data, but with continuous variables (interval or ratio) the histogram is useful for providing a quick assessment of the distribution of the data. A normal distribution line is superimposed over the histogram, providing an easy comparison to see if the data are skewed or multimodal.

Tabulation

tabulation
The orderly arrangement of data in a table or other summary format showing the number of responses to each response category; tallying.

frequency table
A table showing the different ways respondents answered a question.

Tabulation refers to the orderly arrangement of data in a table or other summary format. When this tabulation process is done by hand, the term *tallying* is used. Counting the different ways respondents answered a question and arranging them in a simple tabular form yields a **frequency table**. The actual number of responses to each category is a variable's frequency distribution. A simple tabulation of this type is sometimes called a *marginal tabulation*.

Simple tabulation tells the researcher how frequently each response occurs. This starting point for analysis requires the researcher to count responses or observations for each category or code assigned to a variable. A frequency table showing where consumers generally purchase beer can be computed easily. The tabular results that correspond to the chart would appear as follows:

Response	Frequency	Percent	Cumulative Percentage
Drug store	50	10	10
Convenience store	225	45	55
Grocery store	175	35	90
Specialty	35	7	97
Other	15	3	100

EXHIBIT 20.1
Levels of Scale Measurement and Suggested Descriptive Statistics

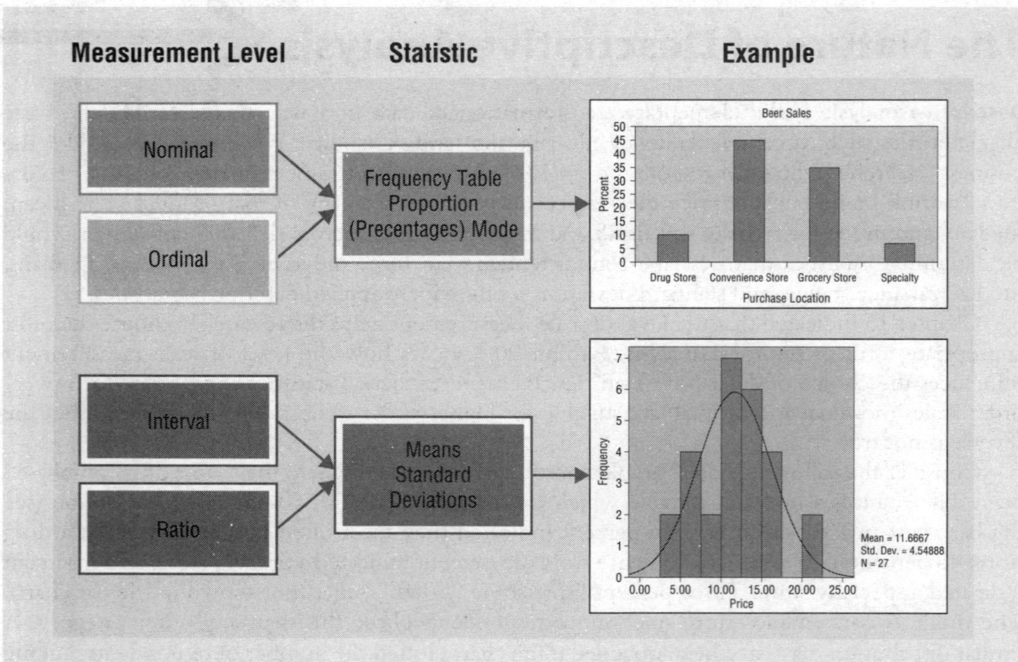

The frequency column shows the tally result or the number of respondents listing each store, respectively. The percent column shows the total percentage in each category. From this chart, we can see the most common outlet—the mode—is convenience store since more people indicated this as their top response than any other. The cumulative percentage keeps a running total, showing the percentage of respondents indicating this particular category and all preceding categories as their preferred place to purchase beer. The cumulative percentage column is not so important for nominal or interval data, but is quite useful for interval and ratio data, particularly when there are a large number of response categories.

Similarly, a recent tabulation of Americans' responses to the simple question of "Who is your favorite TV personality?" revealed the response varied by age. For respondents aged 18–24, Conan O'Brien was listed first. For respondents aged 30–39, Bill O'Reilly was the preferred TV personality, and among consumers 65 and older, Oprah Winfrey was the modal response.[5] The idea that age influences choice of favorite celebrity brings us to cross-tabulation.

Cross-Tabulation

A frequency distribution or tabulation can address many research questions. As long as a question deals with only one categorical variable, tabulation is probably the best approach. Although frequency counts, percentage distributions, and averages summarize considerable information, simple tabulation may not yield the full value of the research. **Cross-tabulation** is the appropriate technique for addressing research questions involving relationships among multiple less-than interval variables. We can think of a cross-tabulation as a combined frequency table. *Cross-tabs* allow the inspection and comparison of differences among groups based on nominal or ordinal categories. One key to interpreting a cross-tabulation table is comparing the observed table values with hypothetical values that would result from pure chance. A statistical test for this comparison is discussed in Chapter 21. Here, we focus on constructing and interpreting cross-tabs.

cross-tabulation

The appropriate technique for addressing research questions involving relationships among multiple less-than interval variables; results in a combined frequency table displaying one variable in rows and another in columns.

Contingency Tables

Exhibit 20.2 shows example cross-tabulation results using contingency tables. A **contingency table** is a data matrix that displays the frequency of some combination of possible responses to multiple variables. Two-way contingency tables, meaning they involve two less-than interval variables, are used most often. A three-way contingency table involves three less-than interval variables. Beyond three variables, contingency tables become difficult to analyze and explain easily. For all practical purposes, a contingency table is the same as a cross-tabulation.

contingency table

A data matrix that displays the frequency of some combination of possible responses to multiple variables; cross-tabulation results.

Two variables are depicted in the contingency table shown in panel A:

- Row Variable: Biological Sex _____M _____F
- Column Variable: "Do you shop at Target? YES or NO"

Several conclusions can be drawn initially by examining the row and column totals:

1. 225 men and 225 women responded, as can be seen in the row totals column.
2. Out of 450 total consumers responding, 330 consumers indicated that "yes" they do shop at Target and 120 indicated "no," they do not shop at Target. This can be observed in the column totals at the bottom of the table. These row and column totals often are called **marginals** because they appear in the table's margins.

marginals

Row and column totals in a contingency table, which are shown in its margins.

Researchers usually are more interested in the inner cells of a contingency table. The inner cells display conditional frequencies (combinations). Using these values, we can draw some more specific conclusions:

EXHIBIT 20.2
Possible Cross-Tabulations of One Question

(A) Cross-Tabulation of Question "Do you shop at Target?" by Sex of Respondent

	Yes	No	Total
Men	150	75	225
Women	180	45	225
Total	330	120	450

(B) Percentage Cross-Tabulation of Question "Do you shop at Target?" by Sex of Respondent, Row Percentage

	Yes	No	Total (Base)
Men	66.7%	33.3%	100% (225)
Women	80.0%	20.0%	100% (225)

(C) Percentage Cross-Tabulation of Question "Do you shop at Target?" by Sex of Respondent, Column Percentage

	Yes	No
Men	45.5%	62.5%
Women	54.5%	37.5%
Total	100%	100%
(Base)	(330)	(120)

3. Out of 330 consumers who shop at Target, 150 are male and 180 are female.
4. Alternatively, out of the 120 respondents not shopping at Target, 75 are male and 45 are female.

This finding helps us know whether the two variables are related. If men and women equally patronized Target, we would expect that hypothetically 165 of the 330 shoppers would be female and 165 would be female. Because we have equal numbers of men and women, the 330 would be equally male and female. The hypothetical expectations (165m/165f) are not observed. What is the implication? Target shoppers are more likely to be female than male. Notice that the same meaning could be drawn by analyzing non–Target shoppers. The Research Snapshot "Contingent Personalities" provides an example of the information provided by cross-tabs.

A two-way contingency table like the one shown in part A is referred to as a *2 × 2 table* because it has two rows and two columns. Each variable has two levels. A two-way contingency table displaying two variables, one (the row variable) with three levels and the other with four levels, would be referred to as a *3 × 4 table*. Any cross-tabulation table may be classified according to the number of rows by the number of columns (*R* by *C*).

Percentage Cross-Tabulations

statistical base
The number of respondents or observations (in a row or column) used as a basis for computing percentages.

When data from a survey are cross-tabulated, percentages help the researcher understand the nature of the relationship by making relative comparisons simpler. The total number of respondents or observations may be used as a **statistical base** for computing the percentage in each cell. When the objective of the research is to identify a relationship between answers to two questions (or two variables), one of the questions is commonly chosen to be the source of the base for determining percentages. For example, look at the data in parts A, B, and C of Exhibit 20.2. Compare part B with part C. In part B, we are considering gender as the base—what percentage of men and of women shop at Target? In part C, we are considering Target shoppers as the base—what percentage of Target shoppers are men? Selecting either the row percentages or the column percentages will emphasize a particular comparison or distribution. The nature of the problem the researcher wishes to answer will determine which marginal total will serve as a base for computing percentages.

TOTHEPOINT

The more we study, the more we discover our ignorance.

—Percy Bysshe Shelley

Fortunately, a conventional rule determines the direction of percentages. The rule depends on which variable is identified as an independent variable and which as a dependent variable. Simply put, *independent variables should form the rows* in a contingency table. The marginal total of the independent variable should be used as the base for computing the percentages. Although survey research does not establish cause-and-effect evidence, one might argue that it would be logical to assume that a variable such as biological sex might predict beverage preference. This makes more sense than thinking that beverage preference would determine biological sex!

Elaboration and Refinement

The *Oxford Universal Dictionary* defines *analysis* as "the resolution of anything complex into its simplest elements." Once a researcher has examined the basic relationship between two variables, he or she may wish to investigate this relationship under a variety of different conditions. Typically, a third variable is introduced into the analysis to elaborate and refine the researcher's understanding by specifying the conditions under which the relationship between the first two variables is strongest and weakest. In other words, a more elaborate analysis asks, "Will interpretation of the relationship be modified if other variables are simultaneously considered?"

Elaboration analysis involves the basic cross-tabulation within various subgroups of the sample. The researcher breaks down the analysis for each level of another variable. If the researcher has cross-tabulated shopping preference by sex (see Exhibit 20.2) and wishes to investigate another variable (say, marital status), a more elaborate analysis may be conducted. Exhibit 20.3 breaks down the responses to the question "Do you shop at Target?" by sex and marital status. The data show women display the same preference whether married or single. However, married men are much more likely to shop at Target than are single men. The analysis suggests that the original conclusion about the relationship between sex and shopping behavior for women be retained. However, a relationship that was not discernible in the two-variable case is evident. Married men more frequently shop at Target than do single men.

elaboration analysis

An analysis of the basic cross-tabulation for each level of a variable not previously considered, such as subgroups of the sample.

The finding is consistent with an interaction effect. The combination of the two variables, sex and marital status, is associated with differences in the dependent variable. Interactions between variables examine moderating variables. A **moderator variable** is a third variable that changes the nature of a relationship between the original independent and dependent variables. Marital status is a moderator variable in this case. The interaction effect suggests that marriage changes the relationship between sex and shopping preference.

moderator variable

A third variable that changes the nature of a relationship between the original independent and dependent variables.

EXHIBIT 20.3

Cross-Tabulation of Marital Status, Sex, and Responses to the Question "Do You Shop at Target?"

	Single		Married	
	Men	Women	Men	Women
"Do you shop at Target?"				
Yes	55%	80%	86%	80%
No	45%	20%	14%	20%

RESEARCH SNAPSHOT

Contingent Personalities

Who is the world's favorite celebrity? This is an important question because the answer helps to determine how much a celebrity endorsement is worth. Sports stars like Tiger Woods are effective in shaping consumers' product preferences worldwide. NBA player Tony Parker is wildly popular in France, where he can be seen endorsing International Watch Company (IWC Schaffhausen) wristwatches. In China, actress Zhang Ziyi helps pitch Maybelline, Garnier, and Asience (Japanese shampoo brand). In other parts of the world, Aishwarya Rai could do the same thing. Perhaps some celebrities are effective nearly everywhere, but others may only be effective in a given country. Their effectiveness is contingent upon region.

Television personalities also influence the public's opinion by giving their own. But all opinions may not be equal. Polling agencies like the Harris interactive poll (**http://www.harrisinteractive.com**) monitor the popularity of celebrities. Who is America's favorite television personality? Oprah Winfrey has achieved the top rating by Americans for several years. But is Oprah's likeability contingent upon other factors? Cross-tabulations can help answer this question. Consider the following 2-by-2 contingency table showing results of 1,000 respondents asked to choose whether they prefer Oprah Winfrey or David Letterman:

	Oprah Winfrey	David Letterman	Totals
Men	150	350	500
Women	380	120	500
	530	470	1,000

© iStock

Or, consider the 3-by-3 contingency table:

	Oprah Winfrey	Bill O'Reilly	Jon Stewart	Totals
Conservatives	60	260	20	340
Liberals	100	20	200	320
Moderates	210	70	60	340
	370	350	280	1,000

In either case, opinions about the preferred celebrity seem to be contingent, or to depend on some characteristic. Results like these would suggest that although Oprah is preferred overall, men prefer David Letterman over Oprah. Also, one's favorite celebrity depends on political orientation. Thus, managers should consider the contingencies when trying to identify preferred celebrities.

Sources: Erdogan, B. Zater, Michael J. Baker, and Stephen Tagg, "Selecting Celebrity Endorsers: The Practitioner's Perspective," *Journal of Advertising Research* 41 (May/June 2001), 39–48; Goetzl, David and Wayne Friedman, "What We're Talking about," *Advertising Age* 73 (December 2, 2002), 51–57; "Harris Poll: Oprah Again Tops America's List of Favorite TV Personalities," *Wall Street Journal Online*, (February 3, 2006), http://online.wsj.com/article/SB113889692780763347.html; "IWC Schaffhausen Appoints Tony Parker as New Friend of the Brand," *PR Newswire* (June 28 2007); Flannery, Russell, "Forbes China Celebrity List," Forbes.com (March 18, 2009).

© D VAN/UPI/LANDOV

In other situations the addition of a third variable to the analysis may lead us to reject the original conclusion about the relationship. When this occurs, the elaboration analysis suggests the relationship between the original variables is spurious (see Chapter 3).

The chapter vignette described data suggesting a relationship between the type of store in which a consumer shops and beverage preference. Convenience store shoppers seem to choose beer over wine, while grocery store shoppers choose wine over beer. Does store type drive drinking preference? Perhaps a third variable, age, determines both the type of store consumers choose to buy in and their preference for adult beverages. Younger consumers both disproportionately shop in convenience stores and drink beer.

How Many Cross-Tabulations?

Surveys may ask dozens of questions and hundreds of categorical variables can be stored in a data warehouse. Using computer programs, business researchers could "fish" for relationships by cross-tabulating every categorical variable with every other categorical variable. Thus, every possible response becomes a possible explanatory variable. A researcher addressing an exploratory research question may find some benefit in such a fishing expedition. Software exists that can automatically search through volumes of cross-tabulations. These may even provide some insight into the business questions under investigation. Alternatively, the program may flag the cross-tabulations suggesting the strongest relationship. CHAID (chi-square automatic interaction detection) software exemplifies software that makes searches through large numbers of variables possible.[7] Data-mining can be conducted in a similar fashion and may suggest relationships that are worth considering further.

However, outside of exploratory research, researchers should conduct cross-tabulations that address specific research questions or hypotheses. When hypotheses involve relationships among two categorical variables, cross-tabulations are the right tool for the job.

Quadrant Analysis

Quadrant analysis is a variation of cross-tabulation in which responses to two rating scale questions are plotted in four quadrants of a two-dimensional table. A common quadrant analysis in business research portrays or plots relationships between average responses about a product attribute's importance and average ratings of a company's (or brand's) performance on that product feature. The term **importance-performance analysis** is sometimes used because consumers rate perceived importance of several attributes and rate how well the company's brand performs on that attribute. Generally speaking, the business would like to end up in the quadrant indicating high performance on an important attribute.

quadrant analysis

An extension of cross-tabulation in which responses to two rating-scale questions are plotted in four quadrants of a two-dimensional table.

importance-performance analysis

Another name for quadrant analysis.

Exhibit 20.4 illustrates a quadrant analysis for an international, mid-priced hotel chain.[8] The chart shows the importance and the performance ratings provided by business travelers. After plotting the scores for each of eight attributes, the analysis suggests areas for improvement. The arrows indicate attributes that the hotel firm should concentrate on to move from quadrant three, which means the performance on those attributes is low but business consumers rate those attributes as important, to quadrant four, where attributes are both important and rated highly for performance.

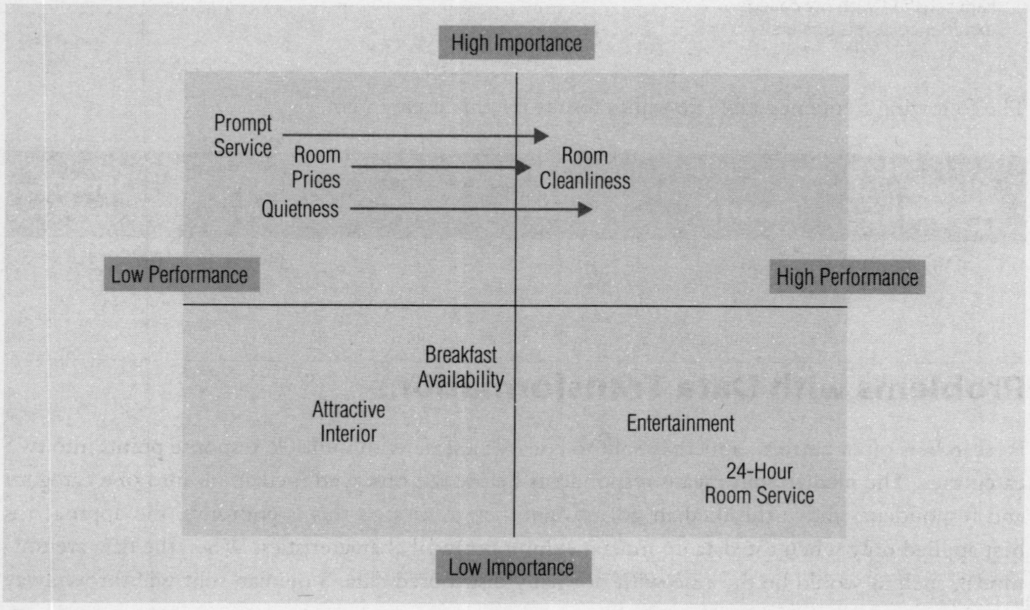

EXHIBIT 20.4
An Importance-Performance or Quadrant Analysis of Hotels

Data Transformation

Simple Transformations

data transformation

Process of changing the data from their original form to a format suitable for performing a data analysis addressing research objectives.

Data transformation (also called *data conversion*) is the process of changing the data from their original form to a format suitable for performing a data analysis that will achieve research objectives. Researchers often modify the values of scalar data or create new variables. For example, many researchers believe that less response bias will result if interviewers ask respondents for their year of birth rather than their age. This presents no problem for the research analyst, because a simple data transformation is possible. The raw data coded as birth year can easily be transformed to age by subtracting the birth year from the current year.

TOTHEPOINT

All that we do is done with an eye to something else.

—Aristotle

In earlier chapters, we discussed recoding and creating summated scales. These also are common data transformations.

Collapsing or combining adjacent categories of a variable is a common form of data transformation used to reduce the number of categories. A Likert scale may sometimes be collapsed into a smaller number of categories. For instance, consider the following Likert item administered to a sample of state university seniors:

The distribution of responses suggests the responses are bimodal. That is, two "peaks" exist in the distribution, one at either end of the scale. Exhibit 20.5 shows an example of a bimodal distribution. Since the vast majority of respondents [80 percent = (110 + 210)/400] indicated either strongly disagree or strongly agree, the variable closely resembles a categorical variable. In general, customers either strongly disagreed or strongly agreed with the statement. So, the research may wish to collapse the responses into two categories. While multiple ways exist to accomplish this, the researcher may assign the value of one to all respondents who either strongly disagreed or disagreed and the value two to all respondents who either agreed or strongly agreed. Respondents marking neutral would be deleted from analysis. In this case, we would end up with 140 (110 + 30) respondents that disagree with this statement and 245 (210 + 35) that agree.

	Strongly Disagree	Disagree	Neutral	Agree	Strongly Agree
I am satisfied with my college experience at this university	☐	☐	☐	☐	☐

The following frequency table describes results for this survey item:

Strongly Disagree	Disagree	Neutral	Agree	Strongly Agree
110	30	15	35	210

Problems with Data Transformations

median split

Dividing a data set into two categories by placing respondents below the median in one category and respondents above the median in another.

Researchers often perform a median split to collapse a scale with multiple response points into two categories. The **median split** means respondents below the observed median go into one category and respondents above the median go into another. Although this is common, the approach is best applied only when the data do indeed exhibit bimodal characteristics. When the data are unimodal, such as would be the case with normally distributed data, a median split will throw away valuable information and lead to error.

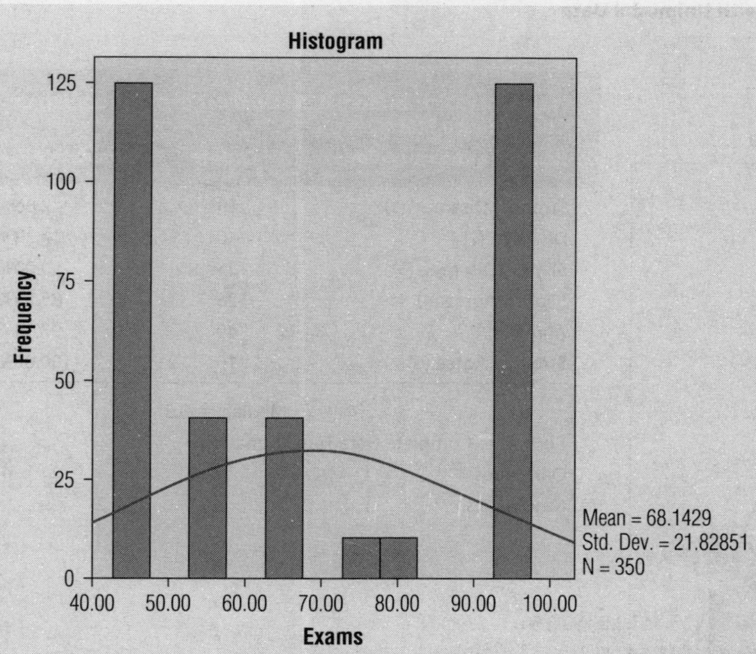

Adapted from 1987 Nielsen Television Report.

EXHIBIT 20.5
Bimodal Distributions are Consistent with Transformations into Categorical Values

Exhibit 20.6 illustrates this problem. Clearly, most respondents either slightly agree or slightly disagree with this statement. The central tendency could be represented by the median of 3.5, a mean of 3.5, and modes of 3 and 4 (3 and 4 each have the same number of responses). The "outliers," if any, appear to be those not indicating something other than slight agreement/disagreement. A case can be made that the respondents indicating slight disagreement are more similar to those indicating slight agreement than they are to those respondents indicating strong disagreement. Yet we can see the recode places values 1 and 3 in the same new category, but places values 3 and 4 in a different category (see the recoding scheme in Exhibit 20.6). The data distribution does not support a median split into two categories and so a transformation collapsing these values into agreement and disagreement is inappropriate.

When a sufficient number of responses exist and a variable is ratio, the researcher may choose to delete one-fourth to one-third of the responses around the median to effectively ensure a bimodal distribution. However, median splits should always be performed only with great care, as the inappropriate collapsing of continuous variables into categorical variables ignores the information contained within the untransformed values. Rather than splitting a continuous variable into two categories to conduct a frequency distribution or cross-tabulation, we have more appropriate analytical techniques that are discussed in the chapters which follow.

Index Numbers

index numbers

Scores or observations recalibrated to indicate how they relate to a base number.

The consumer price index and wholesale price index are secondary data sources that are frequently used by business researchers. Price indexes, like other **index numbers**, represent simple data transformations that allow researchers to track a variable's value over time and compare a variable(s) with other variables. Recalibration allows scores or observations to be related to a certain base period or base number.

Consider the information in Exhibit 20.7. Weekly television viewing statistics are shown grouped by household size. Index numbers can be computed for these observations in the following manner:

EXHIBIT 20.6 **The Problem with Median Splits with Unimodal Data**

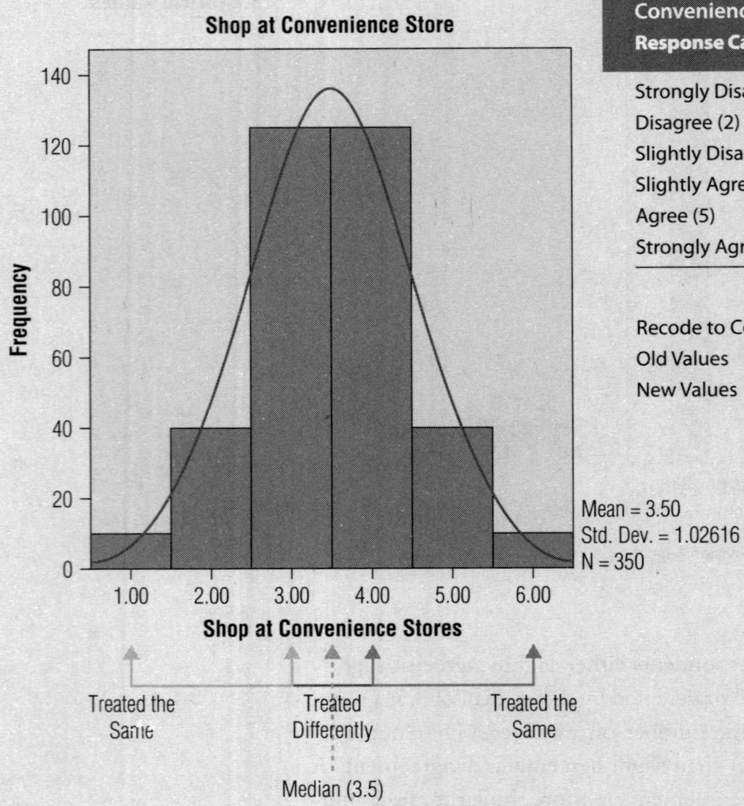

Frequency Distribution: X_1 5 I Do Most of My Shopping at Convenience Stores.

Response Category (Code)	Counts	Cumulative Percentage
Strongly Disagree (1)	10	2.86%
Disagree (2)	40	14.29%
Slightly Disagree (3)	125	50.00%
Slightly Agree (4)	125	85.71%
Agree (5)	40	97.14%
Strongly Agree (6)	10	100.00%

Median = 3.5

Recode to Complete Data Transformation:

Old Values	1	2	3	4	5	6
New Values	1	1	1	2	2	2

1. A base number is selected. The U.S. household average of 52 hours and 36 minutes represents the central tendency and will be used.
2. Index numbers are computed by dividing the score for each category by the base number and multiplying by 100. The index reflects percentage changes from the base:

$$\text{1 person hh:} \quad \frac{41:01}{52:36} = 0.7832 \times 100 = 78.32$$

$$\text{2 person hh:} \quad \frac{47:58}{52:36} = 0.9087 \times 100 = 90.87$$

$$\text{3+ person hh:} \quad \frac{60:49}{52:36} = 1.1553 \times 100 = 115.53$$

$$\text{Total U.S. average:} \quad \frac{52:36}{52:36} = 1.0000 \times 100 = 100.00$$

If the data are time-related, a base year is chosen. The index numbers are then computed by dividing each year's activity by the base-year activity and multiplying by 100. Index numbers require ratio measurement scales. Managers may often chart consumption in some category over time. Relating back to the chapter vignette, grocers may wish to chart the U.S. wine consumption index. Using 1968 as a base year, the current U.S. wine consumption index is just over 2.0, meaning that the typical American consumer drinks about twice as much wine today as in 1968, which is just over 8.7 liters of wine per year.[9] The Research Snapshot "Twitter and the ReTweetability Index" shows another application of data transformation and index creation.

EXHIBIT 20.7
Hours of Television Usage per Week

Household Size	Hours:Minutes
1	41:01
2	47:58
3+	60:49
Total U.S. average	52:36

Adapted from 1987 Nielsen Television Report.

Calculating Rank Order

Survey respondents are often asked to rank order their preference for some item, issue, or characteristic. For instance, consumers may be asked to rank their three favorite brands or employee respondents may provide rankings of several different employee benefit plans. Ranking data can be summarized by performing a data transformation. The transformation involves multiplying the frequency by the ranking score for each choice to result in a new scale.

For example, suppose a CEO had 10 executives rank their preferences for locations in which to hold the company's annual conference. Exhibit 20.8 shows how executives ranked each of four locations: Hawaii, Paris, Greece, and Hong Kong. Exhibit 20.9 tabulates frequencies for these rankings. A ranking summary can be computed by assigning the destination with the highest preference the lowest number (1) and the least preferred destination the highest consecutive number (4). The summarized rank orderings were obtained with the following calculations:

Hawaii: $(3 \times 1) + (5 \times 2) + (1 \times 3) + (1 \times 4) = 20$

Paris: $(3 \times 1) + (1 \times 2) + (3 \times 3) + (3 \times 4) = 26$

Greece: $(2 \times 1) + (2 \times 2) + (4 \times 3) + (2 \times 4) = 26$

Hong Kong: $(2 \times 1) + (2 \times 2) + (2 \times 3) + (4 \times 4) = 28$

Three executives chose Hawaii as the best destination (ranked "1"), five executives selected Hawaii as the second best destination, and so forth. The lowest total score indicates the first (highest) preference ranking. The results show the following rank ordering: (1) Hawaii, (2) Paris, (3) Greece, and (4) Hong Kong. Company employees may be glad to hear their conference will be in Hawaii!

Tabular and Graphic Methods of Displaying Data

Tables, graphs, and charts may simplify and clarify data. Graphical representations of data may take a number of forms, ranging from a computer printout to an elaborate pictograph. Tables, graphs, and charts, however, all facilitate summarization and communication. For example, see how the simple frequency table and histogram shown in Exhibit 20.7 provide a summary that quickly and easily communicates meaning that would be more difficult to see if all 350 responses were viewed separately.

Today's researcher has many convenient tools to quickly produce charts, graphs, or tables. Even common programs such as Excel and Word include chart functions that can construct the chart within the text document. Bar charts (histograms), pie charts, curve/line diagrams, and scatter plots are among the most widely used tools. Some choices match well with certain types of data and analyses.

RESEARCH SNAPSHOT

© iStock

Twitter and the *Re*Tweetability Index

Twitter is one of the fastest growing social networks. A privately funded organization in San Francisco, Twitter's first prototype was developed in March of 2006 and launched publicly five months later. Since then, Twitter has evolved into a real-time messaging service compatible with several different networks and multiple devices:

Simplicity has played an important role in Twitter's success. People are eager to connect with other people and Twitter makes that simple. Twitter asks one question, "What are you doing?" Answers must be under 140 characters in length and can be sent via mobile texting, instant message, or the web.

Twitter's core technology is a device agnostic message routing system with rudimentary social networking features. By accepting messages from sms, web, mobile web, instant message, or from third party API projects, Twitter makes it easy for folks to stay connected.

If you are not familiar with Twitter, a basic understanding of the terminology is necessary. After signing up for a Twitter account, you can *tweet* your 140 character message. *Followers* are people who have signed up to receive someone's Twitter messages. A *retweet* (or RT) occurs when a follower takes a tweet and then tweets that message to everyone in their own Twitter network. Encouraging other Twitter users to retweet your messages is the key in spreading your message across the Twittersphere. Wow!

Dan Zarrella, a self-proclaimed viral marketing scientist, has developed an index to assess the most influential Twitter users. While several sites rank users by their number of followers, and others report the number of RTs, Zarrella has combined these figures with the daily number of tweets to calculate the *Re*Tweetability Index:

(Retweets per Day / Tweets per Day) / Followers

The index is intended to provide a score and ranking of Twitter users based on the power of their tweets. The higher the number, the more influential Twitter you are!

Sources: "About Twitter," Twitter, http://twitter.com/about; Dan Zarrella's *Re*Tweetability Index, http://www.retweetability.com; Saric, Marko, "Make Your Blog Go Viral with Twitter ReTweets," How to Make My Blog.com (January 13, 2009), http://www.howtomakemyblog.com/twitter/make-your-blog-go-viral-with-twitter-retweets.

COURTESY OF TWITTER.COM

EXHIBIT 20.8
Executive Rankings of Potential Conference Destinations

Executive	Hawaii	Paris	Greece	Hong Kong
1	1	2	4	3
2	1	3	4	2
3	2	1	3	4
4	2	4	3	1
5	2	1	3	4
6	3	4	1	2
7	2	3	1	4
8	1	4	2	3
9	4	3	2	1
10	2	1	3	4

EXHIBIT 20.9
Frequencies of Conference Destination Rankings

	Preference Rankings			
Destination	1st	2nd	3rd	4th
Hawaii	3	5	1	1
Paris	3	1	3	3
Greece	2	2	4	2
Hong Kong	2	2	2	4

Bar charts and pie charts are very effective in communicating frequency tabulations and simple cross-tabulations. Exhibit 20.10 displays frequency data from the chapter vignette with pie charts. Each pie summarizes preference in the respective year. The size of each pie slice corresponds to a frequency value associated with that choice. When the three pie charts are compared, the result communicates a cross-tabulation. Here, the comparison clearly communicates that wine preference increased at the expense of beer preference from 1992 to 2005, but has yielded some ground in 2008. In other words, the relative slice of pie for wine became larger, then slightly smaller.

Chapter 25 discusses how these and other graphic aids may improve the communication value of a written report or oral presentation.

Computer Programs for Analysis

Statistical Packages

Just 50 years ago, the thought of a typical U.S. company performing even basic statistical analyses, like cross-tabulations, on a thousand or more observations was unrealistic. The personal computer brought this capability not just to average companies, but to small companies and individuals with limited resources. Today, computing power is very rarely a barrier to completing a research project.

In the 1980s and early 1990s, when the PC was still a relatively novel innovation, specialized statistical software formerly used on mainframe computers made their way into the personal computing market. Today, most spreadsheet packages can perform a wide variety of basic statistical options. Excel's basic data analysis tool will allow descriptive statistics including frequencies and measures of central tendency to be easily computed.[10] Most of the basic statistical features are now menu driven, reducing the need to memorize function labels. Spreadsheet packages like Excel continue to evolve and become more viable for performing many basic statistical analyses.

Despite the advances in spreadsheet applications, commercialized statistical software packages remain extremely popular among researchers. They continue to become easier to use and more compatible with other data interface tools including spreadsheets and word processors. Like any specialized tool, statistical packages are more tailored to the types of analyses performed by statistical analysts, including business researchers. Thus, any serious business

EXHIBIT 20.10 **Pie Charts Work Well with Tabulations and Cross-Tabulations**

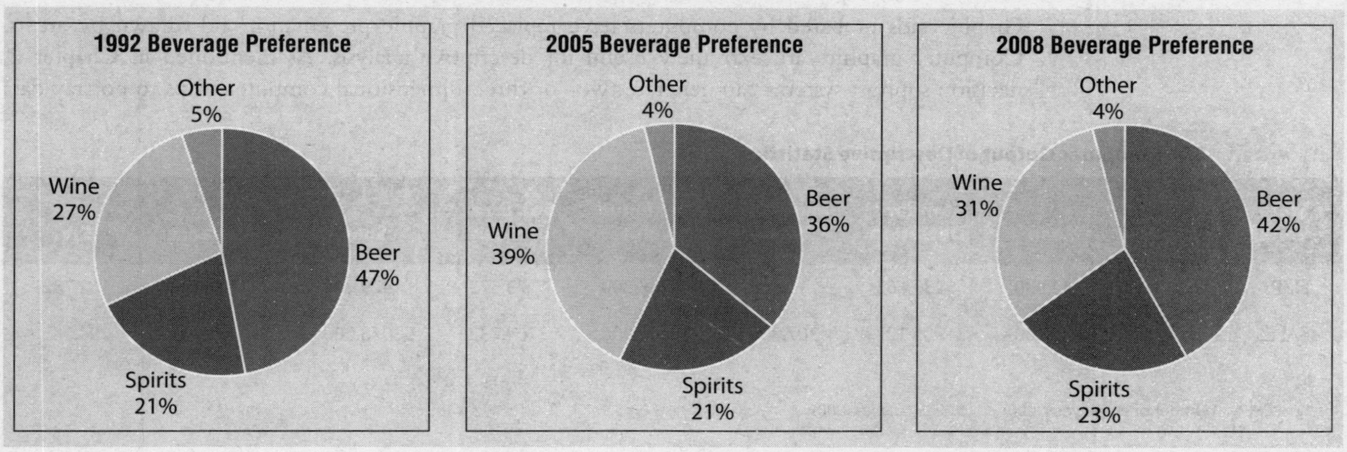

or social science researcher should still become familiar with at least one general computer software package.

Two of the most popular general statistical packages are SAS (**http://www.sas.com**) and SPSS (**http://www.spss.com**). SAS revenues exceed $2.15 billion in 2008 and its software can be found on computers worldwide. SAS was founded in 1976, and its statistical software historically has been widely used in engineering and other technical fields. SPSS stands for *Statistical Package for the Social Sciences*. SPSS was founded in 1968 and sales now exceed $300 million annually. SPSS is commonly used by university business and social science students. Business researchers have traditionally used SPSS more than any other statistical software tool. SPSS has been viewed as more "user-friendly" in the past. However, today's versions of both SPSS and SAS are very user friendly and give the user the option of using drop-down menus to conduct analysis rather than writing computer code.

Excel, SAS, and SPSS account for most of the statistical analysis conducted in business research. University students may also be exposed to MINITAB, which is sometimes preferred by economists. However, MINITAB has traditionally been viewed as being less user-friendly than other choices.

In the past, data entry was an issue as specific software required different types of data input. Today, however, all the major software packages, including SAS and SPSS, can work from data entered into a spreadsheet. The spreadsheets can be imported into the data windows or simply read by the program. Most conventional online survey tools will return data to the user in the form of either an SPSS data file, an Excel spreadsheet, or a plain text document.

Exhibit 20.11 shows a printout of descriptive statistics generated by SAS for two variables: EMP (number of employees working in an MSA, or Metropolitan Statistical Area) and SALES (sales volume in dollars in an MSA) for 10 MSAs. The number of data elements (*N*), mean, standard deviation, and other descriptive statistics are displayed. SAS output is generally simple and easy to read.

As an example of SPSS output, the histograms shown in Exhibits 20.6 and 20.7 were created by SPSS. By clicking on "charts" in the SPSS tool menu, one can see the variety of charts that can be created. The key place to click to generate statistical results in tabular form is "analyze." Here, one can see the many types of analysis that can be created. In this chapter, the choices found by clicking on "analyze" and then "descriptive statistics" are particularly relevant.

Exhibit 20.12 shows an SPSS cross-tabulation of two variables, class status and smoking behavior. The data come from a sample intercepted on an urban university campus. It addresses the research question, "Does smoking on campus vary across groups?" More nonsmokers than smokers are found. However, the results show that graduate students, and to a lesser extent instructors, smoke more than the norm. The SPSS user can ask for any number of statistics and percentages to be included with this output by clicking on the corresponding options.

Computer Graphics and Computer Mapping

Graphic aids prepared by computers have replaced graphic presentation aids drawn by artists. Computer graphics are extremely useful for descriptive analysis. As mentioned in Chapter 2, decision support systems can generate two- or three-dimensional computer maps to portray data

EXHIBIT 20.11 **SAS Computer Output of Descriptive Statistics**

State = NY Variable	*N*	Mean	Standard Deviation	Minimum Value	Maximum Value	Std. Error of Mean	Sum	Variance	C.V.
EMP	10	142.930	232.665	12.800	788.800	73.575	1429.300	54133.0	162.782
SALES	10	5807.800	11905.127	307.000	39401.000	3764.732	58078.000	141732049.1	204.985

Key: EMP = number of employees (000) SALES = Sales (000)

CLASS * SMOKING Cross-Tabulation				
		Smoking		
Count		Smoker	Non-Smoker	Total
Class	high school	7	9	16
	undergraduate	9	22	31
	graduate	15	10	25
	career	6	6	12
Total		37	47	84

EXHIBIT 20.12
Examples of SPSS Output for Cross-Tabulation

about sales, demographics, lifestyles, retail stores, and other features. Exhibit 20.13 shows a computer graphic depicting how fast-food consumption varies from state to state. The chart shows the relative frequencies of eating fast-food burgers, chicken, tacos, or other types of fast food across several states. Computer graphics like these have become more common as common applications have introduced easy ways of generating 3-D graphics and maps. Many computer maps are used by business executives to show locations of high-quality customer segments. Competitors' locations are often overlaid for additional quick and easy visual reference. Scales that show miles, population densities, and other characteristics can be highlighted in color, with shading, and with symbols.

TOTHEPOINT

The thing to do is to supply light.

—Woodrow Wilson

Many computer programs can draw **box and whisker plots**, which provide graphic representations of central tendencies, percentiles, variabilities, and the shapes of frequency distributions. Exhibit 20.15 shows a computer-drawn box and whisker plot for 100 responses to a question measured on a 10-point scale. The response categories are shown on the vertical axis. The small box inside the plot represents responses for half of all respondents. Thus, half of respondents marked 4, 5, or 6. This gives a measure of variability called the **interquartile range**, but the term *midspread* is less complex and more descriptive. The location of the line within the box indicates the median. The dashed lines that extend from the top and bottom of the box are the whiskers. Each whisker extends either the length of the box (the midspread in our example is 2 scale points) or to the most extreme observation in that direction.

box and whisker plots
Graphic representations of central tendencies, percentiles, variabilities, and the shapes of frequency distributions.

interquartile range
A measure of variability.

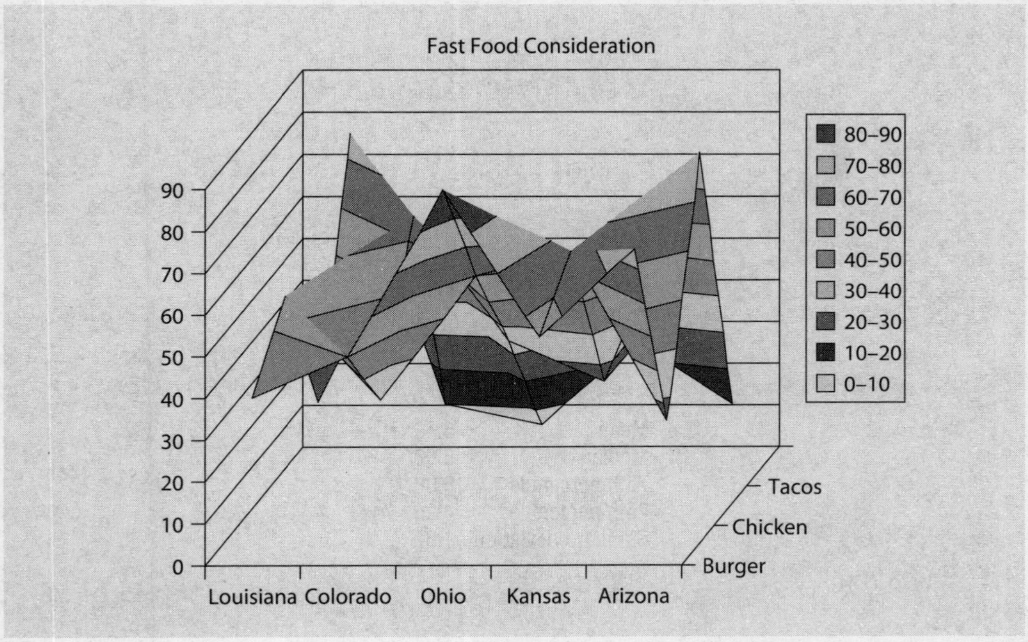

EXHIBIT 20.13
A 3-D Graph Showing Fast-Food Consumption Patterns around the United States

outlier
A value that lies outside the normal range of the data.

An **outlier** is a value that lies outside the normal range of the data. In Exhibit 20.15 outliers are indicated by either a 0 or an asterisk. Box and whisker plots are particularly useful for spotting outliers or comparing group categories (e.g., men versus women).

Interpretation

An interpreter at the United Nations translates a foreign language into another language to explain the meaning of a foreign diplomat's speech. In business research, the interpretation process explains the meaning of the data. After the statistical analysis of the data, inferences and conclusions about their meaning are developed.

interpretation
The process of drawing inferences from the analysis results.

A distinction can be made between *analysis* and *interpretation*. **Interpretation** is drawing inferences from the analysis results. Inferences drawn from interpretations lead to managerial implications. In other words, each statistical analysis produces results that are interpreted with respect to insight into a particular decision. The logical interpretation of the data and statistical analysis are closely intertwined. When a researcher calculates a cross-tabulation of number of dependents of employee with choice of health plan, an interpretation is drawn suggesting that employees with a different number of dependents may be more or less likely to choose a given health place. This interpretation of the statistical analysis may lead to a realization that certain health plans are better suited for different family situations.

From a management perspective, however, the qualitative meaning of the data and their managerial implications are an important aspect of the interpretation. Consider the crucial role played by interpretation of research results in investigating one new product, a lip stain that could color the lips a desired shade semi-permanently and last for about a month at a time:

EXHIBIT 20.14
Computer Drawn Box and Whisker Plot

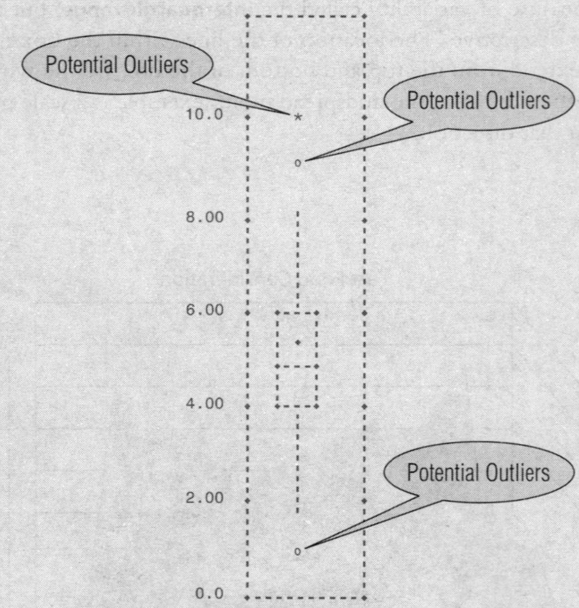

Mean	5.40
Median	5.00
75th percentile	6.00
25th percentile	4.00
Standard deviation	1.62

TIPS OF THE TRADE

- A frequency table can be a very useful way to depict basic tabulations.
- Cross-tabulation and contingency tables are a simple and effective way to examine relationships among less than interval variables.
  - When a distinction can be made between independent and dependent variables (that are nominal or ordinal), the convention is rows are independent variables and columns are dependent variables.
- Importance-performance charts are a good way to illustrate market positioning by showing where brands are strong or weak on important variables. A weakness on an important variable is a call to action.
- A continuous variable that displays a bimodal distribution is appropriate for a median split.
  - Median splits on continuous variables displaying a normal distribution are typically not appropriate and result in a loss of information. If necessary, these should only be performed after deleting one-fourth to one-third of the responses around the median to help prevent logically inconsistent classifications.
- Box and whisker plots can reveal outliers.
  - Outliers can distort statistical analysis. Therefore, they become candidates for deletion.

> *The lip stain idea, among lipstick wearers, received very high scores on a rating scale ranging from "excellent" to "poor," presumably because it would not wear off. However, it appeared that even among routine wearers of lipstick the idea was being rated highly more for its interesting, even ingenious, nature than for its practical appeal to the consumer's personality. They liked the idea, but for someone else, not themselves. . . . [Careful interpretation of the data] revealed that not being able to remove the stain for that length of time caused most women to consider the idea irrelevant in relation to their own personal needs and desires. Use of the product seems to represent more of a "permanent commitment" than is usually associated with the use of a particular cosmetic. In fact, women attached overtly negative meaning to the product concept, often comparing it with hair dyes instead of a long-lasting lipstick.*[11]

This example shows that interpretation is crucial. However, the process is difficult to explain in a textbook because there is no one best way to interpret data. Many possible interpretations of data may be derived from a number of thought processes. Experience with selected cases will help you develop your own interpretative ability.

Data are sometimes merely reported and not interpreted. Research firms may provide reams of computer output that do not state what the data mean. At the other extreme, some researchers tend to analyze every possible relationship between each and every variable in the study. Such an approach is a sign that the research problem was not adequately defined prior to beginning the research and the researcher really doesn't know what business decision the research is addressing. Researchers who have a clear sense of the purpose of the research do not request statistical analysis of data that have little or nothing to do with the primary purpose of the research.

Summary

1. Know what descriptive statistics are and why they are used. Descriptive analyses provide descriptive statistics including measures of central tendency and variation. Statistics such as the mean, mode, median, range, variance, and standard deviation are all descriptive statistics. These statistics provide a summary describing the basic properties of a variable.

2. Create and interpret simple tabulation tables. Statistical tabulation is another way of saying that we count the number of observations in each possible response category. In other words, tabulation is the same as tallying. Tabulation is an appropriate descriptive analysis for less-than interval variables. Frequency tables and histograms are used to display tabulation results.

3. Understand how cross-tabulations can reveal relationships. Cross-tabulation is when we combine two or more less-than interval variables to display the relationship. For example, a cross-tabulation of respondent gender with adult beverage preference (i.e., beer, spirits, wine) would give us two rows (male and female) and three columns (beer, spirits, wine), which would show the preferred beverage for each gender. The key to interpreting a cross-tabulation result is to compare actual observed values with hypothetical values that would result from pure chance. When observed results vary from these values, a relationship is indicated.

4. Perform basic data transformations. Data transformations are often needed to assist in data analysis and involve changing the mathematical form of data in some systematic way. Basic data transformations include reverse coding, summating scales, creating index numbers, and collapsing a variable based on a median split.

5. List different computer software products designed for descriptive statistical analysis. While spreadsheets have improved with respect to their ability to conduct basic statistical analyses, business researchers still rely heavily on specialized statistical software. SAS and SPSS are two of the best known statistical packages. Each is available for even the most basic modern PC and can be used with a drop-down window interface, practically eliminating the need for writing computer code.

6. Understand a researcher's role in interpreting the data. The interpretation process explains the meaning of the data. Interpretation is drawing inferences from the analysis results, providing meaning for the figures which are observed. Inferences drawn from interpretations lead to managerial implications.

Key Terms and Concepts

box and whisker plots, *535*
contingency table, *524*
cross-tabulation, *523*
data transformation, *527*
descriptive analysis, *521*
elaboration analysis, *525*
frequency table, *522*
histogram, *522*
importance-performance analysis, *527*
index numbers, *529*
interpretation, *536*
interquartile range, *535*
marginals, *524*
median split, *529*
moderator variable, *526*
outlier, *536*
quadrant analysis, *527*
statistical base, *525*
tabulation, *522*

Questions for Review and Critical Thinking

1. What are five descriptive statistics used to describe the basic properties of variables?
2. What is a *histogram?* What is the advantage of overlaying a normal distribution over a histogram?
3. A survey asks respondents to respond to the statement "My work is interesting." Interpret the frequency distribution shown here (taken from an SPSS output):
   a. My work is interesting:

Category Label	Code	Abs. Freq.	Rel. Freq. (Pct.)	Adj. Freq. (Pct.)	Cum. Freq. (Pct.)
Very true	1	650	23.9	62.4	62.4
Somewhat true	2	303	11.2	29.1	91.5
Not very true	3	61	2.2	5.9	97.3
Not at all true	4	28	1.0	2.7	100.0
	•	1,673	61.6	Missing	
	Total	2,715	100.0	100.0	
Valid cases	1,042		Missing cases	1,673	

4. Use the data in the following table to
   a. Prepare a frequency distribution of the respondents' ages
   b. Cross-tabulate the respondents' genders with cola preference
   c. Identify any outliers

Individual	Gender	Age	Cola Preference	Weekly Unit Purchases
James	M	19	Coke	2
Parker	M	17	Pepsi	5
Bill	M	20	Pepsi	7
Laurie	F	20	Coke	2
Jim	M	18	Coke	4
Jil	F	16	Coke	4
Tom	M	17	Pepsi	12
Julia	F	22	Pepsi	6
Amie	F	20	Pepsi	2
Dawn	F	19	Pepsi	3

5. Data on the average size of a soda (in ounces) at all 30 major league baseball parks are as follows: 14, 18, 20, 16, 16, 12, 14, 16, 14, 16, 16, 16, 14, 32, 16, 20, 12, 16, 20, 12, 16, 16, 24, 16, 16, 14, 14, 12, 14, 20. Compute descriptive statistics for this variable including a box and whisker plot. Comment on the results.
6. The following computer output shows a cross-tabulation of frequencies and provides frequency number N) and row R) percentages.
   a. Interpret this output including a conclusion about whether or not the row and column variables are related.
   b. Critique the way the analysis is presented.
   c. Draw a pie chart indicating percentages for having read a book in the past three month for those with and those without high school diplomas.

Have You Read a Book in Past 3 Months?	Have High School Diploma? Yes	No	Total
Yes	489 73.8	174 26.2	663
No	473 55.6	378 44.4	851
	……	……	……
TOTAL	962	552	1,514

7. List and describe at least three basic data transformations.
8. What conditions suggest that a ratio variable should be transformed (recoded) into a dichotomous (two group) variable?
9. A data processing analyst for a research supplier finds that preliminary computer runs of survey results show that consumers love a client's new product. The employee buys a large block of the client's stock. Is this ethical?

Research Activities

1. **'NET** Go the Web site for the Chicago Cubs baseball team (**http://chicago.cubs.mlb.com**). Use either the schedule listing or the stats information to find their record in the most recent season. Create a data file with a variable indicating whether each game was won or lost and a variable indicating whether the game was played at home in Wrigley Field or away from home. Using computerized software like SPSS or SAS,
   a. Compute a frequency table and histogram for each variable.
   b. Use cross-tabulations to examine whether a relationship exists between where the game is played (home or away) and winning.
   c. Extra analysis: Repeat the analyses for the Houston Astros baseball team (**http://houston.astros.mlb.com**). What does this suggest for the relationship between playing at home and winning?
2. **'NET** Go to **http://www.spss.com** and click on Industries and Market Research. What services does the company provide?

Case 20.1 Body on Tap

A few years ago Vidal Sassoon, Inc., took legal action against Bristol-Myers over a series of TV commercials and print ads for a shampoo that had been named Body on Tap because of its beer content.[12] The prototype commercial featured a well-known high fashion model saying, "In shampoo tests with over 900 women like me, Body on Tap got higher ratings than Prell for body. Higher than Flex for conditioning. Higher than Sassoon for strong, healthy-looking hair."

The evidence showed that several groups of approximately 200 women each tested just one shampoo. They rated it on a six-step qualitative scale, from "outstanding" to "poor," for 27 separate attributes, such as body and conditioning. It became clear that 900 women did not, after trying both shampoos, make product-to-product comparisons between Body on Tap and Sassoon or between Body on Tap and any of the other brands mentioned. In fact, no woman in the tests tried more than one shampoo.

The claim that the women preferred Body on Tap to Sassoon for "strong, healthy-looking hair" was based on combining the data for the "outstanding" and "excellent" ratings and discarding the lower four ratings on the scale. The figures then were 36 percent for Body on Tap and 24 percent (of a separate group of women) for Sassoon. When the "very good" and "good" ratings were combined with the "outstanding" and "excellent" ratings, however, there was only a difference of 1 percent between the two products in the category of "strong, healthy-looking hair."

The research was conducted for Bristol-Myers by Marketing Information Systems, Inc. (MISI), using a technique known as blind monadic testing. The president of MISI testified that this method typically is employed when what is wanted is an absolute response to a product "without reference to another specific product." Although he testified that blind monadic testing was used in connection with comparative advertising, that was not the purpose for which Bristol-Myers retained MISI. Rather, Bristol-Myers wished to determine consumer reaction to the introduction of Body on Tap. Sassoon's in-house research expert stated flatly that blind monadic testing cannot support comparative advertising claims.

Question

Comment on the professionalism of the procedures used to make the advertising claim. Why do you believe the researchers performed the data transformations described?

Case 20.2 Downy-Q Quilt

The research for Downy-Q is an example of a commercial test that was conducted when an advertising campaign for an established brand had run its course.[13] The revised campaign, "Fighting the Cold," emphasized that Downy-Q was an "extra-warm quilt"; previous research had demonstrated that extra warmth was an important and deliverable product quality. The commercial test was requested to measure the campaign's ability to generate purchase interest.

The marketing department had recommended this revised advertising campaign and was now anxious to know how effectively this commercial would perform. The test concluded that "Fighting the Cold" was a persuasive commercial. It also demonstrated that the new campaign would have greater appeal to specific market segments.

Method

Brand choices for the same individuals were obtained before and after viewing the commercial. The commercial was tested in 30-second, color-moving, storyboard form in a theater test. Invited viewers were shown programming with commercial inserts. Qualified respondents were women who had bought quilts in outlets that carried Downy-Q. The results are shown in Case Exhibits 20.2–1 through 20.2–4.

Question

Interpret the data in these tables. What recommendations and conclusions would you offer to Downy-Q management?

CASE EXHIBIT 20.2–1 **Shifts in Brand Choice before and after Showing of Downy-Q Quilt Commercial**

Question: We are going to give away a sample of fabric softener. You can select the brand you most prefer. Which brand would you chose?

Brand Choice before Commercial	Brand Choice after Commercial (%)	
	Downy-Q (*n* = 23)	Other Brand (*n* = 237)
Downy-Q	78	19
Other brand	22	81

CASE EXHIBIT 20.2–2 Pre/Post Increment in Choice of Downy-Q

Improvement in score based on exposure to commercial.

	"Fighting the Cold"		Norm: All Quilt Commercials	
Demographic Group	**Base**	**Score**	**Average**	**Range**
Total audience	(260)	+15	+10	6–19
By marital status				
Married	(130)	+17		
Not married	(130)	+12		
By age				
Under 35	(130)	+14		
35 and over	(130)	+15		
By employment status				
Not employed	(90)	+13		
Employed	(170)	+18		

CASE EXHIBIT 20.2–3 Adjective Checklist for Downy-Q Quilt Commercial

Question: Which of these words do you feel come closest to describing the commercial you've just seen? (Check all that apply.)

Adjective	"Fighting the Cold" (%)	Norm: All Quilt Commercials (%)
Positive		
Appealing	18	24
Clever	11	40
Convincing	20	14
Effective	19	23
Entertaining	5	24
Fast moving	12	21
Genuine	7	4
Imaginative	7	21
Informative	24	18
Interesting	13	17
Original	7	20
Realistic	8	3
Unusual	3	8
Negative		
Amateurish	9	11
Bad Taste	4	4
Dull	33	20
Repetitious	17	16
Silly	8	19
Slow	8	7
Unbelievable	3	5
Unclear	3	2
Unimportant	14	14
Uninteresting	32	19

CASE EXHIBIT 20.2–4 Product Attribute Checklist for Downy-Q

Question: Which of the following statements do you feel apply to Downy-Q? (Mark as many or as few as you feel apply.)

Attributes	"Fighting the Cold" (%)
Extra warm	56
Lightweight	48
Pretty designs	45
Durable fabrics	28
Nice fabrics	27
Good construction	27

CHAPTER 21 UNIVARIATE STATISTICAL ANALYSIS

LEARNING OUTCOMES

After studying this chapter, you should be able to

1. **Implement the hypothesis-testing procedure**
2. **Use p-values to test for statistical significance**
3. **Test a hypothesis about an observed mean compared to some standard**
4. **Know the difference between Type I and Type II errors**
5. **Know when a univariate χ^2 test is appropriate and how to conduct one**

Chapter Vignette: Well, Are They Satisfied or Not?

Ross has worked for PrecisionMetals for six years, but had really only served as an analyst for the production facility. This was the first corporate-level opportunity to showcase his research skills. His corporate contact was David Green, who currently served as Chief Operations Officer for PrecisionMetals. David had specifically asked to meet with him about the satisfaction survey conducted a month ago.

"Ross, we continue to worry about losing metalwork employees at our Madison plant, but our Richmond plant seems to be OK in terms of turnover," David stated. "What is your take on our employee satisfaction?" Ross replied, "We put together an index of three questions that asked about job satisfaction. We have analyzed the data from the Madison plant, and our average satisfaction is 3.9." David asked, "What does 3.9 mean? How am I supposed to understand that?" Ross responded, "I'm sorry, I should have explained this better. We asked the employees on a scale with five categories, with '1' meaning 'Strongly Disagree,' and '5' meaning 'Strongly Agree.' When the scores were averaged for Madison, our overall satisfaction was 3.9." David continued, "Is that good or bad? Sounds OK I guess. And what about Richmond?" Ross, realizing that he was not communicating the information well, responded, "Our satisfaction score from last year for both plants was 3.5. We can certainly check on this."

© BLEND IMAGES/JUPITER IMAGES

David realized that Ross was getting flustered. It was time to reassure him. "Ross, I'm sorry but I don't know what the scores mean. If 3.5 was a good score for us last time, then great. I just want to know if the new survey shows they are more satisfied or not."

Ross went back to the research section, with two things on his mind. "I've got to compare the last satisfaction score with the new score," he thought. And as he walked into his office and shut the door quietly he said to himself, "I can't just speak about scores. I'm here to help them understand what the scores really mean." It was time to get to work.

Introduction

Empirical testing typically involves inferential statistics. This means that an inference will be drawn about some population based on observations of a sample representing that population. Statistical analysis can be divided into several groups:

- **Univariate statistical analysis** tests hypotheses involving only one variable.
- **Bivariate statistical analysis** tests hypotheses involving two variables.
- **Multivariate statistical analysis** tests hypotheses and models involving multiple (three or more) variables or sets of variables.

univariate statistical analysis
Tests of hypotheses involving only one variable.

bivariate statistical analysis
Tests of hypotheses involving two variables.

multivariate statistical analysis
Statistical analysis involving three or more variables or sets of variables.

The focus in this chapter is on univariate statistics. Thus, we examine statistical tests appropriate for drawing inferences about a single variable. In the chapter vignette, the COO was interested in the satisfaction of a plant, compared to what it was a year ago. This could represent an opportunity to test hypotheses about a single variable—in this case job satisfaction. The survey data regarding job satisfaction will be analyzed and tested against a benchmark of 3.5.

Hypothesis Testing

Descriptive research and causal research designs often climax with hypothesis tests. Hypotheses are defined as formal statements of explanations stated in a testable form. Generally, hypotheses should be stated in concrete fashion so that the method of empirical testing seems almost obvious. Types of hypotheses tested commonly in business research include the following:

1. Relational hypotheses—examine how changes in one variable vary with changes in another. This is usually tested by assessing covariance in some way, very often with regression analysis.
2. Hypotheses about differences between groups—examine how some variable varies from one group to another. These types of hypotheses are very common in causal designs.
3. Hypotheses about differences from some standard—examine how some variable differs from some preconceived standard. The preconceived standard sometimes represents the true value of the variable in a population. These tests can involve either a test of a mean for better-than ordinal variables or a test of frequencies if the variable is ordinal or nominal. These tests typify univariate statistical tests.

The Hypothesis-Testing Procedure

PROCESS

Hypotheses are tested by comparing the researcher's educated guess with empirical reality. The process can be described as follows:

1. First, the hypothesis is derived from the research objectives. The hypothesis should be stated as specifically as possible.
2. Next, a sample is obtained and the relevant variable is measured.
3. The measured value obtained in the sample is compared to the value either stated explicitly or implied in the hypothesis. If the value is consistent with the hypothesis, the hypothesis is supported. If the value is not consistent with the hypothesis, the hypothesis is not supported.

A univariate hypothesis consistent with the chapter vignette would be

H_1: The average satisfaction at the Madison plant is greater than 3.5.

If the average job satisfaction is 3.4, the hypothesis is not supported. If the average job satisfaction is 3.9, the hypothesis is supported.

Univariate hypotheses are typified by tests comparing some observed sample mean against a benchmark value. The test addresses the question, Is the sample mean truly different from the benchmark? But how different is really different? If the observed sample mean is 3.45 and the benchmark is 3.50, would the hypothesis still be supported? Probably not! When the observed mean is so close to the benchmark, we do not have sufficient confidence that a second set of data using a new sample taken from the same population might not produce a finding conflicting with the benchmark. In contrast, when the mean turns out well above 3.5, perhaps 3.9, then we could more easily trust that another sample would not produce a mean equal to or less than 3.5.

In statistics classes, students are exposed to hypothesis testing as a contrast between a *null* and an *alternative* hypothesis. A "null" hypothesis can be thought of as the expectation of findings as if no hypothesis existed (i.e., "no" or "null" hypothesis). In other words, the state implied by the null hypothesis is the opposite of the state represented by the actual hypothesis. A null to the hypothesis listed in the Research Snapshot "The Freshman 7.8" is

H_n: *The average number of pounds gained in the freshman year is equal to 7.8 (not greater than).*

The alternative hypothesis states the opposite of the null, which normally conforms to one of the common types of relationships above. So, the researcher's hypothesis is generally stated in the form of an "alternative" hypothesis. Are you confused?

While this terminology is common in statistical theory, the idea of a null hypothesis can be confusing. Therefore, the use of the term *null hypothesis* will be avoided when at all possible. The reader should instead focus on what the findings should look like if the proposed hypothesis is true. If the hypothesis above is true, an observed sample's mean should be noticeably greater than (or in our case less than) 7.8. We test to see if this idea can be supported by the empirical evidence.

Empirical evidence is provided by test results comparing the observed mean against some sampling distribution. The variance in observations also plays a role because with greater variance, there is more of a chance that the range of values includes 7.8. A statistical test's significance level or p-value becomes a key indicator of whether or not a hypothesis can be supported.

significance level
A critical probability associated with a statistical hypothesis test that indicates how likely an inference supporting a difference between an observed value and some statistical expectation is true. The acceptable level of Type I error.

p-value
Probability value, or the observed or computed significance level; p-values are compared to significance levels to test hypotheses.

SIGNIFICANCE LEVELS AND p-VALUES

A **significance level** is a critical probability associated with a statistical hypothesis test that indicates how likely it is that an inference supporting a difference between an observed value and some statistical expectation is true. The term **p-value** stands for probability-value and is essentially another name for an *observed* or *computed* significance level. Exhibit 21.1 discusses interpretations of p-values in different kinds of statistical tests. The probability in a p-value is that the statistical expectation (null) for a given test is true. So, low p-values mean there is little likelihood that the statistical expectation is true. This means the researcher's hypothesis positing (suggesting) a difference between an observed mean and a population mean, or between an observed frequency and a population frequency, or for a relationship between two variables, is likely supported.

Traditionally, researchers have specified an acceptable significance level for a test prior to the analysis. Later, we will discuss this as an acceptable amount of Type I error. For most applications, the acceptable amount of error, and therefore the acceptable significance level, is 0.1, 0.05, or 0.01. If the p-value resulting from a statistical test is less than the pre-specified significance level, then a hypothesis about differences is supported.

Consider an example where researchers have identified that a successful restaurant should have families with an average of 1.4 children within a 10-minute drive of their location. Exhibit 21.2 illustrates an important property of p-values. In this case, the comparison standard of 1.4 is shown as an orange line. The sample result is shown as an orange line (3.1). The normal curve illustrates what other sample results would likely be. What is most important to realize is that as the observed value gets further from 1.4, the p-value gets smaller, meaning that the chance of the mean actually equaling 1.4 also is smaller. With the observed mean of 3.1 and the observed standard deviation of 1.02, there is very little chance that the researcher would be wrong in concluding the actual number of children per family is greater than 1.4.

RESEARCH SNAPSHOT

The "Freshman 7.8"

There is a common belief that when college freshman students start their first semester away from their families, they gain 15 pounds in the first year. Commonly referred to as the "Freshman 15," few research studies have actually examined if this extra 15 pounds actually appears. In fact, this belief is so prevalent that at an annual meeting of the Obesity Society, the current generation of college students were referred to as "Generation XL."

Researchers at Purdue University conducted a study of freshman-year weight gain, using 907 freshman students. Their results were consistent with another study at Brown University. For both universities, freshman students gained between 6 and 8 pounds, with the Purdue average being 7.8 pounds. Male students were more likely to gain weight than female students. Clearly, students were gaining weight. Many of them placed the blame on their newfound freedom. It was just too easy to eat whatever and whenever they wanted. However, it appears that the belief that new students experience the "Freshman 15" was actually quite a bit higher than reality.

As a test, we asked a freshman class for their own weight gain. Granted, it was certainly a subjective assessment, and students were not weighed before or after they started their university education. But it does allow for a hypothesis test: Given the results of the Purdue University study, do students gain 7.8 pounds in their first year of school?

The test is conducted with 46 male and female students with the results shown below:

	N	Mean	Std. Deviation	Std. Error Mean
Students	46	5.63	2.51	0.369

Was the self-reported weight gain of these students supportive of the hypothesis? The univariate statistic testing this result suggests the answer to this question is no. The p-value for this test is less than 0.0001, which supports the premise that the mean number of pounds gained is less than 7.8 pounds. It certainly suggests that the "Freshman 15" should lose a few pounds.

Test Value = 7.8

					95% Confidence Interval of the Difference	
	T	*df*	p-value (2-tailed)	Mean Difference	Lower	Upper
Pounds	−5.86	45	0.000	−2.166	−2.911	−1.421

Sources: Hellmich, Nancy, "Freshman 15 Drops Some Pounds," *USA Today* (October 23, 2006), accessed April 23, 2009.

Consider the test in the Research Snapshot "The Freshman 7.8." The statistical test is whether or not the mean computed from the 46 observations is different from 7.8. Given the risk associated with being wrong, the researcher uses an acceptable significance level of 0.05. After computing the appropriate test, the research observes a computed significance level or p-value that is less than 0.001. Therefore, the hypothesis is supported.

In discussing confidence intervals, statisticians use the term *confidence level,* or *confidence coefficient,* to refer to the level of probability associated with an interval estimate. However, when discussing hypothesis testing, statisticians change their terminology and call this a *significance level,* α (the Greek letter *alpha*).

An Example of Hypothesis Testing

The example described here illustrates the conventional statistical approach to testing a univariate hypothesis with an interval or ratio variable. Suppose the Pizza-In restaurant is concerned about store image before deciding whether to expand. Pizza-In managers are most interested in how friendly customers perceive the service to be. A sample of 225 customers was obtained and asked to indicate their perceptions of service on a five-point scale, where 1 indicates "very unfriendly" service and 5 indicates "very friendly" service. The scale is assumed to be an interval scale, and experience has shown that the previous distribution of this attitudinal measurement assessing the service dimension was approximately normal.

EXHIBIT 21.1
p-Values and Statistical Tests

Test Description	Test Statistic	
Compare an Observed Mean with Some Predetermined Value	*Z* or *t*-test—Low p-values Indicate the Observed Mean Is Different Than Some Predetermined Value (Often 0)	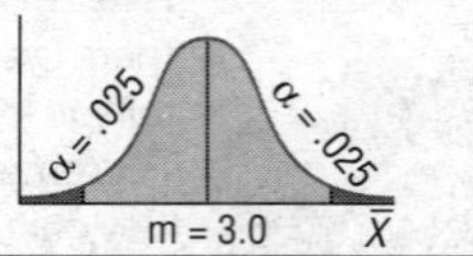
Compare an Observed Frequency with a Predetermined Value	X^2—Low p-values Indicate That Observed Frequency Is Different Than Predetermined Value	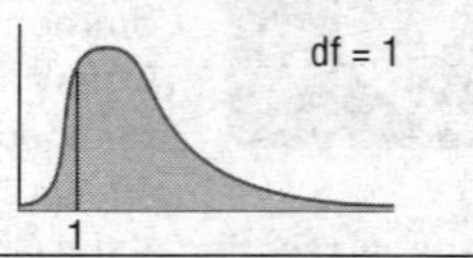
Compare an Observed Proportion with Some Predetermined Value	*Z* or *t*-test for Proportions—Low p-values Indicate That the Observed Proportion Is Different Than the Predetermined Value	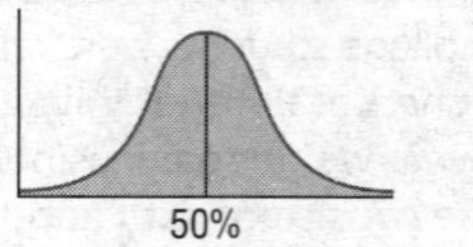
Bivariate Tests:		
Compare Whether Two Observed Means Are Different from One Another.	*Z* or *t*-test—Low p-values Indicate the Means Are Different	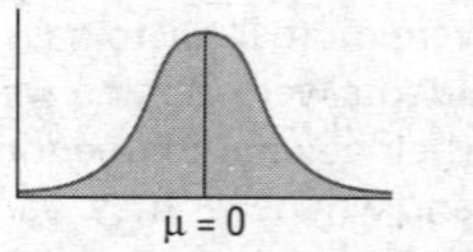
Compare Whether Two Less-Than Interval Variables Are Related Using Cross-tabs	X^2—Low p-values Indicate the Variables Are Related to One Another	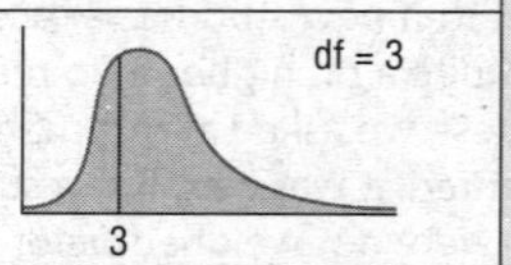
Compare Whether Two Interval or Ratio Variables Are Correlated to One Another	*t*-test for Correlation—Low p-values Indicate the Variables Are Related to One Another	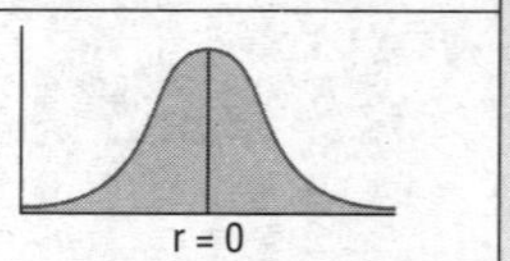

EXHIBIT 21.2
As the observed mean gets further from the standard (proposed population mean), the p-value decreases. The lower the p-value, the more confidence you have that the sample mean is different.

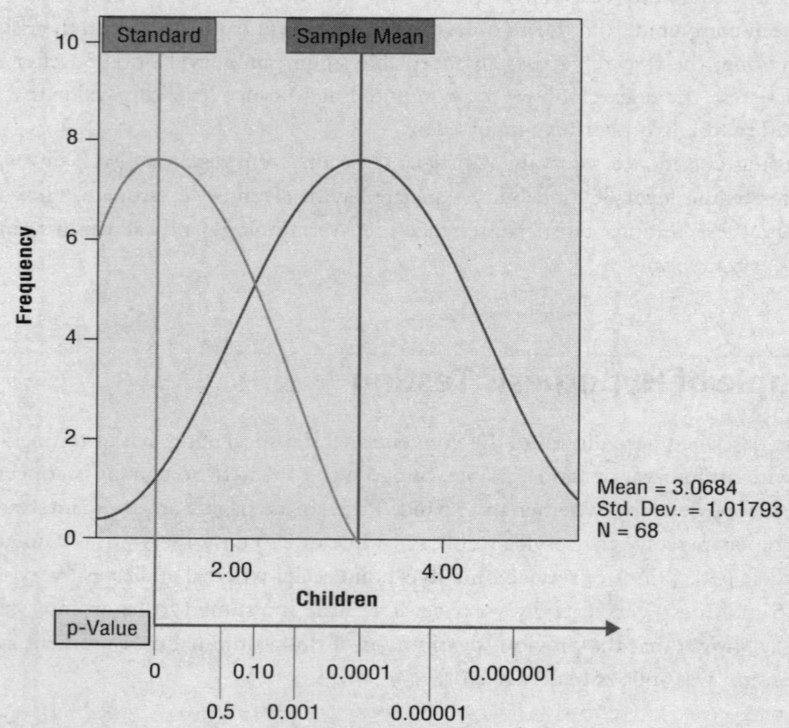

Now, suppose Pizza-In believes the service has to be different from 3.0 before a decision about expansion can be made. In conventional statistical terminology, the null hypothesis for this test is that the mean is equal to 3.0:

$H_0: \mu = 3.0$

The alternative hypothesis is that the mean does not equal 3.0:

$H_1: \mu \neq 3.0$

More practically, the researcher is likely to write the substantive hypothesis (as it would be stated in a research report or proposal) something like this:

H_1: *Customer perceptions of friendly service are significantly greater than three.*

Note that the substantive hypothesis matches the "alternative" phrasing. In practical terms, researchers do not state null and alternative hypotheses. Only the substantive hypothesis implying what is expected to be observed in the sample is formally stated.

Next, the researcher must decide on a significance level. This level corresponds to a region of rejection on a normal sampling distribution as shown in Exhibit 21.1. The peak of the distribution is the theoretical expected value for the population mean. In this case it would be three. If the acceptable significance level is 0.05, then the 0.025 on either side of the mean that is furthest away from the mean forms the rejection zone (shaded dark gray in Exhibit 21.1). The values within the unshaded area are called *acceptable at the 95 percent confidence level* (or 5 percent significance level, or 0.05 alpha level), and if we find that our sample mean lies within this region we conclude that the means are not different from the expected value, 3 in this case. More precisely, we fail to reject the null hypothesis. In other words, the range of acceptance (1) identifies those acceptable values that reflect a difference from the hypothesized mean in the null hypothesis and (2) shows the range within which any difference is so minuscule that we would conclude that this difference was due to random sampling error rather than a false null hypothesis. H_1 would not be supported.

In our example, the Pizza-In restaurant hired research consultants who collected a sample of 225 interviews. The mean friendliness score on a five-point scale equaled 3.78. (If σ is known, it is used in the analysis; however, this is rarely true and was not true in this case.[1]) The sample standard deviation was $S = 1.5$. Now we have enough information to test the hypothesis.

The researcher has decided that the acceptable significance level will be set at 0.05. This means that the researcher wishes to draw conclusions that will be erroneous 5 times in 100 (0.05) or fewer. From the table of the standardized normal distribution, the researcher finds that the Z score of 1.96 represents a probability of 0.025 that a sample mean will be above 1.96 standard errors from μ. Likewise, the table shows that 0.025 of all sample means will fall below −1.96 standard errors from μ. Adding these two "tails" together, we get 0.05.

The values that lie exactly on the boundary of the region of rejection are called **critical values** of μ. Theoretically, the critical values are $Z = -1.96$ and $+1.96$. Now we must transform these critical Z-values to the sampling distribution of the mean for this image study. The critical values are

critical values
The values that lie exactly on the boundary of the region of rejection.

$$\begin{aligned}\text{Critical value} - \text{lower limit} &= \mu - ZS_{\bar{X}} \quad \text{or} \quad \mu - Z\frac{S}{\sqrt{n}} \\ &= 3.0 - 1.96\left(\frac{1.5}{\sqrt{225}}\right) \\ &= 3.0 - 1.96(.1) \\ &= 3.0 - 0.196 \\ &= 2.804\end{aligned}$$

$$\begin{aligned}\text{Critical value} - \text{upper limit} &= \mu + ZS_{\bar{X}} \quad \text{or} \quad \mu + Z\frac{S}{\sqrt{n}} \\ &= 3.0 + 1.96\left(\frac{1.5}{\sqrt{225}}\right) \\ &= 3.0 + 1.96(.1) \\ &= 3.0 + 0.196 \\ &= 3.196\end{aligned}$$

Based on survey results, the sample mean ($\overline{X}$) is 3.78. The sample mean is contained in the region of rejection (see the dark shaded areas of Exhibit 21.3). Since the sample mean is greater than the critical value of 3.196, falling in one of the tails (regions of rejection), the researcher concludes that the sample result is statistically significant beyond the 0.05 level. A region of rejection means that the thought that the observed sample mean equals the predetermined value of 3.0 will be rejected when the computed value takes a value within the range. Here is another way to express this result: If we took 100 samples from this population and the mean were actually 3.0, fewer than five will show results that deviate this much.

What does this mean to the management of the Pizza-In? The results indicate that customers believe the service is pretty friendly. The probability is less than 5 in 100 that this result ($\overline{X}$ = 3.78) would occur because of random sampling error. This suggests that friendliness of the service personnel may not be problem. However, perhaps Pizza-In should compare its friendliness rating with the friendliness rating of a key competitor. That analysis will have to wait until we cover bivariate tests.

EXHIBIT 21.3

A Hypothesis Test Using the Sampling Distribution of $\overline{X}$ under the Hypothesis $\mu = 3.0$

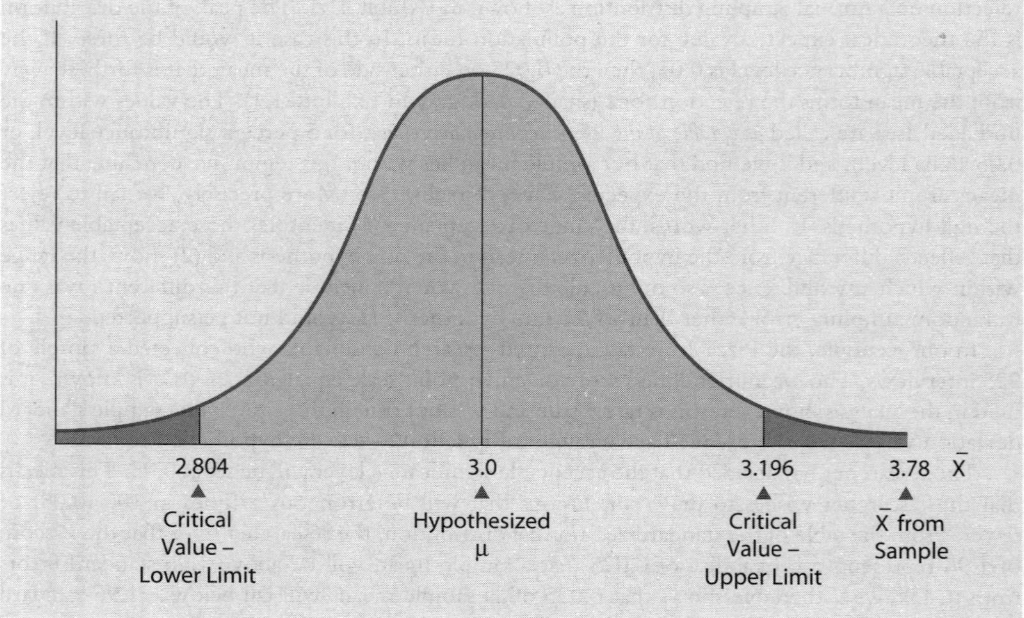

An alternative way to test the hypothesis is to formulate the decision rule in terms of the Z-statistic. Using the following formula, we can calculate the observed value of the Z-statistic given a certain sample mean, ($\overline{X}$):

$$\begin{aligned} Z_{obs} &= \frac{\overline{X} - \mu}{S_{\overline{X}}} \\ &= \frac{3.78 - \mu}{S_{\overline{X}}} \\ &= \frac{3.78 - 3.0}{.1} \\ &= \frac{.78}{.1} \\ &= 7.8 \end{aligned}$$

In this case, the Z-value is 7.8 and we find that we have met the criterion of statistical significance at the 0.05 level. This result produces a p-value of 0.000001. Once again, since the p-value is less than the acceptable significance level, the hypothesis is supported. The service rating is significantly higher than 3.0. This example used the conventional statistical terminology involving critical values and a statistical null hypothesis. Once again, it is rare that researchers have to look up tabled values for critical values anymore since the statistical packages will usually return a p-value for a given test. Thus, the p-value, or a confidence interval associated with the p-value, is the key to interpretation.

Type I and Type II Errors

Hypothesis testing using sample observations is based on probability theory. We make an observation of a sample and use it to infer the probability that some observation is true within the population the sample represents. Because we cannot make any statement about a sample with complete certainty, there is always the chance that an error will be made. When a researcher makes the observation using a census, meaning that every unit (person or object) in a population is measured, then conclusions are certain. Researchers very rarely use a census.

The researcher using sampling runs the risk of committing two types of errors. Exhibit 21.4 summarizes the state of affairs in the population and the nature of Type I and Type II errors. The four possible situations in the exhibit result because the null hypothesis (using the example above, $\mu = 3.0$) is actually either true or false and the observed statistics ($\bar{X} = 3.78$) will result in acceptance or rejection of this null hypothesis.

Type I error

An error caused by rejecting the null hypothesis when it is true; has a probability of alpha. Practically, a Type I error occurs when the researcher concludes that a relationship or difference exits in the population when in reality it does not exist.

TYPE I ERROR

Suppose the observed sample mean described above leads to the conclusion that the mean is greater than 3.0 when in fact the true population mean is equal to 3.0. A **Type I error** has occurred.

EXHIBIT 21.4
Type I and Type II Errors in Hypothesis Testing

Actual State in the Population	Decision: Accept H_0	Decision: Reject H_0
H_0 is true	Correct—no error	Type I error
H_0 is false	Type II error	Correct—no error

TO THE POINT

It is terrible to speak well and be wrong.

—Sophocles

A Type I error occurs when a condition that is true in the population is rejected based on statistical observations. When a researcher sets an acceptable significance level a priori α he or she is determining tolerance for a Type I error. Simply put, a Type I error occurs when the researcher concludes that there is a statistical difference when in reality one does not exist. When testing for relationships, a Type I error occurs when the researcher concludes a relationship exists when in fact one does not exist.

TYPE II ERROR

If the alternative condition is in fact true (in this case the mean is not equal to 3.0) but we conclude that we should not reject the null hypothesis (accept that the mean is equal to 3.0), we make what is called a **Type II error**. A Type II error is the probability of failing to reject a false null hypothesis. This incorrect decision is called beta (β). In practical terms, a Type II error means that we fail to reach the conclusion that some difference between an observed mean and a benchmark exists when in fact the difference is very real. In terms of a bivariate correlation, a Type II error would mean the idea that a relationship exists between two variables is rejected when in fact the relationship does indeed exist. The Research Snapshot "The Law and Type I and Type II Errors" provides further clarification of the Type I and Type II conditions.

Type II error

An error caused by failing to reject the null hypothesis when the alternative hypothesis is true; has a probability of beta. Practically, a Type II error occurs when a researcher concludes that no relationship or difference exists when in fact one does exist.

RESEARCH SNAPSHOT

The Law and Type I and Type II Errors

Although most attorneys and judges do not concern themselves with the statistical terminology of Type I and Type II errors, they do follow this logic. For example, our legal system is based on the concept that a person is innocent until proven guilty. Assume that the null hypothesis is that the individual is innocent. If we make a Type I error, we will send an innocent person to prison. Our legal system takes many precautions to avoid Type I errors. A Type II error would occur if a guilty party were set free (the null hypothesis would have been accepted). Our society places such a high value on avoiding Type I errors that Type II errors are more likely to occur.

Unfortunately, without increasing sample size the researcher cannot simultaneously reduce Type I and Type II errors. They are inversely related. Thus, reducing the probability of a Type II error increases the probability of a Type I error. In marketing problems, Type I errors generally are considered more serious than Type II errors. Thus more emphasis is placed on determining the significance level, α, than in determining β.[2]

Choosing the Appropriate Statistical Technique

Numerous statistical techniques are available to assist the researcher in interpreting data. Choosing the right tool for the job is just as important to the researcher as to the mechanic. Making the correct choice can be determined by considering

1. The type of question to be answered
2. The number of variables involved
3. The level of scale measurement

Today, the researcher rarely has to perform a paper and pencil calculation. Hypotheses are tested by using a correct click-through sequence in a statistical software package. The mathematics of these packages is highly reliable. Therefore, if the researcher can choose the right statistic, know the right click-through sequence, and read the output that results, the right statistical conclusion should be easy to reach.

Type of Question to Be Answered

The type of question the researcher is attempting to answer is a consideration in the choice of statistical technique. For example, a researcher may be concerned simply with the central tendency of a variable or with the distribution of a variable. Comparison of different business divisions' sales results with some target level will require a one-sample *t*-test. Comparison of two salespeople's average monthly sales will require a *t*-test of two means, but a comparison of quarterly sales distributions will require a chi-square test.

The researcher should consider the method of statistical analysis before choosing the research design and before determining the type of data to collect. Once the data have been collected, the initial orientation toward analysis of the problem will be reflected in the research design.

Number of Variables

The number of variables that will be simultaneously investigated is a primary consideration in the choice of statistical technique. A researcher who is interested only in the average number of times

RESEARCH SNAPSHOT

Living in a Statistical Web

Having trouble learning statistical concepts? Do a little surfing and the concepts may become clear. Many sources exist that illustrate statistical problems and provide data for practice. Here are just a few:

STATLIB

http://lib.stat.cmu.edu/

StatLib is a system for distributing statistical software, data sets, and information by electronic mail, FTP, and the World Wide Web.

STAT-HELP

http://www.stat-help.com/

Stat-Help.com provides help with statistics via the Internet and contains spreadsheets for performing many basic calculations.

SURFSTAT.AUSTRALIA

http://surfstat.anu.edu.au/surfstat-home/surfstat-main.html

SurfStat.australia is an online text in introductory statistics from the University of Newcastle and the Australian government.

ELECTRONIC ENCYCLOPEDIA OF STATISTICAL EXAMPLES AND EXERCISES

http://www.stat.ohio-state.edu/~eesee/

The Electronic Encyclopedia of Statistical Examples and Exercises is a resource for the study of statistics that includes real-world examples of the uses and abuses of statistics and statistical inference.

THE RICE VIRTUAL LAB IN STATISTICS

http://onlinestatbook.com/rvls.html

http://davidmlane.com/hyperstat/

The Rice Virtual Lab in Statistics provides hypertext materials such as HyperStat Online.

STATCRUNCH

http://www.statcrunch.com/

Stat-Crunch is a statistical software package via the World Wide Web.

GRAPHPAD

http://www.graphpad.com/quickcalcs/Statratio1.cfm

GraphPad software is a p-value calculator.

a prospective home buyer visits financial institutions to shop for interest rates can concentrate on investigating only one variable at a time. However, a researcher trying to measure multiple complex organizational variables cannot do the same. Simply put, univariate, bivariate, and multivariate statistical procedures are distinguished based on the number of variables involved in an analysis.

Level of Scale of Measurement

The scale measurement level helps choose the most appropriate statistical techniques and appropriate empirical operations. Testing a hypothesis about a mean, as we have just illustrated, is appropriate for interval scaled or ratio scaled data. Suppose a researcher is working with a nominal scale that identifies users versus nonusers of bank credit cards. Because of the type of scale, the researcher may use only the mode as a measure of central tendency. In other situations, where data are measured on an ordinal scale, the median may be used as the average or a percentile may be used as a measure of dispersion. For example, ranking brand preferences generally employs an ordinal scale. Nominal and ordinal data are often analyzed using frequencies or cross-tabulation.

Parametric versus Nonparametric Hypothesis Tests

The terms parametric statistics and nonparametric statistics refer to the two major groupings of statistical procedures. The major distinction between them lies in the underlying assumptions about the data to be analyzed. **Parametric statistics** involve numbers with known, continuous distributions. When the data are interval or ratio scaled and the sample size is large, parametric statistical procedures are appropriate. **Nonparametric statistics** are appropriate when the numbers do not conform to a known distribution.

Parametric statistics are based on the assumption that the data in the study are drawn from a population with a normal (bell-shaped) distribution and/or normal sampling distribution. For example, if an investigator has two interval-scaled measures, such as gross national product (GNP)

parametric statistics

Involve numbers with known, continuous distributions; when the data are interval or ratio scaled and the sample size is large, parametric statistical procedures are appropriate.

nonparametric statistics

Appropriate when the variables being analyzed do not conform to any known or continuous distribution.

and industry sales volume, parametric tests are appropriate. Possible statistical tests might include product-moment correlation analysis, analysis of variance, regression, or a *t*-test for a hypothesis about a mean.

Nonparametric methods are used when the researcher does not know how the data are distributed. Making the assumption that the population distribution or sampling distribution is normal generally is inappropriate when data are either ordinal or nominal. Thus, nonparametric statistics are referred to as distribution free.[3] Data analysis of both nominal and ordinal scales typically uses nonparametric statistical tests.

EXHIBIT 21.5 **Univariate Statistical Choice Made Easy**

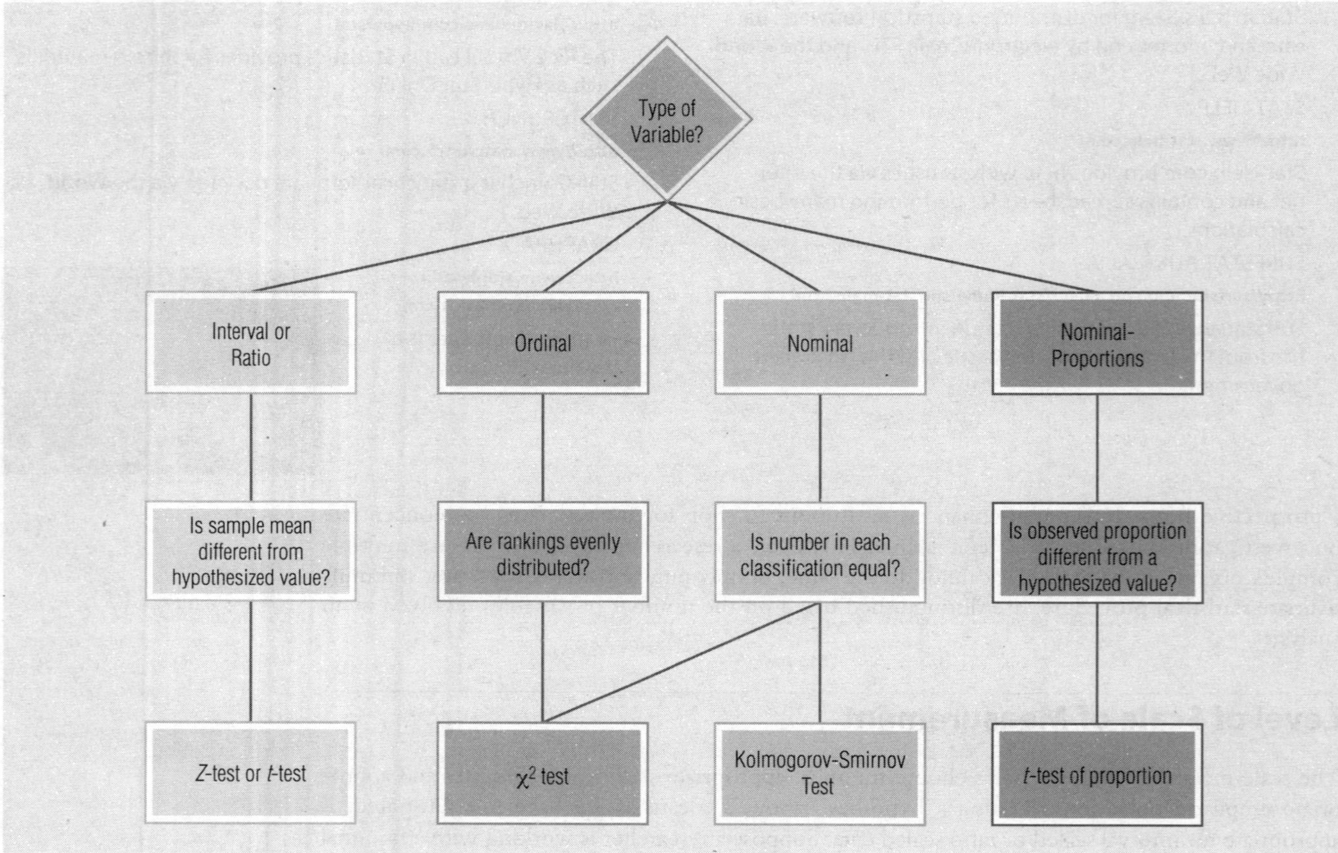

t-test

A hypothesis test that uses the *t*-distribution. A univariate *t*-test is appropriate when the variable being analyzed is interval or ratio.

Exhibit 21.5 illustrates how an appropriate univariate statistical method can be selected. The exhibit illustrates how statistical techniques vary according to scale properties and the type of question being asked. More univariate statistical tests exist than are shown in Exhibit 21.5, but these basic options address the majority of univariate analyses in marketing research. A complete discussion of all univariate techniques is beyond the scope of this text.

The *t*-Distribution

t-distribution

A symmetrical, bell-shaped distribution that is contingent on sample size; has a mean of 0 and a standard deviation equal to 1.

A univariate **t-test** is appropriate for testing hypotheses involving some observed mean against some specified value. The **t-distribution**, like the standardized normal curve, is a symmetrical, bell-shaped distribution with a mean of 0 and a standard deviation of 1.0. When sample size (n) is larger than 30, the *t*-distribution and *Z*-distribution are almost identical. Therefore, while the *t*-test is strictly appropriate for tests involving small sample sizes with unknown standard deviations, researchers commonly apply the *t*-test for comparisons involving the mean of an interval or ratio measure. The precise height and shape of the *t*-distribution vary with sample size. More specifically, the shape of the t-distribution is influenced by its **degrees of freedom (*df*)**. The degrees of freedom are determined by the number of distinct calculations that are possible given a set of information. In the case of a univariate t-test, the degrees of freedom are equal to the sample size (n) minus one.

degrees of freedom (*df*)
The number of observations minus the number of constraints or assumptions needed to calculate a statistical term.

Exhibit 21.6 illustrates t-distributions for 1, 2, 5, and an infinite number of degrees of freedom. Notice that the t-distribution approaches a normal distribution rapidly with increasing sample size. This is why, in practice, marketing researchers usually apply a t-test even with large samples. The practical effect is that the conclusion will be the same since the distributions are so similar with large samples and the correspondingly larger numbers of degrees of freedom.

EXHIBIT 21.6
The *t*-Distribution for Various Degrees of Freedom

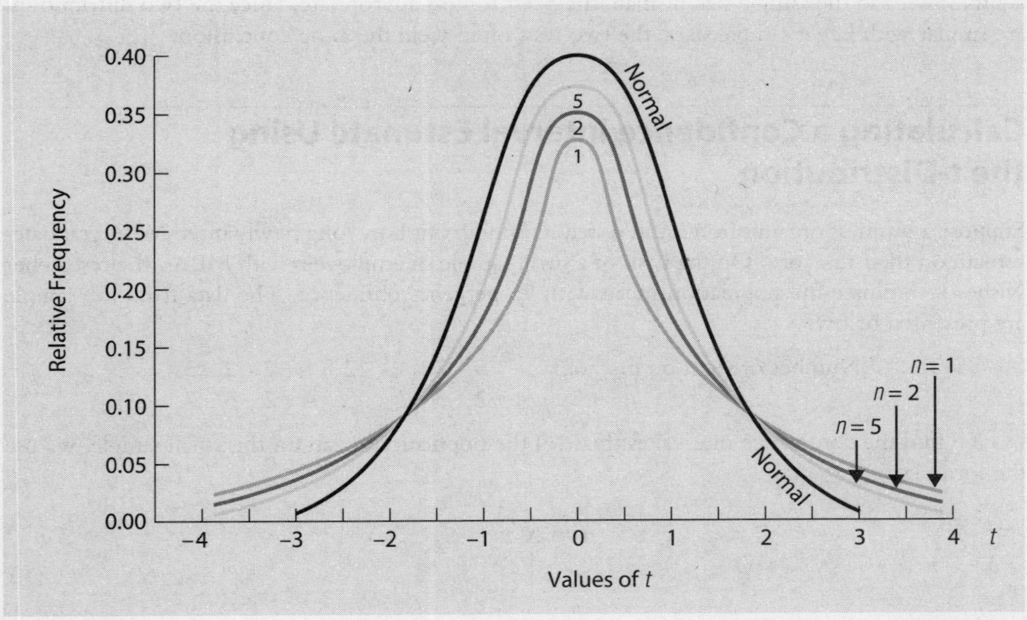

Another way to look at degrees of freedom is to think of adding four numbers together when you know their sum—for example,

$$\begin{array}{r} 4 \\ 2 \\ 1 \\ \underline{+X} \\ 12 \end{array}$$

The value of the fourth number has to be 5. The values of the first three digits could change to any value (freely vary), but the fourth value would have to be determined for the mean to be still equal to 12. In this example there are three degrees of freedom. Degrees of freedom can be a difficult concept to understand fully. For most basic statistical analyses, the user only needs to remember the rule for determining the number of degrees of freedom for a given test. Today, with computerized software packages, even that number is provided automatically for most tests.

Ultra-luxury car makers have sales goals that may involve selling 1,000 cars per year or fewer worldwide. What questions are asked in marketing a car like this that might involve a univariate analysis?[4]

The calculation of t closely resembles the calculation of the Z-value. To calculate t, use the formula

$$t = \frac{\overline{X} - \mu}{S_{\overline{X}}}$$

with $n - 1$ degrees of freedom.

The Z-distribution and the t-distribution are very similar, and thus the Z-test and t-test will provide much the same result in most situations. However, when the population standard deviation (σ) is known, the Z-test is most appropriate. When σ is unknown (the situation in most marketing research studies), and the sample size greater than 30, the Z-test also can be used. When σ is unknown and the sample size is small, the t-test is most appropriate. Since the two distributions are similar with larger sample sizes, the two tests often yield the same conclusion.

Calculating a Confidence Interval Estimate Using the *t*-Distribution

Suppose a business organization is interested in finding out how long newly hired MBA graduates remain on their first jobs. On the basis of a small sample of employees with MBAs, the researcher wishes to estimate the population mean with 95 percent confidence. The data from the sample are presented below.

Number of years on first job:	3	5	7	1	12	1	2	2	5
	4	2	3	1	3	4	2	6	7

To find the confidence interval estimate of the population mean for this small sample, we use the formula

$$\mu = \overline{X} \pm t_{c.l.} S_{\overline{X}}$$

or

$$\text{Upper limit} = \overline{X} + t_{c.l.}\left(\frac{S}{\sqrt{n}}\right)$$

$$\text{Lower limit} = \overline{X} - t_{c.l.}\left(\frac{S}{\sqrt{n}}\right)$$

where

μ = population mean
$(\overline{X})$ = sample mean
$t_{c.l.}$ = critical value of t at a specified confidence level
$S_{\overline{X}}$ = standard error of the mean
S = sample standard deviation
n = sample size

More specifically, the step-by-step procedure for calculating the confidence interval is as follows:

1. We calculate $(\overline{X})$ from the sample. Summing our data values yields $\Sigma X = 70$, and $(\overline{X}) = \Sigma X/n = 70/18 = 3.89$.
2. Since σ is unknown, we estimate the population standard deviation by finding S, the sample standard deviation. For our example, $S = 2.81$.
3. We estimate the standard error of the mean using the formula $S_{\overline{X}} = S/\sqrt{n}$. Thus, $S_{\overline{X}} = 2.81/\sqrt{18}$ or $S_{\overline{X}} = 0.66$.
4. We determine the t-values associated with the desired confidence level. To do this, we go to Table A.3 in the appendix. Although the t-table provides information similar to that in the Z-table, it is somewhat different. The t-table format emphasizes the chance of error, or significance level (α), rather than the 95 percent chance of including the population mean in the estimate. Our example is a two-tailed test. Since a 95 percent confidence level has been selected, the significance level equals $0.05(1.00 - 0.95 = 0.05)$. Once this has been determined, all we have to do to find the t-value is look under the 0.05 column for *two-tailed tests* at the

row in which degrees of freedom (*df*) equal the appropriate value ($n - 1$). Below 17 degrees of freedom ($n - 1 = 18 - 1 = 17$), the *t*-value at the 95 percent confidence level (0.05 level of significance) is $t = 2.12$.

5. We calculate the confidence interval:

$$\text{Lower limit} = 3.89 - 2.12\left(\frac{2.81}{\sqrt{18}}\right) = 2.49$$

$$\text{Upper limit} = 3.89 + 2.12\left(\frac{2.89}{\sqrt{18}}\right) = 5.28$$

In our hypothetical example it may be concluded with 95 percent confidence that the population mean for the number of years spent on the first job by MBAs is between 2.49 and 5.28.

ONE- AND TWO-TAILED *t*-TESTS

Univariate *Z*-tests and *t*-tests can be one- or two-tailed. A two-tailed test is one that tests for differences from the population mean that are either greater or less. Thus, the extreme values of the normal curve (or tails) on both the right and the left are considered. In practical terms, when a research question does not specify whether a difference should be greater than or less than, a two-tailed test is most appropriate. For instance, the following research question could be examined using a two-tailed test:

The number of take-out pizza restaurants within a postal code in Germany is not equal to 5.

A one-tailed univariate test is appropriate when a research hypothesis implies that an observed mean can only be greater than or less than a hypothesized value. Thus, only one of the "tails" of the bell-shaped normal curve is relevant. For instance, the following hypothesis could be appropriately examined with a one-tailed test:

H_1: *The number of pizza restaurants within a postal code in Florida is greater than five.*

In this case, if the observed value is significantly less than five, the hypothesis is still not supported. Practically, a one-tailed test can be determined from a two-tailed test result by taking half of the observed p-value. When the researcher has any doubt about whether a one- or two-tailed test is appropriate, he or she should opt for the less conservative two-tailed test. Most computer software will assume a two-tailed test unless otherwise specified.

Univariate Hypothesis Test Using the *t*-Distribution

The step-by-step procedure for a *t*-test is conceptually similar to that for hypothesis testing with the *Z*-distribution. Suppose a Pizza-In store manager believes that the average number of customers who return a pizza or ask for a refund is 20 per day. The store records the number of returns and exchanges for each of the 25 days it was open during a given month. Are the return/complaint observations different than 20 per day? The substantive hypothesis is

$$H_1: \mu \neq 20$$

1. The researcher calculates a sample mean and standard deviation. In this case, $\overline{X} = 22$ and S (sample standard deviation) $= 5$.
2. The standard error is computed ($S_{\overline{X}}$):

$$S_{\overline{X}} = \frac{S}{\sqrt{n}}$$

$$= \frac{5}{\sqrt{25}}$$

$$= 1$$

3. The researcher then finds the *t*-value associated with the desired level of confidence level or statistical significance. If a 95 percent confidence level is desired, the significance level is 0.05.

4. The critical values for the t-test are found by locating the upper and lower limits of the confidence interval. The result defines the regions of rejection. This requires determining the value of t. For 24 degrees of freedom ($n = 25$, $df = n - 1$), the t-value is 2.064. The critical values are

$$\text{Lower limit} = \mu - t_{c.l.}\, S_{\overline{X}} = 20 - 2.064\left(\frac{5}{\sqrt{25}}\right)$$
$$= 20 - 2.064(1)$$
$$= 17.936$$
$$\text{Upper limit} = \mu + t_{c.l.}\, S_{\overline{X}} = 20 + 2.064\left(\frac{5}{\sqrt{25}}\right)$$
$$= 20 + 2.064(1)$$
$$= 22.064$$

Finally, the researcher makes the statistical decision by determining whether the sample mean falls between the critical limits. For the pizza store sample, $\overline{X} = 22$. The sample mean is *not* included in the region of rejection. Even though the sample result is only slightly less than the critical value at the upper limit, the null hypothesis cannot be rejected. In other words, the pizza store manager's assumption appears to be correct.

As with the Z-test, there is an alternative way to test a hypothesis with the t-statistic. This is by using the formula

$$t_{\text{obs}} = \frac{\overline{X} - \mu}{S_{\overline{X}}}$$
$$t_{\text{obs}} = \frac{22 - 20}{1} = \frac{2}{1} = 2$$

We can see that the observed t-value is less than the critical t-value of 2.064 at the 0.05 level when there are $25 - 1 = 24$ degrees of freedom. As a result, the p-value is greater than 0.05 and the hypothesis is not supported. We cannot conclude with 95 percent confidence that the mean is not 20.

The Chi-Square Test for Goodness of Fit

chi-square (χ^2) test

One of the basic tests for statistical significance that is particularly appropriate for testing hypotheses about frequencies arranged in a frequency or contingency table.

goodness-of-fit (GOF)

A general term representing how well some computed table or matrix of values matches some population or predetermined table or matrix of the same size.

A **chi-square (χ^2) test** is one of the most basic tests for statistical significance and is particularly appropriate for testing hypotheses about frequencies arranged in a frequency or contingency table. Univariate tests involving nominal or ordinal variables are examined with a χ^2. More generally, the χ^2 test is associated with **goodness-of-fit (GOF)**. GOF can be thought of as how well some matrix (table) of numbers matches or *fits* another matrix of the same size. Most often, the test is between a table of observed frequency counts and another table of expected values (central tendency) for those counts.

Consider the following hypothesis that relates back to the chapter vignette:

H_1: *Papa John's Pizza stores are more likely to be located in a stand-alone location than in a shopping center.*

A competitor may be interested in this hypothesis as part of the competitor analysis in a marketing plan. A researcher for the competitor gathers a random sample of 100 Papa John's locations in California (where the competitor is located). The sample is selected from phone directories and the locations are checked by having an assistant drive to each location. The following observations are recorded in a frequency table.

Location	One-Way Frequency Table
Stand-Alone	60 stores
Shopping Center	40 stores
Total	100 stores

These observed values (O_i) can be compared to the expected values for this distribution (E_i) to complete a χ^2 test. The χ^2 value will reflect the likelihood that the observed values come from a distribution reflected by the expected values. The higher the value of the χ^2 test, the less likely it is that the expected and observed values are the same.

In statistical terms, a χ^2 test determines whether the difference between an observed frequency distribution and the corresponding expected frequency distribution is due to sampling variation. Computing a χ^2 test is fairly straightforward and easy. Students who master this calculation should have little trouble understanding future significance tests since the basic logic of the χ^2 test underlies these tests as well.

The steps in computing a χ^2 test are as follows:

1. Gather data and tally the observed frequencies for the categorical variable.
2. Compute the expected values for each value of the categorical variable.
3. Calculate the χ^2 value, using the observed frequencies from the sample and the expected frequencies.
4. Find the degrees of freedom for the test.
5. Make the statistical decision by comparing p-value associated with the calculated χ^2 against the predetermined significance level (acceptable Type I error rate).

These steps can be illustrated with the pizza store location example.

- The data for the location variable (stand-alone or shopping center) are provided in the preceding frequency table.
- The next step asks, "What are the expected frequencies for the location variable?" This is another way of asking the central tendency for each category. Since the sample size is 100, finding the expected values is easy. If no pattern exists in the locations, they should be distributed randomly across the two categories. We would expect that half (50) of the locations would be stand-alone and half (50) would be in a shopping center. This is another way of saying that the expected probability of being one type of location is 50 percent. The expected values also can be placed in a frequency table:

Location	Expected Frequencies
Stand-Alone	100/2 = 50 stores
Shopping Center	100/2 = 50 stores
Total	100 stores

- The actual χ^2 value is computed using the following formula:

$$\chi^2 = \Sigma \frac{(O_i - E_i)^2}{E_i}$$

where

χ^2 = chi-square statistic
O_i = observed frequency in the *i*th cell
E_i = expected frequency in the *i*th cell

Sum the squared differences:

$$\chi^2 = \frac{(O_1 - E_1)^2}{E_i} + \frac{(O_2 - E_2)^2}{E_2}$$

Thus, we determine that the chi-square value equals 4:

$$\chi^2 = \frac{(60 - 50)^2}{50} + \frac{(40 - 50)^2}{50}$$
$$= 4$$

RESEARCH SNAPSHOT

Interested in Retirement? It Often Depends on Your Age

Chi-square tests are used often in business research. Consider a business that sponsors a program to educate employees on retirement issues. They need to plan the number and types of activities that should be the focus of the training and development seminars. One question is whether or not an equal number of younger versus older employees will come to the sessions. They decide to observe the relative frequencies of younger versus older employees based upon the number of sign-ups they receive in the first week since the program was announced, with a cut-off set at 200. The results are shown in the bar chart below:

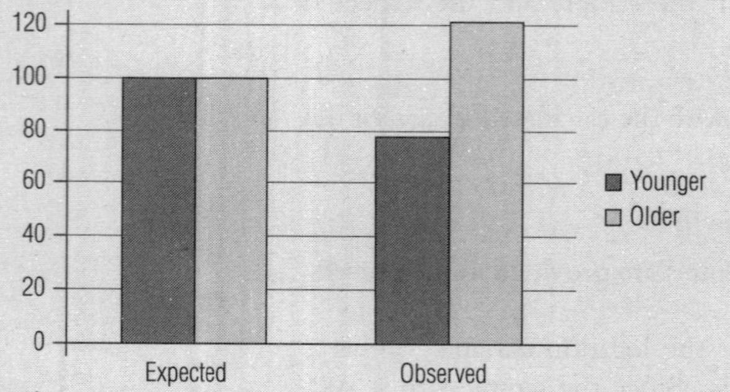

The χ^2 value can be computed as shown below:

	Expected	Observed	*O* − *E*	$(O - E)^2$	$(O - E)^2/E$
Younger	100	78	−22	484	48.4
Older	100	122	22	484	48.4
					96.8

The HR managers want to be sure a difference exists before investing resources into activities designed for younger or older employees only. Therefore, the acceptable level of Type I error is set at 0.01. Rather than referring to a critical value table, the p-value associated with a χ^2 value and the associated degrees of freedom can be found on any one of several statistical calculators found on the Internet. In this case, the researcher uses the calculator found at **http://faculty.vassar.edu/lowry/tabs.html#csq.** By simply plugging in the observed value of 96.8 and the number of degrees of freedom as indicated, 1 in this case, the calculator returns a p-value. In this case, the p-value returned is less than 0.0001. Therefore, since the p-value is less than the acceptable level of risk, the researcher reaches the conclusion that the older workers are much more likely to attend the retirement seminar. They can design the seminar to meet the needs associated with the number and type of attendees.

Alternatively, the calculation can be followed in tabular form:

Location:	O_i	E_i	$(O_i - E_i)$	$\frac{(O_i - E_i)^2}{E_i}$
Stand-Alone	60	50	10	100/50 = 2.0
Shopping Center	40	50	−10	100/50 = 2.0
Total	100	100	0	$\chi^2 = 4.0$

- Like many other probability distributions, the χ^2 distribution is not a single probability curve, but a family of curves. These curves vary slightly with the degrees of freedom. In this case, the degrees of freedom can be computed as

$$df = k - 1$$

where

k = number of cells associated with column or row data.

Thus, the degrees of freedom equal 1 ($df = 2 - 1 = 1$).

- Now the computed χ^2 value needs to be compared with the critical chi-square values associated with the 0.05 probability level with 1 degree of freedom. In Table A.4 of the appendix the critical χ^2 value is 3.84. Since the calculated χ^2 is larger than the tabular chi-square, the conclusion is that the observed values do not equal the expected values. Therefore, the hypothesis is supported. More Papa John's restaurants are located in stand-alone locations.

We discuss the chi-square test further in Chapter 20 as it is also frequently used to analyze contingency tables.

Hypothesis Test of a Proportion

Researchers often test univariate statistical hypotheses about population proportions. The population proportion (π) can be estimated on the basis of an observed sample proportion (p). Conducting a **hypothesis test of a proportion** is conceptually similar to hypothesis testing when the mean is the characteristic of interest. Mathematically the formulation of the standard error of the proportion differs somewhat, though.

hypothesis test of a proportion

A test that is conceptually similar to the one used when the mean is the characteristic of interest but that differs in the mathematical formulation of the standard error of the proportion.

Consider the following example. A state legislature is considering a proposed right-to-work law. One legislator has hypothesized that more than 50 percent of the state's labor force is unionized. In other words, the hypothesis to be tested is that the proportion of union workers in the state is greater than 0.5.

The researcher formulates the hypothesis that the population proportion (π) exceeds 50 percent (0.5):

$$H_1: = \pi > 0.5$$

Suppose the researcher conducts a survey with a sample of 100 workers and calculates $p = 0.6$. Even though the population proportion is unknown, a large sample allows use of a Z-test (rather than the t-test). If the researcher decides that the decision rule will be set at the 0.01 level of significance, the critical Z-value of 2.57 is used for the hypothesis test. Using the following formula, we can calculate the observed value of Z given a certain sample proportion:

$$Z_{\text{obs}} = \frac{p - \pi}{S_p}$$

where

p = sample proportion
π = hypothesized population proportion
S_p = estimate of the standard error of the proportion

The formula for S_p is

$$S_p = \sqrt{\frac{pq}{n}} \quad \text{or} \quad S_p = \sqrt{\frac{p(1-p)}{n}}$$

where

S_p = estimate of the standard error of the proportion
p = proportion of successes
$q = 1 - p$, = proportion of failures

In our example,

$$\begin{aligned} S_p &= \sqrt{\frac{(0.6)(0.4)}{100}} \\ &= \sqrt{\frac{0.24}{100}} \\ &= \sqrt{0.0024} \\ &= 0.04899 \end{aligned}$$

Z_{obs} can now be calculated:

$$\begin{aligned} Z_{\text{obs}} &= \frac{p - \pi}{S_p} \\ &= \frac{0.6 - 0.5}{0.04899} \\ &= \frac{0.1}{0.04899} \\ &= 2.04 \end{aligned}$$

The Z_{obs} value of 2.04 is less than the critical value of 2.57, so the hypothesis is not supported.

TIPS OF THE TRADE

© iStock

The use of hypothesis testing is a critical skill that all business researchers should have experience with. Here are some tips of the trade that may help you build on this skill.

- Business researchers are often brought in to not just conduct survey research and analysis, but to help their stakeholders frame the research questions as well. Approach your research with the goal that hypotheses will be generated to support or reject business decisions. Therefore, carefully work with your sponsor in developing research questions that are, in fact, testable.
- Hypothesis testing is often done using productivity or other performance benchmarks. Select your benchmarks carefully. Make sure that you can justify their selection, and note any instance where a seemingly outlying benchmark is still justifiable.
- Garbage in, garbage out always applies to hypothesis testing. If you don't carefully select variables that are appropriate, the results you obtain will not be reflective of your research question. Also, as you have learned, outlying cases in your data can skew results. Note these cases carefully.
- You have developed an appropriate research question, conducted your data collection, selected appropriate benchmarks, and conducted your hypothesis testing. What happens when your results are NOT supported? Be prepared for when this happens, because it will. You will need to have some way of offering alternative explanations, or find some valid reason to explain your results.

Additional Applications of Hypothesis Testing

The discussion of statistical inference in this chapter has been restricted to examining the difference between an observed sample mean and a population or pre-specified mean, a χ^2 test examining the difference between an observed frequency and the expected frequency for a given distribution, and Z-tests to test hypotheses about sample proportions when sample sizes are large. Other hypothesis tests for population parameters estimated from sample statistics exist but are not mentioned here. Many of these tests are no different conceptually in their methods of hypothesis testing. However, the formulas are mathematically different. The purpose of this chapter has been to discuss basic statistical concepts. Once you have learned the basic terminology in this chapter, you should have no problem generalizing to other statistical problems.

The key to understanding statistics is learning the basics of the language. For this chapter, we begin to adopt a more practical perspective by focusing on the p-values to determine whether a hypothesis is supported rather than discussing null and alternative hypotheses. In more cases than not, low p-values (below the specified α) support researchers' hypotheses.[5] It is hoped that some of the myths about statistics have been shattered and that they are becoming easier to use.

Summary

1. Implement the hypothesis-testing procedure. Hypothesis testing can involve univariate, bivariate, or multivariate statistics. In this chapter, the focus is on univariate statistics. These are tests that involve one variable. Usually, this means that the observed value for one variable will be compared to some benchmark or standard. Statistical analysis is needed to test hypotheses when sample observations are used to draw an inference about some corresponding population. The research establishes an acceptable significance level, representing the chance of a Type I error, and then computes the statistic that applies to the situation. The exact statistic that must be computed depends largely on the level of scale measurement.

2. Use p-values to test for statistical significance. A p-value is the probability value associated with a statistical test. The probability in a p-value is the probability that the expected value for some test distribution is true. In other words, for a t-test, the expected value of the t-distribution is 0. If a researcher is testing whether or not a variable is significantly different from 0, then the p-value that results from the corresponding computed t-value represents the probability that the true population mean is actually 0. For most research hypotheses, a low p-value supports the hypothesis. If a p-value is lower than the researcher's acceptable significance level (α), then the hypothesis is usually supported.

3. Test a hypothesis about an observed mean compared to some standard. Researchers often have to compare an observed sample mean with some specified value. The appropriate statistical test to compare an interval or ratio level variable's mean with some value is either the *Z*- or *t*-test. The *Z*-test is most appropriate when the sample size is large or the population standard deviation is known. The *t*-test is most appropriate when the sample size is small or the population standard deviation is not known. In most practical applications the *t*-test and *Z*-test will result in the same conclusion. The *t*-test is used more often in practice.

4. Know the difference between Type I and Type II errors. A Type I error occurs when a researcher reaches the conclusion that some difference or relationship exists within a population when in fact none exists. In the context of a univariate *t*-test, the researcher may conclude that some mean value for a variable is greater than 0 when in fact the true value for that variable in the population being considered is 0. A Type II error is the opposite situation. When the researcher reaches the conclusion that no difference exists when one truly does exist in the population, the researcher has committed a Type II error. More attention is usually given to Type I errors. Type II errors are very sensitive to sample size.

5. Know the univariate χ^2 test and how to conduct one. A χ^2 test is one of the most basic tests for statistical significance. The test is particularly appropriate for testing hypotheses about frequencies arranged in a frequency or contingency table. The χ^2 test value is a function of the observed value for a given entry in a frequency table minus the statistical expected value for that cell. The observed statistical value can be compared to critical values to determine the p-value with any test. The χ^2 test is often considered a goodness-of-fit test because it can test how well an observed matrix represents some theoretical standard.

Key Terms and Concepts

Questions for Review and Critical Thinking

1. What is the purpose of a statistical hypothesis?
2. What is a *significance level?* How does a researcher choose a significance level?
3. What is the difference between a *significance level* and a *p-value?*
4. How is a p-value used to test a hypothesis?
5. Distinguish between a *Type I* and *Type II error.*
6. What are the factors that determine the choice of the appropriate statistical technique?
7. A researcher is asked to determine whether or not a productivity objective (in dollars) of better than $75,000 per employee is possible. A productivity test is done involving 20 employees. What conclusion would you reach? The sales results are as follows:

a. 28,000	105,000	58,000	93,000	96,000
b. 67,000	82,500	75,000	81,000	59,000
c. 101,000	60,500	77,000	72,500	48,000
d. 99,000	78,000	71,000	80,500	78,000

8. Assume you have the following data: H_1: $\mu \neq 200$, $S = 30$, $n = 64$, and $\overline{X} = 218$. Conduct a two-tailed hypothesis test at the 0.05 significance level.
9. If the data in question 8 had been generated with a sample of 25 ($n = 25$), what statistical test would be appropriate?
10. The answers to a researcher's question will be nominally scaled. What statistical test is appropriate for comparing the sample data with hypothesized population data?
11. A researcher plans to ask employees whether they favor, oppose, or are indifferent about a change in the company retirement program. Formulate a hypothesis for a chi-square test and the way the variable would be created.
12. Give an example in which a Type I error may be more serious than a Type II error.
13. Refer to the pizza store location χ^2 data in the section "The Chi-Square Test for Goodness of Fit." What statistical decisions could be made if the 0.01 significance level were selected rather than the 0.05 level?
14. Determine a hypothesis that the following data may address and perform a χ^2 test on the survey data.
    a. *American Idol* should be broadcast before 9 p.m.

Agree	40
Neutral	35
Disagree	25
	100

    b. Political affiliations of a group indicate

Republicans	102
Democrats	98
	200

15. A researcher hypothesizes that 15 percent of the people in a test-market will recall seeing a particular advertisement. In a sample of 1,200 people, 20 percent say they recall the ad. Perform a hypothesis test.

Research Activities

1. **'NET** What is the ideal climate? Fill in the following blanks: The lowest temperature in January should be no lower than _____ degrees. At least _____ days should be sunny in January.
   a. List at least 15 places where you would like to live. Using the Internet, find the average low temperature in January for each place. This information is available through various weather related Web sites such as **http://www.weather.com** or through each community's local news Web site. Record the data in a spreadsheet or statistical package such as SPSS. Using the benchmark (preferred population low temperature) you filled in above, test whether the sample places that you would like to live have an ideal January minimum temperature.
   b. Using the same Web site, record how many days in January are typically sunny. Test whether or not the number of sunny days meets your standard.
   c. For each location, record whether or not there was measurable precipitation yesterday. Test the following hypothesis:

   H_1: Among places you would like to live, there is less than 33.3 percent chance of rain/snow on a given day (five days out of fifteen).

2. **ETHICS** Examine the statistical choices under "analyze" in SPSS. Click on compare means. To compare an observed mean to some benchmark or hypothesized population mean, the available choice is a one-sample *t*-test. A researcher is preparing a report and finds the following result testing a hypothesis that suggested the sample mean did not equal 14:
   a. What is the p-value? Is the hypothesis supported?
   b. Write the 95% confidence interval which corresponds to an α of 0.05.
   c. Technically, since the sample size is greater than 30, a *Z*-test might be more appropriate. However, since the *t*-test result is readily available with SPSS, the research presents this result. Is there an ethical problem in using the one-sample *t*-test?

One-Sample Statistics

	N	Mean	Std. Deviation	Std. Error Mean
1997–2000	67	14.5337	16.02663	1.95796

Test Value = 14

	t	*df*	Sig. (two-tailed)	Mean Difference	95% Confidence Interval of the Difference: Lower	95% Confidence Interval of the Difference: Upper
1997–2000	0.273	66	0.786	0.53373	−3.3755	4.4429

Case 21.1 Quality Motors

© GETTY IMAGES/ PHOTODISC GREEN

Quality Motors is an automobile dealership that regularly advertises in its local market area. It claims that a certain make and model of car averages 30 miles to a gallon of gas and mentions that this figure may vary with driving conditions. A local consumer group wishes to verify the advertising claim. To do so, it selects a sample of recent purchasers of this make and model of automobile. It asks them to drive their cars until two tanks of gasoline have been used up and to record the mileage. The group then calculates and records the miles per gallon for each year. The data in Case Exhibit 21.1–1 portray the results of the tests.

CASE EXHIBIT 21.1–1 **Miles per Gallon Information**

Purchaser	Miles per Gallon	Purchaser	Miles per Gallon
1	30.9	13	27.0
2	24.5	14	26.7
3	31.2	15	31.0
4	28.7	16	23.5
5	35.1	17	29.4
6	29.0	18	26.3
7	28.8	19	27.5
8	23.1	20	28.2
9	31.0	21	28.4
10	30.2	22	29.1
11	28.4	23	21.9
12	29.3	24	30.9

Questions

1. Formulate a statistical hypothesis appropriate for the consumer group's purpose.
2. Calculate the mean average miles per gallon. Compute the sample variance and sample standard deviation.
3. Construct the appropriate statistical test for your hypothesis, using a 0.05 significance level.

CHAPTER 22
BIVARIATE STATISTICAL ANALYSIS: DIFFERENCES BETWEEN TWO VARIABLES

LEARNING OUTCOMES

After studying this chapter, you should be able to

1. **Recognize when a particular bivariate statistical test is appropriate**
2. **Calculate and interpret a χ^2 test for a contingency table**
3. **Calculate and interpret an independent samples *t*-test comparing two means**
4. **Understand the concept of analysis of variance (ANOVA)**
5. **Interpret an ANOVA table**

Chapter Vignette: Gender Differences and Double Standards in Ethical Perceptions

What if you went to trade in your car, knowing that it had an oil leak "which is not very noticeable and doesn't require immediate attention," but would require $200 to have fixed in the near future?[1] Would you feel a moral obligation to tell the car dealer? How about if you went to buy a car with the same issue? Would it be ethical for the dealer to sell you the car without mentioning the oil leak?

Ethical conduct, both of businesses and consumers, is an important issue in the business world. Recent research conducted in Flanders, a European region that includes parts of Belgium, France, and the Netherlands, investigated two aspects of ethical perceptions with relevance to business.[2] First, is there a difference between women and men in their ethical perceptions? Second, is there an ethical double standard—that consumers view an action performed by a customer as more ethical than the same action performed by a business? The researchers hypothesized that women would report higher ethical standards than men and that the "double standard" would exist with respondents perceiving customer actions as more ethical than business behavior.

© EMIN KULIYEV/SHUTTERSTOCK

While we would need to talk to every man and woman to actually know if their ethical perceptions were different, as researchers we understand that a sample of the population has to be used in most situations. In this case, business researchers asked 127 respondents to evaluate a series of ethical scenarios (short stories with ethical implications) including the car with the oil leak mentioned above (Scenario 2). These scenarios were split so that half of them had a consumer engaging in the act while the other half had a business performing the act. The respondents were presented the scenarios and then asked to indicate how ethical they thought the act described was on a scale from 1 indicating "totally unethical" to 7 indicating "totally ethical." Across the four scenarios, the results show:

Gender	Scenario 1	Scenario 2	Scenario 3	Scenario 4
Male	5.59	4.38	5.83	6.24
Female	5.21	3.12	4.88	5.71

While all four scenarios indicate that men rated the activity as more ethical than women, to generalize these results from the sample to the population we need to perform statistical tests. These tests show that there is not a significant difference in three of the four scenarios, with only Scenario 2 showing a statistically significant difference at the 0.05 level.

When testing for the presence of the proposed double standard, the results show:

Source	Scenario 1	Scenario 2	Scenario 3	Scenario 4
Consumer	5.38	3.70	5.32	5.95
Corporate	3.36	1.67	3.38	4.97

In this case, there is a statistically significant difference on all four scenarios. In other words, people perceive the same act as less ethical when performed by a business than a consumer.

How do we do these statistical tests? How can we determine if the results we see might be unique to the sample, or if these results are likely to be found across the population? This chapter focuses on this question when we are examining differences between two variables.

Introduction

The Chapter Vignette is just one illustration of business researchers' desire to test hypotheses stating that two groups differ. In business research, differences in behavior, characteristics, beliefs, opinions, emotions, or attitudes are commonly examined. For example, in the most basic experimental design, the researcher tests differences between subjects assigned to an experimental group and subjects assigned to the control group. The experiment illustration presented in Chapter 12 on self-efficacy is an example of this approach. A survey researcher may be interested in whether male and female consumers purchase a product in the same amount. Business researchers may also test whether or not business units in Europe are as profitable as business units in the United States. Such tests are bivariate **tests of differences** when they involve only two variables: a variable that acts like a dependent variable and a variable that acts as a classification variable. These bivariate tests of differences are the focus of this chapter.

test of differences

An investigation of a hypothesis stating that two (or more) groups differ with respect to measures on a variable.

What Is the Appropriate Test of Difference?

Exhibit 22.1 illustrates that the type of measurement, the nature of the comparison, and the number of groups to be compared influence the statistical choice. Often researchers are interested in testing differences in mean scores between groups or in comparing how two groups' scores are distributed across possible response categories. We will focus our attention on these issues.[3] The rest of the chapter focuses on how to choose the right statistic for two-group comparisons and perform the corresponding test. Exhibit 22.1 provides a frame of reference for the rest of the chapter by illustrating various possible comparisons involving a few golfers.

Construction of contingency tables for χ^2 analysis gives a procedure for comparing observed frequencies of one group with the frequencies of another group. This is a good starting point from which to discuss testing of differences.

TOTHEPOINT

You got to be careful if you don't know where you're going, because you might not get there.

—Yogi Berra

Cross-Tabulation Tables: The χ^2 Test for Goodness-of-Fit

Cross-tabulation is one of the most widely used statistical techniques among business researchers. Cross-tabulations are intuitive, easily understood, and lend themselves well to graphical analysis using tools like bar charts. Cross-tabs are appropriate when the variables of interest are less-than interval in nature.

As we discussed in Chapter 20, a cross-tabulation, or contingency table, is a joint frequency distribution of observations on two or more variables. Researchers generally rely on two-variable cross-tabulations the most since the results can be easily communicated. Cross-tabulations are much like tallying. When two variables exist, each with two categories, four cells result. The χ^2 distribution provides a means for testing the statistical significance of a contingency table. In other words, the bivariate χ^2 test examines the statistical significance of relationships between two less-than interval variables.

EXHIBIT 22.1 Some Bivariate Hypotheses

	Golfer							
Information	**Dolly**	**Lori**	**Mel**	**Hypothesis or Research Question**	**Level of Measurement Involved**	**Statistic Used**	**Comment**	**Result**
Average Driver Distance (meters)	135	150	185	Lori hits her drives further than Dolly	Golfer = Nominal; Drive Distance = Ratio	Independent Samples *t*-test to compare mean distance	The data for Lori and Dolly are used.	Supported ($t = 2.07$, df = 56, $p < .05$)
σ	30	25	30					
Average 7-Wood Distance (meters)	140	145	150	Mel hits her driver further than her 7-wood	Club = Nominal (7-wood or driver); 7-Wood Distance = Ratio	Paired-Samples *t*-test to compare mean distances for Mel	Only the data for Mel are used (std of diff = 30)	Supported ($t = 6.39$, df = 29, $p < .05$)
σ	30	30	30					
Sample size (number of balls hit)	28 drives 28 7-woods	30 drives 28 7-woods	29 drives 28 7-woods	A relationship exists between golfers and 7-wood distance	Golfer = Nominal; Distance = Ratio	One-Way ANOVA to compare means for the three groups	All data for 7-wood distance are used (MSE = 30)	Not supported ($F = 0.83$, ns)
Number of Drives in Fairway	4	22	11	Mel drives the ball more accurately than Dolly	Golfer = Nominal; Accuracy = Nominal (Right, Fairway, Left)	Cross-Tabulation with χ^2 Statistic	Resulting cross tabulation table is 2 rows × 3 columns (rows = golfer and columns = accuracy (fairway, right left)	Supported ($\chi^2 = 10.3$, df = 3, $p < .05$)
Drives missing right of fairway	16	7	9	A relationship exist between golfers and accuracy	Golfer = Nominal; Accuracy = Nominal (Right, Fairway, Left)	Cross-Tabulation with χ^2 Statistic	Cross-tabulation is now 3 rows × 3 columns	Supported ($\chi^2 = 23.7$, df = 4, $p < .05$)
Drives missing left of fairway	8	1	9					

The χ^2 test for a contingency table involves comparing the observed frequencies (O_i) with the expected frequencies (E_i) in each cell of the table. The goodness- (or closeness-) of-fit of the observed distribution with the expected distribution is captured by this statistic. Remember that the convention is that the row variable is considered the independent variable and the column variable is considered the dependent variable.

Recall that in Chapter 21 we used a χ^2 test to examine whether or not Papa John's restaurants in California were more likely to be located in a stand-alone location or in a shopping center. The univariate (one-dimensional) analysis suggests that the majority of the locations (60 percent) are stand-alone units:

Location	One-Way Frequency Table
Stand-Alone	60 stores
Shopping Center	40 stores
Total	100 stores

Recall that the $\chi^2 = 4.0$ with 1 degree of freedom ($p < 0.01$).

Is there any effect of location of Papa John's restaurants? Suppose the researcher wishes to examine the following hypothesis:

Stand-alone locations are more likely to be profitable than are shopping center locations.

While the researcher is unable to obtain the dollar figures for profitability of each unit, a press release indicates which Papa John's units were profitable and which were not. Cross-tabulation using a χ^2 test is appropriate because

- The independent variable (location) is less-than interval.
- The dependent variable (profitable/not profitable) is less-than interval.

The data can be recorded in the following 2 × 2 contingency table:

Location	Profitable	Not Profitable	Total
Stand-Alone	50	10	60
Shopping Center	15	25	40
Totals	65	35	100

Several conclusions appear evident. One, it seems that more stores are profitable than not profitable (65 versus 35, respectively). Secondly, more of the profitable restaurants seem to be in stand-alone locations (50 of the 65). However, is the difference strong enough to be statistically significant?

Is the observed difference between stand-alone and shopping center locations the result of chance variation due to random sampling? Is the discrepancy more than sampling variation? The χ^2 test allows us to conduct tests for significance in the analysis of the $R \times C$ contingency table (where R = row and C = column). The formula for the χ^2 statistic is the same as that for one-way frequency tables (see Chapter 21):

$$\chi^2 = \sum \frac{(O_i - E_i)^2}{E_i}$$

where

χ^2 = chi-square statistic

O_i = observed frequency in the ith cell

E_i = expected frequency in the ith cell

Again, as in the univariate χ^2 test, a frequency count of data that nominally identify or categorically rank groups is acceptable.

If the researcher's hypothesis is true, the frequencies shown in the contingency table should not resemble a random distribution. In other words, if location has no effect on profitability, the profitable and unprofitable stores would be spread evenly across the two location categories. This is really the logic of the test in that it compares the observed frequencies with the theoretical expected values for each cell.

After obtaining the observations for each cell, the expected values for each cell must be obtained. The expected values are what we would find if there is no relationship between the two variables. In this case, that the location of the pizza store has no relationship with whether or not the store is profitable. The expected values for each cell can be computed easily using this formula:

$$E_{ij} = \frac{R_i C_j}{n}$$

where

R_i = total observed frequency count in the ith row

C_j = total observed frequency count in the jth column

n = sample size

Only the total column and total row values are needed for this calculation. Thus, the calculation could be performed before the data are even tabulated. The following values represent the expected values for each cell:

RESEARCH SNAPSHOT

Chi-Training

When is a cross-tabulation with a χ^2 test appropriate? The answer to this question can be determined by answering these questions:

- Are multiple variables expected to be related to one another?
- Is the independent variable nominal or ordinal?
- Is the dependent variable nominal or ordinal?

When the answer to all of these questions is yes, cross-tabulation with a χ^2 test will address the research question. One common application involves the effect of some workplace change. For instance, this might involve the adoption of a new technology or the effect of training. For instance, consider the following contingency data represented in bar charts to the right.

© COMSTOCK IMAGES/JUPITER IMAGES

The data show whether or not the adoption of a new information system produced accurate or inaccurate information. The 2-by-2 contingency table underlying this bar chart produces a χ^2 value of 5.97 with 1 degree of freedom. The p-value is less than 0.05; thus, the new technology does seem to have changed accuracy. However, we must examine the actual cell counts to see exactly what this effect has been. In this case, the bar chart indicates that the new technology is associated with more incidences of accurate rather than inaccurate information.

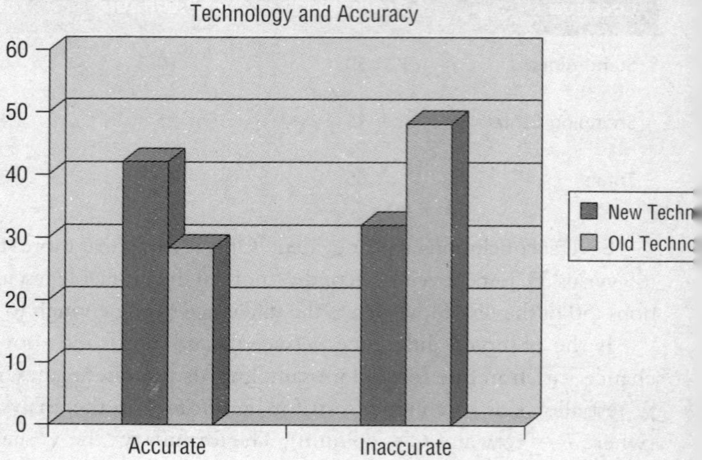

Sources: For examples of research involving this type of analysis, see Gohmann, S. E., R. M. Barker, D. J. Faulds, and J. Guan, "Salesforce Automation, Perceived Information Accuracy and User Satisfaction," *Journal of Business and Industrial Marketing* 20 (2005), 23–32; Makela, C. J. and S. Peters, "Consumer Education: Creating Consumer Awareness among Adolescents in Botswana," *International Journal of Consumer Studies* 28 (September 2004), 379–387.

© iStock

Location	Profitable	Not Profitable	Total
Stand-Alone	(60 × 65)/100 = 39	(60 × 35)/100 = 21	60
Shopping Center	(65 × 40)/100 = 26	(40 × 35)/100 = 14	40
Totals	65	35	100

Notice that the row and column totals are the same for both the observed and expected contingency matrices. These values also become useful in providing the substantive interpretation of the relationship. Significant variation from the expected value indicates a relationship and tells us the direction.

The actual bivariate χ^2 test value can be calculated in the same manner as for the univariate test. The one difference is that the degrees of freedom are now obtained by multiplying the number of rows minus one $(R - 1)$ times the number of columns minus one $(C - 1)$:

$$\chi^2 = \sum \frac{(O_i - E_i)^2}{E_i}$$

with $(R - 1)(C - 1)$ degrees of freedom. The observed and expected values can be plugged into the formula as follows:

$$\chi^2 = \frac{(50-39)^2}{39} + \frac{(10-21)^2}{21} + \frac{(15-26)^2}{26} + \frac{(25-14)^2}{14}$$

$$= 3.102 + 5.762 + 4.654 + 8.643$$

$$= 22.16$$

The number of degrees of freedom equals 1:

$$(R - 1)(C - 1) = (2 - 1)(2 - 1) = 1$$

From Table A.4 in the appendix, we see that the critical value at the 0.05 probability level with 1 *df* is 3.84. Thus, we are very confident that the observed values are not equal to the expected values. Before the hypothesis can be supported, however, the researcher must check and see that the deviations from the expected values are in the hypothesized direction. Since the difference between the stand-alone locations' observed profitability and the expected values for that cell are positive, the hypothesis is supported. Location is associated with profitability. The Research Snapshot "Chi-Training" provides another example of cross-tabs and a χ^2 test.

Thus, testing the hypothesis involves two key steps:

1. Examine the statistical significance of the observed contingency table.
2. Examine whether the differences between the observed and expected values are consistent with the hypothesized prediction.

The examples provided both have 2-by-2 contingency tables (that is, two levels of two variables). However, cross-tabulations and the χ^2 test can be used regardless of the number of levels. For instance, if the Papa John's locations were instead stand-alone, shopping center, and delivery only, we would have a 3-by-2 contingency table. Or, perhaps we want to look at the distribution of our male and female sales reps across our five product lines, which would give us a 2-by-5 contingency table. The number of cells is not limited. However, proper use of the χ^2 test requires that each expected cell frequency (E) have a value of at least 5. If this sample size requirement is not met, the researcher should take a larger sample or combine (collapse) response categories.

The *t*-Test for Comparing Two Means

Cross-tabulations and the χ^2 test are appropriate when both variables are less-than interval level. However, researchers often want to compare one interval or ratio level variable across categories of respondents. The Chapter Vignette describes such a situation. The researchers are interested in comparing the ethical perceptions between genders. When a researcher needs to compare means for a variable grouped into two categories based on some less-than interval variable, a *t*-test is appropriate. One way to think about this is testing the way a dichotomous (two-level) independent variable is associated with changes in a continuous dependent variable. Several variations of the *t*-test exist.

Independent Samples *t*-Test

Most typically, the researcher will apply the **independent samples *t*-test**, which tests the differences between means taken from two independent samples or groups. So, for example, if we measure the price for some designer jeans at 30 different retail stores, of which 15 are Internet-only stores (pure clicks) and 15 are traditional stores, we can test whether or not the prices are different based on store type with an independent samples *t*-test. The *t*-test for difference of means assumes the two samples (one Internet and one traditional store) are drawn from normal distributions and that the variances of the two populations are approximately equal (homoscedasticity).

independent samples *t*-test

A test for hypotheses stating that the mean scores for some interval- or ratio-scaled variable grouped based on some less-than interval classificatory variable.

INDEPENDENT SAMPLES *t*-TEST CALCULATION

The *t*-test actually tests whether or not the differences between two means is zero. Not surprisingly, this idea can be expressed as the difference between two population means:

$$\mu_1 = \mu_2, \text{ which is equivalent to } \mu_1 - \mu_2 = 0$$

However, since this is inferential statistics, we test the idea by comparing two sample means ($\overline{X}_1 - \overline{X}_2$).

A verbal expression of the formula for t is

$$t = \frac{\text{Sample Mean 1} - \text{Sample Mean 2}}{\text{Variability of random means}}$$

In almost all situations, we will see from the calculation of the two sample means that they are not exactly equal. The question is actually whether the observed differences have occurred by chance, or likely exist in the population. The t-value is a ratio with information about the difference between means (provided by the sample) in the numerator and the standard error in the denominator. To calculate t, we use the following formula:

$$t = \frac{\bar{X}_1 - \bar{X}_2}{S_{\bar{X}_1 - \bar{X}_2}}$$

where

$\bar{X}_1$ = mean for group 1

$\bar{X}_2$ = mean for group 2

$S_{\bar{X}_1 - \bar{X}_2}$ = pooled, or combined, standard error of difference between means

pooled estimate of the standard error

An estimate of the standard error for a t-test of independent means that assumes the variances of both groups are equal.

A **pooled estimate of the standard error** is a better estimate of the standard error than one based on the variance from either sample. The pooled standard error of the difference between means of independent samples can be calculated using the following formula:

$$S_{\bar{X}_1 - \bar{X}_2} = \sqrt{\left(\frac{(n_1 - 1)S_1^2 + (n_2 - 1)S_2^2}{n_1 + n_2 - 2}\right)\left(\frac{1}{n_1} + \frac{1}{n_2}\right)}$$

where

S_1^2 = variance of group 1

S_2^2 = variance of group 2

n_1 = sample size of group 1

n_2 = sample size of group 2

Are business majors or sociology majors more positive about a career in business? A t-test can be used to test the difference between sociology majors and business majors on scores on a scale measuring attitudes toward business careers. We will assume that the attitude scale is an interval scale. The result of the simple random sample of these two groups of college students is shown below:

Business Students	Sociology Students
$\bar{X}_1 = 16.5$	$\bar{X}_2 = 12.2$
$S_1 = 2.1$	$S_2 = 2.6$
$n_1 = 21$	$n_2 = 14$

A high score indicates a favorable attitude toward business. We can see in the sample that business students report a higher score (16.5) than sociology students (12.2). This particular t-test tests whether the difference in attitudes between sociology and business students is significant. That is, is the sample result due to chance or do we expect this difference to exist in the population? A higher t-value is associated with a lower p-value. As the t gets higher and the p-value gets lower, the researcher has more confidence that the means are truly different. The relevant data computation is

$$S_{\bar{X}_1 - \bar{X}_2} = \sqrt{\left(\frac{(n_1 - 1)S_1^2 + (n_2 - 1)S_2^2}{n_1 + n_2 - 2}\right)\left(\frac{1}{n_1} + \frac{1}{n_2}\right)}$$

$$= \sqrt{\left(\frac{(20)(2.1)^2 + (13)(2.6)^2}{33}\right)\left(\frac{1}{21} + \frac{1}{14}\right)}$$

$$= 0.797$$

The calculation of the t-statistic is

$$t = \frac{\overline{X}_1 - \overline{X}_2}{S_{\overline{X}_1 - \overline{X}_2}}$$

$$t = \frac{16.5 - 12.2}{0.797}$$

$$= \frac{4.3}{0.797}$$

$$= 5.395$$

In a test of two means, degrees of freedom are calculated as follows:

$$df = n - k$$

where

$n = n_1 + n_2$

k = number of groups

In our example df equals 33((21 + 14) − 2). If the 0.01 level of significance is selected, reference to Table A.3 in the appendix yields the critical t-value. The t-value of 2.75 must be surpassed by the observed t-value if the hypothesis test is to be statistically significant at the 0.01 level. The calculated value of t, 5.39, far exceeds the critical value of t for statistical significance, so it is significant at $\alpha = 0.01$. The p-value is less than 0.01. In other words, this research shows that business students have significantly more positive attitudes toward business than do sociology students.

PRACTICALLY SPEAKING

While it is good to understand the process involved, in practice computer software is used to compute the t-test results. Exhibit 22.2 displays a typical t-test printout. These particular results examine the following research question:

RQ: Does religion relate to price sensitivity?

This question was addressed in the context of restaurant and wine consumption by allowing 100 consumers to sample a specific wine and then tell the researcher how much they would be willing to pay for a bottle of the wine. The sample included 57 Catholics and 43 Protestants. Because no direction of the relationship is stated (no hypotheses is offered), a two-tailed test is appropriate. Although instructors still find some value in having students learn to perform the t-test calculations, this procedure is usually computer generated and interpreted today. Using SPSS, the click-through sequence would be:

Analyze → *Compare Means* → *Independent-Samples t-test*

Then, the variable used to categorize the respondent as either Catholic or Protestant would be entered as the *grouping variable* and the variable with the amount the respondent was willing to pay as the *test variable.*

The interpretation of the t-test is made simple by focusing on either the p-value or the confidence interval and the group means. Here are the basic steps:

1. Examine the difference in means to find the "direction" of any difference. In this case, Catholics are willing to pay nearly \$11 more than Protestants.
2. Compute or locate the computed t-test value. In this case, $t = 0.998$.
3. Find the p-value associated with this t and the corresponding degrees of freedom. Here, the p-value (two-tailed significance level) is 0.321. This suggests a 32 percent chance that the means are actually equal given the observed sample means. In other words, the difference we see may be due to this

EXHIBIT 22.2 **Independent Samples *t*-Test Results**

Group Statistics

	rel	*N*	Mean	Std. Deviation	Std. Error Mean
price	Catholic	57	61.00	43.381	5.746
	Protestant	43	50.27	64.047	9.767

1. Shows mean, standard deviation, and standard error for each group (Catholic and Protestant)

Independent Samples Test

NOTE: Top row shows results assuming equal variances. Bottom row assumes variance is different in each.

		Levene's Test for Equality of Variances		*t*-Test for Equality of Means						
									95% Confidence Interval of the Difference	
		F	Sig.	*t*	d.f.	Sig. (2-tailed)	Mean Difference	Std. Error Difference	Lower	Upper
price	Equal variances assumed	0.769	0.383	0.998	98	.321	10.734	10.752	−10.603	32.070
	Equal variances not assumed			0.947	69.829	.347	10.734	11.332	−11.868	33.336

2. Computed *t*-test value shown in this column ($t = 0.998$).

3. P-value for *t*-value and associated degrees of freedom ($t = 0.998$, 98 d.f.)

4. Confidence intervals for $\alpha = 0.05$ (100% − 95%). In this case, it includes 0.

sample of 100 respondents rather than being found in the population. Assuming a 0.05 acceptable Type I error rate (α), the appropriate conclusion is that the means are *not* significantly different.

4. The difference can also be examined using the 95 percent confidence interval ($-10.603 < \bar{X}_1 - \bar{X}_2 < 32.070$). Since the confidence interval includes 0, we lack sufficient confidence that the true difference between the population means is not 0.

A few points are worth noting about this particular result. First, strictly speaking, the *t*-test assumes that the two population variances are equal. A slightly more complicated formula exists which will compute the *t*-statistic assuming the variances are not equal.[4] SPSS provides both results when an independent samples *t*-test is performed. The sample variances appear considerably different in this case (43.4, 64.0). Nonetheless, the conclusions are the same using either assumption. In business research, we often deal with values that have variances close enough to assume equal variance. This isn't always the case in the physical sciences where variables may take on values of drastically different magnitude. Thus, the rule of thumb in business research is to use the equal variance assumption. In the vast majority of cases, the same conclusion will be drawn using either assumption.

Second, notice that even though the means appear to be not so close to each other, the statistical conclusion is that they are the same. The substantive conclusion is that Catholics and Protestants would not be expected to pay different prices. Why is it that means do not appear to be similar, yet that is the conclusion? The answer lies in the variance. Respondents tended to provide very wide ranges of acceptable prices. Notice how large the standard deviations are compared to the mean for each group. Since the *t*-statistic is a function of the standard error, which is a function of the standard deviation, a lot of variance means a smaller *t*-value for any given observed difference. When this occurs, the researcher may wish to double check for outliers. A small number of wild price estimates could be inflating the variance for one or both groups. An additional consideration would be to increase the sample size and test again.

Third, a t-test is used even though the sample size is greater than 30. Strictly speaking, a Z-test could be used to test this difference. Researchers often employ a t-test even with large samples. As samples get larger, the t-test and Z-test will tend to yield the same result. Although a t-test can be used with large samples, a Z-test should not be used with small samples. Also, a Z-test can be used in instances where the population variance is known ahead of time.

As another example, consider 11 sales representatives categorized as either young (1) or old (2) on the basis of their ages in years, as shown in Exhibit 22.3. The exhibit presents a SAS (pronounced "sass") computer output that compares the mean sales volume for these two groups. We can see that the mean for the young group is 61,879 and that of the old group is 86,962, which appears considerably different. Again, though, this difference is not statistically significant at the 0.05 level as the p-value is 0.3218. In this case, the very small sample size (11 in total) drastically limits the statistical power.

Paired-Samples *t*-Test

What happens when means need to be compared that are not from independent samples? Such might be the case when the same respondent is measured twice—for instance, when the respondent is asked to rate both how much he or she likes shopping on the Internet and how much he or she likes shopping in traditional stores. Since the liking scores are both provided by the same person, the assumption that they are independent is not realistic. Additionally, if one compares the prices the same retailers charge in their stores with the prices they charge on their Web sites, the samples cannot be considered independent because each pair of observations is from the same sampling unit.

paired-samples *t*-test
An appropriate test for comparing the scores of two interval variables drawn from related populations.

A **paired-samples *t*-test** is appropriate in this situation. The idea behind the paired-samples t-test can be seen in the following computation:

$$t = \frac{\bar{d}}{s_d/\sqrt{n}}$$

where $\bar{d}$ is the difference between means, s_d is the standard deviation of the observed differences, and n is the number of observations. Researchers also can compute the paired-samples t-test using statistical software. For example, using SPSS, the click-through sequence would be:

Analyze → Compare Means → Paired-Samples t-test

A dialog box then appears in which the "paired variables" should be entered. When a paired-samples t-test is appropriate, the two numbers being compared are usually scored as separate variables.

Exhibit 22.4 displays a paired-samples t-test result. A sample of 69 young adult consumers was asked to rate how likely they would be to consider purchasing grocery via (a) an online store and (b) a well-known supermarket store in their neighbourhood. Each respondent provided two responses, much as in a within-subjects experimental design. The SPSS output depicts the

EXHIBIT 22.3 **SAS *t*-Test Output**

***t*-Test Procedure Variable: CR Sales**

Age	*n*	Mean	Standard Deviation	Standard Error	Minimum	Maximum	Variances	*t*	d.f.	Prob > |*T*|
1	6	61879.33333	22356.20845	9126.88388	41152.00000	103059.0000	Unequal	−0.9758	5.2	0.3729
2	5	86961.80000	53734.45098	24030.77702	42775.00000	172530.0000	Equal	−1.0484	9.0	0.3218

For H_0: Variances are equal, $F = 5.78$ with 4 and 5 d.f., Prob. $> F = 0.0815$.

EXHIBIT 22.4 Example Results for a Paired-Samples *t*-Test

Paired-Samples Statistics

		Mean	*N*	Std. Deviation	Std. Error Mean
Pair 1	X10 – Will buy from online store	5.24	63	.734	.093
	X11 – Will buy from Supermarket	3.37	63	.955	.120

Paired-Samples Test

	Paired Differences							
				95% Confidence Interval of the Difference				
	Mean	Std. Deviation	Std. Error Mean	Lower	Upper	*t*	d.f.	Sig. (2-tailed)
X10 – Will buy from online store - X11 – Will buy from Supermarket	1.873	1.114	.140	1.592	2.154	13.342	62	.000

means for each variable (Online purchase likelihood and store purchase likelihood). The *t*-test results suggest that the average difference of 1.873 is associated with a *t*-value of 13.342. As can be seen using either the *p*-value (0.000 rounded to 3 decimals) or the confidence interval $1.592 < d < 2.154$), which does not include 0, the difference is significantly different from 0. Therefore, the results suggest a higher likelihood to buy grocery online that a well-known bricks-and-mortar supermarket store.

Management researchers have used paired-samples *t*-tests to examine the effect of downsizing on employee morale. For instance, job satisfaction for a sample of employees can be measured immediately after the downsizing. Some months later, employee satisfaction can be measured again. The difference between the satisfaction scores can be compared using a paired-samples *t*-test. Results suggest that the employee satisfaction scores increase within a few months of the downsizing as evidenced by statistically significant paired-samples *t*-values.[5]

The *Z*-Test for Comparing Two Proportions

Z-test for differences of proportions
A technique used to test the hypothesis that proportions are significantly different for two independent samples or groups.

What type of statistical comparison can be made when the observed statistics are proportions? Suppose a researcher wishes to test the hypothesis that wholesalers in the northern and southern United States differ in the proportion of sales they make to discount retailers. Testing whether the population proportion for group 1 (p_1) equals the population proportion for group 2 (p_2) is conceptually the same as the *t*-test of two means. This section illustrates a **Z-test for differences of proportions**, which requires a sample size greater than 30.

The test is appropriate for a hypothesis of this form:

$$H_0: \pi_1 = \pi_2$$

which may be restated as

$$H_0: \pi_1 - \pi_2 = 0$$

Comparison of the observed sample proportions p_1 and p_2 allows the researcher to ask whether the difference between two *large* (greater than 30) random samples occurred due to chance alone. The Z-test statistic can be computed using the following formula:

$$Z = \frac{(p_1 - p_2) - (\pi_1 - \pi_2)}{S_{p_1-p_2}}$$

where

p_1 = sample proportion of successes in group 1

p_2 = sample proportion of successes in group 2

$\pi_1 - \pi_2$ = hypothesized population proportion 1 minus hypothesized population proportion 2

$S_{p_1-p_2}$ = pooled estimate of the standard error of differences in proportions

The statistic normally works on the assumption that the value of $\pi_1 - \pi_2$ is zero, so this formula is actually much simpler than it looks at first inspection. Readers also may notice the similarity between this and the paired-samples t-test.

To calculate the standard error of the differences in proportions, use the formula

$$S_{p_1-p_2} = \sqrt{\bar{p}\bar{q}\left(\frac{1}{n_1} + \frac{1}{n_2}\right)}$$

where

$\bar{p}$ = pooled estimate of proportion of successes in a sample

$\bar{q} = 1 - \bar{p}$, or pooled estimate of proportion of failures in a sample

n_1 = sample size for group 1

n_2 = sample size for group 2

To calculate the pooled estimator, $\bar{p}$, use the formula

$$\bar{p} = \frac{n_1p_1 + n_2p_2}{n_1 + n_2}$$

Suppose the survey data are as follows:

Northern Wholesalers	Southern Wholesalers
$p_1 = 0.35$	$p_2 = 0.40$
$n_1 = 100$	$n_2 = 100$

First, the standard error of the difference in proportions is

$$S_{p_1-p_2} = \sqrt{\left(\bar{p}\bar{q}\,\frac{1}{n_1} + \frac{1}{n_2}\right)}$$

$$= \sqrt{(0.375)(0.625)\left(\frac{1}{100} + \frac{1}{100}\right)} = 0.068$$

where

$$\bar{p} = \frac{(100)(0.35) + (100)(0.40)}{100 + 100} = 0.375$$

If we wish to test the two-tailed question of no difference, we must calculate an observed *Z*-value. Thus,

$$Z = \frac{(p_1 - p_2) - (\pi_1 - \pi_2)}{S_{p_1 - p_2}}$$

$$= \frac{(0.35 - 0.40) - (0)}{0.068}$$

$$= -0.73$$

In this example the idea that the proportion of sales differs by region is not supported. The calculated *Z*-value is less than the critical *Z*-value of 1.96. Therefore, the p-value associated with the test is greater than 0.05.

Analysis of Variance (ANOVA)

What Is ANOVA?

So far, we have discussed tests for differences between two groups. However, what happens when we have more than two groups? For example, what if we want to test and see if employee turnover differs across our five production plants? When the means of more than two groups or populations are to be compared, one-way **analysis of variance (ANOVA)** is the appropriate statistical tool. ANOVA involving only one grouping variable is often referred to as *one-way* ANOVA because only one independent variable is involved. Another way to define ANOVA is as the appropriate statistical technique to examine the effect of a less-than interval independent variable on an at-least interval dependent variable. Thus, a categorical independent variable and a continuous dependent variable are involved. An independent samples *t*-test can be thought of as a special case of ANOVA in which the independent variable has only two levels. When more levels exist, the *t*-test alone cannot handle the problem.

analysis of variance (ANOVA)

Analysis involving the investigation of the effects of one treatment variable on an interval-scaled dependent variable—a hypothesis-testing technique to determine whether statistically significant differences in means occur between two or more groups.

The statistical null hypothesis for ANOVA is stated as follows:

$$\mu_1 = \mu_2 = \mu_3 = \cdots = \mu_k$$

The symbol k is the number of groups or categories for an independent variable. In other words, all group means are equal. The substantive hypothesis tested in ANOVA is[6]

At least one group mean is not equal to another group mean.

As the term *analysis of variance* suggests, the problem requires comparing variances to make inferences about the means.

The Papa Johns example considered locations that were stand-alone and shopping center, compared to the categorical variable of profitable or not profitable. However, if we knew the exact amount of profit or loss for each store, this becomes a good example of a *t*-test. Specifically, the independent variable could be thought of as "location," meaning either stand-alone or shopping center. The dependent variable is the amount of profit/loss. Since only two groups exist for the independent variable, either an independent samples *t*-test or one-way ANOVA could be used. The results would be identical. This is shown in the Research Snapshot "More Than One-Way."

However, assume further that location involved three group levels. Profit would now be compared based on whether the store was stand-alone, shopping center, or delivery only. The *t*-test would not be appropriate; one-way ANOVA would be the choice for this analysis.

RESEARCH SNAPSHOT

More Than One-Way

An independent samples *t*-test is a special case of one-way ANOVA. When the independent variable in ANOVA has only two groups, the results for an independent samples *t*-test and ANOVA will be the same.

The two sets of statistical results below demonstrate this fact. Both outputs are taken from the same data. The test considers whether men or women are more excited about a new Italian restaurant in their town. Sex2 is dummy coded so that 0 = men and 1 = women. Excitement was measured on a scale ranging from 0 to 6.

Independent Samples *t*-Test Results:

Group Statistics

	Sex2	*N*	Mean	Std. Deviation	Std. Error Mean
Excitement	0.00	69	2.64	2.262	0.272
	1.00	73	2.32	2.140	0.250

Independent Samples Test

		Levene's Test for Equality of Variances		*t*-Test for Equality of Means					95% Confidence Interval of the Difference	
		F	Sig.	*t*	*df*	Sig. (two-tailed)	Mean Difference	Std. Error Difference	Lower	Upper
xcitement	Equal variances assumed	1.768	0.186	0.873	140	0.384	0.323	0.369	−0.408	1.053
	Equal variances not assumed			0.872	138.265	0.385	0.323	0.370	−0.409	1.054

this case, we would conclude that men and women are equally excited—or unexcited as the case may be. The *t* of 0.873 with 140 *df* not significant (p = 0.384).

NOVA Results:

Descriptives

		N	Mean	Std. Deviation	Std. Error	95% Confidence Interval for Mean: Lower Bound	95% Confidence Interval for Mean: Upper Bound	Minimum	Maximum
xcitement	0.00	69	2.64	2.262	0.272	2.09	3.18	0	7
	1.00	73	2.32	2.140	0.250	1.82	2.81	0	7
	Total	142	2.47	2.198	0.184	2.11	2.84	0	7

ANOVA

		Sum of Squares	*df*	Mean Square	*F*	Sig.
Excitement	Between Groups	3.692	1	3.692	0.763	0.384
	Within Groups	677.695	140	4.841		
	Total	681.387	141			

Notice that the *F*-ratio shown in the ANOVA table is associated with the same p-value as is the *t*-value above. This is no accident since the *F* and *t* are mathematical functions of one another. So, when two groups are involved, the researcher can skin the cat either way!

Simple Illustration of ANOVA

ANOVA's logic is fairly simple. Look at the data table below that describes how much coffee respondents report drinking each day based on which shift they work, day shift, second shift, or nights.

Day	1
Day	3
Day	4
Day	0
Day	2
Second	7
Second	2
Second	1
Second	6
Night	6
Night	8
Night	3
Night	7
Night	6

The following table displays the means for each group and the overall mean:

Shift	Mean	Std. Deviation	N
Day	2.00	1.58	5
Second	4.00	2.94	4
Night	6.00	1.87	5
Total	4.00	2.63	14

Exhibit 22.5 plots each observation with a bar. The long vertical line illustrates the total range of observations. The lowest is 0 cups and the highest is 8 cups of coffee for a range of 8. The overall mean is 4 cups. Each group mean is shown with a different colored line that matches the bars

EXHIBIT 22.5 **Illustration of ANOVA Logic**

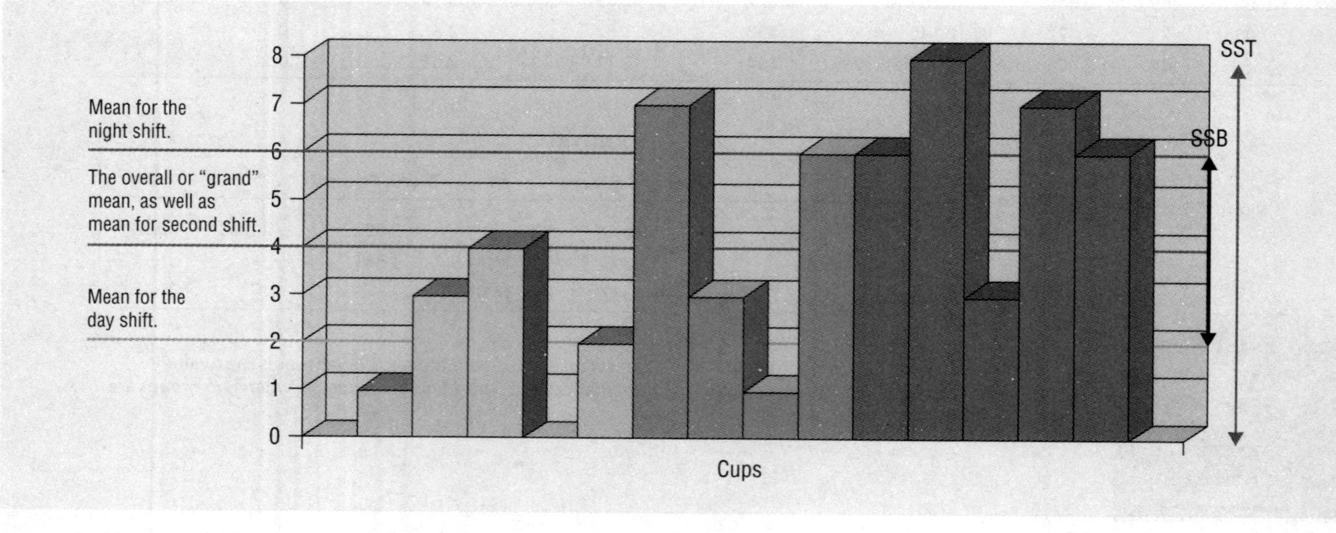

corresponding to the group. The day shift averages 2 cups of coffee a day, the second shift 4 cups, and the night shift 6 cups of coffee per day.

Here is the basic idea of ANOVA. Look at the dark double-headed arrow in Exhibit 22.5. This line represents the range of the differences between group means. In this case, the lowest mean is 2 cups and the highest mean is 6 cups. Thus, the middle vertical line corresponds to the total variation (range) in the data and the thick double-headed black line corresponds to the variance accounted for by the group differences. As the thick black line accounts for more of the total variance, the ANOVA model suggests that the group means are not all the same, and in particular, not all the same as the overall mean. This also means that the independent variable, in this case work shift, explains the dependent variable. Here, the results suggest that knowing when someone works explains how much coffee they drink. Night-shift workers drink the most coffee.

Partitioning Variance in ANOVA

TOTAL VARIABILITY

An implicit question with the use of ANOVA is, "How can the dependent variable best be predicted?" Absent any additional information, the error in predicting an observation is minimized by choosing the central tendency, or mean for an interval variable. For the coffee example, if no information was available about the work shift of each respondent, the best guess for coffee drinking consumption would be four cups. The Sum of Squares Total (SST) or variability that would result from using the **grand mean**, meaning the mean over all observations, can be thought of as

grand mean
The mean of a variable over all observations.

$$\text{SST} = \text{Total of (Observed Value} - \text{Grand Mean)}^2$$

Although the term error is used, this really represents how much total variation exists among the measures.

Using the first observation, the error of observation would be

$$(1 \text{ cup} - 4 \text{ cups})^2 = 9$$

The same squared error could be computed for each observation and these squared errors totaled to give SST.

BETWEEN-GROUPS VARIANCE

ANOVA tests whether "grouping" observations explains variance in the dependent variable. In Exhibit 22.5, the three colors reflect three levels of the independent variable, work shift. Given this additional information about which shift a respondent works, the prediction changes. Now, instead of guessing the grand mean, the group mean would be used. So, once we know that someone works the day shift, the prediction would be that he or she consumes 2 cups of coffee per day. Similarly, the second and night-shift predictions would be 4 and 6 cups, respectively. Thus, the **between-groups variance** or Sum of Squares Between-groups (SSB) can be found by taking the total sum of the weighted difference between group means and the overall mean as shown:

between-groups variance
The sum of differences between the group mean and the grand mean summed over all groups for a given set of observations.

$$\text{SSB} = \text{Total of } n_{\text{group}}(\text{Group Mean} - \text{Grand Mean})^2$$

The weighting factor (n_{group}) is the specific group sample size. Let's consider the first observation once again. Since this observation is in the day shift, we predict 2 cups of coffee will be consumed. Looking at the day shift group observations in Exhibit 22.5, the new error in prediction would be

$$(2 \text{ cups} - 4 \text{ cups})^2 = (2)^2 = 4$$

The error in prediction has been reduced from 3 using the grand mean to 2 using the group mean. This squared difference would be weighted by the group sample size of 5, to yield a contribution to SSB of 20.

Next, the same process could be followed for the other groups yielding two more contributions to SSB. Because the second shift group mean is the same as the grand mean, that group's contribution to SSB is 0. Notice that the night-shift group mean is also 2 different than the grand mean, like the day shift, so this group's contribution to SSB is likewise 20. The total SSB then represents the variation explained by the experimental or independent variable. In this case, total SSB is 40. The reader may look at the statistical results shown in Exhibit 22.6 to find this value in the sums of squares column.

EXHIBIT 22.6 **Interpreting ANOVA**

Tests of Between-Subjects Effects (Dependent Variable: Coffee)

Source	Type III Sum of Squares	d.f.	Mean Square	*F*	Sig.
Corrected Model	40.000[a]	2	20.000	4.400	.039
Intercept	221.538	1	221.538	48.738	.000
Shift	40.000	2	20.000	4.400	.039
Error	50.000	11	4.545		
Total	314.000	14			

[a]R Squared = .444 (Adjusted R Squared = .343)

1. This row shows overall *F*-value testing whether all group means are equal. The sums of squares column calculates the SST, SSE, and SSB (shift row).

Shift	Mean	Std. Error	95% Confidence Interval Lower Bound	95% Confidence Interval Upper Bound
Day	2.000	.953	−.099	4.099
Second	4.000	1.066	1.654	6.346
Night	6.000	.953	3.901	8.099

2. This column shows the group means for each level of the independent variable.

WITHIN-GROUP ERROR

within-group error or variance
The sum of the differences between observed values and the group mean for a given set of observations; also known as total error variance.

Finally, error within each group would remain. Whereas the group means explain the variation between the total mean and the group mean, the distance from the group mean and each individual observation remains unexplained. This distance is called **within-group error or variance** or the Sum of Squares Error (SSE). The values for each observation can be found by

$$\text{SSE} = \text{Total of (Observed Mean} - \text{Group Mean)}^2$$

Again, looking at the first observation, the SSE component would be

$$\text{SSE} = (1 \text{ cup} - 2 \text{ cups})^2 = 1 \text{ cup}$$

This process could be computed for all observations and then totaled. The result would be the total error variance—a name used to refer to SSE since it is variability not accounted for by the group means. These three components are used in determining how well an ANOVA model explains a dependent variable.

The *F*-Test

***F*-test**
A procedure used to determine whether there is more variability in the scores of one sample than in the scores of another sample.

The ***F*-test** is the key statistical test for an ANOVA model. The *F*-test determines whether there is more variability in the scores of one sample than in the scores of another sample. The key question is whether the two sample variances are different from each other or whether they are from the same population. Thus, the test breaks down the variance in a total sample and illustrates why ANOVA is *analysis of variance*.

The F-statistic (or F-ratio) can be obtained by taking the larger sample variance and dividing by the smaller sample variance. Using Table A.5 in the appendix is much like using the tables of the Z- and t-distributions that we have previously examined. These tables portray the F-distribution, which is a probability distribution of the ratios of sample variances. These tables indicate that the distribution of F is actually a family of distributions that change quite drastically with changes in sample sizes. Thus, degrees of freedom must be specified. Inspection of an F-table allows the researcher to determine the probability of finding an F as large as a calculated F.

USING VARIANCE COMPONENTS TO COMPUTE *F*-RATIOS

In ANOVA, the basic consideration for the F-test is identifying the relative size of variance components. The three forms of variation described briefly above are:

1. SSE—variation of scores due to random error or within-group variance due to individual differences from the group mean. This is the error of prediction.
2. SSB—systematic variation of scores between groups due to manipulation of an experimental variable or group classifications of a measured independent variable or between-groups variance.
3. SST—the total observed variation across all groups and individual observations.

Thus, we can partition **total variability** into *within-group variance* (SSE) and *between-groups variance* (SSB).

total variability
The sum of within-group variance and between-groups variance.

The F-distribution is a function of the ratio of these two sources of variances:

$$F = f\left(\frac{SSB}{SSE}\right)$$

A larger ratio of variance between groups to variance within groups implies a greater value of F. If the F-value is large, the results are likely to be statistically significant.

A DIFFERENT BUT EQUIVALENT REPRESENTATION

F also can be thought of as a function of the between-groups variance and total variance.

$$F = f\left(\frac{SSB}{SST - SSB}\right)$$

In this sense, the ratio of the thick black line to the middle line representing the total range of data presents the basic idea of the F-value. Appendix 22A explains the calculations in more detail with an illustration.

Practically Speaking

Exhibit 22.6 displays the ANOVA result for the coffee-drinking example. Again, one advantage of living in modern times is that even a simple problem like this one need not be hand computed. Even though this example presents a small problem, one-way ANOVA models with more observations or levels would be interpreted similarly.

The first thing to check is whether or not the overall model F is significant. In this case, the computed $F = 4.40$ with 2 and 11 degrees of freedom. The p-value associated with this value is 0.039. Thus, we have high confidence in concluding that the group means are not all the same. Second, the researcher must remember to examine the actual means for each group to properly interpret the result. Doing so, the conclusion reached is that the night-shift people drink the most coffee, followed by the second-shift workers, and then lastly, the day-shift workers.

As there are three groups, we may wish to know whether or not group 1 is significantly different than group 3 or group 2, and so on. In a later chapter, we will describe ways of examining specifically which group means are different from one another.

TIPS OF THE TRADE

- The key to being an effective business research analyst is not simply learning the analytical tools, but developing the ability to determine what analytical approach is most appropriate for the circumstances and data. In other words, not only do we need a full box of tools, but we also need to understand when and how to use each tool:
- When we want to examine relationships with two categorical variables (less-than interval level), cross-tabulations are most often appropriate. The bivariate χ^2 test examines statistical significance of the relationships (distributions) between these variables.
- When we have two categories of respondents (for example, gender of the respondent) and want to examine the differences on their attitudes, perceptions, or any other variable measured on an interval or ratio level, a *t*-test is appropriate. The *t*-test will show if there is a significant difference in mean scores between the two groups.
- When we have more than two categories of respondents (for example, five sales regions) and want to examine the differences on their attitudes, perceptions, or any other variable measured on an interval or ratio level, ANOVA is appropriate. ANOVA will show if there is a significant difference in mean scores among the groups.
- Each of these tests determines the statistical significance of the differences we observe in our sample. The test indicates if the results we see are unlikely to have occurred by chance. In other words, that the results are present in the population, not just in the sample, or that they would be repeated if the test was conducted again. For instance, we might test to see if the difference between a score of 4.55 for men and 4.67 for women is statistically significant. We know that 4.67 is higher than 4.55, but we do not know if it is likely we would observe women scoring higher than men if we collected another sample.

Summary

1. Recognize when a particular bivariate statistical test is appropriate. Bivariate statistical techniques analyze scores on two variables at a time. Tests of difference investigate hypotheses stating that two (or more) groups differ with respect to a certain behavior, characteristic, or attitude. Both the type of measurement and the number of groups to be compared influence researchers' choices of the type of statistical test. When both variables are less-than interval level, a contingency table and a χ^2 test are appropriate. When one variable is less-than interval with two levels and the other variable is interval or ratio level, a *t*-test is appropriate. When one variable is less-than interval with three or more levels and the other variable is interval or ratio level, ANOVA is the appropriate statistical technique.

2. Calculate and interpret a χ^2 test for a contingency table. A χ^2 test is used in conjunction with cross-classification or cross-tabs. Thus, when an independent variable is ordinal or nominal and a dependent variable is likewise ordinal or nominal, a χ^2 test can examine whether a relationship exists between the row variable and column variable. A χ^2 test is computed by examining the squared differences between observed cell counts and the expected value for each cell in a contingency table. Higher χ^2 values are generally associated with lower p-values, meaning a greater chance that the relationship between the row and column variable is statistically significant.

3. Calculate and interpret an independent samples *t*-test comparing two means. When a researcher needs to compare means for a variable grouped into two categories based on some less-than interval variable, a *t*-test is appropriate. An independent samples *t*-test examines whether a dependent variable like job satisfaction differs based on a grouping variable like biological sex. Statistically, the test examines whether the difference between the mean for men and women is different from 0. A paired-samples *t*-test examines whether or not the means from two variables that are not independent are different. A common situation calling for this test is when the two observations are from the same respondent. A simple before-and-after test calls for a paired-sample *t*-test so long as the dependent variable is continuous.

4. Understand the concept of analysis of variance (ANOVA). ANOVA is the appropriate statistical technique to examine the effect of a less-than interval independent variable with three or more categories on an at-least interval dependent variable. Conceptually, ANOVA partitions the total variability into three types: total variation, between-groups variation, and within-group variation. As the explained variance represented by SSB becomes larger relative to SSE or SST, the ANOVA model is more likely to be significant, indicating that at least one group mean is different from another group mean.

5. Interpret an ANOVA table. An ANOVA table provides essential information. Most importantly, the ANOVA table contains the model *F*-ratio. The researcher should examine this value along with the corresponding p-value. Generally, as *F* increases, p decreases, meaning that a statistically significant ANOVA model is more likely.

Key Terms and Concepts

analysis of variance (ANOVA), *576*
between-groups variance, *579*
F-test, *580*
grand mean, *579*
independent samples *t*-test, *569*
paired-samples *t*-test, *573*
pooled estimate of the standard error, *570*
test of differences, *565*
total variability, *581*
within-group error or variance, *580*
Z-test for differences of proportions, *575*

Questions for Review and Critical Thinking

1. What tests of difference are appropriate in the following situations?
   a. Average campaign contributions (in $) of Democrats and Republicans are to be compared.
   b. Average campaign contributions (in $) of Democrats, Republicans, and Independents are to be compared.
   c. Human resource managers and chief executive officers have responded "yes," "no," or "not sure" to an attitude question. The HR and CEO responses are to be compared.
   d. One-half of a sample received an incentive in a mail survey while the other half did not. A comparison of response rates is desired.
   e. A researcher believes that married men will push the grocery cart when grocery shopping with their wives. How would the hypothesis be tested?
   f. A manager wishes to compare the job performance of a salesperson before ethics training with the performance of that same salesperson after ethics training.
2. Perform a χ^2 test on the following data:
   a. Regulation is the best way to ensure safe products.

	Agree	Disagree	No Opinion
Managers	58	66	8
Line Employees	34	24	10
Totals	92	90	18

   b. Ownership of residence

	Yes	No
Male	25	20
Female	16	14

3. Interpret the following computer cross-tab output including a χ^2 test. Variable COMMUTE is "How did you get to work last week?" Variable GENDER is "Are you male or female?" Comment on any particular problems with the analysis.

COMMUTE * GENDER Cross-Tabulation

			GENDER		
			Female	Male	Total
COMMUTE	At Home	Count	6	10	16
		% within COMMUTE	37.5%	62.5%	100.0%
		% within GENDER	7.0%	17.9%	11.3%
		% of Total	4.2%	7.0%	11.3%
	Bus	Count	16	16	32
		% within COMMUTE	50.0%	50.0%	100.0%
		% within GENDER	18.6%	28.6%	22.5%
		% of Total	11.3%	11.3%	22.5%
	Drive	Count	32	17	49
		% within COMMUTE	65.3%	34.7%	100.0%
		% within GENDER	37.2%	30.4%	34.5%
		% of Total	22.5%	12.0%	34.5%

(continued)

COMMUTE * GENDER Cross-Tabulation *(continued)*

		GENDER		
		Female	**Male**	**Total**
Passenger	Count	24	9	33
	% within COMMUTE	72.7%	27.3%	100.0%
	% within GENDER	27.9%	16.1%	23.2%
	% of Total	16.9%	6.3%	23.3%
Walk	Count	8	4	12
	% within COMMUTE	66.7%	33.3%	100.0%
	% within GENDER	9.3%	7.1%	8.5%
	% of Total	5.6%	2.8%	8.5%
Total	Count	86	56	142
	% within COMMUTE	60.6%	39.4%	100.0%
	% within GENDER	100.0%	100.0%	100.0%
	% of Total	60.6%	39.4%	100.0%

χ^2 Tests

	Value	*df*	Asymp. Sig. (two-sided)
Pearson Chi-Square	7.751[a]	4	0.101
Likelihood Ratio	7.725	4	0.102
N of Valid Cases	142		

[a]1 cells (10.0%) have expected count less than 5. The minimum expected count is 4.73.

4. A store manager's computer-generated list of all retail sales employees indicates that 70 percent are full-time employees, 20 percent are part-time employees, and 10 percent are furloughed or laid-off employees. A sample of 50 employees from the list indicates that there are 40 full-time employees, 6 part-time employees, and 4 furloughed/laid-off employees. Conduct a statistical test to determine whether the sample is representative of the population.
5. Test the following hypothesis using the data summarized in the table below. Interpret your result:

H1: Internet retailers offer lower prices for Blu-ray players than do traditional in-store retailers.

Blu-ray Player

Retail Type	Average Price	Standard Deviation	*n*
E-Tailers	$371.95	$50.00	25
Multi-Channel Retailers	$360.30	$45.00	25

6. How does an independent sample *t*-test differ from the following?
   a. one-way ANOVA
   b. paired-samples *t*-test
   c. a χ^2 test
   d. a *Z*-test for differences
7. Are *t*-tests or *Z*-tests used more often in business research? Why?
8. A sales force received some management-by-objectives training. Are the before/after mean scores for salespeople's job performance statistically significant at the 0.05 level? The results from a sample of employees are as follows (use your computer and statistical software to solve this problem):

Name	Skill Before	Skill After	Name	Skill Before	Skill After
Ed	4.84	5.43	Kathy	4.00	5.00
Mark	5.24	5.51	Susie	4.67	4.50
Jason	5.37	5.42	Ron	4.95	4.40
Raj	3.69	4.50	Jen	4.00	5.95
Heidi	5.95	5.90	Matt	3.75	3.50
Donna	4.75	5.25	Doug	3.85	4.00
Rob	3.90	4.50	Bob	5.00	4.10

10. Conduct a *Z*-test to determine whether the following two samples indicate that the population proportions are significantly different at the 0.05 level:

	Sample 1	Sample 2
Sample Proportion	0.77	0.68
Sample Size	55	46

11. In an experiment with wholesalers, a researcher manipulated perception of task difficulty and measured level of aspiration for performing the task a second time. Group 1 was told the task was very difficult, group 2 was told the task was somewhat difficult but attainable, and group 3 was told the task was easy. Perform an ANOVA on the resulting data:

Level of Aspiration (10-Point Scale)

Subjects	Group 1	Group 2	Group 3
1	6	5	5
2	7	4	6
3	5	7	5
4	8	6	4
5	8	7	2
6	6	7	3
Cases	6	6	6

12. Interpret the following output examining group differences for purchase intentions. The three groups refer to consumers from three states: Illinois, Louisiana, and Texas.

Tests of Between-Subjects Effects

Dependent Variable: int2

Source	Type III Sum of Squares	*df*	Mean Square	*F*	Sig.
Corrected Model	6681.746[a]	2	3340.873	3.227	0.043
Intercept	308897.012	1	308897.012	298.323	0.000
State	6681.746	2	3340.873	3.227	0.043
Error	148068.543	143	1035.444		
Total	459697.250	146			
Corrected Total	154750.289	145			

[a]R Squared = 0.043 (Adjusted R Squared = 0.030)

Law

Dependent Variable: int2

			95% Confidence Interval	
State	**Mean**	**Std. Error**	**Lower Bound**	**Upper Bound**
IL	37.018	4.339	28.441	45.595
LA	50.357	4.965	40.542	60.172
TX	51.459	4.597	42.373	60.546

Research Activities

1. **ETHICS/'NET** How ethical is it to do business in different countries around the world? An international organization, Transparency International, keeps track of the perception of ethical practices in different countries and computes the corruption perceptions index (CPI). Visit the Web site and search for the latest CPI (**http://www.transparency.org/policy_research/surveys_indices/cpi/2008**). Using the data found here, test the following research questions.
   a. Are nations from Europe and North America perceived to be more ethical than nations from Asia, Africa, and South America?
   b. Are there differences among the corruption indices in the past 5 years (between 2003 and 2008)?
2. **'NET** The Federal Reserve Bank of St. Louis maintains a database called FRED (Federal Reserve Economic Data). Navigate to the FRED database at **http://research.stlouisfed.org/fred**. Randomly select a five-year period between 1970 and 2008 and then compare average figures for U.S. employment in retail trade with those for U.S. employment in wholesale trade. What statistical tests are appropriate?

Case 22.1 Old School versus New School Sports Fans

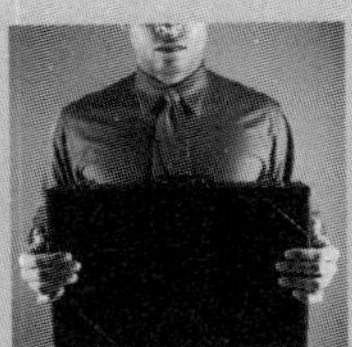

© GETTY IMAGES/ PHOTODISC GREEN

Three academic researchers investigated the idea that, in American sports, there are two segments with opposing views about the goal of competition (i.e., winning versus self-actualization) and the acceptable/desirable way of achieving this goal.[7] Persons who believe in "winning at any cost" are proponents of sports success as a product and can be labeled new school (NS) individuals. The new school is founded on notions of the player before the team, loyalty to the highest bidder, and high-tech production and consumption of professional sports. On the other hand, persons who value the process of sports and believe that "how you play the game matters" can be labeled old school (OS) individuals. The old school emerges from old-fashioned American notions of the team before the player, sportsmanship, and loyalty above all else, and competition simply for "love of the game."

New School/Old School was measured by asking agreement with ten attitude statements. The scores on these statements were combined. Higher scores represent an orientation toward old school values. For purposes of this case study, individuals who did not answer every question were eliminated from the analysis. Based on their summated scores across the ten items, respondents were grouped into low score, middle score, and high score groups. Case Exhibit 22.1–1 shows the SPSS computer output of a cross-tabulation to relate the gender of the respondent (GENDER) with the New School/Old School grouping (OLDSKOOL).

CASE EXHIBIT 22.1–1 **SPSS Output**

OLDSKOOL * GENDER Cross-Tabulation

			GENDER		
			Women	Men	Total
OLDSKOOL	high	Count	9	17	26
		% within OLDSKOOL	34.6%	65.4%	100.0%
		% within GENDER	10.6%	9.2%	9.6%
		% of Total	3.3%	6.3%	9.6%
	low	Count	45	70	115
		% within OLDSKOOL	39.1%	60.9%	100.0%
		% within GENDER	52.9%	37.8%	42.6%
		% of Total	16.7%	25.9%	42.6%
	middle	Count	31	98	129
		% within OLDSKOOL	24.0%	76.0%	100.0%
		% within GENDER	36.5%	53.0%	47.8%
		% of Total	11.5%	36.3%	47.8%
Total		Count	85	185	270
		% within OLDSKOOL	31.5%	68.5%	100.0%
		% within GENDER	100.0%	100.0%	100.0%
		% of Total	31.5%	68.5%	100.0%

Chi-Square Tests

	Value	*df*	Asymp. Sig. (2-sided)
Pearson Chi-Square	6.557[a]	2	.038
Likelihood Ratio	6.608	2	.037
N of Valid Cases	270		

[a]0 cells (.0%) have expected count less than 5. The minimum expected count is 8.19.

Questions

1. Interpret the computer output. What do the results presented above indicate?
2. Is the analytical approach used here appropriate?
3. Describe an alternative approach to the analysis of the original data. Which of these two analyses would you suggest using?

APPENDIX 22A
MANUAL CALCULATION OF AN *F*-STATISTIC

Manual calculations are almost unheard of these days. However, understanding the calculations can be very useful in gaining a thorough understanding of ANOVA. The data in Exhibit 22A.1 are from a hypothetical packaged-goods company's test-market experiment on pricing. Three pricing treatments were administered in four separate areas (12 test areas, A–L, were required). These data will be used to illustrate ANOVA.

Terminology for the variance estimates is derived from the calculation procedures, so an explanation of the terms used to calculate the *F*-ratio should clarify the meaning of the analysis of variance technique. The calculation of the *F*-ratio requires that we partition the total variation into two parts:

$$\underset{(SST)}{\text{Total sum of squares}} = \underset{(SSE)}{\text{Within-group sum of squares}} + \underset{(SSB)}{\text{Between-groups sum of squares}}$$

or

$$SST = SSE + SSB$$

SST is computed by squaring the deviation of each score from the grand mean and summing these squares:

$$SST = \sum_{i=1}^{n}\sum_{j=1}^{c}(X_{ij} - \overline{\overline{X}})^2$$

where

X = individual score—that is, the *i*th observation or test unit in the *j*th group

$\overline{\overline{X}}$ = grand mean

n = number of all observations or test units in a group

c = number of *j*th groups (or columns)

In our example,

$$\begin{aligned} SST = {} & (130 - 119.58)^2 + (118 - 119.58)^2 + (87 - 119.58)^2 \\ & + (84 - 119.58)^2 + (145 - 119.58)^2 + (143 - 119.58)^2 \\ & + (120 - 119.58)^2 + (131 - 119.58)^2 + (153 - 119.58)^2 \\ & + (129 - 119.58)^2 + (96 - 119.58)^2 + (99 - 119.58)^2 \\ = {} & 5{,}948.93 \end{aligned}$$

EXHIBIT 22A.1
A Test-Market Experiment on Pricing

	Sales in Units (thousands)		
	Regular Price, $.99	Reduced Price, $.89	Cents-Off Coupon, Regular Price
Test-Market A, B, or C	130	145	153
Test-Market D, E, or F	118	143	129
Test-Market G, H, or I	87	120	96
Test-Market J, K, or L	84	131	99
Mean	$\overline{X}_1 = 104.75$	$\overline{X}_2 = 134.75$	$\overline{X}_3 = 119.25$
Grand Mean	$\overline{\overline{X}} = 119.58$		

SSE, the variability that we observe within each group, or the error remaining after using the groups to predict observations, is calculated by squaring the deviation of each score from its group mean and summing these scores:

$$SSE = \sum_{i=1}^{n}\sum_{j=1}^{c}(X_{ij} - \overline{X}_j)^2$$

where

X = individual score

$\overline{X}_j$ = group mean for the *j*th group

n = number of observations in a group

c = number of *j*th groups

In our example,

$$\begin{aligned} SSE = {} & (130 - 104.75)^2 + (118 - 104.75)^2 + (87 - 104.75)^2 \\ & + (84 - 104.75)^2 + (145 - 134.75)^2 + (143 - 134.75)^2 \\ & + (120 - 134.75)^2 + (131 - 134.75)^2 + (153 - 119.25)^2 \\ & + (129 - 119.25)^2 + (96 - 119.25)^2 + (99 - 119.25)^2 \\ = {} & 4{,}148.25 \end{aligned}$$

SSB, the variability of the group means about a grand mean, is calculated by squaring the deviation of each group mean from the grand mean, multiplying by the number of items in the group, and summing these scores:

$$SSB = \sum_{j=1}^{c} n_j(\overline{X}_j - \overline{\overline{X}})^2$$

where

$\overline{X}_j$ = group mean for the *j*th group

$\overline{\overline{X}}$ = grand mean

n_j = number of items in the *j*th group

In our example,

$$\begin{aligned} SSB = {} & 4(104.75 - 119.58)^2 + 4(134.75 - 119.58)^2 \\ & + 4(119.25 - 119.58)^2 \\ = {} & 1{,}800.68 \end{aligned}$$

The next calculation requires dividing the various sums of squares by their appropriate degrees of freedom. These divisions produce the variances, or *mean squares*. To obtain the mean square between groups, we divide *SSB* by $c - 1$ degrees of freedom:

$$MSB = \frac{SSB}{c - 1}$$

In our example,

$$MSB = \frac{1{,}800.68}{3 - 1} = \frac{1{,}800.68}{2} = 900.34$$

To obtain the mean square within groups, we divide *SSE* by $cn - c$ degrees of freedom:

$$MSE = \frac{SSE}{cn - c}$$

In our example,

$$MSE = \frac{4{,}148.25}{12 - 3} = \frac{4{,}148.25}{9} = 460.91$$

Finally, the *F*-ratio is calculated by taking the ratio of the mean square between groups to the mean square within groups. The between-groups mean square is the numerator and the within-groups mean square is the denominator:

$$F = \frac{MSB}{MSE}$$

In our example,

$$F = \frac{900.34}{460.91} = 1.95$$

There will be $c - 1$ degrees of freedom in the numerator and $cn - c$ degrees of freedom in the denominator:

$$\frac{c-1}{cn-c} = \frac{3-1}{3(4)-3} = \frac{2}{9}$$

In Table A.5 in the text appendix, the critical value of F at the 0.05 level for 2 and 9 degrees of freedom indicates that an F of 4.26 would be required to reject the null hypothesis.

In our example, we conclude that we cannot reject the null hypothesis. It appears that all the price treatments produce approximately the same sales volume.

The information produced from an analysis of variance is traditionally summarized in table form. Exhibits 22A.2 and 22A.3 summarize the formulas and data from our example.

EXHIBIT 22A.2
ANOVA Summary Table

Source of Variation	Sum of Squares	Degrees of Freedom	Mean Square	F-Ratio
Between groups	$SSB = \sum_{j=1}^{c} n_j(\bar{X}_j - \bar{\bar{X}})^2$	$c - 1$	$MSB = \frac{SSB}{c-1}$	—
Within groups	$SSE = \sum_{i=1}^{n}\sum_{j=1}^{c}(X_{ij} - \bar{X}_j)^2$	$cn - c$	$MSE = \frac{SSE}{cn-c}$	$F = \frac{MSB}{MSE}$
Total	$SST = \sum_{i=1}^{n}\sum_{j=1}^{c}(X_{ij} - \bar{\bar{X}})^2$	$cn - 1$	—	—

where c = number of groups
n = number of observations in a group

EXHIBIT 22A.3
Pricing Experiment ANOVA Table

Source of Variation	Sum of Squares	Degrees of Freedom	Mean Square	F-Ratio
Between groups	1,800.68	2	900.34	—
Within groups	4,148.25	9	460.91	1.953
Total	5,948.93	11	—	—

APPENDIX 22B ANOVA FOR COMPLEX EXPERIMENTAL DESIGNS

To test for statistical significance in a randomized block design, or RBD (see Chapter 12), another version of analysis of variance is utilized. The linear model for the RBD for an individual observation is*

$$Y_{ij} = \mu + \alpha_j + \beta_i + \varepsilon_{ij}$$

where

Y_{ij} = individual observation on the dependent variable

μ = grand mean

α_j = jth treatment effect

β_i = ith block effect

ε_{ij} = random error or residual

The statistical objective is to determine whether significant differences exist among treatment means and block means. This is done by calculating an F-ratio for each source of effects.

The same logic that applies in single-factor ANOVA—using variance estimates to test for differences among means—applies in ANOVA for randomized block designs. Thus, to conduct the ANOVA, we partition the total sum of squares (SS_{total}) into non-overlapping components.

$$SS_{total} = SS_{treatments} + SS_{blocks} + SS_{error}$$

The sources of variance are defined as follows.

Total sum of squares:

$$SS_{total} = \sum_{i=1}^{r}\sum_{j=1}^{c}(Y_{ij} - \bar{\bar{Y}})^2$$

where

Y_{ij} = individual observation

$\bar{\bar{Y}}$ = grand mean

r = number of blocks (rows)

c = number of treatments (columns)

Treatment sum of squares:

$$SS_{treatments} = \sum_{i=1}^{r}\sum_{j=1}^{c}(\bar{Y}_j - \bar{\bar{Y}})^2$$

where

$\bar{Y}_j$ = jth treatment mean

$\bar{\bar{Y}}$ = grand mean

Block sum of squares:

$$SS_{blocks} = \sum_{i=1}^{r}\sum_{j=1}^{c}(\bar{Y}_i - \bar{\bar{Y}})^2$$

where

$\bar{Y}_i$ = ith block mean

$\bar{\bar{Y}}$ = grand mean

Sum of squares error:

$$SS_{error} = \sum_{i=1}^{r}\sum_{j=1}^{c}(Y_{ij} - \bar{Y}_i - \bar{Y}_j - \bar{\bar{Y}})^2$$

*We assume no interaction effect between treatments and blocks.

The SS_{error} may also be calculated in the following manner:

$$SS_{error} = SS_{total} - SS_{treatments} - SS_{blocks}$$

The degrees of freedom for $SS_{treatments}$ are equal to $c - 1$ because $SS_{treatments}$ reflects the dispersion of treatment means from the grand mean, which is fixed. Degrees of freedom for blocks are $r - 1$ for similar reasons. SS_{error} reflects variations from both treatment and block means. Thus, $df = (r - 1)(c - 1)$.

Mean squares are calculated by dividing the appropriate sum of squares by the corresponding degrees of freedom.

Exhibit 22B.1 is an ANOVA table for the randomized block design. It summarizes what has been discussed and illustrates the calculation of mean squares.

EXHIBIT 22B.1
ANOVA Table for Randomized Block Designs

Source of Variation	Sum of Squares	Degrees of Freedom	Mean Squares
Between blocks	SS_{blocks}	$r - 1$	$\frac{SS_{blocks}}{r - 1}$
Between treatments	$SS_{treatments}$	$c - 1$	$\frac{SS_{treatments}}{c - 1}$
Error	SS_{error}	$(r - 1)(c - 1)$	$\frac{SS_{error}}{(r - 1)(c - 1)}$
Total	SS_{total}	$rc - 1$	—

F-ratios for treatment and block effects are calculated as follows:

$$F_{treatment} = \frac{\text{Mean square treatment}}{\text{Mean square error}}$$

$$F_{blocks} = \frac{\text{Mean square blocks}}{\text{Mean square error}}$$

Factorial Designs

There is considerable similarity between the factorial design (see Chapter 12) and the one-way analysis of variance. The sum of squares for each of the treatment factors (rows and columns) is similar to the between-groups sum of squares in the single-factor ANOVA model. Each treatment sum of squares is calculated by taking the deviation of the treatment means from the grand mean. Determining the sum of squares for the interaction is a new calculation because this source of variance is not attributable to the treatment sum of squares or the error sum of squares.

ANOVA for a Factorial Experiment

In a two-factor experimental design the linear model for an individual observation is

$$Y_{ijk} = \mu + \beta_i + \alpha_j + I_{ij} + \varepsilon_{ijk}$$

where

Y_{ijk} = individual observation on the dependent variable

μ = grand mean

β_i = ith effect of factor B—row treatment

α_j = jth effect of factor A—column treatment

I_{ij} = interaction effect of factors A and B

ε_{ijk} = random error or residual

Partitioning the Sum of Squares for a Two-Way ANOVA

Again, the total sum of squares can be allocated into distinct and overlapping portions:

Sum of squares total	=	Sum of squares rows (treatment B)	+	Sum of squares columns (treatment A)	+	Sum of squares interaction	+	Sum of squares error

or

$$SS_{\text{total}} = SSR_{\text{treatment B}} + SSC_{\text{treatment A}} + SS_{\text{interaction}} + SS_{\text{error}}$$

Sum of squares total:

$$SS_{\text{total}} = \sum_{i=1}^{r}\sum_{j=1}^{c}\sum_{k=1}^{n}(Y_{ijk} - \bar{\bar{Y}})^2$$

where

Y_{ijk} = individual observation on the dependent variable

$\bar{\bar{Y}}$ = grand mean

j = level of factor A

i = level of factor B

k = number of an observation in a particular cell

r = total number of levels of factor B (rows)

c = total number of levels of factor A (columns)

n = total number of observations in the sample

Sum of squares rows (treatment B):

$$SSR_{\text{treatment B}} = \sum_{i=1}^{r}(\bar{Y}_i - \bar{\bar{Y}})^2$$

where

$\bar{Y}_j$ = mean of *i*th treatment—factor B

Sum of squares columns (treatment A):

$$SSC_{\text{treatment A}} = \sum_{j=1}^{c}(\bar{Y}_j - \bar{\bar{Y}})^2$$

where

$\bar{Y}_j$ = mean of *j*th treatment—factor A

Sum of squares interaction:

$$SS_{\text{interaction}} = \sum_{i=1}^{r}\sum_{j=1}^{c}\sum_{k=1}^{n}(Y_{ij} - \bar{Y}_i - \bar{Y}_j - \bar{\bar{Y}})^2$$

The above is one form of calculation. However, $SS_{\text{interaction}}$ generally is indirectly computed in the following manner:

$$SS_{\text{interaction}} = SS_{\text{total}} - SSR_{\text{treatment B}} - SSC_{\text{treatment A}} - SS_{\text{error}}$$

Sum of squares error:

$$SS_{\text{error}} = \sum_{i=1}^{r}\sum_{j=1}^{c}\sum_{k=1}^{n}(Y_{ijk} - \bar{Y}_{ij})^2$$

where

$\bar{Y}_{ij}$ = mean of the interaction effect

These sums of squares, along with their respective degrees of freedom and mean squares, are summarized in Exhibit 22B.2.

EXHIBIT 22B.2
ANOVA Table for Two-Factor Design

Source of Variation	Sum of Squares	Degrees of Freedom	Mean Square	F-Ratio
Treatment B	$SSR_{\text{treatment B}}$	$r - 1$	$MSR_{\text{treatment B}} = \frac{SSR_{\text{treatment B}}}{r-1}$	$\frac{MSR_{\text{treatment B}}}{MS_{\text{error}}}$
Treatment A	$SSC_{\text{treatment A}}$	$c - 1$	$MSC_{\text{treatment A}} = \frac{SSC_{\text{treatment A}}}{c-1}$	$\frac{MSC_{\text{treatment A}}}{MS_{\text{error}}}$
Interaction	$SS_{\text{interaction}}$	$(r - 1)(c - 1)$	$MS_{\text{interaction}} = \frac{SS_{\text{interaction}}}{(r-1)(c-1)}$	$\frac{MS_{\text{interaction}}}{MS_{\text{error}}}$
Error	SS_{error}	$rc(n - 1)$	$MS_{\text{error}} = \frac{SS_{\text{error}}}{rc(n-1)}$	
Total	SS_{total}	$rcn - 1$		

CHAPTER 23
BIVARIATE STATISTICAL ANALYSIS: MEASURES OF ASSOCIATION

LEARNING OUTCOMES

After studying this chapter, you should be able to

1. Apply and interpret simple bivariate correlations
2. Interpret a correlation matrix
3. Understand simple (bivariate) regression
4. Understand the least-squares estimation technique
5. Interpret regression output including the tests of hypotheses tied to specific parameter coefficients

Chapter Vignette: Bringing Your Work to Your Home (and Bringing Your Home to Work)

Do you "bring work home?" Do your family experiences and demands affect your work responsibilities? When you think about the stress you may have faced in a particular work situation, it is easy to see how this may, in fact, be the case.

For many years, there was a belief that employees universally separated their work roles from their home/family roles. This belief generally centered on the idea that "what happens at home" doesn't matter in the workplace. As an employee, you were simply there to perform your job, and your family was not part of those responsibilities. Likewise, the responsibilities you have with your family were not affected by work—you left those challenges and stresses "at work." Our understanding of the work and family interface has changed substantially in recent years.

The idea that work roles and family roles could be at odds with one another is nowadays referred to as work-family conflict (WFC).[1] It is typically defined as conflict that results when the demands and responsibilities of one role "spill over" into the other role. For example, it is easy to see how a manager, simultaneously facing a project deadline and a family reunion in the same week, may allow some of his or her frustrations and stress to affect one (or both) of these work and family roles.

There are numerous ways that WFC can be created for an employee. Work demands can include inflexible schedules, project timelines, and even an abusive supervisor. With regard to family demands, any number of family demands can "spill over" into the work role, to include child or elder care and dual career relationships.[2]

Researchers have begun to examine and explore the many different work and family characteristics (i.e., *independent variables*) that can predict WFC (*a dependent variable*), with the goal of providing insights into the causes and consequences of this phenomenon.[3] Think about your own work and family responsibilities. What would be some of the demands on you that lead to WFC? How have these demands affected your job satisfaction and/or family harmony? It is not hard to see that "bringing home work" is a common problem we face in today's society.

Introduction

When business researchers develop and implement a research survey, it is often conducted with several goals in mind. Most important, however, is the goal of answering a particular research question, using survey or other data to justify the result. Finding the "answer" is critically important in this regard. This chapter is designed to familiarize you with how business statistics are used to help accomplish this task.

The Basics

Business research can involve many different professional disciplines. For management, the questions regarding conflict, satisfaction, and employee turnover are often key dependent variables of interest. As the chapter vignette outlines, this question can be a complex one, with many different work and family independent variables affecting work-family conflict. In marketing, sales volume is often *the* dependent variable managers want to predict. Independent variables include marketing-mix elements such as price, number of salespeople, and the amount of advertising related to sales volume. Uncontrollable variables including population, economic conditions, and competitive intensity also affect sales. Most managers would not be surprised to find that sales of baby strollers are associated with the number of babies born in each sales period. In this case the dependent variable is the sales volume of baby strollers, and the independent variable is the number of babies born. The mathematical symbol *X* is commonly used for an independent variable, and *Y* typically denotes a dependent variable.

The chi-square (χ^2) test provides information about whether two or more less-than interval variables are interrelated. For example, a χ^2 test between a measure of package color and product choice provides information about the independence or interrelationship of the two variables. Over the years, psychological statisticians have developed several other techniques that demonstrate empirical association.

Exhibit 23.1 shows that measurement characteristics influence which **measure of association** is most appropriate. This chapter describes simple correlation (Pearson's product-moment correlation coefficient, *r*) and bivariate or simple regression analysis. Correlation analysis is most appropriate for interval or ratio variables. Regression can accommodate either less-than interval independent variables, but the dependent variable must be continuous. Other techniques mentioned are for advanced students who have specific needs.[4]

measure of association
A general term that refers to a number of bivariate statistical techniques used to measure the strength of a relationship between two variables.

Simple Correlation Coefficient

The most popular technique for indicating the relationship of one variable to another is correlation. A **correlation coefficient** is a statistical measure of covariation, or association between two variables. **Covariance** is the extent to which a change in one variable corresponds systematically to a change in another. Correlation can be thought of as a standardized covariance.

correlation coefficient
A statistical measure of the covariation, or association, between two at-least interval variables.

covariance
The extent to which two variables are associated systematically with each other.

When correlations estimate relationships between continuous variables, the Pearson product-moment correlation is appropriate. The correlation coefficient, *r*, ranges from −1.0 to +1.0. If the value of *r* equals +1.0, a perfect positive relationship exists. Perhaps the two variables are one and the same! If the value of *r* equals −1.0, a perfect negative relationship exists. The implication is that one variable is a mirror image of the other. As one goes up, the other goes down in proportion and vice versa. No correlation is indicated if *r* equals 0. A correlation coefficient indicates both the magnitude of the linear relationship and the direction of that relationship. For example, if we find that $r = -0.92$, we know we have a very strong inverse relationship—that is, the greater the value measured by variable *X*, the lower the value measured by variable *Y*.

EXHIBIT 23.1
Bivariate Analysis—Common Procedures for Testing Association

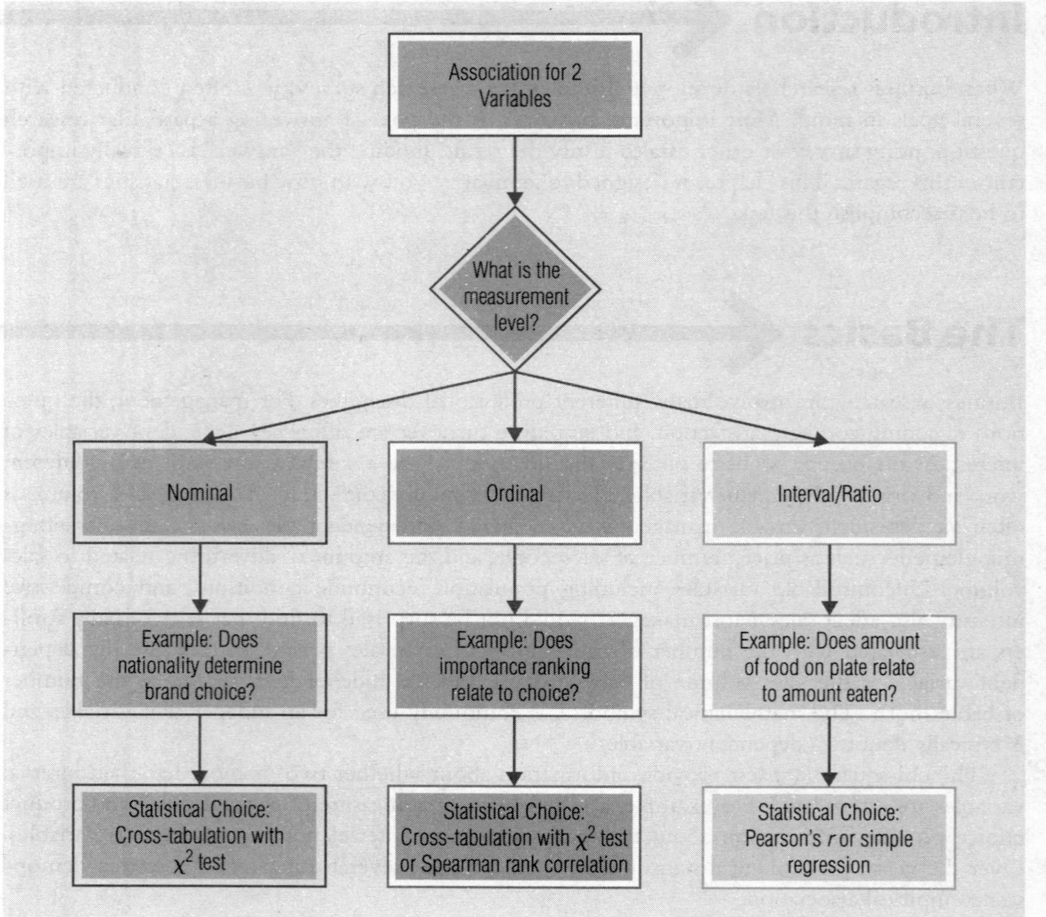

The formula for calculating the correlation coefficient for two variables X and Y is as follows:

$$r_{xy} = r_{yx} = \frac{\sum_{i=1}^{n}(X_i - \overline{X})(Y_i - \overline{Y})}{\sqrt{\sum_{i=1}^{n}(X_i - \overline{X})^2 \sum_{i=1}^{n}(Y_i - \overline{Y})^2}}$$

where the symbols $\overline{X}$ and $\overline{Y}$ represent the sample averages of X and Y, respectively. An alternative way to express the correlation formula is

$$r_{xy} = r_{yx} = \frac{\sigma_{xy}}{\sqrt{\sigma_x^2\ \sigma_y^2}}$$

where

σ_x^2 = variance of X

σ_y^2 = variance of Y

σ_{xy} = covariance of X and Y

with

$$\sigma_{xy} = \frac{\sum_{i=1}^{n}(X_i - \overline{X})(Y_i - \overline{Y})}{n}$$

If associated values of X_i and Y_i differ from their means in the same direction, their covariance will be positive. If the values of X_i and Y_i tend to deviate in opposite directions, their covariance will be negative.

The Pearson correlation coefficient is a standardized measure of covariance. Covariance coefficients retain information about the absolute scale ranges so that the strength of association for scales of different possible values cannot be compared directly. Researchers find the correlation coefficient useful because they can compare two correlations without regard for the amount of variance exhibited by each variable separately.

Exhibit 23.2 illustrates the correlation coefficients and scatter diagrams for several sets of data. Notice that in the no-correlation condition, the observations are scattered rather evenly about the space. In contrast, when correlations are strong and positive, the observations lie mostly in quadrants II and IV formed by inserting new axes though $\overline{X}$ and $\overline{Y}$. If correlation was strong and negative, the observations would lie mostly in quadrants I and III.

An Example

The correlation coefficient can be illustrated with a simple example. Today, researchers do not need to calculate correlation manually. However, the calculation process helps illustrate exactly what is meant by correlation and covariance. Consider an investigation made to determine whether the average number of hours worked in manufacturing industries is related to unemployment. A correlation analysis of the data is carried out in Exhibit 23.3.

The correlation between the two variables is –0.635, indicating an **inverse (negative) relationship.** When number of hours goes up, unemployment comes down. This makes intuitive sense. If factories are increasing output, regular workers will typically work more overtime and new employees will be hired (reducing the unemployment rate). Both variables are probably related to overall economic conditions.

inverse (negative) relationship

Covariation in which the association between variables is in opposing directions. As one goes up, the other goes down.

Correlation, Covariance, and Causation

Recall that concomitant variation is one condition needed to establish a causal relationship between two variables. When two variables covary, they display concomitant variation. This systematic covariation does not in and of itself establish causality. Remember that the relationship would also need to be nonspurious and that any hypothesized "cause" would have to occur before any subsequent effect. Work experience displays a significant correlation with job performance.[5] However, in a retail context, workers with more experience often get assigned to newer stores. Thus, the researcher would need to sort out to what extent age of the store may also be responsible for *causing* store performance.

TOTHEPOINT

Statistics are like a bikini. What they reveal is suggestive, but what they conceal is vital.

—Aaron Levenstein

Coefficient of Determination

If we wish to know the proportion of *variance* in Y that is explained by X (or vice versa), we can calculate the **coefficient of determination (R^2)** by squaring the correlation coefficient:

$$R^2 = \frac{\text{Explained variance}}{\text{Total variance}}$$

The coefficient of determination, R^2, measures that part of the total variance of Y that is accounted for by knowing the value of X. In the example about unemployment and hours worked, $r = -0.635$; therefore, $R^2 = 0.403$. About 40 percent of the variance in unemployment can be explained by the variance in hours worked, and vice versa. As can be seen, R-*squared* really is just r squared!

coefficient of determination (R^2)

A measure obtained by squaring the correlation coefficient; the proportion of the total variance of a variable accounted for by another value of another variable.

EXHIBIT 23.2
Scatter Diagram to Illustrate Correlation Patterns

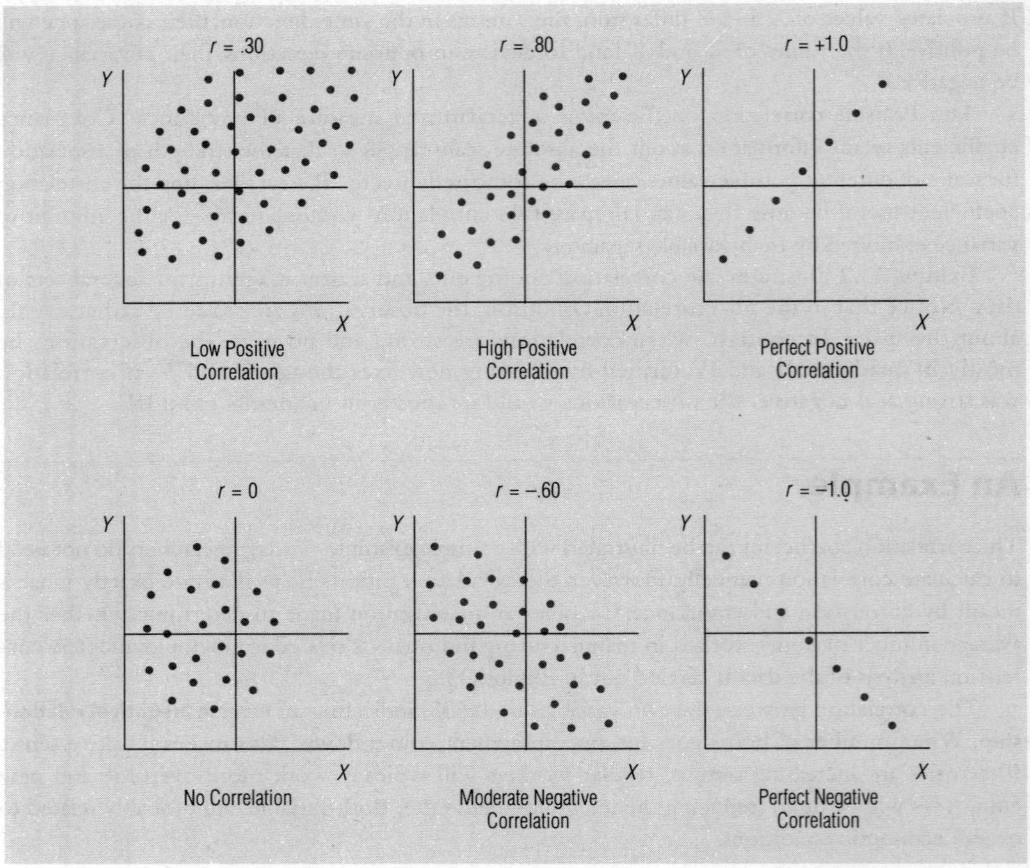

Correlation Matrix

correlation matrix
The standard form for reporting correlation coefficients for more than two variables.

A **correlation matrix** is the standard form for reporting observed correlations among multiple variables. Although any number of variables can be displayed in a correlation matrix, each entry represents the bivariate relationship between a pair of variables. Exhibit 23.4 shows a correlation matrix that relates some measures of salesperson job performance to characteristics of the sales force.[6]

Note that the main diagonal consists of correlations of 1.00. Why is this? Simply put, any variable is correlated with itself perfectly. Had this been a covariance matrix, the diagonal would display the variance for any given variable.

Performance (S) was measured by identifying the salesperson's actual annual sales volume in dollars. Notice that the performance variable has a 0.45 correlation with the workload variable (WL), which was measured by recording the number of accounts in a sales territory. Notice also that the salesperson's perception of job-related tension (JT) as measured by an attitude scale has a –0.48 correlation with performance (S). Thus, when perceived job tension is high, performance is low.

Researchers are also concerned with statistical significance. The procedure for determining statistical significance is the *t*-test of the significance of a correlation coefficient. Typically it is hypothesized that $r = 0$, and then a *t*-test is performed. The logic behind the test is similar to that for the significance tests already considered. Statistical programs usually indicate the p-value associated with each correlation and/or star significant correlations using asterisks. The Research Snapshot "What Makes Attractiveness?" displays the way correlation matrices are often reported.

EXHIBIT 23.3 **Correlation Analysis of Number of Hours Worked in Manufacturing Industries with Unemployment Rate**

Unemployment Rate (X_i)	Number of Hours Worked (Y_i)	$X_i - \bar{X}$	$(X_i - \bar{X})^2$	$Y_i - \bar{Y}$	$(Y_i - \bar{Y})^2$	$(X_i - \bar{X})(Y_i - \bar{Y})$
5.5	39.6	.51	.2601	−.71	.5041	−.3621
4.4	40.7	−.59	.3481	.39	.1521	−.2301
4.1	40.4	−.89	.7921	.09	.0081	−.0801
4.3	39.8	−.69	.4761	−.51	.2601	.3519
6.8	39.2	1.81	3.2761	−1.11	1.2321	−2.0091
5.5	40.3	.51	.2601	−.01	.0001	−.0051
5.5	39.7	.51	.2601	−.61	.3721	−.3111
6.7	39.8	1.71	2.9241	−.51	.2601	−.8721
5.5	40.4	.51	.2601	.09	.0081	.0459
5.7	40.5	.71	.5041	.19	.0361	.1349
5.2	40.7	.21	.0441	.39	.1521	.0819
4.5	41.2	−.49	.2401	.89	.7921	−.4361
3.8	41.3	−1.19	1.4161	.99	.9801	−1.1781
3.8	40.6	−1.19	1.4161	.29	.0841	−.3451
3.6	40.7	−1.39	1.9321	.39	.1521	−.5421
3.5	40.6	−1.49	2.2201	.29	.0841	−.4321
4.9	39.8	−.09	.0081	−.51	.2601	.0459
5.9	39.9	.91	.8281	−.41	.1681	−.3731
5.6	40.6	.61	.3721	.29	.0841	.1769

$$\bar{X} = 4.99$$

$$\bar{Y} = 40.31$$

$$\sum (X_i - \bar{X})^2 = 17.8379$$

$$\sum (Y_i - \bar{Y})^2 = 5.5899$$

$$\sum (X_i - \bar{X})(Y_i - \bar{Y}) = -6.3389$$

$$r = \frac{\sum (X_i - \bar{X})(Y_i - \bar{Y})}{\sqrt{\sum (X_i - \bar{X})^2 \sum (Y_i - \bar{Y})^2}} = \frac{-6.3389}{\sqrt{(17.8379)(5.5899)}} = \frac{-6.3389}{\sqrt{99.712}} = -.635$$

Regression Analysis

Regression analysis is another technique for measuring the linear association between a dependent and an independent variable. Although simple regression and correlation are mathematically equivalent in most respects, regression is a dependence technique where correlation is an interdependence technique. A dependence technique makes a distinction between dependent and

EXHIBIT 23.4 **Pearson Product-Moment Correlation Matrix for Salesperson Example**[a]

Variables	S	JS	GE	SE	OD	VI	JT	RA	TP	WL
Performance (S)	1.00									
Job satisfaction (JS)	.45[b]	1.00								
Generalized self-esteem (GE)	.31[b]	.10	1.00							
Specific self-esteem (SE)	.61[b]	.28[b]	.36[b]	1.00						
Other-directedness (OD)	.05	−.03	−.44[b]	−.24[c]	1.00					
Verbal intelligence (VI)	−.36[b]	−.13	−.14	−.11	−.18[d]	1.00				
Job-related tension (JT)	−.48[b]	−.56[b]	−.32[b]	−.34[b]	.26[b]	−.02	1.00			
Role ambiguity (RA)	−.26[c]	−.24[c]	−.32[b]	−.39[b]	.38[b]	−.05	−.44[b]	1.00		
Territory potential (TP)	.49[b]	.31[b]	.04	.29[b]	.09	−.09	−.38[b]	−.26[b]	1.00	
Workload (WL)	.45[b]	.11	.29[c]	.29[c]	−.04	−.12	−.27[c]	−.22[d]	.49[b]	1.00

[a]Numbers below the diagonal are for the sample; those above the diagonal are omitted.
[b]$p < .001$.
[c]$p < .01$.
[d]$p < .05$.

independent variables. An interdependence technique does not make this distinction and simply is concerned with how variables relate to one another.

Thus, with simple regression, a dependent (or criterion) variable, Y, is linked to an independent (or predictor) variable, X. Regression analysis attempts to predict the values of a continuous, interval-scaled dependent variable from specific values of the independent variable.

The Regression Equation

simple (bivariate) linear regression

A measure of linear association that investigates straight-line relationships between a continuous dependent variable and an independent variable that is usually continuous, but can be a categorical dummy variable.

The discussion here concerns **simple (bivariate) linear regression**. Simple regression investigates a *straight-line relationship* of the type

$$Y = \alpha + \beta X,$$

where Y is a continuous dependent variable and X is an independent variable that is usually continuous, although dichotomous nominal or ordinal variables can be included in the form of a dummy variable. Alpha (α) and beta (β) are two parameters that must be estimated so that the equation best represents a given set of data. These two parameters determine the height of the regression line and the angle of the line relative to horizontal. When these parameters change, the line changes. Regression techniques have the job of estimating values for these parameters that make the line *fit* the observations the best.

The result is simply a linear equation, or the equation for a line, just as in basic algebra! α represents the Y intercept (where the line crosses the Y-axis) and β is the slope coefficient. The slope is the change in Y associated with a change of one unit in X. Slope may also be thought of as rise over run: that is, how much Y rises (or falls if negative) for every one unit change in the X-axis.

Parameter Estimate Choices

The estimates for α and β are the key to regression analysis. In most business research, the estimate of β is most important. The explanatory power of regression rests with β because this is where

RESEARCH SNAPSHOT

What Makes Attractiveness?

What are the things that make someone attractive? Many people are interested in this question. Among these are companies that hire people to sell fashion. The correlation matrix below was computed with SPSS. The correlations show how different characteristics related to each other. Variables include a measure of fit, meaning how well the person matches a fashion retail concept, attractiveness, weight (how overweight someone appears), age, manner of dress (how modern), and personality (warm versus cold). Thus, a sample of consumers rated a model shown in a photograph on

Correlations

		Fit	Attract	Fat	Age	Modern	Cold
Fit	Pearson Correlation	1	0.831**	−0.267*	0.108	−0.447**	−0.583**
	Sig. (2-tailed)		0.000	0.036	0.404	0.000	0.000
	N	62	62	62	62	62	62
Attract	Pearson Correlation	0.831**	1	−0.275*	0.039	−0.428**	−0.610**
	Sig. (2-tailed)	0.000		0.030	0.766	0.001	0.000
	N	62	62	62	62	62	62
Fat	Pearson Correlation	−0.267*	−0.275*	1	0.082	0.262*	0.058
	Sig. (2-tailed)	0.036	0.030		0.528	0.040	0.653
	N	62	62	62	62	62	62
Age	Pearson Correlation	0.108	0.039	0.082	1	−0.019	0.104
	Sig. (2-tailed)	0.404	0.766	0.528		0.882	0.423
	N	62	62	62	62	62	62
Modern	Pearson Correlation	−0.447**	−0.428**	0.262*	−0.019	1	0.603**
	Sig. (2-tailed)	0.000	0.001	0.040	0.882		0.000
	N	62	62	62	62	62	62
Cold	Pearson Correlation	−0.583**	−0.610**	0.058	0.104	0.603**	1
	Sig. (2-tailed)	0.000	0.000	0.653	0.423	0.000	
	N	62	62	62	62	62	62

**Correlation is significant at the 0.01 level (2-tailed). *Correlation is significant at the 0.05 level (2-tailed).

those characteristics. The results reveal the following: Thus, if the model seems to "fit" the store concept, she seems attractive. If she is too big, she is seen as less attractive. Age is unrelated to attractiveness or fit. Modernness and perceived coldness also are associated with lower attractiveness. Using these correlations, a retailer can help determine what employees should look like!

Correlations can be found using SPSS by navigating as shown below:

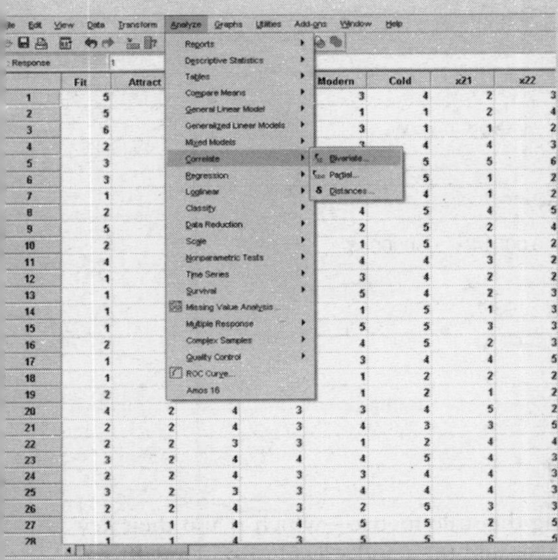

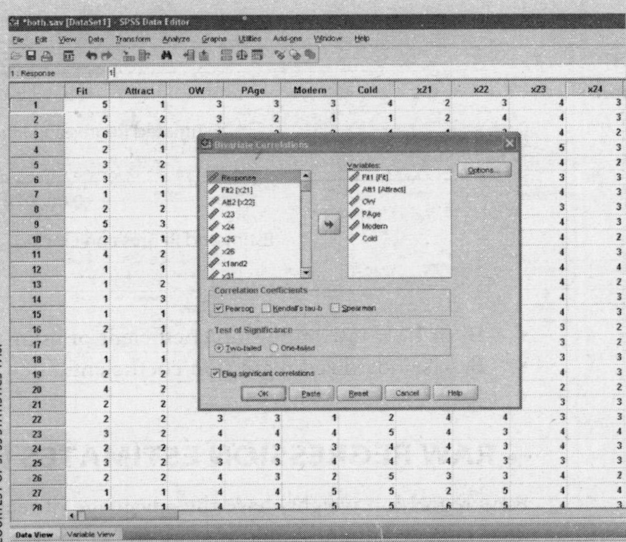

COURTESY OF SPSS STATISTICS 17.0.

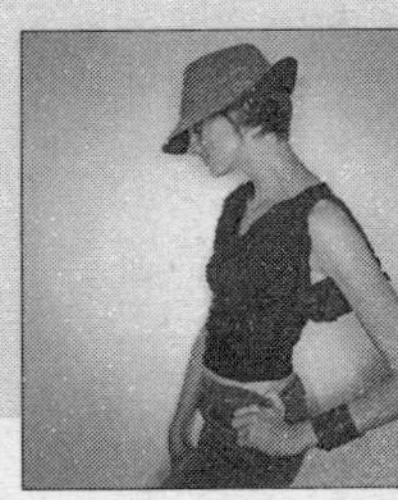

© JILL WENDELL/JUPITER IMAGES

the direction and strength of the relationship between the independent and dependent variable is explained.

A *Y*-intercept term is sometimes referred to as a constant because α represents a fixed point. An estimated slope coefficient is sometimes referred to as a regression weight, regression coefficient, parameter estimate, or sometimes even as a *path* estimate. The term *path estimate* is a descriptive term adapted because of the way hypothesized causal relationships are often represented in diagrams:

$$\boxed{X} \xrightarrow{\beta_1} \boxed{Y}$$

For all practical purposes, these terms are used interchangeably.

Parameter estimates can be presented in either raw or standardized form. One potential problem with raw parameter estimates is due to the fact that they reflect the measurement scale range. So, if a simple regression involved distance measured with miles, very small parameter estimates may indicate a strong relationship. In contrast, if the very same distance is measured with centimeters, a very large parameter estimate would be needed to indicate a strong relationship.

Exhibit 23.5 provides an illustration. Suppose a researcher was interested in how much space was allocated to a specific snack food on a shelf and how it related to sales. Fifteen observations are taken from 15 different stores. The upper line represents a typical distance showing shelf space measured in centimeters. The lower line is the same distance shown in miles. The top frame shows hypothetical regression results if the independent variable is measured in centimeters. The bottom frame shows the very same regression results if the independent variable is measured in miles. Even though these two regression lines are the same, the parameter coefficients do not seem comparable.

standardized regression coefficient (β)

The estimated coefficient indicating the strength of relationship between an independent variable and dependent variable expressed on a standardized scale where higher absolute values indicate stronger relationships (range is from −1 to 1).

Thus, researchers often explain regression results by referring to a **standardized regression coefficient (β)**. A standardized regression coefficient provides a common metric allowing regression results to be compared to one another no matter what the original scale range may have been. Due to the mathematics involved in standardization, the standardized *Y*-intercept term is always 0.[7] The regression equation for the shelf space example would then become:

$$\hat{Y} = 0 + 0.16X_1$$

Even if the distance measures for the 15 observations were converted to some other metric (feet, meters, and so on), the standardized regression weight would still be 0.16.

Researchers use shorthand to label regression coefficients as either "raw" or "standardized." The most common shorthand is as follows:

- $\mathbf{B_0}$ or $\mathbf{b_0}$ = raw (unstandardized) *Y*-intercept term; what was referred to as α above.

EXHIBIT 23.5

The Advantage of Standardized Regression Weights

12.5 cm

Estimated Regression Line: $\hat{Y} = 22 + .07X_1$

0.000078 miles

Estimated Regression Line: $\hat{Y} = 0.00014 + .0000004X_1$

- $\mathbf{B_1}$ or $\mathbf{b_1}$ = raw regression coefficient or estimate.
- β_1 = standardized regression coefficients.

RAW REGRESSION ESTIMATES (b_1)

Raw regression weights have the advantage of retaining the scale metric—which is also their key disadvantage. Where should the researcher focus then? Should the standardized or unstandardized coefficients be interpreted? The answer to this question is fairly simple.

- If the purpose of the regression analysis is forecasting, then raw parameter estimates must be used. This is another way of saying that the researcher is interested only in prediction.

Thus, when the researcher above wants to predict how much will be consumed based on the amount of shelf space, raw regression coefficients must be used. For instance, the forecast for 14 cm of shelf space can be found as follows:

$$\hat{Y} = 22 + 0.07(14) = 23.0$$

The same result can be found by using the equation representing the distance in miles.

STANDARDIZED REGRESSION ESTIMATES (β)

Standardized regression estimates have the advantage of a constant scale. No matter what range of values the independent variables take on, β will not be affected. When should standardized regression estimates be used?

- Standardized regression estimates should be used when the researcher is testing explanatory hypotheses; in other words, when the purpose of the research is more explanation than prediction.

Visual Estimation of a Simple Regression Model

As mentioned above, simple regression involves finding a best-fit line, given a set of observations plotted in two-dimensional space. Many ways exist to estimate where this line should go. Estimation techniques involve terms such as instrumental variables, maximum likelihood, visual estimation, and ordinary least squares (OLS). We focus on the latter two in this text.

Suppose a researcher is interested in forecasting sales for a construction distributor (wholesaler) in Florida. The distributor believes a reasonable association exists between sales and building permits issued by counties. Using bivariate linear regression on the data in Exhibit 23.6, the researcher will be able to explain sales potential (Y) in various counties based on the number of building permits (X).

The data are plotted in a scatter diagram in Exhibit 23.7. In the diagram the vertical axis indicates the value of the dependent variable, Y, and the horizontal axis indicates the value of the independent variable, X. Each single point in the diagram represents an observation of X and Y at a given point in time. The values are simply points in a Cartesian plane.

One way to determine the relationship between X and Y is to simply visually draw the best-fit straight line through the points in the figure. That is, try to draw a line that goes through the center of the plot of points. If the points are thought of as bowling pins, the best-fit line can be thought of as the path that would on average knock over the most bowling pins. For any given value of the independent variable, a prediction can be made by selecting the dependent variable that goes along with that value. For example, if we want to forecast sales if building permits are 150, we simply follow the dotted lines shown in the exhibit to yield a prediction of about 112. The better one can estimate where the best-fit line should be, the smaller will be the error in prediction.

ERRORS IN PREDICTION

Any method of drawing a line can be used to perform regression. However, some methods will obviously have more errors than others. Consider our bowling ball line above. One person may be better at guessing where it should be than another. We would know who was better by determining the total error of prediction.

Let's consider error by first thinking about what value of sales would be the best guess if we had no information about any other variable. In that case, our univariate best guess would be the mean sales of 99.8. If the spot corresponding to 156 building permits (X = 156) were predicted with the

EXHIBIT 23.6
Relationship of Sales Potential to Building Permits Issued

Dealer	*Y* Dealer's Sales Volume (Thousands)	*X* Building Permits
1	77	86
2	79	93
3	80	95
4	83	104
5	101	139
6	117	180
7	129	165
8	120	147
9	97	119
10	106	132
11	99	126
12	121	156
13	103	129
14	86	96
15	99	108

EXHIBIT 23.7
The Best-Fit Line or Knocking Out the Pins

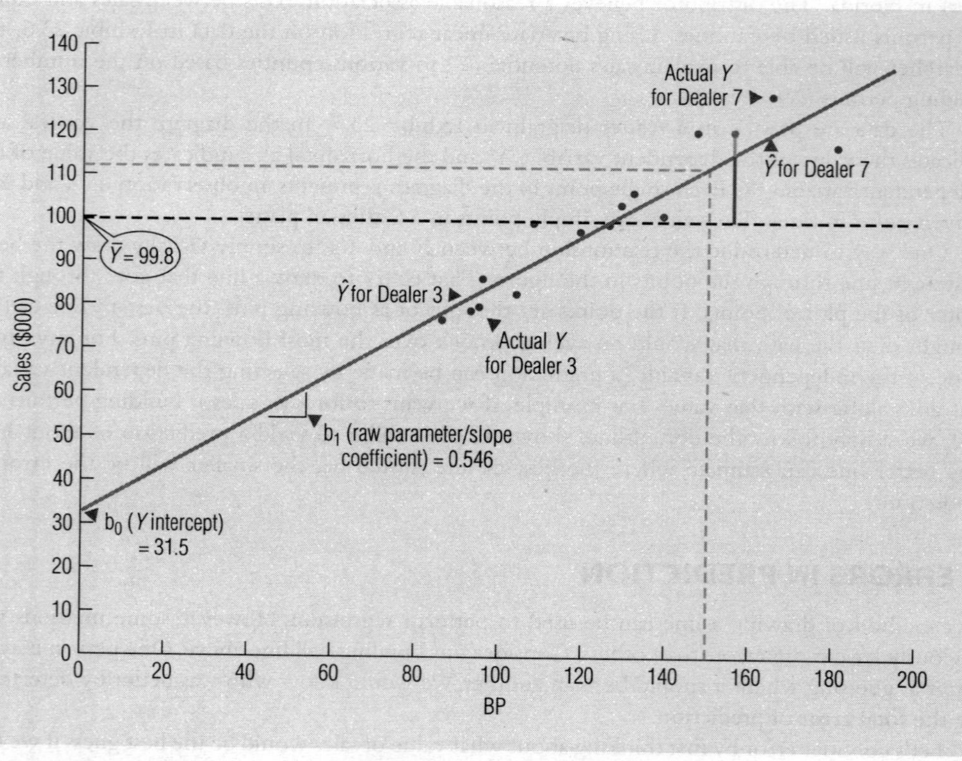

mean, the resulting error in prediction would be represented by the distance of the dark gray and light gray vertical line.

Once information about the independent variable is provided, we can then use the prediction provided by the best-fit line. In this case, our best-fit line is the "bowling ball" line shown in Exhibit 23.7. The error in prediction using this line would be indicated by the vertical line extending up from the regression line to the actual observation. Thus, it appears that at least for this observation, our prediction using the regression line has reduced the error in prediction that would result from guessing with the mean. Statistically, this is the goal of regression analysis. We would like an estimation technique that would place our line so that the total sum of all errors over all observations is minimized. In other words, no line fits better. Although with good guess work, visual estimation may prove somewhat accurate, perhaps there is a more certain way.

Ordinary Least-Squares (OLS) Method of Regression Analysis

The researcher's task is to find the best means for fitting a straight line to the data. OLS is a relatively straightforward mathematical technique that guarantees that the resulting straight line will produce the least possible total error in using X to predict Y. The logic is based on how much better a regression line can predict values of Y compared to simply using the mean as a prediction for all observations no matter what the value of X may be.

Unless the dependent and independent variables are perfectly related, no straight line can connect all observations. More technically, the procedure used in the least-squares method generates a straight line that minimizes the sum of squared deviations of the actual values from this predicted regression line. With the symbol e representing the deviations of the observations from the regression line, no other line can produce less error. The deviations are squared so that positive and negative misses do not cancel each other out. The OLS criterion is as follows:

$$\sum_{i=1}^{n} e_i^2 \text{ is minimum}$$

where

$e_i = Y_i - \hat{Y}_i$ (the residual)

Y_i = actual observed value of the dependent variable

$\hat{Y}_i$ = estimated value of the dependent variable (pronounced "Y-hat")

n = number of observations

i = number of the particular observation

The general equation for any straight line can be represented as $Y = b_0 + b_1X$. If we think of this as the true hypothetical line that we try to estimate with sample observations, the regression equation will represent this with a slightly different equation:

$$Y_i = b_0 + b_1X_1 + e_i$$

The equation means that the predicted value for any value of X (X_i) is determined as a function of the estimated slope coefficient, plus the estimated intercept coefficient plus some error.

The raw parameter estimates can be found using the following formulas:

$$b_1 = \frac{n\left(\sum X_iY_i\right) - \left(\sum X_i\right)\left(\sum Y_i\right)}{n\left(\sum X_i^2\right) - \left(\sum X_i\right)^2}$$

and

$$b_0 = \overline{Y} - b_1\,\overline{X}$$

where

Y_i = ith observed value of the dependent variable

X_i = ith observed value of the independent variable

$\overline{Y}$ = mean of the dependent variable

X = independent variable

$\overline{X}$ = mean of the independent variable

n = number of observations

b_0 = intercept estimate

b_1 = slope estimate (regression weight)

The careful reader may notice some similarity between the correlation calculation and the equation for b_1. In fact, the standardized regression coefficient from a simple regression equals the Pearson correlation coefficient for the two variables. Once the estimates are obtained, a predicted value for the dependent variable can be found for any value of X_i with this equation:

$$\hat{Y}_i = b_0 + b_i X_i$$

Appendix 23A demonstrates the arithmetic necessary to calculate the parameter estimates.

STATISTICAL SIGNIFICANCE OF REGRESSION MODEL

As with ANOVA, the researcher needs a way of testing the statistical significance of the regression model. Also like ANOVA, an F-test provides the answer to this question.

The overall F-test for regression can be illustrated with Exhibit 23.7. Once again examine the gray line showing the predicted value for $X = 156$, which represents the small vertical line located at the upper right of the exhibit.

1. The total vertical line including the dark gray and light gray segments represent the *total deviation* of the observation from the mean:

$$Y_i - \overline{Y}$$

2. The dark gray portion represents how much of the total deviation is *explained* by the *regression* line:

$$\hat{Y}_i - \overline{Y}$$

3. The light gray portion represents how much of the total deviation is not explained by the regression line (also equal to e_i):

$$Y_i - \hat{Y}_i$$

These three components are mathematically related because the total deviation is a sum of what is explained by the regression line and what is not explained by the regression line. This can be expressed mathematically as

$$(Y_i - \overline{Y}) = (\hat{Y}_i - \overline{Y}) + (Y_i - \hat{Y}_i)$$

$$\underset{\text{(SST)}}{\text{Total deviation}} = \underset{\text{(SSR)}}{\text{Deviation explained by the regression}} + \underset{\text{(SSE)}}{\text{Deviation unexplained by the regression}}$$

Just as in ANOVA, the total deviation represents the total variation to be explained. Thus, the partitioning of the variation into components allows us to form a ratio of the explained variation versus the unexplained variation. The corresponding abbreviation for this partitioning is

$$SST = SSR + SSE$$

An **F-test (regression)**, or an *analysis of variance,* can be applied to a regression to test the relative magnitudes of the *SSR* (Sums of Squares – Regression) and *SSE* (Sums of Squared Errors) with their appropriate degrees of freedom. The equation for the *F*-test is

F-test (regression)
A procedure to determine whether more variability is explained by the regression or unexplained by the regression.

$$F_{(k-1)(n-k)} = \frac{SSR/(k-1)}{SSE/(n-k)} = \frac{MSR}{MSE}$$

where

MSR is an abbreviation for Mean Squared Regression

MSE is an abbreviation for Mean Squared Error

k is the number of independent variables (always 1 for simple regression)

n is the sample size

Once again, researchers today need not calculate this by hand. Regression programs will produce an "ANOVA" table, which will provide the *F*-value and a p-value (significance level), and will generally show the partitioned variation in some form. For the sales example, the following table is obtained:

ANOVA

	df	SS	MS	F	p-value
Regression (SSR)	1	3398.48911	3398.489	91.29854	0.0000003
Residual (SSE)	13	483.910892	37.22391		
Total	14	3882.4			

Thus, building permits explain a significant portion of the variation in sales as evidenced by the very low p-value.

R^2

The *coefficient of determination,* R^2, reflects the proportion of variance explained by the regression line. In this example, R^2 can be found with this formula:

$$R^2 = \frac{SSR}{SST} = \frac{3398.5}{3882.4} = 0.875$$

The coefficient of determination may be interpreted to mean that 87.5 percent of the variation in sales was explained by associating the variable with building permits.

What is an "acceptable" R^2 value? This question is asked frequently. However, guidelines for R^2 values are neither simple nor straightforward. Indeed, good and bad values for the coefficient of determination depend on so many factors that a single precise guideline is considered inappropriate. The focus should be on the *F*-test. However, in practice, do not expect to often see a simple regression result with an R^2 anywhere near the value in this example. They will normally be considerably lower.[8]

INTERPRETING REGRESSION OUTPUT

Exhibit 23.8 displays output for the building permit problem. Most computerized software provides similar output for regression analysis. Interpreting simple regression output is a simple two-step process.

1. Interpret the overall significance of the model.
   a. The output will include the "model *F*" and a significance value. When the model *F* is significant (low p-value), the independent variable explains a significant portion of the variation in the dependent variable.
   b. The coefficient of determination or R^2 can be interpreted. As mentioned earlier, this is the percentage of total variation in the dependent variable accounted for by the independent variable. Another way to think of this is as the extent to which the variances of the independent and dependent variables overlap.
2. The individual parameter coefficient is interpreted.
   a. The *t*-value associated with the slope coefficient can be interpreted. In this case, the *t* of 9.555 is associated with a very low p-value (0.000 to 3 decimal places). Therefore, the slope coefficient is significant. For simple regression, the p-value for the model *F* and for the *t*-test of the individual regression weight will be the same.
   b. A *t*-test for the intercept term (constant) is also provided. However, this is seldom of interest since the explanatory power rests in the slope coefficient.
   c. If a need to forecast sales exists, the estimated regression equation is needed. Using the raw coefficients, the estimated regression line is

$$\hat{Y} = 31.5 + 0.546X$$

   d. The regression coefficient (slope) indicates that for every building permit issued, sales increase 0.546. Moreover, the standardized regression coefficient of 0.936 would allow the researcher to compare the explanatory power of building permits versus some other potential independent variable. For simple regression, β_1 equals *r*.

EXHIBIT 23.8
Simple Regression Results for Building Permit Example

R	R Square	Adjusted R Square	Std. Error of the Estimate
.936(a)	.875	.866	6.10114

a Predictors: (Constant), Permits

1. Is model significant?

ANOVA(b)

	Sum of Squares	df	Mean Square	*F*	Sig.
Regression	3398.489	1	3398.489	91.299	.000(a)
Residual	483.911	13	37.224		
Total	3882.400	14			

a Predictors: (Constant), Permits
b Dependent Variable: Sales

2. Interpret parameter estimates?

Coefficients[(a)]

Model	Unstandardized Coefficients: B	Std. Error	Standardized Coefficient: Beta (β)	*t*	Sig.
1.000 (Constant)	31.502	7.319		4.304	0.001
Permits	0.546	0.057	0.936	9.555	0.000

a Dependent Variable: Sales

PLOTTING THE OLS REGRESSION LINE

To draw a regression line on the scatter diagram, only two predicted values of Y need to be plotted. The data for two dealers is used to illustrate how this is done:

$$\text{Dealer 7 (actual } Y \text{ value} = 129\text{): } \hat{Y}_7 = 31.5 + 0.546(165) = 121.6$$

$$\text{Dealer 3 (actual } Y \text{ value} = 80\text{): } \hat{Y}_3 = 31.5 + 0.546(95) = 83.4$$

Using the data for Dealer 7 and Dealer 3, we can draw a straight line connecting the points 121.6 and 83.4. Exhibit 23.9 shows the regression line.

To determine the error (residual) of any observation, the predicted value of Y is first calculated. The predicted value is then subtracted from the actual value. For example, the actual observation for dealer 9 is 97, and the predicted value is 96.5; thus only a small margin of error, $e = 0.5$, is involved in this regression line:

$$e_9 = Y_9 - \hat{Y}_9 = 97 - 96.5 = 0.5$$

where

$$\hat{Y}_9 = 31.5 + .546(119)$$

TOTHEPOINT

Forecasting is like trying to drive a car blindfolded and following directions given by a person who is looking out the back window.

—Anonymous

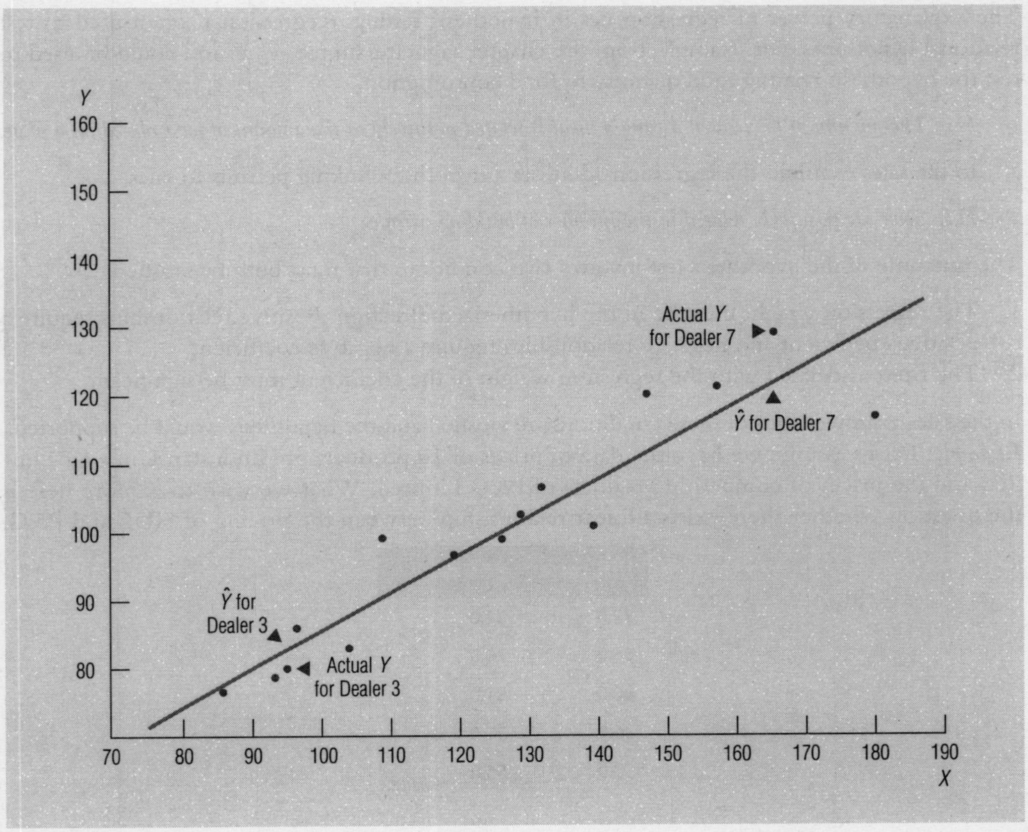

EXHIBIT 23.9
OLS Regression Line

RESEARCH SNAPSHOT

Size and Weight

America seems obsessed with weight control. Thin seems to stay in and the fight to get thin is a multibillion dollar business. Recall in an earlier Research Snapshot correlations between factors related to attractiveness were discussed. What if the following hypothesis were tested?

H1: Perceptions that a female model is overweight are related negatively to perceptions of attractiveness.

Using the scales from the earlier Snapshot, this can be tested with a simple regression. The results can be summarized as shown here:

Model		Sum of Squares	df	Mean Square	F	Sig.
1	Regression	9.228	1	9.227	4.914	0.030
	Residual	112.660	60	1.877		
	Total	121.8870968	61			

Model		Unstandardized Coefficients B	Std. Error	Standardized Coefficients β	t	Sig.
1	(Constant)	4.413	0.952		4.636	0.00002
	x113	−0.582	0.262	−0.275	−2.216	0.030

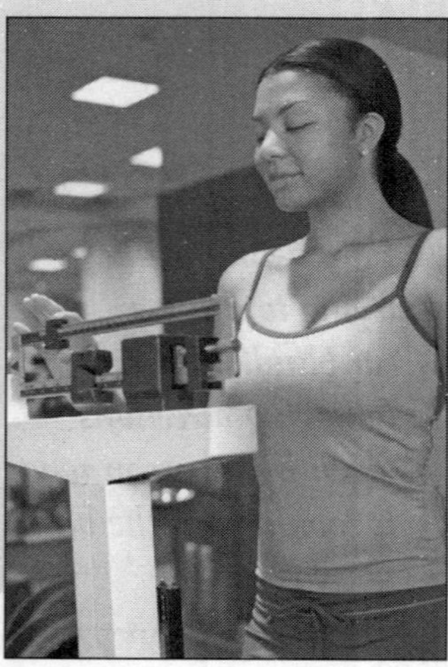

© PHOTODISC/GETTY IMAGES

The results support the hypothesis. The $\beta = -0.275$ is both in the expected direction (negative) and significant ($p < 0.05$). Therefore, if respondents perceived someone as "too fat," they likewise saw the person as less attractive.

© iStock

SIMPLE REGRESSION AND HYPOTHESIS TESTING

The explanatory power of regression lies in hypothesis testing. Regression is often used to test relational hypotheses. For example, from the chapter vignette, simple regression could be used to test the hypothesis relating food quantity to food consumption.

H1: The amount of food eaten during a meal is related positively to the amount of food placed on a plate.

In the sales example, the regression addresses a hypothesis linking permits to sales.

H1: Sales are positively related to the number of building permits.

The outcome of the hypothesis test involves two conditions that must both be satisfied.

1. The regression weight must be in the hypothesized direction. Positive relationships require a positive coefficient and negative relationships require a negative coefficient.
2. The *t*-test associated with the regression weight of the coefficient must be significant.

In the sales example, both of these conditions are satisfied and the hypothesis would be supported.

Example: Let us assume we have the data of prices of 10 products of Hindustan Unilever Limited and the prices of competing products of P&G Limited. What we wish to explore here is the question whether there exists a linear relationship between the pricing of HUL and P&G.

HUL price	P&G price
72.0	78.0
65.0	70.0
80.0	81.0
36.0	31.0
50.0	55.0

Contd..

HUL price	P&G price
21.0	29.0
79.0	74.0
64.0	64.0
44.0	47.0
55.0	53.0

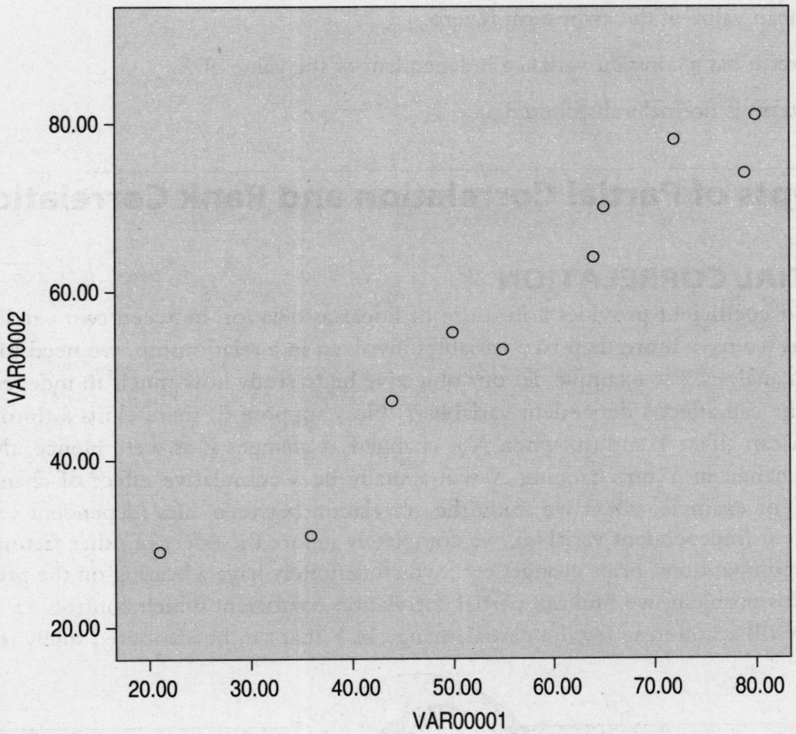

When a scatter plot is plotted for these two variables in SPSS, we get the above graph. It is easily seen from the plot that as the prices of HUL increase, the price of P&G product also goes up. An approximate positive linear relationship seems to exist. Following is the exact correlation coefficient computed using SPSS:

Correlations

		HUL Price	P&G Price
HUL Price	Pearson Correlation	1	0.971**
	Sig. (2-tailed)		0.000
	N	10	10
P&G Price	Pearson Correlation	0.971**	1
	Sig. (2-tailed)	0.000	
	N	10	10

** Correlation is significant at the 0.01 level (2-tailed).

The Pearson correlation coefficient comes out to be 0.971 which being a number close to +1 denotes a very high degree of positive relationship. Also, the significance values (0.000) show that there is overwhelming evidence in the data whereby we can reject the null hypothesis that the correlation between these two variables is zero, or in other words, we accept the alternate hypothesis that a significant relationship between the two variables exists.

Note: The important take in the definition of correlation coefficient above is "linear," i.e., it tests only for the presence of a linear relationship. If an actual relationship exists but it is either non-linear or of a complicated shape, then the correlation coefficient may not be able to capture it.

Assumptions of Regression Model

1. The relationship between dependent and independent variables is linear. The regression line can be extended up to infinity in both directions.
2. The mean value of the error term is zero.
3. Error term has a constant variance independent of the value of *X*.
4. Error term is normally distributed.

Concepts of Partial Correlation and Rank Correlation

PARTIAL CORRELATION

Correlation coefficient provides a measure of linear association between two variables. However, when we have more than two variables involved in a relationship, we need to use partial correlation analysis. For example, let our objective be to study how much an independent variable *X* alone can affect a dependent variable *Y*. Now suppose (i) there exists a third variable *Z* also which can affect *Y* and (ii) when *X* is changed, it changes *Z* as well. Hence, the resulting observed change in *Y* on changing *X* will actually be a cumulative effect of change of both *X* and *Z*. For example, when we study the correlation between sales (dependent variable) and advertisement (independent variable), we completely ignore the effect of other factors like word of mouth, competitions, price change, etc., which definitely have a bearing on the price. To circumvent this problem, we find out partial correlation coefficient which controls for the change in *Z* while still accounting for the partial change in *Y* that can be attributed solely to *X*.

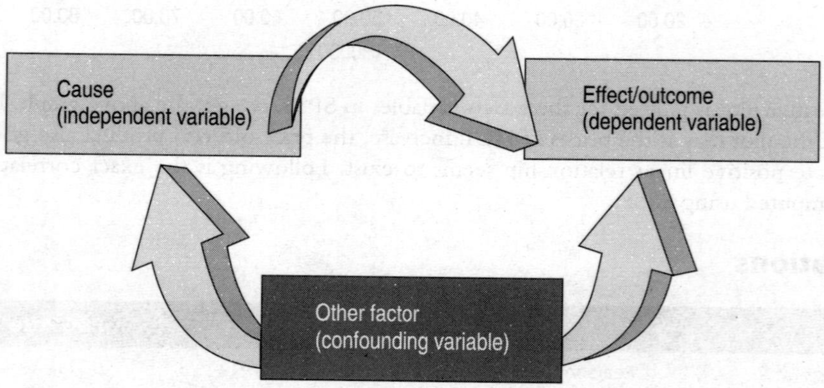

The partial correlation coefficient thus is:

$$r_{XY,Z} = \frac{(r_{XY} - r_{XZ} \times r_{YZ})}{\sqrt{(1-r_{XZ}^2)(1-r_{YZ}^2)}}$$

Visualizing in a geometrical space, the partial correlation relates to the projection of the change in line (3-dimensional) onto the *XY* plane, thus eliminating the effect of the change in *z* variable and retaining only the relationship between *X* and *Y*.

Example: When Coke increases advertising expenditure, it expects an increase in sales. However, an additional variable of simultaneous discount offers can boost up sales as well. Hence, when Coke is trying to account for the increase in sales which was caused by advertising alone, it must control for the effect of discounts, and hence, calculate partial correlation coefficient.

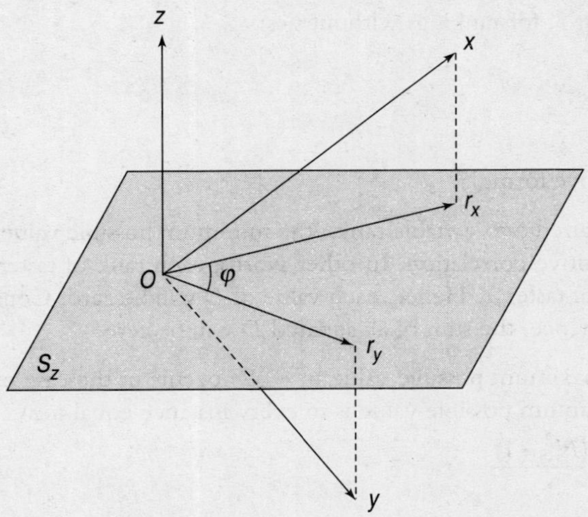

RANK ORDER CORRELATION

Partial correlation uses metric scale to measure the values of *X* and *Y*. It is also possible to apply linear correlation to cases where *X* and *Y* are measured on categorical ranking scale. This is known as rank order correlation (r_s).

Suppose, for example, that two tea tasters *X* and *Y* were asked to rank $N = 8$ types of tea, where rank# 1 = highest and rank# 8 = lowest. Now,

$$r = \frac{SC_{XY}}{\sqrt{SS_X \times SS_Y}}$$

Tea type	Taster X	Taster Y
A	1	2
B	2	1
C	3	5
D	4	3
E	5	4
F	6	7
G	7	8
H	8	6

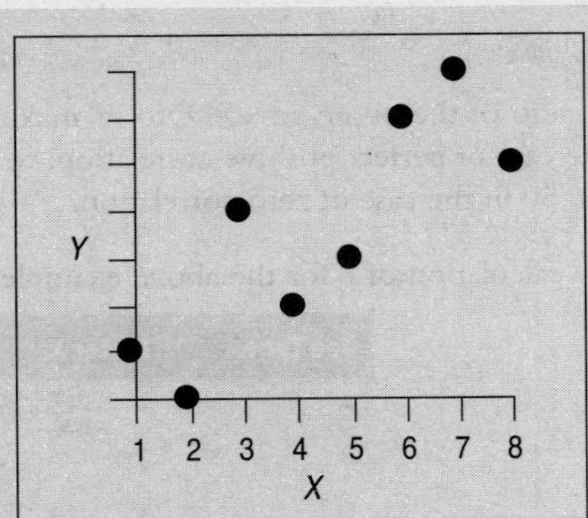

Results are $r = +0.83$ and $r^2 = 0.69$.

These are exactly the same values we will get when we calculate the Spearman coefficient r_s. However, r_s is precisely equal to r only when the rankings within *X* and *Y* are the consecutive integer values: 1, 2, 3, and so on, with no ties.

Tea type	Taster X	Taster Y	D	D^2
A	1	2	−1	1
B	2	1	1	1
C	3	5	2	4
D	4	3	1	1
E	5	4	1	1
F	6	7	−1	1
G	7	8	1	1
H	8	6	2	4

The simple formula for r_s, for rankings without ties:

$$r_s = \frac{1-6\sum D^2}{N(N^2-1)}$$

Explanation to the above formula:

- For any set of N paired two variable ranks, the minimum possible value of $-\Sigma D^2$ occurs in the case of perfect positive correlation. In other words, each rank of taster X will be exactly the same as the ranks of taster Y. Hence, each value of D will be zero. Consequently, their square will be zero, and hence, the sum of all squared D will be zero.
- Conversely, the maximum possible value of $-\Sigma D^2$ occurs in the case of perfect negative correlation. This maximum possible value is in every instance equal to

$$\text{Maximum } \sum D^2 = \frac{N(N^2-1)}{3}$$

Tea Type	Taster X	Taster Y	D	D²	ΣD² = 168
A	1	8	−7	49	
B	2	7	−5	25	
C	3	6	−3	9	8(8² – 1)/3 = 168
D	4	5	−1	1	
E	5	4	1	1	
F	6	3	3	9	
G	7	2	5	25	
H	8	1	7	49	

The ratio of the observed $-\Sigma D^2$ to its maximum possible value will, therefore, be equal to zero in the case of perfect positive correlation, to +1.0 in the case of perfect negative correlation, and to +0.50 in the case of zero correlation.

Now calculation of r_s for the above example:

Tea Type	Taster X	Taster Y	D	D²
A	1	2	−1	1
B	2	1	1	1
C	3	5	−2	4
D	4	3	1	1
E	5	4	1	1
F	6	7	1	1
G	7	8	−1	1
H	8	6	2	4
N = 8, ΣD² = 14				

The meanings of r_s and r_s^2 in a rank order correlation are essentially the same as those of r and r^2 in a correlation when ranks have equal interval. Here, $r_s^2 = 0.69$ means that the covariance between the X and Y rankings is 69% as strong as it possibly could be, and the positive sign of $r_s = +0.83$ signals that this covariance occurs along the upward slant, with higher values of X tending to be associated with higher values of Y and vice versa. However, it is not recommended taking the parallels much farther than this. In particular, it would not make much sense to subject bivariate rankings to the predictive apparatus of linear regression.

TIPS OF THE TRADE

- When designing a survey, build your items with the dependent variables you wish to predict in mind.
- For many researchers, drawing a diagram of the relationships, and whether they are positively or negatively related to your dependent variable or variables, can help you clarify what you would hypothesize.
- Always conduct a correlational analysis before a regression analysis, to get a clearer picture of relationships among all of your variables.
- Remember that in a regression analysis, both the sign of your independent variable and its significance level should be reported to your stakeholders.

Summary

1. Apply and interpret simple bivariate correlations. This chapter covers two approaches for studying relationships among two at-least interval variables. A bivariate correlation is an index that displays how much two variables covary. Another way to think of correlation is as a standardized measure of covariance. When two variables display a correlation of 1.0, they are perfectly correlated. That means that they have no unique variance. Essentially, they are one and the same. When two variables are correlated –1.0 they are perfectly negatively correlated. In this sense they are mirror images of one another. Thus, correlations can range between –1.0 and 1.0. Correlations near 0 indicate a lack of relationship between two variables.

2. Interpret a correlation matrix. A correlation matrix presents all possible bivariate correlations among a set of variables. The statistical significance of each variable can be tested with a *t*-test. Low p-values for this test indicate significant correlations. Patterns of strong correlations among variables indicate variables that share variance in common.

3. Understand simple (bivariate) regression. Simple linear regression investigates a straight-line relationship between one dependent variable and one independent variable. The regression can be done intuitively by plotting a scatter diagram of the *X* and *Y* points and drawing a line to fit the observed relationship. OLS estimation mathematically determines the best-fitting regression line for the observed data. The line determined by this method may be used to forecast values of the dependent variable, given a value for the independent variable. The line's goodness-of-fit may be evaluated with a variant of the analysis of variance (ANOVA) technique or by calculating the coefficient of determination.

4. Understand the least-squares estimation technique. OLS is an estimation technique that minimizes the least-squared error for all observations. Regression models are evaluated based on how much variance they explain. Models with a high SSR relative to SST or SSE explain more variance in the dependent variable. SSR represents the proportion of total deviation from the mean among observations that can be explained by the regression line. SSE, the sums of square error, represents the amount of deviation from the mean for observations that is not accounted for by the regression line. OLS fits the line to minimize SSE.

5. Interpret regression output including the tests of hypotheses tied to specific parameter coefficients. Regression results are interpreted in a two-step process. First, the model's significance is evaluated. The model *F*-ratio, which is a ratio of SSR to SSE, is a key statistic. A significant *F*-ratio means that the independent variable explains a significant portion of the variance in the dependent variable. Second, the individual parameter coefficients are evaluated. When the regression is run for forecasting purposes, the raw parameter coefficients are most useful. When the regression is run for explanatory purposes, the standardized regression weight (β) is most useful.

Key Terms and Concepts

coefficient of determination (R^2), *597*
correlation coefficient, *595*
correlation matrix, *598*
covariance, *595*
F-test (regression), *607*
inverse (negative) relationship, *597*
measure of association, *595*
simple (bivariate) linear regression, *600*
standardized regression coefficient (β), *602*

Questions for Review and Critical Thinking

1. What is *covariance?*
2. How are covariance and correlation different?
3. How does a researcher determine if a correlation coefficient is significant?
4. The management of a regional bus line thought the company's cost of gas might be correlated with its passenger/mile ratio. The data and a correlation matrix follow. Comment.

Year	Average Wholesale Cost of Gas	Passengers/Miles
1	56.5	8.37
2	59.4	8.93
3	63.0	9.15
4	65.6	9.79
5	89.0	11.20

	Year	Price	Mile
Year (*r*)	1.00000	0.87016	0.95127
p-value	*0.00000*	*0.05510*	*0.01280*
Price (*r*)	0.87016	1.00000	0.97309
p-value	*0.05510*	*0.00000*	*0.00530*
Mile (*r*)	0.95127	0.97309	1.00000
p-value	*0.01280*	*0.00530*	*0.00000*

5. Interpret the following data:
   a. $\hat{Y} = 5.0 + .30X_1$
   Where the dependent variable equals turnover intentions for line managers and the independent variable equals number of employees supervised.
   b. $\hat{Y} = 250 - 4.0X_1$
   'NET Where the dependent variable is the number of hits on a new banner ad and the independent variable is the number of weeks the ad has run.
6. What are some different terms used to refer to the slope coefficient estimated in regression analysis?
7. The following ANOVA summary table is the result of a regression of sales on year of sales. Is the relationship statistically significant at the 0.95 significance level? Fill in the value for Sums of Squares in the SST row. Comment.

Source of Variation	Sum of Squares	d.f.	Mean Square	*F*-Value	p-value
SSR	605,370,750	1	605,370,750	3.12	0.115
SSE	1,551,381,712	8	193,922,714		
SST		9			

8. Address the following questions about regression analysis:
   a. Define *simple linear regression.*
   b. When is it most appropriate to rely on raw parameter coefficients and when is it most appropriate to rely on standardized parameter coefficients?
   c. Why is the *Y*-intercept estimate equal to 0 for standardized estimates?
   d. What are the steps in interpreting a regression model?
9. The following table gives a football team's season-ticket sales, percentage of games won, and number of active alumni for the years 1996–2005.

Year	Season-Ticket Sales	Percentage of Games Won	Number of Active Alumni
1996	4,995	40	NA
1997	8,599	54	3,450
1998	8,479	55	3,801
1999	8,419	58	4,000
2000	10,253	63	4,098
2001	12,457	75	6,315
2002	13,285	36	6,860
2003	14,177	27	8,423
2004	15,730	63	9,000
2005	15,805	70	9,500

   a. Compute a correlation matrix for the variables. A software statistical package is recommended. Interpret the correlation between each pair of variables.
   b. Estimate a regression model for sales = Percentage of games won.
   c. Estimate a regression model for sales = Number of active alumni.
   d. If *sales* is the dependent variable, which of the two independent variables do you think explains sales better? Explain.
10. Are the different forms of consumer installment credit in the following table highly correlated?

Debt Outstanding (millions of dollars)

Year	Gas Cards	Travel and Entertainment Cards	Bank Credit Cards	Retail Cards	Total Credit Cards	Total Installment Credit
1	$ 939	$ 61	$ 828	$ 9,400	$11,228	$ 79,428
2	1,119	76	1,312	10,200	12,707	87,745
3	1,298	110	2,639	10,900	14,947	98,105
4	1,650	122	3,792	11,500	17,064	102,064
5	1,804	132	4,490	13,925	20,351	111,295
6	1,762	164	5,408	14,763	22,097	127,332
7	1,832	191	6,838	16,395	25,256	147,437
8	1,823	238	8,281	17,933	28,275	156,124
9	1,893	273	9,501	18,002	29,669	164,955
10	1,981	238	11,351	19,052	32,622	185,489
11	2,074	284	14,262	21,082	37,702	216,572

11. A manufacturer of disposable washcloths/wipes told a retailer that sales for this product category closely correlated with sales of disposable diapers. The retailer thought he would check this out for his own sales-forecasting purposes. The researcher says, "Disposable washcloths/wipes sales can be predicted with knowledge of disposable diaper sales." Is this the right thing to say?
12. Explain how OLS determines where a regression line should be placed among a plot of observations.

Research Activities

1. **'NET** The Federal Reserve Bank of St. Louis maintains a database called FRED (Federal Reserve Economic Data). Navigate to the FRED database at **http://www.stls.frb.org/fred/index.html**. Randomly select a five-year period between 1970 and 2000 and then find the correlation between average U.S. employment in retail trade and U.S. employment in wholesale trade. Which statistical test is appropriate?
2. **'NET/ETHICS** Go to **http://www.transparency.org**. Find the corruption perception indices for 2005. Go to **http://www.geert-hofstede.com/hofstede_dimensions.php**. Create a data set that includes the corruption perception indices for at least 15 countries and the score for one of the Hofstede cultural valued dimensions. Conduct a regression and interpret the relationship between cultural values and corruption perceptions.

Case 23.1 International Operations at CarCare Inc.

CarCare is considering expanding its operations beyond the United States. The company wants to know whether it should target countries with consumers who tend to have a positive attitude toward their current cars. It has gathered data on U.S. and German car owners. The data are included in the "car" data set that can be available from your instructor. Using the data, conduct a correlation and simple regression analysis using spending as the dependent variable and attitude toward the current car as the independent variable.

Questions

1. Test the hypothesis: Attitude toward one's car is related positively to spending for car-care products.
2. Would you recommend CarCare do more research to identify nations with relatively favorable attitudes toward the cars they own? [Note: This data set was referred to for the first time in Chapter 22.]

APPENDIX 23A
ARITHMETIC BEHIND OLS

With simple arithmetic, we can solve for the parameter estimates using the OLS equations. Here, the data from Exhibit 23.6 are used. The different pieces of the equations are calculated and shown in Exhibit 23A.1. To estimate the relationship between the distributor's sales to a dealer and the number of building permits, we insert values from the table as shown below:

$$b_1 = \frac{n(\Sigma X_i Y_i) - (\Sigma X_i)(\Sigma Y_i)}{n(\Sigma X_i^2) - (\Sigma X_i)^2}$$

$$b_1 = \frac{15(193{,}345) - 2{,}806{,}875}{15(245{,}759) - 3{,}515{,}625}$$

$$= 0.546$$

$$b_o = \overline{Y} - b_1\overline{X}$$

$$= 99.8 - 0.546(125)$$

$$= 31.5$$

EXHIBIT 23A.1 **Least-Squares Computation**

	Y	Y^2	X	X^2	XY
1	77	5,929	86	7,396	6,622
2	79	6,241	93	8,649	7,347
3	80	6,400	95	9,025	7,600
4	83	6,889	104	10,816	8,632
5	101	10,201	139	19,321	14,039
6	117	13,689	180	32,400	21,060
7	129	16,641	165	27,225	21,285
8	120	14,400	147	21,609	17,640
9	97	9,409	119	14,161	11,543
10	106	11,236	132	17,424	13,992
11	99	9,801	126	15,876	12,474
12	121	14,641	156	24,336	18,876
13	103	10,609	129	16,641	13,287
14	86	7,396	96	9,216	8,256
15	99	9,801	108	11,664	10,692
	$\Sigma Y = 1{,}497$ $\overline{Y} = 99.8$	$\Sigma Y^2 = 153{,}283$	$\Sigma X = 1{,}875$ $\overline{X} = 125$	$\Sigma X^2 = 245{,}759$	$\Sigma XY = 193{,}345$

The formula $\hat{Y}_1 = 31.5 + 0.546X_1$ is the regression equation used for the prediction of the dependent variable. Suppose the wholesaler is considering opening a new dealership in an area where the number of building permits equals 89. We would need to compute a predicted value for $X = 89$. Sales in this area may be forecasted as

$$\begin{aligned}\hat{Y} &= 31.5 + 0.546(X)\\ &= 31.5 + 0.546(89)\\ &= 31.5 + 48.6\\ &= 80.1\end{aligned}$$

Thus, the distributor may expect sales of 80.1 (or $80,100) in this new area.

Calculation of the correlation coefficient gives an indication of how accurate the predictions are. In this example the correlation coefficient is $r = 0.94$ and the coefficient of determination is $R^2 = 0.88$.

CHAPTER 24
MULTIVARIATE STATISTICAL ANALYSIS

LEARNING OUTCOMES

After studying this chapter, you should be able to

1. **Understand what multivariate statistical analysis involves and know the two types of multivariate analysis**
2. **Interpret results from multiple regression analysis**
3. **Interpret results from multivariate analysis of variance (MANOVA)**
4. **Understand how to use conjoint analysis to design a new product or develop a pricing strategy**
5. **Interpret basic exploratory factor analysis results**
6. **Know what multiple discriminant analysis can be used to do**
7. **Understand how cluster analysis can identify market segments**
8. **Understand how to use multidimensional scaling to develop perceptual map for brand positioning**

Chapter Vignette: Cow-A-Bunga Never Goes Out of Style

As humans, we long to relive the past. This yearning to hold on to the past is a common psychological experience.[1] The psychology of consumption is of interest to many people who are not psychologists, however. The fact is, nostalgia sells, and business researchers are very interested in understanding exactly what nostalgia is, who is most prone to react to it, and how it contributes to business success.

When a boomer or Gen Xer walks through the toy store, he or she is likely to feel right at home. Toy companies like Hasbro have realized that adults buy toys for kids to enjoy. Grown-up consumers like to buy things they feel good about. Thus, the toy shelves are filled with throwback versions of GI Joe, Barbie, and even the Teenage Mutant Ninja Turtles.[2] The game shelves are filled with classic versions of familiar games like Risk, Stratego, and Monopoly.[3]

© AP PHOTO/TAMMIE ARROYO

Not to be outdone, other marketers are also counting on nostalgic consumers. Appliance companies have turned to retro designs with classic 1950s versions of toasters, blenders, and even ovens.[4] Advertisers are also using nostalgia to produce more effective sales appeals. Among others, Coca-Cola has used nostalgic advertising to help consumers relive the past.[5]

This trend is expected to continue, as pointed out by Janet Hsu, President of Sanrio Global Consumer Products, "Inspirational products will be a major trend in 2009 as consumers gravitate towards purchasing products that provide comfort and emotional connection. Evergreen and nostalgic products will continue to sell well. . . ."[6]

How can organizations better integrate nostalgia into their business plans? Researchers are working on numerous issues related to nostalgia:

- How can nostalgia be measured?
- What emotions is nostalgia associated with?[7]
- Can market segments be defined based on the type and amount of nostalgia experienced?
- What happens to consumers when they experience nostalgia?
- What makes a nostalgic consumer different from one who does not experience nostalgia?
- What are the positive outcomes for the business when consumer nostalgia increases?

Nostalgia is a complex experience involving multiple thoughts and feelings. The complexity makes nostalgia somewhat difficult to study. Multivariate research procedures can help address these questions as they consider the effects of multiple variables simultaneously. However, it seems that nostalgic thoughts mean good vibes for the marketer.[8] Cow-a-bunga!

Introduction

If only business problems were really as simple as most textbook examples! Most coursework involves solving problems that have a definite answer. They are usually relatively well-defined problems in which the information provided in the problem can be used to produce *one* correct solution.

Unfortunately, in the real world, most business problems are ill-defined. Not only do they not have a definite answer, but generally information needs to be generated and massaged before any solution can be obtained. Therefore, most business research studies involve many variables that must be organized for meaning. As researchers become increasingly aware of the complex nature of business problems, they gain a greater appreciation for more sophisticated approaches to data analysis. This chapter provides an introduction to some forms of what are known as multivariate data analysis.

TOTHEPOINT

The essence of mathematics is not to make simple things complicated, but to make complicated things simple.

—S. Gudder

What Is Multivariate Data Analysis?

The preceding chapters have addressed univariate and bivariate analyses. Research that involves three or more variables, or that is concerned with underlying dimensions among multiple variables, will involve multivariate statistical analysis. Multivariate statistical methods analyze multiple variables or even multiple sets of variables simultaneously. How do we know when someone has experienced nostalgia and whether or not the experience has altered behavior? Nostalgia itself is a latent construct that involves multiple indicators that together represent nostalgia. As such, the measurement and outcomes of nostalgia lend themselves well to multivariate analysis.[9] Likewise, many other business problems involve multivariate data analysis including most employee motivation research, customer psychographic profiles, and research that seeks to identify viable market segments.

The "Variate" in Multivariate

Another distinguishing characteristic of multivariate analysis is the **variate**. The variate is a mathematical way in which a set of variables can be represented with one equation. A variate is formed as a linear combination of variables, each contributing to the overall meaning of the variate based upon an empirically derived weight. Mathematically, the variate is a function of the measured variables involved in an analysis:

variate

A mathematical way in which a set of variables can be represented with one equation.

$$V_k = f(X_1, X_2, \ldots, X_m)$$

V_k is the kth variate. Every analysis could involve multiple sets of variables, each represented by a variate. X_1 to X_m represent the measured variables.

Here is a simple illustration. Recall that constructs are distinguished from variables by the fact that multiple variables are needed to measure a construct. Let's assume we measured nostalgia with five questions on our survey. With these five variables, a variate of the following form could be created:

$$V_k = L_1X_1 + L_2X_2 + L_3X_3 + L_4X_4 + L_5X_5$$

V_k represents the score for nostalgia, X_1 to X_5 represent the observed scores on the five scale items (survey questions) that are expected to indicate nostalgia, and L_1 to L_5 are parameter estimates much like regression weights that suggest how highly related each variable is to the overall nostalgia score.

While this equation might appear a little intimidating, don't worry! We do not have to manually calculate these scores. We'll rely on the computer to do the heavy lifting. However, this type of relationship is common to multivariate procedures.

Classifying Multivariate Techniques

Exhibit 24.1 presents a very basic classification of multivariate data analysis procedures. Two basic groups of multivariate techniques are *dependence methods* and *interdependence methods.*

Dependence Techniques

dependence techniques
Multivariate statistical techniques that explain or predict one or more dependent variables.

When hypotheses involve distinction between independent and dependent variables, **dependence techniques** are needed. For instance, when we hypothesize that nostalgia is related positively to purchase intentions, nostalgia takes on the character of an independent variable and purchase intentions take on the character of a dependent variable. Predicting the dependent variable "sales" on the basis of numerous independent variables is a problem frequently investigated with dependence techniques. *Multiple regression analysis, multiple discriminant analysis, multivariate analysis of variance,* and *structural equations modeling* are all dependence methods.

Interdependence Techniques

interdependence techniques
Multivariate statistical techniques that give meaning to a set of variables or seek to group things together; no distinction is made between dependent and independent variables.

When researchers examine questions that do not distinguish between independent and dependent variables, **interdependence techniques** are used. No one variable or variable subset is to be predicted from or explained by the others. The most common interdependence methods are *factor analysis, cluster analysis,* and *multidimensional scaling.* A manager might utilize these techniques to determine which employee motivation items tend to group together (factor analysis), to identify profitable customer market segments (cluster analysis), or to provide a perceptual map of cities being considered for a new plant (multidimensional scaling).

Influence of Measurement Scales

As in other forms of data analysis, the nature of the measurement scales will determine which multivariate technique is appropriate for the data. Exhibits 24.2 and 24.3 show that selection of a

EXHIBIT 24.1
Which Multivariate Approach Is Appropriate?

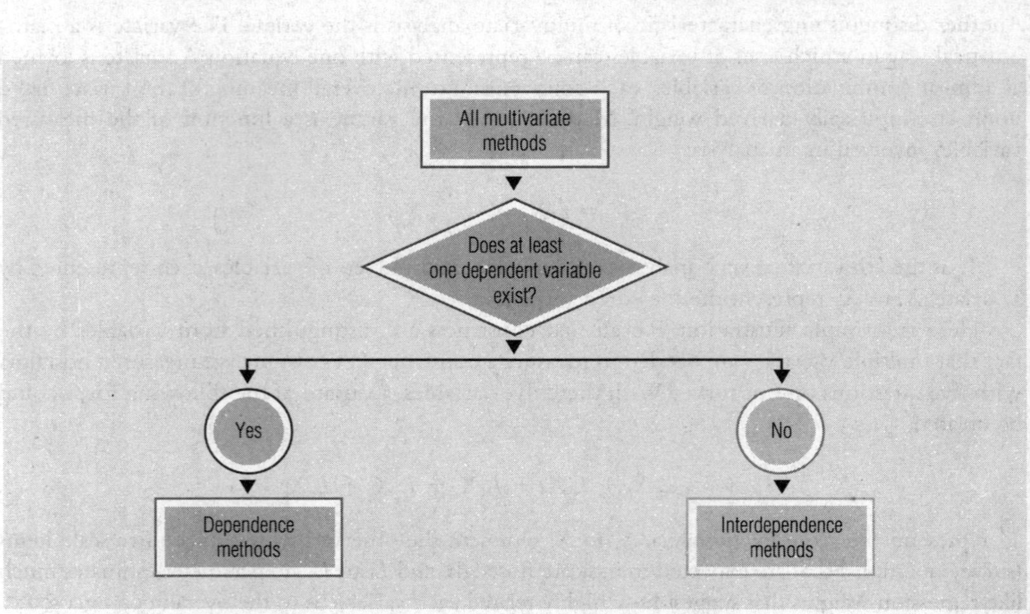

EXHIBIT 24.2
Which Multivariate Dependence Technique Should I Use?

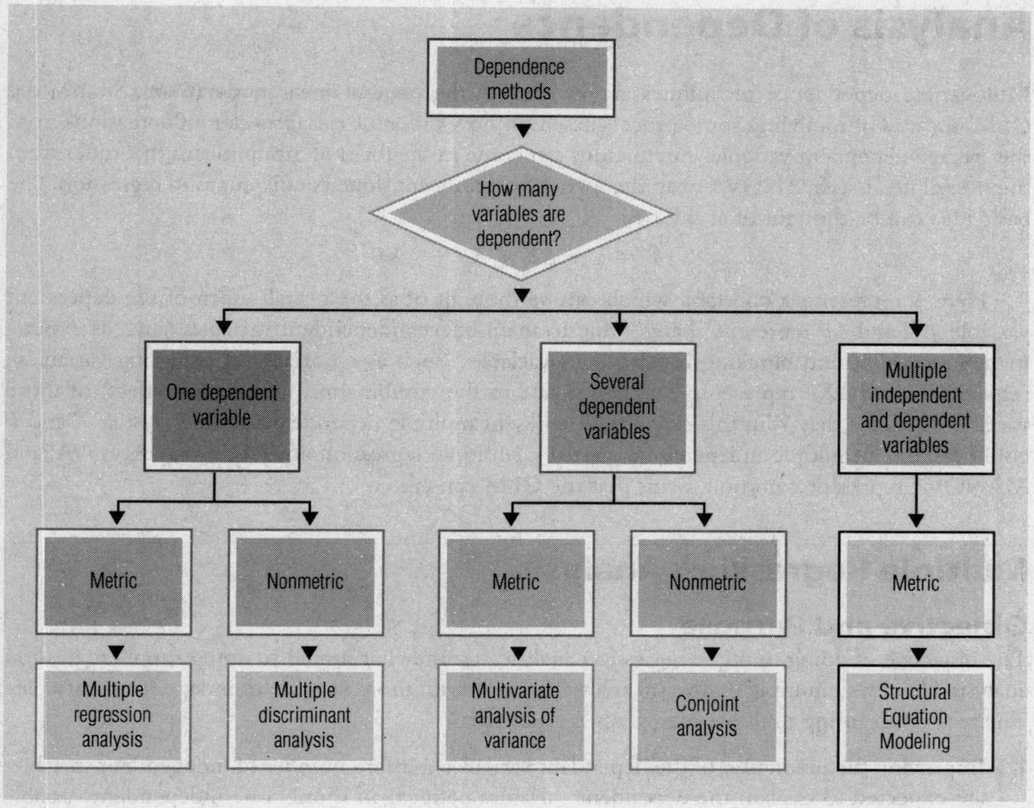

EXHIBIT 24.3
Which Multivariate Interdependence Technique Should I Use?

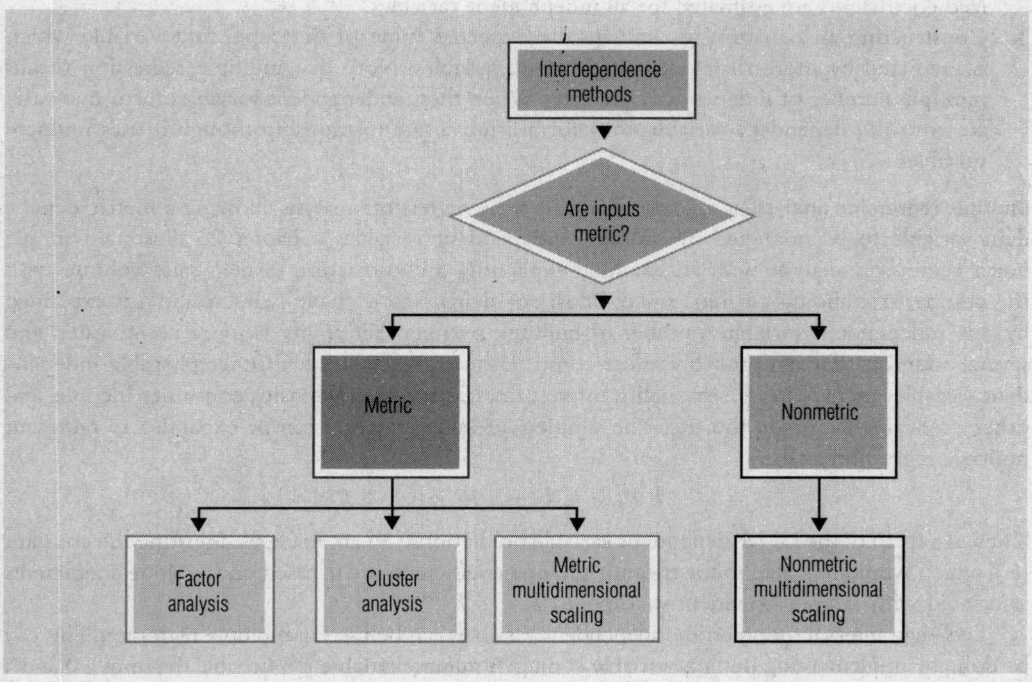

multivariate technique requires consideration of the types of measures used for both independent and dependent sets of variables. These exhibits refer to nominal and ordinal scales as *nonmetric* and interval and ratio scales as *metric.*

Analysis of Dependence

general linear model (GLM)

A way of explaining and predicting a dependent variable based on fluctuations (variation) from its mean. The fluctuations are due to changes in independent variables.

Multivariate dependence techniques are variants of the **general linear model (GLM)**. Simply, the GLM is a way of modeling some process based on how different variables cause fluctuations from the average dependent variable. Fluctuations can come in the form of group means that differ from the overall mean as in ANOVA or in the form of a significant slope coefficient as in regression. The basic idea can be thought of as follows:

$$\hat{Y}_i = \mu + \Delta X + \Delta F + \Delta XF$$

Here, μ represents a constant, which can be thought of as the overall mean of the dependent variable, ΔX and ΔF represent changes due to main effect independent variables (such as experimental variables) and blocking independent variables (such as covariates or grouping variables), respectively, and ΔXF represents the change due to the combination (interaction effect) of those variables. Realize that Y_i in this case could represent multiple dependent variables, just as X and F could represent multiple independent variables. Multiple regression analysis, n-way ANOVA, and MANOVA represent common forms that the GLM can take.

Multiple Regression Analysis

Objective and Purpose

The objective of doing multiple regression analysis is somewhat similar to doing simple regression analysis. However, multiple regression analysis is done with more number of independent variables. The reasons for using multiple regression analysis are:

1. Improving the prediction of the dependant variables, as more number of independent variables are expected to explain the dependent variables better than if only one independent variable was used.
2. Estimating the effect of individual independent variable on dependent variable. Un-standardized coefficients are estimated for all independent variables.
3. Constructing an equation to estimate the expected value of the dependant variable which is predicted by more than one independent variables. Note that multiple regression means multiple number of independent variables. When these independent variables form one variate with the dependent variable, they form a univariate relationship though it uses multiple variables.

multiple regression analysis

An analysis of association in which the effects of two or more independent variables on a single, interval-scaled dependent variable are investigated simultaneously.

Multiple regression analysis is an extension of simple regression analysis allowing a metric dependent variable to be predicted by multiple independent variables. Chapter 23 illustrated simple linear regression analysis with an example explaining a construction dealer's sales volume with the number of building permits issued. Thus, one dependent variable (sales volume) is explained by one independent variable (number of building permits). Yet reality is more complicated and several additional factors probably affect construction equipment sales. Other plausible independent variables include price, seasonality, interest rates, advertising intensity, consumer income, and other economic factors in the area. The simple regression equation can be expanded to represent multiple regression analysis:

$$Y_i = b_0 + b_1X_1 + b_2X_2 + b_3X_3 + \cdots + b_nX_n + e_i$$

Thus, as a form of the GLM, dependent variable predictions ($\hat{Y}$) are made by adjusting the constant (b_o), which would be equal to the mean if all slope coefficients are 0, based on the slope coefficients associated with each independent variable ($b_1, b_2, \ldots, b_n$).[10]

dummy variable

The way a dichotomous (two group) independent variable is represented in regression analysis by assigning a 0 to one group and a 1 to the other.

Less-than interval (nonmetric) independent variables can be used in multiple regression. This can be done by implementing dummy variable coding. A **dummy variable** is a variable that uses a 0 and a 1 to code the different levels of dichotomous variable (for instance, residential or commercial building permit). Multiple dummy variables can be included in a regression model. For example, dummy coding is appropriate when data from two countries are being compared. Suppose the average labor rate for automobile production is included in a sample taken from respondents in the United States and in South Korea. A response from the United States could be assigned a 0 and responses from South Korea could be assigned a 1 to create a country variable appropriate for use with multiple regression.

A SIMPLE EXAMPLE

Assume that a toy manufacturer wishes to explain store sales (dependent variable) using a sample of stores from Canada and Europe. Several hypotheses are offered:

- H1: *Competitor's sales* are related negatively to our firm's sales.
- H2: Sales are higher in communities that have a *sales office* than when no sales office is present.
- H3: *Grammar school enrollment* in a community is related positively to sales.

Competitor's sales is how much the primary competitor sold in the same stores over the same time period. Both the dependent variable and the competitor's sales are ratio variables measured in euros (Canadian sales were converted to euros). The presence of a sales office is a categorical variable that can be represented with dummy coding (0 = no office in this particular community, 1 = office in this community). Grammar school enrollment is also a ratio variable simply represented by the number of students enrolled in elementary schools in each community (in thousands).[11] A sample of 24 communities is gathered and the data are entered into a regression program to produce the following results:

Regression equation: $\hat{Y} = 102.18 + 0.387X_1 + 115.2X_2 + 6.73X_3$

Coefficient of multiple determination (R^2) = 0.845

F-value = 14.6; $p < 0.05$

Note that all the signs in the equation are positive. Thus, the regression equation indicates that sales are positively related to X_1, X_2, and X_3. The coefficients show the effect on the dependent variable of a 1-unit increase in any of the independent variables. The value or weight, b_1, associated with X_1 is 0.387. Thus, a one-unit increase ($1,000) in competitors' sales volume (X_1) in the community is actually associated with an increase of $387 in the toy manufacturer's sales ($0.387 \times \$1,000 = \$387$). The value of $b_2 = 115.2$, which indicates that an increase of $115,200 (115.2 thousand) in toy sales is expected with each additional unit of X_2. Thus, it appears that having a company sales office in a community is associated with a very positive effect on sales. Grammar school enrollments also may help predict sales. An increase of 1 unit of enrollment (1,000 students) indicates a sales increase of $6,730.

Because the effect associated with X_1 is positive, H1 is not supported; as competitor sales increase, our sales increase as well. The effects associated with H2 and H3 are also positive, which is in the hypothesized direction. Thus, if the coefficients are statistically significant, H2 and H3 will be supported.

ASSUMPTIONS OF MULTIPLE REGRESSION

Multiple regression is an estimation process, and there is a certain element of error involved in the process of using the multiple regression equation as the foundation for prediction. This is because we are unable to include all the relevant independent variables that would explain the dependent variable completely. There is a certain variance which occurs in the dependant variable which is estimated or predicted by using multiple regressions. Hence, the technique provides us with a measure of the variance.

Multiple regression model works under the following basic assumptions. These assumptions need to be met to reduce the probabilities of Type I or Type II error. Non-compliance of these assumptions might also lead to overestimation or underestimation of the parameters as well as predictive power of the model.

1. The error term is normally distributed. One of the most important assumptions in multiple regression is that the error term of dependent variable for particular values of independent variables is normally distributed. What it means is that for specific values of independent variables, there could be several values of dependent variables. The difference between the actual value of y and the estimated value of y follows normal distribution. The expectation of this normal distribution of error is zero. For instance, if we generate estimates of footfalls per month in a newly opened retail store of the Aditya Birla Group based on the independent variables of family income and family size, and we subtract the actual footfalls from the expected, then the sum of all the errors obtained should be equal to zero.

2. Dependent variable is normally distributed. For each value of independent variables, the distribution of the dependent variable follows normal distribution. The expected value of distribution is a point on the regression line. Similarly, for every set of specific values of independent variables, corresponding dependent variable values follow normal distributions. Expected values of each of these distributions of dependent variable are estimated values of dependent variable. Consequently, these expected values of dependent variables fall on regression line.

3. Multiple regression model relies on the assumption that there is a linear relationship between dependant variable and multiple number of independent variables. Standard regression can examine accurately if there exists a linear relationship between dependant and independent variables. The linearity of the regression model represents the amount by which the change in dependent variable is associated with the independent variables. However, in many cases, nonlinear relationships may exist. The importance of linearity can be explained by the fact that existence of nonlinear relationships between the independent and dependant variables might cause an underestimation of the actual relationship. Hence, it is important to account the non-linear relationship.

4. Independent variables are measured without error. The variables of our concern are often subjective and can be difficult to measure accurately, causing measurement error. This is an essential apprehension if the objective of the study or analysis is to precisely measure the relationships that exist in the population. Thus, the regression model assumes that independent variables are measured omitting the error. Adding to that, the independent variables do not have any correlation with the error terms in the regression equation.

5. Assumption of homoscedasticity is followed. The variance of errors of dependent variables for each set of specific values of independent variables is constant. This assumption is called homoscedasticity. It implies that since the error is due to the measurement of dependent variables, the variance of dependent variables is also the same as error variance. In case the variances of error values for specific sets of independent variables are different, heteroscedasticity is indicated. If we plot the line that our regression equation generates, then the error terms should be in the form of a cluster near the regression line and should have an equal width above and below the line. But given the situation when the error terms get scattered at places away from the regression line, heteroscedasticity is created.

6. Error terms are not correlated with each other. This assumption states that if we know the error term's value for a particular observation, it is not possible for us to predict in advance the value of the next error term, since one error term is independent of another error term.

REGRESSION COEFFICIENTS IN MULTIPLE REGRESSION

Recall that in simple regression, the coefficient $\mathbf{b}_1$ represents the slope of X on Y. Multiple regression involves multiple slope estimates, or regression weights. One challenge in regression models is to understand how one independent variable affects the dependent variable, considering the effect of other independent variables. When the independent variables are related to each other, the regression weight associated with one independent variable is affected by the regression weight of another. Regression coefficients are unaffected by each other only when independent variables are totally independent.

Conventional regression programs can provide standardized parameter estimates, β_1, β_2, and so on, that can be thought of as *partial regression coefficients.* The correlation between Y and X_1, controlling for the correlation that X_2 has with the Y, is called **partial correlation**. Consider a standardized regression model with only two independent variables:[12]

partial correlation
The correlation between two variables after taking into account the fact that they are correlated with other variables too.

$$Y = \beta_1 X_1 + \beta_2 X_2 + e_i$$

The coefficients β_1 and β_2 are partial regression coefficients, which express the relationship between the independent variable and dependent variable taking into consideration that the other variable also is related to the dependent variable. As long as the correlation between independent variables is modest, partial regression coefficients adequately represent the relationships. When the

RESEARCH SNAPSHOT

Too Much of a Good Thing!

Researchers often test hypotheses by examining regression coefficients. Thus, we are often looking for correlations, sometimes in all the wrong places. Financial data can be problematic to analyze. Consider the case of a financial manager trying to analyze gross margin (dependent variable = margin per employee) using the following independent variables:

- Average sales per square foot per quarter
- Average labor costs per week
- Years of experience for the manager
- Job performance rating for the previous year (100-point scale)

Regression results can be obtained in SPSS by clicking on ANALYZE, REGRESSION, and then LINEAR. The VIF column must be requested by clicking on STATISTICS and then checking COLLINEARITY DIAGNOSTICS. After doing so, the following results are obtained. For the overall model,

ANOVA(b)

Model		Sum of Squares	*df*	Mean Square	*F*	Sig.
1	Regression	142566.5332	4	35641.6333	13.56899	.0000008
	Residual	91934.43848	35	2626.698242		
	Total	234500.9717	39			

A Predictors: (constant), performance, experience, labor, sales
B Dependent Variable: margin

The *F* of 13.57 is highly significant (<0.001), so the variables explain a large portion of the variance in the dependent variable.

Coefficients(a)

Model		Unstandardized Coefficients B	Std. Error	Standardized Coefficients Beta	*t*	Sig.	VIF
1	(Constant)	171.242614	235.9374392		0.725797	0.47279	
	Sales	0.090784631	0.030835442	2.339759409	2.944165	0.00572	56.3836
	Labor	−0.070267446	0.035014493	−1.587938574	−2.00681	0.05254	55.8971
	Experience	−0.488078747	0.955764142	−0.054331204	−0.51067	0.61279	1.0105
	Performance	−1.856084354	3.034080822	−0.068978263	−0.61175	0.54466	1.1351

a Dependent Variable: margin

The model R^2 is 0.61 also supporting this conclusion. The results for the independent variable tests show the following:

Even though the model results appear strong, only one independent variable is significant at a Type I error rate of 0.050 — sales. However, the β coefficients do not make sense. The β coefficients for both sales and labor are beyond the range that β should theoretically take (−1.0 to 1.0). Nothing can be correlated with something more than perfectly (which would be a correlation of 1.0 or −1.0). Notice also that the two VIF factors for sales and labor are in the 50s. Generally, when multiple VIF factors approach 5 or greater, problems with multicollinearity can be expected. The high correlation between sales and labor is a problem illustrating multicollinearity. Multicollinearity (sometimes just referred to as collinearity) in regression analysis refers to how strongly interrelated the independent variables in a model are.

As often occurs with financial data, they can be difficult to use as independent variables. In this case, the researcher may wish to rerun the model after dropping one of the offending variables.

© iStock

© PHOTODISC/GETTY IMAGES

correlation between two independent variables becomes high, the regression coefficients may not be reliable, as illustrated in the Research Snapshot "Too Much of a Good Thing!"

When researchers want to know which independent variable is most predictive of the dependent variable, the standardized regression coefficient (β) is used. One huge advantage of β is that it provides a constant scale. In other words, the βs are directly comparable. Therefore, the greater the absolute value of the standardized regression coefficient, the more that particular independent variable is responsible for explaining the dependent variable. For example, suppose in the toy example above, the following standardized regression coefficients were found:

$$\beta_1 = 0.10$$
$$\beta_2 = 0.30$$
$$\beta_3 = 0.10$$

The resulting standardized regression equation would be

$$Y = 0.10X_1 + 0.30X_2 + 0.10X_3 + e_i$$

Using standardized coefficients, the researcher concludes that the relationship between competitor's sales (X_1) and company sales (Y) is the same strength as is the relationship between grammar school enrollment (X_3) and company sales. Perhaps more important, though, the conclusion can also be reached that the relationship between having a sales office in the area (X_2) and sales is three times as strong as the other two relationships. Thus, management may wish to place more emphasis on locating sales offices in major markets.

R^2 IN MULTIPLE REGRESSION

The coefficient of multiple determination in multiple regression indicates the percentage of variation in Y explained by the combination of *all* independent variables. For example, a value of $R^2 = 0.845$ means that 84.5 percent of the variance in the dependent variable is explained by the independent variables. If two independent variables are truly independent (uncorrelated with each other), the R^2 for a multiple regression model is equal to the separate R^2 values that would result from two separate simple regression models. More typically, the independent variables are at least moderately related to one another, meaning that the model R^2 from a multiple regression model will be less than the separate R^2 values resulting from individual simple regression models. This reduction in R^2 is proportionate to the extent to which the independent variables exhibit multicollinearity.

The R-squared analyses of the pattern of residuals and hypothesis testing are used for assessing a model fit. Statistical significance is checked by an F-test of the overall fit, after which t-tests of individual parameters are conducted.

The coefficient of determination in multiple regression provides the measure of goodness of fit for the estimated regression model. Sum of the errors is the quantity that is minimized by the least squares method that corresponds to the extent to which the regression model fits the data. This quantity of error is known as the sum of squares due to errors (SSE). SSE is the measure of the error in using the estimated regression equation to estimate the values of the dependent variable in the sample.

$$\text{SSE} = (Y_i - \widehat{Y}_i)^2$$

Sum of squares due to regression (SSR) is the measure of how much the regression model fits the data, i.e., how much deviation of actual value from the mean value of dependent variable is estimated by the regression model. Consequently, this is the difference between the estimated values of the dependent variable from the mean value.

$$\text{SSR} = \Sigma(\widehat{Y}_i - \overline{Y})^2$$

The measure of total error involved in using the mean to estimate the dependent variable is provided by the difference between the mean value of dependent variable and its estimated value by the regression model. This is measured using another sum of squares called the total sum of square (SST).

$$\text{SST} = \Sigma(Y_i - \overline{Y})^2$$

Relationship between SST, SSR, and SSE is as follows:

$$SST = SSR + SSE$$

The coefficient of determination is given by:

$$R^2 = \frac{SSR}{SST}$$

STATISTICAL SIGNIFICANCE IN MULTIPLE REGRESSION

Following from simple regression, an *F*-test is used to test statistical significance by comparing the variation explained by the regression equation to the residual error variation. The *F*-test allows for testing of the relative magnitudes of the sum of squares due to the regression (*SSR*) and the error sum of squares (SSE).

$$F = \frac{(SSR/k)}{(SSE)/(n-k-1)} = \frac{MSR}{MSE}$$

where

k = number of independent variables

n = number of observations

MSR = Mean Squares Regression

MSE = Mean Squares Error

Degrees of freedom for the *F*-test (*df*) are:

$$df \text{ for the numerator} = k$$

$$df \text{ for the denominator} = n - k - 1$$

For our toy sales example,

$$df\,(\text{numerator}) = 3$$

$$df\,(\text{denominator}) = 24 - 3 - 1 = 20$$

In the toy example, we have 24 observations (different communities) and 3 independent variables (competitor sales, sales office, and school enrollment). A table of critical *F*-values shows that for 3 and 20 *df*, and a 0.05 Type I error rate, a value of 3.10 or more is necessary for the regression model to be considered significant, meaning that it explains a significant portion of the total variation in the dependent variable. In practice, statistical programs will report the p-value associated with the *F*-test directly. Similarly, the programs report the statistical test for each individual independent variable. Independent variables with p-values below the acceptable Type I error rate are considered significant predictors of the dependent variable.

To find out the standard error of the estimate, we use the following equation:

$$S_e = \left[\sum_{i-1}^{n} \frac{(y_i - \hat{y}_i)^2}{n - p - 1} \right]^{1/2}$$

where

$\hat{y}_i$ = the value of the dependant variable estimated from the regression equation

n = the number of observations taken

p = the numbers of predictors used, common name of independent variable

Let us consider the simple linear regression model $Y = \beta_0 + \beta_1 X + \varepsilon$. For x and y to be linearly related, we must have $\beta_1 \neq 0$. We use *t*-test for this purpose. In multiple regression also, we use the same concept while testing the statistical significance of contribution of each variable in the model. We use *t*-test to check the statistical significance of individual parameter.

We test the following hypothesis:

$$H_0 : \beta_i = 0$$

$$H_a : \beta_i \neq 0$$

If H_0 is rejected, then $\beta_i \neq 0$ and a statistically significant relationship between dependent variable and *i*th independent variable exists. But if H_0 cannot be rejected, then we have insufficient evidence to say that a significant relationship exists. The properties of the sampling distribution of b_i provide the basis for the hypothesis test.

INTERPRETATION OF MODEL PARAMETERS

The partial regression coefficient b_1 in multiple regression is interpreted differently from the regression coefficient b_1 in simple regression due to the correlation that usually exists between X_1 and X_2. In simple linear regression, there is only one independent variable. Hence, X_2 was not considered and the variation in Y that was shared between X_1 and X_2 was attributed only to X_1 in simple regression. This does not hold true in the case of multiple independent variables. Hence, in multiple regression, b_1 represents the expected change in Y for a unit change in X_1, keeping X_2 constant. Similarly, b_2 represents the expected change in Y when X_2 is changed by one unit, keeping X_1 constant. The values of the regression coefficients change when different samples are taken. To measure this variation, standard error associated with each of them is used.

Consider the variance of the random error ε around the true line of regression, i.e., σ_e^2, and the unbiased estimate of σ_e^2 is the mean square error (MSE) denoted by S_e^2.

$$S_e^2 = \frac{\sum (Y_i - \widehat{Y}_i)^2}{(n-2)}$$

where

Y_i = the observed value of Y for the *i*th observation

$\widehat{Y}_i$ = the estimated value of Y for the *i*th observation

S_e = the standard error of estimate (SSE)

The interpretation of the standard error of estimate parallels that for the standard deviation.

STEPS IN INTERPRETING A MULTIPLE REGRESSION MODEL

Multiple regression models often are used to test some proposed theoretical model. For instance, a researcher may be asked to develop and test a model explaining business unit performance. Why do some business units outperform others? Multiple regression models can be interpreted using these steps:

1. Examine the model *F*-test. If the test result is not significant, the model should be dismissed and there is no need to proceed to further steps.
2. Examine the individual statistical tests for each parameter estimate. An independent variable with significant results can be considered a significant explanatory variable. If an independent variable is not significant, the model should be run again with nonsignificant predictors deleted. Often, it is best to eliminate predictor variables one at a time, then rerun the reduced model.
3. Examine the model R^2. No cutoff values exist that can distinguish an acceptable amount of explained variation across all regression models. However, the absolute value of R^2 is more important when the researcher is more interested in prediction than in explanation. In other words, the regression is run for pure forecasting purposes. When the model is more oriented toward explanation of which variables are most important in explaining the dependent variable, cutoff values for the model R^2 are not really appropriate.
4. Examine collinearity diagnostics. **Multicollinearity** in regression analysis refers to how strongly interrelated the independent variables in a model are. When multicollinearity is too high, the individual parameter estimates become difficult to interpret. Most regression programs can compute variance inflation factors (VIF) for each variable. As a rule of thumb, VIF above 5.0 suggests problems with multicollinearity.[13]

multicollinearity
The extent to which independent variables in a multiple regression analysis are correlated with each other; high multicollinearity can make interpreting parameter estimates difficult or impossible.

Exhibit 24.4 illustrates these steps. The regression model explains business unit profitability for a sample of 28 business units for a Fortune 500 company. The independent variables are hours (average hours spent in training for the workforce), budget (the percentage of the promotional budget used), and state (a dummy variable indicating whether the business unit is in Arizona and

EXHIBIT 24.4 **Interpreting Multiple Regression Results**

The SAS System

The REG Procedure
Model: MODEL1
Dependent Variable: Paid

Number of Observations Read 28
Number of Observations Used 28

Analysis of Variance

Source	DF	Sum of Squares	Mean Square	F Value	Pr > F
Model	3	1770668	590223	19.38	<.0001
Error	24	731035	30460		
Corrected Total	27	2501703			

Root MSE	174.52738	R-Square	0.7078
Dependent Mean	654.03571	Adj R-Sq	0.6713
Coeff Var	26.68469		

1. Interpret model *F*-test. Test is significant ($p < .05$).

Parameter Estimates

Variable	DF	Parameter Estimate	Standard Error	t Value	Pr > |t|	Standardized Estimate	VIF
Intercept	1	−109.90538	217.46253	−0.51	0.6179	0	
Hours	1	0.99438	0.27688	3.59	0.0015	0.55433	1.96
Budget	1	6.60121	3.54784	1.86	0.0751	0.28210	1.89
State	1	−66.36397	84.82434	−0.78	0.4416	−0.11073	1.65

3. The model R^2 is interpreted. The IVs explain over 70% of variation in the dependent variable.

2. Interpret individual parameter estimates. In this case, only hours is significant based on a p-value below .05 (0.0015).

4. VIFs are checked for multicollinearity problems. None are indicated here.

coded 0, or in Ohio and coded 1). In this case, the researcher is using a maximum acceptable Type I error rate of 0.05. The conclusion reached from this analysis is that hours spent in training seem to pay off in increased business unit profitability as evidenced by the significant, positive regression coefficient ($\beta = 0.55, p < 0.05$).

Consider a regression equation with two independent variables x_1 and x_2:

$$y = a + b_1x_1 + b_2x_2$$

The interpretation of the regression coefficient b_1 is: when x_1 changes by one unit, b_1 represents the change in y holding x_2 constant. Hence, b_1 can also be called partial regression coefficient. The combined effects are additive, i.e., if x_1 and x_2 are both changed by one unit, the expected change in y would be $b_1 + b_2$. Also, if a regression coefficient is negative, it means that a unit increase in the independent variable will lead to a decrease in the dependent variable by the value of the regression coefficient, i.e., there is a negative correlation. It is important to note that non-standardized regression coefficients have units. So, the magnitude alone does not convey anything without the units.

Standardized regression coefficients are nothing but the partial regression coefficients obtained when all the independent and dependent variables have been standardized to a mean of 0 and a variance of 1 before estimating the regression equation.

$$\beta_i = b_i(s_{x1}/s_y)$$

β weights are useful because two variables that are measured in different units, as height and weight, can be compared.

Multicollinearity

Multicollinearity exists when the independent variables in the regression equation are themselves highly correlated with each other. In such a case, results of multiple regression analysis will seem paradoxical, i.e., although the overall significance of the set of all independent variables seems high, none of them are individually statistically significant. This is because the correlated variables essentially convey the same information, so although they together contribute a lot, one of them will not contribute once the other one has.

Example: In a regression model, let y be the customer satisfaction of restaurant service; and x_1 and x_2 (predictors) be food quality and price of the food, respectively. Now, if x_1 and x_2 are correlated, then both of them will have a positive effect on customer satisfaction. The food quality and price of the food are interrelated. While the F-test will be statistically significant indicating that the model is adequate for predicting customer satisfaction, the individual t-tests for β_1 and β_2 may be insignificant suggesting that none of the two predictors, i.e., food quality and price significantly affect customer satisfaction y.

β_1 is the expected change in the *mean value of customer satisfaction* due to *one unit change in food quality* given *price* is already in the model.

β_2 is the expected change in the *mean value of customer satisfaction* due to *price* given *food quality* is already in the model.

Since both x_1 and x_2, i.e., food quality and price of the food contribute redundant information about y, i.e., *customer satisfaction*, once one of the predictors is in the model, the other one does not have much more to contribute. Due to this reason, F-test may be significant and indicates that at least one of the predictors out of the two is important for predicting customer satisfaction, yet the individual tests for predictors may indicate that the contribution of the predictor, given that the other one has already been included, is not really important.

DETECTION OF MULTICOLLINEARITY

1. F-test indicating that predictor set is significant but individual t-tests not showing significance of predictors

2. Large changes in the estimated regression coefficients when an independent variable is added or deleted

3. Calculation of variance inflation factor (VIF), given by

$$\text{VIF} = 1/(1 - R_j^2),$$

where R_j^2 is the coefficient of determination of a regression of predictor j on all the other predictors. If VIF is greater than 5 or 10 as specified, multicollinearity exists.

WHEN IS MULTICOLLINEARITY A PROBLEM?

If the aim is simply to predict y from a set of x variables, multicollinearity is not a problem, since it does not affect the estimate of the dependent variable y or standard error. The predictions will still be accurate, and the overall R^2 (or the adjusted R^2) quantifies how well the model predicts the Y values. If, however, the aim is to understand how the various x variables impact y, multicollinearity can be a big problem. Individual p-values may be high, although the corresponding x is important or significant.

Remedies to negate the effects of multicollinearity are as follows:

- Combine the correlated variables. For example, if speed and time are the variables, replace them with distance, which is derived from speed and time.
- Drop one of the correlated variables.

- Reduce the impact of multicollinearity by increasing sample size, to get narrower confidence intervals.
- Conduct factor analysis. Factor analysis can be used to bring out underlying factors that depend on two or more of the correlated variables. Further, another regression may be run using these factors.

Heteroscedasticity

In ordinary least squares (OLS) methods for estimating unknown parameters in multiple regression, homoscedasticity, i.e., variance of error terms is constant, is an assumption. If the error terms do not have constant variance, they are said to be heteroscedastic. Heteroscedasticity does not result in biased parameter estimates. Heteroscedasticity biases the standard errors of our estimates, and therefore, affects hypothesis testing by increasing the probability of committing Type I error.

CAUSES OF HETEROSCEDASTICITY

1. Errors may increase as the value of an independent variable (IV) increases. For example, consider a model in which annual family income is the IV and annual family expenditures on dinning out is the dependent variable (DV). Families with low incomes will spend relatively less in dinning out, and the variations in expenditures across such families will be small. But for families with large incomes, the amount they spend in dinning out will be higher and there will also be greater variability among such families, resulting in heteroscedasticity. Any time a high value for an IV is a necessary but not sufficient condition for an observation to have a high value on a DV, heteroscedasticity is likely.
2. Errors may also increase as the values of an IV become more extreme in either direction, e.g., perception about particular store that ranges from extremely negative to extremely positive.
3. Heteroscedasticity can also occur if there are moderation effects due to subpopulation differences or other interaction effects, e.g., the effect of advertisement on the intention to buy may significantly differ between male and female buyers.
4. Measurement error is another cause of heteroscedasticity. If the question is ambiguous, some respondents might provide more erroneous responses than others and the variability differs.
5. Other model misspecifications can produce heteroscedasticity. For example, it may be that instead of using *Y*, log of *Y* should be used. Such case transformation of variable would provide a better result. Important variables may be omitted from the model. If the model were correctly specified, the patterns of heteroscedasticity may disappear.

REMEDIES FOR HETEROSCEDASTICITY

1. **Re-specify the model or transform the variables.** Sometimes, heteroscedasticity results from improper model specification. There may be subgroup differences as explained above or effects of variables may not be linear or perhaps some important variables may have been left out of the model.
2. **Use weighted least squares (WLS) method.** In place of ordinary least square, transformed or weighted values of *X* and *Y* may be used and WLS method may be applied. The weights vary over observations, depending on the changing error variances, but are mostly unknown or hard to estimate.

Prediction of the Model

The principal purpose of a regression model is to predict or estimate the value of one variable from known or assumed values of other variables related to it. The regression equation developed can be used to predict an average value over the range of the sample data. The prediction may be good for short to medium ranges. Predicting a change over time or extrapolating from present conditions to future conditions is not the function of regression analysis. However, to make estimates of the future, time series analysis can be used.

The standard error of estimate (i.e., square root of error mean square) is a good indicator of the "quality" of a prediction model since it adjusts the error sum of squares for the number of predictors in the model as follows:

$$\text{EMS} = \frac{\text{Error Sum of Squares}}{(N - \text{Number of Linearly Independent Predictors})}$$

If one keeps adding predictors that do not contribute to a model, the EMS will become less stable.

Confidence interval also provides a useful way of assessing the quality of prediction. In prediction by regression, often one or more of the following constructions are of interest:

1. **Confidence interval estimate for a future value.** A confidence interval of interest can be used to evaluate the accuracy of a single (future) value of y corresponding to a chosen value of X (say, X_0).
2. **Confidence interval estimate for a single point on the line.** If a particular value of the predictor variable (say, X_0) is of special importance, a confidence interval on the value of the criterion variable (i.e., average Y at X_0) corresponding to X_0 may be used.
   It is of interest to compare the above two different kinds of confidence intervals. The first kind has larger confidence interval that reflects less accuracy resulting from the estimation of a single future value of y rather than the mean value computed for the second kind of confidence interval. The second kind of confidence interval can also be used to identify any outliers in the data.
3. **Confidence region for the regression line as a whole.** When the entire line is of interest, a confidence region permits one to simultaneously make confidence statements about the estimates of Y for a number of values of the predictor variable X. In order that the region adequately covers the range of interest of the predictor variable X, usually, data size must be more than 10 pairs of observations.

ANOVA (n-Way) and MANOVA

As discussed above, regression is a form of the GLM with a single continuous dependent measure and continuous independent measure(s). An ANOVA or MANOVA model also represents a form of the GLM. ANOVA can be extended beyond one-way ANOVA to predict a continuous dependent variable with multiple categorical independent variables. **Multivariate analysis of variance (MANOVA)** is a multivariate technique that predicts multiple continuous dependent variables with multiple independent variables. The independent variables are categorical, although a continuous control variable can be included in the form of a covariate. Statistical programs usually refer to any ANOVA with only one dependent variable as univariate analysis of variance or simply as ANOVA.

multivariate analysis of variance (MANOVA)

A multivariate technique that predicts multiple continuous dependent variables with multiple categorical independent variables.

N-WAY (UNIVARIATE) ANOVA

The interpretation of an n-way ANOVA model follows closely from the regression results described above. The steps involved are essentially the same with the addition of interpreting differences between means:

1. Examine the overall model F-test result. If significant, proceed.
2. Examine individual F-tests for each individual independent variable.
3. For each significant categorical independent variable, interpret the effect by examining the group means (see Chapter 12).
4. For each significant continuous variable (covariate), interpret the parameter estimate (**b**).
5. For each significant interaction, interpret the means for each combination. A graphical representation as illustrated in Chapter 12 can greatly assist in this interpretation.

INTERPRETING MANOVA

Compared to ANOVA, a MANOVA model produces an additional layer of testing. The first layer of testing involves the multivariate F-test, which is based on a statistic called Wilke's Lambda (Λ).

RESEARCH SNAPSHOT

How to Get MANOVA Results

A department store developer gathered data looking at the effect of nostalgia on customer impressions. A field experiment was
set up in which a key department was either given a modern design or a retro design. It was hoped that the retro design would create feelings of nostalgia. Several hundred consumers were interviewed. Since two related dependent variables are involved (Y_1 = interest and Y_2 = excitement), MANOVA is the appropriate technique.

MANOVA can be conducted using SPSS by clicking on ANALYZE, then GENERAL LINEAR MODEL, and then MULTIVARIATE.

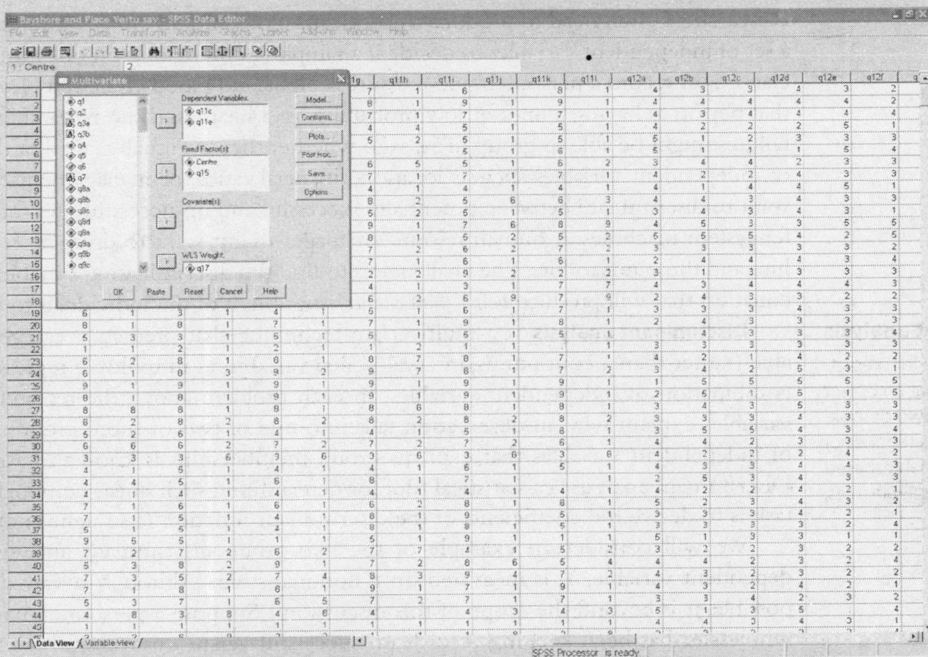

(If only one dependent variable were involved, the choice would be UNIVARIATE.) This opens a dialog box as shown here:

The dialog box includes places to enter dependent variables, fixed factors (between-subjects categorical independent variables), and covariates. In this case, the fixed factors are

1. Experimental variable (0 = modern, 1 = retro)
2. Respondent sex (0 = male, 1 = female)

Respondent age is included as a covariate or control variable (years).

SPSS provided output that can be summarized briefly:

1. Multivariate Results:
   a. Wilke's Lambda = 0.964
   b. Overall multivariate $F = 9.6$ with 2 and 510 *df*
   c. The p-value associated with this result is less than 0.001. Thus the multivariate results are significant, so the research proceeds to interpret the individual univariate ANOVA results for each dependent variable (SPSS provides these results automatically).
2. The univariate model *F* statistics for each dependent variable are both significant ($p < 0.001$) so the researcher moves on to the next step.
3. The individual effects associated with Y_1 (interest) are interpreted. For example, for the experimental variable, the result is:
   a. $F = 0.4$, with 1 and 511 *df* for interest ($p = 0.531$).
   b. Age is not significant.
   c. The interaction is not significant.
4. The individual effects associated with Y_2 (excitement) are interpreted. For example, for the experimental variable, the result is:
   a. $F = 13.4$, with 1 and 511 *df* for excitement ($p < 0.001$).
   b. Sex and age are both significant predictors too ($p < 0.001$).
   c. The interaction of sex and the retro/modern experimental variable is also significant.
5. After carefully reviewing the means for each experimental cell as well as the covariate results, the researcher reaches the following conclusions:
   a. The retro look produced more excitement but not necessarily more interest.
   b. Women are more interested and more excited about shopping.
   c. The effect of the retro condition was stronger for men than for women. That is, the difference in means between the retro and modern condition is larger for men than for women.
   d. Younger consumers are more excited about shopping.

This test examines whether or not an independent variable explains significant variation among the dependent variables within the model. If this test is significant, then the F-test results from individual univariate regression models nested within the MANOVA model are interpreted. The rest of the interpretation results follow from the one-way ANOVA or multiple regression model results above. The Research Snapshot "How to Get MANOVA Results" provides an example of how to run and interpret MANOVA.

Discriminant Analysis

Researchers often need to produce a classification of sampling units. This process may involve using a set of independent variables to decide if a sampling unit belongs in one group or another. A physician might record a person's blood pressure, weight, and blood cholesterol level and then categorize that person as having a high or low probability of a heart attack. A researcher interested in retailing failures might be able to group firms as to whether they eventually failed or did not fail on the basis of independent variables such as location, financial ratios, or management changes. A bank might want to discriminate between potentially successful and unsuccessful sites for electronic fund transfer system machines. A human resource manager might want to distinguish between applicants to hire and those not to hire. The challenge is to find the discriminating variables to use in a predictive equation that will produce *better than chance* assignment of the individuals to the correct group.

discriminant analysis

A statistical technique for predicting the probability that an object will belong in one of two or more mutually exclusive categories of the dependent variable, based on several independent variables.

Discriminant analysis is a multivariate technique that predicts a categorical dependent variable (rather than a continuous, interval-scaled variable, as in multiple regression) based on a linear combination of independent variables. In each problem above, the researcher determines which variables explain why an observation falls into one of two or more groups. A linear combination of independent variables that explains group memberships is known as a discriminant function. Discriminant analysis is a statistical tool for determining such linear combinations. The researcher's task is to derive the coefficients of the discriminant function (a straight line).

We will consider an example of the two-group discriminant analysis problem where the dependent variable, Y, is measured on a nominal scale. (Although n-way discriminant analysis is possible, it is beyond the scope of this discussion.) Suppose a personnel manager for an electrical wholesaler has been keeping records on successful versus unsuccessful sales employees. The personnel manager believes it is possible to predict whether an applicant will succeed on the basis of age, sales aptitude test scores, and mechanical ability scores. As stated at the outset, the problem is to find a linear function of the independent variables that shows large differences in group means. The first task is to estimate the coefficients of the applicant's discriminant function. To calculate the individuals' discriminant scores, the following linear function is used:

$$Z_i = b_1X_{1i} + b_2X_{2i} + \cdots + b_nX_{ni}$$

where

Z_i = ith applicant's discriminant score

b_n = discriminant coefficient for the nth variable

X_{ni} = ith applicant's value on the nth independent variable

Using scores for all the individuals in the sample, a discriminant function is determined based on the criterion that the groups be maximally differentiated on the set of independent variables.

Returning to the example with three independent variables, let us suppose the personnel manager finds the standardized weights in the equation to be

$$\begin{aligned} Z &= b_1X_1 + b_2X_2 + b_3X_3 \\ &= 0.069X_1 + 0.013X_2 + 0.0007X_3 \end{aligned}$$

This means that age (X_1) is much more important than sales aptitude test scores (X_2). Mechanical ability (X_3) has relatively minor discriminating power.

In the computation of the linear discriminant function, weights are assigned to the variables to maximize the ratio of the difference between the means of the two groups to the standard deviation within groups. The standardized discriminant coefficients, or weights, provide information about the relative importance of each of these variables in discriminating between the two groups.

A major goal of discriminant analysis is to perform a classification function. The purpose of classification in our example is to predict which applicants will be successful and which will be unsuccessful based on their age, sales aptitude test score, and mechanical ability, and to group them accordingly. To determine whether the discriminant analysis can be used as a good predictor of applicant success, current employees with known characteristics are used in constructing the model. Each observation (current employee) is placed into one of the groups based on the independent variables. Some will be classified successfully, but some will not. This information is provided in the "confusion matrix," which is similar to cross-tabulations we discussed earlier. Suppose the personnel manager has 40 successful and 45 unsuccessful employees in the sample. The confusion matrix shows that the number of correctly classified employees (72 out of 85) is much higher than would be expected by chance:

Confusion Matrix

	Predicted Group		
Actual Group	**Successful**	**Unsuccessful**	
Successful	34	6	40
Unsuccessful	7	38	45

Again, similar to cross-tabs and χ^2, tests can be performed to determine whether the rate of correct classification is statistically significant.

Exhibit 24.5 summarizes multivariate dependence techniques.

Conjoint Analysis

It is quite imperative that if a researcher asks for direct response on a particular product from the consumer, consumer's response will be highly positive. For example, if a consumer is asked how important the annual fee, the interest rate, or the name of the bank is when he decides to buy a credit card, the responses of such questions will often be very high. However, in practice, consumers don't get product features that give them highest utility. In other words, consumers often go

EXHIBIT 24.5 **Multivariate Dependence Techniques Summary**

Technique	Purpose	Number of Dependent Variables	Number of Independent Variables	Type of Measurement: Dependent	Type of Measurement: Independent
Multiple regression	To investigate simultaneously the effects of several independent variables on a dependent variable	1	2 or more	Interval	Interval
Discriminant analysis	To predict the probability that an object or individual will belong in one of two or more mutually exclusive categories, based on several independent variables	1	2 or more	Nominal	Interval
MANOVA	To determine simultaneously whether statistically significant mean differences occur between groups on several variables	2 or more	1 or more	Interval	Nominal

through trade-offs when they take a buying decision. Conjoint analysis is a technique that is used to determine the relative importance consumers attach to different attributes of a product and the utilities they attach to each level of every attribute of the product. This information is derived from consumer's evaluations of the product profiles composed of several attributes through their levels. The respondents are presented with stimuli or product profiles (called concepts) that consist of combinations of one level of each of all the attributes. Consumers are asked to evaluate these stimuli in terms of their desirability in rating or ranking scale. Conjoint analysis assigns values to the levels of each attribute through a de-compositional technique, so that the resulting values attached to the stimuli match with the input evaluations of the respondents as closely as possible. In other words, just from an overall evaluation of product concepts, the conjoint analysis technique derives internal utility of the respondents with high degree of accuracy. The underlying assumptions are that any set of stimuli, such as products, brands, or stores, is evaluated as a bundle of attributes and utility of the product profile is nothing but the sum of utility of each of these attributes.

HISTORY OF CONJOINT ANALYSIS

The history of conjoint analysis goes far beyond when it was adopted by marketing researchers. Two mathematical psychologists and statisticians, Luce and Tukey (1964), developed conjoint methods in the sixties. Conjoint analysis was then modified through discrete choice methods which were derived from econometrics on the foundation of the work of McFadden (1974) who received Nobel Prize in 2000 in economics. Some researchers say that the word "conjoint" refers to respondents evaluating the features of products or services "considered jointly." Another group of researchers opined that the word "conjoint" came from the verb "to conjoin," meaning "joined together." However, conjoint analysis does the similar activity as is meant by both groups of researchers. The main characteristic of conjoint analysis is that respondents gauge product profiles consisting different levels of multiple attributes or features. Based on how respondents gauge the combined elements, conjoint analysis derives the preference scores that the respondents might have assigned to individual components of the product that would have resulted in those overall evaluations. In other words, conjoint analysis is a decompositional technique to estimate consumers' preferences for features rather than an explicit, compositional approach of simply asking respondents to rate the various features.

OBJECTIVE OF CONJOINT ANALYSIS

Conjoint analysis has been used in marketing for a variety of purposes which include the following:

- Conjoint analysis estimates individual level utilities of each level of each attribute both individual level and aggregate level.
- Conjoint analysis can determine the relative importance of all attributes of consumers both in individual level (for each consumer) and aggregate level (for all consumers together). Conjoint analysis output consists of derived relative importance weight (in percentage form or unit form) for all the attributes of the product profile used in the evaluation task by the consumers.
- Conjoint analysis can estimate market share of brands that differ in attribute levels. Individual level utilities derived from conjoint analysis can be used as input into a choice simulator to determine the share of preference, which can be surrogated as the market share of brands.
- Marketers can determine the composition of the most preferred brand from the corresponding utilities of different attribute levels. The product (attribute level) that yields the highest utility indicates the composition of the most preferred product.

- Conjoint analysis can be used for segmenting the market based on the similarity of preference for the utilities of different levels of all attributes. A cluster analysis may be carried out to determine the number of segments of homogeneous preference, demographic and socio-graphic profile of segments as well as the size of each segment.

CONJOINT ANALYSIS RESEARCH PLAN

The researcher must identify the attributes and attribute levels to formulate conjoint analysis problem that are to be used in constructing the stimuli.. The attributes can be identified through focus group discussions of prospective consumers, discussions with industry experts, previous research on similar products, and pilot surveys. The number of attributes in a conjoint analysis can vary from three to as many as thirty, while a typical conjoint analysis consists of six or seven attributes with three to five levels in each attribute.

After identifying the important attribute, appropriate levels of these attributes should be selected. The number of attribute levels determines the number of parameters (utilities) that will be estimated. The number of attributes and its levels also determines the number of stimuli (product concepts) that will be evaluated by the respondents. To minimize the respondent evaluation task, and yet estimate the parameters with reasonable accuracy, it is desirable to restrict the number of attribute levels.

The utility or part-worth functions for the levels of an attribute may be nonlinear, meaning the utility may not vary with constant slope as the levels change from one to other. The researcher should take into account the attribute levels prevalent in the market place and the objectives of the study. Using attribute levels that are beyond the range reflected in the marketplace will decrease the believability of the evaluation task, but it will increase the accuracy with which the parameters are estimated. Once the input is determined, the conjoint analysis procedure is selected and the results are interpreted. To test the validity of the model, variation between actual responses and modeled responses is determined. The following flow chart shows systematic approach for conjoint analysis research plan.

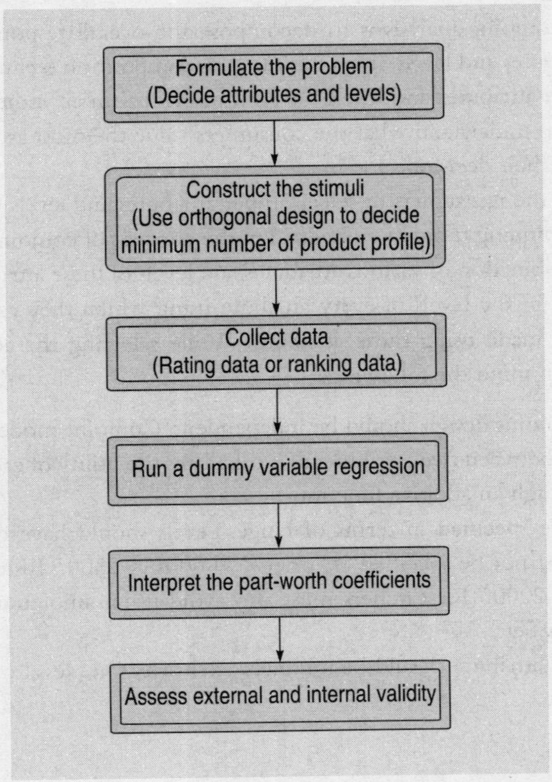

ASSUMPTIONS OF CONJOINT ANALYSIS

Conjoint analysis should only be used when the following assumptions are met:

1. A product can be described by a set of salient attributes that are mutually exclusive.
2. Consumers view the product as a combination of attributes that can be exchanged for others.
3. The total utility of a product is equivalent to the sum of the individual utilities of each attribute.
4. A conjoint analysis model is linear. However, there are some forms of conjoint analysis that relax this restriction.
5. A product that provides higher utility is preferred to a product that provides lower utility.

When these assumptions are met, conjoint analysis provides quantifiable and actionable data that include:

- Relative importance for each product attribute
- Most desirable level of each product attribute
- Potential market share for the product
- Market segmentation information

ATTRIBUTES AND LEVELS

Attributes and levels form the fundamental basis of conjoint analysis. A product or service is broken down into its constituent parts—for instance a laptop has a size, weight, battery life, brand, etc. Each of these elements making up a generic laptop is known as an attribute. In other words, attributes are the features of a product.

When we compare two products, each will have a different specification on each of these attributes. For example, we might have choices in terms of battery life between 9–12 hours. Each of these options is known as a level of that attribute. In other words, levels are the possible values that attributes can take.

The purpose of conjoint analysis is to decompose the overall response about a product or service into their attributes and levels. It is a backdoor decomposition technique that calculates the utility of each of these attributes and levels for each individual in an indirect way. Consequently, it helps the marketer to understand what the consumers value the most as they are forced to do a trade-off while taking their decision.

It is important for the researchers to select proper attributes and levels while designing a conjoint study. The underpinning thought embedded in the concept of conjoint analysis is that buyers view products as a combination of various attributes and levels of these attributes. Consumers have specific utility of each of the levels of every attribute using which they can calculate the overall utility of any product made using those attributes. While selecting the attributes and its levels, researchers may keep in mind the following:

1. Attributes of a conjoint design should be independent. Conjoint model does not account for linear relationship between two attributes as it calculates the utility of each respondent for each attribute level through an additive function.
2. Levels must not be specified in terms of range. Levels should have concrete meaning. For instance, levels must not be specified as "price ₹ 2000 to ₹ 2500." Instead, it should be mentioned as "price ₹ 2200." Researchers must also avoid using ambiguous terms, for example, "often," "frequently," etc.
3. Levels within each attribute should be mutually exclusive. One level must not cover another level.

The basic conjoint analysis model can be modeled as

$$U(X) = \sum_{i=1}^{m} \sum_{j=1}^{k_i} a_{ij} x_{ij}$$

where

$U(X)$ = overall utility of stimuli/product alternative

a_{ij} = utility of individual respondent associated with the jth level (j = 1, 2,..., k) of the ith attri bute (i = 1, 2, 3,..., m) of the product

k_i = number of levels of attribute i considered in the product

m = number of attributes considered in the product

x_{ij} = dummy variables, and can take a value 1 if the jth level of the ith attribute is present in the alternative and the value 0 otherwise

The importance of an attribute W_i can be calculated from the derived part-worth of its levels. Importance is the ratio of the range of part-worth of levels of an attribute to the sum of all ranges of all the attributes. It is mathematically represented as follows:

$$W_i = \frac{I_i}{\sum_{i=1}^{m} I_i}$$

$$I_i = \{\max(a_{ij}) - \min(a_{ij})\}$$

The attribute's importance is normalized to ascertaining its importance relative to other attribute W_i such that $\sum_{i=1}^{m} W_i = 1$.

ESTIMATION OF MODEL

Different procedures are available for estimating the basic model depending upon the type and complexity of conjoint model. These techniques include monotone ANOVA model, logit model, and dummy variable regression. The simplest of these is dummy variable regression. Here the predictor variables consist of dummy variables for the attribute levels. If the attribute has n levels, then we require (n – 1) dummy variables.

Dependent variable used in dummy variable regression is the rating provided by the respondents about their preference or willingness to buy each product profile. Such ratings are captured in interval scale that acts as metric dependent variable. If the data is nonmetric, for instance, captured through a categorical scale, it may be converted to 0 or 1. In such case, a logit analysis is performed instead of the ordinary least square analysis.

Other procedures that are appropriate for nonmetric data include LINMAP and MONANOVA models.

Conjoint analysis can be performed both for individual respondent as well as aggregate level. In individual level conjoint analysis, the analysis of data is done to calculate the utility of each level of every attribute for each respondent. On the other hand, in aggregate level, all respondents belong to the same population and average utility for the group is calculated. Several software are available that perform both individual level as well as aggregate level analysis. It is recommended for the researcher to calculate individual level utilities and then segment the respondents based on their utility structure.

ASSESSMENT OF MODEL FIT

The value of R-square is determined which is the measure of fit in dummy variable regression. R-square value of more than 0.6 is considered to be a good fit. Then, the preference ratings for the validation profiles are predicted, and they are correlated with the input ratings for these profiles obtained from the respondent. If the correlation coefficient is 0.90, it indicates good predictive ability. This correlation coefficient to be tested at significance level of $\alpha = 0.05$.

INTERPRETATION OF RESULTS

Here, the part-worth functions for each attribute are plotted. On the *x*-axis, the attribute is plotted, and on the *y*-axis, the utility is plotted. Depending on part-worth function for each attribute, the greatest and least preferences in terms of their descriptions can be determined. In terms of relative importance of the attributes as determined by the results of conjoint analysis, we can find which attribute is the most preferred one. So, in case price is the most preferred attribute for any respondent, the respondent can be termed as price sensitive one.

INTERNAL AND EXTERNAL VALIDATION

In order to determine the internal validity, the evaluation for holdout or validation stimuli are predicted by part-worth functions. Then, the predicted evaluations are correlated with those obtained from respondents. In case of using aggregate level, the estimated sample is split in several ways, and conjoint analysis can be conducted on each subsample. The obtained results are compared across subsamples to assess its stability.

External validation is similar to internal validation except that combinations other than those included in conducting conjoint analysis are considered for assessing the validity.

In order to assess test–retest reliability, the respondents evaluate selected stimuli, and the two values of these stimuli are then correlated to determine the required reliability.

CONJOINT ANALYSIS MODEL FOR MICROMAX

The aim of this study is to judge what a customer values the most in a high-end mobile. The experiments consist of deducing the preference of consumer to individual attributes of a mobile like brand, screen size, battery life, etc., by obtaining rating for different handsets with different combinations which is known as card.

Attributes and Levels

- *Brand:* *Nokia, Samsung, Micromax*
- *Screen Size:* *2.6", 3"*
- *Price:* *₹ 5000, ₹ 10000, ₹ 15000*
- *Mobile Network:* *CDMA, GSM, Dual*
- *Internet Connectivity:* *GPRS, 3G, Wi-Fi*
- *Camera:* *3.2 MP, 5 MP*
- *Battery:* *4 hours, 7 hours, 12 hours*

Total number of possible combinations = $3 \times 2 \times 3 \times 3 \times 3 \times 2 \times 3 = 972$

Orthogonal Design in SPSS

The list below shows the combinations for estimation.

Eighteen combinations were chosen by SPSS software when data of attributes and levels were fed. Five additional combinations were chosen for external validation. Then a potential customer was asked to give ratings out of 100 to different combinations. These ratings (part-worth utility) were then regressed with dummy variables representing different levels in attributes.

Card List

Card ID	Brand	Display	Network	Connectivity	Camera	Battery	Price
1	Micromax	3"	CDMA	GPRS	5MP	12 hr	Rs 10000
2	Nokia	3"	GSM	3G	5MP	12 hr	Rs 10000
3	Samsung	2.6"	CDMA	3G	3.2MP	12 hr	Rs 5000
4	Micromax	2.6"	CDMA	WiFi	5MP	7 hr	Rs 15000
5	Nokia	3"	CDMA	GPRS	3.2MP	7 hr	Rs 5000
6	Micromax	2.6"	Dual	3G	3.2MP	4 hr	Rs 10000
7	Nokia	2.6"	GSM	WiFi	5MP	4 hr	Rs 5000
8	Micromax	3"	GSM	3G	5MP	7 hr	Rs 5000
9	Samsung	2.6"	GSM	GPRS	5MP	7 hr	Rs 10000
10	Micromax	3"	GSM	GPRS	3.2MP	4 hr	Rs 15000
11	Nokia	3"	Dual	WiFi	3.2MP	7 hr	Rs 10000
12	Samsung	3"	GSM	WiFi	3.2MP	12 hr	Rs 15000
13	Samsung	3"	CDMA	WiFi	5MP	4 hr	Rs 10000
14	Micromax	3"	Dual	WiFi	5MP	12 hr	Rs 5000
15	Nokia	2.6"	Dual	GPRS	5MP	12 hr	Rs 15000
16	Samsung	3"	Dual	GPRS	5MP	4 hr	Rs 5000
17	Nokia	3"	CDMA	3G	5MP	4 hr	Rs 15000
18	Samsung	3"	Dual	3G	5MP	7 hr	Rs 15000
19	Micromax	3"	GSM	GPRS	5MP	7 hr	Rs 5000
20	Nokia	3"	Dual	WiFi	5MP	4 hr	Rs 15000
21	Nokia	3"	GSM	GPRS	5MP	4 hr	Rs 5000
22	Samsung	2.6"	CDMA	WiFi	3.2MP	4 hr	Rs 5000
23	Samsung	2.6"	Dual	3G	3.2MP	12 hr	Rs 10000

Part-Utility Equation

$$\text{Part-worth utility} = \alpha + \beta_{SM} \times SM + \beta_{NK} \times NK + \beta_{S3.0} \times S3.0 + \beta_{GSM} \times GSM + \beta_{DUAL} \times DUAL + \beta_{I3G} \times 3G + \beta_{WIFI} \times WIFI + \beta_{C5} \times C5 + \beta_{B7} \times B7 + \beta_{B12} \times B12,$$

where SM, NK, S3.0, GSM, DUAL, I3G, WIFI, C5, B7, and B12 are dummy variables; α represents part-worth utility of base model of mobile with brand Micromax, screen size 2.6", price ₹ 5000, CDMA network, GPRS, 3.2 MP camera, and 4 hours battery life.

β_{SM} = mean difference of part-worth utilities between brands Samsung and Micromax
β_{NK} = mean difference of part-worth utilities between brands Nokia and Micromax
$\beta_{S3.0}$ = mean difference of part-worth utilities between screen size 3.0" and 2.6"
β_{GSM} = mean difference of part-worth utilities between GSM and CDMA network
β_{DUAL} = mean difference of part-worth utilities between DUAL (GSM+CDMA) and CDMA network
β_{I3G} = mean difference of part-worth utilities between 3G and GPRS connectivity
β_{WIFI} = mean difference of part-worth utilities between Wi-Fi and GPRS connectivity
β_{C5} = mean difference of part-worth utilities between 5MP and 3MP camera
β_{B7} = mean difference of part-worth utilities between 7 hours and 4 hours battery life
β_{B12} = mean difference of part-worth utilities between 12 hours and 4 hours battery life

Results of Experiment

The results showed overwhelming support to the fit of the model. All the beta values and constants are highly significant. Value of *R*-sqaure is 1 which indicates very strong evidence.

Model Summary

Model	R	R Square	Adjusted R Square	Std. Error of the Estimate
1	1.000[a]	1.000	.999	.31623

a. Predictors: (Constant), P15000, B12, C5, WIFI, DUAL, S3.0, NK, P10000, B7, I3G, GSM, SM

ANOVA[b]

Model		Sum of Squares	df	Mean Square	F	Sig.
1	Regression	1537.278	12	128.106	1.281E3	.000[a]
	Residual	.500	5	.100		
	Total	1537.778	17			

a. Predictors: (Constant), P15000, B12, C5, WIFI, DUAL, S3.0, NK, P10000, B7, I3G, GSM, SM

b. Dependent Variable: Score

Coefficients[a]

Model		Unstandardized Coefficients		Standardized Coefficients	t	Sig.
		B	Std. Error	Beta		
1	(Constant)	42.000	.289		145.492	.000
	SM	2.667	.183	.136	14.606	.000
	NK	7.500	.183	.383	41.079	.000
	S3.0	10.083	.158	.514	63.773	.000
	GSM	2.333	.183	.119	12.780	.000
	DUAL	7.333	.183	.374	40.166	.000
	I3G	7.667	.183	.391	41.992	.000
	WIFI	10.000	.183	.510	54.772	.000
	C5	5.083	.158	.259	32.150	.000
	B7	2.667	.183	.136	14.606	.000
	B12	7.500	.183	.383	41.079	.000
	P10000	5.167	.183	.264	28.299	.000
	P15000	-2.500	.183	-.128	-13.693	.000

a. Dependent Variable: Score

Internal and External Validity

Internal and external validities of the model can be tested and percentage variation between estimated scores and actual scores can be found.

Importance of Individual Attributes

Importance of individual attributes was calculated as follows:

$$\text{Importance of individual attribute} = \frac{\text{Individual attribute spread}}{\text{Total spread}}$$

Attributes	Spread	Importance (%)
Brand	7.50	13.60
Screen Size	10.08	18.28
Mobile Network	7.33	13.29
Internet Connectivity	10.00	18.13
Camera	5.08	9.21
Battery	7.50	13.60
Price	7.67	13.90
Total	55.166	100

MANAGERIAL IMPLICATIONS OF RESULTS

- This customer has given medium importance to brand. To target such customers, advertisements highlighting product features will be more useful than just brand building.
- Least valued feature is camera, thus, the company should not spend much on advertising camera features as it will never be better than full fledged digital cameras.
- Craze for big screen size and high-speed Internet connections are emerging trends in premium mobile handset market, and company's product portfolio must be aligned as per new trends.
- Most appropriate price point would be around ₹ 10,000 below which customers will be sceptical about product quality and above which customers will look for cheaper alternatives from competitive brands.

Orthogonal Design using SPSS

To gauge the utilities of different attributes and levels, we need not get consumer ratings for each and every combination. By using orthogonal design, for example, it is possible to generate minimum number of cards or packages which will be sufficient to gauge the utilities or part-worths.

S. No.	Attributes	Levels	Labels
1	Package Cost	1–3 lakhs	Cost_1_3
		3–6 lakhs	Cost_3_6
		6–10 lakhs	Cost_6_10
2	Services at a Function	Only Venue	Event_Venue
		Venue + Catering	Event_V_Cat
		Venue + Catering + Decoration	Event_V_Cat_D
3	Additional Services	Gifts and Cards	Service_Gifts
		Jewellery and Attire	Service_Jewe
		Both	Service_Both
4	Functions Covered	Wedding only	Functions_wed
		Engagement + Wedding	Functions_wed_eng
		Engagement + Wedding + Reception	Functions_wed_eng_Rec

Step 1: Go to data → Orthogonal Design → Generate.

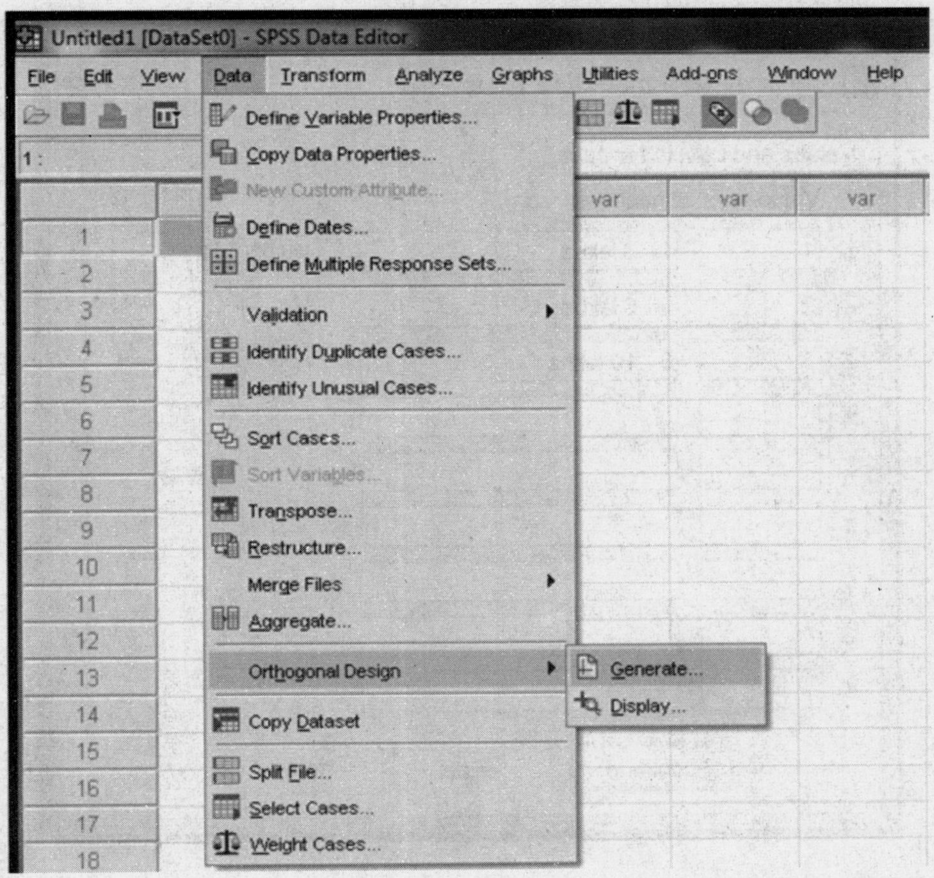

Step 2: Enter the attribute name and label under Factor Name and Factor Label. Then click Add. Select the attribute and then click on Define Values.

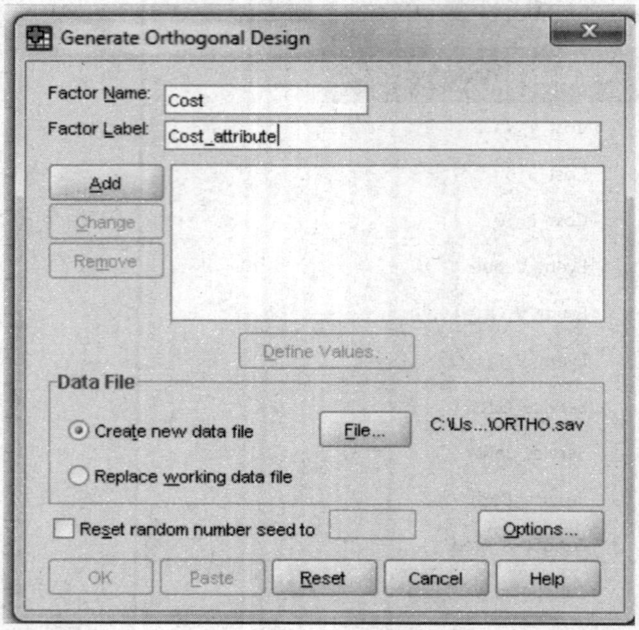

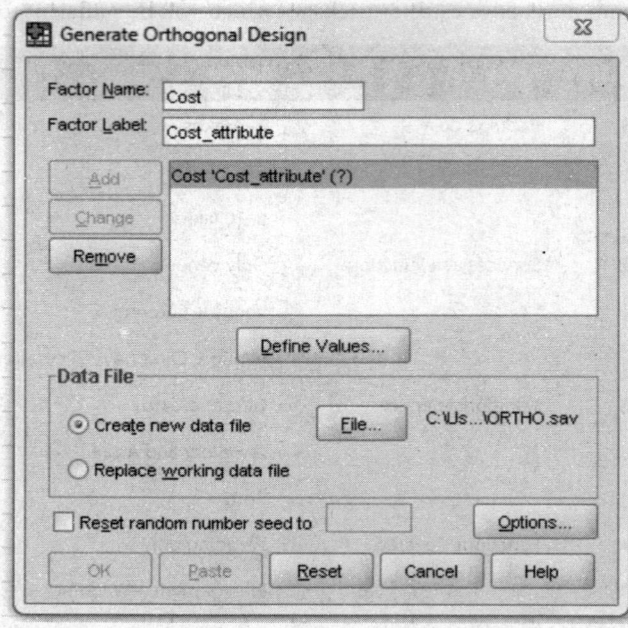

Step 3: Enter the values of levels in a sequential manner and then click Continue.

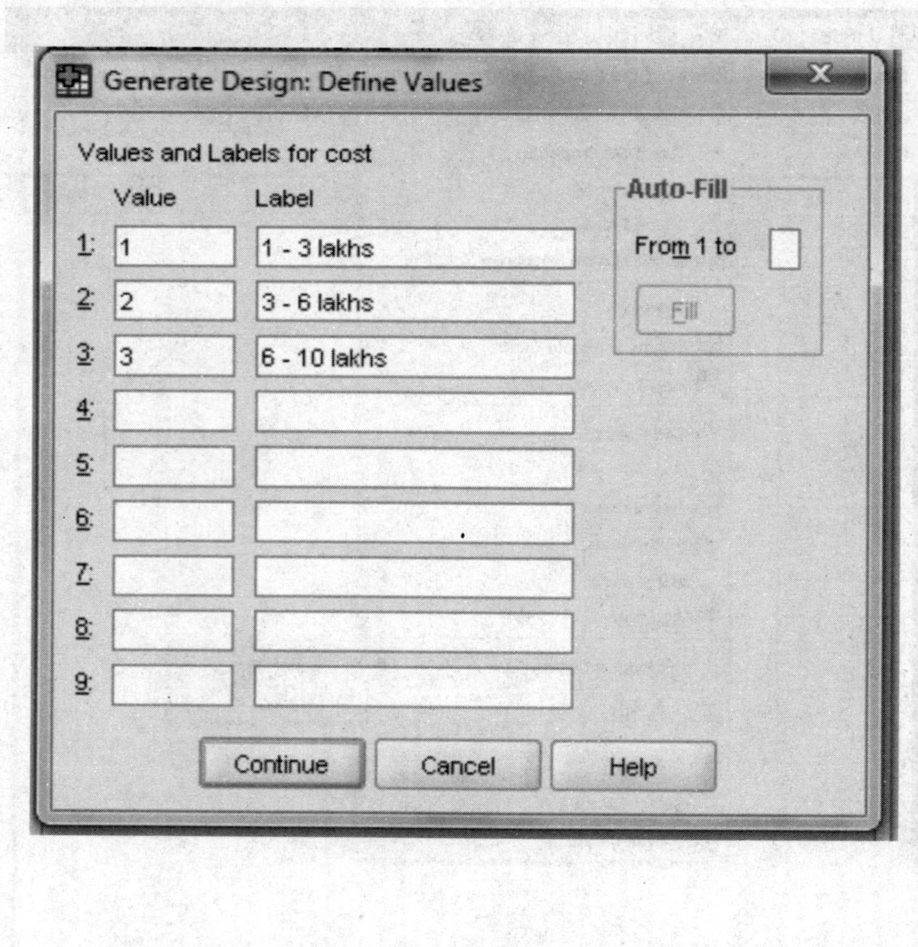

Step 4: Similarly, enter the levels for other attributes and then click OK.

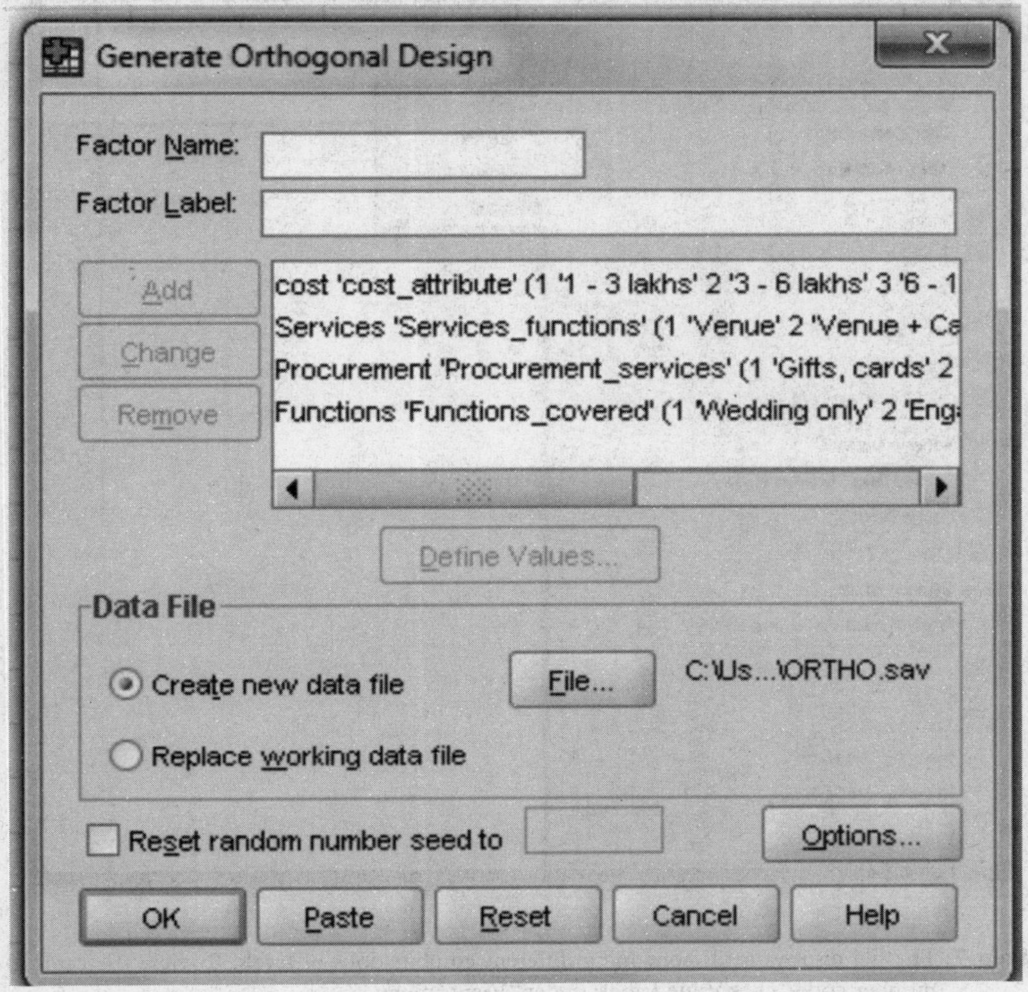

Step 5: The following screen displays the number of cards generated.

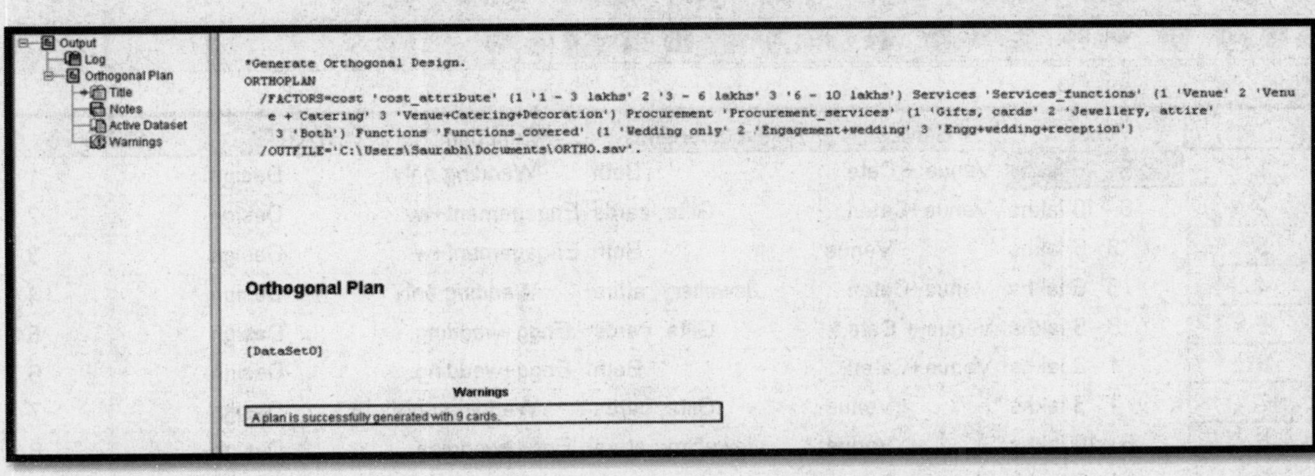

Step 6: Open the file "Ortho.sav."

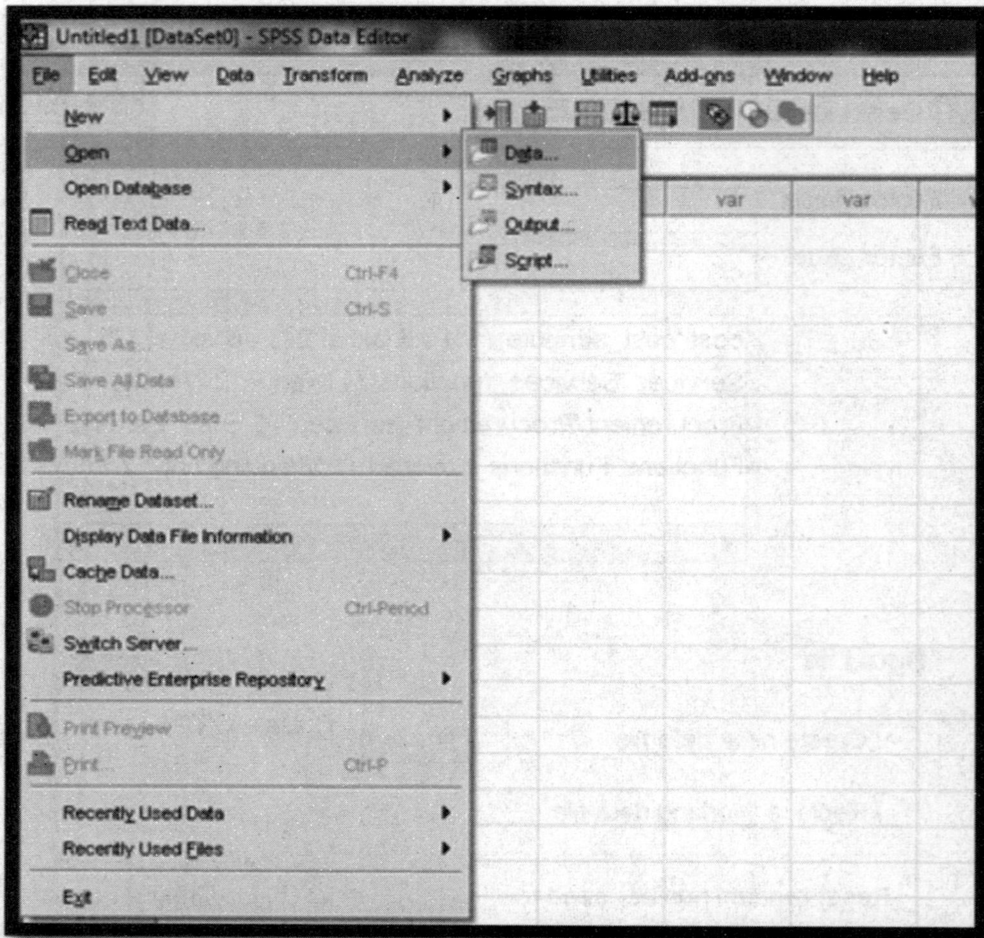

Step 7: The file displays cards containing different combinations of levels. To view the cards in number codes, click Value Labels under "View" menu.

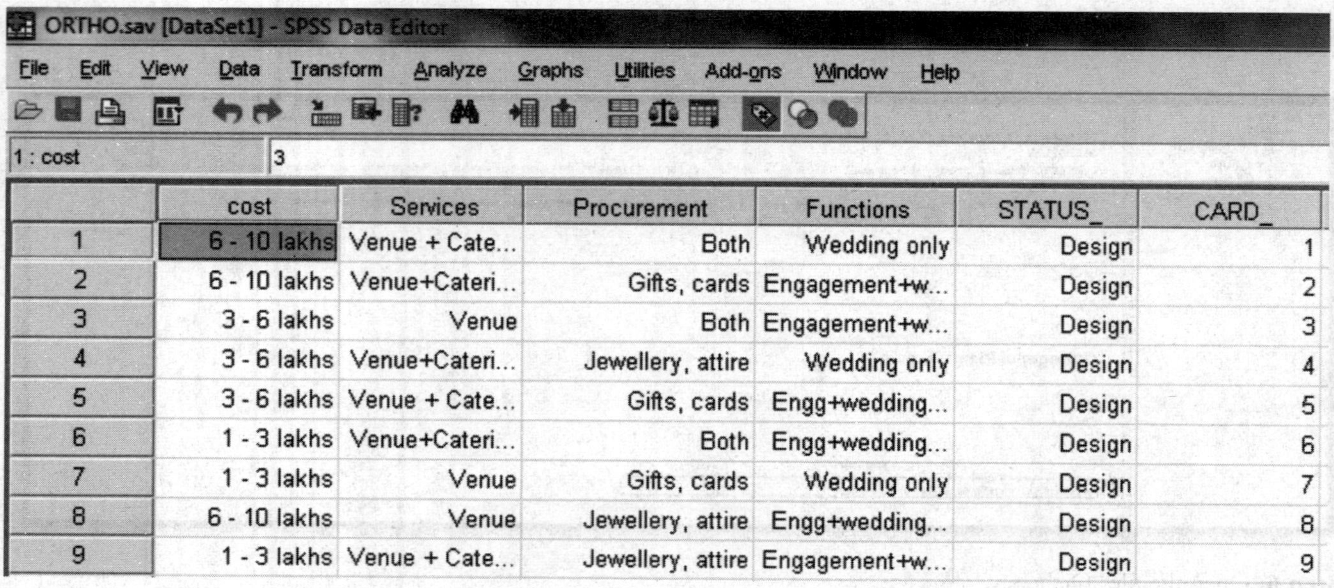

	cost	Services	Procurement	Functions	STATUS_	CARD_
1	6 - 10 lakhs	Venue + Cate...	Both	Wedding only	Design	1
2	6 - 10 lakhs	Venue+Cateri...	Gifts, cards	Engagement+w...	Design	2
3	3 - 6 lakhs	Venue	Both	Engagement+w...	Design	3
4	3 - 6 lakhs	Venue+Cateri...	Jewellery, attire	Wedding only	Design	4
5	3 - 6 lakhs	Venue + Cate...	Gifts, cards	Engg+wedding...	Design	5
6	1 - 3 lakhs	Venue+Cateri...	Both	Engg+wedding...	Design	6
7	1 - 3 lakhs	Venue	Gifts, cards	Wedding only	Design	7
8	6 - 10 lakhs	Venue	Jewellery, attire	Engg+wedding...	Design	8
9	1 - 3 lakhs	Venue + Cate...	Jewellery, attire	Engagement+w...	Design	9

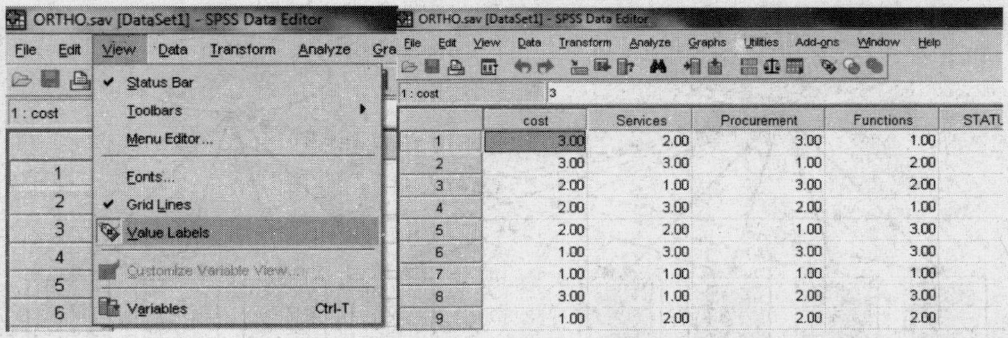

Analysis of Interdependence

Suppose we wished to identify the factors that are associated with pleasant shopping experiences,[14] identify factors that would allow better flexibility and control of logistics programs,[15] or identify groups of students each associated with a unique learning style.[16] Each of these are problems that have been addressed through the use of a multivariate interdependence technique. Rather than attempting to predict a variable or set of variables from a set of independent variables, we use techniques like *factor analysis, cluster analysis,* and *multidimensional scaling* to better understand the relationships and structure among a set of variables or objects.

Factor Analysis

Factor analysis is a prototypical multivariate, interdependence technique. Factor analysis is a technique of statistically identifying a reduced number of factors from a larger number of measured variables. The factors themselves are not measured, but instead, they are identified by forming a variate using the measured variables. Factors are usually latent constructs like attitude or satisfaction, or an index like social class. A researcher need not distinguish between independent and dependent variables to conduct factor analysis. Factor analysis can be divided into two types:

factor analysis
A prototypical multivariate, interdependence technique that statistically identifies a reduced number of factors from a larger number of measured variables.

1. Exploratory factor analysis (EFA)—performed when the researcher is uncertain about how many factors may exist among a set of variables. The discussion here concentrates primarily on EFA.
2. Confirmatory factor analysis (CFA)—performed when the researcher has strong theoretical expectations about the factor structure (number of factors and which variables relate to each factor) before performing the analysis. CFA is a good tool for assessing construct validity because it provides a test of how well the researcher's "theory" about the factor structure fits the actual observations. Many books exist on CFA alone and the reader is advised to refer to any of those sources for more on CFA.

Exhibit 24.6 illustrates factor analysis graphically. Suppose a researcher is asked to examine how feelings of nostalgia in a restaurant influence customer loyalty. Three hundred fifty customers at themed restaurants around the country are interviewed and asked to respond to the following Likert scales (1 = Strongly Disagree to 7 = Strongly Agree):

X_1—I feel a strong connection to the past when I am in this place.
X_2—This place evokes memories of the past.
X_3—I feel a yearning to relive past experiences when I dine here.
X_4—This place looks like a page out of the past.
X_5—I am willing to pay more to dine in this restaurant.
X_6—I feel very loyal to this establishment.
X_7—I would recommend this place to others.
X_8—I will go out of my way to dine here.

Factor analysis can summarize the information in the eight variables in a smaller number of variables. How many dimensions, or groups of variables, are likely present in this case? More than one technique exists for estimating the variates that form the factors. However, the general idea

EXHIBIT 24.6
A Simple Illustration of Factor Analysis

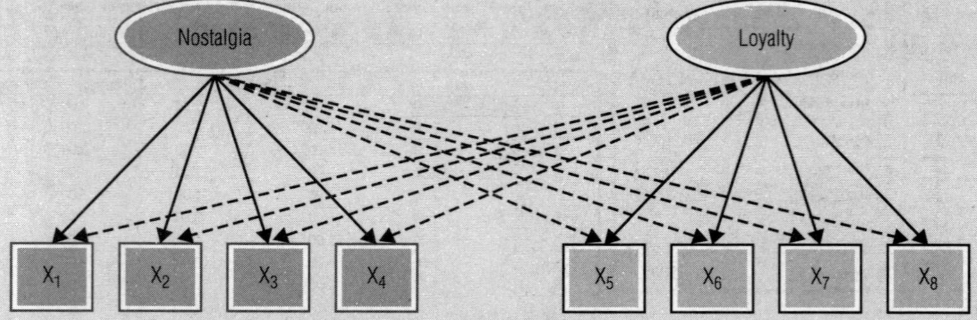

Factor Loading Estimates:

Variable:	Factor 1	Factor 2
X_1	.90	−.02
X_2	.88	.10
X_3	.85	.12
X_4	.70	.31
X_5	−.10	.90
X_6	−.05	.90
X_7	.20	.75
X_8	.21	.72

is to mathematically produce variates that explain the greatest total variance among the set of variables being analyzed. In this example, the factor analysis indicates there are two dimensions, or factors, as shown in Exhibit 24.6. Thus, EFA provides two important pieces of information:

1. How many factors exist among a set of variables?
2. What variables are related to or "load on" which factors?

One of the assumptions in the ordinary least square method in multiple regression is that the independent variables are uncorrelated to each other. However, in business research, there may be a large number of variables; many of them may be correlated. Factor analysis helps to reduce the interrelationships among the variables to a fewer number of variables or factors which are independent of each other. However, unlike dependency techniques namely multiple regression analysis, discriminant analysis, conjoint analysis, etc., no distinction is made between the independent and dependent variables in factor analysis. In other words, factor analysis is an interdependency technique that examines an entire set of interdependent relationships.

The primary purpose of factor analysis is to identify the underlying structure of the variable under consideration. In practice, researchers consider several variables together in the research. Variables are important because they help us to understand business in a manner. However, the number of variables increases to a great extent and we are often required to consider all the variables together. Hence, we use multivariate techniques. In many researches, the number of variables considered together is often more than 50, if not 100. Hence, it becomes difficult to consider all the variables together. But we are likely to find interrelationship among several variables. Variables those are related to each other form a group to represent one underlying dimension; we may label the dimension giving a completely new name that would represent the group of correlated variables. Factor analysis is the multivariate technique which is applied to perform this function.

Factor analysis is broadly classified into four types:

1. **Exploratory factor analysis.** In this type of factor analysis researchers are not aware of how many underlying dimensions (factor) can be found from the variables that are under study. Depending upon the collinearity between the variables, limited number of factors is derived. Exploratory factor analysis searches for the structure among a set of variables and reduces data. That is why it is called data reduction method. Hence exploratory factor analysis does not rely on a priory constraints or number of factors as well as how much information these factors retain of the original variables.

2. **Confirmatory factor analysis.** Unlike exploratory factor analysis, confirmatory factor analysis is conducted by researchers having prior idea about the actual number of structures in the data on the basis of theoretical understanding of previous research. In confirmatory factor

analysis researchers test hypothesis whether the variables under study based on theoretical support actually conform to the factor structure or not.

3. **R-factor analysis**. R-factor analysis involves identifying the number of latent factors from a group of variables. Hence, the variables are the unit of analysis which are grouped together to form a factor.

4. **Q-factor analysis.** Q-factor analysis involves grouping the subjects. In this technique of factor analysis respondents are grouped based on their interrelationship. Members in each group show similar change in behavior and are identified as correlated. Here the unit of analysis is the respondents which are grouped together based on their interrelationship. This application is not used much today since a variety of clustering techniques have been developed that are designed specifically for the purpose of grouping multiple subjects into independent groups

APPLICATIONS OF FACTOR ANALYSIS

Factor analysis is used in many situations in business research. Some of the applications are as follows:

1. **Identifying underlying factors.** Factor analysis helps to explain the correlations among a set of variables (larger in number) and to identify the underlying factors (fewer in number). For example, six psychographic variables, namely frequency of purchase, liking towards formal wear, frequency of business interaction, preference of ethnic versus contemporary, inclination towards savings, and interest towards entertainment, can be represented by two factors: likeliness of different type of wear (Factor 1) and propensity to spend (Factor 2).

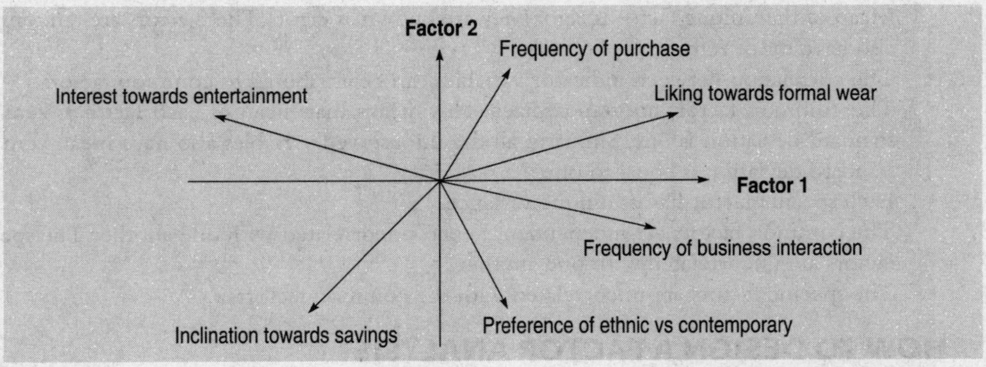

2. **Helps in subsequent data analysis.** Factor analysis identifies a new, smaller set of uncorrelated variables in place of original larger set of correlated variables for subsequent multivariate analysis. For example, the factors identified above—likeliness of different type of wear (Factor 1) and propensity to spend (Factor 2)—may be used as independent variables in explaining the differences between priority and casual customers for a formal garment manufacturing company.

3. **Identifying a smaller set of salient variables from a larger set for use in subsequent multivariate analysis.** For example, few original lifestyle statements that correlate highly with the identified factors may be used as independent variables to explain the difference between priority and casual customers. We can take statements such as "likes saving money," "frequent shopping," and "prefers old versus new" as independent variables and drop other three to avoid problems of multicollinearity.

4. **For interdependency and data delineation.** Factor analysis technique can also be used to delineate complex structure of interrelationship between the variables. It can find out the linear relationship between several sets of interrelated variables which may not be possible for the researcher to identify through observation. In other words, factor analysis untangles the sets of interrelationships among the variables.

5. **Parsimony or data reduction.** Since factor analysis forms less number of factors from a very large number of variables, it is also called a data reduction technique. This process of analyzing data helps the researcher to bring down the complexity of the data structure to a great extent and have a manageable number of underlying dimensions for further analysis.

6. **Scaling.** Factor analysis is also used in the development of scale in behavioral research. Scientists develop skills that measure individual respondents or test unit characteristics. Factor analysis helps in dividing the characteristics into some independent constructs which represent a scale to measure an underlying behavioral dimension.

Factor analysis is also used in business applications. Some of these business applications are:

1. **Market segmentation.** Factor analysis helps in identifying the underlying dimensions from the observed variables which help researcher to group customers based on their homogeneity in the characteristics that are measured.
2. **Identifying dimension.** Factor analysis helps in identifying product or brand attributes that consumers consider important while taking a buying decision. Factors that explain higher varieties contribute highly in factor analysis procedure. This information helps the researcher to figure out which variables account for higher varieties and they may subsequently test its contribution in consumer decision making.

ASSUMPTIONS OF FACTOR ANALYSIS

Following are the assumptions that factor analysis entails:

- The variables included in factor analysis can construct one or more latent factors.
- The variables are interrelated, however, does not assume any causality.
- The sample is representative of the population. Sample is homogeneous and shows diversity in the characteristics across all the respondents uniformly.
- Factors can be represented as a linear combination of the variables.
- Mean of the unique factor is zero. They are known as errors. These errors are random and also have mean zero.
- The correlation between indicator variables can be attributed to common factors.
- The common factors are standardized. This means that mean of each factor is zero and standard deviation is one. Similarly, all the unobserved variables also have mean zero and standard deviation is equal to one.
- Each specific factor has its unique variance.
- The common factors are independent hence, uncorrelated with one another. The specific factors are uncorrelated with one another
- The specific factors are uncorrelated with the common factors.

HOW TO DESIGN A FACTOR ANALYSIS?

Researchers need to think several aspects to design factor analysis to address a research problem. Researchers interested to conduct factor analysis to address the particular problem need to measure the variables in metric scale. They are also to decide which variables could be indicators of some underlying dimension. They also need to decide the number of variables that are due to consider in factor analysis. The researchers then need to decide on the sample size for data collection. Factor analysis requires larger sample to get a clear structure of factors.

Selecting variables and measuring them. It is important for the researchers to know what type of variables can be used in factor analysis and how many variables to be included in the analysis. Since the primary requirement in factor analysis is to calculate a correlation matrix to identify which variables are correlated among each other, it is important for the researchers to measure the variable in a scale that is adequate to calculate correlation matrix among the variables. In most of the instances, it is advisable that the researchers measure variables in metric scale. It is difficult to use a non-metric variable in factor analysis as calculating bivariate correlation between two non-metric variables is often difficult and uninterpretable in the context of conducting factor analysis. In some occasions researchers do use non-metric variables converting them into numbers (that is coding them in 0 or 1) however, it requires a special kind of technique to conduct factor analysis as variables are categorical and non-metric. While deciding on the number of variables to be included in factor analysis, researchers need to ensure that a group of minimum 4 to 5 variables forms one factor. One of the objectives of factor analysis is data reduction, having one variable in one factor does not contribute much to the analysis.

Deciding on sample size. Another important factor in factor analysis is deciding on sample size. Like many other multivariate techniques factor analysis also require a large sample size. However, the number of variables also plays an important role in deciding sample size. In general, it is advisable to have a sample size at least five times of the number of variables. However, minimum sample size has to be more than 100. Some researchers propose that average sample size for factor analysis is to be at least 10 times of the number of variables. In some projects researchers have also considered a sample size of 20 times or more depending upon the need of accuracy of the analysis. It is to be noted that as the number of variables increases, the number of bivariate correlation to be estimated for the analysis also increases exponentially. Considering a 5% level of significance, the number of correlation that might show by chance also increases significantly along with the number of variables. Hence it is always advisable that researchers consider the sample to variable ratio as high as possible.

Deriving factors. The primary objective behind conducting factor analysis is data reduction and summarization. Therefore, it is imperative that we condense the original set of variables into smaller number of factors. Several criteria are examined to determine the number of factors that would ideally represent the data:

1. **A priori determination.** Here, the researcher knows how many factors to expect and thus can specify the number of factors to be extracted beforehand.
2. **Determination based on eigenvalues.** In this approach, only factors with eigenvalues greater than 1.0 are retained. (Eigenvalue represents the total variance explained by each factor.)
3. **Determination based on scree plot.** A scree plot is a plot of eigenvalues against the number of factors in the order of extraction. Typically, the plot consists of a distinct break between the steep slope of factors. Empirically, the number of factors is determined at the point the scree begins.

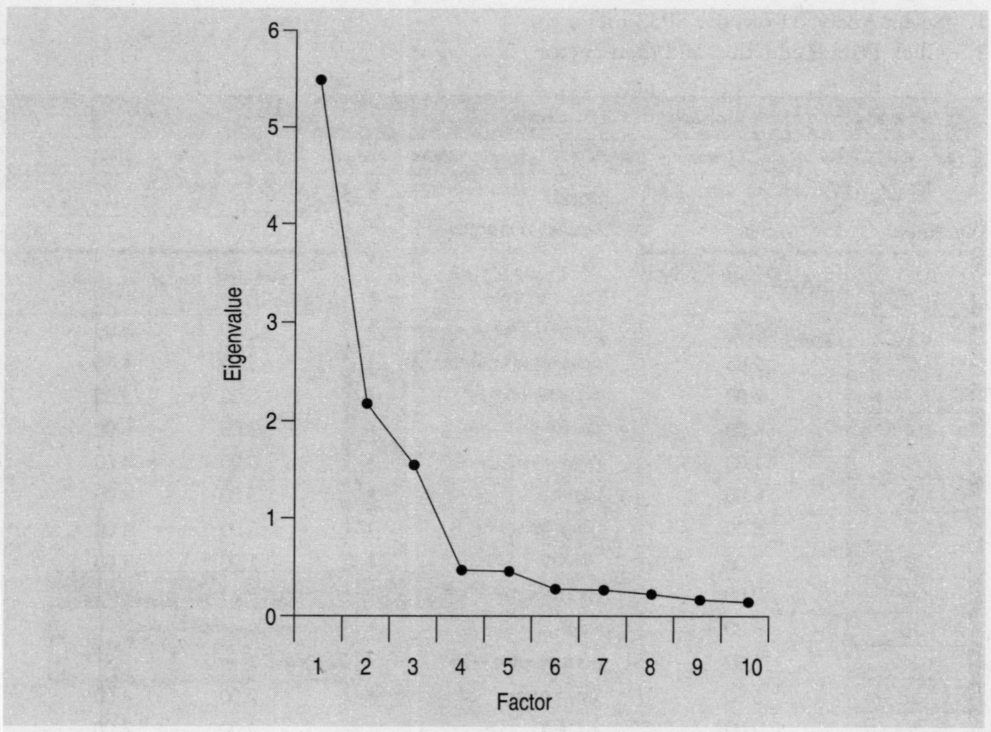

In the above figure, the scree begins at factor 4. So, number of factors to be included is four in the above example.

4. **Determination based on percentage of variance.** In this approach, the number of factors is determined when the cumulative percentage of variance extracted by the factors reaches a satisfactory level. The level of satisfaction depends upon the research problem at hand. But, it is recommended to extract those factors that account for at least 60 percent of the variance.

5. **Determination based on split-half reliability.** Here, factor analysis is performed on two halves of the data set after splitting it into two halves. Then, only factors with high correspondence of factor loadings across the two subsamples are retained.
6. **Determination based on significance tests.** Here, statistical significance of the separate eigenvalues is determined. Then only those factors are retained that are statistically significant. A drawback of this method is observed in case of large samples, wherein many factors are statistically significant, although they represent only small portion of the total variance.

VALIDATING FACTOR ANALYSIS RESULT

In this stage, we are concerned with the issue of generalizability of the factor model we have derived. Herein, two issues are examined:

1. The factor model stable and generalizable
2. The factor solution impacted by outliers, if any

The first issue is examined by using split half validation in SPSS tool.

Split-half validation. The strategy for examining the stability of the model is to do a split-half validation to see if the factor structure and the communalities remain the same.

Identification of outliers. SPSS contains a strategy to identify outliers. SPSS computes the factor scores as standard scores with a mean of 0 and a standard deviation of 1. We can examine the factor scores to see if any are above or below the standard score size associated with extreme cases, i.e., +/−2.5.

DATA ANALYSIS IN SPSS WITH SCREENSHOTS

1. Select Analyze from the SPSS menu bar.
2. Click Data Reduction and then Factor.

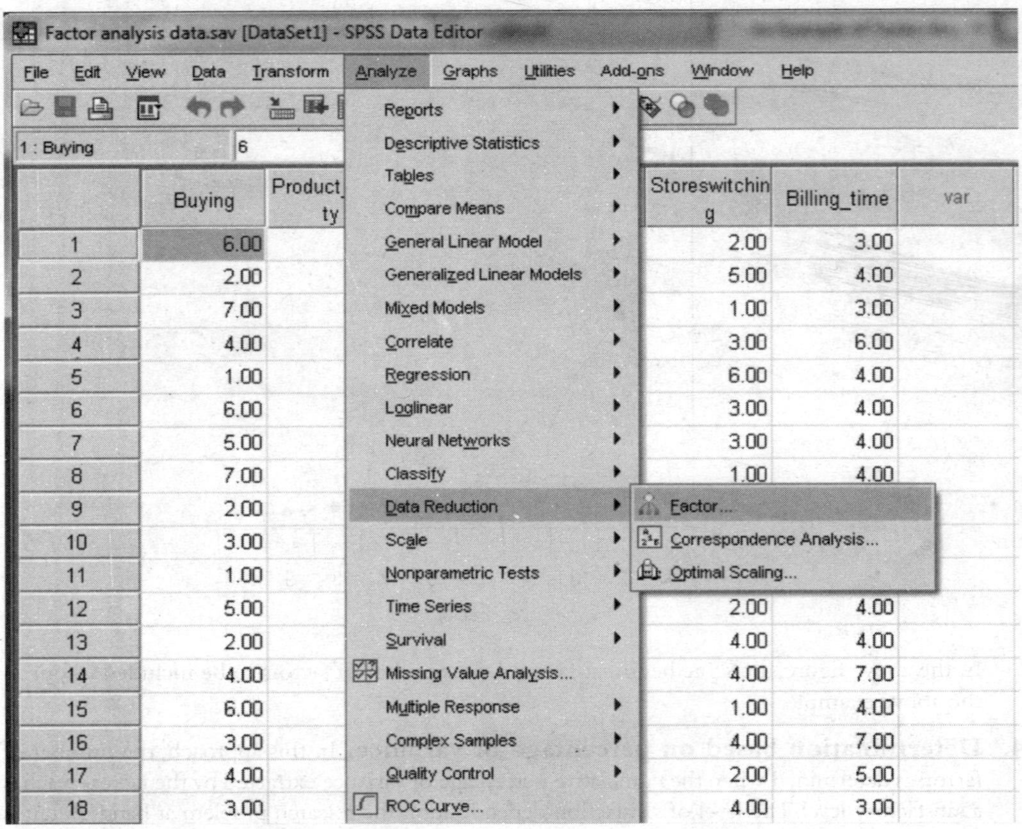

3. Move all the variables in the pop-up that emerges to the other side, i.e., in the Variables box.

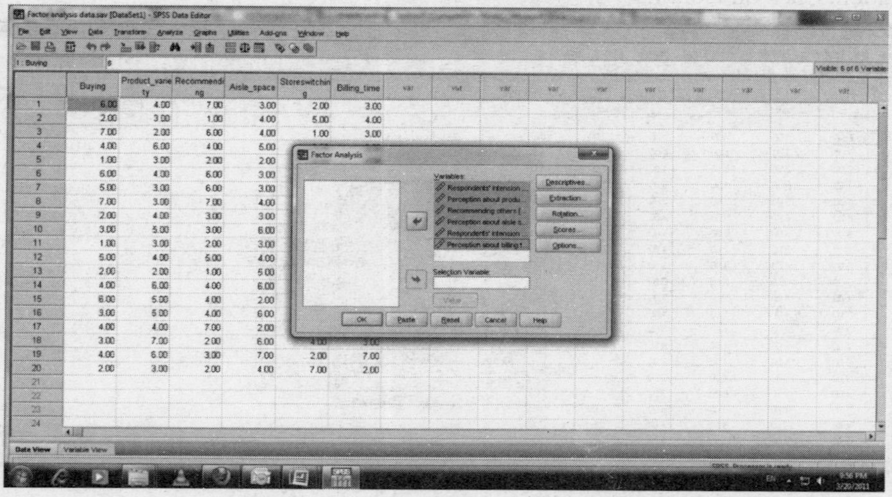

4. Click on Descriptives. In the Statistics box in the pop-up window that emerges, check Initial Solution.
5. In the Correlation Matrix box, check KMO and Bartlett's test of sphericity. Also, check Reproduced. Click on Continue.

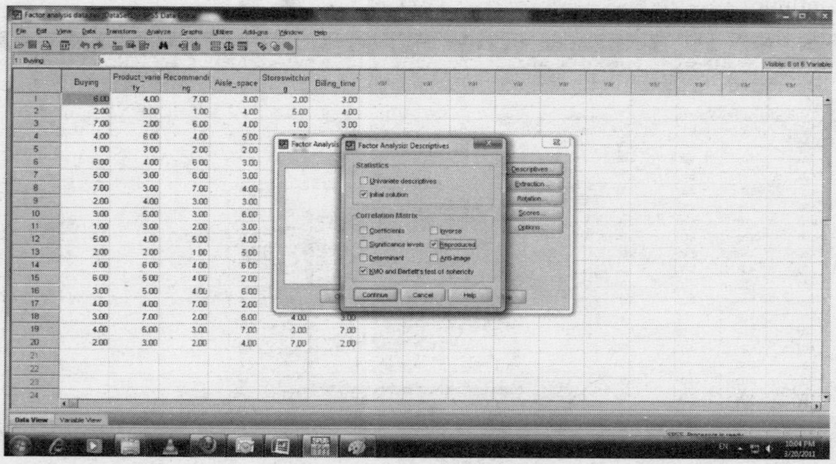

6. Click on Extraction. In the pop-up window that emerges, select Principal Components (default) for Method. In the Analyze box, check Correlation matrix. In the Extract box, select Eigenvalues over and write "1." In the display box, check Unrotated factor solution. Click on Continue.

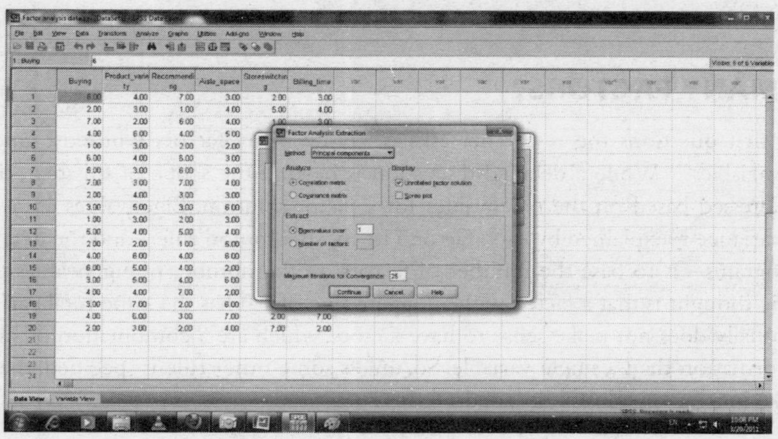

7. Click on Rotation. In the Method box, check Varimax. In the Display box, check Rotated solution. Click on Continue.

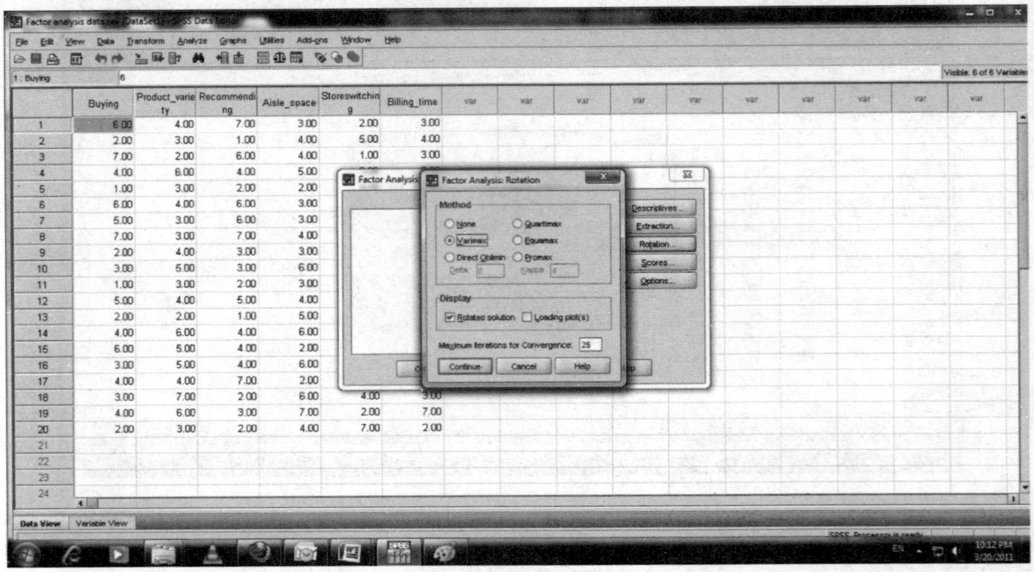

8. Click on Scores. In the pop-up window, check Display factor score coefficient matrix. Click on Continue.

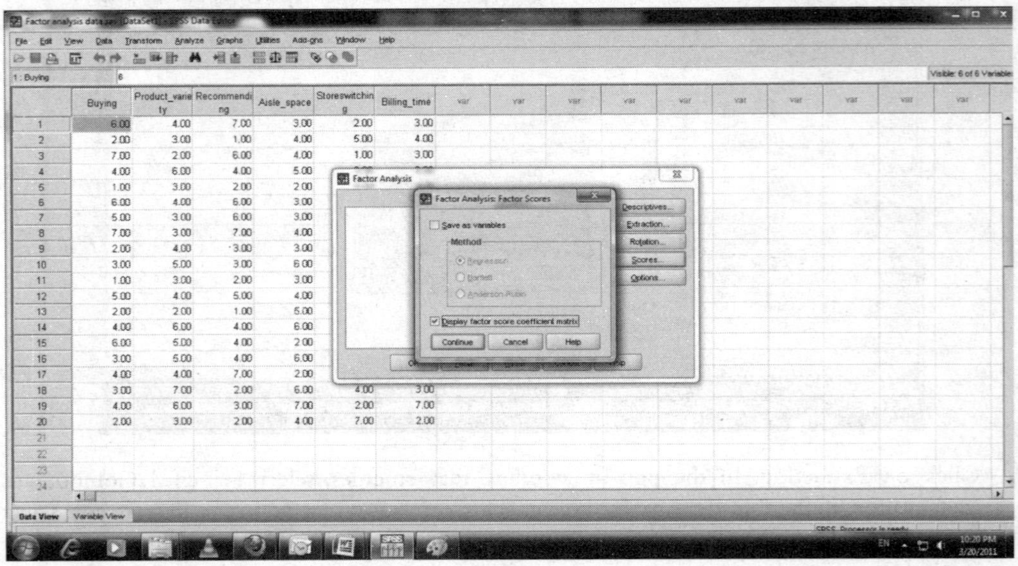

9. Click on OK

HOW MANY FACTORS?

One of the first questions the researcher asks is, "How many factors will exist among a large number of variables?" While a detailed discussion is beyond the scope of this text, the question is usually addressed based on the eigenvalues for a factor solution. Eigenvalues are a measure of how much variance is explained by each factor. The most common rule—and the default for most statistical programs—is to base the number of factors on the number of eigenvalues greater than 1.0. The basic thought is that a factor with an eigenvalue of 1.0 has the same total variance as one variable. It usually does not make sense to have factors, which are a combination of variables, that have less information than a single variable. So, unless some other rule is specified, the number of factors shown in a factor solution is based on this rule.

FACTOR LOADINGS

Each arrow connecting a factor (represented by an oval in Exhibit 24.6) to a variable (represented by a box in Exhibit 24.6) is associated with a **factor loading**. A factor loading indicates how strongly correlated a measured variable is with that factor. In other words, to what extent does a variable "load" on a factor? EFA depends on the loadings for proper interpretation. A latent construct can be interpreted based on the pattern of loadings and the content of the variables. In this way, the latent construct is measured indirectly by the variables.

factor loading

Indicates how strongly a measured variable is correlated with a factor.

Loading estimates are provided by factor analysis programs. In Exhibit 24.6, the factor loading estimates are shown beneath the factor diagram. The thick arrows indicate high loading estimates and the thin dotted lines correspond to weak loading estimates. Factors are interpreted by examining any patterns that emerge from the factor results. Here, a clear pattern emerges. The first four variables produce high loadings on factor 1 and the last four variables produce high loadings on factor 2.

When a clear pattern of factor loadings emerges, interpretation is easy. Because the first four variables all have content consistent with nostalgia and the second four variables all have content consistent with customer loyalty, the two factors can easily be labeled. Factor 1 represents the latent construct nostalgia and factor 2 represents the latent construct customer loyalty.

FACTOR ROTATION

Factor rotation is a mathematical way of simplifying factor results. The most common type of factor rotation is a process called varimax. A discussion of the technical aspects of the concept of factor rotation is far beyond the scope of this book. However, factor rotation involves creating new reference axes for a given set of variables. An initial factor solution is often difficult to interpret. Rotation "clears things up" by producing more obvious patterns of loadings. Users can observe this by looking at the unrotated and rotated solutions in the factor analysis output. An example of how to run factor analysis is provided in the Research Snapshot "Getting Factor Results with SAS or SPSS."

factor rotation

A mathematical way of simplifying factor analysis results so as to better identify which variables "load on" which factors; the most common procedure is varimax.

DATA REDUCTION TECHNIQUE

Factor analysis is considered a **data reduction technique**. Data reduction techniques allow a researcher to summarize information from many variables into a reduced set of variates or composite variables. Data reduction is advantageous for many reasons. In general, the **rule of parsimony** suggests that an explanation involving fewer components is better than one involving more. Factor analysis accomplishes data reduction by capturing variance from many variables with a single variate. Data reduction is also a way of identifying which variables among a large set might be important in some analysis. Thus, data reduction simplifies decision making.

data reduction technique

Multivariate statistical approaches that summarize the information from many variables into a reduced set of variates formed as linear combinations of measured variables.

rule of parsimony

The rule of parsimony suggests that an explanation involving fewer components is better than one involving more.

In our example, the researcher can now form two composite factors representing the latent constructs nostalgia and customer loyalty. These can be formed using factor equations of this form:

$$F_k = L_1X_1 + L_2X_2 + L_3X_3 + L_4X_4 + L_5X_5 + L_6X_6 + L_7X_7 + L_8X_8$$

where

F_k is the factor score for the kth factor (in this case there are two factors)

L represents factor loadings (ith) 1 through 8 for the corresponding factor

X represents the value of the corresponding measured variable

Using this type of equation, the scores for variables X_1–X_8 can be summarized by two scores, one for factor 1 and one for factor 2. This provides an example of the rule of parsimony. If the researcher wanted to analyze the correlation among these variables, now all that needs to be done is to analyze the bivariate correlation between factor 1 (nostalgia) and factor 2 (loyalty). This should prove much easier than analyzing an 8×8 correlation matrix. Statistical programs like SPSS and SAS will produce factor scores automatically if requested.

RESEARCH SNAPSHOT

Getting Factor Results with SAS or SPSS

Although researchers may choose to use a spreadsheet to produce simple or even multiple regression results, they will almost always turn to a specialized program for procedures like factor analysis. As a way of familiarizing readers with the mechanics involved, here are some instructions for getting factor results in each program.

SAS is most typically interfaced by writing short computer programs. SAS can read Excel spreadsheets quite easily. The data simply need to be "imported" into SAS by using the File dialog box (click on File to begin this process—see SAS documentation contained in the help files for more on how to do this). Once the data are set up, a factor program can be easily produced. Suppose we wished to run a factor program including a varimax rotation on eight variables labeled X1–X8. The program would be

```
proc factor rotate = v;
    var X1–X8;
```

After we click "run," the results appear in the output window.

In SPSS, the click-through sequence is as follows:

- ANALYZE
- DATA REDUCTION
- FACTOR ANALYSIS

This produces a dialog box. Now follow the steps below to get results that would match those above:

- Highlight variables X1 to X8 (either individually or in multiples).
- Click the ▶ to move them into the "Variables" window.
- Click "ROTATION."
    - Select VARIMAX.
- Optional: Click "OPTIONS."
    - Select "SORTED BY SIZE."
    - Select "SUPPRESS ABSOLUTE VALUES LESS THAN."
        - These two options make the output easier to read by organizing the output by the size of the loadings on each factor and by not showing loadings below some specified absolute value (0.1 by default). For factor analyses involving many variables, this is particularly helpful.
- Click "CONTINUE."
- Click "OK."

The results will appear in the output window.

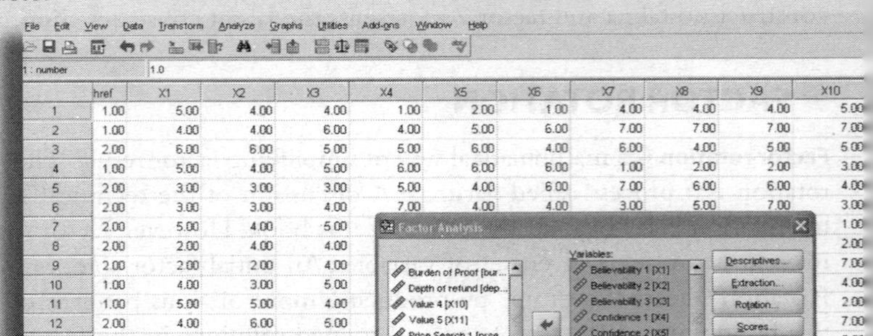

We can see that because F_1 is associated with high values for L_1 through L_4 (and low values for L_5, L_6, L_7, and L_8) and F_2 is associated with high values for L_5 through L_8 (and low for L_1, L_2, L_3, and L_4), F_1 is determined almost entirely by the nostalgia items and F_2 is determined almost entirely by the customer loyalty items. The factor pattern of high and low loadings can be used to match measured variables to factors in this way.

COMMUNALITY

While factor loadings show the relationship between a variable and each factor, a researcher may also wish to know how much a single variable has in common with all factors. Communality is a measure of the percentage of a variable's variation that is explained by the factors. A relatively high communality indicates that a variable has much in common with the other variables taken as a group. A low communality means that the variable does not have a strong relationship with the other variables. The item might not be part of one of the common factors or might represent a separate dimension. Communality for any variable is equal to the sum of the squared loadings for that variable. The communality for X_1 is

$$0.90^2 + 0.02^2 = 0.8104$$

Communality values are shown on factor analysis printouts.

TOTAL VARIANCE EXPLAINED

Along with the factor loadings, the percentage of total variance of original variables explained by the factors can be useful. Recall that common variance is correlation squared. Thus, if each loading is squared and totaled, that total divided by the number of factors provides an estimate of the variance in a set of variables explained by a factor. This explanation of variance is much the same as R^2 in multiple regression. Again, these values are computed by the statistics program so there is seldom a need to compute them manually. In this case, though, the variance accounted for among the eight variables by the nostalgia factor is 0.36 and the variance among the eight variables explained by the loyalty factor is 0.35. Thus, the two factors explain 71 percent of the variance in the eight variables:

$$0.36 + 0.35 = 0.71$$

In other words, the researcher has 71% of the information in two factors that are in the original eight items, another example of the rule of parsimony.

CREATING COMPOSITE SCALES WITH FACTOR RESULTS

When a clear pattern of loadings exists as in this case, the researcher may take a simpler approach. F_1 could be created simply by summing the four variables with high loadings and creating a summated scale representing nostalgia. F_2 could be created by summing the second four variables (those loading highly on F_2) and creating a second summated variable. While not necessary, it is often wise to divide these summated scales by the number of items so the scale of the factor is the same as the original items. For example, F_1 would be

$$((X_1 + X_2 + X_3 + X_4)/4)$$

The result provides a composite score on the 1–7 scale. The composite score approach would introduce very little error given the pattern of loadings. In other words, very low loadings suggest a variable does not contribute much to the factor. The reliability of each summated scale can be tested by computing a coefficient alpha estimate. Then, the researcher could conduct a bivariate regression analysis that would test how much nostalgia contributed to loyalty.

Cluster Analysis

Cluster analysis is a multivariate approach for identifying objects or individuals that are similar to one another in some respect. Cluster analysis classifies individuals or objects into a small number of mutually exclusive and exhaustive groups. Objects or individuals are assigned to groups so that there is great similarity within groups and much less similarity between groups. The cluster should have high internal (within-cluster) homogeneity and high external (between-cluster) heterogeneity.

cluster analysis
A multivariate approach for grouping observations based on similarity among measured variables.

Cluster analysis is an important tool for the business researcher. For example, an organization may want to group its employees based on their insurance or retirement needs, or on job performance dimensions. Similarly, a business may wish to identify market segments by identifying subjects or individuals who have similar needs, lifestyles, or responses to marketing promotions. Clusters, or subgroups, of recreational vehicle owners may be identified on the basis of their similarity with respect to recreational vehicle usage and the benefits they want from recreational vehicles. Alternatively, the researcher might use demographic or lifestyle variables to group individuals into clusters identified as market segments.

We will illustrate cluster analysis with a hypothetical example relating to the types of vacations taken by 12 individuals. Vacation behavior is represented on two dimensions: number of vacation days and dollar expenditures on vacations during a given year. Exhibit 24.7 is a scatter diagram that represents the geometric distance between each individual in two-dimensional space. The diagram portrays three clear-cut clusters. The first subgroup—consisting of individuals L, H, and B—suggests a

EXHIBIT 24.7
Clusters of Individuals on Two Dimensions

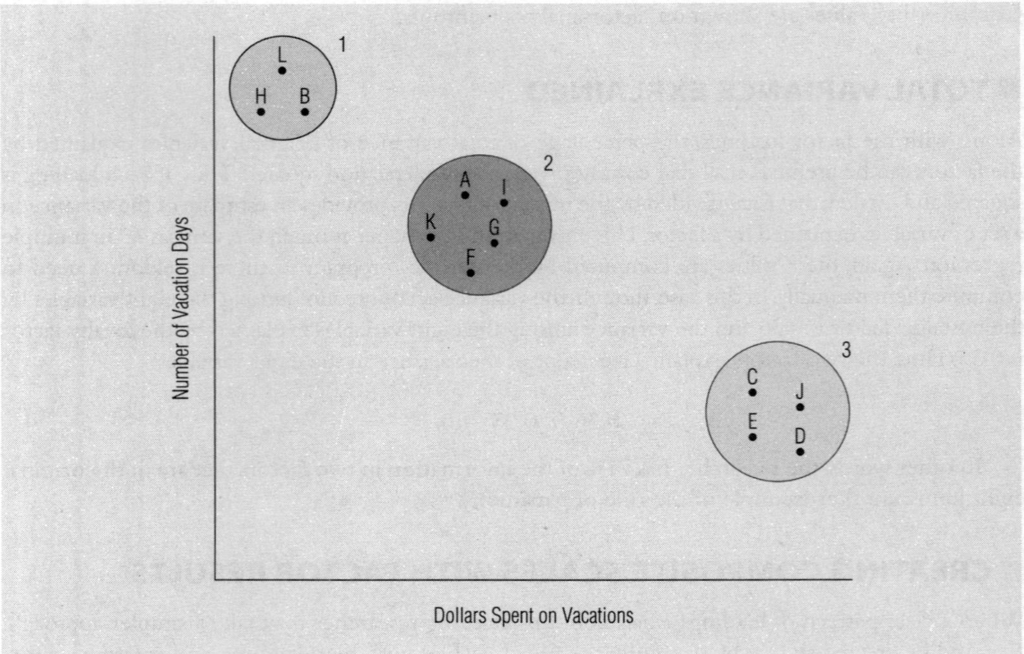

group of individuals who have many vacation days but do not spend much money on their vacations. The second cluster—represented by individuals A, I, K, G, and F—represents intermediate values on both variables: average amounts of vacation days and average dollar expenditures on vacations. The third group—individuals C, J, E, and D—consists of individuals who have relatively few vacation days but spend large amounts on vacations.

In this example, individuals are grouped on the basis of their similarity or proximity to one another. The logic of cluster analysis is to group individuals or objects by their similarity to or distance from each other. The mathematical procedures for deriving clusters will not be dealt with here, as our purpose is only to introduce the technique.

A classic study provides a very pragmatic example of the use of cluster analysis.[17] Managers frequently are interested in finding test-market cities that are very similar so that no extraneous variation will cause differences between the experimental and control markets. In this study the objects to be clustered were cities. The characteristics of the cities, such as population, retail sales, number of retail outlets, and percentage of nonwhites, were used to identify the groups. Cities such as Omaha, Oklahoma City, Dayton, Columbus, and Fort Worth were similar and cities such as Newark, Cleveland, Pittsburgh, Buffalo, and Baltimore were similar, but individual cities within each group were dissimilar to those within other groups or clusters.

This example should help to clarify the difference between factor analysis and cluster analysis. In factor analysis the researcher might search for constructs that underlie the variables (population, retail sales, number of retail outlets); in cluster analysis the researcher would seek constructs that underlie the objects (cities). Cluster analysis differs from multiple discriminant analysis in that the groups are not predefined. The purpose of cluster analysis is to determine how many groups really exist and to define their composition.

Cluster analysis is a multivariate technique that helps researchers to group objects on the basis of similarities. It is a classification technique through which respondents, brands, product categories, etc., can be grouped based on their similarities on the variables used for clustering. Consequently, the objects within each cluster are similar to each other while the objects between two clusters are dissimilar to each other. In other words, a good cluster solution increases within cluster homogeneity and between cluster heterogeneity. A geometrical representation of cluster analysis on cluster variable would show that the objects within the clusters are very close to each other while the objects between the clusters are far apart.

APPLICATION OF CLUSTER ANALYSIS

Cluster analysis is predominantly used in segmenting market. It helps the researcher to find the taxonomy of a given market on the basis of the closeness of consumers on clustering variables. Researchers use these clustering variables for cluster analysis to figure out the number of woody newsgroups present in the market, size of these groups with respect to the total market, and characteristics of these homogeneous groups. Consumption behavior as well as buying pattern may be different for different groups. Cluster analysis helps in identifying these different characteristics of each segment, based on which marketers can take practical decisions. Cluster analysis also helps in identifying new product opportunities and product extensions. Cluster analysis also helps marketers and researchers to carry out segment level analysis instead of aggregate level analysis. While an aggregate level analysis provides an average estimate which might nullify specific behavior of some type of consumers, a segment level analysis helps market to find out the characteristics and behavior of each segment that shows homogeneity.

ASSUMPTIONS OF CLUSTER ANALYSIS

Some of the assumptions made by cluster analysis are:

- The similarity and dissimilarity of clusters can be differentiated by distance between the clusters—often Euclidean distance, the length of the hypotenuse of a right triangle formed between the points.
- The data collected assumes standardization, usually statistical distance (Mahalanobis distance). Standardization of the data is needed if the range or scale of one variable is much larger or different from the range of others. This distance also compensates for intercorrelation among the variables.
- The collinearity among the variables is minimal.
- There are no significant outliers.
- The sample needs to be representative of the population.
- The data ignores the mood of the data provider and other aspects.

DEVELOPING A RESEARCH PLAN FOR CLUSTER ANALYSIS

There are different research plans for different organizations. The plan, hence, must be customized in a particular context. However, the broad guidelines would be as follows:

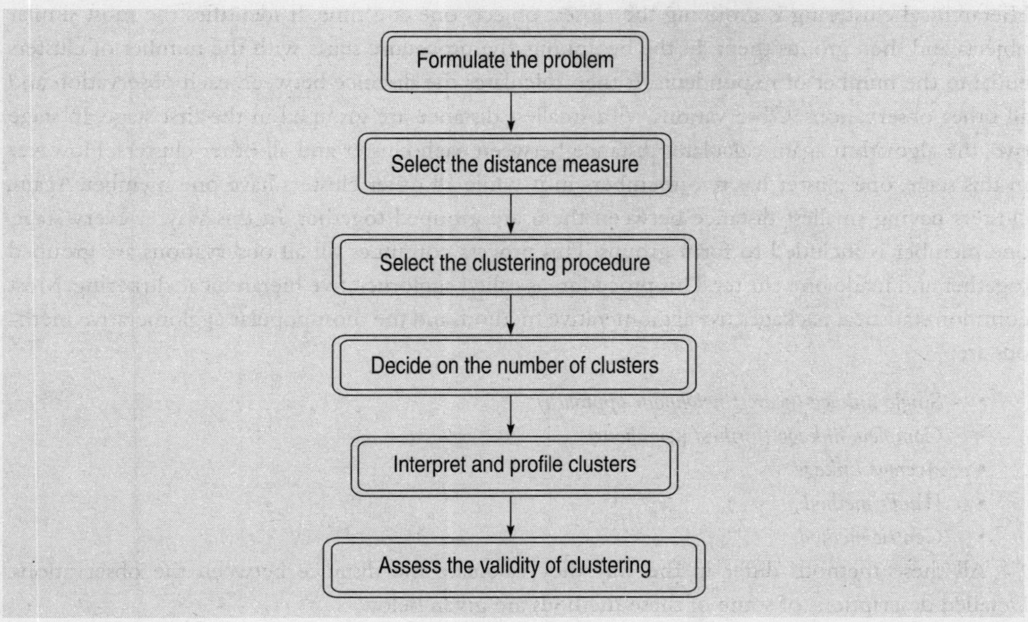

Formulation of the Problem

Formulation of the problem becomes the first step of any research program. In cluster analysis, we need to select the variables on which clustering should be based. We must take measures not to include one or more irrelevant variables that may distort the clustering solution. The variables selected must be relevant to the marketing research problem. The variables can be chosen referring to the literature review.

Selecting a Distance Measure

There are three different methods which are generally used.

- *Euclidean distance*
- *Manhattan distance*
- *Chebychev distance*

The most common way to measure the similarity between any two observational data is by measuring the distance between any two data objects. In most of the cases, Euclidean distance is calculated. Euclidean distance is the square root of the sum of squared differences in values for each of the variable. Another available measure is the City block distance or the Manhattan distance between two objects. It is the sum of the absolute difference in the values for each variable. The Chebychev distance between two objects is the maximum in absolute values for any variable and is also used to measure the distance between any two data objects.

Formation of Clusters

Once the similarity measure is decided by the researchers, there are many methods available to form the clusters. The clustering algorithms are broadly classified into two, namely:

- *Hierarchical algorithms*
- *Non-hierarchical algorithms*

Hierarchical means tree-like structure for understanding the levels of the observations. In the non-hierarchical method, a centroid is chosen and the distance from that centroid is measured. However, identifying the right central position is very difficult. Hence, many people do not use hierarchical procedures.

Hierarchical Clustering

Hierarchical clustering is grouping the closest objects one at a time. It identifies the most similar objects and then groups them. In the beginning, the procedure starts with the number of clusters equal to the number of respondents. It then calculates the distance between each observation and all other observations. Observations with smallest distance are grouped in the first stage. In stage two, the algorithm again calculates distance between each cluster and all other clusters. However in this stage, one cluster has two members in it while all other clusters have one member. Again, clusters having smallest distance between them are grouped together. In this way, at every stage, one member is included to form groups. This process continues till all observations are grouped together and made one cluster. This procedure is called agglomerative hierarchical clustering. Most common statistical packages use agglomerative method, and the most popular agglomerative methods are:

- *Single linkage (nearest neighbour approach)*
- *Complete linkage (furthest neighbour)*
- *Average linkage*
- *Ward's method*
- *Centric method*

All these methods differ in the way they calculate the distance between the observations. Detailed descriptions of some of these methods are given below.

Single linkage. Single linkage is a type of hierarchical clustering which consists of different steps. The number of steps is equal to one less than the total number of respondents included in cluster analysis. Every step consists of adding one new observation in order to form cluster. Therefore, the clusters formed initially will have minimum distance. Next, the second best distance, which is minimum, is included in the previous observation. This procedure is carried on and on till a proper cluster is formed.

Complete linkage. Complete linkage is another type of hierarchical clustering which consists of different steps as it is done in single linkage method. However, in complete linkage, the maximum distance between two observations is considered. The concept behind considering the maximum distance between two observations is that it would be the smallest sphere that would include two observations.

Average linkage. Average linkage is another type of hierarchical clustering procedure where average distance is considered as similarity measure between two observations.

Ward distance. The most commonly used clustering method is Ward's method. This method is different from the other methods since it uses the variance measure for clustering observations. Since conceptually the clusters need to be homogeneous, Ward's method relies on the concept that sums of square within cluster should be minimum. Hence in every step, within cluster variance is calculated between all the observations and cluster with minimum within sums of square value are grouped together. Such agglomerative process continues in every step till all observations are sequentially grouped to form one single cluster.

How Many Clusters to Select?

One of the important decisions researchers have to make is on the number of clusters to select. There is no specific rule to decide the number of clusters, however, researchers may follow several indicators to decide on the number of clusters to select.

1. Depending upon resource available to develop marketing mix for individual segments, marketers may finalize how many segments to target and accordingly how many clusters to select.
2. Depending upon competitions' product offering, marketers may select the segment that they can compete with and accordingly decide on the number of clusters to choose.
3. Size of the clusters often plays a major role in the selection process. Cluster with smaller size may not be attractive for the marketer to target and hence may not be considered. However, it also may be noted that niche segments are often of smaller size with specific requirement which may have large potential in future. Marketing manager with adequate expertize in building a particular product for niche segment may like to select a small cluster having specific needs.

Validating Cluster Solutions

Researchers often recommend validating clusters before using them in practice. Validation of clusters is a process that ensures that the clusters selected are significantly different from each other on the clustering variables considered by the researcher. Validation of cluster solution is also necessary to be sure that such cluster exists in the population. Hence, generalization is an issue in cluster analysis validation process. Validation of cluster solution can be done in the following ways:

1. Separate samples can be collected for analysis and validation purpose. Two separate clustering solutions may be adopted and compared for validation. However, this procedure requires large size of sample to accommodate both analysis as well as validation of sample adequacy.
2. Internal validation of cluster analysis is conducted to determine if the clustering solution is the best option for the data to be analyzed. It is done on the intrinsic information of the data.

   There are several types of internal validation as described below:

1. **Compactness.** Internal validation through compactness is used to measure intra-cluster homogeneity. As the name suggests, compactness determines how compact each cluster is in

terms of its homogeneity. A cluster is homogeneous when the sum of squares within the cluster is minimum compared to the sum of squares between the clusters. Such minimum variance criterion optimizes *K*-means clustering algorithm to find out optimum cluster solution.

2. **Connectedness.** Connectedness, in internal validation of cluster analysis, represents the group of data associated together. It evaluates the partitioning of available data by calculating the local densities. This way it groups the observations together with their nearest observations in the multi-dimensional space.

Researchers may also want to check the predictive validity of cluster solution. In this method, researchers use variables that were not used in cluster analysis though are related to the variables used in cluster analysis. Researchers then carry out the cluster analysis using the second set of variables and compare the cluster solution with the previous cluster solution. However, researchers must be careful that the variables selected for validation should be critically and conceptually related with the previous set of variables used in cluster analysis.

HANDLING OUTLIERS IN CLUSTER ANALYSIS

Similar to selecting suitable variables for cluster analysis, identifying outliers is also an important issue in cluster analysis. The presence of outlier in the data may largely affect the cluster solution. Outliers could be observations that do not represent the population that is being clustered. It may also represent under sampling of actual population as well as biasness in the sample. Actual cluster solution is distorted in the presence of outliers having values significantly different from population values. For this reason, researchers need to identify the outliers in the beginning of the analysis and proper care is to be taken to treat those outliers. It is to be noted with due caution that sometimes outliers may represent the existence of a different segment that might have a special kind of need. For instance, size of the market of innovators in adopting radically innovative products would be very less compared to the total market. In such a case, the number of respondents may be approximately 2% of the whole population. Researchers doing research in those areas must be careful while removing respondents having values significantly different from population value as this may represent a niche segment in the population.

multidimensional scaling
A statistical technique that measures objects in multidimensional space on the basis of respondents' judgments of the similarity of objects.

Multidimensional Scaling

Multidimensional scaling provides a means for placing objects in multidimensional space on the basis of respondents' judgments of the similarity of objects. The perceptual difference among objects is reflected in the relative distance among objects in the multidimensional space.

In the most common form of multidimensional scaling, subjects are asked to evaluate an object's similarity to other objects. For example, a sports car study may ask respondents to rate the similarity of an Acura TSX to a Chevrolet Corvette, then an Acura NSX to the Corvette, followed by a Lotus Elise to the Corvette, a Mustang to the Corvette, and so forth. Then, the comparisons are rotated (i.e., Acura NSX to the TSX, Lotus Elise to the TSX, and so on until all pairs are exhausted). Multidimensional scaling would then generate a plot of the cars, and the analyst then attempts to explain the difference in objects on the basis of the plot. The interpretation of the plot is left to the researcher.

In one study MBA students were asked to provide their perceptions of relative similarities among six graduate schools. Next, the overall similarity scores for all possible pairs of objects were aggregated for all individual respondents and arranged in a matrix. With the aid of a computer program, the judgments about similarity were statistically transformed into distances by placing the graduate schools into a specified multidimensional space. The distance between similar objects on the perceptual map was small for similar objects; dissimilar objects were farther apart.

Exhibit 24.8 shows a perceptual map in two-dimensional space. Inspection of the map illustrates that Harvard and Stanford were perceived as quite similar to each other. MIT and Carnegie also

© REBECCA COOK/REUTERS/LANDOV

© REBECCA COOK/REUTERS/LANDOV

How similar are these cars? This is the input to multidimensional scaling.

were perceived as very similar. MIT and Harvard, on the other hand, were perceived as dissimilar. The researchers identified the two axes as "quantitative versus qualitative curriculum" and "less versus more prestige." The labeling of the dimension axes is a task of interpretation for the researcher and is not statistically determined. As with other multivariate techniques in the analysis of interdependence, there are several alternative mathematical techniques for multidimensional scaling. Likewise, there are multiple ways of using multivariate procedures to generate a perceptual map. For example, factor scores resulting from factor analysis can be plotted along the factor dimensions. Such an approach may show the competitive positioning of several different firms along dimensions related to value and quality.

Exhibit 24.9 summarizes the multivariate techniques for analysis of interdependence.

Multidimensional scaling (MDS) is a class of procedures for representing perceptions and preferences of respondents through a visual display. Perceived or psychological relationships among stimuli are represented as geometric relationships among points in a multidimensional space. These

EXHIBIT 24.8
Perceptual Map of Six Graduate Business Schools: Simple Space

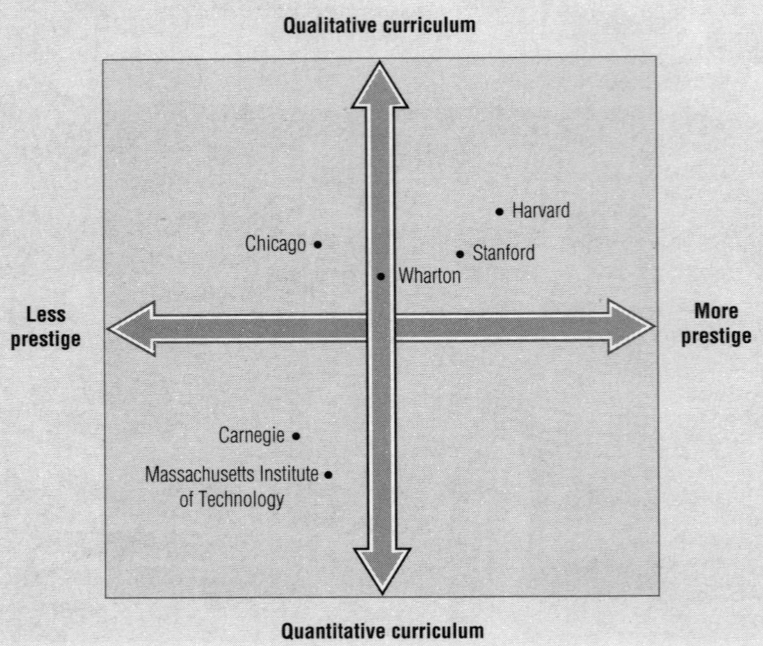

Source: Green, P. E., Carmone F. J., and Robertson, P. J., "Nonmetric Scaling Methods: An Exposition and Overview," *The Wharton Quarterly*, Vol. 2, 1968, pp. 159–173.

EXHIBIT 24.9 **Summary of Multivariate Techniques for Analysis of Interdependence**

Technique	Purpose	Type of Measurement
Factor analysis	To summarize into a reduced number of factors the information contained in a large number of variables	Interval
Cluster analysis	To classify individuals or objects into a small number of mutually exclusive and exhaustive groups, ensuring that there will be as much likeness within groups and as much difference among groups as possible	Interval
Multidimensional scaling	To measure objects in multidimensional space on the basis of respondents' judgments of their similarity	Varies depending on technique

geometric representations are often called spatial maps or perceptual maps. The axes of the spatial map are assumed to denote the psychological bases or underlying dimensions respondents use to form perceptions and preferences for stimuli.

Multidimensional scaling allows a person to measure an object in greater than one dimension at a given time. The virtue of MDS is its ability in scaling these psychological distances called dissimilarities and to convert them into a multidimensional map. The consumers are assumed to have a mental map where they view pairs of objects close to each other as *similar* but pairs of objects not so close to each other as *dissimilar*. The mental map cannot be explicitly visualized and MDS helps in converting this implicit visualization into explicit dimensions and is a very useful tool.

OBJECTIVES AND PURPOSE

Depending upon the relative distances between a pair of points, varying degrees of dissimilarities can be imagined. MDS presumes that the respondent is able to give either numerical measures of his/her perceived degree of dissimilarity for all the pairs of entities or less strictly provide an ordinal measure of dissimilarity. Given the responses, MDS is used to construct a physical map in more than one dimension whose inter-point distances are most consistent and conforming with the input data.

The main purpose of multidimensional scaling is to identify the number and nature of dimensions customers use to perceive different brands in the market place. It also helps in identifying the positions of different brands on these dimensions. Multidimensional scaling also helps in identifying the positions of consumers' ideal brands on these dimensions.

MDS, however, does not explain perception. It only provides useful representation of a set of subjective judgements about the extent to which the respondent views various pairs of entities as being or not being dissimilar.

ASSUMPTIONS OF MDS

The fundamental assumption of MDS is that consumers perceive an object/a set of objects as being similar to each other on a number of dimensions which are usually uncorrelated with each other. MDS also assumes that similar products are close in attribute space than dissimilar ones. Multidimensional scaling approach also depends on the assumption that perception is a function of attributes. The above assumptions are required for interpretation of perceptual map.

SITUATIONS WHERE MDS CAN BE USED

Most MDS studies are of pilot type or diagnostic in nature, which are useful for managers to get the basic hand-on experience for how their brand is positioned in the minds of consumers with respect to competing brands. A few areas in which MDS can be successfully used are perception mapping for beers, cold drinks, fast moving consumer goods, services and sales perceptions, etc. MDS is used in image measurement, brand positioning, market segmentation, new product development, assessing advertising effectiveness, and helping in pricing decision. From the location of the brand in perceptual map, the marketer can figure out the image of their brand in the mind of the prospect. This also helps the marketer in positioning/repositioning the brand depending upon where their brand stays in the mind of the prospect.

NATURE OF INPUT DATA IN MDS

Input data in MDS is a square symmetric matrix that indicates either similarities or dissimilarities among a set of items (for example, brand). These matrices are denoted as similarity matrix or dissimilarity matrix.

Similarity or similar data provided by the respondents do not say about bad aspects of their evaluation judgement. Such comparative aspects can be captured through preference data in MDS analysis. Interpretation of perceptual map generated from these two types of data will be different. Perceptual maps generated using similarity or disimilarity data represent attribute similarities and disimilarities of perceptual map for companies and brands. However, it does not reflect anything on determinants of respondents' choice about the dimensions. On the other hand, perceptual maps generated using preference-based data provide preferred choices of the respondents. However, it will not provide similar dispositions. This is because the respondents might have considered entirely different dimensions while giving similarity of the items vis-a-vis while giving their preference about the items.

Metric versus nonmetric data: Multidimensional scaling technique can be used for both metric and nonmetric data. A metric data is measured in interval ratio scale while nonmetric data are measured in categorical scale. A nonmetric input data in multidimensional scaling produces a nonmetric output which can be interpreted through rank order. Hence, the interpretability of perceptual map generated through nonmetric data is limited. Nowadays, because of the availability of advanced software, metric data are also used in multidimensional scaling. Metric data has the advantage of generating the optimal solution based on measure of similarity between items. Since a metric input data generate a matrix output, it is comparatively robust

TIPS OF THE TRADE

- The analysis stage illustrates the interdependency of the business research steps. How we structured the questionnaire and the level of data we gathered heavily influences the analysis we can conduct. If we know the type of analysis we want to do, then we must construct the survey instrument around this analysis.
- Flow charts—such as those presented in Exhibits 24.1, 24.2, and 24.3—are very useful tools for a business researcher when determining the appropriate analytical technique.
- Multiple regression is used for two purposes.
  - To *predict* something based on known information. For example, consider a fast-food restaurant considering a new location. Information from current restaurants can be used to build a model showing the relationship between independent variables such as population density, traffic flow, average income, population age distributions, distance to competitive restaurants, and so forth. These factors can be regressed on the dependent variable, sales volume. By using the unstandardized coefficients, the *bs* from this model, we can predict sales at potential locations under consideration.
  - To *explain* the drivers of something. Consider the fast-food example above. Which of these factors is most important in determining sales? By examining the standardized coefficients, the βs from this model, we can directly compare the different independent variables. What is the most important driver of restaurant sales?
  - Multicollinearity can be a big problem. It can cause the parameter estimates to take on unreasonable and unreliable values. VIFs of 5 or over are indicative of problems with multicollinearity.
- In a typical data matrix, with the variables as columns and cases as rows, we can think of factor analysis as grouping together the variables (columns) while cluster analysis groups together the respondents (rows).
- After clusters are determined, the cluster members can be "profiled" by examining the makeup (such as attitudes and demographic characteristics) of the group members. This is easily done by using the cluster membership as the factor variable in ANOVA and the variables of interest in the dependent list.

to find the final dimension of the perceptual map. The advantages of metric input data is retained in the output, however, it is difficult to satisfy the assumptions under which a metric data performs well. Often it is found that a perceptual map generated from metric and nonmetric data rarely has difference.

Individual versus Aggregate Level Analysis

Similar and dissimilar data as well as preference data can be used for individual level as well as for aggregate level estimation. The issue here is whether to do the analysis at individual level or at group/aggregate level. There are advantages and disadvantages of these two levels of analysis while drawing perceptual map.

Individual level analysis. Multidimensional scaling is useful for its ability to draw individual level perceptual map. In individual level analyses, the researchers generate perceptual map of the respondents as per their selected dimensions. This helps researchers to produce and interpret unique characteristics of each respondent's perception in a geometric way. The advantage of this technique is that researchers need to identify common dimensions that are to be used by all respondents and then can compare the perceptual map generated for each respondent.

Group/aggregate level analysis. Perceptual maps can also be drawn through multidimensional scaling for a group of respondents. Individual data matrices are arranged one by one in the software and perceptual map is generated for the group of respondents. Such perceptual map is a composite perceptual map and need to be interpreted accordingly.

LIMITATIONS OF MDS

MDS methods still have a number of limitations. For instance, in the case of nonmetric data, the MDS techniques have the problems of local optima and degenerate solutions. In such situations, the output of MDS becomes meaningless, even when statistical validity has been achieved. Metric MDS are a little more robust than nonmetric MDS. They produce good maps in all situations. Dimensional interpretation, the main work of MDS, is based on the highly subjective questioning of the interviewers. The same people under a different investigator may give different results.

Summary

1. Understand what multivariate statistical analysis involves and know the two types of multivariate analysis. Multivariate statistical methods analyze multiple variables or even multiple sets of variables simultaneously. They are particularly useful for identifying latent constructs using multiple individual measures. Multivariate techniques represent data through the use of variates. Variates are mathematical combinations of variables. The two major types of multivariate procedures are interdependence and dependence techniques. Interdependence techniques do not distinguish dependent and interdependent variables, whereas dependence techniques do make this distinction.

2. Interpret results from multiple regression analysis. Multiple regression analysis predicts a continuous dependent variable with multiple independent variables. The independent variables can be either continuous or categorical. Categorical variables must be coded as dummy variables. Multiple regression results are analyzed by examining the significance of the overall model using the *F*-test results, the individual parameter estimates, the overall model R^2, and the model collinearity diagnostics. Standardized regression coefficients have the advantage of a common scale, making them comparable from model to model and variable to variable.

3. Interpret results from multivariate analysis of variance (MANOVA). MANOVA is an extension of ANOVA involving multiple related dependent variables. Thus, MANOVA represents a form of the GLM predicting that multiple categorical independent variables affect multiple, related dependent variables. Interpretation of a MANOVA model is similar to interpretation of a regression model. However, the multivariate *F*-test results associated with Wilke's lambda (Λ) are interpreted first, followed by interpretation of the individual ANOVA results.

4. Interpret basic exploratory factor analysis results. EFA is a data reduction technique in which the variance in multiple variables is represented by a smaller number of factors. The factors generally represent latent factors or indexes. The pattern of loadings suggests both the number of latent factors that may exist and indicates which variables are associated with each factor. Rotated factor solutions are useful in properly interpreting factor analysis results.

5. Know what multiple discriminant analysis can be used to do. Another dependence technique is discriminant analysis. Discriminant analysis uses multiple independent variables to classify observations into one of a set of mutually exclusive categories. In other words, discriminant analysis predicts a categorical dependent variable with multiple independent variables.

6. Understand how cluster analysis can identify market segments. Cluster analysis classifies multiple observations into a smaller number of mutually exclusive and exhaustive groups. These should have as much similarity within groups and as much difference between groups as possible. In cluster analysis the groups are not predefined. However, clusters can be used to represent market segments because market segments also represent consumers who are similar to each other within a segment, but who are different from consumers in other segments.

Key Terms and Concepts

cluster analysis, *659*
data reduction technique, *657*
dependence techniques, *622*
discriminant analysis, *636*
dummy variable, *624*
factor analysis, *649*
factor loading, *657*
factor rotation, *657*
general linear model (GLM), *624*
interdependence techniques, *624*
multicollinearity, *630*
multidimensional scaling, *665*
multiple regression analysis, *624*
multivariate analysis of variance (MANOVA), *634*
partial correlation, *626*
rule of parsimony, *657*
variate, *621*

Questions for Review and Critical Thinking

1. Define *multivariate statistical analysis*.
2. What is the *variate* in multivariate? What is an example of a variate in multiple regression and in factor analysis?
3. What is the distinction between *dependence techniques* and *interdependence techniques*?
4. What is *GLM*? how can multiple regression and n-way ANOVA be described as GLM approaches?
5. What are the steps in interpreting a multiple regression analysis result? Can the same steps be used to interpret a univariate ANOVA model?
6. A researcher dismisses a regression result because the mode R^2 was under 0.70. do you think this was necessarily wise? Explain.
7. Return to the simple example of regression results for the toy company presented in the chapter. Since the data come equally from Europe and Canada, does this represent a potential source of variation that is not accounted for in the researcher's model? How could the researcher examine whether or not sales may be dependent upon country?
8. What is a *factor loading*?
9. How does factor analysis allow for data reduction?
10. How is the number of factors decided in most EFA programs?
11. What is *multidimensional scaling*? When might a researcher use this technique?
12. What is *cluster analysis*? When might a researcher use this technique
13. Name at least two multivariate techniques that can be useful in constructing perceptual maps.
14. A researcher uses multiple regression to predict a client's sales volume based on gross domestic product, personal income, disposable personal income, unemployment, and the consumer price index. What problems might be anticipated with this multiple regression model?

Research Activities

1. Use the multistep process to interpret the regression results below. This model has been run by a researcher trying to explain customer loyalty to a restaurant. The independent variables are customer perceptions of value, atmosphere, quality, and a location variable labeled center. This is a dummy variable that takes the value of 1 if the restaurant is in a shopping center and 0 if it is a standalone location. What substantive conclusions would you recommend to the restaurant company?

Model Summary

Model	*R*	*R* Square	Adjusted *R* Square	Std. Error of the Estimate
1	0.176	0.031	0.027	0.996

DV = Loyalty

ANOVA(b)

Model		Sum of Squares	*df*	Mean Square	*F*	Sig.
1	Regression	27.9731	4	6.9933	7.049	0.0000138
	Residual	876.0469	883	0.9921		
	Total	904.0200	887			

Coefficients(a)

Model		Unstandardized Coefficients B	Std. Error	Standardized Coefficients Beta	*t*	Sig.	VIF
1	(Constant)	−0.306	0.229		−1.338	0.181	
	Value	0.104	0.036	0.099	2.877	0.004	1.087
	Atmosphere	0.048	0.026	0.067	1.883	0.060	1.144
	Quality	0.044	0.028	0.054	1.590	0.112	1.038
	Center	−0.250	0.071	−0.124	−3.508	0.000	1.132

2. Interpret the following GLM results. Following from an example in the chapter, *Performance* is the performance rating for a business unit manager. *Sales* is a measure of the average sales for that unit. *Experience* is the number of years the manager has been in the industry. The variable *dummy* has been added. This variable is 0 if the manager has no advanced college degree and a 1 if the manager has an MBA. Do you have any recommendations?

The SAS System 21:06 Wednesday, April 22, 2009
The GLM Procedure
Dependent Variable: performance

Source	DF	Sum of Squares	Mean Square	F Value	Pr > F
Model	3	173.6381430	57.8793810	13.87	<.0001
Error	36	150.2341040	4.1731696		
Corrected Total	39	323.8722470			

R-Square	Coeff Var	Root MSE	performance Mean
0.536132	2.514731	2.042834	81.23468

Source	DF	Type III SS	Mean Square	F Value	Pr > F
dummy	1	136.9511200	136.9511200	32.82	<.0001
sales	1	22.4950649	22.4950649	5.39	0.0260
Experience	1	2.2356995	2.2356995	0.54	0.4689

Level of		-------performance-------		-----------sales----------		----Experience--------	
dummy	N	Mean	Std Dev	Mean	Std Dev	Mean	Std Dev
0	22	79.4848842	1.78987031	15979.7723	2008.32604	23.8984087	8.27327485
1	18	83.3733171	2.50773844	16432.0080	2015.18863	20.6788050	8.96324112

3. Interpret the following regression results. All of the variables are the same as in number 2. These results are produced with a regression program instead of the GLM-univariate ANOVA program.
   a. What do you notice when the results are compared to those in number 2? Comment.
   b. List the independent variables in order from greatest to least in terms of how strong the relationship is with performance.
   c. When might one prefer to use an ANOVA program instead of a multiple regression program?

The SAS System 21:07 Wednesday, April 22, 2009
The REG Procedure
Model: MODEL1
Dependent Variable: performance

Number of observations Read 40
Number of observations Used 40

Analysis of Variance

Source	DF	Sum of Squares	Mean Square	F Value	Pr > F
Model	3	173.63814	57.87938	13.87	<.0001
Error	36	150.23410	4.17317		
Corrected Total	39	323.87225			

Root MSE	2.04283	R-Square	0.5361
Dependent Mean	81.23468	Adj R-Sq	0.4975
Coeff Var	2.51473		

Parameter Estimates

Variable	Label	DF	Parameter Estimate	Standard Error	t Value	Pr > |t|	Standardized Estimate
Intercept	Intercept	1	72.68459	2.88092	25.23	<.0001	0
dummy	dummy	1	3.80621	0.66442	5.73	<.0001	0.66546
Sales	Sales	1	0.00038324	0.00016507	2.32	0.0260	0.26578
Experience	Experience	1	0.02829	0.03866	0.73	0.4689	0.08475

4. Interpret the following factor analysis results. The variables represent sample results of self-reported emotions while viewing a film. Why are only two factors reported below? What would you name the two summated scales which could be produced based on these results?

Total Variance Explained

Component	Initial Eigenvalues Total	% of Variance	Cumulative %	Extraction Sums of Squared Loadings Total	% of Variance	Cumulative %
1	2.94	36.74	36.74	2.94	36.74	36.74
2	2.51	31.34	68.08	2.51	31.34	68.08
3	0.71	8.84	76.92			
4	0.60	7.53	84.45			
5	0.42	5.20	89.65			
6	0.29	3.67	93.32			
7	0.29	3.64	96.96			
8	0.24	3.04	100.00			

Extraction Method: Principal Component Analysis.

Component Matrix(a)

	Factor 1	Factor 2
Interesting	0.664	−0.327
Anxious	0.444	0.511
Enthusiastic	0.842	−0.332
Worried	0.295	0.828
Exciting	0.812	−0.206
Tired	0.269	0.835
Happy	0.784	−0.383
Guilty	0.398	0.675

Extraction Method: Principal Component Analysis.
A 2 components extracted.

Rotated Component Matrix(a)

	Component Factor 1	Factor 2
Interesting	0.739	−0.024
Anxious	0.194	0.648
Enthusiastic	0.904	0.044
Worried	−0.073	0.876
Exciting	0.825	0.147
Tired	−0.100	0.872
Happy	0.872	−0.025
Guilty	0.084	0.779

Extraction Method: Principal Component Analysis.
Rotation Method: Varimax with Kaiser Normalization.
A Rotation converged in 3 iterations.

5. **'NET** Go to **http://www.census.gov** and examine some of the tables for your area. Cut and paste the table into a spreadsheet or statistical program. Run one dependence and one interdependence technique on the data. Interpret the results.
6. **'NET** Use **http://www.ask.com** to find an *F*-ratio calculator that will return a p-value given a calculated *F*-ratio and the degrees of freedom associated with the test.
7. **'NET** The Federal Reserve Bank of St. Louis maintains a database called FRED (Federal Reserve Economic Data). Navigate to the FRED database at **http://www.stls.frb.org/fred/index.html**. Use the consumer price index, exchange rates, interest rates, and one other variable to predict the consumer price index for the same time period. The data can either be downloaded or cut and pasted into another file.

Case 24.1 The Utah Jazz

The Utah Jazz are interested in understanding the market for the National Basketball Association. A study is conducted as described here.

Data Collection

Data came from a survey of adult residents of a large western metropolitan area. Respondents were selected in accordance with a quota sample of the area that was based on the age and sex characteristics reported in the most recent census. Six age categories for both males and females were used to gain representation of these characteristics in the market. In addition, interviewers were assigned to various geographic regions to ensure representation of the market with respect to socioeconomic characteristics. A total of 225 respondents age 18 and over provided data for the study.

Interviews were conducted by trained interviewers using a self-completion questionnaire. The presence of the interviewers served to answer any questions that might arise as well as to ensure compliance with the instructions.

Measures for the variables in the three categories of AIO (attitudes, interest, and opinions) were obtained using six-point rating scales. For example, the item for price proneness asked, "When you are buying a product such as food, clothing, and personal care items, how important is it to get the lowest price?" This item was anchored with "Not at all important" and "Extremely important."

The broadly defined category of demographics included standard socioeconomic characteristics as well as media preferences and attendance at professional hockey matches and university basketball games. Demographics were obtained using a variety of forced-choice and free-response measures, the natures of which are indicated in the variable information presented in Case Exhibit 24.1–1. The categorical measures of type of dwelling and preferred type of radio programming were coded as dummy variables for analysis. The criterion measure of patronage came from an open-ended question asking how many NBA games the respondent had attended during the past season.

Data Analysis

The distribution of responses to the attendance item was skewed, as might be expected. Thus, 57.3 percent of the respondents reported having attended none of the 41 possible games. Those who attended at least one game were recorded in accordance with specification

CASE EXHIBIT 24.1–1 **Characteristics of the Market for Professional Basketball**

	Means					Loading	
Variables	**None (*n* = 129)**	**Low (*n* = 47)**	**High (*n* = 49)**	***F*-Ratio**	**p**	**I**	**II**
Market Orientation[a]							
Price proneness	3.99	4.04	3.63	1.31	.271		
Quality proneness	4.95	4.74	4.82	.74	.480		
Product awareness	4.45	4.02	4.00	3.71	.026		
Product involvement	4.34	4.43	4.14	.66	.517		
Prepurchase planning	4.21	3.85	3.82	2.03	.134		
Brand loyalty	3.95	4.39	3.92	.96	.384		
Information search	3.83	3.55	3.96	1.06	.347		
Interests in Leisure Pursuits[b]							
Need for change from work routine	4.11	4.34	4.55	1.92	.150	.34	
Need for independence in leisure choice	4.88	4.94	4.96	.09	.911	.08	
Need for companionship during leisure	4.85	5.13	4.88	1.16	.317	.10	
Preference for passive versus active pursuits	3.64	4.15	4.57	7.28	.001	.70	
Self-image as athletic	3.67	4.38	4.47	5.89	.003	.60	
Childhood attendance at sporting events	3.38	3.89	4.18	5.41	.005	.60	
Pleasure from sporting events	3.14	3.66	4.27	10.62	.000	.84	
Opinions about Professional Sports[c]							
Athletes as a reference group	3.51	3.64	4.18	3.90	.022	.30	−.19
Excitement from enthusiastic crowd	4.27	4.72	4.73	2.70	.069	.24	.20
Excitement from animosity between teams	3.29	3.28	4.27	6.94	.001	.36	−.41
Acceptance of alcoholic beverages at games	2.60	3.64	3.39	6.88	.001	.34	.46
Enjoyment from large crowds	3.91	3.85	4.49	3.22	.042	.23	−.32
Enjoyment when standing at games	3.37	3.44	3.90	2.25	.108	.22	−.17
Excitement of professional basketball	4.09	3.91	4.67	5.34	.005	.27	−.49
Satisfaction from professional basketball	3.17	3.70	4.80	24.98	.000	.78	−.26
Importance of a winning team	4.26	4.69	5.07	6.12	.003	.39	.02
Demographics[d]							
Years in local area (number of years)	24.47	23.51	19.04	2.02	.135	−.24	
Sex (0 = female, 1 = male)	.40	.55	.65	5.45	.006	.39	

(Continued)

CASE EXHIBIT 24.1-1 **Characteristics of the Market for Professional Basketball** *(Continued)*

	Means					Loading	
	None	Low	High				
Variables	(*n* = 129)	(*n* = 47)	(*n* = 49)	*F*-Ratio	p	I	II
Demographics[d]							
Marital status (0 = single, 1 = married)	.60	.62	.45	2.00	.138	–.21	
Household size (number of persons)	3.13	3.27	3.14	.11	.896	.01	
Rents apartment (0 = no, 1 = yes)	.18	.32	.35	3.70	.026	.30	
Rents a house (0/1)	.09	.09	.08	.03	.967	–.03	
Owns a house (0/1)	.60	.49	.41	3.08	.048	–.29	
Owns a condominium (0/1)	.05	.02	.06	.50	.607	.01	
Head of household (0/1)	.52	.64	.67	2.19	.115	.24	
Occupational prestige of self (NORC scale)	68.05	69.36	70.63	1.27	.284	.19	
Job leaves evenings free for entertainment (0/1)	.87	.85	.92	.57	.567	.10	
Prefers easy-listening music radio programming (0/1)	.39	.34	.29	.83	.438	–.15	
Prefers contemporary popular music radio (0/1)	.16	.28	.27	1.96	.143	.20	
Prefers rock music radio (0/1)	.14	.11	.27	2.76	.066	.23	
Prefers country-western music radio (0/1)	.15	.19	.08	1.22	.299	–.12	
Prefers talk and news radio programming (0/1)	.09	.04	.06	.52	.597	–.08	
Education (years of schooling)	13.08	13.66	13.56	5.11	.007	.38	
Age (years)	41.51	39.79	33.59	4.21	.016	–.34	
Annual household income (7-point scale)	4.88	5.11	5.16	.65	.523	.13	
Monthly personal expenditures on entertainment for household (dollars)	85.10	112.45	101.29	1.38	.254	.13	
Attendance at university basketball (games last year)	.92	1.89	4.14	15.29	.000	.66	
Attendance at professional hockey (matches last year)	.69	2.28	2.78	5.33	.006	.37	

[a]Canonical discriminant analysis not significant at p = .189; therefore, no loadings are given.
[b]Canonical discriminant analysis significant at p = .004, first function significant. Centroids for the market segment groups are as follows: none, –.29; low, .19; high, .59.
[c]Canonical discriminant analysis significant at p = .000, both functions significant. Centroids for the market segment groups on the first function are as follows: none, –.47; low, .26; high, 1.00. Centroids on the second function are as follows: none, –.10; low, .57; high, –.27.
[d]Canonical discriminant analysis significant at p = .004, first function significant. Centroids for the market segment groups are as follows: none, –.41; low, .14; high, .97.

of the light half and the heavy half of the market. This category of patrons was split as nearly as possible at the median, *giving 20.9 percent who attended one or two games* and *21.8 percent who attended three or more.* The three patronage categories thus used for analysis were subsequently termed the *none, low,* and *high* attendance segments.

Given the categorical nature of the criterion measure and the continuous nature of the predictor variables, both univariate analysis of variance and discriminant analysis were employed for the survey. Each of the four categories of predictor variables was subjected to a *separate discriminant* analysis to test the multivariate hypothesis of relationship between patronage and the predictor set in question. The univariate ANOVAs were used to provide complementary information about the nature of the segments.

Results

Case Exhibit 24.1–1 gives the results of the analyses conducted on the four sets of predictor variables. Each set produced at least one variable that was significant in univariate analysis. Three of the four discriminant analyses were significant.

The first predictor set involving AIOs, "marketing orientation," provided only a single variable that ANOVA showed to differentiate among the members of the three patronage segments. The discriminant analysis was nonsignificant.

"Interests in leisure pursuits" emerged as more predictive. By univariate ANOVA, four variables were found significant at the 0.05 level. The discriminant analysis was significant at $p = 0.004$.

"Opinions about professional sports" provided significant prediction of patronage. Seven of the nine variables reached significance at the 0.05 level in univariate analysis. The discriminant analysis was significant beyond $p = 0.001$, and it produced two significant functions. The first significant function provided 79.8 percent of the explained variance, and the second function provided 20.2 percent.

Finally, the set "demographics" was also found to be related to patronage. Counting the four dummy-coded measures of dwelling type and the five similar preferences for radio programming as separate variables, 7 of the 22 demographics reached significance in univariate analysis. The discriminant analysis was significant at $p = 0.004$.

Question

Interpret the managerial significance of the ANOVA and multiple discriminant analysis results.

Source: Courtesy of the American Marketing Association. Adapted from paper presented at AMA conference, 1984.

Case 24.2 How Do We Keep Them?

Request the data sets for this case from your instructor.

Use the data labeled profit for this case. The data go along with The Research Snapshot "Too Much of a Good Thing!" in addition, management has collected several semantic differential scales from the managers asking them to use emotions to describe the way they feel about their jobs. The emotions include

involved exciting fun satisfied happy pleased

The managers want to understand turnover. So, another variable is included that gives the likelihood a manger will quit within 12 months (labeled turnover in data). After running some initial regression models with eight independent variables predicting turnover, management was confused. They complained that there were too many variables to make sense of.

Thus, the researcher turned to a data reduction technique. Afterwards, a regression model with fewer independent variables gave some clear direction regarding emotions and turnover.

Questions

1. Perform the appropriate multivariate technique to identify underlying dimensions that may exist among the emotion ratings.
2. Create scales for any underlying dimensions.
3. Use these scales as independent variables in a regression model.
4. Interpret the results.

Case 24.3 A Case of Multidimensional Scaling on Telecom Service Providers in India

The case study described here is about telecom service providers in Indian mobile phone market and of five different brands (Airtel, BSNL, Idea Cellular, Reliance, and Vodafone). In this study, there are total five parameters—product, price, distribution, advertisement, and sales promotion—on which researchers have evaluated the above mentioned brands of telecom companies on two dimensions: reliability and value. For multidimensional scaling analysis, each respondent was asked to rate the dissimilarity among the brands by rating all these on a numerical scale. The distance matrix of all respondents was averaged and a single distance matrix was constructed. For the sake of simplicity, integers were used as a distance measure. In the symmetrical 5×5 distance matrix, the columns and rows both denote the brands. It may be noted that individual matrices can also be arranged in a column or in a row to carry out aggregate level analysis in SPSS. In our case, the data used was ordinal in nature, and as per the requirement of MDS method, these data were fitted into the framework of requirement for that. The input data used was ordinal in nature in the form of a 5×5 distance matrix. The respondents were asked to do a pair-wise comparison on a scale of 1–5 between the brands, where 1 denotes less distance and more similarity and 5 denote more distance and less similarity between the brands. There were total five 5×5 distance matrices used as an input data for product, price, advertisement, distribution, and sales promotion, respectively. The input data was analyzed through SPSS 16.0 by using multidimensional scaling method. During the analysis it was observed that the maximum number of dimensions in all the five cases could be two because researchers have only five brands which were compared on two dimensions. The outputs in the form of perceptual map were generated as produced in Case Exhibit 24.3-1 on the basis of which one can position the brands.

From the perceptual map produced we can see that horizontal dimension is *reliability* and vertical dimension is *value*. One can observe that Airtel is perceived as high as reliable service provider followed by Vodafone when they are compared to Reliance and Idea Cellular. It can also be seen that BSNL is perceived as provider of high value compared to their other four counterparts. Marketing manager of specific company may derive the marketing strategy and position future product on this basis.

Questions

1. As a researcher how do you recommend to derive the dimensions of perceptual maps?
2. How do you think the above case to care for the assumptions required to be fulfilled for MDS?
3. What precautions are to be taken while doing an aggregate level multidimensional scaling vis-à-vis an individual level multidimensional scaling?
4. Discuss the procedure to develop a market dimensional scaling with eight telecom brands.

CASE EXHIBIT 24.3-1 **Perceptual Map Produced for Five Brands on Two Dimensions: Reliability and Value**

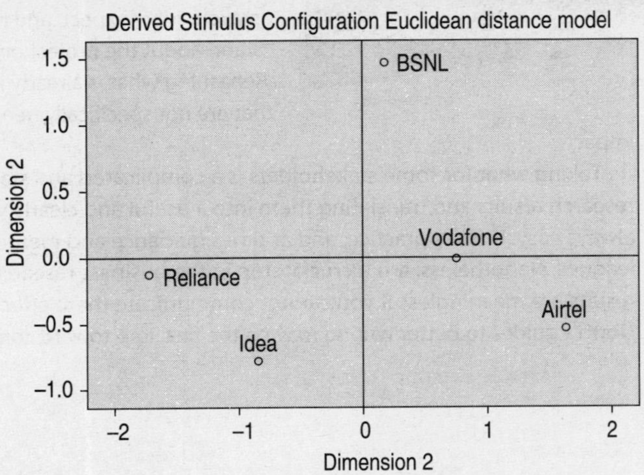

CHAPTER 25
COMMUNICATING RESEARCHRESULTS: REPORT GENERATION, ORAL PRESENTATION, AND FOLLOW-UP

LEARNING OUTCOMES

After studying this chapter, you should be able to

1. **Discuss the research report from the perspective of the communications process**
2. **Define the parts of a research report following a standard format**
3. **Explain how to use tables for presenting numerical information**
4. **Summarize how to select and use the types of research charts**
5. **Describe how to give an effective oral presentation**
6. **Discuss the importance of Internet reporting and research follow-up**

Chapter Vignette: A Business Report Title (and Nothing Else)—Tips to Get Started

A significant part of this text has been devoted to the development and execution of business research, but perhaps the most important component of the business research process has yet to be discussed. Regardless of the research topic or audience, you as a business researcher are faced with communicating your efforts to appropriate stakeholders. This is not a straightforward task for many researchers, who often find themselves staring at a blank computer screen, with a title on the page, and nothing else. To help you get started, you should reflect on a few critical questions regarding your efforts. Fortunately, Tim North of Better Writing Skills (**http://www.betterwritingskills.com**) provides some tips to help you frame this important aspect of your research.[1]

First, you must understand who the readers are, and focus your writing on those stakeholders who are most likely to need your results. It is difficult to satisfy everyone's needs, so identifying the key readers of your business research is a must. Second, you must ask yourself why the readers want your results. Is it for evaluation purposes, to make decisions, or simply for information? Third, as you write your report you should understand what your stakeholders expect, and how much they already understand about the project or program you are writing about. Rehashing what is already known or commenting on results that are not specifically needed will only reduce your report's impact.

Taking what for some stakeholders is a complicated and statistics-heavy set of business research results and translating them into a useful and clearly written research report is not always easy. It takes practice, and at times guidance and mentorship from more experienced colleagues. Nonetheless, it is a crucial step in the business research process. Your elegant research results are meaningless if you cannot communicate them effectively. Taking advantage of Tim North's guides to better writing may be the first step toward completing this journey.

Introduction

Why should a careful researcher have to be a good writer, too? After the researcher has spent days, weeks, or even months working on a project, preparation of the report may feel like an anticlimactic formality. All the "real" work has been done; it just has to be put on paper. This attitude can be disastrous, however. Even if the project was well designed, the data carefully obtained and analyzed by sophisticated statistical methods, and important conclusions reached, unless the reporting is effective all of the earlier efforts will have been wasted. Often the research report is the only part of the project that others ever see. If people who need to use the research results have to wade through a disorganized presentation, are confused by technical jargon, or find sloppiness of language or thought, they will probably discount the report and make decisions without it, just as if the project had never been done. The research report is a crucial means for communicating the whole project. This chapter explains the communication of research results with written reports, oral presentations, and follow-up conversations.[2]

TOTHEPOINT

It is a luxury to be understood.

—Ralph Waldo Emerson

Insights from the Communications Model

Some insights from the theory of communications help to clarify the importance of the research report. Exhibit 25.1 illustrates one view of the **communication process**. Several elements influence successful communication.

communication process
The process by which one person or source sends a message to an audience or receiver and then receives feedback about the message.

- The *communicator*—the source or sender of the message (the writer of the report)
- The *message*—the set of meanings being sent to or received by the audience (the *findings* of the research project)
- The *medium*—the way in which the message is delivered to the audience (the oral or written report itself)
- The *audience*—the receiver or destination of the message (the manager who will make a decision based—we hope—on the report findings)
- *Feedback*—a communication, also involving a message and channel, that flows in the reverse direction (from the audience to the original communicator) and that may be used to modify subsequent communications (the manager's response to the report)

This model may make communication seem simple. Perhaps communication is simple when the message flows smoothly from writer to reader, and then in return, from reader to writer to provide feedback. Actually, communication is more complex. Exhibit 25.2 illustrates one key difficulty. The communicator and the audience each have individual fields of experience. These overlap to some extent; otherwise no communication would be possible. Still, a great deal of experience is not common to both parties. As communicators send a message, they encode it in

EXHIBIT 25.1
The Communication Process

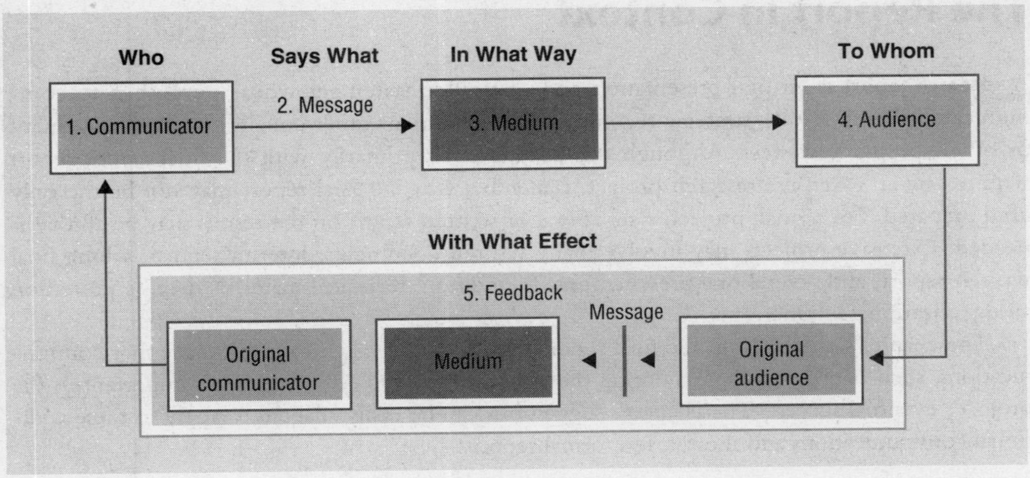

EXHIBIT 25.2
Communication Occurs in a Common Field of Experience

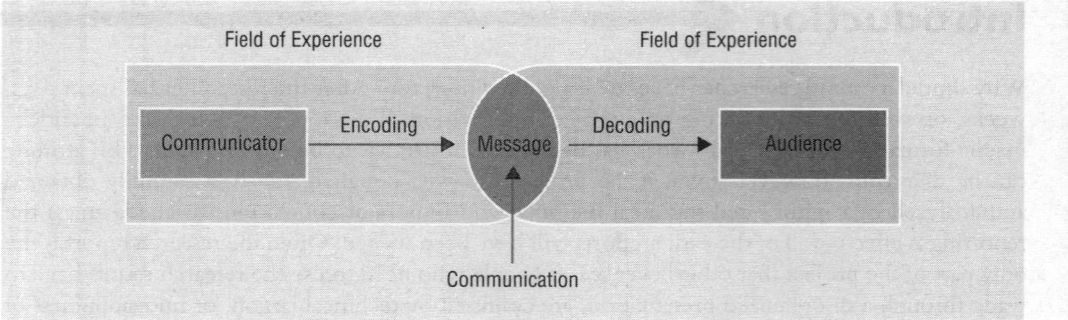

terms that make sense to them based on their fields of experience. As the individuals in the audience receive the message, they decode it based on their own fields of experience. The message is successfully communicated only if the parties share enough common experience for it to be encoded, transmitted, and decoded with roughly the same meaning.

In the research setting, the communicator (the researcher) has spent a great deal of time studying a problem. He or she has looked at secondary sources, gathered primary data, used statistical techniques to analyze the data, and reached conclusions. When the report on the project is written, all this "baggage" will affect its contents. On the assumption that the reader has a lot of background information on the project, the researcher may produce pages and pages of unexplained tables, expecting the reader to unearth from them the same patterns that the researcher has observed. The report may contain technical terms such as *parameter estimate,* F*-distribution, statistical significance, correlations,* and *eigenvalue* on the assumption that the reader will understand them. Another researcher may assume that the reader does not have a lot of background information and may go overboard explaining everything in the report in sixth-grade terms. Although the researcher's intent is to ensure that the reader will not get lost, this effort may insult the reader.

Usually when readers receive a report, they have not thought much about the project. They may not know anything about statistics and may have many other responsibilities. If they cannot understand the report quickly, they may put it on a stack of things to do someday.

Simply delivering a report to its audience is not sufficient to ensure that it gets attention. The report needs to be written so as to draw on the common experience of the researcher and the reader. And the person responsible for making sure that it does so is the writer—not the reader. Unless a report is really crucial, a busy reader will not spend time and effort struggling through an inadequate or difficult-to-read document.

The Report in Context

research report
An oral presentation or written statement of research results, strategic recommendations, and/or other conclusions to a specific audience.

A **research report** is an oral presentation and/or written statement whose purpose is to communicate research results, strategic recommendations, and/or other conclusions to management or other specific audiences. Although this chapter deals primarily with the final *written* report required by an extensive research project, remember that the final report may not be the only kind prepared. For a small project, a short oral or written report on the results may be all that is needed. Extensive projects may involve many written documents, interim reports, a long final written report, and several oral presentations. In addition, technical materials may be posted on an organization's intranet.

The chapter's emphasis on the final report should not be taken to mean that other communications, such as progress reports during the course of the project, are any less important to the project's eventual success. The chapter's suggestions can be easily adapted to apply to these additional communications and shorter, less formal reports.

Report Format

Although every research report is custom-made for the project it represents, some conventions of **report format** are universal. They represent a consensus about the parts necessary for a good research report and how they should be ordered. This consensus is not a law, however. Every book on report writing suggests the use of its own unique format, and every report writer has to pick and choose the section and order that will work best for the project at hand. Many companies and universities also have in-house report formats or writing guides for writers to follow. The format described in this section serves as a starting point from which writers can shape their own appropriate format. It includes seven major elements:

report format
The makeup or arrangement of parts necessary to a good research report.

1. Title page (sometimes preceded by a title fly page)
2. Letter of transmittal
3. Letter of authorization
4. Table of contents (and lists of figures and tables)
5. Executive summary
   a. Objectives
   b. Results
   c. Conclusions
   d. Recommendations
6. Body
   a. Introduction
      1. Background
      2. Objectives
   b. Methodology
   c. Results
   d. Limitations
   e. Conclusions and recommendations
7. Appendix
   a. Data collection forms
   b. Detailed calculations
   c. General tables
   d. Bibliography
   e. Other support material

This format is illustrated graphically in Exhibit 25.3.

Tailoring the Format to the Project

The format of a research report may need to be adjusted for two reasons: (1) to obtain the proper level of formality and (2) to decrease the complexity of the report. The format given here is for the most formal type of report, such as one for a large project done within an organization or one done by a research agency for a client company. This type of report is usually bound in a permanent cover and may be hundreds of pages long.

In less formal reports, each part is shorter, and some parts are omitted. Exhibit 25.4 illustrates how the format is adapted to shorter, less formal reports. The situation may be compared to the way people's clothing varies according to the formality of the occasion. The most formal report is dressed, so to speak, in a tuxedo or long evening gown. It includes the full assortment of prefatory parts—title fly page, title page, letters of transmittal and authorization, and table of contents. Like changing into an everyday business suit, dropping down to the next level of formality involves eliminating parts of the prefatory material that are not needed in this situation and reducing the complexity of the report body. In general, as the report moves down through the sport coat and slacks and then blue jeans stages, more prefatory parts are dropped, and the complexity and length of the report body are reduced.

EXHIBIT 25.3 **Report Format**

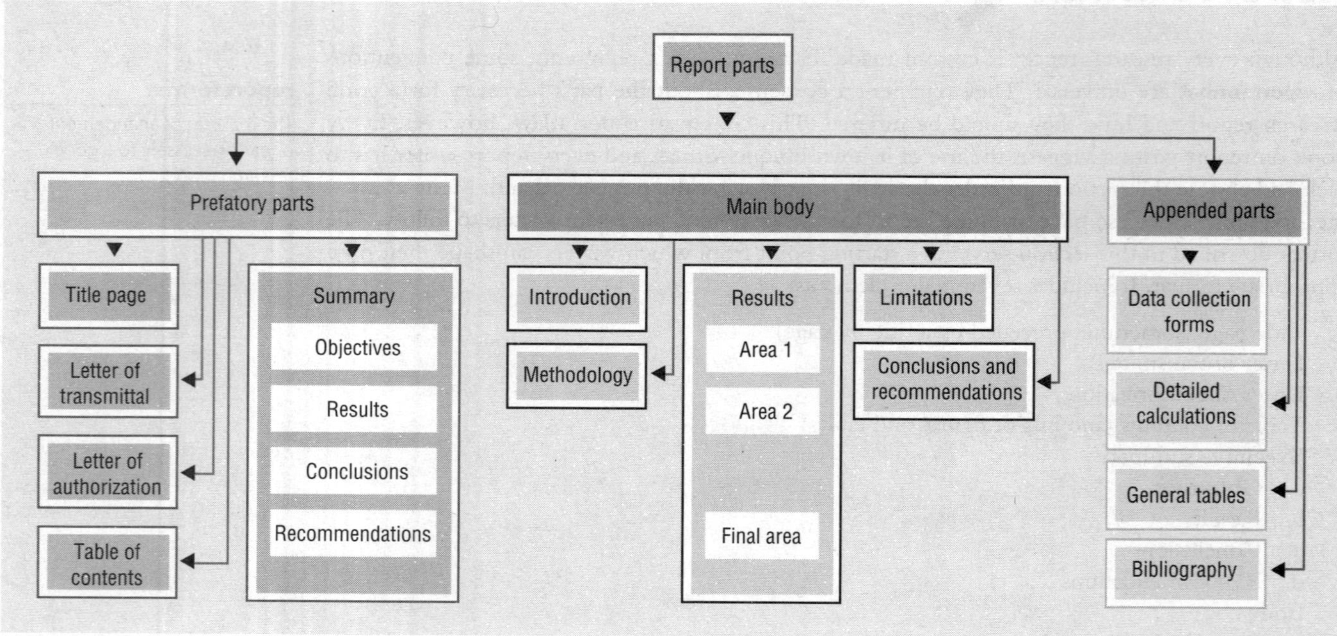

How does the researcher decide on the appropriate level of formality? The general rule is to include all the parts needed for effective communication in the particular circumstances—and no more. This depends on how far up in management the report is expected to go and how routine the matter is. A researcher's immediate supervisor does not need a 100-page, "black-tie" report on a routine project. However, the board of directors does not want a one-page "blue jeans" report on a big project that backs a major expansion program. The formal report to top management may later be stripped of some of the prefatory parts (and thus reduced in formality) for wider circulation within the company.

EXHIBIT 25.4 **Adapting Report Format to Required Formality**

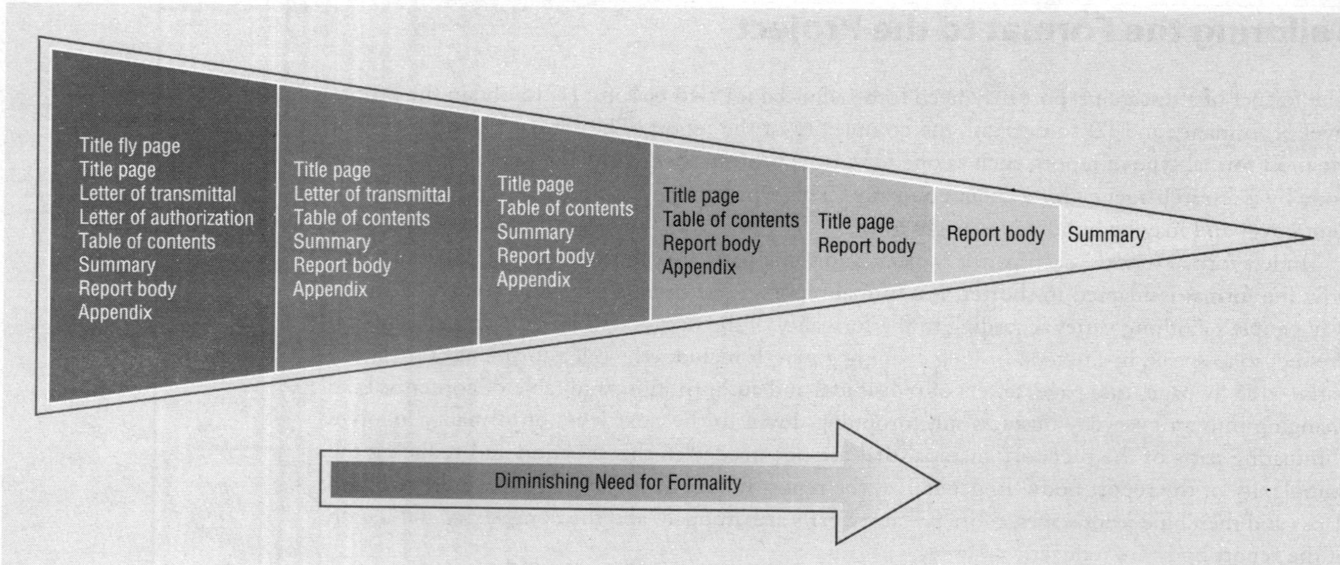

The Parts of the Report

The guidelines that call for each element of the research report also dictate the content of each part.

TITLE PAGE

The *title page* should state the title of the report, for whom the report was prepared, by whom it was prepared, and the date of release or presentation. The title should give a brief but complete indication of the purpose of the research project. Addresses and titles of the preparer and recipient may also be included. On confidential reports, the title page may list the people to whom the report should be circulated. For the most formal reports, the title page is preceded by a title fly page, which contains only the report's title.

TOTHEPOINT

The covers of this book are too far apart.

—Ambrose Bierce

LETTER OF TRANSMITTAL

Relatively formal and very formal reports include a *letter of transmittal.* Its purpose is to release or deliver the report to the recipient. It also serves to establish some rapport between the reader and the writer. This is the one part of the formal report in which a personal or even slightly informal tone should be used. The transmittal should not dive into the report findings except in the broadest terms.

Exhibit 25.5 presents a sample letter of transmittal. Note that the opening paragraph releases the report and briefly identifies the factors of authorization. The letter comments generally on findings and matters of interest regarding the research. The closing section expresses the writer's personal interest in the project just completed and in doing additional, related work.

LETTER OF AUTHORIZATION

The *letter of authorization* is a letter to the researcher that approves the project, details who has responsibility for it, and describes the resources available to support it. Because the researcher would not write this letter personally, writing guidelines will not be discussed here. In many situations, simply referring to the authorization in the letter of transmittal is sufficient. If so, the letter of authorization need not be included in the report. In some cases, though, the reader may be unfamiliar with the authorization or may need detailed information about it. In such cases, the report should include this letter, preferably an exact copy of the original.

THE TABLE OF CONTENTS

A *table of contents* is essential to any report more than a few pages long. It should list the divisions and subdivisions of the report with page references. The table of contents is based on the final outline of the report, but it should include only the first-level subdivisions. For short reports it is sufficient to include only the main divisions. If the report includes many figures or tables, a list of these should immediately follow the table of contents.

THE SUMMARY

The *summary*, also known as executive summary, briefly explains why the research project was conducted, what aspects of the problem were considered, what the outcome was, and what should be done. It is a vital part of the report. Studies have indicated that nearly all managers read a report's summary, while only a minority read the rest of the report. Thus, the writer's only chance to produce an impact may be in the summary.

The summary should be written only after the rest of the report has been completed. It represents the essence of the report. It should be one page long (or, at most, two pages), so the writer must carefully sort out what is important enough to be included in it. Several pages of the full report may have to be condensed into one summarizing sentence. Some parts of the report may

EXHIBIT 25.5
Example Transmittal Letter

EMR ResearchGroup
Moving you forward!

August 30, 2009

Mr. Mario Lagasto
President, Leading Edge Food Group
Columbia, IA 50057

Re: Presentation of Research Identifying Customer Loyalty

Dear Mr. Lagasto:

The report outlined in the research proposal of March 15, 2009, is complete. I have personally supervised the project, conducted the statistical analyses, and prepared this report along with my two senior research associates, Natalia James and David Parker.

The report addresses the key decision statement: In what ways can your restaurants build customer loyalty so that revenues increase through more frequent patronage? The key research questions involve identifying controllable characteristics that end up relating to greater share of wallet. As agreed upon in the proposal, the report offers no specific recommendations for managerial action, but rather, it presents conclusions which should enable you to make informed decisions. Thus, the conclusions conform to the deliverables described in the proposal letter.

We successfully accomplished the research project as described in the outline. We were able to meet our goals for interviewing groups of customers and non-customers in a timely fashion. We are grateful for your business and look forward to working with you as you develop strategic plans of action based on this report. Once you have taken a look at the report, please contact me and we will schedule a formal presentation and question and answer period for your management team.

Sincerely,

Barry J. Babin
President

EMR Research Group
114 Railroad Ave
Choudrant, LA 71272

be condensed more than others; the number of words in the summary need not be in proportion to the length of the section being discussed. The summary should be written to be self-sufficient. In fact, the summary is often detached from the report and circulated by itself.

The summary contains four elements. First, it states the objectives of the report, including the most important background information and the specific purposes of the project. Second, it presents the methodology and the major results. Finally, the conclusions of the report are presented. These are opinions based on the results and constitute an interpretation of the results. Finally come recommendations, or suggestions for action, based on the conclusions. In many

RESEARCH SNAPSHOT

© iStock

Research ROI

The research summary, like the original research design, should be based on the business problem to be solved and the resulting insight into how to address that problem. In today's competitive business environment, companies cannot afford to do research just because it is interesting. They need research that helps them compete as an organization.

Logically, this should mean that companies are measuring whether research helps their bottom line. In practice, however, measuring the return on investment (ROI) for research is still a relatively new idea. Research consultants at a firm called A. Dawn Lesh International surveyed companies to find out how they measure the effectiveness of their research projects. The firm discovered that only 10 to 15 percent of the companies measured research effectiveness at all. Some of those that did measure it simply looked at whether the project's client was satisfied or whether the quality of the work was high. In other cases, researchers determined the expected value of each idea uncovered by the research project.

Lesh International proposes measures that put a dollar value on the research. One of these, which the firm calls ROI Lite, is the dollar value of the decision multiplied by the client's estimate of the increased confidence that the right alternative will be selected, divided by the cost of the research. The second measure, ROI Complete, incorporates the likelihood that the research client will act on the information.

© CREATAS IMAGES/JUPITER IMAGES

Sources: Based on Maddox, Kate, "Market Research Charges Online," *B to B* (April 4, 2005); Maddox, Kate, "The ROI of Research," *B to B*, 89 (April 5, 2005), 25–26; Maddox, Kate, "Market Research Charges Online," *B to B*, 90 (April 4, 2005), 28–31; Hieggelke, Brent, "Marketing & ROI," *iMediaConnection*, (October 19, 2004), http://www.imediaconnection.com, accessed April 1, 2006.

cases, managers prefer not to have recommendations included in the report or summary. Whether or not recommendations are to be included should be clear from the particular context of the report.

An additional element that can be included in the summary is a short justification for the research study and report itself. As seen in the Research Snapshot "Research ROI," the use of ROI to measure research effectiveness is a new way that business researchers are providing this justification.

THE BODY

The *body* constitutes the bulk of the report. It begins with an **introduction section** setting out the background factors that made the project necessary as well as the objectives of the report. It continues with discussions of the methodology, results, and limitations of the study and finishes with conclusions and recommendations based on the results.

introduction section
The part of the body of a research report that discusses background information and the specific objectives of the research.

The introduction explains why the project was done and what it aimed to discover. It should include the basic authorization and submittal data. The relevant background comes next. Background information is important, and may require that you gather additional external data as discussed in the Research Snapshot "How Do We Stack Up? The Value of Business.gov." Enough background should be included to explain why the project was worth doing, but unessential historical factors should be omitted. The question of how much is enough should be answered by referring to the needs of the audience. A government report that will be widely circulated requires more background than a company's internal report on customer satisfaction. The last part of the introduction explains exactly what the project tried to discover. It discusses the statement of the problem and research questions as they were stated in the research proposal. Each purpose presented here should have a corresponding entry in the results section later in the report.

The second part of the body is the **research methodology section**. This part is a challenge to write because it must explain technical procedures in a manner appropriate for the audience. The material in this section may be supplemented with more detailed explanations in the appendix or a glossary of technical terms. This part of the report should address four topics:

research methodology section
The part of the body of a report that presents the findings of the project. It includes tables, charts, and an organized narrative.

1. *Research design.* Was the study exploratory, descriptive, or causal? Did the data come from primary or secondary sources? Were results collected by survey, observation, or experiment? A

RESEARCH SNAPSHOT

How Do We Stack Up? The Value of Business.gov

Many business research projects are designed to capture information on attitudes and behaviors that are reflective of the company. The bigger question to your research stakeholders may be, "How do we stack up with other similar firms?" When writing a research report, it often helps to provide some kind of context, whether it is comparative data from other firms, or general information that the report reader can use to get the big picture.

COURTESY, UNITED STATES GOVERNMENT

Obviously, you can't always get the exact same data from other similar firms. But you may be able to get at least some level of context, if you look in the right place. One place to look is **Business.gov** (**http://www.business.gov**), the clearinghouse Web site that captures governmental and economic statistics from agencies across the United States.

Business.gov includes statistics on employment, consumer spending, production, trade, and other firm-level or industry-level data that may be useful to you as you frame your research results. For example, if your research report is focused on turnover trends in your firm, you may be able to capture industry-wide employment trends to compare your results to the larger picture within an industry or geographic location.

The value of **Business.gov** is the potential to compare how your firm is doing to the "big picture." While it may not have results for every research project or report, it is worth searching through as you develop the body of your report.

Source: Business.gov, http://www.business.gov, downloaded April 28, 2009.

© iStock

copy of the survey questionnaire or observation form should be included in the appendix. Why was this particular design suited to the study?

2. *Sample design*. What was the target population? What sampling frame was used? What sample units were used? How were they selected? How large was the sample? What was the response rate? Detailed computations to support these explanations should be saved for the appendix.
3. *Data collection and fieldwork*. How many and what types of fieldworkers were used? What training and supervision did they receive? Was the work verified? This section is important for establishing the degree of accuracy of the results.
4. *Analysis*. This section should outline the general statistical methods used in the study, but the information presented here should not overlap with what is presented in the results section.

results section
The part of the body of a report that presents the findings of the project. It includes tables, charts, and an organized narrative.

The **results section** should make up the bulk of the report and should present, in some logical order, those findings of the project that bear on the objectives. The results should be organized as a continuous narrative, designed to be convincing but not to oversell the project. Summary tables and charts should be used to aid the discussion. These may serve as points of reference to the data being discussed and free the prose from excessive facts and figures. Comprehensive or detailed charts, however, should be saved for the appendix.

Because no research is perfect, its limitations should be indicated. If problems arose with nonresponse error or sampling procedures, these should be discussed. However, the discussion of limitations should avoid overemphasizing the weaknesses; its aim should be to provide a realistic basis for assessing the results.

conclusions and recommendations section
The part of the body of a report that provides opinions based on the results and suggestions for action.

The last part of the body is the **conclusions and recommendations section**. As mentioned earlier, conclusions are opinions based on the results, and recommendations are suggestions for action. The conclusions and recommendations should be presented in this section in more detail than in the summary, and the text should include justification as needed.

THE APPENDIX

The *appendix* presents the "too . . ." material. Any material that is too technical or too detailed to go in the body should appear in the appendix. This includes materials of interest only to some readers or subsidiary materials not directly related to the objectives. Some examples of appendix materials are data collection forms, detailed calculations, discussions of highly technical questions, detailed or comprehensive tables of results, and a bibliography (if appropriate). Since the advent of company intranets, much appendix material is posted on internal Web pages.

BASIC BUSINESS RESEARCH REPORT

The outline described applies especially to applied business research projects. When basic research reports are written, such as might be submitted and potentially published in an academic business journal, the outline changes slightly since some components become irrelevant. A common outline used in basic business research proceeds as follows:

1. Abstract
2. Introduction
3. Background
   a. Literature Review
   b. Hypotheses
4. Research Methods
5. Results
6. Discussion
   a. Implications
   b. Limitations
   c. Future Research
7. Conclusions
8. References
9. Appendices

The material in the sections does not change very much between different business research problems. So the elements within each section are the same with only the noted exceptions. The basic research report will place a greater emphasis on how the current research is integrated into the previous literature dealing with the research topic. This section finishes with a specific set of theoretical hypotheses. The research methodology and results section may contain more statistical detail and jargon since the reader is expected to be knowledgeable in basic research methodology. A quick look at an academic business journal like the *Journal of Business Research,* the *Journal of Marketing,* the *Journal of Finance,* or the *Journal of Management* will give a reader a feel for this type of writing. Overall, though, both basic and applied business research reports involve technical writing and the principles of good technical writing apply.

Effective Use of Graphic Aids

Used properly, **graphic aids** can clarify complex points or emphasize a message. Used improperly or sloppily, they can distract or even mislead a reader. Graphic aids work best when they are an integral part of the text. The graphics should always be interpreted in the text. This does not mean that the writer should exhaustively explain an obvious chart or table, but it *does* mean that the text should point out the key elements of any graphic aid and relate them to the discussion in progress.

graphic aids
Pictures or diagrams used to clarify complex points or emphasize a message.

Several types of graphic aids may be useful in research reports including tables, charts, maps, and diagrams. The following discussion briefly covers the most common ones, tables and charts. The reader interested in other types of graphic material should consult more specialized sources.

Tables

Tables are most useful for presenting numerical information, especially when several pieces of information have been gathered about each item discussed. For example, consider how hard it might be to follow the information in Exhibit 25.6 with only narrative text and no graphical aids.

Using tables allows a writer to point out significant features without getting bogged down in detail. The body of the report should include only relatively short summary tables, with comprehensive tables reserved for an appendix.

Each table should include the following elements:

- *Table number.* This allows for simple reference from the text to the table. If the text includes many tables, a list of tables should be included just after the table of contents.
- *Title.* The title should indicate the contents of the table and be complete enough to be intelligible without referring to the text.
- *Stubheads and bannerheads.* The stubheads contain the captions for the rows of the table, and the bannerheads (or boxheads) contain those for the columns.
- *Footnotes.* Any explanations or qualifications for particular table entries or sections should be given in footnotes.

EXHIBIT 25.6 Parts of a Table

Table number → Title →

Table 1024. Retail Sales—New Passenger Cars: 1990 to 2003

[In thousands 9,300 represents 9,300,000, except as indicated. Retail new car sales include both sales to individuals and to corporate fleets. It also includes leased cars.]

Bannerheads →

Item	1990	1995	1997	1998	1999	2000	2001	2002	2003
Total retail new passenger car sales	9,300	8,635	8,272	8,142	8,698	8,847	8,423	8,103	7,510
Domestic[1]	6,897	7,129	6,917	6,762	6,979	6,831	6,325	5,676	5,527
Imports	2,403	1,506	1,355	1,380	1,719	2,016	2,098	2,226	2,083
Japan	1,719	982	726	691	758	863	837	923	817
Germany	265	207	297	367	467	517	523	547	544
Other	419	317	332	322	494	637	798	756	722

Stubheads

Footnote → [1] Includes cars produced in Canada and Mexico.

Source: U.S. Bureau of Transportation Statistics, *National Transportation Statistics 2004.* Data supplied by following source: *Motor Vehicle Facts & Figures, 1997.* Southfield. MI: *Ward's Motor Vehicle Facts & Figures, 2002.* Southfield, MI: 2002. See also <http://www.bts.gov>.

↑ Source

— Represents zero. [1]Change from prior year.

Source: U.S. Census Bureau, *Statistical Abstract of the United States,* 2006, table 1024, p. 678.

- *Source notes.* If a table is based on material from one or more secondary sources rather than on new data generated by the project, the sources should be acknowledged, usually below the table.

Tables in a survey research report typically follow the format shown in Exhibit 25.7. This example cross-tabulates demographics with survey responses. Data from a statistical test also might be reported in table form, as shown in Exhibit 25.8.

Suppose an airline asks a question about customers' satisfaction with its baggage-handling service. In addition to showing the simple frequency for each category, most research analysts would cross-tabulate answers to the baggage-handling questions with several demographic variables such as gender, income, education, and age. To present multiple cross-tabulations individually in separate tables requires considerable space. Thus, many research reports use a space-saving format, with either stubheads for rows or bannerheads for columns, to allow the reader to view several cross-tabulations at the same time. Exhibit 25.9 presents several cross-tabulations in a single table with stubheads.

EXHIBIT 25.7 **Reporting Format for a Typical Cross-Tabulation**

Online Activity	Age Group 12–17	18–28	29–40	41–50	51–59	60–69	70+
E-mail	89%	88%	92%	90%	94%	90%	89%
Online games	81%	54%	37%	29%	25%	25%	32%
Instant messaging	75%	66%	52%	38%	42%	33%	14%
Downloading music	51%	45%	28%	16%	14%	8%	5%
Job hunting	30%	62%	51%	40%	36%	17%	2%
Job research	—	44%	59%	59%	54%	31%	13%

Source: Excerpted from Fox, Susannah and Mary Madden, "Generations Online," *Pew Internet and American Life Project*, December 2005, p. 3, http://www.pewinternet.org.

EXHIBIT 25.8 **Reporting Format for a Typical Statistical Test**

Will investors be more cautious about buying stock in companies with questionable advertising?

	Business	Advertising Management
Yes	57%	46%
No	27	35
Not sure	16	19
	$n = 177$	$n = 154$

$x^2 = 4.933$ *d.f.* $= 2$ $p < .08$

Source: *Report to the Federal Trade Commission on the Effects of the STP "Public Notice" Advertising Campaign*, June 1979.

EXHIBIT 25.9 **Using a Stubhead Format to Include Several Cross-Tabulations in One Table**

Characteristic	Total Persons	Level of Highest Degree: Not a High School Graduate	High School Graduate Only	Some College, No Degree	Associate's	Bachelor's	Master's	Professional	Doctorate
All persons*	$37,046	$18,734	$27,915	$29,533	$35,958	$51,206	$62,514	$115,212	$88,471
Age:									
25 to 34 years old	33,212	18,920	26,073	28,954	32,276	43,794	51,040	74,120	62,109
35 to 44 years old	42,475	22,123	31,479	36,038	38,442	57,438	66,264	126,165	101,382
45 to 54 years old	45,908	23,185	32,978	40,291	41,511	59,208	68,344	132,180	92,229
55 to 64 years old	45,154	23,602	31,742	38,131	39,147	57,423	66,760	138,845	98,433
65 years old and over	28,918	17,123	20,618	28,017	23,080	41,323	42,194	77,312	56,724
Sex:									
Male	44,726	21,447	33,286	36,419	43,462	63,084	76,896	136,128	95,894
Female	28,367	14,214	21,659	22,615	29,537	38,447	48,205	72,445	73,516

*For persons 18 years old and over with earnings.
Source: Excerpted from U.S. Census Bureau, *Statistical Abstract of the United States*, 2006, Table 217, p. 148.

Charts

Charts translate numerical information into visual form so that relationships may be easily grasped. The accuracy of the numbers is reduced to gain this advantage. Each chart should include the following elements:

- *Figure number.* Charts (and other illustrative material) should be numbered in a separate series from tables. The numbers allow for easy reference from the text. If there are many charts, a list of them should be included after the table of contents.
- *Title.* The title should describe the contents of the chart and be independent of the text explanation. The number and title may be placed at the top or bottom of the chart.
- *Explanatory legends.* Enough explanation should be put on the chart to spare the reader a need to look at the accompanying text. Such explanations should include labels for axes, scale numbers, and a key to the various quantities being graphed.
- *Source and footnotes.* Any secondary sources for the data should be acknowledged. Footnotes may be used to explain items, although they are less common for charts than for tables.

Charts are subject to distortion, whether unintentional or deliberate. A particularly severe kind of distortion comes from treating unequal intervals as if they were equal; this generally results from a deliberate attempt to distort data.

Another common way of introducing distortion is to begin the vertical scale at some value larger than zero.

PIE CHARTS

One of the most useful kinds of charts is the pie chart, which shows the composition of some total quantity at a particular time. As shown in the example in Exhibit 25.10, each angle, or "slice," is proportional to its percentage of the whole. Companies often use pie charts to show how revenues were used or the composition of their sales. Each of the segments should be labeled with its description

EXHIBIT 25.10
Pie Charts

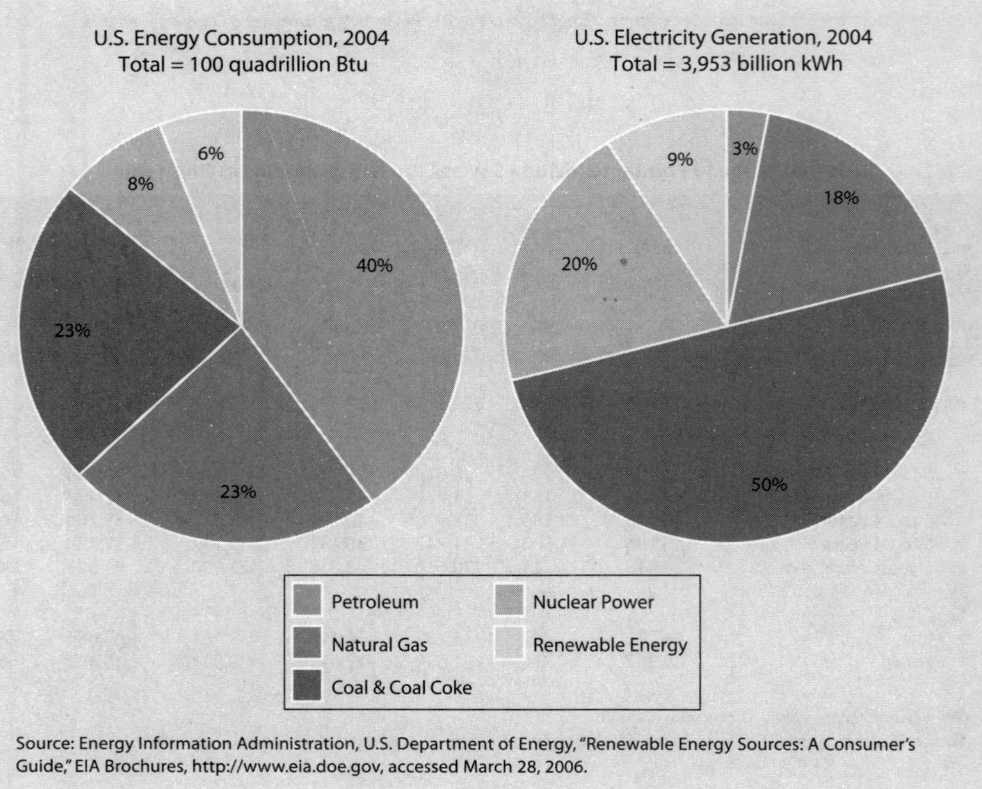

Source: Energy Information Administration, U.S. Department of Energy, "Renewable Energy Sources: A Consumer's Guide," EIA Brochures, http://www.eia.doe.gov, accessed March 28, 2006.

and percentage. The writer should not try to include too many small slices; about six slices is a typical maximum.

LINE GRAPHS

Line graphs are useful for showing the relationship of one variable to another. The dependent variable generally is shown on the vertical axis, and the independent variable on the horizontal axis. The most common independent variable for such charts is time, but it is by no means the only one. Exhibit 25.11 depicts a *simple line graph*.

Variations of the line graph also are useful. The *multiple-line graph*, such as the example in Exhibit 25.12, shows the relationship of more than one dependent variable to the independent variable. The line for each dependent variable should be in a different color or pattern and should

EXHIBIT 25.11
Simple Line Graph

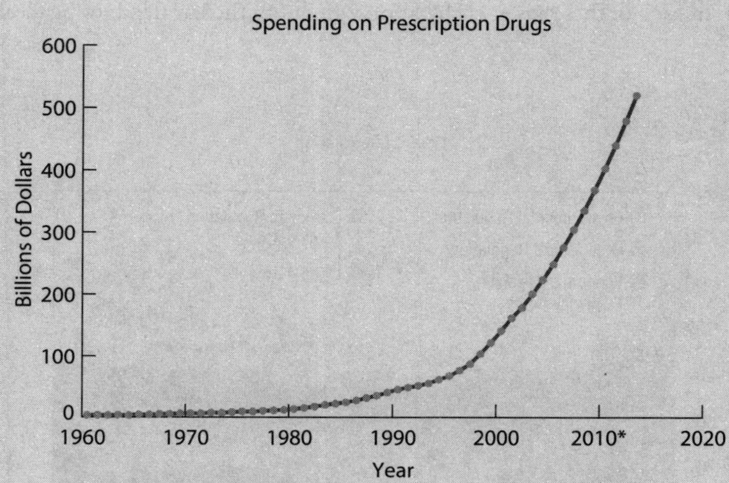

*Projected data for 2004–2014.

Source: Data from U.S. Census Bureau, *Statistical Abstract of the United States*, 2006, Table 118, p. 98.

EXHIBIT 25.12
Multiple-Line Graph

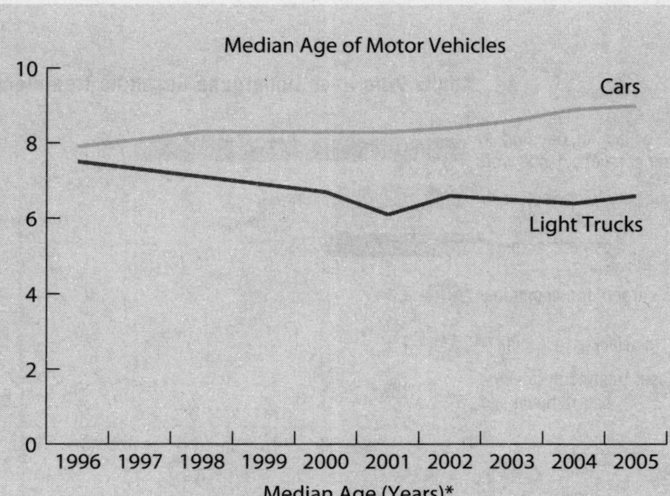

*Age calculated as of July 1.

Source: Data from Dolliver, Mark "Aging of America, Vehicular Division," *Adweek*, March 6, 2006, downloaded from InfoTrac at http://web2.infotrac.galegroup.com.

be clearly labeled. The writer should not try to squeeze in too many variables; this can quickly lead to confusion rather than clarification.

A second variation is the *stratum chart,* which shows how the composition of a total quantity changes as the independent variable changes. Exhibit 25.13 provides an example. The same cautions mentioned in connection with multiple-line graphs apply to stratum charts.

BAR CHARTS

A bar chart shows changes in the value of a dependent variable (plotted on the vertical axis) at discrete intervals of the independent variable (on the horizontal axis). A simple bar chart is shown in Exhibit 25.14.

Like the line graph, the bar chart format has variations. A common variant is the *subdivided-bar chart* (see Exhibit 25.15). It is much like a stratum chart, showing the composition of the whole quantity. The *multiple-bar chart* (see Exhibit 25.16) shows how multiple variables are related to the primary variable. In each of these cases, each bar or segment of the bar needs to be clearly identified

EXHIBIT 25.13
Stratum Chart

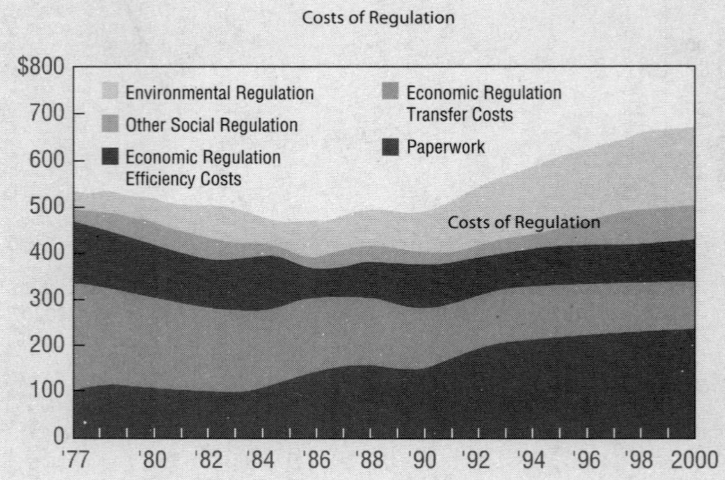

EXHIBIT 25.14
Simple Bar Chart

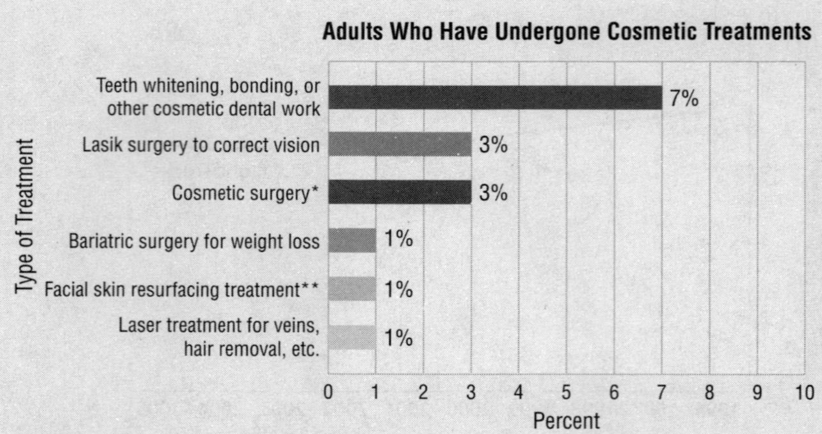

*Includes face lift, chin implant, tummy tuck, etc.
**Includes chemical peels, laser abrasion, etc.

Source: Data from Harris Interactive, "Despite Risks, Adults Not Shying Away from Cosmetic Surgery and Other Treatments," news release, February 13, 2006, http://www.harrisinteractive.com. Accessed April 4, 2006.

with a different color or pattern. The writer should not use too many divisions or dependent variables. Too much detail obscures the essential advantage of charts, which is to make relationships easy to grasp.

EXHIBIT 25.15
Subdivided Bar Chart

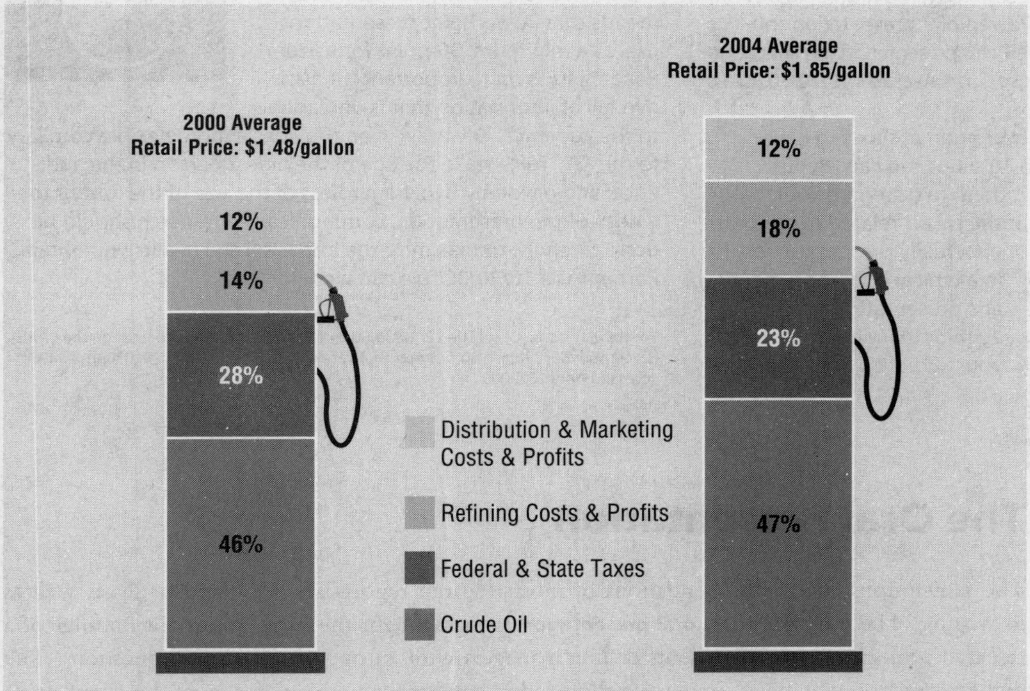

Source: Energy Information Administration, U.S. Department of Energy, "A Primer on Gasoline Prices," EIA Brochures, http://www.eia.doe.gov, accessed March 28, 2006.

EXHIBIT 25.16
Multiple-Bar Chart

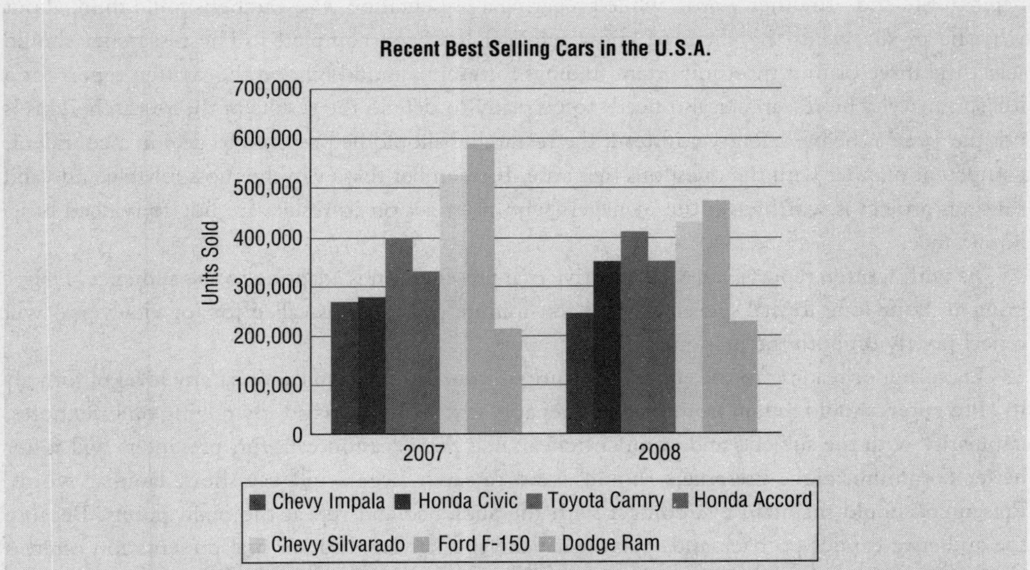

Source: "Forbes.com—10 Best Selling Vehicles of 2007," http://www.autospies.com/news/Forbes-com-10-Best-Selling-Vehicles-of-2007-23985/, accessed December 22, 2008; Mitchell, Jacqueline, "The Year's Best- And Worst-Selling Cars," http://www.forbes.com/2008/12/03/2008-car-sales-forbeslife-cx_jm_1203cars.html, accessed December 22, 2008.

RESEARCH SNAPSHOT

The 10/20/30 Rule of PowerPoint

Many business researchers find themselves being asked to provide a presentation of research findings to different stakeholders. Given today's reliance on visual technology, it is natural to develop a presentation using Microsoft's PowerPoint presentation software. But a poorly developed PowerPoint presentation can limit your impact. One way to avoid this is to use Guy Kawasaki's 10/20/30 Rule of PowerPoint.

The "10" refers to the number of optimal slides to have for your presentation. More than 10 slides can cause your audience to lose interest, causing them to disregard your research findings. The "20" part of the rule is related to the time to actually present the results. In a typical hour-long meeting, any presentation over 20 minutes will start to lose your audience as well, and in many instances the opportunity to discuss or ask questions regarding your research is more valuable than the presentation itself. Finally, Kawasaki recommends that PowerPoint presentations use, as a minimum, 30-point font size. Readability is more important than an overkill of information that is unreadable to the audience. Kawasaki even provides a more flexible corollary to the "30" rule—take the age of the oldest person in the audience, and divide by two! Regardless of the size of the font or the length of the presentation, communicating research should be done carefully, to maximize the impact of the results you obtain. Perhaps the 10/20/30 rule can work for you!

Source: Kawasaki, Guy, "The 10/20/30 Rule of PowerPoint," How to Change the World (December 30, 2005), http://blog.guykawasaki.com/2005/12/the_102030_rule.html, accessed April 28, 2009.

The Oral Presentation

oral presentation
A spoken summary of the major findings, conclusions, and recommendations, given to clients or line managers to provide them with the opportunity to clarify any ambiguous issues by asking questions.

The conclusions and recommendations of most research reports are presented orally as well as in writing. The purpose of an **oral presentation** is to highlight the most important findings of a research project and provide clients or line managers with an opportunity to ask questions. The oral presentation may be as simple as a short video conference with a manager at the client organization's location or as formal as a report to the company board of directors.

In either situation, the key to effective presentation is preparation. The Research Snapshot "The 10/20/30 Rule of PowerPoint" provides some recommendations that can help you as a presenter. Communication specialists often suggest that a person preparing an oral presentation begin at the end.[3] In other words, while preparing a presentation, a researcher should think about what he or she wants the client to know when it has been completed. The researcher should select the three or four most important findings for emphasis and rely on the written report for a full summary. The researcher also needs to be ready to defend the results of the research. This is not the same as being defensive; instead, the researcher should be prepared to deal in a confident, competent manner with the questions that arise. Remember that even the most reliable and valid research project is worthless if the managers who must act on its results are not convinced of its importance.

As with written reports, a key to effective oral presentation is adapting to the audience. Delivering an hour-long formal speech when a ten-minute discussion is called for (or vice versa) will reflect poorly on both the presenter and the report.

Lecturing or reading to the audience is sure to impede communication at any level of formality. Presenters should refrain from reading prepared text word for word. By relying on brief notes, familiarity with the subject, and as much rehearsal as the occasion calls for, presenters will foster better communication. Presenters should avoid research jargon and use short, familiar words. Presenters should maintain eye contact with the audience and repeat the main points. Because the audience cannot go back and replay what the speaker has said, an oral presentation often is organized around a standard format: "Tell them what you are going to tell them, tell them, and tell them what you just told them."

Graphic and other visual aids can be as useful in an oral presentation as in a written one. Presenters can choose from a variety of media. Slides, overhead-projector acetates, and on-screen

TIPS OF THE TRADE

- Much of the research you conduct will generate numerous tables of results. Not all results are necessarily relevant. Make sure you choose carefully what should be reported, and what should not be reported.
- Too often the sophistication of statistics can be off-putting to others. Demonstrating your mastery of complex statistical analyses is not always the best way to draw in your audience. An overreliance on statistical jargon should be avoided.
- Presentation skills mean, at a minimum, practice. To "wing it" at the last minute may reduce your credibility, and possibly the credibility of your research as well.
- The research report is much like your business card—it is a reflection of you to others. Professionalism is reflected in your care and craftsmanship of the report.

computer-generated graphics are useful for larger audiences. For smaller audiences, the researcher may put the visual aids on posters or flip charts. Another possibility is to make copies of the charts for each participant, possibly as a supplement to one of the other forms of presentation.

Whatever medium is chosen, each visual aid should be designed to convey a simple, attention-getting message that supports a point on which the audience should focus its thinking. As they do in written presentations, presenters should interpret graphics for the audience. The best slides are easy to read and interpret. Large typeface, multiple colors, bullets that highlight, and other artistic devices can enhance the readability of charts.

Using gestures during presentations also can help convey the message and make presentations more interesting. Here are some tips on how to gesture:[4]

- Open up your arms to embrace your audience. Keep your arms between your waist and shoulders.
- Drop your arms to your sides when not using them.
- Avoid quick and jerky gestures, which make you appear nervous. Hold gestures longer than you would in normal conversation.
- Vary gestures. Switch from hand to hand and at other times use both hands or no hands.
- Don't overuse gestures.

Some gestures are used to draw attention to points illustrated by visual aids. For these, gesturing with an open hand can seem more friendly and can even release tension related to nervousness. In contrast, a nervous speaker who uses a laser pointer may distract the audience as the pointer jumps around in the speaker's shaky hand.[5]

Reports on the Internet

Many clients want numerous employees to have access to research findings. One easy way to share data is to make executive summaries and reports available on a company Intranet. In addition, a company can use information technology on the Internet to design questionnaires, administer surveys, analyze data, and share the results in a presentation-ready format. Real-time data capture allows for beginning-to-end reporting. A number of companies offer fully Web-based research management systems—for example, WebSurveyor's online solution for capturing and reporting research findings.

The Research Follow-Up

Research reports and oral presentations should communicate research findings so that managers can make business decisions. In many cases, the manager who receives the research report is unable to interpret the information and draw conclusions relevant to managerial decisions. For this reason, effective researchers do not treat the report as the end of the research process. They

research follow-up

Recontacting decision makers and/or clients after they have had a chance to read over a research report in order to determine whether additional information or clarification is necessary.

conduct a **research follow-up**, in which they recontact decision makers and/or clients after the latter have had a chance to read over the report. The purpose is to determine whether the researchers need to provide additional information or clarify issues of concern to management.

Summary

1. Discuss the research report from the perspective of the communications process. A research report is an oral or written presentation of research findings directed to a specific audience to accomplish a particular purpose. Report preparation is the final stage of the research project. It is important because the project can guide management decisions only if it is effectively communicated. The theory of communications emphasizes that the writer (communicator) must tailor the report (message) so that it will be understood by the manager (audience), who has a different field of experience.

2. Define the parts of a research report following a standard format. The consensus is that the format for a research report should include certain prefatory parts, the body of the report, and appended parts. The report format should be varied to suit the level of formality of the particular situation. The prefatory parts of a formal report include a title page, letters of transmittal and authorization, a table of contents, and a summary. The summary is the part of a report most often read and should include a brief statement of the objectives, results, conclusions, and (depending on the research situation) recommendations. The report body includes an introduction that gives the background and objectives, a statement of methodology, and a discussion of the results, their limitations, and appropriate conclusions and recommendations. The appendix includes various materials too specialized to appear in the body of the report.

3. Explain how to use tables for presenting numerical information. Tables present large amounts of numerical information in a concise manner. They are especially useful for presenting several pieces of information about each item discussed. Short tables are helpful in the body of the report; long tables are better suited for an appendix. Each table should include a number, title, stubheads and bannerheads, footnotes for any explanations or qualifications of entries, and source notes for data from secondary sources.

4. Summarize how to select and use the types of research charts. Charts present numerical data in a way that highlights their relationships. Each chart should include a figure number, title, explanatory legends, and a source note for secondary sources. Pie charts show the composition of a total (the parts that make up a whole). Line graphs show the relationship of a dependent variable (on the vertical axis) to an independent variable (horizontal axis). Most commonly, the independent variable is time. Bar charts show changes in a dependent variable at discrete intervals of the independent variable—for example, comparing one year with another or one subset of the population with another. Variants of these charts are useful for more complex situations.

5. Describe how to give an effective oral presentation. Most research projects are reported orally as well as in writing, so the researcher needs to prepare an oral presentation. The presentation should defend the results without being defensive. The presentation must be tailored to the situation and the audience. The presenter should practice delivering the presentation in a natural way, without reading to the audience. Graphic aids are useful supplements when they are simple and easy to read. Gestures also add interest and emphasis.

6. Discuss the importance of Internet reporting and research follow-up. Posting a summary of results online gives clients ready access to that information. Some online survey software processes the data and displays results in a presentation-ready format. In the follow-up stage of a research project, the researchers recontact decision makers after submitting the report. This helps the researchers determine whether they need to provide further information or clarify any issues of concern to management.

Key Terms and Concepts

communication process, *677*
conclusions and recommendations section, *684*
graphic aids, *685*
introduction section, *683*
oral presentation, *693*
report format, *679*
research follow-up, *695*
research methodology section, *683*
research report, *678*
results section, *684*

Questions for Review and Critical Thinking

1. Why is it important to think of the research report from a communications perspective?
2. As a manager, what degree of formality would you want from your research department?
3. What types of tables might be used to describe some of the statistical tests discussed in previous chapters?
4. What is the difference between a *basic business research paper* and *an applied research report?*
5. What is a *pie chart?* What is a *bar chart?* When might one be preferable over the other?
6. What are some basic business research journals? Find some published research reports in these journals. How do they meet the standards set forth in this chapter?
7. What rules should be followed when preparing slides for computer-generated presentations?
8. **ETHICS** What ethical concerns arise when you prepare (or read) a report?
9. **ETHICS** A researcher working for Hi Time prepares a bar chart comparing the number of customers visiting two competing booths at a fashion trade show. One booth is the Hi Time booth, and the other is for a competing company, So Cool. First, the chart is prepared as shown here:

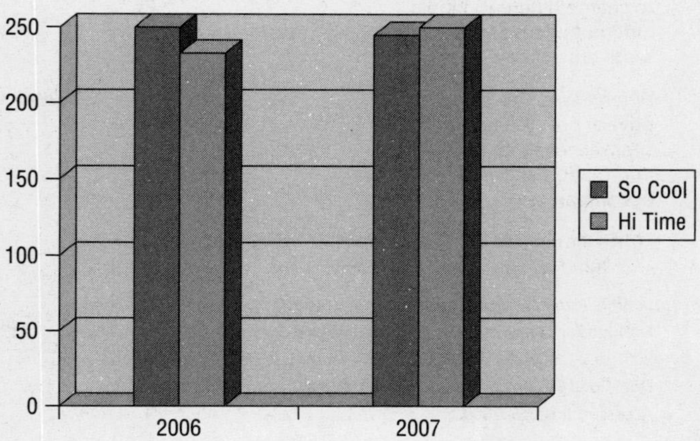

In preparing for a presentation to the Hi Time Board, the client tells the researcher that the chart doesn't seem to reflect the improvements made since 2006. Therefore, the researcher prepares the chart as shown here:

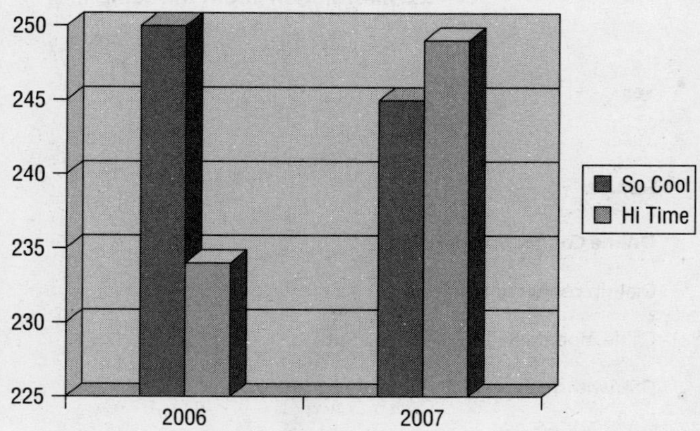

a. What has reformatting the bar chart accomplished?
b. Was it ethical for the client to ask for the bar chart to be redrawn?
c. Would it be ethical for the researcher to use the new chart in the presentation?

Research Activity

1. **'NET** Input "Starbucks" or "McDonald's" in an Internet search engine available through your library's reference service or even a general search engine like Google News. Look at the news and articles for that company. Limit the search by using the word "report." Find one of the articles that actually presents some research reports, such as consumer reactions to a new product. Prepare PowerPoint slides that contain appropriate charts to present the results.

Case 25.1 Annenberg Public Policy Center

© GETTY IMAGES/ PHOTODISC GREEN

A recent study by the Annenberg Public Policy Center investigated one major area of business decisions: pricing practices.[6] Specifically, the study addressed consumer knowledge and attitudes about the practice of online retailers adjusting their prices according to customer characteristics, such as how frequently they buy from the retailer. For example, a Web site selling cameras charged different prices for the same model depending on whether the visitor to the site had previously visited sites that supply price comparisons. In general, charging different prices is called price discrimination and is legal unless it discriminates by race or sex or involves antitrust or price-fixing laws (such as two competitors agreeing to charge certain prices).

The Annenberg study consisted of telephone interviews conducted with a sample of 1,500 adults, screened to find persons who had used the Internet in the preceding 30 days. The questionnaire gathered demographic data and data about Internet usage. In addition, the interviewer read 17 statements about basic laws and practices related to price discrimination and the targeting of consumers according to their shopping behaviors. Respondents were asked whether each of these statements was true or false. Case Exhibits 25.1-1 through 25.1-4 summarize some of the results from this study.

Questions

1. The information provided here is not detailed enough for a formal report, but assume that you are making an informal report in a preliminary stage of the reporting process. Which of these findings do you want to emphasize as your main points? Why?
2. Prepare a written summary of the findings, using at least two tables or charts.
3. Prepare two tables or charts that would be suitable to accompany an oral presentation of these results. Are they different from the visual aids you prepared for question 2? Why or why not?

CASE EXHIBIT 25.1-1 **Selected Information about the Sample**

Sex	
Male	48%
Female	52%
Online Connection at Home	
Dial-up connection only	31%
Cable modem (with/without dial-up)	18%
DSL (with/without dial-up)	25%
Cable or DSL with another method	13%
Don't know	4%
No connection at home	9%
Self-Ranked Expertise Navigating the Internet	
Beginner	14%
Intermediate	40%
Advanced	34%
Expert	12%

Source: Turow, Joseph, Lauren Feldman, and Kimberly Meltzer, "Open to Exploitation: American Shoppers Online and Offline," APPC report, June 2005, p. 15, downloaded at http://www.annenbergpublicpolicycenter.org.

CASE EXHIBIT 25.1-2 **Responses to Selected Knowledge Questions**

	Response*		
Statement	**True**	**False**	**Don't Know**
Companies today have the ability to follow my activity across many sites on the Web.	**80%**	8%	12%
It is legal for an *online* store to charge different people different prices at the same time of day.	**38%**	29%	33%
By law, a site such as Expedia or Orbitz that compares prices on different airlines must include the lowest airline prices.	37%	**32%**	31%
It is legal for an *offline* store to charge different people different prices at the same time of day.	**29%**	42%	29%
When a Web site has a privacy policy, it means the site will not share my information with other websites or companies.	59%	**25%**	16%

*When the numbers do not add up to 100%, it is because of a rounding error. **Boldface** type indicates the correct answer.

Source: Turow, Joseph, Lauren Feldman, and Kimberly Meltzer, "Open to Exploitation: American Shoppers Online and Offline," APPC report, June 2005, p. 20, downloaded at http://www.annenbergpublicpolicycenter.org/Downloads/information_and_society/turow_appc_report_web_final.pdf. Accessed June 15, 2009.

CASE EXHIBIT 25.1-3 **Responses to Selected Attitude Questions**

	Response*			
Statement	**Agree**	**Disagree**	**Neutral**	**Don't Know**
It's okay if a store charges me a price based on what it knows about me.	8%	91%	—	1%
It's okay if an *online* store I use charges different people different prices for the same products during the same hour.	11%	87%	1%	1%
It would bother me to learn that other people pay less than I do for the same products.	76%	22%	1%	1%
It would bother me if websites I shop at keep detailed records of my buying behavior.	57%	41%	2%	1%
It's okay if a store I shop at frequently uses information it has about me to create a picture of me that improves the services it provides for me.	50%	47%	2%	1%

*When the numbers do not add up to 100%, it is because of a rounding error.

Source: Turow, Joseph, Lauren Feldman, and Kimberly Meltzer, "Open to Exploitation: American Shoppers Online and Offline," APPC report, June 2005, p. 22, downloaded at http://www.annenbergpublicpolicycenter.org. Accessed April 7, 2006.

CASE EXHIBIT 25.1-4 **Predicting Knowledge Score from Selected Demographics**

	Unstandardized Regression Coefficient (B)	**Standardized Regression Coefficient (β)**
Education	0.630*	0.200
Income	0.383*	0.150
Self-perceived ability to navigate Internet	0.616*	0.149
Constant	2.687	
R^2	0.148	

*Significance $<$ 0.001 level.

Source: Turow, Joseph, Lauren Feldman, and Kimberly Meltzer, "Open to Exploitation: American Shoppers Online and Offline," APPC report, June 2005, p. 29, downloaded at http://www.annenbergpublicpolicycenter.org/Downloads/information_and_society/turow_appc_report_web_final.pdf. Accessed June 15, 2009.

Part 7
Comprehensive Cases with Computerized Databases

CASE 1
Online Shopping Behavior of Customers in India

CASE 2
Running the Numbers: Does It Pay?

CASE 3
Attiring Situation

CASE 4
Values and the Automobile Market

CASE 5
TABH, INC., Automotive Consulting

CASE 6
The Atlanta Braves

COMPREHENSIVE CASES

Case 1 Online Shopping Behavior of Customers in India

CASE SYNOPSIS

The e-commerce industry has been growing faster in India compared to the average growth rate in the world. Growth in Internet penetration and personal computer market in India drives the growth in e-commerce sector. A mushrooming middle class with higher disposable income and little time due to busy schedules has also resulted in increasing number of people shopping online. A large segment of the population however remains untapped and Indian as well as foreign firms have set their sights on the Indian e-commerce industry.

This research was conducted by a group of researchers. The study is an endeavour to determine the tastes and preferences of online customers both in Tier 1 and Tier 2 cities in India and also perform a comparative analysis to ascertain whether there is a difference between the customers of two segments as penetration of e-commerce remains low in smaller towns and cities. The study is based on an online survey of 300 Indian university students which was conducted after focus group discussions involving respondents from Tier 1 and Tier 2 cities. Several concerns were identified which could help ascertain the potential of e-commerce in India, at the same time an attempt was also made to determine the product groups that customers would be interested in buying online. The study illustrates the importance of the retail brand for expensive purchases and also highlights the importance of online advertisements in driving online purchases.

Introduction: Antecedents and the Role of this Research

The e-commerce industry is growing at 30% CAGR (compound annual growth rate) in India compared to world average of 8–10% (IAMAI, Digital Commerce, 2011). India represents a huge market, and the propensity to purchase online is increasing. The Internet literacy which is a strong driver of online transactions is going up, presently at 100 million in India up by 13% since 2010 (IAMAI, Internet In India, 2011). Internet penetration is on the rise in Tier 2 and Tier 3 cities. Foreign players like EBay have entered the Indian market and the largest online retail in the world, Amazon, plans to foray into Indian market as "Amazon Marketplace." Major Indian players like Flipkart.com are in a mode of rapid expansion (PWC, 2011) aiming to expand into new cities and grow revenues 10–30 times.

At the same time there are many upcoming trends in e-commerce with unconventional products like sales of fresh and cut vegetables going online. New payment modes like cash on delivery and card on delivery are providing convenience and flexibility to the online customer. The growth of online banking (net banking in popular parlance) also contributes to increasing online purchases. Retailers are also trying to customize their offerings to the customer. At the same time, novel services like 3D viewing of the products are being tried out so that the customers concerns of not being able to see the product are assuaged. Thus a thorough understanding of customer's perceptions about these new products and services is essential for success of online retailers as they move to tap huge Indian market.

This research helps in ascertaining the potential of online shopping in India. As stated earlier Flipkart and other retailers in India are planning to expand into new cities; this research shall help determine the acceptability of online commerce in Tier 2 and Tier 3 cities and help compare and contrast their concerns with buyers in the metros. Researchers also attempt to identify the product groups or services which people would want to buy/access online.

Researchers also determine the impact e-tailer's Web site has on the trust that customer places in the retailer and assess the impact of new features like 3D viewing of the products. Researchers also try to address the question of what shall drive a customer to purchase expensive products online given that there is a trust deficit among people when it comes to online purchases.

As e-tailers expand their business, creating awareness and getting customers to visit their sites would be a key step before purchases start happening. This research also tries to find out the appropriate medium of advertising for the online retailers. In this context, this study also examines the difference between visits to an online retailer and purchases from the retailer. A wide gap could be explained by various factors like lack of trust, low discounts, limited opportunities for bargaining, or the customer not being able to find the intended product.

The relative importance that customers attach to product brand, retail brand, prompt delivery, and discount would help the retailers offer best combination to the customers. Researchers attempt to find the importance of these factors for two heavily sold products on the Internet: mobiles and apparels.

Since researchers attempt to discover what product groups other than those currently available could be offered to customers in the online retail space, researchers shall conduct an exploratory research using focus group discussions (FGDs) as their research tool for the initial phase. In order to validate the findings from the FGDs, researchers shall conduct a quantitative research by collecting responses through an online survey.

Previous Work: Theory Building

India is one of the countries with the fastest growing population that uses the Internet (Gupta, Handa, & Gupta, 2008). While most of them use features like emails, social networking, and news portals, a few of them have gradually moved to online shopping. Though the proportion is still quite low, people recognize the potential online shopping has owing to the increasing purchasing power of the Indian middle class and the large number of Internet users from it. Corporations also want to setup online stores as they bring greater flexibility, enhanced market outreach, lower cost structures, faster transactions, broader product lines, greater convenience, and customization (Srinivasan, Anderson, & Ponnavolu, 2002). To realize this and make online shopping a popular medium of purchase, online retailers are required to create the need and also eliminate the apprehensions people have about it.

In the Indian context where personal relations and trust play a crucial role, the online retailers face stiff competition from the traditional stores where interaction between the consumer and seller help in narrowing down the options and final selection of the product. Also trust between them makes it easy for the consumer to feel comfortable that he has purchased the right product at the right price. In this respect it has been said that the intention of a person to purchase online would essentially be based on the information satisfaction of the Web site, which is in respect to contents and navigation ease (Heijden, Verhagen, & Creemer, 2003). Information on a Web site can be classified as *product information* and *service information*. The former consists of information related to product attributes, consumer recommendations, and evaluation reports by third parties, while the latter has membership information, FAQs, and information related to ordering and delivery. Based on these parameters it has been successfully hypothesized that information satisfaction is positively related to the quality of product and service information on the Web site which in turn positively affects security perception of the online seller (Heijden, Verhagen, & Creemer, 2003). Another term coined in this context is relational benefit which relates to the sense of anxiety, trust, and confidence that the customer experiences about the Web site. Quality of product and service information and Web site awareness which can be improved by advertising, promotional events and word to mouth communication is said to positively affect relational benefit. Social media also plays an important role in this especially among the youth (Oracle, 2011). Relational benefit in turn is positively related to the commitment the consumer has towards the Web site. Being the primary mode of communication between the seller and the customer, the quality of the Web site, the information it shows, ease of use, navigation, fast error free browsing, and provision to entertain queries helps to convert an Internet surfer to an online customer (Gupta, Handa, & Gupta, 2008).

Online purchase intentions are affected by attitudes' (attitude towards online shopping) satisfaction. A causal ordering of Satisfaction → Attitude → Intention is also advocated (Abdul-Muhmin, 2010). Factors like personal innovativeness, personal awareness of security, perceived ease of purchasing, and purchase usefulness also affect intentions to purchase (Chiu, Lin, & Tang). To analyze the role of technology in this regard, the Theory of Reasoned Action has been used (Heijden, Verhagen, & Creemer, 2003). According to this theory, a person develops certain attitudes towards a certain object based on certain beliefs and based on these attitudes he forms intentions to behave with respect to that object. As an alternative to personal interaction, technology can be evaluated based on two beliefs based on the user's evaluation of the Web site: perceived usefulness and perceived ease of use. The former could be attributed to the measures taken for effective search, providing a large number of alternative comparisons of such products. The latter corresponds to how less efforts the customer needs to be put to look for a product and arrive at an informed decision. Search that provides results based on previous purchases and searches saves time for the customer. Customized user interface and recommendations also help in this respect. In short, technology plays a very important role in reducing the cost of search and decision making. More significant role is played by trust which needs to be established between the people (consumers) and organizations (online sellers). Trust could be perceived by the size and reputation of the seller and is negatively related to the perceived risk one associates with the selling company (Heijden, Verhagen, & Creemer, 2003).

Having attracted people to purchase online, in order to sustain the business and make profits, it is imperative to retain the customer and develop loyalty towards the store and the brands. In current era many players in the market and online stores providing alternatives and easy comparison make it costly to acquire customers and more difficult to retain them. An effective measure for customer loyalty in this regard (e-loyalty) is the number of repeat purchases done by a customer. Srinivasan, Anderson, & Ponnavolu (2002) present the view that e-loyalty is affected by 8 Cs, viz., customization, contact interactivity, cultivation, care, community, choice, convenience, and character. Customization refers to the extent to which an e-retailer's Web site can recognize a customer and then tailor the choice of products, services, and shopping experience for that customer. This saves customers' time to search for the specific product they need. Contact interactivity refers to the availability and effectiveness of customer support tools on a Web site and the degree to which two-way communication with customers is facilitated. Reviews and recommendations help to improve this. Cultivation is the extent to which an e-retailer provides relevant information and incentives to its customers in order to extend the breadth and depth of their purchases over time. Care refers to the extent to which a customer is kept informed about the availability of preferred products and the status of orders, and the level of efforts expended to minimize disruptions in providing desired services. This is important as a dissatisfied customer makes more noise about the negative experience than a satisfied one speaks about the positives. Community refers to initiatives in terms of the extent to which customers are provided with the opportunity and ability to share opinions among themselves through comment links, buying circles, and chat rooms sponsored by the e-retailer. Choice is the extent to which a store offers wide range of products. Convenience of the Web site is measured in terms of response time, fast completion of a transaction, and minimization of customer effort. Character can be defined as an overall image or personality that the e-retailer projects to consumers through the use of inputs such as text, style, graphics, colors, logos, and slogans or themes on the Web site. According to the researchers, all the above except convenience positively affect e-loyalty. E-loyalty is also positively related to word of mouth behavior of customers and willingness to pay more (Srinivasan, Anderson, & Ponnavolu, 2002).

In order to maintain satisfaction levels with respect to introduction of new products and associated accessories, recommendation agents (RA) are being used. Researchers speculate that RAs are an effective way to influence customer behavior by inducing them to buy products similar to ones they had purchased earlier. Studies show that RAs persuade the customers to consider certain attributes of a product to be more important than others and also enhance the shopping experience. As more studies are conducted to relate the technical aspects of the Web sites to customer satisfaction with features, RAs seem to be an important criterion. According to study done by (Hostler, Yoon, Guo, Guimaraes, & Forgionne, Assessing the impact of recommender agents on online consumer unplanned purchase behavior, 2011), RAs can significantly enhance the effectiveness of product promotion and product searches on the Web site. Because of RAs, customers get to know the availability and status of related products and alternates thereby reducing search and decision costs. They also get an idea of other products that may be of interest to them. Effective search and promotion of products increases the customer satisfaction and increases unplanned purchases, and the study finds them to be positively related.

Having looked at some aspects that are important in attracting and retaining customers, it is worthwhile to note how consumers have accepted new technologies and online shopping. People use the products not only to shop but also to remain updated about new products and research about alternatives. According to a survey conducted by Oracle, 75% of the surveyed people used more than 2 channels for research of a product before they buy. People also visit stores to touch and feel the product before purchasing online. Use of mobile devices is popular, and one-third of the surveyed people use these. 15% of these people had purchased product using the same devices. An encouraging sign for the online retailers is that more than 50% of the people would go to the online shop to view a product, the information for which was sent by email. They look at other products and make them think positively about the site (Oracle, 2011).

Methodology

SAMPLING

The target population were people who purchase from online retailers and all Internet users who don't purchase but can be potential customers for the online retailers. The sample size was over 300 people spread across different cities of the country. Young population in the age group of 18–30 years was targeted as literature survey indicated that they constitute the bulk of online buyers.

Thus the sampling method researchers have used is judgement sampling as researchers were aware that most of the online purchasers were youth who have access to the Internet either at their home or at their workplace. This was also corroborated by the focus group discussions that were conducted. The sampling method helped in concentrating and obtaining appropriate responses from the actual target audience of the online retailers. Also, the sampling technique (Malhotra & Dash, 2011) was low cost and quick. Other probability sampling techniques wouldn't have been practically feasible as the population was very huge, diverse, and spread across different areas. A disadvantage of the sampling method is that it relies on researchers' judgement, and hence, there was a risk of subjectivity entering into researchers' choice of sample.

MEASUREMENT AND SCALING

The research was primarily undertaken to identify the tastes and preferences of online buyers and the key motivators behind an online purchase. Therefore, the questionnaire focused on collecting data on a ratio or ordinal scale so that researchers could run multivariate analysis on the data collected to find causal relationships or dependencies.

Most of the questions were on an interval scale (5 point Likert Scale) as the researchers were trying to gauge the preferences of the respondents, for example, their preference for a particular product/service being available online, their willingness to pay extra shipping charges, etc. Likert scale was used as the respondents easily understand how to use this scale, and hence, it was more suitable for this electronic survey. Also, it is easier to construct and administer. However, Likert scale takes longer to complete than other itemized rating scales and hence there was an increased possibility of the respondent filling in random responses in case of longer surveys.

Researchers took care to remove a few such instances.

Ordinal scale was used for some questions like frequency of visiting an online retailer, online purchase frequency, and annual family income as they were to indicate the relative extent to which some characteristic is present. Demographic information of the respondents like gender, hometown, and marital status was captured using nominal scale. Most of the scales were balanced and odd scales.

QUALITATIVE METHODS

Exploratory research was used to find the underlying motivations of people behind online purchases and their major inhibitions. Four FGDs were conducted by forming homogeneous groups based on age, users/non-users, and people with work experience/fresher. Each FGD lasted for around 1.25 hours and had 8 participants each. The discussions were free flowing and informal and a number of insights were obtained which are summarized below:

- There was a concern about the quality of the product while shopping online and hence brand of the product as well as the retailer played a key role in increasing their trust.
- The brand of the retailer became all the more important in case of expensive purchases.
- Inability to physically touch the product was a concern especially in products like apparels.
- There was a willingness to have services like appointments with doctors and lawyers being available online.
- There was a low preference towards buying fruits and vegetables as quality and freshness created doubts in the minds of the people.
- There was a significant difference between visits to online retailers and actual online purchases.

The FGD was important as it gave insights which helped in preparing the questionnaire. Qualitative analysis of secondary data was also undertaken.

QUESTIONNAIRE

The questionnaire was formed with inputs from FGD and literature review. It was an online survey that captured data from people of Tier 1 and Tier 2/3 cities. The questionnaire was very elaborate and captured data regarding the preference for various products, the Web sites of the retailers, the inclination for expensive purchases, discounts, and shipping charges. Also, data was collected regarding important concerns like security, privacy, quality, and the fact that the consumers are unable to touch the product physically when an online purchase is made.

There were a total of 363 responses. After deleting the incomplete responses and 11 case-wise deletions, researchers were left with a dataset which had responses from 300 people.

QUANTITATIVE METHODS

The full gamut of quantitative techniques was applied to analyze the data starting from simple tools like descriptive statistics to complicated methods like conjoint analysis and cluster analysis. Simple regression and dummy variable regressions were conducted in a number of cases. As researchers wanted to find the differences between the preferences of Tier 1 and Tier 2/3 cities, dummy variable regressions were very suitable for this purpose. Also, researchers conducted factor analysis to group the factors in some cases.

Correlation analysis was also employed, though such an analysis tells us nothing about causality, it gave important insights. Also, researchers employed paired *t*-tests to compare the differences in responses to certain questions (variables).

The following section on analysis will demonstrate the use of each of the techniques discussed above. In the next section researchers highlight just the important hypotheses.

Analysis and Result

1. Testing how the quality concerns of the product influence the purchase behavior of fruits and vegetables

Hypotheses

- H0: Purchase intention of fruits and vegetables online is not influenced by the quality concerns
- Ha: Purchase intention of fruits and vegetables is influenced by the quality concerns

Procedure: Researchers had taken two separate variables, fruits and vegetables, and had tested for the purchase intention on a continuous Likert scale of 1 to 5 with 1 being strongly disagree and 5 being strongly agree to purchase them online.

Combining fruits and vegetables into a single factor got the researchers the following result:

Descriptive Statistics

	Mean	Std. Deviation	Analysis N
6. How would you recommend the following products/services being available for an online purchase?-Fresh cut Vegetables	2.16	1.091	297
6. How would you recommend the following products/services being available for an online purchase?-Fruits	2.34	1.139	297

KMO and Bartlett's Test

Kaiser-Meyer-Olkin Measure of Sampling Adequacy.		.500
Bartlett's Test of Sphericity	Approx. Chi-Square	438.847
	df	1
	Sig.	.000

Anti-image Matrices

		6. How would you recommend the following products/services being available for an online purchase?-Fresh cut Vegetables	6. How would you recommend the following products/services being available for an online purchase?-Fruits
Anti-image Covariance	6. How would you recommend the following products/services being available for an online purchase?-Fresh cut Vegetables	.225	−.198
	6. How would you recommend the following products/services being available for an online purchase ?-Fruits	−.198	.225
Anti-image Covariance	6. How would you recommend the following products/services being available for an online purchase?-Fresh cut Vegetables	.500[a]	−.880
	6. How would you recommend the following products/services being available for an online purchase ?-Fruits	−.880	.500[a]

a. Measures of Sampling Adequacy (MSA)

Component Matrix[a]

	Component
	1
6. How would you recommend the following products/services being available for an online purchase ?-Fruits	.970
6. How would you recommend the following products/services being available for an online purchase?-Fresh cut Vegetables	.970

Extraction Method: Principal Component Analysis.
a. 1 components extracted.

Communalities

	Extraction
6. How would you recommend the following products/services being available for an online purchase?-Fresh cut Vegetables	.940
6. How would you recommend the following products/services being available for an online purchase?-Fruits	.940

Extraction Method: Principal Component Analysis.

Total Variance Explained

	Extraction Sums of Squared Loadings		
Component	Total	% of Variance	Cumulative %
1	1.880	94.007	94.007

Extraction Method: Principal Component Analysis.

Researchers observe from the anti-image correlation matrix that the correlation coefficient of the two variables is 0.5 and that the single factor obtained captures 94% of the total variance of fruits and vegetables. Thus, researchers can conclude that the two variables can be replaced by the single factor variable.

Then this factor score was regressed against quality concerns of the product with the factor as the dependent and the quality concerns as the independent variable. From the result, researchers got the beta value as −0.278 and the standardized beta coefficient as −0.239. Thus, researchers can infer that there is a cause–effect relation between the quality concerns and the purchase intention of fruits and vegetables and thus the null hypothesis is rejected. Further analysis shows that the quality concerns negatively influence the purchase intention of fruits and vegetables which is held true at 1% level of significance.

Testing what is the impact on purchase of jewellery by concerns of security of transactions

The insight for this hypothesis was obtained from the literature review conducted wherein researchers found that users were unwilling to transact online for the large sum of money involved during the purchase of jewellery. The same views were echoed by the FGD participants as well.

Hypotheses

H0: The purchase intention of jewellery is not influenced by concerns of transaction security

Ha: The purchase intention of jewellery is dependent on the transaction security concerns

For this purpose, researchers conducted a simple regression testing on the purchase intention of jewellery online and the security concerns of the consumers and analysis results were obtained. Here, researchers got the beta value as −0.309 and the standardized beta coefficient as −0.444. Thus, the researchers can infer that there is a cause–effect relation between the transaction security concerns and the purchase intention of jewellery online, and thus, the null hypothesis is rejected. Further analysis shows that the security concerns negatively influence the purchase intention of jewellery which is held true at 1% level of significance.

Testing what is the impact on purchase of jewellery by concerns of security of transactions and violation of personal privacy

The reason for taking up this research was not out of FGD and literature review but out of curiosity looking at certain online Web sites selling jewellery who had advertised in bold about the guarantee of personal information confidentiality maintenance.

Procedure: Researchers had taken two separate variables, online transaction security concern and protection of personal privacy concern, on a continuous Likert scale from 1 to 5 with 1 being strongly disagree and 5 being strongly agree, and had tested for the purchase intention on a continuous scale of 1 to 4 combining security and privacy concerns into a single factor. Thus, researchers saw that the factor captures 79.88 % of the information of the individual security and privacy concerns.

Regressing this factor score (independent variable) with the recoded values of jewellery purchase intention (dependent variable) is done using multiple regression. Researchers can thus conclude that the purchase decision of jewellery and the factor for security and privacy concerns have negative effect on the purchase intention of jewellery with the beta value of −0.238 at 1% significance level. Thus, the null hypothesis is rejected.

Testing how the inability to touch objects physically affects the purchase decision of apparels

Most of the respondents in the FGD were of the opinion that the major concern to buying apparels online was that they were unable to touch and feel the texture of the cloth of the apparel. Towards this, researchers had included amongst concerns the inability to physically touch a product.

Hypotheses

H0: The online purchase of apparels is not affected by the lack of physical evidence of the product

Ha: The online purchase of apparels is affected by the lack of physical evidence of the product

Procedure: Researchers conducted a simple regression of the recoded values of the purchase intention of apparels as the dependent variable (refer questionnaire) against the concern of being unable to touch a product physically. The results were interpreted from the output. It was also corroborated by the low preference for fruits and vegetables both among Tier 1 and other cities.

Model Summery

Mode 1	R	R Square	Adjusted R Square	Std. Error of the Estimate
1	.042[a]	.002	−.002	1.00081943

a. Predictors: (Constant), dummy_home

ANOVA[b]

Model	Sum of Squares	df	Mean Square	F	Sig.
1 Regression	.516	1	.516	.515	.473[a]
Residual	295.484	295	1.002		
Total	296.000	296			

a. Predictors: (Constant), dummy_home
b. Dependent Variable: REGR factor score 1 for analysis 1

Coefficients[a]

	Unstandardized Coefficients		Standardized Coefficients		
Model	B	Std. Error	Beta	t	Sig.
1 (Constant dummy_	.047	.088		.538	.591
home	−.084	.117	−.042	−.718	.473

a. Dependent Variable: REGR factor score 1 for analysis 1

2. **Testing whether there is a difference in purchase intention for contraceptives between Tier 1 and Tier 2 cities**

A dummy variable regression was performed as before and following is the SPSS output which shows that the null hypothesis is not rejected. Thus there is no significant difference in the purchase intention of contraceptives between Tier 1 and Tier 2 cities. Also, descriptive statistics showed a high propensity towards buying contraceptives online.

Model Summery

Mode 1	R	R Square	Adjusted R Square	Std. Error of the Estimate
1	.018[a]	.00	−.003	.660

a. Predictors: (Constant), dummy_home

ANOVA[b]

Model	Sum of Squares	df	Mean Square	F	Sig.
1 Regression	.0.40	1	.040	.091	.763[a]
Residual	128.432	295	.435		
Total	128.471	296			

a. Predictors: (Constant), dummy_home
b. Dependent Variable: 6. How would you recommend the following products/services being available for an online purchase?-Contraceptives (with assurance of personal information privacy)

Coefficients[a]

Model	Unstandardized Coefficients		Standardized Coefficients		
	B	Std. Error	Beta	t	Sig.
1 (Constant dummy_	4.192	.058		72.444	.000
home	.023	.077	.018	.301	.763

a. Dependent variable: 6. How would you recommend the following products/services being available for an online purchase?-Contraceptives (with assurance of personal information privacy)

3. **Testing whether there is a difference in fixing appointment with professionals using Internet among Tier 1 and Tier 2/3 respondents**

A dummy variable regression was performed as before and following is the SPSS output which shows that the null hypothesis is rejected.

Thus there is a significant difference among Tier 1 and Tier 2/3 cities when it comes to fixing appointment with professionals like doctors and lawyers. An examination of descriptive statistics shows that Tier 1 respondents are more willing to fix appointments with professionals.

Model Summery

Mode 1	R	R Square	Adjusted R Square	Std. Error of the Estimate
1	.083[a]	.007	.004	.910

a. Predictors: (Constant), dummy_home

ANOVA[b]

Model	Sum of Squares	df	Mean Square	F	Sig.
1 Regression	1.699	1	1.699	2.050	.012
Residual	244.550	295	.829		
Total	246.249	296			

a. Predictors: (Constant), dummy_home
b. Dependent Variable: 6. How would you recommend the following products/services being available for an online purchase?-Appointments with professionals (doctors, lawyers, beauty parlors, etc.)

Coefficients[a]

Model	Unstandardized Coefficients		Standardized Coefficients		
	B	Std. Error	Beta	t	Sig.
1 (Constant dummy_	4.231	.080		52.981	.000
home	.152	.106	.083	1.432	.012

a. Dependent variable: 6. How would you recommend the following products/services being available for an online purchase?-Appointments with professionals (doctors, lawyers, beauty parlors, etc.)

Discussion

The FGD had shown that the preference for online purchase of fruits and vegetables was low. However the participants from Tier 1 cities had been more favourable to the idea of purchasing such items online perhaps because of the busy life in such cities. However a quantitative analysis of the data revealed that both Tier 1 and Tier 2 customers were averse to the idea of buying such products online. This could have been because of the quality concerns and a regression was performed to see the impact of quality and it was found that quality concerns do affect the purchase of fruits and fresh vegetables. Thus selling fruits and vegetables online without adequately addressing the quality concerns of the people is ill advised.

The researchers found a preference for the people to buy contraceptives online. This was observed both in Tier 1 and Tier 2/3 cities. This could have been because ordering online saves the people from awkwardness when they buy from, say, a traditional store. A correlation with privacy concerns showed a low correlation which indicates that people might be more secure while buying contraceptives online than through traditional channels.

The researchers also found that advertising through the online medium is more effective than, say, TV ads and ads in newspapers. Thus advertising in online medium should be pursued by marketers. Also in Tier 2 cities there was a tendency to stick to particular online retail sites while the Tier 1 customers had a tendency to visit and purchase from multiple sites. Hence there is a definite chance of gaining a first mover advantage by tapping into Tier 2 customers. Also both Tier 1 and Tier 2 customers showed a preference when asked whether retailers should take their businesses online.

The impact that retailer brand had on expensive purchases was corroborated by quantitative analysis. This was found in the FGD as well. Thus trust in retailer brand enhanced the likelihood of expensive purchases. Thus established retailers can stock expensive items to cater to this segment. On the other hand product brand did not have a very significant impact on expensive purchases. This was surprising but it could be because people view the retailer as the entity that is selling the product. This was corroborated by an FGD finding where people wanted online retailers to extend services like repair in case of mobiles.

The researchers also found that for expensive items like jewellery, the online transaction security and privacy concerns were major issues. At the same time a well designed Web site was found to increase the trust in the retailer. Thus better authentication systems and secure payment modes might be required to assure the customer so that expensive purchases can be made.

References

1. Abdul-Muhmin, A. G., "Repeat Purchase Intentions in Online Shopping: The Role of Satisfaction, Attitude, and Online Retailers' Performance," *Journal of International Consumer Marketing* (2010), 5–20.
2. Chiu, Y.-B., Lin, C.-P., and Tang, L.-L. (n.d.)., "Gender differs: assessing a model of online purchase intentions in e-tail service," *Journal of Service Industry Management*, 416–435.
3. Gupta, N., Handa, M., and Gupta, B., "Young Adults of India-Online Surfers or Online Shoppers," *Journal of Internet Commerce* (2008), 425–444.
4. Heijden, H. v., Verhagen, T., and Creemer, M., "Understanding online purchase intentions: contributions from technology and trust perspectives," *European Journal of Information Systems* (2003), 41–48.
5. Hostler, R. E., Yoon, V. Y., Guo, Z., Guimaraes, T., and Forgionne, G., "Assessing the impact of recommender agents on online consumer unplanned purchase behaviour," *Information & Management* (2011), 336–343.
6. "Digital Commerce," *Internet & Mobile Association of India* (2011).
7. "Internet in India," *Internet & Mobile Association of India* (2011).
8. "Cross Channel Commerce: A consumer research study," *An Oracle white paper* (2011).
9. "Winning in India's retail sector," *Price Water Coopers* (2011).
10. Srinivasan, S. S., Anderson, R., and Ponnavolu, K., "Customer loyalty in e-commerce: An exploration of its antecedents and consequences," *Journal of Retailing* (2002), 41–50.

Questions

1. Interpret the above outputs in detail keeping the objective of the research in mind.
2. What is your opinion in support of/against the hypothesis tested by the researchers?
3. Suppose that you are asked to extend this research by doing a conjoint analysis to identify the most preferred attributes that influence consumers decision-making; design a conjoint study for (1) apparels and (2) mobile phones.
4. Develop a questionnaire for this study.
5. Do you recommend any change in the sampling plan? Please comment.

Case materials based on research by Arun Narayan, Biswarup Saha, Chandra Sekhar Sathpathy, Debi Prasanna Pati, Kriti Saxena, Mukha Prasad Misra; all are students of Post Graduate Program, Indian Institute of Management Kozhikode, under the guidance of Professor Atanu Adhikari.

Case 2 Running the Numbers: Does It Pay?

(Request the data sets for this case from your instructor.)

Dr. William Ray, a research consultant, has received a government grant of $75,000 to fund research examining how aspects of a student's college experiences relate to his or her job performance. Senator B. I. G. Shot is being lobbied by his constituents that employers are discriminating against people who do not like math by giving them lower salaries. Senator Shot has obtained $50,000 of the $75,000 grant from these constituents. The senator was also instrumental in the selection of Dr. Ray as the recipient and hopes the research supported by the grant will help provide a basis to support the proposed legislation making discrimination against people who do not like math illegal.

The research questions listed in this particular grant proposal include:

RQ1: Does a student's liking of quantitative coursework in college affect his or her future earnings?

RQ2: Do people with an affinity for quantitative courses get promoted more quickly than those who do not?

Dr. Ray has gained the cooperation of a Fortune 500 service firm that employs over 20,000 employees across eight locations. The company allows Dr. Ray to survey employees who have been out of college for three years. Three hundred responses were obtained by sending an e-mail invitation to approximately 1,000 employees who fit this profile. The invitation explained that the research was about various employee attitudes and indicated that employees would not be required to identify themselves during the survey. Respondents were informed that all responses would be strictly confidential. The e-mail provided a click-through questionnaire which directed respondents to a Web site where the survey was conducted using an online survey provider. Each invitation was coded so that the actual respondents could be identified by both e-mail address and name. Dr. Ray, however, kept this information confidential so the company could not identify any particular employee's response.

The following table describes the variables that were collected.

Variables Available from Company Records

Variable Name	Variable Type	Coding
PROM	Nominal indicating whether the employee has been promoted	1 = "Promoted" 0 = "Not Promoted"
GPA	Self-Reported GPA in Last Year of College	0 (lowest) to 4 (highest)
Sex	Nominal	1 = "Female" 0 = "Male"
School	Nominal	School Initials
Salary	Ratio	Actual Annual Salary from Last Year

Questions from Survey

Coding		Strongly Disagree (1)	Disagree (2)	Neutral (3)	Agree (4)	Strongly Agree (5)
X_1	The quantitative courses I took in school were the most useful courses.	☐	☐	☐	☐	☐
X_2	Very few topics can be understood if you do not understand the arithmetic.	☐	☐	☐	☐	☐
X_3	I hated going to math classes in college.	☐	☐	☐	☐	☐
X_4	I learned a great deal from the quantitative projects assigned to me in college.	☐	☐	☐	☐	☐
X_5	Students do not need to study quantitative topics in college to succeed in their careers.	☐	☐	☐	☐	☐

Please use the following items to describe your undergraduate college experience. For each pair of items, choose the check box closest to the adjective that best describes your experience.

Coding		(−3)	(−2)	(−1)	(0)	(1)	(2)	(3)	
S_1	Dull	☐	☐	☐	☐	☐	☐	☐	Exciting
S_2	Laborious	☐	☐	☐	☐	☐	☐	☐	Playful
S_3	Stressful	☐	☐	☐	☐	☐	☐	☐	Relaxing
S_4	Boring	☐	☐	☐	☐	☐	☐	☐	Fun
S_5	Carefree	☐	☐	☐	☐	☐	☐	☐	Responsible

Questions

1. Does this grant present Dr. Ray with an ethical dilemma(s) in any way?
2. Derive at least one hypothesis for each research question listed above. Provide a sound rationale or theoretical explanation that leads to the hypothesis.
3. Use the data that corresponds to this case to perform an adequate test of each hypothesis. Interpret the results.
4. Is there evidence supporting the discrimination claim? Explain.
5. List another hypothesis (unrelated to the research questions in the grant) that could be tested with this data.
6. Test that hypothesis.
7. Considering employees' attitudes about their college experience, does the amount of fun that students had in college or the degree to which they thought quantitative classes were a positive experience relate more strongly to salary?
8. Would the "problem" that led to the grant be a better candidate for ethnographic research? Explain.

Case 3 Attiring Situation

RESERV is a national level placement firm specializing in putting retailers and service providers together with potential employees who fill positions at all levels of the organization. This includes entry-level positions and senior management positions. One international specialty clothing store chain has approached them with issues involving key characteristics of retail employees. The two key characteristics of primary interest involve the appearance of potential employees and problems with customer integrity.

Over the last five years, store management has adopted a very relaxed dress code that has allowed employees some flexibility in the way they dress for work. Casual attire was permitted with the idea that younger customers could better identify with store employees, most of whom are younger than average. However, senior management had just become aware of how some very successful companies tightly control the appearance of their sales force. The Walt Disney Company, for example, has strict grooming policies for all employees, provides uniforms (or costumes) for most *cast members,* and does not permit any employees to work if they have visible tattoos. Disney executives discuss many positive benefits from this policy and one is that customers are more responsive to the employees. Thus, it just may be that the appearance of employees can influence the behavior of customers. This influence can be from the greater identity that employees display—meaning they stand out better and may encourage acquiescence through friendliness.

Senior research associate Michael Neil decides to conduct an experiment to examine relevant research questions including:

RQ1: How does employee appearance affect customer purchasing behavior?

RQ2: How does employee appearance affect customer ethics?

Mr. Neil decides the problem can best be attacked by conducting a laboratory experiment. In the experiment, two variables are manipulated in a between-subjects design. The experiment includes two experimental variables which are controlled by the researcher and by the subjects' biological sex, which was recorded and included as a blocking variable. The experimental variables (and blocking variable) are:

Name	Description	Values
X_1	A manipulation of the attire of the service-providing employee	0 = Professional Attire (Neatly groomed w/ business attire) 1 = Unprofessional Attire (Unkempt hair w/jeans and t-shirt)
X_2	The manner with which the service-providing employee tries to gain extra sales—or simply, the close approach	0 = Soft Close 1 = Hard Close
Gender	Subject's biological sex	0 = Male 1 = Female

Three dependent variables are included:

Name	Description	Range
Time	How much time the subject spent with the employee beyond what was necessary to choose the slacks and shirt.	0–10 minutes
Spend	How much of the $25 the subject spent on extra products offered for sale by the retail service provider	$0–$25
Keep	How much of the $25 the subject kept rather than returning to the researcher	$0–$25

Additionally, several variables were collected following the experiment that tried to capture how the subject felt during the exercise. All of these items were gathered using a 7-item semantic differential scale.

Name	Description
SD_1	Low Quality–High Quality
SD_2	Dislike–Like
SD_3	Unfavorable–Favorable
SD_4	Negative–Positive
SD_5	Easy–Difficult
SD_6	Restful–Tiring
SD_7	Comfortable–Uncomfortable
SD_8	Calm–Tense

The experiment was conducted in a university union. Subjects were recruited from the food court area. RESERV employees approached potential subjects and requested their participation in a study that examined how customers really bought things. Subjects would each receive vouchers that could be exchanged for merchandise in return for their participation. Each potential subject was informed that the participation could take between 20 and 40 minutes to complete. Upon agreeing to participate, subjects were escorted to a waiting area where they were provided with further instructions and mingled with other participants before entering a small room that was set up to resemble an actual retail clothing counter.

Each subject was told to play the role of a customer who had just purchased some dress slacks and a shirt. The employee was to complete the transaction. Once the subject entered the mock retail environment, a research assistant who was playing the role of the retail employee entered the room. As a retail sales associate, one important role was to suggest add-on sales. Several dozen accessory items ranging from socks and handkerchiefs to small jewelry items were displayed at the counter.

As a result of this experimental procedure, each subject was randomly assigned to one of four conditions, each corresponding to a unique combination of the experimental variables described above. In other words, the employee was either:

1. Dressed professionally and used a soft close (i.e., "Perhaps you would like to see some additional accessories") in trying to sell merchandise beyond the slacks and shirt.
2. Dressed unprofessionally and used a soft close.
3. Dressed professionally and used a hard close (i.e., "You really need to match this up with some coordinated accessories which happen to be on sale today only") in trying to sell merchandise beyond the slacks and shirt.
4. Dressed unprofessionally and used a hard close.

Thus, RESERV wishes to use this information to explain how employee appearance encourages shoppers to continue shopping (TIME) and spend money (SPEND). Rather than simply ask purchase intentions, researchers gave each subject $25 (in one-dollar bills) which they were allowed to *spend* on accessories. This allowed each subject to participate in an actual transaction. In addition, the experiment did not provide explicit instructions on what was to be done with the money that was left over. Once the simulated shopping trip was complete, subjects were taken to another small room where they answered a questionnaire containing the semantic differential scales and demographic information which they completed while alone and at their own pace. Because the instructions did not specifically tell subjects what to do with the money they possessed following the experiment, this allowed the researchers to operationalize a behavioral dependent variable (KEEP) that simulated questionable behavior based on the implied assumption that the money was to be either handed to the research assistant when the shopping trip was complete or turned in along with the questionnaire. In other words, subjects who kept money were considered as behaving less ethically than those who left the money behind or turned it in to a member of the research team.

Questions

1. Develop at least three hypotheses that correspond to the research questions.
2. Test the hypotheses using an appropriate statistical approach.
3. Suppose the researcher is curious about how the feelings captured with the semantic differentials influence the dependent variables SPEND and KEEP. Conduct an analysis to explore this possibility. Are any problems present in testing this?
4. Is there a role for factor analysis in any of this analysis?
5. Critique the experiment from the viewpoint of internal and external validity.
6. What conclusions would be justified by management regarding their employee appearance policy?

Case 4 Values and the Automobile Market

(Request the data sets for this case from your instructor.)

In the last decade, the luxury car segment became one of the most competitive in the automobile market. Many American consumers who purchase luxury cars prefer imports from Germany and Japan.

A marketing vice president with General Motors once commented, "Import-committed buyers have been frustrating to us." This type of thinking has led industry analysts to argue that to successfully compete in the luxury car segment, U.S. carmakers need to develop a better understanding of consumers so that they can better target market segments and better position their products via more effective advertising. Insight into the foreign-domestic luxury car choice may result from examining owners' personal values in addition to their evaluations of car attributes, because luxury cars, like many other conspicuously consumed luxury products, may be purchased mainly for value-expressive reasons.

Industry analysts believe it would be important to assess whether personal values of consumers could be used to explain ownership of American, German, and Japanese luxury cars. Further, they believe they should also assess whether knowledge of owners' personal values provides any additional information useful in explaining ownership of American, German, and Japanese luxury cars beyond that obtained from their evaluations of the cars' attributes.

Personal values are likely to provide insights into reasons for ownership of luxury cars for at least two reasons. First, Americans have always had very personal relationships with their cars and have used them as symbols of their self-concepts. For instance, people who value a *sense of accomplishment* are quite likely to desire a luxury car that they feel is an appropriate symbol of their achievement, whereas people who value *fun, enjoyment, and excitement* are likely to desire a luxury car that they perceive as fun and exciting to drive. An advertiser trying to persuade the former segment to purchase a luxury car should position the car as a status symbol that will help its owners demonstrate their accomplishments to others. Similarly, an advertiser trying to persuade the latter segment to purchase a luxury car should position the car as a fun and exciting car to drive. In other words, effective advertising shows consumers how purchasing a given product will help them achieve their valued state, because brands tied to values will be perceived more favorably than brands that deliver more mundane benefits.

Second, when a market is overcrowded with competing brands offering very similar options—as is the case with the luxury car market—consumers are quite likely to choose between brands on the basis of value-expressive considerations.

METHOD

Data were collected via a mail survey sent to 498 consumers chosen at random from a list obtained from a syndicated research company located in an affluent county in a southern state. The list contained names of people who had purchased either an American luxury car (Cadillac or Lincoln Mercury), a German luxury car (Mercedes or BMW), or a Japanese luxury car (Infiniti or Lexus) within the last year. A cover letter explained that the survey was part of an academic research project. People were asked to return the questionnaires anonymously to a university address. (A postage-paid envelope was provided with each survey.) A notice was included that stated that the project was approved by the University Internal Review Board and emphasized the fact that participation was voluntary. Beyond an appeal to help the researchers, respondents were not offered any other incentive to complete the surveys. Of the 498 questionnaires originally sent, 17 were returned by the post office as undeliverable. One hundred fifty-five completed surveys were received, for a response rate of 32.2 percent.

The Survey Instrument

The survey included questions on (1) various issues that people consider when purchasing new cars, (2) importance of car attributes, (3) importance of different values, and (4) demographics (sex, age, education, and family income). Questions relating to the issues that people consider when purchasing new cars were developed through initial interviews with consumers and were measured with a 7-point Likert scale with end anchors of "strongly agree" and "strongly disagree." (See Case Exhibit 4.1.) A list of 12 car attributes was developed from the initial interviews with consumers and by consulting *Consumer Reports*. (See Case Exhibit 4.2.) The importance of each attribute was measured with a 7-point numerical scale with end points labeled "very important" and "very unimportant." The List of Values (LOV) scale in Case Exhibit 4.3 was used to measure the importance of values. Respondents were asked to rate each of the eight values—we combined fun, enjoyment, and excitement into one value—on a 7-point numerical scale with end points labeled "very important" and "very unimportant."

CASE EXHIBIT 4.1 **Issues That Consumers Consider when Buying Luxury Automobiles**

Having a luxury car is a major part of my fun and excitement.[a] (Issue 1)
Owning a luxury car is a part of "being good to myself." (Issue 2)
When I was able to buy my first luxury car, I felt a sense of accomplishment. (Issue 3)
I enjoy giving my friends advice about luxury cars. (Issue 4)
Getting a good deal when I buy a luxury car makes me feel better about myself. (Issue 5)
I seek novelty and I am willing to try innovations in cars. (Issue 6)
I tend to buy the same brand of the car several times in a row. (Issue 7)
I tend to buy from the same dealer several times in a row. (Issue 8)
I usually use sources of information such as *Consumer Reports* in deciding on a car. (Issue 9)
I usually visit three or more dealerships before I buy a car. (Issue 10)
I would read a brochure or watch a video about defensive driving. (Issue 11)
When I buy a new luxury car, my family's opinion is very important to me. (Issue 12)
My family usually accompanies me when I am shopping for a new luxury car. (Issue 13)
I usually rely upon ads and salespersons for information on cars. (Issue 14)
I usually rely upon friends and acquaintances for information on cars. (Issue 15)
When I shop for a car, it is important that the car dealer make me feel at ease. (Issue 16)
Most of my friends drive luxury import cars. (Issue 17)
Most of my friends drive luxury domestic cars. (Issue 18)
I think celebrity endorsers in ads influence people's choices of luxury cars. (Issue 19)
I would not buy a luxury car if I felt that my debt level were higher than usual. (Issue 20)

[a] Note: Subjects' responses were measured with 1 as "strongly agree" and 7 as "strongly disagree."

CASE EXHIBIT 4.2 **Car Attributes**

Attribute	Code	Attribute	Code
Comfort	Comfort	Low maintenance cost	Lomc
Safety	Safety	Reliability	Rely
Power	Power	Warranty	Warrant
Speed	Speed	Nonpolluting	Nonpol
Styling	Styling	High gas mileage	Gasmle
Durability	Durabil	Speed of repairs	Repairs

CASE EXHIBIT 4.3 **List of Values**

Value	Code	Value	Code
Fun-enjoyment-excitement	Fun	Sense of accomplishment	Accomp
Sense of belonging	Belong	Warm relationship	Warm
Being well respected	Respect	Security	Security
Self-fulfillment	Selfful	Self-respect	Selfres

The Sample

Of the 155 respondents in the sample, 58 (37.4 percent) owned an American luxury car, 38 (24.5 percent) owned a European luxury car, and 59 (38.1 percent) owned a Japanese luxury car. The majority of the sample consisted of older consumers (85 percent were 35 years of age or above), more educated consumers (64 percent were college graduates), and economically well-off consumers (87.2 percent earned $65,000 or more).

CODING

Case Exhibit 4.4 lists the SPSS variable names and identifies codes for these variables. (Note that this data set is also available in Microsoft Excel.)

CASE EXHIBIT 4.4 **List of Variables and Computer Codes**

ID—Identification number

AGE (categories are 2 = 35 years and under, 3 = 36–45 yrs, 4 = 46–55 yrs, 5 = 56–65 yrs, 6 = 65+ yrs)

SEX (1 = male, 0 = female)

EDUC—Education (1 = less than high school, 2 = high school grad, 3 = some college, 4 = college grad, 5 = graduate degree)

INCOME (1 = less than $35,000, 2 = $35–50,000, 3 = $50,001–65,000, 4 = $65,001+)

CAR—Type of luxury car (American car, European car, Japanese car)

ISSUES—The sequence of issues listed in Case Exhibit 4.1. (Strongly agree = 1; strongly disagree = 7)

ATTRIBUTES—The sequence of car attributes listed in Case Exhibit 4.2. (Very important to you = 1; very unimportant to you = 7)

VALUES—The sequence of values listed in Case Exhibit 4.3. (Very important = 1; very unimportant = 7)

ADDITIONAL INFORMATION

Several of the questions will require the use of a computerized database. Your instructor will provide information about obtaining the VALUES data set if the material is part of the case assignment.

Questions

1. Is the sampling method adequate? Is the attitude-measuring scale sound? Explain.
2. Using the computerized database with a statistical software package, calculate the means of the three automotive groups for the values variables. Do any of the values variables show significant differences between American, Japanese, and European car owners?
3. Are there any significant differences on importance of attributes?
4. Write a short statement interpreting the results of this research.

Advanced Questions

5. Are any of the value scale items highly correlated?
6. Should multivariate analysis be used to understand the data?

Case materials based on research by Ajay Sukhdial and Goutam Chakraborty, Oklahoma State University.

Case 5 TABH, INC., Automotive Consulting

(Request the data sets for this case from your instructor.)
TABH Consulting specializes in research for automobile dealers in the United States, Canada, Mexico, and Europe. Although much of their work is done on a custom basis with customers such as dealerships and dealership networks selling all major makes of automobiles, they also produce a monthly "white paper" that is sold via their Web site. This off-the-shelf research is purchased by other research firms and by companies within the auto industry itself. This month, they would like to produce a white paper analyzing the viability of college students attending schools located in small college towns as a potentially underserved market segment.

TABH management assigns a junior analyst named Michel Gonzalez to the project. Lacking time for a more comprehensive study, Michel decides to contact the traffic department at Cal Poly University in Pomona, California, and at University of Central Missouri in Warrensburg, Missouri. Michel wishes to obtain data from the students' automobile parking registration records. Although both schools are willing to provide anonymous data records for a limited number of students, Cal Poly offers Michel a chance to visit during the registration period, which just happens to be the following week. As a result, not only can Michel get data from students' registration forms, but she can obtain a small amount of primary data by intercepting students near the registration window. In return, Michel is asked to purchase a booth at the Cal Poly career fair.

As a result, Michel obtains some basic information from students. The information results in a small data set consisting of the following observations for 100 undergraduate college students in Pomona, California:

Variable	Description
Sex	Student's sex dummy coded with 1 = female and 0 = male
Color	Color of a student's car as listed on the registration form
Major	Student's major field of study (Business, Liberal Arts (LA), or Engineering (ENG))
Grade	Student's grade record reported as the mode (A, B, or C)
Finance	Whether the student financed the registered car or paid for it with cash, coded 0 = cash payment and 1 = financed
Residence	Whether the student lives on campus or commutes to school, coded 0 = commute and 1 = on campus
Animal	Michel asks each student to quickly draw a cartoon about the type of car they would like to purchase. Students are told to depict the car as an animal in the cartoon. Although Michel expects to interpret these cartoons more deeply when time allows, the initial coding specifies what type of animal was drawn by each respondent. When Michel was unsure of what animal was drawn, a second researcher was conferred with to determine what animal was depicted. Some students depicted the car as a dog, some as a cat, and some as a mule.

The purpose of the white paper is to offer car dealers considering new locations a comparison of the profile of a small town university with the primary market segments for their particular automobile. For instance, a company specializing in small pickup trucks appeals to a different market segment than does a company specializing in two-door economy sedans. Many small towns currently do not have dealerships, particularly beyond the "Big 3." Although TABH cannot predict with certainty who may purchase the white paper, it particularly wants to appeal to companies with high sales growth in the United States, such as Kia (**http://www.kia.com**), Hyundai (**http://www.hyundai-motor.com**), and potentially European auto dealerships currently without significant U.S. distribution, such as Smart (**http://www.smart.com**), among others. TABH also hopes the white paper may eventually lead to a customized project for one of these companies. Thus, the general research question is:

What are the automobile market segment characteristics of students attending U.S. universities in small towns?

This question can be broken down into a series of more specific questions:

- What segments can be identified based on identifiable characteristics of students?
- How do different segments view a car?
- What types of automobiles would be most in demand?

Questions

1. What types of tests can be performed using the data that may at least indirectly address the primary research question?
2. What do you think the primary conclusions of the white paper will be based on the data provided?
3. Assuming a small college town lacked an auto dealership (beyond Ford, GM, and Chrysler), what two companies should be most interested in this type of location? Use the Internet if necessary to perform some cursory research on different car companies.
4. What are the weaknesses in basing decisions on this type of research?
5. Are there key issues that may diminish the usefulness of this research?
6. What kinds of themes might emerge from the cartoon drawings?
7. Are there any ethical dilemmas presented in this case?

Case 6 The Atlanta Braves

A visit to Turner Field, the Atlanta Braves' state-of-the-art ballpark, feels like a trip back to the future. The stadium blends 1940s tradition with 21st century convenience. The Braves' marketing campaign reflects the charm and nostalgia of baseball's past, but it has a futuristic slogan: "Turner Field: Not just baseball. A baseball theme park."

Fans love the fact that they're closer to the action at Turner Field. It's only 45 feet from either first or third base to the dugouts, with the stands just behind. Besides that, there's a Braves Museum and Hall of Fame with more than 200 artifacts. Cybernauts will find Turner Field awesome because it's a ballpark that makes them a part of the action. At the stadium, built originally for the 1996 Olympics and converted for baseball after the Games, there are interactive games to test fans' hitting and pitching skills, and their knowledge of baseball trivia; electronic kiosks with touch screens and data banks filled with scouting reports on 300 past and present Braves, along with the Braves' Internet home page; a dozen 27-inch television monitors mounted above the Braves' Clubhouse Store, broadcasting all the other major league games in progress, with a video ticker-tape screen underneath spitting out up-to-the-minute scores and stats; a sophisticated communications system, with four miles of fiber-optic cable underneath the playing field that will allow World Series games to be simulcast around the globe, as well as special black boxes placed throughout the stadium to allow as many as 5,500 cell-phone calls an hour.

The marketing of Turner Field is aimed at many types of fans. It is not enough just to provide nine innings of baseball.

Turner Field's theme-park concept was the brainchild of Braves President Stan Kasten. In the early 1990s, as the Braves grew into one of the best teams in baseball, Kasten increasingly became frustrated while watching fans flock to Atlanta–Fulton County Stadium a few hours before games, with little to do but eat overcooked hot dogs and watch batting practice.

As Kasten saw it, they spent too much time milling on the club-level concourse and too little time spending money. What if he could find a way for families to make an outing of it, bring the amenities of the city to Hank Aaron Drive, and create a neighborhood feel in a main plaza at the ballpark? "I wanted to broaden fans' experience at the ballpark and broaden our fan base," Kasten says. "People have no problem spending money when they're getting value. We have one of the highest payrolls in baseball, and I needed to find new ways to sustain our revenues."

Turner Field's main entry plaza opens three hours before games—compared to two hours for the rest of the ballpark—and stays open for about two hours after games. On weekends, there is live music.

Everyone's invited—186 $1 "skyline seats" are available for each game—and that buck gets you anywhere, from the open-air porch at the Chop House restaurant (which specializes in barbecue, bison dogs, Moon Pies, and Tomahawk lager) to the grassy roof at Coke's Sky Field, where fans can keep cool under a mist machine.

Interactive games in Scouts Alley range from $1 to $4, and the chroma-key studios in the East and West Pavilions cost $10–20, where fans can have their picture inserted into a baseball card or into a photo of a great moment in Braves history. Admission to the museum is $2. And it should come as no surprise that there are seven ATMs located throughout the ballpark.

One of the Braves' key marketing objectives is to help build a new generation of baseball fans. The stadium was planned so that fans will find something to love and learn at every turn. The minute a fan's ticket is torn, that person becomes part of what's happening at Turner Field.

Questions

1. What are the key elements of the Turner Field marketing effort?
2. What aspect of the planning of Turner Field, home of the Atlanta Braves, may have been influenced by research using secondary data?
3. What role should business research play in a sporting organization such as the Atlanta Braves, both in making capital decisions and in supporting everyday operational maters?
4. Suppose an executive for the Braves wishes to know whether the stadium has caused employees (including ticket takers, parking attendants, ushers, security personnel, team employees, etc.) to be more committed to the Braves organization than they were playing in an old-fashioned stadium. What would a potential research design involve and what data collection and statistical tests, if any, could be useful?

APPENDIX

APPENDIX

TABLE A.1 **Area Under the Normal Curve**

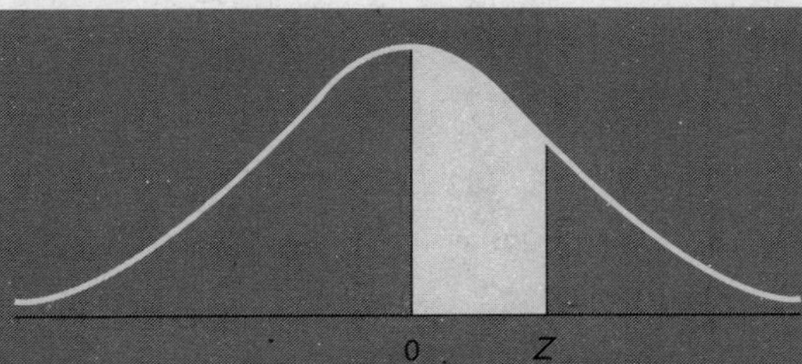

z	.00	.01	.02	.03	.04	.05	.06	.07	.08	.09
0.0	.0000	.0040	.0080	.0120	.0160	.0199	.0239	.0279	.0319	.0359
0.1	.0398	.0438	.0478	.0517	.0557	.0596	.0636	.0675	.0714	.0753
0.2	.0793	.0832	.0871	.0910	.0948	.0987	.1026	.1064	.1103	.1141
0.3	.1179	.1217	.1255	.1293	.1331	.1368	.1406	.1443	.1480	.1517
0.4	.1554	.1591	.1628	.1664	.1700	.1736	.1772	.1808	.1844	.1879
0.5	.1915	.1950	.1985	.2019	.2054	.2088	.2123	.2157	.2190	.2224
0.6	.2257	.2291	.2324	.2357	.2389	.2422	.2454	.2486	.2518	.2549
0.7	.2580	.2612	.2642	.2673	.2704	.2734	.2764	.2794	.2823	.2852
0.8	.2881	.2910	.2939	.2967	.2995	.3023	.3051	.3078	.3106	.3133
0.9	.3159	.3186	.3212	.3238	.3264	.3289	.3315	.3340	.3365	.3389
1.0	.3413	.3438	.3461	.3485	.3508	.3531	.3554	.3577	.3599	.3621
1.1	.3643	.3665	.3686	.3708	.3729	.3749	.3770	.3790	.3810	.3830
1.2	.3849	.3869	.3888	.3907	.3925	.3944	.3962	.3980	.3997	.4015
1.3	.4032	.4049	.4066	.4082	.4099	.4115	.4131	.4147	.4162	.4177
1.4	.4192	.4207	.4222	.4236	.4251	.4265	.4279	.4292	.4306	.4319
1.5	.4332	.4345	.4357	.4370	.4382	.4394	.4406	.4418	.4429	.4441
1.6	.4452	.4463	.4474	.4484	.4495	.4505	.4515	.4525	.4535	.4545
1.7	.4554	.4564	.4573	.4582	.4591	.4599	.4608	.4616	.4625	.4633
1.8	.4641	.4649	.4656	.4664	.4671	.4678	.4686	.4693	.4699	.4706
1.9	.4713	.4719	.4726	.4732	.4738	.4744	.4750	.4756	.4761	.4767
2.0	.4772	.4778	.4783	.4788	.4793	.4798	.4803	.4808	.4812	.4817
2.1	.4821	.4826	.4830	.4834	.4838	.4842	.4846	.4850	.4854	.4857
2.2	.4861	.4864	.4868	.4871	.4875	.4878	.4881	.4884	.4887	.4890
2.3	.4893	.4896	.4898	.4901	.4904	.4906	.4909	.4911	.4913	.4916
2.4	.4918	.4920	.4922	.4925	.4927	.4929	.4931	.4932	.4934	.4936
2.5	.4938	.4940	.4941	.4943	.4945	.4946	.4948	.4949	.4951	.4952
2.6	.4953	.4955	.4956	.4957	.4959	.4960	.4961	.4962	.4963	.4964
2.7	.4965	.4966	.4967	.4968	.4969	.4970	.4971	.4972	.4973	.4974
2.8	.4974	.4975	.4976	.4977	.4977	.4978	.4979	.4979	.4980	.4981
2.9	.4981	.4982	.4982	.4983	.4984	.4984	.4985	.4985	.4986	.4986
3.0	.49865	.4987	.4987	.4988	.4988	.4989	.4989	.4989	.4990	.4990
4.0	.49997									

TABLE A.2 **Distribution of *t* for Given Probability Levels**

	Level of Significance for One-Tailed Test					
	.10	.05	.025	.01	.005	.0005
	Level of Significance for Two-Tailed Test					
df	.20	.10	.05	.02	.01	.001
1	3.078	6.314	12.706	31.821	63.657	636.619
2	1.886	2.920	4.303	6.965	9.925	31.598
3	1.638	2.353	3.182	4.541	5.841	12.941
4	1.533	2.132	2.776	3.747	4.604	8.610
5	1.476	2.015	2.571	3.365	4.032	6.859
6	1.440	1.943	2.447	3.143	3.707	5.959
7	1.415	1.895	2.365	2.998	3.499	5.405
8	1.397	1.860	2.306	2.896	3.355	5.041
9	1.383	1.833	2.262	2.821	3.250	4.781
10	1.372	1.812	2.228	2.764	3.169	4.587
11	1.363	1.796	2.201	2.718	3.106	4.437
12	1.356	1.782	2.179	2.681	3.055	4.318
13	1.350	1.771	2.160	2.650	3.012	4.221
14	1.345	1.761	2.145	2.624	2.977	4.140
15	1.341	1.753	2.131	2.602	2.947	4.073
16	1.337	1.746	2.120	2.583	2.921	4.015
17	1.333	1.740	2.110	2.567	2.898	3.965
18	1.330	1.734	2.101	2.552	2.878	3.922
19	1.328	1.729	2.093	2.539	2.861	3.883
20	1.325	1.725	2.086	2.528	2.845	3.850
21	1.323	1.721	2.080	2.518	2.831	3.819
22	1.321	1.717	2.074	2.508	2.819	3.792
23	1.319	1.714	2.069	2.500	2.807	3.767
24	1.318	1.711	2.064	2.492	2.797	3.745
25	1.316	1.708	2.060	2.485	2.787	3.725
26	1.315	1.706	2.056	2.479	2.779	3.707
27	1.314	1.703	2.052	2.473	2.771	3.690
28	1.313	1.701	2.048	2.467	2.763	3.674
29	1.311	1.699	2.045	2.462	2.756	3.659
30	1.310	1.697	2.042	2.457	2.750	3.646
40	1.303	1.684	2.021	2.423	2.704	3.551
60	1.296	1.671	2.000	2.390	2.660	3.460
120	1.289	1.658	1.980	2.358	2.617	3.373
∞	1.282	1.645	1.960	2.326	2.576	3.291

TABLE A.3 **Chi-Square Distribution**

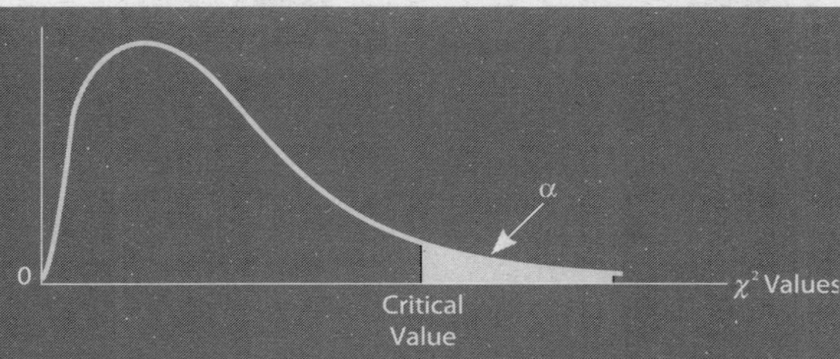

Degrees of Freedom (*df*)	Area in Shaded Right Tail (α) .10	.05	.01
1	2.706	3.841	6.635
2	4.605	5.991	9.210
3	6.251	7.815	11.345
4	7.779	9.488	13.277
5	9.236	11.070	15.086
6	10.645	12.592	16.812
7	12.017	14.067	18.475
8	13.362	15.507	20.090
9	14.684	16.919	21.666
10	15.987	18.307	23.209
11	17.275	19.675	24.725
12	18.549	21.026	26.217
13	19.812	22.362	27.688
14	21.064	23.685	29.141
15	22.307	24.996	30.578
16	23.542	26.296	32.000
17	24.769	27.587	33.409
18	25.989	28.869	34.805
19	27.204	30.144	36.191
20	28.412	31.410	37.566
21	29.615	32.671	38.932
22	30.813	33.924	40.289
23	32.007	35.172	41.638
24	33.196	36.415	42.980
25	34.382	37.652	44.314
26	35.563	38.885	45.642
27	36.741	40.113	46.963
28	37.916	41.337	48.278
29	39.087	42.557	49.588
30	40.256	43.773	50.892

Example of how to use this table: In a chi-square distribution with 6 degrees of freedom (*df*), the area to the right of a critical value of 12.592—i.e., the α area—is .05.

TABLE A.4 *F*-Distribution Table

Level of Significance, $\alpha = 0.05$

Degree of Freedom of Denominator	Degree of Freedom of Numerator																		
	1	2	3	4	5	6	7	8	9	10	12	15	20	24	30	40	60	120	∞
1	161.45	199.5	215.71	224.58	230.16	233.99	236.77	238.88	240.54	241.88	243.90	245.90	248.00	49.10	250.10	251.10	252.20	253.30	254.30
2	18.51	19.00	19.16	19.25	19.30	19.33	19.35	19.37	19.38	19.40	19.41	19.43	19.45	19.45	19.46	19.47	19.48	19.49	19.50
3	10.13	9.55	9.28	9.12	9.01	8.94	8.89	8.85	8.81	8.79	8.74	8.70	8.66	8.64	8.62	8.59	8.57	8.55	8.53
4	7.71	6.94	6.59	6.39	6.26	6.16	6.09	6.04	6.00	5.96	5.91	5.86	5.80	5.77	5.75	5.72	5.69	5.66	5.63
5	6.61	5.79	5.41	5.19	5.05	4.95	4.88	4.82	4.77	4.74	4.68	4.62	4.56	4.53	4.50	4.46	4.43	4.40	4.63
6	5.99	5.14	4.76	4.53	4.39	4.28	4.21	4.15	4.10	4.06	4.00	3.94	3.87	3.84	3.81	3.77	3.74	3.70	3.67
7	5.59	4.74	4.35	4.12	3.97	3.87	3.79	3.73	3.68	3.64	3.57	3.51	3.44	3.41	3.38	3.34	3.30	3.27	3.23
8	5.32	4.46	4.07	3.84	3.69	3.58	3.50	3.44	3.39	3.35	3.28	3.22	3.15	3.12	3.08	3.04	3.01	2.97	2.93
9	5.12	4.26	3.86	3.63	3.48	3.37	3.29	3.23	3.18	3.14	3.07	3.01	2.94	2.90	2.86	2.83	2.79	2.75	2.71
10	4.96	4.10	3.71	3.48	3.33	3.22	3.14	3.07	3.02	2.98	2.91	2.85	2.77	2.74	2.70	2.66	2.62	2.58	2.54
11	4.84	3.98	3.59	3.36	3.20	3.09	3.01	2.95	2.90	2.85	2.79	2.72	2.65	2.61	2.57	2.53	2.49	2.45	2.40
12	4.75	3.89	3.49	3.26	3.11	3.00	2.91	2.85	2.80	2.75	2.69	2.62	2.54	2.51	2.47	2.43	2.38	2.34	2.30
13	4.67	3.81	3.41	3.18	3.03	2.92	2.83	2.77	2.71	2.67	2.60	2.53	2.46	2.42	2.38	2.34	2.30	2.25	2.21
14	4.60	3.74	3.34	3.11	2.96	2.85	2.76	2.70	2.65	2.60	2.53	2.46	2.39	2.35	2.31	2.27	2.22	2.18	2.13
15	4.54	3.68	3.29	3.06	2.90	2.79	2.71	2.64	2.59	2.54	2.48	2.40	2.33	2.29	2.25	2.20	2.16	2.11	2.07
16	4.49	3.63	3.24	3.01	2.85	2.74	2.66	2.59	2.54	2.49	2.42	2.35	2.28	2.24	2.19	2.15	2.11	2.06	2.01
17	4.45	3.59	3.20	2.96	2.81	2.70	2.61	2.55	2.49	2.45	2.38	2.31	2.23	2.19	2.15	2.10	2.06	2.01	1.96
18	4.41	3.55	3.16	2.93	2.77	2.66	2.58	2.51	2.46	2.41	2.34	2.27	2.19	2.15	2.11	2.06	2.02	1.97	1.92
19	4.38	3.52	3.13	2.90	2.74	2.63	2.54	2.48	2.42	2.38	2.31	2.23	2.16	2.11	2.07	2.03	1.98	1.93	1.88
20	4.35	3.49	3.10	2.87	2.71	2.60	2.50	2.45	2.39	2.35	2.28	2.20	2.12	2.08	2.04	1.99	1.95	1.90	1.84
21	4.32	3.47	3.07	2.84	2.68	2.57	2.49	2.42	2.37	2.32	2.25	2.18	2.10	2.05	2.01	1.96	1.92	1.87	1.81
22	4.30	3.44	3.05	2.82	2.66	2.55	2.46	2.40	2.34	2.30	2.23	2.15	2.07	2.03	1.98	1.94	1.89	1.84	1.78
23	4.28	3.42	3.03	2.80	2.64	2.53	2.44	2.37	2.32	2.27	2.20	2.13	2.05	2.01	1.96	1.91	1.86	1.81	1.76
24	4.26	3.40	3.01	2.78	2.62	2.51	2.42	2.36	2.30	2.25	2.18	2.11	2.03	1.98	1.94	1.89	1.84	1.79	1.73
25	4.24	3.39	2.99	2.76	2.60	2.49	2.40	2.34	2.28	2.24	2.16	2.09	2.01	1.96	1.92	1.87	1.82	1.77	1.71
26	4.23	3.37	2.98	2.74	2.59	2.47	2.39	2.32	2.27	2.22	2.15	2.07	1.99	1.95	1.90	1.85	1.80	1.75	1.69
27	4.21	3.35	2.96	2.73	2.57	2.46	2.37	2.31	2.25	2.20	2.13	2.06	1.97	1.93	1.88	1.84	1.79	1.73	1.67
28	4.20	3.34	2.95	2.71	2.56	2.45	2.36	2.29	2.24	2.19	2.12	2.04	1.96	1.91	1.87	1.82	1.77	1.71	1.65
29	4.18	3.33	2.93	2.70	2.55	2.43	2.35	2.28	2.22	2.18	2.10	2.03	1.94	1.90	1.85	1.81	1.75	1.70	1.64
30	4.17	3.32	2.92	2.69	2.53	2.42	2.33	2.27	2.21	2.16	2.09	2.01	1.93	1.89	1.84	1.79	1.74	1.68	1.62
40	4.08	3.23	2.84	2.61	2.45	2.34	2.25	2.18	2.12	2.08	2.00	1.92	1.84	1.79	1.74	1.69	1.64	1.58	1.51
60	4	3.15	2.76	2.53	2.37	2.25	2.17	2.10	2.04	1.99	1.92	1.84	1.75	1.70	1.65	1.59	1.53	1.47	1.39
120	3.92	3.07	2.68	2.45	2.29	2.18	2.09	2.02	1.96	1.91	1.83	1.75	1.66	1.61	1.55	1.50	1.43	1.35	1.29
∞	∞	3	2.60	2.37	2.21	2.10	2.01	1.94	1.88	1.83	1.75	1.67	1.57	1.52	1.46	1.39	1.32	1.22	1.00

TABLE A.4 Continued

Level of Significance, $\alpha = 0.05$

Degree of Freedom of Numerator (columns); Degree of Freedom of Denominator (rows)

	1	2	3	4	5	6	7	8	9	10	12	15	20	24	30	40	60	120	∞
1	647.79	799.48	864.15	899.60	921.83	937.11	948.20	956.64	963.28	968.6	976.72	984.87	993.08	997.27	1001.40	1005.60	1009.79	1014.04	1018.0
2	38.51	39.00	39.17	39.25	39.30	39.33	39.36	39.37	39.39	9.40	39.41	39.43	39.45	39.46	39.36	39.47	39.48	39.49	39.50
3	17.44	16.04	15.44	15.10	14.88	14.73	14.62	14.54	14.47	14.42	14.34	14.25	14.17	14.12	14.08	14.04	13.99	13.95	13.90
4	12.22	10.65	9.98	9.60	9.36	9.20	9.07	8.98	8.90	8.84	8.75	8.66	8.56	8.51	8.46	8.41	8.36	8.31	8.26
5	10.01	8.43	7.76	7.39	7.15	6.98	6.85	6.76	6.68	6.62	6.52	6.43	6.33	6.28	6.23	6.18	6.12	6.07	6.02
6	8.81	7.26	6.60	6.23	5.99	5.82	5.70	5.60	5.52	5.46	5.37	5.27	5.17	5.12	5.07	5.01	4.96	4.90	4.85
7	8.07	6.54	5.89	5.52	5.29	5.12	4.99	4.90	4.82	4.76	4.67	4.57	4.47	4.41	4.36	4.31	4.25	4.20	4.14
8	7.57	6.06	5.42	5.05	4.82	4.65	4.53	4.43	4.36	4.30	4.20	4.10	4.00	3.95	3.89	3.84	3.78	3.73	3.67
9	7.21	5.71	5.08	4.72	4.48	4.32	4.20	4.10	4.03	3.96	3.87	3.77	3.67	3.61	3.56	3.51	3.45	3.39	3.33
10	6.94	5.46	4.83	4.47	4.24	4.07	3.95	3.85	3.78	3.72	3.62	3.52	3.42	3.37	3.31	3.26	3.20	3.14	3.08
11	6.72	5.26	4.63	4.28	4.04	3.88	3.76	3.66	3.59	3.53	3.43	3.33	3.23	3.17	3.12	3.06	3.00	2.94	2.88
12	6.55	5.10	4.47	4.12	3.89	3.73	3.61	3.51	3.44	3.37	3.28	3.18	3.07	3.02	2.96	2.91	2.85	2.79	2.72
13	6.41	4.97	4.35	4.00	3.77	3.60	3.48	3.39	3.31	3.25	3.15	3.05	2.95	2.89	2.84	2.78	2.72	2.66	2.60
14	6.30	4.86	4.24	3.89	3.66	3.50	3.38	3.29	3.21	3.15	3.05	2.95	2.84	2.79	2.73	2.67	2.61	2.55	2.49
15	6.20	4.77	4.15	3.80	3.58	3.41	3.29	3.20	3.12	3.06	2.96	2.86	2.76	2.70	2.64	2.59	2.52	2.46	2.40
16	6.12	4.69	4.08	3.73	3.50	3.34	3.22	3.12	3.05	2.99	2.89	2.79	2.68	2.63	2.57	2.51	2.45	2.38	2.32
17	6.04	4.62	4.01	3.66	3.44	3.28	3.16	3.06	2.98	2.92	2.82	2.72	2.62	2.56	2.50	2.44	2.38	2.32	2.25
18	5.98	4.56	3.95	3.61	3.38	3.22	3.10	3.01	2.93	2.87	2.77	2.67	2.56	2.50	2.44	2.38	2.32	2.26	2.19
19	5.92	4.51	3.90	3.56	3.33	3.17	3.05	2.96	2.88	2.82	2.72	2.62	2.51	2.45	2.39	2.33	2.27	2.20	2.13
20	5.87	4.46	3.86	3.51	3.29	3.13	3.01	2.91	2.84	2.77	2.68	2.57	2.46	2.41	2.35	2.29	2.22	2.16	2.09
21	5.83	4.42	3.82	3.48	3.25	3.09	2.97	2.87	2.80	2.73	2.64	2.53	2.42	2.37	2.31	2.25	2.18	2.11	2.04
22	5.79	4.38	3.78	3.44	3.22	3.05	2.93	2.84	2.76	2.70	2.60	2.50	2.39	2.33	2.27	2.21	2.14	2.08	2.00
23	5.75	4.35	3.75	3.41	3.18	3.02	2.90	2.81	2.73	2.67	2.57	2.47	2.36	2.30	2.24	2.18	2.11	2.04	1.97
24	5.72	4.32	3.72	3.38	3.15	2.99	2.87	2.78	2.70	2.64	2.54	2.44	2.33	2.27	2.21	2.15	2.08	2.01	1.94
25	5.69	4.29	3.69	3.35	3.13	2.97	2.85	2.75	2.68	2.61	2.51	2.41	2.30	2.24	2.18	2.12	2.05	1.98	1.91
26	5.66	4.27	3.67	3.33	3.10	2.94	2.82	2.73	2.65	2.59	2.49	2.39	2.28	2.22	2.16	2.09	2.03	1.95	1.88
27	5.63	4.24	3.65	3.31	3.08	2.92	2.80	2.71	2.63	2.57	2.47	2.36	2.25	2.19	2.13	2.07	2.00	1.93	1.85
28	5.61	4.22	3.63	3.29	3.06	2.90	2.78	2.69	2.61	2.55	2.45	2.34	2.23	2.17	2.11	2.05	1.98	1.91	1.83
29	5.59	4.20	3.61	3.27	3.04	2.88	2.76	2.67	2.59	2.53	2.43	2.32	2.21	2.15	2.09	2.03	1.96	1.89	1.81
30	5.57	4.18	3.59	3.25	3.03	2.87	2.75	2.65	2.57	2.51	2.41	2.31	2.20	2.14	2.07	2.01	1.94	1.87	1.79
40	5.42	4.05	3.46	3.13	2.90	2.74	2.62	2.53	2.45	2.39	2.29	2.18	2.07	2.01	1.94	1.88	1.80	1.72	1.64
60	5.29	3.93	3.34	3.01	2.79	2.63	2.51	2.41	2.33	2.27	2.17	2.06	1.94	1.88	1.82	1.74	1.67	1.58	1.48
120	5.15	3.80	3.23	2.89	2.67	2.52	2.39	2.30	2.22	2.16	2.05	1.94	1.82	1.76	1.69	1.61	1.53	1.43	1.31
∞	5.02	3.69	3.12	2.79	2.57	2.41	2.29	2.19	2.11	2.05	1.94	1.83	1.71	1.64	1.57	1.48	1.39	1.27	1.00

TABLE A.5 **Critical Values of the Pearson Correlation Coefficient**

	Level of Significance for One-Tailed Test			
	.05	.025	.01	.005
	Level of Significance for Two-Tailed Test			
df	.10	.05	.02	.01
1	.988	.997	.9995	.9999
2	.900	.950	.980	.990
3	.805	.878	.934	.959
4	.729	.811	.882	.917
5	.669	.754	.833	.874
6	.622	.707	.789	.834
7	.582	.666	.750	.798
8	.549	.632	.716	.765
9	.521	.602	.685	.735
10	.497	.576	.658	.708
11	.576	.553	.634	.684
12	.458	.532	.612	.661
13	.441	.514	.592	.641
14	.426	.497	.574	.623
15	.412	.482	.558	.606
16	.400	.468	.542	.590
17	.389	.456	.528	.575
18	.378	.444	.516	.561
19	.369	.433	.503	.549
20	.360	.423	.492	.537
21	.352	.413	.482	.526
22	.344	.404	.472	.515
23	.337	.396	.462	.505
24	.330	.388	.453	.496
25	.323	.381	.445	.487
26	.317	.374	.437	.479
27	.311	.367	.430	.471
28	.306	.361	.423	.463
29	.301	.355	.416	.486
30	.296	.349	.409	.449
35	.275	.325	.381	.418
40	.257	.304	.358	.393
45	.243	.288	.338	.372
50	.231	.273	.322	.354
60	.211	.250	.295	.325
70	.195	.232	.274	.303
80	.183	.217	.256	.283
90	.173	.205	.242	.267
100	.164	.195	.230	.254

TABLE A.6 **Critical Values of *T* in the Wilcoxon Matched-Pairs Signed-Ranks Test**

	Level of Significance for Two-Tailed Test		
N	**.05**	**.02**	**.01**
6	1	—	—
7	2	0	—
8	4	2	0
9	6	3	2
10	8	5	3
11	11	7	5
12	14	10	7
13	17	13	10
14	21	16	13
15	25	20	16
16	30	24	19
17	35	28	23
18	40	33	28
19	46	38	32
20	52	43	37
21	59	49	43
22	66	56	49
23	73	62	55
24	81	69	61
25	90	77	68

Adapted from Table 2 of Frank Wilcoxon and Roberta A. Wilcoxon, *Some Rapid Approximate Statistical Procedures* (New York: American Cynamid Company, 1964), p. 28.

Glossary of Frequently Used Symbols

	Greek Letters
α (alpha)	level of significance or probability of a Type I error
β (beta)	probability of a Type II error or slope of the regression line
μ (mu)	population mean
ρ (rho)	population Pearson correlation coefficient
Σ (sigma)	take the sum of
π (pi)	population proportion
σ (sigma)	population standard deviation
χ^2	chi-square statistic
	English Letters
df	number of degrees of freedom
F	F-statistic
n	sample size
p	sample proportion
Pr( )	probability of the outcome in the parentheses
r	sample Pearson correlation coefficient
r^2	coefficient of determination (squared correlation coefficient)
R^2	coefficient of determination (multiple regression)
S	sample standard deviation (inferential statistics)
$S_{\overline{X}}$	estimated standard error of the mean
S_p	estimated standard error of the proportion
S^2	sample variance (inferential statistics)
t	t-statistic
X	variable or any unspecified observation
$\overline{X}$	sample mean
Y	any unspecified observation on a second variable, usually the dependent variable
$\hat{Y}$	predicted dependent variable score
Z	standardized score (descriptive statistics) or Z-statistic

GLOSSARY

GLOSSARY

A

absolute causality Means the cause is necessary and sufficient to bring about the effect.

abstract level In theory development, the level of knowledge expressing a concept that exists only as an idea or a quality apart from an object.

acquiescence bias A tendency for respondents to agree with all or most questions asked of them in a survey.

administrative error An error caused by the improper administration or execution of the research task.

advocacy research Research undertaken to support a specific claim in a legal action or represent some advocacy group.

analysis of variance (ANOVA) Analysis involving the investigation of the effects of one treatment variable on an interval-scaled dependent variable—a hypothesis-testing technique to determine whether statistically significant differences in means occur between two or more groups.

applied business research Research conducted to address a specific business decision for a specific firm or organization.

attitude An enduring disposition to consistently respond in a given manner to various aspects of the world, composed of affective, cognitive, and behavioral components.

attribute A single characteristic or fundamental feature of an object, person, situation, or issue.

B

back translation Taking a questionnaire that has previously been translated into another language and having a second, independent translator translate it back to the original language.

backward linkage Implies that later steps influence earlier stages of the research process.

balanced rating scale A fixed-alternative rating scale with an equal number of positive and negative categories; a neutral point or point of indifference is at the center of the scale.

basic business research Research conducted without a specific decision in mind and that usually does not address the needs of a specific organization. It attempts to expand the limits of knowledge in general and is not aimed at solving a particular pragmatic problem.

basic experimental design An experimental design in which only one variable is manipulated.

behavioral differential A rating scale instrument similar to a semantic differential, developed to measure the behavioral intentions of subjects toward future actions.

between-groups variance The sum of differences between the group mean and the grand mean summed over all groups for a given set of observations.

between-subjects design Each subject in an experiment receives only one treatment combination.

bivariate statistical analysis Statistical test involving two variables.

blocking variables A categorical (less-than interval) variable that is not manipulated as is an experimental variable but is included in the statistical analysis of experiments

box and whisker plots Graphic representations of central tendencies, percentiles, variabilities, and the shapes of frequency distributions.

briefing session A training session to ensure that each interviewer is provided with common information.

business ethics The application of morals to behavior related to the exchange environment.

business intelligence The subset of data and information that actually has some explanatory power enabling effective decisions to be made.

business opportunity A situation that makes some potential competitive advantage possible.

business problem A situation that makes some significant negative consequence more likely.

business research The application of the scientific method in searching for the truth about business phenomena. These activities include defining business opportunities and problems, generating and evaluating ideas, monitoring performance, and understanding the business process.

C

callbacks Attempts to recontact individuals selected for a sample who were not available initially.

case study The documented history of a particular person, group, organization, or event.

categorical variable A variable that indicates membership in some group.

category scale A rating scale that consists of several response categories, often providing respondents with alternatives to indicate positions on a continuum.

causal inference A conclusion that when one thing happens, another specific thing will follow.

causal research Allows causal inferences to be made; seeks to identify cause-and-effect relationships.

cell Refers to a specific treatment combination associated with an experimental group.

census An investigation of all the individual elements that make up a population.

central location interviewing Telephone interviews conducted from a central location, allowing firms to hire a staff of professional interviewers and to supervise and control the quality of interviewing more effectively.

central-limit theorem The theory that, as sample size increases, the distribution of sample means of size *n*, randomly selected, approaches a normal distribution.

check boxes In an Internet questionnaire, small graphic boxes, next to answers, that a respondent clicks on to choose an answer; typically, a check mark or an X appears in the box when the respondent clicks on it.

checklist question A fixed-alternative question that allows the respondent to provide multiple answers to a single question by checking off items.

chi-square (χ^2) test One of the basic tests for statistical significance that is particularly appropriate for testing hypotheses about frequencies arranged in a frequency or contingency table.

choice A measurement task that identifies preferences by requiring respondents to choose between two or more alternatives.

classificatory variable Another term for a categorical variable because it classifies units into categories.

click-through rate Proportion of people who are exposed to an Internet ad who actually click on its hyperlink to enter the Web site; click-through rates are generally very low.

cluster analysis A multivariate approach for grouping observations based on similarity among measured variables.

cluster sampling An economically efficient sampling technique in which the primary sampling unit is not the individual element in the population but a large cluster of elements; clusters are selected randomly.

code book A book that identifies each variable in a study and gives the variable's description, code name, and position in the data matrix.

codes Rules for interpreting, classifying, and recording data in the coding process; also, the actual numerical or other character symbols assigned to raw data.

coding The process of assigning a numerical score or other character symbol to previously edited data.

coefficient alpha (α) The most commonly applied estimate of a multiple item scale's reliability. It represents the average of all possible split-half reliabilities for a construct.

coefficient of determination (R^2) A measure obtained by squaring the correlation coefficient; the proportion of the total variance of a variable accounted for by another value of another variable.

cohort effect A change in the dependent variable that occurs because members of one experimental group experienced different historical situations than members of other experimental groups.

communication process The process by which one person or source sends a message to an audience or receiver and then receives feedback about the message.

comparative rating scale Any measure of attitudes that asks respondents to rate a concept in comparison with a benchmark explicitly used as a frame of reference.

completely randomized design An experimental design that uses a random process to assign subjects to treatment levels of an experimental variable.

composite measures Measurements that assign a value to an observation based on a mathematical derivation of multiple variables.

composite scale A way of representing a latent construct by summing or averaging respondents' reactions to multiple items, each assumed to indicate the latent construct.

computer-assisted personal interviewing (CAPI) Either the interviewer or the respondent answers the interview by sitting at the computer terminal and recording the responses.

computer-assisted self interviewing (CASI) CAPI in the absence of an interviewer.

computer-assisted telephone interviewing (CATI) Technology that allows answers to telephone interviews to be entered directly into a computer for processing.

concept A generalized idea that represents something of meaning.

concept (or construct) A generalized idea about a class of objects that has been given a name; an abstraction of reality that is the basic unit for theory development.

conclusions and recommendations section The part of the body of a report that provides opinions based on the results and suggestions for action.

concomitant variation One of three criteria for causality; occurs when two events "covary," meaning they vary systematically.

conditional causality Means that a cause is necessary but not sufficient to bring about an effect.

confidence interval estimate A specified range of numbers within which a population mean is expected to lie; an estimate of the population mean based on the knowledge that it will be equal to the sample mean plus or minus a small sampling error.

confidence level The range of values for some estimate that accounts for a specified percentage of possibility.

confidentiality The information involved in a research study will not be shared with others.

conflict of interest A condition that occurs when one researcher works for two competing companies.

confound An alternative causal explanation, beyond the intended experimental variable, for any observed differences in the dependent variable.

constancy of conditions Subjects in all experimental groups are exposed to identical conditions except for the differing experimental treatments.

constant Unchanging; this is not useful in addressing research questions.

constant-sum scale A measure of attitudes in which respondents are asked to divide a constant sum to indicate the relative importance of attributes; respondents often sort cards, but the task may also be a rating task.

construct A term used to refer to concepts measured with multiple variables.

construct validity Construct validity exists when a measure reliably and truthfully represents a unique concept; consists of several components including face validity, content validity, criterion validity, convergent validity, and discriminant validity.

consumer panel A longitudinal survey of the same sample of individuals or households to record their attitudes, behavior, or purchasing habits over time.

content analysis The systematic observation and quantitative description of the content of communication.

content providers Parties that furnish information on the World Wide Web.

content validity The degree to which a measure covers the breadth of the domain of interest.

contingency table A data matrix that displays the frequency of some combination of possible responses to multiple variables; cross-tabulation results.

continuous measures Measures that reflect the intensity of a concept by assigning values that can take on any value along some scale range.

continuous variable A variable that can take on a range of values that correspond to some quantitative amount.

contributory causality Means that a cause need be neither necessary nor sufficient to bring about an effect.

contrived observation Observation in which the investigator creates an artificial environment in order to test a hypothesis.

control group A group of subjects to whom no experimental treatment is administered.

convenience sampling The sampling procedure of obtaining those people or units that are most conveniently available.

convergent validity Concepts that should be related to one another are in fact related; highly reliable scales contain convergent validity.

conversations An informal qualitative data-gathering approach in which the researcher engages a respondent in a discussion of the relevant subject matter.

cookies Small computer files that a content provider can save onto the computer of someone who visits its Web site.

correlation coefficient A standardized statistical measure of the covariation, or association, between two at-least interval variables.

correlation matrix The standard form for reporting correlation coefficients for more than two variables.

correspondence rules These indicate the way that a certain value on a scale corresponds to some true value of a concept.

counterbalancing Attempts to eliminate the confounding effects of order of presentation by requiring one-fourth of subjects to be exposed to treatment A first, one-fourth to treatment B first, one-fourth to treatment C first, and finally one-fourth to treatment D first.

counterbiasing statement An introductory statement or preamble to a potentially embarrassing question that reduces a respondent's reluctance to answer by suggesting that certain behavior is not unusual.

covariance Extent to which two variables are associated systematically with each other.

cover letter Letter that accompanies a questionnaire to induce the reader to complete and return the questionnaire.

criterion validity The ability of a measure to correlate with other standard measures of similar constructs or established criteria.

critical values The values that lie exactly on the boundary of the region of rejection.

cross-checks The comparison of data from one source with data from another source to determine the similarity of independent projects.

cross-functional teams Employee teams composed of individuals from various functional areas such as engineering, production, finance, and marketing who share a common purpose.

cross-sectional study A study in which various segments of a population are sampled and data are collected at a single moment in time.

cross-tabulation The appropriate technique for addressing research questions involving relationships among multiple less-than interval variables; results in a combined frequency table displaying one variable in rows and another in columns.

cross-validate To verify that the empirical findings from one culture also exist and behave similarly in another culture.

curb-stoning A form of interviewer cheating in which an interviewer makes up the responses instead of conducting an actual interview.

custom research Research projects that are tailored specifically to a client's unique needs.

customer discovery Involves mining data to look for patterns identifying who is likely to be a valuable customer.

customer relationship management (CRM) Part of the DSS that addresses exchanges between the firm and its customers.

D

data Facts or recorded measures of certain phenomena.

data analysis The application of reasoning to understand the data that have been gathered.

data conversion The process of changing the original form of the data to a format suitable to achieve the research objective; also called data transformation.

data entry The activity of transferring data from a research project to computers.

data file The way a data set is stored electronically in spreadsheet-like form in which the rows represent sampling units and the columns represent variables.

data integrity The notion that the data file actually contains the information that the researcher promised the decision maker he or she would obtain, meaning in part that the data have been edited and properly coded so that they are useful to the decision maker.

data mining The use of powerful computers to dig through volumes of data to discover patterns about an organization's customers and products; applies to many different forms of analysis.

data quality The degree to which data represent the true situation.

data reduction technique Multivariate statistical approaches that summarize the information from many variables into a reduced set of variates formed as linear combinations of measured variables.

data transformation Process of changing the data from their original form to a format suitable for performing a data analysis addressing research objectives.

data warehouse The multitiered computer storehouse of current and historical data.

data warehousing The process allowing important day-to-day operational data to be stored and organized for simplified access.

data wholesalers Companies that put together consortia of data sources into packages that are offered to municipal, corporate, and university libraries for a fee.

database marketing The use of customer databases to promote one-to-one relationships with customers and create precisely targeted promotions.

database A collection of raw data, arranged logically and organized in a form that can be stored and processed by a computer.

data-processing error A category of administrative error that occurs because of incorrect data entry, incorrect computer programming, or other procedural errors during data analysis.

debriefing Procedure in which research subjects are fully informed and provided with a chance to ask any questions they may have about the experiment.

decision making The process of developing and deciding among alternative ways of resolving a problem or choosing from among alternative opportunities.

decision statement A written expression of the key question(s) that the research user wishes to answer.

decision support system (DSS) A computer-based system that helps decision makers confront problems through direct interaction with databases and analytical software programs.

deductive reasoning The logical process of deriving a conclusion about a specific instance based on a known general premise or something known to be true.

degrees of freedom (*df*) The number of observations minus the number of constraints or assumptions needed to calculate a statistical term.

deliverables The term used often in consulting to describe research objectives to a research client.

demand characteristic Experimental design element or procedure that unintentionally provides subjects with hints about the research hypothesis.

demand effect The result that occurs when demand characteristics do indeed affect the dependent variable.

dependence techniques Multivariate statistical techniques that explain or predict one or more dependent variables.

dependent variable A process outcome or a variable that is predicted and/or explained by other variables.

depth interview A one-on-one interview between a professional researcher and a research respondent conducted about some relevant business or social topic.

descriptive analysis The elementary transformation of raw data in a way that describes the basic characteristics such as central tendency, distribution, and variability.

descriptive research A type of research that describes characteristics of objects, people, groups, organizations, or environments and tries to "paint a picture" of a given situation.

descriptive statistics Statistics which summarize and describe the data in a simple and understandable manner.

determinant-choice question A fixed-alternative question that requires the respondent to choose one response from among multiple alternatives.

diagnostic analysis A type of analysis that seeks to diagnose reasons for business outcomes and focuses specifically on the beliefs and feelings consumers have about and toward competing products.

dialog boxes Windows that open on a computer screen to prompt the user to enter information.

direct observation A straightforward attempt to observe and record what naturally occurs; the investigator does not create an artificial situation.

discrete measures Measures that take on only one of a finite number of values.

discriminant analysis A statistical technique for predicting the probability that an object will belong in one of two or more mutually exclusive categories (dependent variables), based on several independent variables.

discriminant validity A type of validity that represents how unique or distinct a measure is; a scale should not correlate too highly with a measure of a different construct.

discussion guide A focus group outline that includes written introductory comments informing the group about the focus group purpose and rules, and then outlines topics or questions to be addressed in the group session.

disguised questions Indirect questions that assume that the purpose of the study must be hidden from the respondent.

disproportional stratified sample A stratified sample in which the sample size for each stratum is allocated according to analytical considerations.

do-not-call legislation Legal action that restricts any telemarketing organization from calling consumers who either register with a no-call list or who request not to be called.

door-in-the-face compliance technique A two-step process for securing a high response rate. In step 1 an initial request, so large that nearly everyone refuses it, is made. Next, a second request is made for a smaller favor; respondents are expected to comply with this more reasonable request.

door-to-door interviews Personal interviews conducted at respondents' doorsteps in an effort to increase the participation rate in the survey.

double-barreled question A question that may induce bias because it covers two issues at once.

drop-down box In an Internet questionnaire, a space-saving device that reveals responses when they are needed but otherwise hides them from view.

drop-off method A survey method that requires the interviewer to travel to the respondent's location to drop off questionnaires that will be picked up later.

dummy coding Numeric "1" or "0" coding where each number represents an alternate response such as "female" or "male."

dummy tables Tables placed in research proposals that are exact representations of the actual tables that will show results in the final report with the exception that the results are hypothetical (fictitious).

dummy variable The way a dichotomous (two group) independent variable is represented in regression analysis by assigning a 0 to one group and a 1 to the other.

E

editing The process of checking the completeness, consistency, and legibility of data and making the data ready for coding and transfer to storage.

elaboration analysis An analysis of the basic cross-tabulation for each level of a variable not previously considered, such as subgroups of the sample.

electronic data interchange (EDI) A type of exchange that occurs when one company's computer system is integrated with another company's system.

e-mail surveys Surveys distributed through electronic mail.

empirical level A level of knowledge that is verifiable by experience or observation.

empirical testing Examining a research hypothesis against reality using data.

environmental scanning A research method that entails all information gathering designed to detect changes in the external operating environment of the firm.

error trapping The use of software to control the flow of an Internet questionnaire—for example, to prevent respondents from returning to previous questions or failing to answer a question.

ethical dilemma A situation in which one chooses form alternative courses of actions, each with different ethical implications.

ethnography The study of cultures through methods that involve becoming highly active within that culture.

evaluation research The formal, objective measurement and appraisal of the extent to which a given activity, project, or program has achieved its objectives.

experiment A carefully controlled study in which the researcher manipulates a proposed cause and observes any corresponding change in the proposed effect.

experimental condition One of the possible levels of an experimental variable manipulation.

experimental group A group of subjects to whom an experimental treatment is administered.

experimental treatment The term referring to the way an experimental variable is manipulated.

experimental variable The proposed cause, controlled by the researcher who manipulates it.

exploratory research A type of research conducted to clarify ambiguous situations or discover ideas that may be potential business opportunities.

external data Data created, recorded, or generated by an entity other than the researcher's organization.

external validity The accuracy with which experimental results can be generalized beyond the experimental subjects.

extraneous variables Variables that naturally exist in the environment and that may have some systematic effect on the dependent variable.

extremity bias A category of response bias that results because some individuals tend to use extremes when responding to questions.

eye-tracking monitor A mechanical device used to observe eye movements; some eye monitors use infrared light beams to measure unconscious eye movements.

F

face validity A scale's content logically appears to reflect what was intended to be measured.

factor analysis A prototypical multivariate, interdependence technique that statistically identifies a reduced number of factors from a larger number of measured variables.

factor loading Indicates how strongly a measured variable is correlated with a factor.

factor rotation A mathematical way of simplifying factor analysis results to better identify which variables "load on" which factors; the most common procedure is varimax.

factorial design A design that allows for the testing of the effects of two or more treatments (experimental variables) at various levels.

fax survey A survey that uses fax machines as a way for respondents to receive and return questionnaires.

field A collection of characters that represents a single type of data—usually a variable.

field editing Preliminary editing by a field supervisor on the same day as the interview to catch technical omissions, check legibility of handwriting, and clarify responses that are logically or conceptually inconsistent.

field experiments Research projects involving experimental manipulations that are implemented in a natural environment.

field interviewing service A research supplier that specializes in gathering data.

field notes The researcher's descriptions of what actually happens in the field; these notes then become the text from which meaning is extracted.

fieldworker An individual who is responsible for gathering data in the field.

filter question A question that screens out respondents who are not qualified to answer a second question.

fixed-alternative questions Questions in which respondents are given specific, limited-alternative responses and asked to choose the one closest to their own viewpoint.

focus blog A type of informal, "continuous" focus group established as an Internet blog for the purpose of collecting qualitative data from participant comments.

focus group A small group that discusses some research topic, led by a moderator who guides discussion among the participants.

focus group interview An unstructured, free-flowing interview with a small group of around six to ten people. Focus groups are led by a trained moderator who follows a flexible format encouraging dialogue among respondents.

foot-in-the-door compliance technique A technique for obtaining a high response rate; compliance with a large or difficult task is induced by first obtaining the respondent's compliance with a smaller request.

forced answering software Software that prevents respondents from continuing with an Internet questionnaire if they fail to answer a question.

forced-choice rating scale A fixed-alternative rating scale that requires respondents to choose one of the fixed alternatives.

forecast analyst Employee who provides technical assistance such as running computer programs and manipulating data to generate a sales forecast.

forward linkage A connection that implies that the earlier stages of the research process influence the later stages.

free-association techniques A technique that records respondents' first (top-of-mind) cognitive reactions to some stimulus.

frequency distribution A set of data organized by summarizing the number of times a particular value of a variable occurs.

frequency table A table displaying a frequency distribution.

frequency-determination question A fixed-alternative question that asks for an answer about general frequency of occurrence.

***F*-test** A statistical test used to determine whether some outcome varies systematically with an independent variable(s).

***F*-test (regression)** A statistical test aimed at determining whether or not a significant amount of variance in a dependent variable is explained by the independent variable(s).

funded business research A type of basic research usually performed by academic researchers and is financially supported by some public or private institution, as in federal government grants.

funnel technique The technique of asking general questions before specific questions in order to obtain unbiased responses.

G

general linear model (GLM) A way of explaining and predicting a dependent variable based on fluctuations (variation) from its mean. The fluctuations are due to changes in independent variables.

global information system An organized collection of computer hardware, software, data, and personnel designed to capture, store, update, manipulate, analyze, and immediately display information about worldwide business activity.

goodness-of-fit (GOF) A general term representing how well some computed table or matrix of values matches some population or predetermined table or matrix of the same size.

grand mean The mean of a variable over all observations.

graphic aids Pictures or diagrams used to clarify complex points or emphasize a message.

graphic rating scale A measure of attitude that allows respondents to rate an object by choosing any point along a graphic continuum.

grounded theory An inductive investigation in which the researcher poses questions about information provided by respondents or taken from historical records; the researcher repeatedly questions the responses to derive deeper explanations.

H

Hawthorne effect The experimental phenomenon whereby people will perform differently from normal when they know they are experimental subjects.

hermeneutic unit A text passage from a respondent's story that is linked with a key theme from within this story or provided by the researcher.

hermeneutics An approach to understanding phenomenology that relies on analysis of texts through which a person tells a story about him or herself.

hidden observation Observation in which the subject is unaware that observation is taking place.

histogram A graphical way of showing a frequency distribution in which the height of a bar corresponds to the observed frequency of the category.

history effect An effect that occurs when some change other than the experimental treatment occurs during the course of an experiment that affects the dependent variable.

host The computer location where the content for a particular Web site physically resides and is accessed.

human subjects review committee An official group that carefully reviews proposed research design to try to make sure that no harm can come to any research participant.

hypothesis Formal statement of an unproven proposition that is empirically testable.

hypothesis test of a proportion A test that is conceptually similar to the one used when the mean is the characteristic of interest but that differs in the mathematical formulation of the standard error of the proportion.

hypothetical constructs Variables that are not directly observable but are measurable through indirect indicators, such as verbal expression or overt behavior.

I

idealism A term that reflects the degree to which one bases one's morality on moral standards.

image profile A graphic representation of semantic differential data for competing brands, products, or stores to highlight comparisons.

importance-performance analysis Another name for quadrant analysis.

impute To fill in a missing data point through the use of a statistical algorithm that provides a best guess for the missing response based on available information.

independent samples *t*-test A test for hypotheses stating the mean scores for some interval- or ratio-scaled variable differ based on some less-than interval classificatory variable.

independent variable A variable that is expected to influence the dependent variable in some way.

index measure An index assigns a value based on how much of the concept being measured is associated with an observation. Indexes often are formed by putting several variables together.

index numbers Scores or observations recalibrated to indicate how they relate to a base number.

index of retail saturation A calculation that describes the relationship between retail demand and supply.

inductive reasoning The logical process of establishing a general proposition on the basis of observation of particular facts.

inferential statistics The use of statistics to project characteristics from a sample to an entire population.

information completeness Having the right amount of information.

information Data formatted (structured) to support decision making or define the relationship between two facts.

informed consent Consent given by an individual who understands what the researcher wants him or her to do and who agrees to participate.

in-house editing A rigorous editing job performed by a centralized office staff.

in-house interviewer A fieldworker who is employed by the company conducting the research.

in-house research Research performed by employees of the company that will benefit from the research.

instrumentation effect A nuisance that occurs when a change in the wording of questions, a change in interviewers, or a change in other procedures causes a change in the dependent variable.

interaction effect Differences in dependent variable means due to a specific combination of independent variables.

interactive help desk In an Internet questionnaire, a live, real-time support feature that solves problems or answers questions respondents may encounter in completing the questionnaire.

interactive medium A medium, such as the Internet, that a person can use to communicate with and interact with other users.

interdependence techniques Multivariate statistical techniques that give meaning to a set of variables or seek to group things together; no distinction is made between dependent and independent variables.

internal and proprietary data Secondary data that originate inside the organization.

internal consistency A measure's homogeneity or the extent to which each indicator of a concept converges on some common meaning.

internal validity A state that exists to the extent that an experimental variable is truly responsible for any variance in the dependent variable.

Internet A worldwide network of computers that allows users access to information from distant sources.

Internet survey A self-administered questionnaire posted on a Web site.

interpretation The process of drawing inferences from the analysis results.

interquartile range A measure of variability.

interrogative techniques Asking multiple what, where, who, when, why, and how questions.

intersubjective certifiability Different individuals following the same procedure will produce the same results or come to the same conclusion.

interval scales Scales that have both nominal and ordinal properties, but that also capture information about differences in quantities of a concept from one observation to the next.

interviewer bias A response bias that occurs because the presence of the interviewer influences respondents' answers.

interviewer cheating The practice by fieldworkers of filling in fake answers or falsifying interviews.

interviewer error Mistakes made by interviewers failing to record survey responses correctly.

intranet A company's private data network that uses Internet standards and technology.

introduction section The part of the body of a research report that discusses background information and the specific objectives of the research.

inverse (negative) relationship Covariation in which the association between variables is in the opposite direction. As one goes up, the other goes down.

item nonresponse Failure of a respondent to provide an answer to a survey question.

J

judgment (purposive) sampling A nonprobability sampling technique in which an experienced individual selects the sample based on personal judgment about some appropriate characteristic of the sample member.

K

keyword search A type of computerized search that takes place as the search engine searches through millions of Web pages for documents containing the keywords.

knowledge management The process of creating an inclusive, comprehensive, easily accessible organizational memory, often called the organization's intellectual capital.

knowledge A blend of previous experience, insight, and data that forms (organizational) memory.

L

laboratory experiment A type of research in which the researcher has more complete control over the research setting and extraneous variables.

ladder of abstraction The organization of concepts in sequence from the most concrete and individual to the most general.

laddering A particular approach to probing, asking respondents to compare differences between brands at different levels that produces distinctions at the attribute level, the benefit level, and the value or motivation level.

latent construct A concept that is not directly observable or measurable, but can be estimated through proxy measures.

leading question A question that suggests or implies certain answers.

Likert scale A measure of attitudes designed to allow respondents to rate how strongly they agree or disagree with carefully constructed statements, ranging from very positive to very negative attitudes toward some object.

literature review A directed search of published works, including periodicals and books, that discusses theory and presents empirical results that are relevant to the topic at hand.

loaded question A question that suggests a socially desirable answer or that is emotionally charged.

longitudinal study A survey of respondents at different times, thus allowing analysis of response continuity and changes over time.

M

mail survey A self-administered questionnaire sent to respondents through the mail.

main effect The experimental difference in dependent variable means between the different levels of any single experimental variable.

mall intercept interviews Personal interviews conducted in a shopping mall.

manager of decision support systems Employee who supervises the collection and analysis of sales, inventory, and other periodic customer relationship management (CRM) data.

managerial action standard A specific performance criterion upon which a decision can be based.

manipulation Means that the researcher alters the level of the variable in specific increments.

manipulation check A validity test of an experimental manipulation to make sure that the manipulation does produce differences in the independent variable.

marginals Row and column totals in a contingency table, which are shown in its margins.

market tracking The observation and analysis of trends in industry volume and brand share over time.

market-basket analysis A form of data mining that analyzes anonymous point-of-sale transaction databases to identify coinciding purchases or relationships between products purchased and other retail shopping information.

marketing-oriented A term describing a firm in which all decisions are made with a conscious awareness of their effect on the customer.

maturation effects Effects that are a function of time and the naturally occurring events that coincide with growth and experience.

mean A measure of central tendency; the arithmetic average.

measure of association A general term that refers to a number of bivariate statistical techniques used to measure the strength of a relationship between two variables.

measurement The process of describing some property of a phenomenon of interest, usually by assigning numbers in a reliable and valid way.

median A measure of central tendency that is the midpoint; the value below which half the values in a distribution fall.

median split Dividing a data set into two categories by placing respondents below the median in one category and respondents above the median in another.

mixed-mode survey A study that employs any combination of survey methods.

mode A measure of central tendency; the value that occurs most often.

model building The use of secondary data to help specify relationships between two or more variables; it can involve the development of descriptive or predictive equations.

moderator variable A third variable that changes the nature of a relationship between the original independent and dependent variables.

moderator A person who leads a focus group interview and ensures that everyone gets a chance to speak and contribute to the discussion.

monadic rating scale Any measure of attitudes that asks respondents about a single concept in isolation.

moral standards Principles that reflect beliefs about what is ethical and what is unethical.

mortality effect (sample attrition) A situation that occurs when some subjects withdraw from the experiment before it is completed.

multicollinearity The extent to which independent variables in a multiple regression analysis are correlated with each other; high multicollinearity can make interpreting parameter estimates difficult or impossible.

multidimensional scaling A statistical technique that measures objects in multidimensional space on the basis of respondents' judgments of the similarity of objects.

multiple regression analysis An analysis of association in which the effects of two or more independent variables on a single, interval-scaled dependent variable are investigated simultaneously.

multiple-grid question Several similar questions arranged in a grid format.

multistage area sampling A type of sampling that involves using a combination of two or more probability sampling techniques.

multivariate analysis of variance (MANOVA) A multivariate technique that predicts multiple continuous dependent variables with one or more categorical independent variables.

multivariate statistical analysis Statistical analysis involving three or more variables or sets of variables.

mutually exclusive A grouping in which no overlap exists among the fixed-alternative categories.

N

neural networks A form of artificial intelligence in which a computer is programmed to mimic the way that human brains process information.

no contacts Members of sampling frame who are not at home or who are otherwise inaccessible on the first and second contact.

nominal scales Ranking scales that represent the most elementary level of measurement in which values are assigned to an object for identification or classification purposes only.

nonparametric statistics A type of statistics appropriate when the variables being analyzed do not conform to any known or continuous distribution.

nonprobability sampling A sampling technique in which units of the sample are selected on the basis of personal judgment or convenience; the probability of any particular member of the population being chosen is unknown.

nonrespondent error An error that the respondent is not responsible for creating, such as when the interviewer marks a response incorrectly.

nonrespondents People who are not contacted or who refuse to cooperate in the research.

nonresponse error The statistical differences between a survey that includes only those who responded and a perfect survey that would also include those who failed to respond.

nonspurious association One of three criteria for causality; any covariation between a cause and an effect is true and not simply due to some other variable.

normal distribution A symmetrical, bell-shaped distribution that describes the expected probability distribution of many chance occurrences.

nuisance variables Items that may affect the dependent measure but are not of primary interest.

numerical scale An attitude rating scale similar to a semantic differential except that it uses numbers instead of verbal descriptions as response options to identify response positions.

O

observation The systematic process of recording the behavioral patterns of people, objects, and occurrences as they are witnessed.

observer bias A distortion of measurement resulting from the cognitive behavior or actions of a witnessing observer.

online focus group A qualitative research effort in which a group of individuals provides unstructured comments by entering their remarks into an electronic Internet display board of some type.

open-ended boxes In an Internet questionnaire, boxes where respondents can type in their own answers to open-ended questions.

open-ended response questions Questions that pose some problem and ask respondents to answer in their own words.

operationalization The process of identifying scales that correspond to variance in a concept to be involved in a research process.

operationalizing The process of identifying the actual measurement scales to assess the variables of interest.

opt in To give permission to receive selected e-mail, such as questionnaires, from a company with an Internet presence.

optical scanning system A data processing input device that reads material directly from mark-sensed questionnaires.

oral presentation A spoken summary of the major findings, conclusions, and recommendations, given to clients or line managers to provide them with the opportunity to clarify any ambiguous issues by asking questions.

order bias Bias caused by the influence of earlier questions in a questionnaire or by an answer's position in a set of answers.

ordinal scales Ranking scales allowing items to be arranged based on how much of some quality they possess.

outlier A value that lies outside the normal range of the data.

outside agency An independent research firm contracted by the company that actually will benefit from the research.

P

paired comparison A measurement technique that involves presenting the respondent with two objects and asking the respondent to pick the preferred object; more than two objects may be presented, but comparisons are made in pairs.

paired-samples *t*-test An appropriate test for comparing the scores of two interval variables drawn from related populations.

parametric statistics Statistics that involve numbers with known, continuous distributions; when the data are interval or ratio scaled and the sample size is large, parametric statistical procedures are appropriate.

partial correlation The correlation between two variables after taking into account the fact that they are correlated with other variables too.

participant-observation An ethnographic research approach where the researcher becomes immersed within the culture that he or she is studying and draws data from his or her observations.

percentage distribution A frequency distribution organized into a table (or graph) that summarizes percentage values associated with particular values of a variable.

performance-monitoring research Research that regularly, sometimes routinely, provides feedback for evaluation and control of business activity.

personal interview Face-to-face communication in which an interviewer asks a respondent to answer questions.

phenomenology A philosophical approach to studying human experiences based on the idea that human experience itself is inherently subjective and determined by the context in which people live.

piggyback A procedure in which one respondent stimulates thought among the others; as this process continues, increasingly creative insights are possible.

pilot study A small-scale research project that collects data from respondents similar to those to be used in the full study.

pivot question A filter question used to determine which version of a second question will be asked.

placebo An experimental tool used to create the perception that some substance or procedure has been administered.

placebo effect The effect in a dependent variable associated with the psychological impact that goes along with knowledge of some treatment being administered.

plug value An answer that an editor "plugs in" to replace blanks or missing values so as to permit data analysis; the choice of value is based on a predetermined decision rule.

point estimate An estimate of the population mean in the form of a single value, usually the sample mean.

pooled estimate of the standard error An estimate of the standard error for a *t*-test of independent means that assumes the variances of both groups are equal.

population (universe) Any complete group of entities that share some common set of characteristics.

population distribution A frequency distribution of the elements of a population.

population element An individual member of a population.

population parameters Variables in a population or measured characteristics of the population.

pop-up boxes In an Internet questionnaire, boxes that appear at selected points and contain information or instructions for respondents.

preliminary tabulation A tabulation of the results of a pretest to help determine whether the questionnaire will meet the objectives of the research.

pretest A small-scale study in which the results are only preliminary and intended only to assist in design of a subsequent study.

pretesting A screening procedure that involves a trial run with a group of respondents to iron out fundamental problems in the survey design.

primary sampling unit (PSU) A term used to designate a unit selected in the first stage of sampling.

probability The long-run relative frequency with which an event will occur.

probability sampling A sampling technique in which every member of the population has a known, nonzero probability of selection.

probing An interview technique that tries to draw deeper and more elaborate explanations from the discussion.

problem A situation that occurs when there is a difference between the current conditions and a more preferable set of conditions.

problem definition The process of defining and developing a decision statement and the steps involved in translating it into more precise research terminology, including a set of research objectives.

product-oriented A term used to describe a firm that prioritizes decision making in a way that emphasizes technical superiority in the product.

production-oriented A term used to describe a firm that prioritizes efficiency and effectiveness of the production processes in making decisions.

projective technique An indirect means of questioning enabling respondents to project beliefs and feelings onto a third party, an inanimate object, or a task situation.

proportion The percentage of elements that meet some criterion.

proportional stratified sample A stratified sample in which the number of sampling units drawn from each stratum is in proportion to the population size of that stratum.

propositions Statements explaining the logical linkage among certain concepts by asserting a universal connection between concepts.

proprietary business research The gathering of new data to investigate specific problems.

pseudo-research A study conducted not to gather information for marketing decisions but to bolster a point of view and satisfy other needs.

psychogalvanometer A device that measures galvanic skin response, a measure of involuntary changes in the electrical resistance of the skin.

pull technology A procedure by which consumers request information from a Web page and the browser then determines a response; the consumer is essentially asking for the data.

pupilometer A mechanical device used to observe and record changes in the diameter of a subject's pupils.

push button In a dialog box on an Internet questionnaire, a small outlined area, such as a rectangle or an arrow, that the respondent clicks on to select an option or perform a function, such as submit.

push poll Telemarketing under guise of research.

push technology A program that sends data to a user's computer without a request being made; software is used to guess what information might be interesting to consumers based on the pattern of previous responses.

p-value Probability value, or the observed or computed significance level; p-values are compared to significance levels to test hypotheses.

Q

quadrant analysis An extension of cross-tabulation in which responses to two rating-scale questions are plotted in four quadrants of a two-dimensional table.

qualitative business research Research that addresses business objectives through techniques that allow the researcher to provide elaborate interpretations of phenomena without depending on numerical measurement; its focus is on discovering true inner meanings and new insights.

qualitative data Data that are not characterized by numbers, and instead are textual, visual, or oral; the focus is on stories, visual portrayals, meaningful characterizations, interpretations, and other expressive descriptions.

quantitative business research Business research that addresses research objectives through empirical assessments that involve numerical measurement and analysis.

quantitative data Data that represent phenomena by assigning numbers in an ordered and meaningful way.

quasi-experimental designs Experimental designs that do not involve random allocation of subjects to treatment combinations.

quota sampling A nonprobability sampling procedure that ensures that various subgroups of a population will be represented on pertinent characteristics to the exact extent that the investigator desires.

R

radio button In an Internet questionnaire, a circular icon resembling a button that activates one response choice and deactivates others when a respondent clicks on it.

random digit dialing The use of telephone exchanges and a table of random numbers to contact respondents with unlisted phone numbers.

random sampling error A statistical fluctuation that occurs because of chance variation in the elements selected for a sample.

random variable A variable that assumes value from a measurement process which is a random process.

randomization The random assignment of subject and treatments to groups; it is one device for equally distributing the effects of extraneous variables to all conditions.

randomized-block design A design that attempts to isolate the effects of a single extraneous variable by blocking out its effects on the dependent variable.

ranking A measurement task that requires respondents to rank order a small number of stores, brands, or objects on the basis of overall preference or some characteristic of the stimulus.

rating A measurement task that requires respondents to estimate the magnitude of a characteristic or quality that a brand, store, or object possesses.

ratio scales Ranking scales that represent the highest form of measurement in that they have all the properties of interval scales with the additional attribute of representing absolute quantities; characterized by a meaningful absolute zero.

raw data The unedited responses from a respondent exactly as indicated by that respondent.

record A collection of related fields that represents the responses from one sampling unit.

refusals People who are unwilling to participate in a research project.

relativism The rejection of moral standards in favor of the acceptability of some action. This way of thinking rejects absolute principles in favor of situation-based evaluations.

relevance The characteristics of data reflecting how pertinent these particular facts are to the situation at hand.

reliability An indicator of a measure's internal consistency.

repeated measures Experiments in which an individual subject is exposed to more than one level of an experimental treatment.

replication Repitition of research to determine whether the same interpretation will be drawn if the study is repeated by different researchers with different respondents following the same methods.

report format The makeup or arrangement of parts necessary to a good research report.

research analyst A person responsible for client contact, project design, preparation of proposals, selection of research suppliers, and supervision of data collection, analysis, and reporting activities.

research assistants Research employees who provide technical assistance with questionnaire design, data analyses, and similar activities.

research design A master plan that specifies the methods and procedures for collecting and analyzing the needed information.

research follow-up Recontacting decision makers and/or clients after they have had a chance to read over a research report in order to determine whether additional information or clarification is necessary.

research generalist A research employee who serves as a link between management and research specialists. The research generalist acts as a problem definer, an educator, a liaison, a communicator, and a friendly ear.

research methodology section The part of the body of a report that presents the findings of the project. It includes tables, charts, and an organized narrative.

research objectives The goals to be achieved by conducting research.

research program Numerous related studies that come together to address multiple, related research objectives.

research project A single study that addresses one or a small number of research objectives.

research proposal A written statement of the research design.

research questions Questions that express the research objectives in terms of questions that can be addressed by research.

research report An oral presentation or written statement of research results, strategic recommendations, and/or other conclusions to a specific audience.

research suppliers Commercial providers of research services.

researcher-dependent Research in which the researcher must extract meaning from unstructured responses such as text from a recorded interview or a collage representing the meaning of some experience.

respondent error A category of sample bias resulting from some respondent action or inaction such as nonresponse or response bias.

respondents People who verbally answer an interviewer's questions or provide answers to written questions.

response bias A bias that occurs when respondents either consciously or unconsciously tend to answer questions with a certain slant that misrepresents the truth.

response latency The amount of time it takes to make a choice between two alternatives, used as a measure of the strength of preference.

response rate The number of questionnaires returned or completed divided by the number of eligible people who were asked to participate in the survey.

results section The part of the body of a report that presents the findings of the project. It includes tables, charts, and an organized narrative.

reverse coding Coding in which the value assigned for a response is treated oppositely from the other items.

reverse directory A directory similar to a telephone directory except that listings are by city and street address or by phone number rather than alphabetical by last name.

reverse recoding A method of making sure all the items forming a composite scale are scored in the same direction. Negative items can be recoded into the equivalent responses for a non-reverse coded item.

rule of parsimony The rule of parsimony suggests an explanation involving fewer components is better than one involving more.

S

sample A subset, or some part, of a larger population.

sample bias A persistent tendency for the results of a sample to deviate in one direction from the true value of the population parameter.

sample distribution A frequency distribution of a sample.

sample selection error An administrative error caused by improper sample design or sampling procedure execution.

sample statistics Variables in a sample or measures computed from sample data.

sample survey A more formal term for a survey.

sampling Any procedure that draws conclusions based on measurements of a portion of the population.

sampling distribution A theoretical probability distribution of sample means for all possible samples of a certain size drawn from a particular population.

sampling frame A list of elements from which a sample may be drawn, also called working population.

sampling frame error An error that occurs when certain sample elements are not listed or are not accurately represented in a sampling frame.

sampling unit A single element or group of elements subject to selection in the sample.

scales A device providing a range of values that correspond to different values in a concept being measured.

scanner data The accumulated records resulting from point of sale data recordings.

scanner-based consumer panel A type of consumer panel in which participants' purchasing habits are recorded with a laser scanner rather than with a purchase diary.

scientific method A set of prescribed procedures for establishing and connecting theoretical statements about events, for analyzing empirical evidence, and for predicting events yet unknown; techniques or procedures used to analyze empirical evidence in an attempt to confirm or disprove prior conceptions.

search engine A computerized directory that allows anyone to search the World Wide Web for information using a keyword search.

secondary data Data that have been previously collected for some purpose other than the one at hand.

secondary sampling unit A unit selected in the second stage of sampling.

selection effect Sample bias from differential selection of respondents for experimental groups.

self-administered questionnaires Surveys in which the respondent takes the responsibility for reading and answering the questions.

self-selection bias A bias that occurs because people who feel strongly about a subject are more likely to respond to survey questions than people who feel indifferent about it.

semantic differential A measure of attitudes that consists of a series of seven-point rating scales that use bipolar adjectives to anchor the beginning and end of each scale.

sensitivity A measurement instrument's ability to accurately measure variability in stimuli or responses.

significance level A critical probability associated with a statistical hypothesis test that indicates how likely an inference supporting a difference between an observed value and some statistical expectation is true; the acceptable level of Type I error.

simple (bivariate) linear regression A measure of linear association that investigates straight-line relationships between a continuous dependent variable and an independent variable that is usually continuous but can be a categorical dummy variable.

simple random sampling A sampling procedure that assures each element in the population of an equal chance of being included in the sample.

simple-dichotomy (dichotomous) question A fixed-alternative question that requires the respondent to choose one of two alternatives.

single-source data Diverse types of data offered by a single company, usually integrated on the basis of a common variable such as geographic area or store.

site analysis techniques Techniques that use secondary data to select the best location for retail or wholesale operations.

situation analysis The gathering of background information to familiarize researchers and managers with the decision-making environment.

smart agent software Software capable of learning an Internet user's preferences and automatically searching out information in selected Web sites and then distributing it.

snowball sampling A sampling procedure in which initial respondents are selected by probability methods and additional respondents are obtained from information provided by the initial respondents.

social desirability bias Bias in responses caused by respondents' desire, either conscious or unconscious, to gain prestige or appear in a different social role.

sorting A measurement task that presents a respondent with several objects or product concepts and requires the respondent to arrange the objects into piles or classify the product concepts.

split-ballot technique The practice of using two alternative phrasings of the same question for respective halves of a sample to elicit a more accurate total response than would a single phrasing.

split-half method A method for assessing internal consistency by checking the results of one-half of a set of scaled items against the results from the other half.

spyware Software placed on a computer without consent or knowledge of the user.

standard deviation A quantitative index of a distribution's spread, or variability; the square root of the variance for a distribution.

standard error of the mean The standard deviation of the sampling distribution.

standardized normal distribution A purely theoretical probability distribution that reflects a specific normal curve for the standardized value, *Z*.

standardized regression coefficient (β) The estimated coefficient indicating the strength of relationship between an independent variable and dependent variable expressed on a standardized scale where higher absolute values indicate stronger relationships (range is from −1 to 1).

Stapel scale A measure of attitudes that consists of a single adjective in the center of an even number of numerical values.

statistical base The number of respondents or observations (in a row or column) used as a basis for computing percentages.

status bar In an Internet questionnaire, a visual indicator that tells the respondent what portion of the survey he or she has completed.

stratified sampling A probability sampling procedure in which simple random subsamples that are more or less equal on some characteristic are drawn from within each stratum of the population.

string characters Computer terminology to represent formatting a variable using a series of alphabetic characters (nonnumeric characters) that may form a word.

structured question A question that imposes a limit on the number of allowable responses.

subjective A term meaning research results are researcher-dependent, meaning different researchers may reach different conclusions based on the same interview.

subjects The sampling units for an experiment, usually human respondents who provide measures based on the experimental manipulation.

summated scale A scale created by simply summing (adding together) the response to each item making up the composite measure.

survey A research technique in which a sample is interviewed in some form or the behavior of respondents is observed and described in some way.

symptoms Observable cues that serve as a signal of a problem because they are caused by that problem.

syndicated service A research supplier that provides standardized information for many clients in return for a fee.

systematic error Error resulting from some imperfect aspect of the research design that causes respondent error or from a mistake in the execution of the research.

systematic or nonsampling error A type of error that occurs if the sampling units in an experimental cell are somehow different than the units in another cell, and this difference affects the dependent variable.

systematic sampling A sampling procedure in which a starting point is selected by a random process and then every *n*th number on the list is selected.

T

tabulation The orderly arrangement of data in a table or other summary format showing the number of responses to each response category; tallying.

tachistoscope A device that controls the amount of time a subject is exposed to a visual image.

***t*-distribution** A symmetrical, bell-shaped distribution that is contingent on sample size, has a mean of 0 and a standard deviation equal to 1.

telephone interviews Personal interviews conducted by telephone, the mainstay of commercial survey research.

television monitoring Computerized mechanical observation used to obtain television ratings.

temporal sequence One of three criteria for causality that deals with the time order of events—the cause must occur before the effect.

tertiary sampling unit A term used to designate a unit selected in the third stage of sampling.

test of differences An investigation of a hypothesis stating that two (or more) groups differ with respect to measures on a variable.

test tabulation Tallying of a small sample of the total number of replies to a particular question in order to construct coding categories.

test units The subjects or entities whose responses to the experimental treatment are measured or observed.

testing effects A nuisance effect occurring when the initial measurement or test alerts or primes subjects in a way that affects their response to the experimental treatments.

test-market An experiment that is conducted within actual market conditions.

test-retest method A reliability approach involving the administration of the same scale or measure to the same respondents at two separate points in time.

thematic apperception test (TAT) A test that presents subjects with an ambiguous picture(s) in which consumers and products are the center of attention; the investigator asks the subject to tell what is happening in the picture(s) now and what might happen next.

themes Meaning identified by the frequency with which the same term (or a synonym) arises in the narrative description.

theory A formal, logical explanation of some events that includes predictions of how things relate to one another.

Thurstone scale An attitude scale in which judges assign scale values to attitudinal statements and subjects are asked to respond to these statements.

time series design A research design used for an experiment investigating long-term structural changes.

timeliness A term indicating that the data are current enough to still be relevant.

total quality management A business philosophy that emphasizes market-driven quality as a top organizational priority.

total variability The sum of within-group variance and between-groups variance.

totally exhaustive A category exists for every respondent in among the fixed-alternative categories.

tracking study A type of longitudinal study that uses successive samples to compare trends and identify changes in variables such as consumer satisfaction, brand image, or advertising awareness.

***t*-test** A hypothesis test that uses the *t*-distribution. A univariate *t*-test is appropriate when the variable being analyzed is interval or ratio.

Type I error An error caused by rejecting the null hypothesis when it is true; it has a probability of alpha. Practically, a Type I error occurs when the researcher concludes that a relationship or difference exits in the population when in reality it does not exist.

Type II error An error caused by failing to reject the null hypothesis when the alternative hypothesis is true; it has a probability of beta. Practically, a Type II error occurs when a researcher concludes that no relationship or difference exists when in fact one does exist.

U

unbalanced rating scale A fixed-alternative rating scale that has more response categories at one end than the other resulting in an unequal number of positive and negative categories.

undisguised questions Straightforward questions that assume the respondent is willing to answer.

uniform resource locator (URL) A Web site address that Web browsers recognize.

unit of analysis What or who should provide the data and at what level of aggregation it should be analyzed (organizations, strategic business units, departments, families, individuals . . .).

univariate statistical analysis Tests of hypotheses involving only one variable.

unobtrusive methods Methods in which research respondents do not have to be disturbed for data to be gathered.

unstructured question A question that does not restrict the respondents' answers.

V

validity The accuracy of a measure or the extent to which a score truthfully represents a concept.

value labels Unique labels assigned to each possible numeric code for a response.

variable piping software Software that allows variables to be inserted into an Internet questionnaire as a respondent is completing it.

variable Anything that varies or changes from one instance to another; variables can exhibit differences in value, usually in magnitude or strength, or in direction.

variance A measure of variability or dispersion. Its square root is the standard deviation.

variate A mathematical way in which a set of variables can be represented with one equation.

verification Quality-control procedures in fieldwork intended to ensure that interviewers are following the sampling procedures and to determine whether interviewers are cheating.

visible observation Observation in which the observer's presence is known to the subject.

voice-pitch analysis A physiological measurement technique that records abnormal frequencies in the voice that are supposed to reflect emotional reactions to various stimuli.

W

welcome screen The first Web page in an Internet survey, which introduces the survey and requests that the respondent enter a password or pin.

within-group error or variance The sum of the differences between observed values and the group mean for a given set of observations, also known as total error variance.

within-subjects design Involves repeated measures because with each treatment the same subject is measured.

World Wide Web (WWW) A portion of the internet that is a system of computer servers that organize information into documents called Web pages.

Z

***Z*-test for differences of proportions** A technique used to test the hypothesis that proportions are significantly different for two independent samples or groups.

ENDNOTES

Chapter 1

1 Grapetime, Terry, "Vote for Me," *Marketing Research* 16 (Winter 2004), 5; "AFLAC's Quacking Duck Selected One of America's Favorite Icons," *Best Review* 105 (October 2004), 119; Gage, Jack, "Waddling Through," *Forbes* 176 (August 15, 2005), 90.

2 Keyo, Michelle "Web Site of the Week: Jelly Belly: Using Sampling to Build a Customer Database," *Inc. Online* (1996), http://www.inc.com, December 9, 1996.

3 Penn, Catherine, "New Drinks Include a Health Benefit for 05," *Beverage Industry*, 96 (January 2005), 45–54.

4 Jelly Belly Candy Company (March 6, 2008). "April Fools' Day: Bamboozle Someone with New Jelly Belly BeanBoozled Jelly Beans: A Fools Errand and Silly Celebrations." Press release.

5 "U.S. Coffee Makers Perky as Consumption Increases," *Nations Restaurant Business* 36 (April 22, 2002), 34; "U.S. Specialty Coffee Market in 30 Year Renaissance," (December 15, 2000), http://www.cnn.com.

6 Kafka, Peter, "Bean-Counter," *Forbes* 175 (February 28, 2005), 78–80.

7 Adapted from "DuPont Employee Survey Finds Eldercare Emerging as Key Work/Life Issues," *PR Newswire* (January 2, 2001), 49–93.

8 Garvin, Andrew P., "Evolve Approach to Serve Complex Market," *Marketing News* (September 15, 2005), 22.

9 Gibson, Lawrence D., "Quo Vadis Marketing Research?" *Marketing Research* 12 (Spring 2000), 36–41.

10 Matthew, Arnold, "FDA Delays DTC Draft Guidance to Study How Consumers Use Brief Summaries," *Medical Marketing and Media* 39 (November 2004), 10.

11 Reyes, Sonia, "Ian Friendly: Groove Tube," *BrandWeek* (October 16, 2000), M111–M116.

12 Garretson, Judith and Scot Burton, "The Role of Spokescharacters as Advertisement and Package Cues in Integrated Marketing Communications," *Journal of Marketing* 69 (October 2005), 118–132.

13 Clancy, Kevin J. and Randy L. Stone, "Don't Blame the Metrics," *Harvard Business Review* 83 (June 2005), 26–28.

14 Honomichl, Jack, "Growth Stunt," *Marketing News* (June 4, 2001), 144.

15 "You Say Tomato, I Say Tomahto," *Express Magazine* (Spring 2006), 19.

Chapter 2

1 Collett, Stacy, "External Business Intelligence Can Be a Powerful Addition to Your Data Warehouse, but Beware of Data Overload," *Computerworld* (April 15, 2002), 34; "Krispy Kreme to Open Stores in China," *Atlanta Business Chronicle* (October 9, 2008), http://atlanta.bizjournals.com/atlanta/stories/2008/10/06/daily56.html.

2 See Albers, Brad, "Home Depot's Special Projects Support Team Powers Information Management for Business Needs," *Journal of Organizational Excellence* 21 (Winter 2001), 3–15; Songini, Marc L., "Home Depot's Next IT Project: Data Warehouse," *Computerworld* 36 (October 7, 2002), 1–2.

3 LaBahn, Douglass W. and Robert Krapfel, "Early Supplier Involvement in Customer New Product Development: A Contingency Model of Component Supplier Intentions," *Journal of Business Research* 47 (March 2000), 173–190.

4 Tay, Nicholas S. P. and Robert F. Lusch, "A Preliminary Test of Hunt's General Theory of Competition: Using Artificial Adaptive Agents to Study Complex and Ill-Defined Environments," *Journal of Business Research* 58 (September 2005), 1155–1168.

5 Knapp, Ellen M., "Knowledge Management," *Business and Economic Review* (July–September 1998), 3–6.

6 Sherman, D. J., D. Berkowitz, and W. E. Soulder, "New Product Development Performance and the Interaction of Cross-Functional Integration and Knowledge Management," *Journal of Product Innovation Management* 22 (September 2005), 399–411.

7 Chonko, L. B., A. J. Dubinsky, E. Jones, and J. A. Roberts, "Organizational and Individual Learning in the Sales Force: An Agenda for Sales Research," *Journal of Business Research* 56 (December 2003), 935–946.

8 "Benefits of RFID Becoming More Visible," *DSN Retailing Today* (August 8, 2005), 22.

9 Hall, Mark, "Seeding for Data Growth," *Computerworld* 36 (April 15, 2002), 52.

10 Angwein, J. and Delaney, K. J., "Top Web Sites Build Up Ad Backlog, Raise Rates," *Wall Street Journal* (November 16, 2005), A1.

11 Gale Annual Directory of Databases, Gale Research Inc.: Detroit.

12 Patrick A. Moore and Ronald Milliman, "Application of the Internet in Marketing Education," (paper presented at the Southwest Marketing Association, Houston, Texas, 1995).

13 Geng, X., M. B. Stinchcombe, and A. B. Whinston, "Radically New Product Introduction Using On-Line Auctions," *Journal of Electronic Commerce* 5 (Spring 2001), 169–189.

14 "A Better Web Through Higher Math" *Business Week Online* (January 2, 2002), http://www.businessweek.com (accessed November 12, 2005).

15 Rangaswamy, Arvind and G. Lilien, "Software Tools for New Product Development," *Journal of Marketing Research* 34 (February 1997), 177–184.

16 Desouza, Kevin and Yukika Awazu, "Maintaining Knowledge Management Systems: A Strategic Imperative," *Journal of the American Society for Information Science and Technology* 56 (May 2005), 765–768.

17 Rangaswamy, Arvind and G. Lilien (1997).

18 Close, A. G., A. Dixit and N. Malhotra, "Chalkboards to Cybercourses: The Internet and Marketing Education," *Marketing Education Review* 15 (Summer 2005), 81–94.

19 Adapted with permission from deJony, Jennifer, "View from the Top," *Technology* 1 (1995), downloaded from the Internet July 3, 1998.

Chapter 3

1 Cox, Reavis, Wroe Alderson, and Stanley J. Shapiro, *Theory in Marketing* (Chicago: American Marketing Association, 1964), 20.

2 Babin, B. J., D. M. Hardesty, and T. A. Suter, "Color and Shopping Intentions: The Effect of Price Fairness and Perceived Affect," *Journal of Business Research* 56 (July 2003) 541–551.

3 Robert Dubin, *Theory Building* (New York: Free Press, 1969), 9.

4 http://the-web-tycoon.com/blog/2009/08/the-budget-constraint-of-consumers-new-release-about-economy-and-business/.

5 Pietrobon, Ricardo, Marcus Taylor, Ulrich Guller, Laurence D. Higgins, Danny O. Jacobs, and Timothy Carey, "Predicting Gender Differences as Latent Variables: Summed Scores, and Individual Item Responses: A Methods Case Study," *Health and Quality of Life Outcomes* (2004), 2–59.

6 Robert Bartels, *Marketing Theory and Metatheory* (Chicago: American Marketing Association, 1970), 6.

7 Hull, Clark L., *A Behavioral System* (New York: John Wiley & Sons, 1952), 1.

8 Based on Ellen J. Jackofsky, "Turnover and Job Performance: An Integrated Process Model," *Academy of Management Review 9*, No. 1 (1984), p. 78; and Paul Solomon, "Reducing Unwanted Staff Turnovers in Public Accounting: An Action Plan," *Northern California Executive Review* (Spring 1986), pp. 22–25.

9 Karl Popper, *Conjectures and Refutations* (London: Routledge and Keagan Paul, 1963).

10 Kerlinger, Fred N., *Behavioral Research: A Conceptual Approach* (New York: Holt, Rinehart and Winston, 1979), 3.

11 From Tucker, W. T., *Foundation for a Theory of Consumer Behavior* (New York: Holt, Rinehart and Winston, 1967), v–vii.

12 Zaltman, Gerald, Christian Pinson, and Reinhart Angelmar, *Metatheory and Consumer Research* (New York: Holt, Rinehart and Winston, 1972), 12–13.

13 From Pirsig, Robert M., *Zen and the Art of Motorcycle Maintenance* (New York: Harper Collins Publishing), (© 1974), 107–111.

Chapter 4

1 This section is based in part on Richard Draft, *Management* (Hillsdale, IL: Dryden Press, 1994).

2 Zahay, Debra, Abbie Griffin, and Elisa Fredericks, "Sources, Uses, and Forms of Data in the New Product Development Process," *Industrial Marketing Management* 33 (October 2004), 658–666.

3 Hara,Yoshika, "New Industry Awaits Human-Friendly Bipeds—'Personal Robots' get Ready to Walk on the Human Side," *Electronic Engineering Times* (September 16, 2002), 157–159.

4 Bocchi, Joe, Jacqueline K. Eastman, and Cathy Owens Swift, "Retaining the Online Learner: Profile of Students in an Online MBA Program and Implications for Teaching Them," *Journal of Education for Business* (March/April 2004), 245–253.

5 Janoff, Barry, "Brands of the Land," *BrandWeek* (April 20, 2001), 28.

6 Bocchi, Eastman and Swift (2004); Carr, S., "As Distance Education Comes of Age, the Challenge Is Keeping the Students," *Chronicle of Higher Education* (2000), 23, A1; Moskal, P. D. and C. G. Dziuban, "Present and Future Directions for Assessing Cybereducation: The Changing Research Paradigm," in L. R. Vandervert, L. V. Chavinina, and R. A. Cornell, Eds., *Cybereducation: The Future of Long-Distance Learning* (New York: P. D. Moskal and C. G. Dziuban, Liebert, 2001), 157–184.

7 Read, Melissa, "Ice Cream Purchases and Murder Rates—Correlation Does Not Imply Causation" Spunlogic Blog (February 5th, 2007), http://blog.spunlogic.com/index.php/2007/02/05/ice-cream-purchases-and-murder-rates-correlation-does-not-imply-causation/.

8 Thomas, Jerry W., "Skipping MR a Major Error," *Marketing News* (March 4, 2005), 50.

9 Einstein, A. and L. Infeld, *The Evolution of Physics* (New York: Simon and Schuster, 1942), 95.

10 Perdue, B. C. and J. O. Summers, "Checking the Success of Manipulations in Marketing Experiments," *Journal of Marketing Research* 23 (November 1986), 317–326.

11 See, for example, Kwok, S. and M. Uncles, "Sales Promotion Effectiveness: The Impact of Consumer Differences at an Ethnic-Group Level," *Journal of Product and Brand Management* 14, no. 3 (2005), 170–186.

12 Approximate exchange rates as of January 25, 2009.

13 Crowley, Michael, "Conservatives (Finally) Rejoice," *New Republic* (2004) 231, 13–14.

Chapter 5

1 Kinnear, Thomas C. and Ann Root, Eds., *Survey of Marketing Research* (Chicago: American Marketing Association, 1994).

2 Blembach, J. and K. Clancy, "Boy, Oh Boy!" *Adweek* 21 (September 25, 2000), 16, Southeastern Edition.

3 See Armstrong, J. S., "Why Do We Know? Predicting the Interests and Opinions of the American Consumer," *Journal of Forecasting* 5 (September 1989), 464.

4 See John, Joby and Mark Needel, "Entry-Level Marketing Research Recruits: What Do Recruiters Need?" *Journal of Marketing Education* (Spring 1989), 68–73.

5 See Izzo, G. Martin and Scott J. Vitell, "Exploring the Effects of Professional Education on Salespeople: The Case of Autonomous Agents," *Journal of Marketing Theory & Practice* 11 (Fall 2003), 26–38; Loe, Terry and William A. Weeks, "An Empirical Investigation of Efforts to Improve Sales Students' Moral Reasoning," *Journal of Personal Selling and Sales Management* 20 (Fall 2000), 243–252.

6 Barnett, Tim and Sean Valentino, "Issue Contingencies and Marketers' Recognition of Ethical Issues, Ethical Judgments and Behavioral Intentions," *Journal of Business Research* 57 (April 2004), 338–346.

7 Robin, D. P., R. E. Reidenbach, and B. J. Babin, "The Nature, Measurement and Stability of Ethical Judgments in the Workplace," *Psychological Reports* 80 (1997), 563–580.

8 Gillin, Donna L., "The Evolution of Privacy Legislation: How Privacy Issues Are Changing Research," *Marketing Research* 13 (Winter 2001), 6–7.

9 Jarvis, Steve, "CMOR Finds Survey Refusal Rate Still Rising," *Marketing News* 36 (February 4, 2002), 4.

10 Gillin, Donna L., "The Evolution of Privacy Legislation: How Privacy Issues Are Changing Research," *Marketing Research* 13 (Winter 2001), 6–7.

11 Spangenberg, E., B. Grohmann, and D. E. Sprott, "It's Beginning to Smell (and Sound) a Lot Like Christmas: The Interactive Effects of Ambient Scent and Music in a Retail Setting," *The Journal of Business Research* 58 (November 2005), 582–589; Michon, Richard, Jean-Charles Chebat, and L. W. Turley, "Mall Atmospherics: The Interaction Effects of the Mall Environment on Shopping Behavior," *Journal of Business Research* 58 (May 2005), 576–583.

12 Carrigan, M. and M. Kirkup, "The Ethical Responsibilities of Marketers in Retail Observational Research: Protecting Stakeholders through the 'Ethical Research' Covenant," *International Journal of Retail, Distribution and Consumer Research* 11 (October 2001), 411–435.

13 "Marketers Value Honesty in Marketing Researchers," *Marketing News* 29 (June 5, 1995), 27.

14 Brennan, M., S. Benson, and Z. Kearns, "The Effect, of Introductions on Telephone Survey Participation Rates," *International Journal of Market Research* 47, no. 1 (2005), 65–74.

15 http://www.cyprusmarketing.com/artcateg_privacy-policy.

16 Mack, Beth, "Online Privacy Critical to Research Success," *Marketing News* 36 (November 25, 2002), 21.

Chapter 6

1 Gibson, Lawrence D., "Defining Marketing Problems: Don't Spin Your Wheels Solving the Wrong Puzzle," *Marketing Research* 10 (Spring 1998), 4–12.

2 "What's New in Your Industry," *Business China* 30 (February 16, 2004), 8–9.

3 Chapman, Randall G., "Problem Definition in Marketing Research Studies," *Journal of Consumer Marketing* 6 (Spring 1989), 51–59; Yang, Yoo S., Robert P. Leone, and Dala L. Aldaen, "A Market Expansion Ability Approach to Identify Potential Exporters," *Journal of Marketing* 56 (January 1992), 84–96.

4 Ackoff, Russell L., *The Scientific Method* (New York: Wiley, 1962), 71.

5 Majchrzak, A., L. P. Cooper, and O. E. Neece, "Knowedge Reuse for Innovation," *Management Science* 50 (February 2004), 174–188.

6 Gibson, Lawrence D. (1988).

7 Gibson, Lawrence D. (1988).

8 Chapman, Randall G. (1989).

9 Holbert, N. B., "Research: The Ways of Academe and Business," *Business Horizons* (February 1976), 38.

10 Honomichl, Jack, "ICR/International Communications Research," *Marketing News* 36 (June 11, 2002), 47.

11 Excerpt reprinted with permission from Paul E. Green, Abba M. Krieger, and Terry G. Varra, "Evaluating New Products," *Marketing Research: A Magazine of Management and Applications* (Winter 1997), 17–18.

Chapter 7

1 Cassidy, Hilary, "Many Paths to Cool, but big Gains for All," *Brandweek* 46 (June 20, 2005), S53.

2 Niemi, Wayne, "Schoenfeld to Leave as Vans CEO; As Its Deal with VF Corp. Closes, the Skate Brand Gains a New President and a New Focus on Apparel," *Footwear News* (July 5, 2004), 2.

3 McLaughlin, Lisa, "The New Roll Model," *Time* 164 (July 26, 2004), 74.

4 Sayre, Shay, *Qualitative Methods for Marketplace Research* (Thousand Oaks, CA: Sage, 2001).

5 Sayre, Shay, (2001); Morse, Janice M. and Lyn Richards, *Readme First for a User's Guide to Qualitative Methods* (Thousand Oaks, CA: Sage, 2002).

6 See, for example, May, Carl, "Methodological Pluralism: British Sociology and the Evidence-Based State: A Reply to Payne et al.," *Sociology* 39 (July 2005), 519–528; Achenbaum, A. A., "When Good Research Goes Bad," *Marketing Research* 13 (Winter 2001), 13–15; Wade, K. R., "We Have Come Upon the Enemy: And They Are Us," *Marketing Research* 14 (Summer 2002), 39; Neill, James, "Qualitative versus

Quantitative Research: Key Points in a Classic Debate," http://wilderdom.com/research/QualitativeVersusQuantitativeResearch.html, accessed February 6, 2009.

7 Babin, Barry J., William R. Darden, and Mitch Griffin, "Work and/or Fun: Measuring Hedonic and Utilitarian Shopping Value," *Journal of Consumer Research* 20 (March 1994), 644–656.

8 Stengal, J. R., A. L. Dixon, and C. T. Allen, "Listening Begins at Home," *Harvard Business Review* (November 2003), 106–116.

9 Semon, Thomas T., "You Get What You Pay for: It May Be Bad MR," *Marketing News* 36 (April 15, 2002), 7.

10 Thompson, Craig J., "Interpreting Consumers: A Hermeneutical Framework for Deriving Marketing Insights from the Tests of Consumers' Consumption Stories," *Journal of Marketing Research* 34 (November 1997), 438–455; Woodside, Arch G., H. M. Pattinson, and K. E. Miller, "Advancing Hermeneutic Research for Interpreting Interfirm New Product Development," *Journal of Business and Industrial Marketing* 20 (2005) 364–379.

11 Thompson, Craig J., "Interpreting Consumers: A Hermeneutical Framework for Deriving Marketing Insights from the Tests of Consumers' Consumption Stories," *Journal of Marketing Research* 34 (November 1997), 438–455 (see pp. 443–444 for quotation).

12 While we refer to a hermeneutic unit as being text-based here for simplicity, they can actually also be developed using pictures, videotapes, or artifacts as well. Software such as Atlas-TI will allow files containing pictures, videos, and text to be combined into a hermeneutic unit.

13 Morse, Janice M. and Lyn Richards (2002).

14 See Feldman, Stephen P., "Playing with the Pieces: Deconstruction and the Loss of Moral Culture," *Journal of Management Studies* 35 (January 1998), 60–80.

15 "Futurespeak," *American Demographics* 26 (April 2004), 44.

16 Louella, Miles, "Living Their Lives," *Marketing* (UK) (December 11, 2003), 27–28.

17 Reid, D. M., "Changes in Japan's Post-Bubble Business Environment: Implications for Foreign-Affiliated Companies," *Journal of International Marketing* 7, no. 3 (1999), 38–63.

18 Morse, Janice M. and Lyn Richards (2002).

19 Strauss, A. L. and J. Corbin, *Basics of Qualitative Research* (Newbury Park, CA: Sage Publications, 1990).

20 Glaser, B. G., and Strauss, A. L., *The Discovery of Grounded Theory: Strategies for Qualitative Research.* (New York: Aldine Publishing Company, 1967).

21 Geiger, S. and D. Turley, "Personal Selling as a Knowledge-Based Activity: Communities of Practice in the Sales Force," *Irish Journal of Management* 26 (2005), 61–70.

22 Beverland, M., "The Components of Prestige Brands," *Journal of Business Research* 59 (February 2006) 251–258; Beverland, M., "Brand Value, Convictions, Flexibility and New Zealand Wine," *Business Horizons* 47 (September/October 2004), 53–61.

23 Harwood, Jonathan, "Philip Morris Develops Smokeless Cigarette," *Marketing Week* 28 (March 31, 2005), 5.

24 Creamer, Mathew, "Slowly, Marketers Learn How to Let Go and Let Blog," *Advertising Age* 76 (October 31, 2005), 1–35.

25 Fass, Allison, "Collective Opinion," *Forbes* 176 (November 28, 2005), 76–79.

26 O'Loughlin, Sandra, "Real Women Have Lingerie," *Brandweek* 46 (November 14, 2005), 22–24.

27. Performance Monitoring and Evaluation Tips, USAID Center for Development Information and Evaluation, http://gametlibrary.worldbank.org/FILES/218_M&E tips Conducting focus group interviews.pdf.

28 See Palan, K. M. and R. E. Wilkes, "Adolescent-Parent Interaction in Family Decision Making," *Journal of Consumer Research* 24 (September 1997), 159–170; Haytko, Diana L. and Julie Baker, "It's All at the Mall: Exploring Adolescent Girls' Experiences," *Journal of Retailing* 80 (Spring 2004), 67–83.

29 Godes, David and Dina Mayzlin "Using On-Line Conversations to Study Word-of-Mouth Communications," *Marketing Science* 23 (2004), 545–560.

30 Babin, Barry J., William R. Darden and James S. Boles, "Salesperson Stereotypes, Consumer Emotions, and Their Impact on Information Processing," *Journal of the Academy of Marketing Science* 23 (Spring 1995), 94–105.

31 Murphy, Ian, "Aided by Research, Harley Goes Whole Hog," *Marketing News* 30 (December 2, 1996), 16–17.

32 Philip Kotler, "Behavioral Models for Analyzing Buyers," *Journal of Marketing* (October 1965), pp. 37–45.

33 Alsop, Ronald, "Advertisers Put Consumers on the Couch," *Wall Street Journal* (May 13, 1998), 19.

34 Huxley, John, "Horrific, but Not the Worst We've Suffered." *Sydney Morning Herald* (February 11, 2009).

Chapter 8

1 The North American Industry Classification System (NAICS), http://www.census.gov/eos/www/naics/.

2 "Breakfast Sandwich Boom," *Chain Leader* (November 2005), http://web2.infotrac.galegroup.com; Perlik, Allison,"Fast Starts," *Restaurants & Institutions* (January 15, 2006), http://web2.infotrac.galegroup.com.

3 Grow, Brian, "Yes, Ma'am, That Part Is in Stock," *BusinessWeek* (August 1, 2005), http://web2.infotrac.galegroup.com; and Servigistics, "Servigistics Pricing: Maximizing the Profitability of Your Service Network," http://www.servigistics.com, accessed February 7, 2006.

4 Prasso, Sheridan, "Battle for the Face of China," *Fortune* (December 12, 2005), http://web2.infotrac.galegroup.com.

5 Charles, Susan K., "Custom Content Delivery," *Online Magazine* (March–April 2004), http://galenet.galegroup.com; Fleming, Lee, "Digital Delivery: Pushing Content to the Desktop," *Digital Information Group* (January 31, 1997); "How Smart Agents Will Change Selling," *Forbes ASAP* (August 28, 1995), 95.

6 "Seeking New Beer Drinkers in the High Andes," *Global Agenda* (July 20, 2005), http://galenet.galegroup.com; "China Ranked Largest Beer Consumer in 2004," *Kyodo News International* (December 15, 2005), http://galenet.galegroup.com.

7 This section is based on Levy, Michael and Barton Weitz, *Retail Management* (Homewood, IL: Richard D. Irwin, 1992), 357–358.

8 Data from the "About Us" section of the Capital One Web site, http://www.capitalone.com, accessed February 9, 2006.

9 Rao, Srikumar S., "Technology: The Hot Zone," *Forbes* (November 18, 1996).

10 IBM Business Intelligence Data Mining Product Discovery, http://www.ibm.com.

11 Wasserman,Todd, Gerry Khermouch and Jeff Green, "Mining Everyone's Business," *Brandweek* (February 28, 2000), 34.

12 "Clients: Case Studies," DataMind Web site, http://www.datamind.com, accessed February 6, 2006.

13 Totty, Michael, "Making Searches Work at Work," *Wall Street Journal* (December 19, 2005), http://online.wsj.com.

14 "Hispanic-Owned Businesses: Growth Projections, 2004–2010," HispanicBusiness.com Store, http://www.hbinc.com, accessed February 7, 2006.

15 Neff, Jack, "Wal-Mart Takes Stock in RetailLink System," *Advertising Age* (May 21, 2001), 6.

16 http://www.usb-port.com/usbscanners.html.

17 See Federal Grants Wire, "National Trade Data Bank (NTDB)," http://www.federalgrantswire.com, accessed February 6, 2006; and STATUSA, "What Information Is Available under GLOBUS and NTBD?" and "GLOBUS & NTDB," http://www.stat-usa.gov, accessed February 6, 2006.

18 Based on Brown, Warren, "Pain at the Pump Doesn't Faze New-Car Buyers," *Washington Post* (January 29, 2006), http://www.washingtonpost.com; Wells, Melanie, "Snowboarding Secrets," *Forbes* (February 14, 2005), http://web5.infotrac.galegroup.com; Halliday, Jean, "Automakers Scrap SUVs, Tout Hybrids," *Advertising Age* (September 26, 2005), http://web5.infotrac.galegroup.com.

Chapter 9

1 "About In-Stat," In-Stat, http://www.instat.com/index.asp; Nissen, Keith, "In-Depth Analysis: The Media Phone Has Arrived!" In-Stat, http://www.instat.com/promos/09/dl/media_phone_3ufewaCr.pdf.

2 http://www.samsung.com/in/consumer/mobile-phone/mobile-phone/index.idx?pagetype=type_p2&.

3 Vascellaro, Jessica E., "Who'll Give Me $50 for This Purse from Nana?" *Wall Street Journal* (December 28, 2005), http://online.wsj.com; "Survey Reveals Majority of Americans Receive Unwanted Gifts," Survey.com news release (December 19, 2005), http://www.survey.com.

4 Excerpts from Arlen, Michael J., *Thirty Seconds* (New York: Farrar, Straus and Giroux, Inc., 1979, 1980), 185–186.This material first appeared in the *New Yorker*.

5 However, the popularity of marketing research has affected the willingness of respondents to participate in surveys. People are increasingly refusing to participate.

6 Tuckel, Peter and Harry O'Neill, "The Vanishing Respondent in Telephone Surveys," (paper presented at the 56th annual conference of the American Association of Public Opinion Research [AAPOR], Montreal, Canada, May 17–20, 2001).

7 Cull, William L., Karen G. O'Connor, Sanford Sharp, and Suk-fong S.Tang, "Response Rates and Response Bias for 50 Surveys of Pediatricians," *Health Services Research* (February 2005), downloaded from http://galenet.galegroup.com.

8 Lee, Eunkyu, Michael Y. Hu, and Rex S. Toh, "Respondent Noncooperation in Surveys and Diaries: An Analysis of Item Non-Response and Panel Attrition," *International Journal of Market Research* (Autumn 2004), downloaded from http://web7.infotrac.galegroup.com.

9 Douglas Aircraft, Consumer Research (undated), p. 13.

10 For an interesting study of extremity bias, see Baumgartner, Hans and Jan-Benedict E. M. Steenkamp, "Response Styles in Marketing Research: A Cross-National Investigation," *Journal of Marketing Research* (May 2001), 143–156.

11 Turner, Charles F., Maria A. Villarroel, James R. Chromy, Elizabeth Eggleston, and Susan M. Rogers, "Same-Gender Sex among U.S. Adults: Trends across the Twentieth Century and during the 1990s," *Public Opinion Quarterly* (Fall 2005), downloaded from http://web7.infotrac.galegroup.com.

12 The term *questionnaire* technically refers only to mail and self-administered surveys, and the term *interview schedule* is used for interviews by telephone or face-to-face. However, we will use *questionnaire* to refer to all three forms of communications in this book.

13 Sobel, Bill, "Poll Reveals Men More Likely Than Women to Keep Their New Year's Resolutions" (December 29, 2008), http://www.sobelmedia.com/2008/12/29/poll-reveals-men-more-likely-than-women-to-keep-their-new-years-resolutions, accessed March 30, 2009.

14 Ohlemacher, Stephen, "Study Finds That Marriage Builds Wealth," Yahoo! News (January 18, 2006), http://news.yahoo.com; Charles Pierret, "The National Longitudinal Survey of Youth: 1979 Cohort at 25," *Monthly Labor Review* (February 2005), 3–7.

15 The Bureau of Business Practice, *Profiles in Quality: Blueprints for Action from 50 Leading Companies* (Boston: Allyn and Bacon, 1991), 113.

16 Weisberg, Karen, "Change Maker," *Food Service Director* (January 15, 2006), downloaded from http://web7.infotrac.galegroup.com.

17 Gavin, David A., "Competing on the Eight Dimensions of Quality," *Harvard Business Review* (November–December 1987), 101–8.

18 Forelle, Charles, "Many Colleges Ignore New SAT Writing Test," *Wall Street Journal* (December 7, 2005), http://online.wsj.com; "Kaplan's New SAT Survey Results," Kaplan Inc., College Admissions, Kaplan Web site, http://www.kaptest.com, accessed February 14, 2006.

Chapter 10

1 Warwick, Donald T. and Charles A. Lininger, *The Sample Survey: Theory and Practice* (New York: McGraw-Hill, 1975), 2.

2 Lockley, L. C., "Notes on the History of Marketing Research," *Journal of Marketing* (April 1950), 733.

3 Hof, Robert D., "The Power of Us," *BusinessWeek* (June 20, 2005), http://web2.infotrac.galegroup.com.

4 For a complete discussion of conducting surveys in Hispanic neighborhoods, see Hernandes, Sigfredo A. and Carol J. Kaufman, "Marketing Research in Hispanic Barrios: A Guide to Survey Research," *Marketing Research* (March 1990), 11–27.

5 Curtin, Richard, Stanley Presser, and Eleanor Singer, "Changes in Telephone Survey Nonresponse over the Past Quarter Century," *Public Opinion Quarterly* (Spring 2005), http://web3.infotrac.galegroup.com.

6 Cuneo, Alice Z., "Researchers Flail as Public Cuts the Cord," *Advertising Age* (November 15, 2004), http://web3.infotrac.galegroup.com.

7 See ibid.; and Jon Kamman, "Cell Phones Put Pollsters 'in a Muddle,'" *USA Today* (December 31, 2003), http://www.usatoday.com.

8 Hembroff, Larry A., Debra Rusz, Ann Rafferty, Harry McGee, and Nathaniel Ehrlich, "The Cost-Effectiveness of Alternative Advance Mailings in a Telephone Survey," *Public Opinion Quarterly* (Summer 2005), http://web3.infotrac.galegroup.com.

9 Brennan, Mike, Susan Benson, and Zane Kearns, "The Effect of Introductions on Telephone Survey Participation Rates," *International Journal of Market Research* 47, no. 1 (2005), 65–74.

10 Dillman, Don A., *Mail and Internet Surveys: The Tailored Design Method* (New York: John Wiley and Sons, 2000), 173.

11 Schaefer, David R. and Don A. Dillman, "Development of a Standard E-Mail Methodology: Results of an Experiment," *Public Opinion Quarterly* 62, no. 3 (Fall 1998), 378.

12 Ibid.

13 For a complete discussion of fax surveys, see the excellent article by Dickson, John P. and Douglas L. Maclachlan, "Fax Surveys: Return Patterns and Comparison with Mail Surveys," *Journal of Marketing Research* (February 1996), 108–113.

14 Merriman, Joyce A., "Your Feedback Is Requested," *American Family Physician* (October 1, 2005), http://web3.infotrac.galegroup.com.

15 Dillmann, D. A. (2000), 369–372.

16 Göritz, Anja S., "Recruitment for On-Line Access Panels," *International Journal of Market Research* 46, no. 4, (2004), 411–425.

17 Fricker, Scott, Mirta Galesic, Roger Tourangeau, and Ting Yan, "An Experimental Comparison of Web and Telephone Surveys," *Public Opinion Quarterly* (Fall 2005), http://web3.infotrac.galegroup.com.

18 See Nielsen, Jakob, "Keep Online Surveys Short," *Alertbox* (February 2, 2004), http://www.useit.com; "About Jakob Nielsen," http://www.useit.com, accessed February 21, 2006; and Nielsen Norman Group, "About Nielsen Norman Group," http://www.nngroup.com, accessed February 21, 2006.

19 See Kilbourne, Lawrene, "Avoid the Field of Dreams Fallacy," *Quirk's Marketing Research Review* (January 2005), 70, 72–73.

20 Mary Lisbeth D'Amico, "Call Security," *Wall Street Journal* (February 13, 2006), http://online.wsj.com.

21 For an interesting empirical study, see Akaah, Ishmael P. and Edward A. Riordan, "The Incidence of Unethical Practices in Marketing Research: An Empirical Investigation," *Journal of the Academy of Marketing Sciences* (Spring 1990), 143–152.

22 Based on "Do-Not-Call List Reduces Telemarketing, Poll Finds," *Wall Street Journal* (January 12, 2006), http://online.wsj.com.

Chapter 11

1 Four Seasons Hotel Chicago, http://www.fourseasons.com/chicagofs/dining.html; Mystery Shopping Providers Association, http://www.mysteryshop.org; Michelson, M., "Taking the Mystery Out of Mystery Shopping," Mystery Shopping Providers Association, www.mspa-eu.org/about/MysteryShopping1.ppt.

2 Selltiz, Claire, Lawrence S. Wrightsman, and Stuart W. Cook, *Research Methods in Social Relations* (New York: Holt, Rinehart and Winston, 1976), 251.

3 Campbell, Angus, Philip E. Converse, and Willard L. Rodgers, *The Quality of American Life* (New York: Russell Sage Foundation, 1976), 112. Although weather conditions did not correlate with perceived quality of life, the comfort variable did show a relationship with the index of wellbeing. This association might be confounded by the fact that ventilation and/or air-conditioning equipment is less common in less affluent homes. Income was previously found to correlate with quality of life.

4 Abrams, Bill, *The Observational Research Handbook* (Chicago: NTC Business Books, 2000), 2, 105.

5 Adapted with permission from the April 30, 1980, issue of *Advertising Age*. Copyright © 1980 by Crain Communications, Inc.

6 "Inside TV Ratings," Nielsen Media Research, http://www.nielsenmedia.com, accessed February 21, 2009.

7 "The Portable People Meter System," Arbitron, http://www.arbitron.com, accessed February 24, 2006.

8 "About the PreTesting Company" and "Television," PreTesting Company, http://www.pretesting.com, accessed February 24, 2006.

9 "Accurate Web Site Visitor Measurement Crippled by Cookie Blocking and Deletion," Jupiter Media news release, (March 14, 2005), http://www.jupitermedia.com; See also Johnson, Steve, "Who's in Charge of the Web Site Ratings Anyway?" *Chicago Tribune* (February 26, 2006), sec. 1, p. 18.

10 Kiley, David, "Google: Searching for an Edge in Ads," *BusinessWeek* (January 30, 2006), downloaded from http://web3.infotrac.galegroup.com; See also Sanders, Pieter and Bram Lebo, "Click Tracking: A Fool's Paradise?" *Brandweek* (June 6, 2005), http://web3.infotrac.galegroup.com.

11 Neff, Jack, "Aging Population Brushes Off Coloring," *Advertising Age* (July 25, 2005), downloaded from http://web5.infotrac.galegroup.com.

12 Stringer, Kortney, "Eye-Tracking Technology for Marketers," *Detroit Free Press* (August 1, 2005), downloaded from http://galenet.galegroup.com.

13 Herbert B. Krugman's statement as quoted in "Live, Simultaneous Study of Stimulus, Response Is Physiological Measurement's Great Virtue," *Marketing News* (May 15, 1981), 1, 20.

14 Based on "Mazda Turns to Eye-Tracking to Assist Revamp of European Site," *New Media Age* (November 3, 2005), downloaded from http://galenet.galegroup.com; and "Persuasion Is the New Focus," *Revolution* (February 21, 2006), downloaded from the Media Coverage page of the Syzygy Web site, http://www.syzygy.co.uk.

15 Adapted with permission from Rayner, Bruce, "Product Development, Now Hear This!" *Electronic Business* (August 1997).

Chapter 12

1 Kohlhoff, C. and R. Steele, "Evaluating SOAP for High Performance Business Applications: Real-Time Trading Systems." Proceedings of WWW2003, May 20–24, 2003, Budapest, Hungary, accessed from http://staff.it.uts.edu.au/~rsteele/EvaluatingSOAP.pdf.

2 Based on McNatt, D. Brian and Timothy A. Judge, "Self-Efficacy Intervention, Job Attitudes, and Turnover: A Field Experiment with Employees in Role Transition," *Human Relations* 61, no. 6 (June 2008), 783–810,

3 Shadish, William R., Thomas D. Cook, and Donald T. Campbell, *Experimental and Quasi Experimental Designs for Generalized Causal Inference* (Geneva, IL: Houghton Mifflin, 2002).
4 Ellingstad, Vernon and Norman W. Heimstra, *Methods in the Study of Human Behavior* (Monterey, CA: Brooks/Cole, 1974).
5 Anderson, Barry F., *The Psychological Experiment: An Introduction to the Scientific Method* (Belmont, CA: Brooks/Cole, 1971), 28, 42–44.
6 Reitter, Robert N., "Comment: American Media and the Smoking-Related Behaviors of Asian Adolescents," *Journal of Advertising Research* 43 (March 2003), 12–13.
7 Lach, Jennifer, "Up in Smoke," *American Demographics* 22 (March 2000), 26.
8 Mitchell, Vincent-Wayne and Sarah Haggett, "Sun-Sign Astrology in Market Segmentation: An Empirical Investigation," *Journal of Consumer Marketing* 14, no. 2 (1997), 113–131.
9 Roethlisberger, F. J. and W. J. Dickson, *Management and the Worker* (Harvard University Press: Cambridge, MA, 1939).
10 Shiv, Baba, Ziv Carmon, and Dan Aneley, "Placebo Effects of Marketing Actions: Consumers May Get What They Pay for," *Journal of Marketing Research* 42 (November 2005), 383–393.
11 Tybout, Alice M. and Gerald Zaltman, "Ethics in Marketing Research: Their Practical Relevance," *Journal of Marketing Research* 21 (November 1974), 357–368.
12 http://telecomtalk.info/bsnl-ties-up-with-indian-railways-to-promote-3g-services/30072/.
13 Peterson, Robert A., "On the Use of Students in Social Science Research: Evidence from a Second Order Meta Analysis," *Journal of Consumer Research* 28 (December 2001), 450–461.
14 Shadish, William R., Thomas D. Cook, and Donald T. Campbell (2002).
15 Reprinted with permission from Lee Martin, Geoffrey "Drinkers Get Court Call," *Advertising Age* (May 20, 1991). Copyright © 1991 Crain Communications, Inc.

Chapter 13

1 Babin, Barry J. and Jill Attaway, "Atmospheric Affect as a Tool for Creating Value and Gaining Share of Customer," *Journal of Business Research* 49 (August 2000), 91–99; Verhoef, P. C., "Understanding the Effect of Customer Relationship Management Efforts on Customer Retention and Customer Share Development," *Journal of Marketing* 67 (October 2003), 30–45.
2 Periatt, J. A., S. A. LeMay, and S. Chakrabarty, "The Selling Orientation-Customer Orientation (SOCO) Scale: Cross-Validation of the Revised Version," *Journal of Personal Selling and Sales Management* 24 (Winter 2004), 49–54.
3 Anderson, Barry F., *The Psychology Experiment*. (Monterey, CA: Brooks/Cole, 1971), 26.
4 Kerlinger, Fred N., *Foundations of Behavioral Research* (New York: Holt, Rinehart and Winston, 1973).
5 Cohen, Jacob, "Things I Have Learned (So Far)," *American Psychologist* 45 (December 1990), 1304–1312.
6 Arnold, Catherine, "Satisfaction's the Name of the Game," *Marketing News* 38 (October 15, 2004), 39–45. Also, see http://www.theacsi.org.
7 In more advanced applications such as those involving structural equations analysis, a distinction can be made between reflective composites and formative indexes. See Hair, J. F., W. C. Black, B. J. Babin, R. Anderson, and R. Tatham, *Multivariate Data Analysis,* 6th ed. (Upper Saddle River, NJ: Prentice Hall, 2006).
8 Bart, Yakov, Venkatesh Shankar, Fareena Sultan, and Glen L. Urban, "Are the Drivers and Role of Online Trust the Same for All Web Sites and Consumers? A Large-Scale Exploratory Study," *Journal of Marketing* 69 (October 2005), 133–152.
9 Cronbach, Lee J. and Richard J. Shavelson, "My Current Thoughts on Coefficient Alpha and Successor Procedures," *Educational and Psychological Measurement* 64 (June 2004), http://epm.sagepub.com/cgi/content/short/64/3/391.
10 Hair et al. (2006).
11 Wells, Chris, "The War of the Razors," *Esquire* (February 1980), 3.
12 Babin, Barry J., William R. Darden, and Mitch Griffin, "Work and/or Fun: Measuring Hedonic and Utilitarian Shopping Value," *Journal of Consumer Research* 20 (March 1994), 644–656.
13 Hair et al. (2006).
14 Cox, Keith K. and Ben M. Enis, *The Marketing Research Process* (Pacific Palisades, CA: Goodyear, 1972); Kerlinger, Fred N., *Foundations of Behavioral Research,* 3rd ed. (Ft. Worth: Holt, Rinehart and Winston, 1986).
15 Headley, Dean E., Brent D. Bowen, and Jacqueline R. Liedtke. This case, originally titled "Navigating through Airline Quality," was reviewed and accepted for publication by the Society for Case Research.

Chapter 14

1 Anhalt, Karen Nickel, "Whiskas Campaign Recruits a Tiny Tiger," *Advertising Age International* (October 19, 1998), 41.
2 Breeden, Richard, "Owners, Executives Cite Small Firms' Advantages," *Wall Street Journal* (January 3, 2006), http://online.wsj.com; "SMB State of the Union Study," AllBusiness.com (Winter 2005), news and press page, http://www.allbusiness.com/press/barometer.pdf.
3 Likert, Rensis, "A Technique for the Measurement of Attitudes," *Archives of Psychology* 19 (1931), 44–53.
4 Osgood, Charles, George Suci, and Percy Tannenbaum, *The Measurement of Meaning* (Urbana: University of Illinois Press, 1957). Seven-point scales were used in the original work; however, subsequent researchers have modified the scale to have five points, nine points, and so on.
5 Menezes, Dennis and Norbert F. Elbert, "Alternative Semantic Scaling Formats for Measuring Store Image: An Evaluation," *Journal of Marketing Research* (February 1979), 80–87.
6 Costanzo, Chris, "How Consumer Research Drives Web Site Design," *American Banker* (April 19, 2005), http://galenet.galegroup.com.
7 "Technology Still Matters to Start-Ups Say Venture Capitalists and Other Industry Influencers," Rôeder-Johnson Corp. news release (January 24, 2006), http://finance.yahoo.com; "Importance of Unique Technology to Start-Up Companies: A Survey," Roeder-Johnson Corp. (January 2006), http://www.roederjohnson.com.

Chapter 15

1 White, Joseph B., "The Price of Safety," *Wall Street Journal* (December 5, 2005), http://online.wsj.com; "J.D. Power and Associates Reports: Premium Surround Sound Systems and HD Radio Garner High Consumer Interest Based on Their Market Price, while Consumers Prefer One-Time Fee over the Monthly Fee Associated with Satellite Radio," J.D. Power and Associates news release (August 18, 2005), http://www.jdpower.com.
2 Smith, Robert, David Olah, Bruce Hansen, and Dan Cumbo, "The Effect of Quesionnaire Length on Participant Response Rate: A Case Study in the U.S. Cabinet Industry," *Forest Products Journal* (November–December 2003), http://galenet.galegroup.com.
3 "Insurers Question Methods in U.S. Treasury Survey on Terror Backstop," *A. M. Best Newswire* (April 12, 2005), http://galenet.galegroup.com.
4 "Mothers Misunderstand Questions on Feeding Questionnaire," medical letter on the CDC and FDA (September 5, 2004), http://galenet.galegroup.com.
5 Donahue, Amy K. and Joanne M. Miller, "Citizen Preferences and Paying for Police," *Journal of Urban Affairs* 27, no. 4 (2005): 419–35.
6 Weber, Nathan, "Research: A Survey Shows How Media Influence Our Decorating and Cooking Choices," *HFN, the Weekly Newspaper for the Home Furnishing Network* (December 5, 2005), http://galenet.galegroup.com.
7 Payne, Stanley L., *The Art of Asking Questions* (Princeton, NJ: Princeton University Press, 1951), 185. The reader who wants a more detailed account of question wording is referred to this classic book on that topic.
8 Roll, Charles W., Jr. and Albert H. Cantril, *Polls: Their Use and Misuse in Politics* (New York: Basic Books, 1972), 106–7.
9 "Hilarious Republican Senate Leadership Survey," The Misanthropic Principle: The Blog of a Bipolar Misanthrope, http://misanthropicscott.wordpress.com/2008/04/19/hilarious-republican-senate-leadership-survey/, accessed March 9, 2009.
10 Payne, Stanley L. (1951), 102–3.
11 Dillman, Don A., *Mail and Internet Surveys: The Tailored Design Method* (New York: John Wiley and Sons, 2000), 357–61.
12 Young, Sarah J. and Craig M. Ross, "Web Questionnaires: A Glimpse of Survey Research in the Future," *Parks & Recreation* 35, no. 6 (June 2000), 30.
13 Michel, Matt "Controversy Redux," CASRO Journal, http://www.decisionanalyst.com/publ_art/contredux.htm, accessed February 8, 2001.
14 Ghaleb Almekhlafi, Abdurrahman, "Preservice Teachers' Attitudes and Perceptions of the Utility of Web-Based Instruction in the United Arab Emirates," *International Journal of Instructional Media* 32, no. 3 (2005): 269–84.
15 Harzing, Anne-Wil, "Does the Use of English-Language Questionnaires in Cross-National Research Obscure National Differences?" *International Journal of Cross Cultural Management* 5, no. 2 (2005): 213–24.
16 Cateora, Philip R., *International Marketing* (Homewood, IL: Richard D. Irwin, 1990), 387–89.
17 "Hospitals, Feds Design Survey to Identify Culture That Encourages Patient Safety," *Health Care Strategic*

Management (February 2005), http://galenet.galegroup.com; "Hospital Survey on Patient Safety Culture," Agency for Healthcare Research and Quality, http://www.ahrq.gov/qual/hospculture, accessed March 7, 2006.

Chapter 16

1 Jones, J. M., "Debt, Money Woes Are Top Family Financial Problems," Gallup Inc. (March 6, 2009), http://www.gallup.com.
2 Kinne, Susan and Tari D.Topolski, "Inclusion of People with Disabilities in Telephone Health Surveillance Surveys," *American Journal of Public Health* 95, no. 3 (March 2005): 512–517.
3 Brock, Sabra E., "Marketing Research in Asia: Problems, Opportunities, and Lessons," *Marketing Research* (September 1989), 47.
4 Yeganeh, Hamid, Zhan Su, Elie Virgile, and M. Chrysostome, "A Critical Review of Epistemological and Methodological Issues in Cross-Cultural Research," *Journal of Comparative International Management* (December 2004), http://web2.infotrac.galegroup.com.
5 Sigenman, Lee, Steven A.Tuch, and Jack K. Martin, "What's in a Name? Preference for 'Black' versus 'African-American' among Americans of African Descent," *Public Opinion Quarterly* (Fall 2005), http://web2.infotrac.galegroup.com.
6 Rideout, Bruce E., Katherine Hushen, Dawn McGinty, Stephanie Perkins, and Jennifer Tate, "Endorsement of the New Ecological Paradigm in Systematic and E-Mail Samples of College Students," *Journal of Environmental Education* (Winter 2005), http://web2.infotrac.galegroup.com.
7 SurveySite, "What We Do: Quantitative Research," http://www.surveysite.com, accessed March 15, 2006.
8 "Frequently Asked Questions about Conducting Online Research: New Methodologies for Traditional Techniques," Council of American Survey Research Organizations (CASRO) (1998), http://www.casro.org.
9 Mellinger, Gloria, "World Opinion Research Profiles," Harris Interactive Inc. (July 18, 2000).
10 Ibid.
11 "Frequently Asked Questions about Conducting Online Research" (1998).
12 "Internet Sampling Solutions," Survey Sampling International, http://www.ssisamples.com, accessed March 15, 2006.
13 Based on Gene Mueller, "It's Hard to Figure Number of Anglers," *Washington Times* (March 20, 2005), http://web3.infotrac.galegroup.com; Atlantic Coastal Cooperative Statistics Program, "About Us: Committees," http://www.accsp.org, accessed March 16, 2006; Atlantic States Marine Fisheries Commission, "About Us," http://www.asmfc.org, accessed March 16, 2006.
14 Material for this case is from *Scientific Telephone Samples User's Manual,* Scientific Telephone Samples, Santa Ana, CA.

Chapter 17

1 Based on Gerdes, Geoffrey R., Jack K. Walton II, May X. Liu, Darrel W. Parke, and Namirembe Mukasa,"Trends in the Use of Payment Instruments in the United States," *Federal Reserve Bulletin* (Spring 2005), http://web2.infotrac.galegroup.com.
2 Most of the statistical material in this book assumes that the population parameters are unknown, which is the typical situation in most applied research projects.
3 The reasons for this are related to the concept of degrees of freedom, which will be explained later. At this point, disregard the intuitive notion of division by n, because it produces a biased estimate of the population variance.
4 In practice, most survey researchers will not use this exact formula. A modification of the formula, $Z = (X - \mu)/S$, using the sample standard deviation in an adjusted form, is frequently used.
5 Hayes, William L., *Statistics* (New York: Holt, Rinehart and Winston, 1963), 193.
6 Wonnacott, Thomas H. and Ronald J. Wonnacott, *Introductory Statistics,* 2nd ed. (New York: Wiley, 1972), 125.
7 Note that the derivation of this formula is (1) $E = ZSX$; (2) $E = ZS/\sqrt{n}$; (3)$\sqrt{n}\ ZS/E$; (4) $(n) = (ZS/E)^2$.
8 Based on Bialik, Carl, "A Survey Probes the Back Seats of Taxis, with Dubious Results," *Wall Street Journal* (January 28, 2005), http://online.wsj.com; "Taxis Hailed as Black Hole for Lost Cell Phones and PDAs, as Confidential Data Gets Taken for a Ride," Pointsec Mobile Technologies news release (January 24, 2005), http://www.pointsec.com.

Chapter 18

1 Askia, http://www.askia.com, accessed April 4, 2009.
2 Sauerbeck, Laura R., Jane C. Khoury, Daniel Woo, Brett M. Kissela, Charles J. Moomaw, and Joseph P. Broderick, "Smoking Cessation after Stroke: Education and Its Effect on Behavior," *Journal of Neuroscience Nursing* (December 2005), downloaded from http://web1.infotrac.galegroup.com.
3 This section relies heavily on *Interviewer's Manual,* rev. ed. (Ann Arbor, MI: Survey Research Center, Institute for Social Research, University of Michigan, 1976).
4 Ibid., p. 11.
5 Ibid., pp. 11–13. Reprinted by permission.
6 Oliver, Daniel G., Julianne M. Serovich, and Tina L. Mason, "Constraints and Opportunities with Interview Transcription: Towards Reflection in Qualitative Research," *Social Forces* (December 2005), downloaded from http://web1.infotrac.galegroup.com,
7 Viewpoint Learning, http://www.viewpointlearning.com, accessed June 22, 2009.
8 Ripley, Birch G. "Confessions of an Industrial Marketing Research Executive Interviewer," *Marketing News* (September 10, 1976), 20.
9 Eng, Susanna and Gardner, Susan, "Conducting Surveys on a Shoestring Budget," *American Libraries*, 36 (February 2005), 38-39.

Chapter 19

1 http://www.tobii.com, Tobii, accessed April 17, 2009.
2 Braunsberger, Karin, B. R. Buckler, and David J. Ortinau, "Categorizing Cognitive Responses: An Empirical Investigation of the Cognitive Intent Congruency Between Independent Raters and Original Subject Raters," *Journal of the Academy of Marketing Science* 33 (Fall 2005), 620–632.
3 These imputation methods are beyond the scope of this text. For more see Hair et al., *Multivariate Data Analysis* (Upper Saddle River, NJ: Prentice Hall, 2006), 39–73, 709–740.
4 Pope, Jeffrey L., *Practical Marketing Research* (New York: AMACOM, 1981), 22 © 1998–1999 VNU Business Media Inc. Used with permission.

Chapter 20

1 Dolliver, Mark, "Plow Under Your Hops and Plant Some Vines," *Adweek* 46 (July 25, 2005), 36–38.
2 Fisher, Mark, "Beer Surges in Popularity—At the Expense of Wine," *Dayton Daily News* (August 1, 2008), http://www.encyclopedia.com/doc/1P2-16950875.html, accessed March 22, 2009.
3 Kirsche, M. L., "Targeting Boomers Could Boost Fizzling Out Beer Sales," *Drug Store News* 27 (June 6 2005), 81.
4 Longo, Don, "Drink Up," *Progressive Grocer* 84 (October 15 2005), 52–58.
5 "Oprah Again Tops American's List of Favorite Personalities," *Wall Street Journal* (February 3, 2006), http://online.wsj.com/article_print/SB113889692780763347.html, accessed February 2, 2006.
6 Rasmussen Reports, National Survey of 1,000 Adults (March 17–18 2009), http://www.rasmussenreports.com/premium_content/econ_crosstabs/march_2009/crosstabs_aig_march_17_18_2009, accessed March 22, 2009.
7 See Dubinsky, Alan J., Rajan Nataraajan, and Wen-Yeh Huang, "Consumers' Moral Philosophies: Identifying the Idealist and the Relativist," *Journal of Business Research* 58 (December 2005), 1690–1701; Deal, Ken, "Deeper into the Trees," *Marketing Research* 17 (Summer 2005), 38–40.
8 Adapted from Yavas, Ugur and Emin Babakus, "What Do Guests Look for in a Hotel? A Multi-Attribute Approach," *Services Marketing Quarterly* 25, no. 2 (2003), 6–14.
9 http://www.wineinstitute.org/communications/statistics, accessed February 6, 2006.
10 The data analysis tool must be added to the conventional Excel install by unpacking the data tool. This can be done by clicking on tools and then clicking on add-ins and following the instructions. See http://www.microsoft.com for more instructions on how to accomplish this.
11 Iuso, Bill, "Concept Testing: An Appropriate Approach," *Journal of Marketing Research* 12 (May 1975), 230.
12 Diamon, Sidney, "Market Research Latest Target in Ad Claim," *Advertising Age* (January 25, 1982), 52. Reprinted with permission by Crain Communications, Inc.
13 Adapted with permission from Prince, Melvin, *Consumer Research for Management Decisions* (New York: John Wiley and Sons, 1982), 163–166.

Chapter 21

1 Technically, the t-distribution should be used when the population variance is unknown and the standard deviation is estimated from sample data. However, with large samples, the t-distribution approximates the Z-distribution, so the two will generally yield the same result.
2 See a comprehensive statistics text for a more detailed explanation.
3 A more complex discussion of the differences between parametric and nonparametric statistics appears in Appendix 22A.
4 Kranz, Rick, "Maybach, Rolls Models Are Far Below Predictions," *Automotive News* 79 (October 18, 2004).
5 In most cases, low p-values support hypotheses. However, if the hypothesis is that the observations will be equal to the theoretical expectations for a given distribution (this would be the null case), then a high p-value would be desired to support the hypothesis.

Generally, this is not good form for a hypothesis. Exceptions to this rule exist. One of the most common is when a researcher compares some matrix of values with some alternative matrix of values with a goodness-of-fit test. Particularly in advanced applications (beyond the scope of this book), the researcher may wish to test whether or not the two matrices are the same within sampling error. In this case, the researcher would need an insignificant p-value (above α) to support the hypothesis.

Chapter 22

1 Vermeir, I. and P. Van Kenhove, "Gender Differences in Double Standards," *Journal of Business Ethics* 81 (2008), 281–295.
2 Vermeir and Van Kenhove (2008).
3 Tests for complex experimental designs are covered in Appendix 22B.
4 The formula is not shown here but it can be found in most basic statistics books.
5 See, for example, Armstrong-Stassen, M., "Designated Redundant but Escaping Lay-Off: A Special Group of Lay-Off Survivors," *Journal of Occupational and Organizational Psychology* 75 (March 2002), 1–13.
6 This is the "statistical alternative" hypothesis.
7 Sukhdial, Ajay, Damon Aiken, and Lynn Kahle, "Are You Old School? A Scale for Measuring Sports Fans' Old-School Orientation," *Journal of Advertising Research* 42 (July/August 2002), 71–81.

Chapter 23

1 Greenhaus, J. H. and N. J. Beutell, "Sources of Conflict Between Work and Family Roles," *Academy of Management Review*, 10, no. 1 (1985), 76.
2 Boyar, S. L., C. P. Maertz Jr., A. W. Pearson, and S. Keough, "Work-Family Conflict: A Model of Linkages Between Work and Family Domain Variables and Turnover Intentions," *Journal of Managerial Issues* 15, no. 2 (2003), 175.
3 Beutell, N. J. and U. Wittig-Berman, "Predictors of Work-Family Conflict and Satisfaction with Family, Job, Career, and Life," *Psychological Reports* 85 (1999), 893–903.
4 For a discussion of the other measures of association, see the appendix to this chapter and J. D. Gibbons, *Nonparametric Methods for Quantitative Analysis* (New York: Holt, Rinehart and Winston, 1976).
5 Bott, J. P., D. J. Svyantek, S. A. Goodman, and D. S. Bernal, "Expanding the Performance Domain: Who Says Nice Guys Finish Last?" *International Journal of Organizational Analysis*, 11, no. 2 (2003), 137–152.
6 Bagozzi, R. P., "Salesforce Performance and Satisfaction as a Function of Individual Difference, Interpersonal and Situational Factors," *Journal of Marketing Research* (November 1978), 517–531.
7 Recall that the mean for a standardized variable is equal to 0.
8 For more on this topic, see Hair, J. F., W. C. Black, B. J. Babin, R. Tathum, and R. Anderson, *Multivariate Data Analysis*, 6th ed. (Upper Saddle River, NJ: Prentice Hall, 2006).

Chapter 24

1 Goulding, Christina, "Romancing the Past: Heritage Visitors and the Nostalgic Consumer," *Psychology and Marketing* 18 (June 2001), 565–592.
2 Tesoriero, H. W., "Babes in 80s Toyland," *Time* 160 (November 11, 2002), 14.
3 "Nostalgia, Education Hot Trends in Toys," *Mass Market Retailers* 21 (February 23, 2004), 47, Thomson-Gale Database.
4 Betts, Kate, "A 1950s State of Mind," *Time* (April 15, 2004), 4.
5 Osborn, Suzanne Barry, "It's Yesterday Once More: Companies Use Nostalgia to Entice Consumers," *Chain Store Age* (June 2001), 32.
6 Peterson, Karyn M., "Entertaining the Future: Licensing Execs on Last Year's Lessons and the Challenge of What's Next," *Playthings* (February 1, 2009), http://www.playthings.com/article/CA6635647.html, accessed April 20, 2009.
7 See Holak, S. L. and W. Havlena, "Feelings, Fun and Memories: An Examination of the Emotional Components of Nostalgia," *Journal of Business Research* 42, no. 3 (1998), 217–226.
8 Muehling, Darrel D. and David E. Sprott, "The Power of Reflection," *Journal of Advertising* 33 (Fall 2004), 25–35.
9 Holak, S. L. and W. Havlena (1998).
10 When the actual regression model is illustrated as an explanation of the actual dependent variable in a population, Y_i is used and an error term (e_i) is included because the sample parameters cannot be expected to perfectly predict and explain the actual value of the dependent variable in the population. When we use a regression equation to represent its ability to predict sample values of the dependent variable from the estimated parameter coefficients, $\hat{Y}_i$ is used to represent predicted values of Y_i and no error term is included since the actual amount of error in any given observation is unknown.
11 School enrollment statistics can often be found using the Internet and either searching through government statistics or examining the Web site for the local school district or school board.
12 The constant term has disappeared since it is equal to 0 when the regression coefficients are standardized.
13 For more on this topic, see Hair, J. F., W. C. Black, B. J. Babin, and R. Anderson, *Multivariate Data Analysis* (Upper Saddle River, NJ: Prentice Hall, 2010).
14 Cox, A. D., D. Cox, and R. D. Anderson, "Reassessing the Pleasures of Store Shopping," *Journal of Business Research* 58 (March 2005), 250–259.
15 Closs, D. J., M. Swink, and A. Nair, "The Role of Information Connectivity in Making Flexible Logistics Programs Successful," *International Journal of Physical Distribution & Logistics Management* 35, no. 4 (2005), 258–277.
16 Morrison, Mark, A. Sweeney, and T. Heffernan, "Learning Styles of On-Campus and Off-Campus Marketing Students: The Challenge for Marketing Educators," *Journal of Marketing Education* 25 (December 2003), 208–217.
17 Paul E. Green, Ronald E. Frank, and Patrick J. Robinson, "Cluster Analysis in Test-Market Selection," *Management Science* 13 (April 1967).

Chapter 25

1 North, Tim, "Business Report Writing Tips," http://www.betterwritingskills.com, downloaded April 28, 2009.
2 The original version of this chapter was written by John Bush, Oklahoma State University, and appeared in William G. Zikmund, *Business Research Methods* (Hinsdale, IL: Dryden Press, 1984).
3 "A Speech Tip," *Communication Briefings* 14, no. 2 (1995), 3.
4 These guidelines, adapted with permission from Marjorie Brody (President, Brody Communications, 1200 Melrose Ave., Melrose Park, PA 19126), appeared in "How to Gesture when Speaking," *Communication Briefings* 14, no. 11 (1995), 4.
5 "Tips of the Month," *Communication Briefings* 24, no. 7 (May 2005), 1.
6 Based on Bridis, Ted, "Study: Shoppers Naïve about Online Pricing," *Information Week* (June 1, 2005), downloaded from http://web2.infotrac.galegroup.com; (APPC),"Annenberg Study Shows Americans Vulnerable to Exploitation in the Online and Offline Marketplace," Annenberg Public Policy Center news release (June 1, 2005), http://www.annenbergpublicpolicycenter.org; Turow, Joseph, Lauren Feldman, and Kimberly Meltzer, "Open to Exploitation: American Shoppers Online and Offline," APPC report, June 2005, downloaded from http://www.annenbergpublicpolicycenter.org.

INDEX

INDEX

S